1794 — 1900

PASICRISIE INTERNATIONALE

INTERNATIONALE

HISTOIRE DOCUMENTAIRE

DES

ARBITRAGES INTERNATIONAUX

PAR

H. LA FONTAINE

SÉNATEUR DE BELGIQUE
AVOCAT A LA COUR D'APPEL DE BRUXELLES
PROFESSEUR DE DROIT INTERNATIONAL

BERNE
IMPRIMERIE STÄMPFLI & CIE.
1902

PASICRISIE

INTERNATIONALE

promis ont été rédigés dans l'idiome national de chacun des Etats intéressés. Certains documents toutefois n'ont été révélés que sous forme de traductions et force nous a été de les reproduire sous cette forme.

* * *

Notre intention première avait été de suivre l'ordre strictement chronologique des différends survenus entre les divers Etats. Mais dès le début de notre travail nous avons rencontré de telles difficultés pour retrouver les documents relatifs à certains arbitrages, qu'il nous a fallu renoncer à notre projet, sinon nous eussions été obligés de remettre à une date de plus en plus éloignée la publication de notre ouvrage. Les recueils de jurisprudence, relatifs au droit interne, ne suivent pas du reste un ordre chronologique et des tables spéciales les complètent à ce point de vue. Nous avons également fait suivre notre recueil d'une table par ordre de dates qui permettra d'envisager l'évolution historique de la procédure arbitrale.

Quant à la date de chacun des arbitrages, nous avons été amenés à la déterminer par celle du compromis qui l'a institué. Il est d'usage, en matière de jurisprudence interne, de classer les contestations soumises aux cours et aux tribunaux d'après les dates des arrêts et des jugements intervenus. Le motif qui nous a incités à renoncer à ce système de classement, c'est que les arbitrages n'ont pas toujours été suivis de sentences ou bien que le nombre des sentences prononcées a été considérable dans un même différend. D'autre part, tout arbitrage international a été précédé soit d'un traité formel, soit d'un échange de notes diplomatiques qui permettent de donner au différend considéré une date unique et absolument certaine. Il n'est que quelques arbitrages pour lesquels il nous a été impossible de fixer la date exacte par suite de l'insuffisance des publications faites à ce jour ou du refus qui nous a été opposé de nous la communiquer.

* * *

De l'ensemble des documents réunis par nous il résulte qu'au cours du siècle dernier cent septante-sept instances arbitrales ont été instituées par les divers Etats. Il est intéressant de constater la progression constante des recours à l'arbitrage spécialement depuis 1820. Voici en effet comment ces recours se répartissent par chaque période de vingt années :

1794—1820	15
1821—1840	8
1841—1860	20
1861—1880	44
1881—1900	90

Il en résulte que le nombre des arbitrages s'est doublé pendant chaque période relativement à celle immédiatement antérieure.

Voici d'autre part dans quelle mesure les divers Etats ont participé aux instances arbitrales :

Grande Bretagne	70	Bolivie	4
Etats-Unis d'Amérique	56	Paraguay	3
Chili	26	Salvador	3
France	26	Transvaal	3
Pérou	14	Autriche	2
Portugal	12	Belgique	2
Brésil	11	Grèce	2
Argentine	10	Saint-Domingue	2
Espagne	10	Siam	2
Nicaragua	9	Suède et Norvège	2
Italie	9	Suisse	2
Mexique	8	Uruguay	2
Venezuela	7	Chine	1
Colombie	6	Congo	1
Guatemala	6	Danemark	1
Honduras	6	Egypte	1
Equateur	6	Japon	1
Costa Rica	5	Orange	1
Pays-Bas	5	Perse	1
Hayti	4	Turquie	1
Russie	4		

Si l'on fait abstraction des deux Etats de langue anglaise, qui ont donné au monde le réconfortant spectacle de cent vingt-six recours à l'arbitrage, ont peut répartir de la manière suivante les participations aux diverses instances :

Amérique méridionale	134
Europe	90
Afrique	6
Asie	5

Malgré toutes les réserves exprimées, malgré tous les doutes émis, le progrès constant de la procédure arbitrale est un fait qui ressort avec une évidence manifeste des quelques chiffres que nous venons d'énumérer.

* * *

Pour fortifier d'une manière plus précise et plus décisive encore la conviction que l'arbitrage s'est imposé aux Etats, comme le mode normal de résoudre les différends qui peuvent naître entre eux, nous avons recherché les traités dans lesquels des clauses compromissoires ont été insérées [1]. Il aurait été fastidieux de reproduire les textes de ces traités : nous nous contentons de donner une liste de ceux que nous avons relevés. Cette liste ne constitue qu'un premier essai ; il est probable qu'un grand nombre de conventions contenant une clause de ce genre, nous ont échappé. Il n'en est pas moins utile de constater le développement continu de l'idée arbitrale chez tous les peuples civilisés.

Nous avons distingué entre les clauses compromissoires générales, qui doivent s'appliquer à tous les différends qui peuvent surgir entre les Hautes Parties Contractantes, et les clauses compromissoires spéciales, limitées à l'interprétation des traités auxquels elles sont incorporées ou à la solution des difficultés nées de l'application de ces traités.

CLAUSES COMPROMISSOIRES GÉNÉRALES

[1]) Cette recherche a été singulièrement facilitée par le *Relevé général des clauses de Médiation et d'Arbitrage concernant les Puissances représentées à la Conférence de la Paix,* réalisé par le Chevalier Descamps et joint en annexe aux procès-verbaux de la Conférence Internationale de la Paix, ainsi que par le document distribué aux membres de la Seconde Conférence Panaméricaine : *Algunos datos sobre Tratados de Arbitraje y Buenos Oficios celebrados por las Naciones Americanas.* Mexico, 1901. In-4°, 66 p.

CLAUSES COMPROMISSOIRES SPÉCIALES

57. 1895—06—18 Belgique, Danemark . . . . Art. 20
58. 1895—12 -31 Norvège, Portugal . . . . » ..
59. 1898—02—25 Japon, Siam . . . . » 3 add.

---

60. 1890—07—02 Acte général relatif au commerce des esclaves . . . Art. 50 à 58
61. 1891—07—04 Union postale universelle . . . . » 23

La progression du nombre des clauses arbitrales préventives est plus considérable encore que celle des recours à l'arbitrage, telle que nous l'avons établie plus haut. Elle se résume en effet comme suit:

1821—1840 10 ▆▆▆▆▆
1841—1860 18 ▆▆▆▆▆▆▆▆
1861—1880 29 ▆▆▆▆▆▆▆▆▆▆▆
1881—1900 79 ▆▆▆▆▆▆▆▆▆▆▆▆▆▆▆▆▆▆▆▆▆▆▆▆▆

Quant au nombre de traités signés par chacune des Hautes Parties Contractantes, il s'élève respectivement pour chacune d'elles aux chiffres qui suivent:

Salvador	21	Orange	4
Italie	20	Pays-Bas	4
Costa Rica	19	Suède	4
Guatemala	16	Uruguay	4
Honduras	15	France	3
Pérou	14	Transvaal	3
Belgique	13	Congo	3
Equateur	13	Danemark	2
Nicaragua	13	Etats-Unis d'Amérique	2
Bolivie	10	Hawaï	2
Mexique	10	Monténégro	2
Espagne	9	Paraguay	2
Colombie	8	République centrale	2
Chili	8	Roumanie	2
Suisse	8	Autriche	1
Norvège	7	Brésil	1
Grande-Bretagne	6	Cap	1
Vénézuéla	6	Japon	1
Argentine	5	Natal	1
Siam	5	Prusse	1
Grèce	4	Sardaigne	1
Nouvelle Grenade	4	Saint-Domingue	1

La répartition des divers Etats par groupes continentaux donne pour résultat:

Amérique méridionale 172
Europe 87
Afrique 12
Asie 6
Amérique septentrionale 4

* * *

Pour compléter cette énumération des instruments diplomatiques, qui ont rendu hommage à l'idée pacificatrice de l'arbitrage, il nous reste à signaler les divers traités qui ont eu pour objet spécial d'organiser une procédure arbitrale permanente.

TRAITÉS D'ARBITRAGE PERMANENT

1880—09—03	Chili, Colombie.		1892—05—23	Guatemala, Honduras, Nicaragua, Salvador.
1880—12—24	Colombie, Salvador.		1898—07—23	Argentine, Italie.
1882—07—03	Saint-Domingue, Salvador.		1899—05—18	Brésil, Chili.
1883—02—07	Salvador, Uruguay.		1899—06—08	Argentine, Uruguay.
1883—10—27	Costa Rica, Salvador.		1899—11—06	Argentine, Paraguay.
1886—01—19	Chili, Suisse.			

Enfin des tentatives importantes ont eu pour objet de faire de l'arbitrage la base d'unions entre de nombreux Etats. Le premier effort en ce sens date de 1883 et essaya de grouper l'Argentine, la Bolivie, la Colombie, l'Equateur, le Mexique, le Pérou, Saint-Domingue, le Salvador et le Vénézuéla.

Le Premier Congrès Panaméricain aboutit également sous la date du 17 avril 1890 à la rédaction d'un projet d'arbitrage permanent, qui ne fut toutefois pas ratifié dans les délais prévus.

D'autre part des pourparlers eurent lieu, dans un but identique, entre les Etats-Unis d'Amérique et la Suisse en 1883 et entre les Etats-Unis d'Amérique et la Grande-Bretagne de 1891 à 1893.

Enfin la dernière et la plus notable tentative a certes été la Conférence Internationale de la Paix, qui siéga à La Haye du 18 mai au 29 juillet 1899 et qui réunit, lors de ses délibérations, les représentants de l'Allemagne, de l'Autriche-Hongrie, de la Belgique, de la Bulgarie, de la Chine, du Danemark, de l'Espagne, des Etats-Unis d'Amérique, de la France, de la Grande-Bretagne, de la Grèce, de l'Italie, du Japon, du

Luxembourg, du Mexique, du Monténégro, de la Norvège, des Pays-Bas, de la Perse, du Portugal, de la Roumanie, de la Russie, de la Serbie, du Siam, de la Suisse et de la Turquie.

*　*　*

Cette rapide revue de l'œuvre accomplie, pour substituer le règne du droit au recours à la force, doit faire pénétrer dans la pensée de tous cette conviction que le vingtième siècle ne se terminera pas sans voir se constituer enfin une Juridiction Internationale Permanente et se promulguer un Code de Droit Public International.

Puisse l'ouvrage que nous offrons à nos contemporains former le premier et modeste recueil d'une Jurisprudence Internationale sans cesse grandissante et pacificatrice. C'est une faible pierre que nous apportons au monument d'entente et de concorde que les peuples, lentement mais inlassablement, élèvent à la Justice.

PASICRISIE INTERNATIONALE.

HISTOIRE DOCUMENTAIRE

DES

ARBITRAGES INTERNATIONAUX.

1794—1900.

I. Etats-Unis d'Amérique, Grande-Bretagne.

19 novembre 1794.

La première convention moderne d'arbitrage a institué en fait trois instances arbitrales, qu'il est utile d'examiner séparément.

A. — Le premier arbitrage a eu pour objet de déterminer exactement une partie de la frontière qui sépare le territoire américain des possessions anglaises du Canada. L'origine des difficultés survenues remonte au traité de Paris du 3 septembre 1783.

Nous croyons, pour la clarté du compromis et de la sentence intervenue, devoir reproduire tout d'abord la stipulation qui donna lieu à la contestation ici examinée.

Treaty of peace and amity, signed at Paris, September 3, 1783.

. . . .

ARTICLE II. And that all disputes which might arise in future on the subject of the boundaries of the said United States may be prevented, it is hereby agreed and declared, that the following are, and shall be, their boundaries, viz:
From the North West angle of Nova Scotia, viz. that angle which is formed by a line drawn due north, from the source of Sainte Croix river to the Highlands, along the said Highlands which divide those rivers that empty themselves into the river St. Lawrence, from those which fall into the Atlantic Ocean, to the north westernmost head of Connecticut river; thence down . . . . .
East, by a line to be drawn along the middle of the river St. Croix, from its mouth in the Bay of Fundy to its source, and from its source directly north to the aforesa'd Highlands, which divide the rivers that fall into the Atlantic Ocean from those which fall into the river St. Lawrence: comprehending all islands . . . . [1]

La commission arbitrale, chargée d'interpréter le texte prémentionné, fut instituée par l'article V du traité d'amitié, de commerce et de navigation du 19 novembre 1794.

Treaty of amity, commerce and navigation between the United Kingdom and the United States of America, signed at London, November 19, 1794.

. . . .

ARTICLE V. Whereas doubts have arisen what river was truly intended under the name of the

---

[1] CH. DE MARTENS et F. DE CURSY. *Recueil manuel et pratique de traités, conventions et autres actes diplomatiques.* Leipzig, F. A. Brockhaus, 1846, tome I, p. 312.

1

river St. Croix, mentioned in the said Treaty of Peace, and forming a part of the boundary therein described, that question shall be referred to the final decision of commissioners to be appointed in the following manner, viz.

One commissioner shall be named by His Majesty and one by the President of the United States, by and with the advice and consent of the senate thereof, and the said two commissioners shall agree on the choice of a third; or if they cannot so agree, they shall each propose one person, and of the two names so proposed, one shall be drawn by lot in the presence of the two original commissioners. And the three commissioners so appointed, shall be sworn impartially to examine and decide the said question according to such evidence as shall respectively be laid before them on the part of the British Government and of the United States. The said commissioners shall meet at Halifax, and shall have power to adjourn to such other place or places as they shall think fit. They shall have power to appoint a secretary, and to employ such surveyors or other persons as they shall judge necessary. The said commissioners shall by a Declaration under their hand and seals decide what river is the river St. Croix intended by the Treaty. The said declaration shall contain a description of the said river, and shall particularize the latitude and longitude of its mouth, and of its source. Duplicates of this declaration, and of the statements of their accounts, and of the journal of their proceedings shall be delivered by them to the Agent of His Majesty, and to the Agent of the United States, who may be respectively appointed and authorized to manage the business on behalf of the respective Governments. And both parties agree to consider such decision as final and conclusive, so as that the same shall never thereafter be called into question, or made the subject of dispute or difference between them [1].

Les commissaires prononcèrent leur sentence, après avoir usé de la faculté de déplacer le siège du tribunal arbitral de Halifax à Providence. Cette sentence, parfaitement explicite et précise, n'appelle aucune observation.

Decision of the British and American Commissioners, under the 5th Article of the Treaty of 1794, relative to the River Sainte Croix. Providence, October 25, 1798.

By Thomas Barclay, David Howell and Egbert Benson, Commissioners appointed in pur-

[1] *Treaties and Conventions between the United States and other Powers*, 1776—1887. p. 382.

suance of the 5th Article of the Treaty of amity, commerce and navigation between His Britannic Majesty and the United States of America, finally to decide the question: « What river was truly intended under the name of the river Sainte Croix, mentioned in the Treaty of Peace between His Majesty and the United States of America, and forming part of the boundary therein described. »

We, the said Commissioners, having been sworn « impartially to examine and decide the said question according to such evidence as should respectively be laid before us on the part of the British Government and of the United States », and having heard the evidence which had been laid before us by the Agent of His Majesty and the Agent of the United States respectively appointed and authorized to manage the business on behalf of the respective Governments, have decided, and hereby do decide:

The river hereinafter particularly described and mentioned to be the river truly intended under the name of the river Sainte Croix in the said Treaty of Peace, and forming a part of the boundary therein described, that is to say, the mouth of the said river is in Passamaquaddy Bay, at a point of land called Ive's Point, about 1 mille northward from the northern part of Sanct Andrew's Island and in the latitude of $45^0 5'$ and $5''$ north, and in the longitude of $67^0 12'$ and $30''$ west from the Royal Observatory at Greenwich in Great Britain, and $3^0 50'$ and $15''$ east of Howard College in the University of Cambridge, in the state of Massachusetts. And the course of the said river up from its source is northerly to a point of land called The Devil's Head, thence turning the said point, is westerly to where it divides in 2 streams, the one coming from the westward and the other from the northward, having the Indian name Chiputnatecook, or Chipnitcook, as the same may be variously spelt, then up the said stream, so coming from the northward to its source, which is at a stake near a yellow birch-tree, hooped with iron, marked « S. T. and J. H., 1797 », by Samuel Titcomb and John Harris, the surveyors employed to survey the above-mentioned stream coming from the northward. And the said river is designated on the map hereunto annexed and hereby referred to as further descriptive of it by the letters A, B, C, D, E, F, G, H, I, K and L, the letter A being at its said mouth, and the letter L being at its said source. And the course and distance of the said source from the island at the confluence of the above-mentioned 2 streams is, as laid down on the said map, north 5^0 and about $15'$ west by the magnet: about $84^1/_2$ miles.

In testimony whereof we have hereunto set

our hands and seals, at Providence, in the State of Rhode Island, the 25th day of october, in the year 1798 [1].

B. — Le second arbitrage institué par le traité de 1794 avait pour objet de fixer les sommes dues à des citoyens anglais par des citoyens américains et devenues irrécouvrables au profit des premiers. Le premier document reproduit par nous est l'article VI du traité du 19 novembre 1794 qui institue la commission arbitrale. Cette commission ne parvint pas à remplir la mission qui lui était dévolue et les deux nations terminèrent le conflit à l'amiable aux termes d'un arrangement conclu en 1802 et dont nous donnons également plus loin les stipulations principales.

Treaty of amity, commerce and navigation between the United Kingdom and the United States of America, signed at London, November 19, 1794.

. . . .

ARTICLE VI. Whereas it is alledged by divers British merchants and others, His Majesty's subjects, that debts to a considerable amount, which were bona fide contracted before the Peace, still remain owing to them by citizens or inhabitants of the United States, and that by the operation of various lawfull impediments since the Peace, not only the full recovery of the said debts has been delayed, but also the value and security thereof have been in several instances, impaired and lessened, so that by the ordinary course of judicial proceedings, the British creditors cannot now obtain, and actually have and receive full and adequate compensation for the losses and damages which they have thereby sustained. It is agreed that in all such cases where full compensation for such losses and damages, cannot, for whatever reason, be actually obtained, had and received by the said creditors in the ordinary course of justice, the United States will make full and complete compensation for the same to the said creditors: But it is distinctly understood, that this provision is to extend to such losses only as have been occasioned by the lawful impediments aforesaid, and is not to extend to losses occasioned by such insolvency of the debtors, or other causes as would equally 'iave operated to produce such loss, if the said impediments had not existed, nor to such losses or damages as have been occasioned by the manifest delay or negligence, or wilful omission of he claimant.

[1] HERTSLET, *A complete Collection* ..., t. IX, p. 761.

For the purpose of ascertaining the amount of any such losses or damages, five Commissioners shall be appointed, and authorized to meet and act in the manner following, viz. Two of them shall be appointed by His Majesty, two of them by the President of the United States by and with the advice and consent of the Senate thereof and the fifth by the unanimous voice of the other four; and if they should not agree in such choice, then the Commissioners named by the two parties, shall respectively propose one person, and of the two names so proposed one shall be drawn by lot in the presence of the four original Commissioners.

When the five Commissioners thus appointed shall first meet, they shall, before they proceed to act respectively, take the following oath or affirmation, in the presence of each other, which oath or affirmation being so taken, and duly attested, shall be entered on the record of their proceedings, viz.:

« I. A. B. one of the Commissioners appointed in pursuance of the 6th Article of the Treaty of Amity, Commerce and Navigation, between His Britannic Majesty and the United States of America do solemnly swear or affirm, that I will honestly, diligently, impartially and carefully examine, and to the best of my judgment, according to justice and equity, decide all such complaints, as, under the said article, shall be preferred to the said Commissioners; and that I will forbear to act as a Commissioner in any case, in which I may be personally interested ».

Three of the said Commissioners shall constitute a board and shall have power to do any act appertaining to the said Commission, provided that one of the Commissioners named on each side, and the fifth Commissioner shall be present, and all decisions shall be made by the majority of the voices of the Comissioners then present. Eighteen months from the day the said Commissioners shall form a board, and be ready to proceed to business, are assigned for receiving complaints and applications; but they are nevertheless authorized, in any particular cases in which it shall appear to them to be reasonable and just, to extend the said term of eighteen months for any term not exceeding six months after the expiration thereof the said Commissioners shall first meet at Philadelphia, but they shall have power to adjourn from place to place as they shall see cause.

The said Commissioners, in examining the complaints and applications so preferred to them, are empowered and required, in pursuance of the true intent and meaning of this Article, to take into their consideration all claims, whether of principal or interest, and (or) balances of principal and interest and to determine the same respectively, according to the merits of the several cases, due regard being had to all the circumstances thereof, and as equity and justice shall appear to them to require. And the said Commissioners shall have power to examine all such persons as shall come before them on oath or affirmation, touching the premises: and also to receive in evidence, according as they may think most consistent, with equity and justice, all written depositions, or books or papers, or copies or extracts thereof; every such deposition, book, or paper, or extract being duly authenticated either according to the legal forms now respectively existing in the two countries, or in such other manner as the said Commissioners shall see cause to require or allow. The award of the said Commissioners, or of any three of them as aforesaid, shall in all cases be final and conclusive, both as to the justice of the claim, and to the amount of the sum to be paid to the creditor or claimant: and the United States undertake to cause the sum so awarded to be paid in specie to such creditor or claimant without deduction, and at such time or times, and at such place or places, as shall be awarded by the said Commissioners: and on condition of such releases or assignments to be given by the creditor or claimant, as by the said Commissioners may be directed: Provided always, that no such payment shall be fixed by the said Commissioners to take place sooner than twelve months, from the day of the exchange of the ratifications of this Treaty [1].

Convention between the United States and Great Britain on the difficulties arisen in the execution of the Treaty of November 19, 1794, signed at London, January 8, 1802.

Difficulties having arisen in the execution of the sixth article of the treaty of amity, commerce and navigation concluded at London on the fourth day of november, one thousand seven hundred and ninety four, between his Britannic Majesty and the United States of America, and in consebuence thereof the proceedings of the Commissioners under the seventh article of the same treaty, having been suspended: the parties to the said treaty being equally desirous, as far may be, to obviate such difficulties, have respectively named Plenipotentiaries to treat and agree respecting the same: that is to say, his Britannic Majesty has named for his plenipotentiary, the right honourable Robert Banks Jenkinson, commonly called Lord Hawkesbury, one of His Majesty's most honourable Privy Council, and his principal secretary of state for foreign affairs: and the President of the United States, by and with the advice and consent of the senate thereof, has named for their plenipotentiary Rufus King, Esquire, minister plenipotentiary of the said Unites States to his Britannic Majesty, who have agreed to and concluded the following Articles:

ART. I. In satisfaction and discharge of the money which the United States might have been liable to pay in pursuance of the provisions of the said sixth article, which is hereby declared to be cancelled and annulled, except so far as the same may relate to the execution of the said seventh article, the United States of America hereby engage to pay, and his Britannic Majesty consents to accept for the persons described in the said sixth article, the sum of six hundred thousand pounds sterling, payable at the times and place, and in the manner following, that is to say: the said sum of six hundred thousand pounds sterling, shall be paid at the city ot Washington in three annual instalments of two hundred thousand pounds sterling each and to such person or persons, as shall be authorized by his Britannic Majesty to receive the same; the first of the said instalments to be paid at the expiration of one year, the second instalment at the expiration of two years, and the third and last instalment at the expiration of three years, next following the exchange of the ratifications of this convention.

And to prevent any disagreement concerning the rate of exchanges, the said payments shall be made in the money of the said United States: reckoning four dollars and forty-four cents to be equal to one pound sterling [1].

C. — La troisième commission arbitrale fut chargée d'évaluer les dommages réciproques soufferts par des citoyens, tant américains qu'anglais, à raison de captures de vaisseaux et de prises de marchandises. Les travaux de cette commission commencés le 16 août 1796 furent interrompus le 20 juillet 1799 à raison des difficultés qui firent échouer la seconde commission. Les deux nations confirmèrent à nouveau les pouvoirs de la troisième commission par une stipulation expresse du traité du 8 janvier 1802.

---

[1] *Treaties and Conventions* ....., 1776-1887, p. 382.

[1] F. DE MARTENS, *Recueil des traités*. Supplément, t. III, p. 202; — *Treaties and Conventions* ....., 1776-1887, p. 398.

Treaty of amity, commerce and navigation, signed at London, November 19, 1794.

. . . .

ARTICLE VII. Whereas complaints have been made by divers merchants and others, citizens of the United States, that during the course of the war in which His Majesty is now engaged, they have sustained considerable losses and damage, by reason of irregular or illegal captures or condemnations of their vessels and other property under colour of authority or commissions from His Majesty, and that from various circumstances belonging to the said cases, adequate compensation for the losses and damages so sustained cannot now be actually obtained, had, and received by the ordinary course of judicial proceedings; it is agreed; that in all such cases where adequate compensation cannot, for whatever reason, be now actually obtained, had, and received by the said merchants and others in the ordinary course of justice, full and complete compensation for the same will be made by the British Government to the said complainants. But it is distinctly understood that this provision is not to extend to such losses or damages as have been occasioned by the manifest delay or negligence, or wilful omission of the claimant.

That for the purpose of ascertaining the amount of any such losses and domages, five Commissioners shall be appointed and authorized to act in London exactly in the manner directed with respect to those mentioned in the proceeding article, and after having taken the same oath or affirmation (mutatis mutandis) the same term of eighteen months is also assigned for the reception of claims, and they are in like manner authorized to extend the same in particular cases. They shall receive testimony, books, papers and evidence in the same latitude, and exercise the like discretion and powers respecting that subject: and shall decide the claims in question according to the merits of the several cases, and to justice, equity and the laws of nations. The award of the Commissioners or any such three of them as aforesaid, shall, in all cases, be final and conclusive, both as to the justice of the claim, and the amount of the sum to be paid to the claimant: and his Britannic Majesty undertakes to cause the same to be paid to such claimant in specie, without any deduction, at such place or places, and at such time or times as shall be awarded by the same Commissioners, and on condition of such releases or assignments to be given by the claimants, as by the said Commissioners may be directed.

And whereas certain merchants and others, His Majesty's subjects complain that in the course

of the War they have sustained loss and damage by reason of the capture of the vessels and merchandise, taken within the limits and jurisdiction of the States, and brought into the ports of the same, or taken by vessels originally armed in parts of the said States:

It is agreed that in all such cases where restitution shall not have been made agreeably to the tenor of the letter from Mr. Jefferson to Mr. Hammond dated at Philadelphia september 5, 1793, a copy of which is annexed to this treaty; the complaints of the parties shall be, and hereby are referred to the Commissioners to be appointed by virtue of this Article, who are hereby authorized and required to proceed in the like manner relative to these as to the other cases committed to them; and the United States undertake, to pay to the complainants or claimants, in specie, without deduction, the amount of such sums as shall be awarded to them respectively by the said Commissioners, and at the times and places which in such awards shall be specified, and on condition of such releases or assignments to be given by the claimants as in the said awards may be directed. And it is further agreed, that not only the now existing cases of both descriptions, but also all such as shall exist at the time of exchanging the ratifications of this Treaty, shall be considered within the provisions, intent and meaning of this Article [1].

Convention between the United States and Great Britain on the difficulties arisen in the execution of the Treaty of November 19, 1794, signed at London, January 8, 1802.

. . . .

ART. III. It is furthermore agreed and concluded that the commissioners appointed in pursuance of the seventh article of the said treaty of amity, commerce and navigation and whose proceedings have been suspended, as aforesaid, shall immediately after the signature of this convention, reassemble and proceed in the execution of their duties according to the provisions of the said seventh article; except only that instead of the sums awarded by the said commissioners being made payable at the time or times by them appointed, all sums of money by them awarded to be paid to American or British claimants, according to the provisions of the said seventh article, shall be made payable in three equal instalments, the first whereof, to be paid at the expiration of one year, the second at the expiration of two years, and the third and last at the expiration of three years next, after the exchange of the ratifications of this convention.

---

[1] *Treaties and Conventions ....*, 1776-1887, p. 384.

ART. IV. This convention, when the same shall have been ratified by His Majesty, and by the President of the United States, by and with the advice and consent of the senate thereof and the respective ratifications duly exchanged, shall be binding and obligatory upon His Majesty and the said United States.

In faith whereof, We the undersigned plenipotentiaries of his Britannic Majesty and of the United States of America, by virtue of our respective full powers, have signed the present convention, and have caused the seals of our arms to be affixed thereto.

Done at London, the eighth day of January one thousand eight hundred and two [1].

La commission se réunit de nouveau du 15 février 1802 au 24 février 1804. Elle statua au sujet de 536 cas et accorda environ 11,650,000 £ à des citoyens de nationalité américaine et 143,428 £ 14 à des citoyens de nationalité anglaise.

II. Espagne, Etats-Unis de l'Amérique du Nord.

11 août 1802.

L'objet de l'arbitrage a été de fixer les indemnités dues par les deux gouvernements à leurs citoyens respectifs pour excès réciproques commis par ces derniers. Ainsi que la lecture des documents diplomatiques le prouve surabondamment, cette affaire n'offre qu'un intérêt fort secondaire.

Convention between Spain and the United States of America for the indemnification of those who have sustained losses, damages or injuries in consequence of the excesses of individuals of either nation during the late war, concluded at Madrid, August 11, 1802.

1. A board of commissioners shall be formed, composed of five commissioners, two of whom shall be appointed by his Catholic Majesty, two others by the government of the United States, and the fifth by common consent; and in case they should not be able to agree on a person for the fifth commissioner, each party shall name one, and leave the decision to lot: and hereafter, in case of the death, sickness or necessary absence of any of those already appointed, they shall proceed in the same manner to the appointment of persons to replace them.

2. The appointment of the commissioners being thus made, each one of them shall take an oath to examine, discuss, and decide, on the claims, which they are to judge, according to the laws of nations and the existing treaty, and with the impartiality justice may dictate.

3. The commissioners shall meet and hold their sessions in Madrid, where, within the term of eighteen months (to be reckoned from the day on which they may assemble) they shall receive all claims, which, in consequence of this convention, may be made, as well by the subjects of his Catholic Majesty as by the citizens of the United States of America, who may have a right to demand compensation for the losses, damages. or injuries, sustained by them, in consequence of the excesses committed by Spanish subjects or American citizens.

4. The commissioners are authorized, by the said contracting parties, to hear and examine, on oath, every question relative to the said demands, and to receive, as worthy of credit, all testimony, the authenticity of which cannot reasonably be doubted.

5. From the decisions of the commissioners there shall be no appeal; and the agreement of three of them shall give full force and effect to their decisions, as well with respect to the justice of the claims, as to the amount of the indemnification which may be adjudged to the claimants; the said contracting parties obliging themselves to satisfy the said awards in specie, without deduction, at the times and places pointed out, and under the conditions which may be expressed by the board of commissioners.

6. It not having been possible for the said plenipotentiaries to agree upon a mode by which the above mentioned board of commissioners should arbitrate the claims originating from the excesses of foreign cruisers, agents, consuls, or tribunals, in their respective territories, which might be imputable to their two governments, they have expressly agreed that each government shall reserve (as it does by this convention) to itself, its subjects or citizens, respectively, all the rights which they now have, and under which they may hereafter bring forward their claims, at such times as may be most convenient to them [1].

Ce traité ne fut jamais exécuté. Bien que ratifié par les Etats-Unis dès 1804, il ne le fut par l'Espagne qu'en 1818. Les ratifications ne furent échangées que le 21 décembre de

[1] F. DE MARTENS, *Recueil des Traités*. Supplément, t. III, p. 202; - *Treaties and Conventions ....*, 1776-1887. p. 398.

[1] JON. ELLIOT. *Diplomatic Code of the United States of America*. Washington, 1827, p. 363. — F. DE MARTENS. *Nouveau Recueil de Traités*. Gœttingue. Dieterich. 1829. Tome V, suppl., p. 400 (402).

cette dernière année. Elles furent du reste suivies presque immédiatement d'un nouveau traité qui annula le traité de 1802.

Traité d'amitié, d'accord et de fixation de limites, conclu entre les Etats-Unis d'Amérique et Sa Majesté Catholique, signé à Washington le 22 février 1819.

ARTICLE X. La convention passée entre les deux gouvernements le 11 août 1802, dont les ratifications ont été échangées le 21 décembre 1818, est annulée.

ARTICLE XI. Les Etats-Unis déchargent l'Espagne de toutes demandes à l'avenir sous le rapport des réclamations de leurs concitoyens, qui sont comprises dans les renonciations déjà spécifiées, et les considérant comme entièrement closes, se chargent de satisfaire à ces réclamations jusqu'à concurrence d'une somme qui n'excèdera pas cinq millions de dollars [1].

L'article prémentionné règle pour le surplus la manière dont seront déterminés le montant et la validité des réclamations : comme ces réclamations n'ont concerné que des citoyens américains indemnisés par le gouvernement américain, il n'y a pas lieu pour nous, au point de vue spécial où nous nous trouvons placés, de nous appesantir davantage au sujet du litige ici examiné.

III. Etats-Unis de l'Amérique du Nord, Grande-Bretagne.

24 décembre 1814.

La convention du 24 décembre 1814 a institué, comme celle du 19 novembre 1794, trois arbitrages distincts, dont l'objet et les résultats seront étudiés séparément par nous.

A. — Le premier arbitrage avait pour but de déterminer auquel des deux pays certaines îles, situées dans la baie de Passamaquoddy, appartenaient en réalité, aux termes du traité du 3 septembre 1783. Nous reproduisons le passage du traité de 1814 qui institue cet arbitrage, ainsi que la décision intervenue le 24 novembre 1817.

[1] CH. DE MARTENS. *Ibid.* Tome III, p. 410 (414). — DE MARTENS. *Nouveau Recueil.* Tome V, p. 328.

Traité de paix et d'amitié entre Sa Majesté Britannique et les Etats-Unis de l'Amérique, signé à Gand le 24 décembre 1814.

ARTICLE IV. Comme il a été stipulé par l'article II du traité de paix de 1783, entre Sa Majesté Britannique et les Etats-Unis d'Amérique, que les limites des Etats-Unis comprendraient « toutes les îles à la distance de 20 lieues d'aucune partie des côtes des Etats-Unis, et situées entre les lignes à tirer directement à l'est des points où lesdites limites, entre la Nouvelle Ecosse d'une part, et la Floride occidentale de l'autre, toucheront respectivement la baie de Fondy et l'Océan Atlantique, excepté les îles qui sont ou ont été jusqu'à présent comprises dans les limites de la Nouvelle Ecosse », et comme les diverses îles de la baie de Passamaquoddy, qui fait partie de la baie de Fondy, et l'île de Grand Monan, dans ladite baie de Fondy, sont réclamées par les Etats-Unis comme étant comprises dans lesdites limites, lesquelles îles sont réclamées comme appartenant à Sa Majesté Britannique, comme étant comprises dans les limites de la Nouvelle Ecosse à l'époque du susdit traité de 1783, et antérieurement ; en conséquence, afin de statuer finalement sur ces réclamations, il est convenu qu'elles seront référées à deux commissaires qui seront nommés de la manière suivante, savoir : un commissaire sera nommé par Sa Majesté Britannique, et un par le président des Etats-Unis, avec l'avis et le consentement du sénat ; et lesdits deux commissaires, ainsi nommés, prêteront serment d'examiner et déterminer impartialement lesdites réclamations, conformément aux preuves qui seront mises sous leurs yeux de la part de Sa Majesté Britannique et de celle des Etats-Unis respectivement. Lesdits commissaires se réuniront à Saint-André, dans la province du Nouveau Brunswick, et ils auront le pouvoir de s'ajourner à tels autres endroits qu'ils jugeront convenables. Lesdits commissaires décideront par une déclaration ou rapport, revêtu de leurs signatures et cachets, à laquelle des deux parties contractantes les diverses îles susdites appartiennent respectivement, en conformité du véritable sens dudit traité de paix de 1783 ; et si lesdits commissaires s'accordent dans leur décision, les deux parties considéreront ladite décision comme définitive et péremptoire.

Il est convenu, en outre, que, dans le cas où les deux commissaires différeraient d'avis sur toutes ou aucunes des matières à eux ainsi référées, ou dans le cas où tous deux ou l'un desdits commissaires refuseraient, ou s'excuseraient, ou négligeraient à dessein d'agir comme tels, ils feront conjointement ou séparément leurs rapports tant au gouvernement de Sa Majesté Britannique qu'à celui des Etats-Unis, dans lesquels ils relateront en détail les points sur lesquels ils diffèrent, et les raisons sur lesquelles leurs opinions respectives ont été formées, et les motifs par lesquels ils ont été ainsi tous deux ou l'un des deux refusé, se sont excusés, ou ont négligé d'agir. Et Sa Majesté Britannique et le gouvernement des Etats-Unis conviennent ici de référer le rapport ou les rapports desdits commissaires à un souverain ou Etat ami, qui sera alors nommé à cet effet et qui sera prié de donner une décision sur les différends qui seront exposés dans lesdits rapports, ou sur le rapport de l'un des commissaires ainsi que sur les motifs par lesquels l'autre commissaire aura refusé, se sera excusé, ou aura négligé d'agir selon le cas. Et si le commissaire qui aura ainsi refusé, se sera excusé ou aura négligé d'agir, néglige aussi à dessein de déduire les raisons pour lesquelles il l'a fait, de même ledit rapport sera déféré audit souverain ou Etat ami, ainsi que le rapport dudit autre commissaire, afin que ledit souverain ou Etat prononce *ex parte* sur ledit rapport seul; et Sa Majesté Britannique et le gouvernement des Etats-Unis s'engagent à considérer la décision dudit souverain ou Etat ami comme définitive et concluante sur toutes les matières ainsi référées [1].

Décision des commissaires nommés par la Grande-Bretagne et les Etats-Unis de l'Amérique septentrionale conformément au quatrième article du Traité de Gand de 1814, datée de New-York du 24 novembre 1817.

By Thomas Barclay and John Holmes, esquires, commissioners, appointed by virtue of the fourth article of the treaty of peace and amity between His Britannic Majesty and the United States of America, concluded at Ghent, on the twenty fourth day of December, one thousand eight hundred and fourteen, to decide to which of the two contracting parties to the said treaty, the several islands in the Bay of Passamaquoddy, which is part of the Bay of Foundy, and the island of Grand Menan, in the said Bay of Foundy, do respectively belong, in conformity with the true intent of the second article of the treaty of peace of one thousand seven hundred and eighty three, between his said Britannic Majesty and the aforesaid United States of America.

We, the said Thomas Barclay and John Holmes, commissioners as aforesaid, having been duly sworn impartially to examine and decide upon the said claims, according to such evidence as should be laid before us on the part of His Britannic Majesty and the United States, respecti-

[1] CH. DE MARTENS. *Ibid.* Tome III, p. 38 (40).

vely, have decided, and do decide, that Moose island, Dudley island and Frederick island, in the Bay of Passamaquoddy, which is part of the Bay of Foundy, do, and each of them does, belong to the United States of America; and we have also decided, and do decide, that all other islands, and each and every of them, in the said Bay of Passamaquoddy, which is part of the Bay of Foundy, and the island of Grand Menan, in the said Bay of Foundy, do belong to his said Britannic Majesty, in conformity with the true intent of the said second article of the said treaty of one thousand seven hundred and eighty three.

In faith and testimony whereof we have set our hands and affixed our seals, at the city of New York, in the State of New York, in the United States of America, this twenty fourth day of November, in the year of our Lord one thousand eight hundred and seventeen [1].

B. — Le second arbitrage, institué par le traité de 1814, a pour origine de nouvelles difficultés survenues relativement aux frontières séparatives des possessions anglaises et américaines, difficultés similaires à celles que le traité du 19 novembre 1794, en son article V, avait eu pour but de solutionner.

Traité de paix et d'amitié entre Sa Majesté Britannique et les Etats-Unis de l'Amérique, signé à Gand le 24 décembre 1814.

ARTICLE V. Comme ni le point des hauteurs situées directement au nord de la source de la rivière de Sainte-Croix, désigné dans le précédent traité de paix entre les deux puissances comme l'angle nord-ouest de la Nouvelle-Ecosse, ni la partie supérieure la plus au nord-ouest de la rivière de Connecticut, n'ont pas encore été constatés; et comme la partie de la ligne frontière entre les possessions des deux puissances qui s'étend depuis la source de la rivière de Sainte-Croix, directement au nord du susdit angle nord-ouest de la Nouvelle-Ecosse, de la longe lesdites montagnes qui divisent les rivières qui se jettent dans le fleuve de Saint-Laurent, de celles qui se jettent dans l'Océan Atlantique dans la partie supérieure la plus à l'ouest de la rivière Connecticut, de là descend au milieu de cette rivière jusqu'au 45° degré de latitude nord, de là par une ligne directe à ladite latitude jusqu'à ce qu'elle touche à la rivière des Iroquois

[1] JON. ELLIOT, *Diplomatic Code of the United States of America.* Washington, 1827. p. 291. - F. DE MARTENS, *Ibid.* Tome V, p. 397.

ou Cataragny, n'a pas encore été reconnûe, il est convenu que pour ses divers objets deux commissaires seront nommés et autorisés, et prêteront serment d'agir exactement de la manière prescrite à l'égard de ce qui est mentionné dans l'article qui précède immédiatement, à moins qu'il ne soit autrement spécifié dans le présent article. Lesdits commissaires se réuniront à Saint-André dans la province du Nouveau-Brunswick, et ils auront le pouvoir de s'ajourner à tels autres endroits qu'ils jugeront convenables. Lesdits commissaires auront le pouvoir de constater et déterminer les points ci-dessus mentionnés, conformément aux dispositions dudit traité de paix de 1783, et ils feront connaître et marquer conformément auxdites dispositions la susdite limite depuis la source de la rivière de Sainte-Croix jusqu'à la rivière des Iroquois ou Cataragny ; lesdits commissaires feront dresser une carte de ladite limite, et y joindront une déclaration revêtue de leurs signatures et cachets, qui certifiera que c'est une carte exacte de ladite limite, et indiquera particulièrement la latitude et la longitude de l'angle nord-ouest de la Nouvelle-Ecosse, de la tête nord-ouest de la rivière de Connecticut et de tels autres points de ladite limite qu'ils jugeront convenables ; et les deux parties conviennent de considérer lesdites cartes et déclaration comme fixant définitivement et péremptoirement ladite limite ; et dans le cas où lesdits commissaires différeraient d'avis, et où tous deux ou l'un des deux refuseraient, s'excuseraient ou négligeraient d'agir, ils feront tous deux, ou l'un d'eux, des rapports, déclarations ou exposés, et il en sera référé à un souverain ou Etat ami à tous égards ainsi qu'il est stipulé dans l'article IV, et aussi pleinement que s'il était ici répété [1].

Les commissaires de 1814, pas plus que les commissaires de 1794, ne parvinrent à accomplir leur mission, et le recours à l'arbitrage d'un souverain ami fut décidé entre les deux nations et réglé par le traité que nous reproduisons ici.

Convention entre la Grande-Bretagne et les Etats-Unis de l'Amérique septentrionale, relative à l'arbitrage sur les points litigieux du cinquième article du traité de Gand, signée à Londres le 29 septembre 1827.

Whereas it is provided by the fifth Article of the Treaty of Ghent, that in case the Commissioners appointed under that Article, for the Settlement of the Boundary Line therein described, should not be able to agree upon such Boundary Line, the Report or Reports of those Commissioners, stating the points on which they

[1] CH. DE MARTENS. *Ibid.* Tome III, p. 38 (41).

had differed, should be submitted to some friendly Sovereign or State; and that the Decision given by such Sovereign or State on such points of difference, should be considered by the Contracting Parties as final and conclusive. That case having now arisen, and it having therefore become expedient to proceed and to regulate the reference as above described, His Majesty the King of the United Kingdom of Great Britain and Ireland, and the United States of America, have for that purpose, named their Plenipotentiaries, that is to say : . . . .
Who after having exchanged their respective Full Powers, found to be in due and proper form, have agreed to and concluded the following Articles.

ART. I.—It is agreed that the Points of Difference which have arisen in the settlement of the Boundary between the British and American Dominions, as described in the fifth Article of the Treaty of Ghent, shall be refered, as therein provided, to some friendly Sovereign or State, who shall be invited to investigate, and make a decision upon such points of difference.

The two Contracting Powers engage to proceed in concert to the choice of such friendly Sovereign or State, as soon as the Ratifications of this Convention shall have been exchanged, and to use Their best endeavours to obtain a decision, if practicable, within two years after the Arbiter shall have signified His consent to act as such.

ART. II.—The reports and documents thereunto annexed, of the Commissioners appointed to carry into execution the fifth Article of the Treaty of Ghent, being so voluminous and complicated, as to render it improbable that any Sovereign or State should be willing or able to undertake the Office of investigating and arbitrating upon them, it is hereby agreed to substitute for those Reports new and separate statements of the respective cases, severally drawn up by each of the Contracting Parties, in such form and terms as each may think fit.

The said statements, when prepared, shall be mutually communicated to each other by the Contracting Parties, that is to say, by Great Britain to the Minister or Chargé d'Affaires of the United States at London; and by the United States to His Britannic Majesty's Minister or Chargé d'Affaires at Washington, within fifteen months after the exchange of the Ratification of the present Convention.

After such communication shall have taken place, each Party shall have the power of drawing up a second and definitive Statement, if it thinks fit so to do, in reply to the statement of the other Party so communicated, which definitive

Statements shall also be mutually communicated, in the same manner as aforesaid, to each other, by the Contracting Parties, within twenty one months after the exchange of the Ratifications of the present Convention.

ART. III.—Each of the Contracting Parties shall, within nine months after the exchange of Ratifications of this Convention, communicate to the other, in the same manner as aforesaid, all the evidence intended to be brought in support in its claims, beyond that which is contained in the Reports of the Commissioners, or Papers thereunto annexed, and other written documents laid before the Commission under the fifth Article of the Treaty of Ghent.

Each of the Contracting Parties shall be bound, on the application of the other Party made within six months after the exchange of the Ratifications of this Convention, to give authentic Copies of such individually specified Acts of a public nature, relating to the Territory in question, intended to be laid as evidence before the Arbiter, as have been issued under the autority, or are in the exclusive possession, of each Party.

No maps, surveys, or topographical evidence of any description shall be adduced by either Party, beyond that which is hereinafter stipulated; nor shall any fresh evidence, of any description, be adduced or adverted to, by either Party, other than that mutually communicated or applied for, as aforesaid.

Each Party shall have full power to incorporate in, or annex to, either its first or second statement, any portion of the Reports of the Commissioners, or Papers thereunto annexed, and other written documents laid before the Commission under the fifth Article of the Treaty of Ghent, or of the other evidence mutually communicated or applied for, as above provided, which it may think fit.

ART. IV.—The map, called Mitchell's map, by which the framers of the Treaty of 1783 are acknowledged to have regulated their joint and official proceedings, and the map A, which has been agreed on by the Contracting Parties, as a delineation of the Water Courses, and of the Boundary Line, in reference to the said Water Courses, as contended for by each Party respectively, and which has accordingly been signed by the above named Plenipotentiaries at the same time with this Convention, shall be annexed to the Statements of the Contracting Parties, and be the only map that shall be considered as evidence, mutually aknowledged by the Contracting Parties, of the topography of the Country.

It shall, however, be lawful for either Party to annex to its respective first Statement, for the purposes of general illustration, any of the maps, surveys, or topographical delineations which were filed with the Commissioners under the fifth Article of the treaty of Ghent heretofore published, and also a transcript of the abovementioned map A, or of a section thereof, in which transcript each Party may lay down the Highlands or other features of the Country, as it shall think fit, the Water Courses, and the Boundary Lines, as claimed by each Party, remaining as laid down in the said map A.

But this transcript, as well as all the other maps, surveys, or topographical delineations, other than the map A and Mitchell's map, intended to be thus annexed by either Party to the respective Statements, shall be communicated to the other Party, in the same manner as aforesaid, within nine months after the exchange of the Ratifications of this Convention, and shall be subject to such objections and observations as the other Contracting Party may deem it expedient to make thereto, and shall annex to his first statement, either in the margin of such transcript, map or maps, or otherwise.

ART. V.—All the statements, papers, maps and documents above mentioned, and which shall have been mutually communicated as aforesaid, shall, without any addition, substraction, or alteration whatsoever, be jointly and simultaneously delivered into the Arbitrating Sovereign or State, within two years after the exchange of Ratifications of this Convention, unless the Arbiter should not, within that time, have consented to act as such; in which case all the said statements, papers, maps and documents shall be laid before him within six months after the time when he shall have consented so to act. No other statements, papers, maps or documents shall ever be laid before the Arbiter, except as hereinafter provided.

ART. VI.—In order to facilitate the attainement of a just and sound Decision on the part of the Arbiter, it is agreed that, in case the Arbiter should desire further elucidation or evidence, in regard to any specific point contained in any of the said statements submitted to him, the requisition for such elucidation or evidence shall be simultaneously made to both Parties, who shall thereupon be permitted to bring further evidence, if required, and to make each a written reply to the specific questions submitted by the said Arbiter, but not further; and such evidence and replies shall be immediately communicated by each Party to the other.

And in case the Arbiter should find the topographical evidence laid, as aforesaid, before him, insufficient for the purposes of a sound and just Decision, he shall have the power of ordering additional surveys to be made of any portions of the disputed Boundary Line or Territory, as he may think fit; which surveys shall be made at the joint expence of the Contracting Parties, and be considered as conclusive by them.

ART. VII.—The Decision of the Arbiter, when given, shall be taken as final and conclusive; and it shall be carried, without reserve, into immediate effect, by Commissioners appointed, for that purpose, by the Contracting Parties[1].

Ce fut le roi de Hollande qui fut choisi comme arbitre. Nous donnons ici le texte de sa sentence :

Nous, Guillaume, par la grâce de Dieu, roi des Pays-Bas, prince d'Orange-Nassau, grand-duc de Luxembourg, etc., etc., etc. ;

Ayant accepté les fonctions d'arbitrateur, qui Nous ont été conférées par la note de l'ambassadeur extraordinaire et plénipotentiaire de la Grande-Bretagne, et par celle du chargé d'affaires des Etats-Unis d'Amérique, à Notre ministre des Affaires étrangères, en date du 12 janvier 1829, d'après l'article V du traité de Gand du 24 décembre 1814 et l'article 1er de la convention conclue entre ces puissances à Londres, le 29 septembre 1827, dans le différend qui s'est élevé entre elles au sujet des limites de leurs possessions respectives ;

Animé du désir sincère de répondre par une décision scrupuleuse et impartiale, à la confiance qu'elles nous ont témoignée, et de leur donner ainsi un nouveau gage du haut prix que nous y attachons ;

Ayant à cet effet dûment examiné et mûrement pesé le contenu du premier exposé ainsi que de l'exposé définitif dudit différend, que nous ont respectivement remis, le 1er avril de l'année 1830, l'ambassadeur extraordinaire et plénipotentiaire de Sa Majesté Britannique, et l'envoyé extraordinaire et ministre plénipotentiaire des Etats-Unis d'Amérique, avec toutes les pièces qui y ont été jointes à l'appui ;

Voulant accomplir aujourd'hui les obligations que nous venons de contracter par l'acceptation des fonctions d'arbitrateur dans le susdit différend, en portant à la connaissance des deux hautes parties intéressées le résultat de notre examen, et notre opinion sur les trois points dans lesquels se divise de leur commun accord la contestation ;

Considérant que les trois points précités doivent être jugés d'après les traités, actes et conventions, conclus entre les deux puissances, savoir, le traité de paix de 1783, le traité d'amitié, de commerce et de navigation de 1794, la déclaration relative à la rivière St-Croix de 1798, le traité de paix signé à Gand en 1811, la convention du 29 septembre 1827, et la carte de

[1] F. DE MARTENS. *Ibid.* Tome VII, p. 491.

Mitchell, et la carte A citées dans cette convention ;

Déclarons que, — Quant au premier point, savoir, la question quel est l'endroit désigné dans les traités comme l'angle nord-ouest de la Nouvelle-Ecosse, et quels sont les Highlands séparant les rivières qui se déchargent dans le fleuve St-Laurent, de celles tombant dans l'Océan Atlantique, le long desquels doit être tirée la ligne de limites depuis cet angle jusqu'à la source nord-ouest de la rivière Connecticut ?

Considérant, — Que les hautes parties intéressées réclament respectivement cette ligne de limites au midi et au nord de la rivière St-John, et ont indiqué chacune sur la carte A la ligne qu'elles demandent ;

Considérant, — Que selon les exemples allégués, le terme Highlands s'applique non seulement à un pays montueux ou élevé, mais encore à un terrain qui, sans être montueux, sépare des eaux coulant dans une direction différente, et qu'ainsi le caractère plus ou moins montueux et élevé du pays, à travers lequel sont tirées les deux lignes respectivement réclamées au nord et au midi de la rivière St-John, ne saurait faire la base d'une option entre elles ;

Que le texte du second article du traité de paix de 1783, reproduit en partie les expressions dont on s'est antérieurement servi dans la proclamation de 1783, et dans l'acte de Quebec de 1774, pour indiquer les limites méridionales du Gouvernement de Quebec, depuis le lac Champlain, "in 45th degrees of North Latitude, along the Highlands which divide the Rivers that empty themselves into the River St-Lawrence from those which fall into the sea, and also along the North Coast of the Bay des Chaleurs" ;

Qu'en 1763, 1765, 1773, et 1782, il a été établi, que la Nouvelle Ecosse serait bornée au nord, jusqu'à l'extrémité occidentale de la Baie des Chaleurs, par la limite méridionale de la province de Quebec, que cette délimitation se retrouve pour la province de Quebec, dans la commission du gouverneur général de Quebec de 1786, où l'on a fait usage des termes de la proclamation de 1763, et de l'acte de Quebec de 1774 ; et dans les commissions de 1786 et postérieures des gouverneurs du Nouveau-Brunswick pour cette dernière province, ainsi que dans un grand nombre de cartes antérieures et postérieures au traité de 1783, et que l'article premier dudit traité cite nominativement les Etats, dont l'indépendance est reconnue ;

Mais que cette mention n'implique point l'entière coïncidence des limites entre les deux puissances, réglées par l'article suivant, avec l'ancienne délimitation des provinces anglaises, dont le maintien n'est pas mentionné dans le traité de

1783, et qui par ses variations continuelles, et par l'incertitude qui continua d'exister à son égard, provoqua de temps à autre des différends entre les autorités provinciales;

Qu'il résulte de la ligne tirée par le traité de 1783 à travers les grands lacs à l'ouest du fleuve St-Laurent, une déviation des anciennes provinciales en ce qui concerne les limites;

Qu'on chercherait en vain à s'expliquer pourquoi, si l'on entendait maintenir l'ancienne délimitation provinciale, l'on a précisément fait usage dans la négociation de 1783 de la carte de Mitchell, publiée en 1755, et par conséquent antérieure à la proclamation de 1763, et à l'acte de Quebec de 1774;

Que la Grande-Bretagne proposa d'abord la rivière Picataque pour limite à l'est des Etats-Unis, et ensuite n'accepta pas la proposition de faire fixer plus tard la limite du Maine, ou du Massachusetts Bay;

Que le traité de Gand stipula un nouvel examen sur les lieux lequel ne pouvait s'appliquer à une limite historique ou administrative, et que dès lors l'ancienne délimitation des provinces anglaises n'offre pas non plus une base de décision;

Que la longitude de l'angle nord-ouest de la Nouvelle-Ecosse laquelle doit coïncider avec celle de la source de la rivière St-Croix, fut seulement fixée par la déclaration de 1798, qui indiqua cette rivière;

Que le traité d'amitié, de commerce et de navigation de 1794 mentionne le doute qui s'était élevé à l'égard de la rivière St-Croix; et que les premières instructions du congrès lors des négociations, dont résulta le traité de 1783, placent ledit angle à la source de la rivière St-John;

Que la latitude de cet angle se trouve sur les bords du St-Laurent, selon la carte de Mitchell, reconnue pour avoir réglé le travail combiné et officiel des négociateurs du traité de 1783; au lieu, qu'en vertu de la délimitation du gouvernement de Quebec, l'on devrait la chercher aux Highlands séparant les rivières qui se déchargent dans la rivière St-Laurent de celles tombant dans la mer;

Que la nature du terrain à l'est de l'angle précité n'ayant pas été indiqué dans le traité de 1783, il ne s'en laisse pas tirer d'argument pour le fixer de préférence dans tel endroit, plutôt que dans un autre;

Qu'au surplus, si l'on croyait devoir le rapprocher de la source de la rivière St-Croix, et le chercher, par exemple, à Mars Hill, il serait d'autant plus possible que la limite du Nouveau-Brunswick tirée de là au nord-est, donnât à cette province plusieurs angles nord-ouest situés davantage au nord, et à l'est, selon leur plus grand éloignement de Mars Hill, que le nombre de degrés de l'angle mentionné dans le traité a été passé sous silence;

Que par conséquent l'angle nord-ouest de la Nouvelle-Ecosse, dont il est ici question, ayant été inconnu en 1783, et le traité de Gand l'ayant encore déclaré non constaté, la mention de cet angle historique dans le traité de 1783, doit être considérée comme une pétition de principe, qui ne présente aucune base de décision, tandis que si on l'envisage comme un point topographique eu égard à la définition "viz that Angle which is formed by a Line drawn due North from the source of the St. Croix River to the Highlands", il forme simplement l'extrémité de la ligne "along the said Highlands, which divide those Rivers that empty themselves into the River St. Lawrence, from those which fall into the Atlantic Ocean", extrémité que la mention de l'angle nord-ouest de la Nouvelle-Ecosse ne contribue pas à constater et qui, étant à trouver elle-même ne saurait mener à la découverte de la ligne qu'elle termine;

Enfin, que les arguments tirés des droits de souveraineté exercés sur le fief Madawaskas de et sur le Madawaska Settlement, admis même que cet exercice fût suffisamment prouvé, ne peuvent point décider la question, par la raison, que ces deux établissements n'embrassent qu'un terrain partiel de celui en litige; que les hautes parties intéressées ont reconnu le pays situé entre les lignes respectivement réclamées par elles, comme faisant un objet de contestation, et qu'ainsi la possession ne saurait être censée déroger au droit, et que si l'on écarte l'ancienne délimitation des provinces alléguée en faveur de la ligne réclamée au nord de la rivière St-John, et spécialement celle mentionnée dans la proclamation de 1763 et dans l'acte de Quebec de 1774, l'on ne saurait admettre à l'appui de la ligne demandée au midi de la rivière St-John, des arguments tendant à prouver que telle partie du terrain litigieux appartient au Canada ou au Nouveau-Brunswick;

Considérant, — Que la question, dépouillée des arguments non décisifs tirés du caractère plus ou moins montueux du terrain, de l'ancienne délimitation des provinces, de l'angle nord-ouest de la Nouvelle-Ecosse, et de l'état de possession, se réduit en dernière analyse à celles-ci : Quelle est la ligne tirée droit au nord depuis la source de la rivière St-Croix, et quel est le terrain, n'importe qu'il soit montueux et élevé ou non, qui, depuis cette ligne jusqu'à la source nord-ouest de la rivière Connecticut, sépare les rivières se déchargeant dans le fleuve St-Laurent, de celles qui tombent dans l'Océan Atlantique; que les hautes parties intéressées ne sont d'accord que sur la circonstance que la limite à trouver doit être déterminée par une telle ligne, et par un tel terrain ; qu'elles le sont encore, *depuis la déclaration de 1798, sur la réponse à faire à la première question, à l'exception de la latitude, à laquelle la ligne tirée droit au nord de la source de la rivière St-Croix doit se terminer ; que cette latitude coïncide avec l'extrémité du terrain, qui depuis cette ligne jusqu'à la source nord-ouest de la rivière Connecticut sépare les rivières se déchargeant dans le fleuve St-Laurent, de celles qui tombent dans l'Océan Atlantique, et ̦que, dès lors, il ne reste qu'à déterminer ce terrain;

Qu'en se livrant à cette opération, on trouve, d'un côté :

D'abord, que si par l'adoption de la ligne réclamée au nord de la rivière St-John, la Grande-Bretagne ne pourrait pas être estimée obtenir un terrain de moindre valeur, que si elle eût accepté en 1783 la rivière St-John pour frontière, eu égard à la situation du pays entre les rivières St-John et St-Croix dans le voisinage de la mer, et à la possession des deux rives de la rivière St-John dans la dernière partie de son cours, cette compensation serait cependant détruite par l'interruption de la communication entre le Bas-Canada et le Nouveau-Brunswick, spécialement entre Quebec et Fredericton, et qu'on chercherait vainement quels motifs auraient déterminé la Cour de Londres à consentir à une semblable interruption ;

Que si, en second lieu, en opposition aux rivières se déchargeant dans le fleuve St-Laurent, on aurait convenablement, d'après le langage usité en géographie, pu comprendre les rivières tombant dans les Baies de Fundy et des Chaleurs, avec celles se jetant directement dans l'Océan Atlantique, dans la dénomination générique de rivières tombant dans l'Océan Atlantique, il serait hasardeux de ranger dans l'espèce, parmi cette catégorie, les rivières St-John et Ristigouche, que la ligne réclamée au nord de la rivière St-John sépare immédiatement des rivières se déchargeant dans le fleuve St-Laurent, non pas avec d'autres rivières coulant dans l'Océan Atlantique, mais seules, et d'appliquer ainsi, en interprétant la délimitation fixée par un traité, où chaque expression doit compter, à deux cas exclusivement spéciaux, et où il ne s'agit pas du genre, une expression générique qui leur assignerait un sens plus large, ou qui, étendue dans l'espèce, aux Scoudiac Lakes, Penobscott et Kennebec, qui se jettent directement dans l'Océan Atlantique, établirait le principe, que le traité de 1783 a entendu des Highlands séparant aussi bien médiatement qu'immédiatement les rivières se déchargeant dans le fleuve St-Laurent de celles qui tombent dans l'Océan Atlantique, principe également réalisé par les deux lignes;

Troisièmement, que la ligne réclamée au nord de la rivière St-John ne sépare pas même immédiatement les rivières se déchargeant dans le fleuve St-Laurent, des rivières St-John et Ristigouche, mais seulement des rivières qui se jettent dans les St-John et Ristigouche, à l'exception de la dernière partie de cette ligne près des sources de la rivière de St-John ; et qu'ainsi, pour arriver à l'Océan Atlantique, les rivières séparées par cette ligne de celles se déchargeant dans le fleuve St-Laurent, ont chacune besoin de deux intermédiaires, les unes de la rivière St-John et de la Baie de Fundy, et les autres de la rivière Ristigouche et de la Baie des Chaleurs ;

Et de l'autre,

Qu'on ne peut expliquer suffisamment, comment, si les hautes parties contractantes ont entendu établir en 1783 la limite au midi de la rivière St-John, cette rivière, à laquelle le terrain litigieux doit en grande partie son caractère distinctif, a été neutralisée et mise hors de cause ;

Que le verbe „divide" paraît exiger la contiguité des objets qui doivent être „divided" ;

Que ladite limite forme seulement à son extrémité occidentale la séparation immédiate entre la rivière Mettjurmette et la source nord-ouest de Penobscott, et ne sépare que médiatement les rivières se déchargeant dans le fleuve St-Laurent, des eaux du Kennebec, du Penobscott et des Scoudiac Lakes ; tandis que la limite réclamée au nord de la rivière St-John sépare immédiatement les eaux des rivières Ristigouche et St-John, et médiatement les Scoudiac Lakes, et les eaux des rivières Penobscott et Kennebec, des rivières se déchargeant dans le fleuve St-Laurent, savoir, les rivières Beaver, Metis, Rimousky, trois Pistoles, Green, du Loup, Kamouaska, Ouelle, Bras, St-Nichalas, du Sud, la Famine et Chaudière ;

Que même en mettant hors de cause les rivières Ristigouche et St-John, par le motif qu'elles ne pourraient être censées tomber dans l'Océan Atlantique, la ligne septentrionale se trouverait encore aussi près des Scoudiac Lakes, et des eaux du Penobscott et du Kennebec que la ligne méridionale des rivières Beaver, Metis, Rimousky, et autres, se déchargeant dans le fleuve St-Laurent, et formerait aussi bien que l'autre une séparation médiate entre celles-ci, et les rivières tombant dans l'Océan Atlantique ;

Que la rencontre antérieure de la limite méridionale, lorsque de la source de la rivière St-Croix on tire une ligne au nord, pourrait seulement lui assurer un avantage accessoire sur l'autre, dans le cas où l'une et l'autre limite réunissent au même degré les qualités exigées par les traités ;

Et que le sort assigné par celui de 1783 au Connecticut, et au St-Laurent même, écarte la supposition que les deux puissances auraient voulu faire tomber la totalité de chaque rivière, depuis son origine jusqu'à son embouchure, en partage à l'une ou à l'autre;

Considérant, — Que d'après ce qui précède les arguments allégués de part et d'autre, et les pièces exhibées à l'appui, ne peuvent être estimés assez prépondérants pour déterminer la préférence en faveur d'une des deux lignes, respectivement réclamées par les hautes parties intéressées, comme limites de leurs possessions depuis la source de la rivière St-Croix, jusqu'à la source nord-ouest de la rivière Connecticut; et que la nature du différend, et les stipulations vagues et non suffisamment déterminées du traité de 1783, n'admettent pas d'adjuger l'une et l'autre de ces lignes à l'une desdites parties, sans blesser les principes du droit et de l'équité envers l'autre;

Considérant, — Que la question se réduit, comme il a été exprimé ci-dessus, à un choix à faire du terrain séparant les rivières se déchargeant dans le fleuve St-Laurent, de celles qui tombent dans l'Océan Atlantique, que les hautes parties intéressées se sont entendues à l'égard du cours des eaux, indiqué de commun accord sur la carte A et présentant le seul élément de décision et que dès lors les circonstances, dont dépend cette décision, ne sauraient être éclaircies davantage, au moyen de nouvelles recherches topographiques, ni par la production de pièces nouvelles:

Nous sommes d'avis, — Qu'il conviendra d'adopter pour limite des deux Etats une ligne tirée droit au nord depuis la source de la rivière St-Croix jusqu'au point où elle coupe le milieu du *Thalweg* de la rivière St-John, de là le milieu du *Thalweg* de cette rivière, en la remontant jusqu'au point où la rivière St-Francis se décharge dans la rivière St-John; de là le milieu du *Thalweg* de la rivière St-Francis, en la remontant jusqu'à la source de sa branche la plus sud-ouest, laquelle source nous indiquons sur la carte A par la lettre X authentiquée par la signature de notre ministre des affaires étrangères; de là une ligne tirée droit à l'ouest jusqu'au point où elle se réunit à la ligne réclamée par les Etats-Unis d'Amérique, et tracée sur la carte A; de là cette ligne jusqu'au point où, d'après cette carte, elle coïncide avec celle demandée par la Grande-Bretagne; et de là la ligne indiquée sur ladite carte par les deux puissances, jusqu'à la source la plus nord-ouest de la rivière Connecticut.

Quant au second point, savoir, la question, quelle est la source la plus nord-ouest (Nord-westernmost Head) de la rivière Connecticut?

Considérant, — Que pour résoudre cette question, il s'agit d'opter entre la rivière du Connecticut Lake, Perry's Stream, Indian Stream et Hall's Stream;

Considérant, — Que d'après l'usage adopté en géographie, la source et le lit d'une rivière sont indiqués par le nom de la rivière attaché à cette source et à ce lit, et par leur plus grande importance relative comparée à celle d'autres eaux, communiquant avec cette rivière;

Considérant, — Qu'une lettre officielle de 1772 mentionne déjà le nom de Hall's Brook, et que dans une lettre officielle postérieure de la même année, du même inspecteur, on trouve Hall's Brook représenté comme une petite rivière tombant dans le Connecticut;

Que la rivière dans laquelle se trouve Connecticut Lake paraît plus considérable que Hall's, Indian ou Perry's Stream; que le Connecticut Lake et les deux lacs situés au nord de celui-ci semblent lui assigner un plus grand volume d'eau qu'aux trois autres rivières; et qu'en l'admettant comme ledit du Connecticut, on prolonge davantage ce fleuve, que si l'on donnait la préférence à une de ces trois autres rivières;

Enfin, que la carte A ayant été reconnue dans la convention de 1827 comme indiquant le cours des eaux, l'autorité de cette carte semble s'étendre également à leur dénomination, ou qu'en cas de contestation tel nom de rivière, ou de lac, sur lequel on n'eût pas été d'accord, eût pu avoir été omis, que ladite carte mentionne Connecticut Lake, et que le nom de Connecticut Lake implique l'application du nom Connecticut à la rivière qui traverse ledit lac;

Nous sommes d'avis, — Que le ruisseau situé le plus au nord-ouest de ceux qui coulent dans le plus septentrional des trois lacs, dont le dernier porte le nom de Connecticut Lake, doit être considéré comme la source la plus nord-ouest (North-westernmost Head) du Connecticut.

Et quant au troisième point, savoir, la question, quelle est la limite à tracer depuis la rivière Connecticut le long du parallèle du 45° degré de latitude septentrionale, jusqu'au fleuve St-Laurent, nommé dans les traités, Iroquois ou Cataraguy?

Considérant, — Que les hautes parties intéressées diffèrent d'opinion, sur la question de savoir, si les traités exigent un nouveau levé de toute la ligne de limite depuis la rivière Connecticut, jusqu'au fleuve St-Laurent, nommés dans les traités Iroquois ou Cataraguy, ou bien seulement le complément des anciens levés provinciaux;

Considérant, — Que le Vᵉ article du traité de Gand de 1814, ne stipule point qu'on lèvera telle partie des limites qui n'aurait pas été levée jusqu'ici, mais déclare que les limites n'ont pas été levées et établit qu'elles le seront;

Qu'en effet ce levé, dans les rapports entre les deux puissances, doit être censé n'avoir pas eu lieu depuis le Connecticut jusqu'à la rivière

St-Laurent, nommée dans les traités Iroquois ou Cataraguy, vu que l'ancien levé s'est trouvé inexact, et avait été ordonné non par les deux puissances d'un commun accord, mais par les anciennes autorités provinciales;

Qu'il est d'usage de suivre, en fixant la latitude, le principe de latitude observée;

Et que le gouvernement des Etats-Unis d'Amérique a établies certaines fortifications à l'endroit dit Rouse's Point, dans la persuasion que le terrain faisait partie de leur territoire, persuasion suffisamment légitimée par la ligne réputée jusqu'alors correspondre avec le 45° degré de latitude septentrionale:

Nous sommes d'avis, — Qu'il conviendra de procéder à de nouvelles opérations pour mesurer la latitude observée, afin de tracer là limite depuis la rivière Connecticut, le long du parallèle du 45° degré de latitude septentrionale, jusqu'au fleuve St-Laurent, nommé dans les traités Iroquois ou Cataraguy; de manière cependant, qu'en tout cas, à l'endroit dit Rouse's Point, le territoire des Etats-Unis d'Amérique s'étendra jusqu'au fort qui s'y trouve établi, et comprendra ce fort et son rayon kilométrique.

Ainsi fait et donné sous Notre sceau royal, à la Haye, ce 10 janvier, de l'an de grâce 1831, et de Notre règne le 18.

GUILLAUME [1].

Cette décision souleva les plus vives protestations du représentant du Gouvernement américain. Ce ne fut qu'en 1842 que les deux nations intéressées parvinrent à conclure un arrangement direct, qui mit fin aux longues discussions que cette question des limites entre leurs territoires respectifs avait provoquées. Bien que la convention intervenue ne constitue pas une solution arbitrale, nous croyons intéressant de la reproduire.

Traité entre les Etats-Unis d'Amérique et la Grande-Bretagne réglant les limites des territoires des Etats-Unis et des possessions de Sa Majesté Britannique dans l'Amérique du Nord, signé à Washington le 9 août 1842.

ARTICLE Ier. Il est convenu que la ligne frontière sera fixée comme suit. Elle commencera au monument et à la source de la rivière Sainte-Croix, ainsi qu'il a été convenu par les commissaires, aux termes de l'art. 5 du traité de 1794, conclu entre les gouvernements des Etats-Unis et de la Grande-Bretagne. Puis, au nord, elle suivra la ligne d'exploration fixée par les ingénieurs des deux gouvernements en 1817 et 1818, par application de l'art. 3 du traité de Gand, jusqu'à son

intersection avec la rivière de Saint-Jean, et jusqu'au milieu du canal; puis, du milieu du canal de ladite rivière Saint-Jean jusqu'à l'embouchure de la rivière Saint-François et des lacs par lesquels elle coule, jusqu'à l'issue du lac de Pohenhagumook; puis, au sud-ouest, en ligne droite jusqu'à un point de la branche nord-ouest de la rivière Saint-Jean, qui sera à 10 milles de la branche principale de la rivière Saint-Jean, en ligne droite et dans la direction la plus rapprochée; mais si ce point se trouvait à une distance de moins de 7 milles du point le plus rapproché ou du sommet des *highlands* qui séparent les rivières qui se jettent dans le Saint-Laurent de celles qui tombent dans le Saint-Jean, la ligne s'étendra jusqu'à un point qui sera à 7 milles en ligne droite dudit sommet; de là, en ligne droite, dans une direction d'environ 8 degrés sud, à l'ouest du point où le parallèle de latitude 46 degrés 25 minutes nord coupe la branche sud-ouest du Saint-Jean; de là, au sud, par ladite branche jusqu'à la source des *highlands* qui séparent les eaux qui se jettent dans le Saint-Laurent de celles qui tombent dans l'Océan Atlantique, à la source du torrent de Hall; de là, en descendant le milieu dudit torrent jusqu'au point où la ligne coupe l'ancienne ligne frontière fixée par Valentine et Collins avant 1774, comme formant la 45° degré de latitude nord, et qui constitue la ligne actuelle de séparation entre les Etats de New-York et de Vermont, d'une part, et le Canada, d'autre part; et, dudit point d'intersection, à l'ouest le long de la ligne de séparation convenue jusqu'à ce jour, jusqu'à l'Iroquois ou rivière Saint-Laurent [1].

. . . .

C. — Le troisième arbitrage consenti en 1814, avait également pour but de fixer une partie de la ligne frontière entre le Canada et les Etats-Unis de l'Amérique septentrionale. Les articles du traité que nous reproduisons spécifient avec soin les points litigieux.

Traité de paix et d'amitié entre Sa Majesté Britannique et les Etats-Unis de l'Amérique, signé à Gand le 24 décembre 1814.

ARTICLE VI. Comme par le précédent traité de paix cette portion de la limite des Etats-Unis depuis le point où le 45° degré de latitude nord touche la rivière des Iroquois ou Cataragny, jusqu'au lac Supérieur, a été déclarée être « au milieu de ladite rivière jusqu'au lac Ontario, au milieu dudit lac jusqu'à ce qu'elle touche la communication par eau entre ce lac et le lac Erié,

[1] F. DE MARTENS. *Nouveau Recueil*. Tome X, p. 306.

[1] CH. DE MARTENS. *Ibid.* Tome V, p. 200.

de là au milieu dudit lac jusqu'à ce qu'elle arrive à la communication par eau entre ce lac et le lac Supérieur ; et comme il s'est élevé des doutes sur ce qui formait le milieu desdits rivière, lacs et communications par eau, et si certaines îles qui y sont situées faisaient partie des possessions de Sa Majesté Britannique, ou des Etats-Unis ; en conséquence, afin de statuer définitivement sur ces doutes, il en sera référé à deux commissaires qui seront nommés et autorisés, et prêteront serment d'agir exactement de la manière prescrite à l'égard de ce qui est mentionné dans l'article qui précède immédiatement, à moins qu'il ne soit autrement spécifié dans le présent article. Lesdits commissaires se réuniront premièrement à Albany, dans l'Etat de New-York, et ils auront le pouvoir de s'ajourner à tels autres endroits qu'ils jugeront convenables. Lesdits commissaires, par un rapport ou déclaration revêtu de leurs signatures et cachets, désigneront la limite dans lesdits rivières, lacs et communications par eau, et décideront à laquelle des deux parties contractantes les diverses îles situées dans lesdits rivières, lacs et communications par eau, appartiennent respectivement, conformément au véritable sens dudit traité de 1783. Et les deux parties conviennent de considérer lesdites indication et décision comme définitives et péremptoires. Et dans le cas où lesdits deux commissaires différeraient d'avis, et où tous les deux ou l'un d'eux refuseraient, s'excuseraient ou négligeraient à dessein d'agir, ils feront tous deux ou l'un d'eux des rapports, déclarations ou exposés, et il en sera référé à un souverain ou Etat ami, à tous égards ainsi qu'il est stipulé dans la dernière partie de l'article IV, et aussi pleinement que s'il était rappelé ici.

ARTICLE VII. Il est convenu en outre que lesdits derniers commissaires, après qu'ils auront exécuté les fonctions à eux assignées par l'article précédent, seront et sont ici autorisés, sur leur serment, à fixer et déterminer impartialement, conformément au vrai sens dudit traité de paix de 1783, la partie de la limite entre les possessions des deux pouvoirs qui s'étend depuis la communication par eau entre le lac Huron et le lac Supérieur, jusqu'au point le plus à l'ouest du lac des Bois ; à décider à laquelle des deux parties les diverses îles situées dans les lacs, communications par eau et rivière formant ladite limite, appartiennent respectivement, conformément au vrai sens dudit traité de paix de 1783, et de faire reconnaître et marquer les parties de ladite limite qui le requerront. Lesdits commissaires, par un rapport ou déclaration, revêtu de leurs signatures et cachets, désigneront la susdite limite, prononceront leur décision sur les points à eux référés ainsi, et indiqueront particulièrement la latitude et la longitude du point le plus au nord

du lac des Bois et de telles autres parties de ladite limite qu'ils jugeront convenable, et les deux parties conviennent de considérer lesdites désignation et décision comme définitives et concluantes. Et dans le cas où lesdits commissaires différeraient d'avis, et où tous les deux ou l'un d'eux refuseraient, s'excuseraient ou négligeraient à dessein d'agir, ils feront tous deux ou l'un d'eux des rapports, déclarations ou exposés, et il en sera référé à un souverain ou Etat ami, à tous égards ainsi qu'il est stipulé dans la dernière partie de l'article IV, et aussi pleinement que s'il était rappelé ici [1].

Les commissaires parvinrent à s'entendre au sujet de la partie de leur mission déterminée par l'article VI reproduit ci-dessus. Nous estimons inutile de donner ici le texte complet de la décision intervenue, en tant qu'elle décrit minutieusement les détails de la ligne frontière : nous nous contentons de signaler les passages qui ont un caractère plus général.

Déclaration des commissaires nommés par la Grande-Bretagne et les Etats-Unis de l'Amérique septentrionale pour régler les frontières, faite à Utica le 18 juin 1822.

The undersigned commissioners, appointed, sworn and authorized, in virtue of the sixth article of the treaty of peace and amity between His Britannic Majesty and the United States of America, concluded at Ghent on the 24th of December 1814, "impartially to examine, and by a report or declaration under their hands and seals, to designate that portion of the boundary of the United States from the point where the 45th degree of north latitude strikes the river Iroquois or Cataragni, along the middle of said river into Lake Ontario, through the middle of said lake until it strikes the communication by water between that lake and Lake Erie; thence along the middle of said lake, until it arrives at the water communication into Lake Huron; thence through the middle of said lake to the water communication between that lake and Lake Superior"; and to „decide to which of the contracting parties the several islands, lying within the said river, lakes and water communications, do respectively belong, in conformity with the true intent of the treaty of 1783"; do decide and declare that the following described line is the true boundary intended by the two before mentioned treaties; that is to say:

Beginning at the stone monument erected by Andrew Ellicott, Esq., in the year 1817 on the southbank, or shore of the said river Iroquois, or Cataragni (now called the St. Lawrence) ....

---

[1] CH. DE MARTENS. *Ibid.* Tome III, p. 38 (42).

...... until it strikes a line passing across the river at the head of St. Joseph's Island, and at the foot of the Neebish Rapid, which line denotes the termination of the boundary directed to be run by the 6th article of the treaty of Ghent.

And the said commissioners do farther decide and declare, that all the islands lying in the rivers, lakes and water communications, between the before described boundary line and the adjacent shore of Upper Canada, do, and each of them does, belong to His Britannic Majesty; and that all the islands lying in the rivers, lakes and water communication, between the said boundary line and the adjacent shore of the United States, or their territories, do and each of them does, belong to the United States of America, in conformity with the true intent of the second article of the said treaty of 1783, and of the 6th article of the treaty of Ghent[1].

Ce furent les articles II du traité du 20 octobre 1818[2] et du traité du 9 août 1842[3] qui terminèrent définitivement et directement cette contestation difficultueuse.

IV. Etats-Unis de l'Amérique du Nord, Grande-Bretagne.

20 octobre 1818.

L'arbitrage de 1818 a eu pour objet de régler les difficultés nées au sujet de la restitution réciproque d'esclaves, telle qu'elle avait été stipulée dans le traité de Gand de 1814. Ce fut l'empereur de Russie qui fut choisi de commun accord par les deux parties en litige.

Convention entre les Etats-Unis de l'Amérique septentrionale et la Grande-Bretagne, concernant la pêche, les limites et plusieurs autres points, signée à Londres le 20 octobre 1818.

. . . .
ARTICLE V. Comme il a été convenu par le premier article du traité de Gand, que « tous territoires, places et possessions quelconques dont l'une ou l'autre partie se serait emparée pendant la guerre, ou après la signature de ce traité, seraient, à l'exception des îles ci-après mentionnées, rendus sans délai et sans y détruire, ou en emporter aucune partie de l'artillerie ou autres propriétés publiques capturées · originellement dans lesdits forts ou places, qui s'y trouveraient encore lors de l'échange des ratifications du présent

traité, ainsi que tout esclave ou autre propriété particulière ; » comme, d'après cet article, les Etats-Unis réclament pour leurs citoyens, et à titre de propriété particulière, la restitution, ou du moins une pleine compensation, de tous les esclaves qui, à la date de l'échange des ratifications dudit traité, se trouvaient dans les territoires, places ou possessions quelconques, dont ledit traité ordonnait la restitution aux Etats-Unis, mais qui, à cette époque, étaient encore occupés par les forces britanniques; et que dans cette restitution ils comprennent les esclaves qui étaient, soit à terre, soit à bord de vaisseaux anglais se trouvant dans les eaux des Etats-Unis; comme enfin il s'est élevé des différends sur l'esprit du susdit article du traité de Gand; les hautes parties contractantes consentent par la présente à référer ces différends à quelque souverain ou Etat ami, qui sera nommé pour cet objet; et les hautes parties contractantes s'engagent de plus à regarder la décision de cette puissance amie comme finale et conclusive sur tous les points référés[1].

Ainsi que le document que nous reproduisons plus loin en témoigne, la sentence prononcée par l'empereur de Russie ne posa qu'un principe assez vague et assez indécis. Les deux nations intéressées se décidèrent à conclure une nouvelle convention et chargèrent deux commissaires et deux arbitres de trancher le différend.

Nous appelons l'attention du lecteur sur la coexistence, dans l'espèce, de commissaires et d'arbitres et sur le surarbitrage du ministre de Russie accrédité près des Etats-Unis.

Convention entre la Grande-Bretagne, la Russie et les Etats-Unis de l'Amérique septentrionale pour mettre à exécution l'arbitrage de S. M. l'Empereur de toutes les Russies, concernant le premier article du traité de Gand, signée à Saint-Pétersbourg le 30 juin/12 juillet 1822.

Sa Majesté le Roi du Royaume-Uni de la Grande-Bretagne et de l'Irlande, et le Président des Etats-Unis d'Amérique, ayant d'un commun accord, en conséquence de l'article cinq de la convention conclue à Londres le 20 octobre 1818, que les différends qui se sont élevés entre les deux Gouvernements sur la construction et le vrai sens du premier article du traité de paix et d'amitié conclu à Gand le 24 décembre 1814, seraient déférés à l'arbitrage amical de Sa Majesté l'Empereur de toutes les Russies ; s'étant en outre engagés réciproquement à regarder Sa décision comme finale et définitive ; et Sa Majesté Impé-

---

[1] F. DE MARTENS. *Ibid.* Tome VI, p. 45. — CH. DE MARTENS. *Ibid.* Tome III, p. 546.
[2] F. DE MARTENS. *Ibid.* Tome IV, p. 571 (573).
[3] CH. DE MARTENS. *Ibid.* Tome V, p. 200 (202).

---

[1] CH. DE MARTENS. *Recueil manuel.* Tome III, p. 393 (395). — JOHN ELLIOT. *Diplomatic Code*, p. 262.

riale, après mûre considération, ayant émis cette décision dans les termes suivants :

« Que les Etats-Unis d'Amérique sont en droit
« de réclamer de la Grande-Bretagne une juste
« indemnité pour toutes les propriétés particulières
« que les forces britanniques auraient emportées,
« et, comme il s'agit plus spécialement d'esclaves,
« pour tous les esclaves que les forces britanniques
« auraient emmenés des lieux et territoires dont
« le traité stipule la restitution, en quittant ces
« mêmes lieux et territoires.

« Que les Etats-Unis sont en droit de regarder
« comme emmenés tous ceux de ces esclaves,
« qui, des territoires indiqués ci-dessus, auraient
« été transportés à bord de vaisseaux britanniques
« mouillés dans les eaux desdits territoires, et qui,
« par ce motif, n'auraient pas été restitués.

« Mais que s'il y a des esclaves américains
« emmenés de territoires dont l'article premier du
« traité de Gand n'a pas stipulé la restitution aux
« Etats-Unis, les Etats-Unis ne sont pas en droit
« de réclamer une indemnité pour lesdits esclaves. »

Comme il s'agit à présent de mettre cette sentence arbitrale à exécution, les bons Offices de Sa Majesté Impériale ont été encore invoqués, afin qu'une convention arrêtée entre Sa Majesté Britannique et les Etats-Unis, stipulât les articles d'un accord, propre à établir, d'une part le mode à suivre pour fixer et déterminer la valeur des esclaves ou autres propriétés privées qui auraient été emmenés en contravention au traité de Gand, et pour lesquels les citoyens des Etats-Unis auraient droit de réclamer une indemnité, en vertu de la décision ci-dessus mentionnée de Sa Majesté Impériale ; de l'autre, à assurer un dédommagement aux individus qui ont supporté les pertes qu'il s'agit de vérifier et d'évaluer. Sa Majesté Impériale a consenti à prêter Sa médiation pour ledit objet, et a fondé et nommé le Sieur Charles Robert Comte de Nesselrode, Son Conseiller Privé....; — Et le Sieur Jean Comte de Capodistrias, Son Conseiller Privé et Secrétaire d'Etat....; — pour Ses Plénipotentiaires à l'effet de négocier, régler, et conclure tels articles d'un accord, qui pourraient faire atteindre la fin indiquée plus haut, conjointement avec les Plénipotentiaires de Sa Majesté Britannique et des Etats-Unis, savoir : — De la part de Sa Majesté le Roi du Royaume-Uni de la Grande-Bretagne et de l'Irlande, le très Honorable Sir Charles Bagot, l'un des Membres du très Honorable Conseil Privé de Sa Majesté.... — Et de la part du Président des Etats-Unis, de l'avis et du consentement de leur Sénat, le Sieur Henry Middleton, Citoyen desdits Etats-Unis, et leur Envoyé extraordinaire et Ministre Plénipotentiaire près Sa Majesté Impériale. — Lesquels Plénipotentiaires, après s'être réciproquement communiqué leurs Pleinspouvoirs respectifs, trou-

vés en bonne et due forme, sont convenus des articles suivants :

ARTICLE I. Pour vérifier et déterminer le montant de l'indemnité qui pourra être due aux Citoyens des Etats-Unis, par suite de la décision de Sa Majesté Impériale, deux commissaires et deux arbitres seront nommés de la manière suivante, savoir : — Un commissaire et un arbitre seront nommés par Sa Majesté Britannique ; — l'autre commissaire et l'autre arbitre seront nommés et accrédités par le Président des Etats-Unis, de l'avis et du consentement de leur Sénat. Les deux commissaires et les deux arbitres ainsi nommés se réuniront en conseil et tiendront leurs séances dans la ville de Washington.

Ils auront le pouvoir de choisir un secrétaire, et, avant de procéder au travail de la commission, ils devront prêter respectivement, et en présence les uns des autres, le serment ou l'affirmation qui suit, et ce serment ou affirmation prêté et formellement attesté, fera partie du protocole de leurs actes, et sera conçu ainsi qu'il suit : — « Moi « A. B., l'un des commissaires (ou arbitres, suivant « le cas), nommés en exécution de la convention « conclue à St-Pétersbourg le 30 juin/12 juillet 1822, « entre Sa Majesté l'Empereur de toutes les Russies, « Sa Majesté Britannique, et les Etats-Unis d'Amé- « rique, jure (ou affirme) solennellement, que j'exa- « minerai avec diligence, impartialité, et solli- « tude, et que je déciderai d'après mon meilleur « entendement, et en toute justice et équité, toutes « les réclamations qui me seront déférées en ma « qualité de commissaire (ou arbitre, suivant le « cas) à la suite de ladite convention. » Les vacances causées par la mort, ou autrement, seront remplies de la même manière qu'au moment de la nomination primitive, et les nouveaux commissaires ou arbitres devront prêter le même serment (ou affirmation) et s'acquitter des mêmes devoirs.

ARTICLE II. Si, lors de la première réunion de ce conseil, le gouvernement de la Grande-Bretagne et celui des Etats-Unis ne sont point parvenus à déterminer d'un commun accord, la valeur moyenne qui devra être assignée comme compensation pour chaque esclave pour lequel il sera dû une indemnité, — dans ce cas les commissaires et les arbitres procèderont conjointement à l'examen de tous les témoignages qui leur seront présentés par ordre du Président des Etats-Unis, ainsi que de tous les autres témoignages valables qu'ils croiront devoir requérir ou admettre, dans la vue d'arrêter la véritable valeur des esclaves à l'époque de l'échange des ratifications du traité de Gand ; et d'après les preuves qu'ils auront ainsi obtenues, ils établiront et fixeront la susdite valeur moyenne. — Dans le cas où la majorité du conseil des commissaires et arbitres ne pourrait pas s'accorder sur cette valeur proportionnelle, alors on aura recours à l'arbitrage du ministre ou autre agent de la puissance médiatrice accrédité auprès du gouvernement des Etats-Unis. Toutes les preuves produites et tous les actes des opérations du conseil à ce sujet lui seront communiqués, et la décision de ce ministre ou agent, basée, comme il vient d'être dit, sur ces preuves et sur les actes de ces opérations, sera regardée comme finale et définitive. C'est sur la valeur moyenne, fixée par un des trois modes mentionnés ci-dessus, que devra être réglée en tout état de cause, la compensation qui sera accordée pour chaque esclave, pour lequel on reconnaîtra par la suite qu'une indemnité est due.

ARTICLE III. Lorsque le prorata aura été ainsi arrêté, les deux commissaires se constitueront en conseil pour l'examen des réclamations qui leur seront soumises, et ils notifieront au secrétaire d'Etat des Etats-Unis, qu'ils seront prêts à recevoir la liste définitive des esclave et autres propriétés privées pour lesquels les citoyens des Etats-Unis réclament une indemnité. Il est entendu que les commissaires ne sauraient examiner ni recevoir, et que Sa Majesté Britannique ne saurait, en vertu des clauses de l'article premier du traité de Gand, bonifier aucune prétention qui ne serait pas portée sur ladite liste. Sa Majesté Britannique s'engage, d'autre part, à ordonner que tous les témoignages que Son gouvernement peut avoir acquis, par les rapports des officiers de Sadite Majesté, ou par tout autre canal, sur le nombre des esclaves emmenés, soient mis sous les yeux des commissaires, afin de contribuer à la vérification des faits. Mais, soit que ces témoignages viennent à être produits, soit qu'ils manquent, cette circonstance ne pourra porter préjudice à une réclamation, ou aux réclamations, qui, par une autre voie, seront légitimées d'une manière satisfaisante.

ARTICLE IV. Les deux commissaires sont autorisés et chargés d'entrer dans l'examen de toutes les réclamations qui leur seront soumises, au moyen de la liste ci-dessus mentionnée, par les propriétaires d'esclaves ou les possesseurs d'autres propriétés, ou par ses procureurs ou mandataires de ceux-ci, et à prononcer sur ces réclamations, suivant le degré de leur mérite, la lettre de la décision impériale citée plus haut, et, en cas de besoin, la teneur des documents ci-annexés, et cotés A et B. En considérant lesdites réclamations, les commissaires sont autorisés à interpeller sous serment ou affirmation, telle personne qui se présentera à eux, concernant le véritable nombre des esclaves, ou la valeur de toute autre propriété pour laquelle il serait réclamé une indemnité. — Ils sont autorisés de même à recevoir, autant qu'ils le jugeront conforme à l'équité et à la justice, toutes les dépositions

écrites qui seraient duement légitimées, soit d'après les formes existantes voulues par la loi, soit dans tout autre mode que lesdits commissaires auraient lieu d'exiger ou d'admettre.

ARTICLE V. Si les deux commissaires ne parviennent pas à s'accorder sur une des réclamations qui seront soumises à leur examen, ou s'ils diffèrent d'opinion sur une question résultant de la présente convention, alors ils tireront au sort le nom d'un des deux arbitres, lequel, après avoir pris en mûre délibération l'objet en litige, le discutera avec les commissaires. La décision finale sera prise conformément à l'opinion de la majorité des deux commissaires et de l'arbitre tiré au sort. Dans des cas semblables, l'arbitre sera tenu de procéder, à tous égards, d'après les règles prescrites aux commissaires par le quatrième article de la présente convention. Il sera investi des mêmes pouvoirs, et censé, pour le moment, faire les mêmes fonctions.

ARTICLE VI. La décision des deux commissaires, ou celle de la majorité du conseil, formé ainsi qu'il a été dit en l'article précédent, sera, dans tous les cas, finale et définitive, soit relativement au nombre et à la valeur, soit pour la vérification de la propriété des esclaves, ou de tout autre bien-meuble privé pour lequel il sera réclamé une indemnité; — et Sa Majesté Britannique prend l'engagement que la somme adjugée à chaque propriétaire, en place de son esclave ou de ses esclaves, ou de toute autre propriété, sera payée en espèces sans déduction, à tel temps ou à tels termes, et dans tel lieu ou tels endroits, que l'auront prononcé lesdits commissaires, et sous clause de telles exemptions ou assignations qu'ils l'auront arrêté; — pourvu seulement, qu'il ne soit pas fixé pour ces payements, de terme plus rapproché que celui de douze mois, à partir du jour de l'échange des ratifications de la présente convention.

ARTICLE VII. Il est convenu en outre, que les commissaires et arbitres recevront, de part et d'autre, un traitement, dont les gouvernements de Sa Majesté Britannique et des Etats-Unis se réservent de déterminer le montant et le mode, à l'époque de l'échange des ratifications de la présente convention. Toutes les autres dépenses qui accompagneront les travaux de la commission, seront supportées conjointement par Sa Majesté Britannique et par les Etats-Unis. Ces dépenses devront d'ailleurs être au préalable vérifiées et admises par la majorité du conseil [1].

Les commissaires, les arbitres et le surarbitre ne parvinrent pas à remplir leur mission. Il fallut une convention nouvelle qui mit fin

[1] CH. DE MARTENS. *Recueil manuel.* Tome III. p. 550.

au litige, moyennant le payement d'une indemnité de 1,204,960 dollars, consentie par la Grande-Bretagne.

Convention entre les Etats-Unis de l'Amérique septentrionale et la Grande-Bretagne, pour l'arrangement définitif des diverses prétentions fondées sur la convention signée à Saint-Pétersbourg le 12 juillet 1822, conclue à Londres le 13 novembre 1826.

ARTICLE I. His Majesty the King of the United Kingdom of Great Britain and Ireland agrees to pay, and the United States of America agree to receive, for the use of the persons entitled to indemnification and compensation, by virtue of the said decision and convention, the sum of twelve hundred and four thousand nine hundred and sixty dollars, current money of the United States, in lieu of, and in full and complete satisfaction for, all sums claimed or claimable from Great Britain, by any person or persons whatsoever, under the said decision and convention.

ARTICLE II. The object of the said convention being thus fulfilled, that convention is hereby declared to be cancelled and annulled, save and except the second article of the same, which has already been carried into execution by the commissioners appointed under the said convention, and save and except so much of the third article of the same, as relates to the definitive list of claims, and has already likewise been carried into execution by the said commissioners.

ARTICLE III. The said sum of twelve hundred and four thousand nine hundred and sixty dollars shall be paid at Washington to such person or persons as shall be duly authorised, on the part of the United States, to receive the same, in two equal payments as follows:—

The payment of the first half to be made twenty days after official notification shall have been made, by the government of the United States, to His Britannic Majesty's minister in the said United States, of the ratification of the present convention by the president of the United States, by and with the advice and consent of the senate thereof.

And the payment of the second half to be made on the first day of August 1827.

ARTICLE IV. The above sums being taken as a full and final liquidation of all claims whatsoever arising under the said decision and convention, both the final adjustment of those claims, and the distribution of the sums so paid by Great Britain to the United States, shall be made in such manner as the United States alone shall determine: and the government of Great Britain shall have no further concern or liability therein.

ARTICLE V. It is agreed that, from the date of the exchange of the ratifications of the present convention, the joint commission appointed under the said convention of St. Petersburgh, of the twelfth of July 1822, shall be dissolved, and, upon the dissolution thereof, all the documents and papers, in possession of the said commission. relating to claims under that convention, shall be delivered over to such person or persons as shall be duly authorised, on the part of the United States, to receive the same. And the british commissioner shall make over to such person or persons, so authorised, all the documents and papers (or authentical copies of the same, where the originals cannot conveniently be made over), relating to claims under the said convention. which he may have received from his government for the use of the said commission, conformably to the stipulations contained in the third article of the said convention[1].

V. France, Mexique.

9 mars 1839.

En 1838, la guerre avait éclaté entre les deux pays à raison de traitements odieux infligés à des citoyens français, pour lesquels il avait été impossible d'obtenir les indemnités stipulées dans un ultimatum présenté le 21 mars 1838. Après un blocus d'une année et la prise du fort Saint-Jean d'Ulloa, un traité fut signé le 9 mars 1839, qui institua l'arbitrage dont nous avons à indiquer ici les conditions et le résultat.

Traité de paix et d'amitié conclu à la Vera Cruz le 9 mars 1839 entre la France et le Mexique.

. . . .

ART. II. Dans le but de faciliter le prompt rétablissement d'une bienveillance mutuelle entre les deux nations, les parties contractantes conviennent de soumettre à la décision d'une tierce puissance les deux questions de savoir :

1° Si le Mexique est en droit de réclamer de la France soit la restitution des navires de guerre mexicains capturés par les forces françaises subséquemment à la reddition de la forteresse d'Ulloa, soit une compensation de la valeur desdits navires, dans le cas où le gouvernement français en aurait déjà disposé :

2° S'il y a lieu d'allouer les indemnités que réclameraient. d'une part, les Français qui ont éprouvé des dommages par suite de la loi d'expulsion, de l'autre, les Mexicains qui ont eu à souffrir des hostilités postérieures au 26 novembre dernier [2].

---

[1] CH. DE MARTENS. *Recueil manuel.* Tome IV, p. 45.
[2] M. DU CLERCQ. *Recueil des traités de la France.* Tome IV, p. 446; CH. DE MARTENS. *Ibid.* Tome IV, p. 564.

Convention conclue à la Vera Cruz, le 9 mars 1839, relativement aux indemnités à régler entre la France et la république du Mexique.

. . . .

ART. II. La question de savoir si les navires mexicains et leurs cargaisons, sequestrés pendant le cours du blocus, et postérieurement capturés par les Français, à la suite de la déclaration de guerre, doivent être considérés comme légalement acquis aux capteurs, sera soumise à l'arbitrage d'une tierce puissance, ainsi qu'il est dit en l'article 2 du traité de ce jour [1].

Ce fut la Reine d'Angleterre qui fut choisie comme arbitre par les deux pays et qui rendit la décision suivante.

Sentence arbitrale, rendue le 1er août 1844, par la Reine d'Angleterre, entre la France et le Mexique, au sujet des réclamations pécuniaires fondées sur le traité du 9 mars 1839.

Nous, Victoria, par la grâce de Dieu, Reine du Royaume-Uni de Grande-Bretagne et d'Irlande, ayant accepté l'office d'arbitre qui nous a été conféré par S. M. le Roi des Français et par le Président de la République mexicaine, en vertu des notes adressées à notre Secrétaire d'Etat pour les Affaires Etrangères, les 26 juin et 8 juillet 1843, par les plénipotentiaires respectifs de Sa Majesté et du Président, pour déterminer les différends survenus entre les gouvernements français et mexicain relativement à certains points réservés par le traité et par la convention spéciale conclus entre ces deux gouvernements le 9 mars 1839, lesquels points sont spécifiés dans lesdits traité et convention de la manière suivante :

. . . .

Ayant attentivement et impartialement examiné les points qui nous ont été ainsi soumis; ayant mûrement pesé tout ce qui s'est passé entre les parties depuis le 16 avril 1838 jusqu'à la conclusion du traité du 9 mars 1839;

Déclarons que :

En ce qui concerne le premier point mentionné dans l'article 2 du traité et de la convention spéciale, à savoir : si le Mexique est en droit de réclamer de la France, soit la restitution des navires de guerre mexicains capturés par les forces françaises subséquemment à la reddition de la forteresse d'Ulloa, soit une compensation de la valeur desdits navires dans le cas où le gouvernement français en aurait déjà disposé; et si les navires mexicains et leurs cargaisons, sequestrés pendant le cours du blocus et postérieurement capturés par les Français à la suite de la déclaration de guerre,

[1] M. DU CLERCQ. *Ibid.* Tome IV, p. 448; CH. DE MARTENS. *Ibid.* Tome IV, p. 566.

doivent être considérés comme légalement acquis aux capteurs;

Nous sommes d'avis qu'après le départ de Mexico du plénipotentiaire français, et la notification qui a accompagné son départ, lesquels furent suivis tant d'opérations hostiles exercées par les Français contre la forteresse de Saint-Jean d'Ulloa et contre la flotte mexicaine, que d'une déclaration immédiate de guerre de la part du gouvernement mexicain, et de l'expulsion du territoire des sujets français, il y avait entre les deux pays un état de guerre dont les termes du traité et de la convention spéciale ont reconnu l'existence ;

Qu'en conséquence, la France n'est pas tenue à restitution ni à compensation pour les navires mentionnés dans le traité ou pour les navires et cargaisons spécifiés dans l'article 2 de la convention.

En ce qui regarde le second point mentionné dans l'article 2 du traité, nous sommes d'avis que ni les sujets français, ni les Mexicains n'ont droit à la moindre indemnité, les actes des deux pays se trouvant justifiés par l'état de guerre qui existait entre eux [1].

VI. Etats-Unis de l'Amérique du Nord, Mexique

11 avril 1839

L'objet du présent arbitrage a porté sur des indemnités réclamées par des citoyens américains à charge du gouvernement du Mexique. Ainsi qu'il résulte du texte reproduit plus loin, le soin de trancher le différend fut confié à quatre commissaires, avec la faculté, en cas de partage, de demander la nomination d'un arbitre au souverain de la Prusse, ou, à son défaut, à Sa Majesté Britannique, ou encore, au défaut de cette dernière, au Roi de Hollande. Ce fut le Roi de Prusse qui confia à son ministre à Washington la mission de siéger comme arbitre.

Convention conclue le 11 avril 1839 à Washington entre les Etats-Unis de l'Amérique septentrionale et la République mexicaine pour régler les réclamations de citoyens de ceux-là contre celle-ci.

ART. I. It is agreed that the claims of citizens of the United States upon the Mexican Government, statements of which, soliciting the interposition of the Government of the United States, have been presented to the Department of State or to the diplomatic agent of the United States at Mexico untill the signature of this convention,

[1] M. DU CLERCQ. *Ibid.* Tome V, p. 195.

shall be referred to four commissioners, who shall form a board and be appointed in the following manner, namely: two commissioners shall be appointed by the President of the United States, by and with the advice and consent of the Senate thereof, and two commissioners by the President of the Mexican Republic. The said commissioners, so appointed, shall be sworn impartially to examine and decide upon the said claims according to such evidence as shall be laid before them on the part of the United States and the Mexican Republic respectively.

Art. II. The said board shall have two secretaries, versed in the English and Spanish languages; one to be appointed by the President of the United States, by and with the advice and consent of the Senate thereof, and the other by the President of the Mexican Republic. And the said secretaries shall be sworn faithfully to discharge their duty in that capacity.

Art. III. The said board shall meet in the city of Washington within three months after the exchange of the ratifications of this convention, and within eighteen months from the time of its meeting shall terminate its duties. The Secretary of State of the United States shall, immediately after the exchange of the ratifications of this convention, give notice of the time of the meeting of the said board, to be published in two newspapers in Washington, and in such other papers as he may think proper.

Art. IV. All documents which now are in, or hereafter, during the continuance of the commission constituted by this convention, may come into the possession of the Department of State of the United States, in relation to the aforesaid claims, shall be delivered to the board. The Mexican Government shall furnish all such documents and explanations as may be in their possession, for the adjustment of the said claims according to the principles of justice, the law of nations, and the stipulations of the treaty of amity and commerce between the United States and Mexico of the 5th of April 1831; the said documents to be specified when demanded at the instance of the said commissioners.

Art. V. The said commissioners shall, by a report under their hands and seals, decide upon the justice of the said claims and the amount of compensation, if any, due from the Mexican Government in each case.

Art. VI. It is agreed that. if it should not be convenient for the Mexican Government to pay at once the amount so found due, it shall be at liberty, immediately after the decisions in the several cases shall have taken place, to issue treasury notes, receivable at the maritime customhouses of the Republic in payment of any duties which may be due or imposed at said customhouses upon goods entered for importation or exportation; said treasury to bear interest at the rate of eight per centum per annum from the date of the award on the claim in payment of which said treasury notes shall have been issued until that of their receipt at the Mexican customhouses. But as the presentation and receipt of said treasury notes at said custom-houses in large amounts might be inconvenient to the Mexican Government, it is further agreed that, in such case, the obligation of said Government to receive them in payement of duties, as above said, may be limited to one half the amount of said duties.

Art. VII. It is further agreed that in the event of the commissioners differing in relation to the aforesaid claims, they shall, jointly or severally, draw up a report stating, in detail, the points on which they differ, and the grounds upon which their respective opinions have been formed. And it is agreed that the said report or reports, with authenticated copies of all documents upon which they may be founded, shall be referred to the decision of His Majesty the King of Prussia. But as the documents relating to the aforesaid claims are so voluminous that it can not be expected, His Prussian Majesty would be willing or able personally to investigate them, it is agreed that he shall appoint a person to act as an arbiter in his behalf; that the person so appointed shall proceed to Washington, that his travelling expenses to that city and from thence on his return to his place of residence in Prussia, shall be defrayed, one half by the United States and one half by the Mexican Republic; and that he shall receive as a compensation for his services a sum equal to one half of the compensation that may be allowed by the United States to one of the commissioners to be appointed by them, added to one half the compensation that may be allowed by the Mexican Government to one of the commissioners to be appointed by it. And the compensation of such arbiter shall be paid, one half by the United States and one half by the Mexican Government.

Art. VIII. Immediately after the signature of this convention the plenipotentiaries of the contracting parties (both being thereunto competently authorized) shall, by a joint note, addressed to the Minister of foreign affairs of His Majesty the King of Prussia, to be delivered by the Minister of the United States at Berlin, invite the said monarch to appoint an umpire to act in his behalf in the manner above-mentioned, in case this convention shall be ratified respectively by the Governments of the United States and Mexico.

Art. IX. It is agreed that, in the event of His Prussian Majesty's declining to appoint an umpire to act in his behalf, as aforesaid, the contracting parties, on being informed thereof, shall, without delay, invite Her Britannic Majesty, and in case of her declining his Majesty the King of the Netherlands, to appoint an umpire to act in their behalf, respectively, as above provided.

ART. X. And the contracting parties further engage to consider the decision of such umpire to be final and conclusive on all the matters so referred.

ART. XI. For any sums of money which the umpire shall find due to citizens of the United States by the Mexican Government, treasury notes shall be issued in the manner afore-mentioned.

ART. XII. And the United States agree for ever to exonerate the Mexican Government from any further accountability for claims which shall either be rejected by the board or the arbiter aforesaid, or which, being allowed by either, shall be provided for by the said Government in the manner before-mentioned.

ART. XIII. And it is agreed that each Government shall provide compensation for the commissioners and secretary to be appointed by it, and that the contingent expenses of the board shall be defrayed, one moiety by the United States and one moiety by the Mexican Republic [1].

La décision des commissaires n'a pas été publiée. Elle n'aurait pas été rendue sans difficultés : notamment des questions de procédure épineuses auraient surgi dès les premières délibérations [2]. Quoi qu'il en soit, les commissaires adjugèrent certaines indemnités ; car le 13 janvier 1843 une convention intervint entre les deux républiques pour régler le payement des sommes allouées. Cette convention contient, en outre, un article par lequel les deux gouvernements s'engagent à conclure un nouveau traité d'arbitrage.

Convention ultérieure entre les Etats-Unis d'Amérique et la République du Mexique sur l'exécution de la convention du 11 avril 1839, signée à Mexico le 13 janvier 1843.

. . . .

ART. VI. A new convention shall be entered into for the settlement of all claims of the Government and citizens of the United States against the Republic of Mexico, which were not finally decided by the late commission which met in the city of Washington, and of all claims of the government and citizens of Mexico against the United States [3].

Il ne fut donné aucune suite, ni à la décision des commissaires, ni au traité de 1843. Ce ne fut qu'après la guerre de 1846 que. le traité de paix, intervenu entre les deux pays, régla définitivement le différend ici examiné.

Traité de paix, d'amitié et de limites entre les Etats-Unis d'Amérique et le Mexique, signé à la Guadaloupe Hidalgo le 2 février 1848.

ART. XIII. The United States engage. moreover. to assume and pay to the claimants all the amounts now due them, and those hereafter to become due, by reason of the claims already liquidated and decided against the Mexican Republic, under the conventions between the two republics severally concluded on the eleventh day of April, eighteen hundred and thirty-nine, and on the thirtieth day of January, eighteen hundred and fortythree; so that the Mexican Republic shall be absolutely exempt, for the future, from all expense whatever on account of the said claims.

ART. XIV. The United States do furthermore discharge the Mexican Republic from all claims of citizens of the United States, not heretofore decided against the Mexican Government, which may have arisen previously to the date of the signature of this treaty : which discharge shall be final and perpetual, whether the said claims be rejected or be allowed by the board of commissioners provided for in the following article, and whatever shall be the total amount of those allowed.

ART. XV. The United States, exonerating Mexico from all demands on account on the claims of their citizens mentioned in the preceding article, and considering them entirely and forever cancelled, whatever their amount may be, undertake to make satisfaction for the same, to an amount not exceeding three and one quarter millions of dollars. To ascertain the validity and amount of those claims, a board of commissioners shall be established by the Government of the United States, whose awards shall be final and conclusive : provided, that in deciding upon the validity of each claim, the board shall be guided and governed by the principles and rules of decision prescribed by the first and fifth articles of the unratified convention, concluded at the city of Mexico on the twentieth day of November, one thousand eight hundred and forty-three; and in no case shall an award be made in favor of any claim not embraced by these principles and rules.

If, in the opinion of the said board of commissioners, or of the claimants, any books, records, or documents in the possession or power

---

[1] F. DE MARTENS. *Nouveau Recueil.* Tome XVI, p. 624.
[2] *Revue de droit international et de législation comparée,* 1874, p. 123, en note.
[3] CH. DE MARTENS. *Recueil manuel.* Tome V, p. 273 (274).

of the Government of the Mexican Republic, shall be deemed necessary to the just decision of any claim, the commissioners, or the claimants through them, shall, within such period as Congress may designate, make an application in writing for the same, addressed to the Mexican Minister for Foreign Affairs, to be transmitted by the Secretary of State of the United States; and the Mexican Government engages, at the earliest possible moment after the receipt of such demand, to cause any of the books, records, or documents, so specified, which shall be in their possession or power (or authenticated copies or extracts of the same), to be transmitted to the said Secretary of State. who shall immediately deliver them over to the said board of commissioners: Provided, that no such application shall be made by, or at the instance of, any claimant, until the facts which it is expected to prove by such books, records, or documents, shall have been stated under oath or affirmation[1].

VII. France, Grande-Bretagne

14 novembre 1842

Les termes de la déclaration qui suit sont suffisamment explicites pour nous dispenser de tout commentaire. Ce qui semblera quelque peu insolite, c'est la manière sommaire dont l'arbitrage a été institué.

Déclaration échangée, le 14 novembre 1842, entre la France et l'Angleterre, pour l'acceptation mutuelle de l'arbitrage du Roi de Prusse sur les réclamations relatives aux blocus de Portendick.

Les mesures adoptées par le Gouvernement français, en 1834 et 1835, sur la côte de Portendick, pendant la guerre qu'il avait à soutenir contre les Maures Trarzas, ont amené de la part des négociants anglais qui faisaient sur cette côte le commerce de la gomme, de nombreuses et pressantes réclamations.

Ces réclamations ont donné lieu, de 1836 à 1840, entre le Gouvernement français et le Gouvernement britannique, à des correspondances et à des discussions prolongées, sans que les deux Gouvernements soient parvenus à s'entendre. En 1840, des commissaires ont été nommés, de part et d'autre, pour examiner lesdites réclamations et chercher les moyens de mettre fin au différend dont elles étaient la cause. Or, les commissaires n'ayant pu arriver à aucun arrangement, le Gouvernement britannique a proposé de soumettre cette affaire à l'arbitrage de S. M. le Roi de Prusse; et le Gouvernement français, voulant

[1] Ch. de Martens. *Ibid.* Tome VI, p. 199 (206).

donner une preuve des sentiments d'équité qui l'animent et portant aux lumières et à la haute impartialité de S. M. le Roi de Prusse une pleine confiance, a adhéré à cette proposition, en déclarant, toutefois, que la décision arbitrale à intervenir, quelles qu'en doivent être la nature et la forme, ne saurait à ses yeux, même par voie d'induction, porter aucune atteinte aux principes qu'il a invariablement professés en matière de blocus et de droit maritime, non plus qu'aux droits inhérents à la souveraineté qu'il a toujours soutenus lui appartenir, d'après les termes des traités, sur la côte de Portendick.

De même, le Gouvernement britannique déclare que cette décision de l'arbitre, quelle qu'elle soit, ne sera pas à ses yeux considérée, même par voie d'induction, comme portant atteinte à aucun des droits qu'il a réclamés ni à aucun des principes qu'il a maintenus.

Les deux Gouvernements sont alors convenus de soumettre à l'examen de S. M. le Roi de Prusse la totalité des réclamations présentées dans cette affaire par des sujets britanniques, et de prier S. M. de vouloir bien se prononcer, comme arbitre, sur la question de savoir si; par suite des mesures et des circonstances qui ont précédé, accompagné ou suivi l'établissement et la notification du blocus de la côte de Portendick, en 1834 et 1835, un préjudice réel a été indûment apporté à tels ou tels sujets de Sa Majesté Britannique, exerçant sur ladite côte un trafic régulier et légitime, et si la France est équitablement tenue de payer, à telle ou telle classe desdits réclamants, des indemnités à raison de ce préjudice.

Si, comme les deux Gouvernements l'espèrent, S. M. le Roi de Prusse veut bien accepter l'arbitrage qu'ils désirent remettre entre ses mains, communication lui sera donnée de toutes les dépêches, notes et autres pièces, qui ont été échangées dans cette affaire entre les deux Gouvernements; et S. M. recevra également tous les renseignements qu'elle demandera et tous ceux que l'un ou l'autre Gouvernement croira avoir besoin de placer sous ses yeux.

Les deux Gouvernements s'engagent en outre réciproquement à accepter la décision arbitrale de S. M. le Roi de Prusse et ses conséquences; et si, d'après cette décision, il est déclaré qu'une indemnité est due à telle ou telle classe de réclamants anglais, des commissaires liquidateurs, l'un Français, l'autre Anglais, lesquels seront départagés au besoin par un commissaire surarbitre Prussien, seront chargés d'appliquer ladite décision aux réclamations individuelles qui ont été présentées par des sujets britanniques, et régleront la somme qui devra être allouée pour chaque réclamation comprise dans les classes de réclamations auxquelles l'arbitre aura déclaré qu'une indemnité devait être allouée.

En foi de quoi, nous, Ministre et Secrétaire d'Etat au Département des Affaires étrangères de S. M. le Roi des Français, et nous, Ambassadeur extraordinaire et Plénipotentiaire de S. M. la Reine du Royaume-Uni de la Grande-Bretagne et d'Irlande près S. M. le Roi des Français, duement autorisés par nos souverains respectifs, avons signé la présente déclaration et y avons apposé nos cachets [1].

L'arbitrage suivit son cours normal : voici la sentence intervenue.

Sentence arbitrale, rendue le 30 novembre 1843, entre la France et la Grande-Bretagne, par S. M. le Roi de Prusse, au sujet des réclamations de Portendick.

Nous, Frédéric Guillaume IV, par la grâce de Dieu, Roi de Prusse,

Ayant accepté l'arbitrage que S. M. le Roi des Français et S. M. la Reine du Royaume-Uni de la Grande-Bretagne et de l'Irlande, en vertu d'une déclaration signée par leurs plénipotentiaires respectifs à Paris le 14 novembre 1842, ont remis entre nos mains afin de terminer par ce moyen le différend qui s'est élevé entre eux au sujet de certaines réclamations formées par des négociants anglais contre le Gouvernement français, en conséquence des mesures adoptées par les autorités françaises en 1834 et 1835 sur la côte de Portendick.

Et ayant, aux termes de ladite déclaration, à nous prononcer comme arbitre sur la question de savoir si, par suite des mesures et des circonstances qui ont précédé, accompagné ou suivi l'établissement et la notification du blocus de la côte de Portendick en 1834 et 1835, un préjudice réel a été indûment apporté à tels ou tels sujets de Sa Majesté Britannique exerçant sur ladite côte un trafic régulier et légitime, et si la France est équitablement tenue de payer à telle ou telle classe desdits réclamants des indemnités à raison de ce préjudice.

Ayant, à cet effet, soigneusement examiné et mûrement pesé le contenu des dépêches, notes et autres pièces que les Envoyés extraordinaires et Ministres plénipotentiaires de leurs dites Majestés près notre Cour ont respectivement transmis, sous la date du 19 avril dernier, à notre Ministre des Affaires étrangères,

Déclarons que :

Quant aux réclamations auxquelles ont donné lieu les procédés du brick de guerre français le *Dunois* à l'égard des bâtiments marchands anglais le *Governor Temple* et l'*Industry*,

Nous sommes d'avis :

Que le gouvernement français devra indemniser les sujets de Sa Majesté Britannique des pertes qu'ils ont essuyées par suite desdits procédés, à l'exception toutefois de celles auxquelles se rapporte la réclamation qui a été élevée relativement à l'adjoint du subrécargue du navire anglais le *Matchless*.

Quant aux pertes occasionnées par la mesure dont le bâtiment anglais l'*Elisa* a été l'objet de la part des bâtiments de guerre français, qui l'ont renvoyé à Portendick sans lui permettre d'y prendre auparavant le chargement de gomme qui lui était dû en échange des marchandises déjà délivrées aux Maures, vendeurs de la gomme,

Nous sommes d'avis :

Que la France est équitablement tenue de payer une indemnité à raison de ces pertes.

Quant aux réclamations relatives à la mise en état de blocus par le Gouvernement français de la côte de Portendick,

Nous sommes d'avis :

Que la France devra indemniser les réclamants des dommages et préjudices auxquels ils n'auraient pas été exposés si ledit Gouvernement, en envoyant au gouverneur du Sénégal l'ordre d'établir le blocus, avait simultanément notifié cette mesure au Gouvernement anglais ; que la France, au contraire, malgré l'omission de cette notification officielle du blocus, ne doit aucune indemnité pour les pertes essuyées à la suite d'opérations commerciales auxquelles les réclamants se sont livrés après que, par autres voies, ils ont positivement eu connaissance de la formation du blocus de Portendick ou qu'ils auraient pu, du moins, en être informés par suite de la nouvelle authentique parvenue à cet égard au Gouvernement britannique de la part de quelque autorité anglaise en Afrique.

Pour ce qui regarde l'application de la décision arbitrale que nous venons de rendre, aux réclamations individuelles, ainsi que la fixation du montant de chacune de celles auxquelles une indemnité doit être allouée, elles devront se faire, conformément à la déclaration du 14 novembre 1842, par des commissaires liquidateurs, l'un Français, l'autre Anglais, départagés par un commissaire surarbitre que nous aurons à nommer [1].

Il nous semble intéressant de reproduire le tableau des indemnités allouées par les commissaires liquidateurs et payées ultérieurement par la France.

---

[1] S. DE CLERCQ. *Recueil des traités de la France.* Tome IV, p. 658.

[1] S. DE CLERCQ. *Ibid.* Tome V, p. 131.

4

Réclamants	Navires	Sommes	
		réclamées	allouées
Forster et Smith	G. Temple	63,957. 60	843. 78
	Gambia . . . . }	316,890. —	18,742. 92
	Columbine . . . . . . }		
R. Harrisson	Industry	38,682. —	3,218. 04
	Chance	238,160. —	—
	Matchless	38,026. 40	—
	Elisa	144,723. 60	6,181. 56
Clavering-Redman	Meta	404,208. —	—
	Meta	212,812. —	—
	Marmion	27,398. —	—
	Matchless et P. Oscar . . .	223,444. 80	12,784. 59
Les trois maisons ci-dessus . .	Marmion et Columbine . . .	163,800. —	—
Frais de poursuites	. . . .	31,525. —	—
	Totaux	2,183,627. 40	41,770. 89

VIII. Espagne, France

15 février 1851

Il avait été convenu, aux termes d'un traité signé le 5 janvier 1824 [1], que les gouvernements d'Espagne et de France considéreraient comme équivalentes les prises faites avant le 1er octobre 1823, que l'on évaluerait d'autre part les navires capturés avant cette date, mais relâchés ultérieurement, qu'enfin les prises faites postérieurement à la date susdite seraient considérées comme nulles et les navires restitués à leurs propriétaires.

C'est au sujet de l'exécution et de l'interprétation de ce traité que des difficultés surgirent et qu'un arbitrage fut institué.

Déclaration préliminaire échangée à Madrid le 15 février 1851, entre la France et l'Espagne, pour le jugement arbitral des captures faites en 1823 et 1824.

Considérant que la voie de la simple discussion diplomatique a été impuissante pour résoudre les divergences qui se sont élevées entre les gouvernements de France et d'Espagne au sujet des affaires des navires la *Velos Mariana*, la *Vigie*,

la *Victoria* et d'autres affaires qui s'y rattachent, et considérant combien il est urgent de mettre un terme convenable à des controverses dans lesquelles se trouvent immédiatement intéressés les sujets des deux pays;

Les soussignés, ambassadeur de la République française et premier secrétaire de Sa Majesté catholique, compétement autorisés à cet effet, reconnaissent au nom de leurs gouvernements respectifs que le meilleur moyen d'arriver à la conclusion amiable que ceux-ci ont en vue pour lesdites questions, est de les soumettre à l'arbitrage d'une puissance amie et alliée.

Dans ce but, ils ont choisi, d'un commun accord, le cabinet néerlandais, et ils proposent l'un et l'autre, dans le plus bref délai possible, de faire les diligences nécessaires pour obtenir de lui l'acceptation dudit arbitrage, et dans le cas où cette demande serait accueillie, de présenter à ce cabinet les propositions arbitrales suivantes, qui devront être résolues par lui comme questions de principe :

1° Si la prise et la vente de la *Velos Mariana* ont été ou non légitimes, et si ce navire est ou non compris dans l'art. 1er de la convention du 5 janvier 1824.

2° Si le navire la *Victoria* doit ou non être compris parmi les prises qui font l'objet de l'art. 1er de la convention de 1824; et il est bien entendu que la sentence arbitrale sera seulement

---

[1] DE CLERCQ. *Recueil des traités de France.* Tome III, p. 304.

applicable à la cargaison de ce navire et non au navire lui-même, qui a été restitué.

3° Si l'Espagne doit ou non considérer comme des affaires analogues, au point de vue de la convention de 1824, les affaires de la *Veloz Mariana* et de la *Vigie*, et si elle est ou non fondée dans son refus de payer l'indemnité qu'elle reconnaît devoir aux propriétaires de ce dernier navire, jusqu'à ce que la France ait consenti à acquitter, par compensation ou de toute autre manière, l'indemnité relative à la *Veloz Mariana*.

Les deux gouvernements s'engagent d'avance à nommer une commission mixte composée de quatre membres, deux Français et deux Espagnols, dont la mission sera d'appliquer les décisions de la puissance arbitrale aux faits jugés et aux réclamations, compensations ou restitutions qui pourront réciproquement être faites.

La commission se réunira à Paris et un de ses membres en qualité de secrétaire, ayant voix délibérative, rédigera les procès-verbaux des séances.

Dans le cas où les votes de la commission se partageraient, les deux gouvernements conviennent de s'adresser à la nation arbitre pour obtenir d'elle la solution définitive des points non résolus par suite de l'absence d'une majorité dans la commission [1].

Le roi de Hollande accepta de siéger comme arbitre et rendit la sentence suivante, dont la teneur est tout spécialement claire et précise.

Décision arbitrale, rendue le 13 avril 1852, par Sa Majesté le roi des Pays-Bas, entre la France et l'Espagne, au sujet de la prise des navires la Veloz Mariana, la Victoria et la Vigie.

Nous, Guillaume III, par la grâce de Dieu, roi des Pays-Bas, prince d'Orange-Nassau, etc., etc.,

Ayant accepté les fonctions d'arbitre qui, par la note de l'envoyé extraordinaire et ministre plénipotentiaire de France, et par celle du ministre résident d'Espagne, à notre ministre des affaires étrangères, respectivement en date du 28 mars et du 27 février 1851, nous ont été conférées en vertu d'une déclaration signée entre ces puissances à Madrid, le 15 février 1851, dans le différend qui s'est élevé entre elles au sujet des navires la *Veloz Mariana*, la *Victoria* et la *Vigie*, saisis de part ou d'autre le 22 février 1823, le 15 juillet de la même année et le 12 janvier 1824;

Animé du désir sincère de répondre, par une décision scrupuleuse et impartiale, à la confiance que les hautes parties intéressées nous ont témoignée et de leur donner un nouveau gage du haut prix que nous y attachons;

---

[1] DE CLERCQ. *Ibid.* Tome VI, p. 81.

Ayant, à cet effet, dûment examiné et mûrement pesé, de concert avec notre conseil des ministres, la convention conclue entre la France et l'Espagne, le 5 janvier 1824, ainsi que les mémoires avec leurs annexes que l'envoyé extraordinaire et ministre plénipotentiaire de France et le ministre résident d'Espagne ont communiqués à notre ministre des affaires étrangères, respectivement sous les dates du 25 juillet et du 21 juin 1851;

Voulant satisfaire aux obligations que nous avons contractées par l'acceptation des fonctions d'arbitre dans le susdit différend, en portant à la connaissance des hautes parties intéressées le résultat de notre examen et de notre opinion sur chacune des trois questions posées dans l'acte signé entre elles, le 15 février 1851, savoir :

1° Si la prise et la vente de la *Veloz Mariana* ont été, ou non, légitimes, et si ce navire est, ou non, compris dans l'article 1er de la convention du 5 janvier 1824;

2° Si le navire la *Victoria* doit, ou non, être compris parmi les prises qui font l'objet de l'article 1er de la convention de 1824.

Le navire ayant été restitué, la question ne s'applique qu'à la cargaison;

3° Et si l'Espagne doit, ou non, considérer comme des affaires analogues, au point de vue de la convention de 1824, les affaires de la *Veloz Mariana* et de la *Vigie*, et si elle est, ou non, fondée dans son refus de payer l'indemnité qu'elle reconnaît devoir aux propriétaires de ce dernier navire, jusqu'à ce que la France ait consenti à acquitter, par compensation ou de toute autre manière, l'indemnité relative à la *Veloz Mariana*.

Quant à la première question, il est de fait que le bâtiment espagnol la *Veloz Mariana*, parti le 24 décembre 1822, du port de Vera Cruz en destination de Cadix, fut poursuivi par le vaisseau de ligne français le *Jean Bart*, se rendant en croisière dans les mers des Antilles pour y protéger le commerce français;

Que le commandant du *Jean Bart* donna pour raison de cette prise qu'il y aurait eu provocation et intention hostile de la part du capitaine espagnol qui, dans les ténèbres, avait fait tirer un coup de canon sur le navire qui lui donnait la chasse sans avoir montré son pavillon;

Que la *Veloz Mariana* fut d'abord conduite à la Martinique, puis à Brest;

Qu'amené dans ce dernier port à l'époque où la guerre était commencée, le navire fut mis en séquestre, et vendu ensuite par ordre des autorités françaises, malgré les protestations des propriétaires et les réclamations du gouvernement espagnol.

Et considérant :

Qu'il est avéré par l'histoire et non contesté

par les hautes parties intéressées, que le commencement de la guerre de 1823, ou de l'intervention armée en Espagne, ne saurait être porté à une date antérieure au 8 avril de cette année, époque à laquelle la Bidassoa fut franchie par l'armée française et que, dès lors, la *Velos Mariana*, saisie le 22 février précédent, n'a pas été capturée pendant cette guerre;

Que l'expression : « bâtiments capturés pendant le cours de l'année précédente (las presas hechas en el ano de 1823) » dont les hautes parties se sont servies dans le préambule de la convention du 5 janvier 1824, eu égard à l'intention manifeste des parties contractantes, et conformément au droit des gens, ne peut être interprétée que dans le sens qu'elle concerne les captures faites pendant la guerre de 1823, dont ladite convention était appelée en partie à régler les conséquences;

Que la saisie d'un bâtiment, avant l'époque où la guerre a éclaté, ne saurait être considérée comme prise maritime de guerre;

Que les motifs qui portèrent le commandant du *Jean Bart* à s'emparer de la *Velos Mariana*, fondés ou non, ne sauraient, en aucun cas, donner à cette arrestation le caractère d'une prise de guerre, ni avoir d'autres suites légales que d'engager la responsabilité personnelle du capitaine de la *Velos Mariana* et de donner lieu à une enquête judiciaire;

Que la mise en séquestre de la *Velos Mariana* dans le port de Brest, à une époque où la guerre était commencée, ne saurait non plus équivaloir, d'après le droit des gens, à une prise maritime.

Nous sommes d'avis que la prise et la vente de la *Velos Mariana* ne sauraient être considérées comme prise et vente légitimes, et que ce navire n'est pas compris dans l'article 1er de la convention du 5 janvier 1824.

Quant à la seconde question, il est de fait :

Que le 15 juillet 1823, la frégate espagnole la *Victoria*, venant de Manille, a été arrêtée en vue de Cadix par l'escadre française, conduite dans le port de San Lucar de Barrameda en Andalousie, alors occupé par les troupes françaises, et mise en séquestre;

Que pendant ce séquestre, une partie de la cargaison du navire a été employée au service de l'armée et de la flotte françaises;

Qu'après la signature de la convention du 5 janvier 1824, le gouvernement espagnol a réclamé en faveur des propriétaires la restitution de la *Victoria* restée en séquestre;

Que le gouvernement français, sans reconnaître le droit qu'alléguait le gouvernement espagnol à l'appui de sa demande, a néanmoins consenti à restituer ce bâtiment, dont le gouvernement espagnol déclarait vouloir se servir pour faire porter des dépêches aux Iles Philippines;

Qu'après la restitution de la *Victoria* et de la partie intacte de sa cargaison, le gouvernement espagnol, à l'appui de sa demande, s'appuyant sur le texte précis de l'article 1er de la convention du 5 janvier 1824, a réclamé un dédommagement pour la partie de la cargaison enlevée durant le séquestre;

Que le gouvernement français a refusé de satisfaire à cette réclamation. soutenant que la prise de la *Victoria* tombait sous l'application de l'article 1er de ladite convention, que, dès lors, aucun dédommagement n'était dû et que nul droit ne pouvait être inféré de la restitution volontaire du bâtiment et de la partie intacte de la cargaison;

Et considérant :

Que par l'article 1er de la convention du 5 janvier 1824, il a été stipulé que les prises réciproquement faites et conduites dans les ports de la puissance qui a fait ces prises, demeurent acquises à chacun des deux gouvernements;

Que la validité de la prise de la *Victoria* n'ayant pas été contestée, il suffit d'examiner si cette prise a été conduite dans un port de la *puissance qui l'a faite*;

Que pour déterminer le sens de cette stipulation d'après la commune intention des hautes parties contractantes, il est indispensable de prendre en considération les circonstances exceptionnelles auxquelles se rapporte la convention du 5 janvier 1824;

Que par cette convention, conclue entre l'ambassadeur de Sa Majesté très chrétienne et le ministre d'Etat de Sa Majesté catholique, les hautes parties contractantes avaient en vue de régler, par rapport aux prises maritimes, les conséquences d'une guerre qui avait existé entre la France et le gouvernement de Sa Majesté catholique, d'une part, et les Espagnols indépendants, d'autre part;

Qu'il résulte de ce fait, constaté par l'histoire, que la question, si le port de San Lucar de Barrameda était un port de la puissance par laquelle la *Victoria* était prise, ne peut être envisagée exclusivement sous le point de vue de la nationalité, mais doit être décidée d'après la situation respective des parties, alors belligérantes, dont l'une (les Espagnols indépendants) fut représentée dans la convention du 5 janvier 1824 par le gouvernement de Sa Majesté catholique, comme son successeur de fait, et l'autre par le gouvernement français, qui venait de combattre, conjointement avec Sa Majesté catholique, lesdits indépendants;

Qu'il est avéré et de notoriété publique que le port de San Lucar de Barrameda, au moment où la *Victoria* y fut conduite, était non seulement soumis à l'autorité du gouvernement de Sa Majesté catholique, alliée à la France, mais aussi sous le pouvoir immédiat de l'armée française, d'où il résulte que la prise de la *Victoria* tombe, d'après la commune intention des hautes parties contractantes, sous l'application de l'article 1ᵉʳ de la convention du 5 janvier 1824 ;

Que cette interprétation, conforme aux principes du droit des gens, qui, sous le rapport des prises de guerre, déclare commune la cause des puissances alliées, n'est point invalidée par la restitution de la *Victoria* et de la partie intacte de la cargaison, un acquiescement tacite à une prétention contestée ne pouvant être inféré de ce fait isolé :

Nous sommes d'avis que le navire la *Victoria* doit être compris parmi les prises qui font l'objet de l'article 1ᵉʳ de la convention du 5 janvier 1824.

Quant à la troisième question, il est de fait :

Que la frégate française la *Vigie* a été capturée, le 12 janvier 1824, sur les côtes du Pérou, par un corsaire espagnol, et conduite au port de San Carlos de Chiloé ;

Qu'une instruction judiciaire ayant été entamée sur la validité de cette prise, elle fut immédiatement déclarée nulle par jugement du tribunal d'Arequipa du 7 juillet 1824 ;

Que ce jugement a été reconnu, par le gouvernement espagnol, comme passé en force de chose jugée ;

Que l'intendance d'Arequipa ordonna en conséquence la restitution du navire et de sa cargaison ;

Que cette ordonnance n'a pu être mise à exécution, parce que les autorités coloniales avaient disposé du chargement pour les besoins publics de la colonie et avaient armé en course le navire, tombé depuis au pouvoir des Péruviens indépendants ;

Et considérant :

Que la capture de la *Vigie*, faite trois mois après la fin de la guerre, était nulle aux termes de l'article 5 de la convention du 5 janvier 1824 ;

Qu'elle a été déclarée non valable par un tribunal compétent, qui a ordonné sa restitution complète et immédiate et que le gouvernement espagnol a reconnu la validité et la force obligatoire de ce jugement ;

Que, dès lors, la créance des propriétaires de la *Vigie* est liquide et non contestée par le gouvernement espagnol et qu'ainsi nulle raison péremptoire n'existe, pour faire dépendre la restitution de ce navire et de sa cargaison, ou le dédommagement de sa perte, de la solution du différend relatif à la *Velos Mariana* :

Nous sommes d'avis que l'Espagne ne peut considérer comme des affaires analogues, au point de vue de la convention de 1824, les affaires de la *Velos Mariana* et de la *Vigie*, et qu'elle n'est pas fondée dans son refus de payer l'indemnité qu'elle reconnaît devoir aux propriétaires de ce dernier navire, jusqu'à ce que la France ait consenti à acquitter, par compensation ou de toute autre manière, l'indemnité relative à la *Velos Mariana*.

Fait et donné en double expédition, sous notre sceau royal, à La Haye, ce 13ᵉ jour du mois d'avril de l'an de grâce 1852 [1].

Le règlement du différend donna lieu à une nouvelle convention dont la teneur n'exige aucun commentaire.

Convention conclue à Paris, le 15 février 1862, entre la France et l'Espagne, relativement aux séquestres et prises maritimes opérés pendant les années 1823 et 1824.

ART. I. Le Gouvernement espagnol renonce par la présente Convention à toutes les sommes qui pouvaient lui être dues pour des navires français capturés ou séquestrés en 1823 ou pour leurs cargaisons, aux termes de l'art. 2 de la Convention du 5 janvier 1824.

Le Gouvernement français renonce, de son côté, à toutes les sommes qui pouvaient lui être dues pour des navires espagnols capturés ou séquestrés en 1823, ou pour leurs cargaisons, aux termes de l'article 4 de la même Convention.

ART. II. Le Gouvernement espagnol se substitue au Gouvernement français, en ce qui concerne l'obligation qu'imposait à ce dernier la décision arbitrale rendue par Sa Majesté le Roi des Pays-Bas, à la date du 13 avril 1852, relativement au navire espagnol la *Veloz Mariana*, et s'engage conséquemment à désintéresser les armateurs et créanciers de ce navire, aussitôt que la liquidation à faire, à ce sujet, aura été arrêtée.

ART. III. Le Gouvernement français mettra entre les mains du Gouvernement espagnol, le jour de l'échange des ratifications de la présente Convention, tous les documents qu'il possède relativement à la capture et à la vente du navire la *Velos Mariana*, afin que le Gouvernement espagnol puisse procéder, en pleine connaissance de cause, à l'évaluation dudit bâtiment et de sa cargaison. Cette liquidation se fera conformément à la législation espagnole.

ART. IV. Le Gouvernement espagnol s'engage à payer aux propriétaires des navires français capturés par suite des événements de 1823, dont les réclamations sont aujourd'hui pendantes, le montant des indemnités qui seraient reconnues leur être légitimement dues.

---

[1] DE CLERCQ. *Ibid.* Tome VI, p. 170.

ART. V. Afin d'assurer l'exécution du précédent article, la commission mixte établie à Paris, en vertu de la déclaration du 15 février 1851, ou toute autre commission qui serait instituée à cet effet, sera chargée d'examiner la valeur des réclamations indiquées dans ledit article. Si les membres de la commission se trouvent d'accord, les résolutions qu'ils adopteront seront exécutoires. Dans le cas où ils ne pourraient parvenir à s'entendre, les deux gouvernements nommeront un arbitre qui statuera définitivement, sa décision devant être exécutoire.

ART. VI. Toutes les dispositions de la Convention du 5 janvier 1824, contraires à la teneur de la présente Convention, sont et demeurent abrogées.

ART. VII. La présente Convention sera ratifiée .... [1]

IX. Etats-Unis d'Amérique, Portugal
26 février 1851

En 1814, des troupes anglaises avaient provoqué la destruction, dans le port de Fayal, d'un navire américain, le *General Armstrong*. Des réclamations furent de ce chef adressées au Gouvernement portugais, sur le territoire neutre duquel les faits avaient eu lieu : elles aboutirent, lors de la conclusion d'une convention relative à d'autres réclamations non contestées, à l'introduction dans ce traité des clauses d'arbitrage suivantes :

Convention entre les Etats-Unis d'Amérique et le Portugal relative au payement de certaines indemnités au profit de citoyens américains, signée à Washington, le 26 février 1851.

. . . .

ART. II. The high contracting parties, not being able to come to an agreement upon the question of public law involved in the case of the American privateer brig *General Armstrong*, destroyed by British vessels in the waters of the island of Fayal, in September 1814. Her Most Faithful Majesty has proposed, and the United States of America have consented, that the claim presented by the American Government, in behalf of the captain, officers, and crew of the said privateer, should be submitted to the arbitrament of a sovereign, potentate, or chief of some nation in amity with both the high contracting parties.

ART. III. So soon as the consent of the sovereign, potentate or chief of some friendly nation, who shall be chosen by the two high contracting parties, shall have been obtained to act as arbiter in the aforesaid case of the pri-

vateer brig *General Armstrong*, copies of all correspondence which has passed in reference to said claim between the two Governments and their respective representatives shall be laid before the arbiter, to whose decision the two high contracting parties hereby bind themselves to submit.

. . . . [1]

Ce fut Louis Napoléon, alors Président de la République française, qui consentit, à la demande des hautes parties intéressées, à siéger comme arbitre, et qui rendit la sentence que nous reproduisons ici.

Sentence arbitrale du Président de la République française, en date du 30 novembre 1852, sur les réclamations pendantes entre le Portugal et les Etats-Unis au sujet du corsaire Général Armstrong.

Nous, Louis Napoléon, Président de la République française; le Gouvernement de Sa Majesté la Reine de Portugal et des Algarves, et celui des Etats-Unis, nous ayant, aux termes d'une Convention, signée à Washington le 26 février 1851, demandé de prononcer, comme arbitre, sur une réclamation relative au corsaire américain le *Général Armstrong*, détruit dans le port de Fayal, le 26 septembre 1814;

Après nous être fait rendre un compte exact et circonstancié des faits qui ont causé le différend, et après avoir mûrement examiné les documents, dûment paraphés au nom des deux parties, qui ont été mis sous nos yeux par les représentants de l'une et de l'autre puissance;

Considérant qu'il est constant, en fait, que les Etats-Unis étant en guerre avec S. M. Britannique, et S. M. T. F. conservant la neutralité, le 26 septembre 1814 le brig américain le *Général Armstrong*, commandé par le capitaine Reid, légalement pourvu de lettres de marque et armé en course, étant sorti du port de New-York, jeta l'ancre dans le port de Fayal, l'une des îles Açores, faisant partie des Etats de S. M. T. F.;

Qu'il est également constant que, le soir du même jour, une escadre anglaise, commandée par le commodore Lloyd, entra dans le même port; qu'il n'est pas moins certain que, durant la nuit suivante, sans respect pour les droits de souveraineté et de neutralité de S. M. T. F., une collision sanglante éclata entre les Américains et les Anglais, et que le lendemain, 27 septembre, un des vaisseaux de l'escadre anglaise vint se placer auprès du corsaire américain pour le canonner; que cette démonstration, accompagnée d'effet, détermina le capitaine Reid, suivi de son équipage, à abandonner son navire et à le détruire;

[1] DE CLERCQ. *Recueil des traités de France.* Tome VIII, p. 390.

[1] *Treaties and Conventions between the United States and other Powers, 1776 à 1887*, p. 896.

Considérant que s'il paraît constant que dans la nuit du 26 septembre des chaloupes anglaises commandées par le lieutenant Robert Faunet, de la marine britannique, s'approchèrent du brig américain le *Général Armstrong*, il ne l'est pas que les hommes qui les montaient fussent pourvus d'armes et de munitions;

Qu'il résulte, en effet, des documents produits, que ces chaloupes s'étant approchées du brig américain, l'équipage de ce brig, après les avoir hêlées et sommées de s'éloigner, fit feu incontinent et que des hommes furent tués sur les chaloupes anglaises, et d'autres blessés, dont quelques-uns mortellement, sans que l'équipage de ces chaloupes ait tenté de repousser immédiatement la force par la force;

Considérant que le rapport du gouverneur de Fayal établit que le capitaine américain ne recourut à la protection du Gouvernement portugais qu'après que le sang avait déjà coulé, et lorsque, le feu ayant cessé, le brig le *Général Armstrong* vint se mettre à l'ancre sous le château, à la distance d'un jet de pierre; que ce gouverneur affirme n'avoir été informé qu'alors de ce qui se passait dans le port;

Qu'il est intervenu à plusieurs reprises auprès du commodore Lloyd pour obtenir la cessation des hostilités et se plaindre de la violation du territoire neutre; qu'il s'est efficacement opposé à ce que des matelots américains, qui étaient à terre, s'embarquassent dans le brig américain pour prolonger une lutte contraire aux lois des nations;

Que la faiblesse de la garnison de l'île et le délabrement constant de l'artillerie qui garnissait les forts, rendaient impossible de sa part toute intervention armée;

Considérant, en cet état des choses, que le capitaine Reid n'ayant pas recouru dès le principe à l'intervention du souverain neutre, et ayant employé la voie des armes pour repousser une injuste agression dont il prétendait être l'objet, a ainsi méconnu la neutralité du territoire du souverain étranger et dégagé ce souverain de l'obligation où il se trouvait de lui assurer protection par toute autre voie que celle d'une intervention pacifique:

D'où il suit que le Gouvernement de S. M. T. F. ne saurait être responsable des résultats d'une collision qui a eu lieu, au mépris de ses droits de souveraineté, en violation de la neutralité de son territoire et sans que les lieutenants ou officiers locaux eussent été requis en temps utile et mis en demeure d'accorder aide et protection à qui de droit;

Pourquoi nous avons décidé et nous déclarons que la réclamation formée par le Gouvernement des Etats-Unis contre S. M. T. F. n'est pas fondée et qu'aucune indemnité n'est due par le Portugal à l'occasion de la perte du brig américain armé en course le *Général Armstrong*.

Fait et signé en double expédition sous le sceau de l'Etat, au Palais des Tuileries, le 30 du mois de novembre de l'an de grâce 1852 [1].

X. Etats-Unis d'Amérique, Grande-Bretagne

8 février 1853

Ainsi qu'il résulte du texte que nous reproduisons plus loin, il s'est agi dans l'espèce de régler d'une manière définitive les réclamations réciproques des associations, corporations ou compagnies, et des individus, soumises à leurs gouvernements respectifs depuis le 24 décembre 1814, date du traité de Gand.

Convention entre les Etats-Unis d'Amérique et la Grande-Bretagne, relative à certaines réclamations, signée à Londres, le 8 février 1853.

Whereas claims have, at various times since the signature of the Treaty of Peace and Friendship between the United States of America and Great Britain, concluded at Ghent on the 24th of December, 1814, been made upon the Government of the United States on the part of corporations, companies, and private individuals, subjects of her Britannic Majesty, and upon the Government of her Britannic Majesty on the part of corporations, companies, and private individuals, citizens of the United States; and whereas some of such claims are still pending, and remain unsettled, the President of the United States of America, and her Majesty the Queen of the United Kingdom of Great Britain and Ireland, being of opinion that a speedy and equitable settlement of all such claims will contribute much to the maintenance of the friendly feelings which subsist between the two countries, have resolved to make arrangements for that purpose by means of a Convention, and have named as their Plenipotentiaries to confer and agree thereupon — that is to say —

The President of the United States of America, Joseph Reed Ingersoll, Envoy Extraordinary and Minister Plenipotentiary of the United States to her Britannic Majesty;

And her Majesty the Queen of the United Kingdom of Great Britain and Ireland, the Rhight Honorable John Russell (commonly called Lord John Russell), a member of her Britannic Majesty's Most Honorable Privy Council, a member of Parliament, and her Britannic Majesty's Principal Secretary of State for Foreign Affairs;

Who, after having communicated to each other

---

[1] DE CLERCQ. *Recueil des traités de France.* Tome VI, p. 237.

their respective full powers, found in good and due form, have agreed as follows:

ART. I. The High Contracting Parties agree that all claims on the part of corporations, companies, or private individuals, citizens of the United States,. upon the Government of her Britannic Majesty, and all claims on the part of corporations, companies, or private individuals, subjects of her Britannic Majesty, upon the government of the United States, which may have been presented to either government for its interposition with the other since the signature of the Treaty of Peace and Friendship, concluded between the United States of America, and Great Britain at Ghent, on the 24th of December, 1814, and which yet remain unsettled, as well as any other such claims, which may be presented within the time specified in article III, hereinafter, shall be referred to two commissioners, to be appointed in the following manner — that is to say: One commissioner shall be named by the President of the United States, and one by her Britannic Majesty. In case of the death, absence, or incapacity of either commissioner, or in the event of either commissioner omitting or ceasing to act as such, the President of the United States, or her Britannic Majesty, respectively, shall forthwith name another person to act as commissioner in the place or stead of the commissioner originally named.

The commissioners, so named, shall meet at London at the earliest convenient period after they shall have been respectively named; and shall, before proceeding to any business, make and subscribe a solemn declaration that they will impartially and carefully examine and decide, to the best of their judgement, and according to justice and equity, without fear, favor, or affection to their own country, upon all such claims as shall be laid before them on the part of the Governments of the United States and of her Britannic Majesty, respectively; and such declaration shall be entered on the record of their proceedings.

The commissioners shall then, and before proceeding to any other business, name some third person to act as an arbitrator or umpire in any case or cases on which they may themselves differ in opinion. If they should not be able to agree upon the name of such third person, they shall each name a person; and in each and every case in which the commissioners may differ in opinion as to the decision which they ought to give, it shall be determined by lot which of the two persons so named shall be the arbitrator or umpire in that particular case. The person or persons so to be chosen to be arbitrator or umpire, shall, before proceeding to act as such in

any case, make and subscribe a solemn declaration in a form similar to that which shall already have been made and subscribed by the commissioners, which shall be entered on the record of their proceedings. In the event of the death, absence, or incapacity of such person or persons, or of his or their omitting, or declining, or ceasing to act as such arbitrator or umpire, another and different person shall be named as aforesaid to act as such arbitrator or umpire in the place and stead of the person so originally named as aforesaid, and shall make and subscribe such declaration as aforesaid.

ART. II. The commissioners shall then forthwith conjointly proceed to the investigation of the claims which shall be presented to their notice. They shall investigate and decide upon such claims, in such order, and in such manner, as they may conjointly think proper, but upon such evidence or information only as shall be furnished by or on behalf of their respective governments. They shall be bound to receive and peruse all written documents or statements which may be presented to them by or on behalf of their respective governments, in support of, or in answer to, any claim; and to hear, if required, one person on each side, on behalf of each government, as counsel or agent for such government, on each and every separate claim. Should they fail to agree in opinion upon any individual claim, they shall call to their assistance the arbitrator or umpire whom they may have agreed to name, or who may be determined by lot, as the case may be; and such arbitrator or umpire, after having examined the evidence adduced for and against the claim, and after having heard, if required, one person on each side as aforesaid, and consulted with the commissioners, shall decide thereupon finally, and without appeal. The decision of the commissioners, and of the arbitrator or umpire, shall be given upon each claim in writing, and shall be signed by them respectively. It shall be competent for each government to name one person to attend the commissioners as agent on its behalf, to present and support claims on its behalf, and to answer claims made upon it, and to represent it generally in all matters connected with the investigation and decision thereof.

The President of the United States of America, and her Majesty the Queen of the United Kingdom of Great Britain and Ireland, hereby solemnly and sincerely engage to consider the decision of the commissioners conjointly, or of the arbitrator or umpire, as the case may be, as absolutely final and conclusive upon each claim decided upon by them or him respectively, and to give full effect to such decisions without any objection, evasion, or delay whatsoever.

It is agreed that no claim arising out of any transaction of a date prior to the 24ᵗʰ of December, 1814, shall be admissible under this Convention.

ART. III. Every claim shall be presented to the commissioners within six months from the day of their first meeting, unless in any case where reasons for delay shall be established to the satisfaction of the commissioners, or of the arbitrator or umpire, in the event of the commissioners differing in opinion thereupon; and then, and in any such case, the period for presenting the claim may be extended to any time not exceeding three months longer.

The commissioners shall be bound to examine and decide upon every claim within one year from the day of their first meeting. It shall be competent for the commissioners conjointly, or for the arbitrator or umpire, if they differ, to decide in each case whether any claim has or has not been duly made, preferred, and laid before them, either wholly, or to any and what extent, according to the true intent and meaning of this Convention.

ART. IV. All sums of money which may be awarded by the commissioners, or by the arbitrator or umpire, on account of any claim, shall be paid by the one government to the other, as the case may be, within twelve months after the date of the decision, without interest, and without any deduction, save as specified in article VI. hereinafter.

ART. V. The High Contracting Parties engage to consider the result of the proceedings of this commission as a full, perfect, and final settlement of every claim upon either government arising out of any transaction of a date prior to the exchange of the ratifications of the present Convention; and further engage that every such claim, whether or not the same may have been presented to the notice of, made, preferred, or laid before the said commission, shall, from and after the conclusion of the proceedings of the said commission, be considered and treated as finally settled, barred, and thenceforth inadmissible.

ART. VI. The commissioners, and the arbitrator or umpire, shall keep an accurate record, and correct minutes or notes of all their proceedings, with the dates thereof, and shall appoint and employ a clerk, or other persons, to assist them in the transaction of the business which may come before them.

Each government shall pay to its commissioner an amount of salary not exceeding three thousand dollars, or six hundred and twenty pounds sterling, a year, which amount shall be the same for both governments.

The amount of salary to be paid tho the arbitrator (or arbitrators, as the case may bet shall be determined by mutual consent at the close of the commission.

The salary of the clerk shall not exceed the sum of fifteen hundred dollars, or three hundred and ten pounds sterling, a year.

The whole expenses of the commission, including contingent expenses, shall be defrayed by a ratable deduction on the amount of the sums awarded by the commission; provided always that such deduction shall not exceed the rate of five per cent, on the sums so awarded.

The deficiency, if any, shall be defrayed in moieties by the two governments.

ART. VII. The present Convention shall be ratified by the President of the United States, by and with the advice and consent of the Senate thereof, and by her Britannic Majesty; and the ratifications shall be exchanged at London as soon as may be within twelve months from the date hereof.

In witness whereof, the respective Plenipotentiaries have signed the same, and have affixed thereto the seals of their arms.

Done at London, the eighth day of February, in the year of our Lord one thousand eight hundred and fifty three [1].

La prolongation des pouvoirs de la commission arbitrale, instituée par le précédent traité, fut convenue par un traité subséquent du 17 juillet 1854 [2].

Cet arbitrage qui portait principalement sur le fait, par les autorités anglaises, d'avoir laissé s'échapper les esclaves révoltés d'un navire américain, donna lieu au surarbitrage d'un jurisconsulte londonien, M. Bates: ce dernier donna raison aux réclamants américains et conclut à la restitution des esclaves ou au paiement d'une indemnité. La décision prononcée par lui n'a pas été publiée jusqu'à ce jour.

XI. Etats-Unis d'Amérique, Nouvelle Grenade
10 septembre 1857

Dans cette affaire, il s'est agi de réclamations faites par des citoyens américains à la charge du gouvernement de la Nouvelle Grenade, à raison principalement des dom-

[1] CHARLES SAMWER. *Nouveau recueil général de traités.* Tome XVI, partie I, p. 491 à 496.
[2] *Treaties and Conventions between the United States and other Powers, 1776 to 1887*, p. 445 et 453.

mages causés lors d'un soulèvement à Panama. Les ratifications du traité d'arbitrage ne furent échangées que le 5 novembre 1860.

Convention entre les Etats-Unis d'Amérique et la République de la Nouvelle Grenade, relative à certaines réclamations, signée à Washington, le 10 septembre 1857.

ART. I. All claims on the part of corporations, companies or individual citizens of the United States, upon the government of New Granada, which shall have been presented prior to the first day of September 1859, either to the Department of State at Washington, or to the minister of the United States at Bogota, and especially those for damages which were caused by the riot at Panama on the fifteenth of April 1856, for which the said government of New Granada acknowledges its liability, arising out of its privilege and obligation to preserve peace and good order along the transit route, shall be referred to a Board of commissioners, consisting of two members, one of whom shall be appointed by the government of the United States and one by the government of New Granada. In case of the death, absence or incapacity of either commissioner, or in the event of either commissioner omitting or ceasing to act, the government of the United States, or that of New Granada, respectively, or the minister of the latter in the United States, acting by its direction, shall forthwith proceed to fill the vacancy thus occasioned. The commissioners so-named shall meet in the city of Washington within ninety days from the exchange of the ratifications of this convention, and, before proceeding to business, shall make and subscribe a solemn oath that they will carefully examine and impartially decide, according to justice and equity, upon all the claims laid before them, under the provisions of this convention, by the government of the United States. And such oath shall be entered on the record of their proceedings. The commissioners shall then proceed to name an arbitrator or umpire to decide upon any case or cases on which they may differ in opinion. And if they cannot agree in the selection, the umpire shall be appointed by the minister of Prussia to the United States whom the two high contracting parties shall invite to make such appointment, and whose selection shall be conclusive on both parties.

ART. II. The arbitrator being appointed, the commissioners shall proceed to examine and determine the claims which may be presented to them, under the provision of this convention, by the government of the United States, together with the evidence submitted in support of them, and shall hear, if required, one person in behalf of each government on every separate claim. Each government shall furnish, upon request of either of the commissioners, such papers in its possession as the commissioners may deem important to the just determination of any claims presented to them. In cases where they agree to award an indemnity, they shall determine the amount to be paid, having due regard, in claims which have grown out of the riot of Panama of April 15, 1856, to damages suffered through death, wounds, robberies or destruction of property. In cases where they cannot agree, the subjects of difference shall be referred to the umpire, before whom each of the commissioners may be heard, and whose decision shall be final.

ART. III. The commissioners shall issue certificates of the sums to be paid by virtue of their awards to the claimants, and the aggregate amount of said sums shall be paid to the government of the United States, at Washington, in equal semi-annual payments, the first payment to be made six months from the termination of the commission, and the wole payment to be completed within eight years from the same date; and each of said sums shall bear interest (also payable semi-annually) at the rate of six per cent. per annum from the day on which the awards, respectively, shall have been decreed. To meet these payments, the government of New Granada hereby specially appropriates one half of the compensation which may accrue to it from the Panama Railroad Company, in lieu of postages, by virtue of the thirtieth article of the contract between the Republic of New Granada and said Company, made April 15, 1850, and approved June 4, 1850, and also one half of the dividends which it may receive from the net profits of said road, as provided in the fifty fifth article of the same contract; but if these funds should prove insufficient to make the payments as above stipulated, New Granada will provide other means for that purpose.

ART. IV. The commission herein provided shall terminate its labors in nine months from and including the day of its organization: shall keep an accurate record of its proceedings, and may appoint a secretary to assist in the transaction of its business.

ART. V. The proceedings of this commission shall be final and conclusive with respect to all the claims before it, and its awards shall be a full discharge to New Granada of all claims of citizens of the United States against that Republic which may have accrued prior to the signature of this convention.

ART. VI. Each government shall pay its own commissioner, but the umpire, as well as the incidental expenses of the commission, shall be paid, one half by the United States, and the other half by New Granada [1].

---

[1] *Treaties and Conventions between the United States and other Powers, 1776 to 1887*, p. 210 et 213.

Les Etats-Unis de Colombie conclurent le 10 février 1864 avec les Etats-Unis d'Amérique un traité qui prolongea les pouvoirs des commissaires. Quant à leurs décisions, aucun recueil ne les a publiées.

XII. Chili, Etats-Unis d'Amérique

10 novembre 1858

Cette contestation, connue sous le nom de l'affaire du Macedonian, ne présente aucune particularité spéciale. L'objet du différend est indiqué, d'une manière fort nette, par les documents reproduits par nous.

Convention entre les Etats-Unis d'Amérique et la République du Chili relative à la constitution d'un arbitrage au sujet de certaines réclamations, signée à Santiago le 10 novembre 1858.

The government of the United States of America and the government of the Republic of Chile, desiring to settle amicably the claim made by the former upon the latter for certain citizens of the United States of America, who claim to be the rightful owners of the silver in coin and in bars forcibly taken from the possession of Captain Eliphalet Smith, a citizen of the United States of America, in the valley of Sitana, in the territory of the former Vice Royalty of Peru, in the year 1821, by order of Lord Cochrane, at the time Vice Admiral of the Chilean Squadron, — have agreed, the former to name John Bigler, Envoy Extraordinary and Minister Plenipotentiary of the United States of America, and the latter Don Géronimo Urmeneta, Minister of State in the Department of the Interior and of Foreign Relations, in the name and in behalf of their respective governments, to examine said claim and to agree upon terms of arrangement just and honorable to both governments.

The aforesaid plenipotentiaries, after having exchanged their full powers, and found them in due and good form, sincerely desiring to preserve intact and strengthen the friendly relations which happily exist between their respective governments, and to remove all cause of difference, which might weaken or change them, have agreed, in the name of the government which each represents, to submit to the arbitration of his Majesty the King of Belgium, the pending question between them, respecting the legality or illegality of the above referred to capture of silver in coin and in bars, made on the ninth day of May, 1821, by order of Lord Cochrane, Vice Admiral of the Chilean squadron, in the valley of Sitana, in the territory of the former Vice Royalty of Peru, the proceeds of sales of merchandise imported into that country in the brig Macedonian, belonging to the merchant marine of the United States of America.

Therefore the above-named ministers agree to name his Majesty the King of Belgium as arbiter, to decide with full powers and proceedings ex aequo et bono, on the following points:

First. Is, or is not, the claim which the government of the United States of America makes upon that of Chile, on account of the capture of silver mentioned in the preamble of this convention, just in whole or in part?

Second. If it be just in whole or in part, what amount is the government of Chile to allow and pay to the government of the United States of America, as indemnity for the capture?

Third. Is the government of Chile, in addition to the capital, to allow interest thereon; and, if so, at what rate and from what date is interest to be paid?

The contracting parties further agree that his Majesty the King of Belgium shall decide the foregoing questions upon the correspondence which has passed between the representatives of the two governments at Washington and at Santiago, and the documents and other proofs produced during the controversy on the subject of this capture, and upon a memorial or argument thereon to be presented by each.

Each party to furnish the arbiter with a copy of the correspondence and documents above referred to, or so much thereof as it desires to present, as well as with its said memorial, within one year at furthest from the date at which they may respectively be notified of the acceptance of the arbiter.

Each party to furnish the other with a list of the papers to be presented by it to the arbiter, three months in advance of such presentation.

And if either party fail to present a copy of such papers, or its memorial, to the arbiter, within the year aforesaid, the arbiter may make his decision upon what shall have been submitted to him within that time.

The contracting parties further agree that the exception of prescription, raised in the course of the controversy, and which has been a subject of discussion between their respective governments, shall not be considered by the arbiter in his decision, since they agree to withdraw it and exclude it from the present question.

Each of the governments represented by the contracting parties is authorized to ask and obtain the acceptance of the arbiter; and both promise and bind themselves in the most solemn manner to acquiesce in and comply with his decision, nor at any time thereafter to raise any question directly or indirectly connected with the subject-matter of this arbitration.

This convention to be ratified by the governments of the respective contracting parties, and the ratifications to be exchanged within twelve months from this date, or sooner, if possible, in the city of Santiago.

In testimony whereof, the contracting parties have signed and sealed this agreement in duplicate; in the English and Spanish languages, in Santiago, the tenth day of the month of November, in the year of our Lord one thousand eight hundred and fifty-eight [1].

Le Roi des Belges, Léopold Ier, rendit sous la date du 15 mai 1863 la sentence suivante :

Nous Léopold, Roi des Belges,

Ayant accepté les fonctions d'arbitre qui Nous ont été conférées par une convention signée à Santiago le 10 novembre 1858, entre le Chili et les Etats-Unis, dans le différend qui s'est élevé entre ces Etats au sujet de la saisie d'une somme d'argent opérée le 9 mai 1821 par ordre de Lord Cochrane, vice-amiral de l'escadre chilienne, dans la vallée de Sitana, sur le territoire de l'ancienne vice-royauté du Pérou, laquelle somme provenait de la vente de marchandises importées par le brick « Macedonian » ;

Animé du désir sincère de répondre par une décision scrupuleuse et impartiale à la confiance que les Hautes Parties contractantes Nous ont témoignée ;

Ayant, à cet effet, dûment examiné et mûrement pesé la susdite convention, ainsi que les mémoires avec leurs annexes que l'*Envoyé extraordinaire et Ministre plénipotentiaire du Chili et le Ministre Résident des Etats-Unis* à Bruxelles ont communiqués à Notre Ministre des affaires étrangères, sous la date du 7 juillet 1861 ;

Voulant, pour remplir le mandat que Nous avons accepté, porter à la connaissance des Hautes Parties contractantes le résultat de Notre examen et Notre opinion sur chacune des trois questions soumises à Notre arbitrage, savoir :

1° La réclamation faite par le gouvernement des Etats-Unis d'Amérique à celui du Chili, au sujet de la saisie de l'argent mentionnée dans le préambule de la convention, est-elle fondée en tout ou en partie ?

2° Si elle est fondée en tout ou en partie, quelle somme le gouvernement du Chili doit-il payer à celui des Etats-Unis pour l'indemniser de cette saisie ?

3° Le gouvernement du Chili, outre le capital, doit-il l'intérêt et, dans l'affirmative, depuis quelle date et à quel taux l'intérêt doit-il être payé ?

Quant à la première question :

Il est de fait que la saisie a eu lieu le 9 mai 1821 dans la vallée de Sitana, à plusieurs lieues des côtes, dans l'intérieur des terres ;

Considérant que, d'après les principes du droit des gens, la propriété privée n'est pas saisissable sur terre, qu'elle appartienne à un neutre ou à un ennemi ;

Considérant toutefois que le gouvernement des Etats-Unis n'a pu réclamer qu'au nom des intérêts représentés par ses nationaux ;

Nous sommes d'avis que la réclamation faite par le gouvernement des Etats-Unis d'Amérique à celui du Chili est fondée en ce qui concerne la partie des valeurs saisies appartenant à des citoyens des Etats-Unis.

Quant à la seconde question :

Il est de fait que la somme saisie s'élevait à 70,400 piastres ou dollars ;

Considérant que cette somme provenait d'une opération entreprise en commun et dont la liquidation devait se faire sur les bases fixées dans le contrat intervenu entre les parties, le 25 novembre 1819 ;

Considérant que, d'après ce contrat, le produit de l'opération devait se répartir de la manière suivante :

3/5 pour Arizmendi, du chef de son permis d'importation et des 50,000 piastres qu'il apportait en capital,

1/5 pour Smith, du chef du navire,

1/5 pour les prêteurs, du chef de leurs avances.

Considérant que les prêteurs étaient des citoyens des Etats-Unis, à l'exception d'un marchand chinois de Canton dont Smith était mandataire ;

Nous sommes d'avis que le gouvernement du Chili doit restituer à celui des Etats-Unis les 3/5 des 70,400 piastres ou dollars saisis, soit 42,240 piastres ou dollars, dont 14,080 pour le cinquième de Smith et 28,160 pour les deux cinquièmes des prêteurs.

Quant à la troisième question :

Il est de fait que les ayants-droit ont été privés depuis le 9 mai 1821 des intérêts de la somme saisie ;

Considérant que la saisie n'étant pas fondée, la restitution du capital saisi doit entraîner celle des intérêts ;

Considérant, toutefois, que jusqu'au 19 mars 1841, le gouvernement des Etats-Unis n'a rien fait pour hâter une solution ;

Considérant, en outre, qu'à partir du 26 décembre 1848, les Hautes Parties contractantes étaient d'accord en principe, sur la nécessité d'un arbitrage ;

Considérant, enfin, que le taux légal de l'intérêt dans l'Etat du Massachusetts, auquel appartenaient le capitaine Smith et les réclamants, est de 6 %,

[1] CH. SAMWER. *Nouveau recueil général des traités.* Tome XVII, première partie, p. 243. — *Treaties and Conventions between the United States and other Powers,* 1776 to 1887, p. 142.

Nous sommes d'avis que, outre le capital de 42,240 piastres ou dollars, le gouvernement du Chili doit payer à celui des Etats-Unis les intérêts de cette somme au taux de 6% par an, depuis le 19 mars 1841 jusqu'au 26 décembre 1848.

Fait et donné en double expédition sous Notre sceau Royal au Château de Laeken, le quinzième jour du mois de mai 1863 [1].

XIII. Etats-Unis d'Amérique, Paraguay

4 février 1859

L'arbitrage portait, dans la présente affaire, sur des indemnités réclamées par une société de navigation américaine, établie au Paraguay, pour des dommages soufferts pendant un conflit entre les deux pays en cause. Voici comment cet arbitrage fut constitué.

Convention spéciale entre les Etats-Unis d'Amérique et la République de Paraguay relative aux réclamations élevées par la Compagnie de navigation des Etats-Unis et du Paraguay contre le gouvernement paraguayen, signée à Assomption le 4 février 1859.

His Excellency the President of the United States of America and his Excellency the President of the Republic of Paraguay, desiring to remove every cause that might interfere with the good understanding and harmony, for a time so unhappily interrupted, between the two nations, and now so happily restored, and which it is so much for their interest to maintain; and desiring for this purpose to come to a definite understanding, equally just and honorable to both nations, as to the mode of settling a pending question of the said claims of the "United States and Paraguay Navigation Company" — a company composed of citizens of the United States — against the government of Paraguay, have agreed to refer the same to a special and respectable commission, to be organized and regulated by the convention hereby established between the two high contracting parties; and for this purpose they have appointed and conferred full powers, respectively, to wit:

His Excellency the President of the United States of America upon James B. Bowlin, a special commissioner of the said United States of America, specifically charged and empowered for this purpose; and his Excellency the President of the Republic of Paraguay upon Señor Nicolas Vasquez, Secretary of State and Minister of Foreign Affairs of the said Republic of Paraguay; who, after exchanging their full powers, which were found in good and proper form, agreed upon the following articles:

---

[1] Cette sentence, qui n'a été publiée jusqu'à ce jour dans aucun recueil, nous a été gracieusement communiquée par le Ministère des Affaires Etrangères de Belgique.

ART. I. The government of the Republic of Paraguay binds itself for the responsibility in favor of the "United States and Paraguay Navigation Company", which may result from the decree of commissioners, who, it is agreed, shall be appointed as follows.

ART. II. The two high contracting parties, appreciating the difficulty of agreeing upon the amount of the reclamations to which the said company may be entitled, and being convinced that a commission is the only equitable and honorable method by which the two countries can arrive at a perfect understanding thereof, hereby covenant to adjust them accordingly by a loyal commission. To determine the amount of said reclamations, it is, therefore, agreed to constitute such a commission, whose decision shall be binding, in the following manner:

The government of the United States of America shall appoint one commissioner, and the government of Paraguay shall appoint another; and the two, in case of disagreement, shall appoint a third, said appointment to devolve upon a person of loyalty and impartiality, with the condition that, in case of difference between the commissioners in the choice of an umpire, the diplomatic representatives of Russia and Prussia, accredited to the government of the United States of America, at the city of Washington, may select such umpire.

The two commissioners named in the said manner shall meet in the city of Washington, to investigate, adjust, and determine the amount of the claims of the above-mentioned company, upon sufficient proofs of the charges and defences of the contending parties.

ART. III. The said commissioners, before entering upon their duties, shall take an oath before some judge of the United States of America that they will fairly and impartially investigate the said claims, and a just decision thereupon render, to the best of their judgment and ability.

ART. IV. The said commissioners shall assemble, within one year after the ratification of the "treaty of friendship, commerce, and navigation" this day celebrated at the city of Assumption between the two high contracting parties, at the city of Washington in the United States of America, and shall continue in session for a period not exceeding three months, within which, if they come to an agreement, their decision shall be proclaimed; and in case of disagreement, they shall proceed to the appointment of an umpire as already agreed.

ART. V. The government of Paraguay hereby binds itself to pay to the government of the United States of America, in the city of Assumption, Paraguay, thirty days after presentation to the government of the republic, the draft which that of the United States of America shall issue for the amount for which the two commissioners concurring, or by the umpire, shall declare it responsible to the said company.

ART. VI. Each of the high contracting parties shall compensate the commissioner it may appoint the sum of money he may stipulate for his services, either by instalments or at the expiration of his task. In case of the appointment of an umpire, the amount of his remuneration shall be equally borne by both contracting parties.

ART. VII. The present Convention shall be ratified within fifteen months, or earlier if possible, by the government of the United States of America and by the President of the Republic of Paraguay within twelve days from this date. The exchange of ratifications shall take place in the city of Washington.

In faith of which, and in virtue of our full powers, we have signed the present Convention in English and Spanish, and have thereunto set our respective seals.

Done at Assumption, this fourth day of February, in the year of our Lord one thousand eight hundred and fifty-nine, being the eighty-third year of the independence of the United States of America, and the forty-seventh of that of Paraguay [1].

La décision qui intervint n'a pas été publiée. Il se serait présenté cette circonstance curieuse que le commissaire américain aurait reconnu que son gouvernement n'était nullement fondé à réclamer n'importe quelle somme au Paraguay [2].

XIV. Costa Rica, Etats-Unis d'Amérique

2 juillet 1860

Cette affaire fort simple donna lieu à un arbitrage dont l'acte constitutif est suffisamment explicite par lui-même. La décision qui intervint n'a pas été publiée.

Convention relative à des réclamations présentées par des citoyens des Etats-Unis d'Amérique, signée à San José le 2 juillet 1860.

ART. I. It is agreed that all claims of citizens of the United States, upon the government of Costa Rica, arising from injuries to their persons,

---

[1] CH. SAMWER, *Nouveau recueil général des traités.* Tome XVII, première partie, p. 255. — *Treaties and Conventions between the United States and other Powers*, 1776 to 1887, p. 828.

[2] W. B. LAWRENCE. Note pour servir à l'histoire des arbitrages internationaux. *Rev. de droit int. et de lég. comp.*, 1874, p. 127.

or damages to their property, under any form whatsoever, through the action of authorities of the Republic of Costa Rica, statements of which, soliciting the interposition of the government of the United States, have been presented to the Department of State at Washington, or to the diplomatic agents of said United States at San José, of Costa Rica, up to the date of the signature of this convention, shall, together with the documents in proof, on which they may be founded, be referred to a Board of commissioners, consisting of two members, who shall be appointed in the following manner: one by the government of the United States of America, and one by the government of the Republic of Costa Rica: Provided however, that no claim of any citizen of the United States, who may be proved to have been a belligerent during the occupation of Nicaragua by the troops of Costa Rica, or the exercise of authority, by the latter, within the territory of the former, shall be considered as one proper for the action of the Board of commissioners herein provided for.

In case of the death, absence or incapacity of either commissioner or in the event of either commissioner's omitting or ceasing to act, the government of the United States of America, or that of the Republic of Costa Rica, respectively, or the minister of the latter, in the United States, acting by its direction, shall forthwith proceed to fill the vacancy thus occasioned.

ART. II. The commissioners so named shall meet at the city of Washington, within ninety days from the exchange of the ratifications of this convention; and, before proceeding to business, thay shall, each of them, exhibit a solemn oath, made and subscribed before a competent authority, that they will carefully examine into, and impartially decide, according to the principles of justice and of equity, and to the stipulations of treaty, upon all the claims laid before them, under the provisions of this convention, by the government of the United States, and in accordance with such evidence as shall be submitted to them on the part of said United States and of the Republic of Costa Rica, respectively. And their oath, to such effect, shall be entered upon the record of their proceedings.

Said commissioners shall then proceed to name an arbitrator, or umpire, to decide upon any case or cases concerning which they may disagree, or upon any point or points of difference which may arise in the course of their proceedings. And if they cannot agree in the selection, the arbitrator or umpire shall be appointed by the minister of His Majesty the King of the Belgium, to the United States, whom the two high contracting parties shall invite to make such appointments, and whose selection shall be conclusive on both parties.

ART. III. The arbitrator or umpire, being appointed, the commissioners shall, without delay, proceed to examine and determine the claims which may be presented to them, under the provisions of this convention, by the government of the United States, as stated in the preceding article; and they shall hear, if required, one person in behalf of each government, on every separate claim.

Each government shall furnish, upon request of either of the commissioners, such papers in its possession as may be deemed important to the just determination of any claim of citizens of the United States, referred to the board, under the provisions of the first article.

In cases, whether touching injuries to the person, limb or life of any said citizens, or damages committed, as stipulated in the first article, against their property, in which the commissioners may agree to award an indemnity, they shall determine the amount to be paid. In cases in which said commissioners cannot agree, the points of difference shall be referred to the arbitrator, or umpire, before whom each of the commissioners may be heard, and his decision shall be final.

ART. IV. The commissioners shall issue certificates of the sums to be paid to the claimants, respectively, whether by virtue of the awards agreed to between themselves, or of those made by them, in pursuance of decisions of the arbitrator, or umpire, and the aggregate amount of said sums, decreed by the certificates of award made by the commissioners, in either manner above indicated, and of the sums also acerning from such certificates of award as the arbitrator, or umpire, may, under the authority hereinafter conferred by the seventh article, have made and issued, with the rate of interest stipulated in the present article, in favor of any claimant or claimants, shall be paid to the government of the United States, in the city of Washington, in equal semi-annual instalments. It is, however, hereby agreed, by the contracting parties, that the payment of the first instalment shall be made eight months from the termination of the labors of the commission; and, after such first payment, the second, and each succeeding one, shall be made semi-annually, counting from the date of the first payment; and the whole payment of such aggregate amount or amounts, shall be perfected within the term of ten years from the termination of said commission; and each of said sums shall bear interest (also payable semi-annually) at the rate of six per cent per annum, from the day on which the awards, respectively, will have been decreed.

To meet these payments, the government of the Republic of Costa Rica, hereby specially appropriates fifty per cent of the net proceeds of the revenues arrising from the customs of the said Republic; but if such appropriation should prove insufficient to make the payments as above stipulated, the government of said Republic binds itself to provide other means for that purpose.

ART. V. The commission herein provided shall terminate its labors in nine months from and including the day of its organization. They shall keep an accurate record of all their proceedings, and they may appoint a secretary, versed in the knowledge of the English and of the Spanish languages, to assist in the transaction of their business. And, for the conduct of such business, they are hereby authorized to make all necessary and lawful rules.

ART. VI. The proceedings of such commission shall be final and conclusive with respect to all the claims of citizens of the United States, which having accrued prior to the date of this convention, may be brought before it for adjustment; and the United States agree forever to release the government of the Republic of Costa Rica from any further accountability for claims which shall be rejected, either by the board of commissioners, or by the arbitrator or umpire aforesaid; or for such as, being allowed by either the Board or the umpire, the government of Costa Rica shall have provided for and satisfied in the manner agreed upon in the fourth article.

ART. VII. In the event, however, that upon the termination of the labors of said commission stipulated for in the fifth article of this convention, any case or cases should be pending before the umpire, and awaiting his decision, it is hereby understood and agreed by the two contracting parties that, though the board of commissioners may, by such limitation have terminated their action, said umpire is hereby authorized and empowered to proceed to make his decision or award in such case or cases pending as aforesaid; and, upon his certificate thereof. in each case, transmitted to each of the two governments, mentioning the amount of indemnity, if such shall have been allowed by him, together with the rate of interest specified by the fourth article, such decision or award shall be taken and held to be binding and conclusive. and it shall work the same effect as though it had been made by both the commissioners under their own agreement, or by them upon decision of the case or of the cases, respectively, pronored by the umpire of said board, during the period prescribed for its sessions: provided, however, that a decision on every case that may be pending at the termination of the labors of the board shall be given by the umpire within sixty days from their final adjournment; and that, at the expiration of the said sixty days, the authority and power hereby granted to said umpire shall cease.

Art. VIII. Each government shall pay its own commissioner; but the umpire, as well as the incidental expenses of the commission, including the defrayal of the services of a secretary, who may be appointed under the fifth article, shall be paid one half by the United States, and the other half by the Republic of Costa Rica.

Art. IX. The present convention shall be approved and ratified by the President of the United States of America, by and with the advice and consent of the Senate of the said States; and by the President of the Republic of Costa Rica, with the consent and approbation of the Supreme Legislative Power of said Republic; and the ratifications shall be exchanged in the city of Washington, within the space of eight months from the date of the signature hereof, or sooner if possible.

In faith whereof, and by virtue of our respective full powers, we, the undersigned, have signed the present convention, in duplicate, and have hereunto affixed our seals.

Done at the city of San José, on the second day of July, in the year one thousand eight hundred and sixty, and in the eighty-fourth year of the independance of the United States of America, and of the independance of Costa Rica the thirty-ninth [1].

XV. Equateur, Etats-Unis d'Amérique

25 novembre 1862

L'arbitrage ici relevé ne réclame aucune explication spéciale; les décisions prononcées n'ont point été publiées.

Convention relative à des réclamations présentées par des citoyens des deux pays à charge de leurs gouvernements respectifs, signée à Quito, le 25 novembre 1862.

The United States of America and the Republic of Ecuador, desiring to adjust the claims of citizens of said States against Ecuador, and of citizens of Ecuador against the United States, have, for that purpose, appointed and conferred full powers, respectively to wit:

The President of the United States on Frederick Hassaurek, Minister Resident of the United States in Ecuador, and the President of Ecuador

on Juan José Flores, General-in-chief of the armies of the Republic;

Who, after exchanging their full powers, which were found in good and proper form, have agreed on the following articles:

Art. I. All claims on the part of corporations, companies or individuals, citizens of the United States, upon the Government of Ecuador, or of corporations, companies or individuals, citizens of Ecuador, upon the Government of the United States, shall be referred to a Board of Commissioners consisting of two members, one of whom shall be appointed by the Government of the United States and one by the Government of Ecuador. In case of death, absence, resignation or incapacity of either Commissioner, or in the event of either Commissioner omitting or ceasing to act, the Government of the United States or that of Ecuador, respectively, or the Minister of the United States in Ecuador, in the name of his Government, shall forthwith proceed to fill the vacancy thus occasioned.

The Commissioners so named shall meet in the city of Guayaquil within ninety days from the exchange of the ratifications of this convention, and before proceeding to business shall make solemn oath that they will carefully examine and impartially decide according to justice, and in compliance with the provisions of this convention, all claims that shall be submitted to them; and such oath shall be entered on the record of their proceedings.

The Commissioners shall then proceed to name an Arbitrator or Umpire, to decide upon any case or cases concerning which they may disagree, or upon any point of difference which may arise in the course of their proceedings. And if they cannot agree in the selection, the Umpire shall be appointed by her Britannic Majesty's Chargé d'Affaires, or [excepting the Minister Resident of the United States] by any other diplomatic agent in Quito whom the two high contracting parties shall invite to make such appointment.

Art. II. The Arbitrator or Umpire being appointed, the Commissioners shall, without delay, proceed to examine the claims which may be presented to them by [either of the two Governments; and they shall hear, if required, one person in behalf of each Government on every separate claim. Each Government shall furnish, upon request of either Commissioner, such papers in its possession as may be deemed important to the just determination of any claim or claims.

In cases where they agree to award an indemnity, they shall determine the amount to be paid. In cases in which said Commissioners cannot agree, the points of difference shall be referred

[1] *Treaties and Conventions between the United States and other Powers*, 1776 to 1887, p. 227.

to the Umpire, before whom each of the Commissioners may be heard, and whose decision shall be final.

ART. III. The Commissioners shall issue certificates of the sums to be paid to the claimants, respectively, whether by virtue of the awards agreed to between themselves or of those made by the Umpire, and the aggregate amount of all sums decreed by the Commissioners, and of all sums accruing from awards made by the Umpire under the authority conferred by the fifth article, shall be paid to the Government to which the respective claimants belong. Payment of said sums shall be made in equal annual instalments, to be completed within nine years from the date of the termination of the labours of the Commission, the first payment to be made six months after the same date. To meet these payments both Governments pledge the revenues of their respective nations.

ART. IV. The Commission shall terminate its labours in twelve months from the date of its organization. They shall keep a record of their proceedings, and may appoint a Secretary versed in the knowledge of the English and Spanish languages.

ART. V. The proceedings of this Commission shall be final and conclusive with respect to all pending claims. Claims which shall not be presented to the Commission, within the twelve months it remains in existence, will be disregarded by both Governments, and considered invalid. In the event that, upon the termination of the labours of said Commission, any case or cases should be pending before the Umpire, and awaiting his decision, said Umpire is hereby authorized to make his decision or award in such case or cases, and his certificate thereof in each case, transmitted to each of the two Governments, shall be held to be binding and conclusive; *Provided, however*, that his decision shall be given within thirty days from the termination of the làbours of the Commission, at the expiration of which thirty days his power and authority shall cease.

ART. VI. Each Government shall pay its own Commissioner; but the Umpire, as well as the incidental expenses of the Commission, shall be paid one half by the United States and the other half by Ecuador.

ART. VII. The present convention shall be ratified and the ratifications exchanged in the city of Quito.

In faith whereof, we, the respective Plenipotentiaries, have signed this convention and hereunto affixed our seals, in the city of Guayaquil, this twenty-fifth day of November, in the year of our Lord one thousand eight hundred and sixty two [1].

XVI. Etats-Unis d'Amérique, Pérou.

20 décembre 1862.

Aucune sentence n'est intervenue dans cette affaire. Le Roi des Belges, Léopold Ier, désigné comme arbitre, déclina, en janvier 1864, la mission dont il avait été honoré : cette décision fut motivée parce que la question de fait et celle d'équité se compliquaient d'une question de droit, fort épineuse à décider de loin et sans une connaissance parfaite des législations locales.

Convention providing for the submission to arbitration of the claims of the owners of the Lizzie Thompson and Georgiana against Peru, concluded at Lima, December 20, 1862.

Whereas differences having arisen between the United States of America and the Republic of Peru, originating in the capture and confiscation by the latter of two ships belonging to citizens of the United States, called the *Lizzie Thompson* and *Georgiana;* and the two Governments not being able to come to an agreement upon the questions involved in the said capture and confiscation, and being equally animated with the desire to maintain the relations of harmony which have always existed, and which it is desirable to preserve and strengthen between the two Governments, have agreed to refer all the questions, both of law and fact, involved in the capture and confiscatior of said ships by the Government of Peru, to the decision of some friendly Power; and it being now expedient to proceed to and regulate the reference as above described, the United States of America and the Republic of Peru have for that purpose named their respective Plenipotentiaries, that is to say:

The President of the United States has appointed Christopher Robinson, their Envoy Extraordinary and Minister Plenipotentiary to Peru, and the President of Peru Dr José Gregorio Paz Soldan, Minister of State in the office of Foreign Relations and President of the Council of Ministers;

Who, after having exchanged their full powers, found to be in due and proper form, have agreed upon the following articles:

ART. I. The two contracting parties agree in naming as arbiter, umpire, and friendly arbitrator, His Majesty the King of Belgium, conferring upon

[1] *Treaties and Conventions between the United States and other Powers*, 1776 to 1887, p. 265.

6

him the most ample power to decide and determine all the questions, both of law and fact, involved in the proceedings of the Government of Peru in the capture and confiscation of the ships *Lizzie Thompson* and *Georgiana*.

ART. II. The two contracting parties will adopt the proper measures to solicit and obtain the assent of His Majesty the King of Belgium to act in the office hereby conferred upon him.

After His Majesty the King of Belgium shall have declared his assent to exercise the office of arbiter, the two contracting parties will submit through their diplomatic agents residing at Brussels, to His Majesty copies of all the correspondence, proofs, papers, and documents which have passed between the two Governments or their respective representatives; and should either party think proper to present to said arbiter any other papers, proofs, or documents in addition to those above mentioned, the same shals be communicated to the other party within four months after the ratification of this convention.

ART. III. Both parties being equally interested in having a decision upon the questions hereby submitted, they agree to deliver to the said arbiter all the documents referred to in the second article within six months after he shall have signified his consent to act as such.

ART. IV. The sentence or decision of said arbiter, when given, shall be final and conclusive upon all the questions hereby referred, and the contracting parties hereby agree to carry the same into immediate effect.

ART. V. This convention shall be ratified and the ratifications exchanged in the term of six months from the date hereof.

In faith whereof the Plenipotentiaries of the two Governments have signed and sealed, with their respective seall, the present convention.

Done in the city of Lima, in duplicate, on the twentieth day of December, in the year of our Lord one thousand eight hundred and sixty two [1].

XVII. Brésil, Grande-Bretagne.

5 janvier 1863.

Cet arbitrage ne fut précédé d'aucun traité : il fut organisé par un simple échange de notes, dont le texte n'a pas été publié. Cet échange aurait eu lieu à Rio de Janeiro, le 5 janvier 1863, entre le marquis d'Abrantès, pour le Brésil, et M. Christie pour la Grande-Bretagne. Lord Russell accepta l'arbitrage, au nom de

---

[1] *Treaties and Conventions between the United States and other Powers, 1776 to 1887*, p. 868.

cette dernière nation, par une lettre du 2 février 1863.

Sentence arbitrale du Roi des Belges dans le différend survenu entre la Grande-Bretagne et le Brésil au sujet de l'arrestation des officiers du bâtiment anglais La Forte, donnée à Laeken, le 18 juin 1863.

Nous Léopold, Roi des Belges, ayant accepté les fonctions d'arbitre qui nous ont été conférées de commun accord par la Grande-Bretagne et par le Brésil, dans le différend qui s'est élevé entre ces Etats au sujet de l'arrestation, le 17 juin 1862, par le poste de la police brésilienne situé à la Tijuca, de trois officiers de la marine britannique, et des incidents qui se sont produits à la suite et à l'occasion de cette arrestation ;

Animé du désir sincère de répondre par une décision scrupuleuse et impartiale à la confiance que les dits Etats nous ont témoignée ;

Ayant à cet effet dûment examiné et mûrement pesé tous les documents qui ont été produits de part et d'autre ;

Voulant, pour remplir le mandat que nous avons accepté, porter à la connaissance des hautes parties intéressées le résultat de notre examen, ainsi que notre décision arbitrale sur la question qui nous a été soumise dans les termes suivants, à savoir :

Si dans la manière dont les lois brésiliennes ont été appliquées aux officiers anglais il y a eu offense envers la marine britannique ;

Considérant qu'il n'est nullement démontré que l'origine du conflit soit le fait des agents brésiliens, qui ne pouvaient raisonnablement pas avoir de motifs de provocation ;

Considérant que les officiers lors de leur arrestation n'étaient pas revêtus des insignes de leur grade, et que dans un port fréquenté par tant d'étrangers ils ne pouvaient prétendre à être crus sur parole lorsqu'ils se déclaraient appartenir à la marine britannique, tandis qu'aucun indice apparent de cette qualité ne venait à l'appui de leur déclaration ; que, par conséquent, une fois arrêtés ils devaient se soumettre aux lois et règlements existants et ne pouvaient être admis à exiger un traitement différent de celui qui eût été appliqué dans les mêmes conditions à toutes autres personnes ;

Considérant que, s'il est impossible de méconnaître que les incidents qui se sont produits ont été des plus désagréables aux officiers anglais et que le traitement auquel ils ont été exposés a dû leur paraître fort dur, il est constant toutefois que, lorsque par la déclaration du vice-consul anglais la position sociale de ces officiers eut été dûment constatée, des mesures ont aussitôt été prises pour leur assurer des égards particuliers, et qu'ensuite leur mise en liberté pure et simple a été ordonnée ;

Considérant que le fonctionnaire qui les a fait relàcher a prescrit leur élargissement aussitôt que cela lui a été possible, et qu'en agissant ainsi, il a été mû par le désir d'épargner à ces officiers les conséquences fâcheuses qui aux termes des lois devaient forcément résulter pour eux d'une suite quelconque donnée à l'affaire;

Considérant que, dans son rapport du 6 juillet 1862, le préfet de police n'avait pas seulement à faire la narration des faits, mais qu'il devait rendre compte à l'autorité supérieure de sa conduite et des motifs qui l'avaient porté à user de ménagements;

Considérant qu'il était, dès lors, légitimement et sans qu'on puisse y voir aucune intention malveillante, autorisé à s'exprimer comme il l'a fait;

Nous sommes d'avis que, dans la manière dont les lois brésiliennes ont été appliquées aux officiers anglais, il n'y a eu ni préméditation d'offense, ni offense envers la marine britannique.

Fait et donné en double expédition, sous notre sceau royal, au château de Laeken, le dix-huitième jour du mois de Juin, 1863[1]. Léopold Ier.

XVIII. Etats-Unis d'Amérique, Pérou.

12 janvier 1863.

Cet arbitrage a été considéré, par plusieurs auteurs, comme une suite donnée à l'arbitrage du 20 décembre 1862, confié au Roi des Belges, Léopold Ier, mais décliné par lui à raison de difficultés matérielles et juridiques spéciales. Mais le fait que la décision prise par le Roi des Belges n'a été communiquée aux chancelleries intéressées qu'en janvier 1864, prouve qu'il s'agit bien dans l'espèce d'une contestation nouvelle. La sentence des arbitres n'a pas été publiée.

Convention for the settlement of claims made by the citizens of each country against the Government of the other, concluded at Lima, January 12, 1863.

The United States of America and the Republic of Peru, desiring to settle and adjust amicably the claims which have been made by the citizens of each country against the Government of the other, have agreed to make arrangements for that purpose by means of a convention, and have named as their Plenipotentiaries to confer and agree thereupon as follows:

The President of the United States, Christopher Robinson, Envoy Extraordinary and Minister Plenipotentiary of said States to Peru, and the President of Peru, Dr José Gregorio Paz Soldan, the Minister of Foreign Relations and President of the Council of Ministers;

Who, after having communicated to each other their respective full powers, found to be in due and proper form, have agreed as follows:

ART. I. All claims of citizens of the United States against the Government of Peru, and of citizens of Peru against the Government of the United States, which have not been embraced in conventional or diplomatic agreement between the two Governments or their Plenipotentiaries, and statements of which, soliciting the interposition of either Government, may, previously to the exchange of the ratifications of this convention, have been filed in the Department of State of Washington, or the Department of Foreign Affairs at Lima. shall be referred to a mixed commission composed of four members, appointed as follows: two by the Government of the United States, and two by the Government of Peru. In case of the death, absence, or incapacity of either Commissioner, or in the event of either Commissioner ceasing to act, the Government of the United States, or its Envoy Extraordinary and Minister Plenipotentiary in Peru, acting under its direction, or that of the Republic of Peru, shall forthwith proceed to fill the vacancy thus occasioned.

ART. II. The Commissioners so named shall immediately after their organisation, and before proceeding to any other business, proceed to name a fifth person to act as an arbitrator or umpire in any case or cases in which they may themselves differ in opinion.

ART. III. The Commissioners appointed as aforesaid shall meet in Lima within three months after the exchange of the ratifications of this convention, and each one of the Commissioners, before proceeding to any business, shall take an oath, made and subscribed before the most Excellent Supreme Court, that they will carefully examine and impartially decide, according to the principles of justice and equity, the principles of international law and treaty stipulations, upon all the claims laid before them under the provisions of this convention, and in accordance with the evidence submitted on the part of either Government. A similar oath shall be taken and subscribed by the person elected by the Commissioners as arbitrator or umpire, and said oaths shall be entered upon the record of the proceedings of said commission.

ART. IV. The arbitrator or umpire being appointed, the Commissioners shall without delay, proceed to examine and determine the claims specified in the first article, and shall hear, if

---

[1] CHARLES SAMWER et JULES HOPF (G. FR. DE MARTENS). *Nouveau recueil général de traités.* Tome XX, p. 486.

required, one person in behalf of each Government on each separate claim. Each government shall furnish at the request of either of the Commissioners, the papers in its possession which may be important to the just determination of any of the claims referred.

ART. V. From the decision of the Commissioners there shall be no appeal; and the agreement of three of them shall give full force and effect to their decisions, as well with respect to the justice of their claims as to the amount of indemnification that may be adjudged to the claimants; and in case the Commissioners cannot agree, the points of difference shall be referred to the arbitrator or umpire, before whom the Commissioners may be heard, and his decision shall be final.

ART. VI. The decision of the mixed Commission shall be executed without appeal by each of the contracting parties, and it shall be the duty of the Commissioners to report to the respective Governments the result of their proceedings; and if the decision of said Commissioners require the payment of indemnities to any of the claimants, the sums determined by the said Commissioners shall be paid by the Government against which they are awarded within one month after said Government shall have received the report of said Commissioners; and for any delay in the payment of the sum awarded after the expiration of said month, the sum of six per cent interest shall be paid during such time as said delay shall continue.

ART. VII. For the purpose of facilitating the labors of the mixed commission, each Government shall appoint a secretary to assist in the transaction of their business and to keep a record of their proceedings, and for the conduct of their business said Commissioners are authorised to make all necessary rules.

ART. VIII. The decisions of the Commission, or of the umpire in case of a difference between the Commissioners, shall be final and conclusive, and shall be carried into full effect by the two contracting parties. The Commission shall terminate its labours in six months from and including the day of its organization; provided, however, if at the time stipulated for the termination of said Commission any case or cases should be pending before the umpire and awaiting his decision, it is understood and agreed by the two contracting parties that said umpire is authorised to proceed and make his decision or award in such case or cases; and upon his report thereof to each of the two Governments, mentioning the amount of indemnity, if such shall have been allowed by him, such award shall be final and conclusive in the same manner as if it had been made by the Commissioners under their own agreement; provided that said decision shall be made by said umpire within thirty days after the final adjournment of said Commission, and at the expiration of the said thirty days the power and authority hereby granted to said umpire shall cease.

ART. IX. Each Government shall pay its own Commissioners and secretary, but the umpire shall be paid, one-half by the Government of the United States and one-half by the Republic of Peru.

ART. X. The present convention shall be ratified, and the ratifications thereof shall be exchanged in the term of four months from the date hereof.

In faith whereof, the respective Plenipotentiaries have signed the same and affixed their respective seals.

Done in the city of Lima this twelfth day of January, in the year of our Lord one thousand eight hundred and sixty-three [1].

XIX. Grande-Bretagne, Etats-Unis d'Amérique.

1er juillet 1863.

Cette affaire a eu pour objet l'évaluation des indemnités dues par le gouvernement des Etats-Unis d'Amérique à la compagnie de la Baie de Hudson et à la compagnie agricole de Puget, du chef de la reprise des territoires occupés par ces deux compagnies. Il leur fut accordé respectivement 450,000 et 200,000 dollars.

Convention entre les Etats-Unis de l'Amérique septentrionale et la Grande-Bretagne, concernant le règlement définitif des réclamations faites par les compagnies de Hudson et de Puget, signée à Washington le 1er juillet 1863.

The United States of America and Her Majesty the Queen of the United Kingdom of Great Britain and Ireland, being desirous to provide for the final settlement of the claims of the Hudson's Bay and Puget's Sound Agricultural Companies, specified in Articles III and IV of the treaty concluded between the United States of America and Great Britain on the 15th of June, 1846, have resolved to conclude a treaty for this purpose, and have named as their Plenipotentiaries that is to say:

The President of the United States of America, William H. Seward, Secretary of State; and Her

---

[1] *Treaties and Conventions between the United States and other Powers, 1776 to 1887*, p. 870.

Majesty the Queen of the United Kingdom of Great Britain and Ireland, the Right Honorable Richard Bickerton Pernell, Lord Lyons, a peer of her United Kingdom, a Knight Grand Cross of her most Honorable Order of the Bath and her Envoy Extraordinary and Minister Plenipotentiary to the United States of America;

Who, after having communicated to each other their respective full powers, found in good and due form, have agreed upon and conclued the following articles.

ART. I. Whereas by the III^d and IVth articles of the treaty concluded at Washington on the 15th day of June, 1846, between the United States of America and her Majesty the Queen of the United Kingdom of Great Britain and Ireland, it was stipulated and agreed that in the future appropriation of the territory south of the 49th parallel of north latitude, as provided in the first article of the said treaty, the possessory rights of the Hudson's Bay Company, and of all British subjects who may be already in the occupation of land or other property lawfully acquiered within the said territory should be respected, and that the farms, lands and other property of every description, belonging to the Puget's Sound Agricultural Company, on the north side of the Columbia River, should be confirmed to the said company, but that in case the situation of those farms and lands should be considered by the United States to be of public and political importance, and the United States Government should signify a desire to obtain possession of the whole or of any part thereof, the property so required should be transferred to the said Government at a proper valuation to be agreed upon between the parties;

And whereas it is desirable that all questions between the United States authorities on the one hand, and the Hudson's Bay and Puget's sound Agricultural Companies on the other, with respect to the possessory rights and claims of those companies, and of any other British subjects in Oregon and Washington Territory, should be settled by the transfer of those rights and claims to the Government of the United States for an adequate money consideration :

It is hereby agreed that the United States of America and her Britannic Majesty shall within twelve months after the exchange of the ratifications of the present treaty, appoint each a Commissioner for the purpose of examining and deciding upon all claims arising out for the provisions of the above quoted articles of the treaty of June 15, 1846.

ART. II. The Commissioners mentioned in the preceding article shall, at the earliest con-

venient period after they shall have been respectively named, meet at the city of Washington, in the District of Columbia, and shall, before proceeding to any business, make and subscribe a solemn declaration that they will impartially and carefully examine and decide, to the best of their judgment, and according to justice and equity, without fear, favor, or affection to their own country, all the matters referred to them for their decision, and such declaration shall be entered on the record of their proceedings.

The Commissioners shall then proceed to name an Arbitrator or Umpire to decide upon any case or cases on which they may differ in opinion; and if they cannot agree in the selection, the said Arbitrator or Umpire shall be appointed by the King of Italy, whom the two high contracting parties shall invite to make such appointment, and whose selection shall be conclusive on both parties. The person so to be chosen shall, before proceeding to act, make and subscribe a solemn declaration, in a form similar to which shall already have been made and subscribed by the Commissioners, which declaration shall also be entered on the record of the proceedings. In the event of the death, absence or incapacity of such person, or of his omitting or declinary or ceasing to act as such Arbitrator or Umpire, an other person shall be named, in the manner aforesaid, to act in his place or stead, and shall make and subscribe such declaration as aforesaid.

The United States of America and Her Britannic Majesty engage to consider the decision of the two Commissioners conjointly, or of the Arbitrator or Umpire, as the case may be, as final and conclusive on the matters to be referred to their decision, and forthwith to give full effect to the same.

ART. III. The Commissioners and the Arbitrator or Umpire shall keep accurate records and correct minutes or notes of all their proceedings, with the dates thereof, and shall appoint and employ such clerk or clerks or other persons as they shall find necessary to assist them in the transaction of the business which may come before them.

The salaries of the Commissioners and of the clerk or clerks shall be paid by their respective Governments. The salary of the Arbitrator or Umpire and the contingent expenses shall be defrayed in equal moieties by the two Governments.

ART. IV. All sums of money which may be awarded by the Commissioners or by the Arbitrator or Umpire, on account of any claim, shall be paid by the one Government to the other in two equal annual instalments, whereof the first shall be paid within twelve months after the date of the award, and the second within twenty-four months after the date of the award, without interest, and without any deduction whatever.

ART. V. The present treaty shall be ratified, and the mutual exchange of ratifications shall take place in Washington, in twelve months from the date hereof, or earlier if possible.

In faith whereof we, the respective Plenipotentiaries, have signed this tretay, and have hereunto affixed our seals.

Done in duplicate at Washington, the first day of July, anno Domini one thousand eight hundred and sixty-three [1].

Les ratifications de ce traité furent échangées le 3 mars 1864 et les commissaires devaient se réunir, aux termes dudit traité, dans les douze mois des ratifications. Ce ne fut pourtant que le 10 septembre 1869 que la décision arbitrale fut prononcée par eux, dans les termes concis et brefs qui suivent.

At a meeting of the Commissioners under the treaty of July 1st, 1863, between the United States of America and Her Britannic Majesty, for the final settlement of the claims of the Hudson's Bay and Puget's Sound Agricultural Companies, held at the city of Washington, on the 10th day of September 1869.

Present: Alexander S. Johnson, Commissioner on the part of the United States of America; John Rose, Commissioner on the part of Her Britannic Majesty.

The Commissioners having heard the allegations and proofs of the respective parties, and the arguments of their respective counsel. and duly considered the same, do determine and award that, as the adequate money consideration for the transfer to the United States of America of all the possessory right and claims of the Hudson's Bay Company, and of the Puget's Sound Agricultural Company, under the first article of the treaty of July 1st, 1863, and the third and fourth articles of the treaty of June 15th, 1846, commonly called the Oregon treaty, and in full satisfaction of all such rights and claims, there ought to be paid in gold coin by the United States of America, at the times and in the manner provided by the fourth article of the treaty of July 1st, 1863, on account of the possessory rights and claims of the Hudson's Bay Company, four hundred and fifty thousand dollars; and on account of the possessory rights and claims of the Puget's Sound Agricultural Company, the sum of two

hundred thousand dollars; and that at or before the time fixed for the first payment to be made in pursuance of the treaty and of this award, each of the said Companies do execute and deliver to the United States of America, a sufficient deed or transfer and release to the United States of America, substantially in the form hereunto annexed.

In testimony whereof we, the said Commissioners, have set our hands to this award in duplicate, on the day and year and at the place aforesaid [1].

XX. Grande-Bretagne, Pérou.

Juillet 1863.

La contestation relative à l'arrestation prétenduement illégale du capitaine Melville White souleva, à l'époque où elle éclata, une polémique ardente et vive, surtout de la part de la nation anglaise. L'arrestation survint le 23 mars 1861; le recours à l'arbitrage toutefois ne fut accepté qu'en juillet 1863, après avoir été proposé par le Pérou, le 27 janvier de cette année. Comme pour l'arbitrage entre la France et la Grande-Bretagne, du 14 novembre 1842, aucun compromis, sous forme de traité, ne fut signé par les hautes parties en cause: il ne fut échangé qu'une simple note verbale.

Note verbale entre la Grande-Bretagne et le Pérou, concernant le règlement des réclamations faites par la Grande-Bretagne à raison de l'arrestation du capitaine Melville White, signée à Londres en juillet 1863.

The Government of Her Britannic Majesty having been engaged in pressing on the Government of Peru the claim of Mr Melville White, a British subject, for a pecuniary compensation on account of sufferings and losses caused to him by the acts of Peruvian authorities, the two Governments have agreed that the question as to the right of Mr Melville White to compensation from the Peruvian Government, as well as the question as to the amount of that compensation, if any should be proved to be due to him, should be referred to the arbitration of a friendly power.

Earl Russel and Mr Sang have accordingly agreed on the following steps with a view to bring about a settlement of the matters in question.

1. Earl Russel, on behalf of Her Majesty's Governments, and Mr Sang, as representing the Government of Peru, will address an invitation

---

[1] *Treaties and Convention between the United States and other Powers*, 1776 to 1887, p. 467.

[1] *Treaties and Conventions between the United States and other Powers*, 1776 to 1887, p. 469.

to the Government of the Free Hanseatic City of Hamburgh, requesting the Senate to pronounce a decision on the points above stated.

2. Should the Senat undertake this responsibility, Earl Russel will cause a statement of what has passed between the two Governments in this matter, as well as Mr M. White's own statement of his case, to be laid before the Senate on the part of Her Majesty's Government.

Copies of these documents will likewise be communicated to Mr Sang to enable him to lay before the Senate such observations thereupon, or rejoinder thereto, as he may think necessary in the interest of his Government.

3. Mr Sang will cause to be laid before the Senate a statement of the case on behalf of the Peruvian Government, and he will communicate a copy of his document to Her Majesty's Government.

4. The decision of the Senate of Hamburgh, or of the arbitrator, whoever he may be, who may be accepted by the two Governments in case the Senate of Hamburgh should decline this responsibility, shall be considered by both parties as final, and immediate effect shall be given thereto.

London, July 1863 [1].

Le capitaine Melville White évalua sa demande à la somme de 59,740 livres sterling ou 1,493,500 francs. L'exagération de cette évaluation était évidente, car le gouvernement de la Grande-Bretagne, dans une lettre du 26 janvier 1863, n'avait exigé, en faveur du réclamant, qu'une indemnité de 4500 livres sterling ou 112,500 francs. Ce fait explique les considérants qui servent de début à la décision intervenue le 13 avril 1864. Cette décision est particulièrement intéressante par le soin avec lequel elle a été rédigée et les motifs détaillés qu'elle contient, contrairement à la plupart des décisions que nous avons reproduites jusqu'ici.

Décision de la commission, chargée, par le Sénat de la Ville libre hanséatique de Hambourg, de prononcer dans la cause du capitaine Thomas Melville White, datée de Hambourg du 13 avril 1864.

The demand of the British Government for an indemnification of 4500 l. in favour of Thomas Melville White from the Republic of Peru, now under consideration, is based on the following points:—

[1] *House of Commons.* Paper 482, 13 July 1864, p. 35.

1. The arrest and the long unjust imprisonment of White, founded on a serious but wholly groundless and unsupported accusation.

2. The suffering and annoyances to which he was subjected during his imprisonment.

3. The neglect of the rules and principles not only of Peruvian but of universal law, which was evinced by delaying the trial, and by the manner in which the preliminary proceedings were conducted.

4. His expulsion from the Peruvian dominions, as the result of these unjust proceedings.

As Captain Thomas Melville White has also communicated a statement drawn up by him as claimant, it is to be observed, in reference to that document, that it can only be taken into consideration as being specially referred to in the representations of the British Government.

It appears to be in general a passionate and partial account, with obvious misrepresentations and exagerations, and wherein candour is wanting; for this reason the British Government could not get a clear idea of its contents. The arbitrator has, therefore, only to keep to the official representations of the Government.

The four above-mentioned complaints will now be examined separately:—

1. With regard to the first complaint, the unjustifiable arrest and long imprisonment, it is first of all to be shown that White was arrested on the 23^d March 1861, and, as his own account of the matter has not been contradicted, he was released on the 9th January 1862. The arrest took place in consequence of a communication made by Romero to the Harbour-Captain at Arica, that he had reliable information that White was the delinquent who had attempted to murder the President of the Republic of Peru, Don Ramon Castilla. Now there can be no doubt that it became the imperative duty of all the authorities—in consequence of the universally known fact that the President Castilla had been wounded, on the evening of the 24th of July 1860, by a pistol-shot, fired by an unknown hand, and that the investigations to discover the author of this attempt had hitherto led to no definite result—to use all means in their power to prosecute inquiries with respect to such a suspected person, after the information given by an official of the Republic.

The crime in question was one of the most serious nature, and the arrest of the suspected person was the less to be avoided, as he was caught travelling and was well known to be without any fixed residence. It therefore remains to be ascertained whether the arrest of White was accomplished according to the precepts of the Peruvian laws applicable to the case.

Now, Art. 18, Tit. IV., of the *"Constitution Politica de Peru Reformada en 1860"* enacts that no person shall be arrested without a written order of the competent judge, or of the authorities whose duty it is to maintain public order, *"excepto in fragrante delito,"* and that in every case the arrested person shall be placed at the disposal of the proper tribunal within 24 hours. In the present case White was arrested at Callao on the 23d of March 1861, and on the same day, on the application of the Préfect Freyre, there came the order from the Minister Morales that he should be kept in custody, sent to Lima, and there placed at the disposal of the criminal judge.

By this the above legal requirement was the more undoubtedly satisfied, as at least a preliminary detention of the person caught on his journey must appear to be demanded at once; and if the Préfect Freyre, who apparently had the power of issuing the written order for the arrest, did not do so himself, but left the decision to the highest authority, it can only be looked upon as a proof of his caution and care in the performance of his duty.

The second part of the first point of complaint advanced on the part of the British Government contains the assertion that the imprisonment of White had taken place in an unjust manner, on a serious but unfounded and in no way supported accusation. As a further proof of this assertion, it is said, at page 4 of the statement drawn up in the name of the British Government, that White was, according to the judgment in First Instance, accused of being the instigator only of the crime of murder, and that no other accusation whatever was brought against him. This single accusation was, however, in the course of the proceedings, not only proved to be quite groundless, but that there was no evidence at all, nor a single fact, to give any apparent ground for it. But herein the British Government, irrespective of the correctness of the facts contained in its statement of the matter, proceeds on the erroneous supposition that the rules of criminal procedure in England are to be held good and applied in the criminal proceedings in Peru; but, little doubt as there can be that the rules of procedure to be observed by the courts in any country are to be judged solely and alone according to the legislation in force there, it is quite as certain that in the proceedings in White's case no fault can be found with the Peruvian courts of justice, or with the Peruvian Government, since they were fully justified according to the Peruvian procedure.

The difference between the English and the Peruvian mode of proceeding, which latter obtains also in other countries, consists in the diversity of the principle observed in the accusation and investigation. In Peru, when there are grounds for suspecting any person, an investigation takes place, during which all means are employed which may lead to the establishment of any crime whatever, without such investigation being limited to the particular crime of which the accused was originally suspected. It is only after the completion of the investigation, which embraces everything that can be elicited during the proceedings, that the Attorney General can proceed to the framing of the formal act of accusation, in which all the facts brought to light in the investigation are to be considered. Then only is the accused put upon his trial, and counsel appointed to defend him; up to this point he has only been the subject of inquisition: the whole of the proceedings, before the time of accusation, are withheld from the public. It is obvious, therefore, that the principles of proceeding on simple accusation, observed in England, cannot, in any way, find application in Peru, and therefore it is not consistent with justice, on the part of the British Government, to reject, as inadmissible, the statements of the Attorney General relating to the first accusation of Romero against White. This view is founded on the erroneous supposition that Romero is the accusing party, and therefore bound by his statements.

It is further, also, to be pointed out, that the assertion that Romero only accuses White of being the instigator of the attempt to murder is in nowise in accordance with the documents; for it was not the first preliminary information given to a subordinate authority, the harbour-captain at Arica (the only object of which was the arrest of White), but his depositions on oath before the judge, that would then have to be considered as the complaint. But herein also is found the accusation that White was associated with open enemies of the country, and implicated in a plot against the Government of Peru, and it was distinctly stated that he was an obstinate conspirator. Although the sworn statements of Romero and Douglas, which fully agreed with each other, were, in regard to White having himself attempted to murder the President Castilla, certainly only suppositions, yet such positive facts were elicited as proved beyond doubt the hostile feeling of White towards the Government, and led to the fear that he might commit acts which would endanger the peace of the country. It was thus the strict duty of the judge to continue the investigation, with all care and exactitude, as long as other disclosures might be expected therefrom; and so all persons who might be supposed to have relations with the person under inquisition, or to be acquainted with him and his doings, were examined, except that unfriendly relations with the Republic of Bolivia rendered the examination of persons residing there impossible.

It may here be observed that probably the testimony of Caro, who for this reason could not be examined, and to whom Douglas referred several times in his depositions, would have been of particular value; it was therefore impossible to avoid waiting, at least a reasonable time, for an answer to a request to the authorities of Bolivia, dated 12ᵗʰ July, concerning the examination of Caro.

A glance at the depositions of the accused himself, and of the witnesses examined, will suffice to prove that the charge of Romero was by no means unsupported.

The accused deposes that he is on friendly terms with General Echenique, and admits that he is without occupation, as he believes he will be able to obtain it at Guayaquil by the interest of his friend. He admits that he is totally without means, as he received pecuniary assistance from the British Chargé d'Affaires, which is confirmed by the latter himself.

The witness Douglas deposes to having heard the accused speak ill of the President Castilla, and wish for his fall; further, that the accused had been present at an assembly at Corocoro, in which a toast had been drunk to the fall of Castilla and the elevation of Echenique, and that it had been stated it would be sufficient for this end to get Castilla out of the way. Caro, a friend of the accused, had told him (the witness), "This man (White) will create a great sensation in Lima". Deponent has seen bills of exchange from Echenique in the hands of the accused, and knows that he has much intercourse with him.

Andrew Wilson deposes that the accused was thought to be a spy. Romero knows that he frequently travelled to visit Echenique, and that he was in connection with him and Linarez, whilst it could never be understood whence he derived the money for his journeys, as he was without occupation.

Calista Peralta suspects him of being connected with a political association hostile to the Government, from his mysterious manners and the frequency with which he tries to alter his appearance. Brain, Isabel, Dorra, Dauling, Worm, Williams, and others testify unanimously that the accused makes frequent journeys to the Republic of Bolivia and to Lima, without having any known business, and that he is in debt.

At the conclusion of the investigation, the accusation of the Attorney General now declares that White is proved to be an individual without means or occupation, in debt, and without any fixed residence, and at the same time a friend

of notorious enemies of the country; that he was strongly suspected of having attempted the murder of President Castilla, and of participating in plots against the Government; but, as such proofs as the law requires for the purpose of conviction were wanting, the Attorney General proposes that the accused be released from the Instance, but that he be banished from the Republic as a foreigner without occupation and means, and of proved bad conduct.

The sentence of the First Instance is fully in accordance with this proposition; the sentence passed in Second Instance by the *Corte Superior*, on the appeal in the name of the accused, annulled the previous sentence, and declared the accused quite free; finally, the sentence in Third Instance of the *Corte Suprema*—which, strange to say, has not been mentioned at all in the statement of the British Government—declares the sentence in Second Instance null and void, and certifies further that White has not only been accused for an attempt to murder, but also of participating in enterprises against the peace of the Republic, and frees him in this latter respect only from the Instance, with the orders that he be placed under the surveillance of the police.

Therefore, not only is the above-mentioned assertion, that the exclusive accusation against White was an attempt to murder, based upon error, but it is evident that the further assertion, namely, that it was proved in the course of the proceedings that this sole accusation was quite groundless, is in manifest contradiction to the documents, which can only be explained by the essential void in the statement of the British Government, occasioned by the omission of the sentence in Third Instance. But it is precisely on this final sentence that a proper understanding of the case depends, whilst all the conclusions drawn by the British Government, being based on the judgment in Second Instance, are valueless, as this sentence itself has been declared void. Moreover, the sentence in Third Instance, in so far as it frees White only from the Instance, is the more justified, as, besides that the accused had by no means fully cleared himself from the grounds of suspicion, the examination of all the witnesses could not take place, on account of the external obstacles which interposed, and it might well be expected that a future examination of the witnesses Caro, Jerr, Maldonado, Pearson, and Ruperto would throw further light on the suspicions against the accused that were not cleared up.

Therefore the first point of complaint is to be pronounced of no force; and now there is to be investigated how far, second, the sufferings and injuries to which the accused was subjected

7

during his imprisonment give just occasion for a complaint.

2. Here it is to be observed, first of all, that in general, when the question concerns complaints made by a person kept long in prison of such injuries as he has endured during his imprisonment, his own assertions are always to be examined with the greatest caution; and unconditional credence is the less to be given to them, as such complaints very frequently arise in cases where the imprisonment was well deserved, and in nowise too severe. Now, it appears incontrovertibly, from the documents, that White, being at the time of the arrest a foreigner, without occupation, income, or any fixed domicile, was by no means a personage who could lay claim to particular credibility for his statements, and especially not when the matter in question was a claim from which he, according to his own view, was to receive a good round sum of money. Numerous contradictions and demonstrable falsehoods which he put forward will be noticed hereafter in their proper places. To prove that the British Government, so far as it has sifted the matter, has always given by far too much weight to the assertions of White, it may suffice here to refer to that part of his statement (*vide* p. 22 ff.) which is described as an extract from the Investigation and Process Documents. It contains, in almost every line, the most evident and grossest misrepresentations of the truth, as, on the one side, everything implicating White is throughout passed over in the extract, whilst what is quoted is often either entirely falsified, or at least so disconnected that the result appears quite contradictory to the documents. For example may be quoted that, according to the statement of White, the sentence in First Instance reads, in its decisive part, word for word as follows:—

"Upon which grounds I ought to acquit, and do acquit, Thomas Melville White, as regards complicity in the crime of which he is accused, and generally from co-operating to upset public order; but he must be expelled," &c.

Whereas in the attested English translation, from the documents which he had before him, the sentence corresponding with the Spanish original is as follows:—"Upon which grounds I ought to acquit, and do acquit, *from this Instance*, Thomas Melville White, as regards," &c.

It is further said, page 30: "Page 139 (of the English translation) contains the sentence passed by the Supreme Court in claimant's case, the substance of which is as follows:—

"*We confirm* the sentence of the Superior Court, acquitting Melville White of the horrible charge of which he has been accused. He must remain under the vigilance of the police."

But it is stated, word for word, on page 139 of that attested English translation:—

"*They declared null* the sentence pronounced by the Most Illustrious Superior Court, in as far as regards that, in absolute manner, it absolves Thomas Melville White, and reforming it, absolved him from the Instance *(Instantia)* as to the rest of the charges that have weighed against him, and have been cited, and he ought to remain subject to the vigilance of the police."

And in the face of such wilful misrepresentations of the truth, Thomas Melville White maintains by declaration, in place of oath, before Major Rosi, on the 25th of September 1863, "that all the statements contained in the subjoined case, written and drawn up by me, are strictly in conformity with truth."

No weight whatever ought, therefore, to be attached to the assertions of a man so wanting in veracity.

On entering upon the second point of complaint, it is, in the first place, scarcely necessary to remark, that the arrest of White, as carried out, was fully justified, and was effected without any resort to force; for the harbour-captain, Benjamin Mariategni, reports that White submitted without resistance to the order for his arrest, and there is nothing that could support a contrary supposition.

The above-mentioned complaint may be thus specified in detail: that White was kept in custody for a long time *incommunicado*; that he had been kept, up to the 27th of August, confined in a dirty loathsome cell, without sufficient food, and, lastly, that he had been subjected to torture and ill-treatment. Now, with regard to the first point, it has not been asserted at all that, according to Peruvian law, the Examining Judge has no power to order the imprisonment of a person under examination debarring communication. It would be unjust to deny the judge such power on the general principles of law; it ought rather to be taken for granted that, when a person has been arrested on suspicion of a serious crime, the judge can often only secure the necessary disclosures by preventing all communication with the prisoner, and thus avoid the danger of collusion, by which the investigation might be prejudiced. Besides, according to the Report of Judge Ponce, White was only in custody *incommunicado* for two days (namely, on the 26th and 27th of March); and Judge Ponce, to prove that the isolation was by no means strict, justly states that even during this time the prisoner found means to elude the order, as, according to his own statement, he received a newspaper from a fellow-prisoner, and found means to have his written complaint printed in the Journal *Comercio* of the 26th of March.

It is, moreover, fully proved by the depositions of Bauda, Carillo, Milan, and Harzu, who were examined upon oath at the beginning of April, that White, at the beginning of the imprisonment, was not *incommunicado*, but received frequent visits from his countrymen, and had, moreover, the opportunity of repeating his complaints and threats before fellow-prisoners.

By the same witnesses it has been proved—and this also has been acknowledged by the British Government, but denied by White—that the sum allowed to political prisoners to procure comforts during their imprisonment (namely, one dollar per day) had been repeatedly offered to White, but was refused by him in an insolent manner. His statement, therefore, that he had for days together received no other food than damaged rice is the less credible, as Judge Ponce declares, in his report of the 29ᵗʰ of April 1861, that the food given to prisoners is, according to the legal regulations, tested by the judges every day, and that strict care is taken that it be good and wholesome. With regard to the locality in which the prisoner was, Judge Ponce declares that, so long as the isolation of the prisoner lasted, a place was assigned to him in the courtyard of the prison, which had formerly been the residence of the keeper *(castellan)*, and was airy and by far better than the locality assigned to political prisoners. Ponce further reports, on the 23ʳᵈ of October 1861, that during the whole of his imprisonment, up to that time, an abode had been assigned to him which freed him from contact with other prisoners, without preventing him from receiving the visits of his friends: in fact, he received frequent visits, amongst others from Colonel O'Gorman. The credibility of these official reports of Ponce does not appear to be at all shaken, for there is nothing whatever against them except the assertions of White, which have been partly refuted by the fullest proof, and which do not appear to be sustained by the slightest probability. The British Government has mentioned nothing that would do so, nor has it referred to the documents contained in his statement, which therefore do not require consideration. But it may be openly stated that the pretended declarations of Henry Cornell, produced in an unattested copy, cannot be attended to at all, since there is no warrant whatever for their genuineness; further, that the voluntary depositions of O'Gorman, on the 28ᵗʰ September 1863, cannot be allowed to have any force as proof, considering that, at that time, two years and a half had elapsed since White's arrest, that nothing was positively known either of the deponent himself or of his relations with White; but these depositions themselves are only calculated to lead to the conjecture that he was too intimately connected with the interests of White to be willing to give altogether the unbiassed truth. Now and then he is guilty of notoriously false statements; for instance, when he asserts:—

"That from the first moment of his incarceration, it was notorious in Lima (where the real perpetrator of the crime was well known), that Captain Thomas Melville White was entirely innocent; and the Government, in a few weeks after his arrest, had positive information, from their own official authorities, that he was, at the time of the attack made in Lima on General Castilla, a thousand miles from that city."

It can only be thought natural that the British Government has not even once appealed to such testimony as this.

An evident refutation of White's statements in regard to the condition of his prison must be found in this: that Mʳ Barton personally visited the prisoner, on the 23ʳᵈ of August 1861, as representative of Mʳ Jerningham, and on the following day wrote the letter before us in reference thereto to the Minister Melgar. He says not a word about having found the prison unfit, but merely requests to be informed whether it was likely that the investigation would soon terminate, as the prisoner complained that he was suffering from an affection of the liver in consequence of his long detention. When therefore, on the following day, a better prison was assigned to White, it only shows how anxious the Government and authorities of Peru were to anticipate the wishes on behalf of the prisoner.

The description of White's sufferings which precedes the above-mentioned letter of Mʳ Barton, who is supposed to have witnessed them, is in evident contradiction with the contents of this document, and appears to be only based on the false statements of White.

The occasion of that visit of Mʳ Barton was the complaints made by White of the tortures that he had suffered in the "barra", in which he had been shut up for a long time. But it is proved by the documents that White, on his examination on the 20ᵗʰ of August, demanded the reading of various documents, which, as is admitted at page 23 of the statement of the British Government, were drawn up in an unbecoming tone, and contained abuse of the Government and of judicial persons.

But it is again a misrepresentation when it is said that the judge on this occasion was not satisfied whit refusing to receive these documents, but ordered White to be put in irons; for he received this punishment for having answered Judge Ponce by personal threats, when cautioned with regard to these documents.

Such contempt of the dignity of the judge demanded punishment, and that inflicted on White does not appear to have been too severe, as, according to the official statement of Ponce, dated 7th of September, he was not shut up in the "barra" for more than 10 minutes.

After all this, there is not the slightest proof that White was treated during his arrest with undue severity; and his unsupported assertions with reference to his treatment have not even probility in their favour, considering his proved untrustworthiness, and in the face of the official reports of the judge and other authorities.

3. The third complaint of the British Government is, that in the present case the rules and principles of Peruvian law, and the universal sense of justice, have been neglected, as is demonstrated by the delay of the trial, and by the course and mode of proceedings which preceded it.

In the first place, with regard to the delay of the trial itself, it has been already stated that the mode of criminal procedure in Peru is a combination of proceedings on investigation and accusation, and that, in conformity therewith, the accusation can only be proceeded with after the preliminary investigation is fully completed.

Now by a decree of the Attorney General of the 8th of August, the penal proceedings were commenced, and the accused was informed of this decree on the same day; on the 11th it was ordered that Judge Carillo should take cognizance in First Instance after the penal accusation had been made, and he gave up the further instruction of the matter on the 14th to Juarez. On the 13th the Attorney General ordered the appointment of an interpreter, on the representation of the accused that he had to make some declarations in his cause. This interpreter was appointed on the 19th; on the 20th the final examination of the accused took place, and on the 23d of August came the public accusation on the part of the Attorney General. On the 26th of September the Advocate Pablo Mora, delivered his written defence; on the 30th Juarez ordered the examination on oath of the President Castilla for the completion of the documents. This examination took place, on the 18th of October. On the 8th of November Juarez ordered the production of an authenticated copy of the *"decreto de interdiction"*, which was obtained on the 10th, and on the 30th of November the sentence in First Instance was delivered. It is evident from this account that no delay had taken place from the delivery of the accusation to the 10th of November; and if the Judge in First Instance was reprimanded by the sentence of the Corte Superior for not having delivered his sentence sooner, this reprimand can only refer to a delay between the 10th and 30th of November, as he had not acted as judge at all in the investigation.

As the sentence in Second Instance was given on the 14th of December, and that of the Corte Suprema on the 23d of that month, it certainly appears that sentences in criminal cases are delivered in Peru with especial promptitude. But as the period of 20 days between the completion of the documents and the finding, in First Instance, cannot be considered a delay of importance, compensation on this ground in favour of the accused can be the less demanded as, according to the Peruvian law, a fine *(Ordnungsstrafe)* only can be imposed in cases of delay in official judicial proceedings. It is, moreover, to be questioned whether the reprimand of the judge by the Corte Superior ever came into operation, as the Corte Suprema has declared the sentence of that tribunal to be null.

It remains, therefore, to investigate how far the above-named third complaint of the British Government appears to be founded on the course of the proceedings during the preliminary examination.

This complaint may be divided, according to the contents of the statement before us, into the following points:—1. That a written order, by virtue of which White was arrested, was never shown or delivered to him; 2. That no document containing an accusation was produced during the investigation; 3. That an interpreter was denied to White, notwithstanding his request; 4. That no counsel was allowed him up to the conclusion of the investigation; 5. That force and intimidation were resorted to in the examinations during the investigation, and that the examinations were altogether of a very inquisitorial character; 6. That White was not confronted with any of the witnesses on whose evidence the accusation of the Attorney General was based; 7. That the investigation and, consequently, the opening of the trial had been delayed.

As regards the first point, it has already been stated that the written order of arrest above mentioned was issued by the Minister Morales, as prescribed by the law. The art. 18 of Tit. 4 of the *Constitucion Politica del Peru* ordains— "Los ejecutores de dicho mandamiento estan obligados á dar copia de el siempre que se les pidiere" (Those who execute this order are bound to give a copy of it whenever they are asked).

Now, it does not appear from the Investigation Documents that White himself ever asked for the communication of such a copy, whilst, according to the above legal provision, it was in that case only that it was usual to give the same; but there can be the less doubt that a copy would have been delivered to him on his asking for it, as from the documents it is evident that the whole of the important judicial decrees had been handed over to him whenever the rules of procedure permitted. A reference to the correspondence between Mr Jerningham and the Minister Melgar shows that the former requested to be informed, on the 17th of April, whether the arrest of White had been legally made on the written order of a competent authority. To this question a perfectly satisfactory answer may be found in the reports of Miguel Bagnero and Manuel Freyre of the 1st of May, communicated to Mr Jerningham. It is, however, certain that from the 20th of August, at any rate, White was aware of the wording of the order of arrest, although he had not asked any official for the production of the copy, as on that day the whole of the documents were read over to him.

Lastly, an irregularity on the part of the authorities against the prescription of Tit. IV., Art. 18, could only entail a fine, as the documents prove that the order of arrest had been made according to law, and that, consequently, no material right of the prisoner had been violated.

The fact of no document containing the accusation having been put before the accused requires no justification. In the preliminary investigation the communication of the accusations and grounds of suspicion takes place regularly and properly only when the investigating judge who has to prepare the accusation considers it necessary.

No less untenable is the complaint that no counsel was allowed to the accused during the investigations. That appears to be utterly inadmissible in preliminary investigation. At the opening of the judicial trial, counsel was granted to White, as the Peruvian law requires, and he conducted the defence with the utmost zeal. It is evident that the granting of counsel in preliminary investigations preceding a criminal trial cannot be claimed by Art. 7 of the Treaty of the 10th April 1850, which stipulates that in no case shall counsel be denied to British subjects any more than to natives, as at this stage counsel is not allowed to natives.

The complaint also that an interpreter was denied to the accused is proved to be unfounded. The report of Banda proves that the accused was asked, before the examination, whether he was acquainted with the Spanish language, and that he replied in the affirmative. White's knowledge of the language may also be inferred from his signing, without protest, the minutes of the examination and it is also proved by the testimony of Calista Peralta. The order, therefore, of the

Attorney General which denied this request as frivolous is fully justified.

The assertion of White that threats and intimidations were used, and that he had even been forced to sign a false document, appears to be a pure invention in the face of the documents and the official reports of Ponce, and the reports of Ponce of the 29th of April and 7th of December 1861.

That White was forced to sign any document is the more evidently untrue, as not only was there no reason whatever fot it, but also because he refused to sign nearly all the documents laid before him; nor was he ever asked to do so a second time, for it was quite immaterial to the course of the proceedings whether his signature was given or not.

Finally, just as little can there be any just complaint that the accused was not confronted with any of the witnesses examined, the order for such confrontation depending solely on the discretion of the investigating judge, and on his conscientious consideration whether it would be desirable for the purpose of ascertaining the true state of the case.

In the present case the Judge could not deem it desirable, as there were no contradictions to be cleared up, for which purpose such confrontations are usually ordered; for White says nothing at all against the evidence of the witnesses, but contented himself by declaring that such testimony did not affect him, and accusing the Peruvian Government of having bought it.

But, as it is stated on page 17 of the statement of the British Government, "It appears that the Judges, when they ascertained from his answers to their own interrogatories that he desired any particular witnesses to be examined on his own behalf, took similar means for procuring the testimony of these witnesses." It is only thereby acknowledged that the Judge did his duty according to the legally inquisitorial character of the preliminary investigation for a penal accusation.

It must be repeated, that the principles of law which obtain in England are not applicable here.

Now, as White was arrested on the 23d of March 1861, and the accusation of the Attorney General was not made until the 28th of August, it appears at first sight that the investigation lasted an unusually long time. But it was necessary, first of all, to examine a great number of witnesses, and at four places far distant from each other —namely, Lima, Arica, Tacna, and Iquiqui; and it appears from the documents that the time up to the 4th of July was fully occupied by that examination, and by the necessary official communications of the various courts with each other, as well as those of the acting judges with the higher authorities for the purpose of obtaining their decision; and there does not appear to be any grounds for charging the courts and authorities with laziness. On the 4th of July it was reported from Arica that the examination of the witnesses, Pedro, Caro, Jerr Thomas Pearson, and Manuel Ruperto could not be obtained, as they resided in the Republic of Bolivia. Then, as it could not well be left undone in the then state of the investigation, the necessary steps were taken to obtain their evidence there; but as no answer had, up to the 8th of August, been given by the Ministry of the Republic of Bolivia to the written request made for that purpose, the Attorney General, in order to avoid a useless delay, decided on the following day that the proceedings should be commenced forthwith. That from this day no delay took place up to the sentence in the Third Instance, with the exception already mentioned as not satisfactorily explained, but at all events of no importance, has been shown above.

This complaint also must, therefore, be considered as disposed of.

4. The last complaint of the British Government—"The expulsion of White from the territory of Peru, as the result and consequence of such unjust proceedings."

As the basis of this complaint, the statement of the British Government says that although the Corte Superior had annulled the sentence in the First Instance, that White should quit the country, the Peruvian Government ordered him to leave the country, and that this order had been transmitted to him through the prefect of the town of Lima, to whom he was ordered to present himself on his release on the 9th of January 1862.

These alleged facts are, however, contradicted by the documents. In the first place, the sentence of the Corte Superior is of no importance, as that sentence was quashed by the Corte Suprema, and only orders a surveillance by the police of the accused, who was freed from the Instance. There is no mention, therefore, of banishment in the sentence. Moreover, there is no foundation whatever for the assertion that the Peruvian Government gave this order of banishment contrary to the final judgment. The circumstance also that this complaint was never pressed at the previous diplomatic proceedings by the British Government against the Peruvian Government does not add to its credibility; but the untruth of this assertion is evident from the letter which White addressed to the criminal judge on the 15th of January, in which he requests to be furnished forthwith with copies of the documents

of the trial, "as he was obliged to quit the Republic on account of urgent private affairs."

As it appears, therefore, from all that precedes, that the British subject, Captain Thomas Melville White, was arrested on Peruvian territory, on occasion of serious suspicions, based upon important infrmation; that the investigation has been conducted with zeal and circumspection, in conformity with the regulations of the Peruvian laws, and without procrastination; that he was publicly accused in consequence of the result of this investigation, and by no means found innocent, and was therefore not absolved by the legally valid sentence of the Supreme Court of Lima, whose jurisdiction is not at all questioned, from the charge of hostile agitation against the Republic, but only freed from the Instance; whilst the assertions that White had been treated during his arrest with cruelty and severity, and expelled the country by the Peruvian Government, contrary to the sentence, when not in direct contradiction to the documents, are wholly destitute of any credible foundation;—the present claim on the part of the British Government for a pecuniary compensation for White appears of no force whatever, and is to be rejected as unfounded.

The costs to which each party has been put with regard to these proceedings are to be borne by themselves. The costs incurred by the Commission in these proceedings are to be paid, a moiety by each party[1].

XXI. Grande-Bretagne, Nicaragua.

28 janvier 1860.

Il s'est agi dans cette affaire de régler définitivement les concessions de terre consenties par les indiens Mosquitos.

Traité conclu entre la Grande-Bretagne et la République de Nicaragua pour le règlement de concessions de terres sur le territoire des indiens Mosquitos, signé à Managua, le 28 janvier 1860.

ART. VIII. All *bona fide* grants of land for due consideration made in the name and by the authority of the Mosquito Indians, since the 1st of January, 1848, and lying beyond the limits of the territory reserved for the said Indians, shall be confirmed, provided the same shall not exceed in any case the extent of 100 Yards square if within the limits of San Juan or Greytown, or 1 league square if without the same, and provided that such grant shall not interfere with other legal grants made previously to that date by Spain, the Republic of Central America, or Ni-

---

[1] *House of Commons.* Paper 482, 13 July 1863, p. 108-117.

caragua; and provided further, that no such grant shall include territory desired by the Government of the latter State, for forts, arsenals, or other public buildings. This Stipulation only embraces those grants of land made since the 1st of January, 1848.

In case, however, any of the grants referred to in the preceding paragraph of this Article should be found to exceed the stipulated extent, the Commissioners hereinafter mentioned shall, if satisfied of the *bona fide* of any such grants, confirm to the grantee or guantees, or to his or their representatives or assigns, an area only equal to the stipulated extent.

And in case any *bona fide* grant, or any part thereof should be desired by the Government for forts, arsenals or other public buildings, an equivalent extent of land shall be allotted to the grantees elsewhere.

It is understood that the grants of land treated of in this Article shall not extend to the westward of the territory reserved for the Mosquito Indians in Article II further than 84° 30' of longitude, in a line parallel and equal with that of the said territory on the same side; and if it should appear that any grants have been made further in the interior of the Republic, the lands acquired *bona fide* shall be replaced with those that are within the limit defined under the regulations agreed upon.

ART. IX. Her Britannic Majesty and the Republic of Nicaragua shall within 6 months after the exchange of the ratifications of the present treaty, appoint each a Commissioner for the purpose of deciding upon the *bona fide* of all grants of land mentioned in the preceding Article as having been made by the Mosquito Indians, of lands heretofore possessed by them, and lying beyond the limits of the territory described in Article I.

ART. X. The Commissioners mentioned in the preceding Article shall, at the earliest convenient period after they shall have been respectively named, meet at such place or places as shall be hereafter fixed, and shall before proceedings to any business, make and subscribe a solemn declaration that they will impartially and carefully examine and decide, to the best of their judgment, and according to justice and equity, without fear, favour or affection to their own country, all the matters referred to them for their decision; and such declaration shall be entered on the record of their proceedings.

The Commissioners shall then, and before proceeding to any other business, name some 3rd person to act as arbitrator or umpire in any case or cases in which they may themselves differ in opinion. If they should not be able to agree upon the selection of such a person, the Commissioners on either side shall name a person; and in each and every case in which the Commissioners may differ in opinion as to the decision which they ought to give, it shall be determined by lot which of the 2 persons so named shall be arbitrator or umpire in that particular case. The person or persons so to be chosen shall, before proceeding to act, make and subscribe a solemn declaration, in a form similar to that which shall already have been made and subscribed by the Commissioners, which declaration shall also be entered on the record of the proceedings. In the event of the death, absence, or incapacity of such person or persons, or of his or their omitting, or declining, or ceasing, to act as such arbitrator or umpire, another person or other persons shall be named as aforesaid to act in his or their place or stead and shall make and subscribe such declaration as aforesaid.

Her Britannic Majesty and the Republic of Nicaragua shall engage to consider the decision of the 2 Commissioners conjointly or of the Arbitrator or Umpire, as the case may be, as final and conclusive on the matters to be referred to their decision, and forthwith to give full effect to the same.

ART. XI. The Commissioners and the arbitrators or umpires shall keep accurate records and correct minutes or notes of all their proceedings, with the dates thereof, and shall appoint and employ such clerk or clerks, or other persons, as they shall find necessary to assist them in the transaction of the business which may come before them. The salaries of the Commissioners and of the clerk or clerks shall be paid by their respective Governments. The salary of the arbitrators or umpires, and their contingent expenses, shall be defrayed in equal moieties by the 2 Governments.

ART. XII. The present Treaty shall be ratified by Her Britannic Majesty, and by the congress of the Republic of Nicaragua, and the ratifications shall be exchanged at London at soon as possible within the space of 6 months.

In witness whereof the respective Plenipotentiaries have signed the same, and have affixed thereto their respective seals.

Done at Managua, this 28th day of January, in the year of our Lord, 1860 [1].

La commission arbitrale siéga à Grey Town du 1er novembre 1861 au 15 avril 1865. Au

---

[1] HERTSLET, *A complete Collection of the Treaties and Conventions* ...., t. XI.

cours de ses délibérations, des difficultés surgirent qui aboutirent aux résolutions déposées dans le document suivant.

The Commissioners have taken into consideration the claims which in due form have been presented to them since their last meeting.

There having arisen a difference of opinion between the Commissioners as to the import of the phrase (Cien Yardas cuaradas) as expressed in Article VIII of the Treaty in the Spanish text of the Treaty compared with the English text which expresses (one hundred Yards square), the Commissioners terminate this question by mutually agreeing to the following resolutions.

ART. I. For reasons of equity duly considered and to sustain the good understanding existing between the Republic and Her Britannic Majesty's Government, the Commissioners do hereby confirm all grants of land situated and lying within the limits of the city of Grey Town, or San Juan del Norte, which have been made and issued under and by the Authority of the Mosquito Indians, from the 1st January, A. D. 1848, to 28th January 1860; subject only to the condition mentioned and set forth in Article VIII of the Treaty of Managua of 28th January 1860 made between the Republic of Nicaragua and Her Britannic Majesty's Government, relating to lands required by the Republic of Nicaragua, for forts, arsenals, and other public buildings.

ART. II. And as the Government of Nicaragua has signified its intention to take for public purposes the one-half of the land granted to John Murphy situated in the city of Grey Town, or San Juan del Norte, the grant is confirmed upon the said condition by the Commissioners, and the secretary is ordered to notify John Murphy or his representative or attorney, of this Decree of the Commissioners, and of the intention to grant a full equivalent for the same as set forth in the Treaty.

ART. III. In virtue of what is set forth in Article I, the owners of said grants, their attorneys or agents shall upon their delivery to such owners or the respective attorneys or agents pay to the Government of Nicaragua, or to its representative the annual tax as is expressed in the same, which payment shall be made only once, and that at the time stated, and is not to be understood as a part of the 1 per cent municipal tax established, and which is now being paid.

ART. IV. The grants of Mr John Leefe and Dr Thomas Cody situated on the River San Juan,

shall be reduced to the league square, within the meaning of the Treaty, and the Secretary will communicate this to the respective owners, or their agents, that within 60 days from this date they shall deliver to the Commissioners in writing the area of their grants, the Commissioners relinquishing the annual tax stated in the respective titles.

Grey Town, or San Juan del Norte, September 27, 1862 [1].

XXII. Etats-Unis d'Amérique, Vénézuéla.

25 avril 1866.

Il s'est agi dans cette affaire du règlement des indemnités réclamées par des citoyens américains à la charge de la République de Vénézuéla. Cet arbitrage donna lieu à de sérieuses difficultés : les commissaires siégèrent à Caracas, mais leurs décisions furent vivement contestées par le gouvernement vénézuélien. A plusieurs reprises, notamment le 25 février 1873 et le 20 juin 1878, le Congrès américain fut saisi de la question de savoir s'il y avait lieu de passer outre et d'exiger l'exécution des sentences prononcées. Toutefois, en 1883, il se rallia à la proposition faite de soumettre les réclamations présentées à de nouveaux arbitres. Un traité fut conclu à cet effet le 5 décembre 1885, mais les ratifications en furent successivement prorogées par deux traités des 15 mars et 5 octobre 1888, dont le premier, au surplus, modifia quelque peu la convention principale. Ce ne fut que le 3 juin 1889 que les ratifications furent définitivement échangées. Aucune des sentences intervenues n'a été publiée.

The conclusion of a convention similar to those entered into with other republics, and by which the pending American claims upon Venezuela might be referred for decision to a mixed commission and an umpire, having been proposed to the Venezuelan Government on behalf of the United States of America, as a mean of examining and justly terminating such claims ; and it having been thought that the adoption of the contemplated course will secure at least some of the

---

[1] HERTSLET, A complete Collection ..., t. XIII, p. 667.

advantages attending arbitration, so strongly recommended in article the 112th of the Federal Constitution of Venezuela, while it will preserve unimpaired as reciprocally desired, the good understanding of both nations: The Citizen First Vice-President in charge of the Presidency has accepted the above proposal, and authorized the Minister for Foreign Relations to negotiate and sign the proper convention.

Thereupon said Minister and Mr E. D. Culver, Minister Resident of the United States of America, also duly empowered for that purpose, have agreed upon the following articles of convention:

ART. I. All claims on the part of corporations, companies, or individuals, citizens of the United States, upon the Government of Venezuela, which may have been presented to their Government or to its legation in Caracas, shall be submitted for examination and decision to a mixed commission, consisting of two members, one of whom shall be appointed by the Government of the United States, and the other by that of Venezuela. In case of death, absence, resignation, or incapacity of either of the Commissioners or in the event of either of them omitting or ceasing to act, the Government of the United States or that of Venezuela, respectively, or the Minister of the United States in Caracas by authority of his Government, shall forthwith proceed to fill the vacancy.

The Commissioners so named shall meet in the city of Caracas within four months from the exchange of the ratifications of this convention, and, before proceeding to business, they shall make solemn oath that they will carefully examine and impartially decide, according to justice, and in compliance with the provisions of this convention, all claims submitted to them, and such oath shall be entered on the record of their proceedings. The Commissioners shall then proceed to appoint an Umpire to decide upon any case or cases concerning which they may disagree, or upon any point of difference that may arise in the course of their proceedings. And if they cannot agree in the selection, the Umpire shall be named by the Diplomatic Representative either of Switzerland or of Russia, in Washington, on the previous invitation of the high contracting parties.

ART. II. So soon as the Umpire shall have been appointed, the Commissioners shall proceed, without delay, to examine the claims which may be presented to them under this convention; and they shall, if required, hear one person in behalf of each Government on every separate claim. Each Government shall furnish, on request of either Commissioner, all such documents and papers in its possession, as may be deemed important to the just determination of any claim.

In cases where they agree to award an indemnity, they shall determine the amount to be paid, and issue certificates of the same. In cases when the Commissioners cannot agree, the points of difference shall be referred to the Umpire, before whom each of the Commissioners may be heard and whose decision shall be final. The Commissioners shall make such decision as they shall deem, in reference to such claims, comformable to justice, even though such decisions amount to an absolute denial of illegal pretensions, since the including of any such in this convention is not to be understood as working any prejudice in favor of any one, either as to principles of right or matters of fact.

ART. III. The Commissioners shall issue certificates of the sums to be paid to the claimants, respectively by virtue of their decisions or those of Umpire, and the aggregate amount of all sums awarded by the Commissioners, and of all sums accruing from awards made by the Umpire, shall be paid to the Government of the United States. Payment of said sums shall be made in equal annual payments, to be completed within ten years from the date of the termination of the labors of the Commission; the first payment to be made six months from same date. Semi-annual interest shall be paid on the several sums awarded, at a rate of five per cent per annum from the date of the termination of the labors of the Commission.

ART. IV. The Commission shall terminate its labors in twelve months from the date of its organization, except that thirty days' extension may be given to issue certificates, if necessary, on the decisions of the Umpire in the case referred to in the following article. They shall keep a record of their proceedings and may appoint a secretary.

ART. V. The decisions of this Commission and those (in case there may be any) of the Umpire, shall be final and conclusive as to all pending claims at the date of their installation. Claims which shall not be presented within the twelve months herein prescribed will be disregarded by both Governments, and considered invalid.

In the event that, upon the termination of the labors of said Commission, there should remain pending one or more cases before the Umpire awaiting his decision, the said Umpire is authorized to make his decision and transmit same to the Commissioners, who shall issue their certificates thereupon and communicate them to each Government, which shall be held binding and conclusive; provided however, that his de-

been mail be given within thirty days from the termination of the action of the Commission, and after the expiration of the said thirty days any decision made shall be void and of no effect.

Art. ... Each Government shall pay its own Commissioner and shall pay one-half of what may be due to the umpire and secretary and one-half the incidental expenses of the Commission.

Art. ... The present convention shall be ratified and the ratifications exchanged so soon as may be practicable at the city of Caracas.

In testimony whereof the Plenipotentiaries have signed this convention and have thereunto affixed the seals of the Ministry of Foreign Relations of the United States of Venezuela and of the Legation of the United States of America at Caracas this twenty-fifth day of July in the year one thousand eight hundred and sixty-six.

Convention pour la réouverture des tribunaux sur les réclamations de citoyens américains à la charge de la République de Vénézuela, votée par le traité du 25 avril 1866, conclue à Washington le 5 décembre 1885.

The President of the United States of America having on the 3rd day of March 1883, approved the following Joint Resolution of Congress:

"Joint Resolution providing for a new Mixed Commission in accordance with the treaty of April twenty-fifth, eighteen hundred and sixty-six, with the United States of Venezuela.

Whereas since the dissolution of the mixed Commission appointed under the treaty of April twenty fifth, eighteen hundred and sixty-six, with the United States of Venezuela, serious charges, impeaching the validity and integrity of its proceedings, have been made by the Government of the United States of Venezuela, and also charges of a like character by divers citizens of the United States of America, who presented claims for adjudication before that tribunal; and

Whereas, the evidence to be found in the record of the proceedings of said Commission, and in the testimony taken before Committees of the House of Representatives in the matter, tends to show that such charges are not without foundation; and

Whereas it is desirable that the matter be finally disposed of in a manner that shall satisfy any just complaints against the validity and integrity of the first Commission, and provide a tribunal under said treaty constructed and conducted so as not to give cause for just suspicion; and

---

[1] *Treaties and Conventions between the United States of America and other Powers, 1776 to 1887, p. 1140.*

Whereas all evidence before said ... Commission was presented in writing and is now in the archives of the State Department; and

Whereas the President of the United States has in a recent communication to Congress solicited its advisory action in the matter:

Therefore—

Resolved by the Senate and House of Representatives of the United States of America in Congress assembled, That the President be and he hereby is requested to open diplomatic correspondence with the Government of the United States of Venezuela, with a view to the revival of the general stipulations of the treaty of April 25, 1866, with said government, and the appointment thereunder of a new Commission, to sit in the city of Washington, which Commission shall be authorized to consider all the evidence presented before the former Commission in respect to claims brought before it, together with such other and further evidence as the claimants may offer; and from the awards that may be made to claimants, any moneys heretofore paid by the Department of State upon certificates issued to them respectively, upon awards made by the former Commission shall be deducted, and such certificates deemed cancelled; and the moneys now in the Department of State received from the Government of Venezuela on account of said awards, and all moneys that may hereafter be paid under said treaty, shall be distributed pro rata in payment of such awards as may be made by the Commission to be appointed in accordance with this resolution."

And the proposal contemplated and authorized by the foregoing joint resolution of Congress having been made by the Government of the United States of America to the Government of the United States of Venezuela, and accepted by the latter through its diplomatic representative in Washington: The Government of the United States of America and the Government of the United States of Venezuela, to the end of effecting by means of a convention arrangements for the execution of the accord thus reached between the two Governments, have named their Plenipotentiaries to confer and agree thereupon, as follows:

The President of the United States of America, Thomas F. Bayard, Secretary of State of the United States of America; and

The President of the United States of Venezuela, Antonio M. Soteldo, Chargé d'Affaires of Venezuela at Washington;

Who after having communicated to each other their respective full powers, found in good and due form, have agreed upon the following articles:

ART. I. The general stipulations of the Convention of April 25th, 1866, between the contracting parties are hereby revived with such alterations as are required in conformity with the aforesaid joint resolution of the Congress of the United States, and with such further modifications as are deemed necessary for the certain and speedy accomplishment of the ends in view, and for the reciprocal protection of the interests of the high contracting parties as hereinafter provided.

ART. II. All claims on the part of corporations, companies, or individuals, citizens of the United States, upon the Government of Venezuela, which may have been presented to their Government or to its legation at Carácas, before the first day of August, 1868, and which by the terms of the aforesaid convention of April 25th, 1866, were proper to be presented to the Mixed Commission organized under said convention shall be submitted to a new Commission, consisting of three Commissioners, one of whom shall be appointed by the President of the United States of America, one by the Government of the United States of Venezuela and the third shall be chosen by these two Commissioners; if they cannot agree within ten days from the time of their first meeting as hereinafter provided, then the diplomatic representative of either Russia or Switzerland at this capital shall be requested by the Secretary of State and the Venezuelan Minister at Washington to name the third Commissioner.

In case of the death, resignation or incapacity of any of the Commissioners, or in the event of any of them omitting or ceasing to act, the vacancy shall be filled within three months by naming another Commissioner in like manner as herein provided for the original appointment.

ART. III. The Commissioners so appointed shall meet in the city of Washington at the earliest convenient time within three months from the exchange of the ratifications of this Convention, and shall, as their first act in so meeting, make and subscribe a solemn declaration that they will carefully examine and impartially decide, according to justice and in compliance with the provisions of this Convention, all claims submitted to them in conformity herewith, and such declaration shall be entered on the record of their proceedings.

ART. IV. The concurring judgment of any two Commissioners shall be adequate for every intermediate decision arising in the execution of their duty, and for every final decision or award.

ART. V. So soon as the Commission shall have organized, notice shall be given to the respective Governments of the date of organization and of readiness to proceed to the transaction of the business of the Commission.

The Commissioners shall thereupon proceed without delay to hear and examine all the claims which by the terms of the aforesaid Convention of April 25th, 1866, were proper to be presented to the Mixed Commission organized under the Convention of April 25th, 1866; and they shall to that end consider all the evidence admissible under the aforesaid Convention of April 25th, 1866, in respect to claims adjuciable thereunder, together with such other and further evidence as the claimants may offer through their respective Governments, and such further evidence as may be offered to rebut any such new evidence offered on the part of the claimant, and they shall, if required, hear one person on behalf of each Government on every separate claim.

All the papers and evidence before the said former Commission, now on file in the archives of the Department of State at Washington, shall be laid before the Commission; and each Government shall furnish, at the request of the Commissioners, or of any two of them, all such papers and documents in its possession as may be deemed important to the just determination of any claim.

ART. VI. The Commissioners shall make such decision as they shall deem, in reference to such claims, conformable to justice.

The concurring decisions of the three Commissioners, or of any two of them, shall be conclusive and final. Said decisions shall in every case be given upon each individual claim, in writing, stating in the event of a pecuniary award being made, the amount or equivalent value of the same, expressed in gold coin of the United States of America; and in the event of interest being allowed for any cause and embraced in such award, the rate thereof and the period for which it is to be computed shall be fixed, which period shall not extend beyond the close of the Commission; and said decision shall be signed by the Commissioners concurring therein.

In all cases where the Commissioners award an indemnity as aforesaid, they shall issue one certificate of the sum to be paid to each claimant, respectively, by virtue of their decisions, inclusive of interest when allowed, and after having deducted from the sum so found due to any claimant or claimants any moneys heretofore paid by the Department of State at Washington upon certificates issued to such claimants, respectively, upon awards made by the former Mixed Commission under the Convention of April 25th, 1866. And all certificates of awards issued by the said former Mixed Commission shall be deemed cancelled from the date of the decision of the present Commission in the case in which they were issued.

The aggregate amount of all sums awarded by the present Commission, and of all sums accruing therefrom, shall be paid to the United States. Payment of said aggregate amount shall be made in equal annual payments to be completed within ten years from the date of the termination of the labors of the present Commission. Semi-annual interest shall be paid on the aggregate amount awarded, at the rate of five per cent. per annum from the date of the termination of the labors of the Commission.

ART. VII. The moneys now in the Department of State actually received from the Government of Venezuela on account of the awards of the said former Mixed Commission under the convention of April 25th, 1866, and all moneys that may hereafter be paid on said former account by the Government of Venezuela to the Government of the United States shall be credited to the Government of Venezuela in computing the aggregate total which may be found due to the Government of the United States under the stipulations of the preceding article, and the balance only shall be considered as due and payable with interest in ten annual payments as aforesaid. *Provided however*, That in the event of the aggregate amount which the present Commission may find due to the Government of the United States being less than the aggregate of the sums actually received from the Government of Venezuela, and remaining undistributed in the Department of State, at Washington, the Government of the United States will refund such excess to the Government of Venezuela within six months from the conclusion of the labors of the Commission.

The payment of moneys due from the Government of Venezuela to the Government of the United States under the former Convention of April 25th, 1866, shall be deemed to have ceased from the first day of April 1883, to be resumed should occasion arise as hereinbefore provided.

ART. VIII. In the event of the annulment of any awards made by the former Mixed Commission under the Convention of April 25th, 1866, the Government of the United States is not to be regarded as responsible to that of Venezuela for any sums which may have been paid by the latter Government on account of said awards, so far as said sums may have been distributed. In like manner, if the awards made by the present Commission and the certificates issued by it shall in any cases be found less than the amount heretofore paid to the claimants from the moneys received from Venezuela, the Government of the United States shall not be regarded as responsible by reason thereof to the Government of Venezuela.

The rehearing provided in the present convention affects, as against the Government of the United States, only the installments of moneys paid to and now held by the United States, and those hereafter to be paid; and the effect of such annulment or reduction in any case shall be to discharge the Government of Venezuela, wholly and forever, from any obligation to pay further installments in such case, except as provided in the present convention.

ART. IX. It is further agreed that if the Commission hereunder organized shall in whole or part annul any money awards made in any cases by the former Mixed Commission under the Convention of April 25th, 1866, it shall be the duty of the Commission to examine and decide whether, under all the circumstances, and with due regard to principles of justice and equity, there are any third parties who have, with the observance of due care and diligence, become possessed, prior to the date of the exchange of ratifications hereof, for a just and valuable consideration, of any portion of the certificates of award heretofore issued in said claims, and whether, under the constitution or laws of either of the contracting parties, said third parties have acquired vested rights, by virtue of the awards of the former Commission under the convention of 1866, imposing the duty on the Government of the United States to collect from Venezuela the amount or proportion of said certificates of awards which may be held and owned by third parties.

If the present Commission shall decide that there are third parties who are possessed of vested rights, then it shall examine and ascertain the sum paid by each and all of said third parties, for their respective interests or shares in said awards, and shall fix the amount of their said interest in said certificates of award or each of them, and shall issue new certificates of award for the sums so adjudged due, which shall be paid by Venezuela to the United States in the manner hereinbefore stipulated, the same as all other certificates issued by the present Commission.

ART. X. Upon the conclusion of the labors of the Commission organized in virtue of this present Convention, the Department of State of the United States of America shall distribute pro rata among the holders of the certificates which may be issued under the present convention, the moneys in the Department of State actually received from the Government of Venezuela on account of the awards of the former Mixed Commission under the Convention of April 25th, 1866; and all moneys that may hereafter be paid to the United States under this present convention shall be in like manner distributed pro rata in payment of such awards as may be made under this present convention.

ART. XI. The decisions of the Commission organized under this present convention shall be final and conclusive as to all claims presented or proper to be presented to the former Mixed Commission.

ART. XII. The Commission appointed under this present convention shall terminate its labors within twelve months from the date of its organization. A record of the proceedings of the Commission shall be kept, and the Commissioners may appoint a Secretary.

ART. XIII. Notwithstanding that the present Commission is organized in consequence of representations made by the Government of Venezuela and that it deals solely with the claims of citizens of the United States (for which reasons the United States might properly claim that all the expenses hereunder should be borne by Venezuela alone), it is agreed that, in continuation of the arrangement made in the former convention of 1866, the expenses shall be shared as follows: Each Government shall pay its own Commissioner and shall pay one-half of what may be due to the third Commissioner and the Secretary, and one-half of the incidental expenses of the Commission.

ART. XIV. Except so far as revived, continued, modified and replaced by the terms and effects of this present convention, the effects of the former convention of April 25th, 1866, shall absolutely cease and determine from and after the date of the exchange of ratifications of this present convention, and the high contracting parties hereby agree that the responsibilities and obligations arising under said former convention shall be deemed wholly discharged and annulled by the substitution therefore of the responsibilities contracted and obligations created under this present convention, to which the high contracting parties mutually bind themselves to give full, perfect and final effect, without any evasion, reservation or delay whatever.

ART. XV. The present convention shall be ratified by the President of the United States by and with the advice and consens of the Senate of the United States of America; and by the President of the United States of Venezuela by and with the advice and consent of the Senate of the United States of Venezuela, and the ratifications shall be exchanged at Washington within twelve months from the date of this present convention, and the publication of the exchange of ratifications shall be noticed to all persons interested.

In testimony whereof the respective pleni-

potentiaries have hereunto affixed their signatures and seals.

Done in duplicate, in the English and Spanish languages, at the city of Washington, this 5th day of December 1885.

La convention du 15 mars 1888 ne contient, au point de vue arbitral, qu'une disposition fort brève qui seule est intéressante à reproduire.

ART. I. It is understood and agreed that in the event of any of the awards of the Mixed Commission under the Convention of April 25th, 1866, being annulled in whole or in part by the Commission authorized and created by Article II of the treaty of December 5th, 1885, no new award shall in any case be made by said Commission, to the holders of certificates of any award or awards annulled as aforesaid, in excess of the sum which may be found to be justly due to the original claimant.

XXIII. Argentine, Grande-Bretagne.

15 juillet 1864.

Le 13 février 1845, le gouvernement de Buenos Ayres promulgait un décret en vertu duquel interdiction était faite aux navires, venant de Montevideo, d'entrer dans les ports argentins. Cette mesure avait été prise pour faciliter, au gouvernement régulier de l'Uruguay, la reprise de la ville de Montevideo, qui se trouvait à cette époque aux mains de rebelles. Elle n'en causa pas moins un préjudice considérable à des navires naviguant sous pavillon anglais. Le gouvernement anglais fit valoir de ce chef des réclamations réitérées qui donnèrent lieu enfin, en 1864, à la conclusion d'un traité d'arbitrage.

Protocole de la Conférence entre la Grande-Bretagne et la Confédération argentine, relativement aux réclamations présentées par des sujets anglais du chef des pertes subies par suite du décret du 13 février 1845, avenue à Buenos Ayres le 15 juillet 1864.

His Excellency Doctor Don Rufino de Elizalde, Minister Secretary of State for Foreign Affairs, and Mr Edward Thornton, Her Britannic Majesty's Minister Plenipotentiary, having met at His Excellency's Office for the purpose of arranging the mode of defining the claims presented to the Argentine Government, by that of Her Britannic Majesty, on account of the losses which subjects of Her Britannic Majesty may have suffered from the vessels and cargoes which touched at the port of Montevideo, having been refused admittance into the port of Buenos Ayres, in accordance with the Decree of February 13, 1845, claims to which the Argentine Government believe they are not bound to accede, have agreed.

1. That the question, whether the Argentine Republic is obliged to pay those losses, shall be submitted to the decision of a friendly government as arbiter.

2. That within the term of 6 months, counting from the day of the acceptance by the arbiter who may be requested to be pleased to take charge of the matter, all the necessary documents shall be presented to him, in order that he may pronounce his sentence.

3. If it be declared that the right to claim exists, the claims shall be settled in accordance with the Conventions in force between the Argentine Republic and Great Britain, of the 21 st of August 1858, and 18th of August 1859.

This arrangement shall be submitted for approval to the Argentine Congress and to Her Britannic Majesty's Government as soon as possible.

Buenos Ayres, July 15, 1864 [1].

Par une convention additionnelle du 18 janvier 1865, le Président de la République du Chili fut choisi comme arbitre. Il rendit, cinq ans plus tard, une sentence fort détaillée qui expose avec une grande précision les points de fait et de droit.

Sentence du Président du Chili, au sujet des réclamations présentées par des sujets anglais à la République argentine pour les pertes provenant du décret du 13 février 1845, rendu à Santiago de Chile, le 1er août 1870.

Jose Joaquin Perez, President of the Republic of Chile, named judge Arbiter by the Government of Her Britannic Majesty and by that of the Argentine Republic, to decide upon various claims for damages sustained by several British subjects against the second of the said Governments. Having accepted the charge and being desirous to put an end to this difference by making known to the High Parties concerned the opinion which I have formed on the matter in dispute:

Having carefully perused and examined all the antecedents in the matter, and having in view the opinion declared by the supreme Court of Justice and by the advocate Don Cosmo Campillo, I proceed to give my opinion as follows:—

On the 13th of February, 1845, the Government of the Argentine Confederation, which was then at war with the Republic of Uruguay, issued

a Decree, by which it declared that, from the 1st of March following, all communication with the port of Montevideo would be closed, and ordained that entrance into the Argentine ports should not be allowed to any ship which might arrive direct from Montevideo, or which might have put into or touched at that place, by whatever accident.

The Representative of Her Britannic Majesty in Buenos Ayres stated to the Argentine Government, in an official note of the 17th of the same month of February, that the immediate execution of the Decree would cause severe losses to British commerce, as many British vessels were already dispatched having part of their cargo for Montevideo and part for Buenos Ayres, and for this reason he proposed that at least some further time should be granted to the British vessels which might arrive from Europe and touch at Montevideo to continue their voyage to Buenos Ayres, and discharge in that port the cargoes destined for it.

The Argentine Government replied, on the 27th of the same month, that the Decree of the 13th had gone to the extreme limit in favour of foreign commerce and that its terms, being general, no change could be made in it in favour of British vessels.

Under these circumstances, 6 British merchant vessels arrived at Buenos Ayres proceeding from Europe. The "Cestus" sailed from the port of Hull on the 30th of December 1844 bound to Montevideo and Buenos Ayres, reached the first of those ports on the 18th of March 1845. On the same day the captain went ashore, in order to entend a protest against wind and weather for damages sustained by the vessel during the voyage. Having transacted his business and, in conformity with the orders he then received from the consignees, he set sail for Buenos Ayres on the 19th of March and, having arrived at that port on the following day, the local authorities prevented her entry.

The "Sultana" weighed anchor from Liverpool on the 14th of January 1845, and anchored in the outer roadstead of Montevideo at half-past eleven, P. M., of the 7th of March of the same year. The captain who had for several days been unwell, landed on the following day, in order to find a pilot to conduct his vessel to Buenos Ayres. But having been informed, on returning on board, that shortly after he had gone on shore, Admiral Brourt, Commander-in-Chief of the Argentine Squadron, had sent a boat to communicate the Decree of the 13th of February; he went on board the said Admiral's ships, and obtained from him a certificate to the effect that his landing had no other object than to procure a pilot. With

[1] HERTSLET, A complete Collection ..., t. XIII, p. 69.

this the vessel proceeded to Buenos Ayres, and having arrived there on the 18th of March it received the same repulse as the preceding one.

The barque "James" left Liverpool on the 17th of February, 1845, for Montevideo and Buenos Ayres with a cargo for both ports.

She arrived at Montevideo on the 24th of April and having discharged that portion of her cargo destined for that port, according to the tenor of his bills of lading, continued his voyage to Buenos Ayres and arrived there on the 31st of May, when she there was refused entry.

The brig "Richard Watson" sailed from Cadiz on the 23rd of February, 1845, with a cargo of salt destined for Montevideo. Having arrived in front of that port on the 28th of April she received the orders of her freighters to proceed to Buenos Ayres, and having, on the 2nd of May, attempted to enter the port she was prevented from doing so by the maritime authorities.

The barque "Jean Baptiste" left Liverpool on the 7th of March, 1845, with a cargo of general merchandise for Montevideo and Buenos Ayres. Having reached the first of those ports on the 29th of April, and left there a part of her cargo, in conformity with her bills of lading, signed in Liverpool, she continued her voyage to Buenos Ayres, and on arriving there on the 25th of May, she was there informed, by the captain of the port, that according to the Decree of the 13th of February, she could not enter from having touched at Montevideo.

The barque "Caledonia" which left Liverpool on the 6th of April 1845, with a cargo of good, assorted for Montevideo and Buenos Ayres, arrived in front of the first of those ports on the 18th of June, and the captain, having there learned the Decree of the 13th of February, stopped there until he had communicated with the Buenos Ayrean authorities. But the representations he addressed to them having been of no avail, in conformity with his bills of lading, he entered the port of Montevideo on the 1st of July, and after leaving part of his cargo there, he proceeded to Buenos Ayres, where he arrived on the 25th of August. He was there denied entry in the same form and for the same reason as the other vessels had been.

Each of the captains of the afore-mentioned 6 vessels entered a protest at the proper time and before the proper Consular authority, in which all that had occurred was recorded.

On the 21st of August 1858, a Convention was concluded between the High Parties interested, in the preamble of which it is stated that they were both desirous "to arrange the means, mode and form of payment which was to be made of the debt which the Argentine nation recognised as due to the subjects of Her Britannic Majesty

for losses sustained during the disorders which occured in the Republic from the civil war, losses which the Argentine nation wished to recognise following a healing and generous policy".

In conformity with this idea, the conditions and form of payment were established and specified in the said Convention. According to one of the stipulations of the Convention, a Commission was appointed, charged with the arrangement, amicably, of all difficulties which might arise in the fulfilment of the compact.

On the 18th of August 1859, another Convention was concluded between the same High Parties, which was styled "Additional" and of which the object was to determine more clearly some of the stipulations contained in that of the 21st of August. In dictating, in this Convention, rules relating to the rates of interest which ought to be allowed according to the various classes of losses, which the British subjects might claim from the Argentine Government, amongst other matters the following was stipulated: "for the claims arising out of the destruction of farm property, sequestration of marchandise, thefts and other losses, 50 per cent interest on the aggregate amount should be paid, however remote the dates of the events which gave rise to the claim might be."

Some years later, the British Legation addressed the Buenos Ayres Government, claiming indemnification for the losses sustained by the 6 vessels mentioned and their cargoes, and sustaining that those losses were included in those that the Argentine Confederation had recognised in favour of British subjects by the Conventions of the 21st of August 1858, and of the 18th of August 1859, and therefore ought to be taken into consideration by the Commission established by the said convention.

The Government of Buenos Ayres not only rejected the idea that the losses claimed were included in the recognition conceded by those Conventions, but also sustained that no responsibility whatever was incurred by it for the results which the Decree of the 13th of February had caused, for the reason that it had been lawfully dictated, and in use of the right which the Argentine nation possessed in consequence of the war in which it was at that time engaged with Montevideo and other towns of the Oriental Republic of Uruguay.

In the Protocol of the 15th of July 1864, the Representatives of the British and Argentine Governments agreed to submit to the arbitrary decision of a friendly Government the question whether the Argentine Republic is obliged to pay the losses sustained by the British subjects in consequence if its having denied the entry into the port of Buenos Ayres to the 6 vessels already mentioned, and in the Protocol of the 18th of January 1865, the Representatives of the same Governments were pleased to name me Arbiter for the solution of the said question.

The Representatives of the High Parties interessed agree, as is expressed in the memorandum which one and the other have presented to me, that the question should be settled in the following manner. 1st Are the losses sustained by the British subjects, in consequence of those vessels having been refused the entry to the port of Buenos Ayres, included or not included in the terms of the Conventions of the 21st of August 1858, and of the 18th of August 1859, and 2ndly, supposing that the said losses are not comprehended in the terms of the said Convention, is the Argentine Government obliged in justice or not obliged to indemnify them?

With respect to the first of these questions, the Government of Her Britannic Majesty sustains that the losses in question are comprehended in the terms of the Convention cited; and gives as the ground for that opinion that the words "and other losses" which are employed in the additional Convention of the 18th of August 1859, refer to those losses; that other claims for losses of an analogous nature, brought forward by British subjects were taken into consideration by the Commission established in Parana in conformity with the stipulations of the two Conventions referred to, and that the Commission decided those claims in favour of the claimants, assigning to them a certain compensation; that in those cases the decisions of the Commission were submitted to the Argentine Government, which confirmed them before the coupons were issued for the payment of that which was found due to the claimants; that, as the first Article of the Convention of the 21st of August 1888, recognised a national debt all the sums due to British subjects for claims that should have been presented previous to the 18th of January 1860, this recognition could not do less than embrace the claims for every class of losses inclusive of those which might have arisen from other causes than the disorders of the civil war; that on the other side the losses claimed ought to be considered as produced from the disorders of the civil war, because the Decree of the 13th of February 1845 was an act of hostility against the authorities established in Montevideo, who were considered as rebels by the Argentine Confederation, which aided General Oribe and which recognised him as the lawful President of the Republic of Uruguay against those who occupied the city of Montevideo; and that this mode of viewing the question is confirmed by the tenor of Article V

of the above-mentioned Decree which says: "The present Decree shall have effect and be acted upon whilst the city of Montevideo continues to be under the sway of the Unitarian savages and cease whenever the army of operations, under the orders of His Excellency Brigadier-General Don Manuel Oribe, lawful President of the Oriental Republic of Uruguay, enters the said city."

On the part of the Argentine Government, it is answered that the Convention of the 21st of August 1858 recognised as national debt only the sums due as indemnification for losses caused by the disorders of the civil war; that, in the Convention of the 18th of August 1859, are classed the losses which the Argentine Government ought to indemnify, and that in none of those classes are comprehended those which are now claimed; that the words "other losses", employed in the same Convention, cannot be applied to losses sustained in consequence of a legitimate act of authority executed within the sphere of its attributes, such as the Decree of the 13th of February; that, if the Commission established in Parana took into consideration claims analogous to those that are now made and if they were admitted by the Government established in Parana, such acts were null, because they exceeded the attributes of the Commission and of the Government, and as acts which are null cannot be cited in order to fix the sense of the compact; that it is not credible that, if the Commission and the Government of Parana had known the true state of affairs, they would have made the recognitions that are cited, and that it is not strange that the Commission and the said Government should be ignorant of the terms of the Conventions because the archives in which they were recorded were at Buenos Ayres, and unknown in Parana; that the claims presented previous to the 1st of January 1860, to which reference is made in the Convention of the 21st of August 1858, do not refer to all kinds of losses, but only to those caused by the disorders of the civil war, as is expressly declared in Article VI of the Additional Convention of the 18th of August 1859, to the effect that "no claim of the nature of those contemplated in the preamble of the Convention of the 21st of August 1858, can be presented after the 31st of December 1860, without prorogation"; that the Decree of the 13th of February, which was the origin of the losses sustained by the British vessels, cannot be viewed as an incident of civil war, but as a measure dictated in war abroad, because that measure was adopted against foreign Powers who refused to recognise the blockade of the port of Montevideo; that the condition of the cessation of the Decree so soon as the city of Montevideo was captured by the army of General Oribe did not give to the Decree the character of a measure taken in civil war; and that the only character which it impressed was, that when once the city of Montevideo was occupied by the army of General Oribe, there would be no reason for the Decree to exist, because, in such a case, the blockade would cease and, with its cessation, the non-recognition of the blockade which had originated the Decree.

Considering, 1st, that in the Convention concluded on the 21st of August 1858, the Argentine Government only recognised as national debt, in favour of British subjects, that which proceeded from losses which the said subjects had sustained in the disorders occuring in the Republic from civil war;

2ndly, that the Additional Convention of the 18th of August 1859, having reference to the principal one of 1858, both ought to be viewed as of the same category, and that the intention of the latter one being to indemnify the losses sustained by British subjects in the disorders of the civil war, it ought necessarily to be identical in its object with that of the first;

3rdly, that, in accordance with the reason just stated, the words "and other losses" which are employed in Article II of the Additional Convention cannot have reference to losses occasioned in a foreign war, because such signification would alter the nature of the object of the said Additional Convention and consequently that of the principal one;

4thly, that although it is said in Article I of the Convention of the 21st of August 1858, that "the Government of the Argentine Confederation recognises as national debt all the sums due to British subjects for claims that may have been presented previous to the 1st of January 1860, and which shall have been settled jointly by the Commissioners of the Argentine Government for that purpose appointed, and by the Minister Plenipotentiary of Her Britannic Majesty or his Representative", such recognition can only have reference to debt arising from losses occasioned by civil war, which were the only ones that the Convention had for object to liquidate and pay, as is specifically declared in its preamble;

5thly, that the signification just given to Article I of the Convention of the 21st of August 1858, is confirmed by the literal tenor of Article VI of the Additional Convention of the 18th of August 1859:

6thly, that, although it is affirmed, on the part of the Government of Her Britannic Majesty, that the Commission appointed in virtue of the Convention of the 21st of August had taken cognizance of several claims analogous to those which have given rise to the present arbitration, and that the decisions of the said Commission have

been accepted and respected by the Government of the Argentine Confederation, such cannot act as a sufficient precedent to establish that the Argentine Government had desired to enlarge the explicit sense of the Convention by extending it to cases not literally comprehended in it, in as much as the claims which are alluded to on the part of the Government of Her Britannic Majesty are not specified, and therefore cannot be duly appreciated by the Judge Arbiter, so as to give them the importance and scope attributed to them by the said Government;

7thly, that, although the fact to which the preceding opinion refers is not contradicted on the part of the Argentine Government, still explanations are given on this point which show that the circumstances in which the said Government found itself, when it gave its acquiescence, to the decisions of the Commission, did not allow it to examine them with the minute attention due, and with relation to the antecedents of each of the cases;

8thly, that, it being explicitly declared in the Convention of the 21st of August that the desire of the High Contracting Parties was solely to establish rules for the liquidation and payment of the debts arising from losses occasioned by the civil war of the Argentine Republic, it is impossible to apply the stipulations of this Convention to other debts of a very different nature and origin, without the intervention of a declaration equally explicit on the part of the same parties, it being impossible to invoke incidents in order to their being applied which, from their vagueness, cannot be subjected to an exact appreciation susceptible, as they are, of divers explanations;

9thly, that although the Oriental Republic of Uruguay was engaged in civil war in the year 1845, the war which the Argentine Government carried on at that time with one of the contending parties, and aiding the other, could not have that character, because it was made between two nations independent of each other;

10thly, that even considering the war of Uruguay to be solely a civil one, the stipulations of the Convention of the 21st of August could not, on that account, be applicable to losses brought forward by the owners and consignees of the 6 British vessels, as the said losses ought to be viewed as caused by the civil war of a country distinct from that of the Argentine Confederation, and in no case as caused by the civil war of the said Confederation, which is a circumstance indispensable in order that indeminification should be granted according to the said Convention.

For all these reasons, I am of opinion that the losses sustained by the British vessels in consequence of the Decree issued by the Argentine Government, under date of the 13th of February 1845, are not comprehended in the terms of the Conventions of the 21st of August 1858, and of the 18th of August 1859.

With respect to the second of the two questions submitted for consideration, the Government of Her Britannic Majesty sustains, that the Argentine Republic is obliged in justice to indemnify the losses in question, and alleges, as a reason, that the Argentine Government could not dictate the Decree of the 13th of February without giving sufficient time for the prohibition established by it to reach opportunely the knowledge of the vessels which were loading in Europe for Montevideo and Buenos Ayres or by making itself responsible for the losses arising from the measure, if reasons of State should counsel its immediate execution; that, from the time when a vessel leaves with its cargo for a fixed port, it acquires tacitly the right to be admitted into it, and no one can deprive it of that benefit without contracting the obligation to allow it compensation; that, of the vessels in question, some left Europe even before the Decree had been issued, and the others before the time had elapsed requisite for its coming to their knowledge; that to none of the vessels was the Decree made known by the blockading squadron, and that all of them reached Montevideo in complete ignorance of what had occurred; that, if it be wished to say that the Decree was issued as a reprisal against Great Britain for not having recognised the strict blockade of Montevideo, the fact is entirely incorrect, because the Decree gives no such reason, nor is it to be believed that if there had been in it the design of acting hostilely against Great Britain, the English packets proceeding from Europe would have been excepted, as they are in Article IV; that, on the other side, the British Government far from refusing to recognise the blockade, Sir T. Pasley, Commandant of the naval forces of Her Britannic Majesty in the waters of Montevideo addressed, on the 29th of January 1845, a letter to the Admiral of the Argentine Squadron, in which he assured him that the blockade would be recognised by the forces under his command; that only later when the Admiral of the Squadron of His Majesty the King of the French refused to recognise the blockade, it was that Sir T. Pasley claimed for English vessels the same immunities that might be conceded to the French; that there being no mention of the present claims in the Convention concluded between the Argentine Republic and the British Government on the 24th of November 1849, in which other claims of the same nature were accepted, is not a proof that the present ones were abandoned by the Govern-

ment of Great Britain, because Mr J. H. Mandeville, Minister Plenipotentiary of Her Britannic Majesty having opportunely presented a demand against the losses which the Decree of the 13th of February might inflict upon English commerce, without his pretentions having obtained any solution, it would have been necessary, in order that they should be considered as renounced by the said convention, that it should have been so expressly stipulated; and finally, that amongst the 6 vessels which were refused entrance into the port of Buenos Ayres there were some of them that in reality had not infringed the Decree of the 13th of February, as they had only stopped in front of Montevideo without entering the port or executing in it any acts whatsoever.

The Argentine Government, accepting the fact of its having impeded the entry of the 6 vessels into the port of Buenos Ayres, to which the claims of the British Government refer, and setting entirely aside the circumstance of whether or not the losses, which on that account are claimed, were actually sustained, maintains that it is not obliged to indemnify them, and gives as its reason that finding itself, as it then did, at war with Montevideo, it could indoubtedly dictate the Decree of the 13th of February, in which it prohibited traffic with that port, and that this being a legitimate act of warfare, neutral nations had no right to complain of its consequences; that although the "Sultana" and other vessels had sailed for Buenos Ayres, and arrived at Montevideo in entire ignorance of the Decree, and although they had not been notified of it by the Argentine Squadron, they were not on that account exempted from the obligation of complying with it, because measures of this nature do not require a term to be fixed for their being executed, and all to which those who are ignorant of those measures can pretend is, not to be captured, instead of being only obliged to execute them, as it is known that, in case of a blockade, although a term is given that vessels entering be not captured, it is never the custom to authorise them to enter; that it was not the duty of the Argentine Squadron, but of that of Her Britannic Majesty, which was in front of Montevideo, to make known the provisions of the Decree to British subjects and notwithstanding this notice was given to the "Sultana" by the Argentine Squadron, as is admitted by the British Legation in its note of the 11th of May 1845; that, if this principle is applicable to neutral commerce, it is so with much more reasons, towards Powers with whom we are not in a state of perfect peace, and that the Decree of the 13th of February was actually issued in consequence of the Chief of the British naval forces having refused to recognise the blockade, as is established by letter which, in reply to the intimation of the same blockade, Commander Pasley, under date, the 29th of January, addressed to Admiral Browne, demanding that execution of the blockade should be postponed until the Chargé d'Affaires of Her Britannic Majesty at Montevideo should have received from the Minister of Her Britannic Majesty at Buenos Ayres a certain communication on the subject which he considered necessary; that in conformity with this pretention Mr Mandeville, on the 30th of January, requested "that the date of strict blockade both as respected entry and departure should be postponed", to which the Government of Buenos Ayres replied "that the blockade, having been ignored by the forces of Her Britannic Majesty without any right to do so, his request could not be taken into consideration"; that all this, at the same time that it confirms the fact of Great Britains having refused to recognise the blockade, clearly shows that this non-recognition was the cause of the issue of the Decree of the 13th of February; that the exception in favour of the English packets from Europe was not an indication of good relations with Great Britain because it proceeded solely from this, that those packets did not at that time bring cargo, and that what it was intended to prevent was, that goods should enter Montevideo; that in the Convention of the 24th of November 1849, in which is expressly stipulated the restoration of the vessels and cargos captured during the blockade of the Argentine ports established by Great Britain, no mention whatever is made of the losses suffered by English vessels in consequence of the prohibition established in the Decree of the 13th of February, which proves that in the opinion of the British Government the measure was perfectly legal; that the Government of Buenos Ayres did not find itself in the case of demanding when concluding that Convention, the abandonment of a right, which in its opinion did not exist, and that it was for the Government of Her Britannic Majesty to solicit the recognition of that right; that instead of doing this, it obliged itself to restore that which it had captured without recording any compact or expression with respect to the losses now claimed; that the Decree of the 13th of February, far from having been at any time impugned by Great Britain has been expressly recognised and respected by its Diplomatic Agents in various instances, in proof of which it cites the note, which, on the 11th of March 1845, on the occasion of what occured to the "Sultana" Mr Mandeville addressed to the Government of Buenos Ayres in which, without making any observation against the legitimacy of the Decree, he asked the admission of the vessel on the ground solely that it had not infringed the said Decree, because its entering into Montevideo had no other object than to seek a pilot; and that his request having been refused by the Argentine Government the British Legation neither insisted on it nor protested, the same thing, having occurred in various other representations of a like nature at that time made to the Government of Buenos Ayres by the English Minister.

Considering 1st. That the Decree issued by the Argentine Government the 13th of February 1845 had for object to cause to be respected the blockade of the port of Montevideo which the same Government had at that time established.

2nd. That the State which resolves to blockade the port of another with which it is at war, has the right to dictate all the measures tending to cause the blockade to be respected by neutrals.

3rd. That it was neither natural nor just to exact from the Argentine Confederation that it should give reception to its ports to vessels that might have violated the blockade and it being on the contrary natural and just that it should refuse to receive them.

4th. That a term is not given to neutral vessels within which they may enter a blockaded port, neither can it be exacted that it be granted to them in order that they may submit themselves to the measures dictated for the purpose of causing an established blockade to be respected.

5th. That the nation, which in a state of war resolves to close its ports to foreign commerce, is the sole judge in determining the conditions under which the entry to them may be permitted, and to decide whether those who claim to enter have complied or not complied with those conditions.

6th. That it is a principle of universal jurisprudence that he who uses his right offends no one.

By the force of these reasons, I am of opinion that the Government of the Argentine Confederation is not obliged to indemnify the losses suffered by the 6 vessels which were refused entry into the port of Buenos Ayres in virtue of the Decree of the 13th of February 1845, issued by the said Government.

Let this friendly decision be communicated to the High Parties interested, to each of whom will be remitted a copy of it.

Given in the hall of my public office, sealed with the seal of the Republic, and countersigned by my Secretary for foreign Affairs in Santiago de Chile, on the 1st of August 1870 [1].

---

[1] HERTSLET, *A complete Collection* ..., t. XIII, p. 211.

XXIV. Grande-Bretagne, Mexique.

26 juin 1866.

Il s'agit dans cette affaire de simples réclamations diverses. La sentence de la commission
arbitrale n'a point été publiée.

Convention conclue entre Sa Majesté la Reine du Royaume-
Uni de Grande-Bretagne et Sa Majesté l'Empereur du
Mexique pour le règlement des indemnités dues à des
citoyens anglais, signée à Mexico, le 26 juin 1866.

Her Majesty the Queen of the United Kingdom
of Great Britain and Ireland, and His Majesty the
Emperor of Mexico being desirous, in consideration
of the friendly relations which subsist between
the two countries, of fixing the mode of arriving
at an equitable settlement of such claims of Her
Britannic Majesty's subjects as are still pending,
have resolved to conclude a Convention with that
object, and for that purpose have named as their
Plenipotentiaries, that is to say:

Her Majesty the Queen of the United Kingdom
of Great Britain and Ireland the Honourable Peter
Campbell Scarlett, Companion of Her Most Ho-
nourable Order of the Bath, Her Envoy Extra-
ordinary and Minister Plenipotentiary to the Em-
peror of Mexico, and the Emperor of Mexico
Don Thomas Murphy, Concillor of State, Grand
Officer of the Imperial Order of Guadalupe, Grand
Cross of the Orders of the Iron Crown, of the
Red Eagle, and of Philip the Magnanimous, and
Commander of that of Francis Joseph;

Who, after having communicated to each other
their respective full powers, found in good and
due form, have agreed upon the following Articles:

ART. I. All claims of British subjects which
have already been presented to the Mexican
Government, as well as any others which may
be presented within the time to be fixed in accordance with the stipulations contained in Article III, save those which are excepted by Article VI of the present Convention, shall be referred for the purpose of proving their validity
and settling the amount to be paid, to 4 Commissioners appointed to the following manner
that is to say:

Two Commissioners shall be appointed by
Her Britannic Majesty's Representative in Mexico,
and the other two by the Government of the
Emperor, with the understanding that the said
Commissioners shall have no claims of their own,
and that they shall no represent any one of the
claimants.

In case of the death, absence or incapacity
of either or both of the Commissioners, or in the
event of either or both of them omitting or
ceasing to act as such, Her Majesty's Representative or the Government of Mexico as the case
may be, shall forthwith name another person or
persons to replace the Commissioner or Commissioners originally appointed.

The Commissioners so appointed shall meet
at Mexico at the earliest convenient period after
they shall have been respectively appointed, and
before proceeding to discharge their functions shall
make and subscribe a solemn declaration that
they will impartially and scrupulously examine
all the claims which are submitted to them and
decide upon them according to conscience, and
principles of justice and equity. This declaration
shall be entered on the record of their proceedings.

Before the meeting of the Commissioners, the
Representative of Her Britannic Majesty at Mexico,
and the Mexican Government, shall select some
third person who shall be neither a British nor
a Mexican subject, in order that in the character
of Arbitrator or Umpire he may act in any case
or cases in which Commissioners may differ in
opinion.

This third person selected as Arbitrator or
Umpire, before entering into the exercise of his
function shall be requested to make and subscribe
a solemn declaration in the same form as the
one made and subscribed by the Commissioners
which shall be alike entered on the record of
their proceedings. In the event of the death,
absence, or incapacity of such person, or if by
omission, resignation, or any other cause, he
should cease to act as such Arbitrator or Umpire, another person shall be appointed in his
stead, who shall replace him in the same capacity, such person being required to make and
subscribe the above mentioned declaration.

ART. II. The Arbitrator having been appointed, the Commissioners shall proceed to examine
and determine the claims which may be presented
to them, as well as to determine the amount
justly due for each of them separately, with the
understanding that the parties interested shall
establish their rights either by means of the
legal investigation which may have been instituted
with regard to the facts upon which their claims
are founded, or, in default of such investigation,
by means of the declarations of trustworthy witness of the facts referred to. It is equally to be
understood that only such claims shall be admitted for which the Mexican Government is
responsible in accordance with generally admitted
principles of international law and which are, in
origin, continuity and actuality, British.

The said Arbitrator or Umpire shall be bound
to give his decision, which shall be final, on any
claim or matter referred to him, within the term
of 15 days, reckoned from the date on which it
was submitted to his consideration, unless he or

the Commissioners should consider a longer period of time to be absolutely necessary.

ART. III. The Commissioners shall fix a reasonable time, which shall not exceed one year, within which all claims must be submitted to them, and they shall give public notice of the period so fixed.

They shall announce, besides, that the said period shall be extended for 12 months more for the reception of claims which on account of special circumstances could not be presented within the time previously fixed, provided that it be proved to the satisfaction of the Commissioners that such circumstances were entirely beyond the control of the claimant, and were unavoidable.

The Commissioners shall hold for the examination of the claims at least 8 sittings each month, from the date of their first sitting until the completion of their labours.

It shall be competent to the Commissioners conjointly or to the Umpire if they differ, to decide, in each case, whether any claim has or has not been duly made, preferred, or laid before them, either wholly, or to any, and what extent.

ART. IV. The proceedings of the Commission shall be final and conclusive with respect to the claims brought before it, and the Commissioners shall issue to the interested parties, certificates of the sums to be paid by virtue of their award, or of that of the Arbitrator.

ART. V. The Government of His Majesty the Emperor of Mexico shall constitue itself responsible for the payment of the total amount awarded to the Claimants, according to the certificates of the Commissioners.

The mode and period of payment shall be subsequently agreed between Her Britannic Majesty's Representative at Mexico and the Government of His Imperial Majesty.

ART. VI. Such claims as may have been already recognized as valid by the Governments of Great Britain and Mexico, whether the payment of the same be secure or not by specific guarantees, shall not be subject to the revision of the Commission.

With respect to those which are provided for as already mentioned, whatever may have been agreed upon between the two Governments shall be observed. With regard to those which are not, ulterior arrangements shall be entered into for the mode of their payment, which shall have precedence over that of those which are the object of the present Convention.

ART. VII. The Commission to be established shall keep an accurate record in English and Spanish of its proceedings and may appoint a Secretary on each side, to assist it in the transaction of its business.

ART. VIII. The salary of the Commissioners and of the Secretaries shall be fixed and paid by their respective Governments.

The contingent expenses, and those which may be occasioned by arbitration, shall be defrayed in moieties by the two Governments.

ART. IX. The present Convention shall be ratified and the ratifications shall be exchanged at Mexico, as soon as may be within 6 months from the date hereof.

In witness, the above-mentioned Plenipotentiaries have signed the same, and have affixed thereto their respective seals.

Done at Mexico the 26th day of June 1866[1].

XXV. Espagne, Grande-Bretagne.

4 mars 1868.

La question soumise aux arbitres commissaires avait pour objet la destruction d'un navire anglais par les batteries de Ceuta. La décision intervenue n'a été publiée nulle part.

Convention relative à la destruction du schooner anglais Mermaid, signée à Madrid, le 4 mars 1868.

The Undersigned, Sir John Fiennes Crampton, Baronet, Knight Commander of the Most Honourrable Order of the Bath, Her Britannic Majesty's Envoy Extraordinary and Minister Plenipotentiary at the Court of Madrid; and Don Lorenzo Arrazola, Knight Grand Cross of the Royal and Distinguished Order of Charles III, Her Catholic Majesty's Minister and Secretary of State for Foreign Affairs; being duly authorized on the part of their respective Governments, have agreed as follows:—

ART. I. The Government of Her Britannic Majesty and the Government of Her Catholic Majesty agree to refer to the decision of a mixed Commission the claim of Her Britannic Majesty's Government on behalf of the owners of the British schooner "Mermaid" of Dartmouth for compensation for the loss of that vessel alleged by the owners to have been sunk by a shot fired from the batteries of Ceuta on the 16th of October 1864.

ART. II. The Commission shall be composed of four individuals, two to be named by the Government of Her Catholic Majesty: the persons to be chosen to belong to the Diplomatic and Naval Services, as already agreed between the two Governments. The Commissioners shall meet as early as may be praticable, either at Cadiz or at Ceuta and before entering upon the execution

[1] HERTSLET, *A complete Collection of Treaties and Conventions* . . . ., t. XII, p. 655.

of their duties shall make and subscribe a solemn declaration that they will carefully examine and impartially decide the question submitted to them; and such declaration shall be entered upon the record of their proceedings.

At the first meeting of the Commissioners, and before they proceed to transact any other business, they shall name some fifth person to act, in case of necessity, as an Arbitrator or Umpire with regard to any point or points on which the Commissioners may differ in opinion. If, however, the Commissioners should not be able to agree upon any such fifth person, the British and Spanish Commissioners shall each name a person; and in case the Commissioners should differ in opinion with regard to any point, it shall then be determined by lot which of the two persons so named shall be the Arbitrator or Umpire for the decision of that particular point; and so on with regard to any other point or points on which the Commissioners may differ in opinion.

The person so to be chosen shall make and subscribe a solemn declaration in a form similar to that made by the Commissioners, and it shall be entered on the record of the proceedings.

In the event of the death, resignation, absence, or of his or their omitting, declining, or ceasing to act, a new person or persons shall be appointed in the same manner as the person or persons originally appointed.

ART. III. The Commissioners shall then forthwith proceed to the investigation of the claim of the owners of the British schooner "Mermaid".

They shall be bound to receive and peruse all written documents or statements which may be presented to them by or on the part of the owners, or by or on behalf of the Spanish Government, and to receive and consider any evidence that may be tendered to them in support of or against the claim, and also to hear if required, one person as Counsel or Agent on either side. If they should fail to agree either as to the validity of the claim, or as to the amount of compensation to be awarded, they shall call to their assistance the Arbitrator or Umpire; and such Arbitrator or Umpire, after having examined the evidence adduced for or against the claim and having heard, if required, one person on each side, as aforesaid, and consulted with the Commissioners, shall decide therupon finally and without appeal.

The decision of the Commissioners, or of the Arbitrator or Umpire, shall be given in writing, and shall be signed by him or them respectively.

The two Governments solemnly and sincerly engage to consider the decision of the Commissioners conjointly or of the Arbitrator or Umpire, as the case may be, as final and conclusive on the question referred and to give full effect thereto without objection or delay. The decision shall, if possible, be given within three months from the first meeting of the Commissioners.

ART. IV. Should the decision be favourable to the claimants and should it be necessary to pay any sum of money, such sum shall be made good by the Spanish Government within the term of ninety days, reckoned from the date of the decision.

ART. V. The Commissioners and the Arbitrator or Umpire shall keep an accurate record of their proceedings with the date thereof and shall appoint and employ a Clerk to assist them in the transaction of their business.

Any salary or gratuity paid to the Commissioners shall be defrayed by their respective Governments. Any salary or gratuity paid to the Arbitrator or Umpire, and to the Clerk, and any contingent expenses, shall be defrayed in moities by the respective Governments.

In witness whereof the respective parties have signed the present agreement, and affixed their seals thereto.

Done in duplicate in Madrid the fourth day of March one thousand eight hundred and sixty-eight.

XXVI. Etats-Unis d'Amérique, Mexique.

4 juillet 1868.

Cet arbitrage est un des plus importants qui aient été organisés au cours de ce siècle. Il a eu pour objet des réclamations réciproques de citoyens des deux pays à raison de déprédations commises par des tribus indiennes. De nombreux incidents marquèrent les débats, qui se prolongèrent de 1868 à 1876 [1]. M. Francis Lieber et M. Edward Thornton furent successivement désignés comme surarbitres et siégèrent respectivement dans 35 et 460 affaires, sur un nombre total de 2015 réclamations. Leur import s'est chiffré par 470,126,613 dollars pour les 1017 réclamations américaines et par 86,661,891 dollars pour les 998 réclamations mexicaines. 1662 affaires furent déclarées irrecevables ou injustifiées; pour les 186 réclamations américaines qui furent admises, il fut accordé aux intéressés 4,125,622 dollars, tandis

---

[1] On trouvera un exposé fort complet de ces incidents dans un article de MM. Matile et de Montluc, paru dans la *Revue de droit international et de législation comparée*, 1875, pag. 65 à 69.

que pour 167 réclamations mexicaines, il fut alloué 150,498 dollars.

Convention pour le règlement de réclamations réciproques, présentées par des citoyens des deux pays à charge de leurs gouvernements respectifs, conclue à Washington, le 4 juillet 1868.

Whereas it is desirable to maintain the friendly feelings between the United States and the Mexican Republic, and so to strengthen the system and principles of Republican government on the American Continent; and whereas since the signature of the treaty of Guadalupe Hidalgo, of the 2ᵈ of February 1848 claims and complaints have been made by citizens of the United States on account of injuries to their persons and their property by authorities of that republic and similar claims and complaints have been made on account of injuries to the persons and property of Mexican citizens by authorities of the United States, the President of the United States of America and the President of the Mexican Republic have resolved to conclude a convention for the ajustment of the said claims and complaints and have named as their Plenipotentiaries, the President of the United States, William H. Seward, Secretary of State; and the President of the Mexican Republic, Matias Romero, accredited as Envoy Extraordinary and Minister Plenipotentiary of the Mexican Republic to the United States; who, after having communicated to each other their respective full powers, found in good and due form, have agreed to the following articles:

ART. I. All claims on the part of corporations. companies, or private individuals, citizens of the United States, upon the Government of the Mexican Republic, arising from injuries to their persons or property by authorities of the Mexican Republic, and all claims on the part of corporations, companies, or private individuals citizens of the Mexican Republic upon the Government of the United States, arising from injuries to their persons or property by authorities of the United States, which may have been presented to either Government for its interposition with the other since the signature of the treaty of Guadalupe Hidalgo between the United States and the Mexican Republic of the 2ᵈ of February 1848, and which yet remain unsettled as well as any other such claims which may be presented within the time hereinafter specified, shall be referred to two Commissioners, one to be appointed by the President of the United States, by and with the advice and consent of the Senate, and one by the President of the Mexican Republic. In case of the death, absence, or incapacity of either Commissioner, or in the event of either Commissioner omitting or ceasing to act as such, the President

of the United States or the President of the Mexican Republic, respectively, shall forthwith name another person to act as Commissioner in the place or stead of the Commissioner originally named.

The Commissioners so named shall meet at Washington within six months after the exchange of the ratifications of this and shall, before proceeding to business, make and subscribe a solemn declaration that they will impartially and carefully examine and decide, to the best of their judgment and according to public law, justice, and aquity, without fear, favor, or affection to their own country, upon all such claims above specified as shall be laid before them on the part of the Governments of the United States and of the Mexican Republic, respectively; and such declaration shall be entered on the record of their proceedings.

The Commissioners shall then name some third person to act as an Umpire in any case or cases on which they may themselves differ in opinion. If they should not be able to agree upon the name of such third person, they shall each name a person, and in each and every case in which the Commissioners may differ in opinion as to the decision which they ought to give, it shall be determined by lot which of the two persons so named shall be Umpire in that particular case. The person or persons so to be chosen to be Umpire shall before proceeding to act as such in any case make and subscribe a solemn declaration in a form similar to that which shall already have been made and subscribed by the Commissioners, which shall be entered on the record of their proceedings. In the event of the death, absence or incapacity of such person or persons, or of his or their omitting or declining, or ceasing to act as such umpire, another and different person shall be named, as aforesaid, to act as such umpire, in the place of the person so originally named, as aforesaid, and shall make and subscribe such declaration as aforesaid.

ART. II. The Commissioners shall then conjointly proceed to the investigation and decision of the claims which shall be presented to their notice, in such order and in such manner as they may conjointly think proper, but upon such evidence or information only as shall be furnished by or on behalf of their respective Governments. They shall be bound to receive and peruse all written documents or statements which may be presented to them by or on behalf of their respective Governments in support of, or in answer to any claim, and to hear, if required, one person on each side on behalf of each Government on each and every separate claim. Should they fail to agree in opinion upon any individual claim, they shall call to their assistance the umpire whom they may have agreed to name or who may be determined by lot, as the case may be; and such umpire after having examined the evidence adduced for and against the claim, and after having heard, if required, one person on each side as aforesaid, and consulted with the Commissioners, shall decide thereupon finally and without appeal. The decision of the Commissioners and of the umpire shall be given upon each claim in writing, shall designate whether any sum which may be allowed shall be payable in gold or in the currency of the United States, and shall be signed by them respectively. It shall be competent for each Government to name one person to attend the Commissioners as agent on its behalf, to present and support claims on its behalf and to answer claims made upon it, and to represent it generally in all matters connected with the investigation and decision thereof.

The President of the United States of America and the President of the Mexican Republic hereby solemnly and sincerly engage to consider the decision of the Commissioners conjointly or of the Umpire, as the case may be, as absolutely final and conclusive upon each claim decided upon by them or him respectively, and to give full effect to such decisions without any objection, evasion, or delay whatsoever.

It is agreed that no claim arising out of a transaction of a date prior to the 2^d of February 1848 shall be admissible under this convention.

ART. III. Every claim shall be presented to the Commissioners within eight months from the day of their first meeting, unless in any case where reasons for delay shall be established to the satisfaction of the Commissioners, or of the Umpire in the event of the Commissioners differing in opinion thereupon, and then and in any such case the period for presenting the claim may be extended to any time not exceeding three months longer. The Commissioners shall be bound to examine and decide upon every claim within two years and six months from the day of their first meeting. It shall be competent for the Commissioners conjointly, or for the Umpire if they differ, to decide in each case whether any claim has or has not been duly made, preferred, and laid before them, either wholly or to any and what extent, according to the true intent and meaning of this Convention.

ART. IV. When decisions shall have been made by the Commissioners and the Arbiter in every case which shall have been laid before them, the total amount awarded in all the cases decided in favor of the citizens of the one party shall be deducted from the total amount awarded to the citizens of the other party, and the balance, to the amount of three hundred thousand dollars, shall be paid at the city of Mexico or at the city of Washington, in gold or its equivalent, within twelve months from the close of the Commission, to the Government in favor of whose citizens the greater amount may have been awarded, without interest or any other deduction than that specified in article VI of this Convention.

The residue of the said balance shall be paid in annual instalments to an amount not exceeding three hundred thousand dollars; in gold or its equivalent, in any one year until the whole shall have been paid.

ART. V. The high contracting parties agree to consider the result of the proceedings of this Commission as a full, perfect, and final settlement of every claim upon either Government arising out of any transaction of a date prior to the exchange of the ratification of the present Convention, and further engage that every such claim, whether or not the same may have been presented to the notice of, made, preferred, or laid before the said Commission, shall, from and after the conclusion of the proceedings of the said Commission, be considered and treated as finally settled, barred, and thenceforth inadmissible.

ART. VI. The Commissioners and the umpire shall keep an accurate record and correct minutes of their proceedings, with the dates. For that purpose they shall appoint two secretaries versed in the language of both countries to assist them in the transaction of the business of the Commission. Each Government shall pay to its Commissioners an amount of salary not exceeding forty-five hundred dollars a year in the currency of the United States, which amount shall be the same for both Governments. The amount of compensation to be paid to the Umpire shall be determined by mutual consent at the close of the Commission, but necessary and reasonable advances may be made by each Government upon the joint recommendation of the Commission. The salary of the secretaries shall not exceed the sum of twenty-five hundred dollars a year in the currency of the United States. The whole expenses of the Commission, including contingent expenses, shall be defrayed by a ratable deduction on the amount of the sums awarded by the Commission, provided always that such deduction shall not exceed five per cent. on the sums so awarded. The deficiency, if any, shall be defrayed in moieties by the two Governments.

ART. VII. The present convention shall be ratified by the President of the United States, by and with the advice and consent of the Senate thereof, and by the President of the Mexican Republic, with the approbation of the Congress of that Republic; and the ratification shall be exchanged at Washington within nine months from the date hereof, or sooner if possible.

In witness whereof the respective Plenipotentiaries have signed the same, and have affixed thereto the seals of their arms.

Done at Washington, the fourth day of July, in the year of our Lord one thousand eight hundred and sixty eight [1].

Plusieurs conventions prorogèrent successivement la durée primitivement fixée pour la terminaison des travaux de la commission : ces conventions ne contiennent que des stipulations qui ne demandent aucun commentaire.

Convention relative à la prolongation des pouvoirs de la commission arbitrale, nommée en vertu du traité du 4 juillet 1868, signée à Mexico, le 19 avril 1871.

Whereas a convention was concluded on the 4th day of July 1868, between the United States of America and the United States of Mexico. for the settlement of outstanding claims that have originated since the signing of the treaty of Guadalupe-Hidalgo, on the 2d of February 1848, by a mixed commission limited to endure for two years and six months from the day of the first meeting, of the commissioners ; and whereas doubts have arisen as to the practicability of the business of the said commission being concluded within the period assigned ;

The President of the United States of America and the President of the United States of Mexico are desirous that the time originally fixed for the duration of the said commission should be extended and to this end have named Plenipotentiaries to agree upon the best mode of effecting this object that is to say: The President of the United States of America, Thomas H. Nelson, accredited as Envoy Extraordinary and Minister Plenipotentiary of the United States of America to the Mexican Republic; and the President of the United States of Mexico Manuel Azpiroz, Chief Clerk and in charge of the Ministry of Foreign Relations of the United States of Mexico; who, after having presented their respective powers, and finding them sufficient and in due form, have agreed upon the following articles:

ART. I. The high contracting parties agree that the term assigned in the convention of the 4th July 1868 above referred to, for the duration of the said commission, shall be extended for a time not exceeding one year from the day when the functions of the said commission would terminate according to the convention referred to, or for a shorter time if it should be deemed

sufficient by the commissioners, or the umpire in case of their disagreement. It is agreed that nothing contained in this article shall in any wise alter or extend the time originally fixed in the said convention for the presentation of claims to the mixed commission.

ART. II. The present convention shall be ratified, and the ratifications shall be exchanged at Washington, as soon as possible.

In witness whereof the above-mentioned Plenipotentiaries have signed the same and affixed their respective seals.

Done in the city of Mexico the 19th day of April, in the year one thousand eight hundred and seventy-one [1].

Convention relative à une nouvelle prolongation des pouvoirs de la commission arbitrale, nommée en vertu du traité du 4 juillet 1868, signée à Washington, le 27 novembre 1872.

Whereas, by the convention concluded between the United States and the Mexican Republic on the fourth day of July 1868 certain claims of citizens of the contracting parties were submitted to a joint commission, whose functions were to terminate within two years and six months, reckoning from the day of the first meeting of the commissioners ; and whereas the functions of the aforesaid joint commission were extended, according to the convention concluded between the same parties on the nineteenth day of April 1871 for a term not exceeding one year from the day on which they were to terminate according to the first convention ; and whereas the possibility of said commission's concluding its labors even within the period fixed by the aforesaid convention of April nineteenth, 1871, is doubtful;

Therefore, the President of the United States of America and the President of the United States of Mexico, desiring that the term of the aforementioned commission should be again extended in order to attain this end, have appointed, the President of the United States Hamilton Fish, Secretary of State, and the President of the United States of Mexico Ignacio Mariscal, accredited to the Government of the United States as Envoy Extraordinary and Minister Plenipotentiary of said United States of Mexico, who, having exchanged their respective powers, which were found sufficient and in due form have, agreed upon the following articles:

ART. I. The high contracting parties agree that the said commission be revived and that the time fixed by the convention of April nineteenth, 1871, for the duration of the commission afore-

---

[1] *Treaties and Conventions between the United States and other Powers*, 1776 to 1887, p. 700.

[1] *Treaties and Conventions between the United States of America and other Powers*, 1776 to 1887, p. 705.

said, shall be extended for a term not exceeding two years from the day on which the function of the said commission would terminate according to that convention, or for a shorter time if it should be deemed sufficient by the commissioners or the umpire, in case of their disagreement.

It is agreed that nothing contained in this article shall in any wise alter or extend the time originally fixed in the said convention for the presentation of claims to the commission.

ART. II. The present convention shall be ratified and the ratification shall be exchanged at Washington as soon as possible.

In witness whereof, the above named Plenipotentiaries have signed the same and affixed their respective seals.

Done in the city of Washington the twenty seventh day of November, in the year one thousand eight hundred and seventy-two [1].

Convention relative à une troisième prolongation des pouvoirs de la commission arbitrale, nommée en vertu du traité du 4 juillet 1868, signée à Washington, le 20 novembre 1874.

Whereas, pursuant to the convention between the United States and the Mexican Republic of the 19th day of April 1871, the functions of the joint commission under the convention between the same parties of the 4th of July 1868 were extended for a term not exceeding one year from the day on which they were to terminate according to the convention last named;

And whereas, pursuant to the first article of the convention between the same parties, of the twenty-seventh day of November, one thousand eight hundred and seventy-two, the joint commission above referred to was revived and again extended for a term not exceeding two years from the day on which the functions of the said commission would terminate pursuant to the said convention of the nineteenth day of April 1871, but whereas the said extensions have not proved sufficient for the disposal of the business before the said commission, the said parties being equally animated by a desire that all that business should be closed as originally contemplated, the President of the United States has for this purpose conferred full powers on Hamilton Fish, Secretary of State, and the President of the Mexican Republic has conferred like powers on Don Ignacio Mariscal, Envoy Extraordinary and Minister Plenipotentiary of that Republic to the United States. And the said Plenipotentiaries having exchanged their full powers, which were found to be in due form, have agreed upon the following articles.

[1] *Ibid.*, p. 706.

ART. I. The high contracting parties agree that the said commission shall again be extended, and that the time now fixed for its duration shall be prolonged for one year from the time when it would have expired pursuant to the convention of the twenty-seventh of November 1872: that is to say until the thirty first day of January in the year one thousand eight hundred and seventy-six.

It is, however, agreed that nothing contained in this article shall in any wise alter or extend the time originally fixed by the convention of the 4th of July 1868 aforesaid, for the presentation of claims to the commission.

ART. II. It is further agreed that, if at the expiration of the time when, pursuant to the first article of this convention, the functions of the commissioners will terminate, the umpire under the convention should not have decided all the cases which may then have been referred to him, he shall be allowed a further period of not more than six months for that purpose.

ART. III. All cases which have been decided by the commissioners or by the umpire heretofore or which shall be decided prior to the exchange of the ratifications of this convention, shall from the date of such exchange be regarded as definitively disposed of, and shall be considered and treated as finally settled, barred, and thenceforth inadmissible. And, pursuant to the stipulation contained in the fourth article of the convention of the fourth day of July one thousand eight hundred and sixty-eight, the total amount awarded in case already decided and which may be decided before the exchange of ratifications of this convention and in all cases which shall be decided within the time in this convention respectively named, for that purpose, either by the commissioners or by the umpire, in favour of citizens of the one party shall be deducted from the total amount awarded to the citizens of the other party, and the balance, to the amount of three hundred thousand dollars shall be paid at the city of Mexico, or at the city of Washington. in gold or its equivalent, within twelve months from the 31st day of January one thousand eight hundred and seventy-six to the government in favour of whose citizens the greater amount may have been awarded, without interest or any other deduction than that specified in article VI of that convention. The residue of the said balance shall be paid in annual instalments to an amount not exceeding three hundred thousand dollars in gold or its equivalent, in any one year until the whole shall have been paid.

ART. IV. The present convention shall be ratified and the ratifications shall be exchanged at Washington, as soon as possible. In witness whereof the above named Plenipotentiaries have signed the same and affixed thereto their respective seals.

Done in Washington the twentieth day of November, in the year one thousand eight hundred and seventy-four [1].

Convention relative à une quatrième et dernière prolongation des pouvoirs de la commission arbitrale, nommée en vertu du traité du 4 juillet 1868, signée à Washington, le 29 avril 1876.

Whereas, pursuant to the convention between the United States and the Mexican Republic of the 19th day of April 1871, the functions of the joint commission under the convention between the same parties of the 4th of July 1868 were extended for a term not exceeding one year from the day on which they were to terminate according to the convention last named;

And whereas, pursuant to the first article of the convention between the same parties, of the twenty-seventh day of November, one thousand eight hundred and seventy-two, the joint commission above referred to was revived and again extended for a term not exceeding two years from the day on which the functions of the said commission would terminate pursuant to the said convention of the nineteenth day of April 1871:

And whereas, pursuant to the convention between the same parties, of the twentieth day of November one thousand eight hundred and seventy-four, the said commission was again extended for one year from the time when it would have expired pursuant to the convention of the twenty-seventh of November, one thousand eight hundred and seventy-two, that is to say, until the thirty-first day of January one thousand eight hundred and seventy-six; and it was provided that if, at the expiration of that time, the umpire under the convention should not have decided all the cases which may then have been referred to him, he should be allowed a further period of not more than six months for that purpose:

And whereas it is found to be impraticable for the umpire appointed pursuant to the convention adverted to, to decide all the cases referred to him, within the said period of six months by the convention of the twentieth of November one thousand eight hundred and seventy-four;

And the parties being still animated by a desire that all that business should be closed as originally contemplated, the President of the United States has for this purpose conferred full powers on Hamilton Fish, Secretary of State. and the President of the Mexican Republic has conferred like powers on Don Ignacio Mariscal,

Envoy Extraordinary and Minister Plenipotentiary of that Republic to the United States; and the said Plenipotentiaries having exchanged their full powers, which were found to be in due form, have agreed upon the following articles:

ART. I. The high contracting parties agree that if the umpire appointed under the convention above referred to, shall not, on or before the expiration of the six months allowed for the purpose by the second article of the convention of the twentieth of November one thousand eight hundred and seventy-four, have decided all the cases referred to him, he shall then be allowed a further period until the twentieth day of November one thousand eight hundred and seventy-six, for that purpose.

ART. II. It is further agreed that so soon after the twentieth day of November one thousand eight hundred and seventy-six, as may be praticable the total amount awarded in all cases already decided, whether by the commissioners or by the umpire, and which may be decided before the said twentieth day of November, in favour of citizens of the one party shall be deducted from the total amount awarded to the citizens of the other party, and the balance, to the amount of three hundred thousand dollars, shall be paid at the city of Mexico, or at the city of Washington, in gold or its equivalents, on or before the thirty-first day of January one thousand eight hundred and seventy-seven, to the government in favour of whose citizens the greater amount may have been awarded, without interest or any other deduction than that specified in article VI of the said convention of July 1868. The residue of the said balance shall be paid in annual instalments on the thirty-first day of January in each year to an amount not exceeding three hundred thousand dollars, in gold or its equivalent, in any one year, until the whole shall have been paid.

ART. III. The present convention shall be ratified, and the ratifications shall be exchanged at Washington, as soon as possible.

In witness whereof the above named Plenipotentiaries have signed the same and affixed thereto their respective seals.

Done in Washington, the twenty-ninth day of April in the year one thousand eight hundred and seventy-six [1].

Des nombreuses sentences prononcées, il n'a été publié, à notre connaissance, qu'une décision du surarbitre, M. Thornton. Il est vrai que cette décision avait une importance considérable, puisqu'elle a statué en fait sur 365

[1] *Ibid.*, p. 707.

[1] *Ibid.*, p. 709.

réclamations similaires d'un import total de 31,813,053 dollars.

Sentence rendue le 16 avril 1874 dans l'affaire de Don Rafaël Aguirre contre les Etats-Unis d'Amérique par le surarbitre nommé en vertu de la convention du 4 juillet 1868 pour le règlement des réclamations américano-mexicaines.

Le surarbitre a parcouru et étudié avec soin tous les documents qui se rapportent à l'affaire de Don Rafaël Aguirre contre les Etats-Unis n° 131, de même que la demande formulée par l'avocat de ces derniers, avec toutes les preuves qui lui ont été communiquées par la commission mixte américano-mexicaine. De l'examen attentif qu'il a fait du cas, résulte pour lui la conviction que les points sur lesquels repose la question du rejet ou de l'admission de la demande énoncée ci-dessus, sont à rechercher dans les causes qui ont conduit à la conclusion du traité du 30 décembre 1853 entre les Etats-Unis et le Mexique, et dans le sens des paroles du traité. Il paraît évident au surarbitre que l'une de ces causes a dû naître des plaintes constamment répétées du gouvernement mexicain à celui des Etats-Unis, depuis une date voisine de la conclusion du traité de Guadalupe-Hidalgo jusqu'à la fin de l'année 1853; que les stipulations du onzième article de ce traité n'avaient pas été remplies par le dernier gouvernement, et que conséquemment il devait des dommages-intérêts tant au gouvernement mexicain qu'aux citoyens du Mexique pour les dommages résultant de ce défaut d'accomplissement. La correspondance entre les deux gouvernements était d'une nature irritante et paraissait devoir exciter l'amertume de part et d'autre. Il était donc de l'intérêt des deux gouvernements, comme aussi c'était leur désir, de mettre fin à cet état de choses; et le surarbitre n'hésite pas à penser que ce fut là une des causes de désaccord auxquelles se référait le préambule du traité de 1853, désaccord que les deux gouvernements cherchaient à éloigner. On ne pouvait certes pas affirmer que toute cause de désaccord serait écartée jusqu'à ce que cette question fut réglée; et d'autre part, l'absence d'une stipulation dans ce but aurait eu pour effet de produire par cette phrase une fausse impression, car toute cause de désaccord n'aurait pas été écartée. Par le traité non ratifié de 1853. négocié par M. Gadsden, à Mexico, cette république cédait aux Etats-Unis une certaine portion de territoire, et consentait à ce que l'article XI du traité de Guadalupe fut annulé et que les Etats-Unis fussent exonérés de toutes réclamations de la part du Mexique ou de citoyens mexicains, que ce fût en raison du prétendu défaut dans l'accomplissement des obligations du onzième article du traité de Guadalupe, ou pour d'autres

causes d'origine postérieure à la date de ce traité. Ce fut en vue de ces stipulations, que les Etats-Unis consentirent à payer 15.000,000 de dollars et s'engagèrent en outre à prendre à leur compte toutes les réclamations des citoyens des Etats-Unis contre le Mexique, et d'y satisfaire jusqu'à concurrence de 5,000,000 de dollars. Mais le Sénat des Etats-Unis changea les termes de ce traité et les amendements qu'il proposa furent acceptés par le Mexique. Par ce traité ainsi amendé, le Mexique cédait une plus petite portion de territoire et relevait les Etats-Unis de toutes obligations (liabilities) résultant de celles renfermées dans le onzième article du traité de Guadalupe-Hidalgo; et consentait à ce que cet article et le 33ᵉ article du traité du 15 avril 1831 fussent annulés. Ce traité amendé ne fait nulle mention des réclamations de nature mixte des citoyens du Mexique contre les Etats-Unis, ni de celles des citoyens des Etats-Unis contre le Mexique. Ce fut en considération de ces stipulations, c'est-à-dire de la cession d'un territoire moindre, de la libération des Etats-Unis de toutes obligations encourues à teneur de l'article onze du traité de Guadalupe-Hidalgo, et du rappel de cet article avec celui du 33ᵉ article du traité du 5 avril 1831, que les Etats-Unis consentirent à payer au Mexique la somme de dix millions de dollars. De la part du demandeur en cause, on prétend que la première phrase de l'article deux du traité ratifié du 30 décembre 1853 ne libère pas les Etats-Unis du paiement de dommages-intérêts qui peuvent être dus envers les citoyens mexicains par suite de défaut d'exécution de la part des Etats-Unis, si défaut il y a eu, de remplir les obligations du onzième article du traité de Guadalupe. Le surarbitre pense au contraire qu'il libère les Etats-Unis, et que le gouvernement qui a accepté les amendements apportés par les Etats-Unis au traité précédent de Gadsden avait compris dans ce sens ces amendements. Il serait inconcevable qu'après toute la correspondance échangée, et les discussions presque aigres qui eurent lieu entre les deux gouvernements au sujet du prétendu non-accomplissement des obligations de l'article XI du traité de 1848 et les réclamations qui suivirent de la part des citoyens du Mexique, les Etats-Unis du Mexique eussent pu se contenter d'un traité qui n'eût pas pourvu à la solution de l'une des grandes questions qui s'agitaient, qu'ils eussent ratifié ce traité et que le Sénat des Etats-Unis l'eût sanctionné.

On prétend que le deuxième article du traité ne libérait pas les Etats-Unis des réclamations auxquelles ils auraient pu être tenus par la suite pour cause de quelque défaut dans l'accomplissement de l'article onze du traité de 1848: mais comme, par l'article deux lui-même, l'article onze du traité de 1848 était annulé, il ne pouvait y avoir lieu de manquer à des obligations, puisqu'il n'y en avait point, et conséquemment il ne pouvait y avoir lieu à des réclamations futures. S'il y avait des réclamations à l'égard desquelles les États-Unis eussent pu être tenus par suite d'un manque d'accomplissement des obligations de 1848 à 1853, ces réclamations les liaient certainement au moment de la signature du traité de 1853, et la responsabilité d'alors n'aurait pas pu être exclue du terme « all liability » de laquelle le gouvernement du Mexique relevait celui des Etats-Unis.

Le contexte de l'article deux vient à l'appui de cette manière de voir. La seconde phrase de l'article onze annule le onzième article du traité de 1848. Ce faisant, elle relève par cela même les Etats-Unis de toutes réclamations futures provenant d'un défaut d'exécution dans les obligations à remplir ; et la première phrase, si elle ne se rapporte qu'à ces futures réclamations, est évidemment un pléonasme. Dans le deuxième article du traité non ratifié de 1853, il avait été convenu que « pour éloigner toute cause de dispute au sujet des réclamations jusqu'à cette date, fondées sur les prétendues incursions d'Indiens », l'article onze du traité de Guadalupe devait être annulé. Si donc l'abolition de cet article avait cet effet-ci au sujet des réclamations jusqu'à la présente date, a fortiori devait il avoir le même effet au sujet de réclamations qui en réalité ne pouvaient avoir lieu. De plus, si l'on eût jugé nécessaire de libérer les Etats-Unis d'une responsabilité qu'ils ne pouvaient encourir, l'ordre des deux phrases dans l'article deux aurait été renversé : l'abolition de l'article onze du traité de Guadalupe aurait été placé en tête et la libération de responsabilité future aurait suivi comme la conséquence manifeste de l'abolition de cet article.

On allègue que le sens du texte espagnol dans la première phrase de l'article deux en question est différent de celui que donne la version anglaise. Le surarbitre pense autrement. La traduction stricte de l'Espagnol serait : « Le gouvernement du Mexique, par cet article, exempte celui des Etats-Unis des obligations de l'article onze du traité de Guadalupe-Hidalgo ». Un des sens du mot « liable » d'après le dictionnaire de Johnson est « non exempt ». Le verbe « eximer » peut être traduit : « relever de non-exemption ou de responsabilité ». Dans le troisième article du traité non ratifié de 1853, il est dit que, en considération des concessions reçues par les Etats-Unis et des obligations (obligaciones) abandonnées par la République mexicaine, les Etats-Unis consentaient à payer une certaine somme d'argent. Dans l'article précédent, une des stipulations était, que toute occasion de dispute au sujet des réclamations jusqu'à cette date sur de prétendues incursions d'Indiens était écartée par l'abolition de l'article onze du traité de Guadalupe.... Le terme « obligaciones » au commencement de l'article suivant doit donc renfermer ces réclamations.

Par suite, il n'y a pas de raisons pour qu'elles soient exclues du sens du même mot dans l'article deux du traité ratifié ; du reste que la traduction en espagnol soit correcte ou non, le gouvernement mexicain seul en était responsable. La version espagnole n'a jamais été soumise au Sénat des Etats-Unis, dont la sanction est nécessaire pour chaque traité. Il est vrai de dire que M. Marcy établit dans sa note au général Rhodes, du 11 décembre 1856, que « l'amendement du Sénat avait été envoyé au général Almonte pour être traduit avant l'échange des ratifications du traité », mais il n'y a aucune preuve quelconque que la traduction ait été envoyée à M. Marcy, qu'il ait été consulté à son sujet, ou qu'il ait émis aucune opinion quand à son exactitude. Au contraire, le général Almonte demandait le 4 mai 1854 que les amendements du Sénat lui fussent transmis, parce qu'il désirait expédier son courrier du Mexique le lendemain soir. Le jour suivant, le 5, M. Marcy, envoya les amendements demandés au général Almonte. Conséquemment il n'aurait pu y avoir que fort peu de temps pour discuter l'exactitude de la traduction, et même il n'aurait pu y avoir de raison pour le faire, puisque les amendements du Sénat étaient définitifs, et qu'on avait donné clairement à entendre que les Etats-Unis n'y admettraient aucune modification. Le général Almonte était connu pour être parfaitement maître de la langue anglaise. La connaissance qu'il en avait, non moins que ce qui s'était passé avant la conclusion du traité, doivent faire admettre qu'il saisissait bien le sens réel de l'anglais dans la phrase en question, et l'arbitre croit qu'il le rendit correctement en espagnol. Vu l'absence de toutes raisons mises en avant par le Sénat pour réduire la somme à payer au Mexique de 15 millions de dollars à 10 millions, l'arbitre considère qu'il n'y a pas lieu d'avoir recours à des suppositions.

D'autre part, il est de fait que, par le traité amendé, le Mexique cédait aux Etats-Unis une portion de territoire plus petite que celle stipulée dans le traité non ratifié, et que ce dernier exonérait les Etats-Unis de toutes réclamations qui auraient pu se produire de la part de citoyens mexicains depuis la date du traité de Guadalupe. La libération dans le traite amendé n'embrassait pas autant. Ces deux faits peuvent expliquer la réduction faite par le Sénat dans le traité amendé.

Toutefois, malgré cette réduction, les Etats-Unis consentaient toujours, par le troisième article, à payer une valeur substantielle en considération des stipulations contenues dans le premier et le deuxième article.

L'arbitre pense que l'une de ces stipulations, c'est-à-dire celle renfermée dans la première phrase de l'article deux, a libéré les Etats-Unis de toute réclamation de la nature de celle avancée par Don Rafael Aguirre dans le cas n° 131, en conséquence il prononce que les conclusions prises devant la commission par l'avocat des Etats-Unis, le 10 octobre 1870, sont bien fondées.

Washington, 16 avril 1874 [1].

XXVII. Grande-Bretagne, Vénézuéla.

21 septembre 1868.

La discussion porta dans cette affaire sur des réclamations présentées par des citoyens anglais à charge du gouvernement vénézuélien.

Convention conclue entre la Grande-Bretagne et la République Vénézuéla, à l'effet de régler les indemnités dues à des sujets anglais, signée à Caracas, le 21 septembre 1868.

With the view of determining the amount of all pending British claims upon the Government of Venezuela, the Undersigned, Guillermo Tell Villegas Minister of Foreign Affairs duly empowered by his Government, has appointed the citizen Dr Juan de Dios Méndez Commissioner on the part of the United States of Venezuela: and George Fargan, Her Britannic Majesty's Chargé d'affaires to the United States of Venezuela duly empowered by his Government, has appointed Lewis Joel Esq. Commissioner on the part of Great Britain, to sit as a Mixed Commission to fix the amount due to those British subjects whose claims have not yet been adjudicated upon. The Commission above-named shall sit in the city of Carácas after the signature of this agreement.

In case of death, absence, resignation, or incapacity of either of the Commissioners, or in the event of either of them omitting or ceasing to act, the Government of the United States of Venezuela or the British Chargé d'affaires at Carácas, shall forthwith proceed to fill the vacancy.

The Commissioners shall appoint some third person as an arbitrator or umpire, to decide upon any case or cases concerning which they may disagree, or upon any point of difference that may arise in the course of their proceedings.

If however, the Commissioners shall not be able to agree upon such third person, they shall each name a person, and in case the Commissioners should differ in opinion with regard to any point, it shall be determined by lot which

[1] *Revue de droit international et de législation comparée*, 1875, p. 67.

of the two persons so named shall be arbitrator or umpire for the decision of that particular point, and so on with regard to any other point or points on which the Commissioners may differ in opinion.

The decision of the Commissioners, or of the arbitrator or umpire, shall be given in writing, and shall be signed by them or him respectively. The two Governments solemnly and sincerely engage to consider the decision of the Commissioners conjointly, or of the arbitrator or umpire, as the case may be, as final and conclusive on the questions referred, and to give full effect thereto without objection or delay.

The Commissioners, and the arbitrator or umpire, shall keep an accurate record of their proceedings, with the date thereof and may, if necessary, appoint and employ a clerk to assist them in the transaction of their business.

Any salary or gratuity paid to the Commissioners shall be defrayed by their respective Governments. Any salary or gratuity paid to the arbitrator or umpire, and the clerk and any contingent expenses shall be defrayed in moieties by the respective Governments. The present arrangement, as well as the awards made in virtue thereof either by the Commission or the umpire shall be submitted for approval to the Venezuelan National Legislature. In witness thereof, the respective Contracting Parties have hereunto set their hands and affixed their seals at Carácas, this 21st day of September, in the year of our Lord, 1868 [1].

Les arbitres ne purent terminer leurs opérations que ce 15 novembre 1869, ainsi qu'il résulte du procès-verbal de leur réunion finale. Le total des indemnités accordées par eux se monta à la somme de 312,587 pesos 2 cents ou 250,069 venezolanos 61 cents.

Protocole de la réunion finale de la commission arbitrale nommée en vertu du traité du 21 septembre 1868, entre le Vénézuéla et la Grande-Bretagne.

The Undersigned Commissioners under the Convention of the 21st of September, 1868, for the adjustment of pending British claims against the Government of Venezuela, herewith respectfully report to their respective Governments their proceedings and awards.

The claims submitted to the Commissioners for their consideration have greatly exceeded the number originally anticipated. The duties of the Commissioners have, therefore been greatly in excess of what was originally contemplated.

[1] HERTSLET, *A complete Collection...*, t. XIII, p. 1009.

In adjudicating upon the claims submitted to them the Commissioners have been fully sensible of the grave responsibility which devolved upon them, and have. therefore, devoted the most patient labour to their investigation. The whole of the claims having been submitted on documentary evidence (in some cases of a very voluminous character) they have required a most careful examination, and many of the cases have been the subject of long and serious discussion between the Commissioners.

In reporting the result of their labours and that of the Umpire as the best they have been able to attain in the discharge of the important and responsible duties intrusted to them, they entertain the hope of obtaining the approval of their respective Governments.

Carácas, November 15, 1869[1].

XXVIII. Espagne, Etats-Unis d'Amérique.

27 octobre 1795.

Cet arbitrage ne semble pas avoir eu de suite. Bien que les ratifications du traité qui l'institua furent échangées dès le 25 avril 1796, il résulte des termes de l'article 12 du traité du 22 février 1819, que l'article 21 du traité du 27 octobre 1795, spécialement consacré à cet arbitrage, fut annulé de commun accord. Il n'en résulte pas moins que la juridiction arbitrale fut acceptée, dès le siècle dernier, par une nation continentale de l'Europe.

Traité d'amitié et de navigation conclu entre l'Espagne et les Etats-Unis de l'Amérique du Nord, à San Lorenzo el Real, le 27 octobre 1795.

. . . .

ART. XXI. In order to terminate all differences on account of the losses sustained by the citizens of the United States in consequence of their vessels and cargoes having been taken by the subjects of His Catholic Majesty, during the late war between Spain and France, it is agreed that all such cases shall be referred to the final decision of Commissioners, to be appointed in the following manner. His Catholic Majesty shall name one Commissioner and the President of the United States, by and with the advice and consent of their Senate, shall appoint another, and the said two Commissioners shall agree on the choice of a third, or if they cannot agree so, they shall each propose one person, and of the two names so proposed, one shall be drawn by lot

in the presence of the two original Commissioners, and the person whose name shall be so drawn shall be the third Commissioner; and the three Commissioners so appointed shall be sworn impartially to examine and decide the claims in question, according to the merits of the several cases, and to justice, equity, and the law of nations.

The said Commissioners shall meet and sit at Philadelphia: and in the case of death, sickness, or necessary absence of any such Commissioner, his place shall be supplied in the same manner as he was first appointed, and the new Commissioner shall take the same oaths, and do the same duties. They shall receive all complaints and applications authorized by this article, during eighteen months from the day on which they shall assemble. They shall have power to examine all such persons as come before them on oath or affirmation, touching the complaints in question, and also to receive in evidence all written testimony, authenticated in such manner as they shall think proper to require or admit. The award of said Commissioners, or any two of them, shall be final and conclusive, both as to the justice of the claim and the amount of the sum to be paid to the claimants, and His Catholic Majesty undertakes to cause the same to be paid in specie, without deduction, at such times and places, and under such conditions as shall be awarded by the said Commissioners[1].

XXIX. Etats-Unis d'Amérique, Pérou.

4 décembre 1868.

Certains auteurs ont supposé que cet arbitrage était une suite donnée aux arbitrages du 12 janvier 1863 et du 20 décembre 1862. Les termes de l'article 2 du traité qui l'institue prouvent qu'il s'agit de réclamations nouvelles et réciproques postérieures au 30 novembre 1863. La décision des commissionnaires n'a pas été publiée.

Convention conclue entre les Etats-Unis d'Amérique et le Pérou, à l'effet de régler les indemnités réclamées par des citoyens des deux pays, signée le 4 décembre 1868.

Whereas claims may have at various times since the Signatures of the decision of the mixed Commission which met in Lima in July 1863, been made upon the Government of the United States of America, by citizens of Peru, and have been made by citizens of the United States of America upon the Government of Peru and whereas

[1] HERTSLET, A complete Collection..., t. XIII, p. 1010.

[1] Treaties and Conventions between the United States and other powers, 1776-1887, p. 1013.

some of such claims are still pending: The President of the United States of America and the Président of Peru, being of opinion that a speedy and equitable settlement of all such claims will contribute much to the maintenance of the friendly feelings which subsist between the two countries have resolved to make arrangements for that purpose by means of a convention and have named as their plenipotentiaries to confer and agree thereupon that is to say:

The President of the United States names Alvin P. Hovey, Envoy Extraordinary and Minister Plenipotentiary of the United States of America near the Government of Peru; and the President of Peru names His Excellency Doctor Don José Antonio Barrenechea, Minister of Foreign Affairs of Peru.

Who after having communicated to each other their respective full Powers, found in good and true form, have agreed as follows.

ART. I. The high contracting parties agree that all claims on the part of corporations, companies, or private individuals, citizens of the United States, upon the Government of Peru, and all claims on the part of corporations, companies, or private individuals citizens of Peru, upon the Government of the United States, which may have been presented to either Government for its interposition since the sittings of the said mixed commission and which remain yet unsettled as well as any other claims which may be presented within the time specified in Article III herein after, shall be referred to the two Commissioners, who shall be appointed in the following manner, that is to say: One Commissioner shall be named by the President of the United States, and one by the President of Peru. In case of the death, absence, or incapacity of either Commissioner or in the event of either Commissioner omitting or ceasing to act as such, the President of the United States or the President of Peru respectively, shall forthwith name another person to act as Commissioner in the place or stead of the Commissioner already named.

The Commissioners so named shall meet at Lima at their earliest convenience after they have been respectively named, not to exceed three months from the ratification of this convention and shall before proceeding to any business, make and subscribe a solemn declaration that they will impartially and carefully examine and decide to the best of their judgment, and according to justice and equity, without fear, favor, or affection to their own country upon all such claims as shall be laid before them on the part of the Governments of the United States and Peru, respectively, and such declaration shall be entered on the record of the Commission.

The Commissioners shall then, and before proceeding to other business, name some third person of some third nation to act as an Arbitrator or Umpire in any case or cases on which they may themselves differ in opinion. If they should not be able to agree upon the name of such third person, they shall each name a person of a third nation and in each and every case in which the Commissioners may differ in opinion as to the decision which they ought to give, it shall be determined by lot which of the two persons so named shall be the Arbitrator or Umpire in that particular case. The person or persons so to be chosen to be Arbitrator or Umpire shall, before proceeding to act as such in any case, make and subscribe a solemn declaration in a form similar to that which shall have already been made and subscribed by the Commissioners, which shall be entered upon the records of their proceedings. In the event of the death, absence, or incapacity of such person or persons, or of his or their omitting or declining, or ceasing to act as such Arbitrator or Umpire another and different person shall be named as aforesaid to act as such Arbitrator or Umpire in the place and stead of the person so originally named as aforesaid, and shall make and subscribe such declaration as aforesaid.

ART. II. The Commissioners shall then forthwith to the investigation of the claims which shall be presented to their notice. They shall investigate and decide upon such claims in such order and in such manner as they may conjointly think proper, but upon such evidence or information as shall be furnished by or on behalf of their respective Governments. They shall be bound to receive and peruse all written documents or statements which may be presented to them by or on behalf of their respective Governments, in support of or in answer to any claim, and to hear, if required, one person on each side on behalf of each Government as counsel or Agent for such Government, on each and every separate claim. Should they fail to agree in opinion on any individual claim, they shall call to their assistance the Arbitrator or Umpire whom they have agreed to name or who may be determined by lot, as the case may be, and such Arbitrator or Umpire, after having examined the evidence adduced for and against the claim, and after having heard as required an person on each side, as aforesaid and consulted with the Commissioners, shall decide thereupon finally and without appeal. The decision of the Commissioners and of the Arbitrator or Umpire shall be given upon each claim in writing, and shall be signed by them respectively.

It shall be competent for each Government to name one person to attend the Commissioners as agent on its behalf and to answer claims made upon it, and to represent it generally in all matters connected with the investigation and decision thereof.

The President of the United States, and the President of Peru, hereby solemnly and sincerely engage to consider the decision of the Commissioners conjointly, or of the Arbitrator or Umpire as they case may be, as absolutely final, and to give full effect to such decision, without any objections, evasion, or delay whatsoever. It is agreed that no claim arising out of any transaction of a date prior to the 30th of November, 1863, shall be admissible under this convention.

ART. III. Every claim shall be presented to the Commissioners within two months from the day of their first meeting unless in any case where reasons for delay shall be established to the satisfaction of the Commissioners, or of the Arbitrator or Umpire, in the event of the Commissioners differing in opinion thereon, and then and in every such case the period for presenting the claim may be extended to any period not exceeding one month longer.

The Commissioners shall be bound to examine and decide upon every claim within six months from the day of their first meeting.

ART. IV. All sums of money which may be awarded by the Commissioners or by the Arbitrator or Umpire on account of any claim, shall be paid by the one Government to the other, as the case may be, whithin four months after the date of the decision, without interest, and without any deduction, save as specified in Article VI, herein after.

ART. V. The high contracting parties agree to consider the result of the proceedings of this Commission as a full, perfect, and final settlement of every claim upon either Government arising out of any transaction of a date prior to the exchange of the ratifications of the present convention ; and further engage that every such claim, whether or not the same may have been presented to the notice of, made, preferred or laid before the said Commissioners, shall, from and after the conclusion of the proceedings of the said Commission, be considered and treated as finally settled, barred, and therefore inadmissible.

ART. VI. The salaries of the Commissioners shall not exceed forty-five hundred dollars in United States gold coin, each, yearly. Those of the secretaires and Arbitrator or Umpire shall be determined by the Commissioners : and in case the said Commission finish its labors in less than six months, the Commissioners, together with their assistants, will be entitled to six months pay and the whole expenses of the Commission shall be defrayed by a ratable deduction on the amount of the sums awarded by the Commissioners provided always that such deduction shall not exceed the rate of five percent, on the sums so awarded. The deficiency, if any, shall be defrayed by the two Governments in moieties.

ART. VII. The present convention shall be ratified by the President of the United States, by and with the consent of the Senate thereof, and by the President of Peru, with the approbation of the Congress of that Republic and the ratification will be exchanged in Lima, as soon as may be, within six months of the date hereof.

ART. VIII. The high contracting parties declare that this convention shall not be considered as a precedent obligatory on them, and that they remain in perfect liberty to proceed in the manner that may be deemed most convenient regarding the diplomatic claims that may arise in the future.

In witness whereof the respective Plenipotentiairies have signed the same in the English and Spanish languages, and have affixed thereto the seals of their arms.

Done in Lima the fourth day of December, in the year of our Lord one thousand eight hundred and sixty eight [1].

XXX. Grande-Bretagne, Portugal.

13 janvier 1869.

Cet arbitrage confié au Président des Etats-Unis de l'Amérique du Nord a eu pour objet d'attribuer définitivement à l'un des deux pays en cause l'île de Bulama et le territoire sur la terre ferme situé en face de cette île. Le conflit fut tranché en faveur du Portugal par une sentence du 21 avril 1876.

Protocol of Conference between Great Britain and Portugal, agreeing to refer to Arbitration their respective claims to the Island of Bulama. Lisbon, January 13, 1869.

Whereas the Government of His Most Faithful Majesty asserts a claim to the Island of Bulama, on the western coast of Africa, and to a certain portion of territory opposite to that island on the mainland ; and whereas the Government of ther Britannic Majesty asserts a claim to the same island and the territory opposite to it on the mainland ; and whereas both parties, being animated by a friendly feeling and nei-

---

[1] *Treaties and Conventions between the United States and other Powers*, 1776—1887, p. 872.

ther of them having any wish to appropriate territory which may lawfully belong to the other, have consented to refer their respective claims to the arbitration of a third Power in whom both repose confidence.

For this purpose they have agreed to apply to the President of the United States of America and it now becomes necessary to place on record certain terms and arrangements with a view to obtaining the speedy and convenient hearing· and determination of the claims in question; and the undersigned, the Marquis de Sà da Bandeira, a peer of the realm, President of the Council of Ministers, Minister and Secretary of State of War and «ad interim» Minister for Foreign Affairs of His Most Faithful Majesty, and the Honourable Sir Charles A. Murray, knight commander of the Bath, etc., and Her Britannic Majesty's Envoy Extraordinary and Minister Plenipotentiary at the Court of Lisbon, being duly authorised by their respective Governments, have agreed as follows:

ART. I. The respective claims of His Most Faithful Majesty's Government and of the Government of Her Britannic Majesty to the island of Bulama, on the western coast of Africa, and to a certain portion of territory opposite to that island on the mainland shall be submitted to the arbitration and award of the President of the United States of America, who shall decide thereupon finally and without appeal.

ART. II. The award of the President of the United States, whether it be wholly in favour of the claim of either party, or in the nature of an equitable solution of the difficulty, shall be considered as absolutely final and conclusive; and full effect shall be given to such award without any objection, evasion or delay whatsoever. Such decision shall be given in writing and dated; it shall be in whatsoever form the President may choose to adopt; it shall be delivered to the Ministers or other Public Agents of Portugal and of Great Britain, who may be actually at Washington and shall be considered as operative from the day of the date of the delivery thereof.

ART. III. The written or printed case of each of the two parties accompanied by the evidence offered in support of the same shall be laid before the President within 6 months from the date hereof and a copy of such case and evidence shall be communicated by each party to the other, through their respective Ministers at Washington. After such communication shall have taken place, each party shall have the power of drawing up and laying before the President a second and definitive statement, if it think fit to do so, in reply to the case of the

other party so communicated, which definitive statement shall be also laid before the Arbiter, and also be mutually communicated, in the same manner as aforesaid, by each party to the other within 5 months from the date of laying the first statement of the case before the Arbiter.

ART. IV. If in the case submitted to the Arbiter, either party shall specify or allude to any report or documents in its own exclusive possession without annexing a copy, such party shall be bound, if the other party thinks proper to apply for it, to furnish that party with a copy thereof, and if the Arbiter should desire further elucidation or evidence with regard to any point contained in the statements laid before him, he shall be at liberty to require it from either party, and he shall be at liberty to hear one counsel or agent for each party, in relation to any matter which he shall think fit; and at such time, and in such manner as he may think fit.

ART. V. The Ministers or other Public Agents of Portugal and of Great Britain at Washington respectively shall be considered as the Agents of their respective Governments to conduct their case before the Arbiter who shall be requested to address all his communications and give all his notices ·to such Ministers or other Public Agents, whose acts shall bind their Governments to and before the Arbiter on this matter.

ART. VI. It shall be competent to the Arbiter to proceed in the said Arbitration and all matters relating thereto, as and when he shall fit either in person or by a person or persons named by him for that purpose, either with closed doors or in public sitting, either in the presence or absence of either or both Agents and either viva voce or by written discussion or otherwise.

ART. VII. The Arbiter shall, if he think fit, appoint a secretary registrar, or clerk, for the purposes of the proposed arbitration, at such rate of remuneration as he shall think proper. This and all other expenses of, and connected with the said arbitration shall be provided for as herein after stipulated.

ART. VIII. The Arbiter shall be requested to deliver, together with his award, an account of all the costs and expenses which he may have been put to, in relation to this matter, which shall forthwith be repaid in two equal portions, one by each of the two parties.

ART. IX. The Arbiter shall be requested to give his award in writing as early as convenient after the whole case on each side shall have been laid before him, and to deliver one copy thereof to each of the said agents.

Should the Arbiter be unable to decide wholly in favour of either of the respective claims, he shall be requested to give such a decision as will, in his opinion, furnish an equitable solution of the difficulty.

Should he decline to give any decision, then everything done in the premises by virtue of this agreement shall be null and void, and it shall be competent for the Portuguese and British Governments to do and proceed in all respects as if the reference to arbitration had never been made.

Done at Lisbon, the 13th of January 1869[1].

Award of the President of the United States, as Arbiter on the Claims of Great Britain and of Portugal to the Island of Bulama, on the Western Coast of Africa, and to a certain portion of territory, opposite to that Island, on the Mainland, Washington, April 21, 1870.

Ulysses S. Grant, President of the United States, to whom it shall concern, greeting:

The functions of Arbiter having been conferred upon the President of the United States, by virtue of a Protocol of a Conference held in Lisbon, in the Foreign Office, on the 13th day of January, in the year of our Lord 1869, between the Minister and Secretary of State for Foreign affairs of His Most Faithful Majesty the King of Portugal, and Her Britannic Majesty's Envoy Extraordinary and Minister Plenipotentiary, whereby it was agreed that the respective claims of His Most Faithful Majesty's Government and of the Government of Her Britannic Majesty to the Island of Bulama on the Western Coast of Africa, and to a certain portion of territory opposite to that island, on the mainland, should be submitted to the arbitration and award of the President of the United States of America, who should decide thereupon finally and without appeal;

And the written or printed case of each of the two parties, accompanied by the evidence offered in support of the same, having been laid before the Arbiter within 6 months from the date of the said Protocol, and a copy of such case and evidence having been communicated by each party to the other through their respective Ministers at Washington, and each party, after such communication had taken place, having drawn up and laid before the Arbiter a second and definitive statement in reply to the case of the other party so communicated, which said definitive statements were so laid before the Arbiter, and were also mutually communicated, in the same manner as aforesaid, by each party to the other, within 6 months from the date of laying the first statement before the Arbiter;

---

[1] HERTSLET, *A complete Collection of the Treaties and Conventions* . . ., t. XIII, p. 688—690.

And it appearing that neither party desires to apply for any report or document in the exclusive possession of the other party, which has been specified or alluded to in any of the cases submitted to the Arbiter, and that neither party desires to be heard by counsel or agent in relation to any of the matters submitted in this arbitration;

And a person named by the Arbiter for that purpose, according to the terms of the said Protocol, having carefully considered each of the said written or printed statements so laid before the Arbiter, and the evidence offered in support of each of the same, and each of the said second or definitive statements;

And it appearing that the said Island of Bulama and the said mainland opposite thereto were discovered by a Portuguese navigator in 1446; that long before the year 1792, a Portuguese settlement was made at Bissao, on the River Jeba, which said settlement has ever since been maintained under Portuguese sovereignty; that in the year 1699, or about that time, a Portuguese settlement was made at Guinala, on the Rio Grande, which last named settlement, in the year 1778, was «a large village, inhabited only by Portuguese, who had been there from father to son for a long time»; that the coast line from Bissao to Guinala, after crossing the River Jeba, includes the whole coast on the mainland opposite to the Island of Bulama; that the Island of Bulama is adjacent to the mainland, and so near it that animals cross at low water; that in 1752 formal claim was made by Portugal to the Island of Bulama, which claim has been ever since asserted; that the island was not inhabited prior to 1792, and was unoccupied, with the exception of a few acres thereof, at the west end, which were used by a native tribe for the purpose of raising vegetables; that the British title is derived from an alleged cession by native Chiefs in 1792, at which time the sovereignty of Portugal had been established over the mainland and over the Island of Bulama; that the Portuguese Government has not relinquished its claim, and now occupies the island with a Portuguese settlement of 700 person; that attempts have been made since 1792 to fortify the British claim by further similar cessions from native Chiefs; and that none of the acts done in support of the British title have been acquiesced in by Portugal;

And no further elucidation or evidence with regard to any point contained in the statements so laid before the Arbiter being required;

Now, therefore, I. Ulysses S. Grant, President of The United States, do award and decide, that the claims of the Government of His Most

Faithful Majesty the King of Portugal to the Island of Bulama on the Western Coast of Africa, and to a certain portion of territory opposite to this island on the mainland, are proved and established.

In testimony whereof I have hereunto set my hand, and have coused the seal of The United States to be hereto affixed.

Done in triplicate, in the city of Washington, on the 21st day of April, in the year of our Lord 1870, and of the Independence of the United States of America the 94th [1].

XXXI. Grande-Bretagne. Portugal.

28 juillet 1817.

Les commissions arbitrales dont il est question dans le traité reproduit plus loin, ont eu pour objet de régler les indemnités dues aux propriétaires de vaisseaux, saisis par les croiseurs anglais pour avoir coopéré au trafic illicite des esclaves. Nous ne reproduisons de ce traité que les articles qui ont directement trait à l'organisation des commissions arbitrales ; par contre nous avons cru devoir reproduire entièrement le règlement qui y a été annexé et qui est des plus intéressants à raison du soin avec lequel il a été rédigé.

Additional convention to the Treaty of the 22th January 1815, between His Britannic Majesty and His Most Faithful Majesty, for the purpose of preventing their Subjects from engaging in any illicit Traffic in Slaves. Signed at London, the 28th July 1817.

. . . .

ART. VIII. In order to bring to adjudication, with the least delay and inconvenience, the vessels which may be detained for having been engaged in an illicit trafic of slaves, there shall be established, within the space of a year at furthest from the exchange of the ratifications of the present Convention, two mixed Commissions, formed of an equal number of individuals of the two nations, named for this purpose by their respective Sovereigns. These Commissions shall reside, one in a possession belonging to His Britannic Majesty, the other within the Territories of His most Faithful Majesty ; and the two Governments at the period of the exchange of the ratifications of the present Convention, shall declare each for its own Dominions in what places the Commissions shall respectively reside. Each of the two High Contracting Parties reser-

----

[1] *State Papers*, vol. LXI, p. 1103.

ving to itself the right of changing, at its pleasure, the place of residence of the Commission held within its own Dominions, provided, however, that one of the two Commissions shall always be held upon the coast of Africa, and the other in the Brazils.

These Commissions shall judge the causes submitted to them without appeal, and according to the Regulations and Instructions annexed to the present Convention, of which they shall be considered as an integral part.

ART. IX. His Britannic Majesty, in conformity with the stipulations of the Treaty of the 22nd of January 1815, engages to grant, in the manner hereafter explained, sufficient indemnification to all the proprietors of Portugueze vessels and cargoes captured by British cruizers between the 1st of June 1814 and the period at which the two Commissions pointed out in Article VIII of the present convention, shall assemble at their respective posts.

The two High Contracting Parties agree that all claims of the nature herein before mentioned, shall be received and liquidated by a mixed Commission, to be held at London, and which shall consist of an equal number of the individuals of the two nations, named by their respective Sovereigns, and upon the same principles stipulated by the VIIIth Article of this Additional Convention, and by the other Acts which form an integral part of the same. The aforesaid Commission shall commence their functions six months after the ratification of the present Convention, or sooner if possible.

The two High Contracting Parties have agreed that the proprietors of vessels captured by the British cruizers cannot claim compensation for a larger number of slaves than that which, according to the existing laws of Portugal, they were permitted to transport, according to the tonnage of the captured vessels.

The two High Contracting Parties are equally agreed that every Portugueze vessels captured with slaves on board for the traffic, which shall be proved to have been embarked within the territories of the coast Africa, situated to the north of Cape Palmas, and not belonging to the Crown of Portugal, as well as all Portugueze vessels captured with slaves on board for the traffic, six months after the exchange of the ratifications of the Treaty of the 22nd of January, 1815, and on which it can be proved that the aforesaid slaves were embarked in the roadsteds of the coast of Africa, situated to the north of the Equator, shall not be entitled to claim any indemnification.

ART. X. His Britannic Majesty engages to pay within the space of a year at furthest, from he decision of each case, to the individuals having a just claim to the same, the sums which shall be granted to them by the Commissions named in the preceeding Articles.

ART. XI. His Britannic Majesty formally engages to pay the £ 300,000 of indemnification stipulated by the Convention of the 21st of January 1815, in favour of the proprietors of Portugueze vessels captured by British cruizers, up to the period of the 1st of June 1814, in the manner following, viz.

The first payement of £ 150,000 six months after the exchange of the ratifications of the present convention, and the remaining £ 150,000 as well as the interest at five per cent, due upon the total sum, from the day of the exchange of the ratifications of the Convention of the 21st of January 1815, shall be paid nine months after the exchange of the ratifications of present Convention. The interest due shall be payable up to the day of the last payement. All the aforesaid payements shall be made in London, to the Minister, His Most Faithful Majesty shall think proper to authorize for that purpose.

ART. XII. The Acts or Instruments annexed to this additional Convention, and which form an integral part thereof, are as follows:

Nº 1. Form of passport for the Portugueze merchant ships destined for the lawful traffic in slaves.

Nº 2. Instructions for the ships of war of both nations, destined to prevent the illicit traffic in slaves.

Nº 3. Regulation for the mixed Commissions, which are to hold their sittings on the coast of Africa, at the Brazils and in London.

ART. XIII. The present Convention shall be ratified, and the ratifications thereof exchanged at Rio Janeiro, within the space of four months at furthest, dating from the day of its signature.

In witness whereof, the respective Plenipotentiaries have signed the same, and have thereunto affixed the seal of their arms.

Done at London, the 28th July 1817[1].

Regulation for the mixed Commissions, which are to reside on the Coast of Africa, in the Brazils, and at London.

ART. I. The mixed Commissions to be established by the Additional Convention of this date, upon the Coast of Africa and in the Brazils, are appointed to decide upon the legality of the detention of such slave vessels as the cruizers of both nations shall detain, in pursuance of this same Convention, for carrying on an illicit commerce in slaves.

---

[1] HERTSLET, *A complete Collection* ..., t. II, p. 89—95.

The above-mentioned Commissions shall judge, without appeal, according to the letter and spirit of the Treaty of the 22nd of January 1815, and of the Additional Convention to the said Treaty, signed at London on this 28th day of July 1817. The Commissions shall give sentence as summarily as possible and they are required to decide, (as far as they shall find it praticable) within the space of twenty days, to be dated from that on which every detained vessel shall have been brought into the port where they shall reside; 1st, upon the legality of the capture; 2nd in the case in which the captured vessel shall have been liberated, as to the indemnification which she is to receive.

And it is hereby provided, that in all cases the final sentence shall not be delayed on account of the absence of witnesses or for want of other proofs, beyond the period of two months: except upon the application of any of the parties interested, when, upon their giving satisfactory security to charge themselves with the expense and risks of the delay, the Commissioners may, at their discretion, grant an additional delay not exceeding four months.

ART. II. Each of the above-mentioned mixed Commissions, which are to reside on the Coast of Africa and in the Brazils, shall be composed in the following manner:

The two High Contracting Parties shall each of them name a Commissary Judge, and a Commissioner of Arbitration, who shall be authorized to hear and to decide, without appeal, all cases of capture of slave vessels which, in pursuance of the stipulation of the Additional Convention of this date may be laid before them. All the essential parts of the proceedings carried on before these mixt Commissions shall be written down in the language of the country in which the Commission may reside.

The Commissary Judges and the Commissioners of Arbitration, shall make oath, in presence of the principal Magistrate of the place in which the Commission may reside, to judge fairly and faithfully, to have no preference either for the claimants or the captors, and to act, in all their decisions, in pursuance of the stipulations of the Treaty of the 22nd January 1815, and of the Additional Convention to the said Treaty.

There shall be attached to each Commission a Secretary or Registrar, appointed by the Sovereign of the Country in which the Commission may reside, who shall register all its acts, and who, previous to his taking charge of his post, shall make oath, in presence of at least one of the Commissary Judges, to conduct himself with respect for their authority, and to act with fidelity in all the affairs which may belong to his charge.

ART. III. The form of the process shall be as follows :

The Commissary Judges of the two nations shall, in the first place, proceed to the examination of the papers of the vessel and recieve the depositions on oath of the captain and of two or three, at least, of the principal individuals on board of the detained vessel, as well as the declaration on oath of the captor, should it appear necessary, in order to be able to judge and to pronounce if the said vessel has been justly detained or not, according to the stipulations of the Additional Convention of this date, and in order that, according to this judgment, it may be condemned or liberated. And in the event of the two Commissary Judges not agreeing on the sentence they ought to pronounce, wether as to the legality of the detention or the indemnification to be allowed, or on any other question which might result from the stipulations of the Convention of this date, they shall draw by lot the name of one of the two Commissioners of Arbitration, who, after having considered the documents of the process shall consult with the above-mentioned Commissary Judges on the case in question, and the final sentence shall be pronounced conformally to the opinion of the majority of the above-mentioned Commissary Judges, and of the above-mentioned Commissioner of Arbitration.

ART. IV. As often as the cargo of slaves found on board of a Portugueze slave ship shall have been embarked on any point whatever of the coast of Africa, where the slave trade continues lawful to the subjects of the Crown of Portugal, such slave ship shall not be detained on pretext that the above-mentioned slaves have been brought originally by land from any other part whatever of the continent.

ART. V. In the authenticated declaration which the captor shall make before the Commission, as well as in the certificate of the papers seized, which shall' be delivred to the captain of the captured vessel, at the time of the detention, the above-mentioned captor shall be bound to declare his name, the name of his vessel, as well as the latitude and longitude of the place where the detention shall have taken place, and the number of slaves found living on board of the slave ship, at the time of the detention.

ART. VI. As soon as sentence shall have been passed, the detained vessel, if liberated, and what remains of the cargo, shall be restored to the proprietors, who may, before the same Commission, claim a valuation of the damages which they may have a right to demand : the

captor himself, and in his default, his Government, shall remain responsible for the above-mentioned damages. The two High Contracting Parties bind themselves to defray, within the term of a year, from the date of the sentence, the indemnifications which may be granted by the above-named Commission, it being understood that these indemnifications shall be at the expense of the Power of which the captor shall be a subject.

ART. VII. In case of condemnation of a vessel for an unlawful voyage, she shall be declared lawful prize, as well as her cargo, of whatever description it may be, with the exception of the slaves who may be on board as objects of commerce and the said vessel, as well as her cargo, shall be sold by public sale, for the profit of the two Governments, and as to the slaves, they shall receive from the mixt Commission a certificate of emancipation, and shall be delivered over to the Government on whose territory the Commission, which shall have to judged them, shall be established, to be employed as servants or free labourers. Each of the two Governments binds itself to guarantee the liberty of such portion of these individuals as shall be respectively consigned to it.

ART. VIII. Every claim for compensation of losses occasioned to ships suspected of carrying on an illicit trade in slaves, not condemned as lawful prize by the mixt Commissions, shall be also heard and judged by the above-named Commissions, in the form provided by the third Article of the present regulation.

And in all cases wherein restitution shall be so decreed the Commission shall award to the claimant or claimants, or his, or their lawful attorney or attornies, for his or their use, a just and complete indemnification :

First, for all costs of suit, and for all losses and damages which the claimant or claimants may have actually sustained by such capture and detention ; that is to say, in case of total loss, the claimant or claimants shall be indemnified :

1st. For the ship, her tackle, apparel and stores ;

2dly. For all freight due and payable ;

3dly. For the value of the cargo of merchandize, if any :

4thly. For the slaves on board at the time of detention, according to the computed value of such slaves at the place of destination ; deducting there from the usual fair average mortality for the unexpired period of the regular voyage; deducting also for all charges and expenses payable upon the sale of such cargoes, including commission of sale when payable at such port; and,

5thly. For all other regular charges in such cases of total loss:

And in all other cases not of total loss, the claimant or claimants shall be indemnified:

First, for all special damages and expenses occasionned to the ship by the detention, and for loss of freight when due or payable;

Secondly, a demurrage when due, according to the schedule annexed to the present Article;

Thirdly, a daily allowance for the subsistence of slaves, of one shilling, or one hundred and eighty reis for each person, without distinction of sexe or age, for so many days as it shall appear to the Commission that the voyage has been or may be delayed by reason of such detention; as likewise:

Fourthly, for any deterioration of cargo or slaves;

Fifthly, for any diminution in the value of the cargo of slaves, proceeding from an increased mortality beyond the average amount of the voyage, or from sickness occasioned by detention: this value to be ascertained by their computed price at the place of destination, as in the above case of total loss;

Sixthly, an allowance of five per cent on the amount of capital employed in the purchase and maintenance of cargo for the period of delay occasioned by the detention; and

Seventhly, for all premium of insurance on additional risks. The claimant or claimants shall likewise be entitled to interest, at the rate of five per cent per annum on the sum awarded until paid by the Government to which the capturing ship belongs: the whole amount of such indemnifications being calculated in the money of the country to which the captured ship belongs, and to be liquidated at exchange current at the time of award, excepting the sum for the subsistance of slaves, which shall be paid at part, as above stipulated.

The two High Contracting Parties wishing to avoid, as much as possible, every species of fraud in the execution of the Additional Convention of this date, have agreed, that if it should be proved, in a manner evident to the conviction of the judges of the two nations, and without having recourse to the decision of a Commissioner of Arbitration, that the captor has been led in to error by a voluntary and reprehensible fault. on the part of the captain of the detained ship. in that case only, the detained ship shall not have the right of receiving, during the days of her detention, the demurrage stipulated by the present Article.

Schedule of demurrage or daily allowance for a vessel of

100 tons to 120 inclusive	£ 5	
121 do. 150 do.	£ 6	
151 do. 170 do.	£ 8	
171 do. 200 do.	£ 10	per diem
201 do. 220 do.	£ 11	
221 do. 250 do.	£ 12	
251 do. 270 do.	£ 14	
271 do. 300 do.	£ 15	

and so on in proportion.

ART. IX. When the proprietor of a ship suspected of carrying on an illicit trade in slaves, released in consequence of a sentence of one of the mixed Commissions (or in the case, as above-mentioned, of total loss) shall claim indemnification for the loss of slaves which he may have suffered, he shall in no case be entitled to claim for more than the number of slaves which is vessel was, by the Portugueze laws, authorised to carry, which member shall always be declared in his passport.

ART. X. The mixt Commission established, in London ·by Article IX of the Convention of this date, shall hear and determine all claims for Portugueze ships and cargoes, captured by British cruizers on account of the unlawful trading in slaves, since the 1st of June 1814, till the period when the Convention of this date is to be in complete execution; awarding to them, conformally to Article IV of the Additional Convention of this date a just and complete compensation, upon the basis laid down in the preceding Articles, either for total loss, or for losses and damages sustained by the owners and proprietors of the said ships and cargoes. The said Commission established in London shall be composed and shall proceed exactly upon the basis determined in Articles 1, 2 and 3 of the present regulation for the Commissions established on the Coast of Africa and the Brazils.

ART. XI. It shall not be permitted to any of the Commissary Judges, nor to the Arbitrators, nor to the Secretary of any of the mixt Commissions, to demand or receive, from any one of the parties concerned in the sentences which they shall pronounce, any emolument, under any pretext whatsoever, for the performance of the duties which are imposed upon them by the present regulation.

ART. XII. When the parties interested shall imagine they have cause to complain of any evident injustice on the part of the mixt Commissions, they may represent in to their respective Governments, who reserve to themselves the right of mutual correspondence for removing, when they think fit, the individuals who may compose these Commissions.

ART. XIII. In the case of a vessel detained unjustly, under pretence of the stipulations of the Additional Convention of this date, and in which the captor should neither be authorised by the tenour of the above-mentioned Convention nor of the instructions annexed to it, the Government to which the detained vessel may belong shall be entitled to demand reparation ; and in such case, the Government to which the captor may belong, binds itself to cause the subject of complaint to be fully examined, and to inflict upon the captor, if he be found to have deserved it, a punishment proportioned to the transgression which may have been committed.

ART. XIV. The two High Contracting Parties have agreed, that, in the event of the death of one or more of the Commissioners, Judges and Arbitrators composing the above-mentioned mixt Commissions, their post shall be supplied, ad interim, in the following manner ; on the part of the British Government, the vacancies shall be filled successively in the Commission which shall sit within the possessions of His Britannic Majesty, by the Governor or Lieutenant Governor resident in that colony, by the principal Magistrate of the place, and by the secretary ; and in the Brazils, by the British Consul and Vice-Consul resident in the city in which the mixt Commission may be established. On the part of Portugal, the vacancies shall be supplied, in the Brazils, by such persons as the Captain General of the Province shall name for that purpose ; and, considering the difficulty which the Portugueze Government would feel in naming fit persons to fill the posts which might become vacant in the Commission established in the British possessions, it is agreed that in case of the death of the Portugueze Commissioners, Judge or Arbitrator, in those possessions, the remaining individuals of the above-mentioned Commission shall be equally authorized to proceed to the judgement of such slave-ships as may be brought before them, and to the execution of their sentence. In this case alone, however, the parties interested shall have the right of appealing from the sentence if they think fit, to the Commission resident in the Brazils ; and the Government to which the captor shall belong shall be bound fully to defray the indemnification which shall be due to them, if the appeal be judged in favour of the claimants : it being well understood that the ship and cargo shall remain, during this appeal, in the place of residence of the first Commission before whom they may have been conducted. The High Contracting Parties have agreed to supply, as soon as possible, every vacancy that may arise in the above-mentioned Commissions, from death or any other contingency. And in case that the vacancy of each of the Portugueze Commissioners residing in the British possessions, be not supplied at the end of six months the vessels which are taken there to be judged, after the expiration of that time, shall no longer have the right of appeal herein before stipulated.

Done at London, the 28th of July 1817[1].

XXXII. Espagne, Grande-Bretagne.

12 mars 1823.

La présente convention a eu pour but de régler les indemnités dues aux citoyens des deux pays dont les navires avaient été capturés ou les propriétés saisies, à partir du 4 juillet 1808.

Convention of claims between Great Britain and Spain signed at Madrid, March 12th, 1823.

His Majesty the King of the United Kingdom of Great Britain and His Majesty the King of the Spains, equally animated by the desire of arriving at an amicable adjustement of the various complaints, which have been from time to time laid before the Spanish Government, of the capture of vessels, and seizure and detention of property belonging to british subjects, by Spanish authorities, as well as of other grievances : their said Majesties have been pleased to name Plenipotentiaries for the conclusion of a Convention for the attainment of this desirable purpose, to wit :—His Britannic Majesty, the Right Honourable Sir William a Court, Baronet, one of His Majesty's most Honourable Privy Council, and His Envoy Extraordinary and Minister Plenipotentiary to the King of the Spains, etc.;—and His Catholic Majesty, His Excellency Don Evaristo de San Miguel, Secretary of State for the Foreign Department, etc., who, after having communicated their full powers, have agreed upon the following articles.

ART. I. A Mixed Commission, English and Spanish, consisting of two Members of each Nation, shall be appointed and meet in London, within 10 weeks after the signature of the present Convention, or sooner if possible, for the purpose of taking into consideration and deciding in a summary manner, according to equity, upon all cases that shall be brought before it, properly authenticated, of the capture or seizure of British vessels, or detention of property belonging to the subjects of His Britannic Majesty, from the Declaration of Peace between England

---

[1] HERTSLET, *A complete Collection of the Treaties and Conventions...*, t. II, p. 105—121.

and Spain of the 4ᵗʰ of July 1808, to the date of the present Convention; and also upon all cases that shall be brought before it, of the capture or seizure of Spanish vessels, or detention of property belonging to the subjects of His Catholic Majesty during the same period.

ART. II. Should any difference of opinion arise amongst the Members of the said Commission, and their votes be equally divided, a reference shall then be made to the Spanish Envoy at the Court of London, and a Law Officer of the Crown to be named by His Britannic Majesty. If these arbitrators should also be divided in opinion, it shall be determined, by lot, which of the two shall definitively decide the question.

ART. III. An assignment of 40,000,000 of reals upon the Great Book, shall, according to the Decree of the Cortes, immediately be made to the said Commissioners, for the payment of such indemnifications as may be awarded by the Commission. This sum shall be increased or diminished, as the Decree points out, according as a greater or lesser number of claims shall be admitted as valid, exceeding, in the one case, or not amounting to, in the other, the whole amount of the sum in the first instance deposited.

ART. IV. The claims of Spanish subjects which shall be acknowlegded just, shall be paid by the British Government, either in stock, or by an equivalent in money.

ART. V. As soon as the Commissioners shall have admitted any claim as valid, and determined the amount due to the claimant, they shall assign or transfer, in favour of such claimant, a portion of the said rentes, equivalent to the amount awarded, estimating the value thereof according to the current price in London of the said rentes, at the time of making such assignment or transfer.

ART. VI. No claim shall be admitted, which shall not be submitted to the Commission within 6 months after its first meeting.

ART. VII. A person shall be named by each Government, for the selection and transmission of whatever papers or documents it may be necessary to forward from Madrid for the consideration of the Commission, and to arrange the transfer of the rentes, as the respective amounts shall be awarded.

In witness whereof, we, the undersigned, Plenipotentiaries of their Britannic and Catholic Majesties, duly authorised by our full powers, have signed two originals of the present Convention, and have affixed thereunto the seals of our arms, in Madrid, this 12ᵗʰ day of March 1823 [1].

--- -- -
[1] HERTSLET, *A complete Collection*..... t. III, p. 381.

Des difficultés naquirent au cours des débats devant les commissaires et, bien que ceux-ci aient attribué 22,500,000 fr. aux réclamants anglais et 5,000,000 fr. aux réclamants espagnols, il fallut cependant recourir à un arrangement amiable pour terminer le conflit.

Convention between His Majesty and the Catholic King for the final settlement of the claims of British and Spanish subjects, under the convention concluded at Madrid, the 12ᵗʰ of March 1823, signed at London the 28ᵗʰ of October 1828.

His Majesty the King of the United Kingdom of Great Britain and Ireland, and His Majesty the King of Spain and the Indies, being equally convinced of the great and almost insuperable difficulties that have presented themselves in carrying into effect, by means of the Mixed Commission appointed under the Convention concluded on the 12ᵗʰ of March 1823, the stipulations of the said Convention, respecting the claims preferred by subjects of both nations, have considered that the most speedy and efficacious manner of obtaining the objects, which their Britannic and Catholic Majesties proposed to themselves in framing the Convention above-mentioned, would be that of a compromise, or amicable adjustment in which their said Majesties, by common consent, should assign fixed and proportionate sums for the indemnification of the claimants of both countries, so that each of the 2 High Contracting Parties should possess the power of adjudging and satisfying the legitimate claims of its own subjects, out of the sums which each Government should, for such purpose, receive from the other, or of distributing those sums among the individuals interested by means of an arrangement mutually agreed upon. With this view, their Britannic and Catholic Majesties have nominated and appointed as their respective Plenipotentiaries, namely: — His Majesty the King of the United Kingdom of Great Britain and Ireland, the Right Honourable George Earl of Aberdeen, Viscount Formartine, Lord Haddo, Methlick, Tarvis, and Kallie, a Peer of the said United Kingdom, a Member of His Majesty's most Honourable Privy Council, Knight of the most ancient and most noble order of the Thistle, and His said Majesty's Principal Secretary of State for Foreign Affairs: — and His Majesty the King of Spain and the Indies, His Excellency Don Narciso de Heredia, Count of Ofalia, actual Knight of the Royal Spanish order of Charles III, Knight Grand Cross of the American order of Isabel the Catholic, and of the Legion of Honour of France, Councillor of State, and His said Majesty's Envoy Extraordinary and Minister Plenipotentiary on a special Mission to the Court of His Britannic Majesty: — who after having communicated to each other their respective fullpowers, found to be in due and proper form, have agreed upon and concluded the following articles:

ART. I. His Catholic Majesty engages to make good to His Britannic Majesty, the sum of £ 900.000, in specie, as the amount of the whole of the English claims presented to and registered by the mixed Commission established by the Convention of the 12th of March 1823.

ART. II. His Britannic Majesty engages to make good, in the same manner, the sum of £ 200,000, as the whole amount of the Spanish claims, presented to and registered by the Mixed Commission, in pursuance of the said Convention.

ART. III. It shall be lawful for either of the High Contracting Parties to cause to be adjudged within its respective territory the claims of its own subjects, in order to satisfy within 12 months from the date of the exchange of the ratifications of the present Convention, such claims as shall appear to be just and legitimate, out of the sums which one of the High Contracting Parties shall receive, for this purpose, from the other or it shall be lawful for the Government of either of the said High Contracting Parties to agree with the person interested, or their assigns, upon any other mode of arrangement which may be deemed most expedient for satisfying them within the same term without the necessity of any previous and formal adjudication.

ART. IV. The Government of His Britannic Majesty shall retain in its possession the sum of £ 200,000, which, by the IInd Article, is to be made good to Spain, in order to set that sum against, or deduct it from, the £ 900,000, which it is to receive from the same: but it is expressly declared, that this compensation is stipulated on the understanding that His Catholic Majesty within the period specified in the preceding Article, shall pay to his own subjects the amount of their legitimate claims against England, preferred under the Convention of the 12th of March 1823, in specie, or in other effective value; and in such a manner that His Britannic Majesty may be exempted from every responsibility for the amount of such claims.

ART. V. His Catholic Majesty shall effectuate the payment of the £ 900,000, in satisfaction of the English claims, by instalments, in the following order:

£ 200,000 shall be delivered over on the day on which the exchange of the ratifications of the present Convention shall take place; and another like sum at the expiration of 3 months from the exchange alluded to.

The compensation mentioned in the preceding Article shall be considered as the payment of £ 200,000 more: and the remaining £ 300,000 shall be made good by two instalments of £ 150,000, the one at 6 months, and the other at 9 months, from the date of the exchange of the ratifications.

ART. VI. The 2 last instalments of £ 150,000 each, His Catholic Majesty reserves to himself the power either of paying up in specie at the time of that sum falling due, or of effectuating the payment by Certificates of Inscriptions in the English and Spanish languages, expressing the purpose for which they are issued, bearing interest at 5 per cent, per annum, payable half, yearly in London, at 50 per cent discount.

For this purpose, His Catholic Majesty shall, within 3 months from the date of the ratifications of this Convention, cause the sum of 60,000,000 of reals of vellon, in such Inscriptions (being equal, at 100 reals of the pound sterling, to the sum of £ 600,000) to be lodged in the Bank of England, or with the Banker of the Court of Spain in London, with Instructions to deliver one half of them to the Government of His Britannic Majesty, for the use of the claimants, on the day of each of the said instalments falling due, provided they shall not be punctually paid in sterling money.

It is likewise hereby agreed that the Government of His Catholic Majesty shall have the power of redeeming the Inscriptions thus created, during the 4 years succeeding, and upon giving 6 months notice, at the rate of £ 60 for every £ 100.

ART. VII. His Catholic Majesty shall be at liberty to effect the payment of the second instalment of £ 200,000, mentioned in Article V by delivering, on its being due, £ 50,000 in ready money, and £ 150,000 in Inscriptions at 50 per cent, making £ 300,000 in Inscriptions: but this arrangement is only to take place on the express condition that the payment of one of the 2 last instalments of £ 150,000, mentioned in Article VI, shall be made in ready money.

ART. VIII. The Inscriptions to be delivered by the Government of His Catholic Majesty, shall be, in all essential points, according to the form which is annexed to the present Convention.

ART. IX. As soon as the said sum of £ 900,000 shall have been paid, all the bills of exchange, libranzas, and other documents, forming and constituting the value represented by the aggregate of the English claims against Spain, shall be given up to the Government of His Catholic Majesty.

ART. X. There shall be given up also, on the part of the Government of His said Catholic Majesty, at the period specified in the preceding

Article, all the documents relative to the Spanish claims against England.

ART. XI. To prevent any of those claims which shall be satisfied by the present Convention, from again being produced under any other form or pretence, it is hereby agreed that the Mixed Commission appointed under the aforesaid Convention of the 12th of March 1823, shall, prior to the cessation of the exercise of its functions, add to the lists already formed of the English and Spanish claims, presented to and registered by the same, such notes or remarks, relating to the documents in support of those claims, as may be deemed necessary, in order that the said lists and notes, after being given up to both Governments in an authentic form, may serve them as a security, till the delivery of the original documents shall take place.

ART. XII. The aforesaid Convention of the 12th of March 1823, and the several Articles and things therein contained, except so far as the same are altered by this present Convention, are hereby declared to be, and shall remain in force.

ART. XIII. The present Convention shall be ratified, and the ratifications shall be exchanged in 40 days from the date hereof, or sooner if possible.

In witness whereof, the respective Plenipotentiaries have signed the same, and have affixed thereto the seals of their arms.

Done at London, the 28th day of October, in the year of our Lord 1828 [1].

XXXIII. Brésil, Grande-Bretagne.

5 mai 1829.

Dans cette affaire il s'est agi des indemnités à payer par le gouvernement brésilien aux propriétaires des navires capturés en 1826 et 1827. Le décret du 21 mai 1828 auquel il est fait allusion dans le compromis portait sur la condamnation de 25 vaisseaux. Le compromis ne fut présenté au Parlement d'Angleterre que le 27 juin 1832.

Agreement between Great Britain and Brazil, relative to the settlement of British claims signed at Rio de Janeiro, May 5th, 1829.

The Commission to be composed of 4 Members, to be named by the respective Governments or Ministers.

The Commissioners to meet for the dispatch of business af least 3 days in every week.

---

[1] HERTSLET, A complete Collection .... t. IV, p. 416.

Three Commissioners being met, or even if only one of those named by each of the Governments should meet, on the days appointed for the dispatch of business, they may proceed to the settlement of such claims as may be before them, and their decision will be as valid as if the whole of the Commissioners had been present.

Any claim being adjusted by a majority of the Commissioners, the same to be final.

In case a majority of the Commissioners should not agree upon the adjustment of any item or items of the claims, the same shall be referred to the Secretary of State for Foreign Affairs of His Imperial Majesty, and the Minister of His Britannic Majesty at this court, for the final decision.

In proceeding to the adjustment of the claims, those for the vessels and cargoes condemned by the Decree of the 21st of May 1828 shall have precedence.

Eight months to be allowed from the installation of the Commission to produce claims, after which period no claim to be received, unless a majority of the Commissioners shall agree to extend the time for 4 months longer. But in cases not yet finally adjudged, the term of 8 months to be reckoned from the date of the final sentence.

The Commissioners to decide upon every matter and thing relating to the premises upon the basis agreed upon, and in case any part of the indemnities is adjuged in Spanish dollars they are to reduce the same to Brazilian currency, at a fair and reasonable rate of exchange.

The following shall be the basis for adjusting the claims for indemnities.

1st. The Brazilian Government to pay the full value of the vessels and cargoes condemned, also of those vessels restored, but found to be unseaworthy; and on that account sold in the state they then were, deducting the net proceeds of the sale.

2nd. Those vessels which have been restored and fitted out for sea, to be paid the full amount of such outfit, with every charge thereon.

3rd. All sums of money paid for port charges and anchorage.

4th. The amount of freight and passage money payable at the port of discharge, but which, in consequence of the detention, has not been paid.

5th. Losses arising to the vessels from non fulfilment of charter-parties.

6th. Demurrage from the date of the detention of the respective vessels until the date of the execution of the respective sentences, the rate of such demurrage to be regulated according to the rates generally paid on English vessels.

7th. All law charges, or commissions, in lieu of the same, in defending the vessels and cargoes, adjusting general averages, etc., and also the same commissions for recovering the indemnities, and the agent's commission for remitting the same to the parties.

8th. The wages and maintenance of the masters and crews remaining in Brazil, for the defence and protection of the vessels and cargoes, from the date of their capture till the date of the execution of the sentences, or sales of the vessels, with the passage of the masters to England.

9th. The indemnities for the cargoes generally, shall be regulated by the invoices, bills of lading, manifests, and other documents which may be presented to the Commissioners, duly attested by the parties or their agents.

10th. The indemnities for the cargoes condemned, to be regulated according to the invoice cost, and all charges, with 10 per cent on such amount for loss of market, etc.

11th. Such part of the cargoes restored as has been embezzled, lost, damaged, perished, or deficient, to be paid for upon the same principles as expressed in the last article.

12th. Those parts of the cargoes restored, and which have been sold at Rio de Janeiro to be valued at the invoice amount, and charges, with 10 per cent as above, from which to be deducted the net proceeds of the sales; the difference to be admitted as the loss to be indemnified.

13th. Those parts of the cargoes restored and which have been exported, to be indemnified according to the invoice value, by such per centage or the same as to the Commissioners may appear to be fair and reasonable, under all the circumstances of each respective invoice, taking into consideration the state of the market of Rio de Janeiro, the description of merchandise, and the place to which it has been shipped, together with the amount of general average paid, and all charges on shipment.

14th. The owners of the respective cargoes to be indemnified for all extra charges of warehouse rent and duties paid, arising from the detention.

15th. Such cargoes as were shipped for discharge at port or ports on the west coast of South Africa; the value of the same, at such port of discharge, to be taken as far as practicable as the basis for estimating the indemnities.

16th. Such cargoes as were carried into Monte Video, and offers there made to the captors to give ample security for their value, but which offers were refused; the value to be estimated at the current market price in Monte Video, as the basis for indemnities.

17th. The amount of indemnities being adjusted in Brazilian money, the same shall bear interest, as respects the vessels, at the rate of 5 per cent per annum, from 6 months after the date of the capture till payment is made.

18th. Interest on the value of the cargoes restored by the Decree of the 21st of May 1828, or by sentence of the Tribunals, to be paid at the rate of 5 per cent per annum from the date of the capture till the execution of the final sentences.

19th. In adjusting the indemnities, the Commissioners shall reduce the accounts from sterling money into Brazilian currency, at the rate of 32 pence per milreis.

20th. The sums which are to be liquidated shall be realized in equal payments made at this court; the first being paid at 12, the second at 24, and the third at 36 months; reckoned from the date of the day on which the liquidation of each prize is settled.

For this object, policies shall be issued by the public treasury, in which the name or names of the parties interested shall be inserted, in favour of whom they shall be drawn, and these shall be placed at the disposal of His Britannic Majesty's Legation at this court, in order that they may be delivered to those to whom they really appartain.

Rio de Janeiro, May 5th, 1829[1].

XXXIV. Argentine, Grande-Bretagne.

19 juillet 1830.

Arbitrage institué pour le règlement de quelques indemnités dues pour dommages causés à des navires privés et à la propriété d'un citoyen anglais. Ainsi qu'il résulte du memorandum joint au compromis il s'est agi dans cette minime affaire d'une somme de 21,030 £, 15 sh., 5 d.

Convention between Great Britain and Buenos Ayres for the settlement of British claims signed at Buenos Ayres, 19th July 1830.

Whereas certain of His Britannic Majesty's subjects have demands pending against the Government of Buenos Ayres for indemnification for illegal acts and violences, committed by privateers commissioned by them during the late war with the Emperor of Brazil and whereas for the liquidation of those claims, a Mixed Commission was appointed by the Government of Buenos Ayres, in the month of October last, which commission, after having proceeded to the examination of some cases presented to them

---

[1] HERTSLET, A complete Collection . . ., t. IV, p. 60.

have experienced considerable difficulty in arriving at a determination thereupon: and the Government of Buenos Ayres desiring to give a proof of their disposition to bring these long standing claim to as speedy a settlement as possible and having consulted with His Britannic Majesty's Chargé d'Affaires thereupon who has been charged by his Government to promote the adjustment of these cases, they have agreed with the said Chargé d'Affaires upon the following mode of providing for the final settlement of the remaining cases, viz:

ART. I. The liquidation of the remaining cases of His Britannic Majesty's subjects against the Government of Buenos Ayres, arising out of the acts of their privateers in the late war, shall be removed to London.

ART. II. For the purpose of giving effect to this article a new Commission shall be named, to consist of 2 individuals one to be appointed by the Government of Buenos Ayres, the other to be named by His Britannic Majesty's Government on behalf of the claimants.

ART. III. The said commission shall meet in London 6 months from this date.

ART. IV. Due notice of the appointment and meeting of the Commission shall be given in the London Gazette, and a limited period shall at the same time be fixed for the reception of claims, after the expiration of which no other shall be entertained.

ART. V. With respect to the form in which the said claims shall be proved and substantiated by the parties interested, the Commissioners shall guide themselves by the General Rules and practice according to the Law of Nations.

ART. VI. So soon as the amount of any claim shall have been determined by the Commission a certificate thereof shall be delivered to the claimant, signed by the Commissioners.

ART. VII. The amount specified in such certificate shall bear interest at the rate of 5 per cent per annum in favour of the claimants, from the date thereof, till finally paid off by the Government of Buenos Ayres.

ART. VIII. The Government of Buenos Ayres engages to autorize the house of Messrs. Baring in London, to provide for the payment of the amounts of the certificates aforesaid, within the following periods, or sooner, from the date of each certificate, viz.

$\frac{1}{8}$ in 6 months
$\frac{1}{8}$ in 12 months
$\frac{1}{8}$ in 18 months

so that each claim shall be paid off at farthest, in 18 months from the date of the amount being declared by the Commission.

ART. IX. The Government of Buenos Ayres further engages, so far as depends upon them, to assist in furthering the production of such documents as may be required from them, in support of the claims submitted to the Commission. In virtue of which, and for the corresponding ends, 2 copies of this Convention have been signed and exchanged in Buenos Ayres, this 19th day of July 1830.

Memorandum of the British claims against the Government of Buenos Ayres.

The innocent part of the cargo of the Huskisson (approximate value) . . . £ 9,068 s. 00 d. 00
Case of the Concord . . . £ 1,064 » 04 » 08
  »   »   »   Anne . . . . £ 1,912 » 18 » 10
  »   »   »   Albuera . . . £ 2,632 » 12 » 00
  »   »   »   Helvellyn . . . £ 2,227 » 01 » 03
  »   »   »   George and James £ 3,821 » 18 » 08
Mr Carvalho's claim, 1351 milreis £   304

Total approximate amount . £ 21,030 s. 15 d. 05 [1]

XXXV. Grande-Bretagne. Portugal.

13 novembre 1840.

Cet arbitrage est particulièrement intéressant par la nature des réclamations qui en ont formé l'objet : il s'est agi en effet des indemnités dues à des sujets anglais qui avaient pris part à la guerre de libération du Portugal et auxquels il a été distribué une somme de £ 162,500 environ.

Minute of the instructions, agreed upon between Viscount Palmerston and Baron Moncows for the guidance of the Mixed British and Portugueze Commission, London, 13th November 1840.

ART. I. The Commission shall be styled the « Mixed British and Portugueze Commission ».

ART. II. The purpose of the Commission shall be to examine and to decide upon the claims of British subjects who served in the Portugueze Army and Navy, during the late war for the liberation of Portugal.

ART. III. The Commission shall consist of 2 Members, 1 British appointed by Her Britannic Majesty's Government, and 1 Portugueze, appointed by the Government of Her Most Faithful Majesty. And these 2 Members shall be co-equal in power in every respect.

ART. IV. The members of the Commission shall receive full powers from their respective Governments, so that, when both are of the same opinion upon any point or matter their proceedings and decisions shall be final, and shall not be dependent upon the approval, confirmation or intervention of any other authority.

ART. V. The Commission shall be authorized to take into consideration any and every claim, arising out of the above-mentioned service which the claimants, their legal representatives, or their heirs, may bring forward and to examine and decide such claims according to their judgment. They shall also have authority to refuse to receive any claim not included in the classes defined in the Articles II, V and VII.

ART. VI. In order to compensate the officers and men for the losses which they have sustained, in consequence of the delay which has occurred in satisfying their just demands and in consequence of the expense which they have incurred, in employing agents to attend the different Commissions, which have sat in Lisbon for the examination of their claims, the present Commission shall be authorized to allow a compensation, at the rate of 5 per cent per annum, on the amount of pay, gratuity, or pension, found to be due to each individual, unless the Portugueze Commissioner shall be able to prove that the delay in the settlement of any particular claim arose from the fault of the claimant himself. The said compensation shall date from the day when each individual ceased to receive pay from the Portugueze Government ; and the certificate, showing the total amount, which will thus be due to each claimant, shall also contain a declaration, stating that the holder of such certificate is to be entitled to compensation at 5 per cent upon the amount therein specified, until such amount shall be paid.

ART. VII. The Commission shall be authorized to examine the accounts, which any of the British subjects mentioned in Article II may have to render, in consequence of their having received an advance of money to be disbursed by them for the public service of Portugal.

ART. VIII. The Commission shall be authorized to fix and to determine by its own decision, and without any control direct or indirect, on the part of either Government, the order of its proceedings, to decide what papers or accounts are to be examined, and in what manner the examination of them is to be made.

The Commission shall also regulate the delivery of bills, titulos, or other documents, by which a settlement of admitted claims may be effected : but it will be incumbent on the Commissioners, in the performance of this, as well as of every other part of their duties, to be strictly just and impartial, and they will therefore be responsible, that any order of proceedings which they may adopt shall in no degree deviate from impartiality and justice.

ART. IX. The decisions of the Commission as to what is due to the claimants, individually and collectively, shall be considered final and binding : and no future question can be entertained by either Government, with respect to claims so decided.

ART. X. The Commissioner of each nation shall be authorized by his Government, to apply directly to the Minister or head of the proper department of his own Government, for any document or information which the Commission may require for the effective discharge of its duties. And the British and Portugueze Governments will authorize the proper department in London and in Lisbon respectively, to furnish the information and documents for which the Mixed Commission may thus apply to those departments.

ART. XI. Considering the temporary nature of the service on which the British officers and men were employed in Portugal, extraordinary difficulties with which that service was attended, and the many causes of confusion and irregularity which prevailed during the war ; as also the long period that has elapsed since the services were performed, and considering, moreover, that during that period several Commissions have set, by which vouchers have been demanded from claimants, it shall be understood, that although to present Commission ought, in the first instance, and as a general rule to require the production of the military service, yet in cases in which there may be found to be irremediable informality in documents sent in to support claims, or in cases in which such documents may be either wanting or imperfect, the Commission is authorized to collect such other evidence as may be attainable ; and if the Commission can arrive at a moral conviction of the justice or of the injustice of a claim, they may, notwithstanding the absence or incompleteness of vouchers, decide such claim according to principles of equity, keeping in view the letter and the spirit of such contracts as may apply to the case.

ART. XII. Neither member of the Commission shall be at liberty to plead instructions from his Government restricting or enlarging the powers herein specified, and hereby conferred ; it being understood that the Commissioners are placed by their respective Governments in the position of arbitrators in all matters falling within the limits of their jurisdiction: and that therefore they are to be left unbiassed and uncontrolled in the discharge of the duties confided to them.

ART. XIII. As it is alleged that several different contracts of service were concluded between the claimants and the Portugueze Government, it will be the first duty of the Commission to enquire into all the circumstances of each contract, and to decide how far any or all of them, or any part of them, shall be deemed applicable to the several claims which may be presented. The Commission shall frame certain general rules founded upon such of those contracts as may be determined to be valid, and upon such other evidence as the Commission may have before it, defining, as far as practicable, the periods of time, and the classes of claimants to which each rule may apply ; and the claims shall be received, classed, and considered according to these general rules.

ART. XIV. The draft of the rules mentioned in the preceding Article, shall be submitted to Viscount Palmerston, and to the Portugueze Minister at this Court, for their joint approval, before the Commissioners shall sign them, and the rules so approved and signed, shall, in conjunction with these instructions, govern the future proceedings of the Commission.

ART. XV. The Commission will make known by public advertissement in the 3 parts of the United kingdom, the day of its installation in office, and the day on which it will commence receiving claims, and with a view to facilitate the regular progress of its labours, the Commission will publish a statement of the order of proceeding which it may have determined to adopt, and of the mode in which, and of the time within which claims should be sent in.

ART. XVI. If any difference of opinion shall arise between the 2 Commissioners, the point in dispute shall be referred by the Commission to an arbitrator who shall be the Minister of some third Power resident at the Court of London, and who shall, at the invitation of the British secretary of state, and of the Portugueze Minister at this Court, have consented to act in that capacity, and the members of the Commission shall state in writing to the said arbitrator, their conflicting opinions, and the reasons and the evidence on which those opinions are founded.

ART. XVII. If either Commissioner should decline giving an opinion on any question or claim. within a period not exceeding 2 months from the time when such claim or question was first taken into consideration then, and in such ise, unless further delay be agreed to by the mutual consent of both the Commissioners, the cision of the other Commissioner shall be carried before the Arbitrator, and shall be confirmed d negatived by him, and the decision of the bitrator shall be as final and conclusive, as if both the Commissioners had taken part in the previous discussion, and had stated their respective opinions on the point at issue.

ART. XVIII. If any doubt or difficulty should arise between the 2 commissioners, as to the extent of the powers of the Commission, or as to the construction to be put upon any part of these Instructions, such doubt or difficulty will be referred by the Commission, for the decision of Her Majesty's secretary of state for Foreign Affaires and of the Minister Plenipotentiary of Her Most Faithful Majesty at the Court of London.

ART. XIX. If any doubt or difficulty as to questions connected with the interpretation of the law of England, should arise out of the performance of the duties of the Commission, the Commission will refer such question to the secretary of state in order that the opinion of the law officers of the Crown may be taken thereupon.

ART. XX. The office of the Commission shall be separate from the residence of either Commissioner, and neither of the members of the Commission shall transact any business, or take any ste) in connection with his functions as Commissioner except in the presence of, and with the knowledge of his colleague. Nor shall it be competent for either, in the absence of the other, to enter into the investigation of any claim, or to receive any claimant on the business of the Commission.

ART. XXI. The clerks, and other persons employed in the office of the Commission, shall be under the orders of both Commissioners equally.

ART. XXII. The minutes of the proceedings of the Commission and an abstract of its decisions, shall be kept in duplicate, and shall be signed by both Commissioners, in order that each Government may have an authentic copy thereof.

ART. XXIII. No interpreter shall be appointed on either side, because the use of an interpreter would subject the Commissioner so obtaining his information from witnesses, to the chance of being biassed by a person not a Commissioner, and who would have no share in the responsebilities attaching to the Commission. No third person in any capacity, or under any plea whatever, shall be allowed to intervene between the 2 Commissioners.

ART. XXIV. The mode in which the allowed claims shall be paid and satisfied, when the Commission has decided upon their respective amounts, shall be determined by the Secretary of State for Foreign Affairs, and by Her most Faithful Majesty's Plenipotentiary at the Court of London.

- 96 -

ART. XXV. All officers, non commissioned officers, and privates who can give satisfactory proof that they were wounded before the enemy while in the Portugueze service, shall be entitled to claim of the Commission an order to appear for examination before a British Army Medical Board: and the decision of Her Britannic Majesty's Secretary at War, as to the compensation, or pension, which such wounded officer, non commissioned officer, and private, may, in conformity with the regulations of the British service, become entitled to, according to the report of the Army Medical Board, shall be final. If any of the wounded officers, or men, should at any previous period have had assigned to them a smaller compensation than shall thus be awarded, the difference between the 2 rates shall be acknowledged by the Commission, as valid claim against the Portugueze Government.

ART. XXVI. It shall be left to the Commission to receive vivâ voce evidence from the claimants, or not, as in each case they may deem expedient.

London, November 13th, 1840 [1].

Agreement between Great Britain and Portugal. London, 26th August 1842.

Preamble. The labours of the Mixed British and Portuguese Commission having advanced sufficiently to enable the Commissioners to form an estimate of the probable amount which will be required for the payment of the whole of the « titulos » to be issued in conformity with the awards having been prepared, the undersigned, Her Britannic Majesty's Secretary of State for Foreign Affairs, and Her Most Faithful Majesty's Minister at this Court, have agreed to direct the Commissioners to issue « titulos » to the claimants, in accordance with Article VI of the minute of Instructions signed on the 13th of November 1840, and they have agreed upon the following Articles, containing regulations for the issue and payment of the above-mentioned « titulos ».

ART. 1. The undersigned having been informed that, according to an estimate made by the Commissioners the sum of £ 162,500 is the probable amount which Her Most Faithful Majesty's Government will be called upon to provide for the payment of the « titulos » to be issued by the « Mixed British and Portuguese Commission », and for the payment of the interest which will accrue thereon, until the amount specified in each « titulo » shall be paid, it is hereby agreed that Her Most Faithful Majesty's Minister at this Court shall deliver to Her Britannic Majesty's Secretary of State for Foreign Affairs, 13 bills drawn by

---
[1] HERTSLET, A complete Collection...., t. VI, p. 726 -732.

the Portuguese Minister of Finance upon the Portuguese Treasury, in favour of Her Britannic Majesty's Secretary of State for Foreign Affairs, for the sum of £ 12,500 each; and when those bills are delivered, the Commissioners will take the necessary steps for the delivery of the « titulos » in the manner hereinafter stated.

ART. II. The first of the above-mentioned 13 bills shall be made payable on the 1st day of October next, the second on the 1st of April 1843, and the remaining 11 bills shall be made payable in succession, each bill being payable 6 months after the preceding one. The payment of an instalment of the claims shall commence so soon as each of the said bills shall be paid, and a day will be fixed, after which the payment of each instalment will cease.

ART. III. The Commissioners shall deliver to each claimant in whose favour a final award shall have been issued, or to his representative or heir a « titulo » or « titulos », for the amount so awarded, and the Commissioners shall take a receipt for the same in duplicate. And notwithstanding the arrangement contemplated in the XXXth Article of the « General Rules » signed on the 22nd of June 1841, the Commissioners are directed to make the said « titulos » payable to the claimant or the « bearer », in order to obviate the necessity of investigating and demanding proofs of the validity of signatures, at each time when the documents an presented for payment.

ART. IV. The time at which each « titulo » is to be paid shall be stated therein. And in conformity with the Article VI of the « Minute of Instructions » and with the XXXIst Article of the « General Rules » each « titulo » shall contain a statement of the interest which the total amount therein specified is to bear, until such amount shall be paid; and such interest shall be paid half yearly, at each period fixed for the payment of instalments.

ART. V. All awards upon claims for « Prize Money » shall be provided for in distinct and separate « titulos » the amount of which shall be paid in full, at the time fixed for the payment of the last instalment.

ART. VI. If any holder of a « titulo » should neglect to present the same during the period announced for the payment of each instalment, the amount due thereon will not be paid until the period next ensuing: and the holder will not be entitled to receive interest upon such « titulo » for the time thus intervening.

ART. VII. If, before the closing of the Commission, it should turn out that the sums awarded to the claimants should exceed the sum of £ 162,500, the Portuguese Government will, on receiving information to that effect, give another bill for the amount required, payable, at the same date as the 13th of the bills mentioned in Article II. And if, on the other hand, the total sum awarded should prove to be less than the sum estimated, the British Government will cancel such 13th or final bill on receiving from the Portuguese Government in exchange for the bill so cancelled, another bill for the exact amount required, and made payable and the same time.

ART. VIII. At the conclusion of the payments, the « titulos » shall be cancelled; and the « titulos » so cancelled shall be delivered to the Portuguese Government, in acquittance of the claims of British subjects who served in the Portuguese Army and Navy during the late war for the liberation of Portugal; but the said acquittance shall not extend to claims on account of pensions, for the regular payment of which suitable permanent provision shall be made ·by the Portuguese Government so soon as the Commissioners shall make known to the Portuguese Government the total amount of such pensions.

ART. IX. The Commissioners are hereby authorised to make, from time to time, such further rules and regulations as they may deem requisite for the protection of the Portuguese Government from fraud, and for the guidance of the claimants; and they will take care to exact from the agents of absent parties, good and sufficient security for the due performance of the trusts undertaken by those agents.

Foreign Office, 26th August 1842 [1].

XXXVI. Deux Siciles. Grande-Bretagne.

17 novembre 1840.

Cet arbitrage a eu pour objet les dommages causés à des maisons anglaises par suite du décret du 9 juillet 1838, par lequel le roi des Deux Siciles introduisit dans les Etats le monopole de l'extraction et de la vente du soufre. Les intéressés réclamèrent £ 65,610; il leur en fut accordé par les arbitres 21,307.

Arrangement between Great Britain and Two Sicilies respecting the claims of British Subjects, for losses consequent upon the Sulphur Monopoly 1840-1841.

1) Viscount Palmerston to the British Commissioners.

Foreign Office, 17th November 1840.

The Government of His Majesty the King of the French having tendered its good offices to

_____
[1] HERTSLET, A complete Collection...., t. VI, p. 745—747.

the Government of Her Majesty, for the settlement of certain differences which had arisen between Her Majesty's Government and the Government of Naples, on the subject of a Monopoly of the Sulphur Trade of Sicily, which was established by a decree of the King of Naples, dated the 9th of July 1838; and Her Majesty's Government having accepted the offers thus made by the Government of France (in July last), a plan of arrangement proposed by the French Government was consented to by the Government of Her Majesty, and by that of His Majesty the King of the Two Sicilies. It was thereby agreed, that the contract concluded on the 9th of July, 1838, between the Neapolitan Government and the House of Taix, Aycard, and Co., with respect to the Sulphur Trade of Sicily, should be immediately abolished;

That a Commission should be appointed and should meet at Naples, to liquidate the claims of British subjects against the Neapolitan Government, for losses sustained by them in consequence of that contract; and that this Commission should be composed of 2 British commissioners, of 2 Neapolitan commissioners, and of 1 other commissioner, to be named by France, but to be previously approved of by Great Britain and Naples, and who should act as umpire between the British and Neapolitan commissioners on points on which they may differ:

Finally, that no claims should be admitted by the above-mentioned commissioners, except such as should come under one of the following heads;

1st. The claims of persons who, having become proprietors or lessees of sulphur mines in Sicily before the 9th of July 1838, the day on which the contract entered into with Messrs. Taix and Co., was dated, shall have been subjected to impediments either in the raising or in the exportation of sulphur, and who shall, in consequence of these impediments, have suffered losses duly substantiated.

2ndly. The claims of persons who, having, before the period above-mentioned, entered into contracts for the delivery of sulphur, shall, by the operation of the monopoly, have been rendered unable to fulfil their engagements, or shall have been deprived of the benefit which ought to have arisen from their transactions.

Lastly. The claims of persons who, having bought sulphur, the exportation of which shall afterwards have been forbidden, limited or subjected to burdensome conditions, shall have thereby suffered losses capable of positive proof.

It was further agreed, that the claimants should bring forward their claims, together with all the vouchers necessary to substantiate the same, within 3 months after the opening of the Commission at Naples ; that the examination of the same by the commissioners should be finished within a further period of 6 months, and that the compensation wh ch may be finally awarded by the commissioners, shall be paid to the parties within a year from the dissolution of the Commission.

The Neapolitan Government, by a decree dated the 21ˢᵗ of July last, abolished the contract with Messrs. Taix and Co., and thus fulfilled the first condition of the arrangement.

2) Notice respecting the Appointment of British Commissioners.

Foreign Office, 17ᵗʰ November 1840.

It having been agreed between Her Britannic Majesty and His Majesty the King of the Two Sicilies, that a Mixed Commission shall meet at Naples, to liquidate certain claims of Her Majesty's subjects against the Sicilian Government, arising out of the late sulphur monopoly; Her Majesty has been graciously pleased to appoint Sir Woodbine Parish, K. G. H. late Her Majesty's Chargé d'Affaires at Buenos Ayres, and Stephen Henri Sulivan, Esq. now Her Majesty's Secretary of Legation at Munich, to proceed to Naples as Her Majesty's Commissioners, in virtue of the agreement aforesaid.

3) Minute of the installation of the Commission.

Naples, le 23 mars 1841.

La Commission établie en conséquence de l'arrangement fait entre Sa Majesté la Reine du Royaume-Uni de la Grande-Bretagne et d'Irlande, et Sa Majesté le Roi du Royaume des Deux Siciles, sous la médiation de Sa Majesté le Roi des Français pour la liquidation des demandes d'indemnité formées par les sujets anglais, s'étant réunie le 23 mars 1841, dans le palais du Ministre des Finances à Naples, les membres qui la composent, après s'être communiqué leurs Pleins Pouvoirs et Lettres de Nomination, ont déclaré que la Commission était légalement instituée dès ce jour même. MM. les Commissaires anglais se sont chargés d'en donner la notification nécessaire aux réclamants Britanniques, pour les mettre à même de produire devant la Commission des titres justificatifs de leurs demandes en indemnité, conformément aux trois catégories stipulées dans le conclusum de juillet 1840, et dans le délai de trois mois, à dater de l'institution de la Commission. Ce terme finira le 24 du mois de juin 1841. En foi de quoi les membres de la Commission ont signé le présent procès-verbal.

4) Notice of the Commissioners to British Claimants.

We have the honour to acquaint you, for the information of the parties interested, that the Mixed Commission appointed to liquidate the claims of British subjects, arising out of the late sulphur monopoly, is now complete. We shall, in consequence, be ready to receive such claims as may be sent to us, from this date to the 24ᵗʰ of June next, being the 3 months prescribed for their presentation, conformally to their arrangement concluded between Her Majesty's Government and the Government of His Sicilian Majesty. We have to request that you will duly notify the same to all such of Her Majesty's subjects as may have claims to bring forward within your Consulate.

5) The British Commissioners to the Earl of Aberdeen.

Naples, 29ᵗʰ December 1841.

We have the honour herewith to transmit to your Lordship the copy of a minute, declaratory of the closing of the Mixed Commission appointed to liquidate the claims of British subjects arising out of the sulphur monopoly which was signed on the 24ᵗʰ instant by the British and Neapolitan Commissioners, as well as by the French arbiter.

We have the honour further to inclose a list of the several claims, and of the awards which have been delivered on each case by the Commission.

From these documents your Lordship will observe, that the claims laid before the Commission amounted to 373,978 ducats, or £ 65,610 5 s. 5 d. sterling, and that the total of the awards of the Mixed Commission amounts to 121,454 ducats, or £ 21,307 14 s. sterling, with interest at 6 per cent thereupon, calculated from the date of the claim to the period at which the payment may be effected. A certificate of each award, signed by the 4 Commissioners has been issued to the claimants, according to the form herewith inclosed ; and we are given to understand that His Sicilian Majesty has caused arrangements to be made for paying off the sums awarded, with as little delay as possible: although, according to the agreement concluded between Her Majesty's Government and the Government of His Sicilian Majesty, a year's delay, calculated from the date of the closing of the Commission, is allowed for their final settlement. According to the terms of the agreement concluded between Her Majesty's Government and the Government of His Sicilian Majesty, the cases to be decided upon were divided under 3 heads, viz :

6ᴵ

1ˢᵗ. Of those parties who, having become mine proprietors or lessees previously to the 9ᵗʰ of July 1838, the date of the contract with Taix and Co., may have experienced impediments in the extraction or exportation of their sulphur and may, in consequence of those impediments, have suffered losses duly substantiated.

2ⁿᵈ. Of those who, previously to the said period, having entered into contracts for the delivery of sulphur may have found it impossible to fulfill their engagements, or may have been deprived of the profits stipulated for on their transactions.

3ʳᵈ. Of those who, having bought sulphur, the exportation of which had been either prohibited or limited, or subjected to more onerous conditions, may have, in consequence, sustained losses capable of positive proof.

With respect to the first of these classes of claims, viz., of mine proprietors or lessees, for impeded production of sulphur the main points to establish were:

1ˢᵗ. The proper quantities of sulphur to be charged for ; and,

2ⁿᵈ. The proper valuation or price at which those quantities were to be paid for.

In order to establish the former point, we determined to admit, in the first instance, the quantities as estimated by the claimants, and then to make a reduction from those quantities of 20 per cent as an allowance for casualties, according to custom il all mining calculations.

We found that the principal claimants under this class had themselves made a similar deduction when they originally submitted an estimate of their losses to Mr. Temple.

With regard to price, we adopted 3 carlins per cantar as the rule, instead of 4 carlins per cantar, as charged by the claimants. In the case of the Favara mine, where the sulphur was of the lowest quality, and where the cost of production amounted only to two thirds of that of the mines of Riesi and of Gallazi, we reduced the price, in proportion to the cost, to 2 carlins per cantar.

The second class of claims, viz., for losses upon pending contracts which could not be fulfilled in consequence of the restrictions imposed by the monopoly, differed from those under the first and third categories, inasmuch as they were capable of positive and satisfactory proof, and most of them were consequently admitted with a very trifling alteration, upon due evidence being given of the loss which had actually accrued to the claimant.

With respect to the third class of claims, comprising those for sulphur, which although purchased previously to the monopoly was not permitted to be exported during the continuance of the monopoly, we laid down the following as a principle for indemnity :

To grant to the claimant the difference between the price paid for the sulphur before the monopoly, and the price at which he was able to sell it, after the abolition of the monopoly. This difference, with the charges for interest of money and warehouse rent, consequent upon the sulphur remaining on hand, constituted the amount of the positive loss incurred by the claimant. We are fully satisfied that the claimants have been fully indemnified for such of their losses as can, strictly speaking, be attributed to the monopoly contract which was abolished in July 1840.

6) Minute of the Closing of the Commission.

Naples, le 24 décembre 1841.

La Commission mixte, établie en conséquence de l'arrangement fait entre Sa Majesté la Reine du Royaume Uni de la Grande-Bretagne et d'Irlande, et Sa Majesté le Roi du Royaume des Deux Siciles, sous la médiation de Sa Majesté le Roi des Français pour la liquidation des demandes d'indemnités formées par les sujets britanniques dans l'affaire des soufres de Sicile, s'étant réunie aujourd'hui le 24 décembre 1841 au Palais du Ministère des Finances, après avoir invité M. le Commissaire Surarbitre à se joindre à elle, a procédé à la signature du procès-verbal de clôture de ses travaux, conformément aux stipulations du conclusum de juillet 1840. En conséquence, se référant :

1º A son procès-verbal du 23 mars 1841 qui établit à partir de ce même jour, l'institution légale de la Commission, accordant aux réclamants britanniques le délai de 3 mois pour la présentation de leurs demandes en indemnités ;

2º A son procès-verbal du 25 juin 1841, par lequel le terme de 3 mois, accordé par le conclusum de juillet 1840, aux réclamants britanniques, pour produire devant la Commission leurs demandes en indemnité, est déclaré expiré le 24 juin 1841.

Les soussignés déclarent que le délai de 6 mois stipulé par le conclusum de juillet 1840, et qui a commencé le 24 juin 1841, jusqu'au jour d'aujourd'hui, pendant lequel espace de temps toutes les réclamations des sujets britanniques présentées en temps utile, ont été examinées, liquidées ou rejetées est écoulé. Un état général de cette liquidation a été dressé et joint au présent procès-verbal sous le titre d'annexe, lettre A.

Cet état ainsi que le présent procès-verbal a été revêtu des signatures des 4 Commissaires, ainsi que de celle du Commissaire Surarbitre.

Les Commissaires de Sa Majesté Britannique et de Sa Majesté Sicilienne ont signé les certificats, qui, selon ce qui avait été réglé dans la séance du 20 décembre 1841, devaient être remis à chacun des réclamants, afin de lui donner un titre dont il pourra se servir pour obtenir le paiement de l'indemnité qui lui a été accordée.

Ce document portant intérêt à 6 pour cent, à partir de la date de la réclamation, jusqu'au jour de paiement inclusivement, devra être soldé, dans le délai d'une année, ainsi qu'il a été spécifié dans le conclusum cité plus haut, de juillet 1840.

En foi de quoi, les soussignés, Commissaires de Sa Majesté Britannique, Commissaires de Sa Majesté Sicilienne, et Commissaire Surarbitre Français ont signé le présent procès-verbal par lequel la Commission établie à Naples pour la liquidation des réclamations des sujets britanniques dans l'affaire des soufres de Sicile est déclarée dûment et réellement close.

ANNEXE A.

LIST OF CLAIMS PRESENTED TO THE COMMISSION FOR LOSSES SUSTAINED BY BRITISH SUBJECTS, FROM BEING IMPEDED IN THE PRODUCTION OR EXPORTATION OF THEIR SULPHUR BY THE MONOPOLY, SHOWING THE QUANTITIES CHARGED FOR AND ALLOWED, AND THE SEVERAL SUMS AWARDED BY THE COMMISSION.

№	Claimants	Class	Sulphur The production or Export of which was impeded		Total Claim		Total Award	
			Quantities charged for	Quantities allowed	Neapolitan	English Exchange 57	Neapolitan	English Exchange 57
			Cantars	Cantars	Ducats Grs.	£ s. d.	Ducats	£ s. d.
1	G. Wood & Co. . .	1	132,478	105,982	81,510 26	14,300 00 10	36,948	6,482 02 01
2	G. Wood & Co. . .	1	105,847	84,678	67,544 95	11,849 19 09	21,688	3,804 14 09
3	G. Wood & Co. . .	1	9,636	7,710	8,895 87	1,560 13 06	3,698	648 15 00
4	G. Wood & Co. . .	3	7,243	7,243	19,875 63	3,486 19 00	6,600	1,157 17 11
5	G. Wood & Co. . .	3	2,847	2,847	7,853 18	1,377 15 00	2,400	421 01 01
6	Morrison & Co. . .	1	26,901	12,913	10,112 28	1,774 01 08	2,900	508 15 05
7	Morrison & Co. . .	1	6,500	6,500	10,916 62	1,915 03 11	4,340	761 08 01
8	Morrison & Co. . .	1	3,288	3,288	4,023 63	705 18 00	1,622	284 11 03
9	Morrison & Co. . .	2	3,000	3,000	1,482 00	260 00 00	1,322	231 18 07
10	Morrison & Co. . .	2	3,000	3,000	4,164 87	730 13 06	4,002	702 02 01
11	Morrison & Co. . .	2	3,000	—	4,775 66	837 16 08	—	—
12	Morrison & Co. . .	3	2,716	2,716	3,821 63	670 09 02	1,814	318 04 10
13	Prior Turner & Co. .	3	21,057	16,056	58,400 31	10,245 13 04	20,000	3,508 15 06
14	W. Leaf & Co. . .	3	26,136	26,136	72,566 81	12,731 00 04	9,000	1,578 19 00
15	Franck Ball . . .	3	2,500	2,500	6,685 68	1,172 18 06	1,500	263 03 02
16	T. & R. Sanderson .	3	2,200	2,200	2,971 16	521 05 01	2,971	521 04 07
17	Mathey, Oates & Co.	2	700	700	1,204 12	211 05 00	300	52 12 08
18	Thurburn Rose . .	3	671	671	904 00	158 12 00	350	61 08 00
19	Samuel Lowell . .	2	6,700	—	6,270 00	1,100 00 00	—	—
	Total		366,420	288,140	373,978 66	65,610 05 05	121,454	21,307 14 00

Naples, 24th December, 1841[1].

[1] HERTSLET, *A complete Collection* . . . ., t. VI, p. 796—804.

XXXVII. Grande-Bretagne. France.
20 novembre 1815.

Cette contestation, bien que relative à la liquidation de simples créances privées, est remarquable à raison de la coexistence de Commissaires dépositaires des fonds à distribuer, de Commissaires liquidateurs et de Surarbitres. Elle mérite aussi l'attention par l'importance des sommes qui furent définitivement attribuées à la Grande-Bretagne et qui se montèrent au total à 130,450,000 francs, ainsi que par le mode de paiement en rentes, inscrites sur le grand livre de la dette publique de France.

Convention entre la Grande-Bretagne et la France, signée à Paris, le 20 novembre 1815, conclue en conformité de l'article 9 du traité principal, relativement à l'examen et à la liquidation des réclamations des sujets de sa Majesté britannique envers le Gouvernement Français.

ART. I. Les sujets de sa Majesté Britannique porteurs de créances sur le Gouvernement Français, lesquels, en contravention à l'article II du Traité de Commerce de 1786 et depuis le 1er janvier 1793, ont été atteints à cet égard, par les effets de la confiscation ou du séquestre décrétés en France, seront conformément à l'article IV additionnel du Traité de Paris de 1814, eux, leurs héritiers ou ayant-cause, sujets de sa Majesté Britannique, indemnisés et payés, après que leurs créances auront été reconnues légitimes, et que le montant en aura été fixé suivant les formes et sous les conditions stipulées ci-après :

. . . .

ART. VIII. Le montant des inscriptions revenant à chaque créancier, pour ses créances liquidées et reconnues, sera partagé par les Commissaires dépositaires en cinq portions égales, dont la première sera délivrée immédiatement après la liquidation faite, la seconde trois mois après et ainsi de suite pour les autres, de trois mois en trois mois. Néanmoins les créanciers recevront les intérêts de leurs créances totales liquidées et reconnues, à dater du 22 mars 1816, inclusivement, aussitôt que les réclamations respectives auront été reconnues et admises.

ART. IX. Il sera inscrit comme fonds de garantie, sur le grand livre de la dette publique de France, un capital de 3,500,000 francs de rente, avec jouissance du 22 mars 1816, aux noms de deux ou de quatre Commissaires, moitié anglais, moitié Français, choisis par leurs Gouvernements respectifs. Ces Commissaires recevront

lesdites rentes, à dater du 22 mars 1816, de semestre en semestre; ils en seront dépositaires, sans pouvoir les négocier et ils seront tenus en outre à en placer le montant dans les fonds publics, et à en percevoir l'intérêt accumulé et composé au profit des créanciers. Dans le cas où les 3,500,000 francs de rente seraient insuffisants, il sera délivré aux dits Commissaires des inscriptions pour de plus fortes sommes, et jusqu'à concurrence de celles qui seront nécessaires pour payer toutes les dettes mentionnées dans le présent acte. Ces inscriptions additionnelles, s'il y a lieu, seront délivrées avec jouissance des mêmes époques que les 3,500,000 fr. ci-dessus stipulés, et administrées par les Commissaires, d'après les mêmes principes; en sorte que les créances qui resteront à solder seront acquittées avec la même proportion d'intérêt accumulé et composé que si le fonds de garantie avait été suffisant dès le commencement; et lorsque tous les paiements dûs aux créanciers auront été effectués, le surplus des rentes non assignées, avec la proportion d'intérêt accumulé et composé qui leur appartiendra sera rendu s'il y a lieu à la disposition du Gouvernement Français.

ART. X. A mesure que les liquidations seront faites, et que les créances seront reconnues, avec distinction des sommes représentant les valeurs capitales et des sommes provenant des arrérages ou intérêts, la commission de liquidation dont il sera parlé aux articles suivants, délivrera aux créanciers reconnus. deux certificats pour valoir inscription avec jouissance du 22 mars 1816, inclusivement; l'un des certificats relatif au capital de la créance, et l'autre relatif aux arrérages ou intérêts liquidés jusqu'au 22 mars 1816, exclusivement.

ART. XI. Les certificats mentionnés ci-dessus seront remis aux Commissaires dépositaires de rentes, qui les viseront afin qu'ils soient inscrits immédiatement sur le grand livre de la dette publique de France, au débit de leur dépôt et au crédit des nouveaux créanciers reconnus et porteurs desdits certificats, en ayant soin de distinguer les rentes perpétuelles des rentes viagères, et lesdits créanciers seront autorisés, dès le jour de la liquidation définitive de leurs créances, à recevoir, de la part desdits Commissaires, les rentes qui leur sont dues, avec les intérêts accumulés et composés, s'il y a lieu à leur profit, et avec une portion du capital qui aura été payé, d'après ce qui a été réglé par les articles précédents.

ART. XII. Un nouveau délai sera accordé après la signature de la présente Convention, aux sujets de Sa Majesté Britannique formant des prétentions sur le Gouvernement Français, pour des objets spécifiés dans le présent Acte à l'effet de faire leurs réclamations et de produire leurs titres. Ce délai sera de 3 mois pour les créanciers résidant en Europe, de 6 mois pour ceux qui sont dans les Colonies Occidentales et de 12 mois pour ceux qui sont dans les Indes Orientales ou dans d'autres pays également éloignés.

Après ces époques, lesdits sujets de Sa Majesté Britannique ne seront plus admissibles à la présente liquidation.

ART. XIII. A l'effet de procéder aux liquidations et reconnaissances de créances mentionnées aux articles précédents, il sera formé une commission composée de deux Français et de deux Anglais, qui seront désignés et nommés par leurs Gouvernements respectifs. Ces Commissaires, après avoir reconnu et admis les titres procèderont, d'après les bases indiquées, à la reconnaissance, liquidation et fixation des sommes qui seront dues à chaque créancier.

A mesure que ces créances auront été reconnues et fixées, ils délivreront aux créanciers les deux certificats mentionnés dans l'article 10, l'un pour le capital, l'autre pour les intérêts.

ART. XIV. Il sera nommé en même temps une commission de Surarbitres, composée de 4 membres, dont deux seront nommés par le Gouvernement Britannique et deux par le Gouvernement Français.

S'il y a nécessité d'appeler les Surarbitres pour vider le partage, les 4 noms des surarbitres Anglais et Français seront mis dans une urne, et le nom de celui des quatre qui sortira sera le Surarbitre de l'affaire spéciale sur laquelle il y aura eu partage.

Chacun des Commissaires Liquidateurs prendra à son tour dans l'urne le billet qui désignera le Surarbitre. Il sera dressé procès-verbal de cette opération et ce procès-verbal sera joint à celui qui sera dressé pour la liquidation et fixation de cette créance spéciale.

S'il survient une vacance, soit dans la commission de liquidation, soit dans celle des Surarbitres, le Gouvernement qui devra pourvoir à la nomination d'un nouveau membre, procédera à cette nomination sans aucun délai, afin que les commissions restent toujours complètes, autant que faire se peut.

Si l'un des Commissaires Liquidateurs est absent, il sera, pendant son absence, remplacé par un des Surarbitres de la même nation; et comme dans ce cas, il ne resterait qu'un Surarbitre de cette nation, les deux Surarbitres de l'autre nation seront de même réduits à un par la voie du sort. Et si l'un des Surarbitres était dans le cas de s'absenter, la même opération aurait lieu pour réduire à un les deux Surarbitres de l'autre nation. Il est généralement entendu

que pour obvier à tout retard dans l'opération, la liquidation soit l'adjudication, ne sera pas suspendue, pourvu qu'il se trouve présent et en activité un Commissaire et un Surarbitre de chaque nation, conservant en tous cas le principe de la parité entre les Commissaires et les Surarbitres des deux nations, et de la rétablir au besoin par la voie du sort. Dans le cas où l'une ou l'autre des Puissances Contractantes aurait à procéder à la nomination de nouveaux Commissaires Liquidateurs, Dépositaires ou Surarbitres lesdits Commissaires seront tenus, avant de procéder de prêter le serment et dans les formes qui sont indiquées dans l'article suivant.

ART. XV. Les Commissaires Liquidateurs, les Commissaires Dépositaires et les Surarbitres prêteront en même temps serment, en présence de l'Ambassadeur de Sa Majesté Britannique, entre les mains de M. le garde des sceaux de France, de bien et fidèlement procéder, de n'avoir aucune préférence ni pour le créancier ni pour le débiteur et d'agir dans tous leurs actes d'après les stipulations du Traité de Paris du 30 mai 1814, des Traités et Conventions avec la France signés aujourd'hui et notamment d'après celles du présent acte.

Les Commissaires Liquidateurs, ainsi que les Surarbitres, seront autorisés, toutes les fois qu'ils le jugeront nécessaire, à appeler des témoins et à les interroger sous serment dans les formes prescrites, sur tous les points relatifs aux différentes réclamations qui font l'objet de cette convention.

ART. XVI. Après que les 3,500,000 francs de rentes, mentionnés dans l'article 9 auront été inscrits au nom des Commissaires Dépositaires et à la première demande du Gouvernement Français, Sa Majesté Britannique donnera les ordres nécessaires pour effectuer la rétrocession des Colonies Françaises telle qu'elle a été stipulée par le Traité de Paris, du 30 mai 1814 y compris la Martinique et la Guadeloupe, qui ont été occupées depuis par les forces Britanniques.

L'inscription mentionnée ci-dessus aura lieu d'ici au 1er janvier prochain au plus tard.

ARTICLE ADDITIONNEL. Les réclamations des sujets de Sa Majesté Britannique, fondées sur la décision de Sa Majesté Très Chrétienne, relativement aux marchandises anglaises introduites à Bourdeaux, par suite du tarif des douanes publié dans ladite ville par son Altesse Royale Monseigneur le Duc d'Angoulême, le 24 mars 1814, seront liquidées et payées d'après les principes et le but indiqués dans cette décision de Sa Majesté Très Chrétienne.

La commission créée par l'article 13 de la Convention de ce jour, est chargée de procéder immédiatement à la liquidation de ladite créance et à la fixation des époques du paiement en argent effectif.

La décision qui sera rendue par les Commissaires, sera exécutée immédiatement, selon sa forme et teneur. Le présent article additionnel aura la même force ou valeur que s'il était inséré, mot à mot, dans la Convention de ce jour, relative à l'examen et à la liquidation des réclamations des sujets de Sa Majesté Britannique envers le Gouvernement Français.

En foi de quoi les Plénipotentiaires respectifs l'ont signé et y ont apposé le cachet de leurs armes.

Fait à Paris le 20 novembre, l'An de Grâce 1815 [1].

Convention entre la Grande-Bretagne et la France pour l'arrangement final des réclamations des sujets de Sa Majesté Britannique envers le Gouvernement Français, signée à Paris, le 25 Avril 1818.

Sa Majesté Britannique et Sa Majesté Très Chrétienne désirant écarter tous les obstacles qui ont retardé, jusqu'à présent, l'exécution pleine et entière de la Convention (n° 7) conclue en conformité de l'Article 9 du Traité du 20 novembre 1815, relative à l'examen et à la liquidation des réclamations des sujets de Sa dite Majesté Britannique envers le Gouvernement Français, ont nommé pour leurs Plénipotentiaires, savoir : Sa Majesté Britannique, le sieur Charles Stuart, G. C. B., son Ambassadeur Extraordinaire et Plénipotentiaire près Sa Majesté Très Chrétienne, etc., etc., et Sa Majesté Très Chrétienne, le sieur Armand Emmanuel Duplessis Richelieu, Duc de Richelieu, son Ministre et Secrétaire d'Etat des Affaires Etrangères, et Président du Conseil de ses Ministres, etc., etc., etc. Lesquels, après s'être communiqué leurs pleins pouvoirs respectifs, sont convenus des articles suivants :

ART. I. A l'effet d'opérer le remboursement et l'extinction totale, tant pour le capital que pour les intérêts, des créances des sujets de Sa Majesté Britannique, dont le paiement est réclamé en vertu de l'Article Additionnel du Traité du 30 Mai 1814 et de la susdite Convention du 20 Novembre 1815, il sera inscrit sur le grand livre de la dette publique de France, avec jouissance du 22 Mars 1818, une rente de 3,000,000 de francs représentant un capital de 60,000,000.

ART. II. La portion de rente qui est encore disponible sur les fonds créés en vertu de l'Article 9 de la susdite Convention du 20 Novembre 1815, y compris les intérêts composés et accumulés depuis le 22 mars 1816, reste également affectée au remboursement des mêmes créances ; en

conséquence les inscriptions des dites rentes seront remises aux Commissaires Liquidateurs de Sa Majesté Britannique, immédiatement après l'échange des ratifications de la présente Convention.

ART. III. La rente de 3,000,000 de francs qui sera créée conformément à l'Article premier ci-dessus, sera divisée en douze inscriptions, de valeur égale, portant toutes jouissance du 22 Mars 1818, lesquelles seront inscrites au nom des Commissaires de Sa Majesté Britannique, ou de ceux qu'ils désigneront, et leur seront successivement remises de mois en mois, à commencer du jour de l'échange des ratifications de la présente Convention.

ART. IV. La délivrance des dites inscriptions aura lieu, nonobstant toute signification de transfert ou oppositions faites au trésor royal de France, ou entre les mains des Commissaires de Sa Majesté Britannique.

La liste des significations et oppositions qui existeraient au trésor royal sera néanmoins remise avec les pièces à l'appui aux dits Commissaires de Sa Majesté Britannique, dans le délai d'un mois, à dater du jour de l'échange des ratifications de la présente Convention ; et il est convenu que le paiement des sommes contestées sera suspendu jusqu'à ce que les contestations qui auraient donné lieu aux dites oppositions ou significations aient été jugées par le tribunal compétent, qui dans ce cas sera celui de la partie saisie. Le terme de rigueur fixé ci-dessus étant expiré, on n'aura plus égard aux oppositions et significations qui n'auraient pas été certifiées aux Commissaires soit par le trésor, soit par les parties intéressées. Il sera toutefois permis de former opposition ou de faire tout autre acte conservatoire entre les mains des dits Commissaires ou du Gouvernement de Sa Majesté Britannique.

ART. V. Le Gouvernement Britannique voulant prendre, dans l'intérêt de ses sujets créanciers de la France, les mesures les plus efficaces pour faire opérer la liquidation des créances et la répartition des fonds auxquels les dits créanciers auront proportionnellement droit, d'après les principes contenus dans les stipulations du Traité du 30 Mai 1814, et de la Convention du 20 Novembre 1815, il est convenu, qu'à cet effet, le Gouvernement Français fera remettre aux Commissaires de Sa Majesté Britannique les dossiers contenant les pièces à l'appui des réclamations non encore payées, et donnera en même temps les ordres les plus précis pour que tous les renseignements et documents, que la vérification de ces réclamations pourra rendre nécessaires, soient fournis, dans le plus court délai possible, aux susdits Commissaires, par les différents ministères et administrations.

[1] HERTSLET. *A complete Collection* ... t. I, p. 276, 286-294, 296.

ART. VI. Les créances des sujets de Sa Majesté Britannique déjà liquidées, et sur lesquelles il reste encore un cinquième à payer, seront soldées aux échéances qui avaient été précédemment fixées, et les cinquièmes coupures seront délivrées sur la seule autorisation des Commissaires de Sa Majesté Britannique.

ART. VII. La présente Convention sera ratifiée et les ratifications en seront échangées à Paris, dans le terme d'un mois ou plutôt, si faire se peut.

ARTICLE SÉPARÉ. Il est bien entendu que la Convention de ce jour entre la Grande-Bretagne et la France ne déroge en rien aux réclamations des sujets de Sa Majesté Britannique fondés sur l'Article Additionnel de la Convention du 20 Novembre 1815, relativement aux marchandises anglaises introduites à Bordeaux, lesquelles réclamations seront définitivement réglées conformément à la teneur du susdit Article Additionnel.

Le présent article aura la même force et valeur que s'il était inséré mot à mot, dans la susdite Convention.

En foi de quoi les Plénipotentiaires respectifs l'ont signé et y ont apposé le cachet de leurs armes.

Fait à Paris le 25 avril 1818.

Convention additionnelle relative aux marchandises introduites à Bordeaux, signée à Paris le 4 Juillet 1818.

Les Cours de la Grande-Bretagne et de France étant convenues de terminer par une transaction à l'amiable, les difficultés qui se sont opposées jusqu'à ce jour à la liquidation complète, et au paiement des sujets de Sa Majesté Britannique, dont les réclamations étaient fondées sur l'Article Additionnel de la Convention du 20 Novembre 1815, confirmé par l'Article Additionnel (Séparé) de la Convention du 25 Avril dernier, les soussignés, Chevalier Charles Stuart, Ambassadeur Extraordinaire et Ministre Plénipotentiaire de Sa Majesté Britannique près la Cour de Sa Majesté Très Chrétienne, etc., etc., etc., et le Duc de Richelieu, Ministre et Secrétaire d'Etat au département des Affaires Etrangères de Sa Majesté Très Chrétienne, et Président du Conseil de ses Ministres, etc., etc., etc., munis de l'autorisation de leurs Gouvernements respectifs, sont convenus de ce qui suit :

ART. I. Le montant total des paiements à faire par la France pour l'acquittement et l'extinction totale des créances des sujets de Sa Majesté Très Chrétienne, relativement aux marchandises introduites à Bordeaux, par suite du tarif des douanes publié le 24 Mars 1814, est fixé à la somme de 450,000 francs. .

ART. II. La dite somme de 450,000 francs sera versée entre les mains des Commissaires désignés à cet effet par Sa Majesté Britannique, par portions égales de 75,000 francs chacune, dont le paiement aura lieu le premier de chaque mo s, à dater du premier Août prochain, de manière à ce que la somme totale soit acquittée au premier Janvier 1819.

ART. III. Les présents Articles seront ratifiés, et les ratifications en seront échangées dans le terme d'un mois, ou plutôt si faire se peut.

En foi de quoi les soussignés les ont signés, et ont apposé le cachet de leurs armes.

Fait à Paris le 4 Juillet 1818.[1]

XXXVIII. Autriche. France. Grande-Bretagne. Prusse. Russie.

20 novembre 1815.

Similaire à la contestation précédente, elle fut comme elle terminée par une transaction définitive, dont l'import considérable fut fixé au total à 240,800,000 francs.

Convention entre les Grandes Puissances et la France, conclue en conformité de l'article 9 du traité principal relativement à l'examen et à la liquidation des réclamations (particulières) à la charge du Gouvernement Français, signée à Paris le 20 novembre 1815.

Pour applanir diverses difficultés qui se sont élevées sur l'exécution de divers Articles du Traité de Paris, du 30 mai 1814, et notamment sur ceux relatifs aux réclamations des sujets des Puissances alliées, les Hautes Parties contractantes, désirant faire promptement jouir leurs sujets respectifs des droits que ces Articles leur assurent, et prévenir en même temps autant que possible, toute contestation qui pourrait s'élever sur le sens de quelques dispositions du dit Traité, sont convenues des Articles suivants :

Art. I. Le Traité de Paris du 3 mai 1814, étant confirmé par l'article 9 du Traité Principal auquel la présente Convention est annexée, cette confirmation s'étend nommément aux Articles 19, 20, 21, 22, 23, 24, 25, 26, 30 et 31 du dit Traité autant que les stipulations renfermées dans ces articles n'ont pas été changées ou modifiées par le présent Acte, et il est expressément convenu que les explications et les developpements que les Hautes Parties Contractantes ont jugé à propos de leur donner par les Articles suivants, ne préjudicieront en rien aux réclamations de toute autre nature, qui seraient autorisées par ledit Traité, sans être spécialement rappelées par la présente convention.

[1] HERTSLET, A complete Collection..., t. 1. p. 328-336.

Art. II. En conformité de cette disposition, Sa Majesté Très Chrétienne promet de faire liquider dans les formes ci-après indiquées, toutes les sommes que la France se trouve devoir dans les pays hors de son territoire tel qu'il est constitué par le Traité auquel la présente Convention est annexée, en vertu de l'article 19 du Traité de Paris du 30 mai 1814, soit à des individus, soit à des communes, soit à des établissements particuliers dont les revenus ne sont pas à la disposition des Gouvernements.

Cette liquidation s'étendra spécialement sur les réclamations suivantes :

1) Sur celles qui concernent les fournitures et prestations de tous genres faites par des communes ou des individus et en général par tout autre que les Gouvernements, en vertu de contrats ou de dispositions émanées des Autorités Administratives Françaises renfermant promesse de paiement ; que ces fournitures et prestations ayant été effectuées dans et pour les magasins militaires en général, ou pour l'approvisionnement des villes et places en particulier, ou enfin aux armées Françaises, ou à des détachements de troupes, ou à la gendarmerie, ou aux Administrations Françaises, ou aux Hopitaux Militaires, ou enfin pour un service public quelconque.

Ces livraisons et prestations seront justifiées par les reçus des gardes magasins, officiers civils ou militaires, commissaires, agents ou surveillants, dont la validité sera reconnue par la Commission de Liquidation dont il sera question à l'article 5 de la présente Convention.

Les prix en seront réglés d'après les contrats ou autres engagements des Autorités Françaises, ou, à leur défaut, d'après les mercuriales des endroits les plus rapprochés de celui où le versement a été fait.

2) Sur les arriérés de solde et de traitement, frais de voyage, gratifications et autres indemnités revenant à des militaires ou employés à l'armée Française, devenus, par les Traités de Paris du 30 Mai 1814 et du 20 Novembre 1815, sujets d'une autre Puissance, pour le temps où ces individus servaient dans les armées Françaises, ou qu'ils étaient attachés à des établissements qui en dépendaient, tels qu'hôpitaux, pharmacies, magasins ou autres.

La justification de ces demandes devra se faire par la production des pièces exigées par les lois et règlements militaires.

3) Sur la restitution des frais d'entretien des militaires Français dans les hospices civils qui n'appartenaient pas au Gouvernement, en tant que le paiement de cet entretien a été stipulé par des engagements exprès.

La quotité de ces frais sera justifiée par les bordereaux certifiés par les chefs de ces établissements.

4) Sur la restitution des fonds confiés aux postes aux lettres Françaises, qui ne sont pas parvenus à leur destination, le cas de force majeure excepté.

5) Sur l'acquit des mandats, bons et ordonnances de payements fournis, soit sur le Trésor Public de France, soit sur la caisse d'amortissement ou leurs annexes ainsi que des bons donnés par cette dernière caisse ; lesquels mandats, bons et ordonnances, ont été souscrits en faveur d'habitants de communes ou d'établissements ; sans que de la part de la France on puisse refuser de les payer par la raison que les objets, pour la vente desquels ces bons, mandats et ordonnances devaient être réalisés, ont passé sous un Gouvernement étranger.

6) Sur les emprunts faits par les Autorités Françaises, civiles ou militaires, avec promesse de restitution.

7) Sur les indemnités accordées pour non-jouissance de biens domaniaux donnés en bail : sur toute autre indemnité et restitution pour fait d'affermage de biens domaniaux, ainsi que sur les vacations, émoluments et honoraires, pour estimation, visite ou expertise de bâtiments et autres objets, faites par ordre et pour compte du Gouvernement Français, en tant que ces indemnités, restitutions, vacations, émoluments et honoraires ont été reconnus être à la charge du Gouvernement et légalement ordonnés par les Autorités Françaises alors existantes.

8) Sur le remboursement des avances faites par les caisses communales, par ordre des Autorités Françaises et avec promesse de restitution.

9) Sur les indemnités dues à des particuliers pour prise de terrain, démolition, destruction de bâtiments qui ont lieu d'après les ordres des Autorités Militaires Françaises, pour l'agrandissement ou la sûreté des places fortes, citadelles, dans le cas où il est dû indemnité, en vertu de la loi du 10 juillet 1791 et lorsqu'il y aura eu engagement de payer résultant : soit d'une expertise contradictoire, réglant le montant de l'indemnité, soit de tout autre acte des Autorités Françaises.

. . . .

Art. V. Les Hautes Parties contractantes animées du désir de convenir d'un mode de liquidation, propre en même temps à abréger le terme, et à conduire dans chaque cas particulier à une décision définitive, ont résolu, en expliquant les dispositions de l'article 20 du traité du 30 Mai 1814, d'établir des Commissions de Liquidation, qui s'occuperont en premier lieu de l'examen des réclamations, et des Commissions d'Arbitrage, qui en décideront dans le cas où les premières ne seraient pas parvenues à s'accorder. Le mode qui sera adopté à cet égard sera le suivant:

1) Immédiatement après l'échange des ratifications du présent Traité, la France et les autres Hautes Parties Contractantes ou intéressées à cet objet, nommeront des Commissaires-Liquidateurs et des Commissaires-Juges, qui résideront à Paris, et qui seront chargés de régler et faire exécuter les dispositions renfermées dans les Articles 18 et 19 du Traité du 30 Mai 1814 et dans les Articles 2, 4, 6, 7, 10, 11, 12, 13, 14, 17, 18, 19, 22, 23, 24 de la présente Convention.

2) Les Commissaires-Liquidateurs seront nommés par toutes les parties intéressées qui voudront en déléguer, au nombre que chacune d'elle jugera convenable. Ils seront chargés de recevoir et d'examiner dans l'ordre d'un tableau qui sera établi pour cela, et dans le plus bref délai, et de liquider, s'il y a lieu, toutes les réclamations. Il sera libre à chaque Commissaire de réunir dans une même Commission tous les commissaires des différents Gouvernements, pour leur présenter et faire examiner par eux les réclamations des sujets de son Gouvernement, ou bien de traiter séparément avec le Gouvernement Français.

3) Les Commissaires-Juges seront chargés de prononcer définitivement et en dernier ressort sur toutes les affaires qui leur seront renvoyées, en conformité du présent Article, par les Commissaires-Liquidateurs, qui n'auront pas pu s'accorder sur elles. Chacune des Hautes Parties Contractantes ou intéressées pourra nommer autant de ces juges qu'elle trouvera convenable; mais tous ces juges prêteront, entre les mains du garde des sceaux de France et en présence des Ministres des Hautes Parties Contractantes résidant à Paris, serment de prononcer sans partialité aucune sur les parties, d'après les principes établis par le Traité du 30 Mai 1814, et par la présente Convention.

4) Immédiatement après que les Commissaires-Juges nommés par la France, et par deux au moins des autres parties intéressées, auront prêté ce serment, tous ces Juges, présents à Paris, se réuniront sous la présidence du doyen-d'âge pour convenir de la nomination d'un ou de plusieurs greffiers et d'un ou de plusieurs commis, qui prêteront serment entre leurs mains, ainsi que pour délibérer s'il y a lieu à un règlement général sur l'expédition des affaires, la tenue des registres et autres objets d'ordre d'intérieur.

5) Les Commissaires destinés à former les Commissions d'arbitrage étant ainsi instituées, lorsque les Commissaires-Liquidateurs n'auront pu s'accorder sur une affaire, il sera procédé devant les Commissaires-Juges, comme il va être dit.

6) Dans les cas où les réclamations seraient de la nature de celles prévues par le Traité de Paris, ou par la présente Convention et où il ne s'agirait que de statuer sur la validité de la demande, ou de fixer le montant des sommes réclamées, la Commission d'Arbitrage sera composée de 6 Commissaires-Juges, savoir : trois Français et trois personnes désignées par le Gouvernement réclamant. Ces six Juges tireront au sort pour savoir lequel d'entre eux devra s'abstenir. Les Commissaires étant ainsi réduits au nombre de cinq, statueront définitivement sur la question qui leur sera présentée.

7) Dans le cas où il s'agirait de savoir si la réclamation contestée peut être rangée parmi celles prévues dans le Traité de Paris du 30 Mai 1814, ou dans la présente Convention, la Commission d'arbitrage sera composée de six membres, dont 3 Français et 3 désignés par le Gouvernement réclamant. Ces 6 Juges décideront à la majorité, si la réclamation est susceptible d'être admise à la liquidation ; en cas de partage égal d'opinions, il sera sursis à l'examen de l'affaire et elle fera la matière d'une négociation diplomatique ultérieure entre les Gouvernements.

8) Toutes les fois qu'une affaire sera portée à la décision d'une Commission d'Arbitrage, le Gouvernement dont le Commissaire-Liquidateur n'aura pu s'accorder avec le Gouvernement Français, désignera trois Commissaires-Juges et la France en désignera autant, les uns et les autres pris parmi tous ceux qui auront prêté et prêteront, avant de procéder, le serment prescrit. On fera connaître ce choix au Greffier, en lui transmettant le dossier des pièces. Le greffier donnera acte de cette désignation et de ce dépôt, et inscrira la réclamation sur le registre particulier qui aura été établi à cet usage. Lorsque, dans l'ordre de ces inscriptions, le tour d'une réclamation sera venu, le greffier convoquera les six Commissaires-Juges désignés.

S'il s'agit d'un des cas énoncés dans le Paragraphe six du présent article, les noms de ces six Commissaires-Juges seront mis dans une urne, et le dernier sortant sera éliminé de droit, de sorte que le nombre des juges soit réduit à cinq. Il sera néanmoins libre aux parties de s'en tenir, si elles en conviennent d'un commun accord, à une Commission de quatre Juges, dont le nombre, pour obtenir un nombre impair, sera réduit de la même manière à trois. Dans le cas prévu par le paragraphe sept du présent Article, les six juges ou les quatre, si les deux parties sont convenues de ce nombre, entrent en discussion sans l élimination préalable d'un de leurs membres. Dans l'un est l'autre cas, les Commissaires-

Juges convoqués pour cet effet, s'occuperont immédiatement de l'examen de la réclamation ou du chef de réclamation dont il s'agit et prononceront, à la pluralité des voix, en dernier ressort. Le greffier assistera à toutes les séances et y tiendra la plume. Si la Commission d Arbitrage n'a point décidé d'un chef de réclamation, mais d'une réclamation même, cette décision terminera l'affaire. Si elle a prononcé sur un chef de réclamation, l'affaire, dans le cas que ce chef est reconnu valable, retourne à la Commission de Liquidation, pour que cette dernière s'accorde sur l'admissibilité de la réclamation particulière et de la fixation de son montant, ou qu'elle la renvoie de nouveau à une Commission d'Arbitrage réduite au nombre de cinq, ou de trois membres. La décision rendue, le greffier donnera à la Commission de Liquidation connaissance de chaque sentence prononcée, afin qu'elle la joigne à ses procès-verbaux, ces jugements devant être envisagés comme faisant partie du travail de la Commission de Liquidation.

Il est au reste bien entendu, que les Commissions établies en vertu du présent Article, ne peuvent point étendre leur travail au-delà de la Liquidation des obligations résultant du présent Traité, et de celui du 30 Mai 1814.

. . . .

ART. XVI. Les Gouvernements qui ont des réclamations à faire, au nom de leurs sujets, s'engagent à les faire présenter à la liquidation dans le délai d'une année, à dater du jour de l'échange des ratifications du présent Traité, passé lequel terme il y aura déchéance de tout droit, réclamation et répétition.

ART. XVII. Tous les deux mois il sera dressé un bordereau des liquidations définitivement arrêtées, agréées ou jugées, indiquant le nom de chaque créancier et la somme pour laquelle sa créance doit être acquittée, soit en principal, soit en intérêts arrérages. Les sommes qui sont à payer en numéraire par le trésor royal, soit pour capitaux, soit pour intérêts seront remises aux Commissaires-Liquidateurs du Gouvernement intéressé, sur leurs quittances visées par les Liquidateurs Français. Quant aux créances qui d'après les articles 4 et 19 de la présente Convention doivent être remboursées en inscriptions, sur le grand livre de la dette publique, elles seront inscrites au nom des Commissaires-Liquidateurs des Gouvernements intéressés ou de ceux u'ils désigneront. Ces inscriptions seront prises lu fonds de garantie établi par l'Article 20 de résente Convention, et de la manière qui est 'ipulée par l'Article XXI.

ART. XX. Il sera inscrit le 1ᵉʳ janvier pro- in au plus tard, comme fonds de garantie,

sur le grand livre de la dette publique de France, un capital de 3,500,000 francs de rente, avec jouissance du 22 Mars 1816, aux noms de deux, quatre ou de six Commissaires, moitié sujets de Sa Majesté Très Chrétienne, moitié sujets des Puissances alliées, lesquels Commissaires seront choisis et nommés savoir : un, deux ou trois par le Gouvernement Français et un, deux ou trois par les Puissances alliées. Ces Commissaires toucheront lesdites rentes de semestre en semestre ; ils en seront dépositaires sans pouvoir les négocier. Ils en placeront le montant dans les fonds publics, et ils en recevront l'intérêt accumulé et composé au profit des créanciers.

Dans le cas où les 3,500,000 francs de rente seraient insuffisants, il sera délivré aux susdits Commissaires des inscriptions pour plus fortes sommes et jusqu'à concurrence de celles qui seront nécessaires pour payer les dettes indiquées par la présente Convention.

Ces inscriptions additionnelles, s'il y a lieu, seront délivrées avec jouissance de la même époque que celle fixée pour les 3,500,000 francs de rente ci-dessus stipulés, et elles seront administrées par les mêmes Commissaires et d'après les mêmes principes ; en sorte que les créances qui resteront à solder seront acquittées avec la même proportion d'intérêts accumulés et composés que si le fonds de garantie avait été suffisant dès le commencement.

Lorsque les paiements dus aux créanciers auront été effectués le surplus des rentes non assignées, s'il .y en a, ainsi que la proportion d'intérêts accumulés et composés qui leur appartiendra, seront remis à la disposition du Gouvernement Français.

ART. XXI. A mesure que les bordereaux de liquidation prescrits par l'Article 17 de la présente Convention seront présentés aux Commissaires dépositaires des rentes, ceux-ci les viseront afin qu'ils puissent être inscrits immédiatement sur le grand livre de la dette publique, au débit de leur dépôt et au crédit des Commissaires-Liquidateurs des Gouvernements réclamants [1].

. . . .

Convention entre les Grandes Puissances et la France pour la liquidation finale des réclamations particulières envers le Gouvernement Français, signée à Paris le 25 avril 1818.

Les Cours de la Grande-Bretagne, d'Autriche, de Prusse et de Russie, Signataires du Traité du 20 Novembre 1815, ayant reconnu que la liquidation des réclamations particulières à la charge de la France, fondée sur la Convention

---

[1] HERTSLET. *A complete Collection* . . . . t. I. pp. 298, 304-310. 320-322, 324-326.

(n°13) conclue en conformité de l'Article 9 du dit Traité, pour régler l'exécution des Articles 19 et suivants du Traité du 30 Mai 1814, était devenue par l'incertitude de sa durée et de son résultat une cause d'inquiétude toujours croissante pour la nation Française, partageant en conséquence avec Sa Majesté Très Chrétienne le désir de mettre un terme à cette incertitude, par une transaction destinée à éteindre toutes ces réclamations moyennant une somme déterminée, les dites Puissances et Sa Majesté Très Chrétienne ont nommé pour leurs Plénipotentiaires savoir:

Sa Majesté le Roi du Royaume Uni de la Grande-Bretagne et d'Irlande; le sieur Charles Stuart G. C. B., Son Ambassadeur Extraordinaire et Plénipotentiaire près de Sa Majesté Très Chrétienne.

Sa Majesté l'Empereur d'Autriche, Roi de Hongrie et de Bohême; le sieur Nicolas Charles Baron de Vincent, Son Envoyé Extraordinaire et Ministre Plénipotentiaire près Sa Majesté Très Chrétienne, etc., etc.

Sa Majesté le Roi de France et de Navarre, le sieur Armand-Emmanuel Duplessis Richelieu, Duc de Richelieu, Son Ministre et Secrétaire d'Etat des Affaires Etrangères et Président du Conseil de Ses Ministres, etc., etc.,

Sa Majesté le Roi de Prusse, le sieur Charles Frédéric Comte de Goltz, Son Envoyé Extraordinaire et Ministre Plénipotentiaire près Sa Majesté Très Chrétienne, etc., etc.

Sa Majesté l'Empereur de toutes les Russies Roi de Pologne: le sieur Charles-André Pozzo de Borgo, Lieutenant-Général de ses Armées, Son Ministre Plénipotentiaires près Sa Majesté Très Chrétienne, etc.

Et attendu qu'elles ont considéré que le concours de Son Excellence Monsieur le Maréchal Duc de Wellington contribuerait efficacement au succès de cette négociation, les Plénipotentiaires Soussignés, après avoir arrêté de concert avec lui et d'accord avec les Parties intéressées, les bases de l'arrangement à conclure, sont convenues des Articles suivants:

ART. I. A l'effet d'opérer l'extinction totale des dettes contractées par la France dans les pays hors de son territoire actuel, envers des individus, des communes ou des établissements particuliers quelconques, dont le paiement est réclamé en vertu des Traités du 30 Mai 1814 et du 20 Novembre 1815, le Gouvernement Français s'engage à faire inscrire sur le grand livre de sa dette publique avec jouissance du 22 Mars 1818, une rente de 12,040,000 fr. représentant un capital de 240,800,000 fr.

ART. II. Les sommes remboursables au Gouvernement Français en vertu de l'Article 21 du Traité du 30 Mai 1814 et des Articles 6 et 22 de la susdite Convention du 20 Novembre 1815, serviront à compléter les moyens d'extinction des susdites dettes de la France envers les sujets des Puissances qui étaient chargées du remboursement de ces sommes. En conséquence le Gouvernement Français reconnaît n'avoir plus rien à réclamer, en raison du dit remboursement. De leur côté, les dites puissances reconnaissent que les déductions et bonifications auxquelles donnaient lieu en leur faveur l'Article 7 de la Convention du 20 Novembre 1815, étant également comprises dans l'évaluation de la somme fixée par l'Article 1 de la présente Convention, ou abandonnées par les Puissances intéressées, toutes réclamations et prétentions à cet égard se trouvent complètement éteintes.

Il est bien entendu que le Gouvernement Français conformément aux stipulations contenues dans les Articles 6 et 22 de la même Convention, continuera à servir la rente des dettes des pays détachés de son territoire qui ont été converties en inscriptions sur le grand livre de la dette publique, soit que ces inscriptions se trouvent entre les mains des possesseurs originaires, soit qu'elles aient été transférées à d'autres personnes. Néanmoins la France cesse d'être chargée des rentes viagères de la même origine dont le paiement doit être à la charge des possesseurs actuels du territoire à partir du 22 Décembre 1813.

Il est de plus convenu qu'il ne pourra être mis aucun obstacle au libre transfert des inscriptions des rentes appartenant à des individus, communautés, ou corporations qui ont cessé d'être Français.

ART. III. Les reprises, que le Gouvernement Français aurait pu être autorisé à exercer sur les cautionnements de certains comptables, dans les cas prévus par les Articles 10 et 24 de la Convention du 20 Novembre 1815, étant également entrées dans la transaction qui fait l'objet de la présente Convention, elles se trouvent par là complètement éteintes. Quant à ceux de ces cautionnements qui auraient été fournis en immeubles ou inscriptions sur le grand livre, il sera procédé à la radiation des inscriptions hypothécaires ou à la levée des oppositions sur la demande des susdits Gouvernements et les dites inscriptions, ainsi que les actes de main levée seront remis à leurs Commissaires respectifs ou à leurs délégués.

ART. IV. Les sommes versées à titre de cautionnements, dépôts ou consignations, par des sujets Français, serviteurs des pays détachés de la France, dans leurs Trésors respectifs et qui devaient leur être remboursés en vertu de l'Article 22 du Traité du 30 Mai 1814, étant comprises dans la présente transaction, les dites

Puissances se trouvent complètement libérées à leur égard, le Gouvernement Français se chargeant de pourvoir à leur remboursement.

ART. V. Au moyen des stipulations contenues dans les Articles précédents, la France se trouve complètement libérée, tant pour le capital que pour les intérèts, prescrits par l'Article 18 du Traité du 20 Novembre 1815, des dettes de toute nature prévues par le Traité du 30 Mai 1814 et la Convention du 20 Novembre 1815 et réclamées dans les formes prescrites la par susdite Convention, de sorte que les dites dettes seront considérées à son égard comme éteintes et annulées et ne pourront jamais donner lieu contre elle à aucune espèce de répétition.

ART. VI. En conséquence des dispositions précédentes, les Commissions mixtes, instituées par l'Article 5 de la Convention du 20 Novembre 1815, cesseront le travail de liquidation ordonné par la même Convention.

ART. VII. La rente qui sera créée en vertu de l'Article Ier de la présente Convention sera répartie entre les Puissances ci-après nommées, ainsi qu'il suit:

	Francs
Anhalt Bernbourg	17,500
Anhalt Dessau	18,500
Autriche	1,250,000
Bade	32,500
Bavière	500,000
Brème	50,000
Danemarck	350,000
Espagne	850,000
Etats Romains	250,000
Francfort	35,000
Hambourg	1,000,000
Hannovre	500,000
Hesse Electorale	25,000
Grand Duché de Hesse y compris Oldenbourg	348,150
Iles Ioniennes, île de France et autres pays sous la domination de S. M. Britannique	150,000
Lubeck	100,000
Mecklenbourg Schwerin	25,000
Mecklenbourg Strelitz	1,750
Nassau	6,000
Parme	50,000
Pays-Bas	1,650,000
Portugal	40,900
Prusse	2,600,000
Reuss	3,250
Sardaigne	1,250,000
Saxe	225,000
Saxe Gotha	30,000
Saxe Meiningen	1,000
Saxe Weimar	9,250
Schwartzbourg	7,500

	Francs
Suisse	250,000
Toscane	225,000
Wirtembourg	20,000
Hannovre, Brunswick, Hesse Electorale et Prusse	8,000
Hesse Electorale et Saxe Weimar	700
Grand Duché de Hesse et Bavière	10,000
Grand Duché de Hesse, Bavière et Prusse	40,000
Saxe et Prusse	110,000

ART. VIII. La somme de 12,040,000 francs de rentes, stipulées par l'Article I, portera jouissance du 22 Mars 1818, elle sera déposée en totalité entre les mains des Commissaires Spéciaux des Cours d'Autriche, de la Grande-Bretagne et de Russie, pour être ensuite délivrée à qui de droit, aux époques et dans les formes suivantes:

1) Le Ier de chaque mois, le douzième de ce qu'il reviendra à chaque Puissance, conformément à la répartition ci-dessus sera remis à ses Commissaires à Paris, ou aux Délégués de ceux-ci: lesquels Commissaires ou Délégués en disposeront de la manière indiquée ci-après.

2) Les Gouvernements respectifs, ou les Commissaires de Liquidation qu'ils établiront, feront remettre à la fin de chaque mois, aux individus dont les créances auraient été liquidées et qui désireraient rester propriétaire des quotités de rentes qui leur seront allouées, des inscriptions du montant de la somme qui reviendra à chacun d'eux.

3) Pour toutes les autres créances liquidées, ainsi que pour toutes les sommes qui ne seraient pas assez fortes pour pouvoir en former une inscription séparée, les Gouvernements respectifs se chargent de les faire réunir en une seule inscription collective, dont ils ordonneront la vente en faveur des parties intéressées par l'entremise de leurs Commissaires ou Agents à Paris.

Le dépôt de la susdite rente de 12,040,000 fr. aura lieu le premier du mois qui suivra le jour de l'échange des ratifications de la présente Convention, par les Cours d'Autriche, de la Grande-Bretagne et de Prusse seulement, attendu l'éloignement de la Cour de Russie.

ART. IX. La délivrance des dites inscriptions aura lieu nonobstant toute signification de transfert ou opposition au trésor royal de France. Néanmoins les oppositions et significations qui auraient été formées soit au Trésor soit entre les mains des Commissaires-Liquidateurs, auront, suivant l'ordre de leur inscription, leur plein et entier effet, au profit des tiers intéressés, pourvu (à l'égard de celles qui ont été inscrites au Trésor) que dans le délai d'un mois à dater du jour de l'échange des ratifications de la présente Convention, la liste en ait été remise aux Commissaires des Puissances respectives, avec les pièces à l'appui, sans néanmoins préjudicier à la faculté que doivent conserver les parties intéressées, d'en justifier directement, en produisant leurs titres. Le terme de rigueur fixé ci-dessus étant expiré, on n'aura plus égard aux oppositions et significations qui n'auraient pas été notifiées aux Commissaires soit par le Trésor, soit par les parties intéressées. Il sera toutefois permis de former opposition ou de faire tout autre acte conservatoire entre les mains des dits Commissaires ou des Gouvernements dont ils dépendent.

Les oppositions dont la notification aura été faite en temps utile, seront pour les demandes en validité ou en main levée, portées devant le Tribunal de la partie saisie.

ART. X. Les Gouvernements respectifs, voulant prendre dans l'intérêt de leurs sujets, créanciers de la France, les mesures les plus efficaces pour faire opérer, chacun en particulier la liquidation des créances et la répartition des fonds auxquels les dits créanciers auront proportionnellement droit, d'après les principes contenus dans les stipulations du Traité du 30 Mai 1814 et de la Convention du 20 Novembre 1815, il est convenu qu'à cet effet, le Gouvernement Français fera remettre aux Commissaires des dits Gouvernements ou à leurs délégués, les dossiers contenant les pièces à l'appui des réclamations non encore payées, et donnera, en même temps, les ordres les plus précis pour que tous les renseignements et documents que la vérification de ces réclamations pourra rendre nécessaires, soient fournis, dans le plus court délai possible, aux susdits Commissaires par les différents Ministères et Administrations. Il est de plus convenu que, dans le cas où il aurait été payé des à comptes, ou si le Gouvernement Français avait eu des imputations ou des reprises à faire sur quelques-unes des dites réclamations particulières, ces à comptes, imputations ou reprises seront exactement indiqués.

ART. XI. La liquidation des réclamations pour services militaires exigeant quelques formalités particulières, il est convenu à cet égard :

1) Que pour le payement des militaires qui ont appartenu à des corps dont les conseils d'administration ont fourni des bordereaux de liquidation, il suffira de produire les dits bordereaux, ou d'en rapporter des extraits dûment certifiés.

2) Que dans le cas où les conseils d'administration des corps n'auraient pas fourni des bordereaux de liquidation, les dépositaires des archives des dits corps devront constater les sommes dues aux militaires qui en auront fait partie, et en dresser un bordereau dont ils ttesteront la vérité.

3) Que les créances des officiers d'Etat-Major, ou officiers sans troupes, ainsi que celles des employés de l'Administration Militaire seront vérifiées dans les Bureaux de la guerre conformément aux règles établies pour les militaires et employés Français, par la circulaire du 30 Décembre 1814, et en joignant aux bordereaux les pièces à l'appui, ou quand cela ne sera pas praticable, en en donnant communication aux Commissaires ou à leurs délégués.

ART. XII. Pour faciliter la liquidation qui doit avoir lieu conformément à l'Article 10 ci-dessus, des Commissaires nommés par le Gouvernement Français serviront d'intermédiaires pour les communications avec les différents Ministères et Administrations. Ce sera de même par eux que se fera la remise des dossiers de pièces justificatives. Cette remise sera exactement constatée et il leur en sera donné acte, soit par émargement soit par procès-verbal.

ART. XIII. Attendu que certains territoires ont été divisés entre plusieurs Etats et que dans ce cas c'est en général l'Etat auquel appartient la plus grande partie du territoire qui s'est chargé de faire valoir les réclamations communes fondées sur les Articles 6, 7, 9, de la Convention du 20 Novembre 1815, il est convenu que le Gouvernement qui aura fait la réclamation, traitera, pour le payement des créances, les sujets de tous les Etats intéressés comme les siens propres. D'une autre part, comme malgré cette division de territoires, le possesseur principal a supporté la déduction de la totalité des capitaux et intérêts remboursés, il lui en sera tenu compte par les Etats compartageants, proportionnellement à la part du dit territoire que chacun possède conformément aux principes posés dans les Articles 6 et 7 de la Convention du 20 Novembre 1815.

S'il survient quelques difficultés relativement à l'exécution du présent Article, elles seront réglées par une Commission d'Arbitrage formé suivant le mode et les principes indiqués par l'Article 8 de la susdite Convention.

ART. XIV. La présente Convention sera ratifiée par les Hautes Parties Contractantes, et les ratifications en seront échangées à Paris dans l'espace de deux mois ou plutôt si faire se peut.

ART. XV. Les Etats qui ne sont pas au nombre des Puissances signataires mais dont les intérêts se trouvent réglés par la présente Convention, d'après le concert préliminaire qui a eu lieu entre leurs Plénipotentiaires et Son Excellence Monsieur le Duc de Wellington réuni aux Soussignés Plénipotentiaires des Cours signataires du Traité du 20 Novembre 1815, sont invités à faire remettre dans le même terme de deux mois leurs Actes d'accession [1].

---

[1] HERTSLET. *A complete Collection* ... t. I, p. 336-352.

XXXIX. France. Pays-Bas.
20 novembre 1815.

Bien que relative aux deux seuls pays intéressés, la difficulté dont il est question ici fut soumise à un arbitrage par une stipulation introduite dans le traité intervenu entre la France et les Puissances alliées. L'article V, auquel il est fait allusion dans l'article VIII reproduit ci-dessous, est celui dont on trouvera le texte plus haut à la page 105.

Convention entre les Puissances alliées et la France conclue en conformité de l'article 9 du traité principal relativement à l'examen et à la liquidation des réclamations à charge du Gouvernement Français, signée à Paris, le 20 novembre 1815.

. . . .

ART. VIII. Le Gouvernement Français ayant refusé de reconnaître la réclamation du Gouvernement des Pays-Bas, relative au paiement des intérêts de la dette de Hollande qui n'auraient pas été acquittés pour les semestres de Mars et de Septembre 1813, on est convenu de remettre à l'arbitrage d'une Commission particulière la décision du principe de la dite question. Cette Commission sera composée de sept membres, dont deux à nommer par le Gouvernement Français, deux par le Gouvernement des Pays-Bas, et les trois autres à choisir dans des Etats absolument neutres et sans intérêt dans cette question, tels que la Russie, la Grande-Bretagne, la Suède, le Danemark et le royaume de Naples. Le choix de ces trois derniers Commissaires se fera de manière qu'un des deux soit désigné par le Gouvernement Français, l'autre par le Gouvernement des Pays-Bas, et le troisième par les deux Commissaires neutres réunis. Elle s'assemblera à Paris le 1er Février 1816, ses membres prêteront le même serment auquel sont astreints les Commissaires-Juges qui sont institués par l'Article 5 de la présente Convention, et de la même manière. Aussitôt que la commission sera constituée, les Commissaires Liquidateurs des deux Puissances lui soumettront par écrit les arguments, chacun en faveur de son opinion, afin de mettre les Arbitres à même de décider lequel des deux Gouvernements, du Gouvernement Français ou du Gouvernement des Pays-Bas, sera tenu à payer les susdits intérêts arriérés en prenant pour base la disposition du Traité de Paris du 30 mai 1814, et si le remboursement, que le Gouvernement des Pays-Bas sera dans le cas de faire à la France des inscriptions les dettes des pays réunis à sa couronne et étachés de la France, peut être exigible sans

déduction des rentes de la dette d'Hollande, arriérées sur les échéances de 1813 [1].

La décision des arbitres du 16 octobre 1816 se prononça en faveur de la France, ainsi qu'il résulte du texte reproduit ci-dessous.

Décision arbitrale rendue le 16 octobre 1816, au sujet des intérêts de la dette de Hollande, par la Commission mixte instituée conformément à l'article 8 de la Convention du 20 novembre 1815, par les Gouvernements de France et des Pays-Bas.

La Commission d'arbitrage nommée, conformément à l'art. 8 de la Convention du 20 novembre 1815, pour décider lequel des deux Gouvernements, du Gouvernement Français ou de celui des Pays-Bas, sera tenu à payer les intérêts arriérés de la dette de Hollande qui n'auraient pas été acquittés pour les semestres de mars et de septembre 1813 en prenant pour base la disposition du Traité de Paris du 30 mai 1814 et si le remboursement, que le Gouvernement des Pays-Bas sera dans le cas de faire à la France des inscriptions de dettes des pays réunis à sa Couronne et détachés de la France, peut être exigible sans déduction des rentes de la dette de Hollande arriérée sur les échéances de 1813; après avoir pris connaissance: 1° du mémoire de M. le Commissaire-Liquidateur de S. M. le Roi des Pays-Bas, en date du 10 juin 1816; 2° du mémoire de MM. les Commissaires-Liquidateurs de S. M. T. C., sous la même date; 3° de la Réplique de M. le Commissaire-Liquidateur de S. M. le Roi des Pays-Bas, en date du 18 juin 1816, ainsi que des pièces justificatives qui ont accompagné ces différents mémoires; ayant pris pour base de sa décision la disposition du Traité de Paris du 30 mai 1814;

A décidé à la pluralité:

Que les intérêts de la dette de Hollande, qui n'auraient pas été acquittés pour les semestres de mars et de septembre 1813, doivent être payés par le Gouvernement des Pays-Bas, et que le remboursement que le Gouvernement des Pays-Bas sera dans le cas de faire à la France des inscriptions de dettes des pays réunis à sa couronne et détachés de la France, peut être exigible sans déduction des rentes de la dette de Hollande arriérées sur les échéances de 1813.

Paris, le 16 octobre 1816 [2].

XL. Auvergne. Rohan.
9 juin 1815.

Cette contestation est particulièrement intéressante par son objet, le droit de succes-

[1] HERTSLET. A complete Collection..., t. I, p. 312.
[2] DE CLERCQ. Recueil des Traités de France, t. III, p. 45.

sion au Duché de Bouillon, ainsi que par la personnalité des deux prétendants, qui ne furent pas, comme dans la plupart des litiges, des Etats souverains.

Acte du congrès de Vienne, signé le 9 juin 1815.

. . . .

Art. LXIX. S. M. le Roi des Pays-Bas, Grand Duc de Luxembourg, possédera à perpétuité pour Lui et Ses successeurs la souveraineté pleine et entière de la partie du Duché de Bouillon non cédée à la France par le Traité de Paris, et sous ce rapport elle sera réunie au Grand Duché de Luxembourg.

Des contestations s'étant élevées sur ledit Duché de Bouillon, celui des compétiteurs dont les droits seront légalement constatés, dans les formes énoncées ci-dessous, possédera en toute propriété ladite partie du Duché, telle qu'elle l'a été par le dernier Duc, sous la souveraineté de S. M. le Roi des Pays-Bas, Grand Duc de Luxembourg.

Cette décision sera portée sans appel par un jugement arbitral. Des arbitres seront à cet effet nommés, un par chacun des deux compétiteurs, et les autres, au nombre de trois, par les Cours d'Autriche, de Prusse et de Sardaigne. Ils se réuniront à Aix-la-Chapelle aussitôt que l'état de guerre et les circonstances le permettront, et leur jugement interviendra dans les six mois à compter de la réunion.

Dans l'intervalle, S. M. le Roi des Pays-Bas, Grand Duc de Luxembourg, prendra en dépôt la propriété de ladite partie du Duché de Bouillon, pour la restituer, ensemble le produit de cette administration intermédiaire, à celui des compétiteurs en faveur duquel le jugement arbitral sera prononcé. Sa dite Majesté l'indemnisera de la perte des revenus provenant des droits de souveraineté, moyennant un arrangement équitable. Et si c'est au Prince Charles de Rohan que cette restitution doit être faite, ces biens seront entre ses mains soumis aux lois de la substitution qui forme son titre.

Décision arbitrale relative au droit de succéder dans le Duché de Bouillon, du 1 juillet 1816.

En exécution de l'art. LXIX de l'acte final du congrès de Vienne du 9 juin 1815, la commission d'arbitres, qui s'était réunie à Leipzig, dès le commencement de juin 1816, pour décider la question du droit de succéder dans le Duché de Bouillon, a terminé le 1er juillet 1816 ses délibérations.

La possession de ce Duché et les indemnités pour la cession des droits de souveraineté, faite au Roi des Pays-Bas, ont été adjugées, à une

majorité absolue, à S. A. le Prince Charles Alain de Rohan-Montbazon, Duc actuel de Bouillon. M. le Baron de Binder, ministre d'Autriche, M. le Comte de Castelalfer, ministre de S. M. le Roi de Sardaigne à la cour de Prusse, et M. le Comte de Fitte de Soucy, nommé arbitre par le Prince de Rohan, ont voté d'une manière pure et simple, d'après les droits de naissance et de famille, en faveur des prétentions du Prince de Rohan, petit fils de la sœur du Duc de Bouillon, mort en 1792. Le jurisconsulte anglais sir John. Sewell, arbitre nommé par le vice-amiral Philippe d'Auvergne, le second des prétendants, s'est déclaré purement et simplement en faveur des prétentions du vice-amiral. M. le Baron de Brokhausen, ministre d'Etat prussien, a reconnu le droit du Prince de Rohan, mais sous la condition que celui-ci paierait au fils adoptif de son grand-oncle l'amiral d'Auvergne, une legitime de six années de revenu de son Duché.

En conséquence, la question proposée par le congrès sur le droit de succession au Duché de Bouillon, a été décidée à une majorité de quatre voix contre une, et la clause proposée par une seule voix a été rejetée à une majorité de trois voix contre deux [1].

XLI. France, Russie.
30 mai 1814.

C'est par un article additionnel au traité de paix du 30 mai 1814 que la commission spéciale, dont il est question ici, a été instituée. Par un article séparé du traité du 20 novembre 1815, la France s'engagea à envoyer à Varsovie un ou plusieurs commissaires. Cet article toutefois demeura inexécuté et fut remplacé par une convention spéciale, conclue à Paris le 27 septembre 1816.

Article additionnel au Traité de Paix signé à Paris le 30 mai 1814, entre la France et la Russie.

Le Duché de Varsovie étant sous l'administration d'un conseil provisoire établi par la Russie, depuis que ce pays a été occupé par ses armes, les deux hautes parties contractantes sont convenues de nommer immédiatement une commission spéciale, composée de part et d'autre d'un nombre égal de commissaires, qui seront chargés de l'examen de la liquidation et de tous les arrangements relatifs aux prétentions réciproques [2].

[1] G. F. de Martens. *Nouveau recueil des traités*, t. II, p. 413, 490.

[2] Ch. de Martens et F. de Cussy. *Recueil manuel et pratique*, t. III, p. 20.

Convention conclue à Paris le 27 septembre 1816 entre la France et la Russie, pour la liquidation des prétentions respectives de la France et du Duché de Varsovie.

S. M. T. C. et S. M. l'Empereur de toutes les Russies, Roi de Pologne, voulant aplanir et terminer les difficultés qui ont retardé jusqu'à ce jour l'exécution de l'article additionnel du Traité du 30 mai 1814, ont autorisé à cet effet les soussignés, lesquels après s'être communiqué leurs Pleins Pouvoirs, trouvés en bonne et due forme, sont convenus de ce qui suit:

ART. I. La Commission qui doit s'occuper de l'examen et de la liquidation des prétentions réciproques de la France et du ci-devant duché de Varsovie s'assemblera aussitôt que faire se pourra à Varsovie, et commencera ses opérations dès que la vérification des Pouvoirs respectifs aura eu lieu.

ART. II. S. M. T. C. s'engage à admettre en compte de liquidation les sommes payées au Trésor de France par le Trésor du Duché de Varsovie, en vertu de la Convention signée à Bayonne le 10 mai 1808.

ART. III. Il ne sera admis en compte dans la dite liquidation aucun intérêt pour les sommes susmentionnées.

ART. IV. Il est bien entendu que la dette qui pourra être le résultat de la dite liquidation sera remboursée de la manière prescrite par le troisième paragraphe de l'art. 19 de la convention du 20 novembre dernier.

ART. V. Le délai fixé par l'art. 16 de la même convention pour la présentation des réclamations respectives se trouvant insuffisant pour la liquidation à opérer entre la France et le ci-devant Duché de Varsovie, les deux Hautes Parties contractantes sont convenues de le proroger de six mois, à partir du jour de l'arrivée à Varsovie des Commissaires de S. M. T. C.

ART. VI. La présente convention, qui remplace l'article séparé du Traité du 20 novembre dernier, sera ratifiée et les ratifications en seront échangées à Paris, dans l'espace de deux mois ou plus tôt si faire se peut.

En foi de quoi, les Plénipotentiaires soussignés l'ont signée et y ont apposé le cachet de leurs armes.

Fait à Paris le 27 septembre 1816 [1].

XLII. Grande Bretagne, Grèce.

18 juillet 1850.

Prétendue perte de documents faite par un sieur Pacifico, par suite du sac de sa maison, pendant son séjour à Athènes de 1828 à

[1] DE CLERCQ. Recueil des Traités de France, t. III, page 44.

1834. Les arbitres ont pu établir que cette perte n'était pas définitive et qu'il était possible pour l'impétrant de réunir à nouveau les documents en question dont les originaux existaient dans les archives du Portugal. Aussi la réclamation évaluée à 21,295 £ 1 sh. 4 d. fut réduite par eux à une indemnité de 150 £.

Convention entre la Grande Bretagne et la Grèce pour terminer les différends entre les deux gouvernements, signée à Athènes le 18 juillet 1850.

Le Gouvernement de Sa Majesté Britannique et le Gouvernement de Sa Majesté Hellénique ayant accepté les bons offices du Gouvernement français en vue de terminer certains différends qui s'étaient élevés entre le Gouvernement de la Grande Bretagne et celui de la Grèce, un projet de convention à conclure entre la Grande Bretagne et la Grèce pour l'arrangement de ces différends avait été préparé à Londres, et expédié le 19 avril pour être proposé au Gouvernement Grec par le Plénipotentiaire de France à Athènes, et être signé par le Plénipotentiaire Anglais, s'il eût été accepté par le Gouvernement Grec. Bien que le cours des événements ait amené le règlement de quelques-uns des points auxquels ce projet de convention avait rapport avant qu'il ait pu arriver à Athènes, il reste cependant quelques-unes des stipulations du projet proposé qui sont encore applicables à la solution de plusieurs questions pendantes; et comme le Gouvernement de Sa Majesté Britannique et le Gouvernement de Sa Majesté Hellénique désirent également que les différends qui se sont élevés entre eux soient définitivement terminés au moyen des bons offices du Gouvernement Français, ils ont mutuellement consenti à appliquer les stipulations du projet ci-dessus mentionné au règlement des points qui restent encore en suspens. Dans ce but le Gouvernement de Sa Majesté Britannique a nommé le Très Honorable Thomas Wyse, Membre du Très Honorable Conseil Privé de sa Majesté, Ministre Plénipotentiaire de Sa Majesté près de Sa Majesté le Roi de Grèce; et le Gouvernement de sa Majesté Hellénique a désigné M. Londos, sénateur, Ministre de la Maison du Roi et des Relations Extérieures, Chevalier de l'Ordre Royal du Sauveur, Grand'Croix de l'Ordre de St Michel de Bavière, Grand'Croix de la Légion d'Honneur, qui, après avoir mutuellement échangé leurs pleins pouvoirs ont, en présence de M. Édouard Thouvenel, Envoyé Extraordinaire et Ministre Plénipotentiaire de la République Française près de Sa Majesté le Roi de Grèce, Officier de l'Ordre National de la Légion d'Honneur, accepté et arrêté les articles suivants.

ART. I. Toutes les demandes, présentées au Gouvernement de la Grèce dans la note de M. Wyse du 17 janvier 1850, sont reconnues par le Gouvernement de la Grande Bretagne comme ayant été satisfaites, à l'exception de la réclamation provenant de la perte faite par M. Pacifico de certains documents relatifs à des réclamations pécuniaires qu'il avait à faire au Gouvernement Portugais. Le Gouvernement de Sa Majesté Hellénique s'engage à indemnifier M. Pacifico du préjudice réel qu'après une enquête complète et de bonne foi il serait prouvé qu'il eut souffert à raison de la destruction ou perte de ces documents.

ART. II. Dans le but de procéder à l'enquête sus-mentionnée il est convenu entre les Parties Contractantes que deux arbitres, avec un surarbitre pour décider entre eux en cas de contestation, seront nommés par le concours des Gouvernements de la France, de la Grande Bretagne et de la Grèce. Cette commission d'arbitrage rapportera au Gouvernement Britannique et au Gouvernement Hellénique, dans le cas où ce serait, quel est le montant du préjudice réel souffert par M. Pacifico à raison de la perte alléguée des documents mentionnés dans l'Article précédent. La somme consignée dans ce rapport sera celle que M. Pacifico recevra du Gouvernement Grec.

ART. III. En considération des engagements, pris par le Gouvernement de Sa Majesté Hellénique dans les Articles précédents I et II, le Gouvernement de Sa Majesté Britannique promet qu'immédiatement après la ratification de la présente Convention par Sa Majesté Hellénique, la somme de 150,000 drachmes déposée par le Gouvernement Grec pour répondre du résultat de l'enquête sur les réclamations précitées de M. Pacifico, sera restituée au Gouvernement de Sa Majesté Hellénique.

ART. IV. Les réclamations du Gouvernement de Sa Majesté Britannique relatives à l'emprunt garanti par les trois Puissances et aux Iles de Sapienza et Cervi, sont exclues de la présente Convention.

ART. V. La présente Convention sera ratifiée, et les ratifications en seront échangées à Athènes aussitôt que possible. En foi de quoi, les Plénipotentiaires respectifs ont signé la présente Convention, et y ont apposé le cachet de leurs armes privées.

Fait à Athènes, le 6/18 juillet 1850.

Report of the Mixed Commission, on the Claims of M. Pacifico upon the Portuguese Government, under the Convention of 1850 between Great Britain and Greece. May 5, 1851

By a Convention signed at Athens on the 18th July 1850, between Her Britannic Majesty and His Hellenic Majesty, it was agreed and concluded that all the demands made on the Government of Greece in a note of the 17th January 1850, having been satisfied, with the exception of the claim arising ont of the loss by M. Pacifico of certain documents relating to money claims which he had to establish against the Portuguese Government, His Hellenic Majesty engaged to make good to M. Pacifico any real (préjudice réel) injury which, upon a full and fair investigation, it should be proved that he had sustained by the destruction of those documents.

For the purpose of conducting the investigation it was further agreed between the Contracting Parties that 2 arbiters, with an umpire to decide between them in case of difference, should be appointed by the joint concurrence of the Governments of France. of Great Britain, and of Greece, and that this Commission of Arbitration should report to the British and Greek Governments whether any, and if any, what amount of real injury had been sustained by M. Pacifico, by reason of the alleged loss of the documents mentioned; and the amount so reported should be the amount which M. Pacifico is to receive from the Greek Government.

In accordance with the above-mentioned Convention, the Government of France appointed M. Léon Béclard, Secretary of the Legation of France at the Court of Lisbon, Commissioner and Umpire, Her Britannic Majesty's Government nominated M. Patrick Francis Campbell Johnston, British Commissioner ; and His Hellenic Majesty's Government named M. George Torlades O'Neill, Consul-General for Greece at Lisbon, as their Commissioner. The Commission, consisting of these 3 members, assembled and met together at Lisbon, in February 1851, and proceeded to investigate a list of claims dated Athens December 21, 1844, and which was enclosed in a letter addressed to Her Britannic Majesty's Principal Secretary of State for Foreign Affairs by M. Pacifico on the 26th September 1850.

This list purposed to be a statement of documents destroyed at Athens, on the 4th April 1847, relating to the claims of M. Pacifico on the Portuguese Government and a copy of it authenticated by the signatures of the 3 Commissioners, is appended to this Report. The Commissioners, in order to facilitate the inquiry have numbered the claims in that list, and divided them into 2 classes :

1ª. Those which relate to losses sustained, and services rendered, by M. Pacifico during the civil war in Portugal ;

2ndly. Those which relate to claims for salary, expenses, voyage to Greece from Portugal, while holding the office of Consul-General of Portugal in Greece.

The Commissioners, in the prosecution of their duties have endeavoured to ascertain whether among those claims there were any which had not been defeated by the loss of documents carried away or destroyed during the sacking of M. Pacifico's house at Athens and which can therefore still be as well established by means of official documents or records now existing in the public offices in Portugal.

The Commissioners have now the honour to report that they have discovered in the archives of the Cortes at Lisbon, a petition adressed by M. Pacifico to the Chamber of Deputies in 1839, and presented in the same year by one of its members, accompanied by a voluminous body of documents to prove his alleged losses, in which petition M. Pacifico prays for compensation for his sufferings.

The Commissioners are satisfied, from inquiries which they established at great length and much difficulty, that the various certificates and papers attached to that petition are the originals or certified copies of the most important documents alleged to have been destroyed at Athens.

That petition has not yet been disposed of by the Chamber of Deputies, M. Pacifico appearing to have taken no steps since its presentation in 1839, either by himself or his agents, to cause it, together with the accompanying documents, to be taken into consideration and decided by that Assembly.

With reference to M. Pacifico's claims, in regard to the destruction of any documents connected with his salary and other expenses during the time he held the office of Consul-General of Portugal in Greece, the Commissioners are of opinion that they have not been prejudiced by any such loss, and that he is still able to establish his rights, if well founded, against the Portuguese Government.

The Commissioners having now stated their unanimous opinion on the above named-points, beg to add that almost all the losses of property, represented by documents alleged to have been destroyed at Athens, took place between the :ars 1828 and 1834 and that M. Pacifico .ppears to have taken no steps, although con-.tantly in Portugal between the years 1834 and 839, to assert his rights and claims in a legal

manner : nor does it appears that any application was ever made by him to the British Minister or Consular authorities in Portugal, to support his rights or to redress his wrongs.

Under all the circumstances of this case, and taking into consideration the possibility that a few documents of no great importance may have been lost when M. Pacifico's house at Athens was pillaged, and the expenses he has incurred during this investigation, the Commissioners think he is entitled to receive from the Government of Greece the sum of 150 £ for the injury he has received.

The Commissioners cannot conclude their Report without taking opportunity of stating that the utmost cordiality and unanimity of sentiment has accompanied every step they have collectively taken in this very important investigation, and they trust the result of this Commission will prove an additional link in the friendly relations which subsist between Great Britain and France, and that the Portuguese and Greek Governments will feel that England has had but one object in view in this inquiry, namely, a fair, impartial, and honest solution of a difficult question.

In witness whereof, the 2 Commissioners and the Commissioner and Umpire have signed this Report, and affixed to it their respective seals.

Lisbon, May 5, 1851 [1].

XLIII. France. Grande Bretagne. Uruguay.

23 juin 1857.

Cette contestation a eu pour objet l'évaluation des dommages causés par la guerre à des sujets français et anglais. Elle fut définitivement réglée par un arrangement amiable qui fixa à 4,000,000 de piastres le préjudice souffert.

Acte conclu à Montevideo, le 23 juin 1857, entre la France, la Grande Bretagne et l'Uruguay, pour le règlement des réclamations des sujets Franco-Anglais.

S. Ex. M. le Docteur Don Joaquin Requena, Ministre du Département des Relations Extérieures et Leurs Seigneuries MM. Martin Maillefer et Edward Thornton, Chargés d'Affaires de France et d'Angleterre, s'étant réunis dans le Cabinet des Relations Extérieures à l'effet de conférer pour la seconde fois sur les moyens d'arriver à ·l'établissement de la Commission mixte pour le règlement des réclamations des sujets franco-anglais touchant les préjudices soufferts pendant la guerre; les dits sieurs soussignés sont convenus d'adopter comme ils ont adopté les bases suivantes.

---

[1] HERTSLET. *A complete Collection*..., t. IX, p. 499-503.

ART. I. Les réclamations des sujets de France et d'Angleterre touchant les préjudices que leur a occasionnés la guerre et auxquels se réfère la loi du 14 juillet 1853, seront définitivement réglées quant à leur justification et à leur quotité, par une Commission mixte ayant le caractère de juge-arbitre.

ART. II. La dite commission se composera de quatre personnes, deux du côté de la République qui les désignera et deux du côté des réclamants, nommés par les Gouvernements de France et d'Angleterre, ou par leurs agents dûment autorisés.

Le juge lettré des finances de la République présidera la dite Commission ; mais il n'aura pas voix délibérative.

ART. III. La présentation des réclamations se fera devant la commission mixte, et les diligences justificatives seront pratiquées par le Juge des Finances en présence des commissaires.

ART. IV. L'instruction terminée chaque dossier sera soumis au jugement de la commission mixte qui décidera sans appel.

ART. V. Les décisions seront prises à la majorité des voix et en cas de partage, le côté décisif appartiendra à une cinquième personne, tirée au sort d'une liste de huit individus, dont quatre citoyens orientaux et quatre franco-anglais désignés à l'avance de même que les arbitres.

ART. VI. Les réclamations seront présentées dans le terme de quatre-vingt-dix jours pour ceux qui résident sur le territoire de la République, et de cent quatre-vingts jours pour ceux qui se trouveront hors de ce territoire, à compter du jour où la commission mixte annoncera publiquement son installation. Passé ce terme aucune réclamation ne sera plus admise, le droit de réclamer demeurant périmé.

ART. VII. Le montant des indemnités que la commission mixte aura admises comme justifiées sera reconnu par le Gouvernement de la République comme une dette nationale dont l'extinction sera réglée par une Convention spéciale.

En foi de quoi les soussignés sont convenus de dresser le présent acte en trois exemplaires pareils qu'ils ont signés et scellés en due forme à Montevideo le 23 juin 1857 [1].

Convention spéciale concernant le paiement des réclamations franco-anglaises pour préjudices de guerre, signée à Montevideo, le 28 juin 1862.

S'étant réunis dans le Cabinet des relations extérieures de la République Orientale de l'Uruguay, leurs seigneuries MM. Martin Maillefer et William Garrow Lettsom, Chargés d'Affaires de leurs Majestés l'Empereur des Français et la Reine de la Grande Bretagne, et Son Excellence Don Antonio Maria Perez, Ministre intérimaire de ce Département à l'effet de fixer le montant total des réclamations des sujets de France et d'Angleterre pour préjudices de guerre auxquels se réfère la Convention du 23 juin 1857, et d'accomplir en même temps la clause 7 de la même Convention, ont arrêté les bases suivantes :

ART. I. La somme de 4,000,000 piastres, monnaie courante, demeure fixée comme montant total et définitif des réclamations Anglo-Françaises ci-dessus indiquées. Cette somme représentée par des bons spéciaux au porteur de 1000, de 200 et de 100 piastres, sera remise à MM. les agents des Gouvernements Français et Anglais qui en feront faire la répartition entre les intéressés.

ART. II. Ces bons spéciaux au porteur jouiront d'un intérêt annuel de 5 % et seront amortis en un maximum de 30 années divisées en 6 périodes de 5 années chacune, l'amortissement étant de 1 % pour la première période, de 2 % pour la seconde, de 3 % pour la troisième, de 4 % pour la quatrième et de 5 % pour la cinquième et sixième.

ART. III. Il est également convenu, que si, dans le cours des 30 années auquel se réfère l'Article antérieur, la République Orientale se trouvait en état de pouvoir payer tout ou partie de ces bons, elle pourra le faire pour une ou plusieurs périodes anticipées, qui dans ce cas ne rapporteraient pas d'intérêts, les Légations des Gouvernements contractants devant être averties 6 mois d'avance du jour où s'effectuerait le paiement, afin que les porteurs de bons spéciaux puissent se présenter pour en percevoir le montant.

ART. IV. Les fonds destinés aux paiements des intérêts et de l'amortissement de la dite somme de 4,000,000 piastres seront garantis par les rentes générales de la République et les annuités seront mensuellement prélevées sur les revenus du papier timbré et des patentes.

Il est entendu que si, par suite de circonstances quelconques, le revenu du papier timbré et des patentes était insuffisant, le Gouvernement de la République Orientale serait dans l'obligation de parfaire les sommes nécessaires aux prélèvements mensuels.

ART. V. Les sommes ainsi prélevées mensuellement seront délivrées par le Gouvernement de la République à une Banque de cette capitale qui en donnera deux reçus, l'un au Gouvernement et l'autre à MM. les Agents de France et d'Angleterre, le Gouvernement de la République restant responsable jusqu'à la réalisation des paiements.

[1] DE CLERCQ. *Recueil des Traités de France*, t. VII, p. 290; — HERTSLET. *A complete Collection...* t. X, p. 1049.

Art. VI. Les intérêts et l'amortissement auxquels se réfère l'art. II commenceront à courir à partir du 1ᵉʳ avril 1863 et, dès cette époque, le Gouvernement délivrera mensuellement à la Banque qui sera chargée du service de cette dette, la somme correspondante à chaque mois, conformément à ce qui est stipulé à l'article IV.

Art. VII. Le paiement de l'intérêt et de l'amortissement s'effectuera dans les 6 mois, proportionnellement à la somme correspondante au semestre échu, par l'intermédiaire de la maison de Banque indiquée, le premier paiement devant avoir lieu dans les 5 premiers jours du mois d'octobre 1863, et le second dans les 5 premiers jours du mois d'avril 1864, les dits mois demeurant fixés pour les paiements successifs.

Art. VIII. Le paiement des intérêts se fera par la Banque à laquelle sera confié le service de cette dette, à Montevideo, à Paris et à Londres; une somme égale à la 4ᵉ partie des bons existants devant être en circulation dans ces deux dernières capitales pour que le dit paiement puisse s'y effectuer, et avis devant être donné, 6 mois d'avance, à la Banque, des numéros et des valeurs des titres destinés à la circulation dans chacune des dites places.

Art. IX. L'amortissement ne pourra s'effectuer qu'à Montevideo et se fera publiquement au moyen de propositions qui seront présentées à la Banque, en pli fermé, aux jours désignés dans l'article VII, et à l'heure qui sera indiquée à cet effet, MM. les agents de France et d'Angleterre ou les personnes qu'ils délégueraient pouvant assister à cet Acte; le Fiscal du Gouvernement devant se trouver présent à l'ouverture des propositions et les plus avantageuses être acceptées séance tenante.

En foi de quoi les soussignés ont signé la présente convention et y ont apposé leurs cachets respectifs.

Fait en triple expédition à Montevideo, le 28 du mois de juin de l'an 1862[1].

XLIV. Grande-Bretagne. Brésil.

2 juin 1858.

Cette convention organise un arbitrage par deux commissaires et un surarbitre pour juger des réclamations réciproques de citoyens des deux pays. Ratifiée dès le 9 septembre 1858, les arbitres se réunirent à Rio de Janeiro le 10 mars 1859.

---

[1] HERTSLET. *A complete Collection*... t. XIII, p. 1007.

Convention between Great Britain and Brazil, for the settlement of outstanding Private Claims by a Mixed Commission. Signed at Rio de Janeiro, June, 2, 1858.

Whereas claims have at various times since the date of the Declaration of Independence of the Brazilian Empire been made upon the Government of Her Britannic Majesty on the part of corporations, companies and private individuals, subjects of His Majesty the Emperor of Brazil, and upon the Government of His Majesty the Emperor of Brazil on the part of corporations, companies and private individuals, subjects of Her Britannic Majesty; and whereas some of such claims are still pending, or are still considered by either of the 2 Governments to remain unsettled; Her Majesty the Queen of the United Kingdom of Great Britain and Ireland, and His Majesty the Emperor of Brazil, being of opinion that the settlement of all such claims will contribute much to the maintenance of the friendly feelings which subsist between the 2 countries, have resolved to make arrangements for that purpose by means of a Convention, and have named as their Plenipotentiaries to confer and agree thereupon, that is to say:

Her Majesty the Queen of the United Kingdom of Great Britain and Ireland, the honourable Peter Campbell Scarlett, Her Britannic Majesty's Envoy Extraordinary and Minister Plenipotentiary to the Court of Rio de Janeiro &c. &c. &c.;

And His Majesty the Emperor of Brazil, the most illustrious and most excellent Sergio Teixeiro de Macedo, Member of His Council, holding rank as his Envoy Extraordinary and Minister Plenipotentiary, Member of the Chamber of Deputies &c. &c.

Who having communicated to each other their respective full powers, found in good and due form, have agreed as follows:

Art. I. The High Contracting Parties agree that all claims on the part of corporations, companies, or private individuals, subjects of Her Britannic Majesty upon the Government of His Majesty the Emperor of Brazil, and all claims on the part of corporations, companies, or private individuals, subjects of His Majesty the Emperor of Brazil, upon the Government of Her Britannic Majesty, which may have been presented to either Government for its interposition with the other since the date of the declaration of Independence of the Brazilian Empire, and which yet remain unsettled, or are considered to be still unsettled, by either of the 2 Governments, as well as any other such claims which may be presented within the time specified in Art. III hereinafter, shall be referred to 2 commissioners, to be appointed in the following manner; that is to say: I commissioner shall be named by Her

Britannic Majesty and 1 by His Majesty the Emperor of Brazil.

Her Britannic Majesty and His Majesty the Emperor of Brazil, respectively, shall appoint a secretary to the commission, who shall be empowered to act as commissioner in case of the temporary incapacity or absence of the commissioner of his Government, and also in case of the death, definite absence, or incapacity of the said commissioner, or in the event of his omitting or ceasing to act as such, until the appointment of, and assumption of his duties by another commissioner in the place or stead of the said commissioner.

In the case of the death, or definite absence, or incapacity of the commissioner on either side, or in the event of the commissioner on either side omitting or ceasing to act as such, Her Britannic Majesty or His Majesty the Emperor of Brazil, respectively, shall forthwith name another person to act as commissioner, in the place or stead of the commissioner originally named.

In case of the Secretary on either side being appointed permanently commissioner, Her Britannic Majesty or His Majesty the Emperor of Brazil, respectively, shall forthwith name another person to be secretary in the place or stead of the secretary originally named.

The commissioners shall meet at Rio de Janeiro, at the earliest convenient period after they shall have been named, and shall, before proceeding to any business, make and subscribe a solemn declaration that they will impartially and carefully examine and decide, to the best of their judgment, and according to justice and equity, whithout fear, favour, or affection to their own country, upon all such claims as shall be laid before them on the part of the Governments of Her Britannic Majesty and His Majesty the Emperor of Brazil respectively; and such declaration shall be entered on record of their proceedings.

The secretary on either side, when called upon to act as commissioner for the first time, and before proceeding to act as such, shall make and subscribe a similar declaration, which shall be entered in like manner as aforesaid.

The commissioners shall, before proceeding to any other business, name a third person to act as an arbitrator or umpire, in any case or cases on which they may themselves differ in opinion.

If they should not be able to agree upon the selection of such a person, the commissioner on either side shall name a person, and in each and every case in which the commissioners may differ in opinion as to the decision which they ought to give, it shall be determined by lot which of the 2 persons so named shall be arbitrator or umpire in that particular case.

The person so to be chosen to be arbitrator or umpire shall, before proceeding to act as such in any case, make and subscribe a solemn declaration, in a form similar to that which shall have already been made and subscribed by the commissioners, which declaration shall be entered on the record of their proceedings.

In the event of the death, absence, or incapacity of such person, or of his omitting, or declining, or ceasing to act as such arbitrator or umpire, another and different person shall be named as aforesaid to act as such arbitrator or umpire in the place or stead of the person so originally named as aforesaid, and shall make and subscribe such declaration as aforesaid.

ART. II. The commissioners shall then forthwith proceed to the investigation of the claims which shall be presented to their notice.

They shall investigate and decide upon such claims in such order and in such manner as they may think proper, but upon such evidence or information only as shall be furnished by or on behalf to the respective Governments.

They shall be bound to receive and peruse all written or printed documents or statements which may be presented to them by or on behalf of the respective Governments in support of, or in answer to, any claim, and to hear, if required, one person on each side on behalf of each Government, as counsel or agent for such Government, on each and every separate claim.

Should they fail to agree in opinion upon any individual claim, they shall call to their assistance the arbitrator or umpire whom they have agreed to name, or who may be determined by lot as the case may be; and such arbitrator or umpire, after having examined the evidence adduced for and against the claim, and after having heard, if required, one person on each side as aforesaid, and consulted with the commissioners, shall decide thereupon finally, and without appeal.

The decision of the commissioners, and of the arbitrator or umpire, shall be given upon each claim in writing and shall be signed by them respectively.

It shall be competent for each Government to name one person to attend the commission as agent on its behalf, to present and support claims, and to answer claims made upon it, and to represent it generally in all matters connected with the investigation and decision thereof.

Her Majesty the Queen of Great Britain and Ireland, and His Majesty the Emperor of Brazil, hereby solemnly and sincerely engage to consider the decision of the commissioners, or of the arbitrator or umpire, as the case may be, as absolutely final and conclusive upon each claim decided upon by them or him respectively, and to give full effect to such decisions without any objection, evasion, or delay whatsoever.

ART. III. Every claim shall be presented to the commission within 12 months from the day of its first meeting, unless in any case where reasons for delay shall be established to the satisfaction of the commission, or of the arbitrator or umpire in the event of the commissioners differing in opinion thereupon: and then and in any such case, the period for presenting the claim may be extened to any time not exceeding 6 months longer. The commissioners shall be bound, under this Convention, to hold, for the consideration of the claims, at least 8 sittings in each month, from the date of their first sitting until the completion of their labours.

The commissioners shall be bound to examine and decide upon every claim within 2 years from the day of their first meeting, unless on account of some unforeseen and unavoidable suspension of the sittings, the 2 Governments may mutually agree to extend the time.

The arbitrator or umpire shall be bound to come to a final decision on any claim within 15 days from the time of such claim being submitted to his consideration, unless the commissioners consider a more extended period absolutely necessary.

It shall be competent for the commissioners, or for the arbitrator or umpire if they differ, to decide in each case whether any claim has or has not been duly made, preferred, or laid before the commission, either wholly or to any and what extent, according to the true intent and meaning of this Convention.

ART. IV. All sums of money which may be awarded by the commission or by the arbitrator or umpire, on account of any claim, shall be paid by the one Government to the other, as the case may be within 12 months after the date of the decision, without any deduction save as specified in Article VI hereinafter.

ART. V. The High Contracting Parties engage to consider the result of the proceedings of this commission as a full, perfect and final settlement of every claim upon either Government, arising out of any transaction of a date prior to the exchange of the ratifications of the present Convention; and further engage that every such claim, whether or not the same may have been presented to the notice of, made, preferred, or laid before the said commission, shall, from and after the conclusion of the proceedings of the said commission, be considered and treated as finally settled, barred, and thenceforth inadmissible.

ART. VI. The commissioners and the arbitrator or umpire, with the assistance of the secretaries, shall keep an accurate record and correct minutes or notes of all their proceedings, with the dates thereof, and shall appoint and employ a clerk, if necessary, to assist them in the transaction of the business which may come before them.

Each Government shall pay to its commissioner an amount of salary not exceeding 6 contos of reis, or 675 £ a year, which amount shall be the same for both Governments.

Each Government shall pay to its secretary an amount of salary not exceeding 3 contos, or 337 £ 10 s. a year, which amount shall be the same for both Governments.

The secretary on either side, when acting as commissioner shall receive the same amount of salary a year as that paid to the commissioner; it being understood that his salary as secretary shall lapse during that time.

The amount of salary to be paid to the arbitrator or umpire shall be the same, in proportion to the time he may be occupied, as the amount paid a year to a commissioner under this Convention.

The salary of the clerk, if one is appointed, shall not exceed the sum of 2 contos, or 225 £ a year.

The whole expenses of the commission, including contingent expenses, shall be defrayed by a rateable deduction on the amount of the sums awarded by the commissioners, or by the arbitrator or umpire, as the case may be; provided always that such deduction shall not exceed the rate of 5 £ per cent on the sums so awarded.

The deficiency, if any, shall be defrayed by the 2 Governments.

ART. VII. The present Convention shall be ratified by Her Britannic Majesty, and by His Majesty the Emperor of Brazil, and the ratifications shall be exchanged at London as soon as may be whithin 6 months from the date thereof.

In witness whereof the respective Plenipotentiaries have signed the same, and have affixed thereto the seals of their arms.

Done at Rio de Janeiro, the 2nd day of June, in the year of our Lord, 1858. [1]

XLV. Argentine, France, Grande-Bretagne, Sardaigne.

21 août 1858.

Cet arbitrage est curieux par le fait qu'il fut institué par trois conventions similaires,

[1] HERTSLET, A complete Collection..., t. X, p. 724—729.

mais séparées ; toutefois une seule commission arbitrale fut formée pour juger les réclamations des citoyens lésés. Des conventions ultérieures mirent fin à l'amiable aux diverses contestations. Nous ne reproduisons ici que la convention conclue entre l'Argentine et la France.

Convention d'indemnité conclue à Parana le 21 août 1858 entre la France et la Confédération argentine.

S. M. l'Empereur des Français et S. Exc. M. le Président de la Confédération Argentine, capitaine général de ses armées, désirant régler les moyens, mode et forme du paiement de la dette que la nation argentine reconnaît en faveur des sujets de S. M. l'Empereur des Français pour les préjudices qu'ils ont soufferts dans les perturbations causées dans la République par la guerre civile, préjudices qu'elle a voulu reconnaître conformément à une politique réparatrice et généreuse, et comprenant la nécessité de fixer cet accord dans une Convention qui établisse les conditions et la forme du paiement, ont résolu de nommer pour leurs Plénipotentiaires, savoir : S. M. l'Empereur des Français, son Ministre Plénipotentiaire près la Confédération argentine, M. Charles Lefebvre de Bécour, officier de l'ordre de la Légion d'Honneur et Commandeur de de l'Ordre du Danebrog ; et S. Exc. M. le Président de la Confédération Argentine, LL. Exc. MM. les Ministres secrétaires d'Etat au département des Relations Extérieures et de l'Intérieur, les docteurs Don Bernabe Lopez et Don Santiago Derqui.

Lesquels, après avoir échangé leurs pleins-pouvoirs qu'ils ont trouvés en bonne et due forme, sont convenus des articles suivants :

ART. I. Le Gouvernement de la Confédération Argentine reconnaît comme dette nationale toutes les sommes dues à des sujets français pour les réclamations qui auront été présentées le ou avant le 1er janvier 1860 et qui auront été examinées et liquidées conjointement par le Ministre Plénipotentiaire de Sa Majesté l'Empereur des Français ou son représentant et par les Commissaires du Gouvernement Argentin nommés à cet effet.

ART. II. Le Gouvernement de la Confédération Argentine s'engage à payer l'intérêt de cette dette au taux de six pour cent l'an à partir du 1er octobre 1858, et à l'amortir par termes annuels dont le premier sera payé le 31 décembre 1860, sur le pied de un pour cent d'une somme totale composée du capital de la dette et de l'intérêt de 6 p. % susmentionné, calculé

jusqu'au 31 décembre 1859, à partir de quelle époque le montant sera augmenté chaque année dans la proportion du décroissement de la partie des intérêts restant à payer, de manière à ce que le total de la dette soit éteint dans une période de trente-quatre ans selon le calcul du tableau annexé à la présente Convention.

ART. III. Le Gouvernement Argentin émettra pour chaque réclamation trente-quatre coupons au porteur représentant la somme annuelle d'amortissement payable le 31 décembre de chaque année jusqu'à la complète extinction de la dette et portant intérêt à raison de six pour cent, lequel intérêt sera payable par semestre, à savoir : le 30 juin et le 31 décembre de chaque année à partir du 30 juin 1860 jusqu'à complet amortissement de la dette.

ART. IV. Tous les coupons pour les réclamations déjà liquidées seront remis à la Légation Française, pour qui de droit, à l'époque de l'échange des ratifications de la présente Convention, et ceux appartenant aux réclamations qui seront liquidées postérieurement, seront livrés dans les délais d'un mois après que chaque liquidation aura été opérée par le Ministre de France ou son représentant et les Commissaires argentins.

ART. V. Ces coupons seront reçus depuis le jour de leur émission à la Trésorerie du Gouvernement argentin, au pair, en paiement des terres publiques, et seront également reçus au pair dans les douanes principales de la Confédération et actuellement dans celles de Mendoça, Rosario, Corrientes et Gualiguaychú, en payement des droits de douane depuis le 1er janvier de l'année où ils devront respectivement échoir. L'intérêt sera compté au porteur sur le coupon jusqu'au jour où il sera reçu, soit en paiement de droits de douane.

ART. VI. Les coupons seront toujours payés en monnaie d'argent ou en onces d'or au change légal de dix-sept piastres l'once, aussi bien que les intérêts.

ART. VII. Tous les revenus du Gouvernement Argentin seront affectés à l'accomplissement de la présente Convention.

ART. VIII. Considérant que des Conventions analogues ont été signées aujourd'hui par les mêmes Plénipotentiaires de la Confédération Argentine et les Plénipotentiaires respectifs de l'Angleterre et de la Sardaigne, le Gouvernement Argentin consent à l'établissement d'une Commission composée des Ministres ou Chargés d'Affaires de France, d'Angleterre et de Sardaigne et de trois membres nommés par le Gouvernement Argentin à l'effet de régler amiablement toutes les difficultés qui pourraient s'élever relativement à quelqu'une desdites Conventions.

ART. IX. Les ratifications de la présente Convention seront échangées à Parana dans le terme de huit mois ou plus tôt si faire se peut.

En foi de quoi, les Plénipotentiaires respectifs l'ont signée et y ont apposé leurs sceaux.

Fait dans la ville de Parana, capitale provisoire de la Confédération Argentine, le 21° jour du mois d'août de l'an de grâce 1858.

Articles additionnels du 18 août 1859 à la Convention d'indemnité du 21 août 1858.

Dans l'intention de déterminer avec plus de clarté quelques unes des stipulations contenues dans les Conventions conclues le 21 août 1858 entre LL. EE. MM. les Ministres Plénipotentiaires de France et d'Angleterre et M. le Chargé d'Affaires de Sardaigne ; et les Ministres Plénipotentiaires de la Confédération Argentine et pour faciliter leur exécution :

Les soussignés, savoir : S. E. Charles Lefebvre de Bécour, Ministre Plénipotentiaire de S. M. l'Empereur des Français près la Confédération Argentine, sous la réserve de l'approbation de son Gouvernement, et S. E. M. le Brigadier-Général et sénateur Don Tomas Guido, en vertu des pleins-pouvoirs que lui a conférés S. E. M. le Vice-Président, sont convenus de ce qui suit :

ART. 1ᵉʳ. Les Articles 2 et 9 de la Convention du 21 août 1857 et le Protocole du même jour demeurent sans effet et sont remplacés par les articles qui suivent additionnels à ladite Convention, lesquels auront la même force et valeur que s'ils y avaient été insérés mot pour mot.

ART. 2. Au principal de chaque indemnité réglée et liquidée comme il est établi dans l'article 1ᵉʳ de la convention sus-mentionnée, seront ajoutés des intérêts dans les proportions ci-après.

Pour les réclamations provenant de destruction et enlèvement violent de bestiaux, destruction de propriétés rurales, séquestre de marchandises, vols et autres pertes il ne sera payé qu'un intérêt de cinquante pour cent en masse, quelque éloignée que soit la date des faits qui motivent la réclamation.

Pour les emprunts forcés et autres dettes originairement liquides, il sera payé un intérêt de cinq pour cent par an calculé depuis la date des faits qui ont donné lieu à l'indemnité, ou depuis la reconnaissance de la dette, jusqu'au 1ᵉʳ octobre 1859, bien que les reçus d'emprunt fixent un intérêt de un pour cent par mois ou douze pour cent par an.

Pour les réclamations provenant des réquisitions faites et autres dettes contractées pendant le siège de Buenos-Ayres depuis le 29 janvier 1853 jusqu'à la levée du siège, et pour celles qui auraient pris naissance dans d'autres provinces

postérieurement à l'année 1852, cinq pour cent par an depuis la date des faits jusqu'à la même époque du 1ᵉʳ octobre 1859.

Il est entendu qu'aucune des réclamations du siège mentionnées dans le paragraphe ci-dessus, ne comprendra celles qui entreront dans les arrangements faits ou à faire entre les Agents de la France et le Gouvernement de Buenos-Ayres.

ART. 3. Le Gouvernement de la Confédération Argentine s'engage à payer l'intérêt de la dette à raison de six pour cent par an à partir du premier janvier 1860, et à l'amortir par termes annuels d'un pour cent par an, dont le premier sera payé avec le premier terme dudit intérêt de six pour cent, le 31 décembre 1860 et à partir du 31 décembre 1860, le fonds d'amortissement sera augmenté chaque année dans la proportion du décroissement des intérêts restant à payer, de manière à ce que le total de la dette soit éteint dans une période de trente-quatre ans selon le calcul du tableau annexé à la Convention.

ART. 4. Toute dette, dont le principal, avec les intérêts liquidés d'après les bases ci-dessus, n'excédera pas la somme de mille piastres, sera intégralement payée en deux termes égaux le 31 décembre 1860 et le 31 décembre 1861, sans être soumise aux termes et conditions de l'article ci-dessus.

ART. 5. Dans le cas où le Gouvernement de la Confédération voudrait amortir tout ou partie des indemnités accordées par la présente Convention, le paiement du capital qui sera resté dû sera accepté par anticipation.

ART. 6. Aucune réclamation, de la nature de celles auxquelles se rapporte le préambule de la Convention du 21 août 1858, ne pourra être présentée passé le 31 décembre 1860, sans que ce délai puisse être prorogé.

ART. 7. Les ratifications de cette Convention seront échangées à Parana dans le terme de huit mois ou plus tôt si faire se peut.

En foi de quoi, les Plénipotentiaires respectifs l'ont signée et scellée du sceau de leurs armes.

Fait en la ville de Parana, capitale provisoire de la Confédération Argentine, le 18° jour du mois d'août de l'an de grâce 1859[1].

XLVI. Grande-Bretagne. Honduras.

28 novembre 1859.

Relatif à des concessions immobilières et à d'autres réclamations de sujets anglais, cet arbitrage n'appelle aucun commentaire spécial.

---

[1] DÉ CLERCQ. *Recueil des traités de France*, t. VII, p. 492—495; — HERTSLET. *A complete Collection ...*, t. XI, p. 50—55. — *Coleccion de Tratados celebrados por la Republica Argentina*, t. I, p. 580-630.

Treaty between Great Britain and Honduras, respecting the Bay Islands, the Mosquito Indians, and the Rights and Claims of British Subjects. Signed in English and Spanish, at Comayagua, November, 28, 1859.

. . . .

ART. IV. Whereas British subjects have, by grant, lease, or otherwise, heretofore obtained, from the Mosquito Indians, interests in various lands situated within the district mentioned in the preceding Article, the Republic of Honduras engages to respect and maintain such interests; and it is further agreed that Her Britannic Majesty and the Republic shall, within 12 months after the exchange of the ratifications of the present Treaty, appoint 2 Commissioners, 1 to he named by each party in order to investigate the claims of British subjects arising out of such grants or leases, or otherwise; and all British subjects whose claims shall by the Commissioners be pronounced well founded and valid shall be quieted in the possession of their respective interests in the said lands.

ART. V. It is further agreed between the Contracting Parties, that the Commissioners mentioned in the preceding Article shall also examine and decide upon any British claims upon the Government of Honduras that may be submitted to them, other than those specified in that Article, and not already in a train of settlement; and the Republic of Honduras agrees to carry into effect any agreements for the satisfaction of British claims already made, but not yet carried into effect.

ART. VI. The Commissioners mentioned in the preceding Articles shall meet in the city of Guatemala, at the earliest convenient period after they shall have been respectively named, and shall, before proceeding to any business, make and subscribe a solemn declaration that they will impartially and carefully examine and decide, to the best of their judgment. and according to justice and equity, without fear, favour, or affection to their own country, all the matters referred to them for their decision; and such declaration shall be entered on the record of their proceedings.

The Commissioners then, and before proceeding to any other business, name some 3rd person to act as an arbitrator or umpire in any case or cases in which they may themselves differ in opinion. If they should not be able to agree upon the selection of such a person, the Commissioner on either side shall name a person: and in each and every case in which the Commissioners may differ in opinion as to the decision which they ought to give, it shall be determined by lot which of the 2 persons so named shall be arbitrator or umpire in that particular case. The person or persons so to be chosen shall, before proceeding to act, make and subscribe a solemn declaration, in a form similar to that which shall already have been made and subscribed by the Commissioners, which declaration shall also be entered on the record of the proceedings. In the event of death, absence or incapacity of such person or persons, or of his or their omitting or declining, or ceasing to act as such arbitrator or umpire, another person or persons shall be named as aforesaid to act as arbitrator or umpire in his or their place or stead, and shall make and subscribe such declaration as aforesaid.

Her Britannic Majesty and the Republic of Honduras hereby engage to consider the decision of the Commissioners conjointly, or of the arbitrator or umpire, as the case may be, as final and conclusive on the matters to be referred to their decision; and they further engage forthwith to give full effect to the same.

ART. VII. The Commissioners and the arbitrator or umpire shall keep an accurate record, and correct minutes or notes, of all their proceedings, with the dates thereof, and shall appoint and employ a clerk or other persons to assist them in the transaction of the business which may come before them.

The salaries of the Commissioners shall be paid by their respective Governments. The contingent expenses of the Commission, including the salary of the arbitrator or umpire and of the clerk or clerks, shall be defrayed in equal halves by the 2 Governments.

ART. VIII. The present Treaty shall be ratified, and the ratifications shall be exchanged at Comayagua, as soon as possible within 6 months from this date.

In witness whereof the respective Plenipotentiaries have signed the same, and have affixed thereto their respective seals.

Done at Comayagua the 28th day of November in the year of our Lord, 1859 [1].

XLVII. Compagnie de Suez. Egypte.

21 avril 1864.

Cet arbitrage est à remarquer à raison de l'intervention directe, dans la contestation, d'une compagnie financière. Dans les différents arbitrages, où des intérêts privés sont en jeu, les gouvernements, dont les intéressés sont les sujets, interviennent seuls dans le litige. Ici on pourrait justifier la participation directe

---

[1] HERTSLET, A complete Collection...., t. XI, p. 369.

de la Compagnie de Suez par le caractère de personne morale internationale que l'on pourrait lui attribuer.

Sentence arbitrale rendue par l'Empereur Napoléon III, le 6 juillet 1864, entre le Vice-Roi d'Egypte et la Compagnie universelle du canal de Suez.

Napoléon, par la grâce de Dieu et la volonté nationale, Empereur des Français,

A tous ceux qui ces présentes lettres verront, salut.

Vu le compromis signé, le 21 avril 1864, par : S. Exc. Nubar Pacha, mandataire spécial de S. A. le Vice-Roi d'Egypte, et M. Ferdinand de Lesseps, au nom et comme président fondateur de la Compagnie universelle du canal de Suez,

Dont l'article 2 est ainsi conçu : « S. M. est suppliée de prononcer sur les questions ainsi formulées :

« 1° La suppression de la corvée étant acceptée en principe, quelle est la nature et la valeur du règlement du 20 juillet 1856, sur l'emploi des ouvriers indigènes ?

« 2° Quelle serait l'indemnité à laquelle l'annulation de ce règlement peut donner lieu, le fondé de pouvoirs du Vice-Roi se déclarant autorisé à promettre que la clause stipulée en l'article 2 du second acte de concession et cahier des charges du 5 janvier 1856 sera rapportée ?

« 3° La portion du canal d'eau douce non rétrocédée au Vice-Roi par la Convention du 18 mars 1863 doit-elle continuer d'appartenir à la Compagnie pendant la durée déterminée par l'acte de concession comme une annexe indispensable du canal maritime ? Dans le cas contraire quelles sont les conditions auxquelles la rétrocession pourrait en être opérée et que les Parties s'engagent dès à présent à accepter ?

« 4° Les cartes et plans qui, aux termes de l'article 11 de celui du 5 janvier 1856, devaient être dressés, ne l'ayant pas été, qu'elle est l'étendue des terrains nécessaires à la construction et à l'exploitation du canal maritime (et du canal d'eau douce s'il est conservé à la Compagnie), dans les conditions propres à assurer la prospérité de l'entreprise ?

« 5° Quelle est l'indemnité due à la Compagnie, à raison de la rétrocession acceptée en principe des terrains dont il est fait mention dans les articles 7 et 8 de l'acte de concessions de 1854 et dans les articles 10, 11 et 12 de celui de 1856 ? »

Vu le rapport de la commission instituée par notre décision, en date du 3 mars 1864 ;

Considérant, sur la première question, que, pour apprécier la pensée qui a présidé au règlement du 20 juillet 1856 et le caractère de cet acte, il convient de rapprocher les dispositions qu'il renferme, de celles qui sont contenues dans les deux firmans de concession en date du 30 novembre 1854 et du 5 janvier 1856 :

Que celles-ci, après avoir autorisé la constitution de la Compagnie, indiquent le but pour lequel elle doit être établie, déterminent les charges et les obligations qui lui sont imposées et lui assurent les avantages dont elle doit jouir ;

Que ces stipulations ont créé pour la Compagnie et pour le gouvernement du Vice-Roi des engagements réciproques, de l'exécution desquels il ne leur a pas été permis de s'affranchir ; que, notamment, l'article 2 du second firman en laissant à la Compagnie, la faculté d'exécuter les travaux dont elle est chargée, par elle-même ou par des entrepreneurs, exige que les quatre cinquièmes au moins des ouvriers employés à ces travaux soient Egyptiens ;

Qu'au moment où cette condition à été imposée par le Vice-Roi et acceptée par la Compagnie, il a nécessairement été entendu, par l'un et par l'autre, que les ouvriers égyptiens nécessaires pour composer les quatre cinquièmes de ceux qui seraient employés aux travaux seraient mis, par le Vice-Roi, à la disposition de la Compagnie ;

Que celle-ci n'aurait pas consenti à se soumettre à une semblable condition si de son côté, le Vice-Roi ne lui avait pas assuré les moyens de l'accomplir ;

Que cette pensée, sous-entendue dans le second firman de concession, a été formellement exprimée dans l'article 1er du règlement du 20 juillet 1856, portant :

« Les ouvriers qui seront employés aux travaux de la Compagnie seront fournis par le « Gouvernement égyptien, d'après les demandes « des ingénieurs en chef et suivant les besoins » :

Que cet article a par lui-même un sens très clair : que d'ailleurs lorsqu'on le rapproche des stipulations des deux firmans, on aperçoit le lien étroit qui les unit, et l'on reconnaît que la disposition du règlement n'est que le corollaire de celles qui l'ont précédée, qu'elle a le même caractère, la même force obligatoire ;

Que toutes les autres parties du règlement sont en harmonie parfaite avec l'article 1er et confirment l'interprétation qui vient de lui être donnée :

Qu'en effet immédiatement après la promesse du Gouvernement égyptien de fournir les ouvriers, l'acte constate l'engagement corrélatif de la Compagnie de leur payer le prix de leur travail, de leur fournir les vivres nécessaires, de leur procurer des habitations convenables, d'entretenir un hôpital et des ambulances, de traiter les malades à ses frais, de payer également les frais de voyage depuis le lieu du départ jusqu'à l'arrivée sur les chantiers ; enfin de rembourser au Gouvernement égyptien, au prix de revient, les couffes nécessaires pour le transport des terres et la poudre pour l'exploitation des carrières que celui-ci devait fournir ;

Que ces diverses obligations détaillées avec soin dans le règlement n'étaient pour la Compagnie que la contre-partie de celles qu'avait prises le Gouvernement égyptien ; qu'ainsi elles présentaient dans leur ensemble des éléments d'un véritable contrat ;

Que l'intitulé de l'acte n'est point incompatible avec le caractère conventionnel qui lui est attribué par la nature des stipulations qu'il renferme ; qu'à la vérité c'est du Vice-Roi seul que le règlement est émané, mais que les deux firmans de concession ont été faits dans la même forme, et que cependant leur caractère contractuel n'a pas été et ne saurait être sérieusement contesté ; qu'enfin le Vice-Roi dit expressément dans le préambule de l'acte que c'est, de concert avec M. de Lesseps, qu'il en a établi les dispositions ; que cette expression n'indique pas seulement qu'un avis a été demandé au Directeur de la Compagnie ; qu'il exprime que le concours de sa volonté a paru nécessaire et a été obtenu ; qu'il est bien évident que, sans ce concours, il eut été impossible d'assujettir la Compagnie aux obligations multipliées qui lui ont été imposées et qu'elle a ensuite exécutées ;

Que de ce qui précède il résulte que le règlement du 20 juillet 1856, notamment dans la disposition de l'article 1er, a les caractères et l'autorité d'un contrat ;

Considérant sur la seconde question, que, lorsque les conventions ont été librement formées par le consentement de parties capables et éclairées elles doivent être fidèlement exécutées ; que celle des parties contractantes qui refuse ou néglige d'accomplir ses engagements est tenue de réparer le dommage qui résulte de son infraction à la loi qu'elle s'est volontairement imposée ; qu'en général et sauf à tenir compte des circonstances et des motifs de l'infraction, la réparation consiste dans une indemnité représentant la perte qu'éprouve l'autre partie et le bénéfice dont elle est privée ; que, sans méconnaître la force et la vérité de ces principes, on a fait remarquer au nom du Gouvernement égyptien, que par une réserve expresse insérée à la fin de chacun des firmans de concession, le commencement des travaux, c'est-à-dire l'exécution des conventions était subordonnée à l'autorisation de la Sublime-Porte ; qu'en fait, cette autorisation n'ayant jamais été accordée, l'inexécution des conventions ne peut être légitimement reprochée

au Vice-Roi d'Egypte et ne saurait justifier une demande en dommages-intérêts dirigée contre lui :

Qu'il est incontestable que la clause suspensive de la Convention aurait dû produire l'effet qui a été indiqué au nom du Vice-Roi, si les choses étaient restées entières, mais que les faits accomplis depuis la date des firmans, et auxquels le Vice-Roi a concouru, au moins avec autant d'activité et de détermination que la compagnie, ont profondément modifié les situations respectives ;

Que la Compagnie s'est engagée dans l'exécution des travaux, non seulement avec l'assentiment du Vice-Roi, mais même en obéissant à l'impulsion qu'elle a reçue de lui ;

Qu'il serait souverainement injuste que les conséquences fâcheuses d'une résolution prise et suivie de concert fussent entièrement laissées à la charge de l'un des intéressés ;

Que, d'ailleurs, les stipulations qui ont réglé les rapports du Gouvernement égyptien et de la Compagnie, considérées dans leur ensemble, constituent la concession d'un grand travail d'utilité publique, en vue duquel ont été accordés des avantages formant une subvention sans laquelle l'entreprise n'aurait pas eu lieu ;

Que lorsque, par suite d'un événement que les deux parties contractantes ont dû prévoir, et dont elles ont, d'un commun accord, consenti à courir les chances, le gouvernement se trouve hors d'état de procurer à la Compagnie les avantages qu'il lui avait assurés, et que celle-ci continue néanmoins les importants travaux dont le pays tout entier doit profiter, il est juste que des indemnités représentatives des avantages inhérents à la concession soient allouées par le Gouvernement égyptien à la Compagnie ;

Que ces bases étant posées, pour parvenir à déterminer le montant de l'indemnité due en raison de la substitution des machines ou des ouvriers européens aux ouvriers égyptiens, il faut comparer la somme à laquelle se seraient élevées les dépenses des travaux s'ils avaient été exécutés par les ouvriers égyptiens, aux conditions énoncées dans le règlement du 20 juillet 1856, et la somme que coûteront les travaux qui devront être exécutés par les moyens que la Compagnie est désormais obligée d'employer ;

Que le cube des terrains à extraire peut être déterminé très approximativement d'après la configuration des lieux, telle qu'elle est établie par les plans, et d'après les dimensions qui ont été assignées au canal ;

Que, déduction faite des travaux qui sont déjà exécutés, il reste 23,700,000 mètres cubes à extraire à sec et 32,000,000 de mètres cubes à draguer ;

Que, d'un autre côté, le changement des moyens d'exécution aura pour résultat d'augmenter le prix du mètre à sec de fr. 1.19 et celui du mètre à draguer de 15 cts.; qu'en multipliant 23,700,000 mètres par fr. 1.19 et 32,000,000 par 15 cts., on trouve que l'accroissement de la dépense pour les travaux à sec sera de fr. 28,200,000 et pour les terrains à draguer de » 4,800,000

Ensemble fr. 33,000,000

Que des calculs analogues appliqués aux travaux d'art démontrent que la Compagnie sera obligée de supporter de ce chef un surcroît de dépenses s'élevant à 5,000,000 de francs;

Que c'est donc à une somme totale de 38,000,000 de francs que doit s'élever cette partie de l'indemnité;

Que, dans le cours des débats, on a fait observer avec raison que la Compagnie n'était pas autorisée à prétendre que les salaires et le prix des denrées n'éprouveraient aucune augmentation pendant la durée des travaux, ou que, du moins, d'après les termes du règlement, elle n'aurait pas à supporter les conséquences de la hausse qui pourrait survenir;

Que, pour justifier une pareille prétention, il n'eût fallu rien moins qu'une stipulation formelle, et le règlement ne la contient pas;

Qu'en tenant compte de l'augmentation qui a déjà eu lieu, et en appréciant les éventualités de l'avenir, le prix de la journée, qui, en moyenne, était, aux termes du règlement, de 86 cts., doit être évaluée à fr. 1.05, mais que cette élévation du prix de la journée a été l'un des éléments des calculs qui ont fait adopter le chiffre de 38,000,000 de francs; qu'ainsi cette fixation ne doit pas être modifiée;

Qu'en second lieu, au nom du Gouvernement égyptien, il a été allégué que, depuis le commencement des travaux, les salaires qui ont été payés aux ouvriers et les rations qui leur ont été fournies ne l'ont pas toujours été au taux déterminé par le règlement, et l'on a soutenu que la Compagnie doit imputer sur l'indemnité les sommes dont elle a pu profiter par l'effet de cette inexécution partielle de sa convention, alors même qu'elle aurait été, comme tout porte à le croire, le résultat d'une erreur;

Que cette réclamation est bien fondée, que la Compagnie ne peut demander à titre d'indemnité que ce qui sera effectivement déboursé par elle en excédant des prévisions qu'autorisait le règlement du 20 juillet 1856; qu'en exigeant la réparation des pertes que peut lui causer l'inexécution du contrat de la part du Vice-Roi, elle doit tenir compte des avantages qui ont pu résulter pour elle des infractions qui lui sont personnelles;

Qu'une somme de 4,500,000 francs a été réellement payée en moins sur les salaires ou sur la fourniture des rations; qu'elle doit être défalquée du montant de l'indemnité, qui se trouverait ainsi réduite à 33,500,000 francs;

Mais qu'une réclamation a été formée par la Compagnie; qu'elle a demandé qu'une somme de 9,000,000 de francs lui fût allouée pour les intérêts d'une année des capitaux engagés dans l'opération, temps durant lequel ces travaux seront prolongés;

Que cette demande devrait être accueillie en entier, si la prolongation de la durée des travaux pouvait être imputée au Gouvernement égyptien; mais qu'en réalité les conditions imposées par la Sublime-Porte sont un fait indépendant de la volonté du Vice-Roi; que c'est par un événement de force majeure que les travaux auront une durée plus longue que celle qui leur avait été assignée; que, dès lors, soit en raison même de la nature de l'événement, soit en raison des rapports qui continuent à subsister entre le Vice-Roi et la Compagnie, il est équitable qu'ils supportent par moitié la somme de 9,000,000, c'est-à-dire 4,500,000 francs chacun; que cette somme de 4,500,000 francs, ajoutée à celle de 33,500,000 francs, porte l'indemnité, pour l'objet spécial qui vient d'être examiné, à 38,000,000 de francs;

Considérant, sur la troisième question, que les firmans du 30 novembre 1854 et 5 janvier 1856, en faisant à la Compagnie la concession du canal d'eau douce, lui assuraient des avantages et lui donnaient des garanties qui ont dû être considérées comme essentielles pour le succès de son entreprise;

Que, dans l'origine et aux termes des firmans, le canal d'eau douce devait prendre naissance à proximité de la ville du Caire, joindre le Nil au canal maritime et s'étendre, par des branches d'alimentation, d'irrigation et même de navigation, dans les deux directions de Péluse et de Suez; mais que, par une convention en date du 18 mars 1863, les conditions de la concession ont été gravement modifiées; que, notamment, la Compagnie a renoncé au droit qui lui avait été conféré d'exécuter par elle-même la portion du canal entre le Caire et le canal du Ouady, déjà ouvert à la navigation;

Que, d'ailleurs, la Sublime-Porte a prétendu que la rétrocession du canal d'eau douce était la conséquence nécessaire de la rétrocession des terrains;

Que, dans cette situation, il convient, tout en reconnaissant les droits des parties, de chercher à concilier leurs intérêts;

Que la concession du canal d'eau douce, au moment où elle a été faite, offrait à la Compagnie un triple avantage: elle lui assurait la libre disposition de l'eau nécessaire à la mise 'en mouvement des machines employées au creusement du canal maritime et à l'alimentation des ouvriers; elle devait lui fournir le moyen d'arroser les terres qui lui étaient concédées; et, enfin, elle devait lui procurer les bénéfices résultant des droits à établir sur la navigation et d'autres taxes de même nature;

Que le maintien de la concession dans toute son étendue et avec toutes ses conséquences ne pourrait être utilement accordé à la Compagnie qu'autant que la Sublime-Porte consentirait à donner son approbation;

Que ce qui, dans la situation où est placée aujourd'hui la Compagnie, a pour elle un intérêt capital, c'est que le canal soit terminé promptement, et dans des conditions telles qu'il fournisse toujours toute l'eau nécessaire à l'exécution des travaux et à l'alimentation des ouvriers;

Que, pour atteindre ce but, il n'est pas absolument indispenable que la concession soit maintenue dans les termes et pour la durée qui avait été fixée par les firmans; qu'il suffit de confier à la Compagnie l'achèvement du canal et de lui en laisser la jouissance et l'entretien;

Que, dans ce nouvel état des choses, les travaux que la Compagnie a déjà faits et ceux qu'elle aura encore à exécuter pour l'achèvement du canal seront à la charge du Gouvernement égyptien;

Que, par conséquent, celui-ci devra rembourser le prix des uns et des autres, en outre de payer les frais d'entretien;

Que, satisfaction étant ainsi donnée à ce premier intérêt, il ne restera plus qu'à régler les indemnités qui peuvent être dues en raison de la privation des autres avantages que la concession devait produire pour la Compagnie;

Qu'avant de s'occuper de cette fixation, il convient de déterminer les sommes dont la Compagnie est dès aujourd'hui créancière pour les travaux faits, et celles qu'elle aura à réclamer ultérieurement pour les travaux qui restent à faire;

Qu'il résulte des documents produits par les parties et des explications qu'elles ont données contradictoirement, que la dépense des ouvrages déjà exécutés s'élève à 7,500,000 francs;

Que dans cette somme est comprise celle de 3,750,000 francs, représentant: 1° la portion des frais généraux de l'entreprise qui doit être supportée par les travaux du canal d'eau douce, et 2° l'intérêt des capitaux engagés dans l'opération pendant le temps durant lequel les travaux seront prolongés;

Que ces deux causes réunies justifient la demande formée par la Compagnie de la somme susénoncée de 3,750,000 francs:

Que, pour les travaux qui ne sont point terminés, la dépense s'élèvera à la somme de 2,500,000 francs, qui, réunie à celle de 7,500,000 francs, donnera un total de 10,000,000;

Que les droits de navigation et les péages de différente nature, dont la jouissance était assurée à la Compagnie par les firmans de concession, et dont elle se trouvera dépouillée, doivent être évalués, afin que l'indemnité due de ce chef soit également allouée;

Que, déduction faite des frais d'entretien, charge naturelle de la jouissance du canal, la valeur de cette jouissance doit être fixée à 6,000,000 de francs;

Considérant, sur la quatrième question, que la Compagnie en cessant d'être concessionnaire du canal d'eau douce, doit ainsi qu'il vient d'être dit, rester chargée de son achèvement et de son entretien; qu'en conséquence il est nécessaire de déterminer pour le canal d'eau douce, comme pour le canal maritime, l'étendue de terrain qu'exigent l'établissement et l'exploitation; que les termes même du compromis indiquent clairement dans quel esprit doit être examinée cette question;

Qu'il y est dit, en effet, que l'étendue des terrains devra être fixée dans des conditions propres à assurer la prospérité de l'entreprise;

Qu'elle ne doit donc pas être restreinte à l'espace qui sera matériellement occupé par les canaux eux-mêmes, par leurs francs bords et par les chemins de halage;

Que pour donner aux besoins de l'exploitation une entière et complète satisfaction, il faut que la Compagnie puisse établir, à proximité des canaux, des dépôts, des magasins, des ateliers, des ports dans les lieux où leur utilité sera reconnue et, enfin, des habitations convenables pour les gardiens, les surveillants, les ouvriers chargés des travaux d'entretien et pour tous les préposés à l'administration;

Qu'il est, en outre, convenable d'accorder, comme accessoires des habitations, des terrains qui puissent être cultivés en jardins et fournir quelques approvisionnements dans des lieux privés de toutes ressources de ce genre;

Qu'enfin il est indispensable que la Compagnie puisse disposer de terrains suffisants pour y faire les plantations et les travaux destinés à protéger les canaux contre l'invasion des sables et à assurer leur conservation:

Mais qu'il ne doit rien être alloué au delà de ce qui est nécessaire pour pourvoir amplement aux divers services qui viennent d'être indiqués; que la Compagnie ne peut avoir la prétention d'obtenir, dans des vues de spéculation, une étendue quelconque de terrains, soit pour livrer à la culture, soit pour y élever des constructions, soit pour les céder, lorsque la population aura augmenté;

Que c'est en se renfermant dans ces limites qu'a du être déterminé surtout le parcours des canaux, le périmètre des terrains dont la jouissance, pendant la durée de la concession, est nécessaire à leur établissement, à leur exploitation et à leur conservation;

Considérant, sur la cinquième question, que la rétrocession des terrains concédés à la Compagnie n'a pu être consentie qu'avec l'intention réciproque d'obtenir et d'accorder une indemnité;

Que la Compagnie n'a dû renoncer aux avantages de la concession qu'en comptant sur la compensation de ces avantages, et que le Gouvernement égyptien n'a pu avoir la pensée de profiter de la valeur qu'auront les terrains lorsqu'ils seront fécondés par l'irrigation, sans en donner l'équivalent.

Qu'il ne faut pas perdre de vue que la concession des terrains était une des conditions essentielles de l'entreprise, une partie importante de la rémunération des travaux;

Que par conséquent, la Compagnie, en y renonçant, à droit d'en exiger la représentation.

Que soit que l'on consulte les termes des firmans, soit que l'on s'attache aux diverses publications qui ont été faites pendant le cours des travaux, on est conduit à reconnaître que le Gouvernement égyptien n'a point entendu concéder et que la Compagnie n'a pas eu la pensée d'acquérir une étendue illimitée de terrains;

Que la commune intention, clairement manifestée, a été de borner l'étendue de la concession aux terrains à l'irrigation desquels pourrait pourvoir l'eau prise dans le canal d'eau douce;

Qu'il est dès lors facile d'en fixer avec certitude le périmètre;

Qu'en effet, d'une part, on connaît le volume d'eau que le canal peut, en raison de ses dimensions et les besoins de la navigation satisfaits, fournir pour l'irrigation des terres;

Que, d'autre part, on sait la quantité d'eau qui est nécessaire pour l'irrigation de chaque hectare;

Que, d'après ces données, la concession doit comprendre 63,000 hectares, sur lesquels doivent être déduits 3000 hectares, qui font partie des emplacements affectés aux besoins de l'exploitation du canal maritime;

Que cette fixation est en harmonie avec celle qui avait été arrêtée entre les représentants de la Compagnie et ceux du Vice-Roi dans les cartes cadastrales dressées en exécution de l'ar-

ticle 8 du firman du 30 novembre 1854 et de l'article 11 du firman du 5 janvier 1856; que si ces cartes ont plus tard, en 1858, été anéanties d'un commun accord, la difficulté qui a déterminé à les annuler, ne portait point sur l'étendue des terrains qui devaient être compris dans la concession comme susceptibles d'être arrosés;

Que l'estimation des 60,000 hectares qui sont, en définitive, rétrocédés au Gouvernement égyptien, présente sans doute de sérieuses difficultés, puisque ce n'est point d'après leur état actuel que les terrains doivent être appréciés, et qu'en recherchant quelle sera leur valeur dans l'avenir, on se trouve en présence de chances fort diverses et de nombreuses éventualités; que cependant il existe certains éléments de calcul auxquels on peut accorder une grande confiance; que, notamment, la quotité de l'impôt des terres cultivées peut servir à déterminer le revenu, lequel capitalisé comme il doit l'être, eu égard à la situation économique et financière de l'Egypte, indique la valeur vénale de la terre;

Qu'en calculant d'après ces données, le prix de l'hectare doit être fixé à 500 francs;

Que, si cette évaluation a été contestée, elle n'a point cependant paru, aux parties intéressées elles-mêmes, s'éloigner beaucoup de la vérité;

Qu'elle n'a d'ailleurs été adoptée qu'après avoir pris en sérieuse considération, d'une part, les sommes qui devront être dépensées, pour la mise en valeur des terres, et, de l'autre, l'augmentation de prix, que doit produire l'exploitation du canal maritime, et en outre, celle qui peut résulter de l'introduction de nouvelles cultures;

Qu'en résumé, l'indemnité due par le Gouvernement égyptien, par suite de la rétrocession des terrains, s'élève à la somme de 30 millons.

Considérant qu'après avoir apprécié les divers éléments dont doit se composer l'indemnité, il n'est pas possible de les assimiler en ce qui touche les époques d'exigibilité;

Que les uns représentent des sommes déjà dépensées, les autres des avances qui doivent être faites à des époques assez rapprochées, et que certaines allocations, qu'il a été juste d'accorder à la Compagnie sont pour elle la compensation d'avantages ou de bénéfices, qui ne devaient se réaliser que dans un avenir éloigné et qui .étaient subordonnés à l'exécution de travaux dispendieux;

Que, par exemple, dans la première catégorie est comprise la somme de 7,500,000 francs qui a été dépensée pour la partie du canal d'eau douce qui est déjà exécutée;

Que dans la dernière, au contraire, doivent évidemment figurer les 30 millions représentant la valeur d'avenir des terrains retrocédés;

Que c'est en tenant compte de ces différences qu'ont été fixées la quotité et l'échéance des annuités, qui, réunies, composent l'indemnité totale de 84 millions de francs, mise à la charge du Gouvernement égyptien ;

Par ces motifs nous avons décidé, et décidons ce qui suit :

Sur la première question : Le règlement du 20 juillet 1856 a les caractères d'un contrat ; il contient des engagements réciproques qui devaient être exécutés par le Vice-Roi et par la Compagnie.

Sur la seconde question : L'indemnité à laquelle donne lieu l'annulation du règlement du 20 juillet 1856 est fixée à trente huit millions de francs (38,000,000 fr.).

Sur la troisième question : La rétrocession du canal d'eau douce est faite dans les termes et avec les garanties ci-après :

1° La partie du canal comprise entre le Ouady, Timsah et Suez est rétrocédée comme la première partie, au Gouvernement égyptien, mais la jouissance exclusive en sera laissée à la Compagnie jusqu'à l'entier achèvement du canal maritime, sans qu'il puisse être pratiqué aucune prise d'eau sans le consentement de la Compagnie.

2° Le Gouvernement égyptien maintiendra l'alimentation de ce canal par celui de Zagasig ; il exécutera en outre, les travaux de la partie qui lui a déjà été rétrocédée, conformément à la Convention du 18 mars 1863 et mettra cette première section en communication avec la seconde au point de jonction du Ouady, pour assurer en tout temps son alimentation.

3° La Compagnie sera tenue de terminer les travaux restant à faire, pour mettre le canal de Ouady à Suez dans toutes les dimensions convenues et en état de réception.

4° Pendant toute la durée de la concession du canal maritime, la Compagnie sera chargée d'entretenir le canal d'eau douce en parfait état, depuis Ouady jusqu'à Suez ; mais l'entretien sera aux frais du Gouvernement égyptien, qui devra indemniser la Compagnie, au moyen d'un abonnement annuel de 300,000 francs, si mieux il n'aime payer les frais d'entretien sur mémoire ; il sera tenu de faire connaître son option à la Compagnie dans l'année qui commencera à courir du jour de la livraison du canal. La Compagnie devra garnir les digues de plantations pour prévenir les éboulements et l'effet de la mobilité des sables.

L'abonnement de 300,000 francs recevra son application au fur et à mesure de l'avancement des travaux et au prorata de la longueur de chacune des parties achevées ; il sera révisé tous les six ans.

5° La hauteur des eaux sera maintenue dans le canal : dans les hautes eaux du Nil, à 2 m 50 ; à l'étiage moyen, à 2 m ; au plus bas étiage, au minimum 1 m.

6° La Compagnie prélèvera sur le débit du canal 70,000 mètres cubes d'eau par jour, pour l'alimentation des populations établies sur le parcours des canaux, l'arrosage des jardins, le fonctionnement des machines destinées à l'entretien des canaux et de celles des établissements industriels se rattachant à leur exploitation, l'irrigation des semis et plantations pratiqués sur les dunes et autres terrains non naturellement irrigables compris dans les zones réservées le long des canaux ; enfin, l'approvisionnement des navires traversant le canal maritime.

La Compagnie aura la servitude de passage sur les terrains que devront traverser les rigoles et conduites d'eau nécessaires au prélèvement des 70,000 mètres.

7° A partir de l'entier achèvement du canal maritime, la Compagnie n'aura plus sur le canal d'eau douce, que la jouissance appartenant aux sujets égyptiens, sans toutefois que jamais ses barques et bâtiments puissent être soumis à aucun droit de navigation ; l'alimentation d'eau douce en ligne directe à Port-Saïd sera toujours amenée par les moyens que la Compagnie jugera convenable d'employer à ses frais.

8° La Compagnie cesse d'avoir les droits de cession de prises d'eau, de navigation, de pilotage, remorquage, halage ou stationnement à elle accordés sur le canal d'eau douce par les articles 8 et 17 de l'acte de concession du 5 janvier 1856.

9° En dehors des écluses en construction à Ismaïlia et des trois autres écluses sur la dérivation de Suez, il ne pourra être établi aucun ouvrage fixe ou mobile sur le canal d'eau douce et ses dépendances que d'un commun accord entre le Gouvernement égyptien et la Compagnie.

10° Le Gouvernement égyptien payera à la Compagnie une somme de 10,000,000 de francs, savoir : 7,500,000 fr. pour les travaux exécutés, la portion des frais généraux et les intérêts des avances, et 2,500,000 francs pour les travaux qui restent à exécuter.

11° Le Gouvernement égyptien payera à la Compagnie une somme de 6,000,000 de francs en compensation des droits de navigation et autres redevances dont la Compagnie est privée.

Sur la quatrième question : Le périmètre des terrains nécessaires à l'établissement, l'exploitation et la conservation du canal d'eau douce et du canal maritime est fixé à 10,264 hectares pour le canal maritime, et à 9,600 hectares pour le canal d'eau douce, lesquels sont répartis ainsi qu'il suit :

CANAL MARITIME.

	Afrique	Asie
	Hect.	Hect.
Nº 1. Port-Saïd	400	—
» 2. Du Port-Saïd à El-Ferdane	1,152	1,152
» 3. Rosel-Ech.	30	30
» 4. Kantara	100	100
» 5. D'El-Ferdane à Timsah .	1,350	270
» 6. Canal de jonction avec le canal d'eau douce . .	200	—
» 7. Ville d'Ismaïlia	450	—
» 8. Port d'Ismaïlia, dans le lac Timsah (canal en Asie)	450	120
» 9. Du lac Timsah aux Lacs-Amers	850	340
» 10. Traversée des Lacs-Amers	700	700
» 11. Des Lacs-Amers aux lagunes de Suez . . .	1,000	400
» 12. Traversée des lagunes de Suez.	60	60
» 13. Chenal du port de Suez.	150	200
Totaux	6,892	3,372

CANAL D'EAU DOUCE.

	Nord	Sud
	Hect.	Hect.
Nº 1. De l'extrémité du canal à construire par le Gouvernement égyptien jusqu'au ras El-Ouady .	500	—
» 2. Du ras El-Ouady à l'extrémité du lac Maxama	200	3,000
» 3. Du lac Maxama à Néfiche	420	2,100
» 4. De Néfiche à Ismaïlia .	300	—
Totaux	1,420	5,100

	Est	Ouest
	Hect.	Hect.
Nº 5. De Néfiche aux Lacs-Amers	—	2,500
» 6 et 7. Contours des Lacs-Amers.	300	200
» 8. Gare de Suez	30	50
Totaux	330	2,750

Sur la cinquième question : L'indemnité due à la Compagnie, à raison de la rétrocession des terrains, est fixée à trente millions de francs (30,000,000 fr.).

RÉSUMÉ.

L'indemnité totale due à la Compagnie, et s'élevant à la somme de 84,000,000 de francs, lui sera payée par le Gouvernement égyptien par annuités, ainsi qu'il suit :

La première somme allouée de 38 millions sera payée en six annuités divisibles par semestres.

Les huit premiers semestres seront de 3,250,000 francs chacun et les quatre derniers de 3 millions chacun. Le premier semestre sera exigible le 1er novembre 1864 et les paiements continueront de semestre en semestre jusqu'à l'entière libération de la somme de 38 millions.

La somme de 30 millions allouée pour l'indemnité des terrains rétrocédés sera divisée en dix annuités de 3 millions chacune. La première annuité sera exigible seulement après l'entière libération de la somme de 38 millions ci-dessus c'est-à-dire le 1er novembre 1870, et les paiements continueront d'année en année, jusqu'à l'entière libération de la somme de 30 millions.

La somme de 6 millions, allouée pour l'indemnité des droits sur le canal d'eau douce, sera divisée en dix annuités de 600,000 francs chacune, payables aux mêmes échéances que les annuités ci-dessus fixées pour l'indemnité de 30 millions.

Enfin, la somme de dix millions, allouée pour les travaux exécutés et à exécuter au canal d'eau douce, sera payée dans l'année de la livraison du dit canal.

Le tout conformément au tableau ci-après : [1]

XLVIII. Etats-Unis d'Amérique, Brésil.

14 mars 1870.

Il s'est agi dans cette affaire du naufrage d'un navire américain dans les eaux brésiliennes, par suite de l'opposition mise au renflouement par les autorités locales. Il fut accordé 100,740 $ 04 par l'arbitre désigné, M. E. Thornton.

Protocol of a Conference held in Rio de Janeiro in the Foreign Office, May 14, 1870, between the Envoy extraordinary and Minister Plenipotentiary of the United States and the Minister and Secretary of State for the Marine Department in charge of Foreign Affairs.

Whereas the Government of the United States have claimed of the Government of His Imperial Majesty the Emperor of Brazil the payment of a certain compensation to the owners of the United States whaleship Canada which is alleged by the Government of the United States to be justly due to the said owners by the Government of His Imperial Majesty; and whereas the Government of His Imperial Majesty deny their liability to make such payment by reason of any of the alleged causes set forth by the Government of the United States; and whereas both parties being animated by a friendly feeling, and each desiring to make an amicable

[1] Voir ce tableau à la page 130.

INDEMNITÉS.

Années	38,000,000 fr. Indemnité pour la substitution des machines et des ouvriers européens aux ouvriers égyptiens	30.000,000 fr. Indemnité pour rétrocession des terrains	6,000,000 fr. Indemnité pour les droits à percevoir sur le canal d'eau douce	10,000,000 fr. Remboursem[t] des sommes dépensées pour les travaux faits ou à faire au canal d'eau douce	Total : 84,000,000 fr. Echéances
1ʳᵉ année	6,500,000	—	—	—	1ᵉʳ novembre 1864 et 1ᵉʳ mai 1865
2ᵉ »	6,500,000	—	—	—	1ᵉʳ » 1865 » 1ᵉʳ » 1866
3ᵉ »	6,500,000	—	—	—	1ᵉʳ » 1866 » 1ᵉʳ » 1867
4ᵉ »	6,500,000	—	—	—	1ᵉʳ » 1867 » 1ᵉʳ » 1868
5ᵉ »	6,000,000	—	—	—	1ᵉʳ » · 1868 » 1ᵉʳ » 1869
6ᵉ »	6,000,000	—	—	—	1ᵉʳ » 1869 » 1ᵉʳ » 1870
7ᵉ »	—	3,000,000	600,000	—	1ᵉʳ » 1870
8ᵉ »	—	3,000,000	600,000	—	1ᵉʳ » 1871
9ᵉ »	—	3,000,000	600,000	—	1ᵉʳ » 1872
10ᵉ »	—	3,000,000	600,000	—	1ᵉʳ » 1873
11ᵉ »	—	3,000,000	600,000	—	1ᵉʳ » 1874
12ᵉ »	—	3,000,000	600,000	—	1ᵉʳ » 1875
13ᵉ »	—	3,000,000	600,000	—	1ᵉʳ » 1876
14ᵉ »	—	3,000,000	600,000	—	1ᵉʳ » 1877
15ᵉ »	—	3,000,000	600,000	—	1ᵉʳ » 1878
16ᵉ »	—	3,000,000	600,000	—	1ᵉʳ » 1879
A ajouter	38,000,000	30,000,000	6,000,000	10,000,000	dans l'année de la livraison du canal

Total général : 84,000,000

Fait à Fontainebleau le 6 juillet 1864 [1].

[1] DE CLERCQ, *Recueil des Traités de France*, t. IX, p. 108.

settlement of the said cause of difference, have agreed to refer the same to the arbitration of Edward Thornton, esq., commander of the bath, the envoy extraordinary and minister plenipotentiary of Her Britannic Majesty at Washington : For this purpose it now becomes necessary to place on record certain terms and arrangements, with a view of obtaining a speedy and convenient hearing and determination of the matters to be submitted ; and the undersigned, Henry T. Blow, envoy extraordinary and minister plenipotentiary of the United States near the court of His Imperial Majesty and the Baron de Cotegipe, minister and secretary of state for the marine department in charge of the foreign affairs, being duly authorised by their respective governments, have agreed as follows :

ARTICLE I. The claim of the Government of the United States against the Government of Brazil for compensation to the owners of the United States whaleship Canada, and of the cargo thereof, shall be submitted to the arbitration and award of Edward Thornton, esq., commander ot the bath, the envoy extraordinary and minister plenipotentiary of Her Britannic Majesty at Washington.

ARTICLE II. The award of the said arbitrator shall be considered as absolutely final and conclusive, and full effect shall be given thereto without any objection, evasion or delay whatsoever. Such decision shall be given in writing and dated. It shall be in whatsoever form the arbitrator shall choose to adopt. It shall be delivered to the minister or other public agent of His Imperial Majesty who may be actually in the United States and to the Secretary of State at Washington, and shall be considered as operative from the date of the delivery thereof.

ARTICLE III. The written or printed case of each ot the two parties with the documents, correspondence, and evidence on which each relies in support of the same, shall be laid before the arbitrator at Washington on or before the 1st day of June next, and the arbitrator shall decide the questions so submitted to him upon such case, documents, correspondance and evidence.

ARTICLE IV. The Secretary of State of the United States and the minister or other public representative of His Imperial Majesty, actually in the United States, shall be considered as the agents of their respective governments, to whom the arbitrator shall address notices and whose acts shall bind their respective governments.

ARTICLE V. The arbitrator may employ a clerk for the purposes of the arbitration at such rate of remuneration as he shall think proper. This and all other expenses of the arbitration shall be repaid in two equal portions, one by each of the two parties, as soon as the arbitrator renders an account of the same.

ARTICLE VI. Should the arbitrator decline to render any decision, everything done by virtue of this agreement shall be null and void and each government shall be at liberty to proceed as if no arbitration had been made.

Done at Rio de Janeiro the fourteenth day of March in the year of our Lord one thousand eight hundred and seventy. [1]

Award transmitted, July 11, 1870, by M. E. Thornton in regard to the claim for compensation to the owners of the whaleship Canada.

The Governments of the United States and of Brazil have done the undersigned the honor of submitting to his arbitration a question at issue between them relative to the loss in December 1856 of the United States whalingvessel Canada, which loss the owners of that vessel claim was due to the improper interference of the Brazilian authorities.

Before entering into an examination of the case the umpire may be allowed to observe that in other similar cases of arbitration it has sometimes been agreed that each party should submit to the other, at the same time as to the umpire, a copy of the statement made, and should be allowed time to offer further observations and documents in refutation to the arguments used by the opponent. The protocol signed at Rio de Janeiro on the 14th of March 1870 contains no such provision and the undersigned therefore considers it incumbent upon him to come to a decision upon the evidence produced, notwithstanding any errors, omissions, or misstatements

which may possibly have been made by one party or the other. The undersigned has accordingly, after having given the subject all the thought and attention of which he is capable, come to the following conclusions :

The case on the part of the United States is supported by the protest signed by the captain, there mates, and twenty two men of the Canada, and sworn to before the United States consul at Pernambuco on December 18, 1856, and by affidavits sworn to by the captain, the second mate, and two of the seamen, after their return to New Bedford. The protest is the usual course followed by shipmasters in case of damage to their vessels, and the depositions seem to be straightforward. They can only be refuted by convincing evidence to the contrary, or by the impossibility of the facts recounted.

In refutation of the contents of the protest there is the evidence of Francisco Rosa, fourth mate of the Canada, said to have been sworn to by him on the 2d of March 1857. But although the name of this man, with a cross, was affixed to the report of the survey of February 14, 1857, it is not so affixed to the deposition of March 2. Neither has a copy of it been furnished to the undersigned by the Brazilian Government, making him suppose that the latter attaches little weight to it. On the other hand, the same Rosa on the 23d of June 1858 made affidavit on oath in the United States that he never signed or swore to any statement whatever in Brazil on the occasion of the loss of the Canada, and that the sworn depositions of the captain were truthful. This affidavit of Rosa does not seem to have been transmitted to the imperial government. In it Rosa either perjured himself or he did not. If the latter, he never gave any evidence in contradiction to the statements of the crew ; and if he perjured himself, such a man's evidence is not to be credited in any case, and the umpire can not consider it at all.

The statement of Manuel José Pequeno, seaman of the Canada, is likewise open to the objection that it is not signed by the deponent, nor is a copy of it even furnished to the undersigned by the Brazilian Government as a part of their case. He is not, therefore, called upon to consider it although he is of opinion that, even if it had been submitted to him by the imperial government in due form, the declaration of a single seaman who had abandoned his captain before his was regularly discharged could not outweigh the evidence of the remainder of the crew.

It appears that the Canada, being nearly under full sail, went on the reef of the Garças, on the 27th of November 1856, at eleven minutes

[1] J. B. MOORE. History and Digest of the International Arbitrations, p. 4687 ; — Relatorio da Repartiçao dos Negocios Estrangieros, 1870, Annexe I, n° 180, p. 249.

before 7 p. m. According to the protest the crew used their best efforts to get the ship off the reef during the next four days, and succeeded in doing so to such an extent that at half past 4 p. m. of the 1st of December they were within a very short distance of deep water, and would, as the captain believed, have reached in about an hour's time an anchor which was laid out in five and half fathoms water.

At that hour Brazilian officer with fourteen armed men came on board. The umpire believes, and the United States Government acknowledges, that the Canada was at the time within Brazilian jurisdictiction. Therefore it matters little whether this force came at the invitation of the captain or without it. But the officer is charged with having, with the assistance of the men under his command, forcibly prevented the crew from continuing to heave the ship off the reef. It is declared that the captain protested against this act, and finally threw the whole responsibility upon the Brazilian authorities; that the guard subsequently let go the hausers, so that the ship fell back on the reef; that on the following morning the captain offered again to take charge of the ship and save her; but that the officer refused to allow the ship to be taken off the reef.

It is possible that the officer thought the ship would have been in danger of sinking if she had got into deep water and deemed it his duty, in the interest of the Brazilian revenue, to prevent her being exposed to such a danger, but he certainly exceeded his duty; for on board his own ship the captain alone is responsible for its navigation and safety, and should be supreme.

In contradiction to these statements, the only eyewitnesses whose evidence is produced by the United States Government, though not by that of Brazil, are Rosa and Pequeno, and the undersigned has shown that their evidence can not be taken into consideration. And yet another ocular evidence might have been obtained. Why were not the officer, Fortunato José de Lima, the soldiers under his command, and the custom-house officers who were on board, examined on oath after the receipt by the imperial government of the protest signed by the crew? Their testimony, as of eyewitnesses with respect to the facts stated to have happened, would have been of great value. The umpire does not therefore consider that the declarations of the crew of the Canada are disproved by evidence.

As to the possibility that the ship would be and actually was nearly heaved off the reef, the undersigned can not give any weight to the opinion of senhor Jacinto da Rocho e Silva, or to his statement, not made on oath, that she could not be and had not been moved at all. Hundreds of vessels stranded and in a far worse position than the Canada have been saved, in spite of the opinions of experienced seamen, and even naval officers of high rank. And senhor Jacinto did not remain on board to see with his own eyes whether the Canada was moved or not.

Neither can the umpire take into consideration the position of the vessel when the survey was made upon her on the 14th of February 1857, seventy-four days after the captain and crew left her. Senhor Paranhos himself says, in his note of August 14, 1868, that the waves which break upon those reefs are violent by reason of the currents and ordinary winds; and when it is remembered that everything which was on board on the 1st of December 1856, had been taken out before the 14th of February following, whereby the vessel was much lightened, it is impossible to suppose that she had not been driven much higher upon the reef.

The Canada went upon the reef at eleven minutes before 7 p. m., not at low tide, as the United States minister states, but an hour and a quarter after high tide; for the undersigned is informed by the United States Naval Observatory at Washington, that on the 27th of November 1856 it was high water at that place at 5 h. 34 m. p. m. The reef is of that nature that it is too soft seriously to injure a vessel going upon it in a smooth sea, and yet too hard to allow the vessel to become deeply embedded as in mud or sand. When it is remembered then, that upward of twelve hundred barrels of water were emptied and pumped out, that heavy anchors and chain cables were taken out, and that all the least valuable articles were thrown overboard, there is no reason why the vessel should not have been lightened from three to four feet, which, even without a little advantage from a higher tide, would have been quite sufficient to have enabled the crew to heave her off the reef.

The umpire is therefore impelled to give credit to the statements of the officers and crew of the Canada, and to believe that the loss of the vessel was owing to the improper interference of the officers of the imperial government, which is therefore responsible for the domage as hereinafter stated.

It has been urged that the claim is barred because a note of imperial government was left unanswered for some years. The undersigned can not acquiesce in this opinion. The claiming government may suspend its action from consideration for the other government, in which it sees no disposition to yield to the influence of reason, and with which it has no wish to have recourse to force, or itself may be engaged with other matters and unable to attend to the claim of its citizens. But this is no proof that the claim has been waived, and the undersigned has too much confidence in the justice of the Brazilian government to suppose that it would avail itself of such an argument; indeed it has itself declared that it does not pretend to do so.

Neither can the umpire be influenced by the fact that the United States Government at one time offered to accept a reduced sum as a compromise for the claim. Such offers are made for various reasons. It may be that the claimant is much in want of the money to which he is entitled, and desires to obtain compensation at once. His government is perhaps wearied of litigation and desires not to embitter the relations between two friendly countries by useless discussion. An offer is therefore made, even involving a sacrifice. But once the offer is refused, and the discussion is continued till at length arbitration is agreed upon, the duty of the umpire is to calculate the amount of damages in accordance with the evidence submitted to him, and without taking into consideration any proposal which may have been made to accept a reduced sum. Indeed, at the time of making the offer, the rights of the claimants were reserved in case the offer should be rejected.

It now becomes the duty of the undersigned to consider the amount of indemnity for which the imperial government is liable, and in doing so he will go through the different items which have been claimed.

The Canada was built in New York in 1823 as a first-class vessel, and was employed as a liner from that port to Liverpool. From that time to 1856 she was constantly kept in thorough repair, and impartial persons acquainted with such matters have estimated her value in 1856 at $ 18,000; the amount claimed therefore, of $ 15,000 is, so far not excessive; but it must be remembered that the imperial government is liable only for her actual value on the 1st December 1856, after she had been considerably damaged by being off the reef. The undersigned can not conceive that Captain Ricketson would have continued his voyage without docking or beaching and repairing his vessel, and from the undersigned's experience of the country, he believes that the vessel could not have been put into a fit state, including all expenses, for less than $ 5000. The umpire therefore fixes the value of the vessel at $ 10,000.

He has also made inquiries as to the expense of fitting a vessel of that class for a four years whaling expedition, and furnishing her with provisions and all other necessaries, and has been assured that te cost would not have been less

in 1856 than $ 45,000. The undersigned has further examined the accounts rendered by the owners, and has found no charge to which he can object; he must therefore admit the sum of $ 41,000 as the value of the outfits, etc. But he must take into account that as acknowledged by the officers and crew, several articles though of little value, were thrown overboard in order to lighten the vessel. The undersigned has no details of these articles, but he supposes that the captain could hardly have replaced them in Brazil under $ 2000. He therefore places the value of the outfits, etc., for which the government of Brazil is liable, at $ 39,000. The charge of $ 3543.75 for the oil which had already been secured, the umpire considers a legitimate claim.

But the undersigned can in no case admit a right to prospective profits; for the ship and the whole capital might have been entirely unsuccessful and without profit. In this particular case the objection is still stronger, because the Canada was commanded by a captain who, very little after sunset, when darkness could have hardly set in, ran his vessel upon a reef with the existence and position of which he ought to have been well acquainted.

The undersigned can not, however, admit the validity of any argument which would exempt the imperial government from the payment of interest. If the claim in itself can be sustained, of which the umpire has no doubt, the claimants are entitled to interest.

Certain expenses incurred for the maintenance and passage home of the crew, as also three months' wages to each of the crew, being the amount which all owners of vessels of the United States are bound to pay to seamen discharged abroad, the undersigned considers to be justly due, but can not allow more than this, on the same principle on which he founds his opinion that prospective profits are inadmissible.

The undersigned therefore lays down the items as follows:

Value of ship Canada on December 1, 1856	$ 10,000. —
Value of her outfits etc. . . .	» 39,000. —
75 barrels of oil, at $ 47.25 per barrel	» 5,543.75
Transit of crew from Rio Grande do Norte to Pernambuco . .	» 227.82
Board and clothing in December and January	» 432.44
Transit to United States, 26 men at $ 10 each	» 260. —
	$ 53,464.01

	$ 53,464. 01
Wages for three months each:	
First mate, at $ 100 per month »	300. —
Second mate, at $ 75 » » »	225. —
Third mate, at $ 60 » » »	180. —
Fourth mate, at $ 50 » » »	150. —
Four men, boat steerers, at $ 40 per month . . . . . . »	480. —
Four men, boat steerers, at $ 30 per month . . . . »	360. —
Fourteen men, at $ 12 per month »	504. —
Thirteen and a half years' interest, at 6 per cent, from December 1, 1856, to June 1, 1870 »	45,077. 03
	$ 100,740. 04

The umpire therefore decides that the imperial government of Brazil is liable to that of the United States, as compensation to the owners of the United States whaleship Canada and of the cargo thereof, in the sum of $ 100,704. 04 payable in coin [1].

XLIX. Espagne, Etats-Unis d'Amérique.

12 février 1871.

Cet arbitrage a eu pour objet de régler les indemnités dues à des citoyens américains pour dommages soufferts par eux au cours d'une insurrection à Cuba. Il fut institué par un simple échange de lettres. En effet, voici ce que le titulaire de la légation des Etats-Unis d'Amérique à Madrid écrivait, sous la date du 11 février 1871, au Ministre d'Etat d'Espagne:

SIR: I have the honour to receive the note of to day's date addressed to me by your Excellency, proposing certain modifications of the plan of arrangement submitted to you on the 7th instant, for the adjustment of the reclamations made by my Government against that of Spain, I take much pleasure in stating that the changes suggested in the memorandum inclosed in your note have my entire concurrence, and have been duly embodied in the following record of the basis upon which we have agreed.

Memorandum of an arbitration for the settlement of the claims of citizens of the United States, or of their heirs, against the Government of Spain for wrongs and injuries committed against their persons and property, or against the persons and property of citizens of whom the

---

[1] J. B. MOORE. *History and Digest....*, p. 1742.

said heirs are the legal representatives, by the authorities of Spain in the island of Cuba or within the maritime jurisdiction thereof, since the commencement of the present insurrection.

1. It is agreed that all such claims shall be submitted to arbitrators, one to be appointed by the Secretary of State of the United States, another by the Envoy Extraordinary and Minister Plenipotentiary of Spain at Washington, and these two to name an umpire who shall decide all questions upon which they shall be unable to agree; and in case the place of either arbitrator or of the umpire shall from any cause become vacant, such vacancy shall be filled forthwith in the manner herein provided for the original appointment.

2. The arbitrators and umpire so named shall meet at Washington within one month from the date of their appointment and shall, before proceeding to business, make and subscribe a solemn declaration that they will impartially hear and determine, to the best of their judgment and according to public law, and the treaties in force between the two countries, all such claims as shall, in conformity with this agreement, be laid before them on the part of the Government of the United States; and such declaration shall be entered upon the record of their proceedings.

3. Each Government may name an advocate to appear before the arbitrators or the umpire, to represent the interest of the parties respectively.

4. The arbitrators shall have full power subject to these stipulations and it shall be their duty, before proceeding with the hearing and decision of any case, to make and publish convenient rules prescribing the time and manner of the presentation of claims and of the proof thereof; and any disagreement with reference to the said rules of proceeding shall be decided by the umpire. It is understood that a reasonable period shall be allowed for the presentation of the proofs; that all claims and the testimony in favor of them shall be presented only through the Government of the United States; that the award made in each case shall be in writing and if indemnity be given, the sum to be paid shall be expressed in the gold coin of the United States.

5. The arbitrators shall have juridiction of all claims presented to them by the Government of the United States for injuries done to citizens of the United States by the authorities of Spain in Cuba since the first day of October, 1868. Adjudications of the tribunals in Cuba, concerning citizens of the United States, made in the absence of the parties interested, or in violation of international law, or of the guarantees

and forms provided for in the treaty of October 27, 1795, between the United States and Spain, may be reviewed by the arbitrators, who shall make such award in any such case as they shall deem just. No judgment of a Spanish tribunal, disallowing the affirmation of a party that he is a citizen of the United States shall prevent the arbitrators from hearing a reclamation presented in behalf of said party by the United States Government. Nevertheless, in any case heard by the arbitrators, the Spanish Government may traverse the allegation of American citizenship and thereupon competent and sufficient proof thereof will be required. The Commission having recognized the quality of American citizens in the claimants, they will acquire the rights accorded to them by the present stipulations as such citizens. And it is further agreed that the arbitrators shall not have juridiction of any reclamation made in behalf of a native-born spanish subject naturalized in the United States if it shall appear, that the same subject-matter having been adjudicated by a competent tribunal in Cuba and the claimant, having appeared therein, either in person or by his duly appointed attorney and being required by the laws of Spain to make a declaration of his nationality, failed to declare that he was a citizen of the United States; in such case and for the purposes of this arbitration, it shall be deemed and taken that the claimant, by his own default, had renounced his allegiance to the United States. And it is further agreed that the arbitrators shall not have jurisdiction of any demands growing out of contracts.

6. The expenses of the arbitration will be defrayed by a percentage to be added to the amount awarded. The compensation of the arbitrators and umpire shall not exceed three thousand dollars each; the same allowance shall be made to each of the two advocates representing respectively the two Governments; and the arbitrators may employ a Secretary at a compensation not exceeding the sum of five dollars a day for every day actually and necessarily given to the business of the arbitration.

7. The two Governments will accept the awards made in the several cases submitted to the said arbitration as final and conclusive, and will give full effect to the same in good faith and as soon as possible.

I avail myself of this opportunity to renew to your Excellency the assurance of my most distinguished consideration. [1]

---

[1] *Treaties and Conventions between the United States and ther Powers*, 1776 to 1887, p. 1025.

Dès le 12 février 1871 le Gouvernement espagnol acquiesçait à l'arrangement proposé. Successivement le 23 février 1881 et le 6 mai 1882 deux nouveaux articles furent ajoutés au memorandum reproduit plus haut dans le but de fixer la date finale de l'arbitrage.

Agreements for extending the time for the termination of the claims commission under the agreement of February 12, 1871.

8. All claims for injuries done to citizens of the United States by the authorities of Spain in Cuba, since the first day of October, A. D. 1868, which have not heretofore been presented by the Government of the United States to the Commission now sitting in Washington under the agreement of February 12, 1871, shall be so presented to the said Commission within sixty days, from this twenty third day of February, 1881, unless in any case where reasons for delay shall be established to the satisfaction of the Arbitrators, and in any such case the period for presenting the claim may be extended by them to any time not exceeding thirty days longer.

The Commission shall be bound to examine and decide upon every claim which may have been presented to it, or which shall hereafter be presented to it in accordance with this article, within one year from the 12th day of May, 1881. Provided, however, that in any particular case in which delay in completing the defense shall make an extension for the claimant's proofs or final argument, or decision, beyond this period, necessary for justice, such extension may be granted, by the Arbitrators, or, on their disagreement by the Umpire.

The Arbitrators shall have full power, subject to these stipulations, to make and publish convenient rules for carrying into effect this additional Article, and any disagreement with reference to such rules shall be decided by the Umpire.

9. It being impossible for the Commission, in consequence of the death of the Arbitrator and of the Advocate on the part of the United States, to examine and decide within one year from the 12th of May 1881 each and every claim which has been presented, it is agreed that the term aforesaid be extented to the 1st of January 1883, for the sole purpose of permitting the Commission to examine and decide the claims actually pending.

And it is further agreed to this end

1st. That no evidence in any case shall be received after the 15th day of June next.

2nd. That no printed or written brief or argument before the Arbitrators shall be filed on behalf of any claimant after the 15th day of July 1882.

3rd. That no printed or written brief or argument shall be filed in reply on behalf of Spain after the 15th day of September 1882.

4th. That no oral arguments shall be heard by the Arbitrators after the 1st day of November 1882.

5th. That no arguments either written or oral shall be made before the Umpire except on his written request addressed to the Commission, specifying the time within which he will hear or receive said arguments.

6th. That the Arbitrators may establish in accordance with the preceding stipulations convenient rules for the better and more rapid despatch of the business of the Commission, and any disagreement which may arise between them as to those rules or their interpretation, shall be decided by the Umpire.

Decisions in every pending case shall be given by both Arbitrators before the 27th day of December next: jointly if they agree, separately when they disagree.

All cases in which on that day the two Arbitrators shall not have agreed, or in which neither Arbitrator shall have rendered a decision, shall go to the Umpire.

All cases in which the American Arbitrator shall have failed to give a decision shall be rejected or allowed, as the case may be in the form determined by the decision of the Arbitrator of Spain if the Spanish Arbitrator shall have given a decision and vice-versa all cases in which the Spanish Arbitrator shall have failed to give a decision shall be allowed or rejected, as the case may be in the form determined by the decision of the American Arbitrator if the American Arbitrator shall have given a decision: it being the purpose of both parties to have the work of the Arbitrators finished before December 27, 1882.

The Umpire is requested to render decisions before January 1, 1883, in all cases submitted to him in order that the work of the Commission may cease on that day. But if the Umpire fails to comply with this request, decisions rendered by him after that day shall be respected by both parties, notwithstanding that the Commission shall be deemed to be terminated and dissolved after the 1st day of January 1883.»

Les arbitres se réunirent pour la première fois le 31 mai 1871 et terminèrent leurs travaux le 27 décembre 1882. Les dernières décisions du surarbitre furent enregistrées le 22 février 1883. Les demandes soumises aux arbitres sont résumées dans le tableau suivant:

[1] *Treaties and Conventions* ... 1776—1887, p. 1033, 1035.

Dates	Number of claims			Total decided	Amounts exclusive of interest	
	Filed	Dismissed	Allowed		Claimed	Awarded
					$	$
February 12, 1871 to June 30, 1872 . . .	96	—	—	—	—	—
June 30, 1872 to June 30, 1873	10	—	—	—	—	—
» 30, 1873 » » 30, 1874	8	43	2	45	1,647,786.93	6,200.—
» 30, 1874 » » 30, 1875	1	1	5	6	772,932.50	117,635.—
» 30, 1875 » » 30, 1876	3	9	3	12	3,216,832.39	756,180.—
» 30, 1876 » » 30, 1877	3	5	2	7	476,348.89	5,585.—
» 30, 1877 » » 30, 1878	2	9	1	10	1,147,092.98	500.—
» 30, 1878 » » 30, 1879	2	2	1	3	154,719.47	60,000.—
» 30, 1879 » » 30, 1880	8	6	2	8	416,258.24	15,100.—
» 30, 1880 » » 30, 1881	7	6	7	13	1,619,257.—	155,690.33
» 30, 1881 » » 30, 1882	—	14	1	15	8,038,910.10	34,000.—
» 30, 1882 » » 30, 1883	—	10	11	21	12,823,442.82	142,559.62
Total	140	105	35	140	30,313,581.32	1,293,450.55

J. B. MOORE. *History and Digest*......, p. 1050.

Nous croyons intéressant de compléter les documents reproduits ci-dessus par les règles de procédure adoptées par les arbitres pour la réalisation de leur mission.

Regulations now in force, of the Commission on claims of citizens of the United States against Spain, by agreement of February 12, 1871, adopted June 10, 1871.

I. In addition to the representation of his claim, and the exhibits or proofs in support thereof, which may have been or shall be presented to or filed in the Department of State of the United States, every claimant shall file, in the office of this Commission, a statement of his claim in the form of a memorial.

II. Every memorial shall show the full name of the claimant, his place of birth, and, if he be a naturalized citizen of the United States, the time and place and the Style of court before which his « declaration of intention » shall have been made, and the time and place and the style of court by which his letters of naturalization shall have been granted: and authenticated copies of both these acts shall be exhibited with the memorial. Secondary evidence will be admitted upon proper foundation according to recognized rules of evidence.

III. If the claim be preferred on behalf of a firm or association of persons the name of each person interested, both at the date the claim accrued and at the date of verifying the memorial, must be stated, with the proportions of the interest of each person.

IV. Each memorial shall state the particulars of the claim, the general ground on which it is founded under the public international law, and the amount claimed. It shall be verified by the oath of the claimant, or, if the claim be by a firm or association of persons, by the oath of one of them; or in the case of a corporation, by the oats of the president, secretary, or other officer thereof: such oaths to be taken, if in the United States, before any officer having power to administer judicial oaths according to the law of the place where administered and the official character of such officer shall be duly authenticated according to the laws of said place. If such oath be taken without the territory of the United States, it may be administered by the legation or nearest consul of the United States.

V. The Arbitrators may, in their discretion, order any claimant to answer on oath such interrogatories as may be submitted to the Commission for the purpose by or on behalf of either government.

VI. Every claimant shall be allowed two months' time, next following the filing of his memorial, in which to take and file his proofs, and three months next following the same shall be allowed for the taking and filing of proofs on the part of Spain; which respective periods may be prolonged by special order on cause shown.

VII. All depositions shall be taken on notice, specifying the time and place of taking, to be filed in the office of the Commission, with a copy of the interrogatories, or upon a statement in writing by the advocate of the government adducing the witness, to be filed in like manner, showing the subject of the particular examination with sufficient precision to be accepted by the advocate of the government against whom such witness is to be produced, to be signified by his indorsement thereon; such interrogatories or statements to be filed in the office of the Commission at least twenty-one days before the day named for the examination. Every deposition taken, either in the United States or in Spain or her possessions shall be taken before some officer competent to administer judicial oaths under the laws of the place, whose official character shall be duly authenticated according to said laws; and each witness shall state whether he is interested, directly or indirectly, and how, in the matter of the claim, and whether he is agent or attorney for any party interested directly or indirectly therein.

Depositions taken outside of the United States, or of Spain and her possessions, may be taken before the legation or nearest consul of either Government, in the election of the advocate thereof.

VIII. Public acts, decrees, orders, laws, and other official instruments and copies, shall be authenticated according to the country from which they emanate.

IX. Such documents and proofs are liable to be impeached for fraud, in any manner recognized in similar cases, by the laws of the country from which they emanate, or by the laws of nations.

X. After the proofs on the part of Spain shall have been closed and filed, the Commission shall, in every case, when the claimant shall desire to take rebutting proof, accord a reasonable time, in its discretion, for the taking of such rebutting proof.

XI. The rules of evidence, as to the competency, relevancy, and effect of the same, shall be determined by the Commission, in view of these regulations, the laws of the two nations, and the public law.

XII. Each memorial, and all exhibits and proofs, shall be filed in original manuscript, and the same, and all matter, including briefs and arguments, shall be printed at the expense of the party adducing or propounding the same; at least thirty printed copies of each being filed.

XIII. All cases will be submitted on printed arguments, but brief oral explanations will be received at all times from the advocate of either government.

Arguments of special counsel will be received in print, when submitted by the advocate of either government and not otherwise.

XIV. All claims filed with the commission be entered in a docket to be kept by the Secretary. On the first Monday in December next the Arbitrators will proceed to call and hear any cases which may be ready for hearing in conformity with these regulation.

XV. The Secretary shall take charge of all the papers belonging to the Commission. He will not allow them to be withdrawn from the office, but will furnish to parties, or special counsel, all convenient opportunity for inspecting the same, and making extracts thereform in his presence.

XVI. In all cases heretofore filed before this Commission, the memorials and exhibits, and testimony now on file in the English language shall be translated into Spanish, and such translations shall be furnished and filed by the respective claimants on or before the first day of June 1872.

In all cases of memorials, or of exhibits and testimony hereafter to be filed, the claimants are required to furnish such translations, and to file the same, together with the English originals. Of the printed copies now required by the rules, fifteen shall be in English and fifteen in Spanish.

Printed briefs and arguments may be filed in the English language only, as heretofore.

By order of the Commission [1].

L. Amérique du Nord, Grande-Bretagne.

8 mai 1871.

Le traité du 8 mai 1871 a eu pour objet d'organiser quatre arbitrages, dont le plus important, celui relatif à l'Alabama, a fixé tout particulièrement l'attention des juristes et de l'opinion publique. Nous consacrons un paragraphe spécial à chacun de ces arbitrages.

A. — Le premier de ces arbitrages a eu pour objet de déterminer les dommages causés par des corsaires, armés ou accueillis dans des ports de la Grande-Bretagne ou de ses colonies, et dont le plus redoutable avait été l'Alabama. Le tribunal arbitral, qui siégea à Genève, était composé de cinq arbitres, qui accordèrent, aux Etats-Unis de l'Amérique du Nord, une indemnité de 15,500,000 $, à répartir entre les citoyens américains préjudiciés.

Treaty concluded at Washington, on May 8, 1871, between Great Britain and the United States of America for the settlement of claims by arbitration.

ARTICLE I. Whereas difference have arisen between the Government of the United States and the Government of Her Britannic Majesty, and still exist, growing out of the acts committed by the several vessels which have given rise to the claims generically known as the « Alabama Claims » :

And whereas Her Britannic Majesty has authorized Her High Commissioners and Plenipotentiaries to express, in a friendly spirit, the regret felt by Her Majesty's Government for the escape, under whatever circumstances, of the Alabama and other vessels from British ports, and for the depredations committed by those vessels :

Now, in order to remove and ajust all complaints and claims on the part of the United States, and to provide for the speedy settlement of such claims which are not admitted by Her Britannic Majesty's Government, the High Contracting Parties agree that all the said claims, growing out of acts committed by the aforesaid vessels, and generically known as the « Alabama Claims » shall be referred to a Tribunal of Arbitration to be composed of five Arbitrators, to be appointed in the following manner, that is to say: one shall be named by the President of the United States; one shall be named by Her Britannic Majesty; His Majesty the King of Italy shall be requested to name one; the President of the Swiss Confederation shall be requested to name one; and His Majesty the Emperor of Brazil shall be requested to name one.

In case of the death, absence, or incapacity to serve of any or either of the said Arbitrators, or, in the event of either of the said Arbitrators omitting or declining or ceasing to act as such, the President of the United States, or Her Britannic Majesty, or His Majesty the King of Italy, or the President of the Swiss Confederation, or His Majesty the Emperor of Brazil, as the case may be, may fortwith name another person to act as Arbitrator in the place and stead of the Arbitrator originally named by such head of a State.

---

[1] F. DE MARTENS. *Nouveau recueil général*, 2ᵐᵉ série, t. I, p. 19; — *Archives de droit international et de législation comparée*, 1874, p. 118.

And in the event of the refusal or omission for two months, after receipt of the request from either of the High Contracting Parties, of His Majesty the King of Italy, or the President of the Swiss Confederation, or His Majesty the Emperor of Brazil, to name an Arbitrator, either to fill the original appointment, or in the place of one who may have died, be absent or incapacitated, or who may omit, decline, or from any cause cease to act as such Arbitrator, His Majesty the King of Sweden and Norway shall be requested to name one or more persons, as the case may be, to act as such Arbitrator or Arbitrators.

ARTICLE II. The Arbitrators shall meet at Geneva, in Switzerland, at the earliest convenient day after they shall have been named and shall proceed impartially and carefully to examine and decide all questions that shall be laid before them on the part of the Governments of the United States and Her Britannic Majesty respectively. All questions considered by the tribunal, including the final Award, shall be decided by a majority of all the Arbitrators.

Each of the High Contracting Parties shall also name one person to attend the Tribunal as its Agent to represent it generally in all matters connected with the arbitration.

ARTICLE III. The written or printed case of each of the two Parties, accompanied by the documents, the official correspondence and other evidence on which each relies, shall be delivered in duplicate to each of the Arbitrators and to the Agent of the other Party as soon as may be after the organization of the tribunal, but within a period not exceeding six months from the date of the exchange of the ratifications of this treaty.

ARTICLE IV. Within four months after the delivery on both sides of the written or printed case, either Party may, in like manner, deliver in duplicate to each of the said Arbitrators, and to the Agent of the other Party, a counter case and additional documents, correspondence, and evidence, in reply to the case, documents, correspondence, and evidence so presented by the other Party.

The Arbitrators may, however, extend the time for delivering such counter case, documents, correspondence, and evidence, when, in their judgment, it becomes necessary, in consequence of the distance of the place from which the evidence to be presented is to be procured.

If in the case submitted to the Arbitrators either party shall have specified or alluded to any report or document in its own exclusive possession without annexing a copy, such Party shall be bound, if the other Party thinks proper to apply for it, to furnish that Party with a copy thereof: and either Party may call upon the other through the Arbitrators, to produce the originals or certified copies of any papers adduced as evidence, giving in each instance such reasonable notice as the Arbitrators may require.

ARTICLE V. It shall be the duty of the Agent of each Party, within two months after the expiration of the time limited for the delivery of the counter case on both sides, to deliver in duplicate to each of the said Arbitrators and to the Agent of the other party a written or printed argument showing the points and referring to the evidence upon which his Government relies; and the Arbitrators may, if they desire further elucidation with regard to any point, require a written or printed statement or argument, or oral argument by counsel upon it; but in such case the other Party shall be entitled to reply either orally or in writing as the case may be.

ARTICLE VI. In deciding the matters submitted to the Arbitrators, they shall be governed by the following three rules, which are agreed upon by the High Contracting Parties as rules to be taken as applicable to the case, and by such principles of international law not inconsistent therewith as the Arbitrators shall determine to have been applicable to the case.

RULES. *A neutral Government is bound:*

FIRST, *to use due diligence to prevent the fitting out, arming, or equipping, within its jurisdiction, of any vessel which it has reasonable ground to believe is intended to cruise or to carry on war against a power with which it is at peace; and also to use like diligence to prevent the departure from its jurisdiction of any vessel intended to cruise or carry on war as above, such vessel having been specially adapted, in whole or in part, within such jurisdiction, to warlike use.*

SECONDLY, *not to permit or suffer either belligerent to make use of its ports or waters as the base of naval operations against the other, or for the purpose of the renewal or augmentation of military supplies or arms, or the recruitment of men.*

THIRDLY, *to exercise due diligence in its own ports and waters, and as to all person within its jurisdiction, to prevent any violations of the foregoing obligations and duties.*

Her Britannic Majesty has commanded Her High Commissioners and Plenipotentiaries to declare that Her Majesty's Government cannot assent to the foregoing rules as a statement of principles of international law which were in force at the time when the claims mentioned in

Article I arose, but that Her Majesty's Government, in order to evince its desire of strengthening the friendly relations between the two countries and of making satisfactory provision for the future, agrees that, in deciding the questions between the two countries arising out of those claims, the Arbitrators should assume that Her Majesty's Government had undertaken to act upon the principles set forth in these rules.

And the High Contracting Parties agree to observe these rules as between themselves in future, and to bring them to the knowledge of other maritime Powers, and to invite them to accede to them.

ARTICLE VII. The decision of the Tribunal shall, if possible, be made within three months from the close of the argument on both sides.

It shall be made in writing and dated, and shall be signed by the Arbitrators who may assent to it.

The said Tribunal shall first determine as to each vessel separately whether Great Britain has, by any act or omission, failed to fulfil any of the duties set forth in the foregoing three rules or recognized by the principles of international law not inconsistent with such rules, and shall certify such fact as to each of the said vessels. In case the Tribunal find that Great Britain has failed to fulfil any duty or duties as aforesaid, it may, if it think proper, proceed to award a sum in gross to be paid by Great Britain to the United States for all the claims referred to it: and in such case the gross sum to awarded shall be paid in coin by the Government of the United States at Washington, within twelve months after the date of the award.

The award shall be in duplicate, one copy whereof shall be delivered to the Agent of the United States for His Government and the other copy shall be delivered to the Agent of Great Britain for His Government.

ARTICLE VIII. Each Government shall pay its own Agent and provide for the proper remuneration of the counsel employed by it and of the Arbitrator appointed by it, and for the expense of preparing and submitting its case to the Tribunal. All other expenses connected with the arbitration shall be defrayed by the two Governments in equal moieties.

ARTICLE IX. The Arbitrators shall keep an accurate record of their proceedings and may appoint and employ the necessary officers to assist them.

ARTICLE X. In case the Tribunal finds that Great Britain has failed to fulfil any duty or duties as aforesaid, and does not award a sum in gross, the High Contracting Parties agree that a Board of Assessors shall be appointed to ascertain and determine what claims are valid, and what amount or amounts shall be paid by Great Britain to the United States on account of the liability arising from such failure, as to each vessel, according to the extent of such liability as decided by the Arbitrators.

The Board of Assessors shall be constituted as follows: one member thereof shall be named by the President of the United States, one member thereof shall be named by Her Britannic Majesty, and one member thereof shall be named by the representative at Washington of His Majesty the King of Italy; and in case of a vacancy happening from any cause, it shall be filled in the same manner in which the original appointment was made.

As soon as possible after such nominations the Board of Assessors shall be organized in Washington, with power to hold their sittings there, or in New-York, or in Boston. The members thereof shall severally subscribe a solemn declaration that they will impartially and carefully examine and decide, to the best of their judgment and according to justice and equity, all matters submitted to them, and shall forthwith proceed, under such rules and regulations as they may prescribe, to the investigation of the claims which shall be presented to them by the Government of the United States, and shall examine and decide upon them in such order and manner as they may think proper, but upon such evidence or information only as shall be furnished by or on behalf of the Governments of the United States and of Great Britain, respectively. They shall be bound to hear on each separate claim, if required, one person on behalf of each Government, as counsel or agent. A majority of the Assessors in each case shall be sufficient for a decision.

The decision of the Assessors shall be given upon each claim in writing, and shall be signed by them respectively and dated.

Every claim shall be presented to the Assessors within six months from the day of their first meeting but they may, for good cause shown, extend the time for the presentation of any claim to a further period not exceeding three months.

The Assessors shall report to each Government, at or before the expiration of one year from the date of their first meeting, the amount of claims decided by them up to the date of such report; if further claims then remain undecided, they shall make a further report at or before the expiration of two years from the date of such first meeting; and in case any claims remain undetermined at that time, they shall make a final report within a further period of six months.

The report or reports shall be made in duplicate, and one copy thereof shall be delivered to the secretary of State of United States, and one copy thereof to the representative of Her Britannic Majesty at Washington.

All sums of money which may be awarded under this article shall be payable at Washington, in coin, within twelve months after the delivery of each report.

The Board of Assessors may employ such clerks as they shall think necessary.

The expenses of the Board of Assessors shall be borne equally by the two Governments and paid from time to time, as may be found expedient, on the production of accounts certified by the Board. The remuneration of the Assessors shall also be paid by the two Governments in equal moieties in a similar manner.

ARTICLE XI. The High Contracting Parties engage to consider the result of the proceedings of the Tribunal of Arbitration and of the Board of Assessors, should such Board be appointed, as a full, perfect and final settlement of all the claims hereinbefore refered to; and further engage that every such claim, whether the same may or may not have been presented to the notice of, made, preferred, or laid before the Tribunal or Board, shall, from and after the conclusion of the proceedings of the Tribunal or Board, be considered and treated as finally settled, barred and thenceforth inadmissible. [1]

Award pronounced by the Tribunal of Arbitration on the Alabama Claims, Geneva, September 14, 1872.

Her Britannic Majesty and the United States of America having agreed by Article 1 of the treaty concluded and signed at Washington the 8th of May 1871 to refer all the claims « generically known as the Alabama claims » to a Tribunal of Arbitration to be composed of five Arbitrators named: one by Her Britannic Majesty, one by the President of the United States, one by His Majesty the King of Italy, one by the President of the Swiss Confederation, one by His Majesty the Emperor of Brazil; and Her Britannic Majesty, the President of the United States, His Majesty the King of Italy, the President of the Swiss Confederation, and His Majesty the Emperor of Brazil, having respectively named their Arbitrators to wit:

Her Britannic Majesty, Sir Alexander James Edmund Cockburn, Baronet, a Member of Her Majesty's Privy Council, Lord Chief Justice of

[1] *Treaties and Conventions* ...., 1776-1887, p. 479-483.

England; the President of the United States, Charles Francis Adams, Esquire; His Majesty the King of Italy, His Excellency Count Frederick Sclopis of Salerano, a Knight of the Order of the Annunciata, Minister of State, Senator of the Kingdom of Italy; the President of the Swiss Confederation, M. Jacques Stæmpfli; His Majesty the Emperor of Brazil, His Excellency Marcos Antonio d'Araujo, Viscount d'Itajubá, a Grandee of the Empire of Brazil, Member of the Council of His Majesty the Emperor of Brazil, and His Envoy Extraordinary and Minister Plenipotentiary in France;

And the five Arbitrators above named having assembled at Geneva (in Switzerland) in one of the Chambers of the Hôtel de Ville on the 15th of December 1871, in conformity whith the terms of the IInd Article of the treaty of Washington of the 8th of May of that year, and having proceeded to the inspection and verification of their respective powers, which were found duly authenticated, the Tribunal of Arbitration was declared duly organized.

The Agents named by each of the High Contracting Parties, by virtue of the same Article II to wit: for Her Britannic Majesty, Charles Stuart Aubrey, Lord Tenterden, a Peer of the United Kingdom, Companion of the Most Honourable Order of the Bath, Assistant Under-Secretary of State for Foreign Affairs; and for the United States of America, John C. Bancroft Davis, Esquire; whose powers were found likewise duly authenticated, then delivered to each of the Arbitrators the printed Case prepared by each of the two Parties, accompanied by the documents, the official correspondence and other evidence, on which each relied, in conformity whith the terms of the IIIrd Article of the said treaty.

In virtue of the decision made by the Tribunal at its first session, the Counter-Case and additional documents, correspondence, and evidence referred to in Article IV of the said treaty were delivered by the respective Agents of the two Parties to the Secretary of the Tribunal on the 15th of April 1872, at the Chamber of Conference, at the Hôtel de Ville of Geneva.

The Tribunal, in accordance with the vote of adjournment passed at their second session, held on the 16th December 1871, reassembled at Geneva on the 15th of June 1872; and the Agent of each of the parties duly delivered to each of the Arbitrators and to the Agent of the other Party the printed Argument referred to in Article IV of the said Treaty.

The Tribunal having since fully taken into their consideration the treaty and also the Cases, Counter-Cases, documents, evidence, and Arguments and likewise all other communications made to them by the two Parties during the progress of their sittings, and having impartially and carefully examined the same,

Has arrived at the decision embodied in the present award:

Whereas, having regard to the VIth and VIIth Articles of the said treaty, the Arbitrators are bound under the terms of the said VIth Article « in deciding the matters submitted to them, to be governed by the three Rules therein specified and by such principles of International Law, not inconsistent therewith, as the Arbitrators shall determine to have been applicable to the case ».

And whereas the « due diligence » referred to in the first and third of the said Rules ought to be excercised by neutral Governments in exact proportion to the risks to which either of the belligerents may be exposed, from a failure to fulfil the obligations of neutrality on their part;

And whereas the circumstances out of which the fact constituting the subject-matter of the present controversy arose, were of a nature to call for the exercise on the part of Her Britannic Majesty's Government, of all possible solicitude for the observance of the rights and duties involved in the proclamation of neutrality issued by Her Majesty on the 13th day of May, 1861;

And whereas the effects of a violation of neutrality, committed by means of the construction, equipment and armament of a vessel, are not done away with by any commission which the Government of the belligerent power, benefited by the violation of neutrality, may afterwards have granted to that vessel; and the ultimate step, by which the offense is completed, cannot be admissible as a ground for the absolution of the offender, nor can the consumation of his fraud become the means of establishing his innocence,

And whereas the privilege of exterritoriality accorded to vessels of war has been admitted into the law of nations, not as an absolute right, but solely as a proceeding founded on the principle of courtesy and mutual deference between different nations, and therefore can never be appealed to for the protection of acts done in violation of neutrality;

And whereas the absence of a previous notice cannot be regarded as a failure in any consideration required by the law of nations in those cases in which a vessel carries with it its own condemnation;

And whereas, in order to impart to any supplies of coal a character inconsistent with the second Rules prohibiting the use of neutral port, or waters, as a base of naval operations for a belligerent, it is necessary that the said supplies should be connected with special circumstances

of time, of persons, or of place, which may combine to give them such character;

And whereas with respect to the vessel called the Alabama, it clearly results from all the facts relative to the construction of the ship at first designated by the number « 290 » in the port of Liverpool, and its equipment and armament in the vicinity of Terceira through the agency of the vessels called the Agrippina and the Bahama, dispatched from Great Britain to that end, that the British Government failed to use due diligence in the performance of its neutral obligations: and especially that it omitted notwithstanding the warnings and official representations made by the diplomatic agents of the United States during the construction of the said number « 290 », to take in due time any effective measures of prevention, and that those orders which it did give at last for the detention of the vessel were issued so late that their execution was not practicable;

And whereas, after the escape of that vessel, the measures taken for its pursuit and arrest were so imperfect as to lead to no result, and therefore cannot be considered sufficient to release Great Britain from the responsibility already incurred;

And whereas, in despite of the violations of the neutrality of Great Britain committed by the « 290 » this same vessel, later known as the Confederate cruizer Alabama, was on several occasion freely admitted into the ports of Colonies of Great Britain, instead of being proceeded against as it ought to have been in any and every port within British jurisdiction in which it might have been found;

And whereas the Government of Her Britannic Majesty cannot justify itself for a failure in due diligence on the plea of the insufficiency of the legal means of action which it possessed;

Four of the Arbitrators for the reasons above assigned, and the fifth for reasons separately assigned by him, are of opinion:

That Great Britain has in this case failed, by omission, to fulfil the duties prescribed in the first and the third of the Rules established by the VIth Article of the treaty of Washington.

And whereas, with respect to the vessel called the Florida it results from all the facts relative to the construction of the Oreto in the port of Liverpool, and to its issue therefrom, which facts failed to induce the authorities in Great Britain to resort to measures adequate to prevent the violation of the neutrality of that nation, notwithstanding the warnings and repeated representations of the Agents of the United States that Her Majesty's Government has failed to use due diligence to fulfil the duties of neutrality;

And whereas it likewise results from all the facts relative to the stay of the Oreto at Nassau, to her issue from that port, to her enlistment of men, to her supplies and to her armament, with the co-operation of the British vessel Prince Alfred, at Green Cay, that there was negligence on the part of the British colonial authorities;

And whereas, notwithstanding the violation of the neutrality of Great Britain committed by the Oreto, this same vessel, later known as the Confederate cruiser Florida, was nevertheless on several occasions freely admitted into the ports of British Colonies;

And whereas the judicial acquittal of the Oreto at Nassau cannot relieve Great Britain from the responsibility incurred by her under the principles of international law; nor can the fact of the entry of the Florida into the Confederate port of Mobile, and of its stay there during four months extinguish the responsibility previously to that time incurred by Great Britain;

For these reasons, the Tribunal, by a majority of four voices to one, is of opinion:

That Great Britain has in this case failed, by omission to fulfil the duties prescribed in the first, in the second and in the third of the Rules established by Article VI of the Treaty of Washington.

And whereas, with respect to the vessel called the Shenandoah it results from all the facts relative to the departure from London of the merchant-vessel the Sea King and to the transformation of that ship into a Confederate cruiser under the name of the Shenandoah near the Island of Madeira, that the Government of Her Britannic Majesty is not chargeable with any failure, down to that date, in the use of due diligence to fulfil the duties of neutrality;

But whereas it results from all the facts connected with the stay of the Shenandoah at Melbourne and especially with the augmentation which the British Government itself admit to have been clandestinely effected of her force, by the enlistment of men within that port, that there was negligence on the part of the authorities at that place;

For these reasons, the Tribunal is unanimously of opinion:

That Great Britain has not failed, by any act or omission to fulfil any of the duties prescribed by the three Rules of Article VI in the Treaty of Washington or by the principles of international law not inconsistent therewith in respect to the vessel called the Shenandoah, during the period of time anterior to her entry into the port of Melbourne. And, by a majority of three to two voices, the Tribunal decides that Great Britain has failed, by omission, to fulfil the duties prescribed by the second and third of the Rules aforesaid in the case of this same vessel, from and after her entry into Hobson's Bay, and is

therefore responsible for acts committed by that vessel after her departure from Melbourne, on the 18th day of February, 1865.

And so far as relates to the vessels called: the Tuscaloosa (Tender to the «Alabama»), the Clarence, the Tacony, and the Archer (Tenders to the «Florida»), the Tribunal is unanimously of opinion:

That such tenders or auxiliary vessels, being properly regarded as accessories, must necessarily follow the lot of their principals, and be submitted to the same decision which applies to them respectively.

And so far as relates to the vessel called Retribution, the Tribunal, by a majority of three to two voices, is of opinion:

That Great Britain has not failed by any act or omission, to fulfil any of the duties prescribed by the three Rules of Article VI in the Treaty of Washington or by the principles of international law not inconsistent therewith.

And so far as relates tho the vessels called: the Georgia, the Sumter, the Nashville, the Tallahassee and the Chickamauga respectively, the Tribunal is unanimously of opinion:

That Great Britain has not failed, by any act or omission to fulfil any of the duties prescribed by the three Rules of Article VI in the Treaty of Washington or by the principles of international law not inconsistent therewith.

And so far as relates to the vessels called: the Sallies, the Jefferson Davis, the Music, the Boston and the V. H. Joy, respectively, the Tribunal is unanimously of opinion:

That they ought to be excluded from consideration for want of evidence.

And whereas, so far as relates to the particulars of the indemnity claimed by the United States, the costs of pursuit of the Confederate cruisers are not, in the Judgment of the Tribunal, properly distinguishable from the general expenses of the war carried on by the United States;

The Tribunal is, therefore, of opinion, by a majority of three to two voices:

That there is no ground for awarding to the United States any sum by way of indemnity under this head.

And whereas prospective earnings cannot properly be made the subject of compensation, inasmuch as they depend in their nature upon future and uncertain contingencies:

The Tribunal is unanimously of opinion:

That there is no ground for awarding to the United States any sum by way of indemnity under this head.

And whereas, in order to arrive at an equitable compensation for the damages which have been sustained, it is necessary to set aside all double claims for the same losses, and all claims for « gross freights », so far as they exceed « nett freights » ;

And whereas it is just and reasonable to allow interest at a reasonable rate;

And whereas, in accordance with the spirit and letter of the Treaty of Washington, it is preferable to adopt the form of adjudication of a sum in gross, rather than to refer the subject of compensation for further discussion and deliberation to a Board of Assessors as provided by Article X of the said treaty;

The Tribunal making use of the authority conferred upon it by Article VII of the said treaty, by a majority of four voices to one, awards to the United Staates a sum of 15,500,000 dollars in gold as the indemnity to be paid by Great Britain to the United States for the satisfaction of all the claims referred to the consideration of the Tribunal conformably to the provisions contained in Article VII of the aforesaid treaty.

And in accordance with the terms of Article XI of the said treaty, the Tribunal declares that « all the claims referred to in the treaty as submitted to the Tribunal are hereby fully, perfectly, and finally settled. »

Furthermore it declares, that « each and every one of the said claims, whether the same may or may not have been presented to the notice of, or made, preferred, or laid before the Tribunal, shall henceforth be considered and treated as finally settled, barred, and inadmissible. »

In testimony whereof this present Decision and Award has been made in duplicate, and signed by the Arbitrators who have given their assent thereto, the whole being in exact conformity with the provisions of Article VII of the said treaty of Washington.

Made and concluded at the Hôtel de Ville of Geneva in Switzerland, the 14ᵗʰ day of the month of September, in the year of our Lord 1872. [1]

B. — Le second arbitrage, institué le 8 mai 1871, a eu pour objet de statuer sur des réclamations réciproques de citoyens des deux pays contractants; la commission arbitrale fut composée de trois arbitres et siégea du 26 septembre 1871 au 25 septembre 1873. Par une convention du 18 janvier 1873, les arbitres furent autorisés à déplacer le siège du tribunal, primitivement fixé à Washington. Nous croyons intéressant de compléter les articles consacrés à cet arbitrage par la reproduction

---

[1] F. DE MARTENS. *Nouveau Recueil Général*, t. XX, p. 767.

des règles de procédure adoptées par les arbitres le 27 septembre 1871.

Treaty concluded at Washington, on May 8, 1871, between Great Britain and the United States of America for the settlement of claims by arbitration.

. . . .

ARTICLE XII. The High Contracting Parties agree that all claims on the part of corporations, companies or private individuals, citizens of the United States, upon the Government of Her Britannic Majesty, arising out of acts committed against the persons or property of citizens of the United States during the period between the thirteenth of April, eighteen hundred and sixty-one, and the ninth of April eighteen hundred and sixty-five, inclusive, not being claims growing out of the acts of the vessels referred to in Article I of this treaty, and all claims, with the like exception, on the part of corporations, companies, or private individuals, subjects of Her Britannic Majesty, upon the Government of the United States, arising out of acts committed against the persons or property of subjects of Her Britannic Majesty during the same period, which may have been presented to either Government for its interposition with the other, and which yet remain unsettled, as well as any other such claims which may be presented within the time specified in Article XIV of this treaty, shall be referred to three Commissioners, to be appointed in the following manner, that is to say: one Commissioner shall be named by the President of the United States, one by Her Britannic Majesty, and a third by the President of the United States and Her Britannic Majesty conjointly ; and in case the third Commissioner shall not have been so named within a period of three months from the date of the exchange of the ratifications of this treaty, then the third Commissioner shall be named by the Representative at Washington of His Majesty the King of Spain. In case of the death, absence, or incapacity of any Commissioner, or in the event of any Commissioner omitting or ceasing to act, the vacancy shall be filled in the manner hereinbefore provided for making the original appointment; the period of three months in case of such substitution being calculated from the date of the happening of the vacancy.

The Commissioners so named shall meet at Washington at the earliest convenient period after they have been respectively named; and shall before proceeding to any business, make and subscribe a solemn declaration that they will impartially and carefully examine and decide, to the best of their judgment, and according to justice and equity, all such claims as shall be laid before them on the part of the Governments of the United States and of Her Britannic Majesty, respectively; and such declarations shall be entered on the record of their proceedings.

ARTICLE XIII. The Commissioners shall then forthwith proceed to the investigation of the claims which shall be presented to them. They shall investigate and decide such claim in such order and such manner as they may think proper, but upon such evidence or information only as shall be furnished by or on behalf of the respective Governments. They shall be bound to receive and consider all written documents or statements which may be presented to them by or on behalf of the respective Governments in support of, or in answer to, any claim, and to hear, if required, one person on each side, on behalf of each Government as counsel or agent for such Government, on each and every separate claim. A majority of the Commissioners shall be sufficient for an award in each case. The award shall be given upon each claim in writing, and shall be signed by the Commissioners assenting to it. It shall be competent for each Government to name one person to attend the Commissioners as its agent to present and support claims on its behalf, and to answer claims made upon it, and to represent it generally in all matters connected with the investigation and decision thereof.

The High Contracting Parties hereby engage to consider the decision of the Commissioners as absolutely final and conclusive upon each claim decided upon by them, and to give full effect to such decisions without any objection, evasion, or delay whatsoever.

ARTICLE XIV. Every claim shall be presented to the Commissioners within six months from the day of their first meeting, unless in any case where reasons for delay shall be established to the satisfaction of the Commissioners, and then, and in any such case, the period for presenting the claim may be extended by them to any time not exceeding three months longer.

The Commissioners shall be bound to examine and decide upon every claim within two years from the day of their first meeting. It shall be competent for the Commissioners to decide in each case whether any claim has or has not been duly made, preferred and laid before them, either wholly or to any and what extent, according to the true intent and meaning of this treaty.

ARTICLE XV. All sums of money which may be awarded by the Commissioners on account of any claim shall be paid by the one Government to the other, as the case may be, within twelve months after the date of the final award without any deduction save as specified in Article XVI of this treaty.

ARTICLE XVI. The Commissioners shall keep an accurate record, and correct minutes or notes of all their proceedings, with the dates thereof, and may appoint and employ a secretary, and any other necessary officer, or officers, to assist them in the transaction of the business which may come before them.

Each Government shall pay its own Commissioner and agent or counsel. All other expenses shall be defrayed by the two Governments in equal moieties.

The whole expenses of the Commission, including contingent expenses, shall be defrayed by a ratable deduction on the amount of the sums awarded by the Commissioners, provided always that such deduction shall not exceed the rate of five per cent on the sums so awarded.

ARTICLE XVII. The High Contracting Parties engage to consider the result of the proceedings of this Commission as a full, perfect, and final settlement of all such claims as are mentioned in Article XII of this treaty upon either Government; and further engage that every such claim, whether or not the same may have been presented to the notice of, made, preferred, or laid before the said Commission, shall from and after the conclusion of the proceedings of the said Commission, be considered and treated as finally settled, barred, and thenceforth inadmissible.

Rules and regulations adopted by the commissioners, September 27, 1871, under Article XII of the Treaty between the United States and Great Britain, concluded and signed at Washington, on the 8ᵗʰ day of May 1871.

1. In addition to the representation of his claim and the proofs in support thereof which shall have been presented to his Government, the claimant shall file in the office of the Commission a statement of his claim in the form of a memorial addressed to the Commission. The memorials in future will be printed at the expense of the Commission [2].

2. Every memorial shall state the full name of the claimant, the place and time of his birth, and the place or places of his residence between the 13ᵗʰ day of April, 1861, and the 9ᵗʰ day of April, 1865, inclusive; if he be a naturalized citizen or subject of the Government by which his claim is presented, an authentic copy of the

---

[1] *Treaties and Conventions....*, 1776-1887, p. 484-486.

[2] Supersedes the rule who was primitively adopted as follows: « In addition .... in the form of a memorial, accompanied by 20 printed copies thereof. In cases where the amount claimed is less than 1000 dollars, the memorials will be printed at the expense of the Commission. One copy of each memorial will, by the Secretary, be furnished to each Commissioner and 5 copies to the agent of each Government. »

record of his naturalisation shall be appended to the memorial, and the memorial shall also state whether he has been naturalised in any other country than that of his birth, and if not so naturalised, whether he has taken any and what steps towards being so naturalised[1].

3. If the claim be preferred in behalf of a firm or association of persons other than a corporation or joint stock company, the names of each person interested, both at the date of the claim accrued and at the date of verifying the memorial, must be stated, with the proportions of each person's interest. And all the particulars above required to be given in the case of individual claimants must be stated in respect of each member of such firm or association, unless the same be dispensed with on special order of the Commission. If any transfer of the claim, or any part thereof, has occurred, the nature and mode of such transfer must be stated.

4. The memorial must state the particulars of the claim, the general grounds on which it is founded, and the amount claimed. It shall be verified by the oath or affirmation of the claimant, or in the case hereinafter provided, of his agent or attorney; or if the claim be by a firm or an incorporate association of persons, then by the oath or affirmation of one of them; or in the case of a corporation or joint stock company, by the oath or affirmation of the president or other officer. Such oaths or affirmations may be taken, if in the United States or Great Britain, before any officer having authority, according to the laws of the place, to administer oaths or affirmations; and they may be taken in the said countries, or elsewhere, before any consul or diplomatic agent of either Government. The verification may be by the agent or attorney only when verification by the claimant is substantially impracticable, and can only be given at great inconvenience. And in case of verification by agent or attorney, the cause of the failure of the claimant to verify it shall be stated. Objection to the jurisdiction of the Commission or to the sufficiency of the case stated in the memorial may be made in the form of a demurrer, stating, without technical nicety, the substantial ground of the objection; any new matter, constituting a special ground of defence, may be stated in a plea, which may be the subject of demurrer, and all demurrers may be set for hearing on a 10 days' notice.

----

[1] Before being amended, this rule was adopted as follows: « Every memorial shall .... appended to the memorial, and he shall state whether he has taken any and what steps towards becoming naturalised in any country other than that of his birth. »

5. Every claimant shall be allowed two months after the filing of his memorial, to complete his proofs, and notice thereof given; two months shall be allowed for taking proofs for the defence, with such further extension of time in each case as the Commission on application may grant for cause shown.

After the proofs on the part of the defence shall have been closed, the Commission will, when the claimant shall desire to take rebutting proof, accord a reasonable time for the purpose.

6. All depositions, after the filing of the memorial, shall be taken on notice, specifying the time and place of taking, to be filed in the office of the Commission, with a copy of the interrogatories, or a statement in writing by the counsel of the Government adducing the witness, showing the subject of the particular examination with sufficient precision to be accepted by the counsel of the Government against whom such witness is to be produced, to be signified by his endorsement thereon.

Such interrogatories or statement to be filed in the office of the Commission at least 15 days before the day named for the examination, with one additional day for every 500 miles of distance from Washington to the place where the disposition is to be taken. When depositions are to be taken elsewhere than in North America, 30 days will be allowed.

7. Every deposition taken in the United States shall be taken before some officer authorised to take dispositions in cases pending in courts of the United States. Depositions in Great Britain and her possessions may be taken before any person authorised to take depositions, to be used in courts of record, or any justice of the peace. Depositions in those countries or elsewhere may be taken before any consul or diplomatic agent of either Government.

In all cases the cross-examination of the witness may be by written interrogatories or orally in the election of the party cross-examining.

8. The Commissioners may at any time issue a special commission for the taking of testimony on the application of either party: such testimony to be taken either in written interrogatories or orally, as the Commissioners may order.

The Commissioners may also, on motion of either party, order any claimant or witness to appear personally before them for examination or cross-examination.

9. When any original papers filed in the State Department of United States or in the archives of British Legation in Washington cannot be conveniently withdrawn from the files, copies thereof will be received in evidence when cer-

tified by the State Government or by the British Legation as the case may be.

10. When the time has expired for taking proofs, or the case has been closed on both sides, the proofs will be printed under the direction of the Secretary, and at the expense of the Commission. The argument for the claimant shall be filed within 15 days after the papers shall have been printed, and the case shall stand for hearing 10 days thereafter.

11. The secretary will prepare, from time to time, lists of cases ready for hearing, either upon demurrer or upon the merits, in the order in which they are entitled to be heard, or in which the counsels for the two Governments shall agree that they shall be heard.

12. All cases will be submitted on printed arguments, which shall contain a statement of the facts proven and references to the evidence by which they are proven, and, in addition, the counsels for the respective Governments will be heard whenever they desire to argue any cause orally. Arguments of counsel for individual claimants will be received, in print, when submitted by the counsel of either Government and not otherwise.

13. Claims against the United States and Great Britain respectively, will be entered in separate dockets kept by the secretary. The dockets shall contain an abstract of all proceedings, motions, and others in each case.

14. The secretary will keep a record of the proceedings of the Commission upon each day of its session which shall be read at the next meeting and will then be signed by him and approved by the signature of the preceding Commission.

15. The secretary will keep a notice book, in which entries may be made by the counsel for either Government, and all entries so made shall be notice to the opposing counsel.

16. The secretary shall provide books of printed forms in which will be recorded the awards of the Commission signed by the Commissioners concurring therein.

The awards against each Government will be kept in a separate book.

17. A copy of each award, certified by the secretary of the Commission, will be furnished, on request, to the party upon whose claim such award shall have been made.

18. The dockets, minutes of proceedings, and records of awards, will be kept in duplicate, one of which will be delivered to each Government at the close of the duties of the Commission.

19. The secretary will have charge of all the books and papers of the Commission, and no papers shall be withdrawn from the files or taken from the office, without an order of the Commission [1].

La commission statua sur 478 réclamations anglaises et 19 réclamations américaines: elles se montaient au total à une somme de 61,000,000 $ environ. Il ne fut accordé d'indemnités qu'à 181 réclamants anglais pour une somme globale de 1,929,819 $.

The Undersigned Commissioners, appointed under the XIIth Article of the treaty signed at Washington on the 8th day of May 1871 between the United States of America and Her Britannic Majesty, do now make their final Award of and concerning the matters referred to them by said treaty as follows, that is to say:

We award that the Government of the United States of America shall pay to the Government of Her Britannic Majesty, within twelve months from the date hereof, the sum of 1,929,819 dollars in gold subject to the deduction provided for by Article XVI of the treaty aforesaid, for and in full satisfaction of the several claims on the part of corporations, companies, or private individuals, subjects of Her Britannic Majesty, upon the Government of the United States, arising out of acts committed against the persons or property of subjects of Her Britannic Majesty, during the period between the 13th day of April 1861 and the 9th day of April 1865 inclusive: said sum being the aggregate of the several separate awards upon such claims made in writing, in duplicate, and signed by us or such of us as assented to said separate awards.

And all other such claims on part of subjects of Her Britannic Majesty against the United States, which have been presented and prosecuted for our award, have been and are hereby disallowed or dismissed in manner and form as will appear by the several separate awards in writing concerning the same signed as aforesaid. Certain other claims on the part of subjects of Her Britannic Majesty against the United States were also presented, but were afterwards, and before any award was made thereon, withdrawn by the Agent of Her Britannic Majesty, as will appear by the record of the proceedings of the Commission kept in duplicate, and which will be delivered to each Government herewith.

---

[1] J. B. MOORE, *History and Digest* ...., p. 2204.

And we award that all claims on the part of corporations, companies, or private individuals, citizens of the United States, upon the Government of Her Britannic Majesty, arising out of acts committed against the persons or property of citizens of the United States, between the 13th day of April, inclusive, not being claims growing out of the acts of vessels referred to in the I[st] Article of said treaty, have been and are hereby disallowed; separate award upon each of said claims having been made in writing, in duplicate and signed by us or such of us as assented to such separate awards.

And we refer to the several separate awards made and signed as aforesaid, as a part of this our final award, it being our intent that the proceedings of this Commission shall have the force and effect named and provided the XVII Article of said treaty [1].

C. — Cet arbitrage, connu sous le nom de commission de Halifax, a eu pour but de déterminer les compensations dues à des citoyens anglais à raison des avantages concédés, par les articles XVIII à XXI, à des citoyens américains, en matière de droit de pêche. La commission, composée de trois arbitres, ne fut constituée que le 15 juin 1877, mais dès le 23 novembre 1877 elle terminait ses travaux et accordait à la Grande-Bretagne, une somme de 5,500,000 $.

Treaty concluded at Washington, on May 8, 1871, between Great Britain and the United States of America for the settlement of claims by arbitration.

. . . .

ART. XXII. Inasmuch as it is asserted by the Government of Her Britannic Majesty that the privileges accorded to the citizens of the United States under Article XVIII of this treaty are of greater value than those accorded by Articles XIX and XXI of this treaty to the subjects of Her Britannic Majesty and this assertion is not admitted by the Government of the United States, it is further agreed that Commissioners shall be appointed to determine, having regard to the privileges accorded by the United States to the subjects of Her Britannic Majesty, as stated in Articles XIX and XXI of this treaty, the amount of any compensation which, in their opinion, ought to be paid by the Government of the United States to the Government of Her

Britannic Majesty in return for the privileges accorded to the citizens of the United States under Article XVIII of this treaty and that any sum of money which the said Commissioners may so award shall be paid by the United States Government, in a gross sum, within twelve months after such award shall have been given.

ART. XXIII. The Commissioners referred to in the preceding article shall be appointed in the following manner, that is to say: one Commissioner shall be named by the President of the United States, one by Her Britannic Majesty, and a third by the President of the United States and Her Britannic Majesty conjointly: and in case the third Commissioner shall not have been so named within a period of three months from the date when this article shall take effect, then the third Commissioner shall be named by the Representative at London of His Majesty the Emperor of Austria and King of Hungary. In case of the death, absence, or incapacity of any Commissioner, or in the event of any Commissioner omitting or ceasing to act, the vacancy shall be filled in the manner, herein before provided, for making the original appointment, the period of three months in case of such substitution being calculated from the date of the happening of the vacancy.

The Commissioners so named shall meet in the city of Halifax, in the province of Nova Scotia at the earliest convenient period after they have been respectively named, and shall before proceeding to any business, make and subscribe a solemn declaration that they will impartially and carefully examine and decide the matters referred to them to the best of their judgment, and according to justice and equity, and such declaration shall be entered on the record of their proceedings. Each of the high contracting parties shall also name one person to attend the commission as its Agent, to represent it generally in all matters connected with the commission.

ART. XXIV. The proceedings shall be conducted in such order as the Commissioner appointed under Articles XXII and XXIII of this treaty shall determine. They shall be bound to receive such oral on written testimony as either Government may present. If either party shall offer oral testimony, the other party shall have the right of cross-examination, under such rules as the Commissioners shall prescribe. If in the case submitted to the Commissioners either party shall have specified or alluded to any report or document in its own exclusive possession without annexing a copy, such party shall be bound, if other party thinks proper to apply for it, to furnish that party with a copy thereof; and either party may call upon the other, through the

---

[1] HERTSLET, *A complete collection* .... t. XIV, p. 1180; — F. DE MARTENS, *Nouveau Recueil Général* ... 2ᵉ série, t. I (1876), p. 37.

Commissioners, to produce the originals or certified copies of any papers adduced as evidence, giving in each instance such reasonable notice as the Commissioners may require.

The case on either side shall be closed within a period of six months from the date of the organization of the Commission, and the Commissioners shall be requested to give their award as soon as possible thereafter. The aforesaid period of six months may be extended for three months in case of a vacancy occuring among the Commissioners under the circumstances contemplated in Article XXIII of this treaty.

ART. XXV. The Commissioners shall keep an accurate record an correct minutes or note of all their proceedings, with the dates thereof, and may appoint and employ a secretary and any other necessary officer or officers to assist them in the transaction of the business which may come before them. Each of the High Contracting Parties shall pay its own Commissioner and Agent or Counsel; all other expenses shall be defrayed by the two Governments in equal moieties [1].

Award of the British, United States and Belgian Commissioners appointed under the Treaty of 8th May 1871, to award the amount of compensation, if any, to be paid by the United States Government to the British Government, in respect of the North American Fisheries. Halifax, November 23, 1877.

The Undersigned Commissioners appointed under Articles XXII and XXIII of the Treaty of Washington of the 8th May 1871, to determine, having regard to the privileges accorded by the United States to the subjects of Her Britannic Majesty, as stated in Articles XIX and XXI of the said Treaty, the amount of any compensation which in their opinion ought to be paid by the Government of the United States to the Government of Her Britannic Majesty, in return for the privileges accorded to the citizens of the United States, under Article XVIII of the said Treaty:

Having carefully and impartially examined the matters referred to them according to justice and equity, in conformity with the solemn declaration made and subscribed by them on the 15th day of June 1877;

Award the sum of 5,500,000 dollars, in gold, to be paid by the Government of the United States to the Government of Her Britannic Majesty, in accordance with the provisions of the said Treaty.

Signed at Halifax, this 23rd day of november 1877.

Maurice Delfosse. A. T. Galt.

The United States Commissioner is of opinion that the advantages accruing to Great Britain under the Treaty of Washington are greater than the advantages conferred on the United States by the said Treaty, and he cannot, therefore, concur in the conclusions announced by his colleagues:

And the American Commissioner deems it his duty to state further that it is questionable whether it is competent for the Board to make an Award under the Treaty, except with the unanimous consent of its members [1].

E. H. Kellogg.

Malgré cette réserve le Gouvernement Américain n'hésita pas à exécuter la sentence prononcée contre lui et le 21 novembre 1878 la somme de 27,500,000 francs était payée à Londres au Gouvernement Britannique par le Ministre Plénipotentiaire des Etats-Unis d'Amérique.

D. — Enfin un quatrième arbitrage fut organisé par le traité du 8 mai 1871, au sujet du tracé de la frontière entre le Canada et les Etats-Unis de l'Amérique du Nord, vers l'Océan Pacifique. Confié à l'Empereur d'Allemagne, ce dernier rendit sa sentence en faveur des Etats-Unis, le 21 octobre 1872.

Treaty concluded at Washington on May 8, 1871, between Great Britain and the United States of America for the settlement of claims by arbitration.

. . . .

ART. XXXIV. Whereas it was stipulated by Article I of the treaty concluded at Washington on the 15th of June, 1846, between the United States and Her Britannic Majesty, that the line of boundary between the territories of the United States and those of Her Britannic Majesty, from the point of the forty ninth parallel of north latitude up to which it had already been ascertained, should be continued westward along the said parallel of north latitude «to the middle of the channel which separates the continent from Vancouver's Island and thence southerly, through the middle of the said channel and of Fuca Straits, to the Pacific Ocean» and whereas the Commissioners appointed by the two High Contracting Parties to determine that portion of the boundary which runs southerly through the middle of the channel aforesaid, were unable to agree upon the same; and whereas the Government of

[1] *Treaties and Convention* ....., 1776—1887, p. 487—488.

[1] HERSTLET. *A complete Collection* ...., t. XIV, p. 1185.

Her Britannic Majesty claims that such boundary line should under the terms of the treaty above recited, be run through the Rosario Straits, and the Government of the United States claims that it should be run through the Canal de Haro, it is agreed that the respective claims of the Government of the United States and of the Government of Her Britannic Majesty shall be submitted to the arbitration and award of His Majesty the Emperor of Germany, who, having regard to the above mentioned article of the said treaty, shall decide thereupon finally and without appeal, which of those claims is most in accordance with the true interpretation of the treaty of June 15, 1846.

ART. XXXV. The award of His Majesty the Emperor of Germany shall be considered as absolutely final and conclusive; and full effect shall be given to such award without any objection, evasion, or delay whatsoever. Such decision shall be given in writing and dated; it shall be in whatsoever form His Majesty may choose to adopt; it shall be delivered to the Representatives or other public Agents of the United States and of Great Britain, respectively, who may be actually at Berlin, and shall be considered as operative from the day of the date of the delivery thereof.

ART. XXXVI. The written or printed case of each of the two parties accompanied by the evidence offered in support of the same, shall be laid before His Majesty the Emperor of Germany within six months from the date of the exchange of the ratifications of this treaty and a copy of such case and evidence shall be communicated by each party to the other, through their respective Representatives at Berlin.

The High Contracting Parties may include in the evidence to be considered by the Arbitrator such documents, official correspondence, and other official or public statements bearing on the subject of the reference as they may consider necessary to the support of their respective cases.

After the written or printed case shall have been communicated by each party to the other, each party shall have the power of drawing up and having before the Arbitrator a second and definitive statement, if it think fit to do so in reply to the case of the other party so communicated, which definitive statement shall be so laid before the Arbitrator, and also be mutually communicated in the same manner as aforesaid, by each party to the other, within six months from the date of laying the first statement of the case before the Arbitrator.

ART. XXXVII. If, in the case submitted to the Arbitrator, either party shall specify or allude to any report or document in its own exclusive possession without annexing a copy, such party shall be bound, if the other party thinks proper to apply for it, to furnish that party with a copy thereof, and either party may call upon the other through the Arbitrator, to produce the originals or certified copies of any papers adduced as evidence, giving in each instance such reasonable notice as the Arbitrator may require, and if the Arbitrator should desire further elucidation or evidence with regard to any point contained in the statements laid before him, he shall be at liberty to require it from either party, and he shall be at liberty to hear one Counsel or Agent for each party, in relation to any matter, and at such time, and in such manner, as he may think fit.

ART. XXXVIII. The Representatives or other public Agents of the United States and of Great Britain at Berlin, respectively shall be considered as the Agents of their respective Governments to conduct their cases before the Arbitrator, who shall be requested to address all his communications and give all his notices to such Representatives or other public Agents, who shall represent their respective Governments generally in all matters connected with the Arbitration.

ART. XXXIX. It shall be competent to the Arbitrator to proceed in the said arbitration, and all matters relating thereto, as and when he shall see fit, either in person or by a person or persons named by him for that purpose, either in the presence or absence of either or both Agents, and either orally or by written discussion or otherwise.

ART. XL. The Arbitrator may if he think fit appoint a Secretary or Clerk for the purposes of the proposed arbitration at such rate of remuneration as he shall think proper. This and all other expenses of and connected with the said arbitration, shall be provided for as hereinafter stipulated.

ART. XLI. The Arbitrator shall be requested to deliver, together with his award an account of all the costs and expenses which he may have been put to, in relation to this matter, which shall forthwith be repaid by the two Governments in equal moieties.

ART. XLII. The Arbitrator shall be requested to give his award in writing as early as convenient after the whole case on each side shall have been laid before him, and to deliver one copy thereof to each of the said Agents [1].

Schiedsspruch gegeben in Berlin, den 21. October 1872, in der Grenzfrage zwischen Gross-Brittannien und den Vereinigten Staaten von America.

Wir, Wilhelm von Gottes Gnaden Deutscher Kaiser, König von Preussen, etc. etc.

---

[1] *Treaties and Conventions...*, 1776—1887, p. 491—493.

Nach Einsicht des zwischen den Regierungen Ihrer Britischen Majestät und den Vereinigten Staaten von Amerika geschlossenen Vertrages de dato Washington, den 8. Mai 1871, Inhalts dessen die gedachten Regierungen die unter ihnen streitige Frage: ob die Grenzlinie, welche nach dem Vertrage de dato Washington, den 15. Juni 1846, nachdem sie gegen Westen längs des 49. Grades nördlicher Breite bis zur Mitte des Kanals, welcher das Festland von der Vancouver-Insel trennt, gezogen worden, südlich durch die Mitte des gedachten Canals und der Fuca-Meerenge bis zum Stillen Ocean gezogen werden soll, durch den Rosario-Canal, wie die Regierung Ihrer Britischen Majestät beansprucht, oder durch den Haro-Canal, wie die Regierung der Vereinigten Staaten beansprucht, zu ziehen sei, Unserem Schiedsspruche unterbreitet haben, damit Wir endgültig und ohne Berufung entscheiden, welcher dieser Ansprüche mit der richtigen Auslegung des Vertrages vom 15. Juni 1846 am meisten in Einklang stehe.

Nach Anhörung des Uns von den durch Uns berufenen Sach- und Rechtskundigen über den Inhalt der gewechselten Denkschriften und deren Anlagen erstatteten Vortrages, Haben den nachstehenden Schiedsspruch gefällt: Mit der richtigen Auslegung des zwischen den Regierungen Ihrer Britischen Majestät und den Vereinigten Staaten von Amerika geschlossenen Vertrages de dato Washington, den 15. Juni 1846, steht der Anspruch der Regierung der Vereinigten Staaten am meisten im Einklange, dass die Grenzlinie zwischen den Gebieten Ihrer Britischen Majestät und den Vereinigten Staaten durch den Haro-Canal gezogen werde.

Urkundlich unter Unserer Höchsteigenhändigen Unterschrift und beigedrucktem Kaiserlichen Insigel.

Gegeben Berlin, den 21. October 1872 [1].

LI. Pays-Bas, Venezuela.
5 août 1857

Il s'est agi en cette contestation de la souveraineté sur l'île Aves que le Gouvernement des Pays-Bas prétendait faire partie des Antilles néerlandaises. La reine d'Espagne, choisie pour arbitre, de commun accord, repoussa cette prétention.

Convention entre les Pays-Bas et la République de Venezuela, pour régler les différends entre les Gouvernements respectifs, conclue à Caracas le 5 août 1857.

Z. M. de Koning der Nederlanden, Groot-Hertog van Luxemburg, en Z. E. de President

---

[1] F. DE MARTENS, *Nouveau Recueil général*, t. XX, p. 775.

van de Rupubliek Venezuela, gelykelyk gezind om de tusschen beide regeringen sedert meer dan twee jaren bestaande geschillen, het eene, nopens het domaniaal regt en de souvereiniteit van het eiland Aves, gelegen op 15° 40' N. B. en 63° 35' W. L., en het andere, met betrekking tot de plaats gevonden hebbende jammerlyke gebeurtenissen te Coro in February 1855, op eene minnelyke wyze te regelen, hebben te dien einde benoemd, te weten:

Z. M. de Koning der Nederlanden, den heer Pieter van Rees, ridder, enz., Hoogstdeszelfs speciaal Commissaris in buitengewoone zending en Consul-Generaal ad interim by de Republiek van Venezuela, en

Z. E. de President der Republiek van Venezuela, den heer Frans Conde, ondervoorzitter van den Raad van State, deszelfs speciaal Commissaris,

Dewelke, na elkander hunne volmagten te hebben medegedeeld, die in goeden en behoorlyken vorm zyn bevonden, omtrent de volgende artikelen zyn overeengekomen.

Art. 1. Het geschil omtrent het regt van domein en van souvereiniteit op het eiland Aves zal worden onderworpen aan de scheidsregterlyke uitspraak van eene bevriende mogendheid, welke vooraf in gemeen overleg zal worden gekozen.

. . . .

Art. 6. Het oogmerk der beide hooge contracterende partyen alleenlyk zynde om al de vorderingen, welke tot hiertoe ter zake hierin vermeld, zyn voortgebragt, bepaaldelyk te beëindigen, zoo verklaren zy uitdrukkelyk, dat de tegenwoordige overeenkomst alleen van toepassing is op de daarin aangewezen onderwerpen, en, vermits zy geen andere bedoeling hebben, dat het verdrag, noch door de eene, noch door de andere party, in de toekomst zal kunnen worden ingeroepen als antecedent of als regel voor den gevolge.

Art. 7. Paragraaf acht van artikel acht en dertig der nieuwe staatsregeling van Venezuela voorschryvende dat « elk door het uitvoerend gezag aangegaan openbaar verdrag of tractaat niet zal kunnen worden bekrachtigd zonder voorafgaande goedkeuring van het Congres », zoo is uitdrukkelyk overeengekomen, dat Z. E. de President der Republiek deze overeenkomst in de eerste dagen der gewone zitting van 1858 aan de goedkeuring van het Congres zal onderwerpen en aanbevelen.

Art. 8. Deze overeenkomst zal door beide partyen worden goedgekeurd en de bekrachtigingen worden uitgewisseld te Caracas, acht dagen of zoo mogelyk vroeger, na de goedkeuring van het Congres.

Ten blyke waarvan de wederzydsche gevolmagtigden de tegenwoordige overeenkomst hebben onderteekend en met hunne wapenen bezegeld.

Gedaan te Caracas den 5ᵉⁿ Augustus, van het jaar Onzes Heeren 1857.

Decision arbitral en la cuestion entre los Paises Bajos y Venezuela referente al derecho de propriedad sobre la isla de Aves, dada en Madrid, Junio 30, 1865.

Nos doña Isabel Segunda, por la gracia de Dios y la Constitución de la Monarquía, Reina de las Españas, habiendo aceptado las funciones de juez árbitro que por notas que el Ministro de Relaciones Exteriores de la República de Venezuela y el Ministro Plenipotenciario de S. M. el Rey de los Paises Bajos respectivamente dirigieron á nuestro Ministro de Estado, nos han sido conferidas en virtud de un convenio entre las dos Naciones expresadas, firmado el día cinco de agosto de mil ochocientos cincuenta y siete, para que por este nuestro laudo se ponga término á la cuestión suscitada entre ambas sobre el dominio y soberanía de la isla de Aves.

Animada del deseo de corresponder dignamente á la confianza que las Altas Partes interesadas nos han manifestado; á cuyo fin hemos examinado escrupulosamente, con la asistencia de nuestro Consejo de Ministros, todos los documentos, memorias y mapas que los referidos Ministros de Relaciones Exteriores de la República de Venezuela y Ministro Plenipotenciario de S. M. el Rey de los Paises Bajos han remitido respectivamente á nuestro Ministro de Estado. Resultando de los expresados documentos que las principales razones alegadas por le Gobierno de los Paises Bajos en apoyo del derecho que dice asistirle son: 1º Que en los antiguos mapas aparece un banco de arena que una la isla de Aves con la de Sabá, posesion holandesa, lo cual deja suponer que ambas fueron en algún tiempo un solo territorio. 2º Que muchos geógrafos, entre ellos algunos venezolanos, citan la isla de Aves entre las Antillas holandesas, dependientes del Gobierno de Curazao, diciendo que está poblada por pescadores holandeses. 3º Que según una información de testigos, vecinos de Sabá y San Eustaquio, posesiones de los Paises Bajos, los habitantes de estas islas tenían y tienen costumbre de ir á pescar tortugas y recoger huevos de aves á las islas de este nombre, donde enarbolaron algunas veces el pabellón de los Paises Bajos; y 4º Que la República de Venezuela, al conceder un privilegio para la extracción del huano que se encuentra en dicha isle de Aves, consignó en una de las cláusulas del con-

trato, que si era desposeída de aquélla, no quedaría obligada al pago de indemnización alguna. Resultando también que los argumentos que á su vez presenta la República de Venezuela en apoyo de su demanda, son: 1º Que no existe banco de arena que úna la isla de Aves con la de Sabá. 2º Que la ocupación material de la primera de dichas por individuos particulares que no obran en representación de su Gobierno, sino movidos por un interés personal, no constituye posesión. 3º Que todas las islas del Mar Caribe, entre las cuales se cuenta la de Aves, fueron descubiertas por los españoles y al constituirse aquella Republica con el territorio de la antigua Capitanía general de Caracas, sucedió á España en todos sus derechos á la isla en cuestión; y 4º Que el continente venezolano es el territorio de consideración mas próximo á la isla de Aves, lo cual le da un derecho de preferencia, haciéndose aplicación del principio establecido en una cuestión análoga entre Inglaterra y los Estados Unidos. Vista la carta geográfica de las Antillas, presentada por el Gobierno de los Países Bajos, en la cual aparece dibujado un banco de arena que va de la isla de Aves á la de Sabá, sin que conste la fecha de este mapa, ni su autor; vistos los calcos de dos mapas ingleses publicados en mil ochocientos seis, en los cuales aparece el mismo banco de arena, bajo la denominación de banco de Aves. Vistos los documentos presentados por el Gobierno de la República de Venezuela, y entre ellos un informe de la dirección hidrográfica de España, en el cual, refiriéndose por error á otras islas de Aves, se asegura que formaron parte de la Capitanía general de Caracas. Vista la Real Orden de trece de Junio de mil setencientos ochenta y seis, en la cual al decretarse la creación de una audiencia en Caracas, para evitar los perjuicios que se originaban á los habitantes de aquello población de tener que acudir para los recursos de apelación á la de Santo Domingo, se disponía que el territorio de esta audiencia se limitase á la parte española de la isla, la de Cuba, y la de Puerto Rico, lo cual indica que la isla de Aves debió quedar sujeta á la audiencia de Caracas. Considerando que si bien algunos geógrafos han dibujado en mapas antiguos el citado banco de arena entre la isla de Aves y la de Seba; las últimas observaciones hechas sobre el banco enunciado demuestran que no se extiende más allá de doce leguas al sur de la isla de esta nombre, en cuyo punto no se encuentra fondo con ciento sesenta brazas, segun consta de un mapa publicado por el Almirantazgo ingles en mil ochocientos cincuenta y siete. Que hallándose la isla de Aves á unas cuarenta leguas al sur de Sabá, y terminando el banco á las doce de esta po-

¹ LAGEMANS. *Recueil des traités et conventions*, t. IV, p. 322.

blación, es indudable que no existe el banco de arena en una extensión de veinte y ocho leguas, y por consiguiente que no hay unión ne enlace entre las dos islas de Aves y de Sabá. Que aun cuando ambas hubiesen en elgún tiempo formado una sola, resulta que al posesionarse el Gobierno de los Países Bajos de la de Sabá, no formaba parte de esta la de Aves, según indican las palabras de Alcedo, autor citado por el Gobierno de los Países Bajos, el cual dice respectado por el Gobierno de los Países Bajos, el cual dice respecto de Sabá..... «pertenecía al principio á los dinamarqueses.... pero los holandeses enviaron allí una colonia desde San Eustaquio, etc. »; y después habla separadamente de la isla de Aves eran dos islas separados cuando los holandeses entraron en posesión de la primera. Considerando que en las citas geográficas que presenta el Gobierno de los Países Bajos en apoyo de su demanda aparece una gran confusión, refiriéndose muchas de ellas á otras islas de Aves distinas de la que es objeto de la cuestión, á la cual no se asigna por la generalidad de los geógrafos una nacionalidad determinada. Considerando que para dar importancia en materia de propriedad á la autoridad de los geógrafos es necesario que todos ó una gran parte estén unánimes y conformes en determinar la nacionalidad de un territorio dado, y faltando está circunstancia en el caso presente, se requieren otros titulos de más fuerza y validez que la opinión de los geógrafos. Considerando que si bien aparece comprobado el hecho de que los habitantes de San Eustaquio, posesión neerlandesa, van á pescar tortugas y recoger huevos á la isla de Aves, este hecho no puede servir de apoyo al derecho de soberania, porque solamente significa una ocupación temporal y precaria de la isla, no siendo la pesca en este caso un derecho exclusivo, sino la consecuencia del abandono de ella por parte de los habitantes de las comarcas immediatas, ó por su legítimo dueño. Considerando que si bien la República de Venezuela, al conceder un privilegio para la extración del huano de la isla de Aves, pactó que no se le pudiera exigir indemnización si era desposeida de aquel territorio, esta condición nada prueba en favor de la pretensión de los Países Bajos, porque solo demuestra una sensata precaución por parte de la Republica y el natural respeto al estado de litígio en que se encuentra la isla. Considerando que en este resúmen el Gobierno neerlandés sólo ha probado que algunos de sus súbditos avecindados en San Eustaquio y Sabá van á pescar tortugas y recoger huevos en la isla de Aves desde mediados del siglo diez y ocho, y que con este objeto suelen habitar la isla tres o cuatro meses al año. Considerando que á su vez funda Venezuela princi-

palmente su derecho en el de España antes de que aquella República quedase constituida como Estado independiente, y si bien resulta que España no ocupó materialmente el territorio de la isla de Aves es indudable que le pertenecía como parte de las Indias Occidentales que eran del dominio de los Reyes de España, según la ley primera, título quince, libro segundo de la Recopilación de Indias. Considerando que la isla de Aves debió formar parte del territorio de la audiencia de Caracas, cuando ésta fué creada en trece de junio mil setecientos ochenta y seis, y que al constituirse Venezuela como Nación independiente, lo hizo con el territorio de la Capitanía general de su nombre, declarando con posterioridad vigentes en el nuevo Estado todas las disposiciones adoptadas por el Gobierno español hasta mil ochocientos ocho, por lo cual pudo considerar la isla de Aves como parte de la Provincia española de Venezuela. Considerando que aun hecha abstracción de lo que antecede, resulta siempre que, si bien puede decirse que la isla Aves nunca fué real y verdaderamente ocupada por España y habitada por españoles, tampoco la residencia temporal en ella de algunos naturales de Sabá y San Eustaquio es más que una ocupación precaria que no constituye posesión; pues aun cuando la isla no es capaz de habitación permanente por razón de las inmersiones á que se halla expuesta, si los holandeses la hubieran ocupado con ánimo de adquirirla, juzgándola abandonada, habrían construido algún edificio y tratado de hacer la isla habitable constantemente, cosas ambas que no llegaron á tener efecto. Y considerando por último que el Gobierno de los Países Bajos no ha hecho otra cosa que utilizar la pesca en dicha isla por medio de sus colonos, al paso que el Gobierno de Venezuela ha sido el primero en tener allí fuerza armada, y en ejercer actos de soberanía, confirmando así el dominio que adquirió por un título general derivado de España. Es nuestro parecer, conforme con el de nuestro Consejo de Ministros, después de oído el dictamen de nuestro Consejo de Estado en pleno, que la propiedad de la isla en cuestión corresponde á la República de Venezuela, quedando á cargo de ésta la indemnización por la pesca que los súbditos holandeses dejarán de aprovechar, si en efecto se les priva de utilizarla, en cuyo caso servirá de tipo para dicha indemnización, el producto líquido anual de la pesca calculado por el último quinquenio, capitalizándolo al cinco por ciente.

Dado en nuestro Palacio de Madrid, á treinta de Junio de mil ochocientos sesenta y cinco.

---

[1] J. B. MOORE. *History and Digest* ..., p. 5037.

LII. Espagne, Etats-Unis d'Amérique.
16 juin 1870.

Cet arbitrage, proposé par les Etats-Unis d'Amérique par dépêche du 25 mai 1870, fut accepté par l'Espagne sous la date du 16 juin suivant: il avait pour objet la fixation de l'indemnité due aux propriétaires d'un navire indûment retenu dans le port de la Havane, par les autorités locales. La somme allouée s'est élevée à 19,702 $ 50 pour 114 jours de détention.

Award of M. Rösing, November 1870, in the arbitration between Spain and the United States of America.

« To Messrs. Juan M. Ceballos, Esqr.
John S. Williams, Esqr.

« Referees in the case of the steamer Col. Lloyd Aspinwall for damages consequent upon her detention by the Spanish Authorities in Cuban Ports. January 1870.

« Gentlemen: The minutes of your meetings for the settlement of this case with exhibits annexed, together with your respective opinions expressed to me independently in writing, have been before me for some time. Apart from the circumstance that the crowded state of the business of my consular office, as I forewarned you, left me little time to reflect on the matter, I soon perceived that a case of considerable difficulty and delicacy was submitted to my decision, on which I was loth to pronounce.

« The very wide discrepancy in the respective awards is hard to conciliate; the remote and occult nature of the transactions upon which the computation must be based and the imperfect state of the evidence before me have made me hesitate more than once. I might have asked for a completion of the evidence, but for remembering that to insist upon such a thing would have belonged to the respective referees and that as arbiter I was called upon simply to pronounce upon the case as it was laid before me.

« I miss particulary any statement as to the engagements the steamer in question was under when interrupted in her voyage, and every estimate of damages has therefore to be made on nalogies and vague computations. While admit-.ing that a government more even than an individual should be held to make most liberal compensation for an unwarranted interference with legitimate business, still the claims for damages would have to be circumscribed either as lucrum cessans or as damnum emergens. From this view I come to the following points for my guidance.

I find that the steamer in question was interrupted in a voyage begun the 17th of January and by consequence of this act prevented from engaging in any other pursuits till, after having been released, she was ready again to sail, which she did, leaving Havana the 10th of May, making, both days included, 114 days to be considered. As to the rate of compensation $ 300 and even higher sums per day have been mentioned as what she might earn under circumstances. It is not asserted, however, much less proved, that she did earn as much when her business was broken up; it seems hardly probable that so small a steamer of 71.40 tons, fit only for a dispatch boat or tug, worth not more than $ 25,000, could expect such returns for any long period. In fact her owner and captain speak of round trips occupying 12 days, which she performed for $ 2000. It is not shown that her trade was ot any regular character, assuring earnings even at this rate for any length of time. It is claimed that in the eight months preceding the seizure the steamer had earned in gross $ 34,700, to which statement no exception is taken. Eight months comprising 240 days, she might have earned under similar favorable circumstances during the 114 days in proportion the sum of $ 16,482. 50. Under this supposition the steamer would have earned in one year more than double her value. I will give her the benefit of these most favorable circumstances; no allowance however can be made at the same time for all ordinary expenses for running the ship and keeping her in proper condition.

« Therefore I cannot award the whole bill of repairs, made out at Havana, but only one half of the same which may be occasioned by the exposure of the ship in her protracted idleness, say $ 1,000. Other expenses I cannot recognize, as rather larger ones of similar character would have been occasioned by her being in service.

« Something would seem to be due to the crew of the vessel as indemnification for their imprisonment, as it were. For although the men may have received their full wages for no work, they have suffered wrong in their forced idleness. I would award to all of them, as per list of Exhibit E, two months of their wages according to the amounts set forth by the master, including $ 175 per month for the latter, making an aggregate of $ 1220.

« To the owners something is due for their trouble, expenses, loss of interest, etc., occasioned by this incident. One thousand dollars may be award on that account. To recapitulate I would determine the indemnification to be made by the Government of Spain for the seizure of the steamship Col. Lloyd Aspinwall as follows:

« I. To the owners of the ship:

1. For 114 days interruption of trade, gold . . . . $ 16,482. 50
2. For repairs of ship, gold » 1,000. —
3. For expenses in prosecuting claim, gold . . . » 1,000. —

Total gold $ 18,482. 50

« II. To the crew of the ship as per list of Exhibit E, annexed, gold . . . . . . » 1,220. —

Total awarded, gold $ 19,702. 50

Copy of Exhibit E.

Key West, May 23[d], 1870.

List of Crew with wages per month:

Charles H. Mc. Carty, master $ 175 per month
George Shaw, mate . . . » 50 » »
John Burns, 2nd mate . . . » 40 » »
John Weeks, seaman . . . » 30 » »
Charles Wilson, seaman . . » 30 » »
George D. Green, cook . . » 30 » »
Hiram Wood, engineer . . » 100 » »
Charles Palmer, 2nd engineer » 65 » »
John Priest, fireman . . . » 40 » »
Anderson Douglas, fireman . » 40 » » [1]

LIII. Brésil, Suède et Norvège.

12 août 1871.

Relatif à l'abordage de la barque *Queen* par le monitor brésilien *Para*, cet arbitrage fut institué par un simple échange de lettres. Il était réclamé une somme de 530 £ 10: l'arbitre se prononça en faveur du Brésil.

Decisao arbitral proferida do M. de Carvalho e Vasconcellos, Rio de Janeiro, aos 26 de Março 1872.

Eu Mathias de Carvalho e Vasconcellos, do conselho de Sua Magestade Fidelissima, seu enviado extraordinario e ministro plenipotenciario junto de S. M. o Imperador do Brazil, etc., etc.: tendo aceitado o convite que me foi dirigido, de commum accôrdo, pelo governo brazileiro e pelo consul geral do Suecia e Noruega nesta côrte para exercer as attribuições de arbitro no reclamação que este funccionario digirio ao mesmo governo ácerca da abalroação que teve logar entre o monitor brazileiro *Pará* e o navio norueguense *Queen*, no porto d'Assumpção, em cinco de Abril de mil oitocentos e setenta ; Havendo examinado com o maximo escrupulo todos os documentos que me fôrão fornecidos

[1] J. B. MOORE. *History and Digest* . . ., p. 1014.

por uma e outra parte, e devidamente ponderado o sua fórma e substancia:

Considerando que ao conhecimento da presente questão deve ser applicado, como regra dominante de decidir, o preceito de jurisprudencia, reconhecido pela legislação de todos os paizes, de que á parte reclamante incumbe a prova da sua pretenção ;

Considerando que os documentos offerecidos pelo consul geral da Suecia e Noruega para justificar a mencionada reclamação não se mostrão, na parte essencial, revestidos das formalidades prescriptas pela legislação que rege os actos dessa natureza ; carecendo por isso de força probatoria ; assim, nem a declaração que em referencia ao accidente devia ser lançada no livro — Diario de bordo -- do *Queen*, nem o protesto apresentado no porto d'Assumpção a 6 de Abril de 1870 pelo capitão deste navio, fôrão feitos de conformidade com as disposições da lei norueguense de 24 de Março de 1860 ; não constando nem se podendo averiguar a data da declaração, nem mesmo si realmente fôra lavrada no livro diario, como se vê do respectivo documento e da que nelle attesta o capitão do porto d'Assumpção ; e dependendo a validade do protesto da inserção, no proprio termo, do conteúdo da referida declaração. Pelo que respeita ao arbitramento, avaliações e syndicancias a que procedeu o capitão do *Queen* reconhecendo-se que não foi notificado, chamado, nem por algum modo ouvido aos respectivos actos o commandante do monitor *Pará*, ou qualquer dos representantes presentes da fazenda brazileira, conforme era de direito corrente ; não tendo, consequentemente, força nem merecimento essas deligencias contra os interessados inscientes ;

Considerando que limitado, nos termos expendidos, o exame da questão a este ponto preliminar, não assentaria em base legal a reclamação do consul geral da Suecia e Noruega para ser julgada directamente no teor do seu pedido e conclusões ; mas,

Considerando que ainda quando os alludidos documentos fôssem attendiveis para o fim que fica indicado, não póde, nem por méra presumpção, ser attribuido com justiça o facto do sinistro a culpa ou falta do commandante ou da tripolação do monitor *Pará*, porquanto ;

Considerando que é regra geral de direito maritimo, dever todo o navio, qualquer que seja a sua posição, achar se sempre apercebido dos necessarios aprestos e apparelhos e de gente sufficiente para a manobra ; entretanto deprehende-se da discussão havida sobre esta materia entre o governo de S. M. o Imperador do Brazil e o consul geral da Suecia e Noruega que o navio

Queen, além de estár ancorado em logar perigoso onde havião occorrido em datas proximas dois sinistros de especie identica, tinha toda a área da primeira coberta sobrecarregada de fardos de alfafa, o que por certo era grave obstaculo para as manobras, accrescendo que a bordo não havia tripolação bastante paro este effeito: emquanto que o monitor *Pará* navegava aguas abaixo obrigado a passar entre a ponta do Chaco e o *Queen*, parte estreita e arriscada do rio;

Considerando que, apezar das circumstancias apontadas, o *Pará* descia em rumo differente da linha do *Queen*, e seguiri sem accidente algum si esse navio tivesse por manobra prompta arriado ou disposto convenientemente as suas amarras.

Considerando, finalmente, que os factos de navegar a vapor o *Pará* e de achar-se o *Queen* ancorado, em nada alterão a face da questão; porquanto na materia vertente a obrigação de evitar a abalroação é, segundo a sã jurisprudencia, imposta principalmente ao navio que póde mais facilmente conseguir esse resultado, recahindo a responsabilidade do sinistro sobre aquelle que não tiver praticado tudo quanto lhe era possivel no referido intuito;

Julgo improcedemente a reclamação feita ao governo de S. M. o lmperador do Brasil pelo consul geral da Suecia e Noruega, pedindo indemnização dos damnos a que désse logar a abalroação de que se trata.

Dada em duplicado, e sellada com o sello das minhas armas. Rio de Janeiro, aos vinte e seis de Março de mil oitocentos setenta e dois. [1]

LIV. Chili, Pérou.

27 septembre 1871.

Lors de la guerre d'indépendance entreprise contre l'Espagne, le Pérou et le Chili avaient confondu leurs flottes à charge de liquider ultérieurement les dépenses. Des difficultés, nées au cours de la liquidation, décidèrent les deux gouvernements à soumettre leurs différends à un arbitrage. Les Ministres de la République Argentine et de l'Empire d'Allemagne furent successivement, mais en vain, invités à remplir la mission d'arbitre. Le Ministre des Etats-Unis de l'Amérique du Nord accepta de départager les deux pays en conflit et condamna le Pérou à payer au Chili $ 1,130,000.

[1] *Relatorio da Repartição dos Negocios Estrangeiros*, 1872, p. 669—685.

Protocolo entre los Gobiernos del Peru e Chile sobre liquidacion de la escuadra aliada, firmado en Lima, el 27 de Setiembre de 1871.

Reunidos en conferencia el 27 de Setiembre de 1871, en la sala de despacho del Ministerio de Relaciones Exteriores del Peru, José J. Loayza, Ministro del Ramo, y Adolfo Ibañez, Enviado Extraordinario y Ministro Plenipotenciario de Chile, se expuso por este que, segun instrucciones y datos suministrados por su Gobierno, estaba en su conocimiento que los comisionados peruanos y chilenos a cuyo cargo se hallaba la liquidacion de las cuentas de la Escuadra aliada, conforme a las estipulationes del pacto de alianza de 5 de Diciembre de 1865, despues de haber practicado en su mayor parte la dicha liquidacion, habian discordado en la apreciacion y resolucion de varias partidas y cuestiones referentes a ella: que convenidos ya los Gobiernos del Peru y Chile en someter a arbitraje los puntos de la discordia como unico medio justo, legal y logico de arribar a un resultado satisfactorio y conveniente para ambas partes, faltaba solo la designacion de la persona a quien conviniere conferir el cargo de arbitro arbitrador conforme a las leyes de ambos paises, y que en consecuencia invitaba al Sr. Loayza, para que, de comun acuerdo, se procediese desde luego al nombramiento indicado.

Tomado en consideracion este asunto por el Sr. Ministro de Relaciones Exteriores, Dr. D. José J. Loayza, empezo por recordar el vivo deseo que siempre ha animado al Gobierno del Peru por dejar terminada la liquidacion de las cuentas de la alianza; deseo comprobado con el nombramiento de distintos comisarios que acredito con tal fin cerca del Gobierno de Chile, entre ellos el Sr. Masias, que llevo ademas el caracter de Enviado Especial con poderes amplios para terminar esa cuestion. Que desintiendo los Comisarios de ambas Republicas en varios puntos de la cuenta y principalmente en lo relativo a la interpretacion del pacto de alianza, cuyas estipulaciones deben servir de regla para fijar las bases de la liquidacion, y no pudiendo arribar a un avenimiento, habia creido necesario el Sr. Masias entenderse con el Sr. Ministro de Relaciones Exteriores de Chile, quien propuso el arbitrajo de un tercero como medio de llegar a una solucion en este asunto. Que, no estando consignado este caso en las instrucciones del Enviado peruano, ese transmitio la proposicion a su Gobierno, el cual deseoso de dar un nuevo testimonio de deferencia al de Chile, la acepto y dio orden a aquel, para que poniendose de acuerdo con este, procediese a la designacion del dirimente. Que interrumpidas las negociaciones entabladas con tal objeto en Santiago por el mes de Agosto ultimo, a causa de las atenciones que occupaban entonces al Gobierno de Chile, con motivo del cambio que acaba de realizarse en el personal de su administracion y de la licencia concedida al Dr. Masias para regresar al Peru, le sera hoy muy grato continuarlas con el senor Ibañez, a fin de dejar constituido el arbitrajo propuesto por Chile y aceptado por el Peru que debe dejar definitivamente canjada una cuestion en que ambas partes estan igualmente interesadas.

En consecuencia, convenieron ambos senores Ministros en lo siguiente:

1° Los Gobiernos del Peru y Chile legalmente representados, el primero por el senor Ministro de Relaciones Exteriores de la Republica, y el segundo por el Enviado Extraordinario y Ministro Plenipotenciario chileno, nombran al Enviado Extraordinario y Ministro Plenipotenciario de la Republica Argentina en Chile, senor D. Felix Frias arbitro arbitrador y amigable componedor, para que con tal caracter dirima las cuestiones pendientes y en que no estan de acuerdo los comisionados chileno y peruano en el arreglo y liquidacion de las cuentas de la escuadra aliada a que es referente el pacto de alianza de 5 de Diciembre de 1865.

2° El arbitro arbitrador nombrado podra no solo dirimir las dichas cuestiones, sino tambien decidir todas las demas que existieren o que en el curso del juicio se suscitaren en orden a las mismas cuentas, pudiendo de igual modo liquidarlas definitivamente y determinar, en consecuencia, el saldo que resultare contra cualesquiera de las partes comprometidas, de manera que el fallo que pronuncie se estimara como sentencia pasada en autoridad de cosa juzgada sin lugar a reclamo de ninguna especie.

3° En el curso de la gestion y en la secuela del juicio, el arbitro podra adoptar el procedimiento que creyere mas conveniente, debiendo si poner en noticia del Ministro Residente peruano en Chile y del Ministro de Relaciones Exteriores de aquella Republica o de la persona que este delegare para el efecto, el hecho de haber aceptado el nombramiento, a fin de que las partes presenten las exposiciones que a su respectivo derecho convengan o manifiesten que se conforman con las alegaciones ya hechas por los comisionados, fijandoles para el efecto el termino que juzgare necesario.

4° Se fija el plazo de un año para que el arbitro arbitrador nombrado pronuncie el laudo y liquidacion definitivos, y este plazo principiara a correr desde la fecha en que aceptare el nombramiento y asi lo comunicare a los representantes de las partes comprometidas.

En fe de lo cual firmaron y sellaron el presente protocolo por duplicado en ejemplares del mismo tenor [1].

Sentence and award of the arbitrator in the matter of the Chili and Peru alliance, pronounced at Santiago, April 7, 1875.

Whereas the respective plenipotentiaries have stipulated at this capital, on the fifth day of December, one thousand eight hundred and sixty-five, between the republics of Chili and Peru, the following treaty of alliance, offensive and defensive, viz:

In the name of Almighty God, the republics of Chili and Peru, in presence of the danger by which America is menaced and of the violent aggression and unjust pretentions with which the Spanish government has begun to attack the dignity and sovereignty of both, have agreed to enter into a treaty of alliance, offensive and defensive; for which purpose they have nominated plenipotentiaries ad hoc: thus, on the part of Chili, Señor Domingo Santa Maria; and on the part of Peru, the secretary for foreign affairs, Señor Torilio Pacheco; who, having deemed their respective powers sufficient, proceeded to frame the present preliminary treaty.

Art. I. The republics of Chili and Peru stipulate between themselves the most intimate alliance, offensive and defensive, in order to repel the present aggression of the Spanish government, as well as any other from the same government that may be directed against the independence, the sovereignty, or the democratic institutions of both republics, or of any other of the South American continent; or that may have originated in unjust claims deemed such by both nations, and which may not be advanced according to the principles of international law, or which may be disposed of in a way contrary to said law.

Art. II. For the present and by the present treaty, the republics of Chili and Peru oblige themselves to unite such naval forces as they have or may in future have disposable, in order to oppose with them such Spanish maritime forces as are to be or may be found on the waters of the Pacific, whether blockading the ports of one of said republics, as now happens, or of both, as it may happen, or in any other way committing hostilities against Chili or Peru.

Art. III. The naval forces of both republics, whether they operate together or separately, shall obey, while the present war provoked by the Spanish government lasts, the government of that republic on whose waters said naval forces be stationed.

The officer of highest rank, and in case of there being many of the same rank, the senior among them, who may be commanding any of the combined squadrons, will assume command of them, provided such squadrons operate together.

Nevertheless, the governments of both republics may confer command of the squadrons when they operate together, to the native or foreign officer they may think most skillful.

Art. IV. Each one of the contracting republics on whose waters the combined naval forces may happen to be, on account of the present war against the Spanish government, shall defray all kinds of expenses necessary for the maintenance of the squadron or of one or more of its ships; but at the termination of the war, both republics shall nominate two commissioners, one on each side, who shall make the definite liquidation of the expenses incurred and duly vouched, and shall charge to each of the republics half of the total amount of said expenses. In the liquidation, such partial expenses are to be comprised for payment, as may have been made by both republics in the maintenance of the squadron or one or more of its ships.

---

[1] PERU, *Coleccion de los Tratados*, t. IV, p. 110.

Art. V. Both contracting parties pledge themselves to invite the other American nations to adhere to the present treaty.

Art. VI. The present treaty shall be ratified by the governments of both republics, and the ratifications shall be exchanged at Lima within forty days, or sooner if possible.

In faith whereof the plenipotentiaries of both republics sign in and seal the present treaty.

Done at Lima on the fifth day of December, one thousand eight hundred and sixty five.

BASES OF THE LIQUIDATION OF THE ALLIED ACCOUNTS.

Upon a careful consideration of the terms of the treaty of alliance, offensive and defensive, between Peru and Chili, hereto prefixed, the arbiter is of the opinion that the liquidation of the accounts of the allies must be made upon the following bases:

First. To consider the treaty of alliance as operative from the 5th of December, 1865, and the vessels then and thereafter placed at the disposal of the allied governments, as being under the common expense from that date, to the cessation of their service.

Second. To place only such vessels upon the common expense as formed the allied fleet proper, viz: the Amazonas, Apurimac, Union, América, Huáscar, Independencia, Esmeralda, Maipú, Covadonga, Abtao, Valdivia, Arauco, and Nuble.

Third. To regard a vessel as being upon the common expense as soon as she was fitted to serve the cause, and was entered so to serve it, upon the prescribed field of operations, viz., the waters of the Pacific, bordering the coasts of Peru and Chili.

Fourth. To regard all kinds of expenses (apart from those of original equipment) necessary for the maintenance of the allied vessels in a condition of effective service as belonging to the common expense, including therein the sums paid for proper transport-service.

Fifth. To regard as valid the Calvo-Reyes liquidation of September 15, 1870, in so far as it rests upon the bases herein set forth.

Sixth. To regard the 31st of October, 1867, as terminating the common expense for such vessels as remained in service up to that period; and the date when a vessel was withdrawn, by capture or entire disability for further service, as the date when the common expense shall cease as to the said vessel.

Seventh. To regard nothing as being due from one party to the other, upon account of prize-captures made by either, except in the case of Thalaba.

Eighth. To regard nothing as being due from one party to the other upon account of interest, until a balance of indebtedness is determined and default of payment occurs.

Ninth. To regard the decision of minor incidental questions as resting upon the general principles of law and equity, these being fully treated of in another portion of this judgment.

In accordance with the foregoing bases the allied service must be computed as follows:

Peruvian vessels.

Frigate Amazonas, from December 5, 1865, to January 16, 1866.

Frigate Apurimac, from December 5, 1865, to October 31, 1867.

Corvette Union, from December 5, 1865, to October 31, 1867.

Corvette América, from December 5, 1865, to October 31, 1867.

Monitor Huascar, from the 6th of June, 1866 (the time of reaching Chiloé), to October 31, 1867.

Frigate Independencia, from the 6th of June, 1866, to October 31, 1867.

Chilian vessels.

Corvette Esmeralda, from December 5, 1865, to October 31, 1867.

Steamer Maipú, from December 5, 1865, to October 31, 1867.

Schooner Covadonga, from December 5, 1865, to October 31, 1867.

Steamer Abtao, from November 20, 1866.

Steamer Valdivia, from April 5, 1867, to October 31, 1867.

Steamer Arauco, from April 5, 1867, to October 31, 1867.

Steamer Nuble, from June 1, 1867, to October 31, 1867.

In conformity with the preceding bases of liquidation, it has been found that the government of Peru is indebted to the government of Chili, upon account of the expense of the allied fleet, in the sum of one million one hundred and thirty thousand dollars.

The arbiter, not having been furnished with an exact statement of the amount of money paid by the Peruvian government to the government of Chili, in abatement of its indebtedness, it must be understood that the foregoing statement of indebtedness is to be reduced to the extent of the payments upon account made by the government of Peru to the government of Chili.

It would have been more in accordance with the desires of the arbiter, if the allies had been able to agree, in a formal manner, upon a few briefly-stated interrogatories, which should embrace the questions at issue between them, and have required his simple opinion thereon.

From the singularly intricate nature of the case, however, with its very numerous ramifications, this was found to be impossible; and in the protocol agreeing to the reference to arbitration, the arbiter was invested with the additional faculties of a judge, and requested to give his opinions in the formal manner of a legal sentence.

This he has endeavoured to do, as briefly as possible, consistently with a fair expression of the reasons which have moved him to the formation of his opinions, and with the expressed desire of the parties; together with an act of simple justice to himself, which is, that in the discharge of duties so extensive, so responsible, and so very delicate in character, he sufficiently acquit himself of any possible imputation of being dogmatic, arbitrary, or careless, in the making of his sentence.

With these remarks the following observations are submitted as the bases upon which the arbiter's conclusions have been reached :

Observations.

The treaty of alliance, offensive and defensive, between Chili and Peru as against Spain, was signed on the 5th day of December, 1865, and was ratified, according to the requirements of the instrument, on the 14th of January, 1866.

In reference to the alliance, it is to be observed, that it was equal; and to the treaty, that, embarking the allies in a common cause and requiring them to act with all their actual strength, however unequal their real strength, it was also equal. (Vattel, 6th Am., 198.)

Considering the treaty in reference to its validity, it is to be remarked, that it has all the elements, and is accompanied with all the requisite formalities, of a valid international contract, no allegation to the contrary being made by either party.

Considered in reference to its construction, it may be said to be indefinite, and in one sense incomplete, and therefore, somewhat ambiguous. It is indefinite or incomplete for several reasons ; the principal of which are, that no specific mention is made as to how many vessels and how many men each ally shall furnish; when they shall be furnished, what class of expenses shall be considered as common to the allies, and what as special; when these common expenses shall begin to accrue, &c.; and it is both incomplete and ambiguous in Article IV, providing for the ultimate settlement of the accounts between the allies.

As to the principal points of difference growing out of the differences of construction of the treaty,

it appears to the arbiter they may be comprised under the following heads:

First, as to the full scope and precise date of becoming operative of the treaty ratified January 14th, 1896, as bearing upon the question, *when* the expense attached to each vessel began to accrue as common expense; as well as the number of vessels embraced in the alliance.

Second, as to the particular class of expenses which should be borne by the parties in their separate and in their allied capacity.

Third, as to the exact character and full powers of the commissioners appointed by the allies under the provisions of Article IV.

Fourth, as to the validity of the agreements made April 8th and 12th, 1869, by the commissioners Calvo and Reyes, fixing the bases of liquidation, together with the partial adjustment of September 15th, 1870.

Fifth, as to when the period of common expense, pertaining to the individual vessels of the alliance, terminated.

Sixth, as to the division of the prize-spoils.

First.

As to the full scope and precise date of becoming operative of the treaty ratified January 14, 1866, as bearing upon the question when the expense attached to each vessel began to accrue as common expense, as well as the number of vessels embraced in the alliance.

A. *At what precise date did the treaty become operative?*

It was signed by the plenipotentiaries December the 5th, 1865, and the ratifications were formally exchanged January 14, 1866.

It therefore became operative from the former date. (‹ The exchange of ratifications has a retroactive effect, confirming the treaty from its date. › Lawrence's Wheaton, page 326).

B. *What was the scope of the treaty in relation to embracing acts of the plenipotentiaries antecedent to its actual date?*

This question, raised by one of the parties with the view of computing the common expense from a much earlier date than the formation of the treaty, viz., the 17th of October, 1865, would become of importance under a certain state of facts. On the 16th of October, 1865, Senor Don Domingo Santa Maria, as confidential agent of Chili in Peru with full powers, adressed a note to the minister of foreign relations of Peru, Senor Don Juan Manuel La Puente, stating his desire to procure the assistance of the naval and land force of Peru against Spain, which latter had already declared hostilities against Chili, by blockading its ports; and solliciting a personal audience, to lay the matter of his mission before him.

It appears by the record that this interview took place on October 17: that, as a result of the interview, the Peruvian government through its minister, issued orders that four of its vessels should at once proceed to Chilian waters, under order of that government, to assist in repelling the Spanish attack; that the Peruvian minister addressed Senor Santa Maria with an official note, dated Octobre 17, 1865, advising him of the fact and inviting the latter, if he desired to frame any treaty with Peru, to state it, and concluded by remarking that « this note, together with the documents referred to » (meaning the order placing the vessels named at the disposition of the Chilian government with the decree of war against Spain) « being the preliminary of the intimate alliance, defensive and offensive, which is established henceforth between both nations. »

On Octobre 18, 1865, Senor Santa Maria adressed an official note to the Peruvian minister, acknowledging the patriotism of Peru; accepting the order and the assistance, and concluding as follows: « The undersigned perfectly understands that the first foundation of the treaty of alliance, offensive and defensive, for opposing Spain which ought to exist between Peru and Chili is already stipulated; but, nevertheless, he thinks it would be convenient to frame some other stipulations to render the proceedings of both governments during the war they are engaged in, more expeditious. »

On the 5th of December, 1865, Senor Santa Maria upon the part of Chili and Senor Toribio Pacheco upon the part of Peru, formally framed and signed the treaty of that date.

The conclusion from this statement of facts is clear; the official preliminaries recited are to be considered as part of the treaty, and, under it, the vessels *Amazonas, Apurimac, America* and *Union* would be considered upon the common expense from October 17, 1865. (« All mere verbal communications » — and, by unavoidable corollary, written communications — « preceding the final signature of a written convention, are considered as merged in the instrument itself. » Lawrence's Wheaton, pag. 318. — « All communications, written or verbal, between the parties to a treaty, preceding its signatures, and relating to the subject thereof, are merged in the treaty. » Field, Outlines of an International Code.)

But the record shows that however good the intention in the matter of dispatching the vessels named may have been, that it was not done by reason of international difficulties connected with a change of government by that republic, that the said vessels did not become « disposable » for the purposes of the treaty until a much later date. There having been no actual compliance with the spirit or letter of the treaty until the date of its signature, the latter must be considered as the true starting-point of the alliance.

C. What were the vessels embraced in the alliance?

It is unfortunate for both governments that the treaty did not specify, in an exact manner, the number of vessels which were to be considered as constituting the alliance at its formation, together with provisions as tho the means of entry of new vessels, as from time to time they became available. The omission to do so proper a thing can only be explained by considering the great and alarming danger the allies were threatened with in the persons of so large and powerful a fleet as Spain then had upon their coasts.

In the face of such an opponent all considerations of mere money were sunk by the allies before the inexorable necessity of pressing every available means into service to avert the common danger.

The question raised in this connection is one of the two so widely separating the allies, and upon its decision rests the issue of a very large sum of money. It is proper, therefore, to consider it with the utmost care and under all the lights possible to be thrown upon it. An attentive reading of the treaty will justify the following analysis:

Article 1 stipulates an alliance for a certain purpose, viz., « In order to repel the present agression, » &c.

Article 2 prescribes the means for the effective carrying out of the purposes of the alliance. It is agreed that both republics shall unite such « naval forces » as at the time (i. e., the date of the treaty) they had « disposable », *disponibles*, or might in future (i. e., during the life of the treaty) have « disposable », for a definite purpose, i. e., « to oppose with them such Spanish maritime forces, » &c.

The simple language of the text of the two articles would seem to settle the whole question. The allies were threatened with the devastation of their sea-ports by a powerful Spanish fleet as a measure « of agression of the Spanish government ». In the inability of either republic to cope alone with so powerful a foe, it was agreed to make common cause against the maritime forces of Spain upon the waters of the Pacific, and unite certain « naval forces », which are exactly defined by the treaty (all those which were *disposable*), for the purpose of opposing with them these « maritime forces » &c. In this the maxim of strength in union was intended to be illustrated and its benefits achieved.

The idea involved comprehends two points: first, to unite the *disposable* vessels of the republics; and second, with such *disposable* vessels so united, to « oppose the Spanish maritime forces, whether blockading their ports, or in any other way committing hostilities against them ». The logical conclusion is that the allies contemplated the formation of a *fleet*, which might successfully cope with the Spanish fleet and thwart its designs. This interpretation gives a force to the alliance which, by creating a substantial entity, makes the article operate to a greater extent than the mere resolution to unite their efforts by contributing all their forces as the incidents of the war might successfully call them into action. This general idea of contributing an effective fleet seems plainly indicated by the treaty in its parts and in its entirety. If, however, there might be a reasonable doubt from the text as to whether it was contemplated forming a fleet to act in concert against the Spanish forces, or whether it purposed to unite *all* the vessels of each country and place them upon the common expense during the war, it must be dispelled by one word in the article — the word *disposable (disponibles)*.

This word is restrictive in its signification. No other « naval forces » than those which are disposable are to be united by the allies. Two distinct classes of naval forces are organized—those disposable and those not disposable. The disposable are to be united under the treaty for a certain purpose; while the undisposable are reserved for an other purpose. What can that purpose be? Is it not manifestly for the individual protection of each country? What other consideration could render them undisposable for the purposes of the alliance? Why unite only the disposable « naval forces », if it were intended to embrace all of the naval forces of both countries and place them upon the common expense?

If the reference to the disposable « naval forces » thus united be followed through the treaty, it appears to confirm the above construction in a conclusive manner.

Article 3 prescribes that the naval forces referred to in article second shall obey that government upon whose waters they be stationed, and this whether they operate together or separately; thus providing for the contingency of the fleet, before combined, being required to separate by the exigencies of the war, and act upon different waters. This article also provides for the assumption of the supreme command of the united squadron

of naval forces of both republics by the officer of highest rank, in case they operate together; but reserves the right to confer command upon any officer the governments may think most skillful when they act in combination; thus preserving the idea of a single body directed by a single officer, except in the event of their not operating together.

Again, article 4 prescribes that « each government upon whose waters the *combined* naval force may happen to be shall defray all kinds of expenses », &c. The adjective *combined* has here a specific meaning, relating to the act of aggregation, and consistently preserves the idea of the treaty.

It cannot signify an *ideal* union, while physical distinctness exists. A material thing is treated of, the maintenance of « the combined naval forces ». It were superfluous to say that a government would naturally pay the expenses of its own ships on its own waters; and the provision must be intended to meet the case of the ships of one of the republics on the waters of the other; and this consideration coupled with the obvious word combined, carries the whole question with it and calls into existence a substantial and material fleet of war-vessels, which in their operations may find themselves upon the waters of one or the other of the republics whose government is to provide for their maintenance.

To gather the fragments of the different articles and put them in a sentence so they shall tell their own story, it may be said that the *disposable* naval forces of both republics shall be united for the purpose of opposing the maritime forces of Spain on the waters of the Pacific; their command shall be intrusted to a certain officer when they act in combination, and, by inference, to the person naturally commanding them when they do not; and the cost of maintaining these combined naval forces shall be borne by that government upon whose waters they happen to be. No warrant is to be found in the treaty for the division of the expenses upon any other basis than this.

The disposable and combined naval forces of both republics shall be maintained by that government upon whose waters they happen to be, and the division of expenses is to be made at the termination of the war. No other expense is common.

Though possessing only a corrobotary value, but tending to show the intention of the parties to the treaty, it may be said, in general terms, that every document of the government officials of the time, presented to the arbiter, bears out the construction of a single combined fleet, created by the allies, for the purpose of opposing the Spanish fleet.

21

Senor Pacheco, one of the makers of the treaty, writes a note to the minister of Peru in Chili, under date of November 2, 1867, in which the character of the *Callao*, as an allied vessel, is denied, and the allied sqadron, which, it is stated, was stationed at *Chiloé*, in May, 1866, is designated by the specific mention of the vessels at that time composing it; thus plainly giving the allied squadron a « local habitation and a name ». And in this connection, another fact may be referred to. The *Callao* and *Sachaca* were, by decree of the Peruvian government, transferred to a private company, on the 31st of December, 1866, for the purpose of « facilitating the coasting-trade » of one of the allies. Had these vessels constituted a part of the allied fleet, whose expenses were to be borne in common by the allies, the act of withdrawing them by one ally without the consent of the other could hardly be considered proper. The treaty of alliance was a pact between two powers, whereby, for certain mutual interests at stake, it was stipulated that the parties should unite their disposable naval forces for their common defense. Each relied upon the assistance and good faith of the other, and neither party could violate his agreements without annulling the contract. An alliance constituted upon the right to withdraw one or more of the contributed elements whenever the interests or caprice of either party might dictate, would have no strength, moral or physical. It is not probable that either of enlightened nations, parties to the contract, would place itself and its fortune at the hazard of such a chance. Quite as specific as the note of Senor Pacheco before referred to, is the expression contained in an agreement between the minister of foreign relations of Chili and the envoy extraordinary of Peru, under date of April 17, 1866, by which a distinguished vice-admiral is intrusted with the « command in chief of the naval forces which the governments of Chili and Peru now control, or may be able to dispose of, during the actual war ».

Again, a prize-convention was held by the representatives of the two republics, on the 26th of December, 1866, by which certain rules for the distribution of prizes were agreed upon, the following words forming part of article 4: « Provided, the capturing vessel makes part of the allied squadron; but if the capturing vessel do not belong to the allied squadron, but have remained detached to the private service of one of the contracting parties », &c.,; thus at once, preserving the distinct entity of the allied squadron, and the retention of certain vessels for the private service of either party under the head of *indisposable*. This convention was not ratified through non-necessity, but has an importance as showing understanding and intention at the time.

Further, in the protocol signed by the minister of foreign relations of Chili, and the envoy extraordinary of Peru in Chili, under direction of their respective governments, dated October 5, 1867, it was plainly agreed to dissolve the allied squadron by placing the Peruvian division forming part of it under command of its own government.

Of this protocol four leading points are to be observed:

1. That the alliance itself should remain intact.

2. That placing the Peruvian division under orders of its own government should operate to dissolve the common expense.

3. That, should the enemy again call the allies into action, the mutual-expense arrangement for the naval divisions of Peru and Chili under consideration should form the subject of a new agreement.

4. That profound silence is maintained as to the common expense ceasing in regard to vessels not under the orders of Chili; and hence, if *all* the naval vessels of one of the allies had been under the common expense, as claimed, they would still remain so, no modification of the treaty in regard to them having ever been made.

This agreement between Senores Pardo and Fortecilla, whereby the common expense was considered terminated, has an important significance, as showing the interpretation given to the treaty in this respect by those gentlemen. This interpretation is only individual opinion, to be sure, and therefore is in no sense conclusive, but nevertheless it has corroborative value, as showing the understanding of the makers of the treaty by those who were co-actors in the events of the time.

The sole object of the agreement, it is admitted, was to terminate the common expense account of the allies; and it will be observed that this was done, not by a direct agreement to terminate said common account, but by the stipulation that, as it was unnecessary for « the Peruvian naval division incorporated into the allied squadron to continue longer under orders of the Chilian government », the said division should, from the date of the agreement, be considered as under orders of the Peruvian government; but, for reasons which do not appear, it was further stipulated that, notwithstanding the said division was placed under orders of its own government, its expenses should be common until the first of November following.

There can be no mistake as to the understanding of the makers of the agreement in regard to the constitution of an allied squadron proper, whose expenses only were to be common. The placing of the ‹ Peruvian naval division incorporated in the allied squadron ›, under orders of its own government, terminated the common expense at a certain date.

No other common expense is provided for: the designation of those vessels whose expense had been common is specific, viz: ‹ The Peruvian naval division incorporated into the allied squadron, under the orders of the Chilian government. › This construction *must* be accepted; there is but one alternative—that of considering the common expense account as *existing to this day*. The latter proposition, as involving a conceded absurdity, leaves only the former for adoption.

Further, the documents are copious, proving that the commissioners, Calvo and Reyes, acted constantly under instructions from their governments, in the liquidation made by them; while their work shows conclusively that they entertained no idea of creating a community of expense in regard of any other vessels than those specifically defined in their joint liquidation.

Finally, no claim to the contrary by either party anywhere appears, until the supreme decree of the government of Peru, June 3, 1869.

These considerations convey to the mind of the arbiter the unavoidable conviction that the treaty of alliance substantially established only two things: first, that the two republics entered into a league to defend themselves, and back each other to the extent of their ability, against Spain; and second, that as the contest was expected to be of a naval character, and neither of the allies possessed a fleet large enough, or strong enough, to cope with the Spanish fleet, they stipulated to put such vessels together as they could dispose of compatibly with their individual interests and safety, to oppose the Spanish fleet; and that the expense account of the vessels composing the allied fleet should be borne by the allies in common.

D. At what time did the common expense begin to cover vessels which entered the alliance subsequently to the date of the treaty?

In the absence of specific mention upon this important point recourse must be had to the general structure and spirit of the treaty. In the solution of the question two points must be kept prominently in view: first, the vessels which were to be embraced in the alliance; and second, the field of operations prescribed by the treaty.

As regards the first, it appears that such naval forces as the republics then had, or might in the future have at their disposal, were to be embraced in the alliance; and accordingly vessels were added to the combined forces by both parties, as from time to time they became available.

As regards the second point, it must be carefully observed that those naval forces were to be united for a particular purpose, about which there can be no doubt whatever—this purpose being ‹ in order to oppose with them such Spanish maritime forces as are to be or may be found on the waters of the Pacific, whether blockading, › etc. Here the field of hostile operations is limited to *the waters of the Pacific*, and, by fair and logical induction, from the concluding sentences of the article, to those portions of the Pacific, bordering the coasts of allies. Therefore, except through the most extensive interpretation, it would not be within the terme of the treaty to transfer the allied fleet to the coast of Spain or the waters of the Atlantic; nor could any vessel properly belong to the alliance until she was not alone ready for the service, but ready for the service upon the field of action, so plainly prescribed by the treaty. Whenever, therefore, a vessel belonging to either of the allies was ready for service upon such parts of the waters of the Pacific as rendered her of substantial aid to the common cause, and brought her under the direction of the naval chief of the allied fleet, she became an allied vessel under the stipulations of the treaty.

SECOND.

As to the particular class of expenses which should be borne by the parties in their separate and in their allied capacity.

The language of the article 4 of the treaty seems plainly enough to interpret the meaning of the makers. The particular government, upon whose waters the naval forces united or combined in a mutual cause, under article 2, may happen to be, shall defray *all kind of expenses necessary for the maintenance* of the squadron or one or more of its ships. The word maintenance has no technical signification in this relationship, meaning simply the upholding, supporting, and keeping up of each particular vessel, that it might sustain its attitude of belligerency. Hence, its provisions, the pay of its men, its fuel, its ammunition, the repairs necessary to maintain it in its belligerent capacity, etc., are legitimate items belonging to the common expense. It must be remarked, however, that while the warrant is sufficiently extensive to cover every item necessary to the accomplishment of the purpose named, there appears no authority for levying expense upon the common treasury, which did not go to the maintenance above spoken of. Neither would it be proper to compute the expenses of original equipment, outfitting, etc., of such vessel as common expense, these being considered the contribution of each nation to the common cause, and in furtherance of the common safety, under the treaty, which regarded the strength of both republics as being equal, though in fact it may not have been so. As no sharp line of division can be drawn as to the class of expenses which, while necessary under the head of maintenance, at the same time added a permanent value to a particular vessel, the determination as to such cases must fall within the domain of equity.

Nor can it be inferred from the treaty that the loss of the exclusive property of one or the other, in conflicts with the enemy, was to be reimbursed by the allies. The alliance was considered equal in that no mention of the respective vessels each was to furnish, the forces being considered equal for the purposes of the alliance, as before remarked. The vessels of each, such as they were, and however acquired, were embarked in the common cause; and the danger to each republic being equal, as repeatedly stated in the papers accompanying the formation of the treaty, and by the treaty itself, each nation assumed the risks and casualties of the war from necessity, the only expenses which were considered as common between them being those connected with the maintenance of the squadron, or one or more of its ships.

THIRD.

As to the exact character and full powers of the commissioners, appointed by the allies, under the provisions of Article VI.

The difference between the allies upon this point seems radical and irreconcilable; but, it would appear from a careful consideration of the language of Article 4, taken in its usual and accepted sense, together with established usage pertaining to such agents, that there should be no difficulty in arriving at the true solution of the question.

The word commissioner (Latin, *committere*, to intrust to) is usually applied to an agent, who has a commission or warrant to perform some special business, or particular branch of duty. When employed by one government, in the transaction of business with another, it usually falls within this definition; and in such cases, the warrant or power of the officer should exactly express the nature and extent of his commission. (Les commissaires, envoyés à l'étranger, n'ont cette qualité, aucune des prérogatives des ministres publics, mais le titre de ministre leur peut être conféré, ainsi que cela se pratique quelquefois pour des commissaires ayant mission de régler des délimitations de frontières ou de procéder à des liquidations. C'est donc à leur constituant à préciser le caractère officiel dont il entend les revêtir. Martens, Guide diplomatique, p. 62.) Vattel contends that an agent sent with credentials on public business, becomes a public minister, his title, whether it be deputy, commissioner or other, making no difference in the case. The real question between the allies, however, is not as to the precise diplomatic character of the commissioners, provided for in Article 4, but the exact power conferred upon them by that article. It is a fair construction of the article, that having ascertained the amount of expense incurred, they were to make report to the two republics, for approval or ratification; or did the article invest them with authority to make a final settlement between the parties?

There can be no question that it was the intention of the allies to bear each an equal portion of the expense of the allied fleet, and the appointment of the commissioners was a simple provision for arriving at the total amount of the legitimate expense that each of the republics might pay the one-half. Their whole duty was to make the definite liquidation of the expenses incurred and duly vouched, and charge to each republic half of the total amount of said expenses. (Los cuales practicaran la liquidacion definitiva de los gastos hechos y debidamente justificados y cargaran a cada una de ellas la mitad del valor total a que estos gastos asciendan.)

The commissioners were authorized by the article to do two things and only two things: first, to make the definite liquidation of the expenses incurred and duly vouched; and second, to charge each of the republics one-half of the total amount of said expenses.

As regards the first duty, there can be no double interpretation. Bouvier in his Law Dictionary defines liquidation as « a fixed and determinate valuation of things, which before were uncertain ». They were, then, to ascertain the expenses incurred, according to the proper vouchers. After having done this, as the second branch of their duties, they were to *charge* one-half of the amount of the expenses so ascertained to each republic. The verb to *charge* has here no technical meaning in the absence of other stipulations, and must be taken in its usual sense. According to Webster, it signifies « to place to the account of, as a debt; to make responsible for ».

The commissioners, then, were expressly authorized by the treaty to ascertain the whole expense, and to put one-half the total to the account of each republic, as a debt.

These were their specific duties as commissioners and the absence of any other conditions in the treaty shows that their acts were to be considered final. If the words « shall charge » have not this meaning, they have none; and having none, there can be no resulting effect. Hence, according to a recognized rule of interpretation, that signification should be adopted which will permit the provision to operate.

Indeed, it does not appear that any contrary understanding was entertained by either party, until the protocol of the conference between the Chilian chargé, Señor Godoi, and the Peruvian minister of foreign relations and of finance, was signed on November 6, 1869, when Señor Angulo made the statement, apparently acquiesced in by Señor Godoi, that the liquidation of the commissioners required the final approbation of both governments. This, however, was some seven months after the commissioners Calvo and Reyes had signed the agreements fixing the bases for the regulation and liquidation of the accounts; in the second of these agreements, dated April 13, 1869, it appears that Señor Calvo had been under instructions from his government as to what items should be allowed; while subsequent papers show that both commissioners in their settlement referred continually to their respective governments.

In the interpretation of this portion of the treaty, usage, as to the officials denominated commissioners, may also have a corroborative bearing. (A clear usage is the best of all interpreters between nations. Phillimore, vol. 2, p. 72.) Without going further than the example of the United States, in its relations with other powers it may be said that the resort to commissioners has been a frequent method of settling differences as to boundaries, the determination of amounts of money to be paid, etc., as — (see the treaty with Great Britain of October 28, 1795, providing for the appointment of three sets of commissioners, whose awards, on the different subjects submitted to them, were to be final; the treaty of Ghent, February 17, 1815, appointing commissioners to decide boundary-lines, whose award was to be final; with Great Britain, January 10, 1823, to ascertain amount of indemnity to be paid for loss of slaves, under the decision of the Emperor of the Russias, the award of the commissioners to be final; the claims convention with Denmark, June 5, 1830, the treaty not specifying that the award should be final, but being so regarded; the claims convention with Mexico, April 7, 1840; the claims convention with Mexico, February 1, 1869; the boundary convention with Mexico, May 30, 1848; the award of the commissioners in all being final; the claims convention with Great Britain, July 26, 1853; with New Granada, November 5, 1860; with Costa Rica, November 9, 1861; with Ecuador, July 27, 1864; with Venezuela, April 17, 1867; and the cele-

brated treaty of Washington, June 17, 1871, all of these providing for the appointment of commissioners whose award was to be considered final).

Reference may also be made to a claims convention between the United States and Peru, April 18, 1863; and one, July 4, 1869; both providing for the appointment of commissioners whose award was to be considered final.

These examples, certainly, go far toward establishing a clear usage of submitting questions of difference to the decision of commissioners, whose decisions have always been accepted as final. In all the instances, save one, by a special article, however, which does not appear in the treaty of alliance of December 5, 1865. In the face of such precedent, and in consideration of the simple duties of the allied commissioners, as mere *auditing* officers the omission cannot be material. (The rule, that the influence and authority of *usage* in the interpretation of private covenants is such that customary clauses, though not expressed, are held to be contained therein, is, in its spirit, applicable to international covenants. Phillmore, vol. 2, p. 77.)

The expression that the duties of the allied commissioners were expected to be simply those of an auditory and arithmetical character is legitimately inferable from the spirit of the treaty as a whole, and the failure to make any provision for the appointment of an umpire to decide cases of disagreement, while the omission to insert a reservation that their acts should be subjected to the approval of both governments, shows that they were invested with full and final power to audit the indebtedness and specify the balance of money due from one to the other of the allies.

FOURTH.

As to the validity of the agreements made April 8th and 12th, by the commissioners, Calvo and Reyes, fixing the basis of liquidation; together with the partial adjustment, September 15, 1870.

From the foregoing consideration it must be clear that these acts of the commissioners must be considered valid, buth with a most important reservation. It is a well established principle of international law that after a treaty possessing all of the elements of validity, has been formally executed, it can only be altered or amended before its proper expiration by the same authority, and under the same formality of procedure as the original; and especially is it not permissible for either party to interpret its provisions according to his own fancy. In the discharge of their duties under Article fourth, the commissioners must, of necessity, keep themselves strictly within the scope of the treaty, in doing which their acts must be held binding on the allies; but in departing from which their acts are null to the precise extent of the departure. In the difficulties of settlement which presented themselves the commissioners, in a spirit of mutual concession, highly creditable to their desire for amity and fair dealing, saw fit to make certain arbitrary arrangements, as, for instance, that a certain class of expenses of particular vessels should begin at a certain time, and certain others at a certain other time; all of which, as being outside of the proper construction of the treaty, could only be made valid by a submission to and ratification by the principals. Hence, the partial liquidation by the commissioners of the date September 15, 1870, can only be held good so far as it conforms itself to what is believed to be the true interpretation here.

FIFTH.

As to when the period of common expenses pertaining to the individual vessels of the alliance terminated.

The withdrawal of the Spanish forces from the contest without the execution of a formal treaty of peace, led the allies to the conclusion of a convention, fixing the 31st day of October, 1867, as a date whereupon the common expense account should cease. Hence, those vessels serving the allied cause continuously up to that date are to be considered upon the common expense until it was reached; while those serving only a portion of the time could be so reckoned only to the cessation of their service.

SIXTH.

As to the division of the prize spoils.

Under this construction of the treaty, the allies derived no common benefit from the captures in the Atlantic by the ironclads *Huascar* and *Independencia*, because these vessels had not reached the Pacific, and hence could not belong to the allied fleet.

Neither did the *Callao* belong to the allied fleet when she captured the *Guiding Star*, and therefore the actual captors were alone entitled to the prize.

As regards the *Thalaba*, captured by the *Covadonga*, the capture must be considered joint. The allied fleet was at anchor in the bay of Valparaiso, and the *Covadonga* was dispatched by the commander to make the capture, which, although it did not occur within actual sight of the rest of the fleet, yet clearly falls within the general laws of prize entitling the whole squadron to joint participation, when a capture is made by one or more of its vessels, not upon a separate and detached service, and close enough to the squadron to be considered as but one of the outstretched arms of the latter.

THE DECISION OF MINOR INCIDENTAL QUESTIONS.

The Paquette del Maule. — This vessel was a transport, and though chartered by one of the allies prior to December 5, 1865, the date of the treaty, she passed into service as a transport into the allied fleet, as near as can now be determined, about December 30, 1865. No evidence, at least, has been presented to the arbiter that she served the common cause prior to that date. As a transport to the combined fleet, the division of her expenses is legitimate, the transport service being absolutely necessary under the head of maintenance, as defined in the treaty. The documentary evidences are sufficiently copious to show that, when captured, she was on a service directly beneficial to one of the allies, with the full knowledge and at least tacit consent of its representative. No objection was made by him at the proper time, either to the terms or service of the vessel, and the right of objection is therefore lost. The expenses of the vessel, as well as her loss, are divisible by the allies from December 30, 1865.

Enlistments. — These cannot be considered divisible under the head of maintenance. The spirit of the treaty contemplates a contribution, by each nation, of certain efficient warlike elements. Ships unmanned cannot be considered; and recruiting at the common expense was not provided for by the treaty. This item is thrown out of the liquidation, and each ally charged with his own expenses in this direction, so far as it has been possible to ascertain them.

Expenses of repairing at Chiloé. — The note of Señor Calvez, dated December 4, 1865, promising to repay, immediately, the expense of repairing the four vessels sent to Chiloé, must be considered part of the treaty, by a rule before stated. Hence, the ally owing the ships must beer the expenses exclusively. Had the account been presented, and default of payment occurred, interest could have been claimed upon the amount. Under the circumstances, it cannot be allowed.

Surplus supplies. — If a surplus of supplies was drawn by one of the allies, it was by the knowledge and act of the other, who, failing to object or protest at the proper time, has lost the remedy.

Wages of court-martialed officers. — When these left the service of the principal (the allied fleet) by their own act, they had no claim to recompense for services unrendered. The local law of one of the allies, allowing half-pay to court-martialed officers, cannot bind the other in the absence of a mutual agreement.

Difference in coin. — If one of the allies paid the salaries of the men of the other in a coin twenty-five per cent more valuable than the home coin of the latter, it does not appear that the latter had any agency or direction in it; and, as being the act of the former, he cannot take advantage of his own wrong. The difference has not been allowed.

Voyage of a minister from one country to another. — This had no connection contemplated by the treaty with « the maintenance of the allied squadron, or one or more of its ships », and has not been allowed.

The Apurimac after leaving the allied fleet. — This vessel was sent to Peru for repairs, which could not be made in Chile, with the knowledge and consent of both parties. Under the plain provisions of the treaty a vessel was not compelled to be bodely present with the allied fleet in order to constitute a part of it, the contingency of separation being expressly provided for; nor can any claim against her seaworthiness lie at this late day. She was accepted as an allied vessel by both parties, sent to Peru for repairs, and the objection now urged should have been made at that time. The failure to do this places the objectors in the position of taking an advantage after the fact. Her expense is computed as common to October 31, 1867. .

The coal amount. — The expense of maintenance in the way of fuel is common. No human intelligence could have forseen the exact amount of fuel to be required during an undetermined period and by an unknown number of consumers. The provision must be large enough to cover the contingency. As both parties incurred a joint expense in the amount purchased, both should share the profits of the residue. It is therefore so computed in this liquidation, the result being arrived at as accurately as circumstances have permitted. Coal consumed in the private use of one of the parties has been put to his exclusive account.

The matter of cannon received by one ally from the other. — This question, carrying with it a large claim, has received the serious attention of the arbiter, and, from a most careful perusal of the document from which he derives his powers, he can arrive at no other conclusion than that it is not within his faculties to decide the question. His whole authority is « to adjust the pending questions on which the Peruvian and Chilean commissioners are not agreed in the arrangement and liquidation of the accounts of the allied squadron, referred to by the pact of alliance of the 5th of December 1865 »; and further, « to decide all the rest which may exist, or which, in the course of judgment, may arise from the same accounts » (i. e., the accounts of the allied squadron). The transactions referred to had no connection with the allied squadron or its accounts, which were to be born in common; but seem the arbiter to involve a question of international ethics, easily arranged, with which, under his present authority, he cannot intervene, or pronounce a binding judgment, should he do so.

The General Lersundi. — So far as this vessel is connected with the transaction of the cannon between the allies, the arbiter, as before stated, can give no valid judgment; but as it plainly appears that she « was afterward sunk at the mouth of the Huito Channel by the common agreement of a council of war, composed of Chilean and Peruvian officers, in order to save the life of the squadron », she certainly falls within the scrutiny of the arbiter, and strict equity would demand that her loss be imputed to the common account, which is accordingly done in this liquidation.

The Callao as a transport. — Though this vessel did not belong to the allied fleet, yet it has been conclusively shown that she performed important transport service to the fleet, and compensation as such, while actually engaged in the service, has been allowed in this liquidation.'

LV. Brésil, Paraguay.

9 janvier 1872.

La commission mixte, organisée par les puissances contractantes, a eu à évaluer les dommages causés par la guerre et mis à la charge du Paraguay. Le nombre des affaires examinées se monta à 805 et les indemnités réclamées à 27,831 : 346 $ 303. Le protocole final du 30 juillet 1881 résume en détail les travaux des commissaires.

Tratado definitivo de paz entre o Imperio do Brazil e a Republica do Paraguay, hecho en la Ciudad de la Asuncion, Enero 9, 1872.

. . . .

ART. III. El gobierno de la República del Paraguay reconocerá como deuda de la misma República :

1º La importancia de lo indemnizacion de los gastos de la guerra que hizo el gobierno de

---

[1] *Foreign Relation of the U. S.*, 1875—1876, vol. I, p. 188—199.

Su Magestad el Emperador del Brasil y de los daños causados o las propiedades publicas que se fijare en la convencion especial en la forma del articulo 4°.

2° La importancia de los daños e perjuicios causados a los personas y cuidadanos del referido Estado.

Esta indemnizacion será fijada en la forma del articulo 5°.

ART. IV. Una convencion especial que será celebrada, á mas tardar dentro de dos años, fijará benevolamente la *cantidad* de las indemnizaciones de que trata el número 1° del articulo antecedente, á vista de los documentos oficiales; regulará la forma del pagamento y las cuotas de interes y de amortizacion del capital; y designará las rentas que hayan de ser aplicadas a ese pagamento.

ART. V. Dos meses despues de trocadas las ratificaciones del presente tratado se nombrará una comision mixta que se compondrá de dos jueces y de dos arbitros para examinar y liquidar las indemnizaciones provenientes de las causas mencionadas en el 2° número del articulo 3°.

Esta comision se reunirá en las ciudades de Rio de Janeiro ó de la Asuncion conforme convinieren los dos gobiernos.

En los casos de divergencia entre los jueces será escogido á la suerte uno de los arbitros y este decidirá la cuestion.

Si aconteciere (lo que no as de esperar) que una de las altas partes contratantes, por qualquier motivo que sea, deje denombrar el comisario y arbitro en el prazo arriba estipulado, ó que, despues de nombrarlos, siendo necessario sostituirlos, los no sostituya dentro de igual plazo; procederón el comisario y el arbitro de la otra parte contradante al examen y liquidacion de las respectivas reclamaciones, y á sus decisiones se sujetará el gobierno cujos mandatarios faltaren.

ART. VI. Queda establecido el plazo de diez y ocho mesas para la presentacion de todas las reclamaciones que deben ser jusgadas por la comision mixta de que habla el articulo antecedente y fenecido ese plazo, ninguna otra reclamacion será atendida.

La deuda de esto procedencia será pagada por el gobierno paraguayo, á medida que se fuere liquidando en apolices á la par que venzan el interes de seis por ciento, y tengan la amortizacion de uno por ciento al año. La amortizacion se hará a la par y á la suerte, pudiendo asistir al acto el consul de la nacion reclamante que residiere en el lugar en que fuere realizada la dicho operacion, y que habiere sido paro eso autorisado [1].

[1] *Relatorio da Repartição* . . ., 1872, p. 236.

Un seul incident important, relatif à l'interprétation du texte de l'article III du traité du 9 janvier 1872, provoqua la conclusion d'une convention additionnelle.

Protocole du 24 Janvier 1874 destiné à interpréter certains termes du traité du 9 Janvier 1872 et à faciliter les travaux de la commission mixte.

Na cidade de Assumpção do Paraguay, aos vinte e quatro dias do mez de Janeiro de mil oitocentos e setenta e quatro, reunidos no ministerio de relações exteriores SS. EExs. os Srs. conselheiro Antonio José Duarte de Araujo Gondim, enviado extraordinario e ministro plenipotenciaro de Sua Magestade o Imperador do Brazil, e D. José del Rosario Miranda, ministro e secretario de Estado no departamento de relações exteriores, afim de recapitularem as suas anteriores conferencias e darem uma solução definitiva as questões controvertidas entre os Srs. juizes commissarios do Brazil e do Paraguay relativamente á significação da phrase *damnos e prejuizos*, empregada no art. 3° do tratado de paz entre o Imperio e a Republica, quando estipula indemnizações a favor das pessoas e cidadãos do primeiro; ao direito de serem contemplados nessas indemnizações os senhores cujos escravos foram mortos, aprehendidos ou extraviados pelas forças que invadiram as provincias de Mato-Grosso e S. Pedro de Rio Grande do Sul; e á necessidade de serem vertidos em castelhano os processos enviados das referidas duas provincias;

Depois de examinarem madura e amigavelmente a letra e o espirito do supracitado tratado em suas estipulações referentes ao assumpto;

Chegaram ao seguinte accôrdo, que resolveram deixar consignado por escripto:

Por damnos e prejuizos, quanto a bens, deve entender-se não só o valor da propriedade destruida ou arrebatada, ou do damno nella causado, como tambem o juro legal de 6 % ao anno sobre esse valor principal, a contar do dia em que foi realizado o mal. Os escravos, para a indemnização estipulada, devem ser equiparados a qualquer outra propriedade legal, cabendo, portanto, aos reclamantes desta ordem os mesmos direitos reconhecidos aos demais prejudicados. Finalmente, quanto ao terceiro ponto, fica dispensada a traducção dos processos, em attenção á perfeita analogia entre as linguas portugueza e hespanhola; á facilidade com que os Srs. juizes commissarias poderão desvanecer-se reciprocamente qualquer duvida sobre palavras ou phrases peculiares a cada uma das duas linguas; e aos sérios embaraços que o prenchimento de similhante formalidade traria ao regular andamento dos trabalhos da commissão mixta.

Em testemunho do que os referidos Srs. ministros mandaram lavrar o presente protocollo, que assignaram e fizeram sellar [1].

Acta de encerramento dos trabalhos da commissao mixta, assignada nesto cidade de Assumpçao do Paraguay, aos 30 de Julho de 1881.

Nesta cidade de Assumpção do Paraguay aos trinta dias do mez de Julho do anno do Nascimento de Nosso Senhor Jesus Christo de mil oitocentos oitanta e um, sendo Imperador do Brasil Sua Magestade o Senhor Dom Pedro II e Presidente interino da Republica do Paraguay o Sr. General Dom Bernardino Caballero, reunidos os Srs. Juizes Commissarios na sala e hora do costume, declararam aberta a sessão. Foi deliberado pelos mesmos Snr⁰ˢ Juizes que, sendo esta a ultima sessão da Commissão, fossem consignados nesta acta os principaes dados da historia e estatistica da Commissão, que são os seguintes: Da acta n. I vê-se que a Commissão installou seus trabalhos em 16 de Dezembro de 1872 e pela presente n. 369, em que são encerrados, verifica-se que no periodo de oito annos sete mezes e quatorze dias de sua duração foram celebradas 369 sessões de que se lavraram actas. Funccionaram nesta commissão por parte do Brasil como Juizes arbitros os Chefes da respectiva Legação que foram: 1º Exm. Sr. Conselheiro Joaquim Maria Nascentes de Azambuja, nomeado por Decreto de 26 de Maio de 1872, e consta da acta n. I — 2º Exm. Sr. Barão de Araguaya, nomeado por Decreto de 5 de Maio de 1873 como consta da acta n. 33 de 9 de Junho de 1873 a fls. 19 — 3º Exm. Sr. Conselheiro Antonio José Duarte de Araujo Gondim, nomeado por Decreto de 29 de Outubro de 1873 consignado na acta n. 66 a fls. 42 em 29 de Dezembro de 1873 — 4º Exm. Sr. Conselheiro Felippe José Pereira Leal, nomeado por Decreto de 11 de Setembro de 1875, como consta da acta n. 98 a fls. 65 em 9 de Novembro de 1875 — 5º e ultimo o Exm. Sr. Dr. Eduardo Callado, nomeado por Decreto de 12 de Julho de 1876 por Sua Alteza Imperial Regente, como consta da acta n. 112 a fls. 72 em 25 de Janeiro de 1877; e Juiz Commissario o actual Sr. João Pereira Silva, nomeado por Decreto de 26 de Maio de 1872, como consta da acta n. 1. Por parte do Paraguay serviram os Srs. Juizes Arbitros: 1º o cidadão Senador Dⁿ Matheo Collar, nomeado por Decreto de 24 de Julho de 1872, como consta da acta n. 1 — e 2º o cidadão Senador Dom Bernardo Recalde, nomeado por Decreto de 11 de Dezembro de 1873, como consta da acta n. 66 a fls. 42 de 29 de Dezembro de 1873 e Juizes Commissarios: 1º o cidadão Senador Dom Miguel Palacios, nomeado por Decreto de 17 de Junho de 1872 como consta da acta n. 1 — 2º o cidadão Dom Carlos Loizaga, nomeado por Decreto de 11 de Abril de 1874 que consta da acta n. 70 de 13 de Abril de 1874 a fls. 45 — 3º o cidadão Dom Juan Bautista Gonzales, nomeado por Decreto de 29 de Maio de 1875 consignado na acta n. 90 a fls. 60 em 17 .de Junho de 1875 — 4º o cidadão Dom José Segundo Decoud, nomeado por Decreto de 30 .de Outubro de 1875 e consta da acta n. 98 a fls. 65 em 9 de Novembro de 1875 — 5º o cidadão Dom José Thomaz Soza, nomeado por Decreto de 27 de Março de 1876 consignado no acta n. 107 de 30 de Março de 1876 a fls. 68 — 6º o cidadão Dignitario da Ordem da Rosa do Brasil Dom Domingo Antonio Ortiz, nomeado por Decreto de 13 de Janeiro de 1877 e consta da acta n. 112 de 25 do mesmo mez e anno a fls. 72 — 7º o cidadão Deputado Dom Augustin Cañete, nomeado por Decreto de 25 de Maio de 1877 inserto na acta n. 129 de 13 de Junho de 1877 a fls. 78 — 8º e ultimo o actual cidadão Deputado Dom José Maria Fretes, nomeado por Decreto de 8 de Outubro de 1877 constante da acta n. 142 de 12 de Outubro de 1877 a fls. 82. De 16 de Dezembro de 1872 a 15 de Junho de 1874 decorreram os dezouto mezes fixados no articulo 6º do Tratado de 9 de Janeiro de 1872 para apresentação das reclamações e da acta n. 81 a fls. 55 em 18 de Junho de 1874, vê-se que a Commissão recebeu nesse periodo 804 processos de reclamações, numero este que foi elevado a 805 por haver-se desannexado do processo n. 31 por accordo dos dois Governos, o de n. 31 A, como consta da acta n. 364 de 29 de Janeiro de 1880 a fls. 363. A cifra reclamada nestes 805 processos foi de 27,831 : 346 $ 303, e sua liquidação foi feita como se passa a demonstrar no quadro que segue [1].

Das 784 julgadas por sentenças definitivas destacam-se 4, na importancia de Rs. 130 : 767 $ 586, que por sentenças de 30 de Abril proximo findo sob ns. A, B, C e D a commissão julgou-se incompetente para tomar conhecimento dellas por pertencerem, duas á liquidação dos gastos de guerra a propriedades do Estado, e as outras duas por tratarem de damnos verificados fóra do territorio do Brasil, restando 780 com a somma de Rs. 26,811 : 124 $ 040 que por sentenças de ns. I a 780 registradas em livro proprio, e consignadas nas actas tiveram a indemnisação de

---

[1] *Relatorio da Repartição* ..., 1874, p. 488.

[1] Voir le tableau à la page suivante.

Deve	A COMMISSÃO MIXTA BRASILEIRO-PARAGUAYA EM C/C COM OS RECLAMANTES					Haver
805	Processos de reclamação no importe de	27,831 : 346 $ 303	11	Duplicatas actas ns. 48, 76, 79, 83, 84, 85, 86 e 89 . .		612 : 672 $ 542
			10	Com despachos interlocutorios que não voltarão . .		276 : 782 $ 135
			784	Julgadas por sentenças definitivas		26,941 : 891 $ 626
	Réis	27,831 : 346 $ 303		Réis		27,831 : 346 $ 303

Rs. 17,919 : 702 $ 185 ou P. F^a 8,959,851—9¼ sendo de capital Rs. 10,059 : 909 $ 797 e de juros contados até a data das sentenças Rs. 7,859 : 792 $ 388, pertencendo 605 a Brasileiros, representado Rs. 19,855 : 937 $ 457 e 175 a estrangeiros com a cifra de Rs. 6,955 : 186 $ 583, sendo 17 allemães, com 316 : 990 $ 088; 20 argentinos com 803 : 651 $ 563; 26 francezes com 724 : 614 $ 205; 37 hespanhóes com 980 : 600 $ 326; 33 italianos com 2,997 : 412 $ 427; 9 orientaes com 219 : 705 $ 537; 1 paraguayo com 2 : 200 $ 000 e 32 portuguezes com 910 : 012 $ 437. A estatistica contém todos os detalhes por provincias e villas que seria por de mais consignar nesta acta. Das actas deste livro compõe-se a historia da marcha da commissão, e por ellas sabe-se as razões por que só funccionou activamente nos annos de 1879 e 1880.

Dos 25 processos em que a commissão proferio despachos interlocutorios, transcriptos nas actas de ns. 15, 16, 17, 21, 22, 25, 28, 29, 32, 38, 39, 40, 43, 44, 46, 47, 50, 51, 56, 57, 100, 231, 287 e 323, voltaram 15 que foram julgadas definitivamente.

As questões debatidas no seio da commissão, constam das actas ns. 13, 31, 35, 37, 45, 63, 69, 92, 94, 109, 111 e 171, sendo sujeitas á decisão dos dous Governos todas as divergencias. O recurso arbitral não foi usado. Em seguido manifestaram os Srs. Juizes Commissarios reciprocas felicitações por terem conseguido a terminação do pesado mandato que lhes foi confiado por seus respectivos Governos com a conclusão dos trabalhos desta commissão, graças á valiosa coadjuvação que se prestaram e harmonia em que viveram. O cumprimento dos artigos do tratado definitivo de paz assignado nesta capital em 9 de Janeiro de 1872, referentes a esta commissão, não póde deixar de concorrer mui directa e poderosamente para mais desenvolver as relações amistosas entre duas Nações vizinhas, tão necessarios para conseguirem o maior progresso e riqueza com a paz.

Os Srs. Escripturarios foram comprimentados pelos Srs. Juizes Commissarios por haverem concorrido com seus importantes contingentes para os trabalhos da commissão. E não havendo mais de que tratar-se foi declarada encerrada a sessão, e com ella ficam igualmente encerrados os trabalhos desta commissão. Em fé do que lavrou-se a presente acta, que depois de lida e approvada vae assignada pelos dous Srs. Juizes Commissarios[1].

LVI. Grande-Bretagne, Portugal.
25 septembre 1872.

Cette affaire fort simple consistait principalement dans la prétention des deux pays à occuper certains territoires et îlots situés dans la baie de Delagoa. L'arbitre se prononça en faveur du Portugal.

Protocol signed at Lisbon on Septembre 25, 1872, to refer to arbitration the respective claims in Delagoa Bay.

Whereas the Government of Her Britannic Majesty asserts a claim to certain territories formerly belonging to the Kings of Tempe and Mapoota, on the eastern coast of Africa, including the Islands of Inyack and Elephant; and whereas the Government of His Most Faithful Majesty asserts a claim to a portion of the same territories, as far as 26 degrees 30 minutes; and whereas both Parties, being animated by a friendly feeling, and neither of them having any wish to appropriate territory which may lawfully belong to the other, have consented to refer their respective claims to the arbitration of a third Power, in whom both repose confidence.

For this purpose, they have agreed to apply to the President of the French Republic; and it now becomes necessary to place on record certain terms and arrangements with a view of obtaining the speedy and convenient hearing and

---

[1] *Relatorio da Repartiçao* . . ., 1882, p. 152.

determination of the claims in question; and the undersigned, William Doria, Her Britannic Majesty's Chargé d'Affaires at the Court of Lisbon, and the Counciller Joao de Andrade Corvo, Minister and Secretary of State for Foreign Affairs of His Most Faithful Majesty being duly authorized by their respective Governments, have agreed as follows:

ARTICLE I. The respective claims of Her Britannic Majesty's Government and of His Most Faithful Majesty, to the territories and islands abovementioned, shall be submitted to the arbitration and award of the President of the French Republic who shall decide thereupon finally and without appeal.

ARTICLE II. The award of the President of the French Republic whether it be wholly in favor of the claim of either Party or in the nature of an equitable solution of the difficulty, shall be considered as absolutely final and conclusive; and full effect shall be given to such award, without any objection, evasion, or delay whatsoever. Such decision shall be given in writing, and dated; it shall be in whatever form the President may choose to adopt; it shall be delivered to the Ambassadors, Ministers, or other public Agents of Great Britain and of Portugal who may be actually at Paris, and shall be considered as operative from the day of the delivery thereof.

ARTICLE III. The written or printed Case of each of the two Parties, accompanied by the evidence offered in support of the same, shall be laid before the President within twelve months from the date hereof; and a copy of such Case and evidence shall be communicated by each Party to the other through their respective Ambassadors or Ministers at Paris.

After such communication shall have taken place, each Party shall have the power of drawing up and laying before the President a second and definitive statement if it thinks fit so to do, in reply to the Case of the other Party so communicated, which definitive statement shall be so laid before the Arbiter, and also be mutually communicated in the same manner as aforesaid by each Party to the other within twelve months from the date of laying the first statement of the Case before the Arbiter.

ARTICLE IV. If, in the Case submitted to the Arbiter, either Party shall specify or allude to any Report or Document in its own exclusive possession, without annexing a copy, such Party shall be bound, if the other Party thinks proper to apply for it, to furnish that Party with a copy thereof. And, if the Arbiter should desire further elucidation or evidence with regard to any point contained in the statements laid before him, he shall be at liberty to require it from either party;

and he shall be at liberty to hear one counsel or agent for each Party in relation to any matters which he shall think fit for argument, and at such time and in such manner as he may think fit.

ARTICLE V. The Ambassadors, Ministers, or other public Agents of Great-Britain and of Portugal at Paris, respectively, shall be considered as the Agents of their respective Governments to conduct their case before the Arbiter, who shall be requested to adress all his communications and give all his notices to such Ambassadors, Ministers, or other public Agents, whose acts shall bind their Governments to and before the Arbiter on this matter.

ARTICLE VI. It shall be competent to the Arbiter to proceed in the said arbitration, and in all matters relating thereto, as and when he shall see fit, either in person, or by a person or persons named by him for that purpose; either with closed doors, or in public sitting; either in the presence or absence of either or both Agents; and either *viva voce*, or by written discussion or otherwise.

ARTICLE VII. The Arbiter shall, if he thinks fit, appoint a Secretary, Registrar or Clerk, for the purposes of the proposed arbitration, at such rate or renumeration as he shall think proper. This, and all other expenses of and connected with the said arbitration, shall be provided for as hereinafter stipulated.

ARTICLE VIII. The Arbiter shall be requested to deliver, together with his award, an account of all the costs and expenses which he may have been put to in relation to this matter, which shall forthwith be repaid in two equal portions, one by each of the two Parties.

ARTICLE IX. The Arbiter shall be requested to give his award in writing as early as convenient after the whole Case on each side shall have been laid before him, and to deliver one copy thereof to each of the said Agents.

Should the Arbiter be unable to decide wholly in favour of either of the respective claims, he shall be requested to give such a decision as will, in his opinion, furnish an equitable solution of the difficulty.

Should he decline to give any decision, then every thing done in the premises by virtue of this agreement shall be null and void; and it shall be competent for the British and Portuguese Government to do and proceed in all respects as if the reference to arbitration had never been made.

Done at Lisbon, this 25th day of September, 1872.[1]

---

[1] *Parliamentary Papers*, 1875. Delagoa-Bay, p. 14—15.

Décision arbitrale du Président de la République Française entre la Grande-Bretagne et le Portugal relative à la baie de Delagoa, en date du 24 juillet 1875.

Nous, Marie-Edme-Patrice-Maurice de Mac-Mahon, duc de Magenta, maréchal de France, Président de la République française,

Statuant en vertu des pouvoirs qui ont été conférés au Président de la République française aux termes du protocole signé à Lisbonne, le 15 septembre 1872, par lequel le gouvernement de S. M. la Reine de la Grande-Bretagne et de l'Irlande et celui de S. M. le Roi de Portugal sont convenus de déférer au Président de la République française, pour être réglé par lui définitivement et sans appel, le litige qui est pendant entre eux depuis l'année 1823 au sujet de la possession des territoires de Tembe et de Maputo, et des îles d'Inyack et des Eléphans, situés sur la baie de Delagoa ou Lorenço-Marques, à la côte orientale d'Afrique;

Vu les mémoires remis à l'arbitre par les représentants des deux parties, le 15 septembre 1873, et les contre-mémoires également remis par eux les 14 et 15 septembre 1874,

Vu les lettres de S. Exc. M. l'ambassadeur d'Angleterre et de M. le ministre de Portugal à Paris, en date du 8 février 1875;

La commission instituée le 10 mars 1873, à l'effet d'étudier les pièces et documents respectivement produits, nous ayant fait part du résultat de son examen;

Attendu que le litige tel que l'objet en a été déterminé par les mémoires présentés à l'arbitrage et en dernier lieu par les lettres ci-dessus citées des représentants à Paris des deux parties, porte sur le droit aux territoires suivants savoir:

1° Le territoire de Tembe, borné au nord par le fleuve Espirito-Santo ou English-Quiver et par la rivière Lorenço-Marques ou Dundas, à l'ouest par les monts de Lolombo, au sud et à l'est par le fleuve Maputo et de l'embouchure de ce fleuve jusqu'à celle de l'Espirito-Santo, par le rivage de la baie de Delagoa ou Lorenço-Marques;

2° Le territoire de Maputo, dans lequel sont comprises la presqu'île et l'île d'Inyack, ainsi que l'île des Eléphans et qui est borné au nord par le rivage de la baie, à l'ouest par le fleuve Maputo, de son embouchure jusqu'au parallèle de 26 degrés 30 minutes de latitude australe, au sud par ce même parallèle et à l'est par la mer;

Attendu que la baie de Delagoa ou Lorenço-Marques a été découverte au seizième siècle par les navigateurs portugais, et qu'au dix-septième et au dix-huitième le Portugal a occupé divers points sur la côte nord de cette baie et à l'île d'Inyack, dont l'îlot des Eléphans est une dépendance;

Attendu que depuis la découverte, le Portugal a en tout temps revendiqué des droits de souveraineté sur la totalité de la baie et des territoires riverains, ainsi que le droit exclusif d'y faire le commerce; que de plus il a appuyé à main armée cette revendication contre les Hollandais vers 1772, et contre les Autrichiens en 1781;

Attendu que les actes par lesquels le Portugal a appuyé ses prétentions n'ont soulevé aucune réclamation de la part du gouvernement des Provinces-Unies; qu'en 1782, ces prétentions ont été tacitement acceptées par l'Autriche, à la suite d'explications diplomatiques échangées entre cette puissance et le Portugal;

Attendu qu'en 1817, l'Angleterre elle-même n'a pas contesté le droit du Portugal, lorsqu'elle a conclu avec le gouvernement de S. M. Très-Fidèle la convention du 28 juillet, pour la répression de la traite, qu'en effet l'article 12 de cette convention doit être interprété en ce sens qu'il désigne comme faisant partie des possessions de la Couronne de Portugal la totalité de la baie, à laquelle s'applique indifféremment l'une ou l'autre des dénominations de Delagoa ou de Lorenço-Marques;

Attendu qu'en 1822, le gouvernement de S. M. Britannique lorsqu'il chargea le capitaine Owen de la reconnaissance hydrographique de la baie de Delagoa et des rivières qui y ont leur embouchure, l'avait recommandé aux bons offices du gouvernement portugais;

Attendu que si l'affaiblissement accidentel de l'autorité portugaise dans ces parages à pu, en 1823, induire en erreur le capitaine Owen et lui faire considérer de bonne foi comme réellement indépendants de la couronne de Portugal les chefs indigènes des territoires aujourd'hui contestés, les actes par lui conclus avec ces chefs n'en étaient pas moins contraires aux droits du Portugal;

Attendu que, presque aussitôt après le départ des bâtiments anglais, les chefs indigènes de Tembe et de Maputo ont de nouveau reconnu leur dépendance vis-à-vis des autorités portugaises, attestant aussi eux-mêmes qu'ils n'avaient pas eu la capacité de contracter;

Attendu que les conventions signées par le capitaine Owen et les chefs indigènes du Tembe et du Maputo, alors même qu'elles auraient été passées entre parties aptes à contracter, seraient aujourd'hui sans effet, l'acte relatif au Tembe stipulant des conditions essentielles qui n'ont pas reçu d'exécution, et les actes concernant le Maputo, conclus pour des périodes de temps déterminées, n'ayant point été renouvelés à l'expiration de ces délais.

Par ces motifs:

Nous avons jugé et décidé que les prétentions du gouvernement de S. M. Très-Fidèle sur les territoires de Tembe et de Maputo, sur la presqu'île d'Inyack, sur les iles d'Inyack et des Éléphans, sont dûment prouvées et établies.

Versailles, le 24 juillet 1875.[1]

LVII. Colombie, Etats-Unis d'Amérique.

14 décembre 1872.

L'origine de cette affaire remontait à 1855: les intéressés avaient eu à souffrir de la forfaiture d'un magistrat, dont les actes avaient été ultérieurement couverts par une amnistie décrétée en 1860. La sentence fut prononcée le 5 novembre 1875 et la Colombie condamnée à payer $ 50,000 aux réclamants: les motifs de la sentence ont seuls été publiés.

Convention for the settlement of the claim of Cotesworth & Powell, signed at Bogota, December 14, 1872.

The undersigned, Señor Don Jil Colunjé, Secretary of the Interior and Foreign Relations of the United States of Colombia, and Charles O'Leary, Esq., Her Britannic Majesty's Acting Consul General, in charge of Her Majesty's Legation in Bogotá, being both specially authorized by their respective Governments to enter into an agreement which shall put an end to the claim of Messrs. Cotesworth and Powell, British subjects, against the Government of Colombia, arising out of certain acts connected with the administration of Justice in the city of Baranquilla, State of Bolivar between the years 1858 and 1860, have agreed upon the following stipulations for that purpose:

ARTICLE 1. The claim of Messrs. Cotesworth and Powell shall be submitted to the arbitration of two Commissioners, one to be named by the Government of the United States of Colombia, the other by Her Britannic Majesty's chargé d'affaires in Bogotá, or, in his absence, by the British Acting Consul General in charge of Her Majesty's Legation. Any vacancy that may arise in the commission, shall be filled in the same manner as the original appointment.

ARTICLE 2. The commissioners, before proceeding to any other business, shall name some third person to act as an umpire, to decide any point on which they may differ in opinion. If they should not be able to agree in regard to the choice of any such person, the appointment shall be made by the person in charge of the French Legation in Bogotá.

ARTICLE 3. The arbitrators shall decide, as a preliminary question, whether the Republic is bound to grant an indemnity to Messrs. Cotesworth and Powell. If that question be decided in the affirmative, they shall fix the amount of the indemnity, both principal and interest.

ARTICLE 4. Any amount which may be allowed by the arbitrators shall be paid in hard cash to the British chargé d'affaires in Bogotá, or, in his absence, to the person in charge of the British Legation, within twelve months from the date of the award.

ARTICLE 5. The arbitrators shall perform the duties of their office in Bogotá, commencing as soon as the present agreement shall have been approved by the Congress of the Union. In arriving at their decisions, they shall hear, if desired, one counsel for each party, and shall duly weigh the proofs which he may adduce.

Done in Bogotá, the 14th of December 1872 [1].

Award pronounced in the case of Cotesworth and Powell, at Bogota, November 5, 1875.

This is a demand for indemnity for losses caused by alleged delays in awarding justice, by denials of justice, and by acts of notorious injustice occurring under the judicial administration of Colombia, in the years 1858, 1859 and 1860. The case may be briefly stated as follows:

In October 1855 the mercantile firm of Powles, Gower & Co., consisting of the firm of Powles Brothers & Co., of London, and Samuel Gower and Miguel Rivas, of New Granada was established in Barranquilla. The Barranquilla house thus constituted subsequently established a branch house in Bogotá.

Between Powles, Gower & Co., of New Granada; Cotesworth & Powell, of London, and Powles Brothers & Co., of London, there were three several contracts, dated respectively January 14, May 2, and May 22, 1856. These contracts, each separate and distinct from the others, were signed in London by Powles Brothers & Co., for and on behalf of their Barranquilla partners, Powles Gower & Co. Their object was the establishment of a separate business or incidental partnership for the purchase & sale of tobacco; the accounts and transactions of which to be distinct from the ordinary business of the three mercantile houses named, and to be known as accounts in participation,

Powles Brothers and Co. failed November 1857: and soon thereafter Cotesworth & Powell sent an agent to represent their interests in New Granada. This agent was recognized by the Barran-

[1] MARTENS, G. FR., *Nouveau recueil général* ...., 2e série, t. III, p. 517; *Annuaire de l'Institut de droit international*, t. II, p. 270.

[1] J. B. MOORE, *History and Digest* ...., p. 4697.

quilla house, who delivered to him the assets pertaining to the incidental partnership.

Meantime the Barranquilla house failed as a consequence of the failure of its London partners; and on the 13ᵗʰ of February 1858 the judge of the circuit court of Barranquilla took cognizance thereof in proceedings in bankruptcy.

A series of incidental proceedings followed in which the claimants took part. The circuit and provincial courts of Barranquilla, the superior court of the State of Bolivar, and the supreme court of the Confederation, all took cognizance of the various questions arising therefrom. During its different stages, the alcalde of the district, the prefect of the department of Savanilla, the attorney-general of the State, the governor and the general-assembly of the State, all figured in the proceeding.

In July 1859 a local·revolution broke out in the State. The legitimate governor abandoned Carthagena, the capital, and retired to Mompox. One Nieto assumed the prerogatives of chief executive and laid siege to Mompox. In August following the judge of the Barranquilla district absented himself, taking with him the papers relating to the bankruptcy case of Powles, Gower & Co. Many of those documents were never returned.

The revolution terminated in December 1859. In January 1860 a new State constitution was formed under which the laws of amnesty of March 3, 1860, and January 3, 1863, were enacted. Upon the first was based the decisions of the court of last resort of the State of April 17, 1860, and May 8, 1860, as also that of the provincial court of Barranquilla of May 1, 1860. Upon the second, the sentence of the superior tribunal of the State, of May 11, 1863, was predicated.

All these judicial decisions affected the. interests of the claimants. The first dismissed the proceedings instituted against the judge of first instance for the illegal abstraction and sale of certain goods pertaining to the incidental partnership, pending action for their possession. By the second, or that of May 8, 1860, the criminal prosecution of the same judge, for the alleged crimes of robbery and falsification of documents was set aside. By the third, or that of May 1, 1860, all proceedings against the assignee *(syndico)*, for crimes and irregularities during the period of his office, were dismissed. By the fourth or that of May 11, 1863, the irregularities and crimes of the judge of first instance, and his abuses of the judicial authority, to the prejudice of the claimants, were declared comprehended in the amnesty laws of the State. In September 1860 the State of Bolivar entered into a compact of union with that of Cauca against the New Granadian Confederation; and the two States thus confederated adopted the name of United States of Granada:

As the result of these political changes the legislation of the State was frequently changed, resulting in more or less confusion.

During this confusion the claimants first asked for redress through the British legation in Bogotá.

In December 1862 their attorney made written representation to the national executive, asking reparation for damages resulting from delays in awarding justice, from denials of justice, and from acts of notorious injustice; alleging that all appellate revision of unjust sentences and all further redress before the legal tribunals, had been taken away by the amnesty laws. To this a response was given promising means of satisfactory redress.

In March 1864 the attorney for claimants made a third representation in consequence of not having received a final decision upon his former petition. And in April 1865 the national executive decided that Colombia was not obligated to indemnify the claimants for damages and losses sustained by them on account of any misconduct on the part of individuals or subordinate officials in the State Bolivar.

In January 1867 a fourth representation was made by their attorney, asking a reconsideration of the decision of April 1865.

The reconsideration was had; and in October 1871 the minister for foreign affaires announced that the decision of April 1865 would be adhered to.

In November 1871 a demand for reclamation (*sic*) on behalf of the claimants was made upon the Colombian Government by Her Britannic Majesty's diplomatic agent in Bogotá. The discussion which followed resulted in an agreement to refer the whole matter to arbitration.

In December 1872 a convention of arbitration was signed by the plenipotentiaries of the two governments. This was sanctionned by a law of the Colombian congress of April 9, 1873.

Dr. Ancizar, a distinguished citizen of Bogotá, was named arbitrator by the Government of Colombia; the German minister resident, Dr. Schumacher, was appointed on the part of Great Britain; and Drs. Sálas and Rubio were retained as counsel respectively for the Governments of Colombia and Great Britain. The recall of Dr. Schumacher and the resignation of Dr. Ancizar, before any decision had been reached rendered the organization of a new commission necessary. The new commissioners, consisting of the Honourable Eustorjio Salgar, an ex-President of the republic, as Colombian arbitrator; the undersigned, minister resident of the United States of America, as British Arbitrator; and the Honorable Casimir Troplong, chargé d'affaires of France, as umpire, in case of disagreement, were installed some months since. Dr. Rubio appeared as counsel for the claimants and the Honorable Ramon Gomez attorney-general of the nation, appeared for the Colombian Government.

Such, in brief is the origin of this case; a controversy extending through a period of nearly eighteen years, and contemporary with some of the most important papers are missing. Others have accumulated which have little relevancy to the question at issue; and these, together with the voluminous pleadings of counsel, have swelled the mass of documents to a magnitude almost bewildering.

Before leaving Bogotá, Dr. Schumacher prepared, as the result of his study of the case, a comprehensive abstract of the great mass of documents submitted, as well as a copious index to the local statutes bearing upon the subject. This has been found of incalculable assistance in arriving at a clear and succinct history of the case, and, upon careful comparison with the original documents, to be remarkably accurate. It is to be regretted that one so patient and thorough in research, and so learned and able as Dr. Schumacher, could not have remained to complete a labor for wich he is so eminently fitted.

I

The preamble to the convention of December 14, 1872, announces as the object of this arbitration « the putting of an end to the claim of Messrs. Cotesworth & Powell, British subjects, against the Government of Colombia, arising out of certain acts connected with the administration of justice in the city of Barranquilla, State of Bolivar, between the years 1858 and 1860 ». Consequently, the following acts are not the objects of this investigation:

1. Those not connected with the *administration of justice*; for example, legislative acts not connected with the judicial administration;

2. Those not connected with the administration of justice in Barranquilla; that is to say, judicial sentences having no connection with the administration of justice in that city; and,

3. Those not connected with the judicial administration in Barranquilla *during the years 1858, 1859 and 1860;* such for instance, as may have occurred before or subsequent to the time mentioned. The convention, then, involves a consideration of the following proposition, as the primary question to be decided:

Whether there were acts connected with the administration of justice, in the place and during the time mentioned, which under the law of nations obligate the national government of Colombia to indemnify nonresident British subjects for damages and losses suffered by them in consequence thereof?

To decide this question, the arbitrators, being wholly independent of both governments, must be the sole judges of the evidence presented. They can not, for instance, be expected to take into consideration documents which, in their opinion, do not merit confidence. But all documents and copies of documents deemed worthy of credence should be carefully considered; likewise all incidental writings relating to or in explanation of the legal papers connected with the history of the case or which may serve to explain the contents of papers that may have been lost or destroyed without fault of the claimants.

As mere bad administration of justice is not, in itself, just ground for reparation, it becomes necessary to investigate separately, and one by one, each act alleged in evidence of the *abuse* of the judicial authority; acts alleged in proof of positive *denials* of justice; charges of undue *delays* in awarding justice; sentences and rulings of the courts contrary to the *laws* of the country; and other acts alleged in proof of *notorious injustice.*

Should these facts be clearly established, it must furthermore appear, in order to make the nation responsible, that the claimants exhausted every means of obtaining redress before the tribunals of the country; and that, all judicial recourse and appellate revision of unjust sentences being closed against them, they appeal as a last resort, through diplomatic channels, against the nation itself.

In order therefore to simplify the case as much as possible, we shall arrange the allegations preferred under six general heads as follows:

First. Abuse of judicial authority in the bankruptcy proceedings against Powles, Gower & Co.;

Second. Abuse of the judicial authority in regard to certain property claimed as pertaining to the incidental partnership;

Third. Abuse of the judicial authority in depriving the claimants of certain documents pertaining to the incidental partnership;

Fourth. An inquiry into the nature and legal character of this incidental partnership, by which certain 'accounts in participation' were created;

Fifth. The revolution and amnesty, and the hearing of each upon the questions involved in this reclamation; and lastly,

Sixth. The rules of international law and precedents applicable to the case under consideration.

Whe shall proceed to the examination of each in the order named.

II

ABUSE OF THE JUDICIAL AUTHORITY IN THE BANKRUPTCY PROCEEDINGS AGAINST POWLES, GOWER & CO.

This charge may be considered in the following order:

1. Failure to cite the absent creditors;
2. Failure to publish sentence of classification;
3. The sentence excluding the claimants;
4. The appeal therefrom, and its consequences;
5. Inutility of the new proceedings ordered; and
6. Criminal proceedings against the judge and the assignee.

We shall consider:

1. The failure of the judge to cite absent creditors.

The first stage of the bankruptcy proceeding against Powles, Gower & Co., of Barranquilla, comprehends the time from its commencement, on the 13th of February 1858, to that in which the attorney of Cotesworth & Powell took part therein, November 4, 1858, a period of over eight months. The facts are as follows.

Clemente Salazar, judge of the Barranquilla district, took cognizance of the bankruptcy of Powels, Gower & Co., *February 12, 1858*. On the next day he declared the firm in a state of bankruptcy, and nominated an assignee *(sindico)* and a treasurer *(depositario)*. On the first of July following he cited the creditors to meet on the 12th day of the same month.

The meeting of creditors took place on the day named, and Manuel Suarez Fortoul was elected assignee. No steps were taken, however, looking to the collection and placing of the assets of the bankrupt estate under bond. In default of such action, this became the duty of the judge, who nevertheless failed to do so. On the same day the judge issued a decree opening the proceedings to proof.

September 7, 1858: The time when the judge is said to have ordered publication of proofs, setting the time, 20 days, for pleadings, etc. There is no evidence, however, that this writ was made known by means of an edict as provided by the laws of New Granada then in force. On the 12th of October following the judge approved the accounts of the treasurer, M. E. A. Isaacs, and on the 4th of November following the attorney of Cotesworth & Powell presented his authority in court, asking to be considered a party to the bankruptcy proceeding.

With regard to the citation of creditors, only the following facts are adduced:

On the 5th March 1859 Cotesworth & Powell's attorney wished to enter appeal from a sentence of the court, but found the office closed. Subsequently the appeal was entered by the parties interested, and in consequence of this appeal on the 30th of December 1861 the superior tribunal of the State annulled all the proceedings in bankruptcy, for want of citation of absent creditors.

(A) With regard to complaints made by the claimants of acts occurring prior to November 4, 1858, the counsel for Colombia says they are unjust, because previous to that time they were not parties to the suit. Dr. Sálas contends furthermore, that the claimants were not interested parties until April 1862, the time when the new proceedings were opened. The honorable attorney-general of Colombia maintains substantially the same opinion.

Great deference is due to the opinions of both the learned counsel named; but the position here assumed by them can not be admitted as correct. The administration of justice, guaranteed to all persons living in a civilized country, interests all. It especially interests all parties who are either mediately or remotely affected by it. To illustrate: If the sentence of a judge, given in a suit of A versus B, be illegal or manifestly unjust, and in its consequence directly affecting the interests of C, the latter may ask a revision of the proceeding; and this although he may not have had previous occasion or necessity to take part in the suit. In the present case, the claimants were not bound to take part in the proceeding which led to the decision. Therefore if irregularities had taken place in the bankruptcy proceeding, before the date mentioned, they directly affected the interests of the claimants; and for this reason they had a right to demand that justice be administered according to the laws of the country.

Moreover, if, in the present case, positive crimes had not been committed, very great irregularities had taken place—irregularities involving the liability of the judge. Such, in fact, was the opinion of the superior court of the State of December 30, 1861. That tribunal not only pronounced the whole bankruptcy proceeding null *ab initio*—mentioning, among other causes of nullity, the failure to cite absent creditors—and ordered a new convocation of creditors and a new proceeding *de novo*, but likewise condemned the judge who made the unjust sentence of classification to the payment of costs. It is clear, therefore, that the want of citation in this case affected all the creditors of the bankrupt estate, and especially those who had not presented themselves.

It is admitted by the Colombian minister for foreign affairs, the Honorable R. Rocha Gutierrez, in his reply to the first demand by claimants for reparation, that in the decree opening the proceedings in bankruptcy the absent creditors were not notified as provided by the law. He insists, however, that such informality does not incur responsibility to the government further than its duty to annul the proceedings for the purpose of correcting the evils referred to.

This opinion of the distinguished gentleman would be correct, were the evils reparable in the manner indicated. But this was not the case with respect to the claimants. The property in dispute had been sold, and the proceeds either done away with or else illegally portioned among the few favored creditors. In either case, there was no redress, as subsequent decisions of the higher tribunals show.

2. *Failure to publish sentence of classification.*

The second stage of the bankruptcy proceeding comprehends the time from the day in which the attorney for claimants took part therein, to that in which the sentence of classification was decreed, a term of nearly one month. The facts are as follows:

On the 4th of November 1858 Cotesworth & Powell's attorney presented his credentials in court and asked to be considered a party to the proceeding. The next day, becoming party to the suit, he entered claim for £ 2,618 16 s. 9 d., complaining that the writ announcing classification of creditors had not been published; that there had been provided no safe deposit of bankrupt assets, as required by law; that the records of the court did not contain the monthly statements of the assignee, as provided by law, etc.

The sentence of classification of creditors is dated November 19, 1858. Three days thereafter claimants' attorney asked that publication of proofs be made. The judge's decision thereon, if ever rendered, is missing. Five days later the judge declared the sentence of November 19th executed, or is said to have done so. There are no proofs, however, of the time of the publication of this decree. In December following the clerk of the court exhibited to claimants' attorney what purported to be a copy of an edict said to have been published, declaring the sentence of November 19th executed.

The above facts appear to be established, although the evidence is somewhat conflicting. There is no proof that the decree of September 7, 1858, ordering publication of proofs, setting time for pleadings, etc., was ever published. On the contrary, there is circumstantial evidence that it was not published as the law required, and this is supported by the affidavits of José Luis Leon, Arriola, Macias, and Duncan.

3. *Sentence excluding the claimants.*

Even if the writ of September 7th had been published, it is questionable whether, at that stage of the proceeding, the judge could issue a sentence excluding the claimants as common creditors of the bankrupt estate. If, however, the writ had not been legally notified, the sentence of November 19, 1858, was so much the more notoriously unjust, since the attention of the judge had been called to this defect.

The sentence of November 19th referred to declared that, although the attorney of Cotesworth & Powell had petitionned to be considered a party to the bankruptcy proceedings, and had solicited the payment of £ 2,618 16 s. 9 d., as common creditors, such claim could not be recognized, because besides having been made after the term for the convocation of creditors, the claim itself was unsupported by proof.

(B) The first reason here given for excluding the claimants, to wit, that 'the application had been made after the time fixed for the meeting of creditors', is not admissible. Article 43 of the law of June 13, 1843, then in force, provided for the admission of any and all creditors in whatever stage the case might be found when presenting themselves.

The second reason given for the exclusion of claimants, to wit, that their demand 'was destitute of all documentary proofs', is equally fallacious. It is clearly provided, in Article 28 of the law above cited, that proofs may be presented up to the time of citation for sentence. This citation, although said to have been made November 2, 1858, was in all probability never made. Such, in fact, is the presumption, supported by circumstantial evidence. Consequently, the reasons given for the decision of November 19, 1858, failed to show that the judge had the right to exclude the claimants.

It is said that the sentence above referred to was published the day after its delivery. But no evidence exists that the publication was ever made. The counsel for Colombia seems to attach little or no importance to this point. He evidently overlooked the fact that the law already cited provides expressly that all such sentences shall be made public by means of an edict; and that such edict must be posted on the court-house door for the term of at least five days.

That such publication was never made scarcely admits of doubt. All the circumstances of the case, as well as much of the direct evidence, render any other opinion impossible. The disorderly condition of the tribunal at the time; the great confusion in which all the papers were found: the fact that many of the most important documents had been taken away by the judge, and left at other places; that the prefect of the department had warned the judge to desist from such practices; and that the judge's salary had been suspended, because he refused to comply with a plain official duty, are circumstances unfavorable to any other presumption. Moreover these circumstances derive additional significance from the fact that the attorney for claimants, on the 12th January following, asked that investigation be made respecting the publication of all the decrees relating to the bankruptcy case of Powles, Gower & Co. from September 7th to November 20th, 1858; that accordingly, two unsuccessful efforts were made by the prefect to make this investigation; that these efforts were unsuccessful because the judge practically defeated them; and that the prefect finally declared such investigation impossible by reason of the continued absence and perversity of the judge. All these circumstances, almost conclusive of themselves that publication was not made at the time and in the manner indicated, are corroborated by the affidavits of Goenaga, the clerk of the court, Benavidez, Ramon, and others.

It is contended by the counsel of Colombia that these affidavits are worthless. In support of this position, article 36 of the law of December 31, 1857, is cited. That article says only that 'no one can be compelled to testify against himself'; it does not say that testimony *already* given, voluntarily against himself, has no value.

4. The appeal from the sentence of November 19, 1858.

The claimants' attorney petitioned for appeal from the sentence above named, January 15, 1859. Up to June 21st of the same year, the court took no action upon this petition. The judge had issued a decree, but its contents were unknown; and the attorney asked in vain that this decree (whatever it was) be made known to the assignee. In July of the same year, the attorney complained that his representation of January preceding had been wholly disregarded. In August following, he prayed decision upon his petition of June 21, 1859. Two days afterwards, the judge, without giving any decision, absented himself from his office and duties.

Subsequently, the superior court of the State admitted an appeal, by certain creditors of the bankrupt estate, against the sentence of November 19, 1858. In this appeal claimants' attorney cooperated, presenting his papers in court, and asking, in consequence of the appeal which had been admitted, that all previous adjudications made to various creditors be declared null.

This resulted in the decision of December 30, 1861, which as we have already seen, annulled the entire proceeding in bankruptcy from its very commencement; ordered a new proceeding, a new convocation of creditors, and condemned Judge Salazar to the payment of costs. This was after a lapse of three years, ten months and seventeen days from the time of the bankruptcy of Powles, Gower & Co.

5. Inutility of the new proceeding.

In order to sustain the case at this stage, it should be premised that the assignee, Manuel Suarez Fortoul, had resigned in August 1859; that his resignation had been accepted; and that one year thereafter, that is to say, in August 1860, the attorney for claimants petitioned the court to appoint a new assignee, since the creditors had failed to elect one.

On the 12th March 1862, the provincial court of Barranquilla ordered a new convocation of creditors. On the 26th of the same month, the clerk of the court certified that there were no first accounts of the late assignee, Manuel Suarez Fortoul. The meeting of creditors took place June 12, 1862, nearly four years after the first meeting, under the former proceeding. On the 18th July 1862, the new assignee, Mr. Jacobo A. Correa, made affidavit that he neither had in his possession nor knew who did have, any sums of money or assets belonging to the bankrupt estate; that there were no goods, assets or effects of any kind in his possession pertaining to said estate, nor had he ever received any; and that he never received any statement, account or explanation of the disappearance of any goods, assets or effects pertaining to said bankrupt estate from his predecessor. This affidavit referred to the assets of the incidental partnership or 'joint account', as well as to those pertaining to the bankrupt estate proper of Powles, Gower & Co.

After October 2, 1862, when the new assignee presented a statement of the general condition of the assets, or rather the absence of all assets, it does not appear that there was ever another meeting of creditors. All the objects of litigation having disappeared, with no one to render an account of, or to be held responsible for their disappearance, the proceeding seems to have been abandoned as useless.

6. Criminal charges and proceedings.

Meantime, criminal proceedings had been instituted against Judge Salazar and the clerk of his court for falsehood and deception in posting the edict announcing the sentence of November 19, 1858. These charges were preferred in due form, December 2, 1858, by claimants' attorney, before the Honorable Buenaventura Salgado, then judge of second district. The attorney, it appears, held himself in readiness to establish the truth of these charges. Subsequently, José A. Benavidez and Luis Ramon made affidavits to the same effect. Very soon thereafter, Judge Salazar's salary was suspended.

In February 1859 claimants' attorney petitioned the judge of the second district to continue the criminal investigation. He had previously asked for certified copies of the affidavits of Benavidez and Ramon; and some days after this he announced that alterations had been made in those affidavits by the clerk of the court in collusion with Judge Salazar. This resulted in a commission by the prefect to the alcalde, to ascertain the whereabouts of the clerk who had the custody of the papers referred to. The clerk was found concealed in a private house, under a bed, and wrapped up in a counterpane. From thence he was conducted to the court room, where he delivered certain papers, but refused to deliver up the affidavits.

When the last-named documents were delivered, some days later, the attorney general and the claimants' attorney noted certain alterations which had been made in them.

The judge of the second district opened proceedings against Judge Salazar and the clerk for the crimes of altering and falsifying public documents; but three days thereafter, that is on the 20ᵗʰ December 1858, the judge of the second district, who had cognizance of the case, was separated from the discharge of his official duties. Meantime all the papers in the case had been delivered by him to the accused, Judge Salazar of the circuit court, who had reclaimed them. The attorney-general protested before the governor of the State, and very soon thereafter Judge Salazar, who still had possession of the papers, absented himself. Claimants' attorney appealed to the governor of the State. This seems to have been unheeded. In June 1860 the attorney-general and the tribunal of the second district declared that the papers had been lost. Nine days later, the governor commissionned an officer to demand the papers of Judge Salazar; but Salazar made affidavit that they were not in his possession. The result was that they were never produced.

(C) It is apprehended that there can be but one opinion respecting the judicial conduct above described. It seems to be almost without precedent in the modern annals of judicial corruption. That there was a clear violation of the penal code of the State, by the judge of the second district in delivering the papers to one of the accused parties, admits of no doubt.

III.

ABUSE OF THE JUDICIAL AUTHORITY IN REGARD TO CERTAIN PROPERTY CLAIMED AND PERTAINING TO THE 'JOINT ACCOUNT' OR INCIDENTAL PARTNERSHIP.

We have seen that, in consequence of the incidental partnership, created by the three several contracts between Powles Brothers & Co., of London; Powles, Gower & Co., of Barranquilla and the claimants, the Barranquilla house delivered to the agent of the latter certain goods pertaining to the 'joint account'.

These goods were afterwards embargoed, first by certain creditors of the bankrupt house in New Granada, and then by the assignee of the bankrupts, as belonging to the common mass of assets. This gave rise to an action for their possession; and it is of the judicial proceeding connected with this action that complaint is made, and which forms the main basis of this reclamation. We shall, therefore, consider,

1. The embargo by certain creditors;
2. The embargo by assignee of the bankrupts;
3. The action for possession; and,
4. Pending such action, the illegal abstraction and sale of the embargoed goods by the assignee.

1. Embargo by certain creditors.

And first, with reference to the embargo by certain Granadian creditors, the facts are as follows:

On the 23ᵈ February 1858, E. A. Isaacs & Co., of Barranquilla, pointed out or libelled, upon their own responsibility, certain quantities of tobacco which had been delivered to Cotesworth & Powell's agent as belonging to the incidental partnership, but which the informants claimed as belonging of right to the common mass of bankrupt assets. The informants took the usual oath provided in such cases, thereby subjecting themselves to the usual liabilities, should their embargo not be made good. The court admitted this action; and in March following, others of the New Granadian creditors became sureties to the informers.

In January 1859, Isaacs & Co. withdrew their embargo, asked that the goods be released, and that they themselves be exonerated from all liability incurred in consequence of the procedure. This petition was granted by the judge, without hearing the other parties interested.

On the 5ᵗʰ March following, the attorney for claimants went to the tribunal for the purpose of entering appeal from this sentence, but found the office closed. He subsequently asked that the informants be put under bond etc., according to legal usage in such cases. On the 1ˢᵗ of June thereafter, Isaacs & Co. entered exceptions to the authority of claimants' attorney. The attorney answered the exceptions on the 10ᵗʰ of the same month.

On the 20ᵗʰ of June of the same year, Judge Salazar decided that the attorney for claimants had no power to interfere; because, as he said, his power as attorney comprehended only 'the ordinary and indispensable acts for the transaction of business; but not cases requiring more diligence, such as the present. This sentence was not notified.

On the 3ᵈ August 1859 the attorney for claimants asked decision (sic) of the court respecting the exception to his powers, made in this case. He asked this in order that his clients might follow the legal course prescribed in such cases. Two days afterward, the judge ceased to discharge his official duties, and no decision had been rendered.

On the 30ᵗʰ January 1860 the claimants' attorney petitioned the prefect of the department to institute measures for compelling Judge Salazar to deliver up the documents pertaining to the case. On the 10ᵗʰ June, of the same year, the sentence of June 19, 1859, was notified; *that is, one year after its delivery!* On the 8ᵗʰ March 1861 the superior court of the State revoked this sentence.

In February 1862 claimants' attorney entered suit against Isaacs & Co., before the provincial court of Barranquilla, for damages resulting from their embargo of certain goods pertaining to the incidental partnership. In March following that tribunal decided that the attorney had no power to institute such proceedings. The attorney took an appeal to the superior court of the State. The last named tribunal confirmed the sentence of the court below, April 2, 1862, without giving any reason therefore. The supreme court rendered a similar decision, June 30, 1862.

(D) In regard to the proceeding above related, it may be noted,

1. That the sentence exonerating Isaacs & Co., without hearing the parties interested, was illegal and notoriously unjust. This is admitted by the Honorable R. Rocha Gutierrez, in one of his official notes, as minister for foreign affairs. He insists, however, that inasmuch as the attorney for the claimants was finally admitted under decision of the superior court revoking the sentence of the inferior judge, justice was not denied. But the question here raised is technically whether there had been an abuse of the judicial authority, resulting in damages unremediable by or-

dinary legal process. There was, moreover, a delay of nearly one whole year in notifying an important sentence, thus showing the claimants to have been kept in ignorance of the proceeding which directly affected their interest; and

2. That between the sentence of the superior tribunal of March 8, 1861, and that of April 2, 1862, by the same tribunal, there is a direct and irreconcilable contradiction. One recognized the authority of the claimants' attorney to bring action; the other as expressly denied it. Dr. Sálas, one of the counsel for Colombia, insists that this contradiction is more apparent than real; but his opinion is evidently based upon a mistake respecting the date of the first sentence, which is 1861, and not 1862.

2. Embargo by the assignee.

In January 1859, when Isaacs & Co. had withdrawn their embargo, Manuel Suarez Fortoul, as assignee of the bankrupt estate, pointed out the same and other lots of tobacco, demanding their embargo as pertaining to the bankrupt estate. This embargo was admitted by the judge, Clemente Salgar. The attorney for claimants protested, declaring that an assignee had no such authority under the commercial code of New Granada.

This protest appears to have been totally disregarded by the judge. In consequence, he was charged by the attorney with wilful neglect of duty. On the 10ᵗʰ of April following, the attorney renewed his protest, and asked decision of the court upon the proposition whether an assignee could legally make such an embargo. This petition being likewise disregarded by the judge, the attorney repeated it on the 5ᵗʰ June following. No action was still taken and the 19ᵗʰ July following the attorney renewed his petition, which being yet disregarded by the judge, was again renewed on the 3ᵈ of August of the same year. Indeed, it does not appear that the court ever decided the point raised, or took any serious notice of the claimants' petition.

(E) The honorable the attorney-general of Colombia deduces that, because assignees are charged with the defense of all the rights of the bankrupts, as prescribed in article 1005 of the *Codigo de Comercio* of 1853, they are therefore competent to embargo goods and effects not embraced in the mass of assets.

This deduction does not seem to be supported by the spirit of the law cited; because,

1. Neither in the law of June 13, 1843, nor in the *Codigo de Comercio* of 1853, is there found among the attributes of the assignee *(syndico)* any authority to make such embargoes. On the

contrary, that authority is clearly reserved to the creditors themselves, who, in all such cases, must proceed upon their own responsibility; and

2. The article of the code cited by the attorney-general says only that ,es atribucion del sindico la defensa de todos los derechos de la quiebra, y el ejercicio de las acciones y excepciones que le competan'; but this is conceived to refer to the goods and assets actually pertaining to the bankruptcy and not to those out of the common mass of assets; and, finally, because,

3. An assignee can not institute any species of judicial proceedings whatever for the business or interests of the bankrupt estate without previous authority from the judge; and in the case under consideration, this condition was not complied with.

Consequently the undersigned is of opinion that the decision of the court admitting the embargo by the assignee and the failure or refusal of the judge to hear the claimants, or to decide upon their petition challenging the authority of the assignee to make such embargo, involved in its consequences a denial of justice.

3. The action for possession.

In consequence of the embargo above referred to, the claimants entered action for possession February 24, 1859. Meantime, some of the New Granadian creditors of the bankrupt house solicited the exportation and sale of the embargoed tobacco, then stored in Barranquilla. Without hearing the claimants, the judge decreed the sale of certain lots of tobacco, likewise under embargo, then stored in the districts of Sambrano, Carmen and San Juan Nepomuceno; goods pertaining to the incidental partnership, and consequently the object of a possessory action by the claimants.

The claimants entered appeal in March 1859. In June following, they notified the superior court of the State that their appeal had not been permitted to take regular course. This notification was repeated in July of the same year.

The provincial court of Barranquilla decided January 27, 1862, that the goods and assets of the 'joint tobacco account' were the exclusive property of the incidental partnership; and that this partnership owed Cotesworth & Powell, of London, the sum of £ 6,682 2 s. 3 d., with interest thereon from the date of the failure of Powles, Gower & Co.

The assignee appealed, which was however withdrawn eight days afterwards; and on the 17th of February the sentence was declared executed.

4. Illegal abstraction and sale of the embargoed goods, pending action for their possession.

Many of the documents relating to this stage of the suit, are missing. Those submitted prove the following facts:

In September 1858, the attorney for claimants asked that Vicente Palacio make oath relative to the sale of certain tobacco, pertaining to the joint account then under embargo, at the instance of the assignee. Two weeks afterward, Señor Palacio made affidavit; affirming that such sales had been made.

On the 12th of February 1859, Dr. José E. Bermudez made affidavit that he had held in his possession 4792 pounds of the tobacco which had been embargoed by the assignee; but that subsequently he had placed the same to the order of Juan Cotren, by direction of the assignee.

On the 8th of February of the same year the assignee asked that the sale of this tobacco be authorized; on the same day he took from the warehouse in Barranquilla several packages of tobacco, then the object of the possessory action, and shipped them to Santa Martha. On the day following, the judge ordered the assignee to take care to maintain in security, and in good condition, all the goods pertaining to the bankrupt estate. This is alleged to have been a false or feigned decree.

A few days later, the claimants' attorney informed the alcalde of the district of this abstraction and removal by the assignee; and five days later he also notified the attorney-general of the district to the same effect. In March following, he complained to the attorney-general of the delay in the administration of justice on the part of the alcalde. Up to the 8th of April of the same year, 1859, the alcalde had taken no action upon the information given, although he had been repeatedly urged to do so.

On the 21st May 1859 the attorney-general of the State delivered an opinion that the abstraction and removal of the tobacco, pending action for its possession, was a fraudulent act on the part of the assignee; that for this act Judge Salazar was responsible as an accomplice, that both he and the assignee ought to be suspended from their respective functions; and that the offices of both should be opened to inspection by the prefect of the department. The attorney-general closes his opinion in this language: This is not the first time that the chief public minister of justice has been under the necessity of demanding the punishment of Judge Clemente Salazar for crimes in the execution of his judicial functions.

The investigation here recommanded was ordered by the superior court of the State on the 10ᵗʰ of June following.

An attempt at investigation was made in July of the same year; and in January 1860 the prefect returned the papers relating to the case to the superior court of the State.

In February 1860 an order was issued by the last-named tribunal, at the instance of the attorney-general, for the investigation of the circumstances connected with the abstractioṇ and removal of the tobacco named; and, pending this investigation, the amnesty law of March 3, 1860, was enacted.

On the 17ᵗʰ April 1860 the superior court decided that the act of abstraction and removal of the tobacco from Barranquilla to Santa Martha, pending action for its possession, was a criminal offense and punishable as such; that for such offense both Judge Salazar and the assignee, Suarez Fortoul, were responsible; that whether both were principals, or whether one was the accomplice of the other, in either case the penalties were embraced in the law of amnesty of March 3, 1860; and hence that all proceedings against the judge be dismissed.

It is said that the tobacco thus abstracted from the warehouse in Barranquilla and removed to Santa Martha was sold to the highest bidder, although the judge had not caused such sale to be advertised. Many creditors of the bankrupts protested against the illegality of this sale. James Wilson, one of the creditors, protested before the British consul at Barranquilla. Diogenes E. de Castro, the reputed purchaser, testified that 338 packages of tobacco had been sold, July, 22, 1859.

The attorney for claimants asked for authenticated copies of the papers relating to this sale. He was told by the clerk of the court that all the papers were missing. In January 1860, the reputed purchaser, De Castro, testified to the sale, saying that the tobacco had been shipped on account of his mercantile firm « De Castro & Son ».

(F.) One of the counsel for Colombia intimates quite plainly that the loss of the papers pertaining to this transaction was not in consequence of the judge's absence, neglect, or official corruption; but that the claimants were interested in their loss, in the hope of recovering damages, etc. The counsel, however, fails to adduce any proof showing probable ground for this suspicion. Indeed, there does not appear the slightest foundation for the insinuation made by him.

It is also maintained by the counsel for Colombia, first, that the removal of the tobacco was a legitimate act in the administration of the bankrupt estate; and, second, that even though it were not, it was at most an irregular act of the assignee, who is not a government official in a strict technical sense.

Besides being in the very face of the sentence of the superior court of the State of April 17, 1860, this opinion is fallacious for the following reasons:

1. The tobacco in question was embargoed in Barranquilla and in consequence there was pending an action for its possession. The very gist of the controversy was whether this tobacco belonged to the bankrupt estate, and therefore to the common mass of assets; or whether it was the property of the claimants exclusively, and therefore to be delivered to them. Until this question was decided, the property in dispute could not be treated by the assignee as other goods pertaining to the mass of bankrupt's assets.

2. This tobacco ought to have been deposited in some secure place, under lock and key; the judge should have had one of the keys in his possession, and the treasurer the other. If the former failed in his duty in this respect, by not demanding one of the keys; or if, having the key, he permitted the illegal abstraction, shipment, and sale, he thereby became an accomplice.

According to the opinion of the Honorable R. Rocha Gutierrez, minister for foreign affairs, it is only necessary to consult the memorials and other documents issued previous to the sale of the 338 packages of tobacco, and the commercial code, in order to be satisfied that the sale was not clandestine. We find, however, upon examination of the vouchers, that the contrary is proven.

The honorable attorney-general of the nation excuses, if he does not justify, this abstraction and sale on the ground that the tobacco was in a damaged condition. But, admitting the goods to have been in a condition liable to damage, their removal and sale should have been according to the legal formalities provided in such cases. So far from this having been the case, the removal was without the knowledge or consent of the parties most interested, and over the repeated protests of other; whilst an examination of the papers relating to what little is known of the sale, shows that transaction to have been more or less clandestine; nor were the proceeds ever satisfactorily accounted for.

IV.

ABUSE OF THE JUDICIAL AUTHORITY IN ORDER TO DEPRIVE CLAIMANTS OF CERTAIN DOCUMENTS PERTAINING TO THE INCIDENTAL PARTNERSHIP, ETC.

This charge comprehends,

1. The illegal dispossession of the documents; and
2. Injustice in refusing to restore them.

1. The illegal dispossession of the documents.

With regard to the first, the facts are as follows:

Julian Osorio represented to the court, December 21, 1858, that Cotesworth & Powell's attorney was in possession of certain documents which related to him, and he therefore demanded their exhibition. Without hearing the defendant, the judge on the same day ordered the documents to be produced. The defendant represented that he had not received them through Osorio, nor from any other person in his name; but that about September 1, 1858, he had received various papers from a Señor Sansum, an employee of the Cármen establishment of Powles, Gower & Co.

The judge, however, ordered the defendant to exhibit the documents. This was on the 15th January 1859. A few days later, Tiberius C. Araujo was named clerk of the court *ad interim*.

The defendant entered objection, under the then existing law. He also entered an appeal from all the proceedings, had up to that time, in reference to the documents in question. The decision of the judge, if ever given, is missing. On the 15th of February of the same year, the defendant submitted a memorandum of the documents then in his possession. In March following, Osorio represented that he was the owner of the documents named. Two days afterwards, the judge decreed that defendant submit the documents mentioned in his memorandum of February 15 preceding.

This decree was notified to the defendant two days afterwards, when he entered written refusal and exceptions. The decision of the court on these points is missing. Afterwards it seems that the defendant presented some of the documents; the judge asked for the others. Defendant appealed; the judge said he would decide upon the motion for appeal at some futur time, but that the documents must be delivered beforehand. Defendant then asked to be protected in the possession of those already presented; the judge said he would decide that point some other time. Finally, in compliance with the order of the judge, the defendant presented the others, whereupon the court immediately adjourned. Defendant refused to sign the record, because the documents had not been returned to him. He also protested before the public notary. The documents, however, remained in Judge Salazar's possession; and on the day following, the defendant published a card charging him with spoliation and robbery.

It also appears that on the day after Osorio's original representation, that is to say, on the 22nd December 1858, the assignee, Suarez Fortoul, informed the court that Cotesworth & Powell's attorney was in possession of various documents which Osorio had given in pledge to the bankrupt house; he therefore asked that they be embargoed and deposited in his possession. The judge said he would decree the embargo when the documents should be specified.

On the 17th March 1859, Osorio represented that the documents in question had been in his possession; that he had been violently deprived of them, etc.; and he therefore petitioned their return to him. In support of this representation, he produced the affidavits of Bustillo, Hilario Rivas, and Adolfo Perez, made in San Juan Nepomuceno, March 2, 1859. The judge, without hearing the defendant issued the following decree:

March 18, 1859: The court considering that, inasmuch as Osorio had been violently dispossessed of the documents in question, decrees their delivery to him « without appeal by the defendant », etc. The judge then delivered them to Osorio.

2. The action for their restitution.

The claimants' attorney, who had petitioned the return of the documents, charged the judge before the prefect of the department with the crimes of falsification, spoliation, and robbery. Criminal proceedings were instituted against him before the superior court. That tribunal decided that the crimes alleged had not been committed.

In the civil action for restitution, an appeal was finally admitted before the superior court. In its sentence of April 16, 1861, that tribunal held that, since the circuit court of Barranquilla had reserved its decision respecting the right of possession until after the documents in dispute should be exhibited, the question should be referred.

This resulted in a decision by the provincial court of Barranquilla, May 16, 1861, that the attorney of Cotesworth & Powell could not be protected in the possession of the documents. The court was, however, of opinion that Judge Salazar had unlawfully dispossessed the attorney of his papers; and that, when the object of their exhibition in court should be subserved, they should be returned to the defendant; nevertheless, the decision of March 18, 1859, should be respected regardless of the consequences, etc. From this singular sentence, an appeal was taken to the superior court; and, in a decision rendered June 18, 1861, that tribunal affirmed the opinion of the court below. This led to the accusation of the judge of the superior court, a Señor Nuñez, before the general assembly of the State. Charges were preferred under article 561 of the code of New Granada, but the general assembly declared the accusation unsupported.

An effort was next made to appeal from the sentence of June 18, 1861. This was unavailing; the motion for appeal being admitted by neither the supreme court of the State, nor that of the Confederation.

(G) The preceding facts show three distinct actions with respect to the documents in dispute, namely: one for the exhibition in court, one for possession by the assignee, and a counter action for possession by Osorio. The first, though an ordinary process, prepared the way for the reclamatory action. Hence the decision of March 18, 1859, if connected with the exhibitory action, was unjust. There was also an abuse of the judicial authority in deciding an important question without hearing the defendant. There was a denial of justice in the judge's refusal to consider a motion for appeal by the defendant. The attorney's challenge of the clerk *ad interim* was legally made; yet it was illegally disregarded.

The action for possession interposed by the assignee invests the case with little or no additional importance. We have already seen that all such actions by an assignee are of very doubtful legality.

The possessory action brought by Osorio was not notified to the defendant; this was an act of notorious injustice. It appears, moreover, that the affidavits produced by Osorio referred not to facts but to mere legal opinions; the case was not therefore made out as alleged in the declaration. In addition to this, Osorio contradicts one demand by the terms of another subsequently made. It is even doubtful whether the documents referred to in the affidavits named were the same which had been produced in court in consequence of the exhibitory action.

Both the provincial court of Barranquilla and the superior tribunal of the State, denied justice to the defendant by declaring it impossible to protect him in the possession of his papers; because the sentence appealed from, based as it was upon the interdictory action, was irregular and unjust for want of citation.

V.

THE INCIDENTAL PARTNERSHIP.

The contracts establishing this partnership, as we have already seen, were dated in London, January 14, May 2, and May 22, 1856. They were signed by Powles Brothers & Co., of London, for and on behalf of their New Granadian partners, Messrs. Powles, Gower & Co. Each contract was drawn up in the form of a 'Memorandum of agreement', and was duly registered by a public notary in London, November 14, 1857.

In accordance with these agreements, large quantities of tobacco had been purchased on joint account, by the Barranquilla house, with funds supplied by Cotesworth & Powell. By the terms of the agreement, the profits and losses resulting from this transaction were to be shared in equal moieties by the two contracting parties.

When the Barranquilla house failed in consequence of the failure of their London partners, this tobacco, as we have already seen, was turned over to an agent of Cotesworth & Powell. The judicial proceedings growing out of the embargo of this property, first by certain Granadian creditors, and than by the assignee of the bankrupt house, have been detailed at length in the preceding pages. But, as those proceedings form perhaps the principal ground for this reclamation, it may be well to examine briefly the nature of the incidental partnership itself. We shall therefore consider,

1. Whether the contracts were *bona fide*;
2. Whether they were legal; and,
3. When and how the partnership formed by them was dissolved.

1. Were the contracts bona fide?

One of the counsel for the Colombian Government intimates, in many places, that these contracts were feigned for the purpose of defrauding the Granadian creditors. In support of this insinuation, he asserts that the claimants made registration of them only the evening before the failure of the London partners of Barranquilla house. He also adduces the circumstance that certain bills of exchange, drawn by Edward Ross as agent of Powles, Gower & Cie., in Jiron, were against Powles Brothers & Co., instead of Cotesworth & Powell.

The undersigned must be permitted to express surprise that such an argument as this should have been advanced by the learned counsel. There does not appear the slightest foundation for his suspicions. He is even mistaken respecting the time of registration, which was two days prior to the failure of the London partners of Powles, Gower & Co., and not the evening before that event. And when it is borne in mind that the books of the bankrupt house, the contracts and the correspondence between the parties and the other papers submitted all show that Cotesworth & Powell had real and practical interests in possession, the notarial act referred to is of easy explanation without involving any presumptions of fraud. The claimants had advanced large sums of money with which tobacco had been purchased in New Granada upon joint account. It was natural, therefore, that from the momen.

of any intimations of failure by Powles Brothers & Co., the claimants should have taken every reasonable precaution to protect their interests.

In regard to the bills of exchange drawn by Ross, we fail to perceive in that circumstance any evidences of a fraudulent transaction. The contracts under consideration gave the Barranquilla house the authority to draw from time to time upon Cotesworth & Powell: but they certainly did not prohibit them from drawing upon their own partners in London; nor were they obligated by the agreement to execute all their drafts against Cotesworth and Powell.

2. Were the contracts legal?

The laws of New Granada then in force expressly provided for just such contracts of incidental partnership as those under consideration. But the counsel for Colombia maintains that they were not binding upon the Barranquilla house; first, because the firm name of Powles Brothers & Co. had not been used; and second, because there is no written evidence of a commission to Powles Brothers & Co. from Powles, Gower & Co.

The reasons are not well founded; because,

1. The firm of Powles, Gower & Co., was formed, as we have seen, by Powles Brothers & Co., of London, of the one part, and by Samuel S. Gower and Miguel Rivas, of New Granada, of the other part, under written agreement dated October 22, 1855, and in accordance with the laws of New Granada. It was both legal and natural, therefore, that, in London, Powles Brothers & Co., as the only resident partners, should use the firm name there in the same manner that the managing partner in New Granada, Samuel S. Gower, used it in Barranquilla.

2. A special commission, from one to the other, was not necessary to enable the respective partners to use their firm name. Their acts are binding upon the firm without this, under the laws of New Granada.

3. When and how the incidental partnership was dissolved.

This incidental partnership ceased, of course, from the date of the bankruptcy of Powles Brothers & Co. and of their Barranquilla partners. This appears from the sentence of a New Granadian court which declares:

1. That between Powles, Gower & Co., of New Granada, and Cotesworth & Powell, of London, there had existed an incidental partnership since the date of January 14, 1856; and

2. That this incidental partnership was dissolved in December 1857, in consequence of the failure of Powles Brothers & Co.

This decision was in accordance with the commercial laws of New Granada, as may be seen by reference to articles 319 and 290 of the Codigo de Comercio of 1853.

VI

THE REVOLUTION AND THE AMNESTY.

These have a most important bearing upon the questions submitted in this case. The first because it has been made a ground of defense by the counsel for Colombia, the second because it forms the chief if not the only reason for making this reclamation an international question. We shall therefore consider,

1. The revolution.

The counsel for Colombia characterises the revolution in Bolivar, as a 'political situation which exempts the national government of Colombia from all responsibility, for want of those obligations which bind it to other nations', etc., and as rendering the national Government 'irresponsible for damages suffered by strangers voluntarily within the belligerent territory', etc.

These opinions of the learned counsel are applicable to a state of war between the two nations interested; but in the present case, there was no such war. Pacific relations between Colombia and Great Britain had not been interrupted. But if they had been, British subjects in Colombia would have still retained all their rigthts under existing treaties and international polity, until official publication of war had been made. And such publication, we may as well remember, could have been made only by the national authorities. The State of Bolivar, even had it been so inclined, which however does not appear to have been the case, could not have changed the relationship between the two countries; because Bolivar was an integral member of the national entity of Colombia, without any international character or any species of foreign relations whatever.

Moreover, the points raised by Dr. Sálas are inapplicable; because,

1. Even admitting that, between the months of July and December 1859, the condition of political affairs in Bolivar was such as to render the administration of justice uncertain or impossible, this could only have delayed justice until the restoration of peace and order. This took place, as we have already seen, in December 1859; after which time, the war could be no longer alleged as an excuse for delay in awarding justice, still less in mitigation of positive denials of justice, or for acts of notorious injustice.

24

2. The frequent and illegal absence of the judge cannot be excused under the plea of political disorder; because, at the time, there was no direct peril to life in Barranquilla, nor was that judicial circuit in a state of war.

And it may be added in this connection, that the absence of the judge from his place of official duty, without providing any substitute, was aggravated by the fact that he carried with him many important documents pertaining to the suit and, never returned them, nor deposited them in a place of safety; thus depriving the claimants of the ordinary and necessary means of obtaining justice.

2. The amnesty.

The amnesty laws of the State, of March 3, 1860, and January 3, 1853, resulted in judicial sentences, as we have seen, which virtually closed the courts of appellate revision against the claimants. The facts are as follows:

1. By the decree of April 17, 1860, the superior tribunal for the State released both the judge of first instance and the assignee from the consequences of their crimes and misdemeanors; declaring the acts of both comprehended in the amnesty of March 3, 1860.

2. By its sentence of May 1, 1860, the provincial court of Barranquilla dismissed all the proceedings against the assignee, Suarez Fortoul, for the same reason.

3. In like manner, the same tribunal by its sentence of May 8, 1860, dismissed the action brought against ex-judge Salazar for robbery and falsification of documents. But in this case, the court held that the accused was not necessarily released from civil responsibility, under the law of March 3, 1860. Hence, on the 30th December 1861, the same tribunal condemned ex-judge Salazar to the payment of costs and damages caused by his illegal and corrupt decisions and rulings which led to the nullity of the whole bankruptcy proceeding. From this sentence an appeal was subsequently taken by Salazar; and,

4. On the 11th of May 1863 the superior tribunal of the State decided that the sentence condemning Salazar to the payment of costs and damages was 'in consequence of his violations of law': that, whether such violations be con sidered as veritable crimes or as mere irregularities, they were, in either case comprehended in the amnesty of January 3, 1863. The court, therefore, decreed his release from all civil responsibility.

(H) It is asserted by one of the counsel for Colombia that the amnesty laws upon which these judicial sentences were predicated were enacted by the State legislature while in ' open rebellion against the public order; to which (rebellion) the national government succumbed before it could be suppressed ', etc.

To wich we observe,

1. That the rebellion terminated in December 1859. This was two months before the first, or more than two years before the last amnesty law was passed.

2. If the learned counsel's assumption be admitted with respect to the amnesty of March 3, 1860 — wich however is not possible — then that of January 3, 1863, upon which the main decision rests, still remains.

If it were possible to waive this point, and admit the assumption of the counsel with respect to both laws, we should be confronted by the proposition, wheter it was not the duty of the national government to annul all illegal acts committed in 'open rebellion against public order', whenever its authority was reestablished.

It has been well said by Dr. Rubio, the counsel for Great Britain, that 'the rebellion triumphed; that the national constitutional convention acknowledged as valid all the acts of the revolutionary legislature of Bolivar; and the amnesty laws of the State were among the acts thus recognized and adopted'. The undersigned quite agrees with him, therefore, that the nation accepted all the consequences of those acts.

But it is maintained both by Dr. Salas and by the honorable the attorney-general of the nation, that the sentence of May 11, 1863, does not necessarily prove that the amnesty laws deprived the claimants of any right to institute civil actions for damages against individuals who may have wrought them injury.

This opinion seems to be supported by the reasons given for the decision of the provincial court of May 8, 1860. It should be borne in mind, however, that that decision was based upon the law of March 3, 1860; whilst that of May 11, 1863, was founded upon the new law of January 3, 1863; that one decision, which was not appealable, construed the law of 1863 to embrace the civil consequences of the crime; that the same tribunal has never so construed the law of 1860; and hence that the reasons given for the one can have no application with respect to the other. With regard to the decision of April 17, 1860, exempting the judge and assignee, the counsel for Colombia contends that it was appealable. This opinion is erroneous, because,

1. There is no higher tribunal within the State, to which appeal might be taken;

2. There was no national court of appellate revision at that time, so far as the State Bolivar was concerned, in consequence of the political changes; but,

3. If there had been, an appeal would have been wholly useless; because we have just seen that the national tribunal, under the terms of the reorganized government, would have had no other alternative than in recognizing both the amnesty laws of Bolivar as legitimate and in full force.

VII.

THE RESPONSIBILITY.

Having examined at some length the leading facts connected with the administration of justice, in the locality and during the period named in the convention, in cases in which the claimants were interested, it only remains to determine whether the facts proven render the national government of Colombia responsible. We should therefore, consider:

1. The conditions under which one government becomes responsible to another for wrongs occurring under its judicial administration; and
2. Whether, in the present case, the facts proven fulfil these conditions.

1. The conditions of the responsibility.

First, then, with regard to the rights and duties of foreigners, the undersigned deduces the following principles:

1. If a nation annexes any special condition to the permission to enter its territory, it should take measures to accoint foreigners with the fact when they present themselves at the frontier. But when admitted, strangers should obey the laws of the place; and in return for such obedience, they are entitled to the protection of the laws. All disputes, therefore, between themselves or between them and the natives, should, where such provision is made, be determined by the tribunals, and according to the laws of the place.

2. Every nation should provide just and reasonable laws for the administration of justice; and it is equally a duty to provide means for their prompt and impartial execution. Reasonable diligence should be exercised in securing competent and honest judges. This done, the nation has no further concern than to see that they do not neglect their duties:

3. The judiciary of a nation should be respected, as well by other nations as by foreigners resident or doing business in the country. Therefore, every definitive sentence of a tribunal, regularly pronounced, should be esteemed just and executed as such. As a rule, when a cause in which foreigners are interested, has been decided in due form, the nation of the defendants cannot hear their complaints. It is only in cases where justice is refused, or palpable or evident injustice is committed, or when rules and forms have been openly violated, or when odious distinctions have been made against its subjects, that the government of the foreigner can interfere.

4. The granting of amnesty and pardon is one of the attributes of sovereignty, resulting from the very nature of government. But in the exercise of this prerogative, there should be no other object than the greater good to society. Justice should be reconciled with clemency; pity for the unfortunate should never banish care for the public safety.

5. One nation is not responsible to another for the acts of its individuals citizens, except when it approves or ratifies them. It then becomes a public concern and the injured party may consider the nation itself the real author of the injury. And this approval, it is apprehended, need not be in express terms; but may fairly be inferred from a refusal to provide means of reparation when such means are possible; or from its pardon of the offender, when such pardon necessarily deprives the injured party of all redress.

6. According to the old authorities, a judicial sentence notoriously unjust, to the prejudice of a stranger, entitles his government to interfere for reparation even by reprisals. The authority of the judge was not considered to be of the same force against strangers as against citizens, because the latter were concluded by the sentence, though it be unjust; they could not lawfully oppose its execution nor by reprisals recover their rigths 'by reason of the controlling efficacy of the authority under which they live'; whereas strangers had the power of reprisal, although it was considered unlawful to exercise it so long as their rights might be obtained by the ordinary course of justice.

7. This doctrine, however, has been greatly modified. According to modern standard authorities, the nation to which a foreigner belongs may interfere for his protection only when he receives positive maltreatment, or when he has been denied ordinary justice in a foreign country. 'In the former case, immediate reparation may be insisted upon. In the latter, the interference is of a more delicate character'; and in order to be justifiable, all means of legal redress 'afforded by the tribunals of the country in which the injury occurred', must have been exhausted. The ground for interference is fairly laid when those tribunals are unable or unwilling to entertain and adjudicate the grievance. But even then 'it behooves the government interfering to have

the greatest care, *first*, that the commission of wrong be clearly established'; and, *second*, that the refusal of the tribunals to decide the case at issue, be no less clearly established.

8. No demand can be founded, as a rule, upon mere objectionable *forms* of procedure or the *mode* of administering justice in the courts of a country; because strangers are presumed to consider these before entering into transactions therein. Still, a plain violation of the substance of natural justice, as, for exemple, refusing to hear the party interested, or to allow him opportunity to produce proofs, amounts to the same thing as an absolute denial of justice.

9. Nations are responsible to those strangers, under the conditions above enumerated, *first* for denials of justice; and *second*, for acts of notorious injustice. The first occurs when the tribunals refuse to hear the complaint, or to decide upon petitions of complainant, made according to the established forms of procedure, or when undue and inexcusable delays occur in rendering judgment. The second takes place when sentences are pronounced and executed in open violation of law, or which are manifestly iniquitous.

10. With respect to the case under consideration, the undersigned concludes that the Government of Colombia is responsible to that of the claimants, if justice had been denied them, or if they have been the victims of notorious injustice, in cases admitting of no doubt; provided all modes of appellate revision were exhausted, and the executive power, representing the nation (irrespective of its internal distribution of governmental functions) to foreign powers, had notice of the fact and refused redress. We should therefore consider:

2. *Whether the facts proven fulfil the above conditions.*

That there were, in the locality and during the time mentioned in the convention of arbitration undue delays, many irregularities, repeated refusals to hear the parties or to decide upon their petitions; positive violations of law in dictating sentences, and even gross criminal conduct on the part of the judge, in certain lawsuits in which the claimants were interested, and greatly to the detriment of their rights and interests, appears from the foregoing investigation. But for the sake of convenience, the facts may be briefly summed up as follows:

1. In the first stage of the proceeding in bankruptcy against Powles, Gower & Co., the failure of the judge to cite the absent creditors was among the irregularities which, four years after-

wards, caused the nullity of the whole proceeding *ab initio*.

2. In the same proceeding, the sentence of classification, besides being itself illegal, was never legally notified. As a consequence, the sentence of November 19, 1858, was unjust for illegally excluding the claimants as common creditors; even if it had been legally notified, which was not the case.

3. The nullification of the entire proceeding in bankruptcy, nearly four years after its commencement, and after all the assets had been either squandered or illegally partitioned, and when there were no means of their recovery, involved undue delay, positive denials of justice and gross criminal conduct on the part of the judge and assignee.

4. In the first criminal proceeding against this judge and his secretary, for falsification of legal documents, the sumarios were lost or destroyed, and the investigation defeated, in consequence of an open violation of law by the judge having cognizance of the case.

5. The sentence releasing Isaacs & Co. from all responsibility, resulting from their embargo of goods pertaining to the incidental partnership, was a denial of justice; because made without hearing the claimants as plaintiffs in the suit. The delay of nearly one whole year in notifying an important judicial sentence was inexcusable. The exclusion of claimants' attorney, or rather the judge's refusal to decide upon his petition was a denial of justice. The conflict between the decisions of the same tribunals is not accounted for; nor has it ever been attempted, except under misapprehension as to dates.

6. The sentence recognizing the pretentions of the assignee, to embargo goods not among the bankrupts' assets, was of very doubtful legality. This, however, could never have arisen among the causes of complaint, had not the judge refused to hear the parties interested, on their petitions repeatedly and formally made, thus denying them ordinary justice. The decree of sale of certain embargoed goods stored out of Barranquilla, pending action for their possession, and without hearing the parties, was a denial of justice if not notorious injustice.

7. The secret abstraction, appraisement, removal, and sale of certain embargoed goods stored in Barranquilla, pending action for their possession, was at least an irregular and illegal act on the part of the assignee and the judge, if not grossly criminal on the part of both; especially as this was done over the protest of such of the parties interested as happened to suspect the fact, and

as the proceeds of the sale were never satisfactorily accounted for.

8. In the exhibitory action by Osorio, the sentence of March 18, 1859, was unjust; because the documents should have been previously returned. The judge's refusal to hear the defendant was a denial of justice. The same is true of his failure to notify the defendant of Osorio's counter action for possesston, whilst the objects of litigation were yet in possession of the court.

9. The judge's absence from his place of official duty, at the times and under the circumstances named, was a violation of the New Granadian laws. Nor can such absence be excused or mitigated on the ground of political disorder, because life was not in peril in the Barranquilla district at the time. His absence was especially prejudicial to the claimants, since he carried with him the most important papers relating to their suit, and neither deposited them in a place of safety nor ever returned them : thus depriving the claimants of the ordinary and necessary means of obtaining their rights before the tribunals.

10. The amnesty laws of the State took away from the claimants all appellate recourse, and all means of redress before the authorities at Bolivar. By subsequently adopting those laws, the national government of Colombia rendered recourse to its tribunals equally useless. The chief executive of the nation was duly informed of these facts; but, after considerable delay, finally refused to provide means for reparation.

The undersigned considers, therefore, that the facts proven in this case clearly fall within the conditions which render one gouvernement responsible to another for wrongs occurring under its judicial administration. Hence, in regard to the preliminary question propounded in Article III of the convention of December 14, 1872, he is left no [other] alternative than to decide in the affirmative. He places this responsibility of Colombia solely upon the consequences of the amnesty, thus adhering, as he conceives, to the well-established principle in international polity, that, by pardoning a criminal, a nation assumes the responsibility for his past acts.

This involves no humiliation to the Colombian people and nation, because every nationality, however enlightened may be its people, however admirable and just its political and judicial systems, is far from being sufficiently perfect to prevent exceptional cases of judicial corruption, or gross-criminal conduct on the part of its high officials. History, both ancient and modern, abundantly attests that every nation, from the humblest to the greatest, has had its experiences in this line; and, whilst Colombia has been justly noted for

its generous hospitality to strangers, it would be remarkable indeed were it to claim exemption from the ordinary frailties of common humanity. On the contrary, to her credit and honor, both at home and abroad, Colombia has fully recognized the principle here involved by her decree of 1868, awarding indemnity, under precisely similar circumstances, to a foreigner residing in Barranquilla [1].

LVIII. Brésil, Grande-Bretagne.

22 avril 1873.

Cet arbitrage, qui donna lieu à une décision remarquable, fut institué par un simple échange de lettres. Nous nous contentons de reproduire ici la réponse du gouvernement brésilien pour fixer la date de l'accord intervenu. La correspondance ne contient aucune stipulation spéciale quant à la procédure à suivre par les arbitres.

Nota do governo imperial á legação britannica, em 22 de Abril de 1873.

Em notas de 11 e 30 de Janeiro ultimo S. Ex. o. Sr. George Buckley Mathew, enviado extraordinario e ministro plenipotenciario de Sua Magestade Britannica referindo-se ás reclamações do conde de Dundonald, filho do finado lord Cochrane pendentes entre os governos do Brazil e do Gran-Bretanha, propõe, de ordem deste, que as mesmas reclamações sejam submettidas ao juizo arbitral.

Respondendo áquellas notas, tenho a honra de communicar ao Sr. ministro que o governo imperial em prova dos sentimento de justiça que o animam, admitte o alvitre proposta por S. Ex.

O numero dos arbitros poderá ser de dois, designando-se um terceiro para o caso de divergencia entre elles : e sobre sua escolha terei muito prazer em entender-me opportunamente com S. Ex. o Sr. Buckley Mathew, a quem renovo os protestos de minha alta consideração.

Décision des arbitres, nommés par les gouvernements du Brésil et de la Grande Bretagne, prononcée le 6 octobre 1873, à Rio de Janeiro.

Les soussignés, ayant accepté, sur proposition du gouvernement impérial du Brésil et de la légation de Sa Majesté Britannique à Rio de Janeiro, la nomination d'arbitres dans le jugement des réclamations présentées par le comte de Dundonald, pour les services rendus au Brésil par son père feu l'amiral lord Cochrane, ont reçu, le 16 Septembre, la demande «Exposé de services»

---

[1] J. B. Moore, *History and Digest* ...., p. 2053 --2085.

et les documents et pièces justificatives que l'agent du comte de Dundonald leur soumet à l'appui de ses réclamations ; ils ont également reçu les documents et pièces justificatives produits, en réponse, par le gouvernement impérial : sur quoi ils ont immédiatement procédé à l'étude et à l'examen de la matière.

Le premier soin des soussignés a été de choisir un troisième arbitre pour les cas de désaccord entre eux : et le choix est tombé sur leur collègue Monsieur Bartholeyns de Fosselaert, Ministre résident de Sa Majesté le Roi des Belges, lequel a accepté la nomination qui lui a été proposée, sous la réserve de l'approbation de son gouvernement.

Toutefois, il n'a pas été le cas de réclamer l'intervention du troisième arbitre, les soussignés ayant émis d'un seul et même accord le même arrêt.

Et après avoir :

Vu et considéré les preuves et un examen approfondi des documents produits de côté et d'autre ;

Ils passent à exposer leur opinion sur les différents articles, ainsi que leur décision et leur arrêt sur la question qui leur est soumise.

Cette réclamation s'appuie aux services rendus par l'amiral Cochrane, pendant la guerre de l'indépendance, services racontés et détaillés dans l'exposé (Narrative of Services) publié en 1859, et aux pétitions adressées ensuite par le comte de Dundonald, en sa qualité de représentant de son père, au gouvernement impérial, et dans sa demande nouvellement présentée par son agent.

Dans sa demande, aux articles déduits pour lesquels il réclame indemnité, l'amiral ajoute la plainte que la violation des droits du demandeur a été rendue plus flagrante, par un déni de justice, et — « par le refus d'admission de preuves et de déclarations, tandis que le gouvernement brésilien choisissait à plaisir celles qui lui convenaient » ; — et que la conduite du gouvernement à l'égard de lord Cochrane a été par trop sévère et même cruelle.

C'est donc avant tout, le devoir des arbitres vis-à-vis du gouvernement impérial de prononcer tout d'abord leur décision à ce sujet et ils déclarent que, dans leur opinion, ni les faits ni les documents produits ne justifient une pareille assertion.

Au contraire, il résulte, d'une manière satisfaisante pour les soussignés, des documents et faits historiques, que, dès l'entrée de lord Cochrane au service du Brésil, le gouvernement se montra très libéral dans la fixation du rang, du traitement et des allocations accordés à l'amiral :

Que dans le règlement des arriérés du traitement et de la pension, fait en 1857, malgré une longue suspension, sans que l'on ait insisté pour la présentation des comptes et justifications des dépenses qu'il avait faites, pour des sommes considérables, l'amiral a été traité avec une grande indulgence ;

Et, finalement, que les titres et les décorations, ainsi que les marques de faveur qu'il a reçus de l'Empereur, prouvent que l'amiral a été traité avec générosité.

Les arbitres, néanmoins, sont convaincus, par les mêmes faits et documents, que, quoique la conclusion qui précède soit prouvée, il est également évident qu'il y eut défaut dans l'accomplissement de certaines promesses : défaut de régularité dans les payements aux dates fixées, défaut de règlement de la quote part des prises ;

Qu'il y eut délai, et délai prolongé, dans le règlement et le payement de la dette qui a été reconnue et payée ; et, finalement, ajournement indéfini de la liquidation générale.

De toutes ces circonstances, et d'autres incidents de la question, il en est résulté pour le demandeur non seulement une déception dans ses espérances et la conviction bien ou mal fondée d'avoir été victime de mauvais procédés, mais aussi un préjudice réel et un dommage pécuniaire, pour lesquels il a évidemment des titres à demander une réparation et une compensation.

C'est avec une telle conviction que les arbitres ont été amenés à porter le jugement sur ces réclamations, au point de vue le plus favorable, en prenant en considération celles qui sont admissibles, avec la même indulgence et les mêmes égards auxquels, dans leur opinion, le gouvernement impérial pourrait être disposé sans se faire à lui-même une véritable injustice.

Les réclamations présentées, selon les deux pétitions du comte de Dundonald et selon la réponse du gouvernement impérial, sont les suivantes :

I. *Primo :* pour défaut de payement de la quote part de l'amiral ($\frac{1}{8}$) sur la somme de 40,000 duros, allouée au capteur de l'*Imperatris*.

II. *Secundo :* pour la somme de £ 2000 sterling, que l'amiral déclare avoir avancée au chevalier Gameiro, ministre du Brésil à Londres, pour subvenir aux frais de la frégate *Ypiranga*.

III. *Tertio :* pour la quote-part de prises de l'amiral, sur toutes les prises faites pendant la guerre, et qu'il prétend avoir été déclarées bonnes *quoad captores*, malgré qu'elles aient été, ensuite, relâchées par le conseil des prises. Sont comprises dans la présente toutes les réclamations pour les déductions injustes que l'amiral prétend avoir été faites dans les payements précédents.

IV. *Quarto :* pour les intérêts des arriérés de son traitement et pension, dont le capital seul a été payé en 1865.

V. *Quinto:* pour la concession de terrains, comme apanage du marquisat que l'amiral déclare lui avoir été promis par l'Empereur D. Pedro I.

VI. *Sexto:* pour la somme de 67,000 duros, due pour solde à l'amiral par la République du Chili, solde, qu'il prétend avoir perdu par le fait de son entrée au service du Brésil, et dont le gouvernement et l'Empereur lui auraient promis le remboursement.

VII. *Septimo:* pour la somme de 308,208 duros, qui a été imputée aux comptes (descontados) du Marquis, comme ayant été reçue pour la distribuer aux gens de l'escadre, et qui n'aurait pas été payée mais retenue par lui.

On ne parle pas de cette somme dans la demande qui nous est soumise aujourd'hui.

L'agent de lord Dundonald réclame pour tous les articles qui précèdent, à l'exception du septième, et il demande, sur les sommes qu'il prétend être dues, les intérêts composés de 6% par an depuis les époques qu'il énonce.

I.

Dans l'examen de la première réclamation ci-dessus énoncée, la tâche des arbitres soussignés a été heureusement assez aisée. Le gouvernement impérial a, d'ailleurs, reconnu que cette réclamation n'a pas encore été payée.

Il résulte, en effet, d'une manière évidente:

De l'exposé sommaire du 23 Novembre 1869, adressé par le chef de section M' Eusebio José Antunes au département de la marine (voir page 3 de la réponse),

Et du memorandum du même département en date du 24 Juillet 1872 (voir page 115),

Qu'il n'a été fait aucun payement de cette somme allouée par le décret du 23 Février 1824.

Dans le memorandum du ministère de la marine, il est également déclaré que, selon les règles de l'équité, on pourrait, tout au plus, compter les intérêts de cette somme *à partir du jour dans lequel la demande a été faite.*

Après tout ce qui précède, les arbitres soussignés sont donc d'avis que, puisque la somme de 5000 duros avait été acceptée comme compromis pour une somme plus grande, qui avait été demandée,

Que cette somme a été allouée par le decret du 23 Février 1824, à titre de récompense pour des services spéciaux d'une très grande importance pour le gouvernement impérial;

Que, par cela, l'on avait reconnu, à cette époque, qu'une somme était due à titre d'argent de prises,

Les soussignés pensent être en droit de déclarer que cette somme, avec les intérêts de 6% par an, est due depuis le 23 Février 1824, c'est à dire avec les intérêts de 49 ans et 8 mois:

Le capital étant . . . $ 5,000

. Et l'intérêt . . . . . $ 14,900

On aura un total de . . $ 19,900

ou de £ 4125, au change de 50 pences, comme les soussignés préfèrent exprimer cette somme.

Par conséquent, ils arrêtent pour cette réclamation la somme de quatre mille cent vingt cinq livres sterling.

II.

La seconde réclamation porte sur les deux mille livres sterling que l'amiral prétend avoir avancées au ministre du Brésil à Londres, pour subvenir aux frais de la frégate *Ypiranga.*

A l'appui de cette demande d'une somme avancée par lord Cochrane, on a produit un reçu dans les termes suivants:

Londres, 2 Août 1825.

Je soussigné déclare avoir reçu, des mains de Mrs. Coutts et Cⁱᵉ et de la part de lord Cochrane, la somme de deux mille livres sterling, sur l'ordre de Sa Seigneurerie, en faveur du Chevalier Gameiro, pour compte duquel je reçois la dite somme.

(Signé) AUGUSTE DE PAIVA.

L'agent de lord Dundonald déclare que le reçu ci-dessus a été délivré contre la somme indiquée dans le document, somme qui aurait été remise au ministre brésilien à titre d'emprunt; un tel document peut très bien s'accorder avec une transaction de la nature que l'on prétend, quoique, en lui-même, il ne puisse constituer la preuve que la somme a été versée à titre d'emprunt.

Or, il résulterait:

De l'exposé sommaire de Mr. Antunes, du 23 Septembre 1869;

Et du *parecer,* ou rapport des sections de la guerre, de la marine et des finances du Conseil d'Etat réunies en date du 11 Décembre 1871, que le gouvernement impérial a été d'abord disposé à considérer cette somme comme constituant réellement un emprunt, et qu'il en a aussi recommandé le payement avec les intérêts qui en découlent (respectivos).

Dans le rapport du ministère des affaires étrangères, par lequel la question a été soumise aux arbitres (15 Septembre 1873) à page IX, il est dit:

Que «tant qu'il a pu exister des doutes sur la nature véritable de la transaction passée entre lord Cochrane et le ministre brésilien à Londres, au sujet de deux mille livres sterling, les autorités brésiliennes préféraient admettre la demande de remboursement de la somme et des intérêts » : mais que, aussitôt mis en possession des éclaircissements donnés par le chevalier Gameiro à l'époque même de cette transaction, — et à un moment où il était impossible de prévoir qu'une réclamation serait présentée à ce sujet — « il a été prouvé d'une manière évidente que le versement de deux mille livres sterling constituait la restitution d'une somme que lord Cochrane s'était engagé à rembourser, et non une avance ou un emprunt qu'il eut effectué ».

Les deux dépêches du ministre du Brésil à Londres ont été imprimées à pages 58 et 59 de la réponse et documents présentés par le gouvernement impérial.

La première de ces dépêches (voir n. 12, page 59) porte la date de Londres 9 Juillet 1825, — près d'un mois, notons-le, avant la date du reçu du 2 Août 1825, — et contient les déclarations suivantes :

« — Et j'ai commencé par envoyer à Portsmouth un agent de confiance (notre compatriote Manoel Antonio de Paiva), avec ordre de payer (à la frégate) deux mois de solde déjà échus, montant à Reis 9:915 $ 060, (voir annexe n. 2) ou £ 2,065-12ˢ-9ᵈ — selon le change de 50 pences. En addition de cette somme j'ai fait aussi payer £ 1,291-13ˢ-4ᵈ dues à une partie de l'équipage qui avait servi sur les frégates *Paraguassú* et *Nictherohy* (voir annexe n. 3), la première de ces sommes représentant l'équivalent d'une part de prises qui devait encore être payée : mais comme le premier amiral a promis de me faire la restitution (restituir) de ces deux sommes de £ 2,991-13ˢ-4ᵈ qu'il avait reçues de la Commission de Finance du Maranhão, sans les porter au compte de frais faits par la frégate, j'ai donné les ordres nécessaires (pour les réparations et les approvisionnements).

Dans la seconde dépêche, à page 58, il est dit : (N. 17, 9 Août 1825) Excellence : « Ayant informé V. Exc. par ma précédente dépêche n. 12, que j'ai payé sur la demande du premier amiral de l'Empire, le marquis de Maranhão, la somme de £ 2,291-13ˢ-4ᵈ qu'il m'a demandée en me promettant de me la rendre (restituir) sitôt qu'il arrivera dans cette capitale, je ne dois point omettre de communiquer à V. Ex. que le dit amiral a rempli sa promesse en me faisant payer ici par ses banquiers la somme susdite, en déduisant de ce qui était dû aux équipages en la somme de £ 2,291-13ˢ-4ᵈ qu'il déclare n'avoir pas reçue de la commission du Maranhão, ainsi que cela résulte du certificat ci-inclus, n. 1. »

Ces déclarations du chevalier Gameiro qui ne contredisent point, mais sont, au contraire, en accord parfait avec la lettre du reçu contenu dans les dépêches de cette époque, et dont les copies sont légalisées par le ministre des affaires étrangères du Brésil, obligent les soussignés à les admettre comme l'historique et l'explication réelle de la question.

Il est prouvé par ces documents que la somme de £ 2,000 maintenant redemandée comme emprunt fait au ministre du Brésil, — a été — dans le fait reçue par le chevalier Gameiro de lord Cochrane, en restitution d'une somme pareille prise sur les valeurs que l'amiral avait reçues au Maranhão.

Que si, en réponse à ce qui précède, on objecte, — que la somme est toujours due à lord Cochrane, si ce n'est à titre d'emprunt effectué par lui, toutefois comme une partie qu'il aurait restituée sur les valeurs qu'il avait reçues au Maranhão, à titre de quote-part de prises, et qui par conséquent était sa propriété, — dans ce cas, les arbitres ont à déclarer qu'ils prennent en considération et qu'ils décident à l'article n. 3 toute réclamation ayant trait à l'argent des prises, y incluse toute déduction provenant de cette source.

Par conséquent les arbitres ne peuvent déclarer que le reçu produit par lord Cochrane, en présence des dépêches du chevalier Gameiro, prouve un emprunt fait par l'amiral au ministre brésilien pour lequel il puisse élever des prétentions spéciales.

Au contraire, les soussignés doivent déclarer que c'est une restitution, telle qu'elle résulte des deux dépêches citées.

Cette réclamation ne peut donc être admise.

III.

Le troisième article de réclamation est pour la part des prises faites par l'amiral pendant la guerre, en y comptant spécialement sa part en certaines prises qui ont été déclarées illégales par le conseil des prises.

L'amiral déclare que, selon la promesse de l'Empereur, et d'après le décret ou déclaration du gouvernement, les saisies opérées de cette manière devaient être considérées de bonne prise *quoad captores*, quand même elles auraient été déclarées (improcedentes) illégales par le conseil des prises ; dans ce cas, le gouvernement s'engageait à en rembourser la valeur sur le trésor impérial.

Par conséquent la réclamation présentée demande dans toutes les prises bonnes ou mauvaises faites pendant la guerre, au nombre de 126, 33 desquelles ont été déclarées bonnes et adjugées aux capteurs pour la valeur déterminée de Reis 521 : 315 $ 980.

Quant à ce qui regarde les 93 autres prises, aucune valeur n'a été fixée, et, vu qu'il n'existe aucun document ou preuve d'après lesquels cette valeur puisse être estimée, l'agent du comte de Dundonald propose que :

Puisqu'il est juste de supposer que les prises non adjugées aient été d'une nature et d'une valeur moyennes égales à celles qui ont été adjugées bonnes, il propose que leur valeur soit déterminée à l'aide d'une règle de proportion : — que, si les 33 prises ont valu 521,315 duros, les 126 doivent être evaluées à 1,990,475 duros ; que cette somme se trouvant être à peu près égale au montant évalué en bloc par l'amiral (2,000,000 duros), — au moment où par cause du délai dans la liquidation de sa quote-part, il offrait, au nom des officiers et des gens de l'escadre, d'accepter la somme de 600,000 duros, comme leur quote-part, à condition qu'elle fût immédiatement payée, — on peut en induire que cette somme représente la juste évaluation.

Et comme la réclamation est faite pour (I) $\frac{1}{8}$ de cette somme (1,990,475 duros), à titre de quote-part de l'amiral sur toutes les prises faites par l'escadre, c'est 248,809 duros que réclame la demande.

Il faut ajouter à celle-ci le (II) $\frac{1}{8}$ additionnel sur toutes les saisies opérées par le vaisseau amiral tout seul, au nombre de 29, évaluées en bloc à 458,125 duros : de manière que ce huitième monterait à 57,265 duros, et la somme totale demandée comme quote-part de l'amiral serait de 306,704 duros.

De cette somme l'agent convient de déduire la somme entière de Reis 115 : 017 $ 086 (papier monnaie au change de 27 pences), que le gouvernement du Brésil déclare avoir payée à lord Dundonald, en 1865, quoique, dans le fait, une déduction de Reis 30 : 000 $ 000 ait été faite sur la somme sus-énoncée, et que, effectivement, il n'avait touché que Reis 84 : 069 $ 017.

La somme de Reis 115 : 017 $ 086 étant équivalente à 57,500 duros, et cette dernière somme étant déduite des 306,704 duros, sus-énoncés, il reste un excédent de 248,574 duros — quote-part de l'amiral, avec les intérêts composés en sus, à raison de 6 % par an, que l'agent semble prétendre depuis 1825, époque de la fin de la guerre.

Comme toute somme avec les intérêts composés de 6 % par an, se double en près de 12 ans, qu'elle monte au quadruple en 24 ans, et qu'elle se double ainsi de suite à chaque période de 12 années, il s'en suit que la somme de 248,574 duros ferait, au taux indiqué en 1873, en près 3,977,000 duros, soit trois millions neuf cent soixante-dix-sept mille duros, et c'est précisément là la somme que lord Dundonald pourrait légalement demander si les comptes proportionnels de son agent pouvaient être admis.

La meilleure réponse à de certaines demandes est de les reproduire textuellement.

Le gouvernement impérial, en répondant à la demande de la quote-part des prises non payée à l'amiral jusqu'ici, nie qu'il existe, ou même qu'il puisse exister des réclamations sur d'autres prises que celles qui ont été déclarées bonnes par le tribunal compétent ;

Qu'il n'existe aucun décret, ni aucune loi qui accorde aux capteurs le droit de retenir ou de se faire payer la valeur de *tous* les navires capturés ;

Que le gouvernement a été forcé de relâcher, et même de payer la valeur d'un grand nombre de navires illégalement saisis par l'escadre, ou par lord Cochrane ; que, en certains cas, les navires amenés dans les ports ont été non seulement jugés de mauvaise prise (improcedentes), mais que les capteurs ont été mis à l'amende et condamnés à payer des dommages-intérêts : de manière que, ils sembleraient mériter une punition plutôt qu'une récompense ;

Que le gouvernement s'est déjà prononcé sur la question entière de la part des prises, et qu'il a déjà payé à lord Dundonald, en 1865, la solde de tout ce qui pouvait être réclamé en justice ;

Que l'amiral a reçu à différentes époques des sommes considérables, soit du gouvernement, soit des intéressés, à titre de rachat des prises, et qu'il n'en a jamais rendu compte ;

Qu'aussi longtemps que les comptes justificatifs n'auront été produits, on pourra considérer cet argent comme pris ou retenu par l'amiral en payement de sa quote-part de prises, ou d'autres versements auxquels il aurait pu avoir droit, — et que l'amiral ne peut réclamer aucun règlement de la quote-part de prises, sans la présentation des comptes susdits ;

Et, finalement, que l'amiral ayant accepté, en 1857, les arriérés de sa pension sans en demander ou recevoir les intérêts, et le gouvernement n'ayant pas demandé les intérêts, il paraîtrait établi que lord Cochrane ait reçu tout ce qui pouvait lui revenir en payement de toutes réclamations pour les prises.

Les arbitres soussignés ont apporté dans l'examen de cette question des prises la plus grande attention, et ils sont forcés d'avouer qu'après toute espèce d'investigations, et en l'absence de toute preuve sur le nombre et la valeur des prises, ils ne sauraient adopter aucun point de départ, pour prononcer un jugement strictement légal et fondé sur des calculs exacts.

Les arbitres pensent que cette absence de preuves ne les justifierait pas, si, pour déterminer le nombre ou la valeur des prises, ils suivaient la règle d'évaluation proposée par l'agent de lord Dundonald.

Il n'y a nul doute que le gouvernement impérial a le droit de prétendre que tout réclamant ait à corroborer sa demande par des preuves; que, dans toute réclamation pour des sommes d'argent, et basée sur le fait que des sommes aient été retenues, le réclamant doit être tenu à produire des preuves positives, que sa demande corresponde à ces valeurs; et, principalement que ces preuves doivent à plus forte raison être produites, quand le gouvernement déclare que le demandeur lui est débiteur de sommes considérables reçues en numéraire et dont le demandeur n'a pas justifié l'emploi.

Mais, il semble aussi que l'application des errements qui précèdent ne peut être faite avec toute rigueur à une question comme l'actuelle où il y a des faits qui, jusqu'à un certain point, sont indiscutables: ainsi, il est certain que des saisies ont été faites; que, quoique bien des prises aient été jugées mauvaises, il y en a d'autres qui auraient pû être déclarées bonnes; et que, dans cette question bien des preuves ne peuvent être produites d'une manière satisfaisante et évidente, par la seule raison que des documents ont été détruits, et que le laps de 50 ans a rendu impossible de les remplacer.

Cependant, malgré l'absence de ces preuves, les arbitres sont convaincus que parmi les 93 navires sur lesquels il n'y a pas eu de jugement prononcé, il y en avait quelques-uns, quoiqu'il leur soit impossible d'en préciser le nombre, qui auraient pu être déclarés de bonne prise et que ceux-ci avaient une valeur considérable quoiqu'il soit aujourd'hui impossible aux soussignés de la déterminer.

Si les preuves d'après lesquelles ce nombre et ces valeurs auraient pu être déclarées avec exactitude ont été détruites ou perdues, la faute n'en est point imputable à lord Cochrane.

S'il y a eu négligence, refus d'action de la part du conseil des prises, ou long délai et ajournement pendant 50 ans, pour vérifier les faits, la faute n'en est certainement pas à lord Cochrane. Et on ne peut, assurément, lui refuser tout espèce de compensation là où il pourrait avoir droit d'en prétendre une, par le seul motif que l'amiral, par la faute d'autrui, n'est pas en position de démontrer le montant du dommage souffert.

Pourtant, ni la réclamation telle qu'elle est présentée par l'agent, ni la réponse telle qu'elle est présentée par le gouvernement impérial ne peuvent être admises par les arbitres.

Admettre, en effet, la somme demandée par l'agent, ou même la dixième partie, ce ne serait autre chose qu'imposer au gouvernement impérial une amende énorme, dans l'intérêt d'une réclamation d'une valeur douteuse, en compensation d'un dommage supposé, évalué suivant une règle inacceptable, et qui n'est appuyée en aucune preuve légale.

Les arbitres ne sauraient pas résoudre un tel procédé. Admettre d'ailleurs complètement le système du gouvernement impérial et prononcer que, par la raison que toute preuve est aujourd'hui impossible, il n'y a pas eu de prises sur lesquelles lord Cochrane puisse réclamer, qu'il n'a aucun droit, et qu'on ne lui doit rien absolument, quand il est moralement prouvé qu'il y a eu des navires, qu'il y a eu des saisies et des valeurs, et par là des droits, ce serait un flagrant déni de justice à l'égard de lord Cochrane.

Les arbitres ne peuvent, par leur arrêt, confirmer une pareille injustice.

Dans une telle situation les arbitres n'ont d'autres ressources que de rechercher dans les précédents de la question un fait, une offre ou un point de départ quelconque, pour formuler un compromis raisonnable, qui s'accorde avec les droits de chacune des parties, droits qui ne pourraient d'autre manière être conciliés.

L'on pourrait prendre, pour base du compromis, la lettre adressée par lord Cochrane le 9 Février 1860 au Ministre du Brésil à Londres (le Baron de Penedo) qui est à page 99 du rapport imprimé.

Dans cette lettre, lord Cochrane déclare qu'à son avis la somme que le gouvernement du Brésil pourrait convenablement lui offrir, et que lui même pourrait accepter avec reconnaissance (com gratidão) en payement de *tous* ses droits, et en récompense de tous les services par lui rendus, serait au plus bas chiffre, de £ 44,000 sterling.

L'offre a été transmise par le ministre, et recommandée au gouvernement impérial, qui ne semble l'avoir prise en considération jusqu'en 1865, à l'occasion du payement d'un règlement d'une quote-part de prises reçue par lord Dundonald, en Reis 84 : 019 $ 017 ou £ 9450 sterling.

Quoique cette offre n'ayant pas été acceptée en 1860, les arbitres peuvent supposer que le montant ait été regardé comme exagéré, en vue surtout des payements faits à une époque antérieure (1857) ils doivent, cependant, croire que cette raison ne saurait être reproduite aujourd'hui après un si long délai, et que toute déduction de ce montant qui aurait pu être justement demandée en 1860, le gouvernement impérial devrait aujourd'hui la regarder comme simplement une compensation raisonnable pour l'ajournement qui a eu lieu.

Par conséquent, en déduisant du montant de l'offre faite en 1860, le payement fait à compte en 1865, de £ 9450, il reste la somme de £ 34,550 sterling.

Et, vu que la somme allouée pour l'*Impératris* n'a jamais été comptée parmi les réclamations pour la part des prises; qu'elle a été accordée à titre du compromis ainsi qu'il est démontré plus haut (voir n° 1),

Les arbitres jugent que la somme arrêtée pour cet article ne doit pas être déduite du restant sous-énoncé de £ 34,550 sterling.

Par conséquent les soussignés arrêtent pour toute réclamation de l'argent des prises (y inclus toute demande pour des sommes qui en aient été déduites, et excepté ce qui a été alloué pour l'*Imperatris*) la somme de £ 34,550 sterling, trente quatre mille cinq cent cinquante livres sterling.

IV.

Le quatrième article de la réclamation est pour les intérêts des différents quartiers de la pension accordée à lord Cochrane, et dont le service à été suspendu par ordre du gouvernement impérial en conséquence du refus de l'amiral de se rendre à Rio en obéissance aux ordres qu'il en avait reçus.

Un règlement de cette pension a été fait le 11 Février 1857, et les arriérés en furent payés à l'amiral. Celui-ci continua ainsi à recevoir sa pension annuelle de 6000 duros jusqu'au moment de sa mort; et cette pension a été également payée durant la vie de lady Cochrane.

La demande de payement des intérêts n'a été présentée qu'en 1865 par le comte de Dundonald. L'amiral ne fit pourtant pas valoir aucune réclamation à propos des intérêts, lors du règlement susdit en 1857.

Il se plaint, toutefois, dans son « Exposé de service » publié en 1859, que la somme qui lui a été effectivement payée, à titre d'arriérés n'était même pas égale à celle qui serait représentée par la moitié des intérêts.

En réponse à cette demande le gouvernement impérial déclare:

Que lord Cochrane refusa constamment de retourner au Brésil, pour y rendre compte de ses actes, comme il en avait été requis par les ordres qui lui avaient été régulièrement transmis: et que malgré cette circonstance, ce n'est que le 11 Avril 1827, c'est-à-dire deux ans plus tard, qu'il fut déposé de ses fonctions:

Que cette désobéissance et le refus de l'amiral de se soumettre au jugement d'une cour militaire, quel qu'ait été le motif de son refus, constituent une faute de service comme officier; et que la suspension de ses appointements étant le résultat nécessaire de cette faute, ce qui d'ailleurs était le seul moyen de contraindre l'amiral à se présenter: c'est donc à sa conduite que lord Cochrane doit, comme conséquence directe, imputer si son traitement ne lui a été régulièrement payé.

Que le 11 Février 1857, par un acte de faveur, les arriérés furent payés à l'amiral, et que nul gouvernement n'est tenu à payer ni ne paye des intérêts sur les traitements ou allocations de ses employés, toutes les fois que le délai dans le payement de ces mêmes traitements est occasionné par la faute de ces mêmes employés.

Les arbitres soussignés pensent que par les raisons sus-exposées le gouvernement impérial est justifié dans son refus d'admettre la demande de payement des intérêts sur les arriérés de la pension.

Ils pensent également que le règlement accepté par lord Cochrane en 1857 a été un règlement définitif de toute réclamation pour traitements et pension, y inclus tout dommage intérêt jusqu'à cette époque.

Ils sont, pourtant, obligés de rejeter la demande de payement des intérêts sur les arriérés de la pension dont le règlement a été fait en 1857.

V.

Le cinquième article de la rèclamation est pour l'accomplissement de la promesse que l'amiral déclare lui avoir été faite, d'une concession de terrains comme apanage du titre de marquis, qui lui avait été conféré.

A ce sujet les arbitres soussignés ont à observer:

Que nul document à l'appui de cette déclaration n'a été produit.

Que s'il y eût promesse, elle n'avait aucune valeur en présence des lois de l'Empire.

Il paraît que, à ce propos, le demandeur n'est pas disposé à insister, et les arbitres soussignés ne sauraient accorder aucune somme comme due à ce titre à lord Cochrane.

VI.

La sixième réclamation est pour la somme de 67,000 duros, que l'amiral lord Cochrane prétend être le montant qui lui était dû comme solde par la République du Chili, solde qu'il dit avoir perdu par le fait de son entrée au service du Brésil, et dont l'Empereur lui même aurait promis le remboursement à lord Cochrane.

En réponse, le gouvernement impérial produit l'argument suivant:

Que nulle raison ne poussait le gouvernement du Brésil, à se porter garant vis-à-vis de lord Cochrane des dettes contractées par un pays étranger, et que l'amiral aurait du régler avec le gouvernement débiteur;

Qu'il n'existe aucune preuve d'une semblable promesse de payer la dette du Chili; et que, dès l'entrée de lord Cochrane au service impérial, les conditions de son engagement avaient été énumérées dans la patente et dans les *portarias* et décrets postérieurs. Dans l'un de ces derniers l'Empereur gratuitement et *motu proprio* accorde à la veuve de lord Cochrane la continuation de la pension qui avait été allouée à l'amiral pour toute sa vie;

Que, cependant, nulle mention n'a été faite, en aucun document, ni en aucune circonstance, de l'intention du gouvernement impérial d'indemniser l'amiral des pertes qu'il aurait pu souffrir par le fait de son abandon du service du Chili;

Par ces raisons:

Les arbitres soussignés déclarent que le représentant de lord Cochrane ne peut justement réclamer du gouvernement impérial le payement des sommes que l'amiral prétend lui être dues par le Chili;

Qu'au moment où lord Cochrane quitta cette République il aurait dû prendre les arrangements nécessaires pour le règlement immédiat ou à venir de sa comptabilité. Et que, dans tous les cas, le Brésil n'est point responsable pour le défaut de ce payement.

VII.

Le septième article est relatif au remboursement de 308,208 duros, qui suivant la pétition de lord Dundonald, en date du 7 Décembre 1868 (voir page 111 de la réponse imprimée du gouvernement impérial) «auraient été débités à l'amiral pour avoir reçus par lui afin d'être distribués aux gens de l'escadre, distribution que le marquis de Maranhão n'aurait pas faite». Il est à remarquer que l'agent, dans la demande qu'il a présentée, ne formule point une réclamation séparée pour cette somme dont il ne fait aucune mention, et que la réponse du gouvernement n'en parle non plus, quoique, des documents produits, cette dernière somme apparaisse ainsi qu'il est dit plus haut. Les soussignés ont donc conclu qu'il n'y avait lieu à insister sur cette réclamation, parce qu'ils ne rencontrent aucune preuve qui puisse en faire une réclamation séparée.

Il est déclaré dans les documents produits que le gouvernement impérial loin d'admettre cette réclamation de la part de lord Dundonald soutient que l'amiral a reçu cette somme, qu'il l'a gardée ou qu'il n'en a pas rendu compte, cette somme contenant le solde de ce qui était dû par l'amiral au gouvernement sur l'argent des prises.

Les arbitres ne rencontrent aucune raison pour admettre la réclamation de cette somme.

Les arbitres étant arrivés à ce point, après avoir prononcé sur chaque article de cette réclamation, la décision qu'ils ont cru juste et équitable, ont pris la détermination de réexaminer, après un court intervalle, leur appréciation. Et, dans le but de rectifier toute erreur qui puisse être advenue, et reprendre en considération toute observation qui puisse être avancée par chacun des arbitres, ces conclusions ont été séparément étudiées par chacun des soussignés; afin que toute observation ou fait, de nature à produire une modification quelle que ce soit sur un article précédemment décidé de plein accord, puisse être reconsidéré avant leur conférence finale et la signature de cet arbitrage.

Le terme fixé s'étant écoulé, les arbitres à leur conférence finale, ont pris en considération toutes les objections et arguments ayant trait à la question, qui se sont présentés à leur mémoire pendant tout ce laps de temps.

Et après avoir conféré mutuellement, ils ont reconnu que dans leur opinion il n'existe aucun nouveau fait ou argument, qui puisse en rien influer sur leur premier jugement, et sur les évaluations énoncées.

Parmi toutes les considérations qui ont été faites, et qui ont amené les soussignés à maintenir leurs conclusions après cet examen final, ils croient devoir en mentionner une, qui, seule, ne manquera pas de produire, selon leur opinion, sur toute personne de bonne foi et désintéressée, qui puisse avoir connaissance de la question, le même effet qu'elle a produit sur eux-mêmes.

Il résulte de l'«Exposé de services» publié par lord Cochrane que l'amiral est entré au service du Brésil, et qu'il arbora son pavillon à bord du *Pedro I* le 21 Mars 1823.

Dans le cours de 27 mois, et sans qu'il y ait eu nécessité de livrer une seule bataille, les opérations de son escadre à Bahia, Ceará, Pernambuco, Pará et Maranhão, ont déterminé l'abandon du Brésil par les forces portugaises.

L'amiral quitta Maranhão sur la frégate *Ypiranga* le 18 Mai 1825, et arriva en Angleterre le 25 Juin 1825; il n'est plus retourné au Brésil depuis cette époque. Cependant, sa démission formelle ne lui a été donnée que le 10 Avril 1827.

De cette manière lord Cochrane n'a été au service actif que depuis le 21 Mars 1823 jusqu'au 25 Juin 1825, c'est-à-dire pendant une période de deux ans et trois mois.

Pour les services rendus par l'amiral pendant ces 27 mois il a reçu durant sa vie (y inclus la pension payée à lady Cochrane, et le payement successif à lord Dundonald) à titres d'appointements, pension et quote-part de prises d'après l'exposé du gouvernement impérial Reis 699 : 375 $ 775; ou, au change de 27 pences £ 78,000 sterling, et d'après le propre exposé de l'amiral près de £ 62,000 sterling.

N'importe laquelle de ces sommes l'on admette, c'est évidemment une belle récompense pour des services, quelqu'importants qu'ils soient, rendus pendant 27 mois. Mais, quand l'on ajoute que, par les conclusions finales, il est encore alloué aux représentants de l'amiral une somme de £ 38,675 sterling, qui parfait en tout £ 100,675 sterling, pour ces deux années et trois mois de service, il sera probablement admis que, en reconnaissant les services de lord Cochrane, le gouvernement impérial a été au delà de toute munificence.

Cette considération fait que les arbitres soussignés n'ont trouvé aucune raison pour augmenter la somme qui a été accordée.

Et si les soussignés ne voient dans l'observation qui précède une cause de réduction dans la somme allouée c'est simplement parce qu'ils sont convaincus que le désir du gouvernement impérial serait certainement que toute erreur (à moins qu'elle n'entraîne un trop grave préjudice à lui-même) soit plutôt en faveur du demandeur, en tous les cas douteux, à la condition de clôre, d'une manière satisfaisante, une question qui a été discutée, ajournée, reconsidérée et reproduite à plusieurs reprises, pendant les dernières vingt années, sans aucun autre résultat que celui d'amener une différence plus sensible entre les prétentions des deux parties.

Les arbitres soussignés, en maintenant, par conséquent leurs conclusions, ont formulé leur arrêt dans les termes suivants:

Arrêt.

Les soussignés:

L'envoyé extraordinaire et ministre plénipotentiaire de Sa Majesté le Roi d'Italie, et l'envoyé extraordinaire et ministre plénipotentiaire des Etats-Unis d'Amérique:

Ayant accepté l'invitation du gouvernement impérial du Brésil et de la légation de Sa Majesté Britannique à Rio de Janeiro, de se prononcer sur les réclamations du Comte de Dundonald pour les services rendus au Brésil par son père, feu l'amiral lord Cochrane pendant la guerre de l'indépendance. réclamations qui ont été soumises à leur décision par le dit gouvernement impérial et par la susdite légation;

Après avoir:

Vu et pris en considération la demande — Exposé de services — et tous les documents présentés par le Comte de Dundonald; et également, la réponse, rapport, et tous les documents produits par le gouvernement impérial;

Après un examen approfondi et une étude impartiale de toute la question;

D'après les raisons et les motifs qui précèdent;

Les soussignés ont prononcé d'un commun accord les décisions suivantes:

Primo: que dans l'opinion des arbitres, il est dû, et qu'il doit être payé par le gouvernement impérial du Brésil au Comte de Dundonald, en sa qualité de représentant feu l'amiral lord Cochrane, la somme de £ 38,675, trente huit mille six cent soixante-quinze livres sterling.

Secondo: que la dite somme est due au Comte de Dundonald, et qu'elle doit être acceptée par lui comme montant et en quittance finale de tous ses droits contre le gouvernement impérial, soit à titre d'appointements, pension, quote-part de prises ou autre quel qu'il soit, provenant des services rendus par lord Cochrane au gouvernement susdit.

En foi de quoi, les soussignés ont rédigé le présent arrêt en duplicata, dont un exemplaire en langue française pour être présenté au gouvernement impérial, et l'autre en langue anglaise pour être présenté à la légation de Sa Majesté Britannique à Rio de Janeiro.

Fait à Rio de Janeiro, le six Octobre, en l'an de grâce mil huit cent soixante-treize [1].

LIX. Japon, Pérou.

19 juin 1873.

Cet arbitrage a eu pour objet une demande d'indemnité de la part du Pérou à raison de l'arrestation prétenduement illégale du navire *Maria Luz*. Il fut organisé par deux protocoles successifs des 19 et 25 juin 1873: l'Empereur de Russie, choisi comme arbitre, déchargea le Japon de toute responsabilité.

Protocol signed at Tokio by the Peruvian and Japanese ministers on the 19th of June 1873.

On the 19th of June, 1873, a conference took place at the department of foreign affairs of Japan, between the undersigned, Captain Aurelio Garcia y Garcia, envoy extraordinary and minister plenipotentiary of Peru, and Wooyeno Kagenori, His Imperial Japanese Majesty's acting minister for foreign affairs, in reference to the discussion pending between the two governments, growing out of the case of the Peruvian bark Maria Luz.

The Peruvian minister opened the conference by referring to Mr. Wooyeno's dispatch of June 14, 1873, stating that he had seen, with great satisfaction, the declaration of the Minister for

[1] *Relatorio da Repartição dos Negocios estrangeiros* 1874, p. 456--470.

foreign affairs that the Japanese government, in the Maria Luz case, had no intention to affront the dignity of Peru, and added that he was sorry to be obliged to say that Mr. Wooyeno's arguments to prove that no injustice had been done to Peruvian citizens did not satisfy him. Captain Garcia then explained at length all the points of disagreement between his views of the case as exposed in his note of 31st March 1873, and those of Mr. Wooyeno's in reply, and concluded that the Japanese government, in his opinion had not proved their irresponsability.

The minister for foreign affairs discussed the several objections presented by the Peruvian minister, and endeavored to demonstrate that in the case of the bark Maria Luz the Japanese government had acted in strict observance of law and the principles of justice.

A long and frank discussion ensued between both ministers each one sustaining his arguments and conclusions. It being evident that each government thought itself in the right, and neither being willing to yield any point to the other, this irreconciliable diversity of opinion, united to the earnest desire expressed by both of cultivating the most friendly relations, led the undersigned in representation of the governments of Peru and Japan to agree to submit the case to the decision of an impartial judge, to be the chief of a friendly state.

The undersigned will, as soon as possible, agree upon the selection of the arbitrator and the manner of submitting the case to him.

In testimony of which the undersigned have subscribed these presents, in quadruplicate, in the city of Yedo, on the 19th of June, 1873 [1].

Protocol signed on the 25th of June 1873 selecting His Majesty the Emperor of Russia as arbitrator.

The undersigned, Captain Aurelia G. y Garcia, envoy extraordinary and minister plenipotentiary of Peru, and Wooyeno Kagenori, His Imperial Japanese Majesty's acting minister for foreign affairs, having stipulated in the agreement of which a protocol was signed on the 19th day of the present month, that the difference pending between the two governments growing out of the Maria Luz case be submitted to the arbitration of the chief of a friendly state, have, at a further conference, held at the Gwaimusho on the 22d day of June, 1873, agreed on behalf of their respective governments to refer the case to the decision of His Majesty the Emperor of all the Russias as arbitrator. They have also agreed —

1st What the note to be addressed by both governments to the government of His Majesty

the Emperor, requesting his acceptance, shall be dispatched by them respectively in the course of the month of December of the present year.

2d Within twelve months after the date of the acceptance by His Majesty, each government shall present its case to the Arbitrator. The evidence to be presented may comprise such documents, official correspondence, and other official or public statement bearing on the subject of the reference as they may consider necessary to the support of their respective cases.

3d Within six months from the date of receiving the notification of the arbitrator's acceptance, the respective parties shall transmit to each other copies of all the papers which they intend to submit to his consideration, but each shall be at liberty to present to the arbitrator any rebutting evidence and such arguments as it may deem proper; for this purpose either government may appoint an agent or agents near the court of His Majesty to conduct its case before the arbitrator.

4th The arbitrator shall be requested to decide if the claim of Peru is well founded, and if it is what indemnity shall be paid by Japan.

5th The award of His Majesty the Emperor of all the Russias shall be considered as absolutely final and conclusive, and full effect shall be given to such award without any objection, evasion, or delay whatsoever.

And whereas the bark Maria Luz, abandoned by her captain, now lies in the Bay of Yokohama, in charge of a guardian placed on board of her by the then representative of Peru, in Japan, the Hon. C. E. De Long, minister of the United States, and with the consent of the Japanese Government; and whereas that guardianship has been and is now the cause of daily expense, the undersigned, equally desirous to bring to an end this state of things, have agreed that the ship shall be sold in public auction for the benefit of all parties interested in the vessel.

Both governments declining to receive the proceeds of the sale, such proceeds, after the payment of the expenses of keeping the ship since her abandonment, are to be deposited in a bank of Yokohama, to await such disposition as may be ordered by a competent court or by the arbitrator.

In testimony of which the undersigned have subscribed and sealed the present agreement, which shall be approved by the President of Peru.

Done in quadruplicate in the city of Taku, (Yedo) on the 25th of June, 1873, corresponding to the Japanese date, the 25th day, 6th month, 6th year of Meiji [1].

---

[1] *Foreign Relations of the U. S.*, 1873—1874, t. I, p. 617.

[1] *Foreign Relations of the U. S.*, 1873—1874., t. I, p. 617.

Décision arbitrale de l'Empereur Alexandre dans l'affaire de la Maria Luz, entre le Japon et le Pérou, donnée à Ems le 29/17 mai 1875.

Nous, Alexandre II, par la grâce de Dieu Empereur de toutes les Russies,

Conformément à la requête qui nous est adressée par les gouvernements du Japon et du Pérou, contenue dans un protocole dressé de commun accord à Tokio par les plénipotentiaires des deux gouvernements le 13-25 juin 1873, correspondant au 25ᵉ jour de 6ᵉ mois de la sixième année de Meiji, nous sommes convenus d'examiner le différend pendant entre les deux gouvernements relativement à l'arrêt du vaisseau « Maria Luz » dans le port de Kanagawa et particulièrement à la réclamation du Gouvernement Peruvien tendant à rendre le gouvernement Japonais responsable de toutes les conséquences résultant de l'action des autorités japonaises par rapport à la « Maria Luz », à son équipage et à ses passagers, à l'époque de l'arrestation de ce vaisseau à Kanagawa, et nous avons consenti à prendre sur nous la tâche de prononcer une sentence arbitrale qui sera définitive et obligatoire pour les deux parties, et contre laquelle il ne sera admis ni objection, ni explication, ni delai quelconque;

Ayant, en conséquence, mûrement posé les considérations et conclusions des jurisconsultes et des personnes compétentes chargées d'étudier l'affaire, d'après les documents et attestations qui nous ont été transmis conformément au protocole ci-dessus mentionné;

Nous sommes arrivés à la conviction que, en procédant comme il l'a fait à l'égard de la « Maria Luz », de son équipage et de ses passagers, le gouvernement a agi bona fide, en vertu de ses propres lois et coutumes, sans enfreindre les prescriptions générales du droit des gens, ni les stipulations des traités particuliers;

Que par conséquent il ne peut être accusé d'un manque volontaire de respect, ni d'une intention malveillante quelconque vis-à-vis du gouvernement péruvien ou de ses citoyens;

Que les diverses espèces d'opinions provoquées par cet incident peuvent inspirer aux gouvernements qui n'ont pas de traités spéciaux avec le Japon le désir de rendre les relations internationales réciproques plus précises afin d'éviter à l'avenir tout malentendu de ce genre; mais qu'elles ne peuvent, en l'absence de stipulations formelles, faire peser sur le gouvernement japonais la responsabilité d'une action qu'il n'a pas sciemment provoquée et de mesures qui sont conformes à sa propre législation;

En conséquence nous n'avons pas trouvé de motifs suffisants pour reconnaître, comme irréguliers, les actes des autorités japonaises dans l'affaire du vaisseau « Maria Luz »; et attribuant les pertes supportées à une malheureuse combinaison de circonstances;

Nous prononçons la sentence arbitrale suivante :

Le gouvernement japonais n'est pas responsable des conséquences produites par l'arrêt du vaisseau péruvien « Maria Luz » dans le port de Kanagawa;

En foi de quoi, Nous avons signé la présente sentence et Nous y avons fait apposer notre sceau impérial.

Fait à Ems, le 17 (29) mai 1875 [1].

LX. France, Grande-Bretagne.

23 juillet 1873.

Ainsi que les termes du traité intervenu le spécifient, il s'est agi d'évaluer des dommages causés à un certain nombre de négociants par suite d'une modification apportée au régime de l'importation des huiles d'origine britannique.

Traité de commerce et de navigation, signé à Versailles le 23 Juillet 1873.

. . . .

ART. IV. A partir du 1ᵉʳ Janvier 1874, ou plus tôt si faire se peut, les huiles minérales d'origine britannique seront admises en France et en Algérie au droit de douane de 5 pour cent, c'est-à-dire au taux du droit en vigueur avant la loi du 8 Juillet 1871. Il demeure cependant convenu que les dites huiles devront, conformément aux dispositions de l'Article IX du Traité du 23 Janvier 1860, remis en vigueur par l'Article I du présent Traité, acquitter en outre les droits de 5 ou 8 fr. par 100 kilog. établis sur les huiles brutes ou raffinées, par la loi du 16 Septembre 1871, ou ceux qui seraient ultérieurement établis sur les mêmes huiles fabriquées en France.

Une commission, qui sera composée d'un membre nommé par chaque gouvernement se réunira à Paris immédiatement après la ratification du présent Traité pour régler, de la manière ci-dessous prévue, les questions relatives aux droits perçus sur les huiles minérales d'origine britannique; et en même temps pour examiner toute autre question que les Hautes Parties Contractantes conviennent ou conviendront de lui soumettre, et en faire l'objet d'un rapport.

Le bénéfice des dispositions précédentes sera étendu aux huiles minérales d'origine britannique,

[1] F. DE MARTENS, *Nouveau Recueil Général*, 2ᵐᵉ série, t. III, p. 516.

ayant fait l'objet de marchés pour la livraison des dites huiles en France avant la promulgation de la loi du 8 Juillet 1871.

La Commission examinera dans quelle mesure il sera possible d'effectuer le remboursement des droits perçus en plus du droit de 5 pour cent et de la taxe de 5 ou 8 fr. par 100 kilog. ci-dessus indiquée, dans le cas ou des huiles minérales d'origine britannique auraient été introduites en France depuis la promulgation de la loi du 8 Juillet 1871, autrement que pour l'exécution de contrats préalablement passés.

En ce qui concerne les contrats ci-dessus visés, le règlement comprendra une indemnité des poursuites exercées pour défaut d'exécution des contrats passés avant l'application de la loi du 8 Juillet 1871.

Les Hautes Parties Contractantes, avant l'échange des ratifications du présent Traité, nommeront une tierce personne destinée à intervenir comme Arbitre sur toute matière en rapport avec les questions ci-dessus désignées qui se rattachent aux huiles minérales et sur lesquelles les Commissaires ne seront pas d'accord.

La Commission déférera toute difficulté de cette nature à l'Arbitre, dont la décision sera obligatoire pour les Commissaires, qui feront leur rapport en conséquence. Les Hautes Parties Contractantes prendront sans retard les mesures nécessaires pour l'exécution des décisions de la Commission ou de l'Arbitre [1].

Il fut accordé au total une somme de 314,393 francs 33. Les arbitres eurent à statuer sur 61 affaires, d'après les principes et les règles, résumés par eux dans une décision finale.

Décision finale de la Commission mixte instituée en vertu de l'article IV du Traité du 23 Juillet 1873, prononcée à Paris, le 5 Janvier 1874.

Les Commissaires désignés respectivement par Sa Majesté la Reine du Royaume Uni de la Grande-Bretagne et d'Irlande et par le Maréchal, Président de la République Française, pour le règlement des réclamations susmentionnées, ont repris à Paris, le 7 Août 1873, l'examen déjà commencé par eux, conformément au Protocole du 5 Novembre 1872.

Après avoir échangé leurs pleins pouvoirs, les Commissaires, afin d'exécuter les dispositions dont les deux Gouvernements sont convenus dans le dit Traité et conformément aux consultations de leurs Conseils judiciaires, ont, d'un commun

accord, arrêté les principes qui devaient les diriger dans l'examen des affaires délicates sur lesquelles ils avaient à statuer en qualité d'arbitres. Ainsi :

1. Les réclamations pour dommages indirects, tels que commissions perdues, manque à gagner, etc., ont été formellement écartées ;

2. Les réclamations pour dommages directs ont été rangées en quatre catégories, savoir :

a) Celles qui ont été l'objet de jugements de la part des tribunaux français.

b) Celles à l'égard desquelles des instances judiciaires ont été commencées et dont la preuve résulte des assignations envoyées par la partie demanderesse ;

c) Celles pour lesquelles aucune instance judiciaire n'a été engagée mais qui sont ou non accompagnées de pièces indiquant l'intention des parties de recourir à la justice;

d) Enfin, les réclamations ne rentrant dans aucune des trois catégories ci-dessus indiquées.

3. Les Commissaires ont pris pour point de départ des indemnités à allouer par eux, les jugements déjà rendus et portant allocation de dommages et intérêts directs fixés par les sentences judiciaires, en raison des éléments d'appréciation possédés par le tribunal lui-même. A l'égard des réclamations qui n'ont pas été l'objet d'un jugement, mais dont la légimité à été établie par les pièces fournies, les commissaires ont supposé qu'il y avait eu sentence rendue, et ils ont alloué une indemnité réglée sur les bases adoptées par les tribunaux qui tous ont suivi la même jurisprudence dans le règlement des dommages et intérêts à donner à la partie demanderesse.

Dans tous les cas et à moins que le réclamant ne puisse justifier par des quittances de Douane qu'il a dû remplacer par des huiles minérales d'origine britannique celles que les premiers vendeurs refusaient de livrer, les Commissaires ont, au profit du Trésor Français déduit, des sommes allouées à titre d'indemnité, le montant des droits suivants établis dans l'Article IV du Traité du 23 Juillet 1873 : 1. Droit de Douane de 5 pour cent sur une valeur commune de 50 fr. soit 2 fr. 50 c. par 100 kilog. ; 2. Droit d'accise, décimes compris, de 6 fr. ou de 9 fr. 60 c. par 100 kilog., représentant les droits d'accise perçus sur les huiles minérales fabriquées en France.

4. Enfin, pour les huiles minérales d'origine britannique, dont l'importation a été effectuée en France depuis la loi du 8 Juillet 1871, et qui ont payé les droits de Douane établis par la dite loi, les Commissaires se sont bornés, comme le veut la section 4 de l'Article IV du Traité du 23 Juillet 1873, à restituer la différence exis-

---

[1] DE CLERCQ, *Recueil des Traités* . . . . t. XI, p. 77.

tant entre les dits droits et celui de 5 pour cent ajouté aux taxes d'accise ou de consommation intérieure fixés par la loi du 16 Septembre 1871, sur les huiles minérales fabriquées en France.

Les quatre tableaux ci-annexés, lesquels indiquent en regard de chaque affaire la décision prise et signée par l'un et l'autre Commissaire, ont été formulés conformément aux principes précités.

Une question délicate sur laquelle des avis opposés nous ont été donnés par le Conseil judiciaire du Ministère de l'Agriculture et du Commerce et par le Conseil de l'Ambassade Britannique n'a été tranchée que par voie de transaction. Il s'agit d'un jugement rendu par le tribunal de Dunkerque, en faveur du sieur Rouzet, Agent de la Compagnie Anglaise Coatbridge. Dans l'espèce le dommage est-il indirect? Ou sans être précisément direct, n'en avait-il pas le caractère vis-à-vis du demandeur? Cette dernière thèse a été soutenue par M. Treitt, qui reconnaissait toutefois que l'indemnité allouée était exorbitante. La thèse contraire a été défendue par M. Josseau, qui a persisté à penser, comme il l'avait déjà déclaré dans la consultation ci-annexée, que le dommage étant indirect, il n'y avait pas lieu de s'arrêter au jugement du tribunal de Dunkerque.

Sans doute, en présence du désaccord survenu entre nos deux Conseils judiciaires, nous aurions pu, comme nous y autorisait le sixième paragraphe de l'Article IV du Traité du 23 Juillet, recourir au tiers arbitre choisi d'un commun accord par les deux Gouvernements, et attendre sa décision, qui aurait mis notre responsabilité à couvert; mais, dans les discussions que nous avons eues pour le règlement des intérêts qui nous étaient confiés, une entente parfaite s'est établie entre nous et nous avons pensé qu'elle devait nous suivre jusqu'a la fin de nos travaux. Cette réclamation était d'ailleurs d'une nature exceptionnelle, et dès lors aucun des principes arrêtés par les Commissaires ne pourrait s'y rattacher.

Quoi qu'il en soit, les détails de la dite réclamation ont été l'objet d'un examen approfondi, et comme, d'un autre côté, la demande du sieur Rouzet avait été reconnue bien fondée par le Tribunal de Dunkerque, nous avons accepté en principe, le jugement de ce Tribunal.

Toutefois nous avons pensé qu'il était de notre devoir d'abord de réduire dans une forte proportion les dommages-intérêts alloués au sieur Rouzet, dont le contrat avec la Compagnie Coatbridge était résilié; et ensuite de ne pas admettre les indemnités qui ne rentrent dans aucune des dispositions du Traité du 25 Juillet 1873. Tels ont été les motifs qui ont décidé les deux Commissaires à agir par voie de transaction.

D'après les jugements rendus, toutes les sommes allouées portent intérêt à 5 pour cent jusqu'à parfait paiement. Conformément à ces décisions, les deux Commissaires ont décidé que les dits intérêts à 5 pour cent devraient, jusqu'à parfait paiement, être ajoutés aux indemnités par eux réglées.

Enfin quant aux frais de justice, ils ont été immédiatement ajoutés aux dites indemnités lorsque la justification de ces frais a été donnée. Toutes réserves sont faites à l'égard des indemnitaires qui produiraient ultérieurement des justifications autres que celles qu'ils sont fournies et qui n'ont pas paru aux deux Commissaires suffisamment régulières pour en tenir compte dans le règlement des indemnités.

A titre de pièces justificatives, nous joignons au présent Protocole: —

1. Les procès-verbaux de nos délibérations;
2. Un état récapitulatif des indemnités demandées et de celles qui ont été allouées par les deux Commissaires.

Fait à Paris, en double expédition, le 5 Janvier 1874 [1].

LXI. Italie, Suisse.

31 décembre 1873.

La question soulevée se rapportait à la frontière entre les deux pays au lieu dit *Alpe Cravairola*. Les arbitres nommés ne purent s'entendre sur la sentence à prononcer et ce fut le Ministre des Etats-Unis de l'Amérique du Nord qui fut appelé à les départager.

Compromis arbitral concernant la fixation définitive de la frontière italo-suisse, conclu, à Berne, le 31 Décembre 1873.

Sa Majesté le Roi d'Italie, et le Conseil fédéral de la Confédération Suisse, animés du désir de fixer définitivement la ligne frontière entre le royaume d'Italie et le canton du Tessin au lieu dit Alpe de Cravairola et de mettre un terme à un débat plusieurs fois séculaire et d'ailleurs suffisament instruit par les négociations diplomatiques et expertises successives dont il a été l'objet, ont reconnu la convenance de le résoudre par la voie d'un compromis arbitral, et dans le but de régler les conditions de ce compromis ils ont nommé pour leurs plénipotentiaires savoir:

Sa Majesté le Roi d'Italie: Monsieur le chevalier Louis Amédée Melegari, Sénateur du Ro-

---

[1] *Parliamentary Paper* [C. 913], p. 3.

yaume, son Envoyé extraordinaire et Ministre plénipotentiaire près la Confédération Suisse;

Le Conseil fédéral de la Confédération Suisse: Monsieur Paul Ceresole, président de la Confédération Suisse;

Lesquels après s'être communiqué leurs pleins pouvoirs trouvés en bonne et due forme ont arrêté et signé les articles suivants:

ART. 1. La fixation définitive de la ligne frontière qui sépare le territoire Italien du territoire de la Confédération Suisse (Canton du Tessin) au lieu dit Alpe de Cravairola, dès le sommet désigné Sonnenhorn $\triangle$ 2788^m sur la carte topographique suisse, jusqu'au sommet du Pizzo del Lago gelato 2578^m sera soumise au prononcé d'un tribunal arbitral sous forme de la question suivante. La ligne frontière sus-mentionnée doit-elle comme l'estime la Suisse suivre le faîte de la chaîne principale en passant par la Corona di Groppo, Pizzo dei Croselli, Pizzo Pioda, Pizzo del Forno, et Pizzo del Monastero; ou bien doit-elle, comme l'estime l'Italie, quitter la chaîne principale au sommet désigné Sonnenhorn $\triangle$ 2788^m pour descendre vers le ruisseau de la vallée di Campo, et, en suivant l'arête secondaire nommée Creta Tremolina (ou Mosso del Lodano, 2356^m sur la carte suisse), rejoindre la chaîne principale au Pizzo del Lago Gelato?

ART. 2. Les Hautes Parties Contractantes admettront la sentence arbitrale qui interviendra et reconnaîtront comme définitive la ligne frontière qu'elle aura déterminée.

Il est bien entendu que l'arbitrage ne portera que sur la question de la frontière d'Etat, sans préjudice aux droits privés des tiers sur le territoire en question. Les contestations qui pourraient naître de la revendication ou de l'exercice de ces droits ressortiront aux tribunaux civils de l'Etat dont le dit territoire sera reconnu faire partie.

ART. 3. Les arbitres seront au nombre de deux. Chacune des Hautes Parties Contractantes en désignera un qui devra être agréé par l'autre partie.

La nomination des arbitres suivra immédiatement l'échange des ratifications du présent compromis. Les arbitres se réuniront dans la ville de Milan, aussitôt que possible après leur nomination et, au jour qui leur paraîtra le plus convenable, ils informeront les deux gouvernements intéressés de la date choisie par eux pour leur réunion.

ART. 4. Avant toute opération, les arbitres éliront un sur-arbitre qui sera appelé à prononcer sur la question qui leur est soumise, dans le cas où eux-mêmes ne pourraient tomber d'accord sur la solution à lui donner.

Le sur-arbitre ne pourra être ni citoyen italien ni citoyen suisse.

Il ne prendra part aux opération des arbitres que lorsque ceux-ci auront constaté expressément l'impossibilité de résoudre eux-mêmes la question qui leur est soumise et la nécessité de recourir au sur-arbitre. Les arbitres communiqueront le choix qu'ils auront fait d'un sur-arbitre aux deux gouvernements intéressés.

ART. 5. Les arbitres tiendront un procès verbal régulier de leurs opérations. Ce procès-verbal sera fait en deux expéditions signées par les arbitres.

Le jugement devra également être rédigé par écrit et signé, en double expédition, pour être communiqué avec le procès-verbal ci-dessus, aux deux gouvernements intéressés.

Les arbitres choisiront dans ce but un secrétaire dont ils fixeront eux-mêmes la rémunération. Ils joindront au procès-verbal de leurs opérations le compte des frais généraux occasionnés par l'arbitrage.

ART. 6. Chacune des Hautes Parties aura la faculté de se faire représenter à ses frais devant les arbitres par un ou deux agents et, par l'intermédiaire de ceux-ci, de présenter les documents mémoires, contre-mémoires et actes quelconques qu'elle croira de nature à éclairer la cause.

Les agents pourront assister à toutes les opérations des arbitres, sauf aux délibérations sur le jugement.

Les Hautes Parties Contractantes s'engagent à se communiquer réciproquement, par l'intermédiaire de leurs agents respectifs, les mémoires documents et actes quelconques qu'elles soumettront aux arbitres.

En général les communications réciproques entre les arbitres et les gouvernements intéressés se feront par l'intermédiaire des agents respectifs des dits gouvernements.

ART. 7. Les frais de l'arbitrage seront répartis par portions égales entre les deux Etats intéressés.

ART. 8. Les Hautes Parties Contractantes s'engagent à procéder aussitôt que faire se pourra à l'exécution du jugement arbitral.

ART. 9. Le présent compromis sera ratifié et les ratifications en seront échangées à Berne, en même temps que celles de la convention signée aujourd'hui, 31 décembre 1873, concernant la rectification de la frontière entre Brusio et Tirano.

En foi de quoi les Plénipotentiaires ont signé ce compromis arbitral et y ont opposé leur cachet.

Fait à Berne, en double expédition, le trente-un décembre mil-huit-cent-soixante-treize [1].

---

[1] F. DE MARTENS, *Nouveau Recueil Général*, t. XX, p. 214.

Lodo pronunziato dal sopra-arbitro G. P. Marsh, 23 Settembre 1874.

L'onorevole Comm. Enrico Giucciardi, Senatore del Regno d'Italia, e l'onorevole Consigliere degli Stati Hans Hold, Colonello dello Stato maggiore federale Svizzero, debitamente nominati dai rispettivi governi d'Italia e della Confederazione Svizzera, arbitri per la definitiva determinazione del Confine Italo-Svizzero nel luogo detto *Alpe Cravairola*, avendo per mezzo di un istrumento in data tredici luglio mille ottocento settanta quattro ed in virtù del quarto articolo del suddetto « Compromis Arbitral » scelto il sottoscritto come Arbitro Supremo pel caso ch' essi non potessero addivenire ad una soluzione di detta questione; ed i medesimi arbitri avendo debitamente dichiarata nel verbale e notificata al detto arbitro supremo l'impossibilità in cui trovavansi di venire ad un accomodamento; il sottoscritto avendo accuratamente considerato gli argomenti e le prove addotte dalle Alte Parti Contrattanti mediante i loro rispettivi agenti, procede e pronunzia sulla propostagli questione la seguente sentenza:

La questione sottoposta a questo Tribunale Arbitrale dai due governi interessati è formulata come segue nel primo articolo del *Compromis Arbitral* dietro l'autorità del quale il Tribunale agisce:

« La ligne frontière susmentionnée (qui sépare le territoire italien du territoire de la Confédération Suisse) doit-elle, comme l'estime la Suisse, suivre le faîte de la chaîne principale en passant par la Corona di Groppo, Pizzo dei Croselli, Pizzo Pioda, Pizzo del Forno e Pizzo del Monastero; — ou bien doit-elle, comme l'estime l'Italie, quitter la chaîne principale au sommet désigné Sonnenhorn △ 2788ᵐ pour descendre vers le ruisseau de la vallée de Campo en suivant l'arête secondaire nommée Creta Tremolina (ou Mosso de Lodano 2356ᵐ sur la carte suisse) rejoindre la chaîne principale au Pizzo del Lago Gelato? »

Non risulta chiaro al sottoscritto se le Alte Parti Contrattanti abbiano inteso di autorizzare gli arbitri a determinare una linea di frontiera dietro considerazioni di mera convenienza ovvero se si aspetti che risolvano la questione secondo i principi dello stretto diritto. Gli Arbitri e gli Agenti nominati dai due Stati hanno trattato la questione sotto ambo i punti di vista. Egli è quindi necessario esaminare le considerazioni e gli argomenti da essi presentati tanto riguardo alla convenienza quanto rispetto al diritto.

In primo luogo adunque riguardando alla semplice convenienza e lasciando da parte per ora la questione del diritto:

Nell' interesse della Svizzera si insiste sul fatto che il territorio conteso è molto più accessibile dalla Valle Maggia che non dal Val Antigorio, che quindi può essere più convenientemente e più vantaggiosamente amministrato dalle autorità svizzere che non dalle italiane, le quali non possono accedervi che per tre mesi dell' anno, e che in conseguenza tutti i diritti e gl' interessi dei possidenti, relativi sì alle persone che alle proprietà, possono essere più efficacemente protetti dalle istituzioni e dalle autorità giudiziarie ed esecutive della Svizzera che non da quelle dell' Italia.

Si adduce inoltre che per mancanza di controllo legale e di sorveglianza degli attuali occupanti il suolo, le condizioni fisiche del territorio corrono rapidamente a rovina, diminuendo la estensione dei pascoli e delle praterie per la invasione dei cespugli alpini, che secondo le regole di una savia amministrazione debbono essere estirpati, e per il continuo diluvio del suolo, dovuto ad un taglio indiscreto dei boschi che debbono essere preservati, ed alla negligenza dei possessori nel prendere le opportune misure per prevenire il male mediante nuove piantagioni, rinzollando la terra sciolta intorno alle sorgenti e sulle rive dei torrenti e costruendo barriere nei letti dei medesimi.

Di più si osserva che la soverchia ed irregolare flottazione dei legnami tagliati su quell' alpe, giù nei torrenti pei quali le acque si scaricano nella Maggia cagiona mediante le numerose chiuse un cumulo straordinario d'acque, le quali precipitandosi giù per la valle, quando si aprono le dette chiuse, recano grave ingiuria non solo alle sponde dei torrenti nell' alpe stessa ma in maggior proporzione a quelle delle Rovana nel comune di Campo.

Si aggiunge che l'azione di questo torrente produce già effetti dannosissimi sul regime della Maggia; che la violenza e le devastazioni del torrente stesso vanno continuamente crescendo per le summentovate cagioni; e si crede perfino che una sensibile influenza ne derivi sul letto del Lago Maggiore allo sbocco della Maggia, quindi sulla navigazione di una parte del medesimo.

Si insiste poi sul fatto che questi danni già tanto contrari agli interessi della popolazione svizzera e del suo territorio, possono essere prevenuti solo mediante l'applicazione all' Alpe di Cravairola dei moderni metodi concernenti l'economia forestale e la regolazione delle acque.

Or questo, dicesi, può difficilmente essere fatto dal Governo Italiano, a motivo dell' inaccessibilità del territorio dalla parte italiana dei monti, e perchè l'Italia non ha sufficiente interesse nel proteggere i boschi ed il suolo di quell' alpe da costituire un motivo adeguato al suo intervento in siffatta impresa; ed infine perchè la spesa per l'applicazione di tali misure, fatta dall'Italia, sarebbe molto maggiore che se venisse compiuta dalla Svizzera come parte del suo regolare sistema forestale.

Forse non è fuori luogo l'osservare qui che quatunque la Svizzera, nel caso ove il conteso territorio venisse assegnato all'Italia, non potesse addottare nessuna misura di sicurezza e di miglioramento nei limiti dell'Alpe medesima, pur nondimeno, nel caso di tale assegnamento, il quarto articolo della convenzione delle Isole Borromee dell'anno 1650 diventerebbe nullo in virtù dell'articolo settimo della medesima convenzione e che in conseguenza la Svizzera sarebbe libera di proibire la flottazione dei legnami da quell'Alpe ed il loro passaggio attraverso il territorio svizzero, e di dar forza a tale proibizione colla confisca del legname stesso o con qualche altro mezzo legale e così proteggere le sponde della Rovana dai danni provenienti da quella cagione.

Per quanto concerne i fatti sovracitati convien ricordare che nell'argomento dell'avvocato Scaciga della Silva, messo innanzi dagli agenti italiani, si asserisce che la forza produttiva dell'Alpe è già diminuita di una metà; e dalle relazioni degli agenti delle due parti risulta che la diminuzione è di gran lunga maggiore. Oltre a ciò riesce evidente da una superficiale ispezione del territorio e dei possessi del Comune di Campo che i danni fisici, i quali sono risultati oppure si temono da una cattiva amministrazione del suolo e dei boschi dell'Alpe, non sono stati esagerati dai rapporti degli agenti della Svizzera.

Si suggerisce infine che dietro i principi generali della politica economia egli è convenientissimo che il conteso territorio sia assegnato a coloro che possono trarne maggior profitto e che l'Alpe di Cravairola sarebbe di maggior valore per gli abitanti dei comuni svizzeri adiacenti di quel che può essere per possessori così distanti come quelli di Crodo. E questo argomento acquista maggior forza dalla già fatta osservazione che cioè sta in potere della Svizzera di addottare severe misure legali per la protezione del suo territorio ed in tal modo di togliere ai legnami dell'Alpe ogni valore mercantile nelle mani degli occupanti italiani.

Queste considerazioni, che sono qui imperfettamente adombrate ed altri analoghi argomenti che si potrebbero addure, paiono al sottoscritto di non lieve peso, ed egli è pienamente convinto che, se si potesse trovare un soddisfacente compenso pei comuni e i particolari italiani, occupanti ora l'Alpe di Cravairola, gl'interessi dei due Stati sarebbero effettivamente promossi dalla cessione alla Svizzera della sovranità e della proprietà del territorio in discorso. Fortunata-

mente i due Stati hanno pochi o nessuni interessi opposti oppur rivali; al contrario vi è solidarietà d'interessi tra di essi. Ciascun dei due trae vantaggio dalla materiale prosperità e dal progresso politico e sociale dell'altro; ed il rimuovere da essi ogni causa di dissentimento e di irritazione è altamente vantaggioso ad ambedue.

Se dunque risultasse chiaro che gli arbitri hanno la facoltà di dirigersi dietro considerazioni di mera convenienza, e se essi od altri arbitri fossero autorizzati a fissare un compenso agli attuali proprietarii del suolo, il sottoscritto non esiterebbe nel dire che la sovranità e la proprietà dell'alpe devono essere accordate alla Svizzera e che un giusto equivalente deve essere accordato agli attuali occupanti per il trasferto della proprietà.

Ma i termini del «Compromis» non implicano in nessun modo in se stessi un siffatto potere degli arbitri, e l'assenza di ogni provvedimento per il compenso degli attuali proprietarii del suolo conduce il sottoscritto a credere che le Alte Parti Contrattanti non intendevano conferire ai loro arbitri una siffatta autorità. Per di più è opinione del sottoscritto che la estensione delle istituzioni, delle leggi e dell'amministrazione svizzere a quel territorio mentre i proprietarii del medesimo continuerebbero a rimanere soggetti del regno d'Italia, e risiederebbero per la massima parte dell'anno in quel paese, condurrebbe a gelosie, dissensi e contese senza fine e più nocive alla pace ed all'armonia dei due Stati che con la presente poco soddisfacente condizione del territorio; e secondo tutte le probabilità darebbe luogo a più questioni internazionali di quel che qualunque decisione di questo tribunale si potrebbe sciogliere nei limiti della sua competenza.

La questione di convenienza non può dunque essere considerata qual base fondamentale per una decisione, ma può solo servire di criterio sussidiario in mancanza di altri mezzi per arrivare ad una fondata conclusione.

Veniamo dunque alla questione di mero diritto È inteso ammettersi che certi comuni di Val dossola o piuttosto di una diramazione di detta valle, il Val Antigorio, ebbero l'incontestato possesso e l'usufrutto di certi parti dell'Alpe di Cravairola per circa quattro secoli, e di altre parti del medesimo per un periodo di tempo più lungo ancora, e ciò sotto pretensione di un titolo di assoluta proprietà sopra un suolo acquistato con danaro, titolo accompagnato da vari atti ufficiali più o meno importanti dell'autorità pubbliche italiane, i quali atti sono interpretati dagli agenti italiani come prove dell'esercizio della sovranità su quel territorio per parte dell'Italia. Certi documenti sono pure addotti allo scopo di provare il riconoscimento per parte della

Svizzera del diritto dell'Italia all'alto dominio sul distretto contestato.

Gli agenti della Svizzera reclamano l'alto dominio sull'Alpe di Cravairola come parte de Val Maggia che i XII cantoni acquistarono per conquista nel 1513 e per trattato nel 1516 ed in appoggio a siffatta pretesa insistono sul principio di geografia politica che, per lo meno in mancanza di evidenza del contrario, lo spartiacqua dev'essere preso come limite di giurisdizione tra gli Stati limitrofi e conseguentemente che la denominazione « Val Maggia » nel trattato del 1516 dev'essere considerata come abbracciante tutti i bacini minori che sboccano nella valle principale.

Di più essi pretendono che nelle circostanze del caso certi procedimenti dell'anno 1554 per la determinazione dei limiti orientali dell'Alpe Cravairola costituiscono da se stesso un riconoscimento obbligatorio della sovranità e dell'alto dominio della Svizzera sul territorio in questione.

Questi sono i punti cardinali presentati al nostro esame. Altri argomenti minori addotti dalle parti saranno indicati nel corso della discussione.

Numerosi documenti sono stati presentati dalle rispettive parti, i quali tutti sono stati ponderati, ma il sottoscritto ne indicherà solo qui quanto gli parrà avere una sostanziale relazione coll'argomento.

I documenti messi innanzi dall'Italia, sono:

« Sentenza del 1° luglio 1367 del Vicario di Matterello annullante per causa di reciprocità una vendita fatta al Comune di Crodo di una parte di Cravairola. »

« Istromento del 24 Febbraio 1406 di vendita di una parte dell'Alpe Cravairola in territorio di Cravairola. »

« Investitura del 10 giugno 1454 di tre parti dell'Alpe di Collobiasco, in territorio di Cravairola. »

« Istromento del 20 aprile 1497 ove si legge: *busco existente et jacente in et supra territorio et dominio de Crodo nell'Alpe Cravairola'.* »

Questi documenti anteriori tutti alla conquista svizzera ed al trattato del 1516 sono presentati dagli agenti italiani con lo scopo di dimostrare per l'esercizio della giurisdizione e per legale descrizione che il *locus in quo* era indipendente dalla giurisdizione del Val Maggia ed apparteneva al Comune di Crodo. L'Italia mette pure innanzi un fascicolo intitolato « *Jura Crodensium et Pontemaliensium contra Campenses Vallis Madiæ* » contenente una relazione dei processi compiutisi nel 1554 per fissare i limiti dell'Alpe di Cravairola, nonchè vari altri documenti relativi a tale delimitazione.

Gli agenti della Svizzera ne appellano all'istromento del 17 marzo 1420 per il quale una terza parte dell'Alpe di Cravairola «*jacente in territorio Vallis Madiæ* » fu venduta al Comune di Crodo; ed all'istromento dell'8 Dicembre 1490 che cede al Comune di Crodo l'Alpe di Collobiasco « *esistente e situata nel dominio delli uomini di 'Valmaggia ove si dice in Cravairola.* »

La Svizzera sostiene che questi termini implicano in sè un riconoscimento della giurisdizione del Val Maggia e adduce inoltre il trattato concluso nel 1516 tra Francesco I e la Confederazione Elvetica nel quale il Val Maggia è riconosciuto appartenere alla Svizzera.

Essa si appoggia pure sopra un documento già accennato, intitolato: « *Copia positionis terminorum anni 1554,* » contenuto nel fascicolo intitolato: « *Jura* », riferentesi alla determinazione dei limiti orientali dell'Alpe di Cravairola, documento che gli Svizzeri dicono provare una sottomissione del Comune di Crodo alla giurisdizione di un tribunale svizzero, in una materia implicante l'alto dominio sul territorio in questione.

Essendo ammesso che soggetti del Regno d'Italia sono in possesso di quel suolo sotto la protezione della giurisdizione italiana conviene anzitutto esaminare le principali prove colle quali questo diritto è impugnato dalla Svizzera e le testimonianze contrarie a dette prove.

Nella « *Copia positionis terminorum anni 1554,* » viene esposto che « *quædam differentia, lis et quæstio juridica* » erano sorte tra le autorità di Crodo e quelle di Campo « *causa et occasione confinium Alpis Cravairolæ ipsorum de Crodo, et dominii ipsorum de Campo, cuinque fuerit, etc. . . . . quod litigando in jure coram Magnific. D. Christophorum Quintoni de Friburgo et Honor. Comm. Vallis Madiæ,* » etc., e che le parti vennero ad accordo alla conclusione che alcuni cittadini di Crodo, nominati nel documento dovessero definire i limiti per mezzo di segni permanenti, il che fù fatto. Nella sottoscrizione o attestato del notaio il documento è chiamato « *Instrumentum definitionis dominii*».

Si sostiene dagli agenti svizzeri che questi procedimenti sono necessariamente un riconoscimento per parte del Comune di Crodo della giurisdizione delle autorità svizzere sulla materia. Su questo punto bisogna osservare che benchè la *differentia et lis* implichi la questione dei limiti dell'Alpe di Cravairola, non siamo informati qual fosse la natura della lite. Forse è stato in origine un processo contro cittadini di Crodo arrestati sopra territorio preteso da Campo, a cagione della violazione del medesimo, ed in tal caso i magistrati svizzeri di Campo dovevano naturalmente insistere sul diritto di giurisdizione.

Molti altri supposti possono essere fatti per dimostrare che una comparsa del Comune di Crodo dinnanzi un magistrato svizzero se può essere presuntivamente non è necessariamente un riconoscimento della competenza di detto magistrato. In questo caso possiamo anche supporre che un componimento amichevole era stato accettato perchè erano sorte delle obbiezioni contro la giurisdizione del magistrato stesso. Comunque sia stato, nessuna adiudicazione dell'oggetto in questione venne fatta dal magistrato, la vertenza essendo stata accomodata mediante un accordo tra le parti.

Nell'abile ed ingegnoso argomento degli agenti svizzeri si sostiene che l'espressione « *ipsorum de Crodo* » indica semplicemente il diritto di proprietà, mentre le parole « *et dominii ipsorum hominum de Campo*, » significano la giurisdizione di *alto dominio* e di più che la stessa voce *dominii* nell'*attestatu* « *Instrumentum definitionis dominii* » è meramente un'espressione casuale usata dal notaio, e non dalle parti nel senso di semplice proprietà.

Se questa costruzione può essere sostenuta essa è importante come ammissione della sovranità del Val Maggia per parte di persone forse non autorizzate dai loro governi, ma pur tuttavia probabilmente ben informate relativamente alla effettiva giurisdizione. Ma il notaio che sottoscrisse il documento, secondo tutte le probabilità, l'ha pure esteso, ed è improbabile ch'egli abbia usata quella espressione in due sensi diversi nello stesso istromento. Secondo i principii generali della legale interpretazione, una stessa parola usata più d'una volta dallo stesso scrittore nello stesso istromento dev'essere presa come avente sempre il medesimo significato, a meno che il contrario apparisca dal contesto. Nel caso attuale, il sottoscritto non trova nel contesto una ragione sufficiente per credere che il notaio intendesse di usare la voce *dominium* in diversi sensi nei due periodi nei quali essa ricorre; quindi s'egli ebbe in mente di parlare di *alto dominio* nel corpo dell'istromento devesi pure ritenere ch'egli volesse alludere all'*alto dominio* nell'*attestatu*.

Seguendo questa interpretazione i procedimenti in questione assumerebbero l'aspetto di un tentativo di una finale definizione della questione di sovranità territoriale e di giurisdizione.

Ma indipendentemente da ciò, il sottoscritto opina che come questione grammaticale le parole *Alpis Cravairolæ* e *dominii* sono nella stessa categoria, essendo ambedue genitivi posti dopo *confinium*, il primo indicante nominatamente un certo territorio, ed il secondo segnante un'altro territorio mediante un termine descrittivo che indica semplicemente *terre di proprietà* senza nessuna allusione alla sovranità e senza includere affatto il primo tratto di territorio. Con altre parole, l'Alpe di Cravairola è una porzione del suolo situato da un lato dei limiti, ed il *dominium de Campo* è un'altra porzione di suolo

situata dall'altro lato dei medesimi limiti. In fatti dall'esame dei diversi documenti addotti e di altri dello stesso periodo il sottoscritto non trova che risulti alcuna differenza bene stabilita tra *territorium* e *dominium*. Questi vocaboli sembrano essere stati usati indistintamente nel senso di proprietà o di sovranità secondo l'argomento ed in conformità col contesto degli atti. Ma qualunque sia la costruzione grammaticale od il senso logico della parola, quale è usata in questo documento, il fascicolo *Jura* contiene altri documenti di grande importanza tendenti a dimostrare che qualunque fosse il sentimento che nutrissero le parti di questa transazione relativamente al valore di essa, i loro superiori, i rispettivi governi di Milano e della Svizzera, le diedero il valore di una Convenzione internazionale per la fissazione dei limiti della giurisdizione territoriale tra i due Stati.

L'istromento, che segue la *Copia partitionis* nel fascicolo *Jura*, è una comunicazione ufficiale del Governo Milanese al Commissario o Podestà di Domodossola in data 16 febbraio 1555. Essa stabilisce che « gli Ambasciatori delli Signori dei XIII Cantoni Svizzeri .... si sono doluti .... come alli mesi passati alcuni di quella terra e sua jurisdizione sono andati in Valle Maggia, jurisdizione di predetti Signori, e violentemente hanno strappato alcuni termini, *posti alli confini tra l'una e l'altra jurisdizione* et piantati più oltre di quelli erano soliti stare ».

Ora in questa frase *i termini* sono evidentemente quelli piantati nel mese di giugno dell'anno antecedente, cioè i limiti tra l'Alpe di Cravairola e le terre del Comune di Campo; e *l'una e l'altra jurisdizione* può difficilmente significare altro che la giurisdizione della Svizzera esercitata dalle autorità del Val Maggia è limitata a ponente dei termini posti nel 1554 e la giurisdizione di Milano esercitata dalle autorità di Domodossola è limitata a levante dei medesimi termini.

Nell'ordine del tempo segue un comunicato ufficiale del Governo di Milano diretto « all'egregio jurisconsulto Castilioneo ed al Podestà di Domodossola » relativo alla disputa « inter Domodossolanos subditos nostros et homines Vallis Madiæ subditos Helvetiorum, de finibus. »

Seguono cinque o sei altre comunicazioni dell'anno 1556 della stessa sorgente e sullo stesso argomento, tutte insistenti sul ristabilimento dei limiti del 1554 e tutte serventesi delle stesse espressioni per indicare le parti litiganti. Tra questi ve n'è uno (n. 14) del 19 giugno 1556 in cui si allude alla « *Controversia finium inter dictum Commune Crodo et Commune loci de Campo* » e si usano le espressioni « *fines inter ipsa Communia* » e « *termini inter ipsa Communia* ».

È cosa molto rimarchevole che in nessuna di queste carte, tranne quella del 1554, è neppure fatta menzione dell' Alpe Cravairola, ma la controversia è sempre indicata come concernente i limiti, non già di possessi esteri di Crodo, ma dei rispettivi comuni; è come già fu detto le lagnanze degli Ambasciatori svizzeri del 16 febbraio 1555 indicavano espressamente i termini posti nel 1554 come limite tra *le rispettive giurisdizioni*.

Da questi fatti pare risultare chiaramente che sebbene non sia evidente se le parti immediate della transazione lo considerassero come argomento di così grave importanza, i due governi supremi del Val Maggia et del Val d'Ossola nel mezzo del secolo XVI e per circa cento anni dopo convenivano nel ritenere l'accordo del 1554 come una definitiva fissazione dei limiti tra i loro rispettivi territori.

Non v'ha prova che in occasione della transazione del 1554 una pretensione di giurisdizione sia stata fatta innanzi dalle autorità di Val Maggia o dei XIII Cantoni, nè apparisce che in alcuna epoca prima o dopo quella data fino all' anno 1641, la Svizzera abbia asserita una supremazia qualunque o l'alto dominio sopra quel territorio. Ma per altra parte risulta che i governi dei due paesi convennero nell' accomodamento del 1554, come definitivo. In relazione con questo fatto di nessun reclamo per parte della Svizzera, egli è bene notare un' analogo stato di cose relativamente al Governo di Val Maggia. Nessun documento di qualsiasi natura è prodotto dai registri del Val Maggia, e non vi è prova che il Comune di Campo, in verun tempo del periodo storico, sia mai stato possessore dell' Alpe di Cravairola.

Havvi una probabilità meramente intrinseca che in qualche remota età quell'Alpe sia stata proprietà di quel comune ed i due documenti nei quali l'Alpe è descritta come appartenente al *dominium* di Val Maggia aggiungono forza a questo supposto. Ma questi documenti non sono atti nei quali il Val Maggia sia stato parte attiva e non v'ha in essi alcuna prova positiva di sorta dimostrante che le autorità di Val Maggia abbiano mai esercitato o reclamato la giurisdizione sull'Alpe di Cravairola fino al 1641. È una supposizione molto probabile che in quei tempi rozzi, in cui generalmente prevaleva la legge del più forte, e pochi proprietari potevano mostrare qualche titolo delle loro terre o della loro giurisdizione, salvo il titolo di possesso, il trasferimento del suolo ad abitanti di Val Antigorio fosse considerato come implicante con sè anche la sovranità. E per quanto abbiamo i mezzi di saperlo, la Svizzera sembra essere convenuta in questo punto di vista per più di cento anni dopo l'acquisto di Val Maggia.

Nel 1641, Oswaldo di Schiaffusa, Commissario, Balivo di Val Maggia, o per ordine dei suoi superiori o per motivi personali, non si sa, convoca un' assemblea di delegati dei Comuni di Crodo, di Pontimaglio e di Campo per comporre le differenze sorte relativamente all' Alpe di Cravairola. Dietro questa convocazione alcuni cittadini di Crodo e di Pontimaglio convennero con lui e co' suoi compagni sull' Alpe addì 2 ottobre 1641, e dichiararono ch'essi non erano autorizzati dai loro Comuni, ma che avrebbero fatta relazione ai medesimi, acciocchè una delegazione fosse nominata per trattare l'argomento. In quella occasione il Commissario Oswaldo « in faccia ai sudditi di Antigorio ha protestato che la giurisdizione sopradetta dell' Alpe è sua che non può nè deve tralasciarne gli atti che si giudicheranno necessari per il mantenimento della giurisdizione dei suoi Illustrissimi Signori dei XIII Cantoni della Serenissima Republica Elevetica ». Questo, come fu osservato, è il primo reclamo formale conosciuto di sovranità su quell' Alpe per parte della Svizzera. Se esso fu fatto dietro ordine della Svizzera e non fu fatto meramente personale del Commissario, si ha diritto di supporre che gli archivi della Svizzera forniscano la prova del fatto; ma nessuna prova di questo genere venne presentata.

Questo reclamo fu sovente ripetuto durante gli anni seguenti e ne risultarono un maggior eccitamento ed una crescente irritazione. Non è necessario seguir la storia di questi fatti perocchè nel 1650, una convenzione tenutasi alle Isole Borromee dalle autorità dei due governi riconobbe i limiti del 1554, fece varie concessioni alle due parti, e specialmente questa, di autorizzare il popolo di Crodo a trasportare i legnami dell' Alpe per mezzo della Rovana nel Val Maggia, provvedimento, osservasi, affatto superfluo se quell' Alpe fosse stata territorio svizzero.

Un altro provvedimento trattava in sostanza tutte le dispute e risse anteriori come non avvenute, ed infine un articolo concepito in questi termini: « *E questa provvisione abbi a durare sin tanto sarà deciso il punto della giurisdizione sopra la detta Alpe al quale per nessuna delle dette cose s'intende far pregiudizio.* »

Il sottoscritto comprende il termine *provvisione* come applicantesi a tutta la materia della Convenzione e non già ad un articolo o ad alcuni articoli particolari. La convenzione non decise nulla relativamente alla giurisdizione, ma lasciò la questione come la trovò, e naturalmente questo punto, nello stato in cui trovavasi allora, dev'essere giudicato dietro i fatti e le leggi connesse colla storia precedente.

Dopo il 1650 vi furono altri numerosi tentativi, più o meno serii, d'ambo le parti di stabilire una giurisdizione sul conteso territorio, ma nell'opinione del sottoscritto, essi non hanno un carattere abbastanza concludente per isciogliere materialmente la causa nè da un lato nè dall'altro, e dobbiamo riferirci per una decisione ai diritti delle parti, quali erano all'epoca della Convenzione del 1650.

Riepilogando. — L'evidenza del titolo dell'Italia consiste nell'acquisto del suolo prima del 1500 da Comuni ora appartenenti al Regno d'Italia e nell'incontestato possesso del territorio per parte dei medesimi Comuni fino al giorno d'oggi; in certi atti di giurisdizione che diconsi essere stati compiuti dalle autorità ufficiali di Domodossola relativamente al suolo dell'Alpe si allegano non già come concludenti nella loro natura, ma che sono considerati come presunzioni di qualche valore per l'evidenza del fatto, finchè non sieno confutati; nei procedimenti del 1554, del 1555 e del 1556, che dicesi trattino della fissazione dei termini per una delimitazione territoriale e giurisdizionale, e sieno stati accettati come tale da ambedue i governi per quasi un secolo senza questione; e finalmente nell'assenza di qualsiasi reclamo di alto dominio o di giurisdizione per parte della Svizzera o dai suoi dipendenti prima dell'anno 1641, quando l'Alpe era in possesso dei comuni italiani per interi secoli.

Il diritto della Svizzera è fondato: sopra considerazioni di convenienza; sull'allegato principio di geografia politica, secondo il quale i limiti degli stati limitrofi nei paesi montuosi sono determinati dallo spartiacqua; sulla conquista del 1513 e sul trattato del 1516 riconoscendo la Val Maggia, di cui fa parte l'Alpe di Cravairola, come appartenente alla Svizzera; e sui provvedimenti per lo stabilimento dei limiti tra l'Alpe di Cravairola ed il comune di Campo.

Dietro considerazioni di tutti quei punti, il sottoscritto è di parere:

In primo luogo: Che il titolo dell'Italia al territorio in questione è stabilito *prima facie* dalle considerazioni sovranotate e quindi valevole, ammenochè sia confutato da prove addotte dalla Svizzera.

In secondo luogo: Benchè ragioni di convenienza e di mutuo interesse consiglino la cessione dell'Alpe di Cravairola alla Svizzera, pur nondimeno per le ragioni già espresse gli arbitri non sarebbero giustificati nell'assegnare quel territorio alla Confederazione sopra questa sola base.

In terzo luogo: Che il principio geografico della divisione politica dei territori dietro lo spartiacqua o displuvio non è abbastanza generalmente riconosciuto dalle leggi pratiche internazionali Europee per costituire un fondamento indipendente di decisione nei casi contestati.

Egli è vero che geograficamente una grande vallata include i suoi rami minori, ma nel discorso ordinario il nome di valle, quando si tratta di un fiume considerevole, è generalmente ristretto al ramo principale, le valli laterali tributarie avendo al solito i loro propri nomi; quindi una tale designazione non include necessariamente le valli minori, ma dev'essere interpretata secondo il possesso od altre circostanze se queste esistono.

Come fu detto non v'è prova di alcun reclamo per parte della Svizzera relativamente alla sovranità sull'Alpe, come parte del Val Maggia, prima dell'asserto di giurisdizione di Oswaldo nel 1641, e se nel periodo mediovale attraverso il quale si estende la storia dell'Alpe di Cravairola, e stato ricevuto come principio di legge che le valli tributarie debbono seguire la giurisdizione della corrente principale delle acque, non si può spiegare perche il Comune di Campo non ha reclamato la sovranità di Cravairola come appartenente al suo proprio territorio, nel periodo, in cui i Comuni italiani l'acquistarono. Ma non vi è indizio di simile reclamo in nessun tempo sino a un secolo dopo la definizione dei limiti del 1554.

In quarto luogo: Che sebbene in un senso scientifico la valle principale di un fiume abbracci quelle dei suoi tributari, pure questi termini, quando sono usati in istrumenti pubblici, specialmente in quelli di antica data, debbono essere interpretati secondo il senso e l'uso contemporanei. Il sottoscritto non vede nessuna prova che alcuna delle parti del trattato del 1516, quindi di nessun periodo susseguente prima del 1641, considerasse l'Alpe di Cravairola come incluso nella denominazione di Val Maggia, e che al contrario la mancanza di ogni reclamo di sovranità della Svizzera e del Comune di Campo sul suolo situato geograficamente nel Val Maggia, ma posseduto e goduto da corpi morali forestieri *prima facie* mostra all'evidenza che la Confederazione ed il Comune di Campo non si ritenevano investiti di tale sovranità, in alcun tempo, prima che siffatto reclamo fosse assunto da un ufficiale svizzero nel 1641.

In quinto luogo: Che i procedimenti del 1554, che il sottoscritto è costretto d'interpretare in armonia coi correlativi documenti ufficiali del 1555 e 1556, tendono piuttosto a negare che a stabilire il diritto della Svizzera alla sovranità del territorio in questione, ed a mostrare, che i limiti da essi stabiliti erano considerati dalle parti immediatamente interessate e dai loro rispettivi governi come una delimitazione territoriale giurisdizionale.

Sull'insieme della questione il sottoscritto è di parere che, per usare le espressioni del *Compromis:* « La ligne frontière qui sépare les territoire italien du territoire de la Confédération Suisse (Canton Tessin), au lieu dit Alpe de Cravairola, doit quitter la chaîne principale des montagnes au sommet désigné Sonnenhorn, pour descendre vers le ruisseau de la Vallée de Campo et en suivant l'arête secondaire nommée Creta Tremolina (ou Mosso del Lodano sur la carte suisse) rejoindre la chaîne principale au Pizzo del Lago Gelato » ed egli pronunzia sentenza conforme.

In conclusione, il sottoscritto si onora d'esprimere il suo alto apprezzamento per l'abiltà, la moderazione e l'imparzialità spiegate da tutti i componenti l'arbitraggio, come pure i suoi sinceri ringraziamenti per la continua cortesia e considerazione manifestategli da tutti coloro con cui il suo ufficio lo pose in contatto.

Dato in Milano in duplicato 23 settembre 1874[1].

LXII. Colombie, Etats-Unis d'Amérique.

17 août 1874.

Cette affaire a eu pour objet la réparation due pour la saisie d'un steamer par des rebelles colombiens, qui s'en servirent pour fomenter une révolution. L'arbitrage fut confié à deux arbitres et à un surarbitre: ce dernier se prononça en faveur des prétentions américaines, qu'il évalua à 33,401 $.

Agreement of arbitration between Colombia and the United States of America, signed at Bogota, August 17, 1874.

The undersigned, to wit, William L. Scruggs, minister resident of the United States of America, and Jacobo Sánchez, secretary of the interior and foreign relations of the United States of Colombia, being especially authorized by their respective governments to submit to the decision of arbitrators the indemnity-claims made by the Government of the United States against that of Colombia for damages resulting from the seizure and detention of the steamer Montijo, within the territory and by certain citizens of Colombia, in April, 1871, have entered into the following agreement:

I. Said claims shall be submitted to arbitrators, one to be appointed by the minister-resident of the United States of America, another by the government of the United States of Colombia, and these two to name an umpire, who shall decide all questions upon which they may be unable to agree. In case the place of either arbitrator or of the umpire shall, from any cause become vacant, such vacancy shall be filled forth, with, in the manner herein provided for the original appointment. If the arbitrators cannot agree in the choice of an umpire, one shall be selected by new commissioners, chosen for and assigned exclusively to this duty.

II. The arbitrators and umpire so named shall meet in Bogotá within one month from the date of their appointment, and shall, before proceeding to business, make and subscribe a solemn declaration that they will impartially consider and determine, to the best of their judgment, and according to public law and the treaties in force between the two countries, and these present stipulations, the claims herein submitted, and such declaration shall be entered upon the record of their proceedings.

III. The official correspondence and documents relative to the case shall be submitted to the arbitrators; but before their decision is rendered, the attorney-general, or lawyer, of the Government of Colombia shall be heard, as well as the one designated by the minister-resident of the United States. The expositions of the attorneys will be made orally or in writing.

IV. The arbitrators shall have jurisdiction of the claims mentioned, and they shall decide, as a primary question, whether the United States of Colombia is obligated to grant indemnification; and if that question should be decided affirmatively, they will fix the amount of indemnification. The award shall be in writing; and, if indemnity be given, the sum to be paid shall be expressed in the legal coin—pesos de ley—of the United States of Colombia, and paid to the minister-resident of the United States, or to such person as he may name, within one year from the date of the decision.

V. The expenses of the arbitration, not to exceed fifteen hundred dollars, shall be borne in equal moieties by the two governments.

VI. The two governments will accept the award made as final and conclusive, and will give full effect to the same; and the Colombian government shall be forever released from any and all further accountability after the decision of the arbitrators shall have been made and its terms faithfully complied with.

In faith whereof the plenipotentiaries of the two governments have signed and sealed the present agreement, in Bogota, on the 17th day of August, in the year of our Lord one thousand eight hundred and seventy four[1].

---

[1] F. de MARTENS. Nouveau Recueil Général, 2me série, t. VIII, p. 560.

[1] Foreign relations of the United States, 1875—1876, p. 427; — J. B. MOORE, History and Digest..., p. 4698.

Award given by the umpire on the case of the Montijo, in Bogota, July 26, 1875.

In virtue of a convention between the United States of America and the United States of Colombia, dated the 17ᵗʰ of August 1874, it was agreed that there should be submitted to a tribunal of arbitration the final resolution and decision of a claim which had been preferred by the first-named republic against the latter for damages accruing from the occupation, in the months of April and May 1871, in the waters of the State of Panama, of the American steamer *Montijo*.

The tribunal was duly constituted in the city of Bogota, and consists of señor Mariano Tanco, as arbitrator on the part of the United States of Colombia, of Mr. Bendix Koppel, as arbitrator on the part of the United States of America, and of the undersigned, Mr. Robert Bunch, Her Britannic Majesty's minister resident to the United States of Colombia as final referee or umpire.

After due examination of the facts and the emission of written opinions by Messrs. Tanco and Koppel, it was found that an entire discrepancy existed between the gentlemen, for which reason the question has been laid before the undersigned for a final decision, which he proceeds to give in the following manner and terms:

The undersigned will begin by enumerating the points on which both arbitrators seem to be agreed:

1. The *Montijo* was a steamer built and registered in New-York but put together in Panama, in the year 1867. She was owned by Messrs. Schuber Brothers, citizens of the United States, residing and doing business for many years in the city of Panama.

Her papers were always in the custody of the consul of the United States in Panama.

2. That from 1867 to the date of seizure in 1871 she was trading under the American flag in the Pacific, generally between the city of Panama and the town of David and intermediate ports of the State, but also between Panama and Buenaventura, and even between Panama and certain ports of Peru and Ecuador.

3. That during the period between 1869 and 1871 the Montijo was engaged in the trade between the city of Panama and the town of David and intermediate ports as aforesaid, under a contract with the government of the State of Panama dated December 15, 1869, by which 'the President of the State, in conformity with his powers' (en uso de sus facultades), grants permission to the Montijo, although sailing under the flag of the United States of America, to enter the ports of the State as a coasting vessel (buque costanero), and declares her to be exempt from all duties

in such ports. By the same contract an exclusive privilege for eight years is granted to the vessel to enter a disused (antiguo) port called Mangote, and certain lots of land are ceded to her owners for the erection of warehouses, etc.

In return for these and other privileges the owners of the *Montijo* pledge themselves to carry the official correspondence of the State gratuitously, and to give passage at reduced rates to the government troops and officials. It is also stipulated that in cases of disturbance of public order special contracts shall be made for the conveyance of troops, and that a sum not exceeding five hundred dollars a day shall be paid to the owners of the Montijo.

4. That early in the month of April, 1871, the *Montijo* was lying in the port of David. Señor Tomas Herrera and other persons, who were desirous of making a revolution against the State government of Panama, endeavored to obtain by negotiation the services of the vessel from one of her owners Mr. John Schuber, who was on board. That the proposal was rejected, and that on the 6ᵗʰ of April the vessel was taken forcible possession of by Herrera, Diaz and others. The particulars of the seizure are fully detailed in the affidavits of the owner, captain, and engineer, and others.

5. That the vessel remained in possession of the captors, and subsequently of the State government of Panama, for a certain period of time, when she was restored to her owners.

6. That a treaty of peace was subsequently made between the President of the State of Panama, Buenaventura Correoso, on the one hand, and Tomas Herrera, chief of the revolutionary forces, on the other, by which a complete amnesty was reciprocally granted, and by Article VII of which 'the government assumes as its own the expense of the steamers and other vehicles which the revolution has had to make use of up to that date'.

7. That up to this day nothing has been paid by the State of Panama for the use of the steamer *Montijo*.

8. That the Government of the United States has preferred a claim against the Government of Colombia for a sum of upward of $ 94,000 for the use of the *Montijo*, and for other matters arising from it, and that the entire question has since been submitted, by mutual consent, to the decision of the arbitrators, who were duly appointed under the terms of a convention between the two republics.

9. That the said arbitrators have been unable to arrive at a common decision, the one holding that Colombia is not responsible for any of the

damages inflicted on the owners of the *Montijo* whilst the other sentences Colombia to pay to the claimants the sum of $ 33,401, with interest at the rate of 5 per cent per annum since the 1ˢᵗ of January 1872, until the day of payment.

10. That the final decision in the case has been left, under the terms of the aforesaid convention, to the undersigned, who now proceeds to the discharge of his duty.

The undersigned commences by examining the reasons alleged by the honorable the Colombian arbitrator for exempting his government from all responsibility to the owners of the *Montijo*.

These seem to be:

First. That the Messrs. Schuber were domiciled in the city of Panama, where they carried on business for many years under the protection of the laws of the country, for which reason they were subject to those laws in every respect in the same manner as the citizens of Colombia.

Second. That the Messrs. Schuber constantly took part in the civil disturbances of the State of Panama, by hiring their vessel indiscriminately to the constitutional government and to rebels; that they made a contract to place their vessel at the disposal of the local government whenever there might be a domestic war (guerra interior); that they were always paid for such services, which fact establishes on their part an organized speculation in all cases of public disturbance; that the use of the flag of the United States does not add force to their claim, but on the contrary, was rather an abuse, particularly as the vessel had only a third part of her crew citizens of the United States, which was a violation of American law.

Third. That in the case now under consideration the seizure of the vessel was only a natural consequence of the conduct of Schuber Brothers, and of the contract with the President of Panama, under which they were acting, because the revolutionists well knew that if they did not take possession of her, she would be used by President Correoso, thus making of the *Montijo* an element of war of the government of Panama.

Fourth. That it has not yet been proved that Herrera and Diaz took the steamer by force and against the will of the owners, because the only proof alleged is to be found in the affidavits of the persons interested in the present claim and therefore invalid, and also because there is a contradiction in the evidence given by John Schuber, one of the owners.

Fifth. That Schuber Brothers navigated their vessel in the waters of Colombia under a foreign flag without obtaining permission, which, under

penalty of confiscation, is required by a decree of the 13ᵗʰ of May 1862. This permission, it is alleged, Schuber Brothers knew to be necessary, as they obtained it to the contract of the 15ᵗʰ of Dezember 1869 from the President of Panama, who, however, had not legal power to grant it, because such authority belongs only to the government of the Union.

Sixth. That the President of Panama, in virtue of his constitutional authority, issued on the 18ᵗʰ of May an amnesty in which were included Herrera, Diaz and other participators in the local revolution; that, in consequence of this amnesty, no judicial proceedings could be instituted against them (as the judge declared) in any case in which a foreigner, even if strictly neutral, might have ground of complaint; that the authority by which the amnesty was granted assumed voluntarily the obligation of paying to Schuber Brothers the sum due by the revolutionists for the use acquiesced in and indirectly authorized (consentido e indirectamente autorizado) by John Schuber of the vessel. That for these reasons the claim of Messrs. Schuber Brothers can only be considered as an attempt to recover from the federal government, in a largely increased form, the account which they could not obtain from the government of Panama, but with which the government of the Union has nothing to do, as it is a private debt, and moreover, one of vicious origin, the recognition of which would establish a ruinous precedent.

The undersigned proceeds to reply to these reasons in their order, with all the deference justly due to the honorable and distinguished gentleman from whom they emanate.

Reply to reason No. 1:

To reason No. 1, as regards the alleged domicil in Panama of the Messrs. Schuber, the undersigned must remark that there is perhaps no point of international law on which more difference of opinion exists than on that of domicil. It is, therefore, extremely difficult to lay down an absolute and invariable rule respecting it. Long and continued residence will not of itself constitute it. On the contrary, it is well understood that domicil may exist for commercial purposes without a person ceasing to be bound by his allegiance to the country of his birth or adoption. That a distinction may be lawfully made between domiciled persons and visitors in and passengers through a foreign country is not to be lost sight of, because it must affect the application of the rule of law which empowers a nation to enforce the claims of its subjects in a foreign State; but even in this case the application of the right is only a matter of decree, as it undoubtedly exists in cases of flagrant violation of justice. It would therefore seem that even in the case of domiciled foreigners the nation to which they belong by birth or adoption, has a right to interfere on their behalf whenever, in its judgment, the ill treatment inflicted is of a sufficiently serious character to warrant it. But in the case of the owners of the *Montijo* the undersigned is not aware of the existence of any evidence that they were or intended to be domiciled in Colombia. That they have lived for many years (it is stated since 1849) in Panama is no doubt true: but it is equally so that they have constantly gone backward and forward between that city and the United States; that one of them at least passes with his family all his summers in New-York, where he pays taxes on a considerable amount of property, and that in the case of neither has there been the *animus manendi*, or evident intention to fix on Colombia as his home, which constitutes one of the chief reasons for determining the question of domicil. The Colombian arbitrator does not allege that they have become naturalized in the republic; it is not said that they have voted at elections or exercised other privileges of citizenship. The undersigned has, therefore, a right to suppose that they have not done so. It is, moreover, certain that in the opinion of the Government of the United States of America the Messrs. Schuber have not ceased to be citizens of the republic. The fact of the presentation of a claim on their behalf by the minister of the United States, after careful examination of the case and discussion between the cabinets of Washington and Bogotá and their agents, respecting it, is sufficient proof that they are still considered as citizens of the United States, and that Colombia has acquiesced in their being so regarded.

Wherefore, as regards the first reason of the Colombian arbitrator, the undersigned decides:

First. That the Messrs. Schuber can not be considered as domiciled in Columbia; and

Second. That even if they were so domiciled the Government of the United States would still have the right, under certain circumstances, to extend to them its protection. He will add, as an illustration of this latter point, that there lives at this moment in Bogotá a foreigner who has resided here for at least forty years, with only one very brief absence. Two years ago it became necessary for that foreigner to invoke the aid of the government of which he is subject in defense of his rights. That assistance was given him without hesitation, and was certainly not objected to by the Government of Colombia on the ground of the domicile of the foreigner.

Reply to reason No. 2:

It is evident that the Messrs. Schuber chartered the *Montijo* to various governments of the State of Panama as described by the arbitrator of Colombia: In April and May 1868 to the constitutional government; in July 1868 to a *de facto* government, and in December 1869 to the constitutional government of Señor Correoso. It is also alleged that in August 1868 the *Montijo* brought to Panama from David, in concealment, José Aristides Obaldia, who was planning a revolutionary movement against the government of the State, and that the said Obaldia returned to David still in concealment in the same vessel. There is no doubt that Messrs. Schuber were paid for such services. But the undersigned fails to see how the character of a vessel to a government of a state or country constitutes a breach of her neutrality. It will surely not be contended that a government is to be the only entity which is debarred from acquiring by hire or purchase any article of which it may stand in need. If this were the case, a government could never buy a musket or a bale of cloth or a barrel of flour for the use of its troops without subjecting the vendor, if a foreigner, to the penalties of violating his neutrality, or, if a native, to those of losing property, should the government be subsequently displaced by a revolutionary movement.

So far the general principle.

In the cases alleged as against the *Montijo* it is to be observed that all the charters were made with what, to the owners, was the government of the state. One of these governments is called, it is true, by the Colombian arbitrator a government *de facto*; but it is not the part of a foreign merchant to decide on the legitimacy or the reverse of the government under which he lives. To do so would be really to interfere in the domestic concerns of the country. He has only to satisfy himself that the government with which he deals is the one actually in possession of supreme power. That done, he is at perfect liberty to enter into contracts with it without losing his neutrality. This is too obvious to require argument. It happens constantly under all sorts of governments, arbitrary, constitutional, monarchical, and republican.

That for political reasons a foreign government may not see fit to recognize, except at its own time and convenience, a change in the administration of public affairs in another country is, of course, true. But the ordinary foreigner resident for purposes of business or pleasure has no such privilege. To him the government *de facto* is the government *de jure*. He owes it obedience and can claim from it protection.

As regards the affidavit of Ricardo Araujo, José Manuel Russel, and José E. Diaz, that José

Aristides Obaldia was a passenger in concealment in the *Montijo* in August 1868, both from and to David, when he was engaged in some revolutionary movement, it would, in the opinion of the undersigned, be necessary, in order to establish a breach of neutrality, to show that on this occasion the *Montijo* was chartered for the purpose of bringing Señor Obaldia to Panama and taking him back to David. That a solitary passenger should embark in a vessel engaged in her regular traffic, should arrive at a certain place, transact his business there (be it peaceful or revolutionary), and return in the vessel on her next trip to the place from which he started, could scarcely justify a charge against the owners of the ship of a breach of neutrality. As to the concealment, it is not alleged, much less proved, that the owners or the captain were parties to it. A passenger might easily, by remaining in his cabin or by keeping out of the way when an inconvenient visit was made, be said to be in concealment, without the captain taking part in or perhaps being even aware of his intentions.

The undersigned can not, therefore, admit that in any of the cases cited by the Colombian arbitrator the *Montijo* has violated her neutrality by taking part in civil contests.

The undersigned has entered into the details of these cases more out of deference to the elaborate argument of the Colombian arbitrator than out of the belief that such minute examination was really called for from him. In his opinion a simpler solution could be found of the point in dispute. This is, that the *Montijo* can not possibly be held responsible in 1871 for events which took place in 1868, with which those of the later date were in no way connected.

Even if it be granted, for the sake of argument, that these contracts with a legitimate or a *de facto* government for the conveyance of troops or munitions of war were of questionable propriety, the time has gone by for making them a ground of complaint against the *Montijo*. That vessel was chartered, as has been above described; she was paid the sums stipulated in the charters. No complaint has ever been made by any of the governments of Panama, or by that of the Union, against her proceedings. If, during the performance of these contracts, she violated her neutrality, she might have been protected against at law, her captain and crew might have been punished; she might, at least, have been prevented from pursuing the same course in the future. But nothing of this has happened. Each party seems to have been satisfied with his bargain. The vessel was chartered for a given time, or for a given purpose, for a given sum. Each party to the contract has complied with its conditions. There is, therefore, no connection between the acts of 1868 and those of 1871.

The undersigned is aware that the object of the Colombian arbitrator has been to show the general character of the *Montijo*, but he is compelled to remark that a good or a bad reputation is not a reason for condemning or acquitting a criminal. It can only be received in mitigation or aggravation of a punishment.

For these reasons the undersigned is obliged to decide that there was no violation of neutrality in the proceedings of the *Montijo* in 1868, and that, had there been, her owner can not be held responsible in 1871 for them, especially as there is no similarity between the one and the other. There remains to be noticed the allegation of the Colombian arbitrator that the *Montijo* was not entitled to be reputed as an American vessel because only a third of her crew were American citizens, and that this is a violation of the law of the United States. The undersigned must remark, first, that this is rather a question for the Government of the United States than for this tribunal of arbitration: and secondly, that it constantly happens that the requirements of such a law can not be carried out, owing to the impossibility of procuring such citizens. The meaning of the law is that the vessel, *when she leaves an American port*, shall have a certain proportion of her crew of the class required by its provisions. It would be absurd to condemn a vessel to enforced idleness in a foreign port because owing to desertion or death or any other cause that proportion has been disturbed, and American citizens could not be obtained to supply their places. Before the repeal of the British navigation laws the same condition was exacted as regards British vessels, but it was always understood that 'circumstances alter cases', and that a vessel might lawfully navigate with such crew as she could get a distance from home. The undersigned can not go behind the undoubted fact that the Government of the United States considers the *Montijo* as an American ship. On this point it is the sole judge.

Reply to reason No. 3:

As the undersigned has been unable to admit that the *Montijo* had forfeited her neutrality, it follows as a matter of course that he can not accept the statement of the Colombian arbitrator that Señores Herrero, Diaz, and others were justified in seizing her. That these gentlemen may have been right in considering her as an 'element of war', which might and probably would have been used against themselves, and that on the principle of selfpreservation they acted on a natural impulse in taking possession of her is freely admitted; but this is surely no reason for not paying for her. Had the government of Panama complied with its engagements to remunerate her owners (Article VII of the treaty of peace), this claim would not have arisen. But the undersigned can see no possible ground for the owners of the *Montijo* being the losers, because first the revolutionists and subsequently the constitutional government of Panama failed in their promises.

He is, therefore, under the necessity of expressing his dissent from the conclusion of the arbitrator of Colombia contained on his third reason for holding his government exempt from responsibility.

Reply to reason No. 4:

The arbitrator of Colombia asserts, in the first place, that it has not been proved that Herrera and Diaz took the steamer by force and against the will of the owners, because the only proof alleged is to be found in the affidavits of the parties interested in the present claim, which are *pro tanto* invalid; and, secondly, because there is a contradiction in the evidence given by John Schuber, one of the owners.

To the first of the allegations the undersigned replies that, although independent testimony of any fact is always desirable, there are many cases in which it can not be procured. But this is no reason for excluding the evidence of eye witnesses and of participators in a transaction on the ground that they may be interested, pecuniarily or otherwise, in its solution. To render such testimony invalid it would be necessary to prove a notorious absence of credibility in the witnesses, or a manifest combination or conspiracy on their part to swear falsely. It would surely not be held that in a trial for mutiny committed on board of a ship on the high sea, the evidence of a portion of the crew could not be received against another portion because the informants might expect a reward from the owners, or a share in the property which they might have contributed to save by their resistance to the mutineers.

But it is to be borne in mind that there is another and independent witness of the capture: the affidavit of Agustin Castellanos, a native of Cuba, but a naturalized citizen of the United States, who was on board of the *Montijo*, and who did not in any way belong to her crew, distinctly states that the hoisting of the American flag by order of Herrero and Diaz as a signal to a schooner which was lying in the offing, and which proved to be laden with men and supplies for the revolutionists, was done in absolute opposition to the wish of the captain of the *Montijo*, who even put the flag away in his own cabin to insure its safety. It is true that the arbitrator

of Colombia asserts that this affidavit, being only made before the Consul of the United States, without the intervention of any Colombian authority, would not be valid before a tribunal of the republic. But this court of arbitration is not a Colombian tribunal, but an international one. It consequently rests with the arbitrators alone to decide what evidence they will receive or reject, and the undersigned, as final referee, can not see any reason for setting aside the declaration, on oath, of a respectable person, entirely impartial in the matter, against whose right to be believed, on oath, no allegation is or has been made. The undersigned is of opinion that, even if there were no other evidence that the *Montijo* was taken possession of against the consent of her owner and commander, the affidavit of the Señor Castellanos would of itself suffice to prove that such was the case.

As regards the contradiction which is stated to exist between the two affidavits of Mr. John Schuber, the undersigned admits that there is some discrepancy, as in the one Schuber declares that the life of the captain was threatened by Herrero and Diaz with revolver in hand, whilst in the other he affirms that neither Herrera nor Diaz threatened the captain with arms, although their companions had them in their possession.

But whilst allowing, as the undersigned does, that the two versions of the same act do not entirely correspond with each other, he must observe that the main fact of the opposition of the captain to the delivery of the flag remains untouched. Whether Herrero or Diaz or their followers were or were not armed; whether, being armed, they or any of them did or did not menace the captain with the use of their weapons, does not affect the point at issue. The volume of proof that the *Montijo* was taken from the owners against their consent is so overwhelming, the facts connected with her retention by the revolutionists so notorious, that the undersigned will eliminate altogether from the record the affidavit of John Schuber. It shall be to him as if it had never existed.

For these reasons the undersigned is compelled to consider the evidence furnished by the captain and engineer of the *Montijo* and by Agustin Castellanos as quite unimpeachable. He has no doubt that the vessel was taken against the wishes of the owner and captain. That no actual violence, in the sense of coercion by deadly weapons was used is doubtless true, but the undersigned is quite convinced that moral pressure was exercised, and that the American flag was only surrendered by Captain Saunders because he could not help himself.

Reply to reason No. 5:

The arbitrator of Colombia lays much stress on the fact that the *Montijo* was navigated in the waters of Colombia under the foreign flag without obtaining the license which, under penalty of confiscation, is required by a decree of the 13th of May 1862. It is true that in the contract of the 15th of December 1869 a permission was given by the President of Panama; but it is contended that this official had no authority to grant it, the power being reserved to the government of the Union. In connection with this branch of the subject it is further urged by the arbitrator of Colombia, supported by the opinion of the honorable the attorney-general, that the 'coasting trade' (comercio de cabotaje) being forbidden to foreign vessels in Colombia and expressly prohibited by Article III of the treaty of 1846, between the United States and Colombia, no claim can be presented by the owners of the *Montijo* for consequences resulting from their violation of this arrangement between the two nations.

The undersigned will examine these arguments in inverse order.

As regards the term coasting trade *(comercio de cabotaje)* it is scarcely correct to say that it is *forbidden* by either party to the vessels of the other. The words of Article III of the treaty are: 'But it is understood that this article does not include the coasting trade of either country, the regulation of which is *reserved* by the parties, respectively, according to their own separate laws.' It is clear from this reservation that it was lawful for each party to the treaty to open the coasting trade to the other if it saw fit at any time to do so. But the undersigned, whilst feeling it a duty of courtesy to advance this opinion in reply to the argument of the Colombian arbitrator, really attaches little importance to the point, as he agrees with the counsel of the United States of America that the voyages of the *Montijo* either in the interior waters of the State of Panama or from Panama to Buenaventura or Tumaco, are not rightly described by the term *comercio de cabotaje*. The argument of the Honorable Mr. Scruggs on this point appears to the undersigned both exhaustive and convincing. For the sake of brevity he does not incorporate it into this decision, but he recommends its study to everyone who takes an interest in this case. He presumes that it will be published with the other papers. The most that the trade of the *Montijo* can be called is one of *comercio costañero*, which is certainly no prohibited or even provided for by the treaty.

But it is further alleged that, in order for a foreign vessel to carry on this limited traffic as described, alone the consent of the Government of the Union was necessary and that the *Montijo* incurred the penalty of confiscation by not obtaining it. The undersigned does not deny that a decree to that effect undoubtedly exists; but he is compelled to ask, why was it not enforced? It is surely too much to expect that a foreign vessel should inform against itself, or insist on complying with the terms of a law or a decree which the authorities of Colombia, federal and State, allowed to be disregarded and violated for a series of years. No one can be allowed to take advantage of his own wrong. The execution of the laws of Colombia clearly belongs to her own officers, and if, as in the present case, these latter failed to enforce them, the blame must rest with the real delinquents and not with the owners of a foreign vessel. For years previous to the events of 1871 the *Montijo* seems to have made her voyages, without the permission above alluded to; for years afterward the undersigned believes that she continued to do the same. She may be doing so now, although the undersigned has heard that she was wrecked some time ago, and he is not aware whether she was subsequently saved. If the laws of Colombia are so loosely administered as to allow, with the full knowledge of the federal and State authorities of Panama, a foreign ship to perform for years acts which are forbidden by those laws, the undersigned can not consent to punish the foreigner and acquit the native. Nay, more, in the contract of 1869 the President of the State of Panama distinctly permitted the *Montijo* to carry on this trade. If, as is alleged, he had no right to do so, he should have been reproved by the general government and his contract declared invalid. But no such steps were taken. The maxim that silence gives consent, is entirely applicable to this case, and so the undersigned must decide.

He will add his belief that the arrangement by which the *Montijo* traded under the flag of the United States was a convenient one to both parties. To the *Montijo*, because it insured to her owners the protection of a great and powerful country; to the authorities and people of Panama, because the flag increased the probabilities that she would not be interfered with by revolutionary movements whilst she was performing a great service to Panama by her traffic with the northern part of the State, especially by supplying the capital with cattle. It is well known to the undersigned, by his experience of this and other countries where constitutional liberty and settled governments are not as yet as firmly consolidated as their friends could wish, that on the slightest appearance of danger property of every kind, from valuable estates down to a horse or a diamond ring, are transferred to the custody of foreigners, who are made to appear as the real owners. The undersigned considers such transactions as those just described as an open fraud, and neither has admitted nor ever will recognize them when, as has been the case, they are brought to his official knowledge; but no one will deny that they exist. In the case of the *Montijo* there was, of course, no such deceit, as she is *bona fide* the property of foreigners.

It, follows that if the law has been broken both parties are in fault, the authorities of Colombia in a greater degree as it was their duty to enforce the laws which were committed to their keeping.

For these reasons the undersigned can not attach weight to the reasoning and deductions of the arbitrator of Colombia.

Reply to reason No. 6:

The ground assumed by the arbitrator of Colombia on this point seems to be that, as a general amnesty in favor of Messrs. Herrera, Diaz, and all other persons concerned in the attempted revolution of April and May 1871 was subsequently granted by the President of the State of Panama, in the exercise of his constitutional powers, no judicial proceedings could be instituted against the revolutionists, and consequently that no compensation for injuries done by them could be recovered from them by either foreigner or native.

To this argument the undersigned sees two objections. The first is that, even in the absence of any express stipulation to that effect, the grantor of an amnesty assumes as his own the liabilities previously incurred by the objects of his pardon toward persons or things over which the grantor has no control. In the present case it will scarcely be contended that the captors of the *Montijo* had any right, beyond that emanating from a revolutionary movement, to take the vessel from the dominion of her owners. By the terms of the treaty with the United States it is clearly stipulated that 'the citizens of neither of the contracting parties shall be liable to any embargo, nor to be detained with their vessels, cargoes, merchandise, or effects for any military expedition, nor for any public or private purpose whatever, without allowing to those interested an equitable and sufficient indemnification.' If, therefore, the captors had no right before the amnesty to take the *Montijo*, it is evident that the President of Panama could not by the terms of that document confer it on them. They, therefore, are liable to the owners for the expenses incurred and damages occasioned. If no amnesty had ever

been granted, and had Herrera, Diaz and their associates been honestly and effectively proceeded against in the courts of the republic, and cast in damages toward the owners, the aspect of the case would have entirely changed. It would have been, at least, an open question whether their possible or even notorious inability to pay those damages would have rendered Colombia at large responsible for their acts. But the amnesty deprived the Messrs. Schuber of the power of trying the question. Therefore the President of Panama, having no right to dispose of interests which were not his property and which, on the contrary, he was bound by a public treaty to protect, assumed the responsibility to the owners of those interests of the persons by whom they had been injured. It is an old saying that one must be just before one is generous. In Spanish the version is, *'La bolsa ajeno es muy franca'* — it is easy to pay one's debts out of another man's purse. This brings the undersigned to the second ground for dissenting from the decision of the Colombian arbitrator on the point under consideration.

This is that the treaty of peace, of which the amnesty forms a part, contains in its seventh article a distinct engagement that the government of Panama will pay for the use of the *Montijo*. The undersigned considers this fact so important and conclusive that he contents himself with putting it on record without further comment. Why the engagement was not carried out the undersigned can not say. That arbitrators were appointed to fix the amount, and that they came to a decision respecting it, is on record. But their sentence was apparently not ratified; at any rate, it was not carried out. The State of Panama therefore remains to this day responsible, both by implication and by express engagement, for the acts of the revolutionists in this matter.

There remains to be considered the concluding portion of the sixth reason advanced by the Colombian arbitrator, which is that the government of the Union can not be held answerable for the failure of that of Panama to compensate the owners of the *Montijo* because the former has no connection *(solidaridad)* with private debts, especially with those which have, as in the present case, a vicious origin.

To this the undersigned replies, first, that in his opinion the government of the Union has a very clear and decided connection with debts incurred by the States of the Union toward foreigners whose treaty rights have been invaded or attacked; and, secondly, that the debts so incurred by the separate States are in no way private, but, on the contrary, entirely public in their character.

As regards the first point, it can not be denied that the treaties under which the residence of foreigners in Colombia is authorized, and their rights during such residence defined and assured, are made with the general government, and not with the separate States of which the Union is composed. The same practice obtains in the United States, in Switzerland, and in all countries in which the federal system is adopted. In the event, then, of the violation of a treaty stipulation, it is evident that a recourse must be had to the entity with which the international engagements were made. There is no one else to whom application can be directed. For treaty purposes the separate States are non-existent; they have parted with a certain defined portion of their inherent sovereignty, and can only be dealt with through their accredited representative or delegate, the federal or general government.

But, if it be admitted that such is the theory and the practice of the federal system, it is equally clear that the duty of addressing the general government carries with it the right to claim from that government, and from it alone, the fulfillment of the international pact. If a manifest wrong be committed by a separate State, no diplomatic remonstrance can be addressed to it. It is true that in such a case the resident consular officer of a foreign power may call the attention of the transgressing State to the consequences of its action, and may endeavor by timely and friendly intervention on the spot to avoid the necessity of an ultimate application to the general government through the customary diplomatic channel; but should this overture fail, there remains no remedy but the interference of the federal power, which is bound to redress the wrong, and, if necessary, compensate the injured foreigner. If this rule, which the undersigned believes to be beyond dispute, be correctly laid down, it follows that in every case of international wrong the general government of this republic has a very close connection with the proceedings of the separate States of the Union. As it, and it alone, is responsible for foreign nations, it is bound to show in every case that it has done its best to obtain satisfaction from the aggressor.

But it will probably be said that by the constitution of Colombia the federal power is prohibited from interfering in the domestic disturbances of the States, and that it can not in justice be made accountable for acts which it has not the power, under the fundamental charter of the republic, to prevent or to punish. To this the undersigned will remark that in such a case a treaty is superior to the constitution, which latter must give way. The legislation of the republic must be adapted to the treaty, not the

treaty to the laws. This constantly happens in engagements between separate and independent nations. For the purposes of carrying out the stipulations of a treaty, special laws are required. They are made *ad hoc*, even though they may extend to foreigners privileges and immunities which the subjects or citizens of one or both of the treaty-making powers do not enjoy at home.

That under such a rule apparent injustice may occasionally be committed is probably true. But it is more apparent than real. It may seem at first sight unfair to make the federal power, and through it the taxpayers of the country responsible, morally and pecuniarily, for events over which they have no control, and which they probably disapprove or disavow, but the injustice disappears when this inconvenience is found to be inseparable from the federal system. If a nation deliberately adopts that form of administering its publics affairs, it does so with the full knowledge of the consequences it entails. It calculates the advantages and the drawbacks, and can not complain if the latter now and then make themselves felt.

That this liability of the federal power for the acts of the States may produce to the nations at large the gravest complications is matter of history. Probably the most serious case of this inconvenience on record is that of a British subject named McLeod, whose arrest and trial by the State of New York nearly involved Great Britain and the United States in a war. During the Canadian rebellion, an American steamer called the *Caroline*, which had been engaged in carrying arms to the rebels, was boarded in the night by a party of loyalists, set on fire, and driven over the Falls of Niagara. In this affray an American citizen lost his life. In January 1841 Alexander McLeod, a British subject, was arrested while engaged in some business in New York State, and imprisoned on a charge of murder because, as was alleged, he was concerned in the attack on the vessel. The British Government demanded his release on the ground that he was acting under orders, and that the responsibility rested with Great Britain and not with the individual. The Secretary of State of the United States replied that his government was powerless in the matter, as it could not interfere with the tribunals of the State of New York. Great Britain then caused it to be distinctly understood that the condemnation and execution of Mr. McLeod would be immediately followed by a declaration of war. Lord Palmerston, then secretary for foreign affairs, told Mr. Stevenson, United States minister in London, that such would be the case. Great efforts were made by the friends of peace, and as much pressure as could properly be applied to the State of New York was brought to bear, and McLeod was acquitted. But two great and powerful nations were on the verge of a disastrous war because the federal power was held liable for the acts of a separate State.

As regards the second point made by the Colombian arbitrator, that the debts incurred by foreigners by the separate States of the Union are private in their character, the undersigned can only express his dissent from the doctrine. If an engagement, pecuniary or other, made by the constitutional head of State, acting, as in the present case, 'in virtue of powers conferred by law' is to be considered in the same light as an ordinary mercantile debt and only to be recoverable in the same manner, the possibility of a State contracting with either native or foreigner would soon be reduced to very narrow limits. The chances of repayment would depend on the stability of the contracting government, and this of itself would introduce an element of considerable uncertainty into such transactions.

The undersigned holds that all debts contracted by duly authorized officers of a given State are essentially public in their character, and that their nonpayment can be made the subject of remonstrance by a foreign nation, should the engagements be contracted with its subjects or citizens. It is quite true that Great Britain, the greatest lender of money in existence, does not feel herself bound to interfere on behalf of her subjects in every case where they may have lent money to foreign countries, as she holds, as a general rule, that they may be left to find their own remedy for their imprudence; but she explicitly declares that this abstention on her part is a mere matter of discretion, and that she has the undoubted right to interfere whenever she may see fit to do so.

As regards the 'vicious origin' of the present debt, the undersigned does not view it in that light; he can not, therefore, agree with any deductions from that assumption. For these reasons the undersigned holds, as a general principle, that the government of the Union is responsible in certain cases for the wrongs inflicted on foreigners by the separate States, and that debts contracted by the constituted authorities of those States are not private in their character. He is compelled, therefore, to dissent from the sixth reason of the Colombian arbitrator.

The undersigned has now reviewed, to the best of his ability, the able and elaborate arguments of the honorable the arbitrator of Colombia on this question. He wishes he could have brought to the task the same brilliant qualities which Señor Tanco has so liberally displayed, and it would have been agreeable to him to have concurred in the views of a gentleman whom he so highly esteems.

The next step in the discharge of the duty which the undersigned has contracted is the examination of the opinion of the honorable the arbitrator of the United States of America.

This, however, is an easy task, as the undersigned fully concurs in and adopts that opinion as in conformity both with public law, as understood by him, and with the justice of the question in dispute.

Mr. Koppel asserts the responsibility, to the claimants, of the Government of the Colombian Union, and fixes the pecuniary amount which results from that responsibility. Although the undersigned may see reason to differ from the arbitrator of the United States on this latter point, he expresses his entire concurrence in the former. He believes, moreover, that the enlightened and moderate views held and ably advocated by Mr. Koppel will be cheerfully accepted by the government and people of Colombia, however unpalatable it may naturally be to them to be found liable in pecuniary damages. This fact, however, reflects no disgrace to the nation; on the contrary, the conduct of Colombia is calculated to advance her reputation in the eyes of the world, as it shows her willingness to adopt, for the solution of difficulties, the enlightened course which has found favor, especially of late years, with powerful countries which could have trusted with confidence to the arbitrament of the sword.

The task of the undersigned approaches its conclusions. He has reviewed, in the one case in considerable detail, in the other in a much briefer from, the opinions of the two honorable arbitrators of Colombia and the United States of America. It remains for him to give his own decision on the two points to which the convention of arbitration limits its labors.

These are:

First. Whether Colombia, as represented by the Government of the Union, is or is not responsible to the owners of the *Montijo*, her captain, officers and crew, for the events which have given rise to this arbitration?

Second. If she be so responsible, then in what sum is she indebted?

As regards the first point, the undersigned *decides*:

That Colombia is responsible to the owners of the *Montijo*.

That Colombia is not responsible to one of the owners (Mr. John Schuber), to the captain, officers, or crew, for personal damages as claimed by them.

As regards the second point, the undersigned *decides:*

That Colombia is responsible to Messrs. Schuber, owners of the *Montijo*, in $ 33,401, being —

For the use of the steamer by Messrs. Herrero, Diaz and their followers for 43 days, at $ 500 a day. . . . $ 21,500

For the use of the steamer by the government of Panama for 20 days before she was restored to her owners, at $ 500 per day 10,000

For certain necessary repairs . . . 1,901

33,401

The undersigned will give his reasons for the above decisions. As to the first point, he is compelled to decree the responsability of the Colombian Government, because (A) it is the natural heir (if the expression may be permitted) of the liabilities of the State of Panama toward the owners of the *Montijo*. That this vessel was, at the time of her capture by Herrera and Diaz, engaged in the prosecution of a perfectly lawful and peaceful voyage there can be no doubt. With what she may have done in years gone by, with what she may have intended to do in some contingency which had not arisen, and did not subsequently arise, this tribunal can have nothing to do. She was on the 5th of April 1871 performing, with the full consent of and under special contract with the constitutional government of the State of Panama a lawful voyage. That voyage was forcibly interrupted ; the dominion of the owners was disturbed; she passed out of their control and was not restored to it for a period of sixty-three days. It is clear, on every principle of the plainest justice, that 'some one' ought to pay for this act and for its consequences. That 'some one' could not be Herrera and Diaz because their responsibility was saved by the treaty of peace and its accompanying amnesty. We have then to fall back on the State of Panama, which granted the amnesty, and stipulated, moreover, as one of the conditions of the treaty of peace, that it would pay for the use of the *Montijo*, but that State has, for its own reasons, failed to do so. It is, then, to the general government alone that the claimants can apply. As the final result of such application, the undersigned decides that the said government is liable. But there is another and a stronger reason for such liability. This is (B) that the general government of the Union, through its officers in Panama, failed in its duty to extend to citizens of the United States the protection which, both by the law of nations and by special treaty stipulation,

it was bound to afford. It was, in the opinion of the undersigned, the clear duty of the President of Panama, acting as the constitutional agent of the government of the Union, to recover the *Montijo* from the revolutionists and return her to her owner. It is true that he had not the means of doing so, there being at hand no naval or military force of Colombia sufficient for such a purpose; but this absence of power does not remove the obligation. The first duty of every government is to make itself respected both at home and abroad. If it promises protection to those whom it consents to admit into its territory, it must find the means of making it effective. If it does not do so, even if by no fault of its own, it must make the only amends in its power, viz., compensate the sufferer.

For these reasons the undersigned holds Colombia liable to the owners of the *Montijo*. The sum of $ 500 a day has been fixed because that amount seems to have been constantly agreed upon by the government of Panama and the Messrs. Schuber as a fair price.

But the undersigned, whilst deciding on the liability to the owners, does not see any necessity for indemnifying either Mr. John Schuber, the captain, the engineer, or the petty officers and crew of the *Montijo*. No personal injury seems to have been suffered by any of these persons, and the inconvenience they experienced appears to have been small. In the case of the officers and crew probably there was none at all. The wages of all these latter have doubtless been paid by the owners, so that it really must have been a matter of indifference to them whether they were sailing under the orders of Captain Saunders or of Señor Herrera. As to Mr. John Schuber, the undersigned can scarcely consider as a case of false imprisonment his retention on board of his own vessel. That he was not a free man is true, and that he suffered some inconvenience, and possibly some loss of business, by the act of which he complains, is probably the case. It is also possible that a court of law might consider him entitled to personal damages. But the undersigned believes that a tribunal such as this is may lawfully exercise considerable discretion of its own, and decide rather on broad general principles than on a strict interpretation of written law. Such being his opinion, he concurs with the arbitrator of the United States in striking out of the account presented by that government the claims for personal damages of all the parties concerned.

As regards the opinion of the arbitrator of the United States that interest at the rate of 5 per cent per annum should be allowed from the 1st of January 1872 to the date of payment of the claim, the undersigned is not prepared to say that such an allowance would not be strictly justifiable. He nevertheless decides against it for the following reasons:

First. Because there is no settled rule as to the payment of interest on claims on countries or governments;

Secondly. Because it seems open to question whether interest should accrue during the progress of diplomatic negotiations, which are often protracted in their character;

Thirdly. That this reason applies with special force to negotiations which result in an arbitration or friendly arrangement;

Fourthly. That, whilst doing what he considers strict justice to the claimants by giving to them the full value of the use of their vessel during her detention, he desires to avoid any appearance of punishing the Colombian people at large for an act with which very few of them had anything to do, and which affected no Colombian interests beyond those of a few speculators in revolutions in Panama.

The repairs rendered necessary*during the occupation of the vessel seem fairly to belong to the claim, for which reason the sum of $ 1,901 is allowed.

The undersigned wishes to point out that the sum now awarded is simply that which the Government of Panama ought to have paid immediately that the vessel was returned to her owners, and for which it and the revolutionists against its authority received full value. If anything is to be paid at all, it can scarcely be less than the amount now awarded. It is true that the duty of payment is transferred from the State of Panama to the government of the Union, but it is, of course, open to this latter, should it see fit to do so, to claim the sum for the national treasury. If this course be pursued, and an offending State be held strictly accountable to the nation at large for all expenses caused by its local disturbances, the undersigned believes that these will become less frequent and less violent in their character. That this of itself will be a great gain to the republic, morally and materially, it requires no argument of the undersigned to point out.

The undersigned has decided, according to the best of his ability, this delicate and interesting question. If by his decision he has contributed to a fair and reasonable understanding of the relations existing, so far as foreigners residing in Colombia under treaty stipulations are concerned, between the separate States and the general government of the Union, he will be satisfied with his work. If, in conjunction with the honorable gentlemen, his colleagues in this tribunal, he has succeeded in removing a cause of misunderstanding between Colombia and the United States, both they and he will feel their labor has not been in vain.

The undersigned desires to remark, in conclusion, that if he has only casually and even incidentally alluded in the course of this decision to the opinions and views of the counsels for the respective parties, the honorable the attorney-general of Colombia and the honorable the minister of the United States, it has not been from a want of appreciation of their distinguished merit, of their learning, or of their forensic ability; it has simply been because he has conceived his duty to lie exclusively in determining between the views of the two arbitrators who did him the high honor to choose him for that purpose. The undersigned acknowledges with profound gratitude the valuable assistance which he has derived from the arguments of the respective counsels, although he has abstained, with two exceptions, from any allusion to them. That he could not agree with both is evident from his position as umpire. But he is fully sensible of the obligations under which he stands to both of those distinguished and learned gentlemen. [1]

LXIII. Bolivie, Chili.

5 décembre 1872.

Aux termes d'un traité du 10 août 1866 les limites des deux Etats furent fixées au degré 24 de latitude sud. Toutefois les territoires compris entre les degrés 23 et 25 de latitude sud furent exploités pour le compte commun, au point de vue minier. Par deux conventions postérieures des 5 décembre 1872 et 6 août 1874 il fut décidé qu'une commission arbitrale trancherait les points litigieux au sujet des mines et filons à exploiter. Malheureusement le conflit armé qui éclata entre le Chili et la Bolivie rendit caduque cette double stipulation. Après la guerre, les territoires prémentionnés furent cédés au Chili.

Tratado de limites firmado en La Paz, Deciembre 5 de 1872.

. . . .

ART. II. Para determinar con señales visibles la ubicacion de las minas i lugares productores de minerales que estan sujetos a la participacion comun de derechos de esportacion, dentro de

---

[1] J. B. MOORE. *History and Digest* . . . ., p. 1427.

los grados 23 al 25, cada parte nombrara un comisionado para que en calidad de peritos procedan a fijar i determinar dechos lugares. Si los Comisionados estuvieren de acuerdo, la operacion pericial se tendra por firme i subsistente, i se respetera como sentencia posada en autoridad de cosa jusgada, sin que sea necesaria la aprobacion de los respectivos Gobiernos. En caso de discordia los mismos peritos Comisionados nombraran un tercero que la dirima, pero si tampoco estuvieren de acuerdo para tal nombramiento, la designation del tercer dirimente se hara por S. M. el Emperador del Brasil. Entendiendose que el territorio de esplotacion comun designado en el art. 2 del mismo tratado es el poligono formado por el grado 23 al norte i el 25 al sur, las cumbres de los Andes al oriente i el mar Pacifico al occidente [1].

Tratado de limites entre Chile y Bolivia, firmado en Sucre, Agosto 6 de 1874.

. . . .

ART. II. Para los efectos de este tratado se consideran firmes y subsistentes las líneas de los paralelos 23 y 24, fijados por les comisionados Pisis y Mugía y de que da testimonio el acta levantada en Antofagasta el 10 Febrero de 1870.

Si hubiere duda acerca de la verdadera y exacta ubicación del asiento minero de Caracoles ó de cualquier otro lugar productor de minerales, por considerarlos fuera de la zona comprendida entre esos paralelos, se procedera á determinar dicha ubicación por una comision de dos poritos nombrados uno por cada una de las Partes Cortratantes, debiendo los mismos peritos nombrar un tercero en caso de discordia; y si no se aviniesen para ese nombramiento, lo efectuará S. M. el Emperador del Brasil. Hasta que no aparezca prueba en contrario relativa a esta determinación, se seguirá entendiendo, como hasta aquí, que ese asiento minero está comprendido entre les paralelos indicados [2].

LXIV. Chili, Etats-Unis d'Amérique.

6 décembre 1873.

Cette affaire a eu pour objet la retention indue d'un navire, opérée en 1832. Le 18 décembre 1874 un arrangement direct termina cette contestation par le payement de 20,000 $.

---

[1] *Memoria de relaciones esteriores* (Chile), 1873, p. 346.
[2] *Recopilacion de Tratados y Convenciones*, 1894, t. II, p. 102.

Convención de arbitraje, relativa á la fregata Good Return, firmada en Santiago, Diciembre 6, 1873.

Reunidos en conferencia el día 6 de Diciembre de 1873, en la sala de Despacho del Ministerio de Relaciones Exteriores de Chile, Adolfo Hañez, Ministro de Estado del citado Departamento y C. A. Logan, Enviado Extraordinario y Ministro Plenipotentiario de los Estados Unidos de Norte América, con el fin de convenir en la manera de poner término á la prolongada discusion que desde años atrás se viene debatiendo entre los Representantes de ambos Gobiernos acerca de la legalidad ò ilegalidad del embargo y detención del brique ballenero norte-americano *Good Return*, verificado por las autoridades del puerto de Talcaguano en 1832 ;

El señor Enviado Extraordinario y Ministro Plenipotenciario de los Estados Unidos expuso: que deseando su Gobierno conservar intactas y estrechar las relaciones amistosas que felizmente existen con el Gobierno de la República de Chile y alejar al mismo tiempo todo motivo de diferencia que pudiero menoscabarlas ó alterarlas, lo habla autorizado para aceptar la proposición hecha á su predecesor por el señor Ministro de Relaciones Exteriores, de someter á un arbitraje la cuestión antes dicha, y que el podía proponer desde luego, sujeto á la aprobación de su Gobierno, al señor Don Carlos F. Levenhagen, Ministro Residente del Imperio Germánico en Chile, como la persona más apta por su imparcialidad, ilustraciòn y experiencia para dirimir los puntos en discordia entre sus respectivos Gohiernos.

El señor Ministro de Relaciones Exteriores contestó, á nombre de su Gobierno que abundaba por su parte en los mismos sentimientos expresados por el señor Enviado Extraordinario y Ministro Plenipotenciario, y que deseoso como el que más de afianzar y perpetuar la buena amistad existente entre los dos Gobiernos, aceptaba con placer tanto la idea del arbitraje, que ha considerado siempre como el único medio justo, legal y lógico de zanjar todas las difficultades internacionales, como la designación hecha en el señor Don Carlos F. Levenhagen, Ministro Residente del Imperio Germánico, para arbitro de la cuestión objeto de esta conferencia. En consecuencia, convinieron ambos señores Ministros en lo síguiente.

ART. Iº. Los Gobiernos de Chile y de los Estados Unidos de Norte América, legalmente representados, el primero por su Enviado Extraordinario y Ministro Plenipotenciario en Santiago, y el segundo por su Ministro de Estado para los Relaciones Exteriores, nombran al señor Don Carlos F. Levenhagen, Ministro Residente del Imperio Germanico en Chile, para que como Arbitro arbitrador y amigable componedor decida con plenos poderes, procediendo *ex æquo* et *bono* sobre los puntos siguientes :

A) Es ó no justo, en todo ó en parte, el reclamo que el Gobierno de los Estados Unidos de América hace al de Chile con motivo del embargo y detención del brique ballenero *Good Return*, efectuado por las autoridades legalmente constituidos del puerto de Talcaguano en 1832 ?

B) Si es justo, en todo ó en parte, qué cantidad debe el Gobierno de Chile pagar al Gobierno de los Estados Unidos de América como indemnización y completa cancelación de dicho reclamo ?

C) Si se decidiere que el Gobierno de Chile debe pagar al de Estados Unidos de América una suma determinada por dicha reclamación, deberá también el citado Gobierno abonar intereses sobre el capital, y en caso de afirmativa, cuál es la tasa del interés y desde qué fecha habra de pagarse ?

D) Deberá pagarse la suma total del fallo, inclusos intereses, en oro americano ó en moneda de Chile ?

Art. II°. Las Partes Contratantes convienen además en que el señor Don Carlos F. Levenhagen decida las anteriores cuestiones en vista de la correspondencia que ha mediado entre los Representantes de los dos Gobiernos en Washington y en Santiago y de los documentos y pruebas aducidos durante la controversia sobre la materia de este embargo y detención, y en vista de un memorial ó alegato que ambos deben presentar. Cada Parte debe suministrar al Arbitro una copia de la referida correspondencia y documentos, ó de aquella parte de ellos que desee presentar, como también el memorial antes aludido, dentro del plazo de un año á mas tardar, contándose éste desde la fecha en que respectivamente se le notificare la aceptación del Arbitro. Cada parte debe asimismo suministrár á la otra una lista de los papeles que va á presentar, con una anticipación de tres meses á dicha presentación.

Y si alguna de las Partes omitiere presentar una copia de tales papeles ó el referido memorial al árbitro dentro de los tres meses estipulados éste procederá á fallar en vista de los documentos que se le hubieren presentado dentro de ese término.

Art. III°. Cada uno de los Gobiernos representados por las Partes Contratantes se compromete y obliga de la manera más solemne á someterse y cumplir la decisión del Arbitro y á no suscitar en ningún tiempo después cuestión alguna directa ó indirectamente relacionada con el asunto que es materia del arbitraje.

Art. IV°. El presente protocolo, una vez aprobada por el Gobierno de los Estados Unidos de América y el de Chile, previa su aceptación por el Congreso Nacional de esta República, tendrá la fuerza y valor de una Convención regular, y las ratificaciones se conjearán dentro de doce meses contados desde esta fecha, ó antes si fuere posible, en esta ciudad de Santiago.

En fe de lo cual, las Partes Contratantes han firmado y sellado este Protocolo, por duplicado, en los idiomas español é inglés, en Santiago, el día seis de Diciembre de mil ochocientos setenta y tres.

Acta adicional al protocolo de 6 de Diciembre de 1873, firmada en Santiago, Mayo 4, 1874.

Reunidos en el Departamento de Relaciones Exteriores de Chile el señor Don Adolfo Háñez, Ministro de Estado en dicho Departamento, y el señor Don Cornelio A. Logan, Enviado Extraordinario y Ministro Plenipotenciario de los Estados Unidos de Norte América, exhibieron los respectivos plenos poderes que les facultaban para celebrar el Protocolo con fuerza de Convención ajustado en Diciembre último, y convinieron en el siguiente artículo, en vista de los motivos que les asistian para creer que degraciadamente no seria posible al señor Levenhagen aceptar el cargo de Arbitro que por el dicho Protocolo se le defiere.

Art. UNICO. En lugar del señor Don Carlos Fernando Levenhagen, Ministro residente del Imperio Germánico, designado en el articulo I° del Protocolo de 6 de Diciembre de 1873 como Arbitro para resolver la cuestión pendiente entre Chile y los Estados Unidos, con motivo de la detención de la fragata *Good Return* las Partes Contratantes acuerdan nombrar al señor Conde Fabio Sanminiatelli, Encargado de Negocios de Italia, para que decida dicha cuestión con las mismas facultades que señala al señor Levenhagen el referido Protocolo.

En fe de lo cual el señor Ministro de Relaciones Exteriores y el señor Enviado Extraordinario y Ministro Plenipotenciario de los Estados Unidos de Norte América firmaron y sellaron por duplicado, en los idiomas español é inglés, la presente Acta, en Santiago, á cuatro días del mes de Mayo de mil ochocientos setenta y cuatro [1].

[1] *Recopilación de Tratados y Convenciones*, 1894, t. II, p. 82-87.

LXV. Argentine, Paraguay.

3 février 1876.

La question ici soulevée avait pour but l'attribution définitive d'un territoire limitrophe des deux pays intéressés. La sentence intervenue attribua ce territoire au Paraguay.

Tratado de limites entre la Republica Argentina y la del Paraguay. Buenos Aires, 3 Febrero de 1876.

Los infrascritos, Ministros Plenipotenciarios de la República Argentina y de la del Paraguay, nombrados por sus respectivos Gobiernos para celebrar el Tratado de limites pendiente entre ambas Repúblicas, habiendo canjeado sus respectivos Plenos Poderes, y halládolos en buena y debida forma, convinieron en lo siguiente:

ART. I. — La República del Paragnay se divide por la parte del Este y Sud de la República Argentina, por la mitad de la corriente del canal principal del Rio Paraná desde su confluencia con el Rio Paraguay hasta encontrar por su márgen izquierda los limites del Imperio del Brasil, perteneciendo la Isla de Apipé á la República Argentina, y la Isla de Yaciretá á la del Paraguay, como se declaró en el Tratado de 1856.

ART. II. — Por la parte del Oeste, la República del Paraguay se divide de la República Argentinia por la mitad de la corriente del canal principal de Rio Paraguay desde su confluencia con el Rio Paraná, quedando reconocida definitivamente como perteneciente á la República Argentina el territorio del Chaco hastá el canal principal del Rio Pilcomayo, que desemboca en el Rio Paraguay en los 25° 20′ de latitud sud, segun el mapa de Mouchez y 25° 22′ segun el de Brayer.

ART. III. — Pertenece al dominio de la República Argentina la Isla del Atajo o Cerrito. Las demás islas firmes o anegadizas que se encuentran en uno u otro rio, Paraná y Paraguay, pertenecen á la República Argentina ó á la del Paraguay, segun sea su situacion mas adyacente al territorio de una ú otra República, con arreglo á los principios de Derecho International que rijen esta materia. Los canales que existen entre dichas islas, inclusa la del Cerrito, son comunes para la navegacion de ambos Estados.

ART. IV. — El territorio comprendido entre el brazo principal del Pilcomayo y Bahiá Negra se considerará dividido en dos secciones, siendo la primera la comprendida entre Bahiá Négra y el Rio Verde, que se halla en los 23° 10′ de latitud sud, segun el mapa de Mouchez; y la segunda, la comprendida entre el mismo Rio Verde y el brazo principal del Pilcomayo, incluyendose en esta seccion la Villa-Occidental.

El Gobierno Argentino renuncia definitivamente a toda pretension ó derecho sobre la primera seccion.

La propriedad ó derecho en el territorio de la segunda seccion, inclusa la Villa-Occidental, queda sometido á la decision definitiva de un fallo arbitral.

ART. V. — Las dos Altas Partes Contratantes convienen en elegir al Exmo. señor Presidente de los Estados Unidos de Norte América, como Arbitro para resolver sobre el dominio á la segunda seccion del territorio á que se refiere el articulo que precede.

ART. VI. — En el termino de sesenta dias, contados desde el canje del presente Tratado, las Partes Contratantes se dirijirán conjunta ó separadamente al árbitro nombrado, solicitando su aceptacion.

ART. VII. — Si el Exmo. señor Presidente de los Estados Unidos no aceptase el cargo de Juez Arbitro, las Partes Contratantes deberón concurrir á elegir otro árbitro, dentro de los sesenta dias siguientes al recibo de la excusacion; y si alguna de las partes no concurriese en el plazo desígnado á verificar el nombramiento, se entenderá hecho definitivamente por la Parte que lo haya verificado y notificado á la otra. En este caso, la resolucion que el árbitro pronuncie será plenamente obligatoria, como si hubiese sido nombrado de comun acuerdo por ambas Partes, pues la omision de una ó de ellas en el nombramiento, importa delegar en la otra el derecho de hacerlo. El mismo plazo de sesenta dias y las mismas condiciones rejirán en el caso de ulteriores excusaciones.

ART. VIII. — Aceptado el nombramiento de árbitro, el Gobierno de República Argentina, y el del Paraguay le presentarón en el termino de doce meses, contados desde la aceptacion del cargo, Memorias que contengan la exposicion de los derechos con que cada uno se considera al territorio cuestionado, acompañando cada Parte todos los documentos, titulos, mapas, citas, referencias y cuantos antecedentes juzguen favorables á sus derechos, siendo convenido que al vencimiento del expresado plazo de doce meses quedárá cerrada definitivamente la discusion para las Partes, cualquiera que sea la razon que aleguen en contrario.

Solo el árbitro nombrado podrá, despues de vencido el plazo, mandar agregar los documentos ó títulos que juzgue necesarios para ilustrar su juicio, ó para fundar el fallo que está llamado á pronunciar.

ART. IX. — Si en el plazo estipulado, alguna de las Partes Contratantes no exhibiese la Memoria, titulos y documentos que favorezcan sus pretensiones, el árbitro fallará en vista de los que haya exhibido la otra Parte y de los Memorandum presentados por el Ministro Argentino y por el Ministro Paraguayo en el año de 1873 y demas documentos diplomaticos cambiados en la negociacion del año citado. Si ninguno los hubiése presentado, el árbitro fallara, teniendo presente en esa eventualidad, como exposicion y documento suficiente, los expresados.

Cualquiera de los Gobiernos Contratantes podrá presentar esos documentos al árbitro.

ART. X. — En los casos previstos en los articulos anteriores, el fallo que se pronuncie será definitivo y obligatorio para Ambas Partes, sin que puedan alegar razon alguna para dificultar su complimiento.

ART. XI. — Queda convenido que durante la prosecucion del juicio arbitral y hasta su terminacion, no se hará innovacion en la seccion sometida á arbitraje, y que, si se produjese algun hecho de posesion ántes del fallo, il no tendrá valor alguno ni podrá ser alegado en la discusion como un titulo nuevo. Queda igualmente convenido que las nuevas concesiones que se hagan por el Gobierno Argentino en la Villa Occidental, no podrán ser invocadas como titulo á su favor, importando unicamente la continuacion del ejercicio de la jurisdiccion que hoy tiene, y que continuara hasta el fallo arbitral, para no impedir el progreso de aquella localidad en beneficio del Estado á quien sea adjudicada definitivamente.

ART. XII. — Es convenido que si el fallo arbitral fuese en favor de la República Argentina, esta respetará los derechos de propriedad y posesion emanados del Gobierno del Paraguay é indemnizará a este el valor de sus edificios públicos, y si fuese en favor del Paraguay, este respetará igualmente los derechos de propriedad y de posesion emanados del Gobierno Argentino, indemnizando tambien á la República Argentina el valor de sus edificios publicos.

El monto de esta indemnizacion y la forma de su pago serán determinados por los Comisarios que nombrarán las Partes Contratantes, á los seis meses de pronunciado el fallo arbitral. Estos dos Comisarios, en caso de desinteligencia, nombrarán por si solos un tercero para dirimir las diferencias.

ART. XIII. — Los reconocimientos de territorios hechos por los dos paises, no podrán desvirtuar los derechos ó titulos que directa ó indirectamente puedan servirle en cuanto al territorio sujeto á arbitraje.

Art. XIV. — El canje de las ratificaciones del presente Tratado tendrá lugar en la ciudad de Buenos-Aires dentro del mas breve plazo posible.

En fe de lo cual los Plenipotenciarios firmaron el presente Tratado por duplicado, y lo sellaron en la ciudad de Buenos-Aires, á los tres dias del mes de Febrero y año de mil ochocientos sententa y seis.[1]

Award pronounced by the President of the United States of America, on the Argentine Paraguayan Boundary, Washington, November 12, 1878.

Rutherford B. Hayes, President of the United States of America, to all to whom these presents may come, Greetings:

Whereas, pursuant to the fourth article of the treaty of limits between the Argentine Republic and the Republic of Paraguay, of the 3d of February, one thousand eight hundred and seventy six, it was stipulated that ownership in or right to the territory between the river Verde and the principal arm of the Pilcomayo river, including the city of Villa Occidental, should be submitted to the definite decision of an arbitration.

And whereas, by the fifth article of the same instrument, the two High Contracting Parties agreed te select the President of the United States of America as umpire to decide as to the right to possess the said above described territory.

And whereas the High Contracting Parties have, within the stipulated time, presented their invitation to the proposed umpire, which was accepted by him, and have, also, duly presented their respective memoirs, and the documents, titles, maps, quotations, references, and all the antecedents which they judge favorable to their rights, as provided in the sixth and eighth articles of the said treaty;

Now, therefore, be it known, that I, Rutherford B. Hayes, President of the United States of America, having duly considered the said statements and the said exhibits, do hereby determine that the said Republic of Paraguay is legally and justly entitled to the said territory between the Pilcomayo and the Verde Rivers, and to the Villa Occidental, situated therein, and I, therefore, do hereby award to the said Republic of Paraguay, the territory on the western bank of the river of that name, between the Rio Verde and the main branch of the Pilcomayo, including Villa Occidental.

In testimony whereof I have hereunto set my hand and caused the seal of the United States to be affixed.

[1] *Coleccion de tratados celebrados por la Republica Argentina*, t. III, p. 79.

Done in triplicate, in the city of Washington, the twelfth day of November, in the year of our Lord one thousand eight hundred and seventy eight, and of the Independence of the United States of America the one hundred and third[1].

LXVI. France, Nicaragua.

15 octobre 1879.

Cette contestation, qui a eu pour objet une confiscation d'armes par les autorités du Nicaragua, est particulièrement intéressante par le fait que la solution du litige a été confiée à une juridiction préexistante, la Cour de Cassation de France. Une indemnité de 40,320 francs fut accordée par elle.

Protocole conclu pour le règlement par voie d'arbitrage d'une confiscation d'armes, signé à Paris, le 15 octobre 1879.

Au mois de novembre 1874, un certain nombre de caisses d'armes ont été confisquées par les autorités du Nicaragua à bord du navire français le *Phare*, mouillé à Corinto ; cette mesure a été confirmée par le pouvoir judiciaire. Le capitaine du bâtiment, M. Alard, a protesté contre la saisie comme contraire au droit des gens et au traité de commerce et d'amitié conclu entre les deux pays. Le gouvernement français a cru devoir intervenir pour appuyer la réclamation et obtenir la réparation du préjudice souffert par son national. Les pourparlers suivis par la voie diplomatique s'étant prolongés sans amener une entente, le gouvernement du Nicaragua a proposé de soumettre le différend à l'arbitrage de la Cour de Cassation de Paris.

Le gouvernement français, voulant témoigner également des sentiments d'amitié et de conciliation qui l'animent, a acquiescé à cette proposition et s'est assuré que la Cour de Cassation de Paris consent à se charger du mandat dont il s'agit. La délibération du 29 avril 1879, dont une copie est annexée à la présente déclaration constate l'adhésion de la Cour en indiquant les formes dans lesquelles elle entend procéder.

En conséquence, les soussignés, dûment autorisés, conviennent, au nom de leurs gouvernements respectifs, de s'en remettre à l'arbitrage de la Cour de Cassation.

La dite Cour aura tout pouvoir pour apprécier l'ensemble des faits qui ont motivé la réclamation et qui, d'après le gouvernement français, engagent la responsabilité de la République du Nicaragua. Elle aura également tout pouvoir

dans le cas où le Nicaragua serait déclaré responsable pour fixer l'indemnité qui devra être payée au capitaine Alard. Les deux gouvernements s'engagent à faire toutes diligences nécessaires pour entamer, aussitôt que possible, la procédure indiquée dans la délibération ci-annexée de la Cour et pour assurer ensuite l'exécution de la sentence arbitrale qui interviendra et qui constituera une décision souveraine et sans recours.

En foi de quoi les parties susmentionnées ont signé le présent compromis. Fait à Paris, en double expédition, le 15 octobre 1879[1].

Décision arbitrale de la Cour de Cassation de France du 29 juillet 1880.

Sur l'exception de chose jugée opposée par la République du Nicaragua et tirée de l'arrêt rendu le 14 juin 1876 par la cour suprême de justice de Léon, dans la procédure suivie contre le capitaine William Alard.

Attendu que le différend, dont le règlement est soumis à l'arbitrage de la cour, s'est produit entre le gouvernement français et la République du Nicaragua à l'occasion de la saisie, pratiquée à bord du navire le *Phare* par les autorités de Corinto, d'armes et de munitions appartenant au capitaine Alard ; que le gouvernement français, considérant cet acte comme contraire aux droits des gens et aux stipulations du traité de commerce conclu le 11 avril 1859 avec le Nicaragua, avait vainement réclamé, dans les conditions voulues par l'article 35 dudit traité, la réparation du dommage causé à l'un de ses nationaux ; et que c'est à la suite d'une longue correspondance et alors que la discussion diplomatique devait être considérée comme épuisée, que le Gouvernement du Nicaragua a proposé, pour terminer le différend, de le soumettre à l'arbitrage de la Cour de Cassation de France ; que la proposition ayant été agréée, il a été passé entre les parties, le 15 octobre 1879, un compromis dont les termes, absolument conformes aux conventions constatées par la correspondance diplomatique fixent nettement l'objet même de l'arbitrage et précisent sans équivoque les pouvoirs que, d'un commun accord les parties ont entendu conférer à la Cour ; qu'il a été expressément convenu par ledit compromis que la Cour aurait tout pouvoir non seulement pour apprécier l'ensemble des faits qui ont motivé la réclamation, mais encore, dans le cas où le Nicaragua serait reconnu responsable, pour fixer l'indemnité qui devait être payée au capitaine Alard ; qu'en présence de telles dispositions, il est impossible de ne pas reconnaitre qu'il a été dans la commune

---

[1] J. B. MOORE, *History and Digest...*, p. 1943.

[1] ROUARD DE CARD, *Destinées de l'Arbitrage International*, 1892. p. 236.

intention des deux gouvernements d'investir le tribunal arbitral de la toute puissance de juridiction à l'effet de reprendre et d'apprécier les faits litigeux dans leur ensemble et de prononcer définitivement sur le différend qui s'est produit entre eux, abstraction faite de ce qui a pu être décidé par l'autorité judiciaire du Nicaragua vis-à-vis du capitaine Alard.

Rejette la fin de non recevoir.

Et statuant au fond :

Attendu qu'il résulte des documents produits que le capitaine Alard, parti de Bordeaux sur le navire le *Phare*, à la fin de l'année 1873, a été rejoint en juin 1874, à Amapala (Honduras), par la barque française le *Jean Pierre* qui lui apportait un certain nombre de caisses contenant des fusils de guerre dits *riffles* avec un approvisionnement de cartouches ; que ces caisses, transbordées sur le *Phare* se trouvaient à son bord lorsqu'à trois reprises différentes, les 18 juin, 6 octobre et 17 novembre, le navire a jeté l'ancre à Corinto, port principal de la République du Nicaragua, que, peu de jours après l'entrée du navire dans le port, lors de cette dernière relâche, ces armes et munitions ont été saisies à bord par les autorités du Corinto ;

Attendu que, suivant la prétention du Nicaragua, la saisie serait justifiée : 1° en ce que, contrairement aux prohibitions de la législation locale, le capitaine Alard aurait introduit lesdites armes et munitions en contrebande dans le port de Corinto ; 2° en ce qu'il aurait tenté de les introduire sur le territoire du Nicaragua ;

Attendu, quant au premier motif, que la législation locale, notamment le décret exécutif du 3 juillet 1849 et la loi fédérale de douane du 27 février 1837 autorisent d'une manière générale la saisie de tous objets non portés au manifeste, et, en outre, que, tenant comme délit de contrebande le commerce des articles dont l'importation est prohibée, ils autorisent spécialement la saisie des armes introduites sans la permission préalable du gouvernement, leur introduction n'étant licite, aux termes desdites lois, qu'autant qu'elle est autorisée ;

Mais attendu qu'il n'est pas établi qu'il y ait eu de la part du capitaine Alard manquement aux prescriptions de la loi, soit en ce qui concerne les obligations relatives au manifeste, soit par rapport au règlement sur l'introduction des armes de guerre ;

Que d'une part, en effet, les armes saisies figuraient au manifeste du 16 novembre 1874, lequel portait expressément « quarante caisses de fusils, deux colis de revolvers, trois caisses de cartouches » ; qu'à la vérité ces indications détaillées ne se trouvent pas dans les manifestes des 18 juin et 6 octobre, relatifs aux deux précédents voyages ; mais qu'en admettant qu'il y ait eu omission et insuffisance dans les deux manifestes, l'irrégularité aurait été couverte par le manifeste ultérieur du 16 novembre et n'aurait pu en tout cas, dès que le capitaine Alard s'était mis en règle, justifier la saisie qui n'aurait été juste et légitime qu'autant qu'elle aurait eu lieu au moment où le délit était commis et aurait pu être constaté ;

Que d'autre part, ce qui constitue l'introduction par les ports ou dans les ports, c'est, non point le fait seul d'entrer dans le port, mais celui de franchir la ligne de douane et de transporter la marchandise dans l'intérieur du pays ; que l'article 11 de la loi fédérale, qui interdit toute communication « avec le port » jusqu'au dépôt du manifeste, indique par lui-même que ce que la loi entend par le port, c'est la ville et non pas l'espace où mouillent les navires ; qu'il ne saurait donc y avoir introduction frauduleuse de la part du navire qui entre dans le port et se soumet aux formalités de la douane maritime ; que telle était la situation du *Phare* aux 22 et 30 novembre, dates de la saisie ; qu'il appartenait sans doute à l'autorité locale, si elle jugeait dangereuse à un titre quelconque la présence des armes dans le port de Corinto, de refuser au capitaine l'autorisation de les y conserver ; mais qu'elle ne pouvait, alors que l'existence de ces armes à bord était régulièrement relevée par le manifeste, en opérer la saisie sous prétexte d'introduction frauduleuse ;

Attendu, quand au motif tiré de la tentative d'introduction clandestine, que l'article 53 du décret du 22 juillet 1861, portant règlement pour le dépôt à la douane de Corinto, rappelle que la saisie aura lieu pour les articles que « l'on tentera » d'introduire clandestinement ; qu'ainsi et en droit, la tentative d'introduction est, aussi bien que l'introduction consommée, susceptible de justifier la saisie ; mais qu'il faut au moins que la tentative soit établie dans ses caractères constitutifs ; que, suivant le Nicaragua, les actes qui imprimeraient ce caractère au fait imputé consisteraient : 1° en ce que les armes, restées à bord du *Phare* depuis le mois de juin jusqu'au 22 novembre 1874, date du premier acte de la saisie, n'ont été manifestées ni le 18 juin, lors de la première relâche du *Phare* à Corinto, ni le 6 octobre, lors du second voyage ; 2° en ce que, lors de ce dernier voyage, au moment où le *Phare* entrait dans le port de Corinto, le capitaine en second se serait avancé dans une embarcation pour demander au commandant du port la permission, qui lui a été refusée, de jeter l'ancre près la pointe de Castanones ; 3° en ce que, enfin, lors de ce même voyage, un fusil aurait été remis au sieur Pedro Brenes et envoyé par ce dernier comme échantillon, au sieur Guyot, commissionnaire du capitaine Alard à Léon, mais que ces faits, même en admettant qu'ils aient été accomplis dans l'intention prêtée par le gouvernement du Nicaragua au capitaine Alard d'introduire clandestinement des armes de guerre dans le port ou sur le territoire de la République, constitueraient de simples actes préparatoires et ne pourraient être considérés comme commencement d'exécution ou comme tentative punissable, qui, seule, aurait pu justifier la saisie que le gouvernement du Nicaragua a cru devoir ordonner ;

Attendu que de tout ce qui précède il résulte que le dommage causé au capitaine Alard, dans sa propriété, n'est expliqué par aucun fait légalement et juridiquement imputable à ce dernier; que si, néanmoins, le gouvernement du Nicaragua s'est déterminé à ordonner la mesure dommageable, il apparaît nettement de toute sa correspondance diplomatique et des témoignages recueillis dans l'instruction suivie à Corinto, que c'est dans un but purement politique, dans une pensée de conservation sociale, en vue d'éviter que les armes saisies tombassent aux mains du parti révolutionnaire dont le gouvernement se préoccupait alors de déjouer les manœuvres et les projets ; que si, prises dans telles conditions, les mesures de cette nature constituent des actes de légitime défense, il reste cependant qu'elles ne sauraient être accomplies que sous la responsabilité du gouvernement qui a cru devoir les prendre et sous l'obligation de réparer vis-à-vis de ceux qui en sont victimes le dommage qu'elles ont pu causer; qu'à ce point de vue, dès lors, et dans cet ordre d'idées, le gouvernement du Nicaragua doit être déclaré responsable;

Attendu, en ce qui concerne l'indemnité à payer au capitaine Alard, que les documents produits et spécialement les expertises, qui ont eu lieu à Corinto, fournissent les éléments nécessaires pour en fixer le chiffre, et qu'en allouant au capitaine Alard : 1° la somme de 39,720 fr. pour le prix des fusils existant à bord du *Phare*, à la date de la saisie à raison de 40 fr. chacun ; 2° celle de 600 fr. à laquelle il a lui-même fixé la valeur des capsules saisies, il lui sera alloué une indemnité suffisante ;

Par ces motifs, déclare le gouvernement du Nicaragua responsable ;

Fixe en conséquence l'indemnité à payer au capitaine Alard à la somme totale de 40,320 francs avec intérêts pour tous dommages, à raison de 12 pour cent par an, à partir du 30 novembre 1874, date du dernier acte de la saisie ;

Met les dépens à la charge du gouvernement du Nicaragua[1].

---

[1] Rouard de Card, *Ibid.*, p. 237.

LXVII. Etats-Unis d'Amérique, France.

15 janvier 1880.

Il s'agit en espèce d'une des nombreuses commissions arbitrales instituées pour l'examen de dommages réciproques soufferts par des citoyens des pays intéressés. Dans la présente affaire 726 réclamations furent dirigées contre les Etats-Unis d'Amérique et 19 seulement contre la France. Pour les premières, il fut accordé 319.595 $ 02 en principal et 305.971 $ 33 pour intérêts; pour les secondes, principal et intérêts se montèrent à 13.659 $ 14. Le montant des réclamations à charge des Etats-Unis d'Amérique avait été de 35.000.000 $ environ.

Convention instituant une commission arbitrale pour statuer sur des demandes réciproques d'indemnités, signée à Washington, le 15 janvier 1880.

La République Française et les Etats-Unis d'Amérique, animés du désir de régler par un arrangement amical les réclamations élevées par les citoyens de chacun des deux pays contre le gouvernement de l'autre et résultant d'actes commis pendant l'état de guerre ou d'insurrection, par les autorités civiles et militaires de l'un ou de l'autre pays, dans les circonstances spécifiées ci-après, ont résolu de prendre des mesures à cet effet, au moyen, d'une convention et ont désigné comme leurs plénipotentiaires pour conférer et établir un accord, savoir : M. le Président de la République Française, M. Georges Maxime Outrey, envoyé extraordinaire et ministre plénipotentiaire de France à Washington, et le Président des Etats-Unis, M. William Maxwell Ewarts, secrétaire d'Etat aux Etats-Unis, lesquels, après s'être communiqué leurs pleins pouvoirs respectifs et les avoir trouvés en bonne et due forme, sont convenus des articles suivant :

ART. I. — Toutes les réclamations élevées par des corporations, des compagnies ou de simples particuliers, citoyens des Etats-Unis, contre le gouvernement français et résultant d'actes commis en haute mer ou sur le territoire de la France, de ses colonies et dépendances, pendant la dernière guerre entre la France et le Mexique ou pendant celle de 1870—71 entre la France et l'Allemagne, et pendant les troubles civils subséquents connus sous le nom « d'insurrection de la commune », par les autorités civiles ou militaires françaises, au préjudice des personnes ou de la propriété de citoyens des Utats-Unis, non au service des ennemis de la France et qui ne leur ont prêté volontairement ni aide ni assistance, et d'autre part, toutes les réclamations élevées par des corporations, des compagnies ou de simples particuliers citoyens français, contre le Gouvernement des Etats-Unis et fondées sur les actes commis en haute mer et sur le territoire des Etats-Unis pendant la période comprise entre le 13 avril 1861 et le 20 août 1866, par les autorités civiles ou militaires du Gouvernement des Etats-Unis, au préjudice des personnes ou de la propriété de citoyens français, non au service des ennemis du Gouvernement des Etats-Unis et qui ne leur ont prêté volontairement ni aide ni assistance, seront soumises à trois commissaires, dont un sera nommé par le Gouvernement français, un autre par le Président des Etats-Unis et le troisième par S. M. l'Empereur du Brésil.

ART. II. — La dite commission ainsi constituée aura compétence et devra statuer sur toutes les réclamations ayant le caractère ci-dessus indiqué, présentées par les citoyens de chacun des deux pays, sauf sur celles que l'un ou l'autre gouvernement aurait déjà fait régler diplomatiquement, judiciairement ou autrement par les autorités compétentes. Mais aucune réclamation ni article de torts ou de dommages fondés sur la perte ou l'émancipation d'esclaves ne seront examinés par la dite commission.

ART. III. — Dans les cas de mort, d'absence prolongée, d'incapacité de servir de l'un des dits commissionnaires, ou dans le cas où l'un des dits commissionnaires négligerait, refuserait ou cesserait de remplir ses fonctions, le Gouvernement français, ou le Président des Etats-Unis, ou S. M. l'Empereur du Brésil suivant le cas, devra remplir la vacance ainsi occasionnée, en nommant un nouveau commissaire dans les trois mois à dater du jour où la vacance se serait produite.

ART. IV. — Les commissaires, nommés conformément aux dispositions précédentes, se réuniront dans la ville de Washington, aussitôt qu'il leur sera possible, dans les six mois qui suivront l'échange des ratifications de cette convention, et leur premier acte, aussitôt après leur réunion, sera de signer une déclaration solennelle qu'ils examineront et décideront avec soin et impartialité, au mieux de leur jugement, conformément au droit public, à la justice et à l'équité, sans crainte, faveur, ni affection, toutes les réclamations comprises dans les termes et la véritable signification des articles 1 et 2, qui leur seront soumises de la part des deux gouvernements de France et des Etats-Unis respectivement; cette déclaration sera consignée au procès-verbal de leurs travaux. Il est entendu d'ailleurs que le jugement rendu par deux commissaires sera suffisant pour toutes les décisions intermédiaires, qu'ils auront

à prendre dans l'accomplissement de leurs fonctions, comme pour chaque décision finale.

ART. V. — Les commissaires devront procéder sans délai, après l'organisation de la commission, à l'examen et au jugement des réclamations spécifiées par les articles précédents; ils donneront avis aux gouvernements respectifs du jour de leur organisation, en leur faisant savoir qu'ils sont en mesure de procéder aux travaux de la commission. Ils devront examiner et juger les dites réclamations en tel ordre et telle façon qu'ils jugeront convenable, mais seulement sur les preuves et informations fournies par les gouvernements respectifs ou en leur nom. Ils seront tenus de recevoir et de prendre en considération tous les documents ou exposés écrits qui leur seront présentés par les gouvernements respectifs ou en leur nom à l'appui de ou en réponse à toute réclamation et d'entendre, s'ils en sont requis, une personne de chaque côté que les deux Gouvernements auront le droit de désigner comme leur conseil ou agent pour présenter et soutenir les réclamations en leur nom dans chaque affaire prise séparément. Chacun des deux Gouvernements devra fournir à la requête des commissaires ou de deux d'entre-eux, les pièces en sa possession qui peuvent être importantes pour la juste détermination de toute réclamation portée devant la commission.

ART. VI. — Les décisions unanimes des commissaires ou de deux d'entre eux seront concluantes et définitives. Les dites décisions devront dans chaque affaire, être rendues par écrit, séparément sur chaque réclamation, et fixer, dans le cas où une indemnité pécuniaire serait accordée, le montant ou la valeur équivalente de cette indemnité en monnaie d'or de France ou des Etats-Unis, suivant le cas, et, si le jugement allouait des intérêts, le taux et la période pour laquelle ils devront être comptés seront également déterminés, cette période ne pouvant s'étendre au-delà de la durée de la commission; les dites décisions devront être signées par les commissaires qui y auront concouru.

ART. VII. — Les hautes parties contractantes s'engagent par le présent acte, à considérer la décision des commissaires ou de deux d'entre eux, comme absolument définitive et concluante dans chaque affaire réglée par eux et à donner plein effet à ces décisons, sans objection ni délai évasifs d'aucune nature.

ART. VIII. — Toutes les réclamations devront être présentées aux commissaires dans une période de six mois à dater du jour où ils se seront réunis pour commencer leurs travaux après avis donné aux gouvernements respectifs, conformément aux dispositions de l'article 5 de cette convention. Toutefois, dans tous les cas où l'on

ferait valoir de justes motifs de délai à la satisfaction des commissaires ou de deux d'entre eux,
le temps, où la réclamation sera valablement
présentée, pourra être étendu par eux à une
période qui ne devra point excéder un terme additionnel de trois mois.

Les commissaires seront tenus d'examiner et
de rendre une décision sur toutes les réclamations,
dans les deux ans à dater du jour de leur première réunion ci-dessus, ce délai ne pourra être
étendu que dans le cas où les travaux de la
commission seraient interrompus par la mort, l'incapacité de servir, la démission ou la cessation
des fonctions de l'un des commissaires. Dans
cette eventualité, le temps, où une pareille interruption aura existé de fait, ne sera point compté
dans le terme de deux ans ci-dessus fixé.

Il appartiendra aux commissaires de décider,
dans chaque affaire, si la réclamation a ou n'a
pas été dûment faite, présentée et soumise, soit
dans son entier soit en partie, conformément à
l'esprit et à la véritable signification de la convention.

ART. IX. — Toutes sommes d'argent qui pourraient être allouées par les commissaires, en vertu
des dispositions précédentes, devront être versées
par l'un des Gouvernements à l'autre, suivant le
cas, dans la capitale du Gouvernement qui devra recevoir le paiement, dans les douze mois
qui suivront la date du jugement final, sans intérêts ni autres déductions que celles spécifiées
dans l'article X.

ART. X. — Les commissaires devront tenir
un procès-verbal exact et conserver des minutes
ou notes correctes et datées de tous leurs travaux;
les Gouvernements de France et des Etats-Unis
pourront chacun nommer et employer un secrétaire versé dans le langage des deux pays, et
les commissaires pourront nommer tels autres
employés qu'ils jugeront nécessaires pour les
aider dans l'expédition des affaires qui viendront
devant eux.

Chaque Gouvernement paiera ses propres
commissaires, secrétaire et agent de conseil, et la
compensation qui leur sera allouée devra être
égale ou équivalente, autant que possible des
deux côtés, pour les fonctionnaires de même
rang. Toutes les autres dépenses, y compris l'allocation du troisième commissaire, seront supportées par les deux Gouvernements en parties
égales.

Les dépenses générales de la commission, y
compris les dépenses éventuelles, seront couvertes
par une déduction proportionnelle sur le montant
des sommes allouées par les commissaires. Il est
bien entendu, toutefois, que cette retenue ne

devra pas excéder cinq pour cent des sommes
accordées.

Si les dépenses générales excédaient ce taux,
le surplus serait supporté conjointement par les
deux Gouvernements

ART. XI. — Les hautes parties contractantes
sont convenues de considérer le résultat de la
commission instituée par cette convention comme
un règlement complet, parfait et définitif, de toutes
et de chacune des réclamations contre l'une d'elles,
conformément aux termes et à la vraie signification des articles 1 et 2, de telle sorte que
toute réclamation de cette nature, qu'elle ait été
ou non portée à la connaissance des commissaires,
qu'elle leur ait ou non été présentée et soumise,
devra à dater de la fin des travaux de la dite
commission, être tenue et considérée comme
définitivement réglée, décidée et éteinte.

ART. XII. — La présente convention sera
ratifiée par le Président de la République Française et par le Président des Etats-Unis, par et
avec l'avis et le consentement du Sénat, et les
ratifications seront échangées à Washington, au
jour le plus rapproché qu'il sera possible dans
les neuf mois à partir de la date du présent acte.

**Convention additionnelle à la convention du 15 janvier 1880
pour le règlement de certaines réclamations pour
dommages de guerre, signée à Washington, le 19 juillet 1882.**

Le Gouvernement de la République Française
et le Gouvernement des Etats-Unis d'Amérique
ayant acquis la conviction que les travaux de la
commission, pour le règlement des réclamations
des citoyens de chacun des deux pays contre le
gouvernement de l'autre, qui a été institué par
la convention entre les deux gouvernements, signée
à Washington, le 15 janvier 1880, ne peuvent
être terminés au terme fixé par cette convention,
ont résolu de conlure une convention supplémentaire pour prolonger le terme de la durée de la
dite convention jusqu'à une époque ultérieure, et
ont nommé, à cet effet, pour leurs plénipotentiaires, savoir:

Le Président de la République Française,
M. Théodore-Justin-Dominique Roustan, envoyé
extraordinaire et ministre plénipotentiaire de
France à Washington, commandeur de l'ordre
national de la Légion d'honneur, etc., etc., etc.

Le Président des Etats-Unis d'Amérique,
M. Frederick T. Frelinghuysen, secrétaire d'Etat
des Etats-Unis,

Lesquels, après s'être communiqué leurs pleins
pouvoirs trouvés en bonne et due forme, sont
convenus de l'article suivant:

F. DE MARTENS, *Nouveau Recueil Général*, 2ᵐᵉ série,
t. VI, p. 493.

ARTICLE UNIQUE. — Le terme de deux ans fixé par le second paragraphe de l'article 8 de la convention entre la République Française et les Etats-Unis, conclue le 15 janvier 1880, dans lequel les commissaires, nommés en vertu de cette convention, sont astreints à examiner et à juger toute réclamation à eux présentée, est prolongé par le présent acte jusqu'au 1er juillet 1883.

Cette disposition ne peut avoir aucun effet pour étendre ou modifier les délais fixés dans le premier paragraphe du dit article 8 pour la présentation des réclamations, ces délais devant demeurer tels qu'ils ont été fixés.

Si les opérations de la commission sont interrompues par la mort, l'incapacité de siéger, le départ ou la cessation de fonctions de l'un des commissaires, dans ce cas le terme jusqu'auquel la durée de la commission a été prolongée par la présente convention sera calculé défalcation faite du temps pendant lequel la cause de l'interruption aura subsisté.

La présente convention sera ratifiée et les ratifications seront échangées à Washington dans le plus bref délai possible.

En foi de quoi, les plénipotentiaires respectifs ont signé la présente convention, en langue française et en langue anglaise, en duplicata, et l'ont revêtue de leurs sceaux respectifs.

Deuxième convention additionnelle à la convention du 15 janvier 1880 pour le règlement de certaines réclamations pour dommages de guerre, signée à Washington, le 8 février 1883.

Le gouvernement de la République Française et le gouvernement des Etats-Unis d'Amérique ayant acquis la conviction que les travaux de la commission pour le règlement des réclamations des citoyens de chacun des deux pays contre le gouvernement de l'autre, qui a été instituée par la convention entre les deux gouvernements signée à Washington, le 15 janvier 1880, laquelle a été prolongée jusqu'au 1er juillet 1883, en vertu de la convention supplémentaire du 19 juillet 1882, ne peuvent être terminés le 1er juillet 1883, ont résolu de conclure une autre convention supplémentaire pour prolonger le terme de la durée de ladite commission jusqu'à une époque ultérieure et ont nommé à cet effet leurs plénipotentiaires, savoir:

Le Président de la République française, M. Théodore-Justin-Dominique Roustan, envoyé extraordinaire et ministre plénipotentiaire de France à Washington, commandeur de l'ordre national de la Légion d'honneur, etc.

Le Président des Etats-Unis, M. Frederick T. Frelinghuysen, secrétaire d'Etat des Etats-Unis.

Lesquels après s'être communiqués leurs pleins pouvoirs trouvés en bonne et due forme, sont convenus des articles suivants:

ART. 1er. — Le terme de deux ans fixé par le deuxième paragraphe de l'article 8 de la convention entre les Etats-Unis et la République Française, conclue le 15 janvier 1880, dans lequel les commissaires, nommés en vertu de cette convention, sont astreints à examiner et à juger toutes réclamations à eux présentées, lequel a été fixé au 1er juillet 1883, en vertu de la convention supplémentaire du 19 juillet 1882, est prolongé par le présent acte jusqu'au 1er avril 1884.

Cette disposition ne peut avoir aucun effet pour étendre ou modifier les délais fixés dans le premier paragraphe dudit article 8 pour la présentation des réclamations, ces délais devant demeurer tels qu'ils ont été fixés.

Si les opérations de la commission sont interrompues par la mort, l'incapacité de siéger, le départ ou la cessation de fonctions de l'un des commissaires, dans ce cas, le terme jusqu'auquel la durée de la commission a été prolongée par la présente convention sera calculé défalcation faite du temps pendant lequel la cause de l'interruption aura subsiste.

ART. 2. — Aucun témoignage ni aucune preuve à l'appui ou en réponse à une réclamation quelconque ne seront présentés à la commission ou reçus par elle après le 1er juillet 1883.

La présente convention sera ratifiée et les ratifications en seront échangées à Washington dans le plus court délai possible.

En foi de quoi les plénipotentiaires respectifs ont signé la présente convention en langue française et anglaise, en duplicata et l'ont revêtue de leurs sceaux respectifs.

Fait en la ville de Washington, ce huitième jour de février de l'an de grâce mil huit cent quatre-vingt-trois [1].

Final award of the French and American Claims Commission, signed at Washington, March 31, 1884.

We the undersigned Commissioners appointed under, and in pursuance of article I of the Convention between the United States of America and the French Republic concluded the fifteenth day of January, 1880... do now make this our final award of and concerning the matters referred to us by said Convention as follows:

I. We award that the Government of the United States of America shall pay to the Government of the French Republic within twelve

---

[1] F. DE MARTENS. *Nouveau Recueil Général*, 2e série, t. IX, p. 700. — *Treaties and Conventions between the United States and other Powers*, p. 360.

months from the date hereof, the sum of six hundred and twenty five thousand five hundred and sixty-six dollars and thirty five cents ($ 625,566.35) without interest, subject to the deduction provided for by Article X of the Convention aforesaid, for and in full satisfaction of the several claims on the part of corporations, companies. or private individuals, citizens of France upon the Government of the United States arising out of acts committed against the persons or property of citizens of France during the period comprised between the thirteenth day of April, 1861, and the twentieth day of August, 1866, said sum being the aggregate of the principal sums and interest allowed to certain claimants by the several separate awards to that effect made in writing and signed by us, or such of us as assented to said separate awards, which are among the records of this Commission, and are hereby referred to, printed copies of which are hereto annexed.

II. All other such claims on the part of citizens of France against the United States, which have been presented and prosecuted for our award, have been and are hereby disallowed or dismissed, in manner and form as will appear by the several separate awards in writing concerning the same, signed as aforesaid, and which are among the records of the Commission.

III. We award that the Government of the French Republic shall pay to the government of the United States within twelve months from the date hereof the sum of thirteen thousand six hundred and fifty nine francs and fourteen centimes (13,659 fr. 14 cent.) without interest, subject to the deduction provided by Article X of the Convention aforesaid, for and in full satisfaction of the several claims on the part of corporation, companies, or private individuals, citizens of the United States, upon the Government of France, arising out of acts comitted against the persons or property of citizens of the United States during the late war between France and Mexico, or during the war of 1870-1871 between France and Germany, and the subsequent civil disturbance known as the « Insurrection of the Commune », said sum being the aggregate of the principal sums and interest allowed to certain claimants by the several separate awards to that effect made in writing and signed by us, or such of us assented to said separate awards, which are among the records of this Commission, and are hereby referred to, printed copies of which are hereto attached.

IV. All other such claims on the part of citizens of the United States against the Government of the French Republic which have been presented and prosecuted for our award have been and are hereby disallowed or dismissed in manner and form as will appear by the several awards in writing concerning the same, signed as aforesaid, and which are among the records of this Commission.

V. Certain other claims and parts of claims on the part of citizens of France against the United States, and on the part of citizens of the United States against France, were also presented but were afterwards, and before any awards was made thereon, withdrawn by the agent of the United States or by the agent of the French Republic, as will appear by the records of the proceedings of the Commission, printed copies of which, duly approved by the Commissioners, will be delivered to each Government herewith.

VI. And we refer to the several separate awards made and signed as aforesaid, as a part of this, our final award, and to a tabulated statement hereto attached, giving the number of each claim, the name of the claimant, the character of the claim, the place where, and the time when it arose, the amount claimed, the disposition of the claim, and, where an allowance has been made, the principal sum and interest in each case allowed; it being our intent that the proceedings of this Commission shall have the force and effect named and provided in Article XI of said Convention.

Signed at Washington, this thirty first day of March, A. D. 1884.

LXVIII. Grande-Bretagne, Transvaal.

3 août 1881.

La convention de 1881 a prévu la constitution d'une commission qui, en fait, n'a eu à examiner que des réclamations à charge du Transvaal. Elle se réunit dans le courant du mois de décembre et termina ses travaux au mois d'avril suivant.

Convention pour régler les relations politiques, signée le 3 août 1881.

. . . .

ART. VI. Her Majesty's Government will make due compensation for all losses or damage sustained by reason of such acts as are in the 8th Article hereinafter specified, which may have been committed by Her Majesty's forces during the recent hostilities, except for such losses or damage as may already have been compensated for, and the Government of the Transvaal state will make due compensation for all losses or

---

[1] J. B. MOORE. *History and Digest...*, p. 1148.

damage sustained by reason of such acts as are in the 8th Article hereinafter specified which may have been committed by the people who were in arms against Her Majesty during the recent hostilities, except for such losses or damages as may already have been compensated for.

ART. VII. The decision of all claims for compensation, as in the last preceding Article mentioned, will be referred to a sub-commission, consisting of the Honourable George Hudson, the Honourable Jacobus Petrus de Wet, and the Honourable John Gilbert Kotzé. In case one or more of such sub-Commissioners shall be unable or unwilling to act the remaining sub-Commissioner or sub-Commissioners will, after consultation with the Government of the Transvaal state, submit for the approval of Her Majesty's High Commissioners the names of one or more persons to be appointed by them to fill the place or places thus vacated. The decision of the said sub-Commissioners, or of a majority of them, will be final.

The said sub-Commissioners will enter upon and perform their duties with all convenient speed. They will, before taking evidence or ordering evidence to be taken in respect of any claim, decide whether such claim can be entertained at all under the rules laid down in the next succeeding Article. In regard to claims which can be so entertained, the sub-Commissioners will, in the first instance, afford every facility for an amicable arrangement as to the amount payable in respect of any claim, and only, in cases in which there is no reasonable ground for believing that an immediate amicable arrangement can be arrived at, will they take evidence or order evidence to be taken. For the purpose of taking evidence and reporting thereon, the sub-Commissioners may appoint Deputies, who will, without delay, submit records of the evidence and their reports to the sub-Commissioners. The sub-Commissioners will arrange their sittings and the sittings of their Deputies in such a manner as to afford the earliest convenience to the parties concerned and their witness. In no case will costs be allowed to either side, other than the actual and reasonable expenses of witness whose evidence is certified by the sub-Commissioners to have been necessary. Interest will not run on the amount of any claim, except as is hereinafter provided for. The said sub-Commissioners will forthwith, after deciding upon any claim, announce their decision to the Government against which the award is made and to the claimant. The amount of remuneration payable to the sub-Commissioners and their Deputies will be determined by the High Commissioners, after all the claims have been decided upon. The British Government and the government of the Transvaal state will pay proportionate shares of the said remuneration and of the expenses of the sub-Commissioners and their Deputies, according to the amount awarded against them respectively.

ART. VIII. For the purpose of distinguishing claims to be accepted from those to be rejected, the sub-Commissioners will be guided by the following rules, viz.: — Compensation will be allowed for losses or damage sustained by reason of the following acts committed during the recent hostilities, viz.: a) commandeering, seizure, confiscation or destruction of property, or damage done to property; b) violence done or threats used by persons in arms. In regard to acts under a), compensation will be allowed for direct losses only. In regard to acts falling under b), compensation will be allowed for actual losses of property or actual injury to the same proved to have been caused by its inforced abandonment. No claims for indirect losses except such as are in this Article specially provided for will be entertained. No claims which have been handed into the secretary of the Royal Commission after the 1st day of July 1881 will be entertained, unless the sub-Commissioners shall be satisfied that the delay was reasonable. When claims for loss of property are considered, the sub-Commissioners will require distinct proof of the existence of the property and that it neither has reverted nor will revert to the claimant.

ART. IX. The Government of the Transvaal state will pay and satisfy the amount of every claim awarded against in within one month after the sub-Commissioners shall have notified their decision to the said Government, and in default of such payment the said Government will pay interest at the rate of six per cent per annum from the date of such default; but Her Majesty's Government may at any time before such payment, pay the amount, with interest, if any, to the claimant in satisfaction of his claim, and may add the sum thus paid to any debt which may be due by the Transvaal state to Her Majesty's Government, as hereinafter provided for.

. . . .[1]

Les décisions de la commission n'ont pas été publiées et c'est indirectement que la somme mise à charge du Tranvaal a été établie. Dans un rapport fait au Volksraad

---

[1] HERTSLET, A complete collection..., t. XV, p. 406-408; — F. DE MARTENS, Nouveau Recueil Général..., 2ᵉ série, t. VIII (1883), p. 212.

elle est fixée à 136,960 £ 2 sh. 1 d., tandis que dans un rapport du Résident Britannique à Pretoria elle est évaluée à 140,839 £ 10 sh. 11 d.[1]

LXIX. Chili, France.

2 novembre 1882.

C'est une des nombreuses contestations, que le Chili a terminées par le recours à l'arbitrage, du chef des dommages causés à des étrangers par la guerre avec le Pérou et la Bolivie. Une transaction finale termina ce différend en 1887 par le paiement de 300,000 $.

Convention pour la réparation des dommages causés aux Français par les opérations des troupes chiliennes durant la guerre contre le Pérou et la Bolivie, signée à Santiago, le 2 novembre 1882.

Le Président de la République française et Son Excellence le Président de la République du Chili, désirant mettre amicalement un terme aux réclamations introduites par des citoyens français, appuyées par la légation de la République française au Chili, et motivées par les actes et opérations accomplis par les forces de la République du Chili sur les territoires et côtes du Pérou et de la Bolivie durant la présente guerre, ont résolu de conclure une convention d'arbitrage ; et, à cet effet, ils ont nommé pour leurs plénipotentiaires respectifs :

Le Président de la République française, le sieur Adolphe baron d'Avril, ministre plénipotentiaire de Ire classe, officier de l'ordre national de la Légion d'honneur, etc., etc. ;

Et Son Excellence le Président de la République du Chili, le sieur Luis Aldunate, ministre des relations extérieures de la République,

Lesquels plénipotentiaires après avoir examiné et échangé leurs pouvoirs et les avoir trouvés en bonne et due forme sont convenus des articles suivants :

ART. 1er. — Un tribunal arbitral, ou commission mixte internationale, jugera, en la forme et suivant les termes qui seront établis dans la présente convention, toutes les réclamations, qui, motivées par les actes et opérations accomplis par les forces chiliennes de mer et de terre, sur

les territoires et côtes du Pérou et de Bolivie durant la présente guerre, ont été introduites jusqu'à présent ou seront introduites ultérieurement par des citoyens français sous le patronage de la légation de la République française au Chili, dans le délai qui sera indiqué ci-après.

ART. 2. — La commission se composera de trois membres, l'un nommé par le Président de la République française, un autre par le Président de la République du Chili, et le troisième par S. M. l'Empereur du Brésil, soit directement, soit par l'intermédiaire de l'agent diplomatique accrédité par Sa Majesté au Chili.

Dans les cas de mort, absence ou incapacité, pour quelque motif que ce soit, d'un ou de plusieurs des membres de la commission, il sera pourvu à son remplacement dans les formes et conditions respectivement exprimées au paragraphe précédent.

ART. 3. — La commission mixte examinera et jugera les réclamations que les citoyens français ont introduites jusqu'à aujourd'hui ou introduiront ultérieurement par leur organe diplomatique, et motivées par les actes et opérations accomplis par les armées et escadres de la République depuis le quatorze février mil huit cent soixante dix-neuf, date de l'ouverture des hostilités, jusqu'au jour où il sera conclu des traités de paix ou des armistices entre les nations belligérantes, ou jusqu'au jour où auront cessé de fait les hostilités entre les trois nations en guerre.

ART. 4. — La commission mixte accueillera les moyens probatoires ou d'investigation qui, d'après l'appréciation et le juste discernement de ses membres, pourront le mieux conduire à l'éclaircissement des faits controversés et spécialement à la détermination de l'état et du caractère neutre des réclamants.

La commission recevra également les allégations verbales ou écrites des deux gouvernements ou de leurs agents ou défenseurs respectifs.

ART. 5. — Chaque gouvernement pourra constituer un agent qui veille aux intérêts de ses commettants et en prenne la défense ; qui présente des pétitions, documents, interrogatoires ; qui pose des conclusions ou y réponde ; qui appuie ses affirmations et réfute les affirmations contraires ; qui en fournisse les preuves et qui, devant la commission par lui-même ou par l'organe d'un homme de loi, verbalement ou par écrit, conformément aux règles de procédure et aux voies que la commission elle-même arrêtera en commençant ses fonctions, expose les doctrines, principes légaux ou précédents qui conviennent à sa cause.

[1] *Parliamentary Papers*, [C. 3381] p. 104 et 106, [C. 3419] p. 18.

30

ART. 6. — La commission mixte jugera les réclamations d'après la valeur de la preuve fournie et conformément aux principes du droit international, ainsi qu'à la pratique et à la jurisprudence établies par les tribunaux récents analogues ayant le plus d'autorité et de prestige, en prenant ses résolutions, tant interlocutoires que définitives, à la majorité des votes.

Dans chaque jugement définitif, la commission exposera brièvement les faits et causalités de la réclamation, les motifs allégués à l'appui ou en contradiction et les bases sur lesquelles s'appuient ses résolutions.

Les résolutions et jugements de la commission seront écrits, signés par tous ses membres et revêtus de la forme authentique par son secrétaire.

Les actes originaux resteront, avec leurs dossiers respectifs, au ministère des relations extérieures du Chili, où il sera délivré des copies certifiées aux parties qui le demanderont.

La commission tiendra un livre d'enregistrement dans lequel on inscrira la procédure suivie, les demandes des réclamants et les jugements et décisions rendus.

La commission fonctionnera à Santiago.

ART. 7. — La commission aura la faculté de se pourvoir de secrétaires, rapporteurs et autres employés qu'elle estimera nécessaires pour le bon accomplissement de ses fonctions.

Il appartient à la commission de proposer les personnes qui auront à remplir respectivement ces emplois et de fixer les traitements et rémunérations à leur assigner. La nomination de ces divers employés sera faite par Son Exellence le Président de la République du Chili. Les jugements de la commission mixte qui devront être exécutés au Chili auront l'appui de la force publique de la même manière que ceux qui sont rendus par les tribunaux ordinaires du pays. Les jugements qui auront été exécutés à l'étranger sortiront leurs effets conformément aux règles et usage du droit international privé.

ART. 8. — Les réclamations seront présentées à la commission mixte dans les six mois qui suivront la date de sa première séance, et celles qu'on présenterait après l'expiration de ce délai ne seront pas admises.

Pour les effets de la disposition contenue dans le paragraphe précédent, la commission mixte publiera, dans le Journal Officiel de la République du Chili, un avis par lequel elle indiquera la date de son installation.

ART. 9. — La commission aura pour terminer sa mission, à l'égard de toutes les réclamations soumises à son examen et décision, un délai de deux années comptées depuis le jour où elle sera déclarée installée.

Passé ce délai, la commission aura la faculté de proroger ses fonctions pour une nouvelle période qui ne pourra excéder six mois, dans le cas que pour cause de maladie ou d'incapacité temporaire de quelqu'un de ses membres ou pour tout autre motif de gravité reconnue, elle ne serait pas parvenue à terminer sa mission dans le délai fixé au premier paragraphe.

ART. 10. — Chacun des gouvernements contractants pourvoira aux frais de ses propres agents ou défenseurs.

Les dépenses d'organisation de la commission mixte, les honoraires de ses membres, les appointements des secrétaires rapporteurs et autres employés et tous frais et dépenses de service commun, seront payés de moitié par les deux gouvernements; mais s'il y a des sommes allouées en faveur des réclamants, il en sera déduit lesdits frais et dépenses communs en tant qu'ils n'excèdent pas les six pour cent des valeurs que le trésor du Chili ait à payer pour la totalité des réclamations admises.

Les sommes que la commission mixte assignera en faveur des réclamants seront versées par le gouvernement du Chili au gouvernement français par l'entremise de sa légation à Santiago ou de la personne à ce désignée dans le délai d'une année à compter de la date de la résolution y afférente, sans que durant ce délai, lesdites sommes soient passibles d'aucun intérêt en faveur des réclamants.

Les hautes parties contractantes s'obligent à considérer les jugements de la commission mixte, organisée par la présente convention, comme une solution satisfaisante, parfaite et irrévocable des difficultés qu'elle a eu en vue de régler, et il est bien entendu que toutes les réclamations des citoyens français, présentées ou non présentées dans les conditions signalées aux articles précédents, seront tenues pour décidées et jugées définitivement et de manière que pour aucun motif ou prétexte, elles ne puissent être l'objet d'un nouvel examen ou d'une nouvelle discussion.

ART. 12. — La présente convention sera ratifiée par les hautes parties contractantes et l'échange des ratifications s'effectuera à Santiago.

En foi de quoi, les plénipotentiaires de la République française et de la République du Chili ont signé la présente convention en double exemplaire et dans les langues française et espagnole, et l'ont scellée de leurs sceaux respectifs.

Fait à Santiago du Chili le deuxième jour du mois de novembre de l'année de N.-S. mil huit cent quatre-vingt-deux.[1]

Protocole additionnel à la convention du 2 novembre 1882, signé à Valparaiso, le 3 mars 1883.

A Valparaiso, le troisième jour du mois de mars de l'année mil huit cent quatre-vingt-trois, M. Ernest Bourgarel, chargé d'affaires de la République française, et M. Luis Aldunate, ministre des relations extérieures du Chili se sont réunis au ministère des relations extérieures.

M. Bourgarel, au nom de son Gouvernement, a exprimé le désir de voir définir le sens précis qui doit être attribué à la disposition contenue dans le premier paragraphe de l'article 8 de la convention d'arbitrage conclue entre les deux gouvernements, le deux novembre de l'année dernière, en ce qui pourrait concerner les réclamations provenant de faits postérieurs à l'expiration du délai établi dans le dit paragraphe.

M. le ministre des relations extérieures à répondu que son gouvernement attribuait à la disposition contenue dans le paragraphe précité, en ce qui touchait le point concret auquel faisait allusion M. le chargé d'affaires, le sens et la portée qui découlent du paragraphe complémentaire ajouté au premier paragraphe de l'article 8 des conventions analogues conclues postérieurement avec les gouvernements de l'Italie et de la Grande-Bretagne, lequel paragraphe est conçu dans les termes suivants :

« Cependant, si, à l'expiration du délai établi dans ce paragraphe, l'état de guerre subsistait et qu'il se produisît de nouvelles réclamations, basées sur des faits qui surviendraient, la commission mixte aura faculté pour connaître de ces réclamations, pourvu toutefois qu'elles lui soient présentées six mois avant le terme fixé par l'article 9 pour la conclusion de ses travaux. »

Cette explication ayant été entendue et acceptée par M. le chargé d'affaires de la République française, le sens qui doit être donné au dit article 8 de la convention d'arbitrage du 2 novembre de l'année dernière reste établi d'un commun accord, conformément aux termes du paragraphe complémentaire cité plus haut.

En foi de quoi, le chargé d'affaires de la République française et le ministre des relations extérieures du Chili signent le présent protocole en double exemplaire et dans les langues française et espagnole, et le scellent de leurs sceaux respectifs.[2]

[1] F. DE MARTENS, *Nouveau Recueil Général*, 2ᵉ série, t. IX, p. 704. — ROUARD DE CARD, 1892, p. 248. — DE CLERCQ. *Recueil des Traités de France*, t. XIV, p. 61. — *Journal officiel* (de France), 20 septembre 1883.
[2] F. DE MARTENS, *Nouveau Recueil Général*, 2ᵉ série, t. IX, p. 704.

Protocolo que prorogó por once meses el funcionamiento del Tribunal Arbitral establecido por la convencion de 2 Noviembre de 1882, firmado en Santiago, el 25 de Octubre de 1886.

Reunidos en este Departamento los señores Joaquin Godoy, Ministro de Relaciones Exteriores de Chile, y Arthur Lanen, Enviado Extraordinario y Ministro Plenipotenciario de Francia, el señor Lanen, expuso :

Que debiendo expirar el dia 17 del mes próximo el plazo señalado al Tribunal Arbitral Franco-Chileno para evacuar su cometido, en conformidad à la Convención de 2 de Noviembre de 1882, y estando por el momento paralizadas sus funciones, tenia el honor de dirigirse al señor Ministro de Relaciones Exteriores rogándole, en cumplimiento de un encargo telegráfico recibido de su Gobierno, se sirva recabar del Residente de esta República una prorroga de plázo hábil para las funciones del Tribunal aludido el cual podria extenderse al mismo periodo de otra meses otorgado à la Comisión Mixta Italo-Chilena por el Protocolo de 2 del que rige.

El señor Godoy contestó que se hallaba instruido por su Excelencia el Presidente de la República para manifestar que, aun cuando el Gobierno de Chile es extraño á las causas que han motivado la paralización de las funciones del Tribunal Franco-Chileno, y aunque, por otra parte, las disposiciones de la Convención de 2 de Noviembre de 1882 previeron taxativamente la posibilidad de entorpecimientos y suspensiones en la marcha del Tribunal, no obstante, en vista del estado inconcluso de los trabajos de éste y en el interés de atestiguar, una vez más, su espiritu de equidad y sus amistosos propósitos para con el Gobierno Francés acepta la sugestión hecha por el señor Lanen.

En consecuencia, la prórroga quedó acordada en los siguientes términos :

1º Los Gobiernos de Chile y de Francia convienen en prorrogar las funciones del Tribunal Arbitral instituído por la Convención de 2 de Noviembre de 1882, por un plazo final que no podrá exceder de once meses, los cuales se contarón desde el dia 17 de Noviembre próximo, para expirar el 17 de Octubre de 1887.

Está prórroga no importará modificación alguna en las demás estipulaciones de la precitada Convención.

2º El presente Protocolo será ratificado por las Partes Contratantes tan luego como fuere posible.

3º La anterior disposición no obstará à que el Tribunal Arbitral Franco-Chileno pueda utilisar para sus funciones la prórroga acordada desde la fecha inicial señalada en el número 1º.

En fe de lo cual el Ministro de Relaciones Exteriores de Chile y el Enviado Extraordinario y Ministro Plenipotenciario de Francia, debidamente autorizados al efecto, firmaron este Protocolo en doble ejemplar y en los idiomas español y francés y lo sellaron con sus sellos respectivos.

Hecho en el Ministerio de Relaciones Exteriores, en Santiago de Chile, o veinticinco dias del mes de Octubre del año mil ochocientos ochenta y seis [1].

Protocolo chileno-francés complementario del protocolo de 25 de Octubre de 1886, firmado en Santiago, el 8 de Enero de 1887.

Reunidos en el Despacho de Relaciones Exteriores de Chile los señores Francisco Freire, Ministro de ese ramo Arthur Lanen, Enviado Extraordinario y Ministro Plenipotenciario de Francia, han declarado que no siendo posible, en vista de la partida del honorable Árbitro Brasilero Señor Lafayette Rodriguez Pereira, determinar desde luego la epoca en que el Tribunal Arbitral Franco-Chileno. pueda reasumir sus funciones, queda entendido que no debe considerarse como final el plazo de once mezes otorgado por el Protocolo de 25 de Octubre de 1886.

En te de lo cual el Ministro de Relaciones Exteriores de Chile y el Enviado Extraordinario y Ministro Plenipotenciario de Francia firmaron este Protocolo en doble ejemplar y lo sellaron con sus sellos respectivos.

Hecho en Santiago de Chile, à los ocho dias del mes de Enero de mil ochocientos ochenta y siete [2].

Protocolo por el cual se puso termino á las reclamaciones pendientes de la resolucion del Tribunal Arbitral Chileno-Francés, firmado en Santiago, el 26 de Noviembre de 1887.

Reunidos en este Departamento los Señores Miguel Luis Amunátegui, Ministro de Relaciones Exteriores de Chile, y Arthur Lanen, Enviado Extraordinario y Ministro Plenipotenciario de la República Francesa, y autorizados por sus Gobiernos respectivos, han acordado lo siguiente:

1º Aprobar el arreglo que los agentes acreditados por los Gobiernos de uno e otro país ante el Tribunal Arbitral han celebrado para cancelar las ochenta y nueve reclamaciones sometidas á su decisión, por la suma de trescientos mil pesos ($ 300,000) fuertes, chilenos, de plata, que el Gobierno de Chile pagará dentro de los

quince dias siguientes á la approbación de este Convenio por el Congreso Nacional, debiendo dedurcirse de esa suma el seis por ciento (6%) que, según la Convención de 2 de Noviembre de 1882, ha de applicarse á los gastos del expresado Tribunal, y quedando, en consecuencia, extinguidas las reclamaciones indicadas.

2º El Enviado Extraordinario y Ministro Plenipotenciario de la República Francesa recibirá la referida suma y la distribuirá entre los dueños de las ochenta y nueve reclamaciones, en la cantidad, modo y forma que estime convenientes, sin que el Gobierno de Chile tengo ninguna responsabilidad por esta distribución.

3º Queda expresamente establecidò que el Gobierno de Chile ha efectuado este arreglo amistoso con el objeto de llevar á pronto desenlace las reclamaciones pendientes, y sin que este arreglo afecte directa ni indirectamente á los principios y jurisprudencia que el Gobierno de Chile ha mantenido y sostenido ante los Tribunales Arbitrales.

En fe de lo cual lo autorizaron con su firma y su sello, en doble ejemplar, en Santiago, á los veintiséis días del mes de Noviembre de mil ochocientos ochento y siete [1].

LXX. Chili, Italie.

7 décembre 1882.

Cette contestation, similaire à celle entre la France et le Chili, fut terminée comme elle en 1888 par transaction, moyennant le paiement de 297,000 $. Les arbitres avaient en outre condamné le Chili à payer 70,326 $ 31 en principal et 21,942 $ 36 pour intérêts. L'ensemble des réclamations italiennes se montaient à 7,576,030 $ 24 en principal et 1,894,007 $ 60 pour intérêts.

Convention d'arbitrage signée à Santiago le 7 décembre 1882.

Sua Maestá il Re d'Italia et Sua Eccellenza il Presidente della Repubblica del Chile, desiderando porre un termine ai reclami dedotti da sudditi italiani ed appogiati dalla legazione di Italia nel Chile in dependenza degli atti al operazioni eseguiti dalle forze della Repubblica nei territori e coste del Perú et della Bolivia durante la presente guerra, hanno determinato di stipulare una Convenzione d'arbitrato, et con questo

[1] *Recopilación de Tratados y Convenciones*, 1894, t. II, p. 285.
[2] *Recopilación de Tratados y Convenciones*, 1894, t. II, p. 290.

[1] *Recopilación de Tratados y Convenciones*, 1894, t. II, p. 323.

scopo hanno nominato per loro rispettivi plenipotenziari:

Sua Maestá il Re d'Italia:

Il signor Roberto Magliano, sua incaricato
d'affari presso il Governo del Chile; e

S. E. Il Presidente della Repubblica del Chile:

Il signor Luigi Aldunate, ministro delle relazioni esteriori della Repubblica;

I quali plenipotenziari, dopo avere esaminato
e scambiato i loro poteri e questi trovati in buona
et debita forma, hanno convenuto nei seguenti
articoli:

ART. 1. -- Un Tribunale arbitrale o Commissione mista internazionale deciderá nella forma
e secondo i termini che si stabiliscono in questa
Convenzione, tutti i reclami che, in dependenza
degli atti ed operazioni eseguiti dalle forze di
mare e di terra della Repubblica nei territori e
coste del Peru e della Bolivia durante la presente
guerra, sono stati dedotti sinora od ulteriormente
si deducessero da sudditi italiani col patrocinio
della legazione d'Italia nel Chile, entre il periodo
di tempo che s'indichera piu innanzi.

ART. 2. La Commissione sará composta
di tre membri: uno nominato da sua Maestá il
Re d'Italia, l'altro da sua Eccellenza il Presidente
della Repubblica del Chile, ed il terzo da sua
Maestá l'Imperatore del Brasile, sia direttamente
sia per mezzo dell' agente diplomatico che tenesse
accreditato nel Chile.

Nei casi di morte, assenza od inabilitazione
per qualunque altro motivo di alcuno od alcuni
dei membri della Commissione, si procederá alla
sua sostituzione nelle forma e nelle condizioni
rispettivamente indicate nell' inciso precedente.

ART. 3. — La Commissione mista esaminerá
e risolverá i reclami che i sudditi italiani hanno
dedotto sino ad oggi od ulteriormente deducessero
per mezzo del corrispondente organo diplomatico,
per causa degli atti ed operazioni eseguite dagli
eserciti e dalla squadre della Repubblica a partire dal 14 febbrajo mille ottocento settantanove,
data del principio delle ostilita, sino al giorno
in cui si addivenga o trattati di pace o patti
di tregua tra le nazioni belligeranti, o cessino di
fatto le ostilitá fra le tre nazioni in guerra.

ART. 4. — La Commissione mista adotterá
quei mezzi di prova et d'investigazione che, secondo il criterio ed il retto discernimento dei
suoi membri, fossero atti a chiarire nel miglior
modo i fatti in controversia e specialmente a qua-
lificare lo stato ed il carattere neutrale del reclamante.

La Commissione amettera altresi le allegazioni
verbali e scritte d'entrambi i Governi o dei loro
rispettivi agenti o difensori.

ART. 5. — Ogni Governo potrá costituire
un agente che curi l'interesse della sua parte ed
attenda alla sua difesa, presenti istanze, documenti ed interogatori, deferisca od accetti giura-
menti, sostenga i propri argomenti e confuti gli
argomenti contrari, presenti le sue prove, ed
esponga dinanzi la Commissione direttamente o
per mezzo d'uno avvocato, verbalmente o per iscrito
in conformitá delle norme di procedura e di tra-
mitazione che la stessa Commissione stabilira all'
iniziare le poprie funzioni, le dottrine, i principi
legali ed i precedenti, che convengano al suo diritto.

ART. 6. La Commissione mista risolvera
i reclami in base alle prove presentate, attenen-
dosi ai principi del diritto internazionale, non
che alla pratica e giurisprudenza stabilite dai
moderni analoghi tribunali di maggior autoritá e
prestigio, ed emettendo le sue risoluzioni interlo-
cutorie o definitive a maggioranza di voti.

La Commissione mista esporra brevemente in
ogni giudizio definitivo i fatti e le cause del reclamo, i motivi allegati pro e contro, ed i fonda-
menti di diritto internazionale che giustifichino
le sue risoluzioni. Le risoluzioni ed i decreti
della Commissione saranno scritti, firmati da tutti
i membri, ed autenticati dal suo segretario, e si
lasceranno in originale, coi relativi incartamenti,
presso il ministro delle relazioni esteriori del
Chile, rimettendosi alle parti gli estratti che venissero
richiesti.

La Commissione terrá un libro o régistro, nel
quale si noteranno i suoi atti e le istanze dei
reclamanti, ed i decreti o decisioni che emettera.

La Commissione mista funzionera in Santiago.

ART. 7. — La Commissione avrá la facoltá
di provvedersi di segretari, relatori ed altri impiegati, che stimi necessari per il buon disim-
pegno di sue funzioni. Spetterá alla Commissione
di proporre le persone che abbiano a disimpegnare rispettivamente quelle funzioni, e di designare gli stipendi e le rimunerazioni che lor si
debbano assegnare.

La nomina dei sovra indicati impiegati sará
fatta da sua Eccellenza il Presidente della Repubblica del Chile. I decreti della Commissione, che
debbono eseguirsi nel Chile, avranno l'appoggio
della forza pubblica come i decreti emanati dai tribunali ordinari del paese. A quelli che abbiano
da eseguirsi all' estero si dara esecuzione confor-
memente alle norme ed agli usi del diritto internazionale privato.

ART. 8. I reclami saranno presentati alla
Commissione mista i sei mesi successivi alla data
della sua prima sessione, e quelli, che si presen-
tassero dopo trascorso questo termine, non saranno ammessi. Tuttavia, se alla scadenza del
termine fissato in questo inciso sussiste lo stato

di guerra, e si producessero nuovi reclami fondati sopra fatti ulteriormente verificatesi, la Commissione mista rimarra abilitata a risolverli sempre che le fossero presentati sei mesi prima del termine indicato dall' articolo IX per l'esaurimento del suo incarico.

Per gli effetti della disposizione contenuta nel precendente inciso la Commissione mista pubblichera nel Giornale officiale della République del Chile un aviso nel quale s'indichi la data della sua istallazione.

ART. 9. — La Commissione per esaurire il suo incarico in tutti i reclami sottoposti al suo esame e decisione avrà due anni di tempo a partire dal giorno in cui si dichiari installata. Trascorso questo termine, la Commissione avrà la facoltà di prorogare le proprie funzioni per un nuovo periodo che non potrà oltrepassare i sei mesi, nel caso che, per infermità ò temporario ripedimento di alcuno dei suoi membri o per altro motivo di accertata gravità, non fosse riuscita a compiere il suo incarico entro il termine fissato nel primo inciso.

ART. 10. — Ognuno dei Governi contraenti avrà rispettivamente a proprio carico le spese dei propri atti non che gli onorari dei rispettivi agenti e difensori.

La spece dell' organizzazione della Commissione mista, gli onorari dei suoi membri, gli stipendi dei segretari, dei relatori e degli altri impiegati e le altre spese e sborsi di servizio comune, saranno pagati per metà fra i due Governi, ma se vi fossero delle somme aggiudicate a favore dei reclamanti, verranno da queste dedotte le suddette spece comuni in quanto non eccedano il sei per cento dei valori, che il tesoro del Chile avrà da pagare per la totalità dei reclami ammessi. Le somme, che la Commissione mista aggiudicasse a favore dei reclamanti, saranno rimesse dal Governo del Chile al Governo d'Italia per il tramite della sua legazione in Santiago, o della persona dalla legazione medesima designata, nel termine di un anno a partire dalla data della rispettiva risoluzione senza che durante questo termine abbia a decorrere alcun interesse a favore dei reclamanti.

ART. 11. — Le Alte Parti contraenti si obbligano a considerare le decisioni della commissione mista, che viene organizzata con questo Trattato, come una soluzione soddisfacente, perfetta ed irrevocabile delle difficoltà il cui componimento si ha avuto in mira, e nella intelligenza che tutti i reclami dei sudditi italiani presentati od ommessi nelle condizioni indicate nei precedente articolo si avranno per decisi e giudicati definitivamente e per modo che per niun motivo o pretesto possano essere materia di nuovo esame o discussione.

ART. 12. — La presente Convenzione verrà ratificata dalle Alte Parti contraenti, e lo scambio di queste ratifiche avrà luogo in Santiago il più presto che sia possibile.

In fede del che i plenipotenziari del Regno d'Italia e della Repubblica del Chile firmarono la presente Convenzione in doppio originale ed in lingua italiana e spagnuola e vi apposero i respettivi suggelli:

Fatta in Santiago del Chile, addi sette del mese di dicembre dell' anno di N. S. mille ottocento ottantadue [1].

Protocolo que prorrogó el funcionamiento del Tribunal Arbitral creado por el protocolo de 7 de Diciembre de 1882, firmado en Santiago el 2 de Octubre de 1886.

Reunidos en este Despacho los señores Joaquin Godoy, Ministro de Relaciones Exteriores de Chile, y Conde Alejandro Fé d'Ostiani, Enviado Extraordinario y Ministro Plenipotenciario en Misión Especial de Su Majestad el Rey de Italia, el señor Fé d'Ostiani expuso:

Que el dia seis del mes que principia vencerá el plazo señalado al Tribunal Arbitral Italo-Chileno para fallar, en conformidad á la Convención de 7 de Diciembre de 1882, las reclamaciones de indemnización que le están sometidas, provenientes de la última guerra entre Chile y el Perú y Bolivia;

Que, como no lo ignora el Gobierno de Chile, el Arbitro Italiano ha sido autorizado, en razón de apremiantes asuntos domesticos, para salir del país en goce de licencia, lo que ha sido causa de que el Tribunal no haya alcanzado a realizar su objeto;

Que, por esta razón, tenia el honor de dirigirse al señor Ministro de Relaciones Exteriores, rogándole recabara de Su Excelencia el Presidente de la República el acuerdo de una prórrogo de plazo hábil para las funciones del Tribunal aludido. Y finalmente, que debiendo transcurrir necesariamente algún tiempo para que el Gobierno de Italia pueda proveer al envio de un nuevo Arbitro, en caso de que el señor Cárcano, hoy ausente, se encontrare inhabilitado para reasumir pronto su cargo, solicitaba que le prórrogo se extendiese al periodo de once meses que aún restan del plazo de un año señalado á las funciones del Tribunal Chileno-Alemán.

---

[1] F. DE MARTENS. *Nouveau Recueil Général*, 2° série, t. X, p. 638. - *Trattati e Convensioni*, t. IX, p. 70.

El señor Ministro de Relaciones Exteriores contestó que se hallaba instruido por su Excelencia el Presidente de la República para manifestar que, aun cuando el Gobierno Chileno es extraño á las causas que motivaron la paralización de las funciones del Tribunal Italo-Chileno, y aunque, por otra parte, las disposiciones de la ya citada Convención de 7 de Diciembre de 1882 previeron taxativamente la posibilidad de entorpecimientos y suspensiones accidentales en la marcha del Tribunal, reconoce, empero, el hecho de la insuficiencia del plazo, y en el interés de atestiguar una vez más su espíritu de equidad y sus amistosos propósitos para con el Gobierno Italiano, acepta la sugestión hecha por el Enviado Extraordinario y Ministro Plenipotenciario de Italia.

En consecuencia, la prórroga quedo accordada en los siguientes terminos:

1° Los Gobiernos de Chile y de Italia acuerdan prorrogar las funciones del Tribunal Arbitral instituido por la Convención de 7 de Diciembre de 1882, por un plazo final que no podra exceder de once meses, que se contarán desde el siete del presente para expirar el siete de Septiembre de 1887.

Esta prórroga no importará modificación alguna en las demás estipulaciones de la precitada Convención.

2° El presente Protocolo será ratificado por las Partes Contratantes, tan luego como fuere posible.

3° La anterior disposición no obstará a que el Tribunal Italo-Chileno pueda reanudar sus funciones tan luego como todos sus miembros estén debidamente habilitados para hacerlo.

En fe de lo cual el Ministro de Relaciones Exteriores de Chile y el Enviado Extraordinario y Ministro Plenipotenciario de Italia, debidamente autorizados al efecto, firmaron este Protocolo, en doble ejemplar y en los idiomas español é italiano, y lo sellaron con sus sellos respectivos.

Hecho en el Ministerio de Relaciones Exteriores, en Santiago de Chile, á dos dias del mes de Octubre del año mil ochocientos ochenta y seis [1].

Protocolo chileno-italiano complementario del protocolo de 2 Octubre de 1886, firmada en Santiago el 5 de Enero de 1887.

Reunidos en el Departamento de Relaciones Exteriores de Chile los señores Francisco Freire, Ministro de ese ramo, y Conde Fé d'Ostiani, Enviado Extraordinario y Ministro Plenipotenciario

en Misión Especial de S. M. el Rey de Italia, debitamente autorizados al efecto, han declarado que no siendo posible, en vista de la partida del honorable Arbitro Brasilero, señor Lafayette Rodriguez Pereira, determinar desde luego la época en que el Tribunal Italo-Chileno pueda reasumir sus funciones, queda entendido que no debe considerarse como final el plazo de once meses otorgado por el Protocolo de 2 de Octubre de 1886.

En fe de lo cual el Ministro de Relaciones Exteriores de Chile y el Enviado Extraordinario en Misión Especial de S. M. el Rey de Italia firman este Protocolo en doble ejemplar y lo sellan con los sellos respectivos.

Hecho en Santiago de Chile, à cinco días del mes de Enero del año mil ochocientos ochenta y siete [1].

Protocolo italo-chileno para transigir las reclamaciones de los súbditos italianos, firmado en Santiago el 12 de Enero de 1888.

Reunidos en este Departamento los señores Miguel Luis Amunátegui, Ministro de Relaciones Exteriores de Chile, y Conde Fabio Samminiatelli, Ministro Residente de Su Majestad el Rey de Italia, y autorizados por sus respectivos Gobiernos han acordado lo siguiente:

1° Transigir, en los terminos que han convenido los Agentes de ambos Gobiernos acreditados ante el Tribunal Arbitral Italo-Chileno, las reclamaciones presentadas y cuyo número llega á doscientos sesenta y una, en doscientos noventa y siete mil pesos ($ 297,000) fuertes, de plata, chilenos, que el Gobierno de Chile pagará dentro de los quince dias siguientes la aprobación de este Convenio por el Congreso de Chile, debiendo deducirse de esta suma el 6 % que según la Convención de Arbitraje debe aplicarse á los gastos del expresado Tribunal: quedando, en consecuencia, canceladas y extinguidas las dichas reclamaciones.

2° El Ministro de Su Majestad el Rey de Italia recibira la predicha suma de doscientos noventa y siete mil pesos ($ 297,000) fuertes, chilenos, de plata, y la distribuirá entre los dueños de las reclamaciones enunciadas, sin que esta distribución afecte ó pueda afectar de ningún modo la responsabilidad del Gobierno de Chile.

3° Queda expresamente establecido que este arreglo voluntario y directo se ha efectuado por el Gobierno de Chile con el propósito de llevar á pronto desenlace las reclamaciones pendientes, y sin que afecte directa ó indirectamente á los

---

[1] *Recopilacion de Tratados y Convenciones*, 1894, t. II, p. 282

[1] *Recopilacion de Tratados y Convenciones*, 1894, t. II, p. 288.

principios y jurisprudencia mantenidos por el Tribunal y sostenidos por el Gobierno de Chile.

En fe de lo cual el Ministro de Relaciones Exteriores de Chile y el Ministro Residente de Italia firmaron el presente Protocolo, en doble ejemplare, y lo sellaron con sus sellos respectivos.

Hecho en Santiago de Chile, á doce dias del mes de Enero de mil ochocientos ochenta y ocho [1].

LXXI. Pays-Bas, Saint-Domingue.

26 mars 1881.

Il s'est agi en l'espèce de la confiscation par les autorités dominicaines d'un navire hollandais, à raison de l'importation clandestine d'armes et de munitions de guerre. L'arbitre accorda une indemnité de 140,000 francs.

Compromis pour soumettre à l'arbitrage la confiscation du Havana Packet, signé à La Haye le 26 mars 1881.

Entre les soussignés, le Baron C. Th. de Lynden de Sandenburg, Chambellan de Sa Majesté le Roi des Pays-Bas et son Ministre des Affaires Etrangères, et Monsieur Alfred Paz, Ministre Plénipotentiaire de la République Dominicaine près Sa Majesté le Roi des Pays-Bas, muni de pouvoirs spéciaux de son Gouvernement à l'effet des présentes, a été dit et convenu ce qui suit :

Au mois de septembre de 1877 le brick néerlandais « Havana Packet », capitaine J. W. Harken, a été confisqué par les autorités de Monte-Cristo, et, le capitaine, ainsi que quelques hommes de l'équipage, ont été emprisonnés sous la prévention d'avoir eu à bord des armes et des munitions de guerre qui auraient été amenées, pendant que le « Havana Packet » opérait son chargement à Manzanillo, par une embarcation appartenant à la dame Isabel Dickenson, sujette britannique, dans le but de les importer dans un des ports de la République Dominicaine contrairement aux dispositions de la loi du 19 mai 1876. La confiscation prononcée par arrêt du Tribunal de première instance à Santo-Domingo du 19 février 1878, confirmé par celui de la Haute Cour de Justice du 15 mai suivant, a fait l'objet d'une réclamation de la part du capitaine du navire « Havana Packet ».

Le Gouvernement Néerlandais, ayant cru devoir intervenir pour appuyer la réclamation et obtenir la réparation du préjudice souffert par son national, le Gouvernement Dominicain a proposé de soumettre le différend à l'arbitrage d'une

[1] *Recopilacion de Tratados y Convenciones*, 1894, t. II, p. 326.

puissance tierce, qui aurait à se prononcer sur l'ensemble des faits motivant la réclamation et qui, suivant l'appréciation du Gouvernement Néerlandais, engagent la responsabilité du Gouvernement Dominicain et, dans l'opinion de celui-ci, celle des deux Gouvernements, le même arbitre ayant la faculté, dans le cas où le Gouvernement Dominicain serait déclaré responsable, de fixer l'indemnité qui doit être payée.

Voulant donc témoigner des sentiments d'équité et de conciliation qui l'animent, le Gouvernement Néerlandais a acquiescé à cette proposition et les deux Gouvernements ont proposé de soumettre le différend à l'arbitrage du Président de la République Française, s'étant assurés que le Président consent à se charger du mandat dont il s'agit. En conséquence, les soussignés dûment autorisés, conviennent au nom de leurs Gouvernements respectifs de soumettre à l'arbitrage du Président de la République Française les questions suivantes ?

1. Est-il prouvé qu'il y ait eu de la contrebande de guerre à bord de l'embarcation de la dame Dickenson ?

2. Le fait du transbordement, pendant quelques heures à bord du « Havana Packet », de colis appartenant à la dame Dickenson, même dans le cas où ces colis auraient contenu de la contrebande de guerre, constituerait-il un des quatre cas énoncés dans la loi Dominicaine de 1876, et les tribunaux Dominicains se fondant sur l'article 2 de cette loi, ont-ils prononcé à juste titre la peine de la confiscation contre le « Havana Packet » ?

3. Le Gouvernement des Pays-Bas est-il fondé à prétendre que, dans le cas où les faits mis à la charge du capitaine Harken seraient dûment prouvés, l'arrestation de ce capitaine et les mauvais traitements infligés à lui, à son équipage et à sa passagère la dame Dickenson, en admettant même résistance de leur part à l'exécution de la loi, et, le pillage des bagages de cette dernière, même dans le cas où ces bagages auraient contenu de la contrebande de guerre, constituent des actes violents et illégaux pour lesquels une réparation leur est due ?

4. Le procédé des autorités Dominicaines, dans le différend qui fait l'objet de cet arbitrage, en vertu de la loi de 1876, est-il compatible avec les principes du droit international en vigueur chez les nations civilisées ou bien les intérêts, lésés par l'application de cette loi, ont-ils droit à une réparation, et quel sera le montant de l'indemnité ?

Les deux Gouvernements s'engagent à faire toutes les diligences nécessaires pour assurer l'exécution de la sentence arbitrale qui interviendra et qui constituera une décision souveraine et sans recours.

En foi de quoi, les soussignés ont signé la présente déclaration qu'ils ont revêtue du sceau de leurs armes.

Fait à la Haye, en triple expédition, le 26 mars 1881 [1].

Sentence prononcée le 16 mars 1883, par Monsieur le Président de la République Française, dans l'arbitrage entre la Hollande et Saint-Domingue.

Nous, Jules Grévy, Président de la République Française, statuant en vertu des pouvoirs qui nous ont été conférés aux termes du compromis signé à la Haye, le 26 mars 1881, par lequel le Gouvernement des Pays-Bas et le Gouvernement de Saint-Domingue sont convenus de déférer au Président de la République Française pour être réglé par lui et sans recours le litige qui est pendant entre eux depuis 1878 au sujet de la saisie du navire «Havana Packet».

Vu les pièces fournies par les deux Gouvernements, notamment :

1. Une lettre en date du 26 septembre 1879, adressée au Ministre des Affaires Etrangères de France par M. le Baron de Zuylen de Nyevelt, Ministre des Pays-Bas à Paris :

2. Une lettre en date du 18 mai 1880, adressée au Ministre des Affaires Etrangères de France par M. Paz, Ministre de la République Dominicaine à la Haye.

3. Une lettre en date du 28 mars 1881, adressée au Ministre des Affaires Etrangères de France par M. le Baron de Zuylen de Nyevelt, et transmettant :

a) le texte du compromis intervenu entre les deux Gouvernements intéressés ;

b) un exposé des faits ;

c) une note sur la loi Dominicaine du 15 mai 1876 ;

d) le dossier du procès du capitaine Harken et la correspondance échangée entre le Consul des Pays-Bas à Santo Domingo et les Autorités Dominicaines.

4. Une lettre en date du 11 octobre 1881, adressée au Ministre des Affaires Etrangères de France par M. Paz, et transmettant :

a) une copie certifiée des pièces de la procédure ;

b) le texte de la loi Dominicaine du 11 août 1875 ;

c) la gazette officielle du 2 juin 1876, contenant le texte de la loi du 15 mai 1876.

5. Une lettre en date du 18 octobre 1881, adressée à M. le Ministre des Affaires Etrangères

de France par M. le Baron de Zuylen de Nyevelt ;

6. Une lettre en date du 21 juillet 1882, adressée au Ministre des Affaires Etrangères de France par M. le Baron de Zuylen de Nyevelt, et relative aux indemnités réclamées par les Pays-Bas ;

7. La réponse faite le 16 octobre 1882, par le Gouvernement Dominicain, à la communication de la lettre précédente ;

La Commission instituée par Nous, à l'effet d'étudier les documents respectivement produits, nous ayant fait part du résultat de son examen ;

Attendu qu'il résulte de la dépêche du 18 octobre 1881, ci-dessus visée, que le Gouvernement des Pays-Bas a retiré la demande d'arbitrage en tant qu'elle concerne une réparation à accorder à la dame Dickinson ;

Que l'arbitre n'a donc plus à s'occuper que des faits relatifs au Capitaine Harken et au navire « Havana Packet » ;

Attendu que des termes exprès du compromis, il résulte que l'Arbitre a d'abord à rechercher, si les faits imputés au Capitaine Harken, qui ont donné lieu à diverses sentences des tribunaux Dominicains, sont établis par les pièces de la procédure ;

Attendu qu'aucune constatation matérielle n'a été relevée à la charge du Capitaine Harken, que le fait qui a motivé son arrestation et la confiscation du navire « Havana Packet » ne résulte que des dépositions de trois ou quatre témoins ;

Attendu que ces dépositions, qui sont contredites par d'autres, qui contiennent des détails invraisemblables, n'ont pas été faites en présence du Capitaine Harken, qui n'a jamais été confronté avec leurs auteurs, alors que rien n'était plus facile que d'opérer cette confrontation, qu'il y a là un vice essentiel de procédure qui ôte toute valeur probante à l'enquête ;

Attendu, en conséquence, que le fait reproché au Capitaine Harken n'est nullement prouvé et que les mesures rigoureuses prises par les Autorités Dominicaines contre lui, contre son second et contre le navire ne sont pas justifiées ;

Qu'il n'y a pas lieu, dès lors, d'examiner si le fait allégué tombait sous le coup de la loi Dominicaine du 19 mai 1876, ni si cette loi est, ou non, conforme aux principes du droit international ;

Attendu que le compromis charge l'arbitre, dans le cas où le Gouvernement Dominicain serait déclaré responsable, de fixer l'indemnité qui doit être payée ;

Attendu qu'en tenant compte de la valeur du navire confisqué, des dépenses diverses néces-

---

[1] Cette convention nous a été gracieusement communiquée par le Gouvernement des Pays-Bas.

sitées par le procès, de l'emprisonnement et des mauvais traitements subis par le Capitaine et son second, du séjour prolongé que le Capitaine a dû faire à Saint-Domingue, et du temps qui s'est écoulé depuis que le dommage a été causé jusqu'à ce jour, il convient de fixer à cent quarante mille francs le chiffre de l'indemnité due par le Gouvernement de Saint-Domingue au Gouvernement des Pays-Bas ;

Par ces motifs,

Jugeons que le Gouvernement Dominicain doit réparation au Gouvernement des Pays-Bas pour les mesures prises contre le Capitaine Harken et le navire « Havana Packet » :

Fixons à cent quarante mille francs l'indemnité due de ce chef par le Gouvernement Dominicain, indemnité qui devra être payée à Paris, en monnaie ayant cours en France.

Paris, le 16 mars 1883 [1].

LXXII. Chili, Grande-Bretagne.

4 janvier 1883.

Relative aux dommages causés par la guerre entre le Chili, le Pérou et la Bolivie, cette contestation aboutit à l'allocation par les arbitres d'une somme de $ 95,000 et à une transaction de $ 100,000 pour les réclamations sur lesquelles les arbitres ne purent statuer. Le total des indemnités exigées s'était monté à $ 6,416,410 et le nombre des réclamations à 118 [2].

Convention between Great Britain and Chile for the settlement of the Claims of British Subjects. Signed at Santiago, January 4, 1883.

The Government of Her Majesty the Queen of United Kingdom of Great Britain and Ireland, and his Excellency the President of the Republic of Chile, desiring to adjust amicably the claims deduced by British subjects and supported by the British Legation in Chile, as growing out of the acts and operations effected by the forces of the Republic in the territories and coasts of Peru and Bolivia during the present war have agreed to enter on a Convention for arbitration, and with this view have named as their respective Plenipotentiaries:

The Government of Her Britannic Majesty, James de Vismes Drummond Hay, Esquire, Compagnon of the Most Honorable Order of the Bath, Her Majesty's Chargé d'Affaires, in Chile; and,

His Excellency the President of the Republic of Chile, Señor Luis Aldunate, Minister for foreign Affairs of the Republic;

Who, after having communicated to each other their respective full powers found in good order and due form, have agreed upon the following Articles:

ART. I. A tribunal of Arbitration or Mixed International Commission, shall judge, in the form and in accordance with the terms established in this Convention, all the claims which, by reasons of the acts and operations effected by the land and maritime forces of Chile in the territories and coasts of Peru and Bolivia during the present war, have been put forward up to the present time, or may hereafter be put forward, by British Subjects, and supported by the Legation in Chile, within the term hereinafter defined.

ART. II. The Commission shall be composed of three membres, one named by the Government of Her Britannic Majesty, the other by the President of the Republic of Chile, and a third by his Majesty the Emperor of Brazil, either directly or through the Diplomatic Agent accredited in Chile.

In case of death, absence or incapacity from any other cause of one or more of the membres of the Commission, the vacancy shall be filled in the respective manner, form, and conditions expressed in the preceeding paragraph.

ART. III. The Mixed Commission shall examine and judge the claims wich British subjects have already or may hereafter put forward, through their Diplomatic Representative, as arising out of the acts and operations effected by the armies and naval forces of the Republic from the 14th of February, 1879, the date on which hostilities commenced until the day on which Treaties of Peace or Covenants of Truce may be concluded between the belligerent nations, or until such time as hostilities cease between the three nations at war.

ART. IV. The Mixed Commission shall admit the verbal or written statements of both Governments, or that of their respective Agents or Counsel.

ART. V. Each Government may appoint an Agent to act on its behalf, present petitions, documents, interrogatories, bring forward or demand evidence, support charges or refute contrary statements, produce proofs and adduce before the Commission personally, or through an advocate, verbally or in writing, in accordance whit the rules of procedure which the Commission shall lay down on commencing its functions, the doctrines, legal principles, or antecedents which he may deem convenient for the furtherance of his cause.

ART. VI. The Mixed Commission shall decide the claims on the merits of the proof rendered, and in accordance with the principles of international law, and the pratices and jurisprudence established by analogous modern tribunals of highest authority and prestige, delivering its intertocutory or definitive resolutions by a majority of votes.

The Mixed Commission shall set forth briefly, in each final sentence the facts and grounds of the claim, the evidence produced for or against the same and the principles of international right on which the sentence are based. The resolutions and judgements of the Commission shall be accorded in writing, signed by all the members and attested by its secretary; and these original documents shall be deposited with their respective covering despatch, at the Ministry for foreign affairs in Chile, copies being given to the interested parties applying for the same. The Commission shall keep a book or register in which its proceedings, the petitions of the claimants, and the decrees and decisions which it may issue are to be noted. The Mixed Commission shall hold its sessions in Santiago.

ART. VII. The Commission shall have the power to employ secretaries, reporters, or other officers which it may deem necessary for the proper fulfilment of its duties.

The Commission is empowered to name the persons who are respectively to fill those posts, and to determine their salaries or remuneration.

The appointment of the said officers shall be made by his Excellency the President of the Republic of Chile. The decrees of the Mixed Commission which have to be carried out in Chile shall have the assistance of the Executive in the same manner as those issued by the ordinary Tribunals of the country.

Those which have to take effect abroad shall do so in accordance with rules and usages of private international right.

ART. VIII. The claims shall be presented to the Mixed Commission within the six months following the date of its first session, and those claims which are presented after that term has elapsed shall not be admitted. If, however on the expiration of the term established in this paragraph, the war should still continue, and fresh claims arise, founded on events which may thereby occur, the Mixed Commission shall be considered as empowered to arbitrate thereon, provided always that those claims are presented six months previous to the time assigned in Article IX for the Commission to fulfil its charge.

For the purposes of the rules embodied in the preceding paragraph, the Mixed Commission shall publish in the "Diario Official", of the Republic of Chile a notice in which the date of its installation shall be expressed.

ART. IX. The term of two years shall be given to the Commission from the day of its first meeting, to examine and decide upon every claim. But if, in consequence of sickness, temporary inability of any of its member, or of other sufficient cause, it may have been unable to fulfil its charge within such term, the Commission shall be empowered to prorogue its sessions for a further term which shall not exceed six months.

ART. X. Each of the Contracting Governments shall defray its own expenses and the remuneration of its respective Agents or Counsel.

The expenses attending the organization of the Mixed Commission, the compensation to its members, and the salaries of its Secretaries, reporters, or other officers; and other expenses and costs of common service, shall be defrayed by the two Governments in equal moieties. But if there be sums awarded in favour of the claimants, the aforementioned expenses and costs shall be deducted therefrom, provided that such deductions do not exceed 6 per cent of the amount which the treasury of Chile may have to pay for the total of the accepted claims. The sums which the Mixed Commission may award in favour of the claimants shall be paid by the Government of Chile to the British legation, or to the party whom it may name, within the term of one year after the date of the respective sentence and during said term no interest shall accrue on the said sums in favour of the claimants.

ART. XI. The High Contracting parties agree to consider the sentences of the Mixed Commission organized by this Convention as a satisfactory, perfect, and irrevocable settlement of difficulties the adjustment of which has been held in view and with the understanding that all the claims of British subjects presented or omitted to be presented in the manner set forth shall be considered as decided and definitively adjuged in such manner as to exclude every motive or pretext for their further examination or discussion.

ART. XII. The present Convention shall be ratified by the High Contracting parties, and the ratifications shall be exchanged in Santiago.

In testimony whereof the Plenipotentiaries of Great Britain and of the Republic of Chile have signed the present Convention in duplicate in the English and Spanish languages, and have affixed their seals.

Thus done in Santiago, Chile, the 4th day of January the year of our Lord 1883. [1]

Protocol between Great Britain and Chile, extending the duration of the Claims Commission appointed under the Convention of January 1883, for a period of six months. Signed at Santiago, August 16, 1886.

The term allowed by the IXth Article of the Convention of the 4th of January, 1883, between Great Britain and Chile, to the mixed Commission of Arbitration appointed under the authority of that Convention to examine and decide upon all the claims of British subjects arising out of the acts and operations effected by the land and maritime forces of Chile in the territories and coasts of Peru and Bolivia during the late war, not having sufficed for the completion of its labours, the High Contracting Parties agree by the present Protocol, signed and sealed by their respective representatives duly authorized for the purpose, to extend the powers of the said Commission, additionally and finally for six full months, to be counted from the 1st of September next without prejudice to the other stipulations of the aforesaid Convention of the 4th of January, 1883, all of which shall remain unaffected and in full force for the purposes and effects of this Protocol. The present Protocol shall be ratified on either side with as little delay as possible.

Done in Santiago, Chile, in duplicate, in the English and Spanish languages the 16th day of August, 1886[2].

Protocolo para transigir las veintiuna reclamaciones que quedaron sin fallarse en el Tribunal anglo-chileno, firmado en Santiago el 29 de Septiembre de 1887.

Reunidos en este Departamento los señores Miguel Luis Amunátegui, Ministro de Relaciones Exteriores de Chile, y Hugh Fraser, Ministro Residente de Su Majestad Británica, y autorizados por sus respectivos Gobiernos, han acordado lo siguiente :

1° Transigir, en los términos que han convenido los Agentes de ambos Gobiernos acreditados ante el Tribunal Arbitral, las veintiuna reclamaciones que aún quedan por fallarse en el Tribunal Anglo-Chileno, y que son los números 2, 43, 48, 53, 66, 87, 90, 91, 92, 93, 94, 96, 97, 101, 102, 103, 104, 106, 108, 113, y 115, por la suma de cien mil pesos (100,000), que el Gobierno de Chile pagará dentro de los quince dias siguientes á la aprobación de este Convenio por el Congreso de Chile, debiendo deducirse de esta suma el seis por ciento (6%) que por la Convención respective debe aplicarse á los gastos del expresado Tribunal, quedando, en consecuencia, canceladas y totalmente extinguidas las dichas reclamaciones ;

2° El Ministro de Su Majestad Británica recibirá la predicha suma de cien mil pesos (100,000) y la distribuirá entre los veintiún reclamantes dueños de las reclamaciones enunciadas, en la cantidad, modo y forma que estimare convenientes, y sin que por ello afecte responsabilidad alguna al Gobierno de Chile ;

3° Queda expresamente establecido que este arreglo voluntario y directo se ha efectuado por el Gobierno de Chile con el propósito de llevar á pronto desenlace las reclamaciones pendientes ; y sin que afecte directa ni indirectamente á los principios y jurisprudencia mantenidos por el Tribunal y sostenidos por el Gobierno de Chile.

En fe de lo cual el Ministro de Relaciones Exteriores de Chile y el Ministro Residente de la Gran Bretaña firmaron el presente Protocolo en doble ejemplar y lo sellaron con sus sellos respectivos.

Hecho en Santiago de Chile á los veintinueve dias de Septiembre de mil ochocientos ochenta y siete [1].

LXXIII. Grande-Bretagne, Transvaal.

27 février 1884.

Question de frontière confiée par les deux pays intéressés à l'arbitrage du Grand Juge de la République d'Orange, qui donna raison au Transvaal.

Convention for the settlement of the Transvaal Territory, signed at London, February 27, 1884.

. . . .

ART. II. ..... Her Majesty's Government and the Government of the South African Republic will each appoint a person to proceed together to beacon off the amended south-west boundary as described in Article 1 of this Convention ; and the President of the Orange Free State shall be requested to appoint a referee to whom the said persons shall refer any questions on which they may disagree respecting the interpretation of the said Article, and the decision of such referee thereon shall be final. The arrangement already made, under the terms of Article 19 of the Con-

[1] HERTSLET, A complete collection . . . , t. XV., p. 542.
[2] HERTSLET, Ibid., t. XVIII, p. 283.

[1] Recopilación de Tratados y Convenciones, 1894, t. II, p. 309.

vention of Pretoria of the 3ᵈ August 1881, between the owners of the farms Grootfontein and
Valleifontein on the one hand, and the Barolong
authorities on the other, by which a fair share
of the water supply of the said farms shall be
allowed to flow undisturbed to the said Barolongs,
shall continue in force [1].

**Award of M. Melius de Villiers, as to the boundary
question between Great Britain and the South African
Republic. Kunana, August 5, 1885.**

« Whereas it is stipulated by Article II of a
convention between Her Majesty the Queen of
the United Kingdom of Great Britain and Ireland
and the South African Republic, signed in London
on the 27ᵗʰ day of February 1884 by the pre-
sentatives of the respective parties to the said
convention, that « Her Majesty's government and
the South African Republic will each appoint a
person to proceed together to beacon off the
amended southwest boundary as described in
Article I of this convention, and the President
of Orange Free State shall be requested to
appoint a referee, to whom the said persons shall
refer any questions on which they may disagree
respecting the interpretation of the said article,
and that ' the decision of such referee shall be
final ' ;

« And whereas Her Majesty's government did
appoint Captain Claude Reignier Conder, R. E.,
and the government of the South African Republic did appoint Tielman Nieuwoudt de Villiers,
esq., as such persons to proceed together to
beacon off the said amended southwest boundary ;

« And whereas thereafter the President of the
Orange Free State, being thereunto requested,
did, on the 5ᵗʰ day of June 1885, appoint Melius
de Villiers, one of the judges of the high court
of justice of the Orange Free State, to be such
referee as aforesaid ;

« And whereas the before mentioned Captain
Claude Reignier Conder R. E., and Tielman
Nieuwoudt de Villiers, esq., did refer to the said
referee the following question on which they
disagree respecting the interpretation of Article I
of the said convention, namely, what extent of
ground to the west of the roads from Lotlakana
to Kunana and from Kunana to Taungs, as such
roads have been accepted and agreed upon by
the commissioners of the governments of Her
Majesty and of the South African Republic respectively, was intended to be included in the
South African Republic by the words skirting
Kunana so as to include it and all its garden
ground, but no more, in the Transvaal ;

« Now therefore I, the said referee, do hereby
decide and declare that the said words denote
the ground included between the said roads and
the following boundaries, namely : A straight line
from a point on the road from Lotlakana to
Kunana, as accepted and agreed upon by the
respective commissioners before mentioned, 1 mile
southwest of the point where the road crosses
the 'spruit' known as 'Tlakayeng' to a point
on the 'kopje' immediately behind Batubatu's
kraal, where the line next to be mentioned reaches
the summit of the 'kopje', thence a straight
line to a point 200 yards northwest of an isolated
hut whereof compass observations were taken by
the British commissioners in the presence of the
referee and of the commissioner of the South
African Republic, this straight line passing immediately behind the huts of Batubatu's kraal so
as to exclude them from the South African
Republic; next a straight line from the said
point 200 yards from the said hut to the northwestern corner of Ramatlane's garden, of which
similar observations were taken ; thence a straight
line skirting the western side of the garden to
its southwestern corner, that point being very
nearly magnetic north of the 'kopje', being
the northernmost of three 'kopjes' forming the
termination of a range of hills wich is crossed
by the road from Kunana to Marebogo, about
6 miles from the former place ; next a straight
line from the said southwestern corner of Ramatlane's garden to the summit of the said
'kopje', thence a line along the ridge of the
said range of hills to the point where the hill
is crossed by the road last mentioned.

« Dated at Kunana this 5ᵗʰ day of August
1885 [1].

LXXIV. Etats-Unis d'Amerique, Haïti.

28 mai 1884.

Cette affaire constitue en fait un double
arbitrage. Les circonstances invoquées par
les intéressés étant absolument différentes et
sans connexité aucune. Aussi l'arbitre a-t-il
rendu deux sentences, toutes deux fort détaillées. Ces sentences ne furent toutefois pas
exécutées par les Etats-Unis de l'Amérique
du Nord, bien qu'elles fussent favorables à
leurs ressortissants, celle relative au sieur
Pelletier parce qu'elle reposait sur une interprétation erronée du droit des gens, celle

[1] HERTSLET, *A complete collection*, t. XVII, p. 17.

[1] HERTSLET, *A complete collection...*, t. XVII, p. 34.

relative au sieur Lazare à raison de la découverte de documents nouveaux. Cette attitude d'une correction et d'une impartialité rares est tout particulièrement digne d'attention.

Protocole des conventions faites en vue de soumettre à un arbitre les réclamations connues sous le nom des réclamations Pelletier et Lazare contre Haïti, signé à Washington, le 28 mai 1884.

Attendu que le Gouvernement des Etats Unis d'Amérique a présenté au Gouvernement d'Haïti les réclamations d'Antonio Pelletier et d'A. H. Lazare afin d'obtenir des indemnités pour actes contre la personne et la propriété qui auraient été commis par des autorités haïtiennes; et

Attendu que le Gouvernement d'Haïti a constamment nié sa responsabilité dans la matière; et

Attendu que l'honorable William Strong, autrefois juge à la Cour Suprême des Etats-Unis inspire aux deux parties contractantes entière confiance dans sa science, son habileté et son impartialité: en conséquence

Les soussignés, Frederick T. Frelinghuysen, Secrétaire d'Etat des Etats-Unis, et Stephen Preston, Envoyé Extraordinaire et Ministre plénipotentiaire de la République d'Haïti, ayant reçu les pouvoirs nécessaires de leurs Gouvernements respectifs, ont arrêté les Conventions contenues dans les articles suivants:

ART. I. Les dites réclamations d'Antonio Pelletier et d'A. H. Lazare contre la République d'Haïti seront référées à l'honorable William Strong, dont il vient d'être parlé, comme seul arbitre en la matière, sous les conditions ci-après exprimées.

ART. 2. Les faits suivants sont admis par le Gouvernement d'Haïti en ce qui regarde ces deux réclamations

Quant à Antonio Pelletier

Que Pelletier était Capitaine de la barque *William*, lequel navire entra dans le port de Fort Liberté à peu près à la date énoncée (le 31 Mars, 1861); que le Capitaine et l'équipage furent arrêtés et jugés comme accusés de piraterie et de tentative de traite des noirs; que Pelletier, le Capitaine, fut condamné à être fusillé et que le second et les autres gens de l'équipage furent condamnés à diverses peines d'emprisonnement; que la Cour Suprême d'Haïti (Tribunal de Cassation) mit à néant le jugement contre Pelletier, et renvoya l'affaire à la Cour de Cap Haïtien où Pelletier fut jugé de nouveau et condamné à cinq ans d'emprisonnement, et que le navire, avec ses agrès, fut vendu et les produits divisés entre le Gouvernement Haïtien et les personnes qui, pré-tendant avoir été les victimes de ses actes, avaient procédé contre le vaisseau devant le Tribunal haïtien.

Quant à A. Lazare

Que Lazare fit un contrat écrit avec le Gouvernement haïtien le 23 septembre 1874, à l'effet d'établir une Banque Nationale au Port-au-Prince, avec des succursales, le capital étant fixé d'abord a Doll. 3,000,000 et ultérieurement réduit à Doll. 1,500,000; le Gouvernement devait en fournir un tiers et Lazare deux tiers; que la Banque devait être ouverte dans un an, à partir de la date du contrat, qu'une prolongation de quarante-cinq jours fut accordée à la demande de A. Lazare, et que le jour où la Banque devait être ouverte, le Gouvernement Haïtien alléguant que Lazare n'avait pas exécuté les obligations qui résultaient de son contrat, déclara, aux termes des stipulations de l'article 24 de la Convention, le contrat nul et non avenu, et Lazare de son côté déchu de ses droits.

ART 3. Le dit arbitre recevra et prendra en considération tous les documents et preuves relatifs aux dites réclamations qui pourront lui être présentées au nom de l'un des deux Gouvernements.

Si, en présence de ces dits documents et preuves ainsi soumis, le dit arbitre demande que des preuves additionnelles écrites ou testimoniales soient produites devant lui ou devant toute personne dûment nommée à cet effet, les deux Gouvernements ou l'un d'eux s'engagent à procurer et à fournir par tous les moyens en leur pouvoir ces preuves additionnelles; et tous les documents pertinents dans les archives de l'un des deux Gouvernements seront accessibles au dit arbitre.

Les deux Gouvernements auront le droit de se faire représenter devant l'arbitre par des Conseils qui pourront présenter des mémoires (briefs) et qui pourront être aussi entendus oralement si l'arbitre le désire.

ART. 4. Avant d'entrer dans l'exercice de ses fonctions, le dit arbitre signera la déclaration suivante:

« Je déclare solennellement que je déciderai avec impartialité les réclamations d'Antonio Pelletier et d'A. H. Lazare présentées au nom du Gouvernement des Etats-Unis contre le Gouvernement de la république d'Haïti; et que toutes les questions qui me seront référées par l'un des deux Gouvernements au sujet des dites réclamations seront décidées par moi d'après les principes du droit international en vigueur à l'époque des évènements qui font le sujet des réclamations. »

ART. 5. Le dit arbitre devra rendre sa décision séparément dans chacune des affaires susdites, dans un an à partir de la date de cette Convention.

ART. 6. Les Hautes Parties Contractantes paye-ront en parts égales les dépenses de l'arbitrage qui est ici convenu; et elles s'engagent à ac-cepter la décision du dit arbitre dans chacun des dits cas comme finale et obligatoire, et à donner à cette décision plein effet et vigueur de bonne foi, sans délais qui ne seraient pas justifiables, sans réserve et sans évasion quelle qu'elle soit.

En foi de quoi, les soussignés ont signé la présente et y ont apposé leurs sceaux le vingt-huitième jour de Mai, 1884. [1]

Award in the claim of Antonio Pelletier against the Republic of Hayti, given in Washington, June 13, 1885.

In pursuance of the protocol, dated May 28, 1884, between the Hon. Frederick T. Frelinghuysen, Secretary of State of the United States, and the Hon. Stephen Preston, envoy extraordinary and minister plenipotentiary of the Republic of Hayti, representing their respective governments, after having taken before the Chief Justice of the United States the oath required by the fourth article of the protocol, I have investigated the claim of Antonio Pelletier against the Republic of Hayti, and I now submit the following state-ment and award:

This claim is large, amounting, as presented to me, to the sum of $2,466,480. It is based upon an alleged wrongful arrest, trial, conviction, and imprisonment of the claimant by the Haytian Government, together with the seizure of a bark, of which the claimant was master, its cargo and money on board, their condemnation and confis-cation. The principal evidence presented in sup-port of the claim consists of memorials and pro-tests of the claimant, as also his sworn testi-mony, together with the testimony of one Thomas Collar, who was ship's mate on the bark during the voyage she made from Mobile to Hayti. There is, however, some other evidence of minor importance.

Pelletier, the claimant, is a native of France, but he was naturalized in New York in 1852. He had acted as sailing master of several small vessels on the coasts of South America and Central America during several years prior to 1851. Between that date and 1859 he appears to have had his residence partly in New York, partly in Chicago, and partly in Troy, some of the time engaged in sailing vessels out of New York. In 1859 he purchased an old bark, named *Ardennes* at Havana, in Cuba, took her to Jack-sonville, Florida, to obtain an American registry,

[1] F. DE MARTENS, *Nouveau Recueil Général*, 2ᵉ série, t. XI, p. 798.

shipped in her a cargo of rum, sugar, etc., and cleared for the Canary Islands, lying in north latitude between the twenty-seventh and twenty-ninth degrees. He did not, however, go to those islands, being driven, as he states, far out of his course by heavy gales. He was discovered at the mouth of the Congo River acting suspiciously. There his bark was seized and sent to New York by an American cruiser. At New York she was libelled for attempted slave dealing, and after a considerable lapse of time the libel was brought to trial. The trial resulted in the dismissal of the libel, but with a certificate that there was pro-bable cause for the seizure.

Meanwhile, in 1860, Pelletier, as he states, through the agency of one Parker, bought at the marshal's sale the bark *William*, which had been condemned at Key West as a slaver and ordered to be sold. His memorial to the Secre-tary of State, made out in 1864, to which he has sworn before me, asserts 'that the price paid to the marshal was, as near as he could recollect, something over $10,000'. He further swears that after the sale some person ran away with the bark and the deputy marshal who was on board, but that she was recovered and brought back in four or five hours by the United States autho-rities, aided by a schooner, and that the salvage he had to pay, together with commissions to Parker, with some repairs and other expenses, made the aggregate of bills for the purchase, salvage, and expenses some hundreds over $16,000.

The statements, as well as others respecting the value of the vessel, appear to me to be in-credible, and they tend strongly to diminish my confidence in other statements and testimony of the claimant. By the marshal's return it appears that the bark, with her tackle and chronometer, was sold to Parker for $1605. That sum there-fore was all that was paid to the marshal, and not $10,000 as the claimant swears. Parker was the claimant's agent to buy. Of course Pelletier paid to the marshal no more, and he had to pay Parker only commissions. Besides, the reliable evidence in the case satisfies me that the bark was not worth more than from five to seven thousand dollars at most. She was an old vessel of 215⁴⁵/₉₅ tons measurement, and she was known as a condemned slaver. So in regard to the $6000 claimed to have been paid for salvage, commissions, and other small expenses. It appears that the bark was recovered by the United States authorities, who charged nothing, and a schooner, on board of which was the claimant, and that she was brought back within four or five hours. So, when, soon after, the bark was taken to Mobile and some repairs were put upon her there, the claimant's statement is that with those repairs the vessel cost him about $ 30,000 as near as he could recollect in 1864, when everything must have been fresh in his memory.

What the repairs at Mobile were, is stated by Thomas Collar, the mate who superintended what was done. The bark was recalked, deck and hold put in order, the cabin was overhauled, and there was some painting. Including the seamen, about fourteen men were employed about two weeks at $ 3 a day. The total cost was therefore less than $ 600. Yet the claimant states on oath that including the repairs, the bark cost him about $ 30,000, and was worth fully $ 35,000. She was as I have said, a bark measuring 215⁴⁵⁄₉₅ tons. A respectable witness who was engaged in shipbuilding between 1855 and 1860, has testified that $ 55 a ton was a high price for new wellbuilt vessels, copper-bottomed and copper-fastened, at that time. At that rate a new vessel of the size of the *William* would not have been worth more than about one-third of what this old bark cost the claimant, as he testifies. His testimony in this particular can not be true.

After the arrival of the bark at Mobile, to which port she was brought from Key West, Pelletier transferred the title he had to one Emile Delaunay, of New Orleans, a member of the firm of Delaunay, Rice & Co., of which, as he alleges, he was a partner, for the purpose, as he states, 'of procuring a New Orleans registry'. The transfer was to Delaunay, and not to the firm. He now alleges that though he made the transfer he retained the actual ownership and had a bill of sale from Delaunay. But in his memorial he did not claim that he had a bill of sale. In that he asserted only that retaining the ownership, he took from Delaunay an irrevocable power of attorney to control and dispose of the vessel as he pleased. The statements do not harmonize, and it is difficult to see why a power of attorney was taken if he had a bill of sale. On the faith of the transfer the bark was registered, not, however, at New Orleans, where Delaunay resided, but at Mobile, where she did not belong, and where neither Pelletier nor Delaunay resided. She was registered, not in the name of Delaunay as owner (his name was Emile Delaunay), but as owned by Edward Lee Launde, or Edward Lee Launa, or Edward de Launa, and the person calling himself by that name swore that he was the only owner. It is not quite clear whether the registry was for Edward Lee Launde, as owner, or for Edward Lee Launa, or Edward de Launa. The duplicate certificate of registry, signed by the register and deputy collector, on file at the Treasury Department at Washington, gives the name 'Edward Lee Launde'. The vessel's duplicate has not been presented. The record at Mobile gives the name Edward de Launa or Edward Lee Launa, it is uncertain which. Neither was Delaunay's name. That, as I have said, appears to have been Emile Delaunay.

Why the register was obtained at Mobile in the name given as owner rather than in Pelletier's name, if he was the owner, when he was in Mobile at the time the registry was made, it would be hard to conjecture, unless it was desired while obtaining a register, at the same time to conceal the true ownership of the bark for some unavowed reason. Delaunay evidently had a very close connection with the bark and with her outfit and voyage, a connection which it is difficult to account for if he was not the real owner of the vessel and of most, if not all, the property on board, and if Pelletier was anything more than the ship's master.

Though Pelletier claims that he purchased the bark at Key West, in his examination before me he has sworn that Delaunay paid for it. It is proved also that the repairs at Mobile were settled for by Delaunay's clerk.

Pelletier paid nothing. It is proved that when the bark sailed for Carthagena, Delaunay came to Mobile and left the ship only when she was in the lower bay, returning in a tug which took her down from the wharf. It is proved also that Pelletier had nothing to do with the tug, and that its services, if settled for at all, must have been paid by Delaunay. He also attended to the outgoing manifest, which described Pelletier only as master of the bark. Delaunay furnished and put on board the 5 franc pieces and gold alleged to have been shipped, and if there was any insurance upon either the vessel or its contents, which does not appear, it must have been obtained by Delaunay without instruction. Pelletier swears that he paid no attention to insurance.

More than this, a witness, Louis Moses, who has been a resident of New Orleans ever since 1852, engaged in exchange brokerage and insurance, has testified before me that in 1860 he was intimately acquainted with the firm of Delaunay, Rice & Co., holding a power of attorney to transact its business; that he furnished to Delaunay money to fit out the bark; that on the 24ᵗʰ day of October 1860, three days before the bark cleared from Mobile, he advanced to Delaunay $ 15,850, for which he took Delaunay's notes, which he now has unpaid, and exhibited to me, and that he and another man, whom he named, each advanced the further sum of $ 5000; that to obtain this money Delaunay told him he had to put money on board the bark; that he expected a great profit from it; that the bark was fitted out to go to some places in Hayti; that Antonio Pelletier was the captain, and was to engage to import some negroes into Louisiana, and that was the reason why money was to be put on board; that the negroes had been already bought, and that Pelletier was to go and pay for them and bring them. The witness testified further that he himself was to have an interest in the venture, and that Delaunay promised that he should have one hundred of the negroes for the money he advanced. He further testified that the scheme was to land the negroes on a desert island west of the Mississippi, near the mainland of Louisiana. This testimony has not been impeached, nor has it been discredited by anything that has appeared before me. I have not been able to discover any inherent contradiction or improbability in it. If believed, it has a direct and potential bearing upon the merits of the claim made on behalf of Pelletier. It bears upon the ownership of the bark, and of the money on board, as well as upon the character of the voyage which the bark made. It accounts for Delaunay's putting the money on board, paying the bills, being present at the bark's departure, taking a registry in the name of Edward Lee Launde, or Edward de Launa, at Mobile instead of New Orleans, where he resided, and when Pelletier was there, and many other things which I shall notice hereafter. It is not to be overlooked, however, that according to his own testimony the witness was a participant in fitting out an illegal voyage to the extent of furnishing a portion of the funds for it, with full knowledge of the uses to which it was planned the money should be devoted. In other words, he was an accomplice. His testimony, therefore, must be weighed with caution, and, if relied upon, should find elsewhere, as I think it does, corroboration.

At Mobile, as the claimant's memorial states, he purchased and put on board the bark a full cargo of about 200,000 feet of pitch-pine lumber, sawed to his order, to fill a contract he had in New Granada, and also took 36 barrels of ship bread to fill an order from Carthagena. The memorial states, also, that he had on board 36,000 5 franc pieces (silver), $ 3000 in American gold, and about $ 2000 in Spanish-American gold ounces and fractions of ounces, meaning to buy gold dust of Antioquia. He also took on board two kegs of powder and some more; also a large number of pistols and some guns or rifles. Neither the powder nor the guns or pistols were mentioned in the ship's outgoing manifest. On the contrary, the manifest which he signed and delivered to the collector, and which he swore contained a full, just, and true account of all the goods, wares, and merchandise on board the vessel, and that if other goods, wares or merchandise should be put on board previous to sailing, he would immediately report the same to the collector, mentioned only 118,000 feet of lumber and 29 barrels of bread, marked 'Various, and J. B. & Co.; value $ 2214. 40'. The manifest was sworn to by Pelletier on the 27th day of October 1860. On the same day a shipper's manifest of the cargo of the 'bark William, Pelletier, master', was signed, verified and filed in the collector's office exhibiting as shipped on the bark 29 barrels of bread and 118,000 feet of lumber, marked 'J. B. & Co.; value $ 2214. 40'. Both manifest, doubtless, describe the same property, but the latter declared the articles to have been shipped by M. S. Charlock & Co., and intended to be landed at Carthagena. Of the lumber 34,000 feet were loaded on deck and only 84,000 feet in the hold. Why it was thus loaded for a contemplated voyage of some 3000 miles, when the capacity of the hold was sufficient for fully twice the whole quantity, is not apparent. It may have been for convenience of loading and unloading, or it may have been to give to the voyage a colorable appearance of legitimate trading.

At Mobile Pelletier had shipped a crew, consisting of fourteen besides himself, including cook, steward, and clerk. Thomas Collar the second mate had been introduced to him at Key West, and had come with him in the bark from Key West to Mobile, where he was given the superintendence of repairs.

At Key West he was known as Thomas Collar, yet at Mobile he signed the shipping articles with the name Samuel Gerdon, was subsequently addressed by Pelletier as Gerdon, and later, in the following voyage, signed a protest with the same name. At first Collar testified before me that he signed in his true name — Thomas Collar — but afterward, when confronted by his protest, he acknowledged that he had used the name Samuel Gerdon, and accounted for the false personation by saying that the shipping master at Mobile had given him a protection paper with that name, alleging that he had no blank to fill otherwise. The seamen, or a portion of them, as Pelletier states, were furnished to him by a shipping master at New Orleans, it may be presumed at the instance of Delaunay, who resided there. They were forwarded from New Orleans to Mobile by steamboat. They were Frenchmen, and they are described by Pelletier 'as rowdies and highbinders, such as are in general only to be found in Southern seaports'. Indeed, in the entire crew, including cook, clerk, and steward, there was but one Ame-

32

rican. Some other shipments of sailors were afterward made at other ports during the voyage, but they also were Frenchmen or Spaniards.

The ship cleared for Carthagena on the 27th of October 1860, and arrived in that port late in November. There, as stated by Pelletier, the lumber on deck was unloaded, some gold dust was purchased, with some other articles, and some of the private stores of the captain were sold. There Meyers, the chief mate, deserted and escaped on board a British man of war. A revolution then in progress having prevented the sale of the remaining lumber, the bark cleared for Rio Hacha, a port some over one hundred miles east-northeast from Carthagena, having shipped at least one seaman, a Spaniard, and taken on board one Bina, a colored refugee, and Juan Cortez, his wife, child, and servant as passengers for Rio Hacha. Cortez had some freight with him. He and his family were dark, probably mulattoes.

Finding the winds and currents contrary, and having lost an anchor, the bark bore away to the northward and continued on that course about 700 miles. Collar testifies that when the anchor was lost, a day or two after leaving Carthagena, Cortez, whose wife was sick, desired to be put on shore. Pelletier's testimony on this subject is inconsistent with itself. At first he stated Cortez desired to be landed at the first accessible port. That was Carthagena, within two hours' sail from the place where the anchor was lost. But he did not go thither. He said he wanted to proceed on his voyage. In his later testimony he represents Cortez as asking, when near Grand Cayman, to be landed in Jamaica or some port in that direction. Whether after he has sailed so far away from Rio Hacha he intended to return on a long tack to that port, I do not deem it necessary to inquire. He had passengers on board whom he had contracted to deliver there with their freight.

But it may well be that Cortez was anxious and alarmed at being carried so far from his place of destination and consented, even desired, to be landed at Grand Cayman. To this Pelletier assented and put into the port of Georgetown, on that island, arriving there December 19, 1860. There he settled with Cortez, taking from him all his freight at a valuation of $ 1000 and deducting $ 500 for his services. I do not find that the settlement was obtained by threats or duress, or that it was any other than amicable, though it was subsequently contended that the freight belonged to one Cano, British vice-consul at Carthagena, that Cortez had only the care of it, and that it had been extorded from him

by Pelletier. I do not find sufficient evidence to justify such a contention.

On the 24th of December the bark cleared for Port au Prince in Hayti. It is not quite apparent why she was cleared for Hayti. She had cleared from Carthagena for Rio Hacha, professedly in order to dispose there of the lumber in her hold. If her course afterward to the vicinity of Grand Cayman was really to obtain offing for a long tack to Rio Hacha it is not apparent why she did not clear again for that port. It was little more distant than Port au Prince, and the bark would have been assisted by wind and currents. The voyage to Port au Prince was to the windward, against strong northeast winds and strong currents. No explanation has been given of this, and none appears, except perhaps a purpose to obtain a cargo of guano at the island of Navassa, eighty or one hundred miles west of Hayti. The claimant testifies that at the beginning of his voyage he had an understanding with Delaunay, that if he found it practicable, he should bring back to New Orleans a cargo of guano, and that at the island of Grand Cayman he arranged with a person to show him guano, and further, that when first at Port au Prince, before he had any trouble with the authorities, he applied to one Vil Maximilian for fifty men and a few women to go with him to the island of Navassa, and there load his vessel with guano. It is evident, however, from what subsequently occurred, that there never was any serious purpose to look for such a cargo.

At Port au Prince, where the bark arrived some time after the middle of January 1861, the remainder of the lumber, or most of it, was sold, but before much of it was delivered several of the crew, alleged to have been disorderly, were sent on shore and imprisoned at Pelletier's instance. Bina, the refugee from Carthagena, also left the ship and denounced it to the Haytian authorities as a slaver. The claimant's testimony is that this charge was made after Bina had demanded $ 100 from him to pay for a passage back to the Spanish Main, with threats in case of refusal, and that the demand was refused. The imprisoned sailors also preferred accusations. Very naturally and reasonably, the police boarded the vessel and made a partial search. They found arms and ammunition on board, an unusual number of hand cuffs, alleged to have been twenty pairs, but which, as Pelletier and Collar testify, were only eight in number, and they found a large number of water casks. Pelletier and Collar swear there were only eight such casks, but the former admits that he had in addition from twenty to twenty-five barrels, which he filled with salt water for ballast. All these things are acknowledged accompaniments of slave trading. The police did not find the kegs of powder, nor any of the pistols that had been on board. These may have been sold before the search was made or have escaped observation. The search does not appear to have been very thorough. In view of the accusation of Bina and the imprisoned sailors, and of the results of the search, as well as of his application to Maximilian for laborers to go to Navassa, the Haytian authorities evidently had strong suspicions, and I think, with much reason, that the bark was a slaver out on an illegitimate cruise. Yet, after a short delay, they gave up the vessel to the claimant, and at his request gave him a clearance for New Orleans. Their suspicions, however, were not wholly allayed. When the bark sailed, the latter part of February, she was followed a considerable distance by an armed vessel, apparently to observe what course she would take. She did not go westward on the most direct course to New Orleans. Had she taken that course she would have had favoring winds and assisting currents, and she might have taken in her course the guano islands of Navassa. Had there been any real design to take a cargo of guano she must have been taken that course. There was nothing to hinder it. The bark was in good order. The islands were in possession of an American company, and laborers were doubtless there to assist in loading vessels. There could have been no need of laborers taken from Hayti. But instead of taking that course the bark turned eastward around Mole St. Nicole, and continued her course, on the north side of Hayti, against fresh breezes and swift currents, on one route indeed, toward New Orleans, but obviously not the best at that season of the year.

According to Pelletier's statement, finding he had not sufficient ballast, though he had more than 50 tons, he put into Man-of-War Bay, in the island of Grand Inagua, to obtain more. There, by drifting on a reef, the fastenings of his rudder were broken, and it hung only on the forward pintle. It needed two new pintles to replace those which were broken. They might, doubtless, have been supplied by any blacksmith at Inagua, but after lashing the rudder with chains the bark put to sea. Still, not steering well, Pelletier, as he states, endeavored to make a port (La Plata) in San Domingo, in an opposite direction from the course to New Orleans, in order in that port to make repairs. He was soon found on the banks of Caicos, east of Inagua, and soon after far to the southwest, off the coast of Hayti, near Mole St. Nicole, where he was endeavoring to beat to the windward. Several days he was in sight from Cape Haytien, where

there was a good harbor open to commerce, which he could easily have entered in a few hours, and where he might have obtained all needed repairs, but he made no attempt to enter there. Even if his chronometer were out of order, as he alleges, he must have known where he was. He claims to have been a good sailor. He had in his hands the Coast Pilot directions. He was all the while in sight of the coast, and it is incredible that he did not recognize his vicinity to Cape Haytien. Instead of entering it he kept along the coast, saluted with a French flag a passing vessel, and entered Fort Liberté, an obscure port of Hayti, not open to commerce and only about twenty miles from Cape Haytien, mistaking it, as he says, for the harbor of La Plata in San Domingo. I am unable to see how his entrance into Fort Liberté could have been due to any such mistake. The distance from Cape Haytien was too short, only about twenty miles. La Plata is nearly one hundred miles east. The approaches to the two ports, as described in the sailing directions, are notably unlike, and as the land all the way from Cape Haytien must have been in sight, he must have known he was far from La Plata.

At Fort Liberté he floated a French flag, never an American; proclaimed his vessel to be the *Guillaume Tell* from Havana, bound to Havre; ordered his men to speak only the French language, and asserted that his own name was Jules Letellier. He even caused a letter to be written to the French consul repeating these false statements, signed Jules Letellier. The excuse given for this attempted deception is that when on entering the port he saw the Haytian flag he was terrified, remembering his trouble at Port au Prince. I think that is a very insufficient excuse. There was no cause for any such scare, and it is difficult to believe that it existed. The bark had been given a clearance from Port au Prince, and, if she was in distress, that accounted fully for her being again in a Haytian port for repairs.

The falsehoods mentioned were not all he told. He said he had been at Guadaloupe, had been obliged to throw part of his cargo overboard, and that he had been aground on those banks. False statements, when attempts to mislead, very naturally awaken the suspicion of those to whom they are made, and they are in some measure evidence of guilt. Pelletier's attempted deception was soon discovered by the French consul and the Haytian authorities, and his arrest and the seizure of the bark followed.

In view of the facts thus mentioned, which I think are established by the evidence, I can hardly escape from the conviction that the voyage of the bark *William* was an illegal voyage; that its paramount purpose was to obtain a cargo of negroes, either by purchase or kidnapping, and bring them into slavery in the state of Louisiana, and that the load of lumber and the profession of a purpose to go for a cargo of guano were mere covers to conceal the true character of the enterprise. In my opinion, it is beyond doubt that had the bark been captured and brought into an American port, when she was seized at Fort Liberté, she would have been condemned by the United States courts as an intended slaver. And I think the Haytian authorities had such reasons for suspecting, even believing, that she was a slaver, with evil designs against their people; that they were justified in seizing her in one of their ports; and arresting the master, at least for examination. If the uncontradicted testimony of Mr. Moses is to be believed, the voyage was concerted between Delaunay and Pelletier; the bark was procured for the illicit use; it was manned and supplied suitably for such a purpose, and its subsequent conduct down to its hovering along the coast and entering an obscure and private harbor of Hayti under false colors when a better one was easily accessible are all consistent with such a purpose. The suspicious circumstances begin at the beginning. The transfer of the title to Delaunay, as stated by Pelletier, in order to obtain registry *at New Orleans*; the registry *at Mobile*, in the name of Lee Launda, or Edward De Launa or Edward Lee Launa; the taking powder, pistols, and guns in quantities on board without mentioning them in the manifest; the loading of about one-third of the lumber on deck when the hold was more than sufficient for it all, the assumption of a false name by the mate; the character of the crew, all foreigners and roughs; the obviously fallacious pretense that a cargo of guano was sought; the concealing the name of the ship, and false representations respecting her nationality, the port from which she sailed, and her destination; the change of the name of the master; the unusual number of manacles on board, the large number of watercasks, including barrels capable of holding water — all speak with one voice. They all tend in the same direction, and collectively they almost force to the conclusion that the voyage was illicit, and that slave trading was its object. Add to these the fact that Pelletier had applied to a Haytian to obtain fifty men and some women (blacks, of course) to assist him in obtaining guano, and I can not avoid thinking the Haytian Government, though all these facts may not have been known at the time, had ample reason for suspecting, if not believing, that the bark was a slaver, and that

the design of Pelletier was to obtain cargo of blacks from their country. Even the representatives of foreign governments then present in Hayti unanimously expressed to the government their opinion that Pelletier had been guilty of piracy, and that the government was authorized to put in force against him judicial proceedings. And Mr. Lewis, commercial agent of the United States, joined Mr. Byron, consul-general and acting chargé d'affaires of Great Britain, in asking that the captain and bark, then under arrest, should not be set at liberty.

. Having now reviewed and stated what, in my judgment, the evidence exhibits respecting the character and conduct of the voyage down to the entrance of the bark into Fort Liberté, and noticed also the false pretenses of the claimant there, I proceed to examine the action of the Haytian Government, of which he complains. Shortly after the bark's arrival, and while the falsity of the assertion that she was a French vessel on a voyage from Havana to Havre was still undiscovered, one Miranda, who had shipped at Port au Prince on the bark as boatswain, escaped to the shore and denounced to the authorities the vessel and the master. What the charge he made was, whether it was of piracy or slave trading, or a false pretense of nationality, does not distinctly appear, though from his subsequent testimony it seems probable that it was an accusation of all those offenses. It led to the discovery that the vessel and the master were not what had been pretended, but that the vessel was the *William*, which had been suspected at Port au Prince, and that her master was Pelletier. He was therefore ordered to come on shore and to bring the ship's papers. This he refused to do. The French consul also sent a similar order, which Pelletier disregarded, and, having obtained the pintles he desired, he endeavored to escape at night out of the harbor. He was then arrested and taken on shore with the ship's papers.

The bark and the crew were also seized. The consul then examined the papers, and, finding that the vessel was American, turned it, together with Pelletier and the crew, over to the Haytian authorities, who committed the master and crew to jail in irons. Some time afterward they were sent to Cape Haytien and imprisoned there, still in irons, and within a few days they were sent to Port au Prince and marched in irons to the criminal prison there. The statements made by Pelletier and Collar, the mate, of abuse and cruelties inflicted upon them during their transfer from Fort Liberté to Port au Prince are extremely sensational, and if they are true they reveal barbarous treatment by the populace and needless severity of the government officers. But the testimony of these two persons, I think, is very highly colored and in many particulars quite unreliable. Doubtless the populace was much excited, and not without reason.

They probably did insult and abuse the captives. There is other evidence to show it. But both Pelletier and Collar assert unqualifiedly as positive facts many things of which they could have had no knowledge, even if they existed, and they assert some things which are proved to have had no existence. One illustration will suffice: Pelletier states that during the march from the landing at Port au Prince to the prison, Louis Legallin, one of his boys, being weak, fainted from fatigue and loss of blood and fell, when the Haytian officers put a stick through his shackles and dragged him over the pavements and rough stones, so that his skull was worn through and he was dead on arrival at the prison, when his body was thrown into the yard and some small boys were allowed to beat out his eyes with sticks for their amusement. This was horrible, if true; but the statement is not true, and it was known by Pelletier to be false when he made it. Legallin was subsequently indicted, tried, and acquitted in Pelletier's presence. Many other assertions of sensational facts have been made by this witness which have been disproved or which were beyond his possible knowledge. The same thing may be said of the testimony of Collar. They tend greatly to impair my confidence in any portion of their testimony where it is not corroborated. Soon after they had been taken to Port au Prince Pelletier and Collar, with ten of the crew, were indicted for piracy and attempted slave dealing on the coast of Hayti. The indictment charged also that Pelletier had at sea extorted from Cortez a promise to pay a large sum of money for consenting to land him on the nearest land, and that at Grand Cayman he had compelled Cortez, by threats of murder, to give him a deed for all the merchandise intrusted to his (Cortez's) care by one Antonio Cano amounting to more than $ 3000. Prior to the presentation of this indictment the accused had been severally subjected to an examination according to the criminal practice of Hayti.

Meanwhile, Cortez and Cano had come to Port au Prince, and the question arose whether they could join in the criminal prosecution in order to recover thereby compensation for the injuries they alleged they had sustained at the hands of Pelletier.

This question came before a court consisting of Judge Boco and two others, and the court decided that Cortez and Cano could not join the prosecution; that the courts of Hayti had no jurisdiction over their claims but that the criminal courts of the country had jurisdiction of the prosecution for piracy and slave trading. Pelletier states that the court decided to release him. This was not so. The decision was directly to the contrary. But as it was decided that the claim of Cortez and Cano could not be joined with the criminal proceeding, an appeal was taken to the court of cassation, where that decision was reversed. The judgment that the Haytian courts had jurisdiction of the criminal proceeding was left undisturbed, and the prosecution was sent down for trial. Pelletier further asserts that the three judges who made the first decision were sent to jail. Of that there is no proof beyond his assertion. The records show no such thing, and the statement is altogether improbable. Allowance should doubtless be made for mistaken assertions of a witness indicted and tried in a foreign country before strange judges, and in accordance with a course of criminal procedure not familiar to him, but positive misrepresentations respecting the trial are hardly excusable.

The court building and the records of judicial proceedings at Port au Prince have been destroyed by fire since 1861, but official reports of the trial of Pelletier and the others indicted, attested, and signed by the judges, and published at the time in the government official journal, are before me. I think them entitled to credit. They reveal a very different conduct of the judicial proceedings anterior to and during the trial from that testified to by him. Waiving, for the present, consideration of the question whether the Haytian courts had jurisdiction, to which I shall return hereafter, I can discover in those proceedings, including the trial, no satisfactory evidence that they were oppressive or unfair, or that they were not conducted temperately and according to the ordinary course of criminal trials. There are statements of Pelletier to the contrary, but I think them unsustained.

The main trial commenced on the 25th of August 1861, and continued five days. It was at no time hurried. At its beginning the court provided an interpreter for Thomas Collar, the only defendant who did not understand the French language, the language of Hayti. Indeed, all the defendants except Collar were natives of France.

Pelletier declined his right to select six of the jury, denying the jurisdiction of the court, though that had previously been decided against him. Counsel were offered to him by the court, but he declined them because he had counsel of his own selection. Very soon, however, he refused to make any defense and requested his counsel to withdraw. Of this he gives two accounts, not quite harmonious. One is that the pilot he had taken from Carthagena, the seaman Lobos he had shipped there, and whom he had caused to be imprisoned, and the boy he had left at Port au Prince were seized without any charge and imprisoned, so that he was unable to procure their attendance, and that he declared, as his defense was thus gagged, he should make no defense, but deny the jurisdiction of the court, and begged his counsel to withdraw.

But the facts were that he had left the pilot he took at Carthagena at Georgetown, in Grand Cayman. He was not, therefore, seized and imprisoned by the Haytian authorities, and Lobos was a witness and testified during the trial Pelletier's presence. At another time Pelletier testifies that he refused to make any defense, and dismissed his counsel because the ship's papers were refused to him. Of this hereafter.

He makes another statement. It is that Mr. Laveau, one of his counsel, was sent to jail for alluding to the extraordinary means resorted to the produce a conviction, and to the abstraction of his papers so that they could not be used in his defense. But the official report gives a different account. It is that 'the acting government attorney again requested the court to appoint a lawyer to defend Pelletier, whereupon the latter arose and reiterated the declaration which he had already made, viz, that he would not accept the services of any lawyer for his defense. « I shall offer no defense », said he; « I have resolved not to defend myself in view of the base intrigues that have been resorted to in order to gag my defense.» The judge of the criminal court requested the accused to be more moderate, and told him he must retract the words « base intrigues ». Mr. Laveau then proceeded to create a disturbance, and was called to order. He again interrupted, whereupon the judge ordered him to be led out of the court room.' It thus appears that he was led out for a contempt. He had been dismissed as counsel previously. There was no order for imprisonment.

Pelletier also states that he was shut up in a box having only a small aperture, through which he could see the court proceedings only imperfectly. There is no other evidence to sustain this statement, and a witness resident in Port au Prince at the time, familiar with the courtroom, and who had served as a juror, has testified that there was no such box or close dock in it. The trial proceeded, numerous witnesses were examined, each in the absence of all others, and at the close of each one's testimony the accused were severally asked whether what had been testified was true. To these questions they all,

except Pelletier, gave affirmative answers. He refused to make any answers. Among the witnesses was Miranda, the boatswain. He testified *inter alia* that Pelletier had told him he intended to take from Hayti 150 men to sell as slaves. There was also evidence that Pelletier had said he intended to give a ball on the bark at Fort Liberté and carry off a number of young men and women. To this Pelletier made no denial, though asked what he had to say in reply to the charge.

His application to Maximilian at Port au Prince was also proved. This was but a part of the evidence. After a trial, lasting five days, the jury returned a verdict convicting Pelletier of piracy, of the fraudulent abstraction of goods at sea, or Grand Cayman Island, and convicting him also of an attempt at piracy and the slave trade committed on the coast of Hayti. Three others of the accused, Collar, Brown, and the captain's clerk, were convicted as accomplices, and the remainder of the accused were acquitted. On this conviction Pelletier was sentenced to death, and the bark and its contents were adjudged to be confiscated. On appeal to the court of cassation the judgment of the criminal court was in all respects affirmed, except so far as it adjudged death to Pelletier.

That was set aside, for the reason that the statutes of Hayti imposed the penalty of death for piracy only in cases when murder has been committed, and the case was sent to the criminal court, sitting at Cape Haytien, that 'without the assistance of a jury, basing its judgment upon the verdict already rendered', it might enforce the penal law of Hayti according to the Haytian statutes of 1815 against piracy. The criminal court thereupon sentenced the claimant to five years imprisonment, and the court of cassation on a second appeal confirmed the judgment.

There are some other averments of Pelletier impugning the fairness of the judicial proceedings against him that require notice. The principal one is that copies of the ship's papers needed for his defense, and to which he was entitled by the Haytian law, were withheld from him. He asserts that application had been made for them before the trial; that the minister of foreign affairs promised he should be present when the package containing them should be opened, and should see them and take what would be necessary; that his lawyers took every means to get the papers, even applying to Judge Boco for an order on the clerk to exhibit them; that on the presentation of the order to the clerk, and his going into another room to get them, a subordinate officer seized them and carried them away.

All this, if it occurred, he could have known only through the report of his counsel. It may be true, but it does not prove that at another time the copies could not have been obtained. There may have been some reason for the officers taking the papers at that time. Certainly no application for them to a judge or to the minister of foreign affairs was ever refused. Permission to have them was always granted, and it was not of this that Pelletier's counsel complained, although they did complain that the papers were withheld from them while the trial was proceeding.

It should require clear evidence to prove that an inferior officer causelessly interfered to defeat the order of the judge, and the ready offer made by the secretary of State and the minister of foreign affairs. Mr. Linstant, the leading counsel of Pelletier, complained of the action of the court respecting the papers at the trial. But the report shows that when the papers were demanded the demand was coupled with an application for delay. The latter application the court refused, *but ordered the papers to be produced forthwith*. This seems not to have been satisfactory. It was then that Pelletier declared, by the advice of this counsel, that his defense was gagged, declined to defend himself, and dismissed his counsel. The papers were not withheld, but a postponement of the trial was denied. Mr. Linstant in a letter to his client, reviewing the trial, says : 'We were offered the communication of the documents while the court was sitting, as if, while we were attending to the debates and while our attention was riveted upon the testimony of the witnesses we could withdraw ourselves from these important cases to read papers of such importance'. That is a complaint without much substance, intended perhaps as an excuse for having advised his client to make no defense.

Pelletier also asserts that attempts were made to bribe witnesses to testify falsely against him. The charge is a serious one, but I think it wholly unsustained by any reliable evidence. It rests upon two *ex parte* affidavits made in 1868 by two of the sailors, who had been indicted and tried with the captain and mate of the bark, and upon testimony of the mate, Collar. The affidavits are loose. They speak of attempted bribery at Port au Prince during the trouble there before the bark cleared for New Orleans, not of efforts to obtain testimony for the trial, and Brown's affidavit is principally, if not wholly, a hearsay statement. Collar has testified before me that the American consul came to see him in the hospital, to which he had been removed from the prison, and told him if he would testify falsely against Pelletier he would receive considerable money and get his liberty. If so, it was not the act of the Haytian Government. But the story is too improbable to be believed. The consul must have been Mr. Lewis, who was the only consul at that time, and it is inconceivable that he attempted bribery. Besides, Collar, when pressed by repeated inquiries whether the consul asked him to testify *falsely*, equivocated, and after some hesitation said 'he wanted me to testify Pelletier had done an injury there'.

There are other statements made by Pelletier respecting alleged wrongs of which he could have had no knowledge beyond hearsay, statements entirely uncorroborated. I do not think it necessary to review them. After his conviction, and some time in May 1862 he was removed to Cape Haytien—marched, as he says, about 250 miles. (The distance from Port au Prince to Cape Haytien is only ninety miles.) At Cape Haytien he was confined in prison until in the following November or December, when, at the request of Mr. Whidden, then American consul, he was sent back by sea to Port au Prince, where for a time he was confined, and then transferred to a hospital, from which he made his escape on the 11th day of November 1863 and succeeded in reaching Kingston in Jamaica.

I now come to consider the question which I have thus far waived. It is whether, in view of the law of nations as it was in 1861, the Haytian Government had jurisdiction to try, condemn, and punish the master and to confiscate the bark and other property. The bark was a vessel of the United States, duly registered as such, and the master was a naturalized American citizen. The ship's papers showed this, and they were in the possession of the Haytian authorities. They knew, therefore, that the bark was American. It is true that on the 3d of May 1861 Mr. Lewis, then commercial agent of the United States, joined the British consul-general in a request to the government that the bark and the captain, then under arrest, should not be set at liberty. It is also true that on the 15th of May 1861, upon being consulted by the secretary of state for foreign relations of the republic, the representatives of the foreign governments then present at Port au Prince, including the English, French, and, six others, unanimously expressed their opinion that the Haytian Government had authority to take jurisdiction and proceed against Pelletier for the crime of piracy, though the bark was American. But this, while it tends to show that the government acted cautiously, without intention to violate the law of nations, was an insufficient warrant for taking jurisdiction, if in fact that law disallowed it. Later, on the 6th of August 1861, after the indictment had been presented, Mr. Lewis protested against the exercise of jurisdiction in the case by Hayti, and demanded that, in accordance with the laws of nations and those of Hayti, Captain Pelletier, his vessel, and effects should be delivered over to him, in order that they might be sent to the United States, there to be tried. This protest and demand, however, did not avail. The Haytian courts had on that day decided, after a protracted discussion, that they had jurisdiction, overruling pleadings to the contrary.

In this judgment, I think, the Haytian courts were mistaken. They seem to have been guided by the statute law of Hayti rather than by the law of nations, which should have been the rule of decision. I do not deem it necessary to inquire what the municipal law of Hayti was respecting piracy or slave trading.

What constitutes piracy by the municipal law of a state may not be piracy as understood by the law of nations. The slave trade has been declared to be piracy by the statutes of several nations. But the slave trade was not piracy in the view of that law in 1861, nor is it now, though repeated efforts have been made to have it so regarded.

It is the general rule of the law of nations that offenses committed by a vessel at sea or on board while in port of a foreign country are justiciable, or triable only in the courts of the country to which the vessel belongs. The rule is founded upon the accepted principle that the vessel is regarded as part of the territory of the country to which it belongs, and criminal laws do not extend outside of the country which has enacted them. There are, it is true, some exceptions to this rule. One is to its applicability to offenses committed in foreign ports. If they are committed against the peace of the country where the vessel lies, disturbing it, they are cognizable in the courts of that country. Not so if they are offenses committed by persons attached to the vessel upon others likewise attached and committed on board. But crimes and offenses committed even on board by persons not belonging to the ship are thus cognizable, so also offenses committed on shore, no matter who may be the offender. And piracy, as understood by the law of nations, is also an exception to the general rule. That is regarded as a crime against all mankind, and it is punishable wherever the offender is found, no matter where the offense was committed, and no matter what was the nationality of the vessel. These are exceptional cases. The present is not within the description of either. It is the general rule which must now be applied. I am of opinion, therefore, that under the law of nations the courts of Hayti had no

jurisdiction to try and punish the master of the bark *William* for any of the offenses he had committed, or to condemn and confiscate the vessel. The offenses charged in the indictment were piracy, misuse of a passenger at sea, extortion by threats from Cortez, at Grand Cayman, a British island, and attempted slave dealing at Fort Liberté, Hayti. The indictment set forth the acts alleged to have been done at sea and at Grand Cayman, which constituted the piracy charged, if there was any. But it is undeniable that none of them were piratical in view of the law of nations. It may be admitted that had any act been done which the law of nations regarded as piratical the Haytian courts would have had jurisdiction, though the bark was American, for the reason I have stated above. But though acts may have been done which by the Haytian law constitute piracy, those courts could have no jurisdiction over a foreign vessel or its master who had committed them, unless the acts were also piratical under the law of nations, or unless the offense had been committed on Haytian territory. Let it be conceded that a government may lawfully seize in its own ports a vessel and her master when there is probable cause for believing that they are piratical or have piratical intentions, yet, if they belong to another nation, they must be sent home for trial, for the courts of the country where they belong have, by the law of nations, the exclusive right to try them. I speak only of cases where no piratical act has been done within the port or territory in which the arrest is made. For an infraterritorial outrage, the vessel and master may be treated as having forfeited their nationality.

There has been one decision made by the court of cassation of France in 1832 that at first sight may appear to be in conflict with some of the opinions I have expressed, but a careful examination of it will reveal that it is in entire harmony with them. I refer to the case of the *Carlo Alberto*, reported in Devilleneuve's General Collection of Laws and Judgments for 1832.

The facts of the case as they appear in the report were as follows : A conspiracy had been formed between persons in Italy and others in France, principally in Marseilles, to execute a plot against the French Government. A commencement had been made by the Italian conspirators in the charter of the steamer *Carlo Alberto* at Leghorn for a pretended voyage to Barcelona. The steamer took on board clandestinely at night the Duchess de Berri and others, in number twelve, who assumed false names, and clandestinely landed the Duchess and six of her suite at night of April 28 or 29, with the aid of a fishing boat, which had watched the passage of the steamer, on the west side of Marseilles, following which and in consequence of it the plot broke out at Marseilles on the morning of the 30ᵗʰ of April. The steamer, with the others conspirators, subsequently put into the French port, claiming to be in distress, when they were arrested. It is apparent that an offense had been committed on French territory by landing a part of conspirators. This was more than an unexecuted intention to perpetrate a crime. The plot broke out almost immediately in consequence of what was done, and what was done was the act of all the conspirators, for they were acting in pursuance of a common design. What the court of cassation decided was that 'the principle of the law of nations, according to which a foreign vessel, allied or neutral, is considered as forming a part of the territory of the nation to which it belongs, and, consequently, entitled to the privilege of the same inviolability with the territory itself, ceases to protect a vessel which commits acts of hostility in the French territory inconsistent with its character of ally or neutral; as if, for example, such vessel be chartered as an instrument of conspiracy against the safety of the state, and, after having landed some of the persons concerned in these acts, still continues to hover near the coast with the rest of the conspirators on board, and at last puts into port under pretense of distress'. (Wheaton, part 2, section 104.)

This case is not at all inconsistent with what I have said, viz, that, to justify the courts of a nation in taking jurisdiction of offenses committed by vessels of other nations, the offenses must have been committed in whole or in part (not merely planned to be committed) within the territory of that nation. To this rule I find no exception beyond those I have mentioned. Slave trading being not rated as piracy by the law of nations, is not one.

Such, without enlargement, I understand to be the universally acknowledged rule of the laws of nations, and they, I think, determine that the Haytian courts were without jurisdiction. Whatever may have been Pelletier's intentions, or the design of the voyage, it is undeniable that there was no piratical act committed, no act recognized as piratical by the laws of nations, and none was attempted. Evil intentions not carried out are not piracy. No law punishes mere intentions without acts. Abuse of a passenger by the master is not piracy, and if it be admitted that Pelletier extorted by threats property from Cortez at Grand Cayman, it was an offense against British authority there, but it was not piracy. Nor was there anything done by him in the ports of Hayti that amounted to piracy recognized

as such by law of nations. As I have said I do not care to inquire what·the law of Hayti defining piracy may have been. It is another law which is to be the rule of decision in this case; so it is stipulated in the protocol. The false personation by Pelletier at Fort Liberté, the change of the name of the bark, the unwarranted use of the French flag, the false assertions respecting the port of clearance and the port of destination, and the other deceptions practiced there, censurable and wicked as they were and indicative of evil intent, were still not *acts* of piracy. Nor was Pelletier's inquiry of Maximilian at Port au Prince whether he could obtain men and women from Hayti to load his bark with guano at the guano islands an act of piracy, though reasonably awakening suspicions that his intent was slave kidnapping. Nor was his later project (if he entertained it) of giving a ball on his vessel at Fort Liberté and carrying off those invited, unexecuted and unattempt as it was, an *act* of piracy or even slave trading. At most, these were evil intentions not carried out. There was in truth no overt act of piracy, amounting to piracy as understood in the law of nations or of slave trading, and none was charged. There was therefore, in my judgment, plainly no jurisdiction in the Haytian courts over the bark or over the master. It follows that having suffered in consequence of the unauthorized and wrongful assumption of jurisdiction by those courts to try and punish him, the Republic of Hayti may be justly required to make reparation to Pelletier for the wrongs he has suffered.

It remains then to consider what sum should be regarded (as) just reparation. The claims submitted on behalf of Pelletier are primarily three. He claims the value of the bark and her tackle and furniture confiscated, the value of the cargo and money alleged to have been on board when the bark was seized, and compensation for the personal wrongs inflicted upon him, including oppression and unfairness in the judicial proceedings, and his imprisonment.

He claims also compensation for the losses which he alleges he sustained in consequence of his detention in Hayti. I notice each of these in their order.

In regard to the first, the claim for the value of the bark and its furniture, I am of the opinion that the claim ought not to be allowed. The evidence satisfies me the claimant was not the owner of the bark. According to his own testimony, though at Key West he took the title in his own name, he afterward, at Mobile, transferred it to Delaunay, in order, as he says, that it might be registered at New Orleans. His memorial, to which he has sworn, made in 1864,

33

states that though he made the transfer to Delaunay, he retained the ownership and took a power of attorney from Delaunay to do with the vessel what he thought proper. He did not then assert that he took a bill of sale, though the memorial was evidently intended to set forth every claim he had in the fullest and largest manner. That assertion was not made until more than twenty years afterward, and not until after Delaunay's death.

It may be conceded that ordinarily a register in which it is asserted that the person named in it as owner had taken an oath that he was the only owner, is not conclusive or evidence in a contest between that person and another claimant of the ownership. Generally, it has reference to the legal title only. There may be a trust, or an equitable ownership, and the true equitable owner may not know that the vessel has been registered by some other person. But in this case the registry was obtained by Delaunay at Pelletier's instance and substantially in his presence. Delaunay had the legal title, for the bark had been transferred to him by Pelletier. He had also the equitable title, for he had paid all that was paid for it. Pelletier having paid nothing, and therefore had no equitable claim. Under these circumstances I do not see how he could have successfully claimed the ownership as against Delaunay. It is a significant fact that the registry, the manifest, and the clearance were all made on the same day, October 27, 1860, the day the ship sailed. Pelletier and Delaunay were together at Mobile on that day. The ship might then have been registered as owned by Pelletier, if he was in fact the owner. There is non conceivable reason why it was not, except that Delaunay owned her.

Moreover, the great body of evidence tends to prove, as I have already noticed that Delaunay was the true and only owner and that Pelletier was only the master. Before the transfer Delaunay paid whatever was paid at Key West. Pelletier paid not a cent. Afterward Delaunay settled for repairs at Mobile. He attended to the insurance, if there was any. He attended to the manifest and to the towing of the bark out to sea. He came from New Orleans to Mobile to see the vessel off. All these are indications of ownership. On the other hand, there is not a particle of proof that Pelletier did anything that owners ordinarily do or anything more than appertained to his duty as master. And more than this, he never asserted any ownership in himself until he sent his memorial to Mr. Seward in July 1864, in which, in order to obtain governmental interference, he magnified his alleged wrongs and claimed compensation.

In his outgoing manifest he styled himself simply master, not master and owner. In his protest at Grand Cayman, December 20, 1860, he denominated himself as 'master', simply. In his letter to Mr. Hubbard, commercial agent of the United States, complaining of the seizure of the bark, dated April 6, 1861, he described himself 'master of the bark *William*, of New Orleans', and signed 'Antonio Pelletier, master', only. In his protest of June 21, 1861, while in prison at Port au Prince, he claimed only to have been master, and signed it 'Antonio Pelletier, master of the bark *William*'. And in his letter to Mr. Lewis of August 25, 1861, the day his trial commenced, he signed 'Pelletier, master'. And finally, in his protest of August 31, 1861, written after his trial and conviction, he made only the same claim. Not until the 16th of July, 1864, when he prepared his memorial to Mr. Seward, Secretary of State, and claimed therein nearly two millions and a half of dollars for the wrongs he alleged he had sustained, did he ever assert (so far as appears) that he was the owner of the bark, or anything more than the master. It is impossible, in view of this state of the proofs, to come to any other conclusion than that he was not the owner, and therefore, that he is not entitled to compensation for the loss of the bark.

And I think, also, he is not entitled to compensation for the loss of the cargo or the money on board. I am convinced that the whole venture was Delaunay's. The lumber that was shipped by Charlock & Co. Pelletier states that he paid for. It may be so, but if he did it is a fair presumption that it was bought for Delaunay and paid for with Delaunay's money. Delaunay certainly paid for everything else. As Pelletier stated, he paid for the bark, when it appears that he did not, but that Delaunay did. So it may well be with the lumber, Pelletier being but the agent for the purchase. If the lumber was his, there is nothing to explain its being shipped by Charlock & Co. In regard to the money, principally 5 franc pieces, the evidence is quite remarkable. Pelletier's first statement was that he had the money on board, not that it was his. In his testimony before me he has stated that the 5 franc pieces were sent from Paris; that they were consigned to him from Paris. This was manifestly not so. He states that when in New York, some time before the bark *William* was bought, he gave an order for them through Delaunay & Co., and that the purpose in ordering them was to exchange them at Carthagena for gold dust of Antioquia, and that for cut money. But when the order was given, if given at all, it was not known that the bark would be obtained, or that there would be any voyage to Carthagena.

Later Pelletier testified that Delaunay got the 5 franc pieces and put them on board the ship. To this statement he added: 'I paid for them in money'. When asked in what manner, he replied: 'By the general transactions between the firm and myself,' explaining that 'the firm were cotton brokers, and collected a pretty large share of money, and his share of the profits they used to pay themselves'. This is a singular explanation. The firm of Delaunay, Rice & Co. as such had no interest in the bark or in the voyage, and it was under no liability for any debt due from Pelletier to Delaunay. It is quite unlikely that such a debt, if it existed, was paid by the firm. The firm could not pay it rightfully. Pelletier himself does not profess to have any knowledge or informations that the 5 franc pieces were thus paid for. He does not state that he was informed he had been or would be charged by the firm with the money paid for him. He gave no directions for such a charge, and there is not a particle of evidence of any arrangement or understanding that the firm would pay. Yet this he swears was paying for the 5 franc pieces in money. In truth he never paid anything for them, either directly or indirectly. Now, if this be considered in connection with the other evidence, that Delaunay owned the vessel, and that the claimant was only the master; that Delaunay obtained whatever money was put on board at New Orleans, not from Paris, only three days before the vessel cleared, and himself put it on board late in the day on which she sailed, and that he insured it, if any insurance was taken, without direction or request from Pelletier, it is difficult to believe that the money was not his. Pelletier's giving not attention to insurance is unexplainable if he was the owner of the large sum of money he claims was on board an old vessel partially loaded with lumber, and destined for a voyage of some 3,000 miles over stormy seas, and at a season of the year when storms may be expected. Such is not the conduct of an owner acquainted with shipping and navigation, as Pelletier sais he was. And then the source from which the money was obtained by Delaunay and the uses for which he said it was intended, if the testimony of Moses is to be believed, contribute to show that Pelletier had no interest other than that of a master. Reviewing the whole evidence bearing upon the subject, the preponderance appears to me to be greatly in favor of the conclusion that the money on board, whatever its amount was, as well as the bark itself, belonged to Delaunay. I do not therefore feel at liberty to award to the complainant compensation for the loss of either.

But I think he is justly entitled to compensation for the personal injuries inflicted upon him; for his trial by a court that had no jurisdiction; for his condemnation and imprisonment, and his consequent sufferings. I do not overlook the fact that his conduct has given rise to reasonable suspicions that he was a slaver, and that he had evil designs against the negroes of Hayti. It is no wonder that the populace was excited and that he was treated with insults and buffetings during his marches to the prisons at Cape Haytien and Port au Prince, as he undoubtelly was. But his treatment by the inferior officers of the government was harsh. His being marched in irons was unnecessary severity.

His imprisonment was severe, even cruel, and his food was scanty and unsuited to his condition.

The cells in which he was confined were small, damp and unhealthy. For a considerable time before his removal to the hospital he was kept in irons in his cell. It matters not that he was treated as it was the habit of the Haytian Government to treat its prisoners. His sufferings were none the less on that account, and they were sufferings that the government had no right to inflict. For all this compensations is due.

And I do not forget that a long time has elapsed since it was due. For all that I make allowance. Pelletier claims also on account of alleged losses of investments of real estate, and claims in consequence of his imprisonment. These are not proved, and if they were, they were too remote consequences, if consequences at all.

Upon the whole, I award to Antonio Pelletier and against the Republic of Hayti, for the claims of the former, the sum of *fifty seven thousand and two hundred and fifty dollars*.

Witness my hand the thirteenth day of June 1885, at the city of Washington.

Award in the claim of A. H. Lazare against the Republic of Hayti, given in Washington, June 13, 1889.

In pursuance of the protocol, dated May 28, 1884, between the Hon. Frederick E. Frelinghuysen, secretary of State of the United States, and the Hon. Stephen Preston, envoy extraordinary and minister plenipotentiary of the Republic of Hayti, representing their respective governments, after having taken before the Chief Justice of the United States the oath required by the fourth article of the protocol, y have investigated the claim of A. H. Lazare against the Republic of Hayti, and I now make the following statement and *award*:

This claim grows out of a contract between the Government of Hayti and Mr. A. H. Lazare (made in September 1874, and amended in some particulars on the 11th of May 1875), which the claimant alleges that the government wrongfully violated and declared annulled. The formation of the contract is admitted by the protocol. The third article of that instrument contains the following:

'The following facts as to the claim of A. H. Lazare are admitted by the Haytian Government:

That Lazare entered into a written contract with the Haytian Government September 23, 1874, for the establishment of a national bank at Port au Prince with branches, the capital being fixed at first at $ 3,000,000, and afterward reduced to $ 1,500,000 of which capital the government was to furnish one-third part and Lazare two-thirds; that the bank was to be opened in one year from the date of the contract, and an extension of forty-five days on this time was granted on Lazare's request, and that on the day on which the bank was to be opened the Haytian Government, alleging that Lazare had not fulfilled his part of the contract, declared, in accordance with the stipulations of article 24, the contract null and void and forfeited on his, Lazare's, part.'

Such is the extent of the admission. The entire contract is before me. Its leading purpose was, as stated, to secure, through the agency of Mr. Lazare, united with the action of the government, the establishment of a national bank at Port au Prince, with branches in other cities of Hayti. By its first article a concession was made to Lazare of an exclusive right for thirty full and consecutive years, commencing at the expiration of the twelve months specified in article 23, to establish in the republic a bank styled Banque Nationale d'Haïti.

The twenty-third article described the twelve months as beginning at the time of the signature of the contract, which was in September 1874. The right granted to establish the bank became operative, therefore, only in September 1875. In this particular the concession was thus of a future right. The contract, however, made provision for various things to be done preparatory to the establishment of the bank. Hence, it is necessary to examine these, which are set forth in several articles. Some of them imposed obligations upon the grantee of the concession; others required from the government the performance of particular duties, and others still-described the privileges to be enjoyed by the bank when established and the duties it should be required to perform.

Though it was not contemplated or allowed that the bank should be established until the expiration of a year from the signature of the contract, it was necessary that preparation should be made for its establishment. For this, several articles made provision. A bank building with outbuildings and buildings for the branches were necessary. Accordingly, Mr. Lazare undertook the duty of procuring the necessary materials, forwarding them to Port-au-Prince and having the bank building and warehouse erected on ground to be furnished by the government.

The government assumed the obligation to pay the regular bills for the articles he would require for the construction of the bank building and warehouse at Port au Prince, and its branches at two other places, to the amount of 200,000 piasters (dollars), which amount, however, was to be carried to the credit of the republic and to be repaid with interest. The contract imposed upon M. Lazare the further duty of having all the articles required for building the bank and warehouse arrive at Port au Prince within seven months from the signing of the contract, and having the buildings finished within four months thereafter; that at the expiration of the last of the twelve months, 'these establishments being finished should be in full operation.' Such was the requirement of the twenty-third article.

By the eighteenth article, as amended, Mr. Lazare was required to pay all the preliminary expenses connected wit the creation and establishment of the bank, and at the end of the thirty years the establishments constructed for the bank and its branches, including the warehouses, were required to be delivered to the Government of Hayti in good repair. Such were the principal duties assumed by Mr. Lazare, to be performed by him preparatory to the opening of the bank, except such as related to providing the necessary capital.

In relation to the capital, the thirtieth and thirty-first articles are important. By the thirtieth the government, acting by Mr. Rameau, its authorized agent, engaged to subscribe to the bank as shareholder for the sum of 1,000,000 piasters (dollars), which amount it bount itself to pay at the office and deliver into the vaults of the main bank 'as soon as the complete organization of the establishment was effected and duly ascertained or lawfully declared' (dûment constatée).

By the thirty-first article M. Lazare bound himself to pay at the office of the main bank in order to be deposited into the vaults, the sum of 2,000,000 piasters (p. 2,000,000), 'so as to complete the amount of stock of bullion', which was fixed at 'three millions of piasters' (p. 3,000,000).

By an amendment of the thirtieth and thirty-first articles, made May 11, 1875, it was agreed that the government and Mr. Lazare should be obliged to deposit in the vaults of the bank only half of the sum subscribed, the other half to be called at such dates as should be fixed by the *direction générale* of the bank.

It is to be observed the thirtieth article fixed the time when the government was required to make its payment into the vaults of the bank. The thirty-first did not expressly declare when Mr. Lazare's payment should be made. I think, however, it may be fairly inferred from the whole contract that it was required to be made before the bank should go into operation that is, before or at the expiration of twelve months from the signing of the contract or before or at the expiration of the forty-five days to which the time for opening the bank was subsequently extended. But it is manifest that Mr.·Lazare was not bound to pay in his share of the capital before the government paid in its share.

His share was to be paid *'to complete'* the capital partially supplied by the government.

It is material also to observe that the contract required all the capital to be paid in metallic currency. In regard to this there is no controversy. The payments are described as bullion, and the twenty-first article declared that the stock of bullion of the bank should consist of coins of gold and American silver and fractions of the same, preference, however, being given to English and French gold and silver subject to suitable agreement, and no agreement to the contrary appears to have been made.

Thus far, I have noticed principally the obligations which Mr. Lazare assumed and to which he was bound by the contract. Before considering other provisions, it may be well to review what he did toward meeting those obligations. Soon after the contract was signed he returned to New-York, abandoned other occupations in which he had been employed and devoted himself to the preparations necessary for the establishment of the bank. He had been prominently connected with a railrood company and had been president of a steamship line. These positions he appears to have given up. He procured the materials needed for the bank buildings, shipped them to Port au Prince, employed an architect, made arrangements with a builder for the erection of the buildings, commenced the work of putting them up and had the main building completed within the time limited by the contract. He also made arrangement for the engraving of the currency needed by the bank. In fact, he appears to have done all that the contract required him to do before opening the bank for business at the expiration of the year and forty-five days from September 1, 1874, when the contract was signed, unless his not paying into the office of the bank his stipulated share of the capital on or before that day was a default. In December 1874 he went to England and there made arrangements with the house of Benson & Co., then bankers of high standing, that they should furnish the $ 2,000,000, the sum he had agreed to pay in for his share of the capital of the bank. Mr. Benson, however thought the capital too large and advised him to return to Hayti and obtain a modification of the contract in relation to the capital. He did, therefore, go again to Hayti in the beginning of May, 1875, and soon after (Mai, 11, 1875) several amendements of the contract, among them the one-reducing one-half the amount of the capital required to be paid in, were agreed to, thus making the governments share p. 500,000 and Mr. Lazare's p. 1,000,000 (dollars). At the same time the statutes or by-laws for the governement of the bank when established were adopted by the contracting parties. Mr. Lazare then returned to London. On his arrival he found that the firm of Benson & Co. had failed.

He then opened negotiations with two other banking houses of London and one of Liverpool and obtained from them an agreement that they would furnish what he needed for his share of the bank capital. Having secured this he engaged a secretary for the bank and a manager, went to Paris, purchased books for the installation of the bank, paper and blank forms in the French language, and all the furniture needed and shipped them to Hayti. In the latter part of July, 1875, he returned to Port au Prince, taking with him his family and also Mr. Verdereau, whom he had engaged as secretary for the bank. When in Paris during the summer he had learned, as it appears, for the first time that the Haytian Government had effected loans and was effecting others, for the payment of which the customs of Hayti had been and were being pledged. These customs were by the fourteenth and fifteenth articles of the contract pledged to secure repayment of the sums which by those articles the bank was required to advance from time to time to the government. This pledge to the bank was a matter of great importance. It might have been of vital importance. By the fourteenth article the bank was bound to furnish the annual budget voted by the legislative chambers of the republic *(à bureaux ouverts)* with open doors, or, as I understand it, at once, promptly, on demand, but to be reimbursed out of the amount *(sur le montant)* or sum total (as the phrase is defined in the dictionary of the French Academy), with interest to be fixed by the bank, but never to exceed 12 per cent per annum.

True that by the amendement of May 11, 1875, it was agreed that the bank should not be compelled to deliver to the government, in pursuance of article 14, any sum that, added to the sums already advanced, should exceed $ 1,000,000. But even this sum was two-thirds of the proposed paid-in capital of the bank, and, in addition to this, the fifteenth article bound the bank, in case the government should find itself in difficulties demanding extraordinary expenses, apart from those voted for the budget, to furnish the government with the amount it might require, at the same time reserving sufficient capital to carry on its operations, on condition of reimbursement, with interest, in the conditions before mentioned; that is, out of the total of the customs. The article made no other limitation of the amount the government was given the right to require.

It need not be said that such obligations resting on the bank might have proved, and probably would have proved ruinous, unless it was assured of ability to obtain prompt reimbursement of its advances out of the customs. The bank could not afford to wait until other creditors of the governement were satisfied. These articles, the fourteenth and fifteenth, raise at least a strong implication that the bank should have the security of the amount or totality of the customs. They practically represented that the government had such security to give; that it still had an unrestricted right to pledge them, as it undertook to do, to the bank.

But the fact was that the government had granted away this right. I think it appears that the customs were then pledged for the payment of what is called the French 'double debt', in amount 80,000,000 of francs, though this is not very distinctly proved. But it is certain that after the contract was made the government pledged the customs, in fact, all the general revenues of the republic, to secure the payment of two other loans negotiated, agreeing in the one case that the amount of duties collected should be paid at Port au Prince into the hand of the representatives of the creditors up to the sums required for the payment of the loan and in the other binding itself to appropriate to no other use the the proceeds of 45 per cent of all the customs duties of the republic given in security of the loan until a complete payment. I cannot but regard these pledges as violations of the contract with Mr. Lazare.

They impaired the value of the concession made to him. They endangered the credit and safety of the bank he was authorized to establish, and in which he and his associates were expected to invest a large capital. It is no wonder that he and those who had agreed with him to take two-thirds of the stock of the bank, and pay for

it $ 1,000,000, were disturbed by the ascertainment of these pledges and led to distrust the good faith of the Haytian Government. As I have said, I do not find that Mr. Lazare had any knowledge of this action of the government until the summer of 1875. His return to Hayti in July was to endeavour to obtain some arrangement of this matter. In this he was unsuccessful. Mr. Rameau, the high officer of the government and its authorized agent in making the contract received him coolly. The evidence convinces me that he (Rameau) was no longer desirous that the bank should be opened.

When Mr. Lazare desired to have some arrangements made respecting the customs and to have the government's share of the capital paid in, in order that the good faith of the government might be assured, Mr. Rameau replied, 'I will see to it when I have time'. He never did see to it. He made no denial that the pledge of the customs for other loans of the government was a breach of faith with the bank and Mr. Lazare. He did not deny that it was the duty of the government to give that subject its immediate attention. For some reasons, into which it is not necessary to inquire at length, Mr. Rameau was not at the time friendly to Americans, and Mr. Lazare was a citizen of the United States. Moreover the Haytian merchants were opposed to the bank. They were doing for the Haytian Government a kind of banking business. Whatever may have been the cause, I think it manifest that there was then no longer any desire of the government that the contract with Mr. Lazare should be carried out. There was rather a purpose to avoid its consummation. if possible. If Mr. Monsanto, who by the statutes of the proposed bank had been appointed to act on the part of the government, is to be believed, Rameau said he had changed his mind and did not want Mr. Lazare to open the bank; that the merchants were opposed to it, and that he wanted the keys of the bank building. Of these there were two, one of which the government had, and Mr. Lazare had the other. It was then — about the last day of September — Rameau sent a government messenger for Mr. Lazare's key. When it was refused, he sent again, the messenger saying, 'You had better not have any trouble. You had better give me the key.' From prudent motives it was surrendered, and thus Mr. Lazare was wrongfully excluded from the bank building.

Thus matters remained till the 15th of October 1875, the day upon which, by the provisions of the contract as amended, the bank was to be ready for going into operation, and when the capital was required to be in the vaults. Then the government ostentatiously made a pretense of paying in its share of capital, and immediately instituted an *ex parte* proceeding *(procès-verbal)* to declare that it had performed its part of the contract. This payment was a mere pretense, an attempted fraud upon Lazare.

What was deposited in the vaults was $ 235,000 only in coin. The remainder of the $ 500,000 (the government's quota, what it was bound to deposit) consisted of bonds, I. O. U.'s and promises of individuals to pay certain sums. It can not be admitted that such a deposit was a fulfillment of the government's obligation imposed by the thirtieth article of the contract. Yet, because Mr. Lazare did not then pay in his share of the capital in specie, though he was ready and able to pay in drafts, the Haytian Government immediately declared the contract null and void, and notified Lazare of the annulment.

It is impossible for me to regard this action of the Haytian Government as either just or warranted by any provisions of the contract. The government had no right to declare the contract at an end, and its action in this particular was a great wrong to the claimant. It was itself in default. It had not performed its part of the contract. Beyond the breach of the agreement in regard to the customs duties, it had not paid into the vaults of the bank its share of the capital, as it had covenanted to pay it. I can not read the contract as allowing one party to it to declare it void if the failure to carry out its provisions was due, either in whole or in part, to that party. It has been contended before me that the action of the government was justified by the twenty-third and twenty-fourth articles of the agreement. They were as follows :

'ART. 23. Twelve months are allowed to Mr. Lazare, dating from the time these presents will be signed, for the *(fonctionnement)* working, or working order of the main bank : that is to say, that within seven months from the same date the whole of the materials necessary for the construction of the said bank and warehouse shall be delivered at Port au Prince ; that within four months afterward the aforesaid buildings shall be finished, and that at the expiration of the last month, those establishments being finished shall be in full operation.

'ART. 24. The nonperformance of this last condition within the twelve months prescribed, even in the case the work should be commenced, would involve of full right the nullity of the present contract and leave the government free to act as it might please.'

The condition referred to in the twenty-fourth article is the one described in the twenty-third.

It is not clear to my mind that the subject of that, in contemplation of the parties, was anything more than the bank building, its completion, furniture, and readiness for banking operations. Those were all in working order before the expiration of the twelve months. It is to be observed, as already noticed in the provisions of the first article, the concession to establish the bank did not come into operation until after the expiration of twelve months. But if it be conceded that the twenty-third article was intended to make it a condition not merely that the bank buildings, called establishments, should be finished and furnished, but that the bank itself should be in operation, doing business immediately at the expiration of the twelfth months, it was a condition imposed upon both parties of *(sic)* the contract. The bank as such could not go into operation — that is, commence business — until its capital was paid in. The condition therefore required the government to pay as certainly as it required Mr. Lazare to pay, and if the condition was broken, it was broken by the government.

I cannot but think it would be unreasonable to construe the twenty-third article as meaning that if the government of Hayti declined or neglected to perform its part of the contract, it should be at liberty to annul the whole agreement and thus release itself without performance. If such be its meaning the contract was no contract at all. Either party could dissolve it at will by simply neglecting to meet its engagements ; such a construction would, in my opinion, be absurd.

The Government of Hayti has, therefore, in my judgement, no justification for its action declaring the contract null and refusing to acknowledge any obligations under it. Of that action Mr. Lazare has a just right to complain. This is especially true, in view of the twenty-sixth article of the contract, which stipulated that 'in case of any difficulties arising in regard to the present contract, or from any other unforeseen cause which might arise in regard to it, arbitration will be the only means of settlement acceptable by the two parties'. That article provided further for the selection of arbitrators, and declared that their decision should be binding and obeyed without appeal. But if the government could lawfully annul the contract, or declare it void its action annulled that article with the others, and took away from Mr. Lazare his right to have the differences between himself and the government passed upon by an arbitration. That difficulties had arisen has already been shown, particularly that arising from the pledges of the customs. There were others proper to be submitted to the arbitrators. Mr. Lazare had claimed that the government was bound to pay its share of the capital before the expiration of the twelve months, and he insisted that the payment should be made when he returned to Port au Prince, after he had discovered that the government had made other pledges of the customs. And it has been strenuously argued before me that the government was at that time in default, in that it had not deposited in the bank vaults its part of the capital in the preceding May (1875), when it is alleged that the complete organization of the bank was effected and duly ascertained, as contemplated by the thirtieth article, to which reference has heretofore been made. It was on the 11th day of May 1875 that the statutes, as they are called, or by-laws for the bank were framed and agreed to, and on the 22d of that month the government published a notice in the official paper of the state declaring *inter alia* that the joint stock company with the name of the National bank of Hayti was formed. The notice stated also the amount or the capital of the company, the number of its shares, the mode of transfer, the sum to be paid on subscribing for shares, the location of the main office; that A. H. Lazare and C. E. Monsanto, jr., were appointed administrators, the latter chosen by the government; that the local directors would be appointed subsequently; that persons skilled in the business would be sent from Europe to direct the operations of the bank, and that a subsequent anouncement would fix the time for opening subscriptions.

I can not agree that all this, although claimed by Mr. Lazare, was such an effecting and ascertaining the complete organization of the establishment as was contemplated by the thirteenth article, and upon which the government was bound to pay in its share of the capital, and I see no evidence that it was so understood by the parties. The formation of the company and the organization of the bank were two entirely distinct things. The statutes, or by-laws, agreed upon May 11, 1875, were intended to operate preparatory to the organization of the bank, as well as to govern its operations after it should come into existence. They, as well as the notice of May 22, contemplated that many things should be done before the bank could be in a condition to commence business or could be regarded as organized. The banking company had then no capital; not a piaster had been paid in; there was not a shareholder; the directors were yet to be chosen, and persons to be sent from Europe to direct the operations of the bank. More than this, the bank had no right to exist until the expiration of a year from September 1875, and

the bank building was not erected or required to be erected until after May of that year. It cannot, therefore, be maintened that the claim of Mr. Lazare in this particular is sound, namely, that the government was bound to deliver in May 1875 into the vaults of the bank any part of the capital it had agreed to furnish. In this particular the government was not in default. It had an entire year from the signing of the contract—afterward extended to October 15, 1875, — within which to make the deposit. But within that period it was bound to deposit in the vaults $ 500,000 in specie, and I think it was under obligation to make that deposit before Mr. Lazare was required to pay in his one million—the remainder of the capital. There is a very observable difference between the thirtieth and the thirty-first articles of the contract. By the thirtieth, which prescribed the duty of the government in that regard, it (the government) bound itself to pay at the office and deliver into the vaults of the main bank, the seat of which is at Port au Prince, the sum of one million of piasters (p. 1,000,000) 'as soon as the complete organization of the establishment is effected and duly ascertained'. Thus the time for the government's payment was expressly fixed. But the language of the thirty-first article which relates to Mr. Lazare's obligation to pay, is noticeably different. It fixed no time for his payment, except by implication. It commenced thus: 'In consequence' *(en conséquence)* (as I understand it, following the deposit by the government). The entire article y quote:

'In consequence, Mr. A. H. Lazare upon his own special guaranty, assumes charge and responsibility, as in fact he has personal charge and responsibility for the balance of shares or bonds to be issued by himself on his own account or his copartners conformably with article second of the present additional contract, and binds himself for his part to pay at the office of the main bank in order to be deposited in the vaults, the sum of two millions of piasters (p. 2,000,000) *so as to complete the amount of stock of bullion, which is fixed at three millions of piasters* (p. 3,000,000)'.

As heretofore seen, these payments were arranged to be reduced one half. No doubt, though no time was designated for his payment, it is a fair construction of this article that Mr. Lazare was bound to pay his share of the capital immediately after the government paid its share; or at least in season for the opening of the bank on the 15th of October. But he was not bound to pay until the government paid. It was the '*balance*' of shares he covenanted to care for. His payment was required to be made to *complete* the stock of bullion in the vaults, to fill up or *complete* the stock of bullion in the vaults, to fill up or complete an aggregate, of which the government's payment was a part. There was a substantial reason for this difference in the covenants of the parties. The bank was intended, primarily for the convenience, of the government. The bank buildings were to be owned by the government, though it was to pay and did pay, for the materials used in their construction. Mr. Lazare was to attend to procuring and forwarding the materials, and to have the buildings completed and furnished. He was to furnish two thirds of the capital of the bank. Had he been required to pay it in at any fixed time, or before the government was required to pay its quota, it could not have been withdrawn unless at the government's pleasure, even though the government neglected to pay its share. That was a hazard it could not have been expected a sane man would have run. It was no more than reasonable security to ask or to give that the government should first pay in its one third of the capital, and its reasonableness becomes additionally evident when the government demanded and obtained both the keys of the bank building, and thus denied to Lazare all access to it except at its will. But if this construction of the thirty-first article be not maintainable, it is still certain that Lazare was not bound to pay before the government paid. Admit that the covenants required contemporaneous payment, the government never paid, as it was required to pay, and therefore Lazare cannot be adjudged to have been in such default as to justify the government for declaring the contract null. Considering what Mr. Lazare had done and expended in preparation for the establishment of the bank, having done everything that he had engaged to do up to the last, and considering the extent of his readiness to meet the only remaining requirement of the contract from him, I think it would be rank injustice in the government to deprive him of the advantages of what he had done and expended, and of the value of the concession, by making a semblance of performance of its engagements and declaring the contract annulled because he did not pay what he was not bound to pay before the government discharged its covenanted duty. Nor can I overlook the fact proven that what the government did in making its pretended payment, and what it claimed to be full performance of its part, was precisely what it refused to accept as performance by Mr. Lazare. The largest part of its deposit consisted of credits.

For the losses and injury sustained by him in consequence of the injustifiable action of the Haytian Government in annulling the contract and thus revoking its concession, I think the

Government of the United States may properly demand that Mr. Lazare shall be compensated. I agree that both at common and in the civil law one of the two parties to an executory contract containing mutual and concurrent engagements cannot generally recover damages against the other for a breach of that others's engagements without full performance on his own part. But a violator of such contract cannot defend himself against responsibility for his violation by pleading that the other party has failed to perform fully his part of the contract, if the failure was caused by the conduct of the defendant. In this case if Mr. Lazare was not bound to pay his share of the capital until the government paid or deposited its share, there was no default on his part, and if he was bound to pay his share regardless of the fact that the government made no payment, or made only a pretense of payment, depositing most of its share in credits, a mode of payment it denied to him, I cannot but think his default was excusable, because caused by the government's conduct. In either case he is, in my judgment, justly entitled to claim compensation for the wrongful annulment of the contract, and his claim is one which the United States may properly assert in his behalf in full accordance with the rules of international law as they existed at the time and as they exist now.

It remains, therefore, to inquire what should be the compensation awarded. The value of the concession made by the contract to Mr. Lazare, and lost by him in consequence of the wrongful action of the Haytian Government, it is difficult to estimate, though it must have been large. The expenditure of time and money he made in procuring and forwarding the materials for the buildings and providing for their erection, the cost and time required in Europe in making arrangements there, as well as in procuring and forwarding the furniture and forms for the bank, the expense of removing his family to Port au Prince and maintaining it there, are all to be considered. Even in regard to these it would be difficult to reach a reliable conclusion.

But, happily, the Government of Hayti, subsequent to its repudiation of the contract, made its own estimate of what was reasonable compensation to Mr. Lazare. Mr. Rameau was a leading officer of the Haytian Government. He was vice-president of the council of secretaries, a nephew of President Domingue, and, according to the evidence before me, in fact more the acting President of Hayti than Domingue himself. As stated by a very intelligent Haytian, a senator of the republic at the time and one who had been treasurer-general and minister of finance, 'he

34

was the ruling spirit of the whole government'. He signed the original contract made with Lazare in the presence of the secretary of state and the secretary of the interior, and the contract was sanctioned by the legislative assembly. He, in conjunction with Lazare, attended to the matters preparatory to the proposed establishment of the bank. The statutes, or by-laws, were framed by him and Lazare, and he appears to have acted throughout and unquestioned on behalf of the government. I cannot doubt that all his acts in relation to the contract must be regarded as acts of the government.

On the 18th of October 1875, after the government had notified Mr. Lazare the contract was void or at an end, practically that it would no longer be bound by its engagements, Mr. Lazare made out a protest against the action of the government, in which he complained that more than half of the deposit made in the vaults of the bank on the 15th consisted of bonds, drafts, and other papers, a mode of payment denied to him, but which he was ready to make. The protest also denied the right of either contracting party to appoint itself judge and, without the consent of the other contracting party, to annul the contract, which right it asserted belonged only to a third party (evidently refering to the provision in the contract for arbitration). This protest was sent to the government. Soon after, before the end of October, Mr. Rameau sent for Lazare, and an interview took place. Rameau then said he was sorry for what had happened, that he would like to have opened the bank, but he could not do it. Pressure was brought to bear, so that he was obliged to break the contract. The merchants were against it, and there was fear that revolution might break out, and the merchants would help the enemies of the government. Such were Mr. Rameau's statements. He made no charge that Mr. Lazare had been in default; none that Mr. Lazare had broken the contract or done anything that justified its annulment. He never afterward made any such charge. On the contrary, he admitted that *he* had broken the contract, and he desired to make reparation. It was to agree upon this that he had sent for Mr. Lazare. Negotiation ensued. Lazare claimed $ 500,000. Mr. Rameau offered less, and it was finally agreed that Lazare should be paid $ 117,500; that he should be appointed consul general at New-York, and be given also two small orders for the purchase of vessels for the government. To induce the acceptance of these it was promised that he should have a contract for building a national palace, and also that the government would purchase an equestrian statue of Domingue at the price of $ 20,000.

To this settlement Lazare agreed and Domingue expressed his assent. The arrangement was partially carried out. The appointment to the consul-generalship was made, and though it was revoked afterward on the incoming of the new revolutionary government, the revocation was not inconsistent with anything that had been agreed. The two orders were given. The contract for the palace does not appear even to have been desired by Lazare, though it was arranged for him. It certainly was not denied to him. The $ 117,500, however, was not paid, though promised to be paid soon, and I think the sum probably would have been paid had not a revolution soon followed the arrangement. The new government repudiated the acts of its predecessor.

I regard this arrangement between Mr. Lazare and Mr. Rameau (who, I think, under the circumstances, had authority to make it) as very significant and of much importance. At least it was practically an acknowledgment that the government owed reparation to Mr. Lazare; that its annulment of the contract for the concession was unjustifiable, and that Mr. Lazare was not in fault, and I think it is fair to regard it as evidence of the government's estimate of the extent of the reparation due. Throwing out the promise to give a contract for building the national palace, the profits upon which, if any, are too speculative to be capable of estimation, and throwing out also the promise to pay for the statute (that having never been delivered) I cannot resist the conclusion that the agreement to pay $ 117,500 was, in view of what was said at the time, an acknowledgment that to that extent Mr. Lazare had been injured by the wrongful annulment of the contract. Moreover, I am much inclined to think that the agreement to pay $ 117,500 should be regarded as a contract and enforceable as such, a compromise of an acknowledged obligation or at least of a doubtful right. It is true that the civil code of Hayti existing in 1875, after defining a compromise as a contract by means of which the parties interested foreclose an existing dispute or prevent a dispute from arising, declared that the contract should be in writing. But the civil code is the law for private parties. It is not clear that the provision referred to is binding upon the government, not mentioned in the statute. This however, (it) is not now necessary to consider at length. It is enough for the present case that what occurred or was said when the agreement was made may reasonably be regarded as an admission by the Government of Hayti of the measure of reparation due to Mr. Lazare.

It matters not that Rameau was shortly afterward killed, and that Domingue, the President, fled the country. Boisrond Canal succeeded to to the administration. But no change of administration could release the government from obligations binding upon it when the change took place.

I am, therefore, of opinion that A. H. Lazare has a just claim upon the Republic of Hayti to the extent of one hundred and seventeen thousand five hundred dollars, with interest from November, 1875, at six per cent, and I award that sum for the claim against the said republic.

Witness my hand the 13ᵗʰ day of June 1885, at the city of Washington.

LXXV. Allemagne, Grande-Bretagne.

21 juin 1884.

Cet arbitrage, relatif à des concessions territoriales accordées à des sujets allemands par les chefs indigènes des Fidji, donna lieu à une longue correspondance. Elle se termina par l'échange de télégrammes en date des 19 et 21 juin 1884 et de lettres confirmatives des 3 juillet, 4 août et 16 septembre 1884. Il fut accordé par les commissaires une somme de 10,620£ ; il était réclamé 140,000£ par les intéressés.

Echange de télégrammes et de lettres, constitutif d'une commission mixte.

London, den 19. Juni 1884.

Auf den Erlass vom 7. Juli beehre ich mich, Folgendes gehorsamst zu berichten.

Ich habe die Fidjiangelegenheit mit Lord Granville wiederholt besprochen, habe ihm vorgestellt, wie ernst Euere Durchlaucht diese Sache auffassen.

Lord Granville hat mir erklärt, die grossbritannische Regierung habe die feste Absicht, Eurer Durchlaucht Wünschen zu entsprechen. Lord Granville schlägt vor, eine Kommission, welche aus einem deutschen und einem englischen Beamten besteht, zu ernennen. Dieselbe soll die einzelnen Entschädigungsansprüche prüfen und das Ergebnis dieser Prüfung den beiderseitigen Regierungen unterbreiten.

(gez.) MÜNSTER.

Berlin, den 21. Juni 1884.

Wir sind mit Lord Granvilles Vorschlag einverstanden.

(gez.) HATZFELDT.

London, Foreign Office, July 3, 1884.

In my letter of the 9ᵗʰ ultimo, I informed your Excellency that a memorandum was in preparation dealing with the various points in the Pro Memoria communicated to me in your letter of the 8ᵗʰ of April, upon the settlement of the German land claims in Fiji.

Since that date the further negotiations which have taken place resulted in an arrangement for the investigation of those claims by Joint Commissioners, and it is unnecessary therefore to prolong the discussion of the points dealt with in the German Pro Memoria, but as Her Majesty's Government are anxious to remove any apprehension which may have hitherto existed that the constitution of the Tribunals, or the course of its proceedings has either directly or indirectly prejudiced the claims of German subjects, I enclose a printed copy of the promised Memorandum furnished to me by the Secretary of State for the Colonies.

I shall be glad to receive any proposals from your Excellency respecting the appointment of Commissioners to proceed with the inquiry into the claims in question.

(Signed) GRANVILLE [1].

London, den 4. August 1884.

Euerer Excellenz gefällige Note vom 3. d. M. in der Fidjilandfrage habe ich nicht unterlassen, zur Kenntnis meiner Hohen Regierung zu bringen. Erhaltenem Auftrage gemäss beehre ich mich, darauf Folgendes zu erwidern.

Meine Regierung nimmt mit Befriedigung davon Akt, dass sich die britische Regierung bereit erklärt hat, die auf den Landbesitz in Fidji bezüglichen Reklamationen deutscher Reichsangehöriger durch eine gemischte Kommission untersuchen zu lassen.

Als Kommissar von deutscher Seite ist der Kaiserliche Generalkonsul in Sidney, Dr. Krauel, in Aussicht genommen.

Bezüglich des britischen Kommissars erscheint der Wunsch gerechtfertigt, dass derselbe nicht aus den an Ort und Stelle befindlichen Beamten entnommen, sondern dass eine unparteiische, den lokalen Beeinflussungen nicht unterworfene Persönlichkeit von England aus entsendet werde.

Als Vereinigungspunkt der Kommission dürfte Levuka oder ein anderer, den Kommissaren besser geeignet erscheinender Ort der Fidji-Inseln ins Auge zu fassen sein.

Die Thätigkeit der Kommission würde nach Auffassung meiner Regierung sich dahin zu richten haben, jede einzelne der anhängig gemachten

---

[1] *Parliamentary Paper* [C—4433], p. 26.

Reklamationen — soweit nicht die betreffenden Reklamanten ihren Ansprüchen bereits entsagt oder mit den Entscheidungen der englischen Behörden sich einverstanden erklärt haben — einer genauen Prüfung zu unterziehen, die erforderlichen Beweisaufnahmen vorzunehmen und in den Fällen beiderseitigen Einverständnisses selbständig die Entscheidung zu treffen. Ueber etwaige streitige Fälle würde die Kommission hinwegzugehen haben und die Erledigung derselben nach London zu transferiren sein, von wo aus Regierungsinstruktionen leichter eingeholt werden können.

Meine Regierung hofft, dass die Vorschläge sich des Beifalls der britischen Regierung erfreuen werden. Im Falle des Einverständnisses glaubt dieselbe demnächst der Bezeichnung des britischen Kommissars, sowie einer Aeusserung darüber, wann voraussichtlich die Kommission würde in Wirksamkeit treten können, entgegensehen zu dürfen.

(gez.) MÜNSTER [1].

London, Foreign Office, September 16, 1884.

I have the honour to inform you that I have been in communication with Her Majesty's Secretary of State for the Colonies on the subject of Count Munster's note of the 4th ultimo, expressing the concurrence of the German Government in the proposed mixed commission to investigate the claims of German subjects in connection with the Fiji land question, and proposing certain arrangements in connection therewith.

In expressing to you, M. le Chargé d'Affaires, the general acquiescence of Her Majesty's Government in the proposals contained in Count Munster's letter, I am to add that effort will be made to arrange for the despatch of the British Commissioner with little delay, and that a further communication will be addressed to you on this subject.

(Signed) GRANVILLE [2].

Joint Minute and General Report on Claims of German Subjects in respect of lands in Fiji. London, April 15 (?), 1885.

We, the undersigned Commissioners appointed to consider and report upon the claims of German subjects in relation to lands in Fiji, concur in recommending the settlement of the said claims as follows:—

1. 9300 l. to be paid to Mr. Sahl.

The claim in respect of Lovoni is withdrawn, Mr. Sahl electing to proceed with his pending appeal in Fiji and to abide by the result. The claim in respect of the foreshore at Levuka is withdrawn.

2. 1200 l. to be paid to Mr. Pfluger.

3. 120 l. to be paid to Mr. Gerold.

4. The claims of F. C. Hedemann to be wholly disallowed.

* * *

1. The claims arise out of the cession of Fiji to Great Britain made by an instrument of cession dated the 10th October 1874.

2. During a period of about 10 years preceding the cession numerous grants or conveyances of land had been obtained by subjects of European governments and of the United States. These grants or conveyances had for the most part been made by Chiefs of tribes without the concurrence of the tribesmen, and even before the cession the question had arisen and had assumed practical importance, how far grants or conveyances so made ought to be recognised. On the one hand, it was maintained that by the law or custom of Fiji, lands belonged wholly or in part to the tribesmen and could not be permanently alienated at all, or if at all, only with the concurrence of the tribesmen. On the other hand it was contended that no such law or custom existed, that if it ever existed, still grants made by the Chiefs who had lately assumed more or less absolute power and who constituted the de facto government of the country ought to be recognised and that even bad titles, if acquired in good faith, ought to be respected, especially if actual occupation had taken place.

Under the government of Cakobau (Thakombau), by whom the cession was made, a commission had been formed for investigating some of the titles which were already in dispute.

3. The importance of these questions was fully understood at the time of the cession; and by the 4th and 7th Articles of the Deed of cession it was declared « that the absolute proprietorship of all lands not shown to be now alienated so as to have become bonâ fide the property [*in another copy* 'the bonâ fide property'] of Europeans or other foreigners, or not now in the actual use or occupation of some Chief or tribe, or not actually required for the probable future support and maintenance of some Chief or tribe, shall be and hereby declared to be vested in her said Majesty, her heir and successors . . . . That all claims to titles of land, by whomsoever preferred . . . . shall in due course be fully investigated and equitably adjusted. »

4. With a view to giving due effect to this declaration Lord Carnarvon on the 4th of March

[1] *Weissbuch.* Zweiter Teil, S. 89—92.
[2] *Parliamentary Paper* [C—4433], p. 87.

1875, instructed Sir Arthur Gordon (who was then proceeding from England to assume office as Governor of the New Colony) as follows:—

The broad principles to be followed in the difficult and very exceptional case of Fiji are:—

(1) That it should be declared that the whole of the land within the limits of Fiji, whether in the occupation of, or reputed or deemed to have been, prior to the cession of the islands, the property of either Europeans or natives, as well as all waste and unclaimed land, has, by virtue of the instrument which ceded to Her Majesty the « possession of and full sovereignty and dominion over the whole of the islands », become absolutely and unreservedly transferred to the Crown, and that the Queen has the full power of disposing of the whole of the land in such manner as to Her Majesty may seem fit; having due regard to such interests as may be entitled to recognition under Article 4 of that instrument.

(2) That, with the view of disturbing as little as possible existing tenures and occupations, and of maintaining (as far as practicable, and with such modifications only as justice and good policy may in any case appear to demand) all contracts honestly entered into before the cession, the Colonial Government, to which the rights of the Crown are delegated in that behalf, should forthwith require all Europeans claiming to have acquired land by purchase, to give satisfactory evidence of the transactions with the natives on which they rely as establishing their title; and if the land appears to have been acquired fairly and at a fair price, should issue to the persons accepted, after due inquiry, as owners, a Crown grant in fee simple of the land to which they may appear entitled, subject to any conditions as to further payments and charges or otherwise, may appear just.

5. In pursuance of these instructions, Sir A. Gordon, on his arrival in Fiji, forthwith (26th June 1875) issued a notification requiring persons having claims to land to send in the particulars of their claims within a limited time (which was afterwards extended), and on 30th October 1875, the appointment of a Land Commission to inquire and report to the Governor in Council on the claims sent in was gazetted in the Colony. The Land Commissioners held their first inquiry on the 10th December 1875, and their labours were not concluded until the end of 1881, having thus occupied a period of six years, during which time they held sittings at 27 places and made 1327 detailed reports on as many cases, each case in many instances comprising a number of distinct claims.

6. The reports made by the Land Commissioners were by them submitted to the Go-

vernor in Council for adjudication. The decision was in each case made by the Governor Council and it did not always give effect to the report of the Land Commissioners.

7. During the progress of the Land Commission a Colonial Ordinance was passed (No. XXV of 1879) providing for the establishment of a board for the re-hearing of claims by way of appeal from the decisions pronounced by the Governor in Council on the reports of the Land Commission. This board of appeal was not however a body entirely distinct from the Governor and his Council, but consisted of the Governor in Council assisted by the Chief justice of the Colony and other extraordinary members. Numerous appeals were presented to this board, which in most cases affirmed the decisions of the Governor in Council, but in not a few instances reversed allowances as well as disallowances of claims. The right of appeal given by this Ordinance was not prospective only but applied to all cases decided at any time since the cession. The value however of the appeal thus retrospectively given was, in the view of the claimants, somewhat reduced by a provision that on an appeal being brought by a claimant the opponents of his claim were let in to contend by way of cross appeal that the claimant had already got too much.

8. On the 2nd February 1882 the Land Commissioners submitted a final and general report to the Governor of Fiji. This report contains a clear account of the principles on which the Commission proceeded. The more important parts are the following:—

« 11. The 1327 reports have been disposed of with the results following:—

Granted as claimed	517
Disallowed as of right, but granted 'ex gratia' wholly or in part, or with modifications	390
Disallowed	361
Withdrawn and otherwise disposed of	56
Not finally decided	11
	1335

« 12. We must, however, point out that these figures are in some respects misleading, and do not represent the relative number with perfect accuracy, as they comprise not only the original transaction between the natives and first purchasers, but also all the subclaims, founded upon the subsequent transactions between the original purchasers and other whites to whom they afterwards sold.

« 13. And further there are reports which, though numbered as only a single case, in fact cover a number of distinct claims, based upon one title common to all or in which the circumstances are similar in all.

‹ 17. We have, of course, endeavoured, so far was possible, to govern our inquiries according to the English rules of evidence; yet we are well aware that if the notes of evidence taken by us were submitted to the scrutiny of any English court of law a great proportion would be rejected as inadmissible.

‹ 18. We can only submit that, had it been imperative upon us to conduct our inquiry according to the strict technical rules of evidence, our task would, we believe, have been all but impossible, and that in dealing with semi-civilized people like Fijians, differing so widely in all their habits of thought from white men, and labouring under the suspiciousness or timidity which is, we believe, a common characteristic of half savage races, a great latitude must be, and was intended to be, allowed.

‹ 19. We are well aware that ,hearsay' evidence appears on probably every page of our notes, but, on the other hand, it must be remembered that the frightful epidemic of measles in 1875 swept away the great majority of original vendors, who were generally the elders of the people, so that, had we refused to listen to what persons now living had heard from their predecessors, we should have excluded one of the only means of obtaining information that was open to us.

‹ 20. All that we can add further is, that we believe and trust we have allowed this latitude to both parties with impartiality, and to express our conviction that without such latitude it would have been in most cases impossible for claimants to have substantiated their claims.

‹ 21. But it has often occurred that claimants have appeared before us, and have claimed to ,stand upon their deeds', or in other words, that the documents or deeds put in by them should be accepted as conclusive without further question. It therefore becomes important to examine the nature and character of such documents.

‹ 22. In many cases the so-called deed has been merely a sale note of the most irregular and informal character, written on any scrap of paper procurable, and by any person who could be found to write it, but the largest allowance has always been made for informalities where no defect graver than informality has attached to them and, considering the class of persons who constituted the majority of the early land purchasers in Fiji, and the rough half savage manner in which they lived, it is perhaps surprising

that the informalities and irregularities have not been even greater than they are. The following remarks, therefore, must be taken to apply equally to the more pretentious documents drawn by persons assuming to be conveyancers and embodied in legal forms; and it is among these that we have detected some of the most scandalous frauds of any that have come under our notice, and we are of opinion, for reasons which will appear herein-after, that the majority of the deeds which have come before us are of very little value as evidence of any particle of the transaction, except, perhaps, of the intentions of the purchaser, and we further are of opinion that in the construction of these documents the well known maxim of English law that a grant should always in case of doubt be construed adversely to the grantor, should, under the very peculiar conditions which formerly prevailed in Fiji, be inverted.

‹ 23. In civilized countries the execution of a deed is of course the most solemn and conclusive form of recording a contract, and consequently courts of law have been very cautious in admitting evidence to explain or modify deeds, and have always viewed with great suspicion any attempt to do so. But in civilized countries a deed is an instrument carefully prepared and fully considered in all its details by all parties who presumably are in a position to deal together upon equal terms, and such is not the case here.

‹ 24. The vendors, being of course unable to read the documents they professed to be executing, were entirely dependent for their comprehension of their acts upon such explanation as was given them from the purchaser or the interpreter supplied by him, paid by him, and who was in many cases himself continually mixed up with similar transactions.

‹ 25. Still less were they able to sign them, and consequently the execution is almost invariably by mark, and we need not point out the great facilities which this fact alone afforded to unscrupulous persons to obtain deeds which are little better than fraudulent. As an instance, we would cite the case when the mark of a young Chief was obtained who at the time of touching the pen was only a child of about five years of age (see case 327) and while the mere fact of an attesting signature appearing on a deed is no evidence of due execution, seeing that we have met with cases of the grossest recklessness on the part even of a respectable man in signing as attesting merely on the assurance of his friend the purchaser that all had been properly done (see cases 1060, 1,2).

‹ 26. In English deeds we may as a rule rely upon the accuracy of a sum stated to have been given as consideration. In Fiji it is quite the reverse. In the vast majority of cases the actual payments have been made in trade and the difficulty we have always had to encounter has been to arrive at an approximate estimate first of what were the articles given, and second, how far such articles fairly represented the consideration alleged upon the face of the deed. In some cases we have detected the grossest and most scandalous untruthfulness as to the sums alleged to have been given, such as when the consideration was written in the sale note as 50 l., but only 5 l. was in fact given; the excuse for this disgraceful untruth being that some one had suggested that 5 l. was a very small sum, and that 'it might as well be set down at 50 l.,' as falsehood which was repeated in drawing the application, with the knowledge and approval of the claimant's solicitor (see evidence in case No. 866).

‹ 27. But in every case value estimated upon the goods as given to the natives is considerably higher than would have been charged in Levuka for cash; we have it in evidence that on the Macuata coast 100 per cent was the enhanced value according to the common estimate of those days, and hence it is always impossible to fix with anything approaching to certainty what really was the consideration given.

‹ 28. This applies in an especial degree to those cases in which the consideration has been the wiping out of debts incurred by vendors at the stores of the purchasers.

‹ 29. A large proportion of the sales were effected in order to obtain arms and ammunition for offensive and defensive purposes. To many this may seem iniquitous in the extreme on the part of the purchasers, but upon reflection we deem the iniquity of the transaction to rest chiefly with those, whoever they may have been, who first introduced such means of warfare into a country then in a state of rampant savageness and cannibalism.

‹ 30. When guns fell thus into the hands of a tribe upon whose shores the vessel conveying the first fire-arms was anchored, their neighbours would soon discover that it was a matter of life and death that they should likewise procure the same means of defence. And when land buying commenced, what easier than to sell a portion of land upon the desire of a white to buy? For before the arrival of whites the absolute alienation of land in our sense of the term must have been unknown, when the families could only understand that they had the usufruct alone of the soil for themselves and their heirs. When there were no buyers there could be no sellers.

‹ 31. In the matter of such sales for firearms we are of opinion that, when all interests were properly consulted before the completion of the contract, it became competent and proper for the people to alienate a part of their land to procure the means of defence against neighbouring tribes and strangers at a time when the term stranger meant also enemy.

‹ 32. By Fijian custom, that is by Fijian law, the absolute alienation of land as understood by us was unknown, and therefore, strictly speaking, illegal; yet can it be doubted they had a perfect right in common prudence to procure by any means in their power the safety of their lives, of their wives and families?

‹ 33. Where would be the utility of preserving land when by so doing they subjected themselves to extinction altogether, and consequently left no posterity to enjoy the lands thus spared by a too rigid adherence to their old customs?

‹ 34. *Descriptions of parcels.* — We are perfectly satisfied that in a great majority of cases the boundaries were a matter of vagueness and uncertainty to both parties, and were not, and indeed could not be, clear to either.

‹ 35. In a civilized land, well surveyed, nothing can of course be more definite than a side line drawn upon a certain bearing and extending a well-defined distance, but such is not the case in a savage and unsurveyed land as Fiji. Therefore, putting out of the question the foolish and preposterous extent of the purchases, such as we found at Macuata, where the depth of side lines varied from 5 to 20 miles, and restricting ourselves to even the more moderate distances of 2000 or 3000 fathoms, such as are common in Nadroga, we equally hold that, apart from the frontage, both parties were acting in the dark.

‹ 36. *Estate.* — We now come to a most important point, viz., what was the estate or interest which the native vendors conceived they were conveying to the purchasers? We mean, of course, in those cases where all parties may be presumed to have been acting bona fide.

‹ 37. According to the deeds, the estate is, with few exceptions (as in the province of Lau), one in fee simple, a tenure the complete nature of which, even at this day, after the Lands Commission has been pursuing its inquiries for six years, we greatly question being realised by the natives.

‹ 38. This reflection opens up, of course, the whole question of the ancient Fijian customs as to land tenure, which have been so ably set forth both by Consul Pritchard (Polynesian Remembrances, p. 242, published in 1866) and more recently by the admirable lecture delivered by the Rev. Lorimer Fison in Levuka in 1880, and reprinted from the Journal of the Antropological Institute, February 1881.

« 39. The opinions enunciated by these gentlemen have been fully corroborated by all our experience, viz., that the tenure of lands according to Fijian custom resembled the condition of estates tail in England between the reigns of Edward I and Edward IV, during which time they were inalienable, and that consequently in strictness the vendors could only have sold the interest which they themselves possessed, viz., a li e estate; and further, we doubt, whether in selling lands the vendors, even when they were the taukeis, ever contemplated parting entirely with their own rights, but merely intended to convey to the purchasers the same communal rights as they themselves enjoyed, but always concurrently with themselves.

« 40. This theory will, we think, explain numerous cases that have come under our notice of violence and even bloodshed, caused by white men regarding the 'taukeis' of the lands they claimed to have purchased in fee as mere tenants at will, and attempting to oust them from certain rights which from what we believe to be their point of view, were inalienable.

« 41. We greatly doubt whether any single Crown grant could ever have been issued in fee had the lands question been dealt with according to native custom only, which, after all, was the only approach to law that existed until within a few years before annexation, and we submit that in forming an opinion upon the land question in this Colony it is impossible to be too careful to bear in mind the fundamental difference of the points of view from which land tenure is regarded by a white man and a Fijian.

« 42. To such a degree does this view of the inalienability of land extend, that although a tribe might be conquered, and driven or removed from its lands by the conqueror, yet their title to their lands was not thereby extinguished, and 'they consider their title to be inextinguishable as long as they themselves are not extinguished. It may be held in abeyance, but it cannot be destroyed'.

« 43. We have, therefore, no doubt that the numerous sales by conquerors of conquered lands which have come under our notice were absolutely wrongful, and must be placed in much the same category as the sales by single powerful Chiefs independently of the consent of the « taukeis » (or commoners), the most notable instances of which are the sales in Taviuni and Cakaudrove by the late Tui Cakau.

« 44. That he and other Chiefs were able by their power or by the prestige of their position as high Chiefs to sell we do not deny, and it is also possible that, at any rate during their lives, they might have been able to have maintained their vendees in occupation, had these attempted to occupy: but, fortunately for them in many cases, the question never did arise, owing to purchasers not attempting to settle, or subsequently abandoning their lands upon which they had for a time been living; still, such transactions were contrary to ancient custom, and were the outcome of what is termed in Fijian, 'Valavala vakaturaya', which Mr. Fison renders 'masterful doings', of such Chiefs, or, in other words, that it was a question between law, as represented by ancient custom, and despotism, a 'might versus right'.

« 45. In such cases, therefore, we have paid especial regard to the extent to which lands bought under such conditions have been actually occupied, and when the sale has been followed by sufficient occupation we have usually recommended the recognition of the title: but where the claim was in respect of a purchase which has never been followed by such occupation the Government was in fact being asked to complete a wrong which had remained incomplete, and such demand we have considered ought not to be conceded ».

9. In May 1879 a remonstrance had been addressed by Count Münster to the British Secretary of State for Foreign Affairs with reference to the length of time occupied in the settlement of claims in which German subjects were interested. Count Münster's letter and the answer of Sir A. Gordon sufficiently show the then position of affairs and the explanation of the apparent delay:—

German Embassy, May 26, 1879

My Lord.

The presence of Sir Arthur Gordon in London affords me the desired opportunity of bringing forward the subject which has been for many years undecided, of the title to land in Fiji, with the hope of making sensible progress in it.

After the annexation by England of the Fiji Islands all properties were, as is known, made over in the first instance to the British Crown, and the proof of private titles to such properties as were claimed by foreigners, and to any important extent by Germans, devolved upon a Commission named *ad hoc*.

This proof has hitherto been delayed to the detriment of those interested.

How great this interest is is evident from the fact that in one firm alone a nominal capital of nearly 125,000 l. is at stake.

It is self evident that so long as the decision of the Commission is deferred realisation of the properties on fair terms is impeded, and that thereby the proprietors suffer direct and indirect losses.

Under these circumstances I am instructed by the Imperial Government to call your Excellency's attention to this matter, and most earnestly to request the earliest possible settlement of it in the interests of the German subjects concerned.

(Signed) MÜNSTER.

48, Upper Grosvenor Street, June 3, 1879.

Sir

I have the honour to return the letter from the Foreign Office relating to the land claims of foreigners in Fiji, enclosed in your letter of the 30th ultimo.

The German Ambassador is misinformed if he supposes no progress to have been made in the settlement of land claims since the date of cession. Between 700 and 800 claims had been investigated and adjudged previous to my departure from Fiji; and among that number were many claims preferred by German subjects, especially by the house of Hennings. the representatives of the great firm of the Godeffroys of Hamburgh.

During the past year the progress of the investigation has slackened, partly in consequence of my absence, partly from the want of sufficient surveyors, and partly because it was known that a scheme making provision for the rehearing of disallowed claims was under the consideration of Her Majesty's Government, the decision of which it was not unnaturally desired in the first instance to ascertain.

It is quite natural that those whose claims have not been yet investigated should be impatient at the apparent delay, but in point of fact the examination in a little more than two years (between January 1876 and June 1878) of nearly 800 claims, many of which were very difficult, complicated, and open to dispute, is by no means an inconsiderable piece of work, and one which, had it been performed mode rapidly, would inevitably have laid the ground for future misunderstanding and litigation.

But it is clearly as much the interests of the Government as of the claimants to bring all these questions to a speedy issue, and the German Ambassador may rely on my constant and earnest efforts to promote the speedy settlement of the claims in question.

(Signed) A. GORDON.

10. The work of the Land Commission having been, as above stated, concluded at the end of 1881, and having resulted in the disallowance of a considerable number of claims, including some which had been preferred by German subjects, Count Münster in June 1882 communicated to Lord Granville certain complaints relating to the treatment of the German claims. Exception was taken (I.) to the composition and competence of the Land Commission and of the Board of Appeal (II.) to the principles on which the decisions were based, and the manner in which those principles had been applied, and (III.) to the delays which it was represented had occasioned serious loss to the German claimants. These communications were followed by others of similar import, and they finally resulted in the appointment of the present Commission.

11. The cases ultimately presented for our examination are 15 in number, out of about 140 claims presented by German subjects, not perhaps a very large proportion considering the difficult and delicate nature of the colonial investigations.

12. The claimants are only four in number, namely:

(I.) Mr. Sahl, whose claims are mostly in right of Messrs. Hennings,

(II.) Mr. Gerold,

(III.) Mr. Pflüger,

(IV.) Mr. Hedemann.

13. Out of these we have excluded altogether the claim of Mr. Hedemann, who states his loss at 26,000 l. in respect of lands in which is own evidence shows that he had no interests, and which, also according to his own evidence, cannot be worth more than a very small sum. The claim of Mr. Gerold is entirely bonâ fide, but of a very peculiar nature and of no importance in principle. He has not put forward any estimate of his own, and we have thought that his case will be fairly met by a small allowance, the land being admittedly of the poorest kind.

The land claimed by Mr. Pflüger was no doubt acquired by him in complete good faith, although his estimate of the value of the land in those cases in which his title was not recognised by the Land Commission was in our opinion somewhat exaggerated. He asked altogether for about 10,000 l. but half of this was claimed in respect of land which we are constrained to find was acquired by him under a British title and cannot therefore be a subject of consideration by us. In

35

respect of his other claims we have to recommend allowances amounting in the aggregate to 1,200 l.

14. The same remark as to the bonâ fides of the purchase of lands applies to the claims preferred by Mr. Sahl, who estimated the losses incurred by his firm in consequence of the adverse decisions of the land-court in Fiji at a sum of about 110,000 l., including an item for interest of more than 48,000 l. We have found it impossible to admit this latter part of the claim, or to accept the valuations given for the land in dispute, although Mr. Sahl has frankly and readily furnished us with all the materials in his possession necessary for enabling us to form a conclusion upon his case.

As regards one of the most important items of his claim, namely a claim in respect of lands in the Lovoni valley, we have formed the conclusion that the claim is substantially a British one (in right of the Bank of New Zealand as assignee of the late Fiji Banking Company, Limited). Mr. Sahl has under those circumstances consented to withdraw this claim which had not yet been finally decided by the Court for rehearing in Fiji. The only other large item in Mr. Sahl's account is a claim for about 30,000 l. in respect of two blocks of land known as Valavala and Natasa. This claim has given us more anxiety than any other of the claims before us, and is the subject of the only serious difference of opinion, but we have been able to concur in recommending a substantial award.

The remaining items are of comparatively small importance, and we have been able to agree in recommending an aggregate allowance of 9300 l. in respect of the whole of Mr. Sahl's claims.

15. It is right that it should be stated that although the sums which we recommend in Mr. Sahl's case fall so far short of his original estimate, there is not, in the opinion of either of us, any ground for regarding it as put forward otherwise than in good faith, though undoubtedly, in fact, excessive.

16. We desire to record our conviction of the fairness and carefulness of the Land Commission presided over since 1879 by Mr. Williamson, with the assistance of Mr. Carew, although we differ as to the correctness of the principles applied; one of us being of opinion that the right of the tribesmen to be consulted in sales of land is established and was properly recognised by the Land Commissioners as an important element to be considered, and that they did not give it undue weight in connexion with other considerations, the other of us thinking that principle was carried too far, and that sufficient weight was not given to the bonâ fides of those who made their purchases in the belief that the Chiefs, in consequence of their increased influence during the time immediately preceding the cession of Fiji, had not only the power, but a customery right, to sell land without the concurrence of the tribesmen.

17. With respect to the few cases in which we concur in venturing to think that the Governor in Council or the Board of Appeal formed a wrong conclusion on evidence before them, we desire to point out that in dealing with so large a number of cases of so difficult a character, it must inevitably happen that in some instances a conclusion will be formed with which another set of persons may be unable to agree.

18. Lastly, we have to add that in the course of our inquiry, we have seen reason to believe that the course which was suggested by Count Münster in the pro memoria enclosed in his letter of the 8th April 1884, addressed to Lord Granville, and which the instructions given to the British Commissioner permit us to recommend, namely, that cases where a ground for relief is made out should be met by compensation in money and not by re-opening titles to the land itself, will be of great advantage to the colony.

London, April, 1885 [1].

LXXVI. Allemagne, Chili.

23 août 1884.

Cet arbitragé ne réclame aucun commentaire. Il n'a été remarquable que par la manière dont il s'est terminé; le Ministre d'Allemagne dans le protocole de transaction, qui a mis fin à la contestation, a, en effet, stipulé non seulement pour l'Allemagne, mais également pour l'Autriche-Hongrie et la Suisse.

Convención para el juzgamientó de las reclamaciones entabladas por súbditos alemanes, firmada en Santiago, el 23 de Agosto 1884.

S. E. el Presidente de la República de Chile y S. M. el Emperador de Alemania y Rey de Prusia, deseando poner un termino amistoso á las reclamaciones deducidas por súbditos alemanes y apoyadas por la Legación de Alemania en Chile, con motivo de los actos y operaciones ejecutados por las fuerzas de la República en los territorios y costas del Perú y Bolivia durante la última guerra, han acordado celebrar una Con-

[1] *Parliamentary Papers* [C — 4433], p. 110.

vención de Arbitraje, y con esta mira han nombrado por sus Plenipotenciarios respectivos:

S. E. el Presidente de la República de Chile, al señor Aniceto Vergara Albano, Ministro de Relaciones Exteriores de la República, y S. M. el Emperador de Alemania y Rey de Prusia, al señor Baron Schenck zu Schweinzberg, Ministro Residente del Imperio en Chile;

Los cuales Plenipotenciarios, después de verificar sus poderes, ha convenido en los siguientes artículos.

ART. 1º. Un Tribunal Arbitral ó Comisión Mixta Internacional decidirá, en la forma y según los terminos que se establecen en esta Convención, todas las reclamaciones deducidas con motivo de los actos y operaciones ejecutados por las fuerzas de la República en los territorios y costas del Perú y Bolivia durante la última guerra, por súbditos alemanes, con el patrocinio de la Legación de Alemania en Chile, dentro del plazo que se indicará más adelante.

ART. 2º. La Comisión se compondrá de tres miembros: uno nombrado por S. E. el Presidente de la República de Chile, otro por S. M. el Emperador de Alemania y Rey de Prusia y el tercero por S. M. el Emperador del Brasil, bien fuere directamente ó por el intermedio del agente diplomático que tuviere acreditado en Chile.

En los casos de muerte, ausencia ó inhabilitación por cualquier otro motivo, de alguno ó algunos de los miembros de la Comisión, se procederá ó su reemplazo en la forma y condiciones respectivamente expresados en el inciso precedente.

ART. 3º. La Comisión Mixta examinará y decidirá las reclamaciones deducidas por súbditos alemanes, por el correspondiente órgano diplomático, con motivo de los actos y óperaciones ejecutados por el ejercito y escuadra de la República desde el catorce de Febrero de mil ochocientos setento y nueve, día del rompimiento de las hostilidades, hasta lo fecha en que se han ajustado respectivamente los Tratados de Paz y de Tregua con el Perú y Bolivia.

ART. 4º. La Comisión Mixta dará á los medios probatorios ó de investigación que, según el criterio y recto discernimiento de sus miembros, fueren conducentes al mejor esclarecimiento de los hechos controvertidós, y especialmente á la calificación del estado y caracter neutral del reclamante.

La Comisión admitirá también las alegaciones verbales ó escritas de ambos Gobiernos ó de sus respectivos agentes ó defensores.

ART. 5º. Cada Gobierno podrá constituir un agente que vigile el interés de su parte y atien-

dra á su defensa, presente peticiones, documentos, interrogatorios, ponga y absuelva posiciones, apoye sus cargos ó redarguya los contrarios, rinda su prueba y exponga ante la Comisión, por si ó por el organó de un letrado, verbalmente ó por escrito, conforme á las reglas de procedimiento y tramitación que la misma Comisión acordare al iniciar sus funciones, las doctrinas, principios legales ó procedentes que convengan á su derecho.

ART. 6º. La Comisión Mixta decidirá las reclamaciones en mérito de la prueba rendida y con arreglo á los principios del derecho internacional y á las prácticas y jurisprudencia establecidas por los tribunales análogos modernos de mayor autoridad y prestigio, librando sus resoluciones interlocutorias ó definitivas por mayoria de votos.

La Comisión Mixta expondrá brevemente en cada juzgamiento definitivo, los hechos y causales de la reclamación, los motivos alegados en su apoyo ó en su contradicción, y los fundamentos de derecho internacional que justifiquen sus resoluciones.

Las resoluciones y decretos de la Comisión serán escritos, firmados por todos sus miembros y autorizados por su secretario, y se dejarán originales, con su respectivo expediente, en el Ministerio de Relaciones Exteriores de Chile, dándose á las partes los traslados que solicitaren.

La Comisión llevará un libro ó registro en que se anoten sus procedimientos y las peticiones de los reclamantes y los decretos y decisiones que librase.

La Comisión Mixta funcionará en Santiago.

ART. 7º. La Comisión tendra la facultad de proveerse de secretarios, relatores y demás oficiales que estime nesesario para el buen desempeño de sus funciones. Corresponde á la Comisión proponer á las personas que hayan de desempeñar respectivamente aquellas funciones, y designar los sueldos ó remuneraciones que hayan de asignárseles.

El nombramiento de los espresados oficiales se hará por S. E. el Presidente de la República de Chile.

Los decretos de la Comisión que hayan de cumplirse en Chile, tendrám el auxilio de la fuerza pública como los expedidos por los tribunales ordinarios del pais. Los que hayan de ejecutarse en el extranjero, se llevarán á efecto conforme á las reglas y usos del derecho internacional privado.

ART. 8º. Las reclamaciones serán presentadas á la Comision Mixta dentro de los tres meses subsiguientes á la fecha de la primera sesión, y las que se presentaren después de transcurrido este plazo no serán admitidas.

Para los efectos de la disposición contenida en el inciso precedente, la Comisión Mixta publicará en el *Diario Oficial* de la República de Chile un aviso en el cual se exprese la fecha de su instalación.

ART. 9°. La Comisión tendra, para evacuar su encargo en todas las reclamaciones sujetas á su conocimiento y decision, el plazo de un año contado desde el día en que se declare instalada.

Transcurrido este plazo, la Comisión tendrá la facultad de prorrogar sus funciones por un nuevo periodo, que no podrá exceder de seis meses, en caso de que por enfermedad ó inhabilitación temporal de alguno de sus niembros ó por otro motivo de calificada gravedad, no hubiese alcanzado á desempeñar su cometido dentro del plazo fijadó en el primer inciso.

ART. 10°. Cada uno de los Gobiernos Contratantes sufragará los gastos de sus proprias gestiones y de los honorarios de sus respectivos agentes ó defensores.

La expensas de la organización de la Comision Mixta, los honorarios de sus míembros, los sueldos de los secretarios, relatores y otros empleados y demós gastós y costos de servicio común, serán pagados entre ambos Gobiernos, por midad: pero si hubiere cantidades juzgadas á favor de los reclamantes, se deducirán de estas la's dichas expensas y gastos comunes, en cuanto no excedan del seis porciento de los valores que haya de pagar el Tesoro de Chile por la totalidad de las reclamaciones aceptadas.

La sumas que la Comisión Mixta juzgue, en favor de los reclamantes, serán entregadas por el Gobierno de Chile al Gobierno de Alemania, por conducto de su Legación en Santiago ó de la persona que ésta designare, en el término de de un año, á contar desde la fecha de su respectiva resolución, sin que durante este plazo devenguen dichas sumas interés alguno en favor de los expresados reclamantes.

ART. 11°. La Altas Partes Contratantes se obligan á considerar los juzgamientos de la Comisión Mixta que se organiza por este Tratado como una terminación satisfactoria, perfecta é irrévocable de las dificultades cuyo arreglo se ha tenido en mira, y en la inteligencia de que todas las reclamaciones de los súbditos alemanes, presentadas ú omitidas en las condiciones señaladas en los articulos precedentes, se tendrán por decididas y juzgadas definitivamente y de modo que por ningún motivo ó pretexto puedan ser materia de nuevo examen ó discusión.

ART. 12°. La presente Convención será ratificada por las Altas Partes Contratantes, y el canje de estas ratificaciones se verificará en Santiago tan luego como fuere posible.

En fe de lo cual, los Plenipotenciarios de la República de Chile y del Imperio Alemán firmaron la presente Convención, en doble ejemplar y en los idiomas español y alemán, y lo sellaron con sus respectivos sellos.

Hecha en Santiago de Chile, á los veintitrés dias del mes de Agosto del año de Nuestro señor mil ochocientos ochenta y cuatro [1].

Protocolo celebrado entre Chile y el Imperio germánico para transigir las reclamaciones de los súbditos alemanes, y de los de Austria Hungria y de la Confederación Suiza, firmado en Santiago, el 22 de Abril de 1887.

Reunidos en este Departamento los señores Francisco Freire, Ministro de Relaciones Exteriores de Chile, y Barón von Gutschmid, Ministro Residente del Imperio Germánico, facultado, además, especialmente para este caso por los Gobiernos de Austria Hungria y de la Confederación Suiza, han acordado cancelar las reclamaciones de súbditos alemanes y austro-húngaros y de ciudadanos suizos, que existen actualmente pendientes ante el respectivo Tribunal de Arbitraje en conformidad á las bases siguientes :

Primera. Se declaran terminadas las funciones del Tribunal Chileno-Germánico instituido por la convención de 23 de Agosto de 1884 para conocer y fallar las reclamaciones deducidas contra el Gobierno de Chile por súbditos alemanes, y habilitado posteriormente, mediante las Convenciones de 11 de Julio de 1885 y 19 de Enero de 1886, para conocer y fallar las reclamaciones deducidas contra el mismo Gobierno por súbditos austro-húngaros y por ciudadanos suizos.

Segunda. Todas las reclamaciones alemanas que aún no han sido falladas y existen pendientes ante el Tribunal, que suman la cantidad de doscientos treinta y siete mil ciento treinta y cinco pesos sesenta y nueve centavos, plata ($ pl. 237,135. 69) por capital, y de ciento veintiún mil setecientos setenta y cinco pesos ($ pl. 121,775), por intereses, — como asimismo todas las reclamaciones austro-húngaros, — que suman, por capital, cincuenta y tres mil trescientos veintitrés pesos, plata ($ pl. 53,323) y diez y nueve mil trescientos ochenta y cuatro pesos cuarenta y cinco centavos, plata ($ pl. 19,348. 45) por intereses, — y todas las

---

[1] *Recopilación de Tratados y Convenciones*, 1894, t. II, p. 176.

reclamaciones suizas — que suman ciento cinco mil ochocientos catorce pesos, plata ($ pl. 105,814), por capital, y diez y ocho mil novecientos veinte pesos cincuenta centavos plata ($ pl. 18,920. 50), por intereses, — que se hallan también pendientes, componiendo un total reclamado de quinientos sesenta y seis mil trescientos cincuenta y dos pesos sesenta y cinco centavos, plata ($ pl. 566,352. 65), quedarán pagadas y completamente extinguidas, cualesquiera que sean su naturaleza, sus antecedentes y su actual estado en el Tribunal, con la suma de veinte mil pesos fuertes de plata, chilenos, ($ pl. 20,000) que el Gobierno de Chile entregará al Representante diplomático del Imperio Alemán en Santiago, dentro de los quince días siguientes á la aprobación de este Convenio por el Congreso de la República, al cual será sometido en el término más breve posible. La expresada suma de veinte mil pesos ($ 20,000) será distribúda entre los reclamantes por los Gobiernos de Alemania, Austria-Hungria y Suiza, en la proporción y forma que ha sido convenido entre el Gobierno de Chile y el Ministro Residente de Alemania, sin que tal distribución afecte en modo alguno á la responsabilidad del Gobierno de Chile ni al carácter definitivo, total y absoluto del fenecimiento de todas las reclamaciones pendientes contra el mismo Gobierno.

En fe de lo cual el Ministro de Relaciones Exteriores de Chile y el Ministro Residente del Imperio Germánico firmaron este Protocolo, en doble ejemplar, y lo sellaron con sus sellos respectivos.

Hecho en el Ministerio de Relaciones Exteriores de Chile, á veintidós de Abril de mil ochocientos ochenta y siete [1].

LXXVII. Belgique, Chili.

30 août 1884.

Par la convention reproduite ci-dessous, les réclamations belges, au total de 5639 $ 80, furent soumises au jugement du tribunal arbitral italo-chilien : elles furent toutes repoussées.

Convention d'arbitrage conclue á Santiago le 30 août 1884.

Sa Majesté le Roi des Belges et son Exellence le Président de la République du Chili, désirant prendre des mesures, pour résoudre amicalement les réclamations présentées par des sujets belges contre le Gouvernement chilien, en conséquence de la récente guerre avec le Pérou et la Bolivie, ont nommé plénipotentiaires :

Sa Majesté le Roi des Belges, M. Adolphe Carion, chargé d'Affaires de Belgique au Chili, et

Son Excellence le Président de la République du Chili, M. Aniceto Vergara Albano, Ministre des Affaires Etrangères de la République :

Lesquels après l'examen de leurs pouvoirs dont ils ont reconnu la bonne et due forme, sont convenus du suivant :

ARTICLE UNIQUE. Les gouvernements de Belgique et du Chili conviennent de porter à la connaissance et de soumettre au jugement du tribunal arbitral établi par la convention italo-chilienne du 7 décembre 1882, les trois réclamations présentées par des sujets belges contre le Gouvernement du Chili en conséquence de la dernière guerre entre le Chili, le Pérou et la Bolivie.

Ces réclamations, qui sont celles de la succession de Pierre Ringo, de Paita, pour quatre mille vingt-quatre soles argent (s. a. 4024); de MM. Ancion, de Liège, et Schull, d'Anvers, pour trois mille neuf cent quatre-vingt-onze francs vingt-cinq centimes (3991 fr. 25 c.); de M. Auguste Schmitz d'Anvers, pour sept cent quatre-vingt-cinq livres sterling, seize, cinq (£ 785 - 16 - 5) seront jugées conformément aux mêmes principes et avec les mêmes formalités et conditions qu'ont établies pour les réclamations des sujets italiens, la convention susdite du 7 septembre 1882 et le règlement adopté par le tribunal italo-chilien. Elles devront être présentées à ce tribunal par le représentant de Belgique, dans le délai de trente jours à compter du jour de l'échange des ratifications de la présente convention.

Toute autre réclamation qui sera faite par un sujet belge ou des sujets belges contre le gouvernement du Chili, en conséquence des actes et des opérations des forces de mer et de terre de la République sur les territoires et sur les côtes du Pérou et de la Bolivie pendant la dernière guerre, devra être présentée au tribunal italo-chilien, dans le délai de quatre-vingt-dix jours, à compter du jour de l'échange des ratifications de la présente convention, et s'il se présente une réclamation après ce délai, elle ne sera pas admise et sera considérée comme rejetée d'avance, de sorte que, pour aucun motif et sous aucun prétexte, elle ne pourra être l'objet d'un nouvel examen ou d'une discussion.

Le gouvernement de sa Majesté le Roi des Belges se charge d'obtenir l'autorisation nécessaire afin que les juges-arbitres d'Italie et du Brésil puissent s'occuper du jugement des réclamations susdites. La présente convention sera

---

[1] *Recopilación de Tratados y Convenciones*, 1894, t. II, p. 295.

ratifiée par les Hautes Parties Contractantes et les ratifications seront échangées à Santiago aussitôt que possible.

En foi de quoi, les plénipotentiaires des deux pays ont signé la présente convention en double exemplaire et dans les langues française et espagnole, et l'ont scellé de leurs sceaux respectifs.

Fait à Santiago du Chili, le 30ᵉ jour du mois d'Août de l'année 1884 [1].

LXXVIII. Allemagne, Grande-Bretagne.

22 septembre 1884.

Le 7 septembre 1884, le Gouvernement allemand chargeait son représentant à Londres de prévenir le Gouvernement britannique de la prise de possession de la côte d'Afrique du 26ᵉ degré de latitude jusqu'au Cap Frio, et d'offrir, pour le règlement des difficultés éventuelles, de constituer une commission mixte. Cette proposition fut acceptée par une lettre du 22 septembre suivant et confirmée par le Gouvernement allemand par une lettre du 8 octobre 1884.

Echange de correspondance constitutive d'une commission mixte relative à l'occupation d'Angra Pequena.

Berlin, den 7. September 1884

Auftrag, unter Bezugnahme auf die frühern, auf Grund des Erlasses vom 19. August gemachten mündlichen Mitteilungen, vertraulich der englischen Regierung davon Kenntnis zu geben, dass die Küstenstrecken von dem 26. Breitengrad bis Kap Frio nördlich, ausgenommen Walfisch-Bai, von S. M. S. «Wolf» durch Flaggenhissen unter Reichsschutz gestellt seien; ferner, zur Regelung dieser Angelegenheit ebenfalls Verhandlung durch Kommissarien vertraulich anzubieten[2].

Berlin, September 22, 1884.

I have the honour to inform your Excellency that Her Majesty's Principal Secretary of State for Foreign Affairs has been in communication with the Secretary of State for the Colonies on the subject of the communication made to Earl Granville by Baron Plessen on the 8ᵗʰ inst., to the effect that the west coast of Africa from the 26ᵗʰ parallel of south latitude to Cape Frio, with the exception of Walfish Bay, had been placed under the protection of the German Empire by the hoisting of the German Flag by the Commander of His Imperial Majesty's Ship «Wolf».

Information to the same effect has also reached Her Majesty's Government from the Cape Colony.

. . . .

The attention of Her Majesty's Government has been called by the Cape Government to the fact that the islands on the coast between the Orange River and 26° south latitude, and also Hollams' Bird Island and Mercury Island off the coast between 26° and Cape Frio, form part of the Cape Colony, and are consequently British Territory. This statement is confirmed by the Colonial Office, and I am instructed to bring this point to the notice of the Imperial Government, who will no doubt take steps to make it understood by their officers and subjects that the Protectorate of Germany does not extend to the islands. A misapprehension on this point might lead to acts by German subjects which would be inconsistent with British rigths and injurious to the persons who have for many years leased these islands from the British Crown.

Her Majesty's Government believe they may infer, from the tenor of Baron Plessen's last communication, that the German Government are willing to make arrangements by means of a mixed Commission, as already proposed, for defining and securing the rights of British subjects already established within the territory to be placed under German protection and they will glady join in this mode of procedure.

. . . .

(Signed) C. S. SCOTT [1].

[London], den [8.] Oktober 1884.

Der Unterzeichnete beehrt sich, im Auftrage seiner Regierung Seiner Excellenz den Empfang des Schreibens zu bestätigen, welches der königlich grossbritannische Geschäftsträger in Berlin unterm 22. v. Mts. in betreff der Unterstellung gewisser Küstenstriche im südwestlichen Afrika unter den Schutz des Deutschen Reichs an den Grafen von Hatzfeldt gerichtet hat.

. . . .

Was die in dem Schreiben vom 22. v. Mts. berührten Punkte im einzelnen anbetrifft, so beehrt sich der Unterzeichnete, folgendes zu bemerken:

Der Unterzeichnete ist ermächtigt, den Vorschlag anzunehmen, dass zur Prüfung und Sicher-

---

[1] *Moniteur belge.* 8 avril 1886. — F. DE MARTENS, *Nouveau Recueil Général*, 2ᵉ série, t. XI, p. 638.
[2] *Weissbuch*, Erster Teil, S. 117.

---

[1] *Parliamentary Paper* [C-4262], p. 36.

stellung der Rechte britischer Unterthanen in dem fraglichen Territorium eine gemischte, aus beiderseitigen Kommissaren bestehende Kommission zusammentrete. Er erlaubt sich, als Ort des Zusammentritts derselben Kapstadt in Vorschlag zu bringen und als Kommissar von deutscher Seite den zum General-Konsul in Kapstadt ausersehenen Herrn Dr. Bieber, der binnen kurzem sich von Berlin nach Kapstadt begeben wird, namhaft zu machen.

Die gemischte Kommission wird nach Ansicht der Regierung Seiner Majestat in den Kreis der ihr obliegenden Aufgaben auch die Prüfung der Frage zu ziehen haben, welche von den längst der in Rede stehenden Küste belegenen Inseln als unter britischer Herrschaft stehend, von dem deutschen Protektoratsgebiete auszunehmen sind.

Der Unterzeichnete hat der Ansicht Ausdruck gegeben, dass die Regierung Seiner Majestät auf einige, den vorliegenden Angaben zufolge, schon im Jahre 1874 der Kapkolonie einverleibte Inseln keinen Anspruch erhebe. Neuere, der Regierung des Unterzeichneten zugegangene Informationen lassen es indess zweifelhaft erscheinen, ob die Voraussetzungen, auf denen die abgegebene Erklärung beruhte, richtige waren, und ob die Thatsachen und Erwerbungstitel, auf welche sich die britischen Ansprüche stützen, als rechtlich feststehende zu erachten sind. Die gemischte Kommission wird nach Ansicht der Regierung Seiner Majestät diese Punkte zu prüfen und unter Beweis zu stellen haben.

. . . .

(gez.) VON PLESSEN [1].

En l'absence d'un compromis détaillé, une instruction fut adressée par le Gouvernement allemand à son commissaire spécial, et cette instruction fut acceptée par le Gouvernement britannique *mutatis mutandis* pour son propre commissaire.

Instructions to the German and British Representatives of the Angra Pequena Commission.

Berlin, 11th march 1885.

The scope of the inquiry of the joint Commission, on which you had been designated to the British Government as our Commissioner, was specified in my Despatch of the 19th October last in accordance with the state of the negotiations between the two Governments at that time.

A difference of opinion which subsequently arose with respect to the islands off the coast of Angra Pequena has been settled in the course of the last month.

By a Despatch from Lord Derby, dated the 17th ultimo, his Excellency Sir Hercules Robinson has been requested to communicate instructions to your British colleague, Mr. Shippard, and the last obstacle to the commencement of the negotiations has been removed by Mr. De Pass renunciation (brought to my knowledge on the 22nd ultimo), of his demand to appear in person before the Commission. You will therefore enter on the same as soon as Mr. Shippard is ready to do so, and the following instructions will serve for your guidance.

On the one side our protectorate between the mouth of the Orange River and Cape Frio, with the exception of Walfish Bay and the small surrounding territory the boundaries of which are laid down on the English Admiralty Chart and in the Annexation Act of the 22nd July 1884, and on the other side, the British Sovereignty over the Islands named in the letters patent of the 27th February 1867 are to be beyond discussion. It will be the duty of the Commission to examine the claims to private property and concessions which subjects of the one power allege they had acquired in the territory of the other before the German protectorate was proclaimed, and to give their opinion on such claims.

An important element in this inquiry will be the investigation of the claims put forward by British subjects on the ground of the lease granted by Sir P. Wodhouse in 1869 with respect to the islands, rocks, and reefs not named in the lettres patent of the 27th February 1867,

You will make arrangement with your British colleague as to the mode of your joint procedure; and if Sir Hercules Robinson causes a notice to be published warning British subjects to file their respective claims with the Commission, you will publish a corresponding notice to German subjects in a suitable Cape Town paper, and also in the German Official Gazette.

The expenses incurred for clerical assistance and for the eventual aid of interpreters will be borne in equal shares by the two Governments.

If it should be necessary for you to repair to the spot, either an English or a German man-of-war will, if possible, be placed at your disposal.

You will report from time to time on the progress of the negotiations.

(Signed) VON BISMARCK [1].

Les commissaires, qui siégèrent pour la première fois à Cape Town, le 27 mars 1885,

---

[1] *Weissbuch*, Erster Teil, S. 120.

[1] *Parliamentary Paper* [C - 5180], p. 20.

ne parvinrent pas à s'entendre sur toutes les réclamations qui leur furent soumises. Les deux gouvernements par un échange de lettres en date des 6 et 8 mars 1886, constituèrent une nouvelle commission qui siégea à Berlin et termina ses travaux par un protocole du 15 juillet 1886.

Protocol containing the joint recommandations of the British and German Commissioners. Berlin, July 15, 1886.

The undersigned Commissioners having met and discussed fully those British claims in the territories placed under German protection in South-west Africa, upon which Mess. Bieber and Shippard, the Commissioners at Cape Town, had disagreed, agree to submit to their Governments the following recommendations:—

1. *Ebony Mines.* That if Robert Lewis or his assigns desire to work this mine, he or they be at liberty to do so, and to convey the ore to the coast until the 21ˢᵗ of September 1893, without payment to and without hindrance or interference by the Colonial Company.

2. *Sandwich Harbour.* That Mr. Anders Ohlson (trading as A. Ohlson and Company), and Messrs. De Pass, Spence and Co., respectively, be held to have acquired a full title in perpetuity for themselves and their assigns to the lands and buildings which they, respectively, have heretofore occupied in Sandwich Harbour for the purposes of the fishery, together with the right to each firm of taking at any time any other sites on the shore of this harbour, and of erecting buildings thereon, should the sand, as has happened before, shift so as to render useless the land wich is now, or at any future time may be, occupied by their buildings; it being understood that any site so taken becomes the absolute property of Messrs. De Pass, Spence and Co. or of Mr. Ohlson, or their respective assigns, as the case requires, and that they have no further claim to the land which they previously occupied; but that neither firm nor their assigns are entitled to take any site occupied by other persons, nor to take any site the occupation of which would interfere with other persons.

That it should be further recognised that the firms of A. Ohlssen and De Pass, Spence & Co. have the right of coast fishery in Sandwich Harbour and along the coast between Sandwich Harbour and the point 23° 20 south latitude, 14° 31 east longitude, with the right of landing on and using for fishery purposes any part of the coast

not in the private possession of third parties, subject always to the observance of any laws and regulations which may be issued by the competent authorities. The said firms shall not, however, have any right to hinder other persons from also fishing there or from establishing themselves in Sandwich Harbour.

3. *Hottentot Bay.* That Messrs. De Pass, Spence and Co. have in like manner acquired a full title in perpetuity for themselves and their assigns to the guano deposits at Hottentot Bay, and to the land which they now occupy there for carrying on fishery or collecting of guano.

4. *Un-named Islets and Rocks.* That Messrs. De Pass, Spence and Co., and their assigns, be free to make use, as they have hitherto done, of these islets and rocks, including Shark Island without payment until the expiry of their lease, that is to say, until the 30ᵗʰ of June 1895, and if the British Government waive all claim to the sovereignty of these islets and rocks and acknowledge the sovereignty of Germany over them, then that the latter power should consent to confer not private rights over them to any persons other than the lessees for the time being of the 12 British Islands named in the Letters Patent of the 27ᵗʰ of February 1867.

Upon this understanding the British Commissioner will recommend his Government to acknowledge forthwith the sovereignty of Germany in these islets and rocks.

5. *Mainland claims.* That Messrs. De Pass, Spence and Co. should be held to have acquired for themselves and their assigns a full title in perpetuity to the Pomona Mine with two English miles of land round the mine on every side, and that they should have the right to use the lagoon for their vessels and to make use of the land round the lagoon for all purposes as they have done hitherto, without payment and without indrance or disturbance by the Colonial Company; and if irreconcilable disputes between the firm and the company should arise as to the proper exercise of these rights on land, then that the Chief Officer of the German Government within the protectorate shall allot to Messrs. De Pass, Spence and Co., or their assigns, sufficient land for the purposes of their business conveniently situated on the shore of the lagoon, and that the land so allotted shall become the absolute property of the persons to whom the same is allotted but that such allotting of land shall in no way affect or lessen their right to use the lagoon for their vessels[1].

[1] HERTSLET, *A complete Collection* ..., t. XVII, p. 1172.

Les recommandations des commissaires furent définitivement acceptées et respectivement par le Gouvernement britannique le 9 août 1886 et par le Gouvernement allemand le 13 novembre 1886.

LXXIX. Espagne, Etats-Unis d'Amérique.

28 février 1885.

Après une interminable correspondance, les deux gouvernements en cause consentirent à soumettre l'évaluation du dommage, causé par les autorités douanières de Manille à raison de la saisie illégale du vaisseau *Masonic*, à l'arbitrage du Ministre d'Italie, accrédité à Madrid. L'arbitrage fut institué par une lettre collective et la somme allouée fut fixé par l'arbitre à 51,674 $ 07.

Collective letter to submit to arbitration the indemnification to the owner of the Masonic. Madrid, February 28, 1885.

Excellency.

The Government of His Majesty the King, my august sovereign, and the Government of the United States of America have agreed to submit to the decision of an arbitrator the sum which, as indemnification, the Spanish treasury must pay to the owner of the North American bark *Masonic*, in virtue of the decreed sentence of the Council of State of the 16th of October 1884, and both Governments, recognizing the gifts of rectitude and justice which adorn your excellency, have not hesitated a moment in indicating you as the most proper person for the discharge of that delicate commission.

We therefore have the honor to invite your excellency to be pleased to accept the power which the Governments of Spain and of the United States grant you in order that, in a period which cannot exceed six months, you may examine the damages and injuries duly proved by the owner of the *Masonic*, and determine the pecuniary indemnification which you justly and equitably believe ought to be assigned to him, in view of the liquidation of the interested party and of the antecedents of the question, which will be furnished to your excellency in the ministries of ultramar and state and in the legation of the United States at this court[1].

---

[1] *Foreign Relations of the U. S.*, 1885, p. 699.

Award given by Baron Blanc in the case of the vessel Masonic. Madrid, June 27, 1885.

The undersigned, requested by a collective note of his excellency the minister of state of His Majesty the King of Spain and of the chargé d'affaires of the United States at Madrid, dated 28th February ultimo, in the name of the respective governments, to decide in justice and equity, as arbiter, within a period not exceeding six months, the amount of the pecuniary indemnity to be paid by the Spanish treasury to the owner of the North American vessel *Masonic* in virtue of the decreed sentence of the council of state of Spain of October 16, 1884, and in accordance with the damages and injuries duly proved by the claimant, has received from the high parties to form his decision the following documents:

From his excellency the minister of state of Spain the note of 30th May ultimo, containing estimates in support of which are produced as proofs three documents, among which is an account of losses and damages claimed by the owner of the *Masonic* by way of compromise and without proofs, the 6th August 1883, and amounting, including interest, calculated up to August 7, 1883, to $ 49,256.59; which claim his excellency the minister of state, in the same note of 30th May, taking as a basis the two other documents produced by him as proofs, that is to say, the *expediente* prepared in the ministry of state, and the sentence of the council of state of October 16, 1884, answers by an offer which he agrees to accept by way of equity, and notwithstanding the omission up to that time by the claimant of legal proofs with regard to the value and profits of the vessel, an offer amounting to $ 9354.32, including interest calculated up to August 7, 1883.

From his excellency the minister of the United States the notes of April 20, May 30, and June 11, containing estimates in support of which are produced as proofs seventeen documents, the knowledge of which has been offered at the same time to the Spanish Government; documents recapitulated besides in a memorandum which concludes with an account of the losses and damages claimed in strict right as being proved to have been suffered by the owner of the *Masonic* through the seizure and embargo of his vessel, this latter account amounting in all, with interest calculated up to the 15th June instant, to $ 64,639.78.

From the conviction which the undersigned has acquired after a careful examination, the differences of estimate manifested in an equal spirit of equity and justice by the high parties, as to the amount of indemnity to be granted,

36

originate almost entirely from the fact that by reason either of the distance or of the different jurisdictions through which the procedures and negotiations have been followed, the documents produced as proofs were not in their totality in the possession of each one of the high parties when their respective estimates were formed.

The undersigned, to discharge in its entire integrity the commission with which both governments have honored him, had therefore to solve these differences of estimate by basing his decision upon the documents produced by both parties as proofs.

The undersigned, having enlightened his conscience in the best possible way by the scrupulous verification of the proofs submitted in the arbitration, in virtue of the powers which have been conferred upon him by both governments, declares in justice and equity that in conformity with the letter and spirit of the decreed sentence of the council of state of Spain of 16th October 1884, according to his personal knowledge and estimation, the sum to be paid as an indemnity to the Spanish treasury to the owner of the *Masonic*, both as capital and interest up to the date of the present decision, is $ 51,674.07.

Done at Madrid, June 27, 1885.

Memoir concerning the reasons for the decision rendered by the arbiter as to the indemnity to be paid by Spain to the owner of the Masonic.

I.—VALUE OF THE VESSEL.

In the account presented in 1883 by the claimant, without proofs and by way of amicable compromise, $ 14,500 are claimed as the value of the *Masonic* when seized.

In the offers made by way of equity by his excellency the minister of state (note memorandum of May 30) the value of the *Masonic* is fixed at $ 6000.

In the account presented at the arbitration on the same date, of 30th May ultimo, by his excellency the minister of the United States, by way of strict right and the proofs, $ 22,000 are claimed as the value of the *Masonic* when seized.

Among the documents in due form, according to the laws of the United States, presented to arbitration, those of disinterested origin in the claim prove that the building of the *Masonic*, done in 1864, cost, rigging and accessories not included, $ 41,000; that the ship, on her departure from New York, was worth from $ 23,000 to $ 25,000, and according to the most precise estimate, $ 45 per register ton 539.80, viz, $ 24,291, the rigging and effects being by themselves worth $ 6838.45, and the copper sheets covering the bottom, $ 2000; that her conditions as to solidity were certified as good on the 16th of May, 1878, on her departure from New York, by the Bureau Veritas, which classed her A1.1, the register of the American Shipmasters' Association classing her on its own part A1.1½.

But after her forced detention at Manila (January, 1879) the *Masonic* had experienced damages which diminished her value. The cost of repairs of those damages was estimated by Captain Nichols (Blanchard?) and by the Mate Genn, in their affidavits, and without other proof, at $ 3000, having reference to the current prices in the Hong-Kong docks; and by official information not produced at the information, but stated by his excellency the minister of state to have been given by the *comandancia de ingenieros* of marine at Manila, where, according to the documents produced by the claimant, the repairs are more difficult and expensive, at $ 20,000.

It appears that the vice-consul of the United States at Manila proposed to sell the ship, but that this proposition was expressly occasioned, not by the seriousness of the damages, but by the wish to avoid her confiscation with the total loss of the value, on account of the refusal of the customs authorities to admit any protest or appeal before the fine should be paid, and on account of the inability on the part of the captain to pay the fine for want of money; besides, the proposition was not accepted by the captain, who affirmed, and the mate also, that there was no authority to sell.

As to the appraisement of damages, the fact does not seem conclusive that after the seizure and the order of sale issued by the administration of the Philippines, and against which the consulate of the United States, supported by his government, openly presented a protest of nullity, the ship did not find a bidder at any price in the public auction which took place; besides, in regard to this transaction, no document was presented at the arbitration, nor were any documents so exhibited relative to the final sale by the Spanish administration of the ship as wreck for $ 1141.90

An official report, not produced at the arbitration, but declared by his excellency the minister of state as having been given by the *comandancia de ingenieros* of marine at Manila, appraises the ship at $ 6000, that is to say less than a third of the sum appraised by the same *comandancia* for the repairs; however, this appraisement is expressly based upon the affirmation that the damages were not caused by bad weather, but by a condition of radical and actual decay of the vessel.

The undersigned, in view of the above, unavoidably considers the offer of $ 6000 as one of those which the Spanish Government makes upon general grounds and before the production of the contrary proofs which were subsequently presented at the arbitration.

On the other hand, with respect to the claim of $ 22,000, based on the appraisement of the damages at $ 3000 the opinion of the undersigned is that the proofs furnished by the claimant, not being unimpeachable as to the latter figure, and the claimant being liable to be considered as bound by the claim of $ 14,500 made by him in 1883, the only one, according to the declaration of his excellency the minister of state, of which the Spanish Government is officially aware, the appraisement of $ 14,500 made upon the investigation at the time the seizure took place, presented by the claimant in 1883 to the Spanish Government, and produced at the arbitration by his excellency the minister of state, remains a document for the benefit of Spain against the appraisement exceeding that amount. In view, therefore, of the principles of equity and of the sense of conciliation which ought to prevail in an arbitral decision, the undersigned reduces the indemnity for the value of the ship to $ 14,500. He does not adjudge any interest on that amount, for reasons to be set forth below.

II.—VALUE OF THE EARNINGS OF THE 'MASONIC'.

The claimant appraises them at $ 5000 annually net. Whilst refusing that indemnity, in consequence of the reports which represented the ship as not being worth being repaired and unable to render profitable service, yet the Spanish Government recognizes in principle the admissibility of proofs of ordinary and reasonable earnings of a vessel in good condition and ready to go to sea.

The proofs produced in the arbitration having established that the Masonic was in a normal state, in good condition of service and ready to go to sea after repairs which it was not been shown would have exceeded an ordinary character, the undersigned considers himself bound to determine the probable value of the earnings lost by the claimant on account of the seizure. It is certified by witnesses not interested in the claim that from 1874 to 1877 the net profits of the Masonic had not been less than $ 5000 a year.

The same valuation presented by the claimant has been incidentally discredited by the Spanish Government as exaggerated, noting that the rates of freight at the time of the seizure were lower than ever before a remark which would give to the earnings of the Masonic in 1897 a decisive importance in the valuation of probable profits for subsequent years.

The charter party, produced in authentic form by the claimant proves that for the transportation by the Masonic from New York to Nagasaki, whither it was bound, of 7500 (16,500?) cases of petroleum, there was paid 47½ cents per case, say $ 7837. 50. It is alleged, but not proved, that the claimant would have received, besides, a supplementary fee of 5 per cent, the customary commission, say $ 391.87.

It is proved that Bursley, a New York merchant, declaring that he considered the Masonic as a ship of good service, was negotiating to charter the Masonic back from the Philippines to New York, offering $ 8 per ton of freight (50 per cent greater than the register tonnage) say about $ 6500; it is alleged but not proved, that the claimant would be entitled to the same 5 per cent customary commission.

The voyage of the Masonic from New York to Nagasaki and back, feasible in one year, would therefore have paid, if the seizure had not intervened, from $ 14,000 to $ 15,000. The valuation of the expenses, for a sailing vessel of 540 tons register, it does not seem ought to exceed two-thirds of that amount.

The documents produced do not furnish the undersigned with data to modify, by reason of the oscillations of the prices of freights after the year the seizure took place, the valuation which would result from the above of the probable earnings for the following years.

In general, it does not appear unreasonable to admit that a well classed vessel, which has not reached the end of her normal duration, produces annually 12 per cent of her cost of construction.

The undersigned must therefore admit the annual payment of $ 5000 as net earnings lost from the 7th of May 1879, that is to say, two months after the seizure, which took place on the 7th of March, a time deemed necessary for the repairs to be made at Hong-Kong, up to the date of the arbitral decision.

With regard to the interest on the annual earnings asked by the claimant from the date of the expiration of each year, it is stated, in opposition to this demand among others, in the note memorandum of the Spanish Government of 30th May ultimo, that the delays which have occurred in the settlement of this matter are chargeable to the claimant, who, bound to submit himself in his petitions to the administrative jurisdiction to the Spanish laws, refused at first to give the legal bond required for the proceeding instituted by Kerr & Co., at Manila, in the name of the captain of the vessel, before the council of administration of the Philippines.

On the other hand, it is established by the documents Nos. 1 and 2, produced by his excellency the minister of state: —

That the decision of the council of state of October 16, 1884, confirms entirely the decision given on the 9th of June, 1882, by the section of contentions of the council of administration of the Philippines, which had decided that, as the fact upon which the fine and seizure had been based, that is to say, the missing on board of 22 cases of petroleum mentioned in the manifest, should have been correctly ascertained, which was not the case (the cargo having been afterwards proved to be complete), the fine imposed and the seizure effected were in every case illegal, and that the owner of the *Masonic* was entitled to an indemnity for the damages and losses which he should duly prove to have been suffered by him.

That the grounds upon which the two decisions above mentioned are based imply the entire confirmation of the proofs of the facts and reasons of right furnished through a diplomatic channel since 1879 by the Government of the United States against the fine and the seizure.

That in 1882 the governor-general of the Philippines had officially acknowledged the reasons for the seizure to be unfounded; that excessive severity had been exercised towards a ship of a friendly nation bound to a port of a third power, and arrived by stress of weather without any intention of or attempt at a commercial operation at Manila.

That an indemnity was unavoidable, which could but increase with the delays; that an immediate solution was desirable, which was within the power of the government; finally, that the refusal of the claimant to give a bond in the pending administrative procedure was admissible.

That, in fact, by royal order of 19th July, 1882, the claimant was excused from furnishing the bond.

That by the resolution of the council of ministers of the same period, the minister of ultramar was authorized finally to settle the question as he might deem most opportune.

In consequence, the undersigned—

Considering the just regard due to the position of the claimant represented by the Government of the United States as being a respectable citizen, almost ruined by the loss of his means of livelihood, who, however, does not ask for compensation for losses which are not correctly appraisable during the past six years;

In conformity with the spirit of impartially which has characterized the opinions of the government of the Philippines and of the two administrative councils which have given their decision in the matter in a contentious way.

In conformity with the sense of high equity of the declarations of his excellency the minister of state, inasmuch as he admits in principle the 6 per cent interest from the 7th March, 1879, on the cash capital which in equity and justice may bear interest, and inasmuch as in the offer of total indemnity made by the note of 30th May he includes the interest on the total capital which he found then proved;

Adjudges the interest asked on the net earnings capitalized at the end of each year from the 7th May, and therefore does not adjudge the supplementary interest for the value of the ship.

III.—EXPENSES OF TELEGRAMS.

The sum of $ 250, admitted by the Spanish Government, is adjudged, besides the interest for six years at 6 per cent.

IV.—PAYMENTS MADE TO CAPTAIN NICHOLS.

The claimant asks $ 3443.41.

The accounts signed by Nichols prove payments made of $ 1967.20, of which $ 484 are for expenses of return from Manila to New York, which the undersigned acknowledges ought to be admitted, and $ 69 for wages, which must be excluded, as already embraced in the calculation of the net annual earnings. Neither does the undersigned deem recoverable an account signed Nichols, amounting to $ 1258.20, for Nichols's journey from New York to Manila, made previous to the seizure, when Nichols was sent to take the place of the deceased captain.

Finally, the balance of the amount claimed on this item is rejected, and it is not established by proofs, the claimant declaring he has lost the vouchers.

On the other hand, the Spanish Government offers $ 500; but the undersigned, inasmuch as the Spanish Government embraces in that amount salary which becomes inadmissible after the adjudication by the arbiter of the net earnings, does not think he ought to allow the claimant the benefit of said offer, and reduces the indemnity for this item to $ 484, in addition to interest for six years at 6 per cent.

V.—EXPENSES PAID TO CAPTAIN GENN.

The claimant asks $ 294 for wages and expenses incurred as a consequence of the seizure.

The wages cannot be admitted as recoverable; but the seizure having prevented Genn from returning to New York on board the *Masonic*, the sum of $ 250, admitted by the Spanish Government for the journey back of ·Nichols, is adjudged by the undersigned for the return expenses of Genn; in addition 6 per cent interest during six years.

VI.—CONSULAR FEES PAID.

The claimant asks $ 83, an amount estimated by the minister of the United States no to be excessive, the consuls of the United States being authorized in such cases to charge for their services as notaries. However, as there is no proof that the whole of that amount was paid for the two consular documents produced before the arbitration, the indemnity is reduced by the undersigned to the $ 25 offered by the Spanish Government, in addition to 6 per cent interest during six years.

VII.—FEES TO THE LAWYERS OF NEW YORK.

The proof not being produced, the indemnity asked of $ 1500 is reduced to the $ 500 offered by the Spanish Government. No interest has been asked.

VIII.—TRAVELING EXPENSES BETWEEN NEW YORK AND WASHINGTON.

In spite of the likelihood and moderation of the amount of $ 360 asked, of the difficulty of the proofs for such expenses, and of the assurance given by the Government of the United States as to the honesty of the claimant, the undersigned does not think that he can deviate from the principle not to admit what is not proved by formal documents. For this item, as it is not admitted by the Spanish Government, the undersigned does not adjudge any reimbursement.

IX.—EXPENSES OF STAMPED PAPER AT MANILA.

The demand of $ 25, admitted by the Spanish Government, is adjudged. No interest has been claimed.[1]

----

[1] J. B. MOORE, *History and Digest* .., p. 1062—1069.

LXXX. Allemagne, Espagne.

... septembre 1885.

Il est peut-être incorrect de considérer cette affaire comme un arbitrage, puisqu'elle n'a pas été, à proprement parler, précédée d'un compromis et que la décision intervenue est moins une sentence qu'une proposition transactionnelle. Mais dans la plupart des contestations internationales auxquelles l'Allemagne a été mêlée, il est certain que la procédure arbitrale a été regrettablement modifiée, bien qu'en fait elle ait abouti à un résultat identique à ceux obtenus dans des arbitrages régulièrement constitués.

La correspondance entre les deux gouvernements n'a pas été entièrement publiée, mais l'acquiescement de l'Espagne à l'intervention du Pape a certainement eu lieu entre les dates du 31 août et du 1er octobre 1885, dans le courant du mois de septembre 1885.

L'avis du Pape a été suivi de la conclusion d'un traité que nous croyons utile de reproduire également.

Protocole d'arbitrage relatif aux Carolines, signé à Rome, le 22 octobre 1885.

La découverte faite par l'Espagne au seizième siècle des îles faisant partie de l'Archipel des Carolines et Palaos, et une série d'actes accomplis, à diverses époques, dans ces mêmes îles, par le Gouvernement espagnol, pour le bien des indigènes, ont créé dans la conviction de ce Gouvernement et de sa nation un titre à la souveraineté, fondé sur les maximes de droit international invoquées et suivies à cette époque dans les cas de conflits analogues.

Quand on envisage, en effet, l'ensemble des actes susdits, dont l'authenticité se trouve confirmée par divers documents des Archives de la Propagande, on ne saurait méconnaître l'œuvre bienfaisante de l'Espagne envers ces insulaires. Il est à remarquer en outre, que jamais nul autre Gouvernement n'a exercé sur eux une action semblable. Cela explique la tradition constante, dont il convient de tenir compte, et la conviction du peuple espagnol relativement à cette souveraineté — tradition et conviction qui, il y a deux mois, se sont fait jour avec une ardeur et une animosité à compromettre, un instant, la paix intérieure et les relations des deux Gouvernements amis.

D'autre part, l'Allemagne comme l'Angleterre ont déclaré expressément en 1875 au Gouvernement Espagnol qu'elles ne reconnaissaient pas la souveraineté de l'Espagne sur lesdites îles. Le Gouvernement · Impérial pense au contraire, que c'est l'occupation effective d'un territoire qui en crée la souveraineté, occupation qui ne s'est jamais effectuée de la part de l'Espagne pour les îles Carolines. C'est conformément à ce principe qu'il a agi dans l'île de Jap, et en cela, comme de son côté l'a fait le Gouvernement Espagnol, le Médiateur se plaît à reconnaître toute la loyauté du Gouvernement Impérial.

En conséquence, et pour que cette divergence de vues entre les deux Gouvernements ne soit pas un obstacle à un arrangement honorable, le Médiateur, après avoir tout bien considéré, propose que dans la nouvelle convention à stipuler on s'en tienne aux formules du protocole relatif à l'Archipel de Sulu (Solo), signé à Madrid le 7 Mars dernier entre les représentants de la Grande-Bretagne, de l'Allemagne et de l'Espagne, et on adopte les points suivants :

I, On affirme la souveraineté de l'Espagne sur les îles Carolines et Palaos.

II. Le Gouvernement Espagnol pour rendre effective la souveraineté s'engage à établir le plus tôt possible dans cet Archipel, une administration régulière avec une force suffisante pour sauvegarder l'ordre et les droits acquis.

III. L'Espagne offre à l'Allemagne la pleine et entière liberté de commerce, de navigation et de pêche dans ces mêmes îles, comme aussi le droit d'y établir une station navale et un dépôt de charbon.

IV. On assure également à l'Allemagne la liberté de faire des plantations dans ces îles et d'y fonder des établissements agricoles, tout comme les sujets espagnols.

Rome du Vatican, le 22 octobre 1885.

Convention d'acquiescement aux propositions du Pape, signée à Rome le 17 décembre 1885.

Les soussignés :

Son Excellence Monsieur de Schlözer, Envoyé extraordinaire et Ministre plénipotentiaire de Sa Majesté le Roi de Prusse auprès du Saint-Siège, et

Son Excellence le Marquis de Molins, Ambassadeur de Sa Majesté Catholique auprès du Saint-Siège, dûment autorisés pour mener à terme les négociations que les Gouvernements d'Allemagne et d'Espagne, sous la médiation acceptée par eux de Sa Sainteté le Pape, ont poursuivies à Berlin et à Madrid au sujet des

droits que l'un et l'autre des dits Gouvernements aurait acquis à la possession des îles Carolines et Palaos, considérant les propositions que Sa Sainteté a faites pour servir de base à leur entente, se sont mis d'accord sur les articles suivants, conformément aux propositions de l'Auguste Médiateur.

ARTICLE I. — Le Gouvernement allemand reconnaît la priorité de l'occupation espagnole des îles dites Carolines et Palaos et la Souveraineté Catholique qui en résulte et dont les limites sont indiquées dans l'article II.

ARTICLE II. — Ces limites sont formées par l'Equateur et par le onzième degré de Latitude Nord et le cent trente-troisième degré et cent soixante-quatrième de Longitude Est (Greenwich).

ARTICLE III. — Le gouvernement espagnol pour garantir aux sujets allemands la pleine et entière liberté de commerce, de navigation et de pêche dans les Archipels des Carolines et Palaos, s'engage à exécuter dans les dits Archipels les stipulations analogues à celles contenues dans les articles I, II et III du Protocole sur l'Archipel de Sulu signé à Madrid le onze Mars mil huit cent soixante-dix-sept et reproduites dans le Protocole du 7 Mars mil huit cent quatre-vingt-cinq ; c'est-à-dire :

1º Le commerce et le trafic direct des navires et des sujets de l'Allemagne avec les Archipels des Carolines et des Palaos, et dans toutes ses parties, ainsi que le droit de pêche, seront absolument libres, sans préjudice des droits reconnus à l'Espagne par le présent Protocole, conformément aux déclarations suivantes :

2º Les Autorités espagnoles ne pourront pas exiger à l'avenir que les navires et les sujets de l'Allemagne se rendant en toute liberté aux Archipels des Carolines et Palaos, ou d'un point à un autre de ces Archipels sans distinction, ou la dans toute autre partie du monde, touchent avant ou après à un point désigné dans les Archipels ou ailleurs, qu'ils payent des droits quelconques ou se procurent une permission de ces Autorités, qui de leur côté s'abstiendront de tout empêchement et de toute intervention dans le trafic susdit.

Il est bien entendu que les Autorités Espagnoles n'empêcheront d'aucune manière et sous aucun prétexte l'importation et l'exportation libre de tous genres de marchandises sans exception, sauf dans les points occupés et conformément à la déclaration 3º et que dans tous les points non occupés effectivement par l'Espagne, ni les navires, ni les sujets précités, ni leurs marchandises ne seront soumis à aucun impôt ou droit ou paiement quelconque, ni à aucun règlement sanitaire ou autre.

3° Dans les points occupés par l'Espagne dans les Archipels des Carolines et des Palaos, le Gouvernement espagnol pourra introduire des impôts et des règlements sanitaires et autres pendant l'occupation effective des points indiqués. Mais de son côté l'Espagne s'engage à y entretenir les établissements et les employés nécessaires pour les besoins du commerce et pour l'application des dits règlements.

Il est néanmoins expressément entendu, et le Gouvernement Espagnol étant résolu de son côté à ne pas appliquer aux points occupés des règlements restrictifs, prend volontiers l'engagement, qu'il n'introduira pas des impôts ni des droits supérieurs à ceux fixés par les tarifs de l'Espagne ou par les Traités et Conventions entre l'Espagne et toute autre Puissance. Il n'y mettra pas non plus en vigueur des règlements exceptionnels applicables au commerce et aux sujets allemands qui jouiront sous tous les rapports du même traitement que les sujets espagnols.

Afin de prévenir des réclamations qui pourraient résulter de l'incertitude du commerce à l'égard des points occupés et régis par des règlements et tarifs, le Gouvernement Espagnol communiquera dans chaque cas l'occupation effective d'un point dans les Archipels des Carolines et des Palaos au Gouvernement Allemand et en informera en même temps le commerce par une notification publiée dans les journaux officiels de Madrid et de Manille. Quant aux tarifs et aux règlements à appliquer aux points qui sont ou seront occupés par l'Espagne, il est stipulé qu'ils n'entreront en vigueur qu'après un délai de huit mois à partir de cette publication dans le journal officiel de Madrid.

Il est convenu qu'aucun navire ou sujet de l'Allemagne ne sera obligé de toucher à un des points occupés, ni en allant ni en revenant d'un point non occupé par l'Espagne, et qu'aucun préjudice ne pourra lui être causé pour ce motif ni pour aucun genre de marchandises à destination pour un point non occupé des Archipels des Carolines et des Palaos.

ARTICLE IV. — Les sujets allemands auront pleine liberté d'acquérir des immeubles et de faire des plantations dans les Archipels des Carolines et Palaos, d'y fonder des établissements agricoles, d'entretenir toute espèce de commerce et de passer des contrats avec les habitants et d'exploiter le sol dans les mêmes conditions que les sujets espagnols. Leurs droits acquis sont sauvegardés.

Les compagnies allemandes qui jouissent dans leur pays des droits des personnes civiles, et notamment les Compagnies anonymes seront traitées au même pied que les susdits sujets.

Les sujets allemands jouiront pour la protection de leurs personnes et de leurs biens, l'acquisition et la transmission de leurs propriétés et pour l'exercice de leurs professions du même traitement et des mêmes droits que les sujets espagnols.

ARTICLE V. — Le Gouvernement Allemand aura le droit d'établir dans une des îles des Carolines ou des Palaos une station navale et un dépôt de carbon pour la Marine Impériale. Les deux Gouvernements détermineront d'un commun accord le lieu et les conditions de cet établissement.

ARTICLE VI. — Si les Gouvernements d'Allemagne et de l'Espagne n'ont pas refusé leur adhésion au présent Protocole dans un délai de huit jours à partir d'aujourd'hui ou s'ils notifient leur adhésion avant ce terme par l'entremise de leurs Représentants respectifs, les présentes déclarations entreront immédiatement en vigueur.

Fait à Rome le 17 Décembre 1885. [1]

LXXXI. Grande-Bretagne, Russie.

10 septembre 1885.

On pourrait au sujet de la présente affaire soutenir avec quelque raison qu'il ne s'est pas agi d'un arbitrage proprement dit. L'avis des commissaires désignés a toutefois été accepté par les gouvernements intéressés et peut dès lors être assimilé à une véritable sentence.

Protocole relatif à la frontière Afghane, signé à Londres, le 10 septembre 1885.

Les soussignés, son Excellence Monsieur Georges de Staal, Ambassadeur Extraordinaire et Plenipotentiaire de Sa Majesté l'Empereur de toutes les Russies près Sa Majesté Britannique, etc., etc., et le Marquis de Salisbury, Chevalier du Très Noble Ordre de la Jarretière, Principal Secrétaire d'Etat pour les Affaires Etrangères de Sa Majesté Britannique, etc., etc., se sont réunis dans le but de consigner au présent Protocole l'arrangement suivant intervenu entre Sa Majesté l'Empereur de toutes les Russies et Sa Majesté la Reine du Royaume Uni de la Grande-Bretagne et d'Irlande :

1. Il est convenu que la frontière afghane entre le Heriroud et l'Oxus sera tracée comme suit :

---

[1] F. DE MARTENS. *Nouveau recueil général*, 2ᵐᵉ série, t. XII, p. 283-296.

La frontière partira du Heriroud à deux verstes environ en aval de la tour de Zoulfagar et suivra jusqu'au point K le tracé indiqué en rouge sur la carte N° 1 annexée au Protocole, de manière à ne pas se rapprocher à une distance moindre de 3000 pieds anglais de l'arête de l'escarpement du défilé occidental (y compris l'arête marquée L M N de la branche nord du même défilé). A partir du point K le tracé suivra la crête des hauteurs bordant au nord le second défilé qu'il coupera un peu à l'ouest de sa bifurcation à une distance d'environ 850 sagènes du point où convergent les routes d'Adam-Ulan, Koungrouéli et d'Ak-Rabat. Plus loin, le tracé continuera à suivre la crête des hauteurs jusqu'au point P marqué sur la carte N° 2 attachée au Protocole. Il prendra ensuite une direction sud-est à peu près parallèle à la route d'Ak-Rabat, passera entre les lacs salés marqués Q-R se trouvant au sud d'Ak-Rabat et au nord de Soumé-Kehriz, et laissant Soumé-Kehriz aux Afghans, se dirigera sur Islim, où la frontière passera sur la rive droite du Egri-Gueuk en laissant Islim en dehors du territoire afghan. Le tracé suivra ensuite les crêtes des collines qui bordent la rive droite du Egri-Gueuk et laissera Tchéméni-Bid en dehors de la frontière afghane. Il suivra de la même manière la crête des collines qui bordent la rive droite du Kouschk jusqu'au Hauzi-Khan. De Hauzi-Khan le tracé suivra une ligne presque droite jusqu'à un point sur le Mourghab au nord de Méroutchak, fixé de manière à laisser à la Russie les terres cultivées par les Saryks et leurs pâturages.

Appliquant ce même principe aux Turcomans sujets de la Russie et aux sujets de l'Emir de l'Afghanistan, la frontière à l'est du Mourghab suivra une ligne au nord de la vallée de Kaïsser et à l'ouest de la vallée de Sangalak (Abi-Andkoï) et, en laissant Andkoï, à l'est, rejoindra Khodja-Saleh sur l'Oxus. La délimitation des pâturages appartenant aux peuplades respectives sera abandonnée aux Commissaires. Dans le cas où ceux-ci parviendraient pas à s'entendre, la délimitation sera réglée par les deux Cabinets, sur la base des cartes dressées et signées par les Commissaires. Pour plus ample clarté, les principaux points de la ligne frontière sont marqués sur les cartes annexées au présent Protocole.

2. Il est convenu que des Commissaires seront nommés de suite par les Gouvernements de Sa Majesté l'Empereur de toutes les Russies et Sa Majesté la Reine du Royaume Uni de la Grande-Bretagne et d'Irlande, qui procéderont à examiner et à tracer sur les lieux les détails de la frontière afghane fixée par l'article précédent. Un Commissaire sera nommé par Sa Majesté l'Empereur et un par Sa Majesté la Reine.

Les escortes de la Commission sont fixées à cent hommes au plus de chaque côté et aucune augmentation ne pourra être admise sauf entente entre les Commissaires. Les Commissaires se réuniront à Zoulfagar dans un délai de deux mois à partir de la date de la signature du présent Protocole et procéderont immédiatement au tracé de la frontière conformément aux stipulations qui précèdent.

Il est entendu que la délimitation sera commencée de Zoulfagar et que, aussitôt que les Commissaires se seront réunis et auront commencé leurs travaux, la neutralité de Pendjé sera limitée au district compris entre une ligne au nord allant de Bendi-Nadiri à Burdj-Uraz-Khan et une ligne au sud allant de Méroutchak à Hauzi-Khan, les postes Russes et Afghans sur le Mourghab étant respectivement à Bendi-Nadiri et à Méroutchak.

Les Commissaires devront terminer leurs travaux aussi vite que possible.

3. Il est entendu qu'en traçant cette frontière et en se conformant, autant que possible, à la description de cette ligne dans le présent Protocole, ainsi qu'aux points marqués sur les cartes ci-annexées, les dits Commissaires tiendront dûment compte et des nécessités et du bien-être des populations locales.

4. A mesure de l'avancement des travaux de délimitation, les parties respectives auront le droit d'établir des postes sur la frontière.

5. Il est convenu que quand les dits Commissaires auront complété leurs travaux, des cartes seront dressées, signées et communiquées par eux à leurs Gouvernements respectifs.

En foi de quoi les soussignés, dûment autorisés à cet effet, ont signé le présent Protocole et y ont apposé le sceau de leurs armes.

Fait à Londres, le 10 septembre 1885. [1]

Protocole final de la commission de délimitation afghane, signé à Saint-Pétersbourg le 10 (22) Juillet 1887.

Le Conseiller Privé Zinoview et le Colonel Sir West Ridgeway s'étant réunis dans le but de s'entendre définitivement sur les termes d'un arrangement destiné à résoudre les difficultés surgies à l'occasion du tracé de la frontière Afghane sur la rive gauche de l'Amou-Daria, ont commencé par récapituler la marche que les négociations engagées entre eux ont suivie jusqu'à ce jour.

Ainsi qu'il résulte des Protocoles précédents, le Cabinet de Londres a été d'avis que l'arran-

---

[1] *Délimitation afghane*, 1872-1885. Pétersbourg, 1886, p. 378.

gement intervenu en 1873 entre les deux Gouvernements avait pour objet de confirmer les droits de l'Amir Afghan sur toutes les contrées dont Schir-Ali-Kan se trouvait à cette époque en possession, et qu'à ce titre le district de Khamiah, qui, conformément à des informations recueillies sur les lieux, avait été incorporé à l'Afghanistan bien avant l'époque de l'arrangement en question, devait également rester soumis à l'autorité de l'Amir Abdourrahman Khan. Cette manière de voir ne pouvait pas être adoptée par le Gouvernement Impérial de Russie qui, se basant sur le texte de l'arrangement de 1873, affirmait que l'état actuel des choses, sur la rive gauche de l'Amou-Daria, ne saurait porter atteinte aux droits du Boukhara résultant du même arrangement.

Le Gouvernement Impérial jugeait d'autant moins possible de sacrifier ces droits que, d'autre part, à la suite de la délimitation effectuée aux termes du Protocole de Londres du 29 août (10 septembre) 1885, les Turcomans Saryks de l'oasis du Pendjé avaient été dépossédés des terres dont ils avaient joui précédemment, et que ces terres avaient été comprises dans le territoire Afghan.

Eu égard à cette divergence de vues et désireux de prouver son respect de la lettre même de l'arrangement conclu entre les deux Gouvernements, le Cabinet de Sa Majesté Britannique a autorisé Sir West Ridgeway à proposer une frontière, qui, en partant de Doukchi — point jusqu'auquel la délimitation avait déjà été effectuée — aboutissait à l'Amou-Daria aux environs d'Islam ; à la suite d'un examen approfondi des informations recueillies par son Commissaire sur les lieux, le Cabinet Britannique était arrivé à la conclusion qu'Islam répondait sous tous les rapports au point frontière Khodja-Saleh dont il est fait mention dans la correspondance relative à l'arrangement.

Cette proposition ne fut pas non plus acceptée par le Cabinet Impérial de Russie, qui, envisageant la question à un point de vue tout à fait différent, soutenait que, vu les contradictions qui s'étaient produites entre les Commissaires respectifs à l'occasion de l'appréciation des données locales, la conformité des noms géographiques pouvait seule servir de base à une délimitation équitable ; que le Seraï Khadja-Saleh, situé à proximité du Ziaret connu sous le même nom, devait être considéré comme point extrême des possessions Afghanes sur l'Amou-Daria, et que la frontière devait être tracée immédiatement en aval du Seraï en question.

Au point de vue du Cabinet de Sa Majesté Britannique une délimitation effectuée dans ces conditions était de nature à offrir de graves inconvénients, surtout en égard à la circonstance que les canaux servant à l'irrigation du territoire compris entre Khodja-Saleh et Islam avaient leur prises d'eau aux environs du Kilif, ce qui ne pouvait manquer de devenir la source de complications continuelles entre les populations des deux côtés de la frontière. Aussi pour remédier à ces inconvénients, le Cabinet de Sa Majesté Britannique jugea-t-il préférable de renoncer à des tentatives ayant pour objet une entente sur une nouvelle frontière sur la rive gauche de l'Amou-Daria, et d'autoriser Sir West Ridgeway à offrir au Gouvernement Impérial de Russie, en échange du territoire qu'il réclamait sur la rive gauche de l'Amou-Daria, une compensation sur une autre partie de la frontière. Cette compensation portait sur le territoire dont les Turcomans Sarycks de Pendjé, ainsi qu'il a été exposé plus haut, avaient été dépossédés à la suite du tracé de la frontière en conformité des dispositions contenues dans le Protocole de Londres du 29 Août (10 Septembre) 1885. Cette proposition ayant obtenu l'adhésion du Gouvernement Impérial de Russie, M. Zinoview et Sir West Ridgeway sont tombés d'accord sur les dispositions suivantes :

I. La frontière dont la description est contenue dans l'Annexe au présent Protocole sous la lettre A, et qui est comprise entre les poteaux N° 1 et N° 19 et les poteaux N° 36 et N° 65 est considérée comme arrêtée définitivement. Les points trigonométriques sur la partie de la ligne frontière décrite ci-dessus et comprise entre les poteaux N° 19 et N° 36 sont également admis comme définitifs ; la description de cette partie de la frontière, ainsi que la partie à l'est du poteau N° 65, pourra être complétée après la démarcation.

Le synopsis de poteaux attaché au Protocole N° 15 en date du 1 (13) Septembre 1886, est reconnu exact et définitif en ce qui concerne les poteaux depuis le N° 1 jusqu'au N° 19 et depuis le N°36 jusqu'au N° 65 ; il sera complété ultérieurement par le synopsis des poteaux depuis le N° 20 jusqu'au N° 35, et de celui des poteaux à l'est du N° 65.

II. A partir du poteau N° 19 la frontière suivra une ligne droite jusqu'au sommet de la colline marquée 2740 sur la Carte N° 1 annexée au présent Protocole. Ce point, où sera placé le poteau N° 20, est connu sous la dénomination de « station trigonométrique de Karo-Tépé » (latitude 35° 17′ 49″, longitude 62° 15′ 17″). Plus loin le tracé descendra la crête des collines, se dirigeant de ce point vers le confluent du Koushk et du Moghur ; le poteau N° 21 sera placé sur un point de cette crête ou de son versant, de manière à être vu du confluent ci-dessus mentionné. Une ligne droite réunira le N° 21 au N° 22 placé dans la vallée du Koushk sur la rive gauche de la rivière, à 900 pieds au nord du confluent du Koushk et du Moghur (à 6300 pieds environ du Mazarishah Alam, indiqué sur la carte N° 2 annexée au Protocole).

A partir du poteau N° 22 le tracé remontera le thalweg du Koushk jusqu'au poteau N° 23, placé à 2700 pieds en amont de la tête du nouveau canal de la rive droite, dont la prise d'eau est située à 6000 pieds environ au nord-nord-ouest du Ziaret de Tchil-Doukhtar. Du poteau N° 23 une ligne droite sera tracée jusqu'au point marqué 2925 sur la Carte N° 3 annexée au présent Protocole (latitude 35° 15′ 53″, longitude 62° 27′ 57″, poteau N° 24), d'où la frontière suivra la ligne de partage des eaux en passant par les points suivants : le point 3017 (Bandi Akhamar, latitude 35° 14′ 21″, longitude 62° 35′ 48″, poteau N° 26), le point 3198 (latitude 35° 14′ 30″, longitude 62° 41′ 0″, poteau N° 27) et le point Kalari 2 (latitude 35° 18′ 21″, longitude 62° 47′ 18″) et aboutira au point marqué N° 29 sur la Carte N° 4 annexée au présent Protocole. La frontière franchira la vallée de la rivière Kashan en ligne droite entre les poteaux N° 29 et N° 30 (station trigonométrique de Tori-Scheikh, latitude 35° 24′ 51″, longitude 62° 59′ 43″), et suivra la ligne de partage des eaux Sanicha jusqu'au point (poteau No 31 de la Carte N° 3) où elle rencontrera la ligne de partage des eaux du Kashan et du Mourghab, passera sur cette dernière et la suivra jusqu'à la station trigonométrique du Kashan (latitude 35° 38′ 13″, longitude 63° 6′ 4″, poteau N° 32). De cette station une ligne droite sera tracée jusqu'à un point sur le Mourghab (poteau N° 35) situé à 700 pieds en amont de la prise d'eau du Canal Yaki-yuz (ou Yaki-yangi). Plus loin la frontière, en descendant le thalweg du Mourghab rejoindra le poteau N° 36 de la frontière démarquée en 1885-1886.

À l'est du poteau N° 65 la frontière suivra la ligne marquée A. B. C. D. sur la Carte N° 8 annexée au présent Protocole, le point A étant situé à la distance de 3500 pieds au sud des puits d'Imam-Nazar ; le point B se trouvant près de Kara-tépé-Khurdkak, qui reste aux Afghans ; le point C à peu près à mi-chemin entre les puits Ali-Kadim et les puits marqués Chahi. Les puits d'Imam-Nazar, Kara-tépé-Khurd, Khata-badji ouest et Ali Kadim restent en dehors du territoire Afghan. Du point D une ligne droite sera tracée jusqu'au commencement de la frontière locale démarquée entre Bosagha et Khamiab, qui continuera à servir de frontière entre ces deux villages avec la seule réserve que les canaux de Bosagha sur tout leur parcours, c'est-à-dire jusqu'à Koïnli (point H) seront compris dans le territoire Russe. En d'autres termes la démarcation actuelle consacrera sur les bords de l'Amou-Daria les droits existants des deux parties, c'est-à-dire que les habitants de Khamiab conserveront toutes leurs terres et tous leurs pâturages, y compris ceux qui se trouvent à l'est de la frontière locale marquée E. F. G. sur les Cartes N°ˢ 9 et 10, annexées au Protocole ; les habitants de Bosagha, d'autre part, conserveront la jouissance exclusive de leurs canaux jusqu'à Koïnli, avec le droit de les réparer et de les alimenter, conformément aux usages existants de ceux de Khamiab, lorsque les eaux de l'Amou-Daria seront trop basses pour alimenter directement les prises d'eau de Koïnli.

Les officiers qui seront chargés d'exécuter sur les lieux les dispositions du présent Protocole entre les poteaux ci-dessus nommés seront tenus de placer un nombre nécessaire de poteaux intermédiaires, en profitant à cet effet autant que possible des points saillants.

III. La clause du Protocole N° 4 du 14 (26) Décembre 1885 défendant aux Afghans de se servir dans la Vallée du Koushk, en aval de Tchil Doukhtar, des canaux d'irrigation qui n'étaient pas en exploitation à ce moment, reste en vigueur, mais il est bien entendu que cette clause ne pourra être appliquée qu'aux canaux dérivés du Koushk. Les Afghans ne pourront pas se servir, pour leurs travaux de culture au nord de Tchil-Doukhtar, des eaux du Koushk ; mais les eaux du Moghur leur appartiennent exclusivement, et ils pourront pour s'en servir exécuter tous les travaux qu'ils jugeraient utiles.

IV. Les clauses des Protocoles N° 4 des 14 (26) Décembre 1885, et N° 15 du 1ᵉʳ (13) Septembre 1886, relatives à la construction d'une digue sur le Mourghab restent en vigueur. M. Zinoview ayant exprimé le désir que l'obligation imposée à l'Emir Afghan de concéder à cette fin sur la rive droite du Mourghab un terrain dans les conditions stipulées dans les dits Protocoles, soit étendue à tout le parcours de la rivière en aval de Yaki-Yuz, le Colonel Ridgeway est d'avis que les démarches nécessaires à cet effet auprès de l'Emir Afghan pourraient retarder la conclusion du présent arrangement ; mais il est néanmoins convaincu que le consentement de l'Emir à la concession, dans les mêmes conditions, d'un terrain sur la rive droite pourra être obtenu sans difficultés, si plus tard le Gouvernement Impérial avisait le Gouvernement de Sa Majesté Britannique de son intention de procéder à la construction d'une digue en amont de la prise d'eau du canal de Bendi-Nadiz.

V. Le Gouvernement Britannique communiquera sans délai les dispositions ci-dessus convenues à l'Emir de l'Afghanistan, et le Gouvernement Impérial de Russie entrera en possession du territoire qui lui est adjugé par le présent Protocole à partir du 1ᵉʳ (13) Octobre de l'année courante.

VI. La ligne frontière convenue sera démarquée sur les lieux par une Commission mixte, conformément aux Cartes signées. Dans le cas où les travaux de démarcation éprouveraient des retards, la ligne tracée sur les Cartes n'en sera pas moins considérée par les deux Gouvernements comme obligatoire. [1]

Dès le 22 Juillet (3 Août) 1887, les deux gouvernements échangèrent des notes établissant leur acceptation des conclusions adoptées par les commissaires.

LXXXII. Etats-Unis d'Amérique, Hayti.

25 janvier 1885.

Relatif à une insurrection qui survint à Port-au-Prince les 22 et 23 septembre 1883, cet arbitrage ne fut consenti qu'après une longue correspondance qui se termina le 25 janvier 1885 par un arrangement verbal. Nous reproduisons ici la lettre qui confirme cet arrangement, ainsi que les instructions données aux commissaires de Hayti et acceptées par le Ministre des Etats-Unis. Il fut accordé 5700 $ aux intéressés.

Port-au-Prince, February 12, 1885.

In accordance with the agreement existing between us since sunday, the 25ᵗʰ of last month, and confirmed by your dispatch of the 11ᵗʰ instant, received yesterday, I have the honour to advise you that, with Messrs. Charles Weymann and Edward Cutts, whom you have named, will be joined Messrs. B. Lallemand, president of tribunal of cassation, and C. A. Preston, designated by the Government of the Republic to form a mixed commission to which shall be submitted the American reclamations growing out of the events of September 22 and 23, 1883. I have the honour in consequence to communicate to you, herewith inclosed, the text of the instructions in conformity with which the commission should examine such reclamations. I do not

___
[1] F. DE MARTENS. *Nouveau Recueil Général*, 2ᵉ série, t. XIII, p. 566.

doubt, Mr. Minister, that you will ratify the instructions, which are drawn up according to justice and equity. Thus have I the hope that your next response to this communication will express your entire compliance.

In that which concerns the sessions of the mixed commission, I would add that it will itself choose its place and will fix the day and hour of its meetings.

Instructions for the haytian commissioners, given at Port-au-Prince, February 12, 1885.

The greatest interests of the nation find themselves placed in your hands by the exalted and delicate mission whereof to day you are charged. The Government has counted in the circumstance upon your patriotism and your intelligence, and it hopes that you will give to its service all the activity of which you are able to dispose to bring to a desirable end the conferences which you are about to open.

I ought not to pretend to mark out in these few lines a complete code of instructions to follow in the exercise of your duty; it imports only that I bring to your attention some essential points of the matter to be settled to tell you how so far it has been met by the Government. That will be to initiate you into its views and its aspirations.

It is sought, as you know, to fix the figures of the indemnities to be accorded to foreigners whose interests has been directly destroyed at the times of the events which took place the 22ᵈ and 23ᵈ September of last year at Port-au-Prince (1883).

While leaving the responsibility of these scenes of disorder, pillage, and conflagration to the rioters of those days, the Government has determined that at present it is its duty to avoid all difficulties, all unhappy complications with the foreign powers, it has itself, in anticipation of reclamations, declared that it recognized the principle thereof, happy to give in the circumstance the most complete affirmation at its firm purpose to offer every security to foreigners and to capital which immigrate into the country. This principle admitted, it remains to approach in unity all the elements of indisputable appreciation the discussion of the figures of the indemnities with the foreign commission, the members of which, Messrs. Weymann and Edward Cutts, have been designated by the chief of the American legation of this city.

The work of the mixed commission shall not be subject to revision. You ought to judge sovereignly and without appeal, and it will suffice to express to you a just idea of the high confidence which is placed in you and which commands you, by consequence, to employ all care, all discernement, all tact, all equity necessary in the solutions to intervene. You are armed with powers of a court of arbitration judging in last resort, and in case of an equal division of votes upon the indemnities to be fixed it will be your duty to name an umpire to give you a casting vote.

From powers so extended, you will permit me to repeat it to you, follows the obligation for you to neglect nothing to furnish you with all the elements of nature to cast the most lively light upon the facts which you are going to examine, and the deplorable consequences which have been the result thereof. It is to sources of information the most fruitful, and at the same time the most pure, that you ought to have recourse to settle your judgments upon a just and equitable basis.

After the preparatory work, which will consist necessarily in making a list of the claimants, in placing opposite each name the figure of the indemnity demanded, you will make an expose of the facts of the reclamation supported by all the proofs. It is then that the debates contradictory can be opened and that a conscientious and profound examination shall fix your judgment.

You ought not to lose from view that the object of your mission consists in determining the figures of the indemnities to be accorded to foreigners whose interests have been directly destroyed by the fact of pillage or conflagration resulting from the events occurring the 22^d and 23^d of September, of the year 1883, at Port-au-Prince.

It is enough to tell you that you ought to be declare the rejection of reclamations founded upon indirect damages resulting from the same facts. There is no further controversy upon the solution of these questions. Recent examples are there to form it.

With your powers already so extended, the Government confers upon you the right of inquiry without limits. This shall be therefore the principal point of your operations, and it imports that you shall exercise that right in the largest manner to be exactly informed in your examination. Seek again carefully, with all the means possible, the proofs which you shall lack ; call and interrogate witnesses; enlighten your judgment by drawing from all the sources worthy of confidence, and notably from official sources, which cannot fail you.

Is the loss of merchandise discussed ? In the absence of valid balance-sheets, or all other sufficient papers, the documents of the custom-house will they not offer you the necessary provisions of a just appreciation of the nature and of the importance of the commerce of the claimant ?

I confine myself to this single example, as it will belong to you, certainly, to generalize in addressing yourselves to other public administrations if necessity should make itself felt in that regard.

Such are, in substance and in a manner evidently abridged, the general instructions which should serve as a guide to your operations. At the close of your conferences you will prepare a report in detail, to which should be annexed all the minutes of your sessions, etc. If, in the course of your investigations, any points of detail, which I have not been able to anticipate, should arise to hinder the progress thereof, you will be good enough to present them to me. I will make haste to have an understanding on such subject with Mr. Langston, minister of the American Government, and I am persuaded, with the spirit of good will, of conciliation, of justice, which animates him, there will be no lack of understanding on his part with me to settle the difficulties and place you in a position to accomplish to the general satisfaction the difficult and important mission with which you are charged.

The present instructions have been communicated to the minister of the United States of America, who entirely adheres to them ; you can then from their reception betake yourself to your labors. [1]

Report of the proceedings of the mixed commission on American claims against the Haytian government. Port-au-Prince, April 22-24, 1885.

Wednesday, April 22, 1885 — 4 p. m.

The members of the mixed commission charged to examine the American claims arising out of the events occurring at Port-au-Prince, 22^d and 23^d september, 1883, Messrs. B. Lallemand, S. Gentil, designated by the Haytian Government, and Weymann and Terres, named by the minister resident of the United States of America, met at the office of the American legation and took cognizance of the proofs submitted in support of the claims presented by

(1) Mr. C. W. Mossel, amounting to the sum of . . . . . . $ 5,551. 50
(2) Mr. E. V. Garrido, amounting to the sum of . . . . . . » 1,791. 00
(3) Mrs. Maria Hamilton, amounting to the sum of . . . . . . » 720. 00

$ 8,062. 50

[1] *Foreign Relations of U. S.*, 1885, p. 501.

In view of this examination and after mature deliberation, the mixed commission decided to fix as follows the indemnity to be awarded to

(1) Mr. C. W. Mossel . . . . . . $ 2,500
(2) Mr. E. V. Garrido . . . . . . » 850
(3) Mrs. Maria Hamilton . . . . . » 550
                                   ――――――
                                   $ 3,900

The mixed commission adjourned the continuation of its labor to Friday the 24th instant at four o'clock in the afternoon. And the members have signed the present minutes in double copy.

――――――

Friday, April 24, 1885 — 4 p. m.

In consequence of the adjournment made the 22[d] instant at the closing of its preceding minute, te mixed commission met at the office of the American legation and proceeded to the examination of the claims made for losses of merchandise and house-hold goods by

(1) Messrs. Bertram Bros. . . . . $ 1,800
(2) Mrs. Isabella Fournier . . . . » 1,000
                                   ――――――
                                   $ 2,800

In view of this examination and after mature deliberation, the mixed commission decided to fix as follows the indemnity to be awarded to

(1) Messrs. Bertram Bros. . . . . $ 1,100
(2) Mrs. Isabella Fournier . . . . » 700
                                   ――――――
                                   $ 1,800

The mixed commission then took cognizance of the two claims for loss of real estate, one presented by Mrs. Evan Williams (widow), for a two-story brick-building, situated in Port-au-Prince, fronts Forts street, amounting to $ 16,000 and the other presented by Mrs. Isabella Fournier, for a house situated in this city at the corner of Centre and Cæsar streets, amounting to $ 1500.

The Haytian commissioners declared that they could not admit these two claims, for the following reasons:

Mrs. Isabella Fournier, being a foreigner, cannot, according to the provision of the constitution and of article 450 of the civil code, be an owner of real estate in Hayti. Mrs. Evan Williams, *née* Rivière, widow, having lost her rights as a Haytian, from the effect of the promulgation of the constitution of 1874, she could not in 1875, at the opening of the succession of Mr. J. J. Rivière, inherit the real estate of that succession, since in virtue of the constitution and articles 450 and 587 of the civil code, a foreigner cannot be owner of real estate, and is only admissible to succeed to personal property in Hayti.

If in 1876 Mrs. Evan Williams, widow, participated in the act of separation of the succession of real estate of Mr. J. J. Rivière, it is probable that she intended to renounce her rights as a foreigner, from which it results that Mrs. Evan Williams, widow, cannot present herself as a foreigner to formulate a claim against the Government of Hayti.

The American commissioners declare their non-participation in this opinion of the Haytian commissioners. They hold that from the sole fact of possession by these claimants an indemnity is due them.

These opinions being contrary, and each of the commissioners persisting in his opinion, the mixed commission has not been able to come to an understandig on a decision in the case Evan Williams, widow, of the two claims for losses of real estate presented by Mrs. Evan Williams and Mrs. Isabella Fournier.

In presence of this divergence of opinion the commissioners have decided that they would notify the high contracting parties thereof.

Whereas there remains nothing further to act upon on the lists presented by the American legation, the mixed commission has closed its sessions.

And the members have signed the present minute made in duplicate copy[1].

LXXXIII. Autriche, Chili.

14 juillet 1885.

Cette affaire, similaire à celle entre l'Allemagne et le Chili, du 23 août 1884, se termina, à l'intervention de l'ambassadeur d'Allemagne, par le paiement d'une somme globale de $ 20,000 à partager entre les ressortissants allemands, autrichiens et suisses.

Convencion de arbitraje entre Chile y el Imperio Austro-Hungaro, firmada en Santiago el 11 de Julio de 1885.

Por cuanto entre la República de Chile y el Imperio Austro-Húngaro, se negoció, concluyó y firmó el once de Julio de mil ochocientos ochenta y cinco, por medio de Plenipotenciarios competentemente autorizados al efecto, una Convención de Arbitrage cuyo tenor literal es como sigue:

Su Excelencia el Presidente de la Republica de Chile y su Majestad el Emperador de Austria, Rey de Bohemia, etc., etc., Rey-Apostólico de Hungría, deseando arbitrar los medios para resolver

――――――

[1] *Foreign Relations of the U. S.*, 1885, p. 519.

amistosamente las reclamaciones presentadas por subditos austriacos ó húngaros contra el Gobierno Chileno, á consecuencia de la última guerra entre Chile y el Perú y Bolivia, han nombrado sus Plenipotenciarios:

Su Excelencia el Presidente de la República de Chile, el señor Aniceto Vergara Albano, Ministro de Relaciones Exteriores de la República; y

Su Majestad el Emperador de Austria, Rey de Bohemia, etc., etc., Rey-Apostólico de Hungría, el señor Barón Schenck zu Schweinsberg, Ministro Residente del Imperio Germánico en Chile;

Los cuales Plenipotenciarios, después de haber. examinado sus plenos poderes y de haberlos encontrado en buena y debida forma, han convenido en lo siguiente:

ARTICULO UNICO. El Gobierno de la República de Chile y el del Imperio Austria-Hungría convienen en deferir al conocimiento y resolución del Tribunal Arbitral establecido por la Convención Chileno-Alemana de 23 de Agosto de 1884, las reclamaciones presentadas por súbditos austriacos ó húngaros contra el Gobierno de Chile, con motivo de los actos y operaciones ejecutados por las fuerzas de mar y tierra de la República en los territorios y costas del Perú y Bolivia durante la última guerra.

Estas reclamaciones serán falladas en conformidad á los mismos principios y bajo los mismos trámites y condiciones que ha establecido para las reclamaciones de súbditos alemanes la ya referida Convención de 23 de Agosto de 1884, y deberán ser presentadas al Tribunal por el Representante diplomático del Imperio Germánico en el termino de noventa días, contados desde aquel en que se verifique el canje de las ratificaciones de la presente Convención.

Toda reclamación que se presentare después de transcurrido el plazo indicado en el inciso precedente, no será admitida, teniéndose desde luego como desechada, de modo que por ningún motivo ó pretexto pueda ser materia de nuevo examen ó discusión.

El Gobierno del Imperio Austro-Hungaro queda encargado de recabar la autorización necesaria para que los jueces árbitros de Alemania y del Brasil puedan concurrir á la resolución de las reclamaciones indicadas. La presente Convención será ratificada por las Altas Partes contratantes, y las ratificaciones se canjearán en Santiago cuanto antes sea posible.

En fe de lo cual los Plenipotenciarios de ambos paises la firmaron en doble ejemplar y en los idiomas español y alemán, y la sellaron con sus sellos respectivos.

Hecha en Santiago de Chile, á los once dias del mes de Julio del año de mil ochocientos ochenta y cinco[1].

LXXXIV. Chili, Suisse.

19 janvier 1886.

Semblable à la convention conclue entre l'Autriche et le Chili, sous la date du 11 juillet 1885, elle se termine de la même manière à l'intervention de l'ambassadeur d'Allemagne.

Convencion de arbitraje chileno-suiza, firmada en Santiago el 19 de Enero de 1886.

S. E. el Presidente de la República de Chile y el Consejo Federal Suizo, deseando arbitrar los medios para resolver amistosamente las reclamaciones presentadas por ciudadanos suizos contra el Gobierno Chileno, á consecuencia de la última guerra entre Chile, el Perú y Bolivia han nombrado por sus Plenipotenciarios:

S. E. el Presidente de la República de Chile el señor Anibal Zañartu, Ministro de Relaciones Exteriores de la República, y el Consejo Federal Suizo el señor Barón Schenck zu Schweinsberg, Consejero de Legación y Ministro Residente de S. M. el Emperador de Alemania en Chile;

Los cuales Plenipotenciarios, después de haber examinado sus plenos poderes y de haberlos encontrado en buena y debida forma han convenido en lo siguiente:

ARTICULO UNICO. El Gobierno de la República de Chile y el Consejo Federal Suizo convienen en deferir al conocimiento y resolución del Tribunal Arbitral establecido por la Convención Germano-Chilena de 23 de Agosto de 1884, las reclamaciones presentadas por ciudadanos suizos contra el Gobierno de Chile, con motivo de los actos y operaciones ejecutados por las fuerzas de mar y tierra de la República en los territorios y costas del Perú y Bolivia durante la última guerra. Estas reclamaciones serán falladas en conformidad á los mismos principios y bajo los mismos trámites y condiciones que ha establecido para las reclamaciones de súbditos alemanes la ya referida Convención de 23 de Agosto de 1884, y deberán ser presentadas al Tribunal por el Representante diplomatico del Imperio Alemán, en el término de noventa días, contado desde aquel en que se verifique el canje de las ratificaciones de la presente Convención.

---

[1] *Recopilacion de Tratados y Convenciones*, t. II, p. 268. — Le traité qui a terminé cette affaire se trouve reproduit plus haut, p. 276.

Toda reclamación que se presentare después de transcurrido el plazo indicado en el inciso precedente, no será admitida, teniéndose desde luego como desechada de modo que por ningún motivo ó pretexto pueda ser materia de nuevo examen ó discussión.

El Consejo Federal Suizo queda encargado de recabar la autorización necesaria para que los jueces árbitros de Alemania y del Brasil puedan concurrir á la resolución de los reclamaciones indicadas.

La presente Convención será ratificada por las Altas Partes contratantes, y las ratificaciones se canjearán en Santiago cuanto antes fuere posible.

En fe de lo cual los Plenipotenciarios de ambos paises la firmaron en doble ejemplar y en los idiomas español y alemán y la sellaron con sus sellos respectivos[1].

LXXXV. Colombie, Italie.

24 mai 1886.

Cette affaire, qui faillit amener la guerre entre les deux pays, fut arrangée grâce à la médiation du gouvernement espagnol. Il s'agissait, en l'occurrence, de la confiscation des biens d'un sieur Cerruti, pour une prétendue participation de ce dernier à des faits insurrectionnels. Le médiateur, chargé d'examiner s'il y avait lieu de réparer le dommage causé au dit sieur Cerruti, résolut cette question par l'affirmative. En, exécution de la convention avenue entre les deux pays, le tribunal arbitral se réunit à Bogota le 5 septembre 1888.

Arrangement destiné à régler d'un commun accord, par médiation, les questions pendantes entre les deux pays, signé à Paris le 24 mai 1886.

Les Gouvernements d'Italie et de Colombie, ayant réglé, au moyen de notes diplomatiques, les questions pendantes entre les deux pays, qui étaient placées hors de la médiation amicale que le Gouvernement de S. M. Catholique leur a offerte, et désirant, pour ce qui concerne les autres questions, fixer d'une manière claire, précise et positive les bases que les deux parties accepteraient d'un commun accord pour la dite médiation,

[1] *Recopilacion de Tratados y Convenciones*, t. II, p. 272. — Voir plus haut, p. 276, le traité qui a terminé la contestation.

S. Exc. le général comte Menabrea, marquis de Valdora, Ambassadeur extraordinaire et plénipotentiaire de S. M. le Roi d'Italie près le Gouvernement de la République française, d'une part, et

S. Exc. D. Francisco de Paula Matéus, Envoyé extraordinaire et ministre plénipotentiaire de Colombie près le Gouvernement de la dite République, de l'autre,

A ce dûment autorisés, ont signé ad referendum le présent protocole, destiné à être soumis, aussitôt après l'approbation de leurs Gouvernements, au Gouvernement de S. M. Catholique :

ART. I. Aussitôt après l'approbation de ce protocole, le Gouvernement de la République de Colombie rendra au sujet italien M. Ernest Cerruti, ou à ses représentants, les biens immeubles lui appartenant, situés sur le territoire de la dite République, qui lui ont été saisis par les autorités de l'Etat de Cauca, ou par d'autres autorités quelconques de la nation colombienne, pendant la dernière guerre civile.

ART. II. Toute autre réclamation, de quelque nature que ce soit, actuellement pendante entre le Gouvernement de S. M. le Roi d'Italie et le Gouvernement de Colombie, dans l'intérêt du sieur Cerruti ou d'autres sujets italiens, reste soumise à la médiation du Gouvernement de S. M. Catholique, par devant lequel les deux Gouvernements présenteront leurs preuves et documents respectifs.

Les questions principales que le médiateur aura à résoudre sont les suivantes :

Le sieur Cerruti, ou d'autres sujets italiens, ont-ils, oui ou non, perdu en Colombie leur qualité d'étrangers neutres ?

Ont-ils, oui ou non, perdu les droits, les prérogatives et les privilèges que le droit commun et les lois de Colombie accordent aux étrangers ?

La Colombie doit-elle, oui ou non, payer des indemnités au sieur Cerruti ou à d'autres sujets italiens ?

ART. III. S'il résulte de la dite médiation que la Colombie doit payer des indemnités, ces indemnités ainsi que les modalités, les termes et les garanties du paiement formeront, sans appel ni réserve quelconque, l'objet d'un jugement arbitral que les deux Gouvernements conviennent dès aujourd'hui de déférer à une commission mixte ainsi composée : le Représentant d'Italie à Bogota, un délégué du Gouvernement Colombien, le Représentant d'Espagne à Bogota. Le travail de la commission mixte doit être achevé dans les six mois après la notification, par le Gouvernement espagnol, de ses conclusions, aux Représentants des deux Parties à Madrid. Cette même commis-

sion mixte aurait·à statuer dans le cas où une
contestation s'élèverait sur l'étendue des biens
immeubles appartenant à M. Cerruti, lesquels,
d'après l'article Ier, devront lui être rendus dans
toute l'extension qu'ils avaient au moment de la
saisie.

ART. IV. Sauf les conclusions, quelles qu'elles
soient, de la médiation, il est expressément
entendu que M. Cerruti ne pourra jamais être
ultérieurement, ni d'aucune façon, molesté à raison
de tout acte qu'il serait accusé d'avoir accompli,
jusqu'à la date du présent protocole.

ART. V. Les rapports diplomatiques et de
bonne amitié seront considérés comme repris dès
le jour où le présent protocole sera approuvé
par les deux Gouvernements. Le Gouvernement
de Colombie accréditera, aussitôt que possible,
un représentant auprès de Sa Majesté le Roi.
Aussitôt après l'approbation du présent protocole,
et comme gage du rétablissement des rapports
amicaux entre les deux pays, le Gouvernement
du Roi accréditera de nouveau un Représentant
de Sa Majesté en Colombie. Ce dernier se rendant à Bogota, sera conduit par un bâtiment de
la marine royale au port de Cartagena, où, après
avis préalable, on échangera alternativement des
saluts par vingt et un coups de canon entre le
bâtiment et les batteries de terre.

ART. VI. Le présent protocole sera soumis
à l'approbation des deux Gouvernements. L'approbation doit être mutuellement notifiée, par
l'organe des Représentants respectifs à Paris,
dans le délai de trois mois, ou plus tôt si faire
se peut.

Fait à Paris, en double exemplaire, le vingtquatre mai 1886[1].

Par suite de divers incidents, le demandeur M. Cerruti se retira et le tribunal arbitral
se considéra dès lors comme dessaisi. De nouveaux pourparlers s'engagèrent entre les deux
gouvernements et aboutirent à l'adoption d'une
convention nouvelle, par laquelle le Président
des Etats-Unis de l'Amérique du Nord était
prié de trancher le différend.

**Protocollo fra l'Italia e la Colombia per sottoporre ad
arbitrato la definizione della vertenza Cerruti, sottoscritto in Castellamare di Stabia, il 18 Agosto 1894.**

Il Governo del Regno d'Italia ed il Governo
della Repubblica di Colombia, desiderando di porre
un termine alle cause di dissenso originate fra
essi dai reclami del signor Ernesto Cerruti contro

[1] F. DE MARTENS. *Nouveau Recueil Général*, 2me série,
t. XVIII, p. 659.

il Governo della Colombia per perdite e danni
alle sue proprietà nello Stato (ora dipartimento)
del Cauca nella detta Repubblica, durante i torbidi politici del 1885, e desiderando inoltre di
fare un giusto componimento dei detti reclami;

Sua Eccellenza il barone Blanc, Ministro degli
affari esteri di Sua Maestà il Re d'Italia, da una
parte, e Don José Marcelino Hurtado, Inviato
straordinario e Ministro plenipotenziario della
Repubblica di Colombia presso Sua Maestà il Re
d'Italia, dall'altra parte, i quali agiscono debitamente autorizzati dai rispettivi loro Governi,
hanno firmato questo protocollo, subordinatamente all'approvazione del Congresso di Colombia, cui sarà sottoposto nell'attuale sessione.

Il Governo d'Italia ed il Governo di Colombia
convengono di sottoporre all'arbitrato le materie
e reclami sopra riferiti, allo scopo di giungere
ad una sistemazione dei medesimi, in quanto
pendono fra i due Governi. A tale effetto, tostochè
questo protocollo avrà ottenuto l'approvazione
del Congresso di Colombia, si uniranno nel domandare a Sua Eccellenza il Presidente degli Stati
Uniti d'America che si compiacci di accettare
la qualità di arbitro nella causa e di disimpegnarne i doveri relativi, a titolo di amichevole
atto verso ambedue i Governi.

Tostochè l'arbitro colla sua accettazione dell'ufficio avrà acquestato titolo per entrare nelle sue
funzioni, resterà investito di pieno potere, autorità
e giurisdizione per fare ed eseguire, e disporre che
si faccia e si eseguisca, ogni cosa, senza alcuna limitazione qualsiasi, che a suo giudizio possa essere
necessaria o conducente al conseguimento in retta
ed equa maniera dei fini e propositi che il presente
accordo è destinato ad assicurare.

Ed Egli, quindi, procederà ad esaminare e
decidere, in base ai documenti e prove che gli
siano sottoposti da ciascuno dei due Governi o
dal reclamante, come una delle parti interessate
nel giudizio, ed ai principii di diritto pubblico
in primo luogo quali, se ve ne siano alcuni fra
i detti reclami del signor E. Cerruti contro il
Governo di Colombia, formino un reclamo o reclami di competenza di un giudizio internazionale;
e secondariamente quali, se ve ne siano dei detti
reclami del signor E. Cerruti contro il Governo
di Colombia, formino un reclamo o reclami di
competenza dei tribunali territoriali della Colombia.

È per quanto riguarda il reclamo o reclami,
se ve ne siano, che a giudizio dell'arbitro avranno
il carattere e faranno parte del primo ordine di
reclami sopra definito, l'arbitro procederà a determinare e dichiarare l'ammontare della indennità,
se alcuna gliene competa, che il reclamante signor E. Cerruti abbia diritto di ricevere dal Governo
di Colombia in via diplomatica. E per quanto
riguarda il reclamo o reclami del signor E. Cer-

ruti, se ve ne siano, che a giudizio dell' arbitro avranno il carattere e faranno parte del secondo ordine di reclami sopra definito, l'arbitro dichiarerà che essi sono tali e non prenderà alcuna ulteriore ingerenza nella materia di tale o di tali reclami. I reclami cui questo protocollo si riferisce saranno presentati, insieme coi documenti e prove in appoggio, all' arbitro ed al medesimo sottoposti, non prima di sei mesi del calendario, nè dopo sette mesi del calendario, calcolati da e dopo la data della accettazione dell' ufficio di arbitro per parte di Sua Eccellenza il Presidente degli Stati Uniti di America.

Ciascuna delle due Parti interessate nel giudizio sopporterà le spese incorse per sua individuale autorizzazione od interesse; ma tutte le spese sostenute per autorizzazione o colla sanzione dell' arbitro per lo scopo di convenientemente disimpegnare le sue funzioni o doveri, o per il vantaggio comune di ambedue le Parti interessate nel giudizio, saranno sopportate in parti eguali da entrambe.

I due Governi solennemente si obbligano a stare alle decisioni dell' arbitro, le quali saranno finali e conclusive e non soggette a discussione od appello. Ed essi inoltre convengono di non riaprire negoziati o discussioni diplomatiche sopra qualsiasi punto o punti sui quali l'arbitro abbia deciso o disposto, o sui quali Egli dichiari essere già stato disposto in conformità al diritto pubblico; nè sopra qualsiasi reclamo o reclami del signor E. Cerruti che l'arbitro dichiari aver carattere interno e territoriale.

In fede di che, sua Eccellenza il barone Blanc, Ministro degli affari esteri di Sua Maestà il Re d'Italia, e don José Marcelino Hurtado, Inviato straordinario e Ministro plenipotenziario della Repubblica di Colombia presso Sua Maestà il Re d'Italia, appongono le loro firme al presente protocollo, a Castellamare di Stabia, il diciotto agosto dell' anno mille ottocento novantaquattro[1].

Lodo arbitrale del Presidente degli Stati Uniti nella vertenza Cerruti fra l'Italia e la Colombia, dato Washington, Marzo 2, 1897.

This protocol concluded August 18th, 1894, between the Kingdom of Italy and the Republic of Colombia was entered into for the purpose of putting an end to the subjects of disagreement between the two Governments growing out of the claims of signor Ernesto Cerruti against the Government of Colombia for losses and damages to his property in the State (now Department) of Cauca in the said Republic, during the political troubles of 1885, and for the further purpose of

making a just disposition of said claims. By the terms of the protocol each Government agreed to submit to arbitration the matters and claims above referred to for the purpose of arriving at a settlement thereof as between the two Governments, and they joined in asking me, Grover Cleveland, President of the United States of America, to accept the position of Arbitrator in the case and discharge the duties pertaining thereto as a friendly act to both Governments, vesting in me full power, authority and jurisdiction to do and perform, and to cause to be done and performed, all things, without any limitation whatsoever, which in my judgment might be necessary or conducive to the attainment in a fair and equitable manner of the ends and purposes the agreement is intended to secure.

Pursuant to the terms of the said protocol the two Governments and the claimant, signor Ernest Cerruti as one of the two parties interested in the suit, have submitted to me within the time specified in said protocol the documents and evidence in support of their several asserted rights.

Now, therefore, be it known that I, Grover Cleveland, President of the United States of America, upon whom the functions of Arbitrator have been conferred, as aforesaid, having duly examined the documents and evidence submitted by the respective parties pursuant to the provisions of said protocol, and having considered the arguments addressed to me in relation thereto, do hereby decide and award:

1. That the claims made by signor Ernesto Cerruti against the Republic of Colombia for losses of and damages to the real and personal property owned by him individually in the said State of Cauca, and the claims of said signor Ernesto Cerruti for injury sustained by him by reason of losses of and damages to his interest in the firm of E. Cerruti and Company, are proper claims for international adjudication.

2. That the claim submitted to me by signor Ernesto Cerruti for personal damages, resulting from imprisonment, arrest, enforced separation from his family, and sufferings and privations endured by himself and family, is disallowed. I therefore make no award on account of this claim.

3. The claim of signor Ernesto Cerruti for moneys expended and obligations incurred for legal expenses in the preparation and prosecution of this claim, including former and present proceedings, is disallowed by me.

4. I award for losses and damages to the individual property of signor Ernesto Cerruti in the State of Cauca and to his interest in the copartnership of E. Cerrruti and Company, of which he was a member, including interest, the

---

[1] *Trattati e Convenzioni . . .*, vol. XIII, p. 348.

net sum of sixty thousand pounds sterling, of which sum ten thousand having been already paid, the Government of the Republic of Colombia will, in addition, pay to the Government of the Kingdom of Italy, for the use of signor Ernesto Cerruti, ten thousand pounds sterling thereof within sixty days from the date hereof, and the remainder, being forty thousand pounds, within nine months from the date hereof with interest from the date of this award at the rate of six per cent per annum until paid, both payments to be made by draft payable in London England, with exchange from Bogota at the time of payment.

5. It being my judgement that signor Ernesto Cerruti is, as between himself and the Government of the Republic of Colombia, which I find has by its acts destroyed his means for liquidating the debts of the copartnership of E. Cerruti and Company for which he may be held personally liable, entitled to enjoy and be protected in the net sum awarded him hereby, I do, under the protocol which vests me with full power, authority and jurisdiction to do and perform, and to cause to be done and performed, all things without any limitation whatsoever which in my judgment may be necessary or conducive to the attainment in a fair and equitable manner of the ends and purposes which the protocol is intended to secure, decide and adjudge to the Government of the Republic of Colombia all rights legal and equitable of the said signor Ernesto Cerruti in and to all property real, personal and mixed in the Department of Cauca and which has been called in question in this proceeding, and I further adjudge and decide that the Government of the Republic of Colombia shall guarantee and protect signor Ernesto Cerruti against any and all liability on account of the debts of the said copartnership, and shall reimburse signor Ernesto Cerruti to the extent that he may be compelled to pay such bona fide copartnership debts duly established against all proper defences which could and ought to have been made, and such guarantee and reimbursement shall include all necessary expenses for properly contesting such partnership debts.

In testimony whereof, I have hereunto set my hand and caused the seal of the United States to be affixed.

Done in duplicate at the city of Washington, on the second day of March in the year one thousand eight hundred and ninetyseven, and of the independence of the United States the 121st [1].

---

[1] *Trattati e Convenzioni . . . .*, vol. XV, p. 9—12.

LXXXVI. Costa Rica, Nicaragua.

24 décembre 1886.

Relatif principalement aux limites des deux pays, cet arbitrage mit fin à une situation tendue entre les deux gouvernements intéressés.

Convencion de arbitraje entre Nicaragua y Costa Rica, firmada en Guatemala, Diciembre 24, 1886.

Los Gobiernos de las Repúblicas de Costa Rica y Nicaragua, animados del deseo de poner termino á la cuestión por ellos delatida desde 1871, á saber: si es ó no válido el Tratado firmado por ambos el día 15 de Abril de 1858, han nombrado respectivemente para Plenipotenciarios al señor don Ascensión Esquivel, Enviado Extraordinario y Ministro Plenipotenciario de Costa Rica ante el Gobierno de Guatemala, y al señor don José Antonio Ramon, Enviado Extraordinario y Ministro Plenipotenciario de Nicaragua ante el mismo Gobierno quienes, después de comunicarse sus plenos poderes, que hallaron en debida forma, y de conferenciar con intervención del señor Ministro de Relaciones Exteriores de la República de Guatemala, Doctor don Fernando Cruz, designado para interponer los buenos oficios de su Gobierno, generosamente ofrecidos á las Partes contendientes, y por estas con gratitud aceptádos, han convenido en los siguientes articulos.

ARTICULO 1. — La cuestión pendiente entre los Gobiernos Contratantes sobre validez del Tratado de límítes de 15 de Abril de 1858, se somete á arbitramento.

ARTICULO 2. —- Será árbitro de esa cuestión el señor Presidente de los Estados Unidos de América.

Dentro de los sesenta días siguientes al canje de ratificaciones de la presente Convención, los Gobiernos Contratantes solicitarán del árbitro nombrado, la aceptación del cargo.

ARTICULO 3. — En el inesperado caso de que el señor Presidente de los Estados Unidos no se digne aceptar, las Partes nombran para árbitro al señor Presidente de la República de Chile, cuya aceptatión se solicitará por los Gobiernos Contratantes, dentro de noventa díaz contados desde aquel en que el señor Presidente de los Estados Unidos notifique su excusa á ambos Gobiernos ó á sus Representantes en Washington.

ARTICULO 4. — Si desgraciadamente tampoco el señor Presidente de Chile pudiera prestar á los Partes el eminente servicio de admitir el cometido, ambos Gobiernos se pondrán de acuerdo para elegir otros dos árbitros, dentro de noventa días contados desde aquel en que el señor Presidente de Chile notifique su no aceptación á ambos Gobiernos, ó á sus Representantes en Santiago.

ARTICULO 5. — Los procedimientos y términos á que deberá sujetarse el juicio arbitral, serán los siguientes:

Dentro de novento días contados desde que la aceptación del árbitro fuere notificada á las Partes, estas le presentarán sus alegatos y documentos.

El árbitro comunicará al Representante de cada Gobiernos, dentro de ocho días después de presentados los alegatos del contrario, para que pueda relatirlos dentro de los treinta días siguientes á aquel en que se le hubieren comunicado.

El árbitro deberá pronunciar su fallo, para que sea valedero, dentro de seis meses á contar de la fecha en que hubiere vencido el termino otorgado para contestar alegatos, háyanse ó no presentado éstos.

El árbitro puede delegar sus funciones, con tal que no deje de intervenir directamente en la pronunciación de la sentencia definitiva.

ARTICULO 6. — Si el laudo arbitral decide la validez del Tratado, la misma sentencia declarará si Costa Rica tiene derecho de navegar el rio San Juan con naves de guerra ó destinadas al servicio fiscal. De igual modo decidirá en caso de ser válida dicha Convencion, todos los demás puntos de dudosa interpretación que cualquiera de las Partes encuentre en el Tratado, y que comunique á la otra dentro de treinta días, contados desde el canje de ratificaciones del presente.

ARTICULO 7. — La decisión arbitral, cualquiera que sea, se tendrá por Tratado perfecto y obligatorio entre las Partes Contratantes; no admitirá recurso alguno, y empezará á ejecutarse treinta días después de haber sido notificada á ambos Gobiernos ó á sus Representantes.

ARTICULO 8. — Si se llegase á declarar la nulidad del Tratado, ambos Gobiernos, dentro de un año contado desde la notificación del laudo arbitral, se pondrán de acuerdo para fijar la línea divisoria de los territorios respectivos.

Si ese acuerdo no fuere posible, celebrarán en el año siguiente una Convención para someter á la decisión de un Gobierno amigo la cuestión de límites entre ambas Repúblicas.

Desde que el Tratado se declare nulo, y mientras no haya acuerdo entre las Partes, ó no recaiga sentencia que fije los derechos definitos de ambos paises, se respetarán provisionalmente los que establece el Tratado de 15 de Abril de 1858.

ARTICULO 9. — Mientras la cuestión de validez del Tratado no sea resuelta, el Gobierno de Costa Rica consiente en suspender el cumplimiento de su acuerdo de 16 de marzo último, en cuanto dispone la navegación del rio San Juan por un vapor nacional.

ARTICULO 10. — En caso de que se decida por el laudo arbitral que el Tratado de límites es válido, los Gobiernos Contratantes, dentro de los noventa dias siguientes á aquel en que sean notificados de la sentencia, nombrarán cuatro comisionados, dos cada uno, que practiquen las medidas correspondientes á la línea divisoria establecida en el articulo 2 del referido Tratado de 15 de Abril de 1858.

Estas medidas y el amojonamiento que á ellas es consiguiente se practicarán dentro de treinta meses contados desde el día en que sean nombrados los comisionados.

Estos comisionados tendran la facultad de apartese de la linea fijada por el Tratado en interés de buscar límites naturales, ó más facilmente distinguibles, hasta una milla; pero esta desviación solo podrá hacerse cuando todos los comisionados se pongan de acuerdo en el punto ó puntos que han de sustituir la línea.

ARTICULO 11. — Este Tratado deberá someterse á la aprobación del Ejecutivo y Congreso de ambas Repúblicas Contratantes; y sus ratificaciones se canjearán en Managua ó en San José de Costa Rica, el treinta de Junio próximo, ó antes si fuere posible.

En fe de lo cual, los Plenipotenciarios y el señor Ministro de Relaciones Exteriores de Guatemala, lo han firmado y sellado con sus sellos particulares en la ciudad de Guatemala, á los veinticuatro días del mes de Diciembre de mil ochocientos ochenta y seis [1].

Award of the Arbitrator, the President of the United States, upon the validity of the Treaty of Limits of 1858 between Nicaragua and Costa Rica. Washington, March 22, 1888.

Grover Cleveland, President of the United States, to whom it shall concern, greeting:

The functions of arbitrator having been conferred upon the President of the United States by virtue of a treaty signed at the City of Guatemala on the 24th day of December, one thousand eight hundred and eighty-six, between the Republics of Costa Rica and Nicaragua, whereby it was agreed that the question pending between the contracting Governments in regard to the validity of their Treaty of Limits of the 15th day of April, one thousand eight hundred and fifty-eight, should be submitted to the arbitration of the President of the United States of America; that if the arbitrator's award should determine

---

[1] *Collección de Tratados.* Costa Rica, 1896, p. 183.

that the treaty was valid, the same award should also declare whether Costa Rica has the right of Navigation of the river San Juan with vessels of war or of the revenue service, and that in the same manner the arbitrator should decide, in case of the validity of the treaty, upon all the other points of doubtful interpretation which either of the parties might find in the treaty and should communicate to the other party within thirty days after the exchange of the ratifications of the said treaty of the 24th day of December, one thousand eight hundred and eighty-six;

And the Republic of Nicaragua having duly communicated to the Republic of Costa Rica eleven points of doubtful interpretation found in the said Treaty of Limits of the 15th day of April, one thousand eight hundred and fifty-eight; and the Republic of Costa Rica having failed to communicate to the Republic of Nicaragua any points of doubtful interpretation found in the said last-mentioned treaty:

And both parties having duly presented their allegations and documents to the arbitrator, and having thereafter duly presented their respective answers to the allegations of the other party as provided in the treaty of the 24th day of December, one thousand eight hundred and eighty-six;

And the arbitrator pursuant to the fifth clause of said last-named treaty having delegated his powers to the honorable George L. Rives, Assistant Secretary of State, who, after examining and considering the said allegations, documents and answers, has made his report in writing thereon to the arbitrator;

Now, therefore, I, Grover Cleveland, President of the United States of America, do hereby make the following decision and award:

First. The above-mentioned Treaty of Limits, signed on the 15th day of April, one thousand eight hundred and fifty-eight, is valid.

Second. The Republic of Costa Rica under said treaty and the stipulations contained in the sixth article thereof, has not the right of navigation of the River San Juan with vessels of war; but she may navigate said river with such vessels of the revenue service as may be related to and connected with her enjoyment of the « purpose of commerce » accorded to her in said article, or as may be necessary to the protection of said enjoyment.

Third. With respect to the points of doubtful interpretation communicated as aforesaid by the Republic of Nicaragua, I decide as follows:

1. The boundary line between the Republic of Costa Rica and Nicaragua, on the Atlantic side, begins at the extremity of Punta de Castilla at the mouth of the San Juan de Nicaragua River, as they both existed on the 15th day of April, 1858. The ownership of any accretion to said Punta de Castilla is to be governed by the laws applicable to that subject.

2. The central point of the Salinas Bay is to be fixed by drawing a straight line across the mouth of the bay and determining mathematically the centre of the closed geometrical figure formed by such straight line and the shore of the bay at low-water mark.

3. By the central point of Salinas Bay is to be understood the centre of the geometrical figure formed as above stated. The limit of the bay towards the ocean is a straight line drawn from the extremity of Punta Arranca Barba, nearly true south to the westernmost portion of the land about Punta Sacate.

4. The Republic of Costa Rica is not bound to concur with the Republic of Nicaragua in the expenses necessary to prevent the bay of San Juan del Norte from being obstructed; to keep the navigation of the river or port free and unembarrassed, or to improve it for the common benefit.

5. The Republic of Costa Rica is not bound to contribute any proportion of the expenses that may be incurred by the Republic of Nicaragua for any of the purposes above mentioned.

6. The Republic of Costa Rica can not prevent the Republic of Nicaragua from executing at her own expense and within her own territory such works of improvement, provided such works of improvement do not result in the occupation or flooding or damage of Costa Rica territory, or in the destruction or serious impairment of the navigation of the said river or any of its branches at any point where Costa Rica is entitled to the same. The Republic of Costa Rica has the right to demand indemnification for any places belonging to her on the right bank of the river San Juan which may be occupied without her consent, and for any lands on the same bank which may be flooded or damaged in any other way in consequence of works of improvement.

7. The branch of the river San Juan known as the Colorado River must not be considered as the boundary between the Republics of Costa Rica and Nicaragua in any part of its course.

8. The right of the Republic of Costa Rica to the navigation of the river San Juan with men-of-war or revenue-cutters is determined and defined in the second article of this award.

9. The Republic of Costa Rica can deny to the Republic of Nicaragua the right of deviating the waters of the river San Juan in case such deviation will result in the destruction or serious impairment of the navigation of the said river or

any of its branches at any point where Costa Rica is entitled to navigate the same.

10. The Republic of Nicaragua remains bound not to make any grants for canal purposes across her territory without first asking the opinion of the Republic of Costa Rica, as provided in Article VIII of the Treaty of Limits of the 15th day of April, one thousand eight hundred and fifty-eight. The natural rights of the Republic of Costa Rica alluded to in the said stipulation are the rights which, in view of the boundaries fixed by the said Treaty of Limits, she possesses in the soil thereby recognized as belonging exclusively to her; the rights which she possesses in the harbors of San Juan del Norte and Salinas Bay; and the rights which she possesses in so much of the river San Juan as lies more than three English miles below Castillo Viejo, measuring from the exterior fortifications of the said castle as the same existed in the year 1858; and perhaps other rights not here particulary specified. These rights are to be deemed injured in any case where the territory belonging to the Republic of Costa Rica is occupied or flooden; where there is an encroachment upon either of the said harbors injurious to Costa Rica; or where there is such an obstruction or deviation of the river San Juan as to destroy or seriously impair the navigation of the said river or any of its branches at any point where Costa Rica is entitled to navigate the same.

11. The Treaty of Limits of the 15th day of April, one thousand eight hundred and fifty-eight, does not give to the Republic of Costa Rica the right to be a party to grants which Nicaragua may make for interoceanic canals; though in cases where the construction of the canal will involve an injury to the natural rights of Costa Rica, her opinion or advice, as mentioned in Article VIII of the Treaty, should be more than 'advisory' or 'consultative'. It would seem in such cases that her consent is necessary, and that she may thereupon demand compensation for the concessions she is asked to make; but she is not entitled as a right to share in the profits that the Republic of Nicaragua may reserve for herself as a compensation for such favors and privileges as she, in her turn, may concede.

In testimony whereof, I have hereunto set my hand and have caused the seal of the United States to be hereunto affixed.

Done in triplicate at the city of Washington, on the twenty-second day of March, in the year one thousand eight hundred and eighty-eight, and of the Independence of the United States the one hundred and twelfth [1].

[1] *Foreign Relations of the U. S.*, 1888, p. 456, 459-468.

Cette décision était accompagnée d'un rapport circonstancié du sieur Georges L. Rives, Secrétaire d'Etat assistant, détaillant les considérations qui ont servi de motifs à la sentence prononcée par M. Cleveland.

Il fallut donner à cette sentence une exécution matérielle: malheureusement la situation tendue, qui exista pendant longtemps entre les deux pays, retarda cette exécution jusqu'en 1896. Une convention nouvelle fut conclue le 27 mars 1896 et institua une nouvelle procédure arbitrale.

LXXXVII. Etats Unis d'Amérique, Hayti.

24 mai 1888.

Cette affaire a eu pour objet l'arrestation prétendument illégale d'un sieur Van Bokkelen. Il fut accordé par l'arbitre une indemnité de $ 60,000. La sentence intervenue est une des plus considérables qui aient été prononcées.

Protocol for the submission to an arbitrator of the claim of Charles Adrien Van Bokkelen, signed at Washington, May 24, 1888.

The United States of America and the Republic of Hayti, being mutually desirous of maintaining the good relations that have so long subsisted between them and of removing, for that purpose, all causes of difference their respective representatives, that is to say: Thomas F. Bayard, Secretary of State of the United States, and Stephen Preston, Envoy Extraordinary and Minister Plenipotentiary of the Republic of Hayti, have agreed upon and signed the following protocol:

1. It having been claimed on the part of the United States that the imprisonment of Charles Adrien Van Bokkelen, a citizen of the United States, in Hayti, was in derogation of the rights to which he was entitled as a citizen of the United States under the treaties between the United States and Hayti, which the Government of the latter country denies, it is agreed that the questions raised in the correspondence between the two Governments in regard to the imprisonment of the said Van Bokkelen shall be referred to the decision of a person to be agreed upon by the Secretary of State of the United States and the Envoy Extraordinary and Minister Plenipotentiary of the Republic of Hayti.

2. The referee so chosen shall decide the case upon such papers as may be presented to him by the Secretary of State of the United States

and the Minister of Hayti respectively, within two months after the date of his appointment; but he shall not take into consideration any question not raised in the correspondence between the two Governments prior to the date of the signature of this protocol.

3. Each Government shall submit with the papers presented by it a brief of argument, and should the referee so desire, he may require further argument, oral or written, to be made within five months from the date of his appointment. He shall render his decision within six months from said date.

4. A reasonable fee to the Referee shall be paid by the Government of Hayti.

5. Any award made shall be final and conclusive and, if in favor of the claimant, shall be paid by the Government of Hayti within twelve months of the date of such award.

Done in duplicate, at Washington this 24ᵗʰ day of May, one thousand eight hundred and eighty-eight[1].

Award of the referee in the matter of the claim of Charles Adrian Van Bokkelen, given in Washington, December 4, 1888.

In pursuance of the protocol, dated May 24, 1888, between Hon. Thos. F. Bayard, Secretary of State of the United States, and the Hon. Stephen Preston, envoy extraordinary and minister plenipotentiary of the Republic of Hayti, representing their respective Governments, after having made a declaration that I would impartially and carefully examine and decide the case submitted to me, in good faith, to the best of my judgment, and, conformably to the principles of law applicable thereto, I have investigated the claim of Charles Adrian Van Bokkelen, a citizen of the United States, against the Republic of Hayti, and I now make the following statement and *award:*

This claim grows out of the imprisonment, during the years 1884 and 1885, at Port au Prince, of Charles Adrian Van Bokkelen, a citizen of the United States, by the authorities of the Republic of Hayti. The imprisonment continued for period of nearly fifteen (15) months; and the claim made on behalf of Van Bokkelen is in the form of a demand upon Hayti, for pecuniary indemnity in the sum of one hundred and thirteen thousand six hundred dollars ($ 113,600).

Although the essential facts are within a small compass and the question submitted for decision to the referee is single and explicit, the case has been the subject of a multiplicity of proceedings and pleadings, judicial, executive,

---

[1] *Foreign Relations of the U. S.,* 1883, p. 986.

and diplomatic; and has given rise to voluminous correspondence and elaborate argumentation on the part of the two Governments. In the disposition of this case I shall confine myself as closely as may be practicable to a presentation of the essential matters, and to the determination of the single and explicit issue suggested by the terms of the protocol. It is proper, however, to state here, that at an early stage of the submission of this case to me as referee, a demurrer was interposed by the defendant Government that there was no provision under the submission for special pleading, and that the protocol specified and indicated in express terms the subject-matter and the question submitted for determination. As a matter of fact, the argument which was entitled « Brief on behalf of the defendant Government in support of demurrer », is a full and exhaustive exposition of the material points relied on by the defense, and covers fifty-five (55) type-written folios.

In addition, the limitation of time within which the referee was required to render his decision precludes the idea of the interposition of special pleading.

And further as to the propriety of a demurrer, general or special, under this arbitration, it is to be said that a state, like an individual, accused of having inflicted wrong upon another, may shape its defense against the charge with reference to the *facts*, or to the *law*. Under the terms of the protocol, as well as from the correspondence heretofore passed between the contracting parties, it seems clear that there is not now and never was any denial by the defendant Government of the substantive *facts* which give rise to this claim.

Subsequently complainant Government and the counsel for the respective Governments were notified that I desired briefs on the subject of the measure of damages. These additional briefs were duly filed and have been considered.

The defense set up by the defendant Government is rested upon a collision between the treaty and certain articles in the municipal codes of Hayti. And this issue may only be determined by reference to the treaty stipulations and to the provisions contained in the municipal statutes.

STATEMENT OF FACTS

Charles Adrian Van Bokkelen was a citizen of the United States, who prior to the year 1872, resided in Brooklyn N. Y. In that or the following year he went to Hayti and established himself in business at Port au Prince. In 1880 he married a Haytian lady, the widow of General P. Lorquet, an owner of real estate in Hayti in her own right. There were two children of this mariage, who with their mother reside at Port au Prince.

On the 15th of February, 1883, having sustained severe losses in his business, and a judgment against him having been affirmed in the court of cassation, which he was unable to pay, and under which he was liable to be imprisoned for one year, he filed a schedule of his assets and liabilities in the civil court of Port au Prince, preparatory to applying for the benefit of judicial assignment, under which, in Hayti, an honest but unfortunate debtor is allowed to surrender all his property for the benefit of his creditors, and is entitled to be discharged from prison, if he has been arrested, and to be free from arrest thereafter on account of his existing indebtedness. At that time, in Hayti, imprisonment for mere debt had not been abolished.

Three other judgments were subsequently recovered against Van Bokkelen, two in favor of the Bank of Hayti and one in favor of J. Archin, under each of which he was liable to three years imprisonment in default of payment, making ten years in all. A fifth judgment was rendered against him in favor of St Aude, jr., which does not seem to have decreed any imprisonment. These judgments are enumerated in Mr. Langston's dispatch of January 14, 1885, to Mr. Frelinghuysen, and it is there stated that the terms of imprisonment fixed in three of the judgments are twice as long as would have been imposed in the case of a Haytian.

After the filing of Van Bokkelen's schedule, which was duly recorded by the clerk of the civil court in Port au Prince, on the 15th of February, 1883, the proceedings seem to have been postponed by notices of writs until the following year.

On or about the 5th of March, 1884, Van Bokkelen was arrested on the judgment of Toeplitz & Co., and confined in the common jail of Port au Prince. Although imprisonment for debts, irrespective of fraud in contracting them or evading their payment, was then lawful in Hayti, there seems to have been no separate prison for debtors. The character of the common jail, and of the military hospital in which Van Bokkelen was confined, and the state of his health when he was incarcerated, will be noticed hereafter in connection with the question of damages.

Van Bokkelen protested against his arrest as illegal, on the ground that by an order of the Haytian authorities, published in the official journal, « it was made obligatory that before a foreigner could be placed in jail the complaint should first be submitted to the attorney for the Government for his examination and approval, and (should be) signed with his signature, with

seal attached ». On the 18th of the same month it was judicially determined that Van Bokkelen's arrest was illegal. But before he was discharged other creditors, availing themselves of a provision of Haytian law under which, when a debtor is imprisoned, they can keep him in jail by « recommending » him, recommended him accordingly, and the jailor refused to discharge him.

It is to be· noted that these creditors took advantage of Van Bokkelen's illegal imprisonment to keep him from getting out of jail by a method which would not have enabled them to put him in.

Van Bokkelen thereupon, through his counsel, applied to the civil court of Port au Prince for the benefit of judicial assignment.

He had been adviced that under the treaty of 1864 between the United States and Hayti he was entitled to the benefit of judicial assignment the same as if he were a citizen of that country. In the proceedings upon Van Bokkelen's petition to the civil court of Port au Prince for the benefit of judicial assignment, twelve of his creditors appeared, and all but two assented.

These opposing creditors raised various objections, but insisted mostly on Article 794 of the Code of Civil Procedure and Article 569 of the Code of Commerce, which expressly exclude foreigners (les étrangers) from the benefit of this provision of Haytian law.

All the objections of the opposing creditors were traversed by the petitioner. His counsel argued that the schedule of his assets and liabilities was sufficient; that his misfortunes and good faith were manifest; that the treaty of 1864 between Hayti and the United States repealed Article 794 of the Code of Civil Procedure and Article 569 of the Code of Commerce so far as the disability attaching to the petitioner in his character of American citizen or foreigner was concerned. This he argued at length, and also claimed that inasmuch as the petitioner had established himself at Port au Prince in business and married a Haytian wife, who owned real property in the city and had borne him children, having thus fixed his home as well as his commercial interests in Hayti with the knowledge of the Government, a just construction of the term « les étrangers » required that he should not be treated as a foreigner or a stranger, but as a domiciled merchant entitled to all civil rights and privileges as distinguished from those that are political ; and in support of the proposition that the exercise of civil rights is independent of the exercise of political rights, and that « the capacity of a citizen resides in the combination of civil and political rights », he cited Article 11 of the Civil Code of Hayti.

The opposing creditors (Toeplitz & Co.) rejoined that they had no knowledge of the treaty and had not been served with a copy ; and therefore moved for information in that regard at the cost of the petitioner. Petitioner's counsel replied that the treaty was not a document, but a law of which no one was supposed to be ignorant.

It appears also that the Government of Hayti, as well as all the parties to these proceedings, was represented by counsel and heard by the court.

The first question that the court decided was « whether the petitioner should be condemned to furnish to Toeplitz & Co. information regarding the treaty concluded between Hayti and the United States of America, and whether such information should likewise be furnished to Louis Nadal ». That question the court decided in favor of Van Bokkelen, as follows :

« Whereas a treaty, concluded between Hayti « and the United States of America, November 3, « 1864, sanctioned by the Senate and promul- « gated by the executive branch of the Govern- « ment, is a law of the State ;

« Whereas Article 75 of the Code of Civil « Procedure renders it obligatory upon the peti- « tioner to furnish a copy of the documents or « of that part thereof upon which the petition is « based ; but it does not provide that a copy « of the law or of the provision of the law on « which the petition is based shall be furnished ;

« Whereas, thus, Mr. C. A. Van Bokkelen is « not obliged to furnish information of the treaty « to Louis Nadal, and can not be condemned to « furnish such information to Toeplitz & Co., « who are under obligations, just as C. A. Van « Bokkelen is, to have knowledge of the law. »

On the main question, involving the rights of Van Bokkelen under the treaty, and deciding upon the objection of his alienage based upon Article 794 of the Code of Civil Procedure and Article 569 of the Code of Commerce, interposed by L. Toeplitz & Co. and by Louis Nadal, the court, after having deliberated, denied Van Bokkelen's application.

His application to make the judicial assignment having been denied by the civil court of Port au Prince, Van Bokkelen was kept in jail. He appealed to the court of cassation — the court of last resort — which rendered its decision affirming the judgment of the civil court on the 26th of February, 1885, almost a year from the time when Van Bokkelen was first imprisoned. It seems that pending his appeal the time within which further objections could be made by his creditors to his petition expired on the 21th of

October, 1884, and that no one, not even the parties upon whose application he had been illegally arrested the previous March, made any opposition. This fact is stated in a letter from Van Bokkelen's father to Mr. Frelinghuysen, who was then Secretary of State, dated November 15, 1884, a copy of which was transmitted by Mr. Davis, Acting Secretary, to Mr. Langston, United States minister at Port au Prince, November 19, 1884.

The Secretary of State of the United States was informed of this decision on the 21st of March, 1885, and on the 28th of the same month he sent a dispatch to the United States minister at Port au Prince, in which, after reviewing the facts and the law, he claimed that there had been a denial of justice in Van Bokkelen's case, and that he should be released from jail forthwith, in the following terms :

« The release of Mr. Van Bokkelen is now « asked on independent grounds. It is maintai- « ned, first, that continuous imprisonment for « debt, when there is no criminal offense imputed, « is contrary to what are now generally recog- « nized principles of international law. It is main- « tained, secondly, that the imprisonment of « Mr. Van Bokkelen is a contravention of articles « 6 and 9 of the treaty of 1865 between the « United States and the Republic of Hayti.

« The Haytian Government has a clear and « ample opportunity to relieve this case from all « difficulty by recognizing the error of their courts « in supposing that the privilege of release of an « imprisoned debtor would be denied to a Hay- « tian citizen by the United States courts upon « making assignment of his property for the be- « nefit of his creditors.

« You are now instructed to earnestly press « the views of this Government, as outlined in « this instruction, on the early attention of the « Government of Hayti by leaving a copy thereof « with the minister of foreign affairs. The res- « ponse of the Government of Hayti should be « promptly communicated to this Department. »

On the 17th of April, 1885, Mr. Langston sent a copy of this dispatch to the Haytian Government and urged the prisoner's immediate release, inviting attention also to his 'feeble and failing health'. The reply of the Haytian Government, twelve days later, was an elaborate defense of Van Bokkelen's imprisonment—solely, however, upon the ground that he was an alien.

Meanwhile, and shortly after the decision of the court of cassation, the prisoner, who, at the request of the United States minister, had been removed to the military hospital on account of his infirm condition, was sent back again to the common jail. On the 15th of May, the United States minister sent another note to the Haytian Government, insisting on Van Bokkelen's immediate release, and on the afternoon of the 27th of that month Van Bokkelen was conducted to the United States legation by an attorney of the Haytian Government, 'on its order, as stated, and thus given his release and liberty'. On the 5th of the following June, Mr. Langston received a note from the Haytian Secretary of State for foreign affairs, maintaining the position which had been held throughout by the Haytian Government, and closing as follows:

‹ I understand that Mr. Van Bokkelen has ‹ been put at liberty. This result, happy for him, ‹ is due, doubtless, to some arrangement made ‹ with his creditors. This, besides, to which I ‹ will not address myself further, as it is not ‹ proper, has itself, as you will unterstand, been ‹ accomplished without interference of the exe- ‹ cutive power; it comes to pass without saying ‹ that it annuls in no wise the considerations ‹ which this department has plead relative to the ‹ case of Van Bokkelen. ›

Pending Van Bokkelen's appeal to the court of cassation, the Department of State, upon representations of the United States minister at Port au Prince in regard to the adjudged illegality of the arrest in the first instance, and the prisoner's unquestionable right under the treaty to make the judicial cession and obtain his release, had instructed the minister to use every proper effort with the Haytian Government to that end.

Mr. Van Bokkelen sailed for the United States shortly after his release, and on his arrival made a statement of his case to the Secretary of State and appeal for his good offices in collecting indemnity from the Haytian Government. In response, Mr. Bayard addressed a note to the United States minister at Port au Prince, dated October 2, 1885, instructing him as follows:

‹ Sir: I herewith inclose a copy of a letter ‹ from Mr. C. A. Van Bokkelen, of the 19th ul- ‹ timo, in reference to his illegal imprisonment ‹ at Port au Prince and his claim for damages ‹ in consequence thereof.

‹ In view of Mr. Van Bokkelen's present sta- ‹ tement of facts and those already before your ‹ legation in regard to his case, I desire that you ‹ will call the attention of the Government of ‹ Hayti to his claim. There can be no doubt ‹ that Mr. Van Bokkelen was wrongfully impri- ‹ soned by the Haytian authorities, and that great ‹ damage accrued to him thereby.

‹ Under these circumstances, therefore, you ‹ are directed to ask and to press for the redress

‹ claimed by Mr. Van Bokkelen or, if the amount ‹ to be paid can not be immediately agreed upon, ‹ for a reference of the question to an arbitrator, ‹ so that the case may be disposed of without ‹ unnecessary delay. ›

To this Mr. Thompson, who had succeded Mr. Langston, made the following reply:

‹ Sir: I have to inform you of the death of ‹ Mr. Charles A. Van Bokkelen, who died on ‹ the first instant, at 2 o'clock in the afternoon, ‹ aged thirty-seven years. He was buried on the ‹ 2^d instant, many Americans and foreigners fol- ‹ lowing the remains to their last resting place. ‹ I attended the funeral, and it was a fact worthy ‹ of note that a sincere feeling of sadness at his ‹ death and sympathy for his wife and two small ‹ children seemed to pervade all present. I had ‹ entered his claim against the Haytian Govern- ‹ ment to the sum of $ 113,000, some time be- ‹ fore his death, and will continue to press the ‹ same, as advised by the Department. ›

Subsequent negotiations between the two Governments have resulted in an agreement to submit the claim to arbitration.

THE QUESTIONS TO BE ARBITRATED.

Two questions arise on the facts:

1. Was Van Bokkelen entitled, by the terms of the treaty between the Republic of Hayti and the United States, concluded November 3, 1864, to be discharged from prison on the same terms as a citizen of Hayti imprisoned for the same cause?

2. If there has been a violation by Hayti of the treaty rights of Van Bokkelen, what should Hayti pay to the United States, by way of damages, for the benefit of the representatives of the deceased?

The first question submitted by the two Governments for the decision of the referee is contained in the first article of the protocol of May 24, 1888, and is in the following words:

It having been claimed on the part of the United States that the imprisonment of Charles Adrien Van Bokkelen, a citizen of the United States, in Hayti, was in derogation of the rights to which he was entitled as a citizen of the United States under the treaties between the United States and Hayti, which the Government of the	Comme il a été soutenu de la part des Etats-Unis que l'emprisonnement de Charles Adrien Van Bokkelen, citoyen des Etats-Unis, en Haïti, en dérogation des droits qui lui appartenaient comme citoyen des Etats-Unis, d'après les traités entre les Etats-Unis et Haïti, ce que nie le Gouvernement du dernier Etat, il est con-

latter country denies, it is agreed that the questions raised in the correspondence between the two Governments in regard to the imprisonment of the said Van Bokkelen shall be referred to the decision of a person to be agreed upon, etc. (English text, article I.)

venu que les questions soulevées dans la correspondance entre les deux Gouvernements au sujet de l'emprisonnement du dit Van Bokkelen, seront référées à la décision d'une personne qui sera désignée, etc. (French text, article I.)

It appears clearly from the language of article I, that the subject-matter of this arbitration is the imprisonment in Hayti of Charles Adrian Van Bokkelen, a citizen of the United States, by the authorities of Hayti.

The contention of the complainant Government is that said imprisonment was in derogation of Van Bokkelen's rights as a citizen of the United States under the treaties, and the answer of the defendant Government, while admitting the American citizenship and the fact of imprisonment of Van Bokkelen by the authorities of Hayti, denies that his imprisonment was in derogation of treaty rights. The contention of the complainant Government is based upon the language of articles 6 and 9 of the treaty between the United States and Hayti, concluded November 3, 1864.

The defendant Government does not deny the existence of the treaty or the guaranty of the rights and privileges which it solemnly announces. But the substance of the contention on the part of the defendant Government is that this right or privilege of free access to the tribunals of justice in Hayti is defeated and nullified by the language and force of Article 794, Civil Code of Procedure, and Article 569, section 2, Code of commerce. This contention has been sustained by the courts of first and last resort of Hayti, and has been proclaimed by the Executive of Hayti. Under this decision of the courts and executive of Hayti, Van Bokkelen was imprisoned in the common jail for nearly fifteen months.

Counsel on behalf of defendant Government submit various propositions of fact and law, from which they proceed to argue, which are founded upon or connected with the preliminary proceedings and pleadings in the courts of Hayti anterior to the judgement and decrees of the Haytian courts. These propositions refer to a multitude of defenses, nearly all of which were regularly interposed in defense in the court of the first instance and the court of last resort. But all these several defenses have been withdrawn from the referee as a result of the action of the courts of Hayti, resting their decisions upon a single specific ground (which has been accepted by the contracting parties as the sole question now at issue), and which has been submitted to the decision of the referee. (Protocol, May 24, 1888.)

In this view of the case the referee is not at liberty to go behind the situation and enter upon an original inquiry as to whether the schedule *(bilan)* was regularly prepared and submitted; whether the circumstances of the case indicated fraud on Van Bokkelen's part; whether a Haytian citizen, under similar circumstances, whould have been discharged from imprisonment upon making a judicial assignment, etc. And if, at any time, I shall incidentally advert to such matters, it will be because it seemed unavoidable in the particular connection in which it occurs.

I proceed now to consider various contentions of counsel for the defendant Government.

The first brief, which is entitled a 'brief on behalf of the defendant Government in support of demurrer', insists:

1. That the language employed by Van Bokkelen in the proceedings before the tribunal at Port au Prince in April 1884, in which he describes himself as an American citizen by birth, « residing at Port au Prince and domiciled at New York, United States of America », « defines exactly the international status of claimant ». In answer to this suggestion it may be admitted that the general proposition is substantially correct. It is taken to mean that Van Bokkelen was a citizen of the United States at the time of the ocurrence out of which his claim against Hayti arose; but it is not understood that Van Bokkelen's description of himself as « residing at Port au Prince and domiciled at New York », has any other or further significance than to place him within the guaranties of protection of articles 6 and 9 of the treaty of November 3, 1864. It is to be observed, however, that « the international status of claimant » must be determined no by description, but by the facts of his case. As a matter of fact, the American citizenship of Van Bokkelen has never been questioned.

2. The contention of counsel for defendant Government, that Van Bokkelen, during the years 1882 and 1883, was a merchant doing brokerage business at Port au Prince may be conceded. And the recital of the details of the litigation in preliminary suits between Van Bokkelen and his various creditors may be accepted as correct without having any controlling influence upon the determination of the claim now submitted to the referee.

3. Counsel for the defendant Government argue « that only one ground of error was assigned and pressed » by Van Bokkelen on his appeal upon

the judgment of the civil court to the court of cassation, while the judgment of the lower court disclosed the fact that « at least twelve questions of law or fact were raised by the various pleadings of the parties ». And counsel say that Van Bokkelen sought to reverse the said judgment upon one sole ground, namely, that article 794 of the Code of Civil Procedure and article 569 of the Code of Commerce excluded aliens from the operation of the laws regulating the *cessio bonorum*, and that said articles were contrary to articles 6 and 9 of the treaty between the United States and Hayti.

In answer to this suggestion, it seems only necessary to say that the court of first instance and the court of last resort based their final decision on the single ground stated by them.

It may be added that by the very language of the protocol, the single ground upon which Van Bokkelen « assigned and pressed » his appeal to the court of cassation has been adopted as the very question constituting the subject-matter of this arbitration. In this view the anterior and intermediary proceedings, whether by way of diplomatic intervention, or as the result of the various procedures of the local courts of Hayti, cannot be held to have any controlling influence so far as the result of the present arbitration is concerned.

In a word, the protocol, which must be the guide and grant of jurisdiction for the referee, crystallizes and formulates the substantial grounds of past discussion and controversy in a single, definite issue, and furnishes the rule of decision. The issue presented by the protocol is whether the acts of the authorities of Hayti in respect to Van Bokkelen, a citizen of the United States, were in derogation of his rights as such citizen, and the rule furnished for the decision of the question raised by the issue are the treaties between Hayti and the United States.

4. The contention of counsel for defendant Government is that « full faith and credit must be given to the tribunals of Port au Prince ».

In answer to this point reference is made to what has just been said in reply to the first point. It may be added that the ground of complaint made by complainant Government is that the judgment of the Haytian courts is in contravention of treaty stipulation, which the defendant Government denies. And to decide this very issue, the question has been, by consent of the contracting parties, referred to international arbitration.

The position of the defendant Government as to this point would, if admitted, preclude any examination or decision by the referee; and

would result in making the referee simply the register or recorder of the acts and decrees of the local courts of Hayti. This may not be, for the reason that the Protocol imposes upon the referee the decision of the question raised in the correspondence and found in the record. For a rule and guide for his decision, he is referred to the treaties between Hayti and the United States. And for the interpretation of treaty language and intention, whenever controversy arises, reference must be had to the law of nations and to international jurisprudence.

It is a general maxim, when it is a question of international controversy, that neither of the contracting parties has a right to interpret a treaty according to its own fancy.

5. Another argument of counsel for defendant Government is, that a citizen of Hayti, who intends to avail himself of the benefit of judicial assignment *(cession de biens)* must establish affirmatively that he has been unfortunate and that he has acted in good faith. This point is elaborated with much detail, both in the brief accompanying the note of the Haytian Minister, addressed to the Secretary of State of the United States, August 15, 1887, as well as in the brief now under consideration. The answer to this proposition and argument is that all this may be conceded without its having any influence upon the present controversy, and for this reason: The acts of the judicial tribunals and of the executive of Hayti, of which the complainant Government complains, are rested upon different and independent grounds. And these grounds are that Van Bokkelen was not permitted free access to the tribunals of Hayti on the same terms as citizens of Hayti, and, as has been before stated, the referee is confined to the decision of the single specific question presented by the terms of the Protocol.

6. The further contention of counsel for the defendant Government is that the jurisprudence of France, Belgium and Hayti has constantly « maintained a distinction as between aliens and citizens, and have held that aliens have enjoyed natural rights, but that they were excluded from civil rights ». The answer to this proposition is, that if any such distinctions between what are here styled « natural » rights and « civil » rights existed in Hayti, they were abolished in respect to citizens of the United States commorant in Hayti at the time of the occurences herein complained of, by virtue of articles 6 and 9 of the Treaty of November 3, 1864. It is not, therefore, necessary to enter into any consideration as to the nice distinction between natural, civil, and political rights. These terms, however, have a

well-understood meaning in the law of nations and in modern international jurisprudence. In addition to protection to life, liberty, and property, the class which exercises *political* rights in a community participates in the governing power either by themselves or representatives.

The class which enjoys *civil rights* is equally entitled to protection to life, liberty, and property; but the individuals composing it can not exercise political rights under any claim founded simply upon possession of civil rights.

But the record and correspondence clearly show that the extent of Van Bokkelen's claim was a demand, formally and regularly submitted to the tribunals and to the executive power of Hayti, that he might be admitted to the enjoyment of those strictly civil rights guarantied to him by the Treaty of November 3, 1864.

And it would appear that even in Hayti the exercise of « civil » rights is independent of the exercise of « political » rights; and that the capacity of a citizen resides in the combination of civil and political rights.

7. The counsel for defendant Government submit that « under the civil law nothing short of a clear, positive treaty stipulation can enable an alien to claim the exercise of civil rights ». All this may be admitted, and yet the concession would not avail the defendant Government upon the case under consideration, and for the following reasons:

a) It is here a question of international and not civil law;

b) And a « clear, positive treaty stipulation » does by express language enable an alien, if he be a citizen of the United States and within the jurisdiction of Hayti, to claim the exercise of civil rights.

8. Counseil for defendant Government make ι point that at one time Van Bokkelen described himself as « *domiciled* in New York ». It can not be perceived how that fact, although it should be conceded—which it is not—could be held to except him from the guaranties contained in the treaty.

The American citizenship of Van Bokkelen being conceded by the terms of the Protocol, the question of domicile cuts no figure in the case.

9. Counsel for defendant Government insist that the true meaning of the second section of article 6 of the Treaty of November 3, 1864, is disclosed by « careful examination of article 794 of the Civil Code of Procedure and article 569, section 2, of the Code of Commerce ».

· Counsel say that the second section of article 6 of the treaty is simply intended to secure to

Americans, against any possible repeal, the rights guarantied them by said articles of the· codes, and the construction given them by the Haytian courts. The answer to this suggestion is obvious. It is negatived by the very language of article I of the Protocol of May 24, 1888: And the guaranty of enjoyment of civil rights *(i. e.,* the admission to the tribunal of justice) by citizens of the United States resident or domiciled in Hayti on the same terms with native citizens was not limited to time, but was to avail them during the existence and operation of the treaty.

By provisions of article 42, Treaty of November 3, 1864, the treaty was to « remain in force for the term of eight years, dating from the exchange of ratifications; and if one year before the expiration of that period neither of the contracting parties shall have given notice to the other of its intention to terminate the same, it shall continue in force, from year to year, until one year after an official notification to terminate the same, as aforesaid ». It is not denied that this treaty is still in force.

Counsel for the defendant Government seek to restrain and confine the treaty guaranty of 'free access to the tribunals of justice' to very narrow limits; and it is insisted that this clause could work no change in the laws of Hayti, either general or special; and it is said that 'the meaning of the words free access, used in the treaty', constituted a guaranty of free access to courts *'upon the same terms as the civil law and a constant practic provided for them'*. But the answer and denial to that proposition is contained in the language of the treaty itself, which provides the conditions, namely, *'on the same terms which are granted by the laws and usage of the country to native citizens'*. And the connection in which this language occurs makes the inference irresistible that it included all the steps and processes of the judicial tribunals of either of the contracting parties.

10. Counsel for defendant Governement lay great stress upon the declaration that 'American citizens sojourning, residing or trading in Hayti', must be held to conform to the municipal laws of Hayti. There can be no question but that such an obligation was imposed upon all citizens of the United States in Hayti. But, in this case, there is no complaint that Van Bokkelen, in respect to this matter, did not yield obedience to the municipal laws in operation in Hayti, except as they were modified or repealed by treaty stipulations. And the converse of the proposition is equally true, namely that American citizens sojourning, residing, or trading in Hayti are under the protection of public law and the

treaty stipulations to which Hayti and the United States are the contracting parties.

11. Counsel for defendant Government devote much space to the consideration of the nature and character of the proceeding known as judicial *cessio bonorum*. And it is submitted 'that the application made to the court to be admitted to the benefit of *cession de biens* can not be regarded in the light of a suit to enforce a right'. To this it may be replied that no such contention is presented in this controversy. In the view of the referee, the judicial *cessio bonorum* does not appear to be in the nature of an independent suit. On the contrary it is, as I shall further on indicate, a dependent process or step in the ordinary procedure.

12. It is further submitted, on behalf of defendant Government, that at the utmost, 'argument that the second section of article 6 of the treaty has repealed the provisions of civil law discriminating against aliens in the matter of judicial *cession de biens*, rests upon a repeal by implication of the aforestated articles of the code of civil procedure and of the code of commerce'.

It may be conceded that the cases agree in saying that repeals by implication are not favored. But the very authorities cited by counsel hold that in case of positive repugnancy between the provisions of new laws and those of the old, the former operate to repeal the latter.

In the case under consideration, the provisions of the municipal codes of Hayti, or rather the interpretation sought to be put upon them by counsel for defendant Government, are absolutely repugnant to the stipulations in the treaty of a later date.

13. It is further contended that if the subdivision of paragraph 2 of article 6 implies the repeal of articles 794 and 569 of the code of civil procedure and the code of commerce, 'it would just as well mean that the fundamental distinction underlying the whole system of civil law, as it exists in France or Hayti, has been repealed by implication, and that at best a few obscure words, which referred exclusively to remedies and not to rights, inserted in the treaty stipulation, operate as a repeal of important parts of the whole municipal legislation of Hayti'.

It is not perceived that such a result would follow, and it is not understood that the contention of complainant Government extends to make any 'such claim or demand that would result in revolutionizing the judicial system of Hayti. On the contrary, as has been indicated, the whole scope and effect of the guaranty clauses in articles 6 and 9 of the treaty of November 3, 1864, stipulating for 'free access to the tribunals

of justice' of the respective States, is to place the citizens of Hayti and the citizens of the United States, as to the administration of justice, upon the same footing. It is not clear what force there is in the suggestion that the guaranties in the treaty stipulations must be confined to 'remedies' and not to 'rights'. For, whether free access to the tribunals of a country for the purpose of prosecuting or defending a suit be described as a remedy or as a right, is unimportant. It is in this relation a matter of description rather than of substance. It is the proceeding with which we are concerned, and not the name of it. The right or privilege to make a judicial assignment, under appropriate circumstances, involves the application of a remedy recognized by the law of Hayti.

'Remedies' says Mr. Justice Story, 'are part of the consequences of contracts'. It is laid down by the same author as a general rule, 'that all foreigners *sui juris*, and not otherwise specially disabled by the law of the place where the suit is brought, may there maintain suits to vindicate their rights and redress their wrongs'. It is true, that until the treaty of November 3, 1864, went into operation, citizens of the United States, in common with other aliens, were excluded by the letter of the municipal law from the benefits of the judicial assignment. But from the date of the exchange of ratifications of that treaty, the benefit of the right or the remedy of judicial assignment was accorded to citizens of the United States. 'Free access to the tribunals of justice, etc.', means a right to stand in court, either voluntarily as plaintif for involuntarily as defendant; and after appearance, the suitors or parties litigant must have a right to invoke all the usual, ordinary, and necessary processes of the tribunal, whether it be for purposes of prosecution or by way of defense. In the case under consideration Van Bokkelen was arraigned before the local courts of Hayti, in some of the suits at least, *in invitum*; and as an incident of compulsory process he was imprisoned. Being within the jurisdiction and power of the Haytian court, the treaty stipulations were intended to secure to him, a citizen of the United States, the right to avail himself of all the instrumentalities and processes of the tribunals of justice.

14. It is further contended on behalf of defendant Government that article 9, treaty November 3, 1864, must be construed in the light of the civil law and certain provisions of the Haytian civil code in regard to the transmission of property.

But the protocol makes the treaties between the United States and Hayti the sources of reference for the guidance of the referee. And consequently the obligations are covenants of a reciprocal character, which are contained in these treaties, constitute the supreme law as between the complainant and defendant Governments. In the view which the referee has taken of the question submitted to him, the stipulations and guaranties contained in article 6 of the treaty are in themselves sufficient to justify the claim of Van Bokkelen to stand in justice in the courts of Hayti on the same terms with native citizens. However, it does not seem to the referee that the cumulative force of the stipulations in article 9 in respect to the transmission of property can be lessened by the argument of the defendant Government insisting upon a restrictive interpretation of the latter article. The construction sought to be put upon article 9 is cramped, narrow, and forced.

15. It is insisted on behalf of defendant Government that the whole scope and purpose of the treaty was plainly not to abrogate any law, but to recognize all existing laws in either country and subject the temporary resident to the operation and protection of these laws.

The answers to this proposition are obvious. The temporary resident was already subject to the operation and the protection of the laws of the respective countries; but this protection was unequal. In the United States the Haytian citizen could not, in the absence of contumacious fraud, be denied the privilege of making a judicial assignment, or what was equivalent to it, for the benefit of his creditors; nor could he be imprisoned under the circumstances in which Van Bokkelen was held in bodily confinement. In Hayti, on the contrary, prior to the treaty of November 3, 1864, a citizen of the United States was liable, by the letter of the Haytian statutes, to be summarily arrested and imprisoned for an indefinite period of time, and was excluded from the benefit of judicial assignment. It was to remedy this and other inequalities that articles 6 and 9 were incorporated into the treaty. And their immediate effect and purpose was to relieve the citizens of either of the contracting parties from odious and harsh discrimination of the local laws and to place them on the same footing. If the contention of the defendant Government should be admitted, it would render null and void the stipulations of articles 6 and 9. The object of the treaty, as expressed in its opening paragraph, is 'to make lasting and firm the friendship and good understanding which happily prevail between both nations, and to place their commercial relations upon the most liberal basis'. The articles defining the reciprocal rights of citizens of each of the two nations residing and doing business in the territory of the other will be hereafter noticed.

16. In regard to the suggestion on behalf of defendant Government, charging Van Bokkelen with falsehood and fraud, because his representations in regard to his financial condition were different at different times, it may be said that there is no proof in the record that Van Bokkelen was endeavoring, or had ever attempted, to keep back or conceal anything or reserve any benefit for himself. And the different estimates which he is charged with having made at different times may be easily reconciled with his changed status and the condition in which he found himself.

But whatever presumptions may have availed against Van Bokkelen during the preliminary proceedings in the court of first instance, they may not, in the absence of positive proof, have any force or weight in the consideration of the question now under arbitration.

The courts of Hayti and the executive have nowhere rested their action denying to Van Bokkelen the right to make a judicial assignment upon any charge or suggestion of fraud or informality in these proceedings. And the starting point for the decision under this arbitration must be the action of the courts and the executive of Hayti.

17. Counsel for the defendant Government say the 'second section, article 6, opens the courts of the country to the alien upon the same terms as they are opened to native citizens: *but it does not change or propose to change any rights pertaining to American citizens*'. And it is insisted that the repeated references to the laws and usages of the country must be taken to mean that American citizens possess no rights in Hayti except those which are specified in the municipal statutes. And the contention then is, that the rule of interpretation which is to be applied in this case is that laid down by Mr. Pradier Fodéré: 'Lastly, treaties and conventions must be construed in the light which agrees with *public order* established among the contracting nations, and more particularly with their principles of *public law* and with the organization of their jurisdiction; *in case of doubt, and unless there are irrecusable proofs, the construction which is in harmony with the civil and public laws of France must prevail over that which would create a privileged and exceptional right*'.

It is not perceived how the contention can be sustained which insists that the treaty does not change or propose to change any rights pertaining to American citizens, when, in view of the language of the treaty, its stipulations provide for the guaranty and protection and vindication of the rights of the citizens of the contracting parties on the same terms. The position of defendant Government does not receive any support from the citation from M. Pradier Foderé, for the reason that the author is referring to the *public order* and the *civil and public laws*, and not to *special* or *private* rights and remedies.

M. Pradier Foderé further on says:

« Il est donc manifeste qu'aucune des nations « n'a le droit d'interpréter à son gré les con- « ditions obscures du contrat, ou d'en déléguer « l'examen à ses tribunaux ; pas plus qu'il n'est « loisible à la partie qui a consenti une conven- « tion synallagmatique d'interpréter elle-même, ou « de faire interpréter par un mandataire à son « choix, les clauses obscures ou ambigues que « contiendrait cette convention. »

18. It is further insisted that it is « upon the claimant to establish as an affirmative proposition that the treaty of 1864 between the United States and Hayti has repealed the provisions of articles 794 of the Code of Civil Procedure and 569 of the Code of Commerce ». This contention has been considered elsewhere in this opinion at some length.

Three cases decided by the court of cassation in France, at long intervals of time, are principally relied upon by counsel for defendant Government in support of the contention that articles 6 and 9 of the treaty may not be interpreted to abrogate or repeal the municipal statutes in repugnance or conflict therewith. The first and most important is the case of Napier and others *vs*. The Duke of Richmond, which is cited in support of the contention that « diplomatic treaties must be construed in the light where they are in harmony with public and civil law in use among the contracting nations ». This decision, which was rendered on the 24th of June, 1839, holds that treaties between nations are not of the character of simple administrative and executive acts, but that they possess the character of laws ; that the courts are competent to interpret treaties between nations on the occasion of private (individual) contests which refer to the particular treaties ; that when a treaty has stipulated for the giving up to an alien of immovable property located in France and subject to its authority, the courts are competent to decide whether this giving up, after (agreeably to) the treaty, should operate to the benefit of a single alien heir who is mentioned in it, or of all the heirs, in the proportion of their hereditary rights and interests ; that in the interpretation of diplomatic treaties the judges should prefer an interpretation which agrees with the common law and the public law of France to that interpretation which conflicts with these principles;

that in particular, the treaty of 30th of May, 1814, which, in one of its additional articles, decides first, that the withdrawal of the sequestration or embargo levied by the decree of Berlin of the 21st of November, 1806, upon the d'Aubigny tract of land belonging to the Third Duke of Richmond ; second, that the restitution to the nephew of the latter should not be considered as a grant of said land in favor of this one alone conformably to the law of primogeniture recognized in England, and to the exclusion of all others having equal right, title or interest, but this grant must be executed with reference to the succession of the Third Duke of Richmond, so that this tract of land should be divided among all those entitled in succession in accordance with the rule established by the Civil Code under the title « successions ».

It is to be observed in the first place of this decision, that the subject-matter was real (immovable) property within the territory and jurisdiction of France, and the court rendering the decision was a court of France. The rule is familiar, that the law which governs as to real (immovable) property is *lex rei sitæ*; and under application of this rule the French court, in a controversy between conflicting individual interests, used the language which occurs in this decision, and which has been copied by the Civil court of Port au Prince as applicable to the question in controversy in Van Bokkelen's case.

As the civil court of Port au Prince, and the court of cassation of Hayti, in stating the rule which must govern in the interpretation of treaty language, have quoted and relied upon isolated expressions of the court of cassation of France in pronouncing judgment in Napier *vs*. Duke of Richmond, it will be necessary to consider the latter case with some particularity. The subject-matter in Napier vs. Richmond was a tract of land described as the d'Aubigny tract, situated in the jurisdiction of France. Like many other estates belonging to the Crown of France it had been granted to a foreign family. This grant reached back to the year 1422, having been made by Charles VII in favor of one of the Stuarts of Scotland, who had rendered signal service to France in her wars with England. In the year 1673 this grant was renewed by Louis XIV in favor of the Duchess of Portsmouth, a French lady in the language of the grant, to be enjoyed by said duchess, and after her decease, by such one of the natural sons of the King of Great Britain whom he might designate, and the male descendants in direct line of this natural son. This grant, which evidently, says the court of cassation of France, had for its object to win over Charles II to the interests of

Louis XIV, does not, however, present in appearance a political character. Charles II designated as the successor of the Duchess of Portsmouth a natural son whom he had by her, named Charles Lennox, who took the title of First Duke of Richmond.

He enjoyed until his death possession of the d'Aubigny tract, and transmitted it successively to his eldest son and to the eldest of his grandsons, second and third dukes of Richmond. This property underwent all of the vicissitudes of the French wars and revolutions. Confiscated during one of the said wars of succession it was restored by the treaty of Utrecht; confiscated again in 1792, during the wars of the revolution, it was restored at the peace of Amiens. Finally, having been confiscated for the third time in 1806, it was again restored by the treaties of 1814 and 1815. When by the decree of Berlin of 21ᵘ of November, 1806, the French Government, availing itself of reprisals against England declared as good prize all the properties belonging to Englishmen in France, the d'Aubigny tract was occupied by Charles Lennox, Third Duke of Richmond, who had taken possession in 1750. This duke died on the 19ᵗʰ of December, 1806, without issue, leaving four sisters and the children of a full brother, who died before him, one of whom took the title of the Fourth Duke of Richmond, who was the father of the defendant in this case. This condition of things continued until the treaty of peace of the 30ᵗʰ day of May, 1814, the fourth article of which stipulated in general terms for the withdrawal of confiscations of the war. However a secret clause of this treaty added :

‹ The confiscation of the Duchy of d'Aubigny ‹ and the property which belongs to it will be ‹ raised, and the Duke of Richmond placed in ‹ possession of the property such as it is now.›

A royal ordinance of the 8ᵗʰ of July, 1814, the terms of which reproduced textually those of the secret clause, and an order of the prefect of Cher, of the 3ᵈ of August following, were forwarded to the Fourth Duke of Richmond who was then in France at the head of a division of the English army, putting him in possession of the d'Aubigny tract. His possession was confirmed by a *procès-verbal* of the 30ᵗʰ of November, 1814. The natural heirs of the Third Duke of Richmond, who did not live in France, being advised later of their rights, addressed themselves in 1830 to the French courts to demand from the Fifth Duke of Richmond, who had succeeded his father in 1819, a division of the d'Aubigny tract, as belonging to the succession of the third duke. To this demand was opposed notably the provision of the secret clause of the treaty of 1814, insisting that it contained a special derogation from article 4 of this treaty which prescribed in a general way the raising of the confiscations of the war. The heirs replied that this article 4 and the secret clause should be interpreted one by the other ; that it was proper to reconcile their provisions ; that the second was only a confirmation of the first, and that it was not reasonable to regard this secret clause as a private and exclusive grant for the benefit of the feudal heir of the third duke. In this condition of the respective claims of the several parties the tribunal of Sancerre having had the controversy submitted to it rendered judgment on the 9ᵗʰ of July, 1834, which decreed the partition of the d'Aubigny tract.

Among other reasons assigned for this judgment were the following :

‹ As to the second question raised in the ‹ argument, that by the literal text the previously ‹ dated treaty raised the confiscation affixed to ‹ the d'Aubigny tract, and stipulated for the res‹ toration of the property to the Duke of Rich‹ mond; that although by this denominative ‹ expression could not be understood the third ‹ duke, against whom the confiscation had been ‹ affixed, since the plenipotentiaries must have ‹ known that this duke, their colleague in the ‹ cabinet and in the House of Lords in England, ‹ had been dead nearly eight years, it must be ‹ understood that the grant was in fact to his ‹ heirs, according to this maxim, *Hæres substinet* ‹ *personam defuncti*; that, moreover, if the treaty ‹ did not say that in default of the third duke, ‹ his representatives should be called to receive ‹ the benefit, it was because in a previous article ‹ it was stated in a general and absolute manner ‹ that the principle of the restoration was in favor ‹ of the former proprietors or their heirs, and that ‹ this general provision applied to the Duchy of ‹ d'Aubigny neither more nor less than to the ‹ other cases of restoration; that the confisca‹ tion of the d'Aubigny tract, by virtue of the ‹ decree of Berlin of 21ᵘ of November, 1806, ‹ must be considered as a spoliation, and that ‹ the treaty of Paris of 1814 stipulated the ‹ restoration of this tract to the proprietor or to ‹ those having a right, but that it was not pos‹ sible to regard the terms of this treaty as expres‹ sed as a personel statute and as a reward to ‹ the fourth duke of Richmond; that the resto‹ ration of the property would not have been ‹ complete if it did not result to the benefit of ‹ those having a right or claim to it; that the ‹ treaty of 1814, understood in such a restricted ‹ sense, would not have been a restoration—a ‹ reparation—but the maintenance and conti‹ nuation of an injust spoliation, which, however,

‹ the high contracting parties declared that they ‹ wished to put an end to after the military events ‹ which had provoked them; that whereas the ‹ succession of the Third Duke of Richmond was ‹ opened 19ᵗʰ of December, 1806, but at that ‹ time the law of the 25ᵗʰ of October, 1792, had ‹ abolished all kinds of substitution, and that ‹ this succession, so far as property situated in ‹ France was concerned, was governed by French ‹ laws, agreeably to article 3 of the civil code; ‹ and that it devolved or descended in five parts ‹ to the brothers and sisters of the deceased or to ‹ their representatives, in accordance with the ‹ terms of article 750, civil code; that in the ‹ treaty of the 30ᵗʰ May, 1894, there is no ‹ expression that leads to the belief that there ‹ was any abrogation of a legislation which had ‹ become fixed in our customs or any failure or ‹ omission of national dignity which would have ‹ resulted in subjecting property situated on ‹ the soil of France to the rules of English legis- ‹ lation. ›

The above decree or judgment of the tribunal of Sancerre was brought by the Duke of Richmond on appeal to the royal court of Bourges, which rendered its decision on the 11ᵗʰ of March, 1835, reversing the judgment of the tribunal of Sancerre. From this decision an appeal was taken by the heirs of the Fourth Duke of Richmond to the court of cassation of France.

When the case came before the court of cassation, the eminent lawyer, M. Dupin, then attorney-general for the Government, made an elaborate argument in support of the position of the heirs of the Fourth Duke of Richmond and in defense of the decree of the tribunal of Sancerre.

The court of cassation of France reversed the decision of the court of Bourges, sustaining in substance the decree of the tribunal of Sancerre, as well as the main argument of the attorney-general. In announcing its judgment the court of cassation, among other propositions, held:

‹ On the first branch of the argument: Whe- ‹ reas the defendant having been summoned to ‹ make partition of the d'Aubigny tract and to ‹ restore the fruits and allowances received by ‹ him, as well as by the Fourth Duke of Rich- ‹ mond, has opposed, as the principal exception ‹ or objection, a secret clause in the treaty of ‹ the 30ᵗʰ of May, 1894, to this effect: ‹ The ‹ confiscation affixed to the Duchy of d'Aubigny ‹ and on the property which belongs to it shall ‹ be raised, and the Duke of Richmond shall be ‹ placed in possession of the property such as ‹ it is presently; › that the defendant has drawn ‹ from this clause the consequence that he had ‹ been invested with the exclusive property of

‹ this immovable by the diplomatic convention ‹ of 1814, and the complainants having disputed ‹ this interpretation, the first question to decide ‹ in the case is that relative to the true sense ‹ and effect of the stipulation above cited; whereas ‹ the tribunals having jurisdiction of the action ‹ were necessarily competent judges of the excep- ‹ tion or objection, since they were not prohibited ‹ by any provision of law; that the defendant ‹ without avail invokes the principle which forbids ‹ the judicial authority to interpret administrative ‹ acts; that the treaties between nations are not ‹ simple administrative and executive acts; that ‹ they possess the character of law and can not ‹ be applied and interpreted but in the forms ‹ and by the authorities intrusted with applying ‹ all the laws within their jurisdiction whenever ‹ disputes which give rise to this interpretation ‹ have private interest for their object; that the ‹ action of complainants, founded upon their ‹ character as heirs, raised the questions of pri- ‹ vate succession and of property, which is allotted ‹ by the law to the judicial power; whereas the ‹ decrees attacked instead of pronouncing judg- ‹ ment on the questions determining the true ‹ sense of this clause, which was never published ‹ nor inserted in the Bulletin des Lois, declared ‹ that the royal court had not the right to seek ‹ out the sense of the treaty, and that the com- ‹ plainants should go before the competent autho- ‹ rity who executed this act before availing ‹ themselves of their character, pretended or real, ‹ as heirs in equal proportion of the Third Duke ‹ of Richmond; that it resulted from these reasons ‹ that the royal court refused to pronounce judg- ‹ ment as well on the principal action and as to ‹ the title of the heirs, which was the main ques- ‹ tion, as also on the exception and the meaning ‹ of the clause; that it referred all the points of ‹ which it was regularly seized to another autho- ‹ rity, which it did not indicate; that the com- ‹ plainants would be deprived by this dismissal ‹ of all means of obtaining a legal decision upon ‹ their demand; whereas the royal ordinance of ‹ the 8ᵗʰ of July, 1814, and the prefect's decree ‹ of the 31ˢᵗ of August following are only acts ‹ in execution of the treaty, and of the obliga- ‹ tions which article 4 of the additional clauses ‹ imposed upon each of the contracting powers ‹ to raise several confiscations which had been ‹ affixed; that moreover these acts, which did not ‹ add anything to the treaty, and with which they ‹ are identified, can not be considered as acts ‹ belonging to the exercise of the administrative ‹ powers, cognizance of which was forbidden to ‹ the tribunals.

‹ As to the second branch of the argument: ‹ Whereas the decrees denounced, after having

40

‹ in their reasons declared the incompetency of
‹ the tribunals and referred to another authority,
‹ had meanwhile decided that the complainants
‹ could not sustain their action, for the reason
‹ that the treaty invested the defendant with the
‹ property of the immovable claimed by them;
‹ that the reasons for these decrees and their
‹ provisions imply a contradiction; that they have,
‹ in addition, ignored: First, the text of the laws
‹ which govern immovables situated in France
‹ and their transmission to the heirs; second,
‹ the true meaning of the treaty and of the secret
‹ clause; third, the rules established by the Civil
‹ Code for the interpretation of conventions;
‹ finally, the d'Aubigny tract being situated in
‹ France, was governed as to the succession of
‹ the Third Duke of Richmond, by the law of
‹ France; that substitutions were abolished and
‹ the privilege of the oldest male was suppressed,
‹ and that the heirs of this duke were entitled
‹ to receive this property in equal portions, and
‹ that they were invested with it by the mere
‹ operation of law; that the defendant can not
‹ invoke the law of nations to claim the grant
‹ of an exclusive right; that the transmission of
‹ property by way of succession is governed by
‹ the civil law of each State; whereas, if the text
‹ of this stipulation left any doubt of its true
‹ meaning, it would be disposed of by the rules
‹ of law in reference to the interpretation of con-
‹ ventions; that the first is to seek out the com-
‹ mon or ordinary intention of the contracting
‹ parties, rather than to stop at the literal mea-
‹ ning of the terms; that it is impossible to sup-
‹ pose that the intention of the plenipotentiaries
‹ was to regulate the law of succession between
‹ co-heirs; to grant to one the whole property
‹ in the estate or land to the exclusion of the
‹ others, without any indemnity whatever to these
‹ latter; that this grant to the Fourth Duke of
‹ Richmond alone would have been in derogation
‹ of French legislation, and would have created
‹ in France a property or estate governed by
‹ privileged and exceptional law; that such an
‹ intention which would be in opposition to all
‹ the provisions of the treaty, can not be admitted
‹ without unexceptionable proofs; that it would
‹ have been expressed in positive terms if it had
‹ existed; that all the clauses should be inter-
‹ preted one by the other so as to give to each
‹ the meaning which results from the whole text,
‹ and the secret clause should be understood in
‹ the sense of a restoration to the one who was
‹ entitled, or to his heirs, in accordance with the
‹ spirit of the treaty; that diplomatic treaties
‹ should be understood in the sense which places
‹ them in accord with the civil and public law
‹ recognized by the contracting parties; that the
‹ interpretation given to the clause by the decrees
‹ which are attacked put them in opposition to
‹ all the laws, the civil as well as the public
‹ law, of France. That in not designating by
‹ name which Duke of Richmond should be pla-
‹ ced in possession, the clause could only have
‹ had in view the one who was dispossessed, or
‹ his representatives; that in admitting the fourth
‹ duke to restoration it was for the benefit of
‹ his co-heirs as well as for himself. It results
‹ from the considerations which precede, that the
‹ decrees which are attacked for refusing to take
‹ into consideration the rights of the parties in
‹ accordance with the interpretation of diplomatic
‹ conventions, and in deciding that the apparent
‹ text of these conventions had dispossessed the
‹ heirs of the Third Duke of Richmond of their
‹ rights to the d'Aubigny tract, have violated
‹ and misapplied the laws above cited. ›

It seems to the referee that the above exposition of facts and of law which were involved in
the case of Napier vs. The Duke of Richmond,
and the decision of the court of cassation of
France thereon, make it clear that the case does
not justify the use or application which the Haytian courts have attempted to make of it by incorporating in their judgments isolated expressions,
which are withdrawn from the context in the
decision of the former case. The court of cassation of France simply decided that they
would not put such a construction upon treaty
language as would result in the abrogation of
the law of descent of France in respect to real
(immovable) property; that as to such property
the *lex rei sitæ* governed; and that it was impossible to suppose that the intention of the
plenipotentiaries was to abrogate the laws of descent of France in this respect, and that such an
intention would be in conflict with all the provisions of the treaty.

In the view taken of that case there does not
seem to be room for complaint or criticism.
And there is no evidence that the action of the
Government of France, as expressed in the decree of its supreme court, has been ever excepted or objected to by Great Britain. If, however,
Great Britain had considered, that as a consequence of this decree injustice had been done to
one of her citizens, or a treaty stipulation had
been violated by France, she would, no doubt,
have made it the subject of international settlement.

The second case cited by counsel for defendant Government in this connection is Challier
vs. Ovel, which was decided by the court of
cassation of France on the 17th of March, 1830.
The extent to which the court went was to hold

that, although Article 22 of the treaty of the 24th of March, 1760, between France and Sardinia, had abrogated a principle sanctioned by Article 121, ordinance 1629, as also by Articles 21-23 and 21-28 Civil Code and 646 Code of Procedure, it did not follow that the execution of these judgments rendered by the Sardinian tribunals should be decreed in France, when they were contrary to the maxims of the *public law of France* or to the *public order of jurisdiction*, and that in refusing to decree in France the execution of the judgment and decrees rendered in the cause by the Piedmontese tribunal, the decree attacked only conformed to the principles of the public law, *and did not violate either the treaty of 1760 or any law*. Challier vs. Ovel was a case where a citizen of France, having been arraigned before one of the courts of Sardinia, demurred to the jurisdiction of that court, and claimed exemption from suit in the foreign jurisdiction, insisting that he could only be sued in the jurisdiction of his domicile, which was France. The Sardinian court, notwithstanding his plea, proceeded with the cause and rendered judgment against him. It was such a judgment against a citizen of France so obtained that the court of cassation of France declined to put into execution. This case has nothing in common with Van Bokkelen vs. Hayti.

The third case cited by counsel for defendant Government in this connection is Alberto Balestrini vs. Aubert and others. The conclusion reached was, that international treaties are not simple administrative acts; that they may be applied and even interpreted by judicial authority, when it is a question of conventions having for their object individual interests. The case of Balestrini vs. Aubert presented a controversy between contesting associates, one of whom had a concession under the provisions of a treaty which gave him a right to establish and operate a telegraph line under a new system of electric cable between France and the United States. The contest was as to the respective interests of these several associates, and the provisions of the grant or concession in the treaty came thus for consideration incidentally before the court. It was in such a case that the court of cassation of France held that the stipulations of a treaty could be applied and interpreted by judicial authority whenever it was a question of agreements or conventions having private or individual interests for their object. It must be perceived that there is no similarity between that case and the one under consideration.

The *ratio decidendi* in all these cases is very plain. It is this, that the judicial tribunals of a country when called upon to decide controversies between individuals which grow out of or are dependent upon treaty stipulations, will not hesitate to construe the language of those treaties according to the rules of law which apply to all instruments. They will construe the provisions so as to give effect to rather than to defeat the intention of the contracting parties; and they will reconcile apparent conflicts of particular parts by reference to the context in which they occur and to the whole instrument. They will not impute to the plenipotentiaries in the negociation of a treaty an intention which is in conflict with the fundamental law of the State. They will not lend their sanction to execute a treaty stipulation when it is in violation of the fundamental law of the jurisdiction; and they do this upon the ground that it is beyond the competency of the treaty-making power to enter into stipulations which are in conflict with the public law or the public policy of the jurisdiction.

‹ The treaty-making power is necessarily and
‹ obviously subordinate to the fundamental laws
‹ and constitution of the State, and it can not
‹ change the form of the Government or annihi-
‹ late its constitutional powers. ›

This language has been used by distinguished American jurists in relerence to the Government of the United States. It applies equally to the public policy and limitations of all constitutional States.

In every civilized State two divisions of law are recognized: First, the law which regulates the public order and right of nations, which is *jus publicum*; second, the law which determines the private rights of men, which is called *jus civile*. The law of procedure (the adjective law) is distinguished from the fundamental law ol a State, and includes remedial law, which is a law whereby a method is pointed out to recover a man's private rights or redress his private wrongs. And the instrument by which the individual vindicates his rights and remedies his wrongs is an action or suit at law. In this sense an action is not a right; but it is the means which the law affords for pursuing the right. ‘*Actio non est jus, sed medium jus persequendi.*’

‘I consider’, says Lord Bacon, ‘that it is a true and received division of law into *jus publicum* and *jus privatum*, the one being the sinews of property, and the other of Government.’ Law defines the rights which it will aid, and specifies the way in which it will aid them. So far as it defines, thereby creating, it is ‘substantive law’; so far as it provides a method of aiding and protecting, it is ‘adjective law’ or procedure.

It would seem to be clear from the cases decided by the court of cassation of France, heretofore cited, that the decisions do not sustain the position taken by the Haytian courts and by the counsel for defendant Government. In the case under consideration Van Bokkelen petitioned the court for the purpose of availing himself of the law of procedure guaranteed to him by the treaty. The pretension that Articles 6 and 9 of the treaty of November 3, 1864, contained any stipulation that was violative of the fundamental law of Hayti is without any foundation.

The article 1054 (civil code of Hayti) which Van Bokkelen invoked for his protection belongs to the law of procedure or the adjective law of Hayti. And the article 794 (Haytian code of civil procedure) and article 569 (Haytian code of commerce) which the Haytian authorities opposed in denying Van Bokkelen's petition, are also a part of the law of procedure or adjective law of Hayti. They do not form a part of the constitutional, fundamental, or national law of Hayti. And the attempt by the judicial and executive authorities of Hayti to characterize a simple judicial assignment as an institution of civil law, or an institution of civil right, in the sense intended, is a missuse of language and a misapplication of terms.

The counsel for defendant Government invite attention to 'the leading English case on this subject', upon which they place some reliance. This was an action between private litigants upon several policies of insurance on a certain ship and cargo, upon which the defendant in error had effected insurance. While on a trading voyage, ship and cargo were captured by a British squadron and thus became a total loss to the owners and insurers. Demand was then made by the insured upon the insurer to make good his proportion of the loss so incurred. He refused to do so, and when sued, set up the defense that the voyage on which ship and cargo were lost was illegal. On the trial before King's Bench and Exchequer Chamber it was admitted that the voyage was illegal and *unless* it was within the protection of certain articles of the treaty between Great Britain and the United States, concluded the 19th of November, 1794. Defendant insisted that the voyage was not within the letter of the treaty, and therefore it was illegal. But the Exchequer Chamber held that the voyage was within the spirit, though not the letter of the treaty; and, in deciding the case, used the language quoted in the argument for defendant Government. Chief-justice Eyre, in deciding the case, said:

« There may be reason to apprehend that « this treaty will open a door to many of our « own people whom the policy of our laws has « shut out from a direct trade to the East Indies. « In truth, it can hardly be expected that the « spirit of commerce too often found eluding laws « made to keep it within bounds, that the *lucri* « *bonus odor* should not embark British capital « in this trade. This ought to have been foreseen « and therefore I conclude it was foreseen, and « that it was found that the balance of advantage « and disadvantage preponderated in favor of the « treaty. If not, those who advised it will have « to answer for it; responsibility is not with us. « We are not even expounders of treaties. This « treaty is brought under our consideration inci- « dentally as an ingredient in a cause in judgment « before us; we only say how it is to be under- « stood between the parties to this record.

« This we are bound to do; we have but « one rule by which we are to govern ourselves. « We are to construe this treaty as we would « construe any other instrument, public or private. « We are to collect from the nature of the sub- « ject, from the words and from the context, « the true intent and meaning of the contracting « parties, whether they are A and B, or happen « to be two independent States. The judges who « administer the municipal laws of one of those « States would commit themselves upon very « disadvantageous ground—ground which they « could have no opportunity of examining—if « they were to suffer collateral considerations to « mix in their judgment on a case circumstanced « as the present one is. Whether the trade should « have been conceded under any qualifications « or restrictions is one thing; it having been « conceded, now to attempt to cramp it by « narrow, rigorous, forced construction of the « words of the treaty is another and a very « different consideration. We can not suppose « that an indirect advantage was intended to be « reserved to the East India Company by so « framing the treaty that the *American* trade « might by construction be put under disadvan- « tage, because this would be chicanery unworthy « of the *British* Government and contrary to the « character of its negociations, which have been « at all times distinguished by their good faith « to a degree of candor which has been supposed « sometimes to have exposed it to the hazard of « being made the dupe of more refined politicians. « The nature of the trade granted, in my opinion, « fixes the construction of the grant. If it were « necessary to go further, strong arguments may « be drawn from the context of this article and « the contrast, which the comparing it with the « preceding article will produce. »

Far from advancing the argument of counsel for defendant Government, the conclusions and the reasoning of the Chief-Justice in Marryat *vs.*

Wilson are strongly opposed to the contention of the defendant Government, and sustain the position of the complainant Government in this case. Marryat *vs.* Wilson is strong authority for the proposition that the municipal tribunals of a country may not nullify the purpose and effect of treaty language by imposing upon it a cramped, narrow, and forced construction. And it is to be observed that in the case before the Exchequer Chamber, the judgment of the court sustaining interpretation of treaty stipulations which would give effect to the spirit, if not to the letter of the treaty, was rendered in a case where the beneficiaries were aliens, that is citizens of the United States, and in denial of defenses set up by British subjects before one of the superior courts of Great Britain.

It is to be noted that these several decisions of the highest courts of France and Great Britain, which are cited and relied upon by the defendant Government on this branch of the argument, are cases in which the conclusions of the courts were in support of the protective and private property rights of individuals. The result of all these decisions was to work out substantial justice between the parties. In the case under consideration, the result of the judgments of the Haytian courts and the action of the Executive of Hayti was to defeat the efforts of Van Bokkelen to protect himself from wrong and injustice, and to secure to himself rights plainly guarantied to him, in common with all other citizens of the United States, by the treaty.

Counsel for defendant Government cites a decision of the Supreme Court of the United States, referred to as the Head Money Cases, to the effect that so far as a treaty made by the United States with any foreign nation can become the subject of judicial cognizance in the United States, it is subject to such acts as Congress may pass for its enforcement, modification, or repeal.

On this point there is not room for much controversy. But an act of the Congress of the United States in derogation of treaty rights has always been held to be a ground for diplomatic intervention. In the case under consideration, the converse of the proposition announced by the Supreme Court in the Head Money Cases is presented. Here the collision or conflict is between provisions contained in prior municipal statutes of Hayti and stipulations of a treaty between the United States and Hayti of a subsequent date. The rule is universal that a prior statute is repealed by a subsequent statute which is absolutely repugnant ; *leges posteriores priores contrarias abrogant.* The same principle applies when a municipal statute and a treaty stipulation is in competition. A treaty stipulation of a later date repeals a prior statute with whose provisions it is repugnant. And the reverse of the proposition is maintained by the Supreme Court of the United States. In the Head Money Cases the Supreme Court of the United States laid down the following propositions :

‹ A treaty is primarily a compact between ‹ independent nations. It depends for the enfor- ‹ cement of its provisions on the interest and the ‹ honor of the governments which are parties to it.

‹ If these fail, its infraction becomes the subject ‹ of international negotiations and reclamations, ‹ so far as the injured party chooses to seek ‹ redress, which may in the end be enforced by ‹ actual war. It is obvious that with all this the ‹ judicial courts have nothing to do and can give ‹ no redress. But a treaty may also contain pro- ‹ visions which confer certain rights upon the ‹ citizens or subjects of one of the nations resi- ‹ ding in the territorial limits of the other, which ‹ partake of the nature of municipal law, and ‹ which are capable of enforcement as between ‹ private parties in the courts of the country. ‹ An illustration of this character is found in ‹ treaties which regulate the mutual rights of ‹ citizens and subjects of the contracting nations ‹ in regard to rights of property and descent or ‹ inheritance, when the individuals concerned are ‹ aliens. The Constitution of the United States ‹ places such provisions as these in the same ‹ category as laws of Congress by its declaration ‹ that 'this Constitution and the laws made in ‹ pursuance thereof, and all treaties made or ‹ which shall be made under authority of the ‹ United States, shall be the supreme law of the ‹ land'. A treaty, then, is a law of the land as ‹ an act of Congress is, whenever its provisions ‹ prescribe a rule by which the rights of the ‹ private citizen or subject may be determined. ‹ And when such rights are of nature to be ‹ enforced in a court of justice, that court resorts ‹ to the treaty for a rule of decision for the case ‹ before it, as it would to a statute. ›

It will be seen from the above review of the several arguments on behalf of defendant Government, that many of the propositions which are still strenuously urged in defense are addressed to the consideration and support of subsidiary and collateral issues which are, by the terms of the protocol, excluded from the consideration of the referee.

THE TREATY OF NOVEMBER 3, 1864.

It becomes, therefore, necessary to examine the provisions of the treaty upon which complainant Government relies in its intervention on behalf of Van Bokkelen, and to the application of which defendant Government objects. Section 2, article 6, stipulates :

The citizens of the contracting parties shall have free access to the tribunals of justice, in all case to which they may be a party, on the same terms which are granted by the laws and usages of the country to native citizens, etc.	Les citoyens des parties contractantes auront libre accès près des tribunaux de justice dans toutes les causes où ils seront intéressés, aux mêmes conditions que les lois et les usages du pays font aux nationaux, etc.

In view of the explicit language in both texts, it would seem clear that the guaranty to the citizens of contracting States of 'free access to the tribunals of justice, in all cases to which they may be a party, on the same terms which are granted by the laws and usage of the country to native citizens', mean that they shall be entitled to the exercise of all the processes of the courts of the respective countries, whether they concern rights or remedies. And the extent to which these processes of the courts may be invoked is expressed in language equally free from doubt: 'On the same terms which are granted by the laws and usage of the country to native citizens'. It is not denied that a citizen of Hayti in the situation which Van Bokkelen was, would have been entitled to release from imprisonment upon making a judicial assignment. Indeed, the language and reasoning of the Haytian courts and of the Executive of Hayti admit as much.

Article 9 stipulates :

The citizens of each of the high contracting parties within the jurisdiction of the other shall have power to dispose of their personal property by sale, donation, testament, or otherwise; and their personal representatives, being citizens of the other contracting party, shall succeed to their personal property, whether by testament or ab intestato. They may take possession thereof, either by themselves or by others acting for them, at their pleasure, and dispose of the same, paying such duty only as the citizens of the	Les citoyens de chacune des hautes parties contractantes auront, dans la juridiction de l'autre, la faculté de disposer de leurs biens mobiliers, par vente, donation, testament ou autrement; et leurs successeurs, citoyens de l'autre partie contractante, pourront hériter de leurs biens mobiliers soit par testament, soit ab intestat. Ils pourront en prendre possession soit par eux-mêmes, soit par des tiers agissant pour eux, comme ils le voudront, et en disposer sans payer d'autres droits que ceux auxquels sont assujettis, dans
country wherein the said personal property is situated shall be subject to pay in like cases, etc.	les mêmes circonstances, les citoyens du pays où sont situés les dits biens mobiliers, etc.

There would seem to be no ambiguity in the language of these articles; and the best way to construe them is to follow the words thereof.

But the civil court of Port au Prince, and the court of cassation affirming the decision of the civil court, denying Van Bokkelen's petition to execute a judicial assignment, decide that there is nothing in articles 6 or 9 of the treaty of November 3, 1864, which guaranties to Van Bokkelen, or any citizen of the United States, the right to release from imprisonment upon the execution of a judicial assignment · conformally to the terms of the civil procedure of Hayti. The civil court decided, among other things, that the 'reason which causes the exclusion of foreigners is that the benefit of an assignment has always been regarded as *an institution of civil law* which should benefit native citizens only'; and 'it is impossible to suppose that it was the intention of the contracting plenipotentiaries to abrogate or modify, by article 9 or by article 6 of the treaty, as those articles are worded, article 794 of the civil code of procedure and article 569 of the code of commerce which exclude a foreigner from the benefit of making an assignment'; and further, that 'whereas, although the text of this stipulation (article 9), and even that of article 6, which grants to the citizens of the two contracting parties free access to the courts of justice, in all cases in which they shall be interested, on the same terms that are granted by the laws and usage of the country to native citizens, might leave some doubt with regard to their true meaning, it would be dispelled by the rules of law concerning the interpretation of conventions which are applicable to treaties'; and this court then proceeds as follows :

« Whereas the first of these rules is to seek « out the common intention of the contracting « parties rather than to be guided by the literal « meaning of the terms. »

From this decision of the civil court of Port au Prince, rendered May 27, 1884, Van Bokkelen appealed to the court of cassation, which rendered its decision, affirming the decision of the civil court, on February 26, 1885, almost a year from the time Van Bokkelen was first imprisoned.

The court of cassation, affirming the judgment of the civil court, held :

« Whereas the judicial assignment of property « is *an institution of civil right*, the articles 769 « (794) of the Code of Civil Procedure and 569

‹ of the Code of Commerce, excepting foreigners ‹ from the benefit of this institution since they ‹ do not exercise in Hayti all rights, they can ‹ only enjoy privileges derived from natural ‹ rights or of mankind, and not those which ‹ are derived from purely civil law. ›

If, as I shall hereafter endeavor to show, the judicial assignment *(cession de biens)* is simply a step in the procedure of the courts in bankruptcy proceedings, it is not perceived how the description of it 'as an institution of the civil law' can have the effect of withdrawing it from the guaranty expressed in the treaty grant of 'free access to the tribunals of justice', unless it was excepted in terms from the treaty stipulations.

Of the decree of the court of cassation, affirming the decision of the civil court of Port au Prince, it is to be observed that the latter court follows substantially, though not literally, the reasoning of the former.

A careful reading of the decree of the court of cassation indicates that the court has, in its attempt to justify the authorities of Hayti, indulged in the same peculiar reasoning as the civil court of Port au Prince; and it is consequently open to the same criticism.

The extreme to which the court has gone in search of reasons to justify its judgment indicates the absence of that good faith which should characterize the interpretation of treaty stipulations. And in view of the language of articles 6 and 9 of the treaty of November 3, 1864, it is difficult to understand by what process of reasoning the court reached the conclusion that a citizen of the United States, within the jurisdiction of Hayti, *'can only enjoy privileges derived from natural rights or of mankind and not those that are derived from purely civil law'*.

Equally illogical and untenable is the reasoning of the court of cassation in holding that nowhere in the treaty of November 3, 1864, is there to be found a provision which may be held to confer upon the citizens of the contracting States other and additional rights; *i. e.* full right to exercise the 'judicial assignment' of property. Under the public law or law of nations aliens enjoy purely natural rights in whatever State they may be. And in the absence of any treaty, a citizen of the United States would have enjoyed natural rights in Hayti; but the terms of the treaty of November 3, 1864, stipulate, in effect, that such citizen further enjoy civil rights.

The court of cassation, although admitting that the treaty stipulates that 'the citizens of the contracting parties should have free access to the courts of justice in all cases wherein they may be interested, on the same conditions that the laws and usage of the country give to their citizens, furnishing security required in the case', maintains 'that this provision of article 6 is not intended to grant to the citizens of these two nations the enjoyment of civil rights'. The court of cassation is in error in assuming that the privilege of release of an imprisoned debtor would be denied to the Haytian citizen by the United States courts circumstanced as Van Bokkelen was when he invoked the protection of the treaty. In such a case, assuming that other and ordinary applications for release had failed, the writ of habeas corpus would lie to the courts of the United States, and would avail to secure his release from imprisonment.

In view of the treaty language and terms of the protocol, it is impossible for the referee to sustain the reasoning or the conclusions reached by the civil court of Port au Prince or by the court of cassation. It is not perceived how the nature or character of the remedy or right expressly guarantied to citizens of the United States within the jurisdiction of Hayti can be withheld from them by describing it, as the judgment of the civil court of Port au Prince does, 'as an institution of civil law', or as the decree of the court of cassation does, 'an institution of civil right'. The 'judicial assignment' (cession de biens), as I have elsewhere pointed out, is simply an incident or step in the judicial procedure, in the courts of Hayti in bankruptcy proceedings. And if it be not included within the guaranty of 'free access to the tribunals of justice', the language is without meaning and inoperative. 'Free access to the tribunals of justice' that was limited to admission to the courts, without the privilege to plaintiff or defendant of employing the usual, ordinary processes of the court, would be a delusion and a snare. Such an intention or purpose may not, in the absence of plain language, be imputed to the high contracting parties.

The attempt of the courts of Hayti and of the Executive to exclude a citizen of the United States from the benefit of a judicial assignment, on the ground that the treaty of November 3, 1864, makes no mention of it in express terms, does not seem to call for serious consideration. Such a strained objection would only be satisfied by incorporating the body of the Haytian codes in the treaty articles. With equal force and soundness the courts of Hayti and the executive power might have denied this right, remedy, or privilege to Van Bokkelen on the ground that he was not mentioned or particularly named in the treaty. When the treaty said 'free access to the tribunals of justice on the same terms which are granted by the laws and usages of the country to native citizens', it included the whole class of citizens, and fixed the terms upon which the laws and usage of the country were to be applied to them. Among the international rules proposed by the Institute of International Law of Geneva, 1877, with the view to negotiation of international treaties, the following rules, among others, were adopted;

« 1. *L'étranger sera admis à ester en justice aux mêmes conditions que le regnicole.*»

« 2. Les formes ordinaires de l'instruction et de la procédure seront régies par la loi du lieu où le procès est instruit. Seront considérées comme telles, les prescriptions relatives aux formes de l'assignation (sauf ce qui est proposé ci-dessous, 2ᵐᵉ al.), aux délais de comparution, à la nature et à la forme de la procuration *ad litem,* au mode de recueillir les preuves, à la rédaction et au prononcé du jugement, à la passation en force de chose jugée, aux délais et aux formalités de l'appel et autres voies de recours, à la péremption de l'instance.»

Reference is here made to the language of the above rules to show that when a alien is admitted to stand in justice on the same terms as a citizen, he must necessarily be entitled to invoke in his behalf all the customary and civil processes of the courts which are open to citizens.

JUDICIAL ASSIGNMENT.

In view of the fact that the executive and judicial authorities of Hayti have placed their refusal to admit Van Bokkelen to the benefits of the judicial assignment upon the ground that by the letter of the municipal codes of Hayti all aliens are excluded from its privileges, and that it is confined to native citizens, and that it is a civil institution of the State, it becomes necessary to inquire into the real nature and character of the proceeding known as judicial assignment *(cession de biens).* This is of the first importance, because the fallacy in the reasoning of the courts and of the Executive of Hayti and of counsel for the defendant Government consists in attributing exceptional characteristics and functions to the act of judicial assignment.

The provisions of the Haytian code which have been cited are here below inserted.

There is nothing exceptional, unusual or extraordinary in this proceeding. It is not, as the language of the courts and the executive of Hayti, and the argument of counsel for defendant Government implies, a law unto itself of such supreme authority as to negative the purpose and effect of a treaty stipulation.

The judicial assignment *(cession de biens)* of the Haytian codes is described under title 5 of the Civil Code of Hayti, and 12 of the Code of Civil Procedure, and title 2 of the Code of Commerce.

There is nothing hidden or mysterious about it; it possesses no cabalistic power. And the execution of a judicial assignment is simply a step in the ordinary procedure and practice of the courts of Hayti. It is a familiar and well-known incident in the jurisprudence of the civil law. The provisions in the Haytian code were transferred bodily from the civil code of France; and France incorporated them in her code from the corresponding title *(cessio bonorum)* of the Justinian code, whence they are traced back to the Lex Julia.

« The Lex Julia, probably passed in the reign of Augustus at length, exempted insolvent debtors from the penalty of imprisonment and infamy and secured to them the *beneficium competentiæ* or right to maintenance; provided they made an immediate and complete *cessio bonorum* to their creditors.

« The surrender was made by solemn declaration, either judicial or extrajudicial. The property thus given up was sold and the price distributed among the creditors. The debtor was not released from his debts unless the creditors were fully paid, but he was protected from imprisonment at their instance. If the debtor subsequently acquired property, his creditors were entitled to attack it, except in so far as it was necessary for his own subsistence. This latter privilege was called 'exceptio' or 'benificium competentiæ'. The *Lex Julia de cessio bonorum* introduced a *new procedure* in relation to a bankrupt's estate *(venditio bonorum)* which theretofore was governed by the '*missio in bona*'.»

The rule of the interpretation of treaty stipulations suggested in the jugdment of the civil courts of Port au Prince, as has been pointed out, was taken from its appropriate context in the decision of the court of cassation, in Napier *vs.* Duke of Richmond, which case has been considered. As it is sought to be used in relation to the case under consideration, it is without relevance or authority. The language of all the authorities repudiates such a strained and singular construction, whether it be in application to private contracts or to international covenants.

It may be said of the treaty of November 3, 1864, as was said of the Constitution of the United States by Mr. Justice Story, with the approval of Chancellor Kent, that:

« The instrument furnishes essentially the means of its own interpretation.»

‹The first and fundamental rule in the inter‹pretation of all instruments is to construe them ‹according to the sense of the terms and the ‹intention of the parties. The intention of a law ‹is to be gathered from the words, the context, ‹the subject-matter, the effects and consequence, ‹or the reason and spirit of the law.

‹And the only case in which a literal mea‹ning is not to be adopted is limited to the ‹exception when such construction would involve ‹a manifest absurdity.

‹When the words are plain and clear, and the ‹sense distinct and perfect arising on them, there ‹is generally no necessity to have recourse to ‹other means of interpretation. In literal inter‹pretation the rule observed is to follow the sense ‹in respect both of the words and construction ‹of them which is agreeable to common use ‹without attending to etymological fancies or ‹grammatical refinements.

‹All international treaties are covenants bona ‹fide and are therefore to be equitably and not ‹technically construed. The principal rule has ‹already been adverted to, namely to follow the ‹ordinary and usual acceptation, the plain and ‹obvious meaning of the language employed. ‹This rule is, in fact, inculcated as a cardinal ‹maxim of interpretation equally by civilians and ‹by writers on international law.

‹Vattel says that it is not allowable to inter‹pret what has no need of interpretation. If the ‹meaning be evident and the conclusion not ab‹surd, you have no right to look beyond or ‹beneath it, to alter or to add to it by conjec‹ture. Wolf observes that to do so is to remove ‹all certainty from human transactions. Treaties ‹are to be interpreted according to their plain ‹sense. Publicists are generally agreed in laying ‹down certain rules of construction as being ap‹plicable when disagreement takes place between ‹the parties to a treaty as to the meaning or ‹intention of stipulations. Some of these rules are ‹either unsafe in their application or of doubt‹ful applicability; and rules tainted by any shade ‹of doubt, from whatever source it may be derived, ‹are unfit for use in international controversy.

‹Those against which no objection can be ‹urged, and which are probably sufficient for ‹all purposes, may be stated as follows:

‹When the language of a treaty, taken in ‹the ordinary meaning of the words, yields a ‹plain and reasonable sense, subject to the quali‹fications, that any words which may have a ‹customary meaning in treaties differing from ‹their common signification must be understood ‹to have that meaning, and that a sense can

‹not be adopted which leads to an absurdity or ‹to incompatibility of the contract with an ac‹cepted fundamental principle of law.

‹Treaties of every kind, when made by the ‹competent authority, are as obligatory upon ‹nations as private contracts are binding upon ‹individuals, and these are to receive a fair and ‹liberal interpretation, according to the intention ‹of the contracting parties, and to be kept with ‹the most scrupulous good faith. Their meaning ‹is to be ascertained by the same rules of con‹struction and course of reasoning which we apply ‹to the interpretation of private contracts.›

Applying these rules to the words, the context, and the subject-matter found in articles 6 and 9 of the treaty of November 3, 1864, there would seem to be no difficulty in ascertaining their precise intention and meaning. The infirmity of fallacy disclosed in the reasoning of the decrees of the Haytian courts and in the message of the executive of Hayti, referring to this case and adopting the views of the courts, is that the judges and President Salomon reason about the competition which exists between the treaty and the municipal law of Hayti, as if the question of relative authority and comparative precedence was between a municipal statute of the United States and a municipal statute of Hayti. In doing this they lose sight of the important fact that the competition is between provisions contained in municipal statutes of Hayti and stipulations in a treaty of subsequent date, to which Hayti is one of the contracting parties. It would seem, from the character of the arguments submitted on behalf of Hayti, that counsel did not fail to recognize this infirmity in the reasoning of the judicial and executive authorities. And this seems to have embarrassed counsel for defendant Government, and accounts for the shifting positions upon which the defense in this case has, at different times, rested. It seems to be forgotten that the operation of treaty stipulations within the jurisdiction of a contracting party is not a foreign interference, nor is it the application of extraterritorial or foreign law. By the constitution and law of Hayti a treaty is a law of the State.

The treaty of November 3, 1864, is within Lorimer's category of the third class of treaties 'as sources of international law'; treaties which, among other things, recognize the equal rights of foreigners and natives before the municipal law:

‹The value of treaties, as a source of the ‹positive law of nations, is supposed to have ‹been greatly enhanced by the annex to Protocol ‹No. 1 of the conferences held in London in

« 1871 respecting the clauses of the treaty of « Paris of 1856, which have reference to the « neutralization of the Black Sea. The protocol « is in the following words:

« The plenipotentiaries recognize that it is an « essential principle of the law of nations that « no power can liberate itself from the engage- « ments of a treaty, nor modify the stipula- « tions thereof, unless with the consent of the « contracting powers by means of an amicable « arrangement. »

Some of the inconsistencies in the positions assumed, at different times, by the defendant Government have been pointed out in the brief on behalf of complainant.

It was first maintained that the case of Van Bokkelen in the Haytian courts was decided only on an exception; that is to say, that the court of cassation, affirming the judgment of the court below, held that Van Bokkelen, being an alien, the said court had no jurisdiction over the subject-matter.

At a later date, referring to the decision of the courts, it was argued that 'at the utmost the Haytian judges erred in resting their decision upon grounds erroneous, or open to discussion; and the only error, if any which may possibly be charged to them, was to set forth as a ground for their judgment that Van Bokkelen's case did not fall within the scope of the treaty, *instead of stating simply that petitioner had not taken the steps required to be entitled to the rights guarantied him by said treaty stipulations'.*

As has been said, 'such a decision would, indeed, have created an entirely different situation'.

In the second argument or note the Haytian minister maintained that under article 148 of the Haytian code of civil procedure judgment in the Van Bokkelen case was null and void. His first proposition in regard to the action of the court is, that it dismissed Van Bokkelen's case for want of jurisdiction. His second proposition is, that the judgment of the tribunal of Port au Prince must be regarded as a final decision against Van Bokkelen of all the questions raised by the pleadings; and his third proposition is, that Van Bokkelen did not exhaust the legal remedies afforded by municipal law, because, on account of an omission on the part of the judges to 'pass upon' all the questions raised, the judgment was null and void, and Van Bokkelen was therefore entitled to the extraordinary remedy known as « la requête civile ».

It is quite clear from an examination of article 148 of the Haytian code of civil proce-

dure, referred to by Mr. Preston, that the judges are not required to 'pass upon' all the points raised in the pleadings in the sense of judicially determining them, but only of taking notice or mentioning them in the judicial summary of the proceedings, which in Haytian procedure constitutes the judgment. And one of the objects of this requirement seems to be to furnish evidence to the parties in the judgment itself that none of their points have been overlooked. It further appears that the re-opening of the judgment under that article can be had only 'upon the request of those who have been parties, or of those who have been duly brought into court'.

Reference is again made to the conflicting and contradictory positions assumed, at different stages of the proceedings, by the defendant Government, for the purpose of showing how important and necessary it has been for the referee to confine himself to the narrow ground furnished in the single issue suggested by the terms of the arbitration. The language of the protocol necessarily fixed the decision of the Haytian courts and the action of the executive of Hayti as the starting point for the referee's examination and decision. And the treaties between the high contracting parties were made the supreme law for his consideration and guidance.

IN CONCLUSION

Whether the literal, natural meaning of the language, or of the spirit of the treaty of November 3, 1864, or the common intention of the contracting parties be regarded, I am of opinion, first, that the imprisonment of Charles Adrian Van Bokkelen, a citizen of the United States in Hayti, was in derogation of the rights to which he was entitled as a citizen of the United States under stipulations contained in the treaty between the United States and Hayti; second, that the record of the case and the correspondence between the two Governments fails to disclose any extenuating circumstances or sufficient justification for the harsh treatment and protracted imprisonment of Van Bokkelen by the constituted authorities of the Republic of Hayti, notwithstanding the earnest and repeated protests of the representatives of the United States; and I award that the Republic of Hayti pay to the United States, on behalf of the representatives of Charles Adrian Van Bokkelen, the sum of sixty thousand dollars ($ 60,000).

Witness my hand this 4th day of December, A. D. 1888, at the city of Washington.

---

[1] *Foreign Relations of U. S.,* 1888, p. 1007-1036.

LXXXVIII. Bolivie, Chili.

4 avril 1884.

Après la guerre, qui divisa les deux pays, la convention de trève a prévu la constitution d'une commission arbitrale pour fixer les indemnités dues à des citoyens du Chili. Cette disposition fut confirmée implicitement par un protocole complémentaire du 30 mai 1885.

Pacto de tregua entre Chile y Bolivia, firmado en Valparaiso, Abril 4, 1884.

. . . .

TERCERA. — Los bienes secuestrados en Bolivia á nacionales chilenos por decretos del Gobierno ó por medidas emanadas de autoridades civiles y militares, serán devueltos immediatamente á sus dueños ó á los representantes constituidos por ellos con poderes suficientes.

Los será igualmente devuelto el producto que el Gobierno de Bolivia haya recibido de dichos bienes, y que aparezca justificado con los documentos del caso.

Los perjuicios que por las causas expresadas ó por la destruccion de sus propiedades hubieron recibido los ciudadanos chilenos, serán indemnizados en virtud de las gestiones que los interesados entablaron ante el Gobierno de Bolivia.

CUARTA. — Si no se arribase á un acuerdo entre el Gobierno de Bolivia y los interesados, respecto del monto é indemnización de los perjuicios y de la forma del pago, se someterán los puntos en disidencia al arbitraje de una comisión compuesta de un miembro nombrado por parte de Chile, otro por la de Bolivia y de un tercero que nombrará en Chile, de comun acuerdo, de entre los representantes neutrales acreditados en este país. Esta designación se hará á la posible brevedad [1].

Protocolo complementario del tratado de tregua, firmado en Santiago, Mayo 30, 1885.

. . . .

3° — Para los efectos de la disposición contenida en el Articulo 4° del mencionado tratado de tregua, se declara que el tercer miembro de la Comisión Arbitral que habrá de estimar y decidir las reclamaciones deducidas por ciudadanos chilenos contra el Gobierno de Bolivia, sé le entrará en el ejercicio de sus funciones cuando en la apreciación de alguno de los reclamos se produzca desacuerdo entre los comisionados nombrados por parte de Chile y Bolivia [1].

[1] *Recopilación dos Tratados*, p. 167, 255.

Il ne semble pas avoir été donné de suite à cette convention d'arbitrage. Les longues discussions, qui aboutirent au traité définitif de paix du 18 mai 1895, ne font aucune allusion à l'arbitrage convenu et le texte du traité est muet sur ce point.

LXXXIX. Colombie, Equateur, Pérou.

1er août 1887.

Dans cet arbitrage la question des limites contestées des républiques de l'Equateur et du Pérou fut soumise à l'arbitrage du Roi d'Espagne. Ce n'est qu'ultérieurement par une convention du 15 décembre 1894 que la Colombie accéda au compromis accepté par les deux Etats voisins.

Convenio para la resolucion de la cuestion de limites por medio del arbitraje, firmado en Quito, Agosto 1 de 1887.

Deseando los Gobiernos del Perú y del Ecuador poner un termino amistoso á las cuestiones de límites pendientes entre ambas Naciones, han autorizado para celebrar un arreglo con tal fin, á los infrascritos, quienes, despues de haber exhibido sus poderes, han convenido en los articulos siguientes:

ART. I. — Los Gobiernos del Perú y del Ecuador someten dichas cuestiones á Su Majestad el Rey de España, para que los decida como Arbitro de derecho de una manera definitiva é inapelable.

ART. II. — Ambos Gobiernos solicitarán simultáneamente, por medio de Plenipotenciarios, la aquiescencia de Su Majestad Católica á este nombramiento, dentro de ocho meses contados desde el canje de las ratificaciones de la presente Convencion.

ART. III. — Un año despues de la acceptacion del Augusto Arbitro presentarán los Plenipotenciarios á Su Majestad Católica, ó al Ministro que Su Majestad designe, una exposicion en que consten las pretensiones de sus respectivos Gobiernos, acompañada de los documentos en que las apoyen y en la que harán valer las razones juridicas del caso.

ART. IV. — Desde el día en que se presenten dichas exposiciones ó alegatos, quedarán autorizados los Plenipotenciarios para recibir y contestar, en el término prudencial que se les fije, los traslados que el Augusto Arbitro crea conveniente pasarles, así como para cumplir las providencias que dicte con el objeto de esclarecer el derecho de las partes.

ART. V. — Una vez pronunciado el fallo arbitral y publicado oficialmente por el Gobierno de Su Majestad, quedará ejecutoriado y sus decisiones serán obligatorias para ambas partes.

ART. VI. — Antes de expedirse el fallo arbitral, y, á la mayor brevedad posible despues del canje, pondrán ambas partes el mayor empeño en arreglar, por medio de negociaciones directas, todos ó algunos de los puntos comprendidos en las cuestiones de límites, y, si se verifican tales arreglos y quedan perfeccionados, segun las formas necesarias para la validez de los tratados públicos, se pondrán en conocimiento de Su Majestad Católica, dando por terminado el arbitraje, ó limitandolo á los puntos no acordados, segun los casos. A falta de acuerdo directo, quedará expedito el arbitraje en todo su extension como lo fija el articolo I.

ART. VII. — Aun cuando ambas partes contratantes abrigan la intima persuasion de que Su Majestad Católica se prestará á aceptar el arbitraje que se le propone, desde ahora designan como Arbitros, para el caso contrario, á S. E. el Presidente de la República francesa, ó á Su Majestad el Rey de los Belgos, ó al Excmo. Consejo Federal Suizo, en el órden en que quedan nombrados, á fin de que ejerzon el cargo conforme á lo estipulado en los articulos que preceden.

ART. VIII. — Despues de aprobarse la presente Convencion por los Congresos del Perú y del Ecuador, se canjearán las ratificaciones en Quito ó Lima en el menor tiempo posible.

En fé de lo cual los infrascritos Plenipotenciarios la han firmado y sellado con sus respectivos sellos, en Quito, á 1º de Agosto de mil ochocientos ochenta y siete [1].

Convención adicional para la resolucion de la cuestion de límites, firmado en Lima, Diciembre 15 de 1894.

Los Gobiernos del Perú, Colombia y Ecuador, deseosos de poner fraternal y decoroso término á la cuestion pendiente entre los tres Estados respecto á sus límites territoriales, y animados nel propósito de remover toda causa ó motivo de desavenencia que queda perturbar la amistad que felizmente mantienen, han creido oportuno provocar un acuerdo entre ellos, y han nombrado, con tal fin, sus respectivos Plenipotenciarios, á saber:

S. E. el Presidente de la República del Perú:

Al Dr D. Louis Felipe Villarán, Abogado y Plenipotenciario especial del Perú.

S. E. el Presidente de la República de Colombia:

Al Dr D. Anibal Galindo, Abogado especial de límites y Plenipotenciario especial,

Y al señor D. Luis Tanco, Encargado de Negocios de Colombia en el Perú.

Y S. E. el Presidente de la República del Ecuador:

Al Dr D. Julio Castro, Enviado Extraordinario y Ministro Plenipotenciario del Ecuador en el Perú.

Quienes, como resultado de la conferencia tenida en Lima, y despues de haber canjeado sus plenos poderes y haberlos hallado en buena y debida forma, han acordado la Convencion adicional de arbitraje que se contiene en los siguientes articulos:

ART. I. — Colombia se adhiere á la Convencion de arbitramento entre el Perú y el Ecuador de 1º de Agosto de 1887, canjeada en Lima en 14 de Abril de 1888; pero las tres altas partes contratantes estipulan que el Real Arbitro fallará las cuestiones materia de la disputa, atendiendo, no solo á los titulos y argumentos de derecho que se le han presentado y se le presenten, sino tambien á las conveniencias de las partes contratantes, conciliándolas de modo que la linea de frontera este fundada en el derecho y en la equidad.

ART. II. — El Gobierno de Colombia cumplirá los deberes que á las partes contratantes impone el Articulo 2º de la referida Convencion, dentro de ocho meses contados desde la ratificacion de la presente; y el del Articulo 3º de aquella, dentro de seis meses, contados desde la aceptacion del Real Arbitro. A partir de eso fecha, se arreglará en todo á los procedimientos pactados en la Convencion á la cual se adhiere.

ART. III. — Los gastos que ocasione al Arbitro la sustanciacion del proceso, los reembolsarán los Gobiernos contratantes, erogando cada uno la tercera parte de la suma á que dichos gastos asciendan.

ART. IV. — Si esta Convencion fuere desaprobada por la República de Colombia, producirá no obstante sus efectos entre las Repúblicas del Perú y del Ecuador, cuyas cuestiones sobre límites serán decididas con arreglo á lo estipulado en el articulo 1º.

ART. V. — Si dicha Convencion fuese desaprobada por el Perú, por el Ecuador, ó por ambos, continuará vigente entre las dos Naciones el Convenio de arbitraje de 1º de Agosto de 1887, y Colombia quedará en libertad para adherirse pura y simplemente á el, dentro de noventa días, contados desde que oficialmente le sea notificada la improbacion.

[1] *Tratados del Perú*, t. V, p. 803.

ART. VI. — La presente Convencion será ratificada por los Congresos de las tres Repúblicas contratantes y las ratificaciones se canjearán en Lima, Bogotá ó Quito, en el menor tiempo posible. En fé de lo cual, los Plenipotenciarios de las altas partes contratantes han firmado la presente Convencion y la han sellado con sus sellos particulares, en triple ejemplar, en Lima, á los quince días del mes de Diciembre de mil ochocientos noventa y cuatro [1].

Aucune décision n'est encore intervenue.

XL. Guatemala, Mexique.

26 janvier 1888.

Simples réclamations réciproques, soumises à deux commissaires avec un surarbitre. Les réclamations mexicaines se montèrent à $ 2,954,421.28 et les réclamations guatémaliennes à $ 2,139,379.25; il fut accordé respectivement $ 39,044.30 et $ 49,100.

Convencion sobre reclamaciones firmada el 26 Enero 1888, con las alteraciones aprobadas el 15 Febrero 1889.

En vista de que ciudadanos de la República Mexicana han presentado quejas y hecho reclamaciones por perjuicios sufridos en sus personas y propiedades, y de los cuales consideran responsables á autoridades de la República de Guatemala, y de que se han presentado quejas y reclamaciones semejantes por perjuicios causados á ciudadanos guatemaltecos en sus personas y propiedades, y de los cuales se considera responsables á autoridades mexicanas, el Presidente de la República Mexicana y el Presidente de la República de Guatemala han determinado celebrar una Convención para el arreglo de dichas reclamaciones y han nombrado sus Plenipotenciarios :

El Presidente de la República Mexicana al Sr. D. Ignacio Mariscal, Secretario de Estado y del Despacho de Relaciones Exteriores;

Y el Presidente de la República de Guatemala al Sr. D. José Salazar, Enviado Extraordinario y Ministro Plenipotenciario en la República Mexicana ;

Quienes, despúes de haberse mostrado sus respectivos plenos poderes y encontrádolos en buena y debida forma, han convenido en los artículos siguientes :

ARTICULO I. Todas las reclamaciones pendientes de corporaciones, compañias ó individuos particulares de nacionalidad guatemalteca, en los términos que después se especificarán, por perjuicios sufridos en sus personas y propiedades, y de los cuales se considere responsables á autoridades de México; y todas las reclamaciones pendientes de corporaciones, compañias ó individuos particulares de nacionalidad mexicana en los mismos términos, por perjuicios sufridos en sus personas y propiedades, y de los cuales se considere responsables á autoridades guatemaltecas, como también todas las reclamaciones de esa clase que se presentaren dentro del término que se fija más adelante en este Convenio, serán remitidas á dos Comisionados, de los cuales uno será nombrado por el Presidente de la República de Guatemala y otro por el Presidente de la República Mexicana. En caso de muerte, ausencia ó impedimento de cualquiera de los Comisionados, ó en caso de que uno de ellos dejar de ejercer sus funciones, el Presidente de la República de Guatemala ó el Presidente de la República Mexicana, en su caso, nombrará desde luego á otra persona para que funcione como Comisionado en lugar del nombrado originalmente.

ARTICULO II. Queda establecido que, con arreglo á esta Convención, no serán admitidas las reclamaciones que se funden en acontecimientos anteriores al año de 1873. Cuando las reclamaciones procedan de hechos anteriores al año de 1873, ó de daños y perjuicios causados en terrenos disputados antes de fijarse de un modo definitivo los límites de ambas Repúblicas, siempre que fuere imposible resolver sobre la legalidad de los hechos sin determinar á cuál de las dos pertenecía el terreno, los Comisionados se declararán incompetentes y las remitirán á sus respectivos Gobiernos para que sean resueltas, á solicitud de la parte interesada, por las autoridades ordinarias, conforme á la ley, sin haber lugar á la vía diplomática sino en caso de denegación de justicia. La Comisión mixta, en su caso, conocera de las excepciones legales que se opongan, inclusive la de prescripción, y las resolverá de conformidad con los principios generales de derecho.

ARTICULO III. Cuando la queja de un reclamante suponga su derecho de propiedad en bienes raíces, esta propiedad se comprobará ante los Comisionados conforme á las leyes del país donde estén situados dichos bienes, y que hayan estado vigentes al verificarse los hechos que servan de fundamento á la reclamación.

ARTICULO IV. Los Comisionados nombrados se reunirán en la ciudad de México dentro de seis meses contados desde el canje de las ratificaciones de esta Convención, y antes de dar principio á sus trabajos harán y firmarán una declaración solemne de que examinarán cuida-

---

[1] *Tratados del Perú*, t. V, p. 989.

dosamente y fallarán según su mejor saber y conforme al derecho público, la justicia y equidad, y sin temor, favor ni inclinación hacia su respectivo país, sobre todas aquellas reclamaciones que respectivamente les fueren presentadas por los Gobiernos de las Repúblicas de México y Guatemala; y dicha declaración será asentada en el acta de sus procedimientos.

En seguida los Comisionados nombrarán una tercera persona para que funcione como Arbitro en el caso ó casos en que opinen de distintos modos. Si no pudieren ponerse de acuerdo respecto del nombramiento de esa tercera persona, el Secretario de Relaciones Exteriores de la República Mexicana y el Ministro de Guatemala en México harán dicho nombramiento. La persona que así se eligiere para ser Arbitro hará y firmará, antes de proceder á obrar como tal, una declaración solemne en forma semejante á la que deberá haber sido ya hecha y suscrita por los Comisionados, la cual se asentará también en el acta de sus procedimientos. En caso de muerte, ausencia ó impedimento de tal persona, ó en caso de que, por cualquier motivo, deje de obrar como Arbitro, otra persona será nombrada de la manera indicada anteriormente para sustituirla y hará y firmará la declaración mencionada.

Artículo V. Después de haber suscrito las protestas respectivas, procederán los Comisionados juntos á examinar y resolver las reclamaciones que se les presenten, en el orden y de la manera que de común acuerdo juzguen oportuno; pero aceptarán solamente aquellos informes ó pruebas que les fueren ministrados por sus respectivos Gobiernos ó en nombre de éstos. Tendrán obligación de recibir y leer todas las manifestaciones ó documentos escritos que se les presenten por sus respectivos Gobiernos ó en su nombre, en apoyo ó respuesta á cualquiera reclamación, y de oir, si necesario fuere, á una persona por cada parte en cada caso separado de reclamación, á una persona por cada parte en nombre de cada uno de los dos Gobiernos. Si no estuvieren conformes respecto de alguna reclamación particular, llamarán en su auxilio al Arbitro que se haya nombrado de común acuerdo; y el Arbitro, después de haber examinado las pruebas producidas en favor y en contra de la reclamación, y después de haber oído, si necesario fuere, á una persona por cada parte, como antes se ha dicho, y de haber consultado con los Comisionados la fallará definitivamente y sin apelación.

Artículo VI. El fallo de los Comisionados y del Arbitro se dará por escrito en cada caso de reclamación; especificará que la candidad que se concede debe ser pagada en moneda mexicana, y será firmado por ellos.

Artículo VII. Cada Gobierno podrá nombrar una persona para que, obrando en su nombre, presente y apoye reclamaciones, responda á las que se hicieren contra él, y lo represente en general en todos los asuntos relacionados con el examen y fallo de las mismas.

Artículo VIII. El Presidente de la República Mexicana y el Presidente de la República de Guatemala se comprometen solemne y sinceramente á considerar de todo punto definitivo y final el fallo dado de común acuerdo por los Comisionados, ó por el Arbitro en su caso, sobre cada una de las reclamaciones; y á dar cumplimiento á esos fallos sin objeción, excusa ni demora.

Artículo IX. Todas las reclamaciones serán presentadas á los Comisionados dentro de cuatro meses contados desde el día de su primera junta, con excepción de cualquier caso en que las razones de la demora habida fueren satisfactorias, á juicio de los Comisionados, ó del Arbitro si los Comisionados no estuvieren de acuerdo; y entonces podrá alargarse el periodo fijado para presentar la reclamación por un término que no exceda de tres meses.

Los Comisionados tendrán la obligación de examinar y fallar todas las reclamaciones, dentro de un año contado desde la fecha de su primera junta. De conformidad con el objeto y sentido verdadero de esta Convención, podrán los Comisionados, ó el Arbitro si no estuvieren de acuerdo, decidir en cada caso si la reclamación ha sido ó non hecha y presentada debidamente, ya sea en todo ó en parte.

Artículo X. Después de haberse fallado por los Comisionados y el Arbitro en todos los casos sometidos á su resolución, la suma de las cantidades concedidas á los ciudadanos de una parte, será rebajada de la suma de las cantidades concedidas á los ciudadanos de la otra parte; y la diferencia, hasta la cantidad de sesenta mil pesos de moneda mexicana, sin rédito ni otra rebaja que la especificada en el artículo XIII de esta Convención, será pagada en la ciudad de México ó en la de Guatemala, dentro de doce meses contados desde el término de los trabajos de la Comisión, al Gobierno á cuyos ciudadanos se hubiere concedido mayor cantidad. El resto de dicha diferencia se pagará en abonos anuales que no excedan de sesenta mil pesos demone da mexicana cada uno, hasta que la suma total de esa diferencia esté pagada.

Artículo XI. Las Altas Partes Contratantes convienen en considerar el resultado de los trabajos de esta Comisión como arreglo completo, perfecto y definitivo de todas las reclamaciones contra los dos Gobiernos, motivadas por hechas ocurridos antes de la fecha del canje de las ratificaciones de la presente Convención; y se comprometen, en consecuencia, á considerar y tratar cualquiera de esas reclamaciones, aunque no hubiere sido presentada á dicha Comisión como definitivamente arreglada, excluída é inadmisible desde la conclusión de los trabajos de la citada Comisión.

Artículo XII. Los Comisionados y el Arbitro llevarán un registro minucioso con apuntes exactos de sus procedimientos y con especificación de las fechas: con este fin nombrarán dos secretarios para que les auxilien en el despacho de los asuntos de la Comisión.

Artículo XIII. Cada Gobierno pagará á su Comisionado un sueldo anual que non exceda de tres mil pesos de moneda mexicana; y cada uno de los dos Gobiernos pagará la cantidad que de común acuerdo se fije.

La remuneración que se hubiere de pagar al Arbitro será determinada de común acuerdo al concluir los trabajos de la Comisión; pero en virtud de recomendación hecha por los Comisionados, podrá cada Gobierno hacer á cuenta de ella los anticipos que fueren necesarios ó equitativos.

El sueldo anual de los secretarios no excederá de dos mil pesos de moneda mexicana.

La suma total de los gastos de la Comisión, inclusos los imprevistos, será satisfecha, rebajándola proporcionalmente de las cantidades que la Comisión haya concedido por indemnización á los reclamantes, siempre que esa rebaja no exceda del cinco por ciento sobre las cantidades fijadas por indemnización.

En caso de que los gastos importaren más ese cinco por ciento, cada Gobierno cubrirá la mitad de la demasía.

Artículo XIV. La presente Convención será ratificada conforme á las leyes vigentes en cada una de las dos Repúblicas; y el canje de las ratificaciones se hará en la ciudad de México, tan pronto como fuere posible.

En fé de lo cual, los respectivos Plenipotenciarios la hemos firmado y sellado.

Hecho en México, en dos originales, el dìa veintiseis de Enero de mil ochocientos ochenta y ocho.[1]

Tratado para renovar la convencion sobre reclamaciones, firmado en Guatemala, Diciembre 22, 1891.

Considerando: que con fecha veintiséis de Enero de mil ochocientos ochenta y ocho, fué concluida una Convención entre los Estádos Uni-

dos Mexicanos y la República de Guatemala, para el arreglo de reclamaciones de una y otra República, por medio de una Comisión Mixta cuya duración fué limitada por el término de un año contado desde la fecha de su primera junta, y considerando que ese término ha sido insuficiente para fallar todas las reclamaciones presentadas en tiempo oportuno;

El Presidente de los Estados Unidos Mexicanos y el Presidente de la República de Guatemala, animados del mismo deseo de no perjudicar los intereses reciprocos de los reclamantes de ambas naciones, y de que todos esos negocios queden terminados como se estipuló originalmente, manteniendo así los sentimientos amistosos que unen á las dos Repúblicas, han nombrado sus Plenipotenciarios, á saber:

El Presidente de los Estados Unidos Mexicanos, al Sr. Lic. D. Carlos Américo Lera, Encargado de Negocios *ad interim* de México en las Repúblicas de Centro-América; y El Presidente de la República de Guatemala, al Sr. Lic. D. Emilio de Léon, su Ministro de Relaciones Exteriores. Quienes, después de haberse mostrado sus respectivos Plenos Poderes y halládolos en buena y debida forma, han convenido en los artículos siguientes:

Art. I. Las altas Partes Contratantes convienen en renovar por una sola vez y por un término que no exceda de seis meses, la Convención del veintiséis de Enero de mil ochocientos ochenta y ocho, con el exclusivo objeto de que la Comisión Mixta que se nombre se ocupe en fallar los casos que le fueron sometidos en tiempo hábil, y quedaron sin resolverse el treinta y uno de Julio del corriente año.

Art. II. Los Comisionados se reunirán dentro de cuatro meses, contados desde el canje de las ratificaciones de esta Convención.

Los seis meses de que habla el articulo anterior se contarán desde la fecha de la primera junta que celebren los Comisionados. Dentro del primero de estos meses los Comisionados recibirán los alegatos que les presenten los respectivos Gobiernos ó sus Procuradores en apoyo ó descargo de las reclamaciones, y dentro de los cuatro siguientes fallarán, sin más trámites, todos los asuntos objeto de la presente Convención. Si no estuvieren conformes respecto de algún caso particular, fundarán por escrito su respectivo parecer y posarán inmediatamente al Arbitro todos los antecedentes del negocio, para que lo falle después de haber examinado las pruebas presentadas en pro ó en contra y de haber oído, si necesario fuere, á los Procuradores de los dos Gobiernos.

[1] *Tratados y Convenciones concluidos... por la República Mexicana*, 1896, p. 278.

El último mes se concede al Arbitro para resolver los asuntos que aun estuvieren pendientes de su decisión.

ART. III. Con la sola excepción de lo dispuesto en los dos artículos anteriores, se renueva in todas sus partes la citada Convención del veintiseis de Enero de mil ochocientos ochenta y ocho.

ART. IV. La presente Convención será ratificada de conformidad con las leyes vigentes en cada una de las dos Repúblicas, y el canje de las ratificaciones se hará en la ciudad de Guatemala tan pronto como fuere posible.

En fé de lo cual, los respectivos Plenipotenciarios han firmado por duplicado la presente Convención y puesto en ella sus sellos, el día veintidós de Diciembre de mil ochocientos noventa y uno[1].

XCI. France, Hollande.
29 novembre 1888.

Un des multiples arbitrages relatifs aux limites des diverses Guyanes. Il fut confié à l'Empereur de Russie, qui prononça la sentence en 1891.

Convention d'arbitrage relative aux limites des Guyanes, signée à Paris, le 29 novembre 1888.

Le Président de la République Française et Sa Majesté le Roi des Pays-Bas, voulant mettre fin à l'amiable au différend qui existe touchant les limites de leurs colonies respectives de la Guyane Française et de Surinam, en amont du confluent des rivières de l'Awa et du Tapanahoni qui forment ensemble le Maroni, ont nommé pour leurs plénipotentiaires: le Président de la République Française: M. René Goblet, député, ministre des affaires étrangères, etc. etc.; S. M. le Roi des Pays-Bas, M. le Jonkheer Alphonse-Lambert-Eugène de Stuers, son envoyé extraordinaire et ministre plénipotentiaire près le Gouvernement de la République française; lesquels dûment autorisés à cet effet sont convenus des articles suivants:

ART. I. Le gouvernement de la République française et le gouvernement de S. M. le roi des Pays-Bas conviennent de remettre à un arbitre le soin de procéder à la délimitation sus-mentionnée. Les deux gouvernements se mettront d'accord sur le choix de l'arbitre, auquel ils communiqueront tous les documents et tous les dossiers dont ils disposent.

ART. 2. Les deux gouvernements s'engagent à accepter comme jugement suprême et sans appel la décision que prendra l'arbitre et à s'y soumettre sans aucune réserve.

ART. 4. La présente convention aura un effet dès que les Chambres françaises et les Etats-Généraux des Pays-Bas l'auront approuvée, et dès que les ratifications en auront été échangées dans le plus bref délai possible.

En foi de quoi, les soussignés ont dressé la présente convention et y ont apposé leurs cachets.

Fait en double exemplaire, à Paris, le 29 novembre 1888.[1]

Convention complémentaire relative aux limites des Guyanes, signée à Paris le 28 avril 1889.

Le gouvernement de la République française et le gouvernement des Pays-Bas ont été informés que l'auguste souverain invité, conformément aux termes de la convention du 28 novembre 1888, à régler comme arbitre le différend concernant la délimitation de la Guyane Française et des colonies de Surinam, a cru, avant tout examen du litige, devoir décliner cette mission.

Considérant qu'il y a lieu d'espérer qu'il serait disposé à l'accepter encore si des pouvoirs plus étendus lui étaient dévolus, de manière à ne pas l'astreindre à désigner exclusivement comme limite une des deux rivières mentionnées dans la susdite convention, le gouvernement de la République française et le gouvernement des Pays-Bas, désireux d'assurer promptement l'arrangement du litige, se sont entendus par la présente déclaration pour accorder, à l'arbitre désigné avec l'assentiment des Parlements respectifs pour autant que nécessaire, le pouvoir subsidiaire d'adopter et de fixer éventuellement, comme solution intermédiaire, une autre limite sur l'étendue du territoire contesté, pour le cas où il ne parviendrait pas, après examen du différend, à fixer comme frontière une des deux rivières mentionnées dans la convention précitée.

En foi de quoi, les soussignés, Alexandre Ribot, député, ministre des affaires étrangères de la République française, et le chevalier de Stuers, envoyé extraordinaire et ministre plénipotentiaire de S. M. le roi des Pays-Bas près le gouvernement de la République française, ont dressé la présente déclaration et y ont apposé leurs cachets.[2]

---

[1] *Tratados y Convenciones concluidos ... por la República Mexicana*, 1896, p. 289

[1] F. DE MARTENS, *Nouveau Recueil Général*, 2ᵉ série, t. XVI, p. 730.

[2] ROUARD DE CARD. *Les Destinées de l'Arbitrage*, pag. 233.

Nous Alexandre III, par la grâce de Dieu empereur de toutes les Russies.

Le Gouvernement de la République française et le Gouvernement des Pays-Bas, ayant résolu, aux termes d'une convention conclue entre les deux pays, le 29 novembre 1888, de mettre fin à l'amiable au différend qui existe touchant les limites de leurs colonies respectives de la Guyane française et de Surinam, et de remettre à un arbitre le soin de procéder à cette délimitation, nous ont adressé la demande de nous charger de cet arbitrage.

Voulant répondre à la confiance que les deux puissances litigantes nous ont ainsi témoignée, et après avoir reçu l'assurance de leurs gouvernements d'accepter notre décision comme jugement suprême et sans appel, et de s'y soumettre sans aucune réserve, nous avons accepté la mission de résoudre comme arbitre le différend qui les divise et nous tenons pour juste de prononcer la sentence suivante :

Considérant que la convention du 28 août 1817, qui a fixé les conditions de la restitution de la Guyane française à la France par le Portugal, n'a jamais été reconnue par les Pays-Bas ;

Qu'en outre, cette convention ne saurait servir de base pour résoudre la question en litige, vu que le Portugal qui avait pris possession, en vertu du traité d'Utrecht de 1713, d'une partie de la Guyane française, ne pouvait restituer à la France en 1815 que le territoire qui lui avait été cédé ; or les limites de ce territoire ne se trouvent nullement définies par le traité d'Utrecht de 1713.

Considérant d'autre part :

Que le Gouvernement hollandais, ainsi que le démontrent des faits non contestés par le Gouvernement français, entretenait à la fin du siècle dernier des postes militaires sur l'Awa ;

Que les autorités françaises de la Guyane ont maintes fois reconnu les nègres établis sur le territoire contesté comme dépendant médiatement ou immédiatement de la domination hollandaise, et que ces autorités n'entraient en relations avec les tribus indigènes habitant ce territoire que par l'entremise et en présence des représentants des autorités hollandaises ;

Qu'il est admis sans conteste par les deux pays intéressés que le fleuve Maroni à partir de sa source, doit servir de limites entre leurs colonies respectives ;

Que la commission mixte de 1861 a recueilli des données en faveur de la reconnaissance de l'Awa comme cours supérieur du Maroni,

Par ces motifs :

Nous déclarons que l'Awa doit être considéré comme fleuve limitrophe devant servir de frontière entre les deux possessions.

En vertu de cette décision arbitrale, le territoire en amont du confluent des rivières Awa et Tapanahoni doit appartenir désormais à la Hollande, sans préjudice toutefois des droits acquis bona fide par les ressortissants français dans les limites du territoire qui avait été en litige.

Fait à Gatchina, le 13/25 mai 1891 [1].

XCII. Danemark, Etats-Unis d'Amérique.

6 décembre 1888.

Cette contestation a eu pour objet l'arrestation par les autorités danoises de deux navires appartenant à un citoyen américain. L'arbitre déclara qu'aucune responsabilité n'était encourue et refusa dès lors d'accorder une indemnité quelconque.

Agreement to submit to arbitration the claim against
Denmark of Carlos Butterfield & Co., concluded at
Copenhagen. December 6, 1888.

Whereas the Government of the United States of America has heretofore presented to the Kingdom of Denmark the claim of Carlos Butterfield and Company, of which Carlos Butterfield now deceased was the surviving partner, for an indemnity for the seizure and detention of the two vessels, the steamer Ben Franklin and the bark Catherine Augusta, by the authorities of the Island of St. Thomas of the Danish West India Islands in the years 1854 and 1855; for the refusal of the ordinary right to land cargo for the purpose of making repairs; for the injuries resulting from a shot fired into one of the vessels, and for other wrongs;

Whereas the said Governments have not been able to arrive at a conclusive settlement thereof; and

Whereas each of the parties hereto has entire confidence in the learning, ability and impartiality of Sir Edmund Monson, Her British Majesty's Envoy extraordinary and Minister plenipotentiary in Athens;

Now therefore the undersigned, Rasmus B. Anderson, Minister Resident of the United States of America at Copenhagen, and Baron O. D. Rosenörn-Lehn, Royal Danish Minister of Foreign Affairs, duly empowered thereto by their respective Governments have agreed upon the stipulations contained in the following articles:

[1] F. DE MARTENS, *Nouveau Recueil Général*, 2ᵉ série, t. XVIII, p. 100.

42

ARTICLE I. The said claim of Carlos Butterfield and Company shall be referred to the said Sir Edmund Monson, Her British Majesty's Envoy extraordinary and Minister plenipotentiary in Athens, as sole arbitrator thereof in conformity with the conditions hereinafter expressed, to which end the High Contracting Parties agree to communicate to him in writing their common desire to commit the matter to his arbitration.

ARTICLE II. The Arbitrator shall receive in evidence before him duly certified copies of all documents, records, affidavits, or other papers heretofore filed in support of or against the claim in the proper department of the respective Governments, copies of which shall at the same time be furnished to the other Government.

Each Government shall file its evidence before the arbitrator within seventy-five days after its receipt of notice of his acceptance of the position conferred upon him.

Each party shall be allowed seventy-five days thereafter to file with the arbitrator a written argument. The arbitrator shall render his award within sixty days after the date at which the arguments of both parties shall have been received.

ARTICLE III. The expenses of such arbitration, which shall include the compensation of a clerk at the rate of not more than two hundred dollars a month, should the arbitrator request such aid, shall be borne by the two Governments jointly in equal moeties.

ARTICLE IV. The High Contracting Parties agree to accept the decision of the arbitrator as final and conclusive and to abide by and perform the same in good faith and without unnecessary delay.

ARTICLE V. This agreement shall be ratified by each Government and the ratifications exchanged at Washington as soon as possible.

In witness whereof, the respective Plenipotentiaries have signed and sealed the present agreement in duplicate, in the English and Danish languages.

Done at Copenhagen this 6th day of December in the year of our Lord, one thousand eight hundred and eighty-eight[1].

Award in the case of Carlos Butterfield and Co., given in Athens, January 22, 1890.

The undersigned, Her Britannic Majesty's envoy extraordinary and minister plenipotentiary to His Majesty the King of the Hellenes, having

been nominated by a convention signed at Copenhagen on the 6th of December, 1888, arbitrator in respect of the claim preferred by the Government of the United States against that of Denmark for compensation due by the latter to the former on account of the alleged seizure and detention in the years 1854 and 1855 of the steamer *Ben Franklin* and the bark *Catherine Augusta* by the authorities of the island of St. Thomas, in the Danish West Indian Islands has had before him, and was duly considered, the evidence tendered by the respective parties to the said convention, and has carefully studied the arguments in which the merits of the case are set forth according to the views of the two Governments.

The argument of the United States places the question before the arbitrator as follows: What indemnity is due from the Government of Denmark for losses and injuries growing out of the following wrongful acts committed by the Danish authorities at the island of St. Thomas, West Indies:

First. The seizure and detention of the American bark *Catherine Augusta*.

Second. The refusal to her of the ordinary right to land her cargo for the purpose of making repairs, and herein of the exaction of unusual, onerous, and illegal conditions.

Third. The seizure and detention of the steamer *Ben Franklin*.

Fourth. The wrongful firing of a shot into the last-named steamer, and the injuries resulting therefrom.

The argument of the United States contends that, as it is indubitable that a vessel injured by the elements has a right to put into a friendly port for repairs, and a further right to land her cargo in order to effect such repairs, and as it is equally indubitable that a peaceful vessel may not, under ordinary circumstances, be fired into and the lives of those on board imperiled, the mere statement of the case, with regard to the facts of which there is no material divergence in the evidence presented by the respective parties, establishes under the principles of international law, an indubitable ground upon which the claim of indemnity may safely be permitted to rest.

The Danish Government, on the other hand, argues, in the first place, that, setting aside the original merits of the case altogether, the amount of time which was allowed to elapse before the claim was first presented, and the intermittent manner in which it was subsequently pressed constitute in themselves a conclusive objection to the validity of the claim.

[1] F. DE MARTENS, *Nouveau Recueil Général*, 2me série, t. XV, p. 790.

It appears convenient to settle this preliminary point at once; and the arbitrator has no difficulty in deciding that, although neither Butterfield and Company nor the United States Government have used due diligence in the prosecution of the claim, and have thereby exposed themselves to the legitimate criticism of the Danish Government on their dilatory action, the delay caused thereby can not bar the recovery of just and reasonable compensation for the alleged injuries, should the further consideration of the merits of the case result in the decision that such compensation is due.

Those merits depend, as is legitimately stated in the Danish argument, upon the answers which the arbitrator must return to three questions which relate to the legality of the measures adopted by the Danish authorities with regard to the two vessels—measures which, as aforesaid, are described by the argument of the United States as 'seizure and detention'. The question of the firing upon the *Ben Franklin* will be treated separately.

The three questions above referred to are:

1. Had the local authorities legitimate grounds of suspicion warranting them in taking precautions?

2. Is there reasonable ground for objecting to the nature and extent of the measures taken by those authorities?

3. Where those measures allowed to remain in force for a longer period than necessary?

First. The careful consideration of the whole correspondence set forth in the evidence submitted by the respective parties had led the arbitrator to decide the first question in the affirmative, and he consequently declares that the authorities of St. Thomas were warranted in taking precautions to prevent the possible violation of the neutrality of the port by acts of the nature of an equipement of armed vessels intended to operate against a friendly power.

Second. In deciding the second question, the arbitrator must point out that the words 'seizure and detention' constitute an erroneous description of the measures taken by the Danish authorities. Those measures consisted in exacting from the consignees a bond of moderate amount, for which their personal guaranty was accepted, that the vessels, if allowed to be repaired, would not be employed for purposes of aggression against a power with which Denmark was at peace; and in a subsequent guaranty that the cargo, consisting of munitions of war, which had to be landed in order that the ships might be repaired, should not be replaced on board or reexported without satisfactory proof being given

to the authorities as to its destination being a legitimate one, this latter precaution being obligatory on the governor in virtue of the law which forbids the free export of arms. The ships were in no sense seized nor detained, and the precautionary measures proposed by the governor of the island were cheerfully acquiesced in by the consignees and the commercial agent of the United States. The arbitrator is of opinion that these measures were reasonable, and in no sense oppressive, and that they can not be considered to have been extorted under duress.

Third. It appears from the correspondence that no request for permission to reload the cargo was made to the governor of St. Thomas until the 7th of May, 1855, and that that permission was almost immediately granted; nor is there in the evidence presented to the arbitrator anything to warrant the presumption that, had such a request been preferred at an earlier date, it would have been refused. The arbitrator must therefore decide that the precautionary measures were not maintained longer than was necessary.

The conclusions arrived at by the arbitrator on these points will, therefore, have the effect of disallowing all claim for compensation for the measures taken by the Danish authorities of St. Thomas in regard to the vessels *Ben Franklin* and *Catherine Augusta* conjointly.

There remains the question of the firing upon the *Ben Franklin*. The arbitrator is of opinion that the temporary engagement of the steamer by the representatives of the Royal Mail Steamship Company to convey passengers and mails to Barbadoes did not *ipso facto* entitle her to the enjoyment of those privileges accorded by the Danish Government to the regular packets of the company, in virtue of which they were allowed to leave the port of St. Thomas at night without complying with the formalities imposed on all other merchant vessels, including even Danish mail packets. It is clear that the captain of the *Ben Franklin* neglected to comply with these formalities, and consequently the Danish Government can not be fixed with the responsibility of what unfortunately ensued. It is pertinent to add that the assertion that the action of the commandant of the fort was subsequently disapproved by his superiors and that he was dismissed from his appointment is absolutely erroneous.

The arbitrator has therefore only further to declare that neither in respect of the firing upon the steam ship *Ben Franklin*, any more than in the treatment of that steamer and of her consort, the *Catherine Augusta*, is any compensation due from the Danish Government.

In testimony of which the arbitrator has hereto set his hand and seal, in duplicate, on the twenty second day of January, in the year of our Lord one thousand eight hundred and ninety [1].

XCIII. Costa Rica, Nicaragua.

10 janvier 1889.

Cet arbitrage porte sur une question accessoire relative à l'interprétation du traité de 1858, qui a fait l'objet de la convention de 1886 et de la sentence de 1888 : notamment sur la question de savoir si le Nicaragua peut traiter au sujet du canal interocéanique sans l'intervention du Costa Rica. Les ratifications de la convention ne furent pas échangées dans les délais stipulés et les deux gouvernements ont considéré qu'elle avait, par ce fait, perdu sa vigueur.

Convención de arbitraje celebrada entre las Repúblicas de Costa Rica y Nicaragua, en la ciudad de San José Enero 10, 1889.

Los Gobiernos de las Repúblicas de Costa Rica y Nicaragua, en el proposito de terminar de una manera cordial la cuestión que ultimamente ha surgido con motivo de haber celebrado el Gobierno Costarricense un contrato para la excavación del Canal Interoceánico, con la *Asociación del Canal de Nicaragua*, han nombrado sus Plenipotenciarios, á saber :

El Gobierno de Costa Rica, al Excelentísimo señor don Manuel J. Jiménez, su Secretario de Relaciones Exteriores ; y el Gobierno de Nicaragua, al Excelentísimo señor General don Isidro Urtecho, Enviado extraordinario y Ministro Plenipotenciario en el Congreso Centroamericano.

Quienes, canjeados los plenos poderes y habiendo conferenciado, estuvieron en desacuerdo formal y ocurrieron á la mediación oportunamente ofrecida y aceptada de las Repúblicas de Guatemala, Honduras y Salvador, y que respectivamente estuvieron representadas por sus Enviados Extraordinarios y Ministros Plenipotenciarios cerca del Gobierno Costarricense y Ministros Plenipotenciarios en el Congreso Centroamericano, los Excelentísimos señores Licenciado don José Farfán H. ; Licenciado don Jerónimo Zelaya, Ministro de Relaciones Exteriores de Honduras, y Doctor don Francisco E. Galindo, Enviado Extraordinario y Ministro Plenipotenciario cerca del Gobierno de Nicaragua.

[1] *Foreign Relations of the U. S.*, 1889, p. 158.

Y habiendo continuado las conferencias con la intervención de los mediadores, cuyas credenciales fueron también reconocidas, los Plenipotenciarios de Costa Rica y Nicaragua han convenido en lo siguiente :

ART. 1. Se somete á la decisión arbitral del Excelentísimo señor Presidente de los Estados Unidos de América, la cuestión suscitada por el Gobierno de Nicaragua contra el de Costa Rica, con motivo de haber celebrado éste con la *Asociación del Canal de Nicaragua* el contrato denominado *Zeledón-Menocal*, que lleva la fecha del 31 de Julio del año próximo pasado.

ART. II. El arbitro decidirá :

Si Costa Rica, de conformidad con el Tratado de límites celebrado con Nicaragua el 15 de abril de 1858 y el laudo que lo declara vigente y lo aclara, dictado por el Excelentísimo señor Presidente de los Estados Unidos de América el 22 de marzo del año próximo pasado, tuvo facultad ó no para celebrar el contrato Zeledón-Menocal.

En el caso de decidirse que Costa Rica tuvo facultad para celebrar el referido contrato, el arbitro decidirá :

Si los derechos que le reconocen á la República de Costa Rica el tratado de límites y el laudo ya citados, fueron traspasados ó no por el Gobierno Costarricense, en perjuicio de los derechos de Nicaragua, al pactar con la Asociación del Canal de Nicaragua, alguno ó algunos de los articulos de que consta el contrato Zeledón-Menocal ?

El arbitro senalará el articulo ó articulos en que Costa Rica hubiese traspasado sus derechos en perjuicio de los de Nicaragua, é indicará, en todo caso, el sentido en que tales derechos hubieren sido traspasados.

ART. III. El contrato Zeledón-Menocal ya referido, será considerado nulo si el laudo le negare en absoluto a Costa Rica la facultad de celebrarlo.

Serán considerados nulos los articulos del contrato, respecto de los cuales el laudo declare que Costa Rica traspase sus derechos en perjuicio de Nicaragua.

Las declaraciones que el arbitro hiciere contra la validez del contrato o contra la validez de alguno ó algunos de sus articulos, sentarán precedente entre Costa Rica y Nicaragua.

Por el contrario, la declaración de la validez del contrato y los articulos que no fueren impugnados por el arbitro, sentarán asimismo precedente entre Costa Rica y Nicaragua para el caso de no ejecutarse el contrato.

ART. IV. Dentro de los treinta días siguientes al canje de las ratificaciones de la presente

Convención, los Gobiernos contratantes solicitarán la aceptación del arbitro.

ART. V. Si el arbitro elegido no podiere desempeñar el cargo, ambos Gobiernos se pondran de acuerdo para nombrar otro dentro de noventa dias, contados desde aquel en que el Excelentísimo señor Presidente de los Estados Unidos de América notificare su excusa á ambos Gobiernos o á sus Representantes en Washington.

ART. VI. Los procedimientos y términos á que deberá sujetarse el juicio arbitral serán los siguientes:

a) Dentro de los treinta días siguientes á la fecha en que la aceptación del arbitro hubiere sido notificada á las partes, estas le presentarán sus alegatos y documentos en idioma español, pudiendo acompañar en idioma ingles la traduccion correspondiente.

b) El arbitro comunicará al Representante de cada Gobierno el alegato del contrario dentro de los ocho días siguientes á la presentación.

c) Cada Gobierno tendrá el derecho de rebatir el alegato de la parte contraria dentro de los noventa días siguientes á la fecha en que el respectivo alegato le fuere comunicado, y con las replicas podrán también presentarse documentos.

d) El arbitro deberá pronunciar su fallo, para que sea valedero, dentro de los ciento veinte días siguientes á la fecha en que se hubiere vencido el término para contestar alegatos, hayanse ó no presentado estos.

ART. VII. La decisión arbitral, cualquiera que sea, se tendrá como tratado perfecto, obligatorio y perpetuo entre las Altas Partes contratantes, y no admitirá recurso alguno.

ART. VIII. Esta convención será sometida en Costa Rica y Nicaragua á las ratificaciones constitucionales, y el canje de estas se verificará en las ciudades de San José de Costa Rica ó Managua, a más tardar al 30 de abril del corriente año.

En fé de lo cual la firman y le ponen sus sellos respectivos en dos ejemplares, también firmados y sellados por los Excelentísimos señores Enviados Extraordinarios y Ministros Plenipotenciarios de las Repúblicas mediadoras.

Hecho en la ciudad de San José de Costa Rica á los diez días del mes de enero de mil ochocientos ochenta y nueve, sexagesimo octavo de la Indepencia de Centro-América. [1]

---

[1] *Memoria de la Secretaria de Relaciones Exteriores* (Costa Rica) 1889.

XCIV. Etats-Unis d'Amérique, Mexique.

1er mars 1889.

La commission, désignée par la convention de 1889 et devenue permanente depuis 1900, a plus spécialement pour objet de régler les questions de frontière nées du déplacement du lit du Rio Grande et du Colorado. Ce n'est que dans les cas où les commissionnaires sont d'accord que leurs décisions ont un caractère définitif.

Convention between the United States of America and the United States of Mexico to facilitate the carrying out of the principles contained in the Treaty of November 12, 1884, and to avoid the difficulties occasioned by reason of the changes which take place in the beds of the Rio Grande and Colorado Rivers, signed at Washington, March 1, 1889.

The United States of America and the United States of Mexico, desiring to facilitate the carrying out of the principles contained in the treaty of November 12th, 1884, and to avoid the difficulties occasioned by reason of the changes which take place in the bed of the Rio Grande and that of the Colorado River, in that portion thereof where they serve as a boundary between the two Republics, have resolved to conclude a treaty for the attainment of these objects and have appointed as their respective Plenipotentiaries:

The President of the United States of America, Thomas F. Bayard, Secretary of State of the United States of America; and

The President of the United States of Mexico, Matias Romero, envoy extraordinary and minister plenipotentiary of the United States of Mexico, at Washington,

Who, after having exhibited their respective full powers, and having found the same to be in good and due form, have agreed upon the following articles:

ARTICLE I. All differences or questions that may arise on that portion of the frontier between the United States of America and the United States of Mexico where the Rio Grande and the Colorado River form the boundary line, whether such differences or questions grow out of alterations or changes in the bed of the aforesaid Rio Grande and that of the aforesaid Colorado River, or of works that may be constructed in said rivers, or of any other cause affecting the boundary line, shall be submitted for examination and decision to an International Boundary Commission, which shall have exclusive jurisdiction in the case of said differences or questions.

ARTICLE II. The International Boundary Commission shall be composed of a Commissioner appointed by the President of the United States of America, and of an other appointed by the President of the United States of Mexico, in accordance with the constitutional provisions of each country, of a Consulting Engineer, appointed in the same manner by each Government, and of such Secretaries and Interpretes as either Government may see fit to add to its Commission. Each Government separately shall fix the salaries and emoluments of the members of its Commission.

ARTICLE III. The International Boundary Commission shall not transact any business unless both Commissioners are present.

It shall sit on the frontier of the two contracting countries, and shall establish itself at such places as it may determine upon; it shall, however, repair to places at which any of the difficulties or questions mentioned in this convention may arise, as soon as it shall have been duly notified thereof.

ARTICLE IV. When, owing to natural causes, any change shall take place in the bed of the Rio Grande or in that of the Colorado River, in that portion thereof wherein those rivers form the boundary line between the two countries, which may affect the boundary line, notice of that fact shall be given by the proper local authorities on both sides to their respective Commissioners of the International Boundary Commission, on receiving which notice it shall be the duty of the said Commission to repair to the place where the change has taken place or the question has arisen, to make a personal examination of such change, to compare it with the bed of the river as it was before the change took place, as shown by the surveys, and to decide whether it has occurred through avulsion or erosion for the effects of Articles I and II of the convention of November 12th, 1884; having done this it shall make suitable annotations on the surveys of the boundary line.

ARTICLE V. Whenever the local authorities on any point of the frontier between the United States of America and the United States of Mexico, in that portion in which the Rio Grande and the Colorado River form the boundary between the two countries, shall think that works are being constructed, in either of those rivers, such as are prohibited by Article III of the convention of November 12th, 1884, or by Article VII of the treaty of Guadalupe Hidalgo of February 2, 1848, they shall so notify their respective Commissioner, in order that the latter may at once submit the matter to the International Boundary Commission, and that said Commission may proceed, in accordance with the provisions of the foregoing article, to examine the case, and that it may decide whether the work is among the number of those which are permitted, or of those which are prohibited by the stipulations of those treaties.

The Commission may provisionally suspend the construction of the works in question pending the investigation of the matter, and if it shall fail to agree on this point, the works shall be suspended, at the instance of one of the two Governments.

ARTICLE VI. In either of these cases, the Commission shall make a personal examination of the matter which occasions the change, the question or the complaint and shall give its decision in regard to the same in doing which it shall comply with the requirements established by a body of regulations to be prepared by the said Commission and approved by both Governments.

ARTICLE VII. The International Boundary Commission shall have power to call for papers and information, and it shall be the duty of the authorities of each of the two countries to send it any papers that it may call for, relating to any boundary question in which it may have jurisdiction in pursuance of this convention.

The said Commission shall have power to summon any witnesses whose testimony it may think proper to take, and it shall be the duty of all persons thus summoned to appear before the same and to give their testimony, which shall be taken in accordance with such by-laws and regulations as may be adopted by the Commission and approved by both Governments. In case of the refusal of a witness to appear, he shall be compelled to do so and to this end the Commission may make use of the same means that are used by the courts of the respective countries to compel the attendance of witnesses, in conformity with their respective laws.

ARTICLE VIII. If both Commissioners shall agree to a decision, their judgment shall be considered binding upon both Governments, unless one of them shall disapprove it within one month reckoned from the day on which it shall have been pronounced. In the latter case, both Governments shall take cognizance of the matter and shall decide it amicably, bearing constantly in mind the stipulation of Article XXI of the treaty of Guadalupe Hidalgo of February 2, 1848.

The same shall be the case when the Commissioners shall fail to agree concerning the point which occasions the question, the complaint or the change, in which case each Commissioner shall prepare a report in writing, which he shall lay before his Government.

ARTICLE IX. This convention shall be ratified by both parties, in accordance with the provision of their respective constitutions, and the ratifications thereof shall be exchanged at Washington, as speedily as possible, and shall be in force from the date of exchange of ratifications for a period of five years.

In testimony whereof the undersigned Plenipotentiaries have signed and sealed it.

Done in duplicate, in the city of Washington, in the English and Spanish languages, on the 1st day of March one thousand eight hundred and eighty-nine [1].

Des prorogations successives s'imposèrent et les deux Gouvernements, par une convention du 21 novembre 1900, ainsi que nous l'avons indiqué plus haut, prolongèrent les pouvoirs de la commission arbitrale pour une période indéfinie.

Convention extending for an indefinite period the treaty of March 1, 1889, signed at Washington, November 21, 1900.

Whereas the United States of America and the United States of Mexico desire to give full effect to the provisions of the Convention concluded and signed in Washington, March 1, 1889, to facilitate the execution of the provisions contained in the Treaty signed by the two High Contracting Parties on the 12th of November 1884, and to avoid the difficulties arising from the changes which are taking place in the beds of the Bravo del Norte and Colorado Rivers in those parts which serve as boundary between the two Republics;

And whereas the period fixed by Article XI of the Convention of March 1, 1889, extended by the Conventions of October 1, 1895, November 6, 1896, October 29, 1897, December 2, 1898, and December 22, 1899, expires on the 24th of December 1900;

And whereas the two High Contracting Parties deem it expedient to indefinitely continue the period fixed by Article IX of the Convention of March 1, 1889, and by the sole Article of the Convention of October 1, 1895, that of November 6, 1896, that of October 29, 1897, that of December 2, 1898, and that of December 22, 1899, in order that the International Boundary Commission may be able to continue the examination and decision of the cases submitted to it, they have, for that purpose, appointed their respective Plenipotentiaries, to wit:

The President of the United States of America, John Hay, Secretary of State of the United States of America; and

The President of the United States of Mexico, Manuel de Aspiroz, Ambassador Extraordinary and Plenipotentiary of the United States of Mexico at Washington;

Who after communicated to each other their respective full powers, found in good and due forme, have agreed upon and concluded the following article:

The said Convention of March 1, 1889, as extended on the several dates above mentioned, and the Commission established thereunder shall continue in force and effect indefinitely, subject, however, to the right of either contracting party to dissolve the said Commission by giving six months-notice to the other; but such dissolution of the Commission shall not prevent the two governments from thereafter agreeing to revive the said Commission, or to reconstitute the same, according to the terms of the said Convention; and the said Convention of March 1, 1889, as hereby continued, may be terminated twelve months after notice of a desire for its termination shall have been given in due form by one of the two contracting parties to the other.

This Convention shall be ratified by the two High Contracting Parties in conformity with their respective Constitutions, and the ratifications shall be exchanged in Washington as soon as possible.

In testimony whereof, we the undersigned, by virtue of our respective power, have signed this Convention in duplicate, in the English and Spanish languages and have affixed our respective seals.

Done in the City of Washington on the 21st day of November, one thousand nine hundred [1].

XCV. Allemagne, Grande-Bretagne.

.... avril 1889.

Il a été impossible d'obtenir l'indication exacte de la date de cet arbitrage, ni les termes du compromis qui a précédé la sentence que nous reproduisons.

Sentence rendue au sujet du différend de Lamu, par le Baron Lambermont, prononcée à Bruxelles le 17 août 1889.

Nous, baron Lambermont, Ministre d'Etat de Sa Majesté le Roi des Belges,

Ayant accepté les fonctions d'arbitre qui nous ont été conférées par le gouvernement de S. M.

l'Empereur de l'Allemagne, Roi de Prusse, et par le gouvernement de S. M. la Reine de Grande-Bretagne et d'Irlande, Impératrice des Indes, au sujet d'un différend survenu entre la Compagnie allemande de Witu et la Compagnie impériale anglaise de l'Afrique orientale;

Animé du désir sincère de répondre par une décision scrupuleuse et impartiale à la confiance que les deux gouvernements nous ont témoignée;

Ayant, à cet effet, dûment examiné et mûrement pesé les documents qui ont été produits de part et d'autre;

Et voulant statuer sur l'objet du litige qui est l'affermage des douanes et de l'administration de l'île de Lamu, située à la côte orientale d'Afrique;

L'une des parties revendiquant pour la Compagnie allemande de Witu la priorité du droit quant à cette prise à ferme;

L'autre soutenant que le feu Sultan et le Sultan actuel de Zanzibar se sont engagés à concéder ce même affermage à la Compagnie impériale anglaise de l'Afrique orientale et que les objections élevées du côté de l'Allemagne ne sont pas de nature à mettre obstacle à ce que le Souverain de l'île de Lamu remplisse les obligations contractées par son prédécesseur et par lui-même envers cette société.

I.

Considérant que le mémoire présenté par le gouvernement impérial allemand fait, en premier lieu, dériver le droit de la Compagnie de Witu de la convention intervenue, les 29 octobre et 1er novembre 1886, entre l'Allemagne et l'Angleterre et de la portée qui aurait été attachée à cet accord par les puissances contractantes;

Attendu que la dite convention a circonscrit le terrain sur lequel elle devra recevoir son application dans des limites expressément déterminées, à savoir, en partant de la mer, la Rowuma au sud et le Tana au nord;

Qu'elle a ensuite divisé cet espace en deux zones, séparées par une ligne de démarcation suivant la Wanga ou Umbe;

Que, de ces deux zones, l'une est attribuée exclusivement à l'influence allemande qui s'exercera au *sud* de la ligne de démarcation, et l'autre exclusivement à l'influence anglaise qui s'exercera au *nord* de la même ligne;

Que les limites respectives des deux zones d'influence sont ainsi nettement fixées et sont formées par la ligne de démarcation et le périmètre au delà duquel elles ne pourraient s'étendre sans sortir du territoire régi par l'arrangement;

Attendu que, pour tirer de l'esprit ou du sens de la convention une conséquence qui ne naît

pas de son texte et qui attribuerait à l'Allemagne une liberté exclusive d'action sur les territoires situés au nord du Tana, il faudrait qu'une entente spéciale et nouvelle se fût, à cet effet, établie entre les puissances contractantes et qu'elle fût dûment constatée;

Qu'il n'est produit aucun acte justifiant de l'existence d'une telle entente, et

Que cette constatation ne résulte point de la note du gouvernement britannique en date du 7 septembre 1888, puisque, en reconnaissant que la sphère d'influence anglaise ne s'étend pas jusqu'à la rivière Osi, ce document est en parfaite concordance avec les termes de l'accord de 1886, qui limite son application aux territoires compris entre la Rowuma et le Tana,

Par ces motifs:

Nous sommes d'avis que, sauf la clause qui reconnaît comme appartenant au territoire de Witu la bande côtière entre Kripini et l'extrémité septentrionale de la baie de Manda, l'accord anglo-allemand des 29 octobre et 1er novembre 1886 n'étend pas plus ses effets au delà du Tana qu'au delà de la Rowuma et ne donne à aucune des parties un droit de préférence quant à l'affermage des douanes et de l'administration de l'île de Lamu, située en dehors des limites dans lesquelles cet arrangement doit, d'après ses propres termes, recevoir son application.

II.

Considérant que, selon le mémoire allemand, les îles de la baie de Manda, au point de vue géographique, appartiennent au pays de Witu dont elles formeraient le prolongement; que, envisagée sous le rapport commercial, l'île de Lamu est le lieu de dépôt des marchandises qui arrivent du pays de Witu ou qui sont destinées à cette possession allemande, et enfin que sa dépendance du continent apparaît encore dans l'ordre juridique ou politique à raison des relations multipliées des habitants de l'île avec le continent et des questions de propriété ou de culture qui s'y rattachent, l'ensemble de ces faits démontrant que l'administration de l'île doit être confiée aux mains qui détiennent celle du continent;

Considérant que, de son côté, le mémoire anglais représente l'île de Lamu comme étant, depuis longtemps, un entrepôt du commerce britannique, un lieu d'escale pour les bateaux à vapeur de la Compagnie des Indes britanniques desservant l'Afrique orientale, et un centre de commerce qui est presque exclusivement entre les mains de négociants anglais;

Attendu qu'aucune déduction tirée du voisinage du continent ne saurait, en ce qui concerne l'île de Lamu, prévaloir contre la clause formelle de l'accord anglo-allemand des 29 octobre et 1er novembre 1886, qui range cette île parmi les possessions dont la souveraineté est reconnu au Sultan de Zanzibar, et

Que, si des considérations basées sur l'intérêt économique et administratif ou sur des convenances politiques peuvent mettre en lumière les avantages ou les inconvénients qu'offrirait une solution conforme aux vues de l'une ou de l'autre des parties, de telles raisons ne tiennent pas lieu d'un mode d'acquisition reconnu par le droit international,

Par ces motifs :

Nous sommes d'avis que ni la dépendance géographique, ni la dépendance commerciale, ni l'intérêt politique proprement dit ne mettent aucune des parties en position de réclamer, à titre de droit, la cession des douanes et de l'administration de l'île de Lamu.

III.

Les questions d'un caractère préjudiciel ainsi résolues et le débat étant amené sur le terrain des engagements qu'auraient pris les Sultans de Zanzibar envers les deux parties :

Considérant qu'il y a lieu de rechercher si, et jusqu'à quel point, les engagements invoqués par les deux parties réunissent les conditions nécessaires à la justification de leur existence et de leur validité ;

En ce qui concerne la Compagnie allemande de Witu :

Considérant que, le 10 décembre 1887, le consul général d'Allemagne et M. Töppen, représentant de la Compagnie de Witu, ont été reçus en audience par le Sultan Sayd Bargash, audience dont le consul général a rendu compte à son gouvernement par un rapport qui n'est pas produit, mais dont le mémoire allemand termine l'analyse en ces termes : « Le résultat de cet entretien développé peut être résumé en ce sens que le Sultan se déclarait être immédiatement prêt (sofort sich bereit erklärte) à accorder la concession pour les îles de la baie de Manda à la Compagnie de Witu aussitôt que l'autre arrangement avec la Compagnie orientale africaine allemande serait conclu, et qu'il ne désirait conserver sa liberté d'action que pour la fixation de l'un ou de l'autre mode de l'indemniser en argent » ; et que, dans sa lettre du 16 novembre 1888 au Sultan Sayd Khalifa, le consul général s'exprime ainsi : « Je me permets de rappeler que sous Sayd Bargash déjà des négociations se sont poursuivies tendant à une concession des îles de la baie de Manda à la Compagnie allemande de Witu, dont M. Töppen est le représentant à Lamu ; Sayd Bargash a reçu M. Töppen en ma présence et il s'est montré prêt à prendre un

semblable engagement (Sayd Bargash hat seine Bereitwilligkeit, ein derartiges Abkommen zu treffen, ausgesprochen) aussitôt que la convention avec la Compagnie orientale africaine serait arrivée à conclusion » ;

Attendu que les termes dont se serait servi le Sultan, pris dans leur sens naturel, impliqueraient l'intention de conclure une convention ;

Que, pour transformer cette intention en une promesse unilatérale valant convention, l'accord des volontés aurait dû se manifester par la promesse expresse de l'une des parties, jointe à l'acceptation de l'autre, et que cet accord de volontés aurait dû porter sur les éléments essentiels qui constituent l'objet de la convention ;

Attendu que, dans une espèce telle que celle dont il s'agit, la prise à ferme des douanes et de l'administration d'un territoire ou d'un port devait être un contrat synallagmatique, comprenant de la part du bailleur la cession de l'exercice de droits souverains qui peuvent être formulés de manières très diverses quant à leur objet et leur durée et consistant de la part du preneur en une redevance fixe ou proportionnelle ;

Que dans les paroles attribuées au Sultan, telles qu'elles sont résumées par le mémoire allemand et reproduites par la lettre du consul général d'Allemagne du 16 novembre 1888, les conditions essentielles du contrat à intervenir ne se trouvent pas déterminées ;

Attendu que, si aucune loi ne prescrit une forme spéciale pour les conventions entre Etats indépendants, il n'en est pas moins contraire aux usages internationaux de contracter verbalement des engagements de cette nature et de cette importance ;

Que l'adoption de la forme écrite s'impose particulièrement dans les rapports avec les gouvernements de nations peu civilisées, qui souvent n'attachent la force obligatoire qu'aux promesses faites en une forme solennelle ou par écrit ;

Que, surtout dans l'espèce, l'existence d'une convention verbale devrait résulter de stipulations formelles et qu'on ne pourrait, sans grave détriment pour la sécurité et la facilité des rapports internationaux, la déduire de la simple déclaration qu'on est prêt à accorder une concession ;

Attendu qu'il n'est produit d'autres pièces écrites vers l'époque dont il s'agit que la lettre, en date du 21 novembre 1887, par laquelle le consul général d'Allemagne a transmis au Sultan Sayd Bargash la proposition de M. Töppen et l'accusé de réception du Sultan, daté du même jour, et qui ne se prononçait pas sur le fond ;

Que, entre le 10 décembre 1887, date de la promesse qu'aurait faite le Sultan, et le 28 mars 1888, date de sa mort, il n'est fourni aucun document, aucune indication écrite ou verbale

43

émanant de Sa Hautesse et constatant ou impliquant son assentiment à la proposition du représentant de la Compagnie Witu ;

Que, d'après les assurances réitérées du Sultan actuel et données soit au consul général d'Allemagne, soit au consul général d'Angleterre, on n'aurait découvert, ni dans les archives du sultanat, ni dans les souvenirs des employés, aucune trace de cet acquiescement et que, eût-on retrouvé les pièces écrites qui viennent d'être mentionnées, l'accusé de réception du Sultan Sayd Bargash aurait témoigné qu'à leur date Sa Hautesse n'avait rien préjugé ;

Que, dès lors, quel que soit le sens que l'on attache aux paroles du Sultan Sayd Bargash, la preuve de l'ouverture de la négociation a seule été administrée ; qu'en ce qui concerne l'engagement lui-même, s'il en est fait mention dans la lettre que le consul général d'Allemagne a écrite au Sultan, le 16 novembre 1888, et s'il est rapporté dans la dépêche adressée par le même agent à son propre gouvernement à la suite de l'audience du 10 décembre 1887, il doit être de principe, en matière internationale comme en toute autre, et toute question de bonne foi à part, qu'on ne peut se créer de titre à soi-même ;

Attendu enfin, quelque digne de confiance que soit l'agent consulaire et sa bonne foi étant absolument mise hors de cause, que les paroles du Sultan Sayd Bargash ont été prononcées en arabe, recueillies et traduites par un drogman sans qu'il soit possible de contrôler la fidélité de cette traduction et que leur interprétation n'a été ni confirmée par le défunt Sultan, ni reconnue par son successeur,

Par ces motifs :

Nous sommes d'avis que la preuve de l'engagement qu'aurait contracté le Sultan Sayd Bargash au 10 décembre 1887 d'affermer les douanes et l'administration de l'île de Lamu à la Compagnie allemande de Witu n'est pas fournie à suffisance de droit, et

Que, en conséquence, la dite compagnie ne peut fonder aucun droit de préférence ou de priorité sur les déclarations du Sultan au cours de l'entretien qui a eu lieu à cette date ;

Considérant qu'il y a lieu d'examiner si les faits accomplis depuis l'avènement du Sultan actuel ne sont pas venus modifier le bien-fondé de ces conclusions ;

Attendu que, d'après le mémoire allemand, le Sultan Sayd Khalifa aurait déclaré au consul général d'Allemagne, en juin 1888, qu'il n'accorderait plus aucune concession sans s'être entendu avec les représentants de l'Allemagne et de l'Angleterre et que, d'après la lettre du consul général d'Allemagne au Sultan, en date du

16 novembre suivant, ce dernier l'aurait assuré qu'il n'existait pas encore de proposition anglaise et que, s'il s'en produisait, il demanderait à l'avance l'opinion du consul général d'Allemagne ;

Attendu que, dans sa lettre du 12 janvier 1889 au dit consul général, Sayd Khalifa se défend d'avoir fait ou pu faire ces déclarations, l'erreur pouvant dans son opinion provenir d'un malentendu attribuable au drogmanat et que, dans sa lettre du 16 du même mois au consul général d'Angleterre, lettre insérée au mémoire anglais, Sa Hautesse a répété ses dénégations ;

Que, sans mettre en question la bonne foi des parties, on peut et on doit reconnaître que les déclarations dont il s'agit n'auraient pu conférer par elles-mêmes aucun droit à la Compagnie de Witu sur l'île de Lamu, et

Que, au surplus, quant à leur portée à d'autres égards, elles tomberaient par leur forme sous l'application des principes ci-dessus développés,

Par ces motifs :

Nous sommes d'avis que les faits postérieurs à l'entretien du 10 décembre 1887 n'ont pas changé sa portée, telle qu'elle est définie dans les conclusions précédentes ;

En ce qui concerne la Compagnie impériale anglaise de l'Afrique orientale :

Considérant que, dans le système du mémoire anglais, les Sultans de Zanzibar auraient, dès 1877, constamment tenu à la disposition de M. William Mackinnon, de ses associés et de la future compagnie britannique une concession de territoires comprenant l'île de Lamu, que la dite concession, loin d'être jamais rejetée ou retirée, aurait été acceptée de temps en temps pour ce qui concerne certaines parties de ces territoires, le reste, et particulièrement celle-ci, ayant été réservé à la disposition ultérieure des dites personnes et de la dite compagnie ;

Attendu que le contrat de cession qui doit servir de base à ces promesses n'est représenté qu'en un projet qui ne porte ni date ni signature ;

Que, dans cette forme, on ne peut y voir qu'une proposition faite au Sultan Sayd Bargash, sans qu'il soit prouvé que celle-ci ait été transformée en une concession de Sa Hautesse à M. Mackinnon ou en une promesse générale de céder l'administration du sultanat à la compagnie anglaise, promesse que cette société aurait successivement acceptée pour les diverses parties des territoires appartenant au Sultan ;

Qu'aucun des actes postérieurs allégués par la compagnie anglaise ne mentionne directement et clairement ce projet, qui n'a reçu aucun commencement d'exécution ;

Que le témoignage du général Mathews, commandant des troupes du Sultan, témoignage inscrit au mémoire anglais et reçu sous serment, le 23 janvier 1889, rappelle des *négociations* entamées environ neuf ans auparavant et poursuivies jusqu'au commencement de 1887, mais ne cite aucune convention conclue pendant cette période ;

Que l'écrit en forme solennelle remis par le Sultan Sayd Bargash au consul général d'Angleterre, à la date du 6 décembre 1884, eût été inutile si le projet de 1877 avait eu la valeur d'une promesse contractuelle liant absolument le Sultan à l'égard de la Compagnie impériale anglaise ;

Qu'il n'est pas possible, à l'aide des documents produits, de rattacher à ce projet, par un lien direct d'où résulterait l'exécution d'une convention antérieure parfaite et valable, les négociations qui ont été reprises par M. Mackinnon au printemps de 1887 ;

Attendu que, à la date du 22 février 1887, le Sultan Sayd Bargash adressa à M. Mackinnon un télégramme par lequel Sa Hautesse se déclarait prête à lui accorder les concessions qu'il (M. Mackinnon) avait antérieurement proposées et que cette offre a été suivie, le 24 mai, de la conclusion d'un accord concédant à la Compagnie impériale anglaise la bande côtière de la Wanga à Kipini ;

Que, dans cet accord, il n'est fait aucune mention des territoires situés au nord de Kipini et comprenant l'île de Lamu ;

Que, à l'égard de ceux-ci, la Compagnie impériale anglaise se borne à invoquer le témoignage du général Mathews, déclarant qu'à sa connaissance ces territoires ont été offerts par le Sultan à M. Mackinnon en 1887 ; qu'il a toujours compris qu'ils ont été réservés, selon le désir de M. Mackinnon, pour une concession ultérieure, et qu'il fut envoyé, comme représentant du Sultan, faire à M. E.-N. Mackensie, agent de la Compagnie impériale anglaise, une communication verbale l'autorisant à informer M. Mackinnon que tous les territoires au nord de Kipini lui seraient offerts de préférence quand ils viendraient à être affermés ou cédés ;

Attendu qu'on ne peut trouver dans le message verbal dont a été chargé le général Mathews, quelque considération d'ailleurs que puisse mériter son témoignage, les éléments d'une promesse actuelle et positive de faire une concession dont les conditions essentielles seraient suffisamment déterminées, et

Que, quant à l'acceptation réservée ou anticipée de M. Mackinnon, elle ne fait l'objet de la part du général que d'une appréciation purement personnelle ;

Attendu que le témoignage du général Mathews est en concordance avec le télégramme ci-dessus cité du Sultan Sayd Bargash quant à l'in-

tention de traiter avec les Anglais et que cette intention se retrouve et prend corps dans la lettre adressée par son successeur, le 26 août 1888, au consul général d'Angleterre ;

Que toutefois, si cette dernière lettre constitue un engagement politique de gouvernement à gouvernement de ne point céder l'administration du sultanat à d'autres qu'à des sujets du Sultan ou à des Anglais ou à M. Mackinnon pour ce qui concerne Zanzibar et Pemba, on n'y rencontre pas encore la promesse directe et actuelle de céder à la Compagnie impériale anglaise elle-même tous les ports du Nord ;

Attendu que l'intention de traiter avec les Anglais est, d'autre part, exprimée d'une manière évidente dans la lettre de Sayd Khalifa au consul général d'Allemagne, en date du 12 janvier 1889, et

Qu'il n'y a pas lieu de s'arrêter à l'objection que cette détermination serait viciée pour avoir eu une cause fausse, à savoir que le Sultan Sayd Khalifa ne l'aurait prise qu'en raison d'une promesse qu'il croyait avoir été faite par son prédécesseur à la société anglaise, la connaissance de la communication faite, le 22 février 1887, par son prédécesseur, ainsi que des démarches faites au nom de celui-ci par le général Mathews ayant pu légitimement influer sur la résolution, et le Sultan ayant pu d'ailleurs ne pas se décider d'après un mobile unique, ainsi qu'il ressort de sa dite lettre au consul général d'Allemagne et de celles qu'il a, dans le cours du même mois, adressées au consul général d'Angleterre et qui sont reproduites au mémoire anglais ;

Attendu que l'intention itérativement manifestée par le Sultan Sayd Khalifa s'est traduite en fait par les négociations qui s'ouvrirent au mois de janvier 1889 entre Sa Hautesse et M. Mackensie, mandataire de M. Mackinnon ;

Que, dans ces négociations, les conditions essentielles de la reprise de l'administration et des douanes de l'île de Lamu ont été posées et débattues pour la première fois entre les parties ;

Que l'accord des volontés s'est établi sur tous les points, ainsi que cela résulte de l'échange des lettres du 19 et du 20 janvier 1889 entre le Sultan et M. Mackensie, combiné avec le télégramme du Sultan à M. Mackinnon en date du 30 du même mois ;

Mais attendu que l'acte ainsi préparé n'a pas reçu la signature du Sultan et que celui-ci l'a subordonnée à la levée d'un obstacle qui arrêtait sa détermination définitive,

Par ces motifs :

Nous sommes d'avis que le Sultan est resté maître de disposer de l'exercice de ses droits souverains dans les limites tracées par la lettre de son prédécesseur à sir John Kirck du 6 décembre 1884 et par celle qu'il a lui-même adressée au consul général d'Angleterre le 26 août 1888, et

Que la Compagnie impériale anglaise de l'Afrique orientale ne produit aucun engagement valablement pris envers elle par l'un des Sultans de Zanzibar et créant en sa faveur un droit exclusif à la reprise des douanes et de l'administration de l'île de Lamu;

Considérant enfin que la signature de la convention formulée entre le Sultan Sayd Khalifa et le représentant de la Compagnie impériale anglaise de l'Afrique orientale n'a été différée qu'à raison de l'opposition du consul général d'Allemagne;

Et attendu que cette opposition se fonde sur le droit de priorité réclamé par la Compagnie allemande de Witu, droit dont la réalité a fait l'objet de conclusions précédentes,

Par ces motifs:

Nous sommes d'avis que l'accord projeté entre le Sultan Sayd Khalifa et le représentant de la Compagnie impériale anglaise de l'Afrique orientale au sujet de l'île de Lamu peut être signé sans donner prise à une opposition fondée en droit.

Fait à Bruxelles, en double original, le 17 août 1889[1].

XCVI. Argentine, Brésil.

7 septembre 1889.

Il s'est agi dans ce différend du territoire des missions d'une superficie de 30,621 kilomètres carrés, revendiqué par les deux pays. L'arbitre émit un avis favorable au Brésil.

Tratado para someter al arbitraje la cuestion de limites pendiente entre lo Brasil e la Republica Argentina. Buenos Ayres, 7 setiembre 1889.

Su Magestad el Emperador del Brazil y Su Excelencia el Presidente de la República Argentina, deseando resolver con la mayor brevidad posible la cuestion de limites pendiente entre los dos Estados, acordaron, sin perjuicio del Tratado de 28 de setiembre de 1885, en fijar plazo para concluir la discusion de derecho, y, no consiguiendo entenderse, en someter la misma cuestion al arbitraje de un Gobierno amigo, y siendo necesario para esto un tradado, nombraron sus Plenipotenciarios, a saber:

Su Magestad el Emperador del Brasil al Baron de Alencar, de Su Consejo, y Su Enviado Ex-

[1] *Moniteur Belge*, 1890, p. 2461.

traordinario y Ministro Plenipotenciario en la República Argentina; Su Excelencia el Presidente de la República Argentina al Dr. D. Norberto Quirno Costa, Su Ministro secretario en el Departamento del Interno en el de Relaciones Exteriores.

Los cuales, habiéndose canjeado sus Plenos Poderes que fueron hallados en buena y debida forma convinieron en los articulos siguientes:

ARTICULO I. La discusion del derecho que cada una de las Altas Partes Contratantes juzga tener al territorio en litijio entre ellas, quedará cerrada en el plazo de noventa dias contados desde la conclusion del reconocimiento del terreno en que encuentran las cabeceras de los rios Chapéco ó Pequiri-Guazú y Jangada ó San Antonio-Guazú. Entiendese concluido este reconocimiento el dia en que las comisiones nombladas en virtud del tratado de 28 de setiembre de 1885 presentasen a sus Gobiernos las memorias y los planos á que se refiere el articulo 4° del mismo tratado.

ARTICULO II. Terminado el plazo del articulo precedente, sin solucion amigable, la cuestion sera sometida al arbitraje del Presidente de los Estados Unidos de América, a quien, dentro de los sesenta dias siguientes se dirijiran las Altas Partes Contratantes pidiendole que acepte ese encargo.

ARTICULO III. Si el Presidente de los Estados Unidos de América se escusase, las Altas Partes Contratantes elejiron otro Arbitro, en Europa ó en América, dentro de los sesenta dias siguientes al recibo de la escusacion, y en el caso de cualquiere otra, procederan del mismo modo.

ARTICULO IV. Aceptado el nombramiento, en el término de doce meses contados desde la fecha en que fuere recibida la respectiva comunicacion, présentará cada una de las Altas Partes Contratantes al Arbitro su exposicion con los documentos y titulos que convinieren á la defensa de su derecho. Presentada ella, ninguna agregacion podró ser hecha, salvo por exijencia del Arbitro, el cual tendrá la facultad de mandar que se le presten los esclarecimientos necesarios.

ARTICULO V. La frontera hade ser constituida por los rios que el Brasil ó la República Argentina han designado, y el Arbitro será invitado à pronunciarse por una de las Partes, como jusgase justo en vista de las razones y de los documentos que produjerem.

ARTICULO VI. El laudo será pronunciado en el plazo de doce meses contados desde la fecha en que fueren presentadas las exposiciones, ó desde la mas reciente si la presentacion no fuere hecha al mismo tiempo por ambas Partes. Será definitivo y obligatorio y ninguna razon podrá alegarse para dificultar su complimiento.

ARTICULO VII. El presente tratado será ratificado y las ratificaciones seran canjeadas en la ciudad de Rio de Janeiro en al menor plazo posible.

En testimonio de lo cual los Plenipotenciarios del Imperio del Brasil y de la Republica Argentina firmam el mismo tratado y le ponen sus sellos en la ciudad de Buenos Aires à los siete dias del mes de setiembre de 1889 [1].

Award of the President of the United States of America under the Treaty of Arbitration concluded September 7, 1889, between the Argentine Republic and the Empire (now United States) of Brazil.

The Treaty concluded September 7, 1889, between the Argentine Republic and Brazil for the settlement of a disputed boundary question provides, among other things, as follow:

ARTICLE I. The contention about the right that each one of the High Contracting Parties judges to have to the territory in dispute between them, shall be closed within the term of ninety days to be counted from the ending of the survey of the land in which the head water of the rivers Chapeco or Pequiri-guazu and Jangada or San Antonio-guazu are found. The said survey is understood to end the day on which the commissions appointed by virtue of the Treaty of September 28, 1885, shall present to their gouvernments their reports and plans referred to in Article 4 of the same Treaty.

ARTICLE II. Should the time specified in the preceding article expire without an amicable solution being reached, the question shall be submitted to the Arbitration of the President of the United States of America, to whom the High Contracting Parties shall address themselves within the next sixty days, requesting him to accept that Commission.

ARTICLE V. The boundaries shall be established by the rivers that either Brazil or the Argentine Republic has designated, and the Arbitrator shall be invited to decide in favor of one of the parties, as he may deem just, and in view of the reasons and the documents they may produce.

ARTICLE VI. The decision shall be pronounced within the term of twelve months, counting from the date of the presentation of the expositions,

---

[1] *Relatorio do Ministerio das Relações exteriores*, 1891-1892, p. 40, — *Foreign Relations of the United States*, 1892, p. 2.

or from the latest one, if the presentation be not made at the same time by both Parties. It shall be final and obligatory, and no reason shall be alleged to obstruct its enactment. The High Contracting Parties having failed to arrive at an amicable solution within the time stipulated as aforesaid, have, in accordance with the alternative provisions of the Treaty, submitted the controverted question to me, Grover Cleveland, President of the United States of America, for Arbitration and award under the conditions in said Treaty prescribed. Each party has presented to me, within the time and in the manner specified in Article IV of the Treaty, an argument with evidence, documents and titles in support of its asserted right.

The question submitted to me for decision under the Treaty aforesaid is, which of two certain systems of rivers constitutes the boundary of Brazil and the Argentine Republic in that part of their adjoining territory wich lies between the Uruguay and Iguazu Rivers. Each of designated boundary systems is composed of two rivers having their sources near together and flowing in opposite directions one into the Uruguay and the other into the Iguazu.

The two rivers designated by Brazil as constituing the boundary in question (which may be denominated the Westerly system) are a tributary of the Uruguay and a tributary of the Iguazu which were marked, recognized and declared as boundary rivers in 1759 and 1760 by the joint Commission appointed under the Treaty of January 13, 1750 between Spain and Portugal to locate the boundary between the Spanish and Portuguese possessions in South America. The affluent of the Uruguay is designated in the report of those commissioners as the Pepiri River (sometimes spelled Pepiry). In certain later documents put in evidence it is called the Pepiri-guazu. The oposite river flowing into the Iguazu was named the San Antonio by the said commissioners, and it retains that name.

The two rivers claimed by the Argentine Republic as forming the boundary (which may be denominated the Easterly system) lie more to the east and are by that Republic called the Pequiri-guazu (flowing into the Uruguay) and the San Antonio-guazu (flowing into the Iguazu). Of these two rivers last aforesaid the first is by Brazil called the Chapeco and the second the Jangada.

Now, therefore, be it known that I, Grover Cleveland, President of the United States of America, upon whóm the functions of arbitration have been conferred in the premises, having duly examined and considered the arguments, documents and evidence to me submitted by the respective Parties pursuant to the provisions of said Treaty, do hereby make the following decision and award:

That the boundary line between the Argentine Republic and the United States of Brazil in that part submitted to me for arbitration and decision is constitued and shall be established by and upon the rivers Pepiri (also called Pepiriguazu) and San Antonio, to wit, the rivers which Brazil has designated in the argument and documents submitted to me as constituing the boundary, and herein before denominated the Westerly System.

For convenience of indentification, these rivers may be further described as those recognized, designated, marked and declared as the Pepiri and San Antonio respectively, and as the boundary rivers in the years 1759 and 1760, by the Spanish and Portuguese Commissioners in that behalf appointed pursuant to the Treaty of Limits concluded January 13, 1750 between Spain and Portugal, as is recorded in the official report of the said commissioners. The mouth of the affluent of the Uruguay last aforesaid, to wit, the Pepiri (also called Pepiri-guazu), which with the San Antonio is hereby determined to be the boundary in question, was reckoned and reported by the said commissioners who surveyed it in 1759, to be one and one-third leagues up stream from the Great Falls (Salto Grande) of the Uruguay and two-thirds of a league above a smaller affluent on the same side called by the said commissioners the Itayoa. According to the map and report of the Survey made in 1887 by the Brazilian-Argentine Joint Commission in pursuance of the Treaty concluded september 28, 1885 between the Argentine Republic and Brazil, the distance from the Great Falls of the Uruguay to the mouth of the aforesaid Pepiri (also called Pepiri-guazu) was ascertained and shown to be four and one half miles as the river flows. The mouth of the affluent of the Iguazu last aforesaid, to wit, the San Antonio, was reckoned and reported by the said commissioners of 1859 and 1760 to be nineteen leagues up stream from the Great Falls (Salto Grande) of the Iguazu, and twenty-three leagues from the mouth of the latter river. It was also by them reported as the second important river that empties itself on the south bank of the Iguazu above its Salto Grande; the San Francisco, about seventeen and one fourth leagues above the Great Falls, being the first. In the report of the Joint Survey made in 1788 under the Treaty of October 1, 1777, between Spain and Portugal, the location of the San Antonio with reference to the mouth and the Great Falls of the Iguazu agrees with that above stated.

In testimony whereof I have hereunto set my hand and caused the seal of the United States to be affixed.

Done in triplicate at the city of Washington on the fifth day of February, in the year one thousand eight hundred and ninety-five and of the independence of the United States the one hundred and nineteenth [1].

XCVII. Italie. Perse.
5 juin 1890.

Arbitrage ayant pour objet l'indemnité réclamée par un sujet italien du chef de la préemption de ses marchandises par la douane persane. Il fut accordé à l'intéressé une somme de 78,000 francs.

Agreement of June 5, 1890, entered by the governments of Italy and Persia.

The government of His Imperial Majesty the Shah of Persia and the Government of His Majesty the King of Italy, being equally animated with the desire to settle in a friendly manner the difference which arose at Recht in November 1882 between the administration of the Imperial Persian customs and M. Joseph Consonno, an Italian subject, on account of the importation by the latter of ninety-two cases of merchandise, have decided to submit the question to the judgment of an arbitrator, who has been chosen in the person of His Ex. Sir W. White, ambassador of Her Majesty the Queen of Great Britain at Constantinople.

For this purpose the two high contracting parties have agreed that:

1. The documents, information, examinations and proofs of every nature which the parties shall judge it their interest to present to the arbitrator shall be submitted to His Excellency within the term of two months and a half from the date of the signature of the present protocol. After this period no production of documents or proofs shall be admitted;

2. His Ex. Sir William White is requested to have the goodness to pronounce his opinion within the period of a month from the date of the production of the last documents by the parties;

3. The arbitral opinion shall be without appeal and the parties pledge themselves to recog-

[1] *Relatorio do Ministerio das Relações exteriores*, 1895. Annexo I, p. 5; — *Foreign Relations of the United States*, 1895, p. 1.

— 343 —

nize it and execute it within the space of forty-five days from the date of its delivery.

In faith whereof, His Highness Aminé-Sultan, Grand Vizier and Minister of the Court of His Imperial Majesty the Shah of Persia, and His Excellency Alexander, Count of Rege di Donato, Minister of His Majesty the King of Italy, at Teheran, have signed the present act, in quadruple original, in the French language, accompained by a translation in the Persian language, and have affixed thereto the seal of their arms.

Done at Teheran, the 5th day of the month of June, in the year one thousand eight hundred and ninety of the Christian era, the 16th of the month of Chowal of the year one thousand three hundred and seven of the Hegira [1].

Award rendered on June 12, 1891, by the arbitrators in the case between Italy and Persia.

The government of His Majesty the King of Italy and the government of His Majesty the Shah having agreed, in virtue of a protocol signed at Teheran the 5th of June 1890, to request the British ambassador at Constantinople, the very honorable Sir William White, to consent to be arbitrator in a litigation arising between M. J. Consonno, an Italian subject of the one part, and the administration of the Persian customs on the other, and the British ambassador having accepted this mandate;

The British ambassador, having subsequently asked the said governments to authorize him to associate with himself two assessors of his own choice, and the said governments having consented to that purpose M. Emile de Borchgrave, minister and envoy of Belgium to Constantinople, and M. Egmont de Winkler, counsellor of the German embassy in the same place, equally accepting;

The said arbitrator and the assessors having received the assurance of the two above-mentioned governments that their decision would be without appeal, have considered it just, after hearing the advocates of both parties, and having sought every means of enlightening their conscience to pronounce the following sentence:

Whereas the Persian customs at Recht had the right to examine and stamp the merchandise contained in the ninety-two cases imported on the 28th of November 1882, by Mr. Consonno, and that the latter acted illegally in opposing that examination;

Whereas the Persian Government had the right, on the refusal of M. Consonno to submit

to the customs formalities at Recht, to confiscate the said goods;

Whereas, however, the Persian Government, by not using its right immediately and by leaving the dispute unsettled for nearly eight years, caused a manifest injury to M. Consonno;

Whereas, besides, if it is just, on the one hand, to abandon to the Persian Government the said goods contained in the ninety-two above-mentioned cases, it seems equitable, on the other hand, to pay the value of them to M. Consonno according to the valuation made by him at the customhouse;

For these reasons the arbitrator and assessors decide and declare:

That the Persian Government remains and shall remain in possession of the ninety-two above-mentioned cases which it seized;

That the Persian Government shall pay to M. Consonno the sum of seventy-eight thousand francs, representing both the value of the goods, as it was declared by M. Consonno, and all the interest on this principal sum, of which M. Consonno was deprived during nearly eight years;

That there is no ground to admit the reservations formulated during the pleadings, and since, by the advocate of the applicant, nor any others whatsoever;

That each of the two governments shall pay the expenses occasioned by its own procedure, and divide in common the fees of the engrossing clerk and the translation of the documents required during the course of the arbitration;

That the payments shall be effected within the space of forty-five days from the notification of the first sentence; that the sum adjudged to M. Consonno shall be paid to the embassy of His Majesty the King of Italy at Constantinople, and the above-mentioned expenses to whom due, also in Constantinople;

This done and decided at Therapia the twelfth (12) of June one thousand eight hundred and ninety-one [1].

XCVIII. France, Venezuela.

24 février 1891.

Cette contestation a eu pour objet de réparer le préjudice causé au sieur Fabiani par les agissements des autorités judiciaires et administratives du Vénézuéla. Il fut accordé une indemnité de fr. 4,346,656. 51.

[1] J. B. MOORE, History and Digest . . ., p. 5019.

[1] J. B. MOORE, History and Digest . . ., p. 5019.

Convention d'arbitrage, signée à Caracas
le 24 février 1891.

Le Gouvernement de la République Française et le Gouvernement des Etats-Unis du Vénézuéla, sont convenus de soumettre à un arbitre les réclamations de M. Antoine Fabiani, contre le Gouvernement Vénézuélien.

L'arbitre devra :

1° Décider si, d'après les lois du Vénézuéla, les principes généraux du droit des gens et la Convention en vigueur entre les deux Puissances contractantes, le Gouvernement Vénézuélien est responsable des dommages que Fabiani dit avoir éprouvés, pour dénégation de justice ;

2° Fixer, au cas où cette responsabilité serait reconnue pour tout ou partie des réclamations dont il s'agit, le montant de l'indemnité pécuniaire que le Gouvernement Vénézuélien devra verser entre les mains de M. Fabiani, et qui s'effectuera en titres de la dette diplomatique du Vénézuéla 3 %.

Les deux Gouvernements sont d'accord pour prier M. le Président de la Confédération suisse, de vouloir bien se charger de cet arbitrage.

La présente déclaration restera soumise à l'approbation du Congrès de Vénézuéla.

Fait en double exemplaire à Caracas, le 24 février 1891 [1].

Sentence prononcée, en cause du sieur Fabiani, par le Président de la Confédération Suisse. Berne, 30 Décembre 1896.

Le Président de la Confédération Suisse, arbitre désigné pour trancher le différend existant entre le Gouvernement de la République Française, partie demanderesse, et le Gouvernement des Etats-Unis du Vénézuéla, partie défenderesse;

Vu les exposés et les conclusions des parties, ainsi que les preuves administrées;

Considérant qu'il en résulte :

A. — EN FAIT.

I. Les Gouvernements de la République Française et des Etats-Unis du Vénézuéla sont convenus, par compromis signé à Caracas le 24 février 1891, de soumettre à l'arbitrage du Président de la Confédération Suisse la question de savoir si : « d'après les lois du Vénézuéla, les principes généraux du droit des gens et la Convention (26 novembre 1885) en vigueur entre les deux Puissances contractantes, le Gouvernement vénézuélien est responsable des dommages que

[1] F. DE MARTENS. *Nouveau Recueil Général*, 2ᵐᵉ série, t. XX, p. 705.

Fabiani dit avoir éprouvés pour dénégation de justice », et de charger l'arbitre « de fixer, au cas où cette responsabilité serait reconnue pour tout ou partie des réclamations dont il s'agit, le montant de l'indemnité pécuniaire que le Gouvernement vénézuélien devrait verser entre les mains de M. Fabiani, et qui s'effectuerait en titres de la dette diplomatique de Vénézuéla 3 % ».

L'arbitrage ayant été accepté, la procédure fut instruite par voie d'échange de mémoires et par l'administration de preuves tant littérales que testimoniales offertes par les Gouvernements intéressés.

II. Les faits allégués dans la demande sont les suivants :

M. Antoine Fabiani épousa, en Avril 1867, la fille de M. Benoît Roncayolo, chef d'une maison d'armement de voiliers à Marseille. Roncayolo suspendit ses payements, le 31 août de la même année, et fut déclaré en état de faillite. Son gendre Fabiani, qui était avocat près la cour de Bastia, s'efforça de sauver la situation. Au bout de deux ans il put informer son beau-père, établi à Maracaïbo, qu'il avait obtenu un concordat pour ce dernier ; il paya lui-même le dernier dividende de 10 %.

Fabiani fixa son domicile à Marseille. Un oncle lui avança de fortes sommes d'argent, et lui-même chercha désormais à reconquérir la fortune perdue par Benoît Roncayolo. Dans ce but, et afin de conserver le monopole presque exclusif des rapports maritimes et commerciaux de Maracaïbo avec la France, monopole exercé naguère par Roncayolo, il acheta d'abord le navire Pauline ; il développa ensuite ses affaires d'exportation et d'importation et affecta cinq trois-mâts à ce service, sans parler d'un puissant remorqueur destiné à la barre et au lac de Maracaïbo. Trois maisons furent successivement fondées au Vénézuéla, à Caracas, à Maracaïbo, à La Guayra ; Fabiani y intéressa son beau-père et son beau-frère André Roncayolo, qui reçurent l'attribution de la moitié des bénéfices.

Mais bientôt Fabiani découvrit que les Roncayolo avaient commis des malversations à son préjudice, au Vénézuéla. Il se vit obligé d'interdire à son beau-père toute participation officielle aux opérations de la maison Fabiani et de restreindre les pouvoirs du Roncayolo. Le 7 décembre 1874, B. Roncayolo n'en renouvela pas moins, en son nom, le contrat de remorquage passé avec le président de l'Etat vénézuélien de Zulia, en engageant la responsabilité de « ses » établissements de commerce fondés sous la raison sociale Antoine Fabiani & Cⁱᵉ. Fabiani arrêta net toutes les affaires d'exportation, prohiba tous tirages de traites, exigea la restitution de ses avances et la prompte liquidation de ses intérêts. Il dut néanmoins se convaincre que les Roncayolo travaillaient à « une spoliation qui serait facilitée par la vénalité des pouvoirs judiciaires du Vénézuéla ». Il se disposait à recourir aux tribunaux français, les conditions de l'association ayant été arrêtées à Marseille, quand, sur les instances de Roncayolo fils, il consentit à une solution amiable du conflit.

La transaction, signée à cette occasion, date du 31 janvier 1878. Intervenue entre Antoine Fabiani et André Roncayolo, elle constate que B. Roncayolo n'a jamais fait d'apports en argent, elle défère au Tribunal de Marseille toutes les difficultés qui pourraient s'élever au sujet de son exécution, elle constitue Roncayolo fils débiteur de la somme de 617,895 fr. 10, valeur 31 janvier 1878. D'autre part, la maison Roncayolo de Maracaïbo devait être remplacée par une succursale de la maison Fabiani de Marseille, succursale qui serait dirigée par A. Roncayolo, à l'exclusion de toute ingérence de Roncayolo père.

Les anciennes irrégularités reprochées aux Roncayolo se renouvelèrent. Fabiani révoqua les pouvoirs de Roncayolo fils et lui substitua un sous-agent, auquel Roncayolo père s'empressa de marier sa fille cadette. Il y avait 6 à 700,000 fr. de traites à payer. Fabiani comprit que sa présence au Vénézuéla était nécessaire. Il partit le 3 novembre 1879, non toutefois sans avoir introduit une instance, à Marseille, contre ses deux fondés de procuration; les tribunaux de Marseille étaient compétents, en effet, et du reste B. Roncayolo, avait écrit, le 14 juin 1879, que la justice vénézuélienne se laissait corrompre à prix d'argent.

Au Vénézuéla, Fabiani réclama, en toute première ligne, le paiement d'une somme de 105,458 fr. 75, représentée par cinq traites qui lui avaient été délivrées, pour des transports d'émigrants, par les consuls du Vénézuéla à Marseille et à Ténériffe. MM. Roche & Cⁱᵉ, auxquels ces traites avaient été remises pour l'encaissement, refusèrent de les restituer, sous prétexte qu'elles avaient été données en gage par acte du 6 mars 1877, acte frauduleux d'après la demande. Le dossier de ces traites avait d'ailleurs disparu et le cabinet de Caracas annula ses ordres de paiement antérieurs. Si Fabiani ne poursuivit pas l'affaire au criminel, c'est qu'on l'en dissuada vivement. Les Roncayolo, le Directeur du Ministère des Finances et un comparse auraient collaboré à cette machination.

On méconnut également les droits de Fabiani, comme propriétaire du vapeur Pauline, pour services rendus à l'Etat par ce navire pendant la révolution qui ramena M. Guzman Blanco au pouvoir. B. Roncayolo avait touché 55,000 fr.

sur ce qui était dû à Fabiani, au lieu de 30,000 fr. qu'il avouait avoir perçus; le Ministère des Finances ne permit pas au véritable créancier de faire constater ce détournement. Fabiani tenta en vain d'obtenir du tribunal de commerce de Caracas la nullité du gage invoqué par MM. Roche & Cⁱᵉ. La restitution des traites fut bien ordonnée, mais, aussitôt après, le tribunal rejeta une requête à fin d'exécution provisoire du jugement, par la raison que Fabiani, étranger au pays, devait, au préalable, fournir un cautionnement. Fabiani annonça qu'il était en mesure d'offrir toutes les garanties désirables, son vapeur Pauline étant arrivé à La Guayra. Mais quand il voulut verser au dossier sa patente de navigation, il découvrit qu'elle était au nom de « Roncayolo-Fabiani », bien qu'elle lui eût été accordée à lui comme propriétaire unique, en avril 1879. Il y avait là un audacieux abus de pouvoir commis par A. Roncayolo junior, au mépris de la transaction de 1878.

Le vapeur Pauline, réquisitionné par le Gouvernement vénézuélien pour aider à la répression d'une émeute, allait regagner son port d'attache. B. Roncayolo, comme représentant de Roncayolo-Fabiani, sollicitait le paiement d'une somme de 63,000 fr. due de ce chef. Fabiani s'y opposa et le montant de la réclamation, arrêté par l'Etat au chiffre de 57,780 fr., fut consigné en mains tierces pour le compte de la maison Antoine Fabiani de Maracaïbo, car, selon la demande, les Roncayolo étaient plus sûrs des autorités judiciaires de cette dernière ville que de celles de Caracas. Au demeurant, M. Guzman Blanco, chef de l'Etat, qui était associée dans de grandes entreprises avec B. Roncayolo, son agent politique, s'apprêtait à intervenir directement dans le conflit. De graves soucis appelant Fabiani à Maracaïbo, il s'y rendit en avril 1880, mais il y trouva presque vide la caisse de son agence; André Roncayolo l'avait pillée. Après bien des pourparlers et des démêlés avec celui-ci, Fabiani comprit qu'il serait obligé de capituler, tant le terrain était bien préparé contre lui à Maracaïbo.

En revanche, B. Roncayolo était de plus en plus en faveur auprès de M. Blanco, avec lequel il était intéressé dans la grosse affaire du chemin de fer de la Ceïba à Sabana de Mendoza; l'obstination que Fabiani mettait à défendre ses droits dérangeait des combinaisons politico-financières importantes. M. Stamman, ministre plénipotentiaire d'Allemagne à Caracas, aura, à la demande, renseigné son Gouvernement sur les attentats et les injustices dont Fabiani fut victime durant ce séjour à Maracaïbo.

En attendant, on lui avait enlevé le service du remorquage, on s'était emparé de ses navires, et la cour suprême avait confirmé la sentence qui dépossédait Fabiani. Il ne restait plus à ce dernier qu'à retourner en France et à implorer la protection de son Gouvernement, si les autorités judiciaires et administratives du Vénézuéla continuaient à se liguer contre lui. C'est alors qu'un ami vint lui proposer de le sortir d'embarras, moyennant qu'il consentit à une revision de la transaction de 1878 par un arbitrage. Fabiani, cédant à la force majeure, accepta de suspendre toutes poursuites et actions, et de signer un compromis qui sauverait peut-être l'avenir de son commerce au Vénézuéla.

Le tribunal arbitral, réuni à Marseille, statua en date du 15 décembre 1880 ; ses décisions, aux termes du compromis, étaient exécutoires au Vénézuéla, sans délai et sans qu'on pût admettre contre elles aucun recours. La sentence qu'il rendit, peut se résumer ainsi :

1° Les comptes de Fabiani furent reconnus exacts ; le débit d'André Roncayolo fut fixé à la somme de 538,359 fr. 07 cent., toute réclamation lui étant interdite au sujet des dits comptes ;

2° L'entreprise du remorquage fut déclarée la propriété exclusive de Fabiani, depuis le 30 novembre 1877, comme aussi les vapeurs Éclair, Mara, Pauline et les engins et accessoires destinés au service du remorquage. Fabiani fut autorisé à reprendre l'administration de ce service, « pour en régler la gestion à sa convenance, sans que M. Benoit Roncayolo, ni M. André Roncayolo, ni aucun tiers puissent s'y immiscer directement ou indirectement », l'insertion du nom de B. Roncayolo dans l'acte de concession « ayant été la conséquence d'une faute ». B. Roncayolo était tenu cependant, à peine de dommages et intérêts, de laisser son nom figurer dans l'entreprise, si Fabiani le jugeait plus conforme à ses intérêts, ou si le Gouvernement vénézuélien se refusait à modifier la concession sur ce point ;

3° Tous les produits du remorquage, depuis le 30 novembre 1877, y compris les bénéfices du pilotage dès la même date, furent attribués à Fabiani ; les personnes qui les avaient touchés avaient l'obligation de les restituer ;

4° B. et A. Roncayolo furent condamnés solidairement au coût de l'enregistrement de la sentence arbitrale et de ses annexes.

Le compromis liait Fabiani de même que Roncayolo père et fils, qui y avaient adhéré tous les deux. La sentence, rendue par deux arbitres, qui étaient, l'un, le frère et créancier de B. Roncayolo, l'autre, l'oncle et créancier de Fabiani, fut enregistrée à Marseille le 17 décembre 1880 et déclarée exécutoire le 21 du même mois, par le président du tribunal de première instance de cette ville.

Les Roncayolo formèrent opposition à l'exécution de la sentence arbitrale, en requérant l'annulation du compromis de Caracas et la révocation de l'ordonnance d'exequatur. Déboutés par jugement du tribunal de première instance de Marseille, du 1er avril 1881, ils interjetèrent appel ; mais la cour d'appel d'Aix confirma la décision du tribunal de Marseille par son arrêt du 25 juillet suivant, et il n'y eut pas de pourvoi en cassation.

Avant le prononcé de l'arrêt d'appel, Fabiani, qui était retourné en Europe, repartit pour Caracas dans le but d'introduire et de diriger la procédure d'exécution. Mais divers indices et renseignements lui firent craindre de nouvelles difficultés. Trois jours après son arrivée à Caracas, vers la fin de mai 1881, Fabiani écrivit à M. Guzman Blanco pour lui annoncer que le paiement d'une somme de plus de 40,000 fr., réclamé au Gouvernement par B. Roncayolo, devait être effectué entre ses mains à lui, Fabiani, en vertu de la sentence arbitrale du 15 décembre 1880 ; il le priait, en même temps, de différer le paiement de la dite somme. Cette lettre demeura sans réponse. Le 7 juin 1881, il déposa au greffe de la haute cour fédérale l'original et la traductioe du dossier d'arbitrage, ainsi qu'une demande d'exequatur.

Il ne s'agissait, en l'espèce, que d'une simple formalité, à moins d'une véritable dénégation de justice de la part de la haute cour (art. 556 et suiv. C. proc. civ. vénéz.). Des renvois, des incidents, des intrigues retardèrent la solution de l'affaire. En fin de compte, bien qu'il eût été établi au cours des plaidoyers, par des documents irrécusables, que l'ordonnance d'exécution du président du tribunal de Marseille avait été confirmée aussi bien en appel qu'en première instance, la haute cour fédérale, le 11 novembre 1881, se déclara, par cinq voix contre quatre, incompétente pour donner force exécutoire à la sentence arbitrale, attendu « qu'on ne peut considérer comme un tribunal de France la réunion des arbitres qui a eu lieu à Marseille », et qu'une ordonnance judiciaire d'exécution « ne peut convertir en juges, ceux qui ne le sont pas, et en sentence d'un tribunal étranger ce qui est simplement le complément d'un contrat » (Annexe I de la défense, p. 23 et suiv.). Les quatre juges formant minorité protestèrent dans des « réserves » motivées, la sentence arbitrale satisfaisant, selon eux, à toutes les conditions prescrites par l'art. 557 du Code de procédure civile vénézuélien et son assimilation à un jugement ordinaire n'étant pas contestable.

Une nouvelle instance fut introduite, et, le 6 juin 1882, la haute cour fédérale, dont la composition avait partiellement changé dans l'intervalle, « déclarait exécutoire au Vénézuéla la sentence de la cour d'appel d'Aix ».

Fabiani, sur le conseil d'un ami, communiqua ce résultat à M. Blanco, qui, au lieu de respecter les décisions judiciaires intervenues, commença par mander à son ministre des finances de verser à B. Roncayolo une somme de 28,000 fr. due à Fabiani pour emploi récent du vapeur Pauline dans l'intérêt de l'Etat. Fabiani ne s'empressa pas moins, malgré l'hostilité du pouvoir, de requérir l'exécution effective du jugement arbitral. Il s'embarqua pour Maracaïbo; une inscription hypothécaire fut prise, dès le 14 juin 1882, contre B. et A. Roncayolo sur tous les droits leur appartenant dans le chemin de fer et sur la douane de la Ceïba, et une autre inscription, de 120,000 fr., sur la section Trujillo du chemin de fer. Mais les Roncayolo, soutenus au reste par le président de l'Etat de Trujillo, venaient par un contrat frauduleux, de céder tous leurs droits à un tiers.

Le juge de première instance, à Maracaïbo, ordonna l'exécution de la sentence au bénéfice de laquelle se trouvait Fabiani; les Roncayolo demandèrent alors sa récusation. Il se récusa d'abord, puis se ravisant, débouta les opposants de leurs conclusions formulées contre sa dernière décision et décréta l'envoi en possession des navires, le 14 juillet 1882.

Sur ces entrefaites, Fabiani tomba malade de la fièvre jaune. La procédure d'exécution fut suspendue sans raisons plausibles; en particulier, le juge, qui n'aurait dû admettre aucun pourvoi contre le mandat d'exécution par lui décerné, accueillit, avec effet dévolutif seulement, il est vrai, l'appel interjeté contre son décret. Les adversaires de Fabiani recoururent au juge supérieur, qui attribua à l'appel un double effet, dévolutif et suspensif. Tout acte de procédure était interdit jusqu'à ce qu'il eût été prononcé en instance d'appel.

L'admission de l'appel à deux effets violait la loi, ainsi que la haute cour fédérale le reconnut, dans son arrêt du 8 décembre 1883, en déclarant que l'exécution avait été interrompue par « des recours illégaux lorsqu'il s'agit de l'exécution d'une sentence ». Aux yeux de Fabiani, le juge président de la cour supérieure était l'instrument des Roncayolo. Fabiani souleva le recours de fait devant la décision supérieure contre la décision de ce magistrat et le récusa du même coup. Il rentra bientôt après en Europe, en confiant la garde de ses intérêts à ses amis et représentants.

Trois motifs de récusation avaient été invoqués. Les ennemis de Fabiani, désireux d'en finir, parvinrent à faire modifier la constitution de l'Etat de Falcon-Zulia, dans le sens que,

« pour le cas de récusation du juge supérieur, son suppléant n'aurait plus besoin d'être docteur en jurisprudence », et que, pour connaître de la récusation, la cour suprême formerait une liste d'avocats et de citoyens, parmi lesquels le gouverneur — qui était le frère d'un des avocats de Roncayolo — choisirait le suppléant.

Le juge suppléant désigné pour statuer sur le premier motif de récusation, l'écarta et se retira dès qu'il eut à se prononcer sur le deuxième. Il fut remplacé par une créature des Roncayolo et de leurs alliés, qui débouta Fabiani. Une troisième récusation ayant été proposée pour manifestation d'opinion, le magistrat la déclara irrecevable, parce qu'une formalité de procédure ne fut pas remplie ensuite d'un oubli. La décision fut aussitôt frappée d'appel; il refusa d'admettre le pourvoi et la cour suprême fut saisie.

Entre temps, les autorités, à en croire les lettres des fondés de pouvoir de Fabiani, considéraient les vapeurs de celui-ci comme leur bien. On escomptait l'annulation du mandat d'exécution et l'on se promettait d'écraser Fabiani en exigeant de lui le remboursement immédiat des recettes du remorquage, les frais judiciaires et les honoraires des avocats poursuivants.

Il y avait un moyen encore de conjurer les efforts des Roncayolo: provoquer l'intervention de l'exécutif fédéral, qui, d'après le § 17 de l'art. 13 de la constitution, devait veiller à l'exécution « des décrets et ordres » que les « tribunaux de la fédération rendraient dans l'exercice de leurs attributions et de leurs facultés légales ». Le ministre de l'Intérieur, invité à agir, le 2 juillet 1883, répondit, le 9 même mois, que « l'exécutif national a décidé que c'est à la haute cour fédérale qu'il appartient de faire observer ses dispositions et que c'est à elle que doit s'adresser l'intéressé ».

Fabiani revint devant la haute cour. Mais, dans l'intervalle, pour détruire par anticipation l'effet d'une décision nouvelle, le Président de la République, M. Guzman Blanco, par une résolution du 21 août 1883, approuva la cession frauduleuse du contrat de chemin de fer de la Ceïba consentie par B. Roncayolo, soustrayant ainsi les biens d'un débiteur à l'action d'un créancier. Enfin, le 8 décembre 1883, la haute cour décida que le juge de première instance devait continuer une exécution illégalement arrêtée depuis le 14 juillet 1882.

Le 28 janvier 1884 le juge compétent décerna un mandat d'exécution, qui visait spécialement les droits et actions de B. Roncayolo dans le chemin de fer et sur la douane de la Ceïba. Cette décision du juge de Maracaïbo devait précipiter les événements. La Gaceta Official, du 21 février 1884, notifia que, par un contrat daté de la veille, le service du remorquage, des bouées et du pilotage dans la lagune et sur la barre de Maracaïbo, dont Fabiani venait d'être remis en possession paisible, était concédé à un prête-nom de B. Roncayolo. Or, ce contrat apparaissait comme un acte de vengeance; coïncidence singulière, il fut signé le jour même où M. Blanco avait dû résigner ses fonctions présidentielles entre les mains de son successeur.

Dès qu'on connut à Maracaïbo le contrat du 20 février 1884, qui causait un préjudice matériel et moral considérable à Fabiani, le crédit de celui-ci fut sérieusement ébranlé et la maison menacée d'une catastrophe.

Bien plus, au même moment, le 23 février 1884, la cour suprême de Falcon-Zulia, soulevant un conflit de compétence, déniait à la haute cour fédérale le droit de faire exécuter la sentence arbitrale et ordonnait la transmission du dossier à un tribunal spécial, pour voir annuler l'arrêt du 8 décembre 1883.

Cet arrêt de conflit, suivant de si près le retrait du remorquage, mettait Fabiani en présence d'un tribunal qui n'avait jamais fonctionné et dont la composition était à la discrétion du pouvoir exécutif; il était d'ailleurs entaché d'arbitraire, comme le Gouvernement et la haute cour l'avaient reconnu implicitement, l'un le 9 juillet, l'autre le 8 décembre 1883. Mais on espérait ramener ainsi la procédure à son point de départ, anéantir tous les actes postérieurs au 9 juillet 1883 et livrer Fabiani à des juges complaisants.

Le 4 mars 1884, le Gouvernement accordait en outre à M. B. Roncayolo, pour le chemin de fer de la Ceïba, une subvention mensuelle de 2000 fr. qui, toute minime qu'elle fut, n'en était pas moins destinée à montrer où allaient les sympathies officielles. Le chemin de fer avait bien été cédé par Roncayolo six semaines auparavant, mais la cession, revêtue cependant de l'approbation du chef de l'Etat, s'évanouissait, car Roncayolo avait toujours été en fait le propriétaire de la ligne. Seulement, il n'avait plus rien à craindre de Fabiani, et, par un subterfuge, les droits de Roncayolo pouvaient être rendus illusoires, s'il le fallait, pour contrecarrer son adversaire.

Fabiani retourna au Vénézuéla en mai 1884. Le tribunal d'exception, qui aurait dû statuer d'office et sans délai sur l'arrêt de conflit, ne se réunissait point. L'influence de M. Blanco demeurait prépondérante et sa haine s'acharnait contre Fabiani. Tout était perdu d'autant plus que, le 26 octobre 1885, B. Roncayolo devait céder à nouveau ses droits sur la ligne de la Ceïba pour la somme de 298,600 fr., dont 178,600 déjà reçus, en sorte qu'il ne restait plus que 120,000 fr., juste la valeur de l'inscription hypothécaire incomplète prise au nom de Fabiani le 16 juin 1883, et des terrains qu'on eût vendus pour rien au cours d'une expropriation forcée. Seule, une donation déguisée, ou toute autre machination, pouvait expliquer l'abandon, à ce prix, d'une ligne de 50 kilomètres qui avait été construite à grands frais et qui devait donner pour l'exercice de 1890 à 1891 un bénéfice net de 400,000 fr.

Le Gouvernement approuva ce transfert, bien qu'il fût notoire au Vénézuéla que Fabiani avait des réclamations très considérables à faire valoir contre les Roncayolo et que le contrat du 26 octobre 1885 dépouillât ses débiteurs. Il ne fallait pas, poursuit la demande, songer à intenter une action paulienne devant les tribunaux de l'Etat de Trujillo, au fond des Cordillières, puisque après des années Fabiani n'avait pu obtenir à Caracas et Maracaïbo l'exécution de jugements inattaquables. Plus tard, B. Roncayolo réussit à se faire octroyer une autre concession de chemin de fer, qui a présenté, pour lui, un bénéfice annuel de 225,000 fr. en 1892.

La demande rappelle encore que, le 21 novembre 1885, la France et Vénézuéla signèrent une convention pour la reprise des négociations diplomatiques et que Fabiani fut, quelque temps après, déclaré en état de faillite au Vénézuéla, pour défaut de paiement immédiat d'un montant inférieur au tiers des sommes indûment retenues par le Gouvernement défendeur. Elle cherche à prouver que la convention de 1885 est inapplicable au différend Fabiani et conclut à la réparation du dommage causé, pour faits du prince et dénis de justice par les autorités administratives et judiciaires de l'Etat de Vénézuéla, dommage dont l'Etat est responsable, et qui comprend :

1° La réparation du tort éprouvé;

2° Le gain manqué;

3° Les intérêts calculés dès la date des actes dommageables;

4° Les intérêts composés;

5° Les sacrifices faits par la partie lésée pour le maintien de son industrie;

6° Le préjudice résultant des dépenses faites et du temps perdu pour arriver à l'exécution des sentences;

7° Les dommages à considérer comme la suite nécessaire des délits;

8° Le dommage causé par la privation du travail à l'avenir;

9° La réparation du préjudice moral.

L'état des réclamations Fabiani est spécifié comme suit dans la demande en capital et intérêts capitalisés:

Etat A. Liquidation des sentences.

Francs

1° Solde créditeur au 31 août 1879, réduit à 509,183. 70

     Intérêts 630,966. 02

2° Annuités totales en vertu du contrat de mariage du 20 avril 1877, du 24 avril 1877, à pareille date de 1892, la transaction de 1878 ayant liquidé la situation antérieure, en capital . . . .   150,000. —

     Intérêts . . . . . .   96,701. —

3° Perte éprouvée sur la vente de la moitié des marchandises qui restaient à liquider à Marseille, poste dû d'après la transaction du 31 janvier 1878 .   24,296. 72

     Intérêts 33,926. 58

4° Recettes du pilotage suivant sentence arbitrale:

   a. du 1ᵉʳ décembre 1877 au 30 novembre 1878 . . .   16,000. —

     Intérêts 21,428. 58

   b. du 1ᵉʳ décembre 1878 au 30 novembre 1879 . . .   16,000. —

     Intérêts . . . . .   19,310. —

   c. du 1ᵉʳ décembre 1879 au 30 novembre 1880 . . .   16,000. —

     Intérêts . . . . .   17,311. —

   d. du 1ᵉʳ décembre 1880 au 30 novembre 1881 . . .   12,500. —

     Intérêts 12,051. 38

   e. du 1ᵉʳ décembre 1881 au 15 juillet 1882 . . . .   7,812. 45

     Intérêts 6,981. 23

5° Indemnité pour emploi du vapeur Pauline, solde (abus de confiance B. Roncayolo), année 1879 . . . . .   25,000. —

     Intérêts 31,517. 50

6° Indemnité pour services rendus par les vapeurs de Fabiani (abus de confiance B. Roncayolo), année 1879 . . .   45,385. —

     Intérêts 56,239. 80

7° Rémunération due pour vapeur Pauline, ensuite du sauvetage du navire anglais Angel (abus de confiance B. Roncayolo) année 1879 . . . . .   47,653. 32

     Intérêts 59,563. 63

Francs

8° Somme payée pour le compte de B. Roncayolo et comprise dans le montant des condamnations pécuniaires prononcées par le tribunal de commerce de Marseille, mais ne faisant pas double emploi avec des sommes dues en vertu de la transaction de 1878, année 1879 . . . . .   8,363. 84

     Intérêts 10,724. 38

9° Détournement d'une somme payée par l'Etat, pour vapeur Pauline (voyage de mai 1879 à La Guayra). . . . .   10,000. —

     Intérêts 12,176. 38

10° Détournement d'une somme payée par l'Etat de Zulia pour vapeur Pauline (voyage à Coro), année 1879 . . .   9,100. —

     Intérêts 11,080. 49

11° Frais du vapeur Pauline employé à la répression de l'insurrection de Pio-Rebello (détournement B. Roncayolo), année 1880 . . . . . .   28,000. —

     Intérêts 31,716. 67

12° Intérêts 1 % par mois du 1ᵉʳ juillet au 31 octobre 1880, perçus sur les 30,000 fr. de titres détournés par B. Roncayolo (p. 639 et 647 de la demande) . . . . . .   4,800. —

     Intérêts 5,242. 14

13° Assurance du vapeur Pauline du 1ᵉʳ janvier 1880 au 15 juillet 1882, pendant la spoliation   19,333. 33

     Intérêts 19,238. 45

14° Produit de remorquage en 1880 . . . .   100,000. —

     Intérêts 107,180. 33

15° Produit net du remorquage en 1881 . . . .   100,000. —

     Intérêts 95,453. 13

16° Produit net du 1ᵉʳ janvier au 15 juillet 1882 . . . .   54,166. 51

     Intérêts 48,403. 73

17° Somme détournée par les Roncayolo pour service des vapeurs, en 1879 . . . .   42,550. —

     Intérêts 38,023. 10

Francs

18° Somme allouée pour services du vapeur Pauline, pendant l'insurrection d'avril et mai 1882 . . . . 28,000. —
   Intérêts 25,485.07

19° Solde restant dû sur les 17,880 fr. alloués par l'Etat pour le vapeur Pauline, année 1880 . . . . . . 9,780. —
   Intérêts 10,084.94

20° Frais judiciaires jusqu'au 30 juin 1882, réduits à . . . 100,000. —
   Intérêts 89,712.96

   Total de l'Etat A . . . 2,877,129.10
Déduction à faire, avec intérêts, et comprenant, entre autres, une somme de 79,536 fr. 12 relative au poste n° 1 ci-dessus 204,954.96

   Montant du compte des sentences 2,672,174.14

Etat B.

Cet état forme plus ou moins un supplément du précédent; il se réfère aussi en partie à des décisions judiciaires non connexes avec la sentence arbitrale, mais demeurées sans effet par la faute des pouvoirs publics de Vénézuéla.

Francs

1° Versement du capitaine Santi non entré en caisse, année 1878 8,000. —
   Intérêts 11,385.58

2° Montant de traites fournies de Maracaïbo et Caracas sous la signature de Fabiani et non versé à la caisse de l'agence, année 1878 . . . . . . 90,701.64
   Intérêts 128,867.36

3° Débours détournés par B. Roncaloyo, année 1879 . . . . 31,009.24
   Intérêts 38,545.56

4° Débit personnel de B. Roncaloyo envers l'agence Fabiani, année 1879 . . . . . . 24,985.80
   Intérêts 30,154.74

5° Déficit de caisse imputable à A. Roncayolo, 31 janvier 1879 29,610.44
   Intérêts 39,198.47

Francs

6° Prélèvements avoués et illicites de A. Roncayolo, 31 mars 1880 35,136.44
   Intérêts 43,161.83

7° Surprimes payées à la caisse générale des familles, 1er octobre 1879 et 1er mai 1881, de 4000 fr. l'une, pour les risques résultant des voyages de Fabiani au Vénézuéla . . 8,000. —
   Intérêts 9,038.28

8° 5 novembre 1880, frais de séjour à Caracas avec famille 11,250. —
   Intérêts 12,267.78

9° Même date, frais de voyage de retour avec famille . . . 18,000. —
   Intérêts 19,629.38

10° 31 août 1880, frais de voyage et séjour à Caracas, avec M. Tedeschi, en juillet et août 1880 . . . . 4,800. —
   Intérêts 5,339.63

11° 7 novembre 1882, frais de séjour à Caracas avec famille pendant 14 mois. . . . . 37,000. —
   Intérêts 35,317.65

12° Frais de voyage aller et retour avec famille, 5 novembre 1882 18,500. —
   Intérêts 17,658.80

13° Crédits réels ou supposés faits indûment par B. Roncayolo et dont le recouvrement a été impossible, année 1880 . . 120,000. —
   Intérêts 139,657.79

14° Staries et surestaries du Mathieu-Orenga, du 24 mai au 15 août 1880, sur 166 tonnes de jauge, suivant tarif légal . 12,948. —
   Intérêts 14,535.18

15° Staries et surestaries du César-Etienne, 318 tonnes, du 24 juin au 1er octobre 1880 . . 29,910. —
   Intérêts 32,968.96

16° Staries et surestaries des Deux-Amis, 24 juillet au 9 octobre 1880, 186 tonnes . . . . 13,734. —
   Intérêts 15,105.91

17° Staries et surestaries des Deux-Amis, 1er avril au 15 juillet 1882, 186 tonnes . . . . 18,786. —
   Intérêts 16,706.92

18° Remise à A. Roncayolo, 5 novembre 1880 . . . . . — Francs 4,800. —

Intérêts 5,185. 24

19° Complément de frais judiciaires de 1883 à 1886 . . 160,000. —

Intérêts 135,023. 56

20° Perte des capitaux détenus par Roche et Cⁱᵉ et montant des traites d'immigration (assignations, 23 mai 1877) . . 347,814. 32

Intérêts, y compris ceux du poste n° 21 ci-dessous . 583,716. 68

21° Frais judiciaires, etc. (les intérêts sont portés au numéro précédent) . . . . 28,000. —

Total de l'Etat B 2,386,451. 18

Déductions consenties (avec intérêts) 234,304. 96

Montant du compte B 2,152,146. 22

L'*Etat C* concerne le service du remorquage, il se monte, valeur au 30 juin 1893, à la somme de 1,916,948. 35

Le retrait du service du remorquage équivaut à une dénégation de justice, puisque le Gouvernement restituait, par l'intermédiaire d'un prête-nom, aux Roncayolo une source de revenus annuels considérables que le jugement arbitral avait attribués à Fabiani. Le contrat de remorquage du 7 décembre 1874 avait été conclu pour une durée de dix ans ; le non-renouvellement du contrat, en 1884, ne fut qu'un acte de représailles dirigé par les pouvoirs publics contre l'adversaire des Roncayolo.

Etat D { En capital . . . . . 4,200,000. — / En intérêts . . . . 3,544,369. 12 } Francs

Les dommages et intérêts compris dans cet état correspondent aux sacrifices faits pour le maintien de l'industie de Fabiani et au gain dont il a été frustré. Les frais généraux de la maison de Maracaïbo étaient de 52,720 fr. par an, soit plus de 350,000 fr. pour sept années. A cela il faut ajouter, par 172,571 fr. 93, les frais généraux de la maison de Marseille, par 102,660 fr. 18, les dépenses personnelles du ménage Fabiani, par 589,425 fr. 39, le compte d'agios et intérêts, plus le frêt de plusieurs milliers de tonnes perdu par suite du mauvais vouloir des autorités, soit 100,000 fr. au minimum, le déficit de 100,000 fr. sur le produit de la vente des navires, le maintien de l'industrie huilière exploitée par Fabiani (au moins 100,000 fr.) et d'autres pertes et sacrifices pécuniaires représentant un capital de plus d'un million et demi

et de près de 2,800,000 fr. avec les intérêts calculés dès le 1ᵉʳ janvier 1883. D'un autre côté, Fabiani aurait pu, dans des conditions ordinaires, réaliser un bénéfice net de 200,000 fr. par an, si son commerce d'importation n'avait pas été arrêté par l'acte délictueux du 7 décembre 1874 jusqu'à la transaction de 1878 et repris ensuite dans des circonstances particulièrement difficiles. L'industrie huilière aurait rapporté, en outre, près de 200,000 fr. par an.

Etat E { En capital . . . . . 5,500,000. — / En intérêts . . . . 2,847,995. 01 } Francs

Ce poste se réfère à la réparation du préjudice immédiat et direct, causé depuis le 30 avril 1886, époque à laquelle Fabiani était prêt à réduire amiablement ses réclamations aux pertes éprouvées, en éliminant tous les dommages et intérêts qui dérivaient des actes de M. Blanco. Celui-ci refusa d'entrer en matière. La faillite de Fabiani fut déclarée pour non paiement d'une somme de 70,000 fr. au plus, alors qu'on lui devait des millions au Vénézuéla, et les juges de Maracaïbo allèrent même jusqu'à solliciter les présidents des tribunaux de première instance de Paris et de Marseille de faire publier l'avis de faillite dans les journaux les plus répandus de ces deux villes. Cette faillite a eu de désastreuses conséquences et le Gouvernement vénézuélien est responsable des dénis de justice qui l'ont déterminée.

Etat F. Frais du procès international . 200,000 Francs

Dans cette somme sont compris, entre autres, les frais d'installation de Fabiani et de sa famille à Paris, depuis 1886. A ces préjudices commerciaux vient s'ajouter le dommage éprouvé dans l'affaire du chemin de fer de la Ceïba ; l'exécution des sentences aurait permis à Fabiani de se substituer, dès 1881, à ses débiteurs, en exerçant tous leurs droits et actions (concession de la ligne, exploitation de la douane, etc.).

Cette entreprise, que Fabiani eût menée à bien, a produit, dans les conditions les plus défavorables, un bénéfice net supérieur à 250,000 fr. par an ; le revenu net a été de 389,164 fr. 87 pour l'exercice 1890 à 1891 et il doit être aujourd'hui de plus d'un million. Or la concession était accordée pour une période de plus d'un siècle.

La partie demanderesse récapitule ses états de dommages et intérêts et arrive aux totaux suivants, valeur au 30 juin 1893 :

Francs

1° Préjudices commerciaux . . 22,944,563. 17

2° Affaire de la ligne de la Ceïba 24,000,000. —

Total général 46,944,563. 17

III. Dans sa défense, le Gouvernement vénézuélien relève d'abord le fait que l'objet du litige est le « déni de justice allégué par Fabiani, pour non-exécution, selon lui, de la sentence arbitrale rendue en sa faveur à Marseille, le 15 décembre 1880, homologuée par le tribunal civil de première instance et confirmée par la cour d'appel d'Aix ; et le point de départ ne peut être autre que. l'arrêt par lequel, à la date du 6 juin 1882, la haute cour fédérale du Vénézuéla a donné force exécutoire dans le pays à la sentence de la cour d'appel d'Aix ».

Or la sentence arbitrale décidait : 1° que l'entreprise du remorquage devait être mise sous le nom de Fabiani ; 2° que les vapeurs Eclair, Mara et Pauline et tout l'outillage de l'entreprise du remorquage appartenaient à Fabiani ; 3° que pour règlement de compte, André Roncayolo restait débiteur de Fabiani de la somme de 538,359 fr. 07 cent. Les faits antérieurs à la décision de la haute cour fédérale du 6 juin 1882 ne rentrent point dans l'objet du litige actuel, en sorte que toute la question à trancher tient, en somme, dans ces mots : la sentence arbitrale a-t-elle été exécutée conformément aux lois vénézuéliennes, et la suspension de la procédure d'exécution est-elle imputable aux autorités de l'Etat défendeur, ou à Fabiani ?

En particulier, Fabiani a tort de considérer comme un déni de justice l'arrêt du 11 novembre 1881, émané de la haute cour fédérale. La jurisprudence française elle-même reconnaît que, l'arbitre volontaire étant un mandataire et non un magistrat, cette circonstance enlève à sa sentence le caractère d'un jugement proprement dit. Et, si cet arrêt reposait sur de fausses appréciations juridiques, il ne faut pas oublier, qu'à la date du 6 juin 1882, la haute cour fédérale déclara les sentences françaises exécutoires, lorsque Fabiani eut déposé en forme authentique la décision de la cour d'appel d'Aix (art. 558 C. proc. civ. vénéz.).

Les clauses du compromis de Caracas, du 7 août 1880, qui, en prescrivant l'exécution immédiate et sans recours possible au Vénézuéla, rendaient, d'après la demande, toute comparution inutile devant la haute cour fédérale, sont manifestement contraires aux principes généraux du droit, car aucun Etat ne renonce, en faveur des institutions d'un autre Etat ou de conventions entre parties, aux règles fondamentales de sa législation. L'exequatur doit être ordonné, dès lors, suivant la procédure fixée par la loi du pays dans lequel il est requis. La cour avait l'obligation de citer l'adversaire de Fabiani, et, s'il l'exigeait, de l'entendre. Quant aux dénis de justice rentrant dans les termes du compromis, ils n'existent pas. L'arrêt du 6 juin 1882 a été exécuté ; les tribunaux vénézuéliens ont accordé à Fabiani tout ce qu'il a réclamé ; s'il y a eu des retards, c'est qu'il s'en produit dans toute exécution entravée par un défendeur qui cherche à faire valoir ses droits ou à gagner du temps, et que Fabiani les a provoqués lui-même, soit par des récusations intempestives, soit par son ignorance des lois applicables en l'espèce ; et enfin, la sentence arbitrale a été exécutée en conformité du droit vénézuélien, jusqu'au moment où Fabiani déserta la procédure. Effectivement, le 6 juillet 1882, le juge Mendez ordonne l'exécution à Maracaïbo, sur requête de Fabiani. Les Roncayolo forment opposition, mais ils sont déboutés dès le 11 juillet, et le magistrat dispose : « Ce jour étant le quatrième depuis que l'ordonnance d'exécution a été rendue (art. 301 C. proc. civ.), un mandement sera adressé au juge du municipe de San-Raphaël en désignant les immeubles et autres objets que Roncayolo père et fils doivent remettre à Fabiani... pour qu'il le mette en possession des dits objets, faisant usage de la force en cas de nécessité ». Le 12 juillet, le tribunal du municipe de San-Raphaël met Fabiani en possession des vapeurs Eclair, Mara et Pauline ; le 14, même mois, l'entreprise du remorquage passe entre ses mains. Si le juge de première instance admit l'appel d'André Roncayolo avec effet seulement dévolutif, si le juge supérieur l'accueillit, lui, à deux effets, et si l'exécution demeura naturellement suspendue jusqu'au jugement sur l'incident, il n'y a là rien d'illégal. Ce sont les récusations non motivées de Fabiani qui ont entraîné des retards, en arrêtant toute la procédure pendant près d'une année. Après avoir tenté, par trois fois, de récuser le juge supérieur, il récusait encore le président de la cour suprême qui venait d'autoriser son appel à l'égard de la sentence prononcée sur la troisième récusation.

En somme, Fabiani envisagea qu'il avait tout gain à interrompre la procédure et il n'exerça contre les juges dont il flétrit après coup les actes prétendument illégaux et criminels, aucun des recours donnés par les lois nationales. Les erreurs qu'il a pu commettre n'engagent pas non plus la responsabilité de l'Etat défendeur ; l'art. 2 du Code civil vénézuélien porte que « l'ignorance des lois ne dispense pas de l'obligation de les observer ».

Fabiani affirme bien, sans preuves sérieuses, que le pouvoir exécutif fédéral intervenait abusivement dans la procédure d'exécution. Mais, c'est lui-même qui sollicita l'intervention du Gouvarnement, en se basant sur une interprétation erronée du § 17 de l'art. 13 de la constitution. La séparation des pouvoirs existe au Vénézuéla comme en Suisse et ailleurs. Fabiani a été mal conseillé ou mal inspiré.

Le 10 juillet 1883, le fondé de pouvoirs de Fabiani s'adresse de nouveau à la haute cour fédérale pour qu'elle enjoigne au juge d'exécuter l'arrêt du 6 juin 1882; le 8 décembre, la cour fait droit à ses conclusions. C'était, au dire de Fabiani, la condamnation du système de tergiversations inauguré par le juge supérieur; s'il en est ainsi, il devait procéder contre ce dernier en application de l'art. 341 du Code pénal vénézuélien, sous peine de perdre son recours. Les étrangers ne sauraient se réclamer de privilèges que les nationaux n'ont point. D'ailleurs, le 19 janvier 1884, le tribunal de Maracaïbo ordonne l'exécution des sentences françaises; le 8 février, le représentant de Fabiani requiert l'embargo sur les droits et actions de Roncayolo dans la douane et le chemin de fer de la Ceïba; le lendemain, le mandataire d'André Roncayolo forme opposition, en alléguant que la haute cour fédérale n'était pas compétente; le 13 février, le tribunal de 1re instance écarte la demande de l'opposant; le 23 cependant, sur requête d'André Roncayolo, la cour suprême de justice de l'Etat rend son arrêt de conflit, et, en se basant sur l'art. 50 C. proc. civ. vénéz., le tribunal suspend l'exécution.

Au lieu de faire trancher le conflit de compétence par le tribunal extraordinaire que prévoit l'art. 16 de la loi du 16 mai 1882, Fabiani abandonna la procédure, en prétextant qu'il cherchait en vain à obtenir justice au Vénézuéla. Or la cour suprême de l'Etat Falcon avait uniquement revendiqué (cfr. art. 89 de la Const. vénéz.) l'autonomie judiciaire d'un des Etats confédérés, comme elle en avait le droit; tant que la question de compétence n'était pas résolue, Fabiani ne pouvait se plaindre d'un déni de justice. Et il avait, au surplus, la faculté de rechercher le tribunal en dommages et intérêts, si l'arrêt de conflit avait été injustement rendu (art. 57 C. proc. civ. vénéz.). A ce moment, en effet, il n'avait pas d'action contre le Vénézuéla, mais contre la cour suprême de l'Etat Falcon. Il avait à suivre la voie que la loi trace aux étrangers comme aux nationaux; et il lui était interdit d'exiger une indemnité de la nation, avant d'avoir épuisé les recours légaux.

Relativement au service du remorquage, le Vénézuéla pouvait dénoncer le contrat du 7 décembre 1874 pour son échéance; ce qu'il a fait, en disposant que le nouveau contrat n'entrerait en vigueur qu'à l'expiration des dix années de la concession antérieure, soit dès le 8 décembre 1884. L'Etat n'avait pas perdu son droit souverain, parce que Fabiani avait des contestations judiciaires au Vénézuéla avec des particuliers.

L'hypothèque prise sur la douane de Ceïba, même en admettant que les droits des Ronçayolo — au reste, cédés à un tiers — fussent susceptibles d'hypothèque, ne pouvait produire d'effets légaux avant un jugement rendu sur l'opposition formée par le gouvernement de la section de Zulia. L'inscription hypothécaire de 120,000 frs., radiée le 3 septembre 1887, par les syndics définitifs de la faillite Fabiani, n'entre plus en ligne de compte, d'autant plus qu'une inscription résultant d'une sentence étrangère ne saurait être la conséquence immédiate de celle-ci, mais seulement de l'exequatur accordé par les tribunaux nationaux. Quant au contrat du 21 octobre 1885, Fabiani devait l'attaquer au moyen de l'action paulienne s'il le tenait pour frauduleux; il s'en est bien gardé, et il crie au déni de justice avant même d'avoir saisi les autorités judiciaires.

En outre, la convention franco-vénézuélienne de 1885 n'est nullement contraire au principe de la non-activité des lois. Conforme à tous les égards aux lois antérieures (art. 10 de la Const., art. 5 du décret du 14 février 1873), elle ne donne ouverture à l'action diplomatique que lorsque les étrangers ont épuisé les recours légaux. Le ministre de France à Caracas, dans sa note du 3 août 1887, a reconnu « que les réclamations élevées de ce chef (pour dénis de justice) rentrent dans les prévisions de l'art 5 de la convention du 26 novembre 1885 ». Cet acte est, de plus, réservé au compromis du 24 février 1891, et, s'il n'était pas applicable à l'affaire Fabiani, toutes les réclamations de ce dernier seraient, aux termes du décret du 14 février 1873, justiciables de la haute cour fédérale.

Le Gouvernement défendeur critique aussi l'état de dommages et intérêts de la partie des manderesse. La plupart des indemnités réclamées sont exclues par les termes mêmes du compromis. Fabiani n'est, au demeurant, créancier que des Roncayolo. La faute des autorités vénézuélienne n'est pas mieux établie que la responsabilité de l'Etat. Toute la demande repose sur des affirmations de Fabiani qui n'ont aucune valeur, ni en fait ni en droit.

La défense conclut dès lors à ce qu'il plaise à l'arbitre de décider que le Vénézuéla n'est pas responsable des dommages que Fabiani dit avoir éprouvés pour dénégations de justice.

IV. Dans sa réplique, le Gouvernement demandeur constate, entre autres, qu'il appartient à l'arbitre de déterminer souverainement le point de départ des dénégations de justice prétendues par Fabiani, le compromis étant rédigé en termes très généraux. Le déni de justice est nettement défini à l'art. 288 du C. pén. vénéz., et la définition en est très large.

Il convient de remarquer encore que l'arrêt du 11 novembre 1881, qui est en contradiction flagrante avec celui du 6 juin 1882, équivaut à

45

une dénégation de justice dont les conséquences ont été très graves; les motifs de cet arrêt sont inadmissibles. Il y a eu violation des art. 556 à 558 C. proc. civ. vénéz. et refus d'exécution d'une sentence définitive dans le sens de la convention du 26 novembre 1885. L'arbitre, en consultant le Diario de la haute cour fédérale, pourra vérifier même si elle a tenu du 12 au 31 octobre 1881 les deux audiences prévus par la loi (art. 111, ibid. et 288 C. pén. vénéz.).

Tout ce que dit la défense au sujet de l'opposition des Roncayolo et des récusations de Fabiani, est sans concluance au vu de l'arrêt de la haute cour fédérale du 8 décembre 1883, qui déclare que l'exécution des sentences françaises a été interrompue par des recours illégaux. Grâce à des retards contraires aux lois, Fabiani n'a pu mettre l'embargo sur les droits et actions de ses débiteurs. Il a fallu des années pour ne pas rendre une ordonnance d'exécution, qui devait être prononcée séance tenante.

Il n'était pas possible de rechercher, au préalable, en responsabilité le juge supérieur de Maracaïbo et la cour suprême de l'Etat de Falcon, puisque, depuis près de quatre ans, Fabiani réclamait vainement l'exequatur d'un jugement inattaquable.

Suit un « état définitif » des preuves invoquées.

V. Le Gouvernement défendeur insiste, dans sa duplique, sur la circonstance que des négociations auxquelles le compromis a donné lieu et de ses termes mêmes il résulte que cet acte se réfère exclusivement aux faits postérieurs à à l'arrêt du 6 juin 1882. L'arrêt du 11 novembre 1881 était parfaitement correct, puisque l'homologation de la sentence arbitrale n'était pas définitive, le 7 juin précédent, date du dépôt de la requête à fin d'exequatur.

En ce qui concerne le conflit de compétence, ni Fabiani lui-même, ni sa partie adverse ne se sont adressés à la cour de cassation ou à la haute cour fédérale, pour provoquer la solution du conflit, et ils n'ont pas fourni le papier timbré nécessaire à la procédure, qui a été abandonnée. La duplique pose en principe: qu'il n'y a pas eu de déni de justice, pas plus d'après les lois vénézuéliennes que d'après l'art. 506, C. proc. civ. fr., ou les lois allemandes et suisses; que l'Etat n'est point responsable des actes de ses fonctionnaires de l'ordre judiciaire, si cette responsabilité n'est formellement consacrée par la loi, et que le droit vénézuélien ne la proclame pas, tant que les étrangers lésés n'ont pas porté leurs demandes d'indemnité devant la haute cour fédérale; que l'intervention diplomatique enfin est inadmissible, aussi longtemps que les recours prévus par les lois territoriales n'ont pas été épuisés.

VI. Par son ordonnance de juillet 1895, l'arbitre a invité le Gouvernement demandeur à produire divers documents et renseignements complémentaires, et prescrit l'audition de différents témoins invoqués en demande. De ces témoins trois seulement, MM. Plumacher, R. Seijas et F. Osio ont pu être entendus, en présence des parties, par les soins de M. le représentant des Etats-Unis d'Amérique à Caracas; il a fallu près d'une année pour recueillir ces témoignages. Des quatre autres témoins, l'un est décédé au cours du procès, deux n'ont pu être atteints et le quatrième a refusé de répondre aux questions qui lui étaient posées, vu sa qualité d'ancien président de l'un des deux Etats en cause.

Une partie des documents et renseignements complémentaires requis par l'ordonnance de juillet 1895 ont été fournis. Il n'a pas été pris de conclusions contre l'authenticité des pièces produites de part et d'autre; l'arbitre appréciera librement, en conséquence, leur valeur probante et leur force obligatoire. Les difficultés soulevées par l'apport même des preuves littérales ont été écartées, ainsi que cela ressort des déclarations des Gouvernements intéressés.

VII. La procédure a été déclarée close par l'arbitre le 21 octobre 1896.

B. EN DROIT.

Il importe, en toute première ligne, de déterminer exactement l'objet du différend soumis à l'arbitrage. Aux termes du compromis du 24 février 1891, la question litigieuse est de savoir si, « d'après les lois du Vénézuéla, les principes généraux du droit des gens et la convention (du 26 novembre 1885) en vigueur entre les deux puissances contractantes, le Gouvernement vénézuélien est responsable des dommages que Fabiani dit avoir éprouvés pour dénégation de justice ». Indépendamment même de l'intention des parties, manifestée durant les négociations auxquelles a donné lieu la convention franco-vénézuélienne de 1885, il résulte à l'évidence, du texte même du compromis et de l'ensemble des faits de la cause, que le Gouvernement défendeur est actionné uniquement à raison de la non-exécution, par les autorités vénézuéliennes, du jugement arbitral rendu à Marseille, en date du 15 décembre 1880, entre Antoine Fabiani, d'une part, Benoit et André Roncayolo d'autre part. L'Etat demandeur semble même reconnaitre que la dénégation de justice initiale est l'arrêt du 11 novembre 1881 (Réplique p. 2): et, comme on le verra plus loin, il est inutile de rechercher s'il faut considérer plutôt l'arrêt du 11 novembre 1881 que celui du 6 juin 1882 comme point de départ des responsabilités éventuelles encourues dans le sens du compromis.

D'un autre côté la signification du mot « dénégation de justice » veut être précisée. Il convient d'entendre par là que tout acte devra être envisagé comme une dénégation de justice, soit d'après les lois du Vénézuéla, soit d'après les principes généraux du droit des gens, soit d'après la convention du 26 novembre 1885, le compromis n'exigeant pas la concordance absolue de ces trois sources juridiques et des différences essentielles ou même notables n'existant d'ailleurs pas entre elles sur la matière.

La législation vénézuélienne ne fournit pas une définition directe de la dénégation de justice. Cependant, le décret du 14 février 1873, sur les droits et devoirs des étrangers, dispose à cet égard, dans son art. 5, que les étrangers ont le droit de recourir à l'intervention diplomatique « lorsque, ayant épuisé les recours légaux devant les tribunaux compétents, il apparaît clairement qu'il y a eu déni de justice ou injustice notoire ». Et les art. 282 et 288 du C. pén. vénéz., du 27 avril 1873, sont ainsi conçus :

« Tout juge exécuteur d'une sentence rendue exécutoire, qui refusera ouvertement de l'accomplir, sera puni de la même peine édictée par l'article précédent (amende ou détention), sans préjudice des poursuites auxquelles il y aura lieu de procéder de ce fait (282). Les magistrats d'un tribunal agrégé et autres juges qui n'expédieront pas les affaires avec la célérité prescrite par les lois, qui n'édicteront point les ordonnances et sentences dans les délais accordés aux parties, ou qui, d'une manière quelconque, retarderont la solution des procès civils ou criminels, seront punis de la suspension de l'emploi pendant une durée de un à six mois » (288). ·

On peut prétendre que le décret de 1873 ne saurait être invoqué dans ce cas, attendu qu'entre la France et le Vénézuéla, la question du droit à l'intervention diplomatique a été réglée par la convention précitée de 1885. En vérité, un acte international a été substitué, sur ce point, à une loi purement nationale (cfr. art. 10 de la Const. vénéz. de 1881), et, bien que le compromis réserve l'application des lois vénézuéliennes, il ne vise que celles de ces lois opposables au Gouvernement demandeur ; or, celle de 1873 a été modifiée, pour les ressortissants français, dans son art. 5 du moins, par une convention postérieure, obligatoire pour les deux Etats signataires du compromis.

S'il en est ainsi, la seule définition dont il est possible de tenir compte, en droit vénézuélien, est celle des art. 282 et 288 du Code pénal de 1873, qui assimilent à une dénégation de justice,

tout fait d'une autorité judiciaire, constituant un refus d'exécution d'une sentence rendue exécutoire, un retard illégal dans l'expédition des affaires, un défaut de prononcer les ordonnances et sentences dans les délais fixés, une prorogation ou une réduction indue des délais établis par la loi, ou encore tout retard quelconque apporté à la solution d'un procès. Les refus d'exécution, l'inobservation de délais péremptoires et les retards illégaux qui peuvent être reprochés aux juges dans l'exercice de leurs fonctions sont donc les trois ordres de faits caractéristiques de la dénégation de justice, dans la législation du Vénézuéla.

La convention du 26 novembre 1885 porte ce qui suit, en son art. 5 : « Afin d'éviter à l'avenir tout ce qui pourrait troubler leurs relations amicales, les hautes parties contractantes conviennent, que leurs représentants diplomatiques n'interviendront point en matière de réclamations ou de plaintes de particuliers dans les affaires qui sont de la compétence de la justice civile ou pénale, conformément aux lois locales ; à moins cependant qu'il ne s'agisse de déni de justice ou de retard dans la procédure contraire à la coutume ou à la loi, ou d'inexécution d'un arrêt définitif, ou enfin de la violation évidente des traités ou des règles du droit des gens, malgré l'accomplissement de toutes les formalités légales. » On a paru, dans la demande tout au moins, contester l'applicabilité de la dite convention au litige actuel, en invoquant le principe de la nonrétroactivité des lois et en rappelant que l'affaire Fabiani remonte à une période antérieure à la date du 26 novembre 1885. Mais, en l'espèce, ce n'est point Fabiani personnellement qui est partie du procès, l'arbitrage est conclu non pas entre lui, mais entre la République Française et le Vénézuéla. L'Etat demandeur est lié par l'acte international susmentionné, pour toutes les interventions diplomatiques à venir. Au demeurant, la convention est expressément reconnue applicable à la présente contestation par le compromis du 24 février 1891 ; elle fait loi entre les deux pays.

Une définition directe du déni de justice n'est point donnée par l'art. 5 de la convention franco-vénézuélienne ; le texte le signale seulement parmi les causes d'une intervention diplomatique, et on pourrait même croire qu'il le distingue en quelque sorte des autres causes d'intervention — retards, inexécution d'un arrêt définitif, etc. — ou qu'il l'en sépare nettement. Mais sans qu'il soit besoin d'examiner si les parties ont employé, dans le compromis, l'expression de « dénégation de justice » comme équivalent exact du terme de déni de justice, qui est généralement adopté par la législation, la jurisprudence et la doctrine, il est permis d'affirmer que l'art. 5 ci-dessus assimile pleinement au déni de justice, quant à leurs effets, les retards illégaux de procédure, l'inexécution d'arrêts définitifs, les violations flagrantes du droit commises sous l'apparence de la légalité; dans tous ces cas, l'intervention diplomatique est déclarée admissible, pourvu qu'il s'agisse d'affaires rentrant dans « la compétence de la justice civile ou pénale ». La condition, posée par le décret de 1873, de l'épuisement des pourvois légaux devant les tribunaux, n'est pas rappelée dans la convention de 1885, et il serait excessif de dire que l'art. 5, in fine, de cet acte international (« malgré l'accomplissement de toutes les formalités légales ») se rapporte aux actions en responsabilité dirigées contre les autorités fautives; ces « formalités légales » s'intendent de celles à l'observation desquelles est subordonné l'accomplissement de l'acte judiciaire qui peut avoir déterminé un déni de justice, ou l'une des autres causes de l'intervention diplomatique; elles sont, par conséquent, antérieures au déni de justice lui-même.

En consultant les principes généraux du droit des gens sur le déni de justice, c'est-à-dire les règles communes à la plupart des législations ou enseignées par la doctrine, on arrive à décider que le déni de justice comprend non seulement le refus d'une autorité judiciaire d'exercer ses fonctions, et, notamment, de statuer sur les requêtes qui lui sont soumises, mais aussi les retards obstinés de sa part à prononcer ses sentences (cfr. arrêts du tribunal fédéral suisse des 11 juin 1880 et 7 mai 1884, dans le Journal des Tribunaux, année 1880, p. 801, et année 1884, p. 402; Code proc. civ. français, art. 506 et 507; Garsonnet, Traité théorique et pratique de procédure, vol. I, p. 225 et 229; Huc, Commentaire théorique et pratique du Code civil, vol. I, n° 180; Holtzendorff, Rechtslexikon, article « Rechtsverweigerung »; Wetzell, System des ordentlichen Civilprocesses, 5ᵉ éd., p. 815 et 463; Laband, Das Staatsrecht des deutschen Reichs, vol. II, nᵒˢ 242 et 243; Holtzendorff, Handbuch des Völkerrechts, vol. II, p. 74 et note 5 p. 75).

En réalité, les puissances compromettantes semblent avoir voulu attribuer aux mots « dénégation de justice » leur signification la plus étendue (justitia denegata vel protracta) et y faire rentrer tous les actes d'autorités judiciaires impliquant un refus direct ou déguisé de rendre la justice. Au lieu de reproduire textuellement les termes de la Convention de 1885, elles ont choisi une formule générale embrassant, dans les limites de ladite Convention, les griefs judiciaires de Fabiani contre le Vénézuéla, griefs qui, s'ils sont fondés, ont, en partie du moins, la portée de dénis de justice, tant d'après l'art. 5 de cet acte international que d'après les lois vénézuéliennes

et le droit des gens. Ce sont, effectivement, les réclamations de Fabiani, communiquées à son gouvernement, qui devaient inspirer la rédaction du compromis; et la mission de l'arbitre consiste précisément à décider si le Vénézuéla est « responsable des dommages que Fabiani dit avoir éprouvés pour dénégations de justice ».

Il n'est pas douteux qu'à l'époque où le compromis a été signé, les réclamations de Fabiani reposaient, entre autres, à la fois sur les dénis de justice *sensu stricto*, et sur d'autres faits, tels que les dénis de justice *sensu lato* indiqués dans la Convention de 1885. Et l'Etat défendeur, après avoir cité une note du 3 août 1887, où la légation française à Caracas, réduisant les prétentions de Fabiani à « ce qu'elles comportent en droit », ainsi que le défaut « d'exécution des sentences en temps utile » — l'Etat défendeur ajoute ceci: « Le Gouvernement du Vénézuéla trouva sans fondement les prétentions de Fabiani à réclamer une réparation, parce qu'il n'y avait pas eu de déni de justice, ni lieu de recourir à l'intervention diplomatique » (Défense, p. 3).

Ainsi, l'objet du différend et ses origines sont reconnus des parties; c'est pour refus d'exécution du jugement arbitral du 15 décembre 1880 que Fabiani possédait contre deux débiteurs domiciliés au Vénézuéla, ou pour défaut d'exécution par suite de l'admission de moyens illégaux, que la France a pris en mains les intérêts de son national. Le gouvernement vénézuélien conteste le droit de son adversaire de l'actionner en responsabilité, non point parce qu'il n'envisagerait pas les faits judiciaires allégués par Fabiani, s'ils étaient vrais, comme emportant des dénis de justice, mais parce qu'il voit l'absence de dénis de justice dans l'inexactitude de ces faits, ou dans la désertion de la procédure avant l'épuisement des recours légaux. Les parties en s'appuyant, dans le traité d'arbitrage, sur la Convention de 1885, ont, quoiqu'elles ne parlassent au compromis que de « dénégations de justice », considéré que l'arbitre pouvait retenir comme des éléments du procès les faits rentrant dans le cadre de la Convention prérappelée et constitutifs de dénis de justice en droit vénézuélien comme d'après le droit des gens: de l'avis même des intéressés, dès lors, et conformément aux textes applicables, les dénégations de justice, dans le sens du compromis, s'entendent de tous refus directs ou déguisés de juger, de tous retards de procédure illégaux et de toutes inexécutions d'arrêts définitifs, moyennant que ces faits concernent des affaires de la justice civile ou pénale, soient imputables à des autorités judiciaires du Vénézuéla et se soient produits « malgré l'accomplissement de toutes les formalités légales » par la partie lésée.

En revanche, le Vénézuéla n'encourt aucune responsabilité, selon le compromis, à raison de faits étrangers aux autorités judiciaires de l'Etat défendeur. Les réclamations que le demandeur fonde sur des « faits du prince », qui sont, soit des changements de législation, soit des actes arbitraires du pouvoir exécutif, sont absolument soustraites à la décision de l'arbitre, qui élimine de la procédure tous les allégués et moyens de preuve y relatifs, en tant qu'il ne pourrait pas les retenir en vue d'établir d'autres faits concluants et connexes relatifs aux dénégations de justice.

II. Ce sont bien les dénégations de justice, commises au cours de la procédure d'exécution de la sentence arbitrale du 15 décembre 1880, et l'appréciation éventuelle de leurs conséquences pécuniaires, qui forment le litige actuel. Il est cependant nécessaire de relever encore une objection de la demande.

La situation judiciaire de Fabiani au Vénézuéla fut liquidée d'abord par la transaction du 31 janvier 1878. Après une série d'incidents Fabiani renonçait au bénéfice de cet acte et signait le compromis qui a donné naissance à la sentence arbitrale du 15 décembre 1880. La partie demanderesse a exposé qu'elle avait adhéré à ce compromis sous l'empire d'une force majeure et qu'il ne couvrait pas les dénégations de justice antérieures. Mais elle reconnaît sans détour (Demande, p. 142 et s.) que Fabiani, qui aurait pu faire casser le compromis par les tribunaux français, préféra réserver l'avenir de son commerce au Vénézuéla en épuisant tous les moyens de conciliation; Fabiani se contentait ainsi de l'état de choses créé par l'acceptation de la juridiction arbitrale, et d'ailleurs, depuis ce moment, ses efforts judiciaires au Vénézuéla tendirent uniquement à l'exécution du jugement du 15 décembre 1880. Le motif tiré de la vis major, qui aurait affecté le compromis de 1880 et qui reculerait le point de départ des dénégations de justice comprises dans la présente instance, ne saurait donc être pris en considération. Des dénégations de justice, en vertu desquelles il serait possible de rechercher le Vénézuéla en responsabilité devant l'arbitre, n'ont pu se produire avant l'introduction de la procédure d'exécution de la sentence du 15 décembre 1880, soit avant 7 juin 1881, date de la demande d'exequatur formée auprès de la haute cour fédérale.

Aussi l'arbitre n'a-t-il pas admis à la preuve, outre « les faits du prince », tous les faits étrangers à l'inexécution et aux effets de l'inexécution de la sentence prérappelée.

III. La procédure d'exécution, introduite par Fabiani au Vénézuéla, remonte aux premiers jours du mois de juin 1881; interrompue à plusieurs reprises par des incidents divers, elle fut définitivement suspendue par l'arrêt de conflit du 23 février 1884 et l'inaction du tribunal extraordinaire chargé par la loi de trancher la question de compétence que souleva la cour suprême de l'Etat de Falcon, en sorte qu'à cette heure, la sentence arbitrale du 15 décembre 1880 n'est point exécutée. Les dénégations de justice dont Fabiani peut avoir été victime, ont, en conséquence, dû se produire depuis le commencement de juin 1881 jusque dans les premiers mois de l'année 1884.

C'est par une requête à fin d'exequatur des 3 et 7 juin 1881 que Fabiani accomplit le premier acte de sa procédure; celle-ci n'était, suivant la demande (p. 165), « qu'une simple formalité ». Assurément le compromis de 1880 stipulait que la sentence qui serait rendue par les arbitres deviendrait immédiatement exécutoire au Vénézuéla, sans qu'on pût admettre contre elle aucun recours. Mais les conventions des parties ne peuvent déroger à des règles d'ordre public, comme le sont celles relatives à l'exécution de jugements étrangers; cette manière de voir se rattache à la souveraineté, et les principes qui la régissent sont du droit le plus strict (cfr. Calvo, Le droit international théorique et pratique, 5e éd., vol. III, p. 366).

A d'autres égards, ce sont les lois territoriales qui déterminent exclusivement les formalités et conditions nécessaires pour obtenir l'exequatur. Ces formalités et conditions se trouvaient fixées, en l'espèce, par les art. 557 et 558 C. proc. civ. vénéz. et en particulier par l'art. 558, ainsi conçu :

« Pour que la sentence soit déclarée exécutoire, il faut citer le jour la personne contre laquelle la sentence a été prononcée, et que les parties soient admises à discuter verbalement, en audience publique, ce qu'elles croient convenable pour la défense de leurs droits. La partie qui introduit l'affaire doit présenter la sentence en forme authentique. » C'est à tort que la demande critique la procédure suivie par la haute cour fédérale, à laquelle s'était adressé Fabiani et qui a, de par l'art. 556 C. proc. civ. vénéz. « fonction de donner force exécutoire aux sentences rendues par les autorités étrangères » : la haute cour avait l'obligation de citer et d'entendre les adversaires de Fabiani, nonobstant les termes du compromis de 1880, et, ce faisant, elle ne s'est point rendue coupable d'une dénégation de justice.

Il n'est pas possible non plus de voir un déni de justice dans la décision sur l'incident du 27 septembre 1881, car le fond de la contestation n'était pas abordé et il n'y a pas de contradiction insoluble entre elle et l'arrêt du 11 novembre, ni dans la circonstance que la haute cour n'a pas siégé, du 14 octobre 1881, jour de la clôture des débats, jusqu'au 31 du même mois, l'art. 111 C. proc. civ. vénéz. ne prescrivant aux juges de rendre leurs sentences dans les deux jours à compter de celui où « sont terminés les exposés des parties », que « sous réserve de dispositions spéciales », auxquelles il a fallu recourir (Annexe I de la défense, p. 20 et s.).

L'arrêt du 11 novembre 1881 ne constitue pas davantage un déni de justice, un refus déguisé de statuer. Fabiani s'adressait à la haute cour fédérale, pour qu'elle déclarât exécutoire au Vénézuéla l'ordonnance du président du tribunal de première instance de Marseille du 21 décembre 1880, mise au pied de la sentence arbitrale du 15 même mois. Benoît et André Roncayolo contestaient la compétence de la cour et la valeur juridique de l'ordonnance du juge français. Au moment même où la procédure d'exécution fut introduite par Fabiani, celui-ci ne possédait, ni ne pouvait posséder, une copie authentique du jugement définitif dont il requérait l'exécution, puisque l'ordonnance du 21 décembre 1880, portée par voie d'opposition devant le tribunal de 1re instance de Marseille puis confirmée le 1er avril 1881, mais déférée aussitôt après à l'instance supérieure, ne devenait définitive que par l'arrêt de la cour d'appel d'Aix du 25 juillet de cette dernière année.

Aussi longtemps que la question de la validité de l'ordonnance d'exécution du 21 décembre 1880 restait en suspens, la haute cour fédérale n'était pas tenue d'accorder l'exequatur requis. Il est vrai, qu'en terminant ses plaidoiries, l'avocat de Fabiani a produit une expédition de l'arrêt rendu par la cour d'Aix (Annexe I de la défense, p. 18, 27, 32); mais le Gouvernement demandeur n'a mis sous les yeux de l'arbitre aucun texte légal qui pût faire considérer ce complément du dossier comme n'étant pas tardif, et Fabiani lui-même ne paraît pas y avoir attaché d'importance; effectivement, le 12 novembre 1881, il priait la haute cour fédérale de « donner exécution à l'arrêt de la cour d'appel d'Aix » du 25 juillet, après avoir été débouté, comme il le rappelle, des fins de sa requête tendant à obtenir l'exequatur de la sentence arbitrale déclarée exécutoire par l'ordonnance du 21 décembre 1880. Si l'arrêt d'Aix rentrait dans l'objet de la décision de la haute cour fédérale, du 11 novembre 1881, la nouvelle requête du lendemain aurait dû être forcément écartée, attendu qu'il y aurait eu res judicata sur ce point comme sur les autres; s'il n'y rentrait pas, la haute cour n'avait point, le 11 novembre 1881, l'obligation d'accorder l'exequatur à une sentence qui n'avait pas encore la valeur d'un jugement étranger passé en force de chose jugée. Partant, il est superflu de dis-

cuter le mérite des motifs invoqués, à l'appui de l'arrêt précité de la haute cour fédérale, par la majorité des membres de celle-ci. Il ne pouvait, au reste, y avoir de dénégation de justice dans le cas particulier, spécialement en vertu de la Convention franco-vénézuélienne de 1885, qu'autant que toutes les formalités légales — soit, notamment, le dépôt régulier d'une sentence arbitrale munie d'une ordonnance d'exécution non frappée de recours — auraient été préalablement accomplies par Fabiani, ce qui n'a pas eu lieu, ainsi que les actes ultérieurs de la procédure permettent de le constater.

Il n'est pas indispensable de rechercher si l'arrêt de la haute cour fédérale, du 6 juin 1882, qui décréta l'exécution de l'arrêt de la cour d'appel d'Aix du 25 juillet 1881, a été rendu dans un sens favorable à Fabiani, parce qu'on redoutait, au Vénézuéla, que la question internationale ne fût posée. Cette décision n'implique évidemment aucune dénégation de justice; mais il convient d'examiner si ses effets n'ont pas été compromis d'une manière illicite par les autorités judiciaires de l'Etat défendeur.

Certains faits exposés dans la demande (p. 285 et s.) laissent supposer que l'arrêt du 6 juin 1882 n'aurait donné qu'en apparence gain de cause à Fabiani et qu'on se réservait de rendre illusoire, à Maracaïbo, où elle devait être exécutée, la décision de la haute cour fédérale. Mais ces faits, que devaient prouver les déclarations de MM. Palacios et Rojas Paül, ne sont pas établis, l'un des témoins ayant refusé de répondre et l'autre n'ayant pu être atteint.

Quoi qu'il en soit, la série des dénégations de justice commence presque dès l'instant où Fabiani tenta d'obtenir, à Maracaïbo, l'exécution de la sentence arbitrale pourvue désormais d'une ordonnance d'exequatur en due forme; il sied de remarquer, avant tout, que la défense n'a pas même allégué que Fabiani n'eût point satisfait à toutes les « formalités légales » prévues par la Convention de 1885, pour arriver à l'exécution de ses sentences de la part des autorités judiciaires auxquelles il s'est adressé, et que celles-ci n'en ont pas signalé l'insuffisance ou l'absence.

L'existence de dénégations de justice, à compter de cette époque, résulte, entre autres, de l'arrêt de la haute cour fédérale, du 8 décembre 1883, reconnaissant que l'exécution a été arrêtée par « l'admission de recours illégaux » (Annexe II de la défense, p. 187). Il est clair que l'incident soulevé à Maracaïbo par la partie adverse de Fabiani, à savoir que le jugement à exécuter n'était pas la sentence arbitrale mais bien l'arrêt de la cour d'appel d'Aix, « était certainement absurde » comme le dit la défense (Duplique, p. 34): l'autorité judiciaire chargée de l'exécution aurait dû passer outre. Mais, si André Roncayolo est débouté de son opposition, si le Tribunal de première instance au civil de Maracaïbo refuse de se récuser, le même tribunal n'en accueille pas moins, avec effet simplement dévolutif d'abord, l'appel interjeté contre ses décisions, pour le recevoir à double effet, sur l'ordre du juge supérieur.

Or, l'opposition et le pourvoi de Roncayolo devaient être écartés sans examen, ainsi que la haute cour fédérale l'a proclamé dans son arrêt du 8 décembre 1883. En permettant aux adversaires de Fabiani d'entraver sans droit l'exécution des sentences françaises, les autorités judiciaires du Vénézuéla ont commis à l'encontre de ce dernier des dénégations de justice, consacrées essentiellement par l'admission de l'appel des Roncayolo avec effet suspensif; il y a eu refus déguisé de statuer. Et cette opinion est fortifiée encore par le fait de la démission du juge Mendez: il est au moins vraisemblable que ce magistrat, qui avait ordonné les premières mesures d'exécution, se sera démis de ses fonctions pour sortir d'une situation fausse dans laquelle il ne voulait pas assumer plus longtemps une part de responsabilité.

Le défendeur reproche vivement à Fabiani d'avoir causé lui-même de graves retards, à raison des demandes de récusation qu'il a présentées contre le juge supérieur. Abstraction faite du bien-fondé de l'une au moins des causes de récusation (Annexe II de la défense, p. 61 et s.; cfr. art. 59, § 18 et art. 60 C. proc. civ. vénéz.), et du désir tout naturel que devait éprouver Fabiani de ne pas accepter la justice d'un magistrat qui, tout en se rendant l'auteur d'illégalités manifestes, s'obstinait à exercer son mandat, il suffit de rappeler que toute la procédure était arbitrairement arrêtée, contrairement aux vœux de Fabiani, par l'admission de moyens irrecevables; la faute originaire retombait, en tous cas, sur les autorités judiciaires qui n'avaient pas repoussé a limine de semblables moyens.

Des mois se passaient sans qu'il fût possible à Fabiani d'exercer les droits dérivant pour lui de la sentence arbitrale du 15 décembre 1880. Il sollicita, sur ces entrefaites, l'intervention du pouvoir exécutif, en se basant sur le § 17 de l'art. 13 de la Constitution, par lequel l'Etat est tenu « d'accomplir et de faire accomplir et exécuter . . . . les décrets et ordres que . . . . les tribunaux de la Fédération rendraient dans l'exercice de leurs attributions et de leurs facultés légales ». Cette démarche, longuement critiquée dans la défense, était à la fois prudente et correcte, puisque aussi bien l'ordonnance d'exequatur de la haute cour fédérale n'était pas respectée, et qu'en pareil cas le Gouvernement a le devoir constitutionnel d'assurer l'administration de la justice. Si même le § 17 de l'art. 13 précité n'avait point cette portée et si l'on se refusait à voir, avec la demande, de la malveillance ou de l'incurie dans la résolution du Pouvoir exécutif du 9 juillet 1883, l'arrêt de la haute cour fédérale du 8 décembre suivant prescrivit la continuation de la procédure d'exécution suspendue par des « recours illégaux », et décréta implicitement que toute la responsabilité des retards incombait aux autorités judiciaires qui étaient entrées en matière sur ces recours. En réalité, les retards considérables éprouvés par la procédure d'exécution sont bien le fait des juges, et si Fabiani a pu ou dû en occasionner lui-même, il ne serait pas équitable de les lui imputer à faute, parce qu'il il a tenté de modifier une situation contraire aux lois qui était l'œuvre des tribunaux vénézuéliens.

Divers indices donnent à penser que le Gouvernement défendeur prenait ouvertement parti contre Fabiani, et que cette attitude pouvait inciter ou encourager l'autorité judiciaire du moins dans des provinces éloignées de. le capitale et soustraites au contrôle d'une opinion publique vigilante, à méconnaître les droits d'un demandeur étranger auquel des personnes influentes de l'Etat ne ménageaient point leur hostilité. Telle est l'approbation officielle du 21 août 1883 donnée à la cession, consentie par B. Roncayolo, du contrat de chemin de fer de la Ceïba, bien qu'il fût notoire, au Vénézuéla, que cette cession avait pour but de diminuer ou d'anéantir les gages d'un créancier; telle paraît être encore la modification adoptée par la législation de l'Etat Falcon aux art. 5 et 7 de la loi organique du pouvoir judiciaire, en janvier 1883; tel sera encore le retrait du service du remorquage qui, dans les circonstances et à l'époque où il fut décidé, devait être interprété comme un acte de représailles dirigé contre Fabiani.

Une nouvelle dénégation de justice du caractère le plus grave allait se produire. Le juge de première instance de Maracaïbo, se conformant à l'arrêt de la haute cour fédérale du 8 décembre 1883, avait ordonné la continuation de la procédure d'exécution, lorsque, le 9 février 1884, André Roncayolo demanda que le dossier fût transmis à la cour suprême de l'Etat Falcon, qui, seule, était investie légalement de la juridiction en la matière. Cette requête fut repoussée, mais Roncayolo saisit directement la cour suprême; celle-ci, par arrêt du 23 du même mois, et d'office, « décida, en représentation du pouvoir judiciaire de l'Etat Falcon, de contester, comme elle le fait dès à présent, à la haute cour, par devant la cour de cassation, constituée en la forme susmentionnée, la compétence de connaître dans l'affaire de l'exécution de la sentence de la cour d'appel d'Aix, rendue exécutoire au Vénézuéla, dans la cause poursuivie par Antoine Fabiani contre André et Benoît Roncayolo ».

Cet arrêt de conflit suspendait, une fois de plus, le cours de la procédure. Il se fondait sur l'art. 88 de la Constitution du 27 avril 1881, disposant que « tout ce qui n'est pas expressément attribué à l'Administration générale de la Nation, par cette constitution, est de la compétence des Etats ». L'autonomie judiciaire des Etats qui font partie de la Fédération vénézuélienne n'existe toutefois, d'après ce texte, qu'autant qu'elle n'est pas restreinte par la Charte du Pays. Mais elle est limitée, notamment, par le § 17 déjà cité de l'art. 13 de la Constitution, par les art. 556 et suiv. du code de procédure civile, qui, bien que promulgués antérieurement, n'ont été abrogés — le gouvernement défendeur le reconnait d'une manière implicite — ni formellement, ni virtuellement, par celle-ci, et par la loi constitutionnelle du 2 juin 1882 relative à l'organisation de la haute cour fédérale (cfr. Const. du 27 avril 1881, art. 80, chiffre 11).

C'est bien aussi la doctrine consacrée par la haute cour, dans ses deux arrêts du 6 juin 1882 et du 8 décembre 1883, ainsi que par le Gouvernement dans sa résolution du 9 juillet de cette dernière année. Assurément, une minorité des membres de la haute cour opina, et la défense a repris son argumentation, que la compétence de ce tribunal cessait dès le moment où il avait accordé l'exequatur aux sentences françaises. Cette théorie cependant est contredite par la loi organique du 2 juin 1882, qui porte en son article 8, chiffre 11, que la haute cour a mission de « provoquer la plus prompte administration de la justice — sans doute aussi de la justice qu'elle est appelée à prononcer — afin qu'elle soit strictement rendue par les juges et les tribunaux nationaux inférieurs » (cfr. la dite loi art. 18, chiffres 4 et 5, art. 5, chiffre 9, combinés avec les art. 556 et suiv. C. proc. civ. vénéz.). Et le ministre de l'intérieur, par sa résolution du 9 juillet 1883, a expressément déclaré que « c'est à la haute cour fédérale qu'il appartient de faire observer ses dispositions ». Au surplus, le § 17 de l'art. 13 de la Constitution existe; comme les autorités judiciaires supérieures, le pouvoir exécutif était averti des illégalités commises et il n'a rien fait pour les empêcher, ni alors, ni plus tard, quoiqu'il eût le devoir d'assurer l'exécution des « décrets et ordres » émanés des « tribunaux de la Fédération ». La partie défenderesse prétend bien que raisonner ainsi c'est confondre l'exequatur, matière fédérale, avec l'exécution, matière de la juridiction de l'Etat requis. L'exécution est déférée, à la vérité, aux autorités judiciaires des divers Etats de la Fédération, mais, en tant que

chargées de faire exécuter des sentences étrangères ensuite de décisions de la haute cour, elles se trouvent placées sous le contrôle de ce tribunal et elles en apparaissent comme les organes d'exécution. Accepter une thèse différente équivaudrait à convertir en décrets illusoires les ordonnances d'exequatur de la haute cour, qui n'aurait aucun moyen de leur prêter un effet quelconque et qui remplirait à cet égard des fonctions de pure forme. Il est plus logique, et il est dans l'esprit de la législation vénézuélienne, de considérer comme des juges et des tribunaux de la nation placés sous la surveillance de la haute cour et agissant sur ses ordres (loi organique de 1882, art. 8, chiffre 11), les autorités judiciaires auxquelles est déléguée, dans les Etats, l'exécution des jugements étrangers (ibid. art. 18, chiffres 4 et 5).

La cour suprême de l'Etat Falcon, en soulevant un conflit de compétence dans une procédure dont la partie adverse de Fabiani entravait le cours, pour un motif que l'Etat défendeur qualifie de « certainement absurde », a commis une dénégation de justice dans le sens du compromis; en encourageant l'opposition mal fondée d'un débiteur, elle a, si non déterminé un refus de statuer, du moins provoqué un retard injustifié, et après tant d'autres faits de même nature, la décision qu'elle a prise a dû fortifier en Fabiani la conviction que l'évidence de son droit ne le protégeait pas contre l'arbitraire des juges.

Fabiani, dit la défense, déserta la procédure; elle ajoute qu'il ne pouvait se plaindre de dénégations de justice aussi longtemps qu'il n'avait pas épuisé ses moyens d'action judiciaire au Vénézuéla, et provoqué, en particulier, une solution du conflit de compétence, ou invoqué les dispositions légales qui permettent de faire condamner les magistrats fautifs à « rembourser les dommages et préjudices causés ». Mais d'abord, si Fabiani s'était prévalu de ces dispositions légales, il se serait heurté à l'objection que le tribunal extraordinaire, auquel est attribuée la connaissance des conflits de compétence et qui doit les trancher d'office, n'avait pas rendu sa décision; ce tribunal ne s'est d'ailleurs jamais réuni. Ensuite, Fabiani avait des raisons de croire que, s'il ne pouvait obtenir justice au Vénézuéla contre des débiteurs étrangers au pays, il l'obtiendrait moins encore contre des autorités judiciaires même de l'Etat. L'art. 16 de la loi organique de la cour de cassation, du 16 mai 1882, règle la composition du Tribunal extraordinaire (cour de cassation et haute cour fédérale siégeant ensemble) qui avait à liquider le conflit de compétence. Les art. 54 et suiv. du Code de procédure civile prescrivent que « l'autorité supérieure que cela concerne procédera aussitôt qu'elle aura reçu les actes des juges, à la détermination de la compétence dans les vingt-quatre heures, de préférence à toute autre affaire », et que « l'arrêt sur la compétence sera prononcé sans citation ni mémoires ». Conformément à ces textes, l'arrêt du 23 février 1884 ordonne (Annexe II de la défense, p. 338) que « le dossier sera envoyé à la cour de cassation et la présente décision notifiée à la haute cour fédérale *aux effets de la compétence provoquée* » ; la cour de cassation a reçu le dossier le 24 mars 1884 (Ibid., p. 379) et Fabiani devait admettre que l'arrêt du 23 février avait été communiqué immédiatement à la haute cour fédérale. Il n'est nullement établi, ni même allégué, dans la défense, que le tribunal extraordinaire eût besoin, avant de pouvoir statuer, de renseignements complémentaires, qu'il est autorisé à réclamer en vertu de l'art. 55 du Code de procédure civile, ni qu'il se soit jamais réuni. La procédure instituée par la loi du 16 mai 1882, et les art. 54 et suiv. du Code précité, qui sont applicables en l'espèce aux termes de l'art. 12 de la même loi, est une procédure d'office. La cour de cassation et la haute cour réunies devaient prononcer, dans les vingt-quatre heures, à compter du 24 mars 1884, sur le conflit de compétence. En ne le faisant pas, elles se sont rendues coupables d'une dénégation de justice bien caractérisée.

Quant à l'argument du Gouvernement défendeur (Duplique, p. 50), d'après lequel les art. 54 et 55 du Code de procédure civile ne seraient pas applicables, la procédure étant tracée par l'art. 16 de la loi organique de la haute cour fédérale, elle est réfutée par l'arrêt même du 23 février 1884 ; et le dit article 16 ne corrobore pas davantage cet argument que les dispositions transitoires de la loi dont il s'agit.

Il n'y a pas lieu d'attacher plus d'importance à un autre moyen avancé dans la duplique : le tribunal extraordinaire dont il a été question n'aurait eu l'obligation de juger qu'une fois que les parties auraient fourni le « papier timbré nécessaire » (Ibid., p. 50). La formalité du timbre exigée par l'art. 16 de la loi organique, du 2 juin 1882, se rapporte uniquement aux affaires traitées devant la haute cour fédérale ; elle dérive d'une prescription légale qui ne peut être étendue, par analogie, aux conflits de compétence déférés au tribunal extraordinaire souvent mentionné, car l'analogie, exclue en principe dans une pareille matière, l'est formellement par la nature même de la procédure déterminée aux art. 54 et suiv. du code de procédure civile ; on ne concevrait point, à défaut de disposition contraire expresse, que les parties eussent à supporter, en acquittement de droits de timbre, les frais d'une instance qui est ouverte d'office, à raison du fait de juges qui se seraient déclarés faussement compétents ou dont la compétence aurait été contestée à tort par d'autres juges, et qui se déroule en dehors de toute participation des plaideurs. Fabiani, qui n'a pas été cité devant la cour suprême de l'Etat Falcon, qui ne pouvait ni ne devait être assigné devant le tribunal extraordinaire, était absolument étranger au conflit de compétence ; ce tribunal avait l'obligation de statuer d'office, dans les vingt-quatre heures, sans que les parties eussent à accomplir quelque diligence ou formalité que ce fût.

En somme Fabiani a été victime de plusieurs dénégations de justice, consommées par celles qu'implique l'inaction illégale de la cour de cassation et de la haute cour fédérale ; cette dernière dénégation de justice seule suffisait à créer, au profit de Fabiani, le droit à l'intervention diplomatique et à lui assurer un recours en dommages et intérêts contre le Gouvernement défendeur, s'il doit être reconnu que celui-ci est responsable des fautes de ses autorités judiciaires et si Fabiani prouve qu'il a subi un préjudice de ce chef.

Dans les circonstances qui ont été exposées, l'intervention diplomatique était autorisée déjà par les termes formels de l'art. 5 de la Convention franco-vénézuélienne de 1885, et elle n'avait rien de contraire aux décisions de la doctrine (cfr. notamment, Holtzendorff, Handbuch des Völkerrechts, vol. II, p. 74 ; Fiore, Droit international codifié, n°° 339 et 340 ; voir aussi Calvo, op. cit., vol. I, n° 348 ; Pradier-Foderé, Traité de droit international public, vol. I, n°° 402 et suiv. ; Bluntschli, op. cit., n° 380). Il serait effectivement inadmissible d'exiger de Fabiani qu'il eût fait, en outre, constater ces dénégations de justice notoires par les tribunaux vénézuéliens compétents, lui qui, pendant des années, avait demandé en vain l'exécution d'une sentence inattaquable et pourvue de l'exequatur requis par les lois territoriales, bien que les autorités administratives et judiciaires supérieures de surveillance eussent été averties des illégalités commises. L'inexécution des sentences françaises, provoquée par les magistratures inférieures, tolérée par la haute cour fédérale et le Gouvernement, consacrée par le tribunal extraordinaire, enlevait à Fabiani la disposition d'une fortune considérable, l'entraînait dans des procès coûteux et sans issue, l'amenait finalement à la faillite et justifiait amplement une action internationale.

Il semble bien, à considérer la série des dénis de justice dont Fabiani avait le droit de se plaindre, et même l'une ou l'autre de ces décisions judiciaires lui donnèrent momentanément gain de cause en apparence, que ses adversaires étaient protégés, au Vénézuéla, par des influences assez puissantes pour entraver l'activité normale des tribunaux du pays. Cette hypothèse repose, au surplus, sur trois faits précédemment rappelés : approbation officielle due

21 août 1883, modification des art. 5 et 7 de la loi organique du pouvoir judiciaire de l'Etat Falcon, et retrait du service de remorquage. Elle est fortifiée par d'autres circonstances, parmi lesquelles il suffira de mentionner les suivantes :

Deux des trois témoins dont les déclarations ont été recueillies pendant l'instruction de l'affaire, en présence des parties, n'ont fourni aucun renseignement de nature à faire douter de l'impartialité des tribunaux vénézuéliens ; mais le troisième témoin, M. E.-H. Plumacher, consul des Etats-Unis d'Amérique à Maracaïbo, qui a bien été chargé par intérim du consulat de France dans cette ville et qui fut un temps le mandataire spécial de Fabiani, contre lequel toutefois aucune cause de suspicion n'a été relevée et qui est le ressortissant d'un Etat non impliqué dans le litige actuel, a déposé devant le ministre d'une nation neutre chargé de l'entendre au nom de l'Arbitre : qu'il avait « l'impression », qu'en 1880, M. Guzman Blanco avait provoqué ou suggéré des démarches destinées à exercer une pression sur Fabiani, à l'occasion des démêlés de celui-ci avec les Roncayolo ; qu'à ce moment, « M. Blanco était le pouvoir dans le pays » ; « qu'il arriva des choses qui donnèrent lieu de douter de l'impartialité des tribunaux vénézuéliens » ; qu'il avait « entendu de M. William Mollmann, précédemment employé dans la maison Roncayolo, ensuite employé du consulat américain, que M. Guzman Blanco et Benoît Roncayolo avaient des intérêts d'affaires ensemble et que M. Guzman Blanco aiderait Roncayolo en toute circonstance » ; qu'au reste, « tout le monde à Maracaïbo savait cela, et qu'on disait couramment parmi les étrangers que M. Roncayolo gagnerait le procès puisqu'il avait la protection de M. Guzman Blanco » ; qu'il est, lui témoin, « positivement convaincu que M. Fabiani n'était pas bien vu par les tribunaux et autorités ». Ces déclarations sont très générales, il est vrai, et ne reposent pas sur des faits précis dont M. Plumacher aurait eu la perception directe ; elles n'en sont pas moins l'opinion d'un observateur compétent et désintéressé, en sorte qu'à ce titre, elles ne laissent pas d'avoir une certaine valeur.

Enfin, la conviction morale de l'Arbitre est que les dénégations de justice qui se sont produites à l'encontre de Fabiani ont un caractère exceptionnel de gravité, en ce qu'elles ne sont pas la suite de simples négligences ou d'interprétations erronées de textes légaux, mais apparaissent comme intentionnelles. Certes, en droit commun allemand comme en droit français (cfr. Wetzell, op. cit., 3ᵉ édit., § 43 ; Holtzendorff, Rechtslexikon, article « Prozessleitung » ; von Bar, dans l'Encyclopädie der Rechtswissenschaft d'Holtzendorff, 3ᵉ édit., p. 779 ; Garsonnet, op.

cit., vol. II, § 211 et vol. I, § 55 in fine ; Aubry et Rau, 4ᵉ édit., vol. VIII, § 749, n° 2), il est de principe que le juge ne doit prendre en considération que les faits articulés et les moyens de preuves invoqués par les parties. Cependant la doctrine moderne va plus loin (cfr. Kohler, Gesammelte Beiträge zum Civilprozess, p. 361 et suiv. ; Encyklopädie der Rechtswissenschaft, d'Holtzendorff, l. c.) et l'on admet entre autres, que les tribunaux ordinaires peuvent retenir des faits assez notoires pour qu'ils jugent inutile d'en administrer la preuve (C. proc. civ. allem., art. 264 ; cfr. Wetzell, op. cit., § 43 ad note 30, et § 20, ad notes 40 à 43). A plus forte raison en est-il ainsi en matière d'arbitrage, surtout lorsque les parties n'ont point prescrit à l'arbitre la procédure à suivre (cfr. Wach, Handbuch des deutschen Civilprozesses, vol. I, p. 73 et Fuchsberger's Entscheidungen, Reichscivilprozessordnung, Suppl.-Band, note 1 ad art. 866, et notes 4 et 6 ad art. 867, C. proc. civ. allem.).

L'arbitre est investi d'un pouvoir discrétionnaire, limité seulement par l'obligation de se conformer aux principes essentiels de la procédure civile (Bluntschli, Droit international codifié, n° 495) ; il n'est pas forcé de s'en tenir aux allégués et moyens de preuve des parties, ni d'indiquer tous les éléments dans lesquels il puise sa conviction. La maxime des débats et le principe de la publicité, qui lient les juges permanents, et dont l'inobservation pourrait constituer un danger, ne lient pas dans la même mesure un arbitre, qui remplit des fonctions temporaires et qui est investi d'une magistrature de confiance.

Spécialement lorsque le compromis est muet sur la question de la procédure à suivre, comme en l'espèce, on peut envisager que, dans l'intention même des parties, une grande liberté lui est laissée quant au choix des éléments dont il formera sa conviction. Cette conviction dictée déjà par les résultats de l'administration de la preuve, a été renforcée, dans le sens marqué plus haut, par l'étude de documents que l'Arbitre s'est fait un devoir de consulter et d'apprécier au plus près de sa conscience.

Des dénégations de justice ayant été commises, à l'égard de Fabiani, par des autorités judiciaires du Vénézuéla, dont les exposés et les circonstances relatées ci-dessus, il y a lieu d'examiner si l'Etat défendeur en est responsable et, dans l'affirmative, quelle est l'étendue de sa responsabilité.

C'est une question très controversée, en droit public, que celle de savoir si un Etat répond du préjudice causé par ses agents, et spécialement par ses autorités judiciaires, à raison d'actes rentrant dans l'exercice de leurs fonctions. En

France, la doctrine et la jurisprudence sont divisées. La jurisprudence elle-même n'est pas unanime dans l'opinion, généralement consacrée toutefois, que les fautes commises par des fonctionnaires, dans les limites de leurs attributions légales, n'engagent pas la responsabilité de l'Etat, du moins d'une manière absolue et en l'absence de lois positives sur ce point (cfr. Fuzier-Herman, Code civil annoté, vol. III, ad art. 1382 et 1383, n° 767 et suiv.) ; mais la cour de cassation, par exemple, a reconnu dans un arrêt du 1er avril 1845 (cfr. arrêts des 30 juillet et 16 août 1877, ainsi que Pandectes françaises, année 1896, IVe partie, p. 8, note 1, et Laurent, vol. XX, n° 592) que l'Etat, représenté par les différentes branches de l'administration publique, est passible des condamnations auxquelles le dommage causé par le fait, la négligence ou l'imprudence de ses agents peut donner lieu. En tout cas, les fonctionnaires de l'ordre judiciaire n'étant pas tenus de leurs fautes légères (cfr. Fuzier-Herman, op. cit., vol. III, ad art. 1382 et 1383, n°s 505 et suiv. ; Demolombe, vol. XXXI, n° 519; Garsonnet, op. cit., vol. I, § 57, notes 12 et 18), la responsabilité de l'Etat ne pourrait s'étendre au delà. La doctrine enseigne, de son côté, (Aubry et Rau, op. cit., vol. IV, § 447, n° 2 ; Demolombe, vol. XXXI, n° 63 ; Baudry-Lacantinerie, op. cit., vol. III, n° 1352), que l'Etat, représenté par les divers ministères et administrations publiques, doit à l'égal de tout commettant répondre du préjudice occasionné par ses employés ou agents dans l'exercice de leurs fonctions ou services, indépendamment de l'existence d'une loi spéciale, ou encore (cfr. Laurent, vol. XX, n°s 419 et suiv., 444, 591 et suiv.), que la responsabilité de l'Etat est exclue lorsque le fonctionnaire agit, non comme préposé et instrument de l'Etat, mais comme accomplissant la mission sociale qui lui est déléguée.

S'il règne en France une assez grande incertitude, notamment en ce qui concerne la responsabilité de l'Etat pour les dommages causés par ses fonctionnaires de l'ordre judiciaire, et si cette responsabilité paraît plutôt devoir être déniée en thèse générale, il n'en est pas autrement en Allemagne. La question est résolue négativement par Lœning (Die Haftung des Staates, etc., 92 et suiv.), affirmativement par H.-A. Zachariæ (Zeitschrift für die gesamte Staatswissenschaft, année 1865, p. 582 et suiv.), par Stobbe (Handbuch des deutschen Privatrechts, vol. III, § 201, n° 6), par Gerber (Grundzüge des deutschen Staatsrechts, 2° édit., p. 207 et suiv.), par Bluntschli (op. cit., n° 467), par Windscheid (Pandekten, vol. II, § 470, note 4 ; cfr. les auteurs cités dans cette note), avec cette réserve que Windscheid, dans la sixième édition de son

traité, expose, en modifiant son opinion première, que la responsabilité de l'Etat, ensuite de préjudices imputables à ses fonctionnaires, n'est pas un principe de droit commun en Allemagne, et que, d'après Holtzendorff (Encyklopädie der Rechtswissenschaft, p. 1113), cette responsabilité n'est admissible que dans certains cas. Mais la jurisprudence allemande, qui était plutôt favorable à la solution affirmative jusqu'en 1884, applique aujourd'hui la théorie du tribunal de l'Empire, selon laquelle l'Etat n'est responsable qu'en vertu d'une disposition légale expresse (Entscheidungen des Reichsgerichts in Civilsachen, vol. XI, p. 206; cfr. Windscheid, op. cit., vol. II, § 470, note 4).

Cette dernière théorie est adoptée par la jurisprudence et la doctrine suisses (cfr. Blumer-Morel, Handbuch des schweizerischen Bundesstaatsrechts, 2° éd., vol. III, p, 230, et s. ; Hafner, Das schweizerische Obligationenrecht, 2° éd., ad art. 64, note 4, ainsi que les arrêts du Tribunal fédéral cités dans ces deux ouvrages), tandis qu'en Italie la doctrine contraire semble prévaloir (cfr. Fuzier-Herman, op. cit., vol. III, ad art. 1382 et 1383, n° 786). On peut ajouter que les auteurs qui ont fait du droit international leur spécialité, reconnaissent que l'Etat est responsable des dénis de justice commis par ses autorités judiciaires, à tout le moins lorsque duement informé ou averti, il n'aura rien entrepris, ni pour en empêcher les effets, ni pour en suspendre le cours (cfr. Holtzendorff, Handbuch des Völkerrechts, vol. II, p. 74 ; Fiore, Droit international codifié, n°s 339 et 340; voir aussi Calvo, op. cit., vol. I, n° 348 in fine; Pradier-Fodéré, Traité de droit international public, vol. I, n° 402 et s.; Bluntschli, op. cit., n° 340).

En droit vénézuélien, la question est résolue par la loi ; elle l'est également, entre les parties en cause, par la Convention de 1885. Le décret du 14 février 1873, sur les indemnités à allouer aux étrangers, n'a pas été abrogé par l'acte international précité, en ce qui touche les conditions générales de la responsabilité de l'Etat pour des dommages occasionnés par ses fonctionnaires; il dispose en son art. 1er : « Tous les individus, soit nationaux ou étrangers, qui intenteront contre la Nation des actions en dommages et intérêts ou expropriations, provenant d'actes d'employés de la Nation ou des Etats .... devront s'en tenir aux formalités établies par la présente loi » — formalités qui, entre la France et le Vénézuéla, sont réglées aujourd'hui, en ce qui concerne notamment les préjudices dérivant de dénis de justice, par la Convention de 1885. L'art. 7 prévoit que la « Nation aura le droit de se faire rembourser par l'employé responsable, ou par l'Etat duquel relèverait le dit employé au moment de la faute, la somme que le Trésor national débourserait par suite de l'arrêt condamnatoire ». Il ressort de ces textes que le Vénézuéla reconnaît expressément, en principe, sa responsabilité pour des dommages imputables, soit à des fonctionnaires nationaux, soit à des fonctionnaires de l'un ou l'autre des Etats de la Fédération; cette responsabilité est directe, elle donne action contre l'Etat devant la Haute Cour fédérale. Quant aux fonctionnaires (empleados), la loi entend par là non point seulement les agents du pouvoir exécutif ou les préposés dans le sens de l'art. 1384 C. civ. fr., mais toutes les autorités qui, investies d'une part de la puissance publique, représentent l'Etat et le personnifient. L'art. 9 du décret de 1873 le montre clairement: « Dans aucun cas, dit-il, on ne pourra prétendre que la Nation ou les Etats indemnisent à raison des dommages et intérêts ou expropriations qui n'auraient pas été causés par des autorités légitimes agissant en vertu de leur caractère public. » Cette interprétation est confirmée, en outre, par le Code pénal du 27 avril 1873, qui, après avoir traité, en ses art. 258 et 259, des infractions dont les juges peuvent se rendre coupables, ajoute en son article 260 : « Les employés publics d'une autre administration quelconque, etc. ».

En matière de responsabilité de l'Etat, il n'y a donc pas lieu d'établir de distinction, en droit vénézuélien, entre les fonctionnaires de l'ordre judiciaire et ceux de l'ordre administratif, puisque la loi les assimile expressément les uns aux autres, et qu'au même degré, bien que dans les sphères d'activité diverses, ils agissent au nom de l'Etat. Et, à un point de vue général, on ne voit pas pourquoi l'Etat répondrait, dans une mesure différente, des préjudices causés par ses fonctionnaires, selon que les auteurs du dommage seraient employés dans l'administration proprement dite ou dans la justice (cfr. Stobbe, op. cit., vol. III, § 201, ad note 53 ; H.-A. Zachariæ, op. cit., p. 637 ; Windscheïd, op. cit., vol. I, § 59 in fine; Blumer-Morel, op. cit., vol. III, p. 230 et suiv.).

Un décret vénézuélien de même date que le précédent, sur les droits et les devoirs des étrangers, tout en disposant, en son art. 6, que « les étrangers n'ont le droit de demander des indemnités au Gouvernement, que dans les mêmes cas que les Vénézuéliens » — ceci est toutefois modifié envers les Français par la Convention de 1885 — proclame aussi, en principe, la responsabilité de l'Etat défendeur pour les actes de ses fonctionnaires. Il la reconnaît même expressément, à raison des faits illicites des autorités judiciaires, en réservant dans son art. 5 la voie diplomatique pour le cas de « déni de justice ou injustice notoire », et la condition de l'épuisement préalable de toutes les voies légales de re-

cours a été supprimée par la Convention de 1885 à l'égard des Français. Cette responsabilité directe de l'Etat, édictée par la législation vénézuélienne, n'est pas contraire au droit des gens, elle est, de plus, affirmée dans la Convention du 26 novembre 1885, qui permet l'intervention diplomatique et consacre implicitement la responsabilité de l'Etat pour toute la série des irrégularités judiciaires énumérées dans l'art. 5 de ce document.

L'Etat, d'autre part, ne saurait décliner sa responsabilité par le motif que les fautes de ses agents ou fonctionnaires ne représenteraient pas un certain caractère de gravité (voir, d'ailleurs, sub V ci-après). L'art. 1 du décret du 14 février 1873, sur les indemnités à allouer aux étrangers, est conçu en termes si généraux, que l'Etat y apparaît responsable exactement comme ses employés, et rien n'est plus rationnel, puisque l'acte dommageable est alors censé provenir de l'Etat lui-même (cfr. H. A. Zachariæ, op. cit., p. 632 ; Stobbe, op. cit., vol. III, § 201, note 53). Le déni de justice, sous quelque forme qu'il se produise, constitue un cas de responsabilité du fonctionnaire, partant de l'Etat. Dès lors, Fabiani, victime de dénégations de justice dûment prouvées, pouvait actionner le Gouvernement défendeur, sans observer d'ailleurs l'art. 5 du décret du 14 février 1873 concernant les devoirs et les droits des étrangers qui pose comme condition de l'intervention diplomatique l'épuisement préalable « des voies légales auprès des autorités compétentes » (cfr. Convention de 1885, art. 5), et la mesure de son action contre l'Etat est la même que contre les fonctionnaires fautifs.

V. Les dénégations de justice qu'a éprouvées Fabiani sont pour le moins des délits civils ou des quasi-délits. En droit moderne, l'auteur d'une faute aquilienne est, en principe, tenu de réparer tout le préjudice qui peut raisonnablement en être envisagé comme la conséquence directe ou indirecte *(dammum emergens et lucrum cessans)*, certaines législations, comme celles de la France et de l'Allemagne, ne faisant pas dépendre la quotité des dommages et intérêts de la gravité de la faute, d'autres, comme le Code civil autrichien et le Code fédéral des obligations, n'accordant la réparation intégrale qu'en cas de dol ou de faute lourde. Au demeurant, les dommages et intérêts ne doivent pas être la source d'un profit pour celui qui les obtient (cfr. *Fuzier-Herman*, op. cit., vol. III, ad art. 1382 et 1383, n°° 1065 et suiv.; *Aubry et Rau*, vol. IV, § 445 et 446; *Demolombe*, vol. XXXI, n°° 685 et suiv.; *Laurent*, vol. XX, n° 529; *Zachariæ, Handbuch des französischen Civilrechts*, 7° éd., § 443 et 445; *Windscheid*, op. cit., 6° éd., vol. II, § 451, n° 1, 155, n° 5, 258, notes 10 et suiv.; *Stobbe*, op. cit., vol. III, § 200, n° 6; Holtzendorff, *Rechts-lexikon*, article « Schadensersatz »; Holtzendorff, *Handbuch des Völkerrechts*, vol. II, p. 74, 75; *Motive* du projet du Code civil allemand, vol. II, p. 724 et suiv.; Schneider et Fick, *Das schwei-zerische Obligationenrecht*, 3° éd., notes ad articles 50 et 51 C. féd. des obl.; *Hafner*, op. cit., 2° éd., notes ad art. 50 et 51 C. féd. des obl.; Rossel, *Manuel du droit fédéral des obligations*, p. 88 et suiv.)

En ce qui regarde spécialement les fonctionnaires de l'ordre judiciaire, leur responsabilité embrasse, en droit commun allemand, tout le dommage résultant de leur dol ou d'une faute lourde de leur part; le point de savoir si cette responsabilité existe également dans les cas de faute légère est controversé, mais la solution affirmative prévaut (cfr. *Windscheid*, op. cit., vol. II, p. 470; Dernburg, *Pandekten*, 3° éd., vol. II, § 135; *Wetzell*, op. cit., § 36, note 14). La responsabilité du pouvoir judiciaire est aussi admise en France (C. proc. civ. fr., art. 505; cfr. *Garsonnet*, op. cit., vol. I, § 54; *Laurent*, op. cit., vol. XX, n° 447), mais, comme il a été expliqué plus haut, elle n'est pas entraînée par une faute légère.

Au Vénézuéla, ce sont les art. 341, 255 à 259, 282, 288, 297 et 339 du Code pénal du 27 avril 1873 qui règlent, d'une manière spéciale, la matière de responsabilité civile des autorités judiciaires. Les juges peuvent être actionnés en dommages et intérêts, non seulement ensuite de leur dol ou de leurs fautes lourdes, mais encore pour des fautes légères; le texte de l'art. 341 semble indiquer que la réparation doit être complète dans tous les cas. Il n'est pas besoin, au reste, d'appuyer sur cette dernière question, attendu que les dénégations de justice dont se plaint Fabiani procèdent, à tout le moins, de fautes lourdes et que, dans ces circonstances, le préjudice à réparer s'entend et du *damnum emergens*, et du *lucrum cessans*; il comporte, en outre, le tort moral comme le dommage matériel *(Laurent*, vol. XX, n° 393—395 et suiv.: Aubry et Rau, vol. IV, § 445; *Huc*, op. cit. VIII, n° 413; Demolombe, vol. XXXI, n° 672; Code fédéral des obligations, art. 55 et les ouvrages cités de *Schneider et Fick, Hafner* et *Rossel*; C. civ. autr. art. 1329, 1330). Relativement au dommage indirect cependant et à la nécessité d'établir un rapport de cause à effet entre le fait illicite et le dommage prétendu, le demandeur prouvera que, soit en consultant le cours ordinaire des choses, soit en s'attachant aux affaires de la partie lésée ou aux dispositions prises par elle, il est probable — non pas seulement possible — que celle-ci aurait réalisé tel ou tel profit si le fait illicite ne s'était pas produit, la preuve étant d'ailleurs soumise à des conditions moins strictes en cas de faute lourde ou de dol et le juge conservant une entière liberté d'appréciation.

Si l'on doit décider que le Gouvernement défendeur est responsable des conséquences des dénégations de justice imputables aux autorités judiciaires vénézuéliennes envers Fabiani, il reste à déterminer l'étendue de ces conséquences en application des principes exposés plus haut.

Le dommage matériel direct subi par Fabiani comprend les valeurs non recouvrées et les biens perdus, dont il serait rentré en possession, si la sentence arbitrale du 15 décembre 1880 avait pu être exécutée contre les Roncaloyo ; il comprend également, en principe, les frais de la procédure d'exécution (voir sub VI, litt. *a*, chiffre 3). Fabiani n'eût-il pas été victime de dénis de justice, et l'exécution de la dite sentence n'eût-elle pas été entravée, puis rendue illusoire, il aurait pu obtenir paiement de toutes les condamnations prononcées contre ses débiteurs. Effectivement B. et A. Roncaolo étaient solvables jusqu'à concurrence au moins des restitutions diverses ordonnées par le jugement du 15 décembre 1880. Ce fait découle déjà de ce que le Gouvernement vénézuélien n'a jamais allégué même que les réclamations de Fabiani fussent irrécouvrables contre les Roncayolo, et qu'il s'est borné à contester l'existence des dénégations de justice, ainsi que la responsabilité de l'Etat. En outre, B. Roncayolo, de l'aveu de la partie défenderesse, a été agréé par les pouvoirs publics du Vénézuéla comme concessionnaire d'importantes entreprises, et il était fermier de la douane de la Ceïba. André Roncayolo a pu, lui, pendant plus de trois ans, tant en son nom personnel que comme fondé de procuration de son père, faire les frais de nombreuses et coûteuses oppositions à l'exécution de la sentence arbitrale, choisir ses avocats parmi les jurisconsultes notoirement les plus renommés du pays, sans compter qu'il s'était enrichi d'une somme de plus d'un demi-million de francs au détriment de Fabiani. Et c'est vraisemblablement pour mettre à l'abri des poursuites de leur créancier les droits et intérêts considérables qu'ils avaient au Vénézuéla, que les adversaires de Fabiani ont empêché avec tant d'acharnement l'exécution de la sentence du 15 décembre 1880. La solvabilité de B. et A. Roncayolo, partant la recouvrabilité des valeurs au remboursement desquelles ils avaient été condamnés, ne sauraient être sérieusement mises en doute, d'autant plus que, comme on vient de le dire, le Vénézuéla ne les a point déniées. En dehors du dommage matériel direct, Fabiani a éprouvé un tort matériel et surtout moral très grave, en ce que les dénégations de justice ont porté à tous les égards une profonde atteinte à sa situation personnelle et ont même été la cause de la faillite prononcée contre lui au Vénézuéla (voir sub VI, litt. *a*, chiffre 6 ci-après).

Le dommage indirect, enfin, a sa source dans le fait que les sommes payables par les Roncayolo en vertu de la sentence arbitrale ont été soustraites au créancier pendant un grand nombre d'années et qu'il n'a pu ni les employer dans son commerce, ni les faire fructifier d'une manière quelconque ; il ne s'agit pas ici de bénéfices ou de pertes purement hypothétiques, dans lesquelles certains publicistes (*Calvo*, op. cit., IV, 477) se refusent à voir « la matière d'une action pécuniaire de gouvernement à gouvernement », mais d'un manque à gagner dont les éléments reposent sur des faits concluants, et il serait souverainement contraire à l'équité et à la justice de n'en point tenir compte dans le présent procès (voir sub VI, litt. *b*).

Et maintenant, deux éventualités pouvaient se présenter : ou bien, les débiteurs de Fabiani s'acquittaient envers lui, ou bien, soit à l'amiable, soit par voie d'exécution, il se substituait à tous les droits de concessions, de douanes et autres qu'ils possédaient au Vénézuéla. Entre ces deux hypothèses, plausibles l'une et l'autre, il faut nécessairement choisir celle qui est la moins défavorable à l'Etat défendeur et qui est aussi la plus admissible, d'après le cours ordinaire des choses, c'est-à-dire l'hypothèse du paiement. Ceci d'autant plus qu'il n'a été ni offert, ni administré aucune preuve tendant à établir que cette hypothèse de la solution la plus normale du différend Fabiani-Roncayolo ne se serait point réalisée ; il résulte même de l'exposé du Gouvernement demandeur, que les débiteurs de Fabiani avaient un intérêt majeur, s'ils étaient contraints d'exécuter la sentence arbitrale, à se libérer purement et simplement entre ses mains, plutôt qu'à se laisser enlever les droits d'une valeur bien supérieure à celle des condamnations prononcées — sans parler même des obstacles auxquels se serait heurté sans doute le transfert de tous ou partie de ces droits à Fabiani, et sans apprécier l'efficacité des sûretés réelles obtenues au cours de la procédure d'exécution.

La question du mode de payement de l'indemnité a été discutée dans la demande, mais elle n'est point litigieuse ; le compromis l'a réglée d'une manière obligatoire pour les parties et pour l'arbitre.

VI. La liquidation, d'après les principes ci-dessus, de l'état de dommages et intérêts, présenté par le Gouvernement demandeur, fournit les résultats suivants :

a) *Dommage direct et tort moral.*

1° La sentence arbitrale fixait à la somme de 538,359 fr. 07, valeur au 31 janvier 1878, le débit d'André Roncayolo envers Fabiani. Ce poste est réduit, en capital, d'après la demande à . . . . Fr. 429,668. 10

Il y a lieu de tenir compte d'un versement de. . . . . » 5,490. 55

Reste Fr. 424,177. 55

2° Outre cette somme, due par A. Roncayolo, la sentence arbitrale confère à Fabiani le droit de réclamer « tous les produits, sans aucune exception et sans aucune réserve, donnés par l'entreprise du remorquage depuis le 30 novembre 1877, y compris les bénéfices du pilotage », dès la même époque, en tant que ces produits auraient été encaissés par B. ou A. Roncayolo ; les autres condamnations dérivant de la sentence du 15 décembre 1880 ont été exécutées, au moins dans une certaine mesure, puisque Fabiani a repris, dès le mois de juillet 1882, soit avant le début des dénégations de justice, le service du pilotage et du remorquage, et que des preuves positives concernant les effets de l'inexécution de ces autres condamnations font défaut dans la procédure.

Du chef du dispositif précité de la sentence arbitrale, la demande porte au compte de « liquidation des sentences » en capital :

	Francs
Recettes du pilotage du 1er décembre 1877 au 30 novembre 1878 . .	16,000. —
Recettes du pilotage du 1er décembre 1878 au 30 novembre 1879 . .	16,000. —
Recettes du pilotage du 1er décembre 1879 au 30 novembre 1880 . .	16,000. —
Recettes du pilotage du 1er décembre 1880 au 30 novembre 1881 . .	12,500. —
Recettes du pilotage du 1er décembre 1881 au 15 juillet 1882 . . .	7,812. 45
Total	63,312. 45

Le Gouvernement défendeur n'a ni contesté le bien-fondé de cette dette, provenant des encaissements faits sans droit par la partie adverse de Fabiani, ni critiqué ces chiffres, qui ne paraissent pas exagérés.

Il en est de même, pour les restitutions qui se rapportent au remorquage ; elles sont ainsi formulées dans la demande, en capital :

	Francs
Produit net de l'année 1880 . . .	100,000. —
Produit net de l'année 1881 . . .	100,000. —
Produit du 1er janvier au 15 juillet 1882	54,165. 51
Total	254,165. 51

Le produit net, évalué annuellement à 100,000 francs, n'est qu'approximatif ; mais ce chiffre, qui n'a pas été contesté dans la défense, peut être admis au vu des documents produits. Quant aux « abus de confiance » et « détournements » des Roncayolo, qui ne visent pas directement le pilotage ou le remorquage, ils ne sont pas compris dans la sentence arbitrale, ni, par conséquent, dans le compromis de 1891.

3° Il y a lieu d'ajouter au compte de « liquidation des sentences » les frais importants occasionnés par la procédure d'exécution depuis le 15 décembre 1880, frais que le gouvernement demandeur fait figurer sous diverses rubriques de son état de dommages et intérêts ; les autres frais judiciaires réclamés ne peuvent rentrer dans l'indemnité à fixer par l'Arbitre. Ce poste embrasse les frais d'enregistrement de la sentence arbitrale, les frais de justice et de partie, tant de la procédure devant les tribunaux français que devant les tribunaux vénézuéliens, soit que la partie adverse de Fabiani eût l'obligation de les rembourser, soit qu'ils aient été causés inutilement à ce dernier.

Une somme, intérêts compris, de fr. 200,000 ne semble pas excessive, si l'on tient compte, entre autres, des nombreux et coûteux déplacements que la sauvegarde de ses droits a imposés à Fabiani, et même, si l'on porte en déduction les frais qui peuvent être envisagés comme ayant été faits sans motifs légitimes.

Toutes les autres réclamations de l'état consacré à la « liquidation des sentences » sont étrangères au litige actuel ; c'est le cas des « abus de confiance » et « détournements » dont il a été parlé plus haut, ainsi que des « annuités dotales » en vertu du contrat de mariage du 20 avril 1867, de la perte éprouvée sur la vente des marchandises d'après la transaction du 31 janvier 1878, etc. Ces sommes n'étant pas comprises dans la sentence arbitrale n'ont pu provoquer, de la part des tribunaux vénézuéliens, des dénégations de justice dont le Gouvernement défendeur serait responsable aux termes du compromis de 1891.

La question des intérêts est réservée (voir sub litt. b ci-après).

4° Parmi les réclamations figurant dans l'état B, dommages et intérêts, les seules qui puissent être prises en considération, dans l'espèce, sont celles mentionnées sous chiffres 11, 12 et 19 de l'exposé des faits qui précède ; or elles sont entrées en ligne de compte déjà lors de la fixation (voir sub 3) des frais d'exécution de la sentence arbitrale. Les autres indemnités n'ont pas leur source dans la dite sentence, ni, par conséquent, dans son défaut d'exécution ensuite de dénéga-

tions de justice imputables aux tribunaux du Vénézuéla ; il est superflu, dans ces conditions, de s'occuper des déductions consenties dans l'état B, attendu qu'elles ont trait à des postes éliminés par l'Arbitre.

5° L'état C se réfère au service du remorquage, et les dommages et intérêts qu'il comporte ont leur origine dans le retrait de ce service en 1884. Cette question a été tranchée à propos de celle des « faits du prince » ; sans discuter même le point de savoir si le Gouvernement défendeur n'était pas en droit de dénoncer le contrat du 7 décembre 1874, il est évident que les gains que Fabiani prétend avoir été frustré par cet acte ne lui ont pas été enlevés à raison de dénégations de justice qui, seules, peuvent engager la responsabilité du Vénézuéla dans l'instance actuelle. Il s'agit ici précisément d'un de ces « faits du prince », sur la légitimité et les effets duquel l'Arbitre n'a pas à se prononcer ; il ne lui était permis de l'apprécier que comme un indice des dispositions de l'autorité vénézuélienne envers Fabiani (voir sub III ci-devant).

6° Un tort considérable, matériel et surtout moral (état E), a été causé à Fabiani par sa déclaration de faillite au Vénézuéla, la fermeture de ses établissements commerciaux à Maracaïbo, les embarras financiers dans lesquels il a été fatalement plongé et l'abandon forcé de ses entreprises. Ce dommage peut être envisagé comme la conséquence immédiate des dénégations de justice, puisque aussi bien Fabiani a été mis en faillite à Maracaïbo pour défaut de paiement de sommes inférieures de beaucoup à celles que l'exécution de la sentence arbitrale lui aurait fait recouvrer. Le Gouvernement défendeur ne conteste pas que Fabiani possédait des maisons prospères au Vénézuéla et à Marseille, du moins avant les démêlés judiciaires dont est né le présent litige, et les motifs de la sentence arbitrale, ainsi que d'autres éléments de la cause, montrent que le ressortissant dont l'Etat demandeur a pris les intérêts en mains, était un négociant sérieux et honnête, auquel le recouvrement de ce que les Roncayolo lui devaient aurait permis d'escompter largement l'avenir. Sa faillite déterminée par les dénégations de justice souvent rappelées, l'a profondément atteint, tant dans sa situation économique que dans sa personnalité tout entière, si bien que l'allocation d'une indemnité proportionnée au dommage subi s'impose de ce chef. Au reste, Fabiani, grâce à ses connaissances, à son activité, à ses moyens d'action, ne pouvait manquer, dans des conditions normales, d'accroître encore la considération et le crédit dont il jouissait, de donner à ses entreprises un plus grand essor, et, très probablement, de faire en sus du gain perdu et dont il sera parlé ci-après, d'autres bénéfices par l'exploitation d'autres sources de revenus ; par la faute des autorités judiciaires du Vénézuéla, il a perdu tout ensemble ses biens et son honneur, et il a traversé de très pénibles épreuves. Ce sont là des circonstances exceptionnelles, dont il serait injuste de méconnaître la gravité et d'écarter les conséquences dommageables, en invoquant le caractère international de la contestation actuelle.

Des renseignements précis font nécessairement défaut sur certains points, pour établir avec une exactitude absolue le montant de la réparation qui est légitimement due à Fabiani, dans les limites de l'état E de la demande. L'arbitre, appréciant librement les faits de la cause, évalue à frs. 1,800,000 le chiffre des dommages et intérêts représentant le préjudice éprouvé, indépendamment de celui reconnu sous litt. *b*.

b) Dommage indirect.

1º Les dommages et intérêts réclamés dans l'état D correspondent aux sacrifices faits pour le maintien de l'industrie de Fabiani et au gain dont il a été frustré. La non-exécution de la sentence arbitrale, non-exécution provoquée par des dénis de justice a causé à Fabiani un préjudice indirect fixé dans la demande à la somme de 4,200,000 francs ; mais il importe de ne pas confondre ce préjudice et dommage avec celui dont il vient d'être parlé sous litt. *a*, chiffre 6.

Aussi bien, il y a lieu d'admettre ici, à titre de compensation, uniquement l'équivalent du dommage qui peut être considéré comme une suite de l'impossibilité dans laquelle s'est trouvé Fabiani, à raison de l'inexécution du jugement du 15 décembre 1880, de faire fructifier les capitaux importants qui lui étaient dus et qu'il aurait recouvrés. Le moyen le plus sûr d'arriver à une évaluation certaine, eût été de consulter les livres de la maison Fabiani et de vérifier jusqu'à quel point ses bénéfices avaient successivement diminué par l'effet du refus, déguisé mais persistant, des autorités vénézuéliennes, de procéder ou de laisser procéder à l'exécution de la sentence arbitrale. Ces livres n'ont pas été produits, et quoique le défaut de production de ces documents paraisse excusable, les indications fournies dans l'état D ne constituent pas des justifications suffisantes de toute l'indemnité réclamée. L'existence d'un dommage indirect n'en n'est pas moins indubitable. Ce préjudice consiste essentiellement, non pas dans les sacrifices, prouvés d'une manière incomplète, que Fabiani aurait faits pour le maintien de son industrie et dans des profits plus ou moins probables, mais dans la circonstance que les sommes dues en vertu de la sentence arbitrale sont demeurées improductives pendant nombre d'années, et par les dénégations de justice commises à son encontre au Vénézuéla.

Dans la demande, on a ajouté constamment au capital des réclamations formulées, les intérêts composés qui rentrent plutôt dans les indemnités à allouer pour dommage indirect. Il convient, à ce propos, de faire observer que les arguments invoqués par le gouvernement défendeur (Défense, p. 97 et suiv.) contre la prétention de la partie adverse d'exiger des intérêts ne sont nullement fondés ; la renonciation que l'on oppose au Gouvernement de la République française ne concerne pas la présente contestation et ne saurait être étendue au delà de ses termes ; de plus, les considérations juridiques développées à l'appui de la thèse de l'Etat vénézuélien ne sont pas concluantes pour les motifs précédemment exposés et qui montrent que la mesure de la responsabilité de l'Etat est adéquate à celle de la responsabilité des autorités fautives elles-mêmes.

S'il en est ainsi, on doit reconnaître que Fabiani aurait pu faire fructifier, dans ses entreprises, les intérêts simples du montant des condamnations de la sentence arbitrale, dans l'éventualité où il n'aurait pas été victime de dénégations de justice. La capitalisation d'intérêts est autorisée en matière de comptes-courants et d'opérations analogues parce que le législateur présume que, dans le commerce, l'argent ne reste pas improductif (cfr. art. 335, C. féd. des oblig. et *Laurent*, op. cit., vol. XVI, nº 348). Mais Fabiani n'a droit à des intérêts composés que pour les réclamations admises sous litt. *a*, chiffres 1 et 2, qui s'élèvent à la somme totale de frs. 746,656. 51 ; car il n'en saurait être question, ni à l'égard des 200,000 francs alloués pour frais judiciaires, ni à l'égard de l'indemnité ferme de 1,800,000 francs accordée sous litt. *a*, chiffre 6. Les intérêts composés de la somme de frs. 746,656. 55 ne représentent toutefois pas, dans l'opinion de l'Arbitre, le gain intégral dont Fabiani a été frustré par le non-recouvrement des sommes comprises dans la sentence arbitrale. Si Fabiani avait pu tirer parti de ces sommes et les employer dans son négoce, il est vraisemblable qu'il aurait fait des bénéfices supérieurs aux intérêts composés de ce capital pendant le laps de temps durant lequel il serait autorisé à les porter en compte. Ainsi qu'il résulte de circonstances déjà relatées, il avait des maisons de commerce prospères, son crédit était bien établi, ses ressources étaient considérables, toutes ses entreprises paraissaient assurées d'un rapport exceptionnellement élevé ; les dénégations de justice dont il a été victime lui ont causé les pertes très graves qui viennent d'être rappelées. Ici, de nouveau, l'Arbitre doit apprécier librement, suivant la conviction qu'il a pu se former, et il juge équitable d'évaluer à frs. 1,500,000 le dommage indirect subi par Fabiani, en tenant compte de la réalisation de l'hypothèque de 120,000 francs.

2° Sur les préjudices commerciaux de Fabiani viendrait se greffer, suivant la demande, le dommage éprouvé dans l'affaire du chemin de fer de la Ceïba. Comme le montrent les considérations développées sous chiffre V in fine, il n'est point établi que B et A. Roncayolo ne se seraient pas libérés, afin précisément d'arrêter toute procédure dirigée contre des droits et actions d'une grande valeur. Il n'est pas prouvé davantage que le transfert de ces droits et actions, à défaut même de payement, se serait fait nécessairement et pour leur totalité au profit de Fabiani. L'hypothèse sur laquelle repose cette réclamation de 24,000,000 de francs ayant été écartée, il convient de faire complètement abstraction de l'indemnité qui s'y rapporte.

c) Frais de l'instance.

En ce qui concerne *les frais de la présente instance*, l'Arbitre, constatant que les conclusions de la demande sont adjugées en principe, mais que l'exagération des réclamations formulées a entraîné des dépens inutiles, met les frais du Gouvernement demandeur, liquidés à la somme de 100,000 frs. à la charge du Gouvernement défendeur et compense entre les parties les dépens de l'Arbitrage.

IX. De ce qui précède, il résulte que le chiffre intégral de l'indemnité allouée s'établit comme suit :

		Francs.
1. Débit A. Roncayolo		424,177.55
2. Recettes du pilotage		68,312.45
3. Recettes du remorquage . .		254,166.51
4. Frais d'exécution		200,000.—
5. Dommage causé par la faillite		1,800,000.—
6. Dommage indirect		1,500,000.—
7. Frais du demandeur		100,000.—
En tout		4,346,656.51

Par ces motifs,

Prononce :

Le Gouvernement des Etats-Unis du Vénézuéla paiera à Fabiani, à titre d'indemnité, dans les termes du compromis du 24 février 1891, tous frais compris, la somme totale de *quatre millions, trois cent quarante-six mille six cent cinquante-six francs cinquante et un centimes* (Fr. 4,346,656.51), avec intérêts à cinq pour cent l'an dès la date de la présente sentence.

Les dépens de l'arbitrage sont compensés entre les parties.

Ainsi fait à Berne, le trente décembre 1896 [1].

---

[1] *Différend franco-vénézuélien.* Jugement arbitral. Genève, impr. centrale.

XCIX. France, Grande-Bretagne.

11 mars 1891.

Relatif aux pêcheries des homards sur les côtes de Terre-Neuve, l'arbitrage convenu n'a pas eu de suites jusqu'à ce jour.

Arrangement concernant les pêcheries de Terre-Neuve, conclu le 11 mars 1891, entre la France et l'Angleterre.

Le Gouvernement de la République Française et le Gouvernement de Sa Majesté Britannique ayant résolu de soumettre à une Commission Arbitrale la solution de certaines difficultés survenues sur la partie des côtes de Terre-Neuve comprise entre le Cap Saint-Jean et le Cap Raye, en passant par le nord, sont tombés d'accord sur les dispositions suivantes :

1. La Commission Arbitrale jugera et tranchera toutes les questions de principe qui lui seront soumises par l'un ou l'autre Gouvernement ou par leurs Délégués, concernant la pêche du homard et sa préparation sur la partie susdite des côtes de Terre-Neuve.

2. Les deux Gouvernements s'engagent, chacun en ce qui le concerne, à exécuter les décisions de la Commission Arbitrale.

3. Le modus vivendi de 1890, relatif à la pêche du homard et à sa préparation, est renouvelé purement et simplement pour la saison de pêche 1891.

4. Une fois que les questions relatives à la pêche du homard et à sa préparation auront été tranchées par la Commission, elle pourra être saisie d'autres questions subsidiaires relatives aux pêcheries de la partie susdite des côtes de Terre-Neuve et sur le texte desquelles les deux Gouvernements seront préalablement tombés d'accord.

5. La Commission Arbitrale sera composée :

1° De trois spécialistes ou jurisconsultes désignés d'un commun accord par les deux Gouvernements.

2° De deux délégués de chaque pays qui seront les intermédiaires autorisés entre leurs Gouvernements et les autres Arbitres.

6. La Commission Arbitrale ainsi formée de sept membres statuera à la majorité des voix et sans appel.

7. Elle se réunira aussitôt que faire se pourra.

Fait à Londres, le 11 mars 1891 [1].

---

[1] *Parliamentary Papers*, C. 6703, p. 4.

C. Grande-Bretagne, Portugal.

11 juin 1891.

La convention reproduite ici organise le recours à l'arbitrage pour toute une série de questions : limites, concessions minières, construction de routes, liberté de navigation du Zambèse, lignes télégraphiques. Il ne semble pas avoir été donné de suite au traité.

Treaty between Great Britain and Portugal, defining the Spheres of Influence of the two Countries in Africa. Signed at Lisbon, June 11, 1891.

. . . .

ART. IV. It is agreed that the western line of division separating the British from the Portuguese sphere of influence in Central Africa shall follow the centre of the channel of the Upper Zambesi, starting from the Katima Rapids up to the point where it reaches the territory of the Barotse Kingdom.

That territory shall remain within the British sphere ; its limits to the westward, which will constitute the boundary between the British and Portuguese spheres of influence, being decided by a Joint Anglo-Portuguese Commission, which shall have power, in case of difference of opinion, to appoint an Umpire.

It is understood on both sides that nothing in this Article shall affect the existing rights of any other State. Subject to this reservation, Great Britain will not oppose the extension of Portuguese administration outside of the limits of the Barotse country.

ART. V. Portugal agrees to recognize, as within the sphere of influence of Great Britain on the north of the Zambesi, the territories extending from the line to be settled by the Joint Commission mentioned in the preceding Article to Lake Nyassa, including the islands in that lake south of parallel 11° 30′ south latitude, and to the territories reserved to Portugal by the line described in Article I.

. . . .

ART. IX. Commercial or mineral concessions and rights to real property possessed by Companies or individuals belonging to either Power shall, if their validity is duly proved, be recognized in the sphere of the other Power. For deciding on the validity of mineral concessions given by the legitimate authority within 30 miles of either side of the frontier south of the Zambesi, a Tribunal of Arbitration is to be named by common agreement.

It is understood that such Concessions must be worked according to local regulations and laws.

. . . .

ART. XI. The transit of goods across Portuguese territories situated between the East Coast and the British sphere shall not, for a period of 25 years from the ratification of this Convention, be subjected to duties in excess of 3 per cent, for imports or for exports. These dues shall in no case have a differential character, and shall not exceed the customs dues levied on the same goods in the above-mentioned territories.

Her Majesty's Government shall have the option, within five years from the date of the signature of this Agreement, to claim freedom of transit for the remainder of the period of 25 years on the payment of a sum capitalizing the annual duties for that period at the rate of 30,000 l. a year.

Coin and precious metals of all descriptions shall be imported and exported to and from the British sphere free of transit duty.

. . . .

All materials for the construction of roads, railways, bridges, and telegraph-lines shall be admitted free of charge.

. . . .

ART. XIII. Merchant-ships of the two Powers shall in the Zambesi, its branches and outlets, have equal freedom of navigation, whether with cargo or ballast, for the transportation of goods and passengers. In the exercise of this navigation the subjects and flags of both Powers shall be treated in all circumstances on a footing of perfect equality, not only for the direct navigation from the open sea to the inland ports of the Zambesi, and vice-versâ, but for the great and small coasting trade, and for boat trade on the course of the river. Consequently, on all the course and mouths of the Zambesi there will be no differential treatment of the subjects of the two Powers ; and no exclusive privilege of navigation will be conceded by either to companies, corporations, or private persons.

The navigation of the Zambesi shall not be subject to any restriction or obligation, based merely on the fact of navigation. It shall not be exposed to any obligation in regard to landing-station or depôt, or for breaking bulk, or for compulsory entry into port. In all the extent of the Zambesi the ships and goods in process of transit on the river shall be submitted to no transit dues, whatever their starting place or destination.

No maritime or river toll shall be levied based on the sole fact of navigation, nor any tax on goods on board of ships. There shall only be collected taxes or duties which shall be an equivalent for services rendered to navigation itself. The tariff of these taxes or duties shall not warrant any differential treatment. The affluents of the Zambesi shall be in all respects subject to the same rules as the river of which they are tributaries.

The roads, paths, railways, or lateral canals which may . be constructed with the special object of correcting the imperfections of the river route on certain sections of the course of the Zambesi, its affluents, branches, and outlets shall be considered, in their quality of means of communication, as dependencies of this river, and as equally open to the traffic of both Powers. And, as on the river itself, so there shall be collected on these roads, railways, and canals only tolls calculated on the cost of construction, maintenance, and management, and on the profits due to the promoters. As regards the tariff of these tolls, strangers and the natives of the respective territories shall be treated on a footing of perfect equality.

Portugal undertakes to apply the principles of freedom of navigation enunciated in this Article on so much of the waters of the Zambesi, its affluents, branches, and outlets as are or may be under her sovereignty, protection, or influence. The rules which she may establish for the safety and control of navigation shall be drawn up in a way to facilitate, as far as possible, the circulation of merchant-ships.

Great Britain accepts, under the same reservations, and in identical terms, the obligations undertaken in the preceding Articles in respect of so much of the waters of the Zambesi, its affluents, branches, and outlets, as are or may be under her sovereignty, protection, or influence.

Any questions arising out of the provisions of this Article shall be referred to a Joint Commission, and in case of disagreement, to arbitration.

Another system for the administration and control of the Zambesi may be substituted for the above arrangements by common consent of the Riverain Powers.

. . . .

ART. XV. Great Britain and Portugal engage to facilitate telegraphic communication in their respective spheres.

The stipulations contained in Article XIV, as regards the construction of a railway from Pungwe Bay to the interior, shall be applicable in all respects to the construction of a telegraph line for communication between the coast and the British sphere south of the Zambesi. Questions as to the points of departure and termination of the line, and as to other details, if not arranged by common consent, shall be submitted to the arbitration of experts under the conditions prescribed in Article XI.

Portugal engages to maintain telegraphic service between the coast and the River Ruo, which service shall be open to the use of the subjects of the two Powers without any differential treatment.

Great Britain and Portugal engage to give every facility for the connection of telegraph lines constructed in their respective spheres.

Details in respect of such connection, and in respect to questions relating to the settlement of through-tariffs and other charges, shall, if not settled by common consent, be referred to the arbitration of experts under the conditions prescribed in Article XI [1].

CI. Grande-Bretagne, Portugal.

9 juillet 1855.

Cette réclamation était basée sur un prétendu déni de justice de la part des tribunaux administratifs du Portugal. Le Sénat de Hambourg, choisi comme arbitre, repoussa la demande.

Memorandum pour soumettre au Sénat de Hambourg en qualité d'arbitre la réclamation Croft.

O abaixo assignado Enviado Extraordinario e Ministro Plenipotenciario de S. M. Britannica, não perdeu tempo em communicar ao Governo de S. M. a nota que teve a honra de receber em 6 de Novembro de S. Exa. o Visconde d'Athouguia, Ministro e Secretario d'Estado dos Negocios Estrangeiros de S. M. Fidelissima, manifestando o assentimento do Governo de S. M. Fma. á proposta que o abaixo assignado teve a honra de submetter por ordem do seu Governo, em nota datada de· 24 de Julho ultimo, para que o negocio de M. Croft fosse decidido por meio de arbitragem.

O abaixo assignado não deixou em occasião opportun de manifestar á S. Exa. o Visconde d'Athouguia a satisfação com que o Governo de S. M. recebera aquella communicação da parte do Governo de S. M. Fma., como tendente á terminar de uma maneira honroza para ambas as partes e ao mesmo tempo justa para com

---

[1] HERTSLET, *A complete collection* ..., t. XIX, p. 777.

M. Croft, uma questão que havia suscitado tão enfadonha e desagradavel discussão entre os dous Governos, e que parecia dar tão poca esperança de ser decidida de uma maneira condigna com os sentimentos de amizade e benevolencia que o Governo de S. M. tanto deseja manter nas suas relações com este paiz.

S. Exa. o Visconde d'Athouguia lembrar-se-ha igualmente das diversas conversações que tem tido logar entre S. Exa. e o abaixo assignado sobre pontos mais minuciozos em relação a esta pretendida arbitragem, taes como a escolha de um arbitro, a maneira pela qual a arbitragem deveria ser levada a effeito e outros assumptos preliminares cujas conversações finalisaram, como S. Exa. estará lembrado, na escolha de commum accordo, com a annuencia de M. Croft, do Senado da Cidade Livre e Anseatica de Hamburgo, como a corporação a cuja arbitragem o negocio deveria ser submettido.

E tendo o Senado de Hamburgo obsequiosamente annuido a aceitar o cargo de arbitro, torna-se agora necessario assentar em certos termos e disposições, afim de obter um prompto e conveniente andamento e resolução das queixas, reclamações e pedidosfeitos pelo Governo de S. M. a favor de M. Croft para cujo fim o abaixo assignado teve instrucções para propôr á acceitação do Governo de S. M. F. ás seguintes bases de um accordo que é de esperar obterão o assentimento do referido Governo, e as quaes, quando aceitas, se propõe sejam consideradas como um ajuste obrigatorio para ser fiel e honrosamente cumprido por ambas as partes sem dolo ou hesitação.

Fica entendido que as varias queixas, reclamações e pedidos, que teem sido feitos pelo Governo de S. M. ao Governo de S. M. F. a favor de M. Croft, subdito britannico residente em Portugal e de sua mulher D. Maria Luciana d'Oliveira Croft, ou de cada um d'elles e o direito ou reclamação d'elles, ou de cada um d'elles, para receber qualquer indemnisação ou compensação do Governo de S. M. F. formarão o assumpto que deve ser submettido á decizão do Senado da Cidade Livre de Hamburgo conforme as condições seguintes :

1. A decizão do Senado sobre os assumptos que assim lhe forem submettidos será considerada como absolutamente final e concludente, e será cumprida sem a menor objecção, evasive ou demora qualquer.

2. Pedir-se-ha ao Senada que haja de dar a sua decisão por escripto e datada : será formulada da maneira que o dito Senado entenda dever adoptar ; será entregue ao Consul ou Agente publico de cada um dos dous Governos que actualmente esistir em Hamburgo, e será considerada obrigatoria desde a sua data e entrega. Pedir-se-ha especialmente ao Senado que haja de declarar a importancia em moeda ingleza de quaesquer sommas que possa arbitrar.

3. A exposição por escripto ou impressa por parte do Governo de S. M. Britannica será apresentada ao Senado devendo uma copia ser entregue ao Governo de S. M. F. dentro de dous mezes da data d'esta nota, e o Governo de S. M. F. no prazo de dous mezes depois da recepção d'esta copia do Governo de S. M. apresentará a sua contestação perante o dito Senado e dará uma copia d'ella ao Governo de S. M. Britannica.

Independentemente da exposição apresentada pelo Governo de S. M. Britannica será permittido a M. Croft a presentar ao Senado uma exposição preparada por elle, cuja copia será igualmente entregue ao Governo de S. M. Fma.

Quando haja fal a na devida transmissão d'esta contestação ao dito Senado o mesmo procederá sem demora e *ex-parte*.

Deixar-se-ha ao arbitrio do dito Senado pedir algun outro documento ou exposição, ou qualquer prova oral ou documental, ou qualquer outra informação de cada uma das partes e o dito Senado terá o poder de ouvir um advogado ou agente de cada um dos Governos em relação a qualquer ponto que julgar conveniente na occasião e da maneira que o julgar opportuno.

4. Propõe-se que o Encarregado de Negocios, Consul, ou qualquer outro agente publico da Grã-Bretanha e de Portugal actualmente em Hamburgo, sejam considerados agentes dos seus respectivos Governos para guiar este negocio perante o dito Senado, que dirigirá todas as suas communicações e dará todos os seus avisos ao dito Encarregado de Negocios, Consul ou outro agente publico, por cujos actos n'esta materia o seu Governo ficará responsavel para com o dito Senado.

5. Fica entendido que o Senado terá a faculdade de proceder na proposta arbitragem e em todas as materias que lhe são relativas, como e quando o julgar opportuno, quer seja á porta cerrada ou em sessão publica, em plena assembléa ou por uma commissão para esse fim delegada por aquella corporação, quer na presença ou na ausencia de um ou de ambos os Agentes, ou de viva voz ou por discussão escripta ou de qualquer outra maneira que julgue conveniente.

Terá a faculdade de obter copias ou traducções d'aquelles documentos que lhe sejam precisos, e admittir ou recusar qualquer outro documento que não seja a exposição e contestação acima mencionadas e ouvir ou deixar de ouvir quaesquer testemunhas que julgue necessarias serem presentes ou interrogadas.

6. O Senado nomeará, se o julgar conveniente, um Secretario, official de registo ou amanuense para a proposta arbitragem, concedendo-lhe a remuneração que julgar conveniente. Esta e todas as outras despezas da dita arbitragem ou a ella relativas serão satisfeitas da maneira que adiante se propõe.

7. Pedir-se-ha ao Senado que haja de dar por escripto a sua sentença no prazo de trez mezes a contar da epoca em que começar a dar andamento a este negocio, ou antes se fôr possivel, e de entregar uma copia d'essa sentença a cada um dos agentes acima mencionados.

Se isto se não praticar dentro do prazo referido, tornar-se-ha nullo e de nenhum valor tudo quanto em virtude d'este accordo houver sido feito e será da competencia do Governo de S. M. B. obrar e proceder a todos os respeitos como se nunca se tivesse entrado em tal accordo.

No cazo que o Senado não venha a uma decisão e não a entrengue proceder-se-ha á escolha de um novo arbitro.

8. Todas e quaesquer quantias que hajam de ser arbitradas pelo Senado a alguma pessoa ou pessoas, em consequencia das ditas reclamações, serão pagas pelo Governo de S. M. Fma. ao Ministro ou Encarregado de Negocios de S. M. B. em Lisboa dentro de um mez depois de recebida a dita arbitragem, ou em letras a seis mezes contados d'aquella data com o juro de seis por cento ao anno.

9. O Senado será instado para que juntamente com a sua sentença haja de ·apresentar uma conta de todas as custas e das despezas que tiver feito em relação a este negocio as quaes lhe serão logo satisfeitas em duas porções iguaes, uma por cada um dos ditos Governos.

10. Será competente o Senado e pelo presente lhe é pedido haja de arbitrar e determinar por qual das duas Partes e em que proporção serão pagas as custas da dita arbitragem, como distinctas da importancia da indemnisação (se alguma houver) e fixar e determinar a importancia de taes custas, e se isto se não obtiver cada um dos Governos pagará as suas proprias custas e despezas, sem fazer nenhuma reclamação ao outro por esse motivo.

O Governo de S. M. espera e acredita que nada ha nos termos e condições em que assim se propõe seja levado a effeito a arbitragem que se tem em vista, que estaja em opposição com as ideas do Governo de S. M. F., e que havendo-se concordado no principio d'arbitragem, tornando-se

de obvia conveniencia de ambos os Governos que as formulas preliminares sejam determinadas o mais breve possivel, para que o negocio principal tenha o devido andamento e se conclua com a desejada promptidão [1].

Schiedsrichterliche Entscheidung vom 7. Februar 1856 der vom Senate der freien und Hansestadt Hamburg zur Aburteilung der Kompromissache zwischen den Regierungen Ihrer Majestät der Königin von Grossbritannien und Irland und Seiner Majestät des Königs von Portugal, die Angelegenheit des Mr. Croft, niedergesetzten Commission.

Die von dem Mr. Croft gegen die portugiesische Regierung gerichtete und von dem englischen Gouvernement unterstützte Beschwerde ist darauf gegründet, dass die portugiesischen Administrativbehörden, indem sie dem Mr. Croft die Alvará de Insinuação versagten, diejenigen Rechte, welche ihm durch rechtskräftige Urteile zugesprochen worden seien, verletzt, und somit, der konstitutionellen Charte des Königsreichs zuwider, den Akten der Justizgewalt die schuldige Anerkennung versagt hätten, als wofür der portugiesichen Regierung die Pflicht des Schadenersatzes obliege. Dieser Anspruch beruht also auf der gedoppelten Behauptung: 1. dass die Administrativbehörden rechtswidrig gehandelt, und 2. dass die Regierung für die Folgen dieser rechtswidrigen Handlungen verantwortlich sei. Beide Sätze können nicht zugegeben werden.

Die Administrativbehörden, indem sie die Erteilung der Alvará verweigerten, haben in Gemässheit der ihre Verhältnisse regulierenden Codigo Administrativo und der speciellen Gesetze über die Insinuation von Schenkungen gehandelt: denn ihnen steht nach Art. 254 und 280 des genannten Codigo de Function zu, über die Insinuation und deren Zulässigkeit zu entscheiden, und die Insinuation war im vorliegenden Fall, auch abgesehen von dem Gesetze vom 25. Januar 1775, welches vielleicht auf denselben nicht anwendbar ist, jedenfalls nach den Vorschriften von Ordonn. I. IV. t. 62, wegen des bereits erfolgten Todes des Schenkers unzulässig. Wenn über letzteres auch Meinungsverschiedenheiten möglicherweise obwalten konnten, und wirklich früher einmal in dem Fall des Visconde das Picoas in einem anderen Sinn entschieden wurde, so sind demungeachtet, bei genauerer Erwägung der Sache, selbst diejenigen Juristen, welche eine solche Meinung früher geäussert hatten (der General-Prokurator Ottolini und dessen Adjunkt Rangel de Quadros), wie das einstimmige Kon-

---

[1] Nous devons la communication du texte du compromis à la gracieuse bienveillance du gouvernement portugais.

ferenzgutachten vom 16. Oktober 1850 anweist, davon wieder zurückgekommen, und ein einzelnes Präjudicat oder Precedent, welches früher unrichtig abgegeben ward, kann kein Recht für alle folgenden Fälle machen, zumal wo es sich um einen Widerspruch mit bestimmten geschriebenen Gesetzen handelt. Die Kommission ist der Meinung, dass von den Administrativbehörden die Insinuationsbewilligung mit Recht abgelehnt wurde. Sie würde dieser Meinung selbst dann sein, wenn die in der Sache des Mr. Croft gegen die Familie Barcellinhos ergangenen, gerichtlichen Erkenntnisse den Administrativbehörden solche Bewilligung vorgeschrieben hätten. Denn bei der Trennung, welche zwischen den ordentlichen Tribunalen und den Tribunalen der Administrativjustiz nach der Verfassung der portugiesischen Monarchie besteht, kommt jenen überall nicht die Befugniss zu, den letzteren Vorschriften, wie sie zu entscheiden haben, zu erteilen, vielmehr haben sich die letzteren nur nach den für sie bestehenden gesetzlichen Bestimmungen zu richten. Wenn ein Gericht in einem Civilprozess einer Partei zur Pflicht gemacht hat, eine gewisse Handlung vor den Administrativbehörden zu vollziehen, welche zu der Zeit, wo sie gefordert wird, nach den Reglementen der Administrativbehörden gar nicht mehr erfolgen kann, so ist die von den Gerichten gemachte Auflage zu einer Unmöglichkeit geworden, man darf aber nicht den Administrativbehörden daraus einen Vorwurf machen. Es kommt nun aber hinzu, dass die rechtskräftig ergangenen richterlichen Urteile eine solche Vorschrift durchaus niemals erteilt haben. Das massgebende Erkenntnis des Appellhofs von Oporto vom 31. März 1843 sagt durchaus nicht, dass die Insinuation der Schenkung, sei es bei Lebzeiten oder nach dem Tode des Barons de Barcellinhos, erfolgen solle, sondern es sagt nur, dass, wenn sie nicht erfolgen sollte, die Aussteuer sich beim Tode des Barons nur insoweit gültig zeigen werde, als sie nicht die legitima und die gesetzliche Taxe übersteige, für den etwaigen Überschuss aber alsdann als ungültig zu revocieren und rückgängig zu machen sein werde. Dieser Sinn des Oporto-Erkenntnisses geht nicht nur aus den Worten desselben und aus den tenções der Richter, die dasselbe abgaben, hervor, sondern er wird auch durch alle späteren richterlichen Entscheidungen (die Erkenntnisse des Lissaboner Appellhofs vom 12. März 1844, des Richters Novaes vom 15. Juli 1850, des Lissaboner Appellhofs vom 4. Oktober 1851, und die diese Erkenntnisse motivierenden tenções) unzweideutig anerkannt, so dass die Behauptung, als hätte das Erkenntniss von Oporto eine Zwangspflicht zur Insinuation, sei es zu irgend einer Zeit, oder gar zu der bestimmten Zeit nach dem Tode des Barons, ausgesprochen, nicht begründet ist. Vielmehr hat jenes Erkenntniss, ebenso wie alle späteren gerichtlichen Entscheidungen, mit Recht die Frage über die Zulässigkeit und den Zeitpunkt der Insinuation lediglich dem vor den Administrativbehörden zu stellenden Antrage und dort ergehenden Urteil überlassen, und sich nur auf den Ausspruch beschränkt, dass, wenn eine Insinuation nachgewiesen werde, die Aussteuer ihrem ganzen Umfange nach rechtsgültig sei, während sie im entgegengesetzten Fall für den die legitima und taxa dabei übersteigenden Betrag sich als rescissibel darstellen würde.

Der erste der beiden aufgestellten Sätze muss daher verneint werden. Nicht minder ist dies aber auch rücksichtlich des zweiten Satzes der Fall.

Denn angenommen selbst, dass die Administrativbehörden, welche die Alvará verweigerten, darin völlig Unrecht gehabt hätten, so würde demungeachtet eine Verpflichtung des portugiesischen Staates, den dadurch etwa dem Mr. Croft zugefügten Schaden zu ersetzen, nicht gefolgert werden können. Die thätig gewesenen Administrativbehörden, der Administrador do Concelho in erster Instanz, der Concelho do Districto in zweiter, und der Staatsrat, auf dessen Gutachten das königliche Dekret vom 4. Dezember 1849 abgegeben wurde, in dritter Instanz, haben in einer kontentiösen Sache eine Entscheidung abzugeben gehabt, und in diesem Zweige ihrer Thätigkeit handeln sie nicht in der Eigenschaft als blosse Ausführer von Befehlen der Regierung, sondern als wirkliche rechtsprechende Behörden, wie solche nach der portugiesischen Verfassung auch auf dem Gebiete der Administration bestehen. Wenn nämlich eine gewisse Klasse von Rechtsfragen nach den Anordnungen dieser und vieler ähnlicher konstitutioneller Staatsverfassungen den ordentlichen Gerichten entzogen und einer eignen für dergleichen in der Administration vorkommende Rechtsfragen niedergesetzten Jurisdiktion zugewiesen sind, so involviert die Handhabung dieser Jurisdiktion darum nicht minder eine wirkliche richterliche Thätigkeit, indem es bei deren Ausübung lediglich auf die freie und unabhängige rechtliche Überzeugung der dazu gesetzmässig berufenen Individuen, nicht aber auf einen Gehorsam höherer Befehle ankommt, und schon hieraus folgt, dass unmöglich eine Verantwortlichkeit der höheren Regierungsbehörde oder des Staates für Urteile, die von jenen gesprochen wurden, stattfinden kann. Ausnahmefälle von derjenigen Art, wie sie nach der Meinung von Vattel (II, 7, § 84) die Reklamation einer fremden Regierung selbst gegen richterliche Urteile, von denen einer ihrer Unterthanen betroffen wurde, rechtfertigen sollen, kommen hier nicht in Betracht, da keine der von Vattel aufgezählten Voraussetzungen bei den in der gegenwärtigen Sache abgegebenen völlig richtigen Entscheidungen zutrifft. Es muss daher auch der zweite Satz, auf welchen die englische Regierung die Ansprüche des Mr. Croft basieren will, als nicht begründet bezeichnet werden.

Nun hat freilich die portugiesische Regierung selbst, nachdem sie eine lange Zeit hindurch standhaft die Richtigkeit des Verfahrens der administrativen Tribunale in Verweigerung der Alvará behauptet hatte, dennoch gegen Ende des Jahres 1851, um der englischen Regierung entgegenzukommen, und infolge der dringlichen Instanzen derselben, den Versuch gemacht, noch nachträglich eine entgegengesetzte Verfügung herbeizuführen, indem die Minister Ihrer Majestät am 17. November 1851 einen Rekursantrag, vermittelst eines nach Art. 94 des Reglements des Staatsrats an den Präsidenten der kontentiösen Sektion gerichteten Relatorio, stellten, damit der Staatsrat die Sache nochmals in Erwägung ziehe und seinen früheren, die Entscheidung des Distriktsrats bestätigenden Beschluss, auf welchem das Dekret vom 4. Dezember 1849 abgegeben war, wieder aufhebe: und in diesem Rekursantrage haben sich die Minister aller der Argumente bedient, welche bis dahin die englische Regierung gegen das Verfahren der Administrativbehörden geltend gemacht hatte, und welche, wie oben ausgeführt, die Kommission nicht für gegründet erachten kann. Als aber darauf der Staatsrat in vereinten Sektionen seine Consulta über diesen Regierungs-Rekurs aus Gründen, welche der Kommission in allen Punkten richtig erscheinen, dahin abgab, dass dieser Rekurs weder formell noch materiell statthaft erscheine, ist die Regierung noch weiter gegangen, und hat am 3. Januar 1852 ein Dekret erlassen, welches in der Form, die bei Entscheidung von Rekurssachen in kontentiösen Sachen beobachtet wird, aber unter ausdrücklich ausgesprochener Beiseitesetzung der entgegenstehenden Consulta des Staatsrats, das Dekret vom 4. Dezember 1849 annullierte und auf den wider die Verfügung des Distriktsrats vom 10. Mai 1849 erhobenen Rekurs nunmehr dahin entschied, dass die Alvará zu gewähren sei, was denn auch demnächst geschehen ist.

Aus diesem Verhalten der portugiesischen Regierung im November 1851 und Januar 1852 will die englische Regierung entnehmen, dass die portugiesische Regierung selbst die Unrechtmässigkeit der früheren administrativen Entscheidungen anerkannt und die Verpflichtung eingeräumt habe, den Mr. Croft schadlos zu halten und in die Lage zu versetzen, in welcher er sich befunden haben würde, wenn schon am 18. No-

vember 1848, wo der Administrador de Concelho seinen abschlägigen Bescheid abgab, dieser Beamte ihm die Alvará bewilligt hätte.

Wäre das, was der Rekursantrag vom 17. November 1851 enthält, in einer an die englische Regierung gerichteten Note oder sonstigen diplomatischen Mitteilung als die Ansicht der portugiesischen Regierung von der letzteren ausgesprochen worden, so würde man mit Recht sagen, dass darin der Akt eines Geständnisses und einer Einräumung liege, welchen die eine Regierung der anderen gegenüber von sich gegeben habe, und durch welchen diese letztere nun alles Beweises darüber überhoben wäre, dass die Sache sich wirklich so, wie dort dargestellt, verhalte. Aber ein solcher Charakter kann nicht den Äusserungen jenes Relatorio beigelegt werden, welches vielmehr seiner Natur nach nur einen Antrag an den Staatsrat bildete, um denselben zu einer Abänderung seiner früheren Entscheidung, wie die portugiesische Regierung solche des freundschaftlichen Verhältnisses zu England wegen wünschte, wo möglich zu bewegen. Aus dem was in einem solchen Antrage zur Begründung des Gesuches gesagt wurde, kann nicht diejenige Partei, in deren Interesse und zu deren Gunsten es vorgetragen ward, Geständnisse für sich entnehmen. Wenn daher in dem Relatorio aufgestellt worden ist, dass die von den Administrativbehörden abgegebenen Entscheidungen einen «déni de justice» enthielten, weil sie die rechtskräftigen richterlichen Urteile nicht respektierten und «presque une distinction odieuse» zum Nachteil eines Engländers involvierten, weil im Jahre 1838 im Falle des Visconde das Picoas anders entschieden sei, so sind dies in Wahrheit nur Argumente, welche gebraucht wurden, um eine Entscheidung des Staatsrats im Sinne des Begehrens von Mr. Croft zu erwirken, nicht aber Einräumungen, welche, diesem oder der englischen Regierung gegenüber, animo confitendi gemacht wären oder als solche benutzt werden dürften. Ein Gleiches gilt von der ganzen übrigen in jenem Relatorio enthaltenen Darstellung, die sich ersichtlich darauf zweckte, die Gründe, welche das englische Gouvernement für die von ihm verteidigte Sache bisher geltend gemacht hatte, möglichst vollständig und mit angelegentlicher Unterstützung dem Staatsrate vorzutragen. Der Staatsrat hat jedoch in seinem Beschlusse vom 10. Dezember 1851 jene Argumentationen, und zwar, wie die Kommission befindet, mit vollem Recht, als nicht gegründet zurückgewiesen.

Ebensowenig wie aus dem Relatorio vom 17. November 1851 kann aber aus dem Dekrete vom 3. Januar 1852, zu dessen Erlassung sich die portugiesische Regierung demnächst entschloss, die Anerkennung einer Ersatzpflicht ab seiten derselben hergeleitet werden; denn einerseits ist auch dies Dekret keine internationale Verhandlung zwischen beiden Regierungen, sondern ein Urteil, welches in einer kontentiösen Angelegenheit abgegeben wurde, und andernteils würde, wenn selbst aus diesem Dekrete irgend eine Einräumung zu entnehmen wäre, dieselbe doch immer nur die sein, dass die Administrativbehörden früher unrechtmässig verfahren hätten, nicht aber die, dass der portugiesische Staat den aus diesem Verfahren entstandenen Schaden zu ersetzen verpflichtet sei, was etwas überaus Verschiedenes und nach dem oben Ausgeführten keineswegs sich von selbst Verstehendes ist, was aber dennoch wesentlich erforderlich sein würde, um behaupten zu können, dass die portugiesische Regierung die jetzt an sie gestellte Reklamation anerkannt habe.

In dem Dekrete vom 3. Januar 1852 kann auch nicht etwa die Übernahme einer neuen Verbindlichkeit ab seiten der portugiesischen Regierung gegen die englische gefunden werden, da dies nur der Fall sein könnte, wenn entweder in demselben eine Zusage enthalten, oder durch dasselbe dem Mr. Croft ein Schaden zugefügt wäre. Wenn zu irgend einer Zeit die portugiesische Regierung oder deren legitimer Vertreter der englischen Regierung in den Formen des internationalen Verkehrs die Zusage gegeben hätte, dass dem Mr. Croft zur Erfüllung seiner Ansprüche verholfen oder er für dieselben schadlos gehalten werden solle, so würde es keinen Zweifel leiden, dass daraus ein vollgültiges Recht auf Befriedigung oder Ersatz gegen den portugiesischen Staat entstehen würde, weil jenes die konstitutionsmässigen und völkerrechtlichen Formen sind, in denen internationale Verpflichtungen des einen Landes gegen das andere übernommen werden. Aber ein Gleiches lässt sich nicht von einem Falle behaupten, wo nichts anderes vorliegt als eine Verfügung, welche die Regierung an ihre eigenen Behörden zu gunsten eines fremden Unterthans erliess, ohne dass irgend eine Zusage an die Regierung des letzteren voranging. Wenn sich in einem solchen Falle der erlassenen Verfügung konstitutionelle Hindernisse in den Weg stellen, welche ihre Ausführung unmöglich machen, so kann kein völkerrechtlich begründeter Anspruch an die Regierung gestellt werden, dass sie einen Schadenersatz deshalb zu leisten habe, weil jene ihre Verfügung nicht in Ausführung gebracht sei. Es wäre daher selbst denkbar, dass die in dem Dekrete vom 3. Januar 1852 getroffene Anordnung, nämlich die darin anbefohlene Ausfertigung der Alvará, vermöge eines von dem Willen der Regierung unabhängigen gesetzlichen Widerstandes, gar nicht zu realisieren gewesen wäre, und dennoch wäre kein Ersatzanspruch

an den portugiesischen Staat von der englischen Regierung oder ihrem Unterthan darauf zu gründen gewesen. Nun ist aber dieser Fall gar nicht eingetreten, sondern die Verfügung von 3. Januar 1852 ist in Ausführung gekommen, und die Alvará ist dem Mr. Croft erteilt. Er hat somit das, was er verlangte, wirklich erhalten, und der Zweck seines Verlangens war immer nur der, die Alvará demnächst den Gerichten zu präsentieren und auf Grund derselben von diesen einen Rechtspruch gegen die Familie Barcellinhos zu erwirken. Diesen Weg muss er auch jetzt weiter verfolgen und das Ergebniss der richterlichen Entscheidungen erwarten, in denen er, wie sie auch ausfallen mögen, sein alleiniges Rechtsmittel zu erkennen hat. Am wenigsten wird er behaupten können, dass ihm durch das Dekret vom 3. Januar 1852 irgend ein Schaden erwachsen sei.

Im Gegenteil ist ihm durch das neueste der Kommission vorliegende richterliche Erkenntniss, welches in seiner Sache gegen die Familie Barcellinhos erfolgt ist, nämlich durch das Erkenntniss des höchsten Justiztribunals vom 14. August 1854, die Aussicht eröffnet, dass er nach der nunmehr auf Grund jenes Dekretes erfolgten Ausfertigung der Alvará einen günstigen Ausgang seines Prozesses gewärtigen dürfe. Wie dem aber auch sei, und wie immer in dem Prozess gegen die Familie Barcellinhos endgültig entschieden werden möge (da jenes Erkenntniss des höchsten Justiztribunals noch nicht die Kraft einer definitiven Entscheidung hat), jedenfalls ist es nicht das Dekret vom 3. Januar 1852, dem Mr. Croft den etwaigen ungünstigen Ausgang seiner Rechtsstreitigkeit zuzuschreiben haben wird.

Wenn irgend jemand einen Schaden geltend machen könnte, der ihm aus jenem Dekrete erwachsen wäre, so würde es nur die Familie Barcellinhos sein können, in dem Falle nämlich, dass sie in Übereinstimmung mit dem vorgedachten Ausspruche des höchsten Justiztribunals auf Grund der nunmehr beigebrachten Alvará zur Zahlung der vollen Aussteuer rechtskräftig verurteilt werden sollte. Denn insofern in der Erlassung jenes Dekretes eine Rechts- und Gesetzwidrigkeit liegen mag, wird alsdann von der Familie Barcellinhos eine Regressförderung, in Gemässheit der portugiesischen Gesetze, und soweit selbige es, sei es nun gegen den portugiesischen Staatsschatz oder gegen die Urheber des Dekretes zulassen, erhoben werden können. Nicht aber kann die Kommission wegen einer möglicherweise von der portugiesischen Regierung zum Nachteil der Familie Barcellinhos begangenen Gesetzwidrigkeit dem Mr. Croft, zu dessen Gunsten dieselbe begangen wurde, einen Anspruch auf Schadensersatz an eben diese Regierung zugestehen.

Aus diesen Gründen giebt die Kommission den geforderten Schiedspruch dahin ab: dass die portugiesische Regierung von den seitens der englischen Regierung zu Gunsten des Mr. oder der Mrs. Croft wider sie erhobenen Reklamationen, sowie von den Ansprüchen, welche Mr. und Mrs. Croft wider sie aufgestellt haben, freizusprechen sei; die Kosten, welche eine jede der beiden Parteien zum Behuf des gegenwärtigen Kompromissverfahrens aufgewandt hat, sind von ihr selbst zu tragen; die von der Kommission für dieses Verfahren aufgewandten Kosten sind von jeder Partei zur Hälfte zu erstatten.

Hamburg, den 7. Februar 1856.

CII. Grande-Bretagne. Portugal.

8 mars 1861.

Dans cette affaire il s'est agi d'une indemnité réclamée par les sieurs Yuille, Shortridge & Cie. du chef de frais de procédure occasionnés par une fausse interprétation des traités existant entre les deux pays intéressés, et de dommages causés à leur crédit par suite du procès qui leur avait été infligé. Il fut accordé par le Sénat de Hambourg, choisi comme arbitre, une somme de £ 20,296.

Memorandum para ser transmittido ao Senado da Cidade Livre de Hamburgo, para se encarregar da arbitragem relativamente á reclamações dos Snres Yuille, Shortridge e Cia.

O Governo de S. M. Britannica e o S. M. Fidelissima tendo estado em negociações desde o anno 1840 a respeito das reclamações apresentadas pelos subditos britannicos Yuille, Shortridge e Cia. contra o Governo Portuguez para indemnisação das perdas por elles soffridas em virtude de uma allegada infracção de tratado, e não tendo até agora chegado a uma amigavel solução d'essas reclamações, concordaram submetter á arbitragem do Governo da Cidade Livre de Hamburgo *toda a questão, inclusive a que diz respeito á importancia das perdas*.

Os Governos de S. M. Britannica e de S. M. Fidelissima julgão ser este o unico meio que lhes resta para terminarem de um modo honroso para ambas as partes estas reclamações que ha tanto tempo estão pendentes, e que teem dado logar a uma discussão tão fastidiosa e desagradavel entre os dous Governos, e que parece estão tão pouco encaminhadas a ter por outro modo

---

¹ BORGES DE CASTRO. *Collecção dos Tratados...*, t. VIII, supplemento, p. 34-60.

uma solução de uma maneira conforme aos sentimentos de amizade e boa vontade de que ha tanto tempo subsiste entre elles, e que é seu commum desejo que continuem a existir nas relações dos seus respectivos paizes e concordaram que a dita materia em questão fosse submettida ao Senado da Cidade Livre de Hamburgo debaixo das seguintes condições;

1. A decisão do Senado sobre os assumptos que assim lhe forem submettidos será considerada como absolutamente final e concludente e será cumprida sem a menor objecção ou demora qualquer.

2. Pedir-se-ha ao Senado que haja de dar a sua decisão por escripto e datada; será formulada da maneira que o dito Senado entenda dever adoptar; será entregue ao Consul ou Agente publico de cada um dos dous Governos que actualmente esistir em Hamburgo e será considerada obrigatoria desde a sua data e entrega. Pedir-se-ha especialmente ao Senado que haja de declarar a importancia em moeda ingleza de quaesquer sommas de dinheiro que possa arbitrar.

3. Este Memorandum com uma nota que o acompanhe por parte de ambos os dous Governos será immediatamente enviado ao Senado de Hamburgo, e dentro de dous mezes da sua data a exposição por escripto ou impressa por parte de Governo de S. M. Britannica será apresentada ao dito Senado simultaneamente com a que ao diante se menciona por parte do Governo portuguez e uma copia d'ella será dada ao Governo de S. M. Fidelissima dentro de dous mezes da dada da Nota que deve acompanhar este Memorandum.

O Governo de S. M. Fidelissima pela sua parte deverá egualmente apresentar ao dito Senado, por escripto ou impressa, uma exposição da sua questão, e dar uma copia d'ella ao Governo de S. M. Britannica dentro do mesmo periodo: e cada um dos dous Governos deverá dentro do periodo de dous mezes depois da respectiva recepção de taes copias, apresentar as suas respostas perante o mesmo Senado, e dar cada um ao outro copia das ditas respostas.

Não se realisando a devida transmissão das mencionadas respostas, ou de uma d'ella ao dito Senado, procederá este sem demora e *ex-parte*.

Deixar-se-ha ao arbitrio do mesmo Senado pedir algum outro documento ou exposição ou qualque prova oral ou documental ou qualquer outra informação de cada um dos Governos, e o dito Senado terá o poder de ouvir um advogado ou agente por parte de cada um dos Governos; em relação a qualquer ponto que julgar conve-

48

niente, e na occasião e da maneira que julgar opportuna.

4. Propõe-se que o Encarregado de Negocios, Consul ou outro agente publico da Grã-Bretanha e de Portugal actualmente em Hamburgo sejam considerados agentes do seus respectivos Governos para encaminhar este negocio perante o dito Senado, que deve dirigir todas as suas communicações e dar todos os seus avisos ao dito Encarregado de Negocios, Consul, ou outro agente publico, por cujos actos n'esta materia o seu Governo ficará responsavel para com o dito Senado.

Fica comtudo entendido que se tornar necessario, durante a presente arbitragem, fazer alguma mudança de uma ou ambas as pessoas que agora funccionam em Hamburgo como agentes dos dous Governos respectivamente, nenhum dos dous Governos poderá escolher um Letrado para o fim de funccionar como tal agente.

5. Fica entendido que o Senado terá a faculdade de proceder na proposta arbitragem e em todas as materias que lhe são relativas, como e quando o julgar opportuno, quer seja á porta fechada ou em sessão publica, quer em plena assemblêa ou por uma commissão para esse fim delegada por toda a corporação; quer em presença ou na ausencia de um ou de ambos os agentes; quer de viva voz ou por discussão escripta, ou por qualquer outro modo que julgue conveniente.

Terá a faculdade de obter copias o traducções de quaesquer documentos que lhe forem precisos, e receber ou recusar qualquer documento que não seja algum d'aquelles que acima se mencionaram, e ouvir ou recusar-se a ouvir quaesquer testemunhas que se peça sejam produzidas e interrogadas.

6. O Senado nomeará, se o julgar conveniente, um Secretario, official de registro ou amanuense para o fim da proposta arbitragem, com a remuneração que julgar conveniente.

Esta e todas as outras despezas da dita arbitragem ou a ella relativas serão satisfeitas da maneira que adiante se propõe.

7. Pedir-se-ha ao Senado que haja de dar por escripto a sua sentença no prazo de trez mezes, a contar da epoca em que effectivamente começar a dar andamento a este negocio, ou antes se fôr possivel, ou dentro de outro maior prazo que fôr convencionado entre os dous Governos; e de entregar uma copia d'ella a cada um dos agentes acima mencionados.

Se isto se não fizer dentro do prazo acima referido, tornar-se-ha nullo e de nenhum effeito tudo quanto em virtude d'este accordo houver sido feito, e poderá o Governo de S. M. Britan-

nica obrar e proceder a todos os respeitos como se nunca se tivesse entrado em tal accordo.

8. Todas ou quaesquer sommas de dinheiro que forem arbitradas pelo Senado a qualquer pessoa ou pessoas em consequencia das ditas reclamações, serão pagas pelo Governo de S. M. Fidelissima ao Ministro ou Encarregado de Negocios de S. M. Britannica em Lisboa, a razão de quatro mil e quinhentos reis por cada libra esterlina do dinheiro inglez, dentro de um mez depois da recepção da dita arbitragem ou em letras a vencer a oito mezes quando muito, a contar da data da recepção da dita arbitragem, com o accrescimo do juro a razão de seis por cento ao anno.

9. O Senado será instado par que juntamente com a sua sentença haja de apresentar uma conta de todas as custas e despezas que tiver feito em relação á este negocio, das quaes será immediatamente embolsado em duas partes iguaes, uma por cada um dos ditos Governos.

10. Poderá o Senado, e pelo presente se lhe pede, haja de arbitrar e determinar por qual das partes e em que proporção deverão ser pagas as custas da dita arbitragem, como distinctas da importancia da compensação (se alguma houver), e fixar e determinar a importancia de taes custas, e se isto se não obtiver, cada um dos Governos pagará as suas proprias custas e despezas, sem fazer reclamação alguma ao outro por esse motivo.

Sentence arbitrale prononcée par le Sénat de Hambourg, le 21 octobre 1861.

Dans l'affaire de compromis entre le Gouvernement royal de la Grande-Bretagne et le Gouvernement royal de Portugal, touchant les réclamations élevées par le premier en faveur de ses sujets Yuille, Shortridge & Cie., la commission, désignée par le Sénat de la Ville libre et hanséatique de Hambourg à l'effet de prononcer une sentence arbitrale, a statué en droit: que le Gouvernement royal de Portugal est obligé envers le Gouvernement royal de la Grande-Bretagne de veiller à ce que le jugement prononcé le 1er décembre 1838 par le Tribunal de commerce de première instance de Lisbonne dans la cause du sieur Manuel Jose d'Oliveira contre Murdoch, Shortridge & Cie. soit traité comme définitif et exécutoire, ainsi que de payer les dommages-intérêts dus aux susdits sujets anglais en indemnisation du préjudice résultant de ce que le susdit jugement n'a pas été traité comme définitif (final), savoir: 20,296 £, 0 sh., 2 d., soit: Livres Sterling vingt mille deux cent quatre-vingt-seize et deux pence suivant le mode de paiement fixé par le compromis.

Pour ce qui regarde les frais, chacun des deux ~~Gouvernements supportera ceux qu'il aura~~ faits de son côté pour amener ce procédé de compromis. Ceux de la commission, se montant à Ctf. 420,12, seront remboursés de moitié par chaque ~~gouvernement~~.

Motifs.

Le Gouvernement royal de la Grande-Bretagne soutient que le jugement du Tribunal de commerce de seconde instance de Lisbonne du 1ᵉʳ décembre 1838 doit être regardé comme un arrêt vidant et terminant le procès entre Oliveira et la raison anglaise de Murdoch, Shortridge & Cie. En conséquence il signale comme injuste toute la procédure commencée par le recours en cassation et continuée en vertu de l'arrêt de renvoi, et exige que le susdit jugement soit reconnu avoir force de chose jugée, ainsi que l'indemnisation de ses sujets de tout dommage résultanpour eux de la non-reconnaissance.

A l'appui de cette assertion il invoque :

1. le traité de 1654, art. 7 et la convention de 1810, art. 10 ;

2. le fait que le décret du 7 mai 1835 a été émis sans l'assentiment des Cortes, dont il est inféré que l'art. 1116 du Codigo commercial (que ce décret abrogeait en partie) est resté en vigueur : la Cour de Relação avait été, aussi par cette raison, incompétente dans ce procès ;

3. la criante injustice du jugement du 15 novembre 1840 prononcé par la Cour de Relação.

Il y avait donc : I. à examiner la question, sous les trois rapports indiqués ci-dessus, si le jugement du 1ᵉʳ décembre 1838 devait être regardé comme définitif ; II. dans l'affirmative à déterminer les conséquences de l'affirmation de cette question.

En ce qui touche Ad I.

A. La prétendue « criante injustice » du jugement du 15 novembre 1840. Ce motif des réclamations du Gouvernement royal de la Grande-Bretagne doit être rejeté :

1. Tout en admettant sans hésiter que ce jugement est incorrect (erroné). La reversale de A. Wardrop, du 31 décembre 1812, se rapporte (de l'aveu même d'Oliveira dans sa lettre à Yuille du 26 janvier 1827) à une dette privée de Wardrop à Oliveira, née en partie d'une créance de ce dernier sur la maison de Madère, en partie, de lettres de change remises par Oliveira à Wardrop. Il est même très probable que cette créance et les £6000 (environ) dont Oliveira était crédité en 1810, 30 juin, sur les livres de la raison et lesquelles (témoins ces livres mêmes), par suite du transfert sur le compte privé de Wardrop,

furent portées au débit d'Oliveira le 30 juin 1810, étaient identiques. Si cela était constaté, la susdite lettre d'Oliveira prouverait directement que cette dette de la raison fut convertie en dette privée de Wardrop avec l'assentiment d'Oliveira, et même dans le cas de non-accomplissement de la reversale du 31 décembre 1812 la dette de la raison n'aurait aucunement pu revivre. Car l'art. 693, nᵒ 4, du Codigo commercial n'y peut guère faire exception par la seule raison qu'il n'est pas applicable à l'espèce, puisqu'il s'agit ici de la substitution d'un nouveau débiteur à la place du précédent, sans aucune condition quelconque, et ce n'est que deux ans après que le nouveau débiteur et le créancier s'entendent sur le mode de paiement. La bonification d'intérêt sur £10,000 (faite par la raison à Oliveira) portée sur un extrait de compte du 31 janvier 1813, isolée comme elle est, et en contradiction avec l'extrait de compte fait par A. Wardrop pour les années de 1806—1826, ne prouverait rien quand même cet extrait ne serait pas falsifié. Quant au capital de £4000, qui ne figure nulle part sur les livres comme dette de la raison, le titre d'Oliveira manquerait de base même dans la supposition que le transfert des £6000 se soit effectué sans son consentement. Mais, quoi qu'il en soit, il est constant du moins que Oliveira, en appuyant, en première ligne, son action sur la reversale de 1826, a par cela même reconnu indubitablement l'identité de cette créance qu'il fait valoir et de la dette reversale. La conséquence évidente c'est que tous les arguments décisifs tendant à dépouiller la reversale de toute vertu obligatoire par rapport à la raison prouvent en même temps que l'action entière contre la raison est insoutenable.

L'absence de toute vertu obligatoire de la reversale de 1826 pour la raison est tellement mise en évidence, par l'extrait de la correspondance joint au dossier, par les arguments développés dans la sentence arbitrale et celle du Tribunal de commerce (première instance) et par sa reconnaissance énoncée dans le jugement du 15 novembre 1840 même, qu'il serait inutile d'appuyer davantage sur ce point.

Mais si, par les raisons ci-dessus alléguées, le jugement du 15 novembre 1840 peut être regardé comme erroné,

2. Ce défaut de justesse ne suffit pas pour justifier les prétentions du Gouvernement royal de la Grande-Bretage.

Il serait de toute injustice de demander compte au Gouvernement royal de Portugal des fautes commises par les Tribunaux du pays. En vertu de la constitution du royaume de Portugal, ces Tribunaux sont parfaitement indépendants du gouvernement qui par conséquent ne peut exercer aucune influence sur leurs décisions; on ne peut donc pas lui en imposer la responsabilité. Le Gouvernement royal de la Grande-Bretagne ne saurait se refuser à reconnaître cette vérité sans refuser en même temps de reconnaître toute l'organisation du Portugal comme celle d'un Etat policé — ce qui, évidemment, est loin de la pensée du Gouvernement royal de la Grande-Bretagne.

Ceci est reconnu par tous les écrivains sur le droit des gens. Voir Vattel: Droit des gens, livre 2, chap, 7, parag. 84: «C'est à la nation ou à son Souverain de rendre la justice dans tous les lieux de son obéissance... Les autres nations doivent respecter ce droit. Et comme l'administration de la justice exige nécessairement que toute sentence définitive, prononcée régulièrement, soit tenue pour juste et exécutée comme telle, dès qu'une cause dans laquelle des étrangers se trouvent intéressés a été jugée dans les formes, le Souverain de ces plaideurs ne peut écouter leurs plaintes. Entreprendre d'examiner la justice d'une sentence définitive c'est attaquer la jurisdiction de celui qui l'a rendue.»

Or, cet auteur admet en effet une exception à cette interdiction d'intercéder «dans le cas d'un déni de justice ou d'une injustice évidente et palpable ou d'une violation manifeste des règles et des formes ou enfin d'une distinction odieuse faite au préjudice de ses sujets».

Mais ces suppositions ne pourront être regardées comme réalisées qu'en cas de déni de justice, ou d'un simulacre de formes pour masquer la violence. C'est dans ce sens aussi qu'il faut interpréter le cas d'injustice palpable et évidente, puisque autrement le gouvernement étranger pourrait prétendre relativement à toute sentence reconnue erronée, que c'était «une injustice palpable et évidente», ce qui mènerait tout droit à cette «examination de la justice d'une sentence» qu'on vient de déclarer inadmissible.

Or, il est clair que dans le procès en question il ne s'agit ni d'un déni de justice ni d'un simulacre de formes, puisque c'est la Cour de Relação qui a jugé et que dans son jugement elle a suivi des principes de droit, quoique mal appliqués aux faits.

Au reste, ces doctrines ne sont justes qu'avec la restriction indiquée par Martens, Droit des gens, parag. 96, savoir: «l'impossibilité de combattre une sentence évidemment erronée par les moyens ordinaires de procédure en justice». Mais les lois portugaises admettaient non seulement, dans le cas d'une injustice palpable, une requête en revision contre le jugement du 15 novembre 1840 (Codigo, art. 1116), mais, si les circonstances s'y était prêtées, une action contre les juges (Action de syndicat). Or, puisque cette dernière n'a pas été intentée et que la requête a été rejetée comme mal fondée, le Gouvernement royal de la Grande-Bretagne ne peut aucunement être admis à revenir aujourd'hui sur l'examen de l'injustice du jugement en question.

Les mêmes considérations mènent:

B. Au rejet du second moyen (argument) sur lequel le Gouvernement royal de la Grande-Bretagne appuie sa demande.

La question de savoir si le décret du 7 mai 1835, pour avoir été émis sans l'assentiment des Cortes, ne pouvant être regardé comme obligatoire en droit, ne devait pas non plus servir de base à la décision de la Cour suprême, est de nature à ne pouvoir être résolue sur-le-champ. Le Gouvernement royal de Portugal, pour soutenir la validité du décret, fait valoir ces deux arguments: d'abord, qu'il avait été regardé comme légal par toutes les autorités et tous les tribunaux; puis, qu'il n'avait servi qu'à supprimer une disposition du Codigo commercial qui se trouvait en contradiction avec la charte constitutionelle et avec le décret qui instituait la Cour de cassation et en définissait les facultés.

Mais quoi qu'on pense de la justesse de cette argumentation, il faudra toujours convenir que la Cour suprême, en renvoyant la cause à la Cour de Relação a sanctionné la validité du décret.

Ce renvoi à la Cour de Relação, n'est donc pas une conséquence du décret du 7 mai 1835, mais de ce que la Cour suprême regardait ce décret comme obligatoire. Aussi faut-il revenir pour celà aux mêmes principes qui viennent d'être discutés par rapport au premier chef de la demande (plainte) et ces principes, ici comme auparavant, amènent également le rejet de ce (second) chef.

Il ne reste donc maintenant que:

C. D'examiner le troisième chef. L'assertion que, d'après les traités de 1654, art. 7, et de 1810, art. 10, le jugement du 1er décembre 1838 devait être regardé comme définitif, est-elle juste? A cette question il faut répondre affirmativement.

L'interprétation du traité de 1654 de la part du Portugal se trouve en flagrante contradiction avec les propres termes du traité. La disposition: «a Judice Conservatore nulla dabitur provocatio nisi ad Relationis Senatum ubi controversæ artæ interpositis appellationibus intra quattuor mensium spatium ad summum finiantur», est parfaitement claire et doit certainement s'interpréter dans ce sens que: 1. l'unique remède admissible contre les décisions du Juiz Conservator, c'est l'appel au Relationis Senatum, et 2. devant celui-ci les causes seraient mises à fin dans le terme de quatre mois.

Ainsi, quand même le Gouvernement royal de Portugal aurait raison de dire que la première de ces dispositions n'aboutissait qu'a exclure les exceptions (admises alors par la jurisprudence portugaise) de la règle suivant laquelle les appellations des jugements de première instance devaient se diriger à une Cour de Relação, la seconde disposition n'en serait pas moins incompatible avec l'admission d'un remède ultérieur contre le jugement de la Cour de Relação.

Que si, à l'époque du traité, le remède de la revision était déjà sous certaines conditions admis contre les jugements de la seconde instance, celà ne servirait qu'à confirmer cette interprétation, attendu que c'est une raison de plus, pour supposer que le mot « finiantur » tendait à exclure tout procédé ultérieur.

On ne peut pas non plus faire valoir contre des termes si précis la garantie d'une décision juste que devait offrir le recours en revision (et) qu'on n'aurait pas probablement voulu écarter dans un traité fait exprès pour assurer aux Anglais une bonne administration de justice; puisque, surtout pour l'époque du traité (ainsi qu'en général), on pourrait alléguer bien des raisons pour démontrer que le recours à la justice est tout aussi sûr et, par la prompte terminaison des procès, aussi conforme à l'intérêt des plaideurs, avec un nombre restreint d'instances qu'avec l'admission d'une série interminable de remèdes contre les jugements.

Le Gouvernement royal de Portugal en appelle aussi à une pratique maintenue pendant de longues années et offrant des exemples innombrables de recours en revision, mais d'abord, à l'égard du procès entre M. Croft et Oliveira qu'elle évoque, cet appel porte à faux, puisqu'il n'était pas question d'un procès devant un Juiz Conservador.

En résumé, il est évident que tout celà ne saurait donner au traité une portée différente des termes précis dans lesquels il est conçu. De ce seul fait (s'il est exact) il s'ensuit tout au plus que dans beaucoup d'occasions les sujets britanniques n'ont pas tiré parti du droit que leur attribuait le traité.

Néanmoins, de ce que plusieurs Anglais (quel que soit leur nombre) n'ont pas voulu invoquer leur privilège, on ne saurait déduire un préjudice pour les autres qui le revendiquent. Ceux-là n'ont pas le droit d'établir un usage que ceux-ci seraient forcés d'accepter comme obligatoire. La question changerait de caractère si le Gouvernement royal de la Grande-Bretagne avait réitérativement refusé l'intercession par la raison que le traité était tombé en désuétude, ou qu'il eût renoncé à une intercession intentée par la même raison. Car il est certain qu'il appartient aux Gouvernements d'abroger expressément ou de suspendre l'usage d'un traité, ce qui devra être regardé par leurs sujets comme une désuétude dérogeant au traité.

Mais ce non-usage devrait émaner du Gouvernement et se manifester par le refus d'intercéder nonobstant les requêtes de ses sujets à cet effet, ou par l'abandon d'une intercession intentée, par suite de réclamations de la part du Portugal fondées sur la nullité du traité.

Cependant dans ce cas même on ne devrait admettre la vertu suspensive de l'usage relativement au traité qu'avec une extrême précaution. Car dans les cas où de la violation du traité il ne résulterait que peu ou point de préjudice pour les sujets britanniques, l'intercession de leur Gouvernement serait oiseuse et une impolitesse gratuite envers un Gouvernement ami; s'en abstenir serait donc une courtoisie et non une renonciation. Mais le Gouvernement royal de Portugal n'invoque pas ce non-usage. On ne pourra donc pas prétendre, non plus, qu'un usage contraire avait dérogé à l'art. 7 du traité de 1654. Les autres arguments produits contre son application actuelle ne sont pas plus concluants.

Il va sans dire que les édits des souverains portugais ou les lois promulguées en Portugal ne peuvent en rien altérer les obligations contractées de la part du Gouvernement de Portugal. Celà résulte de la nature du traité, c'est-à-dire d'une convention qui astreint les contractants à son accomplissement. Il est vrai que rien n'empêche le Gouvernement royal du Portugal de se mettre dans le cas de ne pouvoir exécuter le traité sans violer les lois de son pays. Mais celà n'affecte aucunement les droits stipulés en faveur de l'autre partie contractante.

Les édits, les décrets ou les lois portugais ne seront donc pris en considération que lorsqu'il serait prouvé que ces lois s'opposent réellement au traité et que le Gouvernement royal britannique y avait déféré expressément ou tacitement.

Ni l'une ni l'autre de ces suppositions ne se rencontre dans les décrets invoqués; ils ne sauraient donc rien décider en faveur du Gouvernement royal de Portugal.

On prétend que l'Alvará du 16 septembre 1665 déclarait : que les Anglais seront sujets au Tribunal fiscal dans toutes les affaires du ressort de ce dernier. Il n'est pas constaté que cette disposition ait été acceptée par l'Angleterre et, quand même, celà ne tirerait guère à conséquence relativement aux autres causes et, par suite, à celle en litige.

L'Alvará du 31 mars 1790, à la requête des sujets anglais, modifie les formalités (procédés) relativement aux griefs proférés contre les décisions du Juiz Conservador en remplaçant l'appellation par le remède de l'« aggravo ordinario para a Casa da Supplicação ». Mais celà n'affecte aucunement le traité et change uniquement les formes de la procédure, la « Casa da Supplicação » étant également une Cour composée de Sénateurs, une des Cours de Relação, par conséquent ce même Relationis Senatus (Paschalis Josephi Mellii Freirii Institutionis Juris Civilis Lusitani, Lissabon, 1789, lib. I, tit. 20, parag. 257 ; lib. IV, tit. 23, parag. 22, 23).

Le susdit décret n'altère pas même la disposition qui prescrit la décision dans le terme de quatre mois, et quand même il serait censé le faire par son silence à cet égard, on n'en pourrait tirer aucune conclusion relativement aux autres dispositions de l'art. 7.

Le Codigo commercial n'y a rien changé non plus. Ceci paraît, en effet, un point épineux : puisque ni le Gouvernement royal britannique, ni les défendeurs n'ont fait aucune opposition, lorsque au lieu d'appeler du jugement du Juiz Conservador directement au Tribunal de commerce de seconde instance, on a, conformément aux dispositions du Codigo, porté l'appellation d'abord au Tribunal de commerce de première instance (qui ne se compose pas de Sénateurs) et seulement de celui-ci au Tribunal de commerce de seconde instance, comme un Tribunal voulu par l'art. 7 du traité. Néanmoins, le raisonnement du Gouvernement royal de Portugal : que quiconque accepte le Codigo pour une de ses parties, ne pourrait en récuser l'autorité pour les autres, est erroné, quoiqu'on ait accepté quelques dispositions qu'en vertu du traité il aurait fallu repousser. Et celà par la raison que ces dispositions au fond n'excluaient pas la jouissance du privilège accordé par le traité, la substitution d'un autre Tribunal n'altérant en rien la juridiction du Tribunal indiqué par le traité. On a donc, il est vrai, permis que l'appellation n'arrivât au Tribunal du traité que par un détour, mais par là, on ne s'est aucunement engagé à regarder le jugement de ce Tribunal comme susceptible de remèdes ultérieurs.

Enfin l'omission des stipulations touchant l'appellation dans les traités de 1810 et 1842 ne justifierait pas la supposition que ces stipulations aient été regardées comme impraticables. Pour le traité de 1842 qui abrogeait la jurisdiction privilégiée, il n'y avait aucun motif de faire mention particulière du privilège des remèdes contre les jugements des Juizes Conservadores parce qu'avec leur abrogation ce privilège tombait de lui-même. Et dans le traité de 1810 il n'est dit nulle part qu'il devait former la source des droits des Anglais par rapport à leur juris-

diction ; il n'annulle point le traité de 1654 et ne contient aucune disposition contraire.

En revanche on y trouve que : « These Judges shall try and decide all causes brought before them by British subjects *in the same manner as formerly* », et le passage : « The laws, decrees and customs of Portugal respecting the jurisdiction of the Judge Conservator are declared to be recognised and received by the present treaty » ne se rapporte aucunement aux remèdes contre les décisions de ces juges.

Ainsi, s'il faut supposer que le traité de 1654, art. 7, devait être interprété dans le sens des Anglais et qu'à l'époque décisive il était encore en vigueur, il s'ensuit que le privilège des Anglais fondé sur ce traité fut lésé par le recours en revision contre le jugement du 1er décembre 1838. Car le Tribunal de commerce de seconde instance est d'un caractère analogue au Relationis Senatus du traité (Codigo commercial, art. 1004, 1005) et le raisonnement : que la Cour de cassation, attendu qu'elle casse et ne juge pas, ne forme point une troisième instance et que par conséquent son intervention ne dérogeait pas à la disposition du traité qui en prescrivait seulement deux, est parfaitement insoutenable, d'autant plus qu'il est parfaitement incompatible avec le mot « finiantur » du traité.

Il pourrait paraître plus difficile de répondre à la question : si, par leur acquiescement, sans protêt, à un litige ultérieur, après le jugement du Tribunal de commerce de première instance du 1er décembre 1838, Murdoch, Shortridge & Cie. ont renoncé à leur droit d'invoquer le traité.

Si Murdoch, Shortridge & Cie., dès l'ouverture des nouveaux débats devant la Cour de cassation, avaient, en vertu des traités en vigueur, requis l'intervention du Gouvernement britannique, on leur aurait répondu avec raison : attendez pour voir si les Tribunaux du pays vous léseront ; ce n'est que dans ce cas que le Gouvernement anglais peut intervenir.

La Cour de cassation ayant renvoyé la cause à la Cour de Relação, c'est le jugement rendu par cette dernière qui fournit au Gouvernement royal britannique des motifs légitimes de griefs.

A celà s'ajoute, que l'évidente injustice des jugements subséquents des Tribunaux portugais (comme il a été démontré plus haut) pouvait bien former, en faveur de Murdoch, Shortridge & Cie., un titre à une « in integrum restitutio » contre cette omission, d'autant plus que des arbitres ne peuvent être considérés aussi strictement liés aux formes juridiques que les tribunaux ordinaires.

Le Gouvernement royal de la Grande-Bretagne devait donc être censé, en vertu du traité de 1654, avoir le droit d'exiger de la part du

Gouvernement royal de Portugal, de reconnaître pour définitif le jugement du 1ᵉʳ décembre 1838; il fallait donc pronocer comme celà s'est fait dans le jugement (la sentence) : que le Gouvernement royal de Portugal est obligé envers le Gouvernement royal de la Grande-Bretagne de veiller à ce que le jugement prononcé le 1ᵉʳ décembre 1838 par le Tribunal de commerce de première instance de Lisbonne, dans la cause du sieur Manoel José d'Oliveira contre Murdoch, Shortridge & Cie., soit traité comme définitif (final) et exécutoire.

Mais de là s'ensuit de soi-même Ad II : son obligation de payer les dommages-intérêts en indemnisation du préjudice résultant de ce que le susdit jugement n'a pas été traité jusqu'ici comme tel, pour les sujets britanniques.

Il semblait répondre aux intentions de l'acte de compromis de fixer dès à présent la somme à laquelle s'élèveraient d'après les calculs ces dommages-intérêts. Et quoique, avec les données actuelles, il soit impossible de les préciser rigoureusement, on croyait ne pas devoir différer cette tàche, attendu qu'il sera toujours difficile de supputer les conséquences de procédures vicieuses, et que, en fin de compte, on sera toujours réduit à consulter les principes d'équité dans l'évaluation des dommages-intérêts même avec de plus amples données.

Ce qu'il y avait d'abord d'irrécusable, c'était :

A. La restitution des frais déboursés par les défenseurs jusqu'au jugement du 1ᵉʳ décembre 1838. Parce que cette restitution aurait eu lieu dès lors, en vertu de ce jugement, qui condamnait le demandeur aux dépens, si, comme de raison, le procès avait été regardé comme terminé.

Le Gouvernement royal de Portugal n'est pas seulement tenu à garantir subsidiairement le paiement actuel de ces frais par les héritiers du demandeur. En effet, on ne saurait de bonne foi imposer aux défenseurs, qui à l'époque indiquée auraient indubitablement recouvré les frais, la tàche ingrate d'affronter toutes sortes de désagréments en essayant d'obtenir ce paiement de la part des héritiers du demandeur aujourd'hui, c'est-à-dire, lorsque, par le décès du demandeur et par les disputes nées depuis relativement à la succession, les procédures seraient infiniment plus compliquées. Il faut au contraire abandonner au Gouvernement royal de Portugal le soin de soutenir ses droits vis-à-vis des héritiers d'Oliveira; de même que la présente sentence qui en vertu du traité de 1654 établit pour ce Gouvernement l'obligation de la restitution n'exclut nullement son droit de prendre à partie Oliveira, respectivement ses héritiers, ou tel autre auteur de ces procédures irrégulières, pour en avoir satisfaction.

Les susdits frais n'étant pas contestés, in quanto, de la part du Gouvernement portugais il y avait d'abord la somme de £ 2589, 14, 1 à mettre en ligne de compte. Il paraît également équitable d'adjuger au Gouvernement royal de la Grande-Bretagne les intérêts sur ce montant, de 6%, à partir de 1839. Cependant puisque, suivant le droit commun, seul applicable à cette question, le cumul des intérêts arriérés s'arrête, lorsqu'ils arrivent à la hauteur du capital (D. de conditione indebiti 12, 6; C. de usuris IV, 32), il fallait resteindre les intérêts dus au Gouvernement royal britannique, sur cette partie, à £ 2589, 14, 1.

B. En ce qui touche les frais déboursés depuis 1838, la somme exigée de £ 5400, 8 (non plus contestée de la part du Portugal), par des raisons ci-dessus développées, doit également être mise à la charge du Gouvernement royal de Portugal.

Les intérêts de cette somme comptés par le Gouvernement royal britannique depuis le mois de juillet de 1852 lui sont adjugés par £ 2916, 4.

Enfin restait à déterminer :

C. Le titre et l'importance des dommages-intérêts dus aux défendeurs en compensation du préjudice porté à leur commerce par la poursuite du procès. A cet égard

1. il y avait à considérer que la partie perdante n'est pas tenue de réparer le dommage causé à un plaideur par les inconvénients et la perte de temps qu'entraîne le litige, ce dommage devant être considéré comme un préjudice indirect, et qu'en général, la restitution des frais par le perdant satisfait toutes les prétentions de la partie victorieuse. Néanmoins

2. on ne pouvait disconvenir que dans le procès en question, par la suite de la procédure viciée, les défendeurs ont dù essuyer des préjudices directs dont l'équité exige la réparation.

Il est en effet hors de doute que l'existence d'une sentence finale, entrainant le paiement de £ 25,000 ne pouvait manquer de compromettre sérieusement le crédit et le commerce des défendeurs; et bien qu'on ne saurait soutenir que ce fâcheux effet n'étant dû qu'à des circonstances particulières et individuelles, ne devait pas être pris en considération; attendu qu'il est évident que tout autre établissement de l'étendue et de la nature de celui des défendeurs, aurait subi les mêmes conséquences. Que si en considération de cet effet de la procédure il y avait une compensation à accorder, il fallait toutefois.

3. se rappeler qu'une demande en indemnisation n'est légitime qu'en tant que le préjudice éprouvé serait une conséquence réelle et inévitable des procédures judiciaires illégalement continuées; relativement à quoi, il y a trois points à discuter:

a) que, comme il résulte des actes, les procédures judiciaires ont été mises à fin au commencement de l'année 1848, d'où il suit que la supposition des dommages-intérêts ne doit pas s'étendre au delà de ce terme;

b) que les effets préjudiciables des procédures n'ont pas pu commencer avant la fin de 1840, parce que c'est seulement alors que fut prononcé le jugement condamnatoire de la Cour de Relação lequel par son caractère extraordinaire justifie l'adjudication de dommages-intérêts, tandis que la procédure depuis le 1er décembre 1838 jusqu'au 15 novembre 1840 n'offre rien de particulier qui pût justifier une déviation du principe établi sub 1;

c) qu'il est constant, qu'avec le procès d'autres causes concouraient, pour réduire les bénéfices du commerce des défendeurs. Tout en admettant, à cet égard, qu'une de ces causes concourantes indiquée par le Gouvernement britannique (savoir l'absence de l'associé Shortridge par suite de son séjour à Lisbonne) était motivée par le procès et par conséquent digne de considération et même en écartant la réflexion que la décadence du crédit des défenseurs doit s'attribuer en partie aux lettres de Shortridge à J. Denyer, lesquelles à l'occasion du procès furent généralement connues; il n'en est pas moins vrai que la conjoncture de l'époque a dû porter un préjudice considérable au commerce des défenseurs. On en voit la preuve spéciale pour le point en question, dans les pièces à l'appui du «Report from the Select Comittee of the House of Commons» sur l'affaire en question, fait en 1854. On a consulté ce rapport avec d'autant plus de confiance pour la sentence, qu'il renferme des documents exhibés par MM. Yuille, Shortridge & Cie. eux-mêmes. Tels sont les comptes de gain et de pertes dans l'appendice N° 2 sub A et B. On voit par le compte sub B, que les mauvais résultats de certaines consignations de vins ainsi que la décadence de la production entraînaient pendant les années de 1839 à 1852 des pertes considérables qui, certes, doivent s'attribuer plutôt à la situation générale des affaires qu'au procès. La même pièce atteste que certaines dépenses faites à Londres ont englouti des sommes considérables sans qu'on puisse découvrir de quelle manière elles se rattachent au procès.

Il va sans dire que des pertes dues à la conjonction générale des affaires et à d'autres causes

étrangères ne pouvaient entrer dans la supputation des dommages-intérêts;

4. restait à déterminer d'après quel principe devait se former le compte des dommages-intérêts.

Il fallait d'abord rejeter celui qu'avait adopté le Gouvernement royal de la Grande-Bretagne, savoir: qu'on devait tenir compte de la valeur des immeubles et de l'établissement au moment de la vente en 1839, d'autant plus qu'il n'y a aucune raison de supposer que, sans le procès, l'établissement eût été réellement vendu. Mais quand même on prendrait cette valeur pour base du calcul, il faudrait d'autre part envisager la valeur qu'aurait eu l'établissement en 1848, époque où, comme on le voit plus haut, le procès fut mis à fin. Mais il n'y a aucun document pour éclairer ce point. On ne peut non plus supposer avec le Gouvernement de la Grande-Bretagne que les immeubles estimés en 1839 à £ 10,000, aient été sans valeur ou même d'une valeur considérablement réduite en 1848 (époque déterminante pour la supputation des pertes) et cela par suite du procès; parce qu'il n'y a aucune pièce à l'appui et qu'on ne saurait admettre une pareille supposition sans preuve. Enfin, il paraît que la perte de la clientèle ne devrait être comptée qu'en tant que, pendant les années de 1840 à 1848 (les seules qu'il faille prendre en considération ici), elle aura contribué à réduire le revenu annuel, parce que, plus tard, c'était à l'activité des défenseurs de réparer ces pertes qui ne se rattachent que très indirectement au procès. D'après tout ce qui vient d'être exposé ci-dessus il n'y avait que la différence des bénéfices nets des années antérieures à 1838 d'avec celles de 1840 à 1848 qui put servir de base au calcul.

Suivant le relevé du Gouvernement royal de la Grande-Bretagne le chiffre moyen des bénéfices annuels depuis 1830 jusqu'à 1838 était de . . . . £ 1931, 15 sh. et plus tard (£ 5768 en 14 ans) de . » 412,— »

Baisse £ 1519, 15 sh.

Eu égard à toutes les considérations alléguées ci-dessus, on prendra sur cette somme £ 500 (ce qui ne paraît pas un chiffre trop bas) pour frais de procédure, ce qui pour les sept années depuis la fin de 1840 jusqu'au commencement de 1848, porte le total des pertes en affaires à . . . . . £ 3,500,—sh.,—d. plus les intérêts à 6%, savoir:

1re année, fin de 1841
jusqu'au milieu de
1861 (sur £ 500,
19 1/2 ans). . . £ 500

<table>
<tr><td>Report</td><td>£ 500</td><td>£ 3,500,— sh.,— d.</td></tr>
</table>

2ᵉ année, fin de 1842
jusqu'au milieu de
1861 (sur £ 500,
18 ¹/₂ ans) . . . » 500

3ᵉ année, fin de 1843
jusqu'au milieu de
1861 (sur £ 500,
17 ¹/₂ ans) . . . » 500
(Par les raisons
indiquées sub II,
les intérêts de ces
trois années ne
pouvaient se por-
ter à un taux d'in-
térêt plus élevé);

4ᵉ année, fin de 1844
jusqu'au milieu de
1861 (sur £ 500,
16 ¹/₂ ans) . . . » 495

5ᵉ année, fin de 1845
jusqu'au milieu de
1861 (sur £ 500,
15 ¹/₂ ans) . . . » 465

6ᵉ année, fin de 1846
jusqu'au milieu de
1861 (sur £ 500,
14 ¹/₂ ans) . . . » 435

7ᵉ année, fin de 1847
jusqu'au milieu de
1861 (sur £ 500,
13 ¹/₂ ans) . . . » 405
——————
£ 3,300,- sh.,— d.

de sorte que cette partie
s'élève à un total de . » 6,800,— » - »

En résumé:

1. Frais de procédure jus-
qu'en 1838 avec intérêts . » 5,179,08 » 02 »

2. Frais de procédure après
1838 avec intérêts . . » 8,316,12 » — »

3. Pertes en affaires avec intérêts . . . . . . » 6,800,— » — »
——————
Total £ 20,296,— sh., 2 d.

que le Gouvernement royal de Portugal a dû être condamné à payer.

Par suite de la réduction nécessaire des prétentions du demandeur il a fallu prononcer sur les frais du compromis comme on le voit dans la sentence.

Hambourg, 21 octobre 1861 [1].

¹ Le compromis et la sentence, reproduits par nous, nous ont été gracieusement communiqués par le Gouvernement portugais.

CIII. Grande Bretagne, Nicaragua.

... janvier 1879.

Il nous a été impossible de fixer la date exacte du compromis, ni de déterminer si un compromis a été signé dans le présent conflit. Soumis à l'Empereur d'Autriche-Hongrie, ce dernier rendit une sentence longuement motivée.

Schiedsspruch zur Aburteilung der Kompromissache zwischen Grossbritannien und Nicaragua, in Wien gefällt, den 2. Juli 1881.

Wir, Franz Joseph der Erste, von Gottes Gnaden Kaiser von Österreich, König von Böhmen, &c., und Apostolischer König von Ungarn, &c.:

Haben, nachdem die Regierungen Ihrer Britischen Majestät und der Republik Nicaragua übereingekommen sind, die unter ihnen streitige Frage der Auslegung einiger Artikel des am 28. Jänner, 1860, zu Managua zwischen ihnen geschlossenen Vertrages Unserer schiedsrichterlichen Entscheidung zu unterstellen, und Wir Uns bereit erklärt haben, das Amt eines Schiedsrichters in dieser Angelegenheit auszuüben, — auf Grund eines von drei durch Uns berufenen Rechtsverständigen Uns erstatteten Gutachtens, — den nachstehenden Schiedsspruch gefällt:

ARTIKEL I. Die in Artikel I und II des Vertrages von Managua ddo. 28. Jänner, 1860, anerkannte Souveränität der Republik Nicaragua ist in Ansehung des durch Artikel II dieses Vertrages den Mosquito-Indianern zugewiesenen Gebietes nicht eine volle und unbeschränkte, sondern durch die den Mosquito-Indianern im Artikel III dieses Vertrages zugestandene Autonomie («self-government») eingeschränkte.

ARTIKEL II. Die Republik Nicaragua ist berechtigt, zur Ersichtlichmachung ihrer Souveränität auf dem den Mosquito-Indianern zugewiesenen Gebiete die Fahne der Republik aufzupflanzen.

ARTIKEL III. Die Republik Nicaragua ist berechtigt, zur Wahrnehmung ihrer Souveränitätsrechte in dem den Mosquito-Indianern zugewiesenen Gebiete einen Commissär zu bestellen.

ARTIKEL IV. Den Mosquito-Indianern ist es gestattet, auch fernerhin ihre eigene Flagge zu führen, sie müssen jedoch mit derselben ein Emblem der Souveränität der Republik Nicaragua verbinden.

ARTIKEL V. Die Republik Nicaragua ist nicht berechtigt, Concessionen zur Gewinnung von Naturprodukten des den Mosquito-Indianern zu-

49

gewiesenen Territoriums zu ertheilen. Dieses Recht steht der Mosquito-Regierung zu.

ARTIKEL VI. Die Republik Nicaragua ist nicht berechtigt, den Handel der Mosquito-Indianer zu regeln und von Waaren, welche in das den Mosquito-Indianern vorbehaltene Gebiet eingeführt, oder aus demselben ausgeführt werden, Einfuhr- oder Ausfuhrzölle zu erheben. Dieses Recht steht der Mosquito-Regierung zu.

ARTIKEL VII. Die Republik Nicaragua ist schuldig, die Rückstände der im Artikel V des Vertrages von Managua den Mosquito-Indianern zugesicherten Jahresrente im Betrage von 30,859 dol. 3 c. denselben auszubezahlen. Zu diesem Ende ist die von der Republik Nicaragua in der Bank von England deponirte Summe von 30,859 dol. 3 c. sammt den mittlerweile daselbst aufgelaufenen Zinsen der Regierung Ihrer britischen Majestät auszufolgen.

Die Republik Nicaragua ist nicht schuldig, Verzugszinsen von der rückständigen Summe zu bezahlen.

ARTIKEL VIII. Die Republik Nicaragua ist nicht berechtigt, von Waaren, welche in das Gebiet des Freihafens San Juan del Norte («Greytown») eingeführt, oder aus demselben ausgeführt werden, Ein- oder Ausfuhrzölle zu erheben.

Die Republik Nicaragua ist jedoch berechtigt, von Waaren, bei ihrem Übertritt aus dem Gebiete des Freihafens San Juan del Norte («Greytown») in das Gebiet der Republik Einfuhrzölle und bei ihrem Übertritt aus dem Gebiete der Republik in das Gebiet des freihafens San Juan del Norte («Greytown») Ausfuhrzölle zu erheben.

Urkundlich dessen Unsere höchsteigenhändige Unterschrift und beigedrücktes Kaiserliches Insiegel.

Gegeben Wien, am 2 Juli, 1881.

———————

I. Um die Differenzen, welche sich zwischen den Regierungen Ihrer Britischen Majestät und der Republik Nicaragua in Betreff der Auslegung einiger Artikel des von ihnen am 28. Januar, 1860, zu Managua geschlossenen Vertrages ergeben haben, würdigen und schlichten zu können, ist es nöthig die verwickelten Verhältnisse und widerstreitenden Ansprüche, welche vor Aufrichtung dieses Vertrages bestanden und zur Abschliessung desselben geführt haben, insoweit sie für die Fällung des Schiedsspruches von Belang sind, in gedrängtester Kürze sich zu vergegenwärtigen.

Die rechtliche Herrschaft über das von den Mosquito-Indianern bewohnte, nach Innen nicht genau abgegrenzte Gebiet an der Ostküste Centralamerika's längs des Caraibischen Meerbusens war seit langer Zeit streitig. Auf der einen Seite wurde dieselbe von jenen Republiken in Anspruch genommen, welche sich von Spanien im dritten Decennium dieses Jahrhunderts losgerissen hatten und ihr Anrecht auf das Mosquito-Gebiet auf ihre Succession und die Rechte des Mutterlandes gründeten. Die Krone Spanien hatte sich von Alters her die Herrschaft über die Mosquito-Indianer zugesprochen und derselben im Jahre 1803 mittelst eines Decrets, das die territoriale Abgrenzung und die administrative Zutheilung des Küstengebiets regelte, bestimmenden Ausdruck gegeben. Da aber weder Spanien noch die von ihm abgefallenen und zur Unabhängigkeit gelangten Colonien die prätendirte rechtliche Herrschaft über das Mosquito-Gebiet factisch ausgeübt hatten und somit der behaupteten Occupation das wesentliche Element der thatsächlichen Besitzergreifung fehlte; so konnten andererseits die Mosquito-Indianer wie ihre factische Selbstandigkeit so ihre rechtliche Unabhängigkeit behaupten und sich als eigenes Gemeinwesen benehmen. Als solches traten die Mosquito-Indianer in commercielle und völkerrechtliche Beziehungen, namentlich zu England. Die Beziehungen zu dieser Macht reichen bis in die Zeit unmittelbar nach der Eroberung Jamaica's in der zweiten Hälfte des 17. Jahrhunderts hinauf, führten im Jahre 1720 zu einem förmlichen Vertrage zwischen dem Gouverneur von Jamaica und dem «König» betitelten Häuptling der Mosquito-Indianer, und gestalteten sich endlich zu einem völkerrechtlichen Schutzverhältniss. Dieses Protectorat England's wurde jedoch nicht nur von den centralamerikanischen Republiken, sondern auch von den Vereinigten Staaten Nordamerika's um so lebhafter angestritten, als die vielumworbenen Gegenden um die Mündung des San Juan-Flusses im Hinblick auf die beabsichtigte Errichtung eines interoceanischen Canals der Verbindung des Atlantischen und des Stillen Meeres in handelspolitischer Beziehung an Wichtigkeit sehr gewonnen hatten.

Als die Mosquito-Indianer im Jahre 1848 mit Hilfe England's sich der an der Mündung des San Juan-Flusses gelegenen wichtigen Hafenstadt San Juan del Norte (Greytown) nach manchen Wechselfällen bemächtigt hatten, drohten kriegerische Verwicklungen mit den Vereinigten Staaten auszubrechen, unter deren Schutz die Republik Nicaragua sich gestellt hatte. Um diesen Gefahren vorzubeugen, und um die Basis für eine gleichmässige Enthaltungspolitik England's und der Vereinigten Staaten in Ansehung der Gegenden längs des beabsichtigten interoceanischen Canals zu gewinnen, schlossen beide Staaten im April 1850 den sogenannten Bulwer-Clayton-Vertrag (Case, Appendix, p. 69 sq.), der aber selbst wieder zum Ausgangspunkte neuer Streitigkeiten wurde. England suchte nunmehr durch Verhandlungen mit den Vereinigten Staaten die Grundlagen für ein Arrangement der centralamerikanischen Angelegenheiten zu erlangen und insbesondere das Schicksal der Mosquito-Indianer und die staatsrechtliche Stellung der wichtigen Hafenstadt San Juan del Norte (Greytown) zu regeln und in dieser Beziehung zunächst mit den Vereinigten Staaten zu bestimmten vertragsmässigen Resultaten zu gelangen, zu deren Annahme beide Staaten hierauf die Republik Nicaragua zu bewegen suchen sollten. Auf diese Weise entstand im April 1852 der sogenannte Crampton-Webster'sche Vertrag (Martens-Samwer, «Recueil de Traités», tome XV, pp. 195 sq.), worin England auf das Protectorat über die Mosquito-Indianer stillschweigend verzichtete und wonach das ganze innerhalb der Grenzen Nicaragua's gelegene Mosquito-Gebiet unter die Souveränität der Republik gelangen sollte, mit Ausscheidung jedoch eines genau abgegrenzten Territoriums, das den Mosquito-Indianern zu selbständiger und unabhängiger Herrschaft überlassen bleiben sollte (Artikel I). Diese Vertragsgrundlagen wurden jedoch von Nicaragua nicht angenommen, welches den Mosquito-Indianern ein unabhängiges Gebiet auch nicht theilweise belassen, sondern die ganze Küste seiner eigenen Souveränität unterstellt wissen wollte. Da weitere Verhandlungen mit den Vereinigten Staaten nicht zum Ziele führten, und insbesondere ein im Jahre 1856 geschlossener Vertrag (sogenannter Clarendon-Dallas'scher Vertrag — Case, Appendix, pp. 72 sq.) nicht ratificirt wurde, so schlug England den Weg directer Negociationen mit der Republik Nicaragua ein und schloss endlich am 28. Januar, 1860, den Vertrag zu Managua ab, der eine Ausgleichung der widerstreitenden Interessen und Ansprüche enthält und für dessen historisches Verständnis und richtige Gesammtauffassung der vorausgegangenen Vertragsverhandlungen zwischen England und den Vereinigten Staaten nicht ohne Bedeutung sind.

II. In dem Vertrage von Managua wurde von England das Protectorat über die Mosquito-Gebiet ausdrücklich aufgegeben (Art. I, Alin. 2), die Souveränität der Republik Nicaragua über das ganze innerhalb ihrer Grenzen gelegene Gebiet der Mosquito-Indianer unter den im Vertrag specificirten Bedingungen und Verpflichtungen anerkannt (Art. I, Alin. 1), zugleich aber den Mosquito-Indianern ein genau abgegrenztes Territorium zugewiesen und vorbehalten (Art. II, VIII), innerhalb desselben sie das Recht der Selbstregierung («self-government») zu geniessen haben (Art. III).

Der Streit zwischen den beiden Regierungen betrifft das Verhältniss der nebeneinander bestehenden Souveränität und Selbstregierung («self-government») zu einander, den Inhalt und Umfang der einerseits der Republik zustehenden Herrschaft und der andererseits den Mosquito-Indianern eingeräumten Selbstbestimmung.

Eine unbefangene Erwägung der Sachlage führt zu folgenden Ergebnissen: —

Die von der Republik Nicaragua zu allen Zeiten in Anspruch genommene Souveränität über das ganze Küstengebiet ist vertragsmässig anerkannt worden. Die Ausscheidung eines Teiles dieses Gebietes zur Erhaltung oder Constituirung eines völlig unabhängigen, in staats- und völkerrechtlicher Beziehung selbständigen Gemeinwesens der Mosquito-Indianer, wie sie noch in den Vertragsverhandlungen zwischen England und den Vereinigten Staaten in Aussicht genommen war, hat nicht stattgefunden.

An die Stelle des bisherigen völkerrechtlichen Schutzverhältnisses ist ein staatsrechtliches Unterwerfungsverhältniss getreten: die Mosquito-Indianer haben an Stelle ihres bisherigen Beschützers (England) einen Beherrscher (die Republik Nicaragua) erhalten, dessen staatsrechtlicher Gewalt und Autorität sie unterstellt sind.

Aber auf der anderen Seite ist den Mosquito-Indianern ein genau abgegrenztes Territorium zugewiesen und ihnen die Selbstregierung innerhalb desselben überlassen worden.

Dieses den Mosquito-Indianern vorbehaltene Territorium, welches daher gemeiniglich «Reserva Mosquita» genannt wird, bildet einen integrirenden und untrennbaren Bestandtheil des Gesammtterritoriums der Republik, eine staatsrechtliche Pertinenz des Hauptlandes.

Auf diesem geschlossenen und aparten Gebiete haben die Mosquito-Indianer ihr eigenes Leben und nationales Dasein zu führen; dieses Territorium ist, obgleich es bleibend zu der Republik Nicaragua gehört, als zunächst und unmittelbar den Indianern gehörig, als ihr Territorium, als das Land der Mosquitos, anzusehen. Dies ergibt sich indirect auch aus dem Verbot der Abtretung dieses Landstrichs durch die Mosquito-Indianer an eine fremde Person oder Macht (Art. II, Alin. 3). Die Mosquito-Indianer dürfen ihr Land nicht einem Anderen zur Herrschaft auftragen.

Innerhalb dieses Territoriums und auf demselben ist den Mosquito-Indianern zugestanden: «the right of governing, according to their own customs and according to any regulations which may from time to time be adopted by them, not inconsistent with the sovereign rights of the Republic of Nicaragua, themselves and all persons residing within such district. Subject to the abovementioned reserve, the Republic of Nicaragua agrees to respect and not to interfere with such customs and regulations so established, or to be established, within the said district» (Art. III). Bei vorurtheilsloser Prüfung und Auslegung dieser Vertragsbestimmung kann man wohl nicht umhin anzunehmen, dass darin das Zugeständniss der Selbstregierung (« self-government ») im Sinne von Selbstgesetzgebung und Selbstverwaltung enthalten sei. Zu diesem Resultate führt mit Nothwendigkeit auch die Bestimmung des Artikels IV, wonach die Mosquito-Indianer zu keiner Zeit verhindert sein sollen « from agreeing to absolute incorporation into the Republic of Nicaragua on the same footing as other citizens of the Republic, and from subjecting themselves to be governed by the general laws and regulations of the Republic, instead of by their own customs and regulations ». Solange dies nicht geschehen ist — und die Bemühungen der Republik Nicaragua in dieser Beziehung sind bisher vergeblich gewesen — sind die Mosquito-Indianer der Republik Nicaragua nicht vollständig einverleibt, sie stehen nicht auf demselben Fusse wie die anderen Unterthanen der Republik, sie unterliegen nicht den allgemeinen Gesetzen und Verordnungen der Republik, sondern sie regieren sich selbst nach eigenen Gewohnheiten und Gesetzen: bis zum Zeitpunkt jener freiwilligen Vereinbarung, einem *dies incertus an et quando*, ist die Incorporation des Mosquito-Gebietes in das Territorium der Republik eine relative und unvollständige. Die Mosquito-Indianer befinden sich sonach in einer vertragsmässig gewährleisteten Sonderstellung: ihr Territorium ist ein von der Gesetzgebung und Verwaltung der Republik exemtes Gebiet und bildet eine eigene, selbständige Gesetzgebungs- und Verwaltungssphäre. Diese locale Autonomie (« local self-government ») ist der letzte Rest der von den Mosquito-Indianern durch Jahrhunderte beanspruchten und ausgeübten Unabhängigkeit und Selbständigkeit.

Diese Selbstregierung (« self-government ») kann sich naturgemäss nicht auf die auswärtigen Angelegenheiten beziehen, da die « Reserva Mosquita » mit der Republik Nicaragua ein staats- und völkerrechtliches Ganzes bildet. Die Mosquito-Indianer haben daher nicht das Recht mit fremden Staaten in Beziehungen zu treten und Verträge zu schliessen, Gesandte abzusenden oder zu empfangen, Krieg zu führen und Frieden zu machen. Wohl aber erstreckt sich ihre Selbstregierung bei der allgemein lautenden Fassung des Artikels III auf den ganzen Umkreis der inneren Angelegenheiten, in deren Regelung sich nicht einzumischen die Republik Nicaragua zugesagt hat.

Der Standpunkt, welchen die Regierung der Republik Nicaragua einnimmt und in ihrer Streit-

schriften zu vertreten sucht, lässt sich nicht rechtfertigen.

Die Regierung der Republik stellt in Abrede, dass den Mosquito-Indianern « une autonomie véritable, une autonomie séparée du reste de la République » eingeräumt worden sei (Réponse, pp. 9, 12). Nach ihrer Ansicht wäre die der Republik zustehende Souveränität auch in Ansehung des Mosquito-Gebietes eine absolute und vollständige (« pleine et absolue », Réponse, pp. 4, 10) und die Republik berechtigt auch auf dem Mosquito-Boden die Herrschaft in ihrem vollen Inhalt und Umfang geltend zu machen (« d'être pratiquement souverain », Exposé, pp. 4, 49—51, 63), die ganze Fülle der in der Souveränität enthaltenen Hoheits- und Regierungsrechte auszuüben (« de nommer ses employés, d'ouvrir des ports de mer, de déterminer les droits de douane . . . . en un mot d'y établir comme dans toutes les autres parties de la nation la constitution et les lois de la République », Réponse, p. 10), und hätte sie sich nur aller Eingriffe in die nationalen Sitten und municipalen Gebräuche (« us et coutumes ») der Mosquito-Indianer zu enthalten (Exposé, pp. 5, 43; Réponse, p. 12).

Diese Behauptung steht in directem Widerspruch mit den Artikeln I—IV, worin die Souveränität der Republik nur in limitirter Weise anerkannt (« subject to the conditions and engagements specified in the present Treaty »), die Unverbindlichkeit der « general laws and regulations of the Republic » für die Mosquito-Indianer stipulirt und diesen die Berechtigung nicht nur sich selbst, sondern überhaupt alle in Mosquitia residirenden Personen zu regieren, zugestanden ist. Sie steht ferner in indirectem Widerspruch mit Artikel V, wonach die von der Republik zu leistende Subvention auch gewährt wird für die Erhaltung der Regierungsbehörden der Mosquitos: « for the maintenance of the authorities to be constituted under the provisions of Article III ». Die Behauptung der Regierung der Republik enthält eine durchaus unberechtigte und nicht zu rechtfertigende Anticipation der in Artikel IV einer zukünftigen freien Vereinbarung vorbehaltenen absoluten Incorporation und durchgängigen Gleichstellung der Mosquito-Indianer mit den übrigen Unterthanen der Republik.

Wenn die Regierung der Republik die Ansicht ausspricht, dass der Stamm der Mosquito-Indianer eine verkommene, entartete, bildungs- und entwicklungsunfähige Race sei, und dass ihm daher alle zur Selbstregierung erforderlichen Anlagen und Voraussetzungen fehlen (Réponse, pp. 4, 9), so ist dagegen zu bemerken, dass unbefangene und mit den Verhältnissen wohl vertraute Schriftsteller diese Ansicht nicht unbedingt theilen; dass die Republik Nicaragua die zehnjährige Subvention auch zu dem Ende zugesagt hat, um « the social improvement » der Mosquito-Indianer zu befördern (Art. V); dass dieselben im Fall der von der Republik Nicaragua so sehr angestrebten absoluten Incorporation sofort die gleichen Rechte wie alle andern Bürger der Republik geniessen sollen (Art. IV) und dass nach der Aussage (« statement ») ihres Chef's bereits eine Anzahl von Schulen, u. s. w. errichtet wurde (Case, p. 52) während für die Verbesserung der Lage der ausserhalb des reservirten Territoriums wohnenden, der Republik Nicaragua vollständig einverleibten Mosquito-Indianer angeblich nichts geschehen sei. Wie dem aber auch sei, dieses Bedenken hätte seinerzeit die Regierung der Republik abhalten müssen den Vertrag zu Managua auf solchen Grundlagen abzuschliessen: sie hätte dann dem Beispiel der Republik Honduras folgen müssen, in deren mit England zu Comayagua am 28. November, 1859, geschlossenem Vertrag den auf dem Gebiet dieser Republik befindlichen Mosquito-Indianern ein besonderes Territorium zur Selbstregierung nicht vorbehalten, sondern deren absolute Incorporation und sofortige unbedingte Gleichstellung mit den übrigen Unterthanen der Republik Honduras festgesetzt wurde (Art. II und III).

Die Berufung der Regierung Nicaragua's auf die rechtliche Lage der Indianer innerhalb der Vereinigten Staaten Nordamerika's ist gleichfalls unzutreffend. Nach dem Zeugniss von Kent (« Commentaries on American Law », 5 edit., 1844, vol. iii, p. 378 sq.) wurden die Indianerstämme in Nordamerika stets behandelt « as free and independent tribes, governed by their own laws and usages, under their own Chiefs, and competent to act in a national character and exercise self-government, and while residing in their own territories owing no allegiance to the municipal laws of the whites » (p. 384). Sie standen zu den Vereinigten Staaten in einem Schutzverhältniss und wurden als « dependent allies » angesehen und behandelt. (Kent, pp. 383, 385; Wheaton, « Eléments de Droit International », 1848, i, p. 50 sq.; Beach-Lawrence, « Commentaire sur les Eléments de Droit International de H. Wheaton », 1868, i, p. 264 sq.; Calvo, « Le Droit International », 3° édit. 1880, i, § 69, p. 178 sq.; Rüttimann, « Das Nordamerikanische Bundesstaatsrecht », i, 1867, S. 1 fg.) Erst in neuester Zeit (3. März 1871) wurde vom Congress zu Washington beschlossen, dass die Indianerstämme in Hinkunft nicht mehr als unabhängige Völkerschaften zu betrachten seien und dass mit ihnen, unbeschadet der Gültigkeit und Wirksamkeit der bereits abgeschlossenen Verträge, keine Allianzverträge mehr abzuschliessen seien (« Revised Statutes of the United States », 1873—74, § 2079,

p. 366). Es ist übrigens schon mit Rücksicht auf die Verschiedenheit der geographischen und ethnographischen Verhältnisse ganz unthunlich eine Parallele zu ziehen. Während die Indianerstämme in den Vereinig.en Staaten allerwärts in enclavirten Gebieten wohnen und einer sie erdrückenden immensen und ungemischten weissen Bevölkerung gegenüber stehen, bewohnen die Mosquito-Indianer (ungefähr 6,000 an der Zahl) einen abgesonderten Küstenstrich, und hat die Republik Nicaragua selbst nur eine schwache und gemischte Bevölkerung (circa 250,000 bis 300,000 Einwohner, wovon ½ Ladinos, ⅛ Indianer, ⅙ Mulatten und Schwarze). (Martin, « The Statesman's Year-book », 1874, pp. 543, 544; Wappäus, « Handbuch der Geographie des Ehemaligen Spanischen Mittel- und Südamerika », 1879, S. 335; Meyer, « Conversations-Lexicon », 3. Auflage, Art. Nicaragua und Mosquito-Küste.) Aus der vorstehenden Erörterung und Darstellung ergibt sich als Resultat, dass die Souveränetät der Republik Nicaragua auf dem Gebiet der Mosquito-Indianer nicht eine volle und unbeschränkte ist, sondern dass dieselbe durch das dem Mosquito-Indianern eingeräumte Recht der Selbstregierung beschränkt und begrenzt ist (Art. I des Entwurfs).

Dieses Verhältniss der Republik Nicaragua zu der « Reserva Mosquita » lässt sich in Kürze durch den Satz charakterisiren: « La République règne, mais elle ne gouverne pas. »

Als Souverain des Mosquito-Gebietes muss die Republik Nicaragua ohne weiteres für berechtigt erkannt werden, zum Zeichen ihrer Herrschaft (« en signe de souveraineté ») die Fahne der Republik auf dem Territorium der Mosquito-Indianer aufzupflanzen (Entw., Art. II). Diesem Anspruch der Regierung der Republik (Exposé, p. 55) setzt auch die englische Regierung keinen Widerstand entgegen (Counter-Case, p. 8, No. 19), obwohl derselbe einen Beschwerdepunkt in dem Mémoire des Häuptlings der Mosquito-Indianer bildet (Case, p. 52). Ebenso muss der Republik Nicaragua das Recht zuerkannt werden einen Commissär zu bestellen, der darüber zu wachen hat, dass die Mosquito-Regierung ihren Wirkungskreis nicht überschreite und in die Souveränitätsrechte der Republik (Art. III) nicht übergreife (Entw., Art. III). Dieser Commissär darf sich jedoch in die inneren Angelegenheiten der Mosquito-Indianer nicht mischen und keinerlei Jurisdiction auf dem Mosquito-Gebiet ausüben. Insoweit das Nicaraguanische Präsidial-Decret, vom 6. Januar, 1875 (Case, p. 82), hiemit in Widerspruch steht, wird dasselbe daher ausser Kraft zu treten haben.

Den Mosquito-Indianern kann es füglich nicht verwehrt werden ihre alte Flagge auch fernerhin zu führen. Sie müssen jedoch ein Zeichen der Souveränität der Republik Nicaragua, der sie unterworfen sind, damit verbinden, um dieses Herrschaftsverhältniss zum allgemein erkennbaren Ausdruck zu bringen (Entw., Art. IV). Dies ist umsomehr geboten, als selbst Staaten, welche nur ein Protectorat ausüben, darauf gedrungen haben, dass der beschützte Staat an seiner Flagge ein Zeichen dieses Schutzverhältnisses (« as a mark of the protection ») anbringe.

So mussten die Jonischen Inseln, solange sie sich unter dem Protectorate England's befanden, dieses Verhältniss an ihrer Flagge ersichtlich machen (Phillimore, « Commentaries upon International Law », i, p. 96 sq.).

III. Die Selbstverwaltung begreift die eigene Verwaltung der wirthschaftlichen Angelegenheiten in sich. Gerade auf dem Gebiete der materiellen Interessen gelangt das Recht der Selbstregierung zu besonderer praktischer Bedeutung.

Die Mosquito-Indianer sind darauf angewiesen die gesammten Bedürfnisse ihrer nationalen Sonderexistenz und alle Kosten ihrer Selbstregierung aus eigenen Mitteln zu bestreiten. Sie haben für die Herbeischaffung dieser Mittel selbst zu sorgen und können dieselben nur durch Gewinnung der Naturproducte ihres Territoriums und möglichst vortheilhaften Absatz derselben aufbringen. In der Ueberlassung eines eigenen Territoriums liegt von selbst die Ueberlassung desselben zu eigener Ausnützung. In Folge der den Mosquito-Indianern eingeräumten territorialen und gouvernementalen Sonderstellung bildet das ihnen vorbehaltene Gebiet ein eigenes selbständiges Wirthschaftsgebiet.

Eine nothwendige Consequenz hiervon ist es, dass der Mosquito-Regierung das Recht zustehen muss Licenzen zur Gewinnung der Naturproducte ihres Territoriums (Holz, Kautschuk, Gummi, Cocosnüsse, Mineralien, u. s. w.) zu ertheilen und Gebühren dafür zu erheben.

Es würde gegen allgemeine Rechtsgrundsätze verstossen, wenn derjenige, dem der Boden gehört, nicht berechtigt wäre die Früchte desselben selbst zu ziehen oder die Gewinnung derselben gegen Entgelt Anderen zu überlassen. Die Ausnützung des Mosquito-Bodens kann nur den Mosquitos zustehen und die Republik Nicaragua kann dahin nicht für berechtigt erkannt werden « de délivrer des patentes pour l'exploitation des produits naturels de la Mosquitia » und den Mosquitos hiemit diese Einnahmsquelle zu entziehen (Entw., Art. V). Die Inanspruchnahme dieser Berechtigung seitens der Regierung der Republik (Exposé, p. 49 sq.) beruht auf einer Verwechslung des staatsrechtlichen Begriffs der Souveränität mit dem privatrechtlichen Begriff des Eigenthums.

Da die Mosquito-Indianer unter der Herrschaft der Republik Nicaragua ein eigenes mit « selfgovernment » ausgestattetes Gemeinwesen ausmachen, so müssen sie auch für berechtigt erkannt werden ihren Handel durch eigene Anordnungen (« Regulations ») zu regeln (Art. III) und, falls es ihnen zweckmässig scheint, von Waaren, die in ihr Gebiet eingeführt oder aus demselben ausgeführt werden, Zölle zu erheben und sich dadurch eine Einnahmsquelle zu eröffnen.

Wenn die Regierung der Republik Nicaragua diese Rechte für die Republik « en sa qualité de Souverain » in Anspruch nimmt und derselben die Befugniss vindicirt « de réglementer le commerce extérieur de la Reserva Mosquita, de réglementer le cabotage, d'ouvrir et de fermer ceux des ports pour lesquels l'une ou l'autre de ces mesures lui parait opportune » (Exposé, pp. 51, 63), « d'imposer les droits généraux d'importation et d'exportation dans le territoire de la Reserva » (Exposé, pp. 52, 53), so ist dies nur eine Consequenz ihrer irrigen principiellen Auffassung, wonach die Republik Nicaragua die volle und unbeschränkte Ausübung der Souveränitätsrechte auch auf dem Mosquito-Territorium zustehen soll. Die Behauptung, dass der Republik das Recht zustehe « d'appliquer dans le territoire de la Reserva les droits généraux qui régissent les autres parties de la République » (Exposé, p. 63), steht vollends im Widerspruch, sowohl mit den Artikeln III und IV des Vertrags, wonach die « General Laws and Regulations of the Republic » auf dem Mosquito-Gebiet nicht gelten sollen, als mit dem den Mosquitos gewährleisteten Rechte der Selbstregierung, da darin unzweifelhaft das ausschliessliche Recht der Selbstbesteuerung, der directen wie der indirecten, enthalten ist.

Die Regierung der Republik Nicaragua beruft sich für ihre Berechtigung die in Greytown importirten, zum Verbrauch im Mosquito-Gebiet bestimmten Waaren bei deren Wiederausfuhr zur See aus diesem Hafen mit einem Zoll zu belegen, auf den Schlusssatz des Artikels VII, wonach die Constituirung von San Juan del Norte (Greytown) zu einem Freihafen die Republik Nicaragua nicht hindern soll die üblichen Zölle von Waaren, die zum Verbrauch innerhalb des Territoriums der Republik bestimmt sind, zu erheben: zu dem Gebiet der Republik gehöre aber auch das Mosquito-Gebiet, die Republik müsse daher berechtigt sein von den aus dem Freihafen Greytown nach Mosquitia exportirten Waaren einen Zoll zu erheben (Exposé, pp. 52, 53; Réponse, p. 18). Allein in dem Schlusssatz des Artikels VII, der überhaupt nicht das Verhältniss Nicaragua's zur Mosquitia betrifft, können ebenso wie im Artikel V, Alinea 2, die Worte « territory of the Republic » nicht die Bedeutung von Gesammtterritorium der Republik haben, sondern es ist darunter das eigentliche Territorium der Republik mit Ausschluss des « territory reserved for the Indians » (Art. VIII) zu verstehen. Ueberdies aber ist die Erhebung eines Zolles unverträglich mit dem Freihafencharakter von Greytown (Nr. V).

Der Besorgniss der Regierung der Republik Nicaragua, dass die zollfreie Einfuhr von Waaren in den Mosquito-District Schmuggel in die übrigen Gebietstheile der Republik zur Folge haben oder befördern würde (Exposé, p. 51), begegnet die Regierung Ihrer Britischen Majestät mit der Einwendung, dass die Grenzgegenden des Mosquito-Gebietes ganz unwegsam seien (Counter-Case, p. 28, Nr. 93). Wäre dies nicht der Fall, so bliebe der Republik Nicaragua nichts übrig, als eine Zwischenzoll-Linie zu errichten. Die Schwierigkeit oder Unausführbarkeit einer solchen Unternehmung vermag dem Recht der Mosquito-Indianer, wie es sich nun einmal, aus dem Vertrag von Managua ergibt, keinen Abbruch zu thun.

Es muss daher erkannt werden, dass die Republik Nicaragua nicht berechtigt ist den Handel der Mosquito-Indianer zu regeln und von Waaren, die in das Mosquito-Gebiet eingeführt oder aus demselben ausgeführt werden, Einfuhr- oder Ausfuhrzölle zu erheben (Entw., Art. VI). Die hiemit im Widerspruch stehenden Artikel 1 und 2 des Nicaraguanischen Präsidial-Decrets vom 4. October, 1864 (Case, p. 82), werden sonach ausser Kraft zu treten haben.

IV. In Artikel V des Vertrags von Managua übernahm die Republik Nicaragua auf die Dauer von 10 Jahren die Verpflichtung den Mosquito-Indianern zum Zweck der Aufbesserung ihrer socialen Lage und der Erhaltung ihrer auf Grund des Artikels III constituirten Regierungsbehörden eine jährliche Rente von 5000 dol. zu zahlen. Diese Rente sollte halbjährig zu Greytown einer vom Häuptling der Mosquitos zum Empfang bevollmächtigten Person ausbezahlt und die erste Rate sechs Monate nach Austausch der Ratificationen des Managua-Vertrages entrichtet werden.

Dieser Austausch erfolgte am 2. August, 1860, in London.

Die Zahlung der Rente geschah unregelmässig und gerieth bald völlig ins Stocken. Als im November 1865 der Häuptling der Mosquito-Indianer starb und dessen Vetter, ein elfjähriger Knabe, als Nachfolger proclamirt wurde, verweigerte die Republik Nicaragua die Anerkennung desselben. Es braucht hier nicht untersucht zu werden, ob diese Verweigerung auf standhaften Gründen beruhte, oder ob sie nur den willkommenen Vorwand bieten sollte, um die Zahlungen der Subvention zurückzuhalten. Jener Häuptling ist seither (nach 1875) gestorben und gegen die Legitimität seines Nachfolgers kein Anstand erhoben worden. Da nun die Zwecke, zu deren Erreichung die Subvention zugesagt wurde, nach wie vor fortbestehen, und da die Zahlung derselben an keinerlei Bedingungen geknüpft ist, so kann es keinem Zweifel unterliegen, dass die Republik Nicaragua schuldig erkannt werden muss die rückständige Summe im Betrage von 30,859 dol. 3 c. zu bezahlen. Diese Summe ist mittlerweile von der Republik Nicaragua bei der Bank von England mit der Bestimmung hinterlegt worden (Case, p. 78), dass dieselbe nach Fällung eines auf Zahlung lautenden Schiedsspruches der britischen Regierung zu Gunsten der Mosquito-Indianer ausgefolgt werde. (Entw., Art. VII.)

Wenn die Regierung der Republik Nicaragua das Begehren stellt, dass die in der Bank von England deponirte Summe ihr ausgefolgt werde, um dieselbe in entsprechender Weise zum Besten der Mosquito-Indianer zu verwenden, da Niemand besser in der Lage sei zu beurtheilen, was zu thun sei als « le Souverain dans ses domaines, et que le territoire de Mosquitia se trouvant dans les limites et sous la juridiction de la République, il est de son devoir de s'enquérir de ses besoins pour y subvenir autant que possible, prenant toutes les mesures qui peuvent contribuer à l'avancement moral et au progrès matériel de ce district » (Réponse, p. 16), — so übersieht sie zunächst, dass die Subvention nicht nur zur Verbesserung der socialen Lage der Mosquitos, sondern auch zur Erhaltung ihrer eigenen Regierungsbehörden dienen soll. Sie sucht sich hiedurch aber auch in principiell unzulässiger Weise an die Stelle der Mosquito-Regierung zu setzen, die zur eigenen und selbständigen Wahrnehmung und Besorgung der Angelegenheiten und Interessen der Mosquitos berufen ist. Ist doch selbst in dem Vertrag, den die Republik Honduras mit Grossbritannien am 28. November, 1859, zu Comayagua geschlossen hat, stipulirt worden, dass die von dieser Republik der vollständig einverleibten Mosquitos zum Zwecke der Verbesserung ihrer intellectuellen und materiellen Lage zu entrichtende zehnjährige Subvention von 5,000 dol. pro Jahr dem Häuptling derselben ausbezahlt werden solle (Art. III, Alin. 2).

Die Republik Nicaragua kann jedoch nicht verhalten werden von der rückständigen Subventionssumme Verzugszinsen zu zahlen. Die Subvention ist zwar nicht, wie die Regierung der Republik Nicaragua meint (Réponse, p. 18) eine reine Schenkung (« un don gratuit, un présent »), da sie vielmehr mit Rücksicht (« in consideration ») auf die mannigfachen Vortheile versprochen worden ist, welche der Republik in dem Vertrag zugesichert und aus demselben erwachsen sind, wie das Aufgeben des Protectorats seitens England's und die Anerkennung der Souveränität der Republik über das ganze Mosquito-Gebiet, die Stadt San Juan del Norte (Greytown) mit inbegriffen. Wenn aber die Subvention auch nicht den Charakter einer reinen Schenkung hat, so hat sie doch immerhin den Charakter einer remuneratorischen Liberalität, und die aus der Natur eines solchen Rechtsverhältnisses sich ergebende Billigkeit schliesst die Verpflichtung zur Zahlung von Verzugszinsen aus (Entw., Art. VII).

V. Wie in Theorie und Praxis allgemein anerkannt ist, besteht das Wesen eines Freihafens darin, dass daselbst alle frei und ohne Entrichtung von Zöllen ein- und ausgeführten Waaren im Gebiet des Hafens selbst verbleiben, um daselbst verkauft oder verbraucht zu werden, oder ob sie aus demselben nach einem im Inland oder im Ausland gelegenen Orte wieder ausgeführt werden. Ein Freihafen, der zu einem bestimmten Staatsgebiet gehört und unter der Souveränität dieses Staates steht, ist eben in Bezug auf Zollsachen als Ausland anzusehen. Sobald jedoch die Waaren aus dem Gebiete des Freihafens in das übrige Staatsgebiet eingeführt werden, können dieselben bei ihrem Eintritt in dieses Gebiet, also ausserhalb des Freihafengebietes, mit einem Einfuhrzoll belegt werden. Nur in diesem Sinne können die Schlussworte des Artikels VII des Vertrags von Managua verstanden werden, welche ihr rechtes Licht durch die unmittelbar vorhergehende Bestimmung erhalten, wonach es der Republik Nicaragua nicht gestattet sein soll, von Waaren, welche von Meer zu Meer durch das Gebiet der Republik auf dem projectirten interoceanischen Kanale gehen, Durchfuhrzölle zu erheben. Desgleichen können die aus dem Inland ausgeführten Waaren (« les articles du pays ») zwar nicht bei ihrem Austritt aus dem Freihafen, wohl aber bei ihrem Uebertritt aus dem Staatsgebiet in das Gebiet des Freihafens mit einem Ausfuhrzolle belegt werden (Entw., Art. VIII). Das mit diesen Grundsätzen in Widerspruch stehende Nicaraguanische Präsidial-Decret vom 22. Juni, 1877 (Case, pp. 92, 93), welches für die Dauer der Litispendenz durch Präsidial-Decret vom 10. April 1878 (Case, pp. 93, 94) für San Juan del Norte (Greytown) bereits suspendirt ist, wird daher für diesen Freihafen definitiv ausser Kraft zu setzen sein.

Da in einem Freihafen Zölle von Waaren überhaupt nicht erhoben werden dürfen, so ist es auch unstatthaft Zölle von daselbst ein- oder ausgeführten Waaren zu dem Zwecke zu erheben, um die Kosten der Verwaltung der Hafenstadt und der Erhaltung des Freihafens zu bestreiten. Die Mittel zur Bedeckung solcher localer Bedürfnisse müssen durch Localbesteuerung in anderen Formen aufgebracht werden, wie z. B. durch Auflegung einer Steuer auf den Verbrauch von zollfrei eingeführten Waaren. Das durch Präsidial-Decret vom 20. Februar 1861 (Case, pp. 88, 89) eingeführte System der Aufbringung der Kosten für die Verwaltung der Stadt und die Erhaltung des Freihafens Greytown durch einen Einfuhrzoll auf die daselbst importirten Waaren wird daher durch ein anderes System zu ersetzen sein.

Ueber das Recht der Republik Nicaragua im Freihafen San Juan del Norte (Greytown) von Schiffen Abgaben (« duties and charges ») zu Zwecken des Hafens zu erheben (Art. VIII) herrscht kein Streit.

Auf die übrigen von der Regierung Ihrer Britischen Majestät zur Urteilsfällung verstellten Punkte (Counter-Case, pp. 32, 33, Nr. 15—19) kann füglich nicht eingegangen werden, da einige derselben theils Administrations-Angelegenheiten, civilrechtliche Rückforderungs-Ansprüche einzelner Privatpersonen betreffen, rücksichtlich anderer Punkte aber das zur Entscheidung nöthige statistische und rechnungsmässige Materiale nicht zu Gebote steht.

VI. Die Regierung der Republik Nicaragua bestreitet das Recht der Regierung Ihrer Britischen Majestät sich der Angelegenheiten, welche die Mosquito-Indianer und den Freihafen San Juan del Norte (Greytown) betreffen, anzunehmen, und in der vorliegenden Streitsache die Rolle des Beschwerdeführers zu übernehmen, da hierin eine unbefugte Einmischung in die innern Angelegenheiten Nicaragua's und eine vertragswidrige Geltendmachung des aufgegebenen Protectorates über Mosquitia liege (Exposé, pp. 53, 54, 63; Réponse, pp. 16, 17).

Diese Bestreitung der Legitimation England's *ad causam* kann nicht für begründet erkannt werden.

Was zunächst den Hafen von San Juan del Norte (Greytown) betrifft, so hat die Republik Nicaragua in Artikel VII des mit England abgeschlossenen Vertrags von Managua die Verpflichtung übernommen denselben zu Freihafen zu constituiren und zu erklären. Diese Constituirung und Erklärung ist durch Präsidial-Decret vom 23. November 1860 (Case, p. 87) denn auch erfolgt. Aber England hat ein vertragsmässiges Recht auch darauf zu dringen, dass diese Constituirung und Erklärung nicht blos eine nominelle sei, sondern dass von der Regierung der Republik Nicaragua keine Verfügungen und Anordnungen getroffen werden, welche mit dem Wesen und dem Charakter eines Freihafens unverträglich sind. Wenn nun die in Greytown ansässigen oder dahin Handel treibenden englischen Kaufleute den Schutz und das Einschreiten der englischen Regierung gegen Massregeln der Regierung Nicaragua anrufen, welche den Freihafencharakter Greytown's und dadurch ihre Handelsinteressen beeinträchtigen, und wenn Angehörige dritter Staaten sich solchen Schritten anschliessen, so liegt hierin kein Vorgang, der mit den Normen des Völkerrechts und der allgemein üblichen und für zulässig erkannten Praxis im Widerspruche stünde.

Was aber die Angelegenheiten der Mosquito-Indianer betrifft, so hat England in dem Vertrag von Managua zwar die Souveränität der Republik Nicaragua anerkannt und auf sein Protectorat verzichtet, aber dies doch nur unter vertragsmässiger Ausbedingung gewisser staatsrechtlicher und pecuniärer Vortheile für die Mosquitos gethan (« subject to the conditions and engagements specified in the Treaty, Art. I »). England hat ein eigenes Interesse an der Erfüllung dieser zu Gunsten seiner ehemaligen Schutzbefohlenen stipulirten Bedingungen und deshalb auch ein eigenes Recht auf die Erfüllung dieser Zusagen wie aller übrigen Vertragsclauseln zu dringen. Mit Unrecht nennt das die Regierung Nicaragua's eine unzulässige « Intervention », da in die Kategorie der allerdings verpönten Einmischung in die inneren Angelegenheiten eines fremden Staates das Andringen auf Erfüllung von demselben vertragsmässig übernommener Verpflichtungen nicht gehört. Nicht minder unrichtig ist es, wenn die Regierung Nicaragua's diese Geltendmachung vertragsmässiger Ansprüche als eine fortgesetzte Ausübung des aufgegebenen Protectorates zu qualificiren sucht und England's Einschreiten aus diesem Grunde für unzulässig erklären will.

Die Regierung der Republik Nicaragua stellt endlich auch das Begehren (Réponse, p. 17): es werde im Schiedsspruch ausgesprochen, dass der Vertrag von Managua, nachdem er seinen Zweck erfüllt habe, in Ansehung der Mosquitia annullirt sei und dass in Hinkunft die betheiligten Parteien sich in dieser Beziehung lediglich an die im Schiedsspruch getroffenen und aufgezählten Bestimmungen zu halten verpflichtet seien. Dieses Begehren verstösst gegen allgemeine Rechtsgrundsätze und kann demselben daher nicht stattgegeben werden. Die Auslegung eines Vertrages kann nimmermehr an die Stelle des ausgelegten Vertrages treten und das richterliche Urtheil schafft nicht neues Recht, sondern bringt nur das vorhandene Recht zur Feststellung und Anerkennung.

CIV. Colombie, Costa Rica.

25 décembre 1880.

Simple question de délimitation de frontière, cette contestation ne fut terminée qu'après de longs et interminables délais. Soumise dès 1880 à l'arbitrage du Roi d'Espagne, il fallut, par suite de la mort de ce dernier, renouveler la convention en 1886; le Gouvernement espagnol ne consentit toutefois à siéger qu'après la solution du conflit pendant entre la Colombie et le Vénézuéla. Ce dernier conflit ne fut résolu qu'en 1891, et la Colombie prétendit alors que le traité de 1886 était devenu caduc. Une nouvelle convention fut signée en 1896 pour revivifier les actes antérieurs et le Président de la République française fut désigné pour siéger désormais en qualité d'arbitre.

Convención de arbitraje entre los Estados Unidos de de Colombia y la República de Costa Rica, firmada en San José, Diciembre 25, 1880.

La República de Costa Rica y la República de los Estados Unidos de Colombia, igualmente animadas del sincero deseo de mantener y consolidar sus amistosas relaciones; convencidas de que, para obtener este bien tan importante á su prosperidad y buen nombre, es preciso cegar la única fuente de las diferencias que entre ellas ocurren, la cual no es otra que la cuestión de límites que, prevista en los artículos 7 y 8 de la Convención de 15 marzo de 1825 entre Centro América y Colombia, ha sido posteriormente objeto de diversos tratados entre Costa Rica y Colombia ninguno de los cuales llegó á ser ratificado; y entendidas ambas naciones de que este antecedente aconseja la adopción hoy día de otro medio más expedito, pronto y seguro de terminar la expresada cuestión de límites mediante la designación, á perpetuidad, de una línea divisoria, clara é incontrovertible, por toda la extensión en que colindan sus respectivos territorios; en consecuencia, el Presidente de la República de Costa Rica, en uso de las facultades de que se halla investido, ha conferido plenos poderes al Excelentísimo señor Doctor don José María Castro, Secretario de Estado y del Despacho de Relaciones Exteriores, y el Presidente de los Estados Unidos de Colombia, especial y competentemente autorizado por las Cámaras Legislativas de aquella nación, al Honorable señor Doctor don José María Quijano Otero, Encargado de Negocios cerca de este Gabinete; quienes después de haberse comunicado sus respectivos plenos poderes, y de encontrarlos en buena y debida forma, han convenido en los articulos siguientes:

ARTICULO 1. La República de Costa Rica y los Estados Unidos de Colombia comprometen en arbitraje la cuestión de límites existente entre ellas, y la designación de una línea que divida para siempre y con toda claridad, el territorio de la primera del territorio de la segunda, quedando cada una en pleno, quieto y pacifico dominio, por lo que respecta á ellas entre sí, de todo el terreno que á su lado deje la expresada línea, el cual no ha de quedar con carga ni gravamen alguno especial en favor del otro.

ARTICULO 2. El árbitro que, dignándose aceptar el cargo de tal, hubiere de ejecutar lo estipulado en el artículo anterior, ha de verificarlo, para que sea valedero, dentro de diez meses, á contar desde la fecha de su aceptación, sin que obste el que alguna de las Partes Contratantes no concurra á deducir sus derechos por medio de representante ó abogado.

ARTICULO 3. Para que la aceptación del árbitro se tenga por debidamente notificada á las Altas Partes Contratantes, y éstas no puedan alegar ignorancia de ella, basta que se publique en periódico oficial de la nación del árbitro, ó de lo de alguna de las Altas Partes Contratantes.

ARTICULO 4. El árbitro, oídas de palabra ó por escrito las Partes ó Parte que se presenten, y considerados los documentos que pongan de manifiesto, ó las razones que expongan, emitirá su fallo sin otra formalidad, y ese fallo, cualquiera que sea, se tendrá desde luego por tratado concluído, perfecto, obligatorio é irrevocable, entre las Altas Partes Contratantes, las cuales renuncian formal y expresamente á toda reclamación, de cualquiera naturaleza, contra la decisión arbitral, y se obligan á acatarla y cumplirla pronta, fielmente y para siempre, empeñando en ello el honor nacional.

ARTICULO 5. En consonancia con los precedentes articulos, y para su ejecución, las Altas Partes Contratantes nombran por árbitro á Su Majestad el Rey de los Belgas; para el caso inesperado de que éste no se digne aceptar, á su Majestad el Rey de España, y para el evento igualmente inesperado de que también éste se niegue, al Excelentísimo señor Presidente de la República Argentina; en todos los cuales las Altas Partes Contratantes tienen, sin diferencia alguna, la más ilimitada confianza.

ARTICULO 6. Aquel de los Altos Arbitros nombrados, que llegare á ejercer el arbitraje, puede delegar sus funciones, no dejando de intervenir directamente en la pronunciación de la sentencia definitiva.

ARTICULO 7. Si desgraciadamente ninguno de los Altos Arbitros nombrados pudiera prestar á las Altas Partes Contratantes el eminente servicio de admitir el cometido, ellas, de común acuerdo, harán nuevos nombramientos y así sucesivamente, hasta que alguno tenga efecto, porque está convenido, y aquí formalmente se estipula, que la cuestión de límites y la designación de una línea divisoria entre los territorios limitrofes de Costa Rica y Colombia, jamás se decidan por otro medio que el civilizado y humanitario del arbitraje, conservándose entre tanto el *statu quo* convenido.

ARTICULO 8. La presente Convención será sometida á la aprobación del Gran Consejo Nacional, en la República de Costa Rica, y de las Cámaras Legislativas, en la de Colombia; y será canjeada en la ciudad de Panamá, dentro del más breve termino posible.

En fe de lo cual, los Plenipotenciarios arriba mencionados firman y ponen sus respectivos sellos en dos originales de la presente Convención.

Hecha en ciudad de San José, capital de la República de Costa Rica, á veinticinco de diciembre de mil ochocientos ochenta.

Convención adicional a la de 25 de diciembre de 1880, entre los Estados Unidos de Colombia y la República de Costa Rica, firmada en París, Enero 20, 1886.

Los infrascritos, á saber:

Léon Fernández, Enviado Extraordinario y Ministro Plenipotenciario de la República de Costa Rica en España, Francia y la Gran Bretaña; y Carlos Holguin, Enviado Extraordinario y Ministro Plenipotenciario de los Estados Unidos de Colombia en España, deseando obviar las dificultades que pudieran suscitarse con respecto á la ejecución de la Convención de arbitraje concluída entre sus Gobiernos respectivos, en 25 de diciembre de 1880, y considerando

1º Que Su Majestad el Rey de España don Alfonso XII se había dignado aceptar verbalmente la designación de árbitro que los infrascritos le propusieron en nombre de sus respectivos Gobiernos, para dirimir las cuestiones territoriales pendientes entre ambas Repúblicas, y que, por tanto, la Convención de arbitraje de 25 de diciembre de 1880 ha tenido ya un principio de ejecución ante el Gobierno de España;

2º Que está en el interés de entrambas Repúblicas continuar allí el juicio arbitral propuesto, tanto porque en los archivos de España se encuentran la mayor parte de los documentos originales que han de servir para fallar con acierto y pleno conocimiento de causa las cuestiones de límites pendientes, como porque allí existe un competente número de personas dedicadas especialmente á estudios sobre América, cuya opinión y consejo contribuerán eficazmente á hacer que el fallo se ajuste cuanto es posible á la verdad y á la justicia; y

3° Que la muy sensible y prematura muerte de Su Majestad don Alfonso XII pudiera dar lugar á dudas respecto á la competencia de su sucesor ó sucesora para continuar conociendo del mencionado juicio arbitral hasta sentencia definitiva, han convenido en celebrar la siguiente Convención ad referendum, Adicional á la suscrita en San José, el 25 de diciembre de 1880, por los Plenipotenciarios de Costa Rica y los Estados Unidos de Colombia, para el arreglo de la cuestión de límites pendiente entre ambas Repúblicas.

ARTICULO 1. La República de Costa Rica y los Estados Unidos de Colombia reconocen y declaran que, no obstante la muerte de Su Majestad don Alfonso XII, el Gobierno de España es competente para seguir conociendo del arbitraje propuesto por ambas Repúblicas, y para dictar con el cárácter de irrevocable é inapelable, fallo definitivo en el litigio pendiente sobre límites territoriales entre las dos Altas Partes Contratantes.

ARTICULO 2. El límite territorial que la República de Costa Rica reclama, por la parte del Atlántico, llega hasta la isla del Escudo de Veraguas y río Chiriqui (Calobebora) inclusive; y por la parte del Pacifico hasta el río Chiriqui Viejo, inclusive al Este de Punta Burica.

El límite territorial que los Estados Unidos de Colombia reclaman, llega por la parte del Atlántico hasta el cabo de Gracias á Dios inclusive; y por el lado del Pacifico hasta la desembocadura del rio Golfito en el Golfo Dulce.

ARTICULO 3. El fallo arbitral deberá circunscribirse al territorio disputado que queda dentro de los límites extremos ya descritos y no podrá afectar en manera alguna los derechos que un tercero que no ha intervenido en el arbitraje pueda alegar á la propiedad del territorio comprendido entre los límites indicados.

ARTICULO 4. Si, por cualquier causa, el árbitro no pudiere dictar su fallo, dentro del término fatal que le señala el articulo 2 de la Convención de arbitraje de 25 de diciembre de 1880, las Altas Partes Contratantes convienen en prorrogar dicho término por otros diez meses más, que se contarán desde el día de la fecha en que haya de espirar el primero.

ARTICULO 5. Salvas las adiciones y modificaciones anteriores, queda vigente en todas sus partes la Convención de Arbitraje de 25 de diciembre de 1880.

En fe de lo cual, firmamos dos en un tenor autorizados con nuestros respectivos sellos, en la ciudad de París, á veinte de enero de mil ochocientos ochenta y seis [1].

Convención para revalidar las convenciones de arbitraje entre la República de Costa Rica e la República de Colombia, firmada en Bogota, Noviembre 4, 1896.

La República de Costa Rica y la República de Colombia, deseando poner término á la cuestión de límites pendiente entre ellas, y alcanzar una definitiva delimitación territorial, han convenido en llevar á efecto, con las adiciones y modificaciones que se van á expresar, las Convenciones de arbitraje que celebraron en San José de Costa Rica el veinticinco de diciembre de mil ochocientos ochenta, por medio de sus Plenipotenciarios Doctor don José María Quijano Otero y Doctor don José María Castro, y en París el veinte de enero de mil ochocientos ochenta y seis por medio de los plenipotenciarios Doctor don Carlos Holguín y Licenciado don León Fernández, y para realizar tal propósito han acreditado como Plenipotenciarios, el Gobierno de Costa Rica al señor don Ascensión Esquivel, su Enviado Extraordinario y Ministro Plenipotenciario en Colombia, y el Gobierno de Colombia al señor General don Jorge Holguín, Ministro de Relaciones Exteriores; quienes después de haberse exhibido sus plenos poderes y de hallarlos en debida forma, han convenido en los artículos siguientes:

ARTICLE I. Decláranse revalidadas las Convenciones de Arbitraje que se han indicado, las cuales serán observadas y cumplidas con las modificaciones que se expresan en los articulos siguientes.

ARTICLE II. Las Altas Partes Contratantes nombran para Arbitro al Excelentísimo señor Presidente de la República Francese; para el caso inesperado de que éste no se dignare aceptar, al Excmo. señor Presidente de los Estados Unidos Mexicanos; y para el caso, igualmente inesperado, de que éste también rehusare el encargo, el Excelentísimo señor Presidente de la Confederación suiza; en todos los cuales tienen las Altes Partes contratantes, sin diferencia alguna, la más illimitada confianza.

Las Altas Partes contratantes hacen constar que si al revalidar las Convenciones de arbitramento, no han designado como Arbitro al Gobierno de España, que había aceptado anteriormente este encargo, ha sido en consideración á la dificultad que experimenta Colombia en exigir de

---

[1] *Memoria de Relaciones esteriores*, Costa-Rica, 1885-1886.

dicho Gobierno tantos servicios seguidos, habiendo ha poco suscrito con el Ecuador y el Perú un tratado de límites en que se nombra Arbitro á su Majestad Católica, después del laborioso juicio de la frontera colombiana-venezolana.

ARTICLE III. La aceptación del primer Arbitro se solicitará dentro de tres meses después de verificado el canje de las ratificaciones del presente Convenio, y si por excusa de alguno de los árbitros hubiere de ocurrirse al que le sigue en orden, la solicitud de aceptación se hará dentro de tres meses después del día en que la excusa haya sido notificada á las Partes.

Si pasados los tres meses dichos no hubiere ocurrido alguna de las Partes á solicitar la aceptación, la que estuviere presente queda autorizada para pedirla, y la aceptación será valedera, como si las dos Partes la hubieran solicitado.

ARTICLE IV. El arbitraje se surtirá conforme á las reglas siguientes:

Dentro del término de dieciocho meses, contados desde que la aceptacion del Arbitro fuere notificada á las Altas Partes contratantes, estas le presentarán sus alegatos y documentos.

Para que lo aceptación se tenga por debitamente notificada á las Partes, de modo que no puedan alegar ignorancia de ella, basta que se publique en el periódico oficial de la Nación del Arbitro.

El Arbitro comunicará al Representante de cada Gobierno los alegatos del contrario, dentro de tres meses después de presentados, para que pueda rebatirlos en el curso de los seis meses siguientes.

El Arbitro deberá pronunciar su fallo, para que sea valedero, dentro del plazo de un año, a contar de la fecha en que hubiere vencido el término otorgado para contestar alegatos, hayan ó no presentado éstos.

El Arbitro puede delegar sus funciones con tal que no deje de intervenir directamente en la pronunciación de la sentencia definitiva.

La decisión arbitral, cualquiera que sea, se tendrá por tratado perfecto y obligatorio entre las Altas Partes contratantes, y no admitirá recurso alguno. Ambas Partes se comprometen á su fiel cumplimiento, y renuncian á todo reclamo contra la decisión, empeñando en ello el honor nacional.

ARTICLE V. Los artículos 2° y 4° del presente Convenio sustituyen los artículos 2° á 6° inclusive de la Convención de veinticinco de diciembre de mil ochocientos ochenta, y 1° y 4° de la de veinte de enero de mil ochocientos ochenta y seis. Salvas las modificaciones y adiciones ex-

presadas, que deben ser cumplidas, las Convenciones de arbitraje ya referidas quedan revalidadas y vigentes en todas sus demás partes.

ARTICLE VI. La presente Convención será sometida á la aprobación del Congreso de Colombia en sus actuales sesiones, y del Congreso de Costa Rica en sus sesiones próximas; y será canjeada en Panamá, San José de Costa Rica ó Wáshington, en el más breve término posible.

En fe de lo cual, los Plenipotenciarios arriba expresados firman y sellan el presente Convenio, en Bogotá, a cuatro de noviembre de mil ochocientos noventa y seis [1].

Sentence arbitrale prononcée par Monsieur le Président de la République Française, à Paris, le 11 Septembre 1900.

Nous, Président de la République Française, arbitre en vertu du traité signé le 4 novembre 1896 à Bogota, par les républiques de Colombie et de Costa-Rica, acte qui nous a conféré pleins pouvoirs en vue d'apprécier, suivant les principes de droit et les précédents historiques, la délimitation à intervenir entre les deux Etats susnommés;

Ayant pris connaissance de tous les documents fournis par les parties en cause, et notamment:

1° En ce qui concerne la Colombie:

De l'exposé de Don François Silvela, avocat de la légation de Colombie en Espagne;

Des deuxième et troisième mémoires, présentés au nom de la république de Colombie, par M. Poincaré, avocat à la cour d'appel de Paris;

D'une consultation de M. Maura, député aux Cortès espagnoles, président de l'académie royale de jurisprudence de Madrid, sur la question de limites entre la Colombie et le Costa-Rica;

D'une autre consultation de MM. le docteur Simon de la Rosa y Lopez, professeur de droit politique à l'université de Séville, et ses collaborateurs;

Du résumé chronologique des titres territoriaux de Colombie;

Et des nombreuses cartes géographiques et textes, tant originaux que traduits et annotés, à nous remis par le représentant de la Colombie, spécialement accrédité auprès de nous pour le litige actuel;

2° En ce qui concerne le Costa-Rica:

Des ouvrages de M. Manuel M. de Peralta, envoyé extraordinaire et ministre plénipotentiaire de cette république à Paris, intitulés:

---

[1] *Memoria de Relaciones exteriores*, Costa Rica, 1897, p. 43.

Limites de Costa-Rica et de Colombie;
Costa-Rica y Costa de Mosquitos;
Juridiction territoriale de Costa-Rica;

De l'exposé des titres territoriaux de la république de Costa-Rica;

De la réplique à l'exposé de la république de Colombie;

De l'atlas historico-geografico de Costa-Rica, Veragua y costa de Mosquitos;

Du volume de M. de Peralta: *Géographie historique et droits territoriaux du Costa-Rica;* Etc., etc.;

Et, en général, de tous et toutes décisions, capitulations, ordres royaux, provisions, cédules royales, lois, édictés et promulgués par l'ancienne monarchie espagnole, souveraine absolue et libre dépositrice des territoires qui ont fait partie, dans la suite, des deux républiques;

Ayant procédé à une étude minutieuse et approfondie des dits actes, à nous soumis par les parties, notamment: des cédules royales du 27 juillet 1513, du 6 septembre 1521, de la provision royale du 21 avril 1529, des cédules royales du 2 mars 1537, des 11 janvier et 9 mai 1541, du 21 janvier 1557, des 23 février et 18 juillet 1560, des 4 et 9 août 1561, du 8 septembre 1563, du 28 juin 1568, du 17 juillet 1572, de la capitulation du Pardo du 1er décembre 1573, de la Recopilación de las Leyes de Indias de 1680, particulièrement des lois IV, VI et IX de ce recueil, des cédules royales des 21 juillet et 13 novembre 1722, du 20 août 1739, du 24 mai 1740, du 31 octobre 1742, du 30 novembre 1756, des différentes instructions émanant du souverain espagnol et adressées tant aux autorités supérieures de la vice-royauté de Santa-Fé qu'à celles de la capitainerie générale de Guatemala au cours du dix-huitième siècle et dans les années suivantes; des ordres royaux de 1803 et 1805, des stipulations du traité conclu en 1825 entre les deux républiques indépendantes, etc., etc.;

Et conscient de l'importance de notre haute mission, ainsi que du très grand honneur qui nous a été fait d'être choisi comme juge dans le présent débat, n'ayant rien négligé pour nous rendre un compte exact de la valeur des titres invoqués par l'un et l'autre pays,

Arrêtons:

La frontière entre les républiques de Colombie et de Costa-Rica sera formée par le contrefort de la Cordillère, qui part du cap Mona sur l'océan Atlantique et ferme au nord la vallée du Rio-Tarire ou Rio-Sixola, puis la chaîne de partage des eaux entre l'Atlantique et le Pacifique jusqu'à par 9 degrés environ de latitude; elle suivra ensuite la ligne de partage des eaux entre le Chiriqui-Viejo et les affluents du golfe Dulce, pour aboutir à la pointe Burica sur l'océan Pacifique.

En ce qui concerne les îles, groupes d'îles, îlots, bancs, situés dans l'océan Atlantique, à proximité de la côte, à l'est et au sud-est de la pointe Mona, ces îles, quels que soient leur nombre et leur étendue, feront partie du domaine de la Colombie. Celles qui sont situées à l'ouest et au nord-ouest de la dite pointe appartiendront à la république de Costa-Rica.

Quant aux îles les plus éloignées du continent et comprises entre la côte de Mosquitos et l'isthme de Panama, nommément: Mangle-Chico, Mangle-Grande, Cayos-de-Albuquerque, San-Andrés, Santa-Catalina, Providencia, Escudo-de-Veragua, ainsi que toutes autres îles, îlots et bancs relevant de l'ancienne province de Cartagena, sous la dénomination de canton de San-Andrés, il est entendu que le territoire de ces îles, sans en excepter une, appartient aux Etats-Unis de Colombie.

Du côté de l'océan Pacifique, la Colombie possédera également, à partir des îles Burica et y compris celles-ci, toutes les îles situées à l'est de la pointe du même nom, celles qui sont sises à l'ouest de cette pointe étant attribuées au Costa-Rica [1].

CV. Etats-Unis d'Amérique, Grande-Bretagne, Portugal.

13 juin 1891.

Il s'agit en cette affaire de la rescision d'une concession de chemin de fer, cédée par le concessionnaire primitif à une compagnie anglaise. Il était réclamé par les intéressés une somme totale de 1,898,500 £; il leur fut accordé 15,314,000 francs, en plus des 28,000 £ versées à compte par le Portugal en 1890.

Protocole signé à Berne le 13 juin 1891, pour soumettre à l'arbitrage l'indemnité résultant de la rescision de la concession du chemin de fer de Lourenço Marques.

Le président de la Confédération suisse ayant fait connaître au Gouvernement des Etats-Unis de l'Amérique du Nord, de la Grande-Bretagne et du Portugal que le Conseil fédéral suisse avait pris en considération la demande que ces gouvernements lui ont faite, de bien vouloir nommer trois jurisconsultes, choisis parmi les plus distingués, pour composer un tribunal arbitral chargé

[1] *Journal officiel de la République française*, 1900, p. 6184.

de fixer le montant de l'indemnité due par le Portugal aux ayants droit des deux autres pays à raison de la rescision de la concession du chemin de fer de Lourenço Marques et de la prise de possession de ce chemin de fer par le gouvernement portugais, les soussignés Envoyés extraordinaires et Ministres plénipotentiaires des Etats-Unis de l'Amérique du Nord, de la Grande-Bretagne et du Portugal, accrédités auprès de la Confédération suisse, dûment autorisés par leurs gouvernements respectifs, sont convenus de ce qui suit :

ARTICLE I. Le mandat que les trois gouvernements sont convenus de confier au Tribunal arbitral est de fixer, comme il jugera le plus juste, le montant de la compensation due par le gouvernement portugais aux ayants droit des deux autres pays, par suite de la rescision de la concession du chemin de fer de Lourenço Marques et de la prise de possession de ce chemin de fer par le gouvernement portugais, et de trancher ainsi le différend existant entre les trois gouvernements à cet égard.

ARTICLE II. Le Tribunal arbitral fixera aux gouvernements des Etats-Unis de l'Amérique du Nord et de la Grande-Bretagne, le délai dans lequel ceux-ci devront lui remettre les mémoires, conclusions et documents à l'appui des réclamations de leurs ressortissants.

Ces pièces seront transmises en deux doubles au gouvernement portugais avec invitation de produire, également en deux doubles, sa réponse, ses conclusions et les documents à l'appui, dans le délai qui lui sera fixé.

Le Tribunal arbitral fixera lui-même, après avoir entendu les parties ou leurs représentants, et d'accord avec elles, le mode de procédure, notamment les délais ci-dessus mentionnés et ceux à fixer pour la remise de la réplique et de la duplique, les règles à suivre pour l'audition des parties ou de leurs représentants, la production des documents, la délibération dans son sein, le prononcé du jugement et la rédaction du protocole.

Chacun des trois gouvernements s'engage à faire tout ce qui dépendra de lui pour que les pièces et renseignements demandés par le Tribunal arbitral lui soient fournis en due forme et dans le délai fixé par lui.

ARTICLE III. Le Tribunal arbitral aura pleine compétence pour connaître des conclusions présentées par chacune des parties dans toute leur étendue et dans toutes leurs dépendances ou incidents, il rendra son jugement sur le fond de la cause et prononcera comme il jugera le plus juste sur le montant de l'indemnité due par le Portugal aux ayants droit des deux autres pays

par suite de la rescision de la concession du chemin de fer de Lourenço Marques et de la prise de possession de ce chemin de fer par le même gouvernement.

ARTICLE IV. Le jugement sera définitif et sans appel.

Le président du Tribunal arbitral délivrera aux représentants de chacun des trois gouvernements une expédition authentique de la sentence.

Les trois gouvernements s'engagent d'avance, pour leur propre part et pour la part de leurs ressortissants respectifs, à accepter et exécuter la sentence, comme règlement final de tous leurs différends sur cette question.

Il est entendu que, bien qu'il appartienne au Tribunal arbitral de désigner les personnes privées ou les personnes morales ayant droit à l'indemnité, le montant de cette indemnité sera remis par le gouvernement portugais aux deux autres gouvernements pour qu'ils en fassent la distribution aux ayants droit.

La quittance délivrée par ces deux gouvernements constituera pour le gouvernement portugais une décharge complète et valable.

Le montant sera remis par le gouvernement portugais aux deux autres gouvernements dans le délai de six mois à compter du prononcé du jugement.

ARTICLE V. Le président du Tribunal arbitral sera prié de présenter le compte de tous les frais occasionnés par l'arbitrage, et les trois gouvernements s'engagent à les faire payer à l'époque que le président désignera.

En foi de quoi, les soussignés ont dressé ce protocole et y ont apposé leurs signatures et leurs sceaux.

Fait à Berne, en triple expédition, le 13 juin 1891[1].

Sentence finale du Tribunal arbitral du Delagoa, prononcée à Berne, le 29 mars 1900.

I. OBJET DU JUGEMENT ARBITRAL.

Le différend sur lequel les arbitres sont appelés à statuer et qui fait l'objet de leur jugement est déterminé par le compromis arbitral. L'article premier de celui-ci leur donne pour mandat « le montant de la compensation due par le gouvernement portugais aux ayants droit des deux autres pays par suite de la rescision de la concession du chemin de fer de Lourenço Marques et de la prise de possession de ce chemin de fer par le gouvernement portugais ».

---

[1] *Sentence finale du Tribunal arbitral du Delagoa*, p. 88.

Il résulte des termes ci-dessus que la rescision de la concession et la prise de possession du chemin de fer par le gouvernement portugais sont considérées comme des faits acquis et irrévocables. Il n'est plus question de rapporter ces mesures ; il s'agit uniquement de fixer la somme à attribuer aux demandeurs en compensation de la perte de leur concession et de leur propriété.

II. LE DROIT APPLICABLE.

Aux termes de l'article premier du compromis, le Tribunal arbitral a pour mandat de fixer le montant de la compensation en question « comme il jugera le plus juste ».

Cette clause n'exclut pas, elle implique, au contraire, pour lui l'obligation de déterminer au préalable quelle est la législation qui devra le guider dans la recherche de la solution «juste».

Or, l'entreprise qui, en vertu du contrat du 26 mai 1884, est devenue concessionnaire au lieu et place de Mac Murdo, était et devait être, conformément à l'article 51 de l'acte de concession, « une société anonyme siégeant à Lisbonne » et « portugaise pour tous les effets ». En réalité, c'est cette société portugaise qui est demeurée concessionnaire jusqu'à la rescision. En effet, le gouvernement portugais s'est opposé au transfert de la concession à la compagnie anglaise, qui devint simplement propriétaire de la presque totalité des actions de la compagnie portugaise. Cette dernière a subsisté de droit et c'est elle seule qui est demeurée en rapport avec le gouvernement.

L'entreprise n'ayant ainsi jamais cessé d'être portugaise, il en suit qu'elle est régie par le droit portugais ainsi que le statue d'ailleurs expressément l'article 50 de la concession. C'est donc aussi le droit portugais qui fait loi dans le présent litige. Mais cette question, qu'il importait de trancher d'entrée de cause, n'a pour ainsi dire qu'une portée théorique. En effet, la loi portugaise ne contient sur les points décisifs et pertinents aucune disposition particulière qui s'écarterait des principes généraux du droit commun des nations modernes.

III. NATURE JURIDIQUE DE LA «COMPENSATION» A ALLOUER.

Pour fixer d'une manière «juste» le chiffre de la «compensation» à allouer, il importe avant tout d'en établir la nature juridique, autrement dit de déterminer les principes du droit qui doivent présider à son allocation.

Ici se posent diverses questions correspondant à tout autant d'alternatives juridiques distinctes. La «compensation» doit-elle représenter la réparation d'un dommage causé sans droit ? ou bien doit-elle former l'équivalent de l'intérêt que les demandeurs avaient à l'exécution d'un engagement contractuel ? ou bien encore les demandeurs ont-ils simplement droit au remboursement d'une valeur dont le Portugal, s'il ne la restituait pas, se trouverait illégitimement enrichi ?

Le mode de calculer la compensation, et, partant, le chiffre de celle-ci devront évidemment varier suivant que l'on s'arrêtera à l'une ou l'autre de ces solutions. Dans la première alternative, la compensation aura le caractère de dommages et intérêts, c'est-à-dire qu'elle devra former l'équivalent du préjudice éprouvé et du bénéfice manqué.

D'après la seconde alternative, la compensation représenterait l'intérêt qu'avaient les demandeurs à l'accomplissement de l'engagement qu'avait contracté le Portugal (art. 42 de la concession) de remettre aux ayants droits le produit de la mise aux enchères de la ligne.

Enfin d'après le troisième système, la compensation devrait équivaloir au prix d'estimation du bien approprié, calculé soit au moyen d'une évaluation, soit sur la base des dépenses utiles et effectives faites par l'ancien propriétaire pour la création ou l'acquisition de ce bien, avec ou sans déductions.

Le Portugal a soutenu, à cet égard, que le choix entre ces diverses solutions se trouve déjà préjugé par l'emploi du terme de *«compensation»* qui, selon lui, « s'oppose à la théorie des dommages et intérêts ».

Tel n'est pas l'avis du tribunal arbitral. Rien dans le texte du compromis n'indique que les parties aient entendu restreindre en quoi que ce soit la liberté d'appréciation des arbitres quant à la nature juridique de la « compensation » à allouer aux demandeurs. Ce terme qui, dans le compromis, alterne indifféremment avec celui « d'indemnité », est dépourvu, dans l'intention de ceux qui l'ont employé, d'une acception technique précise ; c'est un terme vague et général, choisi comme à dessein pour s'adapter à toutes les constructions juridiques possibles. Si, dans l'esprit des parties, le terme de compensation n'avait dû signifier que l'enrichissement ou le prix de revient, on ne voit guère quelle eût été la mission d'arbitres que les parties s'accordaient à choisir « parmi les jurisconsultes », comme il est dit au préambule du compromis ; une estimation des travaux et du matériel par des experts impartiaux eût rendu, et mieux rendu, le même service.

Cela admis, la question primordiale et dont la solution décidera du choix entre les trois systèmes susénoncés, est celle-ci :

Le décret de rescision a-t-il été rendu et la prise de possession de la ligne a-t-elle été opérée, oui ou non, en conformité de l'acte de concession ?

Cet acte, en effet, prévoit des cas où l'Etat aura le droit de résilier la concession de sa seule autorité. Ce sont — à part la faculté de rachat après 35 ans (art. 28) qui n'est pas en cause ici — les deux cas énoncés aux articles 42 et 45 :

Défaut de continuer les travaux sur une échelle proportionnelle à l'étendue de la ligne, ou défaut de terminer le chemin de fer « dans les termes et les délais fixés à l'art. 40 » (art. 42) ;

Interruption totale ou partielle de l'exploitation pendant plus de trois mois, après une sommation de la part du gouvernement (art. 45) ;

« Les cas de force majeure dûment justifiée » faisant exception dans l'un comme dans l'autre de ces cas.

La partie défenderesse s'est, au cours du présent procès, prévalu cumulativement de l'art. 42 et de l'art. 45. Mais le décret de rescision, du 25 juin 1889, n'a point fait état de l'art. 45 ; il a invoqué uniquement l'art. 42.

L'art. 45 et les conséquences qu'on eût pu en tirer ne doivent pas être pris en considération, puisqu'aussi bien le décret de rescision lui-même, à tort ou à raison, en a fait complètement abstraction et que le gouvernement avait d'ailleurs omis de remplir les formalités spéciales prévues par cet article.

La question se réduit donc à ces termes : le gouvernement était-il, lors de la rescision, oui ou non, fondé à affirmer que l'entreprise n'avait point continué les travaux sur une échelle proportionnelle à l'étendue de la ligne ou qu'elle n'avait pas terminé le chemin de fer « dans les termes et les délais fixés à l'art. 40 » ?

L'examen de cette question appelle nécessairement celui d'une autre qui forme à proprement parler le nœud du litige : la question de savoir ce qu'était et quand expirait le délai que l'art. 40 a circonscrit en ces termes : « Un délai de trois ans à partir du jour où les plans soumis par elle (l'entreprise) au gouvernement auront été approuvés. »

C'est sur ce point essentiel que les avis des parties diffèrent du tout au tout.

En fait, il y a eu deux approbations de plans : celle du 30 octobre 1884, pour les 82 premiers kilomètres, « donnée sans préjudice de la présentation du projet concernant la dernière partie de la voie ferrée jusqu'à la frontière », et celle du 23 février 1889, pour les huit derniers kilomètres.

La partie défenderesse fait courir les trois ans « bénévolement » prolongés par elle de la première de ces dates ; les demandeurs les comp-

tent à dater de la seconde. La défenderesse, pour justifier sa manière de voir, soutient que le concessionnaire avait l'obligation de se renseigner lui-même sur la longueur réelle de la ligne et que, dès lors, si les plans présentés par lui la première fois, dans les cent jours visés à l'art. 38 de la concession, ont été incomplets, ce défaut qui fit l'objet d'une réserve insérée dans l'arrêté d'approbation lui demeurait imputable et engageait sa responsabilité : c'était, dit le Portugal, à lui, et à lui seul, d'y remédier en présentant le complément de plans et en exécutant le complément de travaux avant l'expiration du délai qui courait, une fois pour toutes, du 30 octobre 1884.

Cette argumentation ne paraît compatible ni avec le texte ni avec l'esprit de l'art. 38 précité. Le texte de cet article vise « un tracé déjà étudié par ordre du gouvernement portugais et dont les projets devront être fournis » au concessionnaire, qui n'aurait plus qu'à étudier, dans les cent jours, les modifications désirables. Or, un prolongement de huit à neuf kilomètres est plus qu'une simple modification ; et l'interprétation logique corrobore ici le sens littéral ; car il serait par trop malaisé, sinon impossible, de livrer dans les cent jours les plans d'un tracé de 90 kilomètres, étudié directement sur le terrain.

Il faut donc admettre que, suivant l'article 38, le gouvernement portugais était tenu de fournir au concessionnaire les plans de la ligne intégrale, que ce dernier n'avait plus qu'à contrôler. En tout cas, le concessionnaire était fondé à admettre de bonne foi que les plans, tels qu'ils lui avaient été fournis, représentaient le tracé dans toute sa longueur, et le gouvernement portugais lui-même paraît avoir été de cet avis, du moins à l'époque de la conclusion du contrat de concession.

Le gouvernement défendeur objecte, il est vrai, que le concessionnaire, renseigné par l'ingénieur Machado, avait su d'emblée ce qui en était réellement. Mais ce fait, dont la preuve incomberait à la partie portugaise, n'est pas suffisamment établi. Et le fût-il, qu'il ne serait pas pertinent, puisqu'il ne suffisait pas que le gouvernement renseignât le concessionnaire : il fallait qu'il lui fournît les plans, et aucun délai ne courait tant que les plans n'étaient pas fournis.

Or, il est avéré que les plans de la dernière section n'ont été livrés que le 23 juillet 1887, et le major Machado, dans la même lettre du 2 août où il annonçait au gouvernement les avoir communiqués à l'entreprise, constatait d'autre part, qu'il était impossible de fixer le point final de la ligne sans un accord préalable avec le Transvaal. Que devait faire le gouvernement dans ces conditions ? Le Tribunal estime qu'il avait le choix entre deux modes de procéder : ou bien renoncer, comme il le fit plus tard, à l'entente préalable avec le Transvaal et fixer, de son propre chef, le point terminus, sauf à indemniser l'entreprise si, dans la suite, le déplacement de ce point venait à lui causer quelque préjudice, et inviter celle-ci à lui soumettre, pour approbation, les plans de la dernière section ; ou bien laisser les choses en suspens jusqu'à ce que l'entente avec le Transvaal intervint. C'est à ce dernier parti que s'arrêta d'abord le gouvernement, parce qu'il attendait d'un moment à l'autre la réussite des négociations entamées. Et le ministre de la marine et des colonies déclarait expressément que « la délimitation de la frontière une fois arrêtée, le gouvernement ne s'opposera pas à ce qu'il soit établi un délai raisonnable pour l'achèvement de la ligne ». Le ministre ajoutait, il est vrai, qu'il serait « *possible et convenable* » de soumettre dès à présent au gouvernement le projet des sept kilomètres à l'abri de tout changement, mais il n'insistait pas et il émit même l'avis, sinon à l'adresse de l'entreprise, du moins vis-à-vis de son collègue des affaires étrangères, « qu'il ne serait pas raisonnable d'obliger la Compagnie à construire 7 ou 8 kilomètres pour renvoyer jusqu'au moment où la frontière serait fixée la construction de la petite partie restante ».

L'inaction de l'entreprise pendant cette période se trouvait donc couverte par l'acquiescement pour le moins tacite du gouvernement.

Celui-ci, cependant, finit par se lasser d'attendre que l'accord avec le Transvaal aboutît et il prit sur lui d'arrêter de son seul chef le point terminus devant faire règle pour l'entreprise : acte parfaitement légitime et que les parties demanderesses ont critiqué à tort ; car elles n'avaient pas à s'immiscer dans les relations internationales du Portugal, et si cet Etat, sous sa responsabilité, désignait une ligne de frontière, cette désignation devait être tenue pour valable, sauf à la compagnie à lui demander dans la suite la réparation du préjudice qu'aurait pu causer, le cas échéant, le déplacement ultérieur de cette ligne.

Mais le gouvernement portugais ne s'en tint pas là. Il fixa en même temps, par son arrêté du 24 octobre 1888, unilatéralement, un délai global péremptoire de huit mois pour la présentation des plans de la dernière section, pour leur approbation et pour leur exécution, et il maintint ce délai en dépit des remontrances de la compagnie concessionnaire.

Cette mesure prise unilatéralement se renfermait-elle dans les limites des droits attribués au gouvernement défendeur par l'acte de concession, ou les excédait-elle ? Telle est la question de droit, primordiale et décisive, que ce tribunal est appelé à trancher.

Or, il est indéniable que la concession ne contient aucune clause quelconque autorisant le gouvernement à fixer de son chef un délai d'achèvement et à décréter que le délai ainsi fixé « *remplacera* pour tous les effets la période indiquée à l'art. 40 du contrat ».

Cette période, le gouvernement pouvait, à la vérité, *la prolonger* de son plein gré ; aussi s'est-il efforcé, depuis, d'interpréter son acte comme une *prolongation* de délai ; mais cette explication est inadmissible puisque, comme il vient d'être démontré, le délai pour la construction du dernier tronçon n'avait pas même commencé à courir tant que les plans n'en étaient pas approuvés.

Il s'agissait donc bien, en l'espèce, d'*impartir* et non de *prolonger* un délai.

Aussi bien, pour rester dans le cadre de la concession, qui formait sur ce point la loi des parties et attribuait notamment à la compagnie des garanties de nature civile, la fixation du délai d'achèvement ne pouvait-elle avoir lieu qu'en conformité de l'art. 40.

Est-ce à dire que, en vertu de cet article, l'entreprise eût dû absolument bénéficier en droit strict, ainsi que l'affirment les demandeurs, pour la construction de ces huit derniers kilomètres, du délai de *trois ans pleins* statué par l'art. 40 en vue d'un tracé dix fois plus long ?

Le Tribunal ne le pense pas. Il estime que pour ce cas non spécialement prévu d'un tronçon complémentaire à construire, l'art. 40 n'eût été applicable que *par analogie* ; c'est-à-dire que de même que les parties avaient convenu à l'origine d'un délai de trois ans pour construire environ 80 kilomètres de ligne, elles auraient dû s'entendre à nouveau au sujet du temps nécessaire pour construire la section finale ; ou à défaut d'entente provoquer sur ce point une décision des arbitres prévus par l'article 53 du contrat. En revanche, il était décidément inadmissible et contraire au texte de la concession, ainsi qu'au caractère bilatéral de celle-ci, que le gouvernement portugais, cumulant les rôles de juge et de partie, fixât le délai lui seul, *en remplacement* de celui indiqué dans la concession. Il suit de là qu'en procédant ainsi qu'il l'a fait, le gouvernement a agi en dehors de la concession et notamment de l'art. 42 de celle-ci. Il n'était dès lors pas fondé à déclarer, comme il l'a fait dans le préambule de son décret du 25 juin 1889, que l'entreprise n'avait pas terminé la construction... « dans les termes et aux époques convenus » et à se prévaloir expressément dudit art. 42 pour prononcer la résiliation du contrat de concession.

51

Et si le gouvernement du Portugal soutient aujourd'hui que même dans le premier tronçon, soi-disant achevé, de 82 kilomètres, il manquait beaucoup d'ouvrages essentiels, ce fait ne saurait non plus être invoqué par lui comme un motif de rescision, attendu que lors de l'ouverture de la première section de la ligne, le 14 septembre 1887, il n'a été dressé aucun protocole officiel indiquant les ouvrages manquants ou défectueux; aussi est-il absolument impossible de distinguer les défectuosités originaires de celles occasionnées plus tard par les crues du mois de janvier de 1889. Les imperfections originaires se confondent dès lors avec les causes d'interruption ultérieures dont il n'y a pas à tenir compte, puisque, comme il a déjà été exposé plus haut, l'article 45 de la concession traitant des cas d'interruption n'a pas été allégué dans le décret de rescision.

Il résulte de toutes ces considérations que la question primordiale posée plus haut doit être résolue en ce sens que le décret de rescision et la prise de possession du chemin de fer n'ont pas été opérés en conformité du contrat de concession.

Il n'est dès lors pas nécessaire de spécifier la nature juridique de ces actes. Du moment qu'ils ne peuvent se justifier par des clauses mêmes de la concession et qu'on ne peut pas dire que le concessionnaire les ait encourus en vertu même de celle-ci, il ne reste plus qu'un seul principe de droit qui puisse être appliqué à la fixation de la « compensation » à allouer par ce Tribunal; ce principe ne peut être que celui des dommages et intérêts, du *id quod interest*, comprenant d'après les règles de droit universellement admises, le *damnum emergens* et le *lucrum cessans:* le préjudice éprouvé et le gain manqué.

Que l'on veuille, en effet, taxer l'acte gouvernemental de mesure arbitraire et spoliatrice ou d'acte souverain dicté par la raison d'Etat à laquelle toute concession de chemin de fer demeurerait subordonnée, voire même qu'on considère le cas actuel comme un cas d'expropriation légale, toujours est-il que cet acte a eu pour effet de déposséder des particuliers de leurs droits et privilèges d'ordre privé à eux conférés par la concession, et que, à défaut de dispositions légales contraires — dont l'existence n'a pas été alléguée dans l'espèce — l'Etat, auteur d'une telle dépossession, est tenu à la réparation intégrale du préjudice par lui causé.

Il convient cependant de relever dès maintenant que l'incorrection constatée à la charge du Portugal et qui engage inéluctablement sa responsabilité, réside plutôt dans la forme que dans le fond. Le Tribunal s'est convaincu par l'étude du dossier que le délai que des arbitres eussent réputé équitable et nécessaire pour l'achèvement

de la ligne, n'eût pas ou n'eût guère excédé les huit mois qui ont été accordés, et que, nonobstant les pluies qui survinrent, la ligne eût pu être achevée dans ce laps de temps, si les travaux de la première section avaient été solidement exécutés et si, financièrement, la compagnie avait été assise sur des bases convenables.

Du reste, à la forme même, l'incorrection de l'acte gouvernemental apparaît comme atténuée par le fait que la compagnie, questionnée au préalable sur le temps qu'elle jugeait strictement indispensable pour l'achèvement de la ligne, resta muette à ce sujet et que, informée dans la suite du délai à elle imparti, elle répondit même au début que, pourvu que le terminus indiqué coïncidât avec la frontière, elle n'avait rien à objecter.

Toutes ces circonstances qui peuvent être alléguées à la charge de la compagnie concessionnaire et à la décharge du gouvernement portugais atténuent la responsabilité de ce dernier et justifient, comme il va être exposé plus loin, une réduction de la réparation à allouer. Elles excluent notamment d'emblée l'allocation de dommages et intérêts *exemplaires* et de *nature pénale*, tels que, à la rigueur, en eût pu réclamer une personne victime d'un traitement arbitraire absolument immérité.

IV. Les principes régissant la fixation des dommages et intérêts.

D'après le système des demandeurs, le préjudice éprouvé par les ayants droit serait représenté par la valeur des titres de la compagnie anglaise : valeur nominale des obligations et valeur marchande attribuée aux actions, à l'époque qui précéda l'arrêté assignant le délai de huit mois. Cette dernière valeur est indiquée à £ 20 pour les actions en général et à £ 25 environ pour le lot d'actions réuni entre les mains de Mac Murdo.

Ce mode de calculer l'indemnité paraît inadmissible pour plusieurs raisons.

Tout d'abord il se heurte au motif de forme suivant, qui a été invoqué à bon droit par le Portugal. Les ayants droit demandeurs, quels qu'ils soient d'ailleurs, ne font pas valoir un droit qui soit né en leur personne, mais seulement un droit dérivé. Ils ne sont parties au procès qu'en leur qualité de représentants de la compagnie portugaise ; or, celle-ci n'a rien de commun avec les titres de la compagnie anglaise.

Mais voulût-on même, avec les demandeurs, identifier les deux compagnies, que l'on ne saurait qualifier de préjudice réel ni la perte d'un capital-actions purement nominal, sur lequel, notoirement, pas un liard n'a été versé, ni celle d'un capital-obligations de £ 750,000 dont une partie seulement a profité effectivement à l'entreprise, puisque, même d'après les informations incontrôlées des demandeurs, il n'y aurait eu que £ 599,816 employées à des buts intéressant de près ou de loin le chemin de fer (dont £ 117,500 versées d'emblée à Mac Murdo), tandis que les £ 150,000 qui manquent, si tant est qu'elles aient jamais été versées, ont passé on ne sait où.

D'autre part, le fait qu'un millier environ d'actions sur 50,000 aurait été négocié au cours de £ 20 et qu'on aurait même offert davantage pour un lot d'actions détenues par une seule personne, prouve tout au plus que certaines personnes nourrissaient à un moment donné des espérances robustes quant à la future prospérité de la ligne ou quant au profit indirect à tirer de sa possession ; mais il n'y a aucune conclusion à en déduire pour l'appréciation du plus ou moins de fondement de ces prévisions. Il va de soi que la valeur spéculative des titres d'une entreprise encore en voie de formation, aussi bien que leur valeur nominale, versée ou non, peut s'écarter considérablement, en plus ou en moins, de leur valeur intrinsèque et effective telle qu'elle résultera du rendement moyen qui, lui seul, fait la valeur réelle de l'entreprise.

Le rendement moyen, à la vérité, était encore inconnu à l'époque de l'ouverture du procès ; quels que fussent les chiffres qu'on eût pu avancer à cet égard, ils n'eussent pu prétendre à une exactitude même approximative, puisqu'ils ne pouvaient refléter que la situation provisoire et passagère d'une ligne encore sans issue et sans trafic. Aussi bien comprend-on aussi que les demandeurs, appelés à préciser le chiffre de leurs conclusions, aient fait abstraction de données qui étaient alors aussi peu sûres et, qu'ils aient eu recours, faute de mieux, à l'expédient très critiquable consistant à réclamer le montant du capital-actions et du capital-obligations.

Mais depuis, grâce aux longueurs qui ont été inséparables de l'instruction du procès et qui en cela ont été tout à l'avantage des parties demanderesses, il a pu être procédé en 1897 et 1898 à une expertise dont les résultats, pour imparfaits et incertains qu'ils soient, fournissent cependant un critère bien meilleur et bien plus sûr, si ce n'est la base relativement la plus exacte pour la détermination de la valeur commerciale du chemin de fer, attendu qu'au lieu d'en être réduits à des évaluations purement hypothétiques, les experts ont pu tenir compte du résultat financier effectif des exercices postérieurs à 1895, année du raccordement avec le Transvaal. C'est donc à la lumière du rapport des experts techniques qu'il doit être procédé à l'évaluation de la ligne et à la fixation de l'indemnité due à ceux qui en ont été dépossédés, indemnité qui, en principe, devra être calculée d'après le rendement capitalisé.

Or d'après une loi économique qui repose sur les données de l'expérience et qui, ainsi que les experts l'ont vérifié, est aussi applicable au cas particulier, le rendement du chemin de fer litigieux, comme celui des chemins de fer en général, paraît sujet à une augmentation constante. L'expérience prouve en effet qu'une telle augmentation se produit régulièrement, encore qu'il ne soit guère possible d'apprécier sûrement, à l'avance, quel sera l'angle d'inclinaison de la courbe ascendante qui la représente. En d'autres termes, et bien que le fait de l'augmentation du trafic et du rendement corresponde à la règle, la proportion dans laquelle elle se produit est éminemment variable, ce qui se traduit alors graphiquement par des ondulations et des inflexions imprévues de la courbe. Le tribunal ne peut dès lors se dispenser de faire entrer en ligne de compte, dans l'évaluation du chemin de fer objet du litige, la perspective d'une augmentation graduelle de son rendement. En l'espèce, cela s'impose tout particulièrement, puisqu'il s'agit d'une ligne jouissant d'un monopole et aboutissant dans un pays neuf, susceptible d'un grand développement. Il convient toutefois de ne pas perdre de vue qu'un pareil calcul, fait d'avance sur la base de données purement théoriques, ne saurait prétendre à une certitude rigoureuse, mais seulement à une vraisemblance relative. Aussi bien le tribunal doit-il se réserver de tenir tel compte que de juste, dans ce calcul de probabilités, de toutes les autres chances favorables ou défavorables qui pourront influer à l'avenir sur la valeur commerciale de la ligne.

Ces réserves faites, la durée théorique de la période qui doit être prise en considération à cet égard peut, tout d'abord, se déduire de la concession même : l'Etat du Portugal ayant, aux termes de l'article 28, le droit de racheter la ligne au bout de 35 ans, ce n'est que pendant cette période de 35 ans que la compagnie concessionnaire avait la perspective certaine et justifiée en droit d'exploiter la ligne dont la concession lui avait été accordée et de bénéficier de la plus-value due à une augmentation graduelle de son trafic. En d'autres termes, la prise de possession de la ligne par le gouvernement portugais ensuite du décret du 29 juin 1889 apparaît comme un rachat anticipé qui prive les ayants droit des bénéfices qu'ils auraient recueillis pendant cette période de 35 ans. L'indemnité intégrale consistera donc dans la bonification :

1° des bénéfices réels ou, du moins, vraisemblables de ces 35 exercices (sous déduction des pertes éprouvées dans les premiers exercices qui, on le sait, soldèrent par un déficit);

2° du prix que le Portugal devrait payer dans 35 ans pour racheter la ligne. A teneur de l'article 28 de la concession, ce prix serait égal au rendement moyen des sept dernières années multiplié par 20.

Pour fixer, sur cette double base, le chiffre de l'indemnité globale due à une date déterminée, celle de la rescision par exemple, il suffit d'additionner les diverses sommes échelonnées sur les 35 ans après les avoir toutes ramenées à une date unique par la déduction de l'escompte correspondant aux années intermédiaires.

Ce mode de calculer l'indemnité en prenant en considération toute la période de 35 ans ne s'impose à la vérité que si l'on admet que la marche ascendante du rendement se maintiendra et se poursuivra sans interruption jusqu'à l'année du rachat concessionnel. Les experts se sont toutefois refusés à tirer de leurs hypothèses des conséquences aussi osées: on a vu qu'ils s'arrêtent à la limite de la capacité de transport réalisable avec la simple voie actuelle, limite qu'ils supposent atteinte déjà en 1907.

Ce procédé a suscité les critiques des deux parties: le Portugal taxe d'exagéré le coefficient d'augmentation annuelle que les experts ont fixé à 10 %. Cette proportion, dit-il, serait déjà démentie par les faits et ne tiendrait d'ailleurs pas compte des aléas de toute sorte auxquels est exposé le trafic d'une ligne dans un pays neuf, sujet à des bouleversements imprévus. Les parties demanderesses, au contraire, affirment que le Transvaal dédoublera certainement sa voie, une fois la limite de capacité de la ligne simple atteinte, et en tirent cette conséquence que la capacité de transport doit être considérée comme illimitée et la progression de 10 % acceptée comme vraisemblable jusqu'à l'expiration du terme de 35 ans.

Le Tribunal a le sentiment que les arguments pour et contre que font valoir ces critiques se contrebalancent; s'il est, d'une part, assez plausible que les propriétaires de la ligne du Transvaal se prêteront, le moment venu, à un dédoublement de la voie, le coefficient de 10 % semble, d'autre part, n'avoir été admis que sous l'impression immédiate des résultats de l'année 1896, année de prospérité exceptionnelle, et être plutôt exagéré, en ce sens du moins qu'il ne sera pas toujours atteint et qu'il ne se maintiendra en tous cas pas indéfiniment.

La seule chose qui paraisse hors de doute, en revanche, c'est que, tôt ou tard, la capacité actuelle de transport et le maximum de rendement qu'elle comporte seront atteints, et cela avant l'arrivée du terme du rachat concessionnel. Et si, avec les experts, on suppose que ce résultat sera acquis déjà en 1907, l'admission de cette hypothèse, peut-être trop favorable aux demandeurs, trouve sa compensation dans le fait, qu'en revanche l'hypothèse d'un dédoublement de la voie a été jugée trop problématique par les experts pour être prise en considération par eux.

C'est que, comme l'ont fait observer les experts (p. 6 de leur rapport complémentaire) leurs différentes hypothèses sont liées entre elles, qu'elles concordent ensemble et ne peuvent être modifiées isolément.

Le Tribunal se rallie en conséquence au système des experts, d'après lequel le maximum de rendement, qui devra servir de base au calcul du prix de rachat, sera déjà atteint en 1907, de telle sorte qu'à partir de cette date le rendement sera constant et que, par conséquent, la valeur de la ligne et son prix de rachat resteront, dès lors, stationnaires.

L'admission de cette hypothèse a pour effet que l'on peut prendre comme année de rachat n'importe quelle année postérieure à 1906 et faire abstraction des bénéfices des années suivantes, le bénéfice de chaque année subséquente étant compensé par l'escompte qu'il faudrait déduire en plus du capital de rachat pour tenir compte du fait que le paiement est effectué d'une manière anticipée. En d'autres termes, on peut, en faisant abstraction de la période postérieure à 1907, dont les résultats financiers ne modifieraient plus en rien le calcul, supposer le rachat opéré déjà au 31 décembre 1906 sur la base du rendement maximum admis par les experts, c'est-à-dire sur les résultats de 1907. La valeur intégrale du chemin de fer, établie de cette façon, se trouvera ainsi être équivalente au prix que le gouvernement portugais aurait à payer dans le cas d'un rachat concessionnel opéré à l'expiration de la 35ᵉ année sur la base du rendement capitalisé de l'année 1907 (égal au produit moyen capitalisé des sept dernières années précédant l'année de rachat, sous déduction des deux années les moins productives), plus les bénéfices, supputés ou réels, des années intermédiaires de 1891 à 1906, et moins les déficits de 1889 à 1891, le tout ramené, par déduction de l'escompte, du 31 décembre 1906 et des années intermédiaires au 25 juin 1889. La somme ainsi obtenue, représentant la valeur intégrale du chemin de fer, reviendrait, de droit, tout entière à la compagnie dépossédée, si le capital dépensé pour l'établissement de la ligne provenait d'elle seule. Or, tel n'est pas le cas. D'après le rapport des experts, le capital provenant de la Compagnie au moment de la rescision n'était que de fr. 5,690,000 ; c'est à cette somme que se réduisaient les dépenses utiles faites par la Compagnie anglaise au nom de la Compagnie portugaise. La ligne se trouvait dans un état si précaire que le gouvernement portugais dut affecter fr. 2,310,000 à des réfections et parachèvements de la première section. La construction de la seconde section lui coûta fr. 1,560,000, l'achat du matériel roulant fr. 1,200,000 et diverses améliorations et agrandissements en vue du trafic futur fr. 700,000. Total des dépenses du gouvernement portugais, au dire des experts, pour la mise en état de la ligne, fr. 5,770,000. De plus, le Portugal devra encore, suivant l'expertise, dépenser dix millions de francs pour donner à la ligne la capacité de transport de 400,000 tonnes qui a servi de base au calcul des experts.

La valeur de la ligne, calculée comme il vient d'être exposé, se trouve donc représenter le produit d'une mise de fonds de fr. 21,460,000 dont fr. 5,690,000 seulement fournis par la Compagnie concessionnaire, fr. 5,770,000 fournis par le Portugal dans les années qui suivirent la rescision et fr. 10,000,000 à fournir par lui de 1897 à 1907.

Il est évident que le Portugal, appelé à payer la ligne dont il a pris possession, a droit à ce qu'il lui soit tenu compte des apports qu'il a faits pour la mettre en état.

A première vue, la façon normale de lui en tenir compte consisterait, semble-t-il, à le traiter comme un bailleur de fonds, soit comme ayant revêtu la qualité de gérant de l'affaire d'autrui et à le rembourser, en capital et intérêts, par des prélèvements répartis sur les bénéfices des exercices soldant en boni, de façon à achever avec l'année 1907 l'amortissement du capital. Le Portugal serait, en d'autres termes, réputé avoir prêté ce capital à l'entreprise et en avoir successivement reçu le remboursement, sur les bénéfices de celle-ci, de 1892 à 1907.

Cette méthode peut parfaitement être acceptée en tant qu'il s'agit des dix millions que le Portugal est censé devoir avancer de 1897 à 1906 en vue du perfectionnement de la ligne. Les rendements probables de ces dix années sont, en effet, tels que l'entreprise, en quelques mains qu'elle se trouve, doive être considérée comme pouvant aisément obtenir ces capitaux aux conditions ordinaires du marché, soit qu'elle puisse les prélever sur ses bénéfices annuels, soit qu'elle doive les emprunter à n'importe qui. Le rôle du Portugal, pour cette période, est donc celui d'un prêteur ou gérant d'affaires quelconque qui n'a, du fait de son prêt, d'autre action que celle en remboursement de la somme versée, avec les intérêts usuels. Il n'en va pas de même, en revanche, des fr. 5,770,000 dépensés par le Portugal au début, c'est-à-dire dans les premières années de son intervention. La Compagnie, portugaise ou anglaise — car, au point de vue financier, c'était pratiquement tout un —, se trouvait, au moment où cette intervention se produisit, dans une situation extrêmement critique, même voisine de la faillite : son capital-actions était et avait toujours été nul, une dette consolidée et privilégiée de £ 750,000 (fr. 18,750,000) n'avait pour toute contrevaleur que des ouvrages incomplets et mal faits, estimés par les experts à moins de six millions de francs ; à cela s'ajoutaient encore des dettes chirographaires criardes et une caisse vide, à telles enseignes que les administrateurs affirment avoir dû avancer de leurs deniers l'argent nécessaire au rapatriement des employés. Enfin, comme garantie à offrir aux prêteurs en retour des millions nécessaires pour l'achèvement et la mise en état de la ligne, elle n'avait que le rendement, déjà hypothéqué d'ailleurs pour le moment, très problématique si ce n'est négatif, d'un chemin de fer sans trafic local et non relié à son *hinterland*. Vrai est-il qu'on pouvait admettre que le raccordement avec le Transvaal ne serait qu'une affaire de temps ; il n'en demeurait pas moins assez probable que cet Etat, mal disposé envers la Compagnie concessionnaire et son dictateur, continuerait à temporiser pour l'avoir à sa merci.

Si l'on tient compte des faits qui viennent d'être exposés, on ne peut guère admettre comme vraisemblable qu'une compagnie placée dans une pareille situation eût trouvé aux conditions ordinaires les capitaux dont elle avait absolument besoin. Les capitalistes disposés à la sauver de la faillite imminente, si tant est qu'elle en eût trouvé, lui eussent dicté leurs conditions ; ils auraient, selon toute probabilité, réclamé au minimum, comme récompense de leur appui et du risque assumé, une part de propriété et de bénéfices aussi grande que celle des propriétaires dont ils sauvaient la situation.

Il est donc évident que si, malgré la non-intervention du Portugal, la Compagnie concessionnaire avait réussi à se maintenir comme propriétaire de l'entreprise, elle n'eût obtenu ce résultat qu'en faisant à ses sauveteurs une très large part dans ses bénéfices, ce qui eût diminué d'autant la proportion pour laquelle elle y participait elle-même. Il suit de là, que, pour la Compagnie concessionnaire, le *lucrum cessans* résultant de la rescision est loin d'équivaloir aux bénéfices qui se sont produits lorsque, grâce à l'intervention du Portugal, la ligne a pu être mis en état et achevée des deniers de celui-ci.

Or, s'il est juste, d'un côté, de restituer à la Compagnie concessionnaire, à titre d'indemnité, tous les bénéfices dont elle a été réellement privée par la rescision, il serait en revanche contraire à l'équité la plus élémentaire de faire de cette mesure une source d'enrichissement pour elle et de lui attribuer de ce chef les sommes qui, sans la rescision, eussent profité, non pas à elle, mais à des tiers prêteurs quelconques.

La constitution défectueuse de la Compagnie concessionnaire, l'absence d'un fonds social, l'emploi des fonds empruntés à des largesses diverses, sa situation financière précaire sont tout autant de faits qui ne peuvent être imputés qu'à sa faute à elle seule et dont les conséquences doivent retomber sur elle et non sur le Portugal.

Un autre fait qui démontre qu'il serait contraire à la situation vraie des parties d'envisager le Portugal comme un simple *negotiorum gestor*, c'est que les parties demanderesses n'ont jamais demandé à rentrer en possession de la ligne.

Dès leurs premières démarches, en 1889, elles ont toujours entendu en laisser la propriété et l'exploitation, avec tout son aléa, au Portugal, et elles se sont bornées, quant à elles, à réclamer une indemnité en argent, presque heureuses, semble-t-il, d'être débarrassées du souci de devoir exploiter la ligne, avec tous les risques et les obligations que cette exploitation leur eût imposés. Les demandeurs ont donc eux-mêmes assigné au Portugal un rôle autre que celui d'un simple gérant d'affaires, et ils ne sauraient prétendre aujourd'hui qu'appelé à leur payer la valeur de la chose dont il a profité, il n'aurait que le droit d'en déduire ses dépenses utiles.

Cet ensemble de circonstances amène le Tribunal, jugeant comme il estime être « le plus juste », à traiter les 5,770,000 francs dépensés par le Portugal non comme une avance faite par un simple gérant d'affaires ou bailleur de fonds, mais à l'instar d'un apport d'associé, en appliquant par analogie les principes de la *communio incidens*. Le Tribunal attribue en conséquence à cet apport la part proportionnelle des bénéfices que tout autre capitaliste eût réclamée dans les circonstances données; ce faisant, il estime tenir un compte équitable d'une part de la faute concurrente imputable à la Compagnie en raison des vices graves de sa constitution, en second lieu du risque assumé par le Portugal et que les parties demanderesses ont toujours entendu laisser à sa charge, enfin aussi du service que le Portugal a rendu à l'entreprise en assurant ou, tout au moins, en avançant le raccordement avec le Transvaal.

L'application du système qui vient d'être exposé a, dans l'espèce, les conséquences suivantes :

1° Les fr. 10,000,000 dépensés ou à dépenser par le Portugal de 1897 à 1907 doivent être restitués sous forme de défalcations successives sur les bénéfices des exercices de ces dix années. Pour simplifier le calcul, on supposera que les fr. 10,000,000 ont été dépensés en bloc à la date moyenne du 31 décembre 1901, ce qui, ramené au 31 décembre 1896, sous déduction de l'escompte à 6 %, donnera une défalcation à opérer, sur les bénéfices de 1897 à 1906, de fr. 7,473,000.

2° Les fr. 5,770,000 dépensés par le Portugal de 1889 à 1896 ne doivent pas lui être restitués purement et simplement; cette somme doit, au contraire, être traitée, non comme une avance de fonds de sa part, mais comme un apport fait à la *communio incidens*. Le gouvernement défendeur participe dès lors, au prorata de cet apport, au capital représentant la valeur du chemin de fer, lequel capital sera, par conséquent, réparti entre lui et les ayants droit de la Compagnie dépossédée dans la proportion de fr. 5,770,000 au Portugal et de fr. 5,690,000 auxdits ayants droit.

V. CALCUL DE L'INDEMNITÉ DUE POUR LA PRISE DE POSSESSION DU CHEMIN DE FER.

En application des principes exposés au chapitre qui précède l'indemnité due pour le chemin, de fer doit se calculer comme suit:

1. Calcul du prix de rachat au 31 décembre 1906.

Aux termes de l'art. 28 de la concession, le prix de rachat est égal au produit net moyen des sept dernières années précédant le rachat (sous déduction des résultats des deux années les moins productives) multiplié par vingt. Ce produit moyen étant réputé égal au produit net de l'exercice de 1907, il y a lieu de déterminer d'abord ce dernier.

Les experts évaluent le rendement de l'an 1907 à fr. 3,216,000. Pour obtenir le produit net, il y a lieu de déduire de ce chiffre :

a. l'annuité pour amortissement,
b. le 5 % revenant au gouvernement portugais.

a. L'annuité pour amortissement.

Aux termes des art. 20, § 1er, et 25 de la concession, la Compagnie devait céder au bout de 99 ans, gratuitement, sa ligne (matériel roulant non compris) au gouvernement portugais. Cette stipulation imposait théoriquement à la Compagnie l'obligation de mettre de côté chaque année une certaine somme pour amortir son capital d'établissement avant l'expiration de la concession. Ce capital atteignait en 1907 le chiffre de fr. 21,460,000 dont à déduire la valeur du matériel roulant, non sujette à l'amortissement, de fr. 4,610,000. Le capital à amortir étant ainsi de fr. 16,850,000, l'annuité à placer à intérêts composés, à 6%, pour amortir cette somme en 86 ans, l'amortissement commençant à parir du 1er janvier 1900, sera de fr. 6,800 à prélever sur le rendement annuel.

b. Le 5% du gouvernement.

A teneur de l'art. 26 de la concession, l'entreprise devait verser au gouvernement portugais le 5% du dividende distribué à ses actionnaires. Cette redevance grevant le rendement de l'entreprise doit également en être déduite pour le calcul du produit net.

Le Tribunal se trouvant ainsi obligé de déterminer quel aurait dû être, sans la rescision, le dividende de l'année 1907, ne peut naturellement procéder, ici aussi, que par conjectures.

L'hypothèse ci-après, qui fait abstraction des conditions extraordinaires dans lesquelles les Compagnies portugaise et anglaise ont été financées, lui paraît répondre assez exactement à la constitution *normale* d'une compagnie de chemin de fer établie sur des bases solides.

On suppose que le capital d'établissement de fin 1907 (fr. 21,460,000) devait être représenté pour 3/5 par des obligations et pour 2/5 par des actions, ce qui donne un capital obligations de fr. 12,876,000 et un capital-actions de fr. 8,584,000. Le service de la dette, supposée contractée à 6%, exigerait donc en 1907 une dépense de fr. 772,600.

En déduisant du rendement de 1907, qui est de fr. 3,216,000, cette somme de fr. 772,600 requise par le service de la dette, et les fr. 6,800 de l'annuité d'amortissement, il reste à la disposition des actionnaires une somme de fr. 2,436,600 dont l'Etat prélève 5% soit fr. 122,000.

c. Résumé.

Il résulte des calculs exposés aux lettres *a* et *b* ci-dessus que:

Du rendement 1907 estimé à . fr. 3,216,000 viennent en déduction:

a. l'annuité d'amortissement de . . fr. 6,800
b. la redevance de 5% au gouvernement de . . . . » 122,000

Total des déductions » 128,800

Ce qui laisse un *produit net* de fr. 3,087,200

Cette somme, capitalisée à 5% c'est-à-dire multiplié par 20, donne comme *prix de rachat au 31 décembre 1906* la somme de *fr. 61,744,000.*

2. Calcul de la valeur du chemin de fer au 31 décembre 1896.

On obtient la valeur du chemin de fer au 31 décembre 1896 en ajoutant au prix de rachat de fin 1906 le produit net des dix années intermédiaires, tel que l'ont évalué les experts, le tout ramené par déduction de l'escompte au 31 décembre 1896. Puis de la somme ainsi obtenue, on déduit les fr. 10,000,000 de dépenses de construction présumées qui sont censées remboursées au Portugal, sur le produit net de cette période, par un paiement de fr. 10,000,000 à la date moyenne du 31 décembre 1901.

Cette déduction, ramenée à la date initiale du 31 décembre 1891 (escompte 6%) représente une somme de fr. 7,473,000.

Le taux de 6% pour le calcul de l'escompte ramenant les valeurs jusqu'en 1906 à une époque antérieure se justifie par le fait qu'il constitue une moyenne entre le taux de 7% consenti aux obligations de la Compagnie anglaise et celui de 5% admis pour le rachat concessionnel de la ligne.

L'opération qui vient d'être relatée donne les chiffres que voici:

Valeur de rachat au 31 décembre 1906 fr. 61,744,000.

Ce capital ramené au 31 décembre 1896 (escompte 6%) donne . . . 34,478,000

Produits nets annuels de 1897 à 1900 :

Année.	Rendement.	Annuité d'amortissement et de Redevance de 5%.	Différence Produit net.	Produit net ramené au 31 décembre 1896.
	fr.	fr.	fr.	fr.
1906	3,014,000	118,500	2,895,500	1,617,000
1905	2,823,000	110,800	2,712,200	1,605,000
1904	2,646,000	103,700	2,542,300	1,595,000
1903	2,478,000	97,100	2,380,900	1,583,000
1902	2,322,000	91,100	2,230,900	1,573,000
1901	2,176,000	85,600	2,090,400	1,562,000
1900	2,039,000	80,600	1,958,400	1,551,000
1899	1,901,000	69,000	1,832,000	1,538,000
1898	1,644,000	58,000	1,586,000	1,411,000
1897	1,402,000	47,700	1,354,300	1,278,000
			Total	15,313,000
				49,791,000

A déduire: Dépenses de construction présumées pendant cette période, soit fr. 10,000,000 à la date moyenne du 31 décembre 1901, soit au 31 décembre 1896 (escompte 6%) . . . 7,473,000

Valeur au 31 décembre 1896 . 42,318,000

3. Calcul de la valeur du chemin de fer au 25 juin 1889.

(Date de la rescision.)

Pour obtenir finalement la valeur du chemin de fer à la date de la rescision, le procédé est le même que pour le cacul précédent, ainsi qu'il appert du tableau ci-après.

Valeur de la ligne au 31 décembre 1896 fr. 42,318,000.

Ce capital ramené au 31 décembre 1890 (escompte 6 %) est de . 29,833,000

Produits nets annuels de 1891 à 1896 :

Année.	Rendement.	Redevance de 5 °/°.	Produit net.	Ramené au 31 décembre 1890.
	fr.	fr.	fr.	fr.
1896	1,404,000	49,600	1,354,000	955,000
1895	714,700	15,700	690,000	522,000
1894	521,300	6,700	514,600	408,000
1893	684,000	15,500	668,500	561,000
1892	23,600	—	23,600	21,000
1891	−539,000	—	−539,000	−539,000
			Total	1,928,000

Valeur au 31 décembre 1890 . 31,761,000

Ce capital ramené au 31 décembre 1889 équivalait à 29,965,000

A déduire : Pertes sur l'exploitation de 1890 694,000

Valeur au 31 décembre 1889 . 29,271,000

Ce capital ramené au 25 juin 1889 équivalait à 28,418,000

A déduire : Pertes sur l'exploitation de 1889 262,000

Valeur au 25 juin 1889 . . . 28,156,000

4. Répartition.

Comme il a été exposé plus haut, la somme de fr. 28,156,000, représentant la valeur de la ligne ramenée à la date de la rescision (25 juin 1889), doit être répartie entre la Compagnie concessionnaire et le Portugal au prorata de leurs apports de fonds respectifs, soit dans la proportion de fr. 5,690,000 à la Compagnie, et de fr. 5,770,000 au Portugal.

Cette répartition donne pour *la part revenant à la Compagnie concessionnaire, valeur au 25 juin 1889, la somme de fr. 13,980,000.*

VI. INDEMNITÉ POUR LES TERRAINS.

Le fait que, de l'avis du Tribunal, la rescision de la concession a eu lieu contrairement aux clauses de l'acte du 14 décembre 1883, implique pour le Portugal l'obligation de payer aussi une indemnité pour les terrains que l'entreprise concessionnaire avait choisis en vertu de l'article 21 de la concession ou qu'elle avait le droit de choisir à teneur dudit article.

Les experts ont estimé ces terrains (100,000 ha) en bloc à la somme de fr. 200,000, et ils ont maintenu cette appréciation très basse en dépit des critiques des parties demanderesses, en affirmant catégoriquement qu'en dehors du périmètre de 2 km. — qui est expressément exclu du choix — les terrains n'ont de valeur ni pour la construction, ni pour l'agriculture, ni pour l'exploitation minière.

Le Tribunal n'a pas de motif de mettre en doute la justesse d'une appréciation puisée sur les lieux par un expert objectif et impartial. Il croit cependant devoir tenir un certain compte du fait que les terrains en question étaient concédés pour un temps illimité et que la Compagnie concessionnaire a par conséquent été privée par la rescision de la possibilité de spéculer sur une plus-value à réaliser dans un avenir plus ou moins éloigné.

Guidé par cette considération toute d'équité, le Tribunal a fait sien le système d'évaluation que la partie américaine, dans son résumé final, a préconisé comme étant le plus juste : prendre d'abord la moyenne des séries de prix fournies par les experts des demandeurs, ce qui donne £ 1, 14, 0 ou fr. 42.50 l'hectare, soit en tout fr. 4,250,000 ; prendre ensuite la moyenne entre ce chiffre et celui de fr. 82,000, montant de l'estimation du major Machado. On arrive ainsi à une valeur de fr. 2,116,000 que le Tribunal, vu le caractère empirique du procédé, arrondit à la somme de *deux millions de francs*, valeur au 25 juin 1889.

Le Tribunal ne saurait allouer de ce chef une somme plus considérable, étant donné que les parties demanderesses elles-mêmes, dans leurs écritures, n'avaient traité la question des terrains que comme un point purement secondaire et qu'elles ne lui ont attribué une importance majeure que dans une phase du procès où l'allégation de nouveaux faits n'était plus loisible.

VII. DÉCOMPTE.

Suivant les exposés (V et VI) qui précèdent, l'indemnité, arrêtée à la date du 25 juin 1889, se chiffre comme suit :

Part à la valeur du chemin de fer . 13,980,000

Indemnité pour les terrains . . 2,000,000

Total 15,980,000

Report 15,980,000

Le Portugal a versé en juillet 1890 à valoir sur cette somme un acompte de £ 28,000, soit, au cours de fr. 25.20, de fr. 705,600. Ce paiement ramené, lui aussi, au 25 juin 1889, représente à la dite date un montant, à déduire, de 666,000

La somme redue par le Portugal en vertu du présent jugement est donc de 15,314,000

VIII. CONSIDÉRATIONS ACCESSOIRES.

1. L'exposé des motifs qui précède ne s'est, à dessein, point occupé du mémorandum au Transvaal, du 17 mai 1884, dont les demandeurs font un grief à la partie défenderesse.

Il n'est point établi, en effet, que cet acte, auquel la partie américaine elle-même n'attribue que l'importance d'un « fait secondaire », ait un rapport de cause à effet avec le préjudice occasionné par la rescision.

Si la Compagnie portugaise a échoué pendant plusieurs années dans ses tentatives d'emprunt, cet échec peut fort bien être attribué à son manque absolu de surface financière.

Mais à supposer même que le mémorandum ait été la cause maîtresse des retards qu'a subis la réunion des fonds nécessaires à l'entreprise, ce fait n'aurait de l'importance que s'il devait servir à disculper la Compagnie de n'avoir pas achevé la ligne dans le délai imparti par la concession. Le Tribunal ayant, déjà pour d'autres motifs, déclaré mal fondé ce grief fait à la Compagnie, le mémorandum en question est devenu un fait sans portée dans la cause.

2. Il en est de même du grief fait au Portugal d'avoir, une fois la rescision prononcée, omis de mettre le chemin de fer aux enchères.

Le Tribunal tient pour plausible l'explication donnée à ce sujet par l'Etat défendeur : le fait que les demandeurs eurent d'emblée recours à la voie diplomatique pour réclamer une indemnité en argent semblait, en effet, impliquer de leur part la renonciation à la voie de la mise aux enchères, tracée par l'article 42 de la concession.

Le Tribunal est d'ailleurs convaincu que la mise en adjudication, opérée en 1889, eût en tout cas produit une somme très sensiblement inférieure à celle allouée par le présent jugement.

3. La conclusion de la partie défenderesse en déduction d'un cautionnement de £ 15,000, effectué par le concessionnaire et restitué depuis à la Compagnie, ne saurait être accueillie, du moment qu'il n'a pas été jugé que la rescision était justifiée par une inexécution du contrat de la part de l'entreprise concessionnaire.

IX. INTÉRÊTS.

La somme de fr. 15,314,000 représentant la valeur du chemin de fer et des terrains à la date de la rescision étant allouée à titre de dommages et intérêts, il est juste qu'elle soit productive d'intérêts jusqu'au jour du paiement, cela d'autant plus que le Portugal a bénéficié dans l'intervalle de la contre-valeur en nature dont la productivité considérable n'a plus à être démontrée.

Le taux de ces intérêts moratoires doit être fixé à 5 % en conformité du code de commerce portugais du 28 juin 1888 (art. 102, § 2):

« Lorsque des intérêts ... sont dus en vertu d'une disposition de loi, ils seront de 5 % en matière commerciale.»

Il ne peut d'ailleurs s'agir que d'intérêts *simples*, la loi portugaise n'admettant pas en pareil cas l'allocation d'intérêts composés. Au surplus, c'est là le mode de calculer généralement adopté en matière d'intérêts moratoires.

X. ATTRIBUTION ET RÉPARTITION DE L'INDEMNITÉ.

Il a déjà été relevé que la seule personne qui, en droit strict, aurait qualité pour se porter demanderesse vis-à-vis du gouvernement portugais est la Compagnie concessionnaire du chemin de fer; car c'est elle seule qui était en relations contractuelles avec l'Etat défendeur et c'est elle qui a été dépossédée par la rescision.

Le Gouvernement défendeur ayant, cependant, déclaré lui-même ne fonder aucune exception sur le fait que la personne réellement légitimée à l'action n'est pas partie au procès, le Tribunal arbitral doit prendre acte de ce que les parties ont convenu, d'un commun accord, de lui substituer la Delagoa Bay Company. Au reste, celle-ci avait, de fait, assumé la tâche incombant à la Compagnie portugaise, demeurée concessionnaire en la forme, et était devenue propriétaire de la presque totalité de ses actions, propriété grevée, il est vrai, d'un droit de gage en faveur de ses créanciers obligataires. Aussi bien, le montant alloué par le présent jugement ne peut-il être attribué à la Compagnie anglaise qu'à la condition que celle-ci l'affecte au paiement de ces créanciers obligataires gagistes, et autres s'il y a lieu, selon leur rang. Ces créanciers n'étant pas représentés directement dans ce procès et n'ayant par conséquent pas eu l'occasion de formuler leurs moyens et conclusions, le Tribunal n'est pas en mesure d'opérer lui-même cette répartition, mais doit abandonner ce soin à qui de droit, en se bornant à ordonner, en principe, qu'il soit dressé un état de distribution.

C'est dans cet état de distribution que la partie américaine, comme tout autre créancier, devra faire valoir ses droits. Il est impossible de lui reconnaître un droit direct contre le Portugal, en concurrence avec la Compagnie anglaise et au même titre que celle-ci. L'héritière de feu Mac Murdo est intervenue dans ce procès à titre de propriétaire d'actions et d'obligations de la Compagnie anglaise, acquises en échange d'actions de la Compagnie portugaise, et, de plus, en qualité de titulaire du « droit de contrôle » qu'elle estime également être en mesure d'exercer dans la Compagnie anglaise. Or, aucun de ces titres ne saurait lui conférer une action directe contre le Portugal; elle ne possède, de ces différents chefs, que des prétentions à faire valoir contre la Compagnie anglaise. Ce sont là des questions de ménage intérieur qu'il est matériellement impossible de trancher dans un procès lié entre la Compagnie anglaise d'une part, comme ayant droit de la Compagnie concessionnaire, et le gouvernement du Portugal, d'autre part. On chercherait vainement un motif plausible qui permît juridiquement de faire une situation spéciale à Madame Mac Murdo, en sa qualité d'actionnaire la plus forte de la Compagnie anglaise et de porteuse d'obligations de celle-ci, et de la traiter, en cette qualité, sur un autre pied que n'importe quel autre actionnaire ou obligataire de la Compagnie anglaise.

Tout ce qu'il est au pouvoir du Tribunal de faire à cet égard pour tenir compte de la situation spéciale concédée à Madame Mac Murdo par le compromis arbitral, c'est d'ordonner que la somme qui lui reviendra suivant l'état de distribution à dresser sera versée directement au gouvernement des Etats-Unis.

Il est bien entendu que le Portugal n'est point tenu d'attendre que l'état de distribution soit arrêté, mais qu'il peut déjà auparavant, comme tout débiteur, se libérer en consignant la somme globale entre les mains d'un tiers dépositaire présentant des garanties indiscutables.

XI. FRAIS.

Quant à la répartition des frais, le Tribunal croit devoir tenir compte de ce que les parties demanderesses ont obtenu environ le tiers de ce qu'elles réclamaient et que le Portugal est condamné à payer environ le triple de ce qu'il offrait. Il n'y a donc, à proprement parler, aucune partie qui obtienne l'entier de ses conclusions. Aussi bien convient-il de compenser les

dépens des parties, c'est-à-dire de laisser à la charge de chacune d'elles les frais extrajudiciaires qu'elles ont été appelées à faire, et de leur faire supporter par parts égales, savoir chacune un tiers, les frais de l'arbitrage.

Par ces motifs, le Tribunal dit et prononce:

1º Le Gouvernement du Portugal, partie défenderesse, est condamné à payer aux Gouvernements des Etats-Unis de l'Amérique du Nord et de la Grande-Bretagne, parties demanderesses, ensemble, en plus des £ 28,000 versées à compte en 1890, la somme de quinze millions trois cent quatorze mille francs (15,314,000 fr.) en monnaie légale suisse, avec, en plus, les intérêts simples de cette somme, au taux de 5 % l'an, du 25 juin 1889 jusqu'au jour du paiement.

2º Cette somme, après déduction de ce qui sera nécessaire pour couvrir les frais de l'arbitrage incombant aux parties demanderesses, et de plus, le reliquat des £ 28,000 versées à compte en 1890 seront affectés au paiement des créanciers obligataires, et autres, s'il y a lieu, de la Delogoa Bay Company, selon leur rang.

Les parties demanderesses dresseront à cet effet un état de distribution.

Le Gouvernement du Portugal aura à verser entre les mains du Gouvernement des Etats-Unis la somme qui, suivant le dit état, reviendra à Madame Mac Murdo représentée par ce dernier gouvernement, en sa qualité de créancière obligataire en 1ᵉʳ et en 2ᵐᵉ rang.

Il versera le surplus au gouvernement de la Grande-Bretagne pour le compte de tous les autres ayants droit.

3º Le délai de six mois fixé par le dernier alinéa de l'article IV du compromis arbitral courra à partir de ce jour.

4º Quant aux frais:
Les dépens des parties sont compensés. Les frais de l'arbitrage, suivant état à fournir en conformité de l'art. V du compromis, seront supportés, par parts égales, par les trois parties en cause, soit pour un tiers par chacune d'elles.

5º Les conclusions des parties, pour autant qu'elles diffèrent du dispositif ci-dessus, sont écartées.

6º Une expédition authentique de la présente sentence sera délivrée par l'intermédiaire du Conseil fédéral suisse à chacune des trois parties en cause.

Ainsi délibéré en séance du Tribunal arbitral et expédié à Berne le 29 mars 1900.

Les motifs ont été approuvés à Berne le 30 mai 1900[1].

[1] Sentence finale du Tribunal arbitral de Delogoa, p. 153-200.

CVI. Italie, Portugal.

1 septembre 1891.

Réclamation d'un citoyen italien qui se plaignait des mesures prises à son égard par les autorités sanitaires de Saint-Vincent du Cap Vert. Il lui fut acordé une indemnité de 12,347 lires 68.

Convention entre l'Italie et le Portugal pour soumettre à un arbitrage la réclamation d'un sujet italien, signée à La Haye, le 1 Septembre 1891.

Les gouvernements de Sa Majesté le Roi de Portugal et de Sa Majesté le Roi d'Italie, étant tombés d'accord pour soumettre la réclamation du sujet italien Michelangelo Lavarello, pour dommages qu'il dit avoir subis aux mois d'août et d'octobre 1884, comme propriétaire de marchandises transportées à bord du bateau Adria, à l'arbitrage d'un jurisconsulte, nommé par le gouvernement de Sa Majesté la Reine des Pays-Bas, et le gouvernement néerlandais ayant procédé à la nomination de l'arbitre en la personne de S. E. Mr. J. Heemskerk, docteur en droit, ministre d'Etat, membre du conseil d'Etat, les soussignés, envoyés extraordinaires et ministres plénipotentiaires de Portugal et d'Italie, dûment autorisés à cet effet par leurs gouvernements respectifs, s'engagent par le présent compromis à soumettre à la décision du dit arbitre, dont les lumières et le caractère impartial inspire pleine confiance, les trois questions suivantes:

1° Les autorités sanitaires du Cap Vert ont elles causé au sujet italien Michelangelo Lavarello, les dommages et les préjudices pour lesquels il réclame?

2° Lui ayant causé ces dommages et ces préjudices, les autorités sanitaires du Cap Vert ont-elles procédé en conformité des lois et des règlements en vigueur à Cap Vert à l'époque où le vapeur Adria y a mouillé et y a été ancré, et sans manquer aux droits et aux obligations internationaux, établis par les traités existant entre l'Italie et le Portugal?

3° Ont-elles causé ces dommages et ces préjudices par leur procédé irrégulier, illégal ou injustifiable?

En cas de décision affirmative sur le premier et sur le troisième point, il appartiendra à l'arbitre de fixer le montant de l'indemnité qui serait due à Michelangelo Lavarello.

En outre, il est convenu entre les soussignés:

Que, par l'entremise de leurs légations respectives et dans un délai de douze mois à partir de la date du présent compromis, les deux gouverne-ments intéressés pourront présenter à S. E. Mr. Heemskerk les mémoires et les documents tendant à justifier leur cause. Ce délai écoulé, il ne sera admis aucune allégation ni aucun document, à moins qu'il ne soit demandé par l'arbitre, lequel après avoir examiné les preuves des faits allégués et les dispositions légales applicables, prononcera, sans appel, son arrêt motivé, dont il remettra une copie à chacune des deux légations;

Que la langue française sera adoptée dans la procédure, et tous les documents qu'on y joindra seront traduits en français,

Et en dernier lieu, que les honoraires de l'arbitre seront fixés par le gouvernement des Pays-Bas et seront payés par la partie dont le droit n'aura pas été reconnu.

En foi de quoi les plénipotentiaires sous-signés ont muni le présent compromis de leurs signatures et y ont apposé le cachet de leurs armes.

La Haye, le 1er septembre 1901 [1].

Sentence prononcée à La Haye par M. Heemskerk, le 12 mars 1893, dans la cause de M. Lavarello.

Sa Majesté le Roi d'Italie et Sa Majesté Très-Fidèle le Roi de Portugal étant convenus de soumettre à la décision arbitrale d'un jurisconsulte à nommer par le gouvernement des Pays-Bas, le différend existant entre les Hautes Parties, par suite des réclamations du sujet italien Michel-angelo Lavarello contre le gouvernement de Portugal, Sa Majesté la Reine Régente des Pays-Bas a daigné désigner le soussigné, Jean Heems-kerk, docteur en droit et en lettres, ministre d'Etat et membre du conseil d'Etat, comme arbitre.

Dès lors messieurs les envoyés extraordinaires et ministres plénipotentiaires des Hautes Parties à La Haye, agissant d'après les instructions de leurs gouvernements respectifs, ont réglé l'objet de la décision arbitrale et les formes de la procédure par un acte de compromis fait à La Haye le 1er septembre 1891, portant en substance que les Hautes Parties soumettent à la décision de l'arbitre les questions suivantes:

1° Les autorités sanitaires du Cap Vert ont-elles causé au sujet italien M. A. Lavarello les dommages et les préjudices pour lesquels il réclame?

2° Lui ayant causé ces dommages et ces préjudices, les autorités sanitaires du Cap Vert ont-elles procédé en conformité des lois

---

[1] *Negocios externos. Documentos apresentados ao Cortes*, 1891. Secção II, p. 63.

et des règlements en vigueur à Cap Vert à l'époque où le vapeur *Adria* y a mouillé et y a été ancré, et sans manquer aux droits et aux obligations internationaux établis par les traités existant entre l'Italie et le Portugal ?

3° Ont-elles causé ces dommages et ces préjudices par leur procédé irrégulier, illégal et injustifiable ?

Que l'arbitre, en cas de décision affirmative sur les première et troisième questions, fixera le montant de l'indemnité due à M. A. Lavarello;

Que les mémoires et les pièces justificatives des Hautes Parties seront remises à l'arbitre avant le 1er septembre 1892 et qu'après cette date il ne sera admis aucun document et aucune allégation, à moins d'être demandés par l'arbitre;

Que l'arbitre prononcera un arrêt motivé, sans appel, et en remettra une copie à chacune des deux légations; et que les honoraires de l'arbitre seront fixés par le gouvernement des Pays-Bas et payés par la partie dont le droit n'aura pas été reconnu.

Les mémoires et documents justificatifs ont été remis à l'arbitre en temps utile par les chefs des légations respectives à La Haye.

Conformément à l'acte de compromis, l'arbitre a demandé, par sa lettre du 15 novembre 1892, à M. le ministre plénipotentiaire d'Italie à La Haye la production d'un connaissement ou de connaissements de la cargaison de maïs dans 6000 sacs à bord du vapeur *Adria* que M. A. Lavarello a dit avoir voulu débarquer à Saint-Vincent en octobre 1884; de cette demande de documents il a été immédiatement fait part à M. le chargé d'affaires du Portugal à La Haye.

Par sa lettre du 10 janvier 1893, M. le premier secrétaire faisant fonctions de chef de légation d'Italie à La Haye a fait savoir à l'arbitre que les documents demandés n'existent pas et lui a remis trois nouveaux documents, savoir une déclaration de témoin faite sous serment devant un des préteurs à Gênes et deux lettres missives, à l'effet de suppléer à la preuve qui aurait résulté ou pu résulter du connaissement ou des connaissements faisant défaut. M. le chargé d'affaires du Portugal à La Haye, étant informé de l'existence de ces nouveaux documents, a déclaré verbalement et par sa lettre du 12 janvier 1893, ne pas juger utile d'en prendre connaissance, à moins de nouveaux ordres de son gouvernement.

Des mémoires et documents justificatifs des Hautes Parties, dûment examinés, il résulte ce qui suit:

En fait:

Feu M. A. Lavarello, négociant, ayant demeuré à Recco, province de Gênes, sujet italien,

maintenant représenté par ses ayant cause, et dont le gouvernement d'Italie a fait sienne la réclamation contre celui de Portugal, a demandé réparation de dommages soufferts par lui.

(*a*) Parce que, étant parti le 19 août 1884 de Gênes, à bord du pyroscaphe postal italien *Adria*, lequel faisait le voyage à l'Amérique du sud avec escale aux îles de Cap Vert, ayant patente nette délivrée par le consul de Portugal à Gênes, et sans aucun cas de maladie à bord, il est arrivé le 28 du même mois à Saint-Vincent de Cap Vert et que, dans ce port, les autorités sanitaires et civiles ont refusé à lui Lavarello et à d'autres voyageurs destinés au même port, ainsi qu'au navire entier, la libre pratique; que non seulement ces autorités ont imposé à l'*Adria* et aux voyageurs et marchandises que ce navire portait, la quarantaine de rigueur, mais qu'il fut refusé à lui Lavarello de purger sa quarantaine et de débarquer les 37 colis de marchandises qu'il avait apportées, soit à Saint-Vincent même dans une embarcation qu'il aurait louée à cet effet, soit au lazaret existant à Porto-Praia dans l'île de Santhiago. Par suite de ces mesures, par lui qualifiées d'illégales et d'arbitraires, il fut dans la nécessité de rester à bord de l'*Adria* avec les dites marchandises et de faire le voyage aux ports de la république de La Plata et retour à Saint-Vincent de Cap Vert; et il dit avoir éprouvé de grandes pertes sur les marchandises; à ces causes il réclama pour dommages, consistant en ces pertes et en faux frais la somme de livres 15,500.

(*b*) Que dans le même voyage du même pyroscaphe *Adria* lui Lavarello ayant acheté et embarqué à Buenos Ayres et à Montevideo 6000 sacs de maïs pour la somme de livres 55,552. 20, le fret pour Saint-Vincent compris, il arriva de nouveau à ce port le 18 octobre (effectivement c'était le 16 octobre) 1884; que l'*Adria* y fut mis en quarantaine quoique n'ayant aucun cas de maladie à bord et venant d'un port indemne; que le même jour les dites autorités de Saint-Vincent permirent que lui et les autres voyageurs à même destination louassent une barque (schooner) pour les transporter eux et leurs bagages et marchandises au lazaret de Porto-Praia, à l'effet d'y purger la quarantaine; qu'en même temps la permission fut accordée au capitaine de l'*Adria*, M. Caffarena, de décharger les sacs de maïs qui se trouvaient à bord, pour les importer à la douane de Saint-Vincent après qu'ils eussent été exposés à l'air pendant vingt-quatre heures dans des gabares ouvertes; que lui Lavarello loua à cet effet deux gabares de messieurs Cory Brothers à Saint-Vincent; mais qu'après que 512 sacs de maïs eussent été transbordés, un contre-ordre fut donné et l'*Adria* se trouva forcé de continuer le voyage, de sorte que 5448 sacs de maïs restant à bord durent être transportés à Gênes, où ils furent vendus au meilleur prix possible, savoir de lires 39,284, tous frais déduits, de sorte que lui Lavarello éprouva une perte, au lieu du gain espéré sur cette marchandise, laquelle, d'après lui, valait dans ce même temps à Cap Vert environ lires 33 le sac, et aurait donc pu rapporter lires 198,000; il estima le dommage souffert à cette cause à lires 134,000.

c) Que les 512 sacs de maïs débarqués par suite des ordres mentionnés ci-dessus, restèrent pendant quelques jours exposés à la pluie dans une ou deux gabares ouvertes, avant d'être emmagasinés en douane à Saint-Vincent; qu'à cette cause le maïs fut avarié en partie, et que, lors de l'entrée en douane de cette marchandise, il manqua 38 sacs, probablement volés; que les 474 sacs restants durent être vendus à bas prix et ne rapportèrent que 390,300 réis, ou environ lires 2000 (ce compte a depuis été rectifié par le plaignant, et le rendement des 474 sacs de maïs reconnu avoir été 663,385 reis); le dommage qu'il a souffert de ce chef a été évalué par lui à lires 14,688. 20.

En total la réparation de dommages demandée s'élève à lires 164,188. 20.

A ces plaintes et réclamations le gouvernement de Portugal, dans son mémoire accompagné de documents justificatifs, oppose (en substance) les moyens de défense suivants:

(ad a) Qu'il est vrai que le 28 août 1884 les autorités de Saint-Vincent de Cap Vert ont refusé à l'Adria, venant de Gênes, la libre pratique et ont appliqué la quarantaine de rigueur aux voyageurs et aux marchandises se trouvant à bord de ce navire, même qu'elles ont refusé aux voyageurs destinés aux îles de Cap Vert de louer une embarcation à l'effet de se faire transporter avec leurs bagages au lazaret de Porto-Praia, mais que les autorités portugaises à Saint-Vincent, savoir le gouverneur des îles de Cap Vert et le délégué de la Junta de santé, n'ont pas défendu au capitaine de l'Adria de se rendre à Porto-Praia; qu'ils lui ont seulement fait entendre qu'il ne pouvait pas compter y être admis pour purger la quarantaine; que d'ailleurs les autorités de Saint-Vincent ont agi en cette affaire en conformité aux lois existantes, tout au moins aux instructions données par le gouvernement, parce que le port et la ville de Gênes étaient infecté de choléra, ce qui n'était pas encore officiellement porté à la connaissance des autorités de Cap Vert, mais ce qu'elles avaient appris par lettres et télégrammes particuliers; mais que, depuis lors, ces nouvelles se sont trouvées confirmées par un bulletin de la santé ma-

ritime de Lisbonne, du 6 août 1884, inséré dans le Diario do governo, n° 177, et reçu à Saint Vincent le 12 septembre 1884, vu que cet organe officiel a déclaré le port de Gênes infecté de choléra depuis le 31 juillet 1884; que la patente nette, délivrée par le consul portugais à Gênes, ne donnait aucun droit au navire pour être admis en libre pratique, mais ne valait qu'à titre d'information pour les autorités de Saint-Vincent; que d'ailleurs, les pertes subies par Lavarello sur les 37 colis de marchandises n'étaient pas prouvées, mais que, s'il avait subi des dommages par le fait des mesures sanitaires, celles-ci avaient été appliquées à bon droit et seulement pour des motifs de salut public.

(ad b) Que le 16 octobre 1884, l'Adria, en revenant au port de Saint-Vincent, après un voyage à Buenos-Aires et Montevideo, a été mis en quarantaine, quoique ces deux ports fussent indemnes et qu'il n'eût pas de malades à bord, à cause de sa provenance de Gênes, laquelle ville était alors officiellement déclarée infectée de choléra; que vu la longueur du voyage (58 jours en tout) et les patentes nettes délivrées dans l'Amérique du sud, les mesures sanitaires furent moins rigoureuses qu'au mois d'août; qu'à cette cause Lavarello et les autres voyageurs destinés aux îles de Cap Vert purent se rendre avec leurs bagages et marchandises au lazaret de Porto-Praia dans une embarcation (le schooner Maria) par eux louée; que de même leur fut donnée la permission de débarquer une cargaison de maïs, seulement sous la condition d'être exposée à l'air dans des gabares ouvertes pendant un jour; que cette dernière clause était motivée par ce que le maïs pouvait s'être trouvé en contact avec les marchandises chargées à Gênes.

Que, quant au contre-ordre qui aurait empêché le déchargement de la plus grande partie des 6000 sacs de maïs, le gouvernement de Portugal considère la réclamation de Lavarello comme mal fondée, parce qu'il n'a pas prouvé être propriétaire de cette quantité de maïs, ni que ce maïs avait été chargé à Buenos-Aires ou à Montevideo avec destination pour Saint-Vincent, ni qu'un contre-ordre au déchargement ou un ordre pour précipiter le départ de l'Adria au 17 octobre 1884 aient été donnés; qu'au contraire le capitaine de ce navire a déchargé autant de maïs qu'il a voulu, savoir 512 sacs, dont un connaissement se trouve parmi les pièces justificatives de Lavarello, et qu'ensuite ce capitaine est parti librement du port de Saint-Vincent après avoir pris des vivres et du charbon à bord.

(ad c) Que ni l'avarie qui aurait été causée par la pluie pendant que les 512 sacs de maïs étaient exposés à l'air dans une ou deux gabares ouvertes, ni le prétendu vol de 38 sacs n'ont été prouvés; qu'au contraire il n'a pas plu à Saint-Vincent pendant les 17ᵉ et 18ᵉ jours d'octobre et en petite quantité le 19ᵉ de ce mois, auquel jour on avait fini d'emmagasiner le maïs en douane; que 512 ou même 514 sacs de cette céréale ont été dédouanés en bon état, excepté quelque coulage d'un petit nombre de sacs; que les droits d'entrée ont été payés sur le nombre entier par Lavarello ou son mandataire; qu'ainsi il n'y a pas lieu d'admettre qu'il serait dû au plaignant une réparation de dommages éprouvés par lui à ce sujet.

En droit:

Considérant qu'il y a lieu de poser les trois questions mentionnées dans le compromis séparément à l'égard de chacun des griefs mis en avant par le plaignant; et ainsi:

Quant à la plainte *sub a:*

Considérant que les Hautes Parties sont d'accord sur les faits qui se sont passés en août 1884 à Saint-Vincent, excepté en ce que le Gouvernement de Portugal ne reconnait pas que les autorités de Saint-Vincent aient empêché l'Adria de purger la quarantaine de rigueur, qui lui avait été imposée;

Considérant, sur ce point, que le capitaine de l'*Adria* faisait escale à Saint-Vincent à la seule fin de débarquer 15 passagers et leurs bagages et marchandises, parmi lequels était M. A. Lavarello avec les 37 colis de marchandises, chargées par lui à cette destination; que d'après le journal de bord du 30 et 31 août 1884 (*pièce justificative*, n° 33) le pyroscaphe fut déclaré en quarantaine et on ne lui permit de débarquer ni voyageurs ni marchandises pour le lazaret, pas même de conduire ou faire conduire ces voyageurs à Porto-Praia, dans l'île de Santhiago, ce qui avait été demandé expressément, mais ce qui fut refusé; que n'ayant pas moyen de faire autrement, l'*Adria* partit le 31 août après midi pour Montevideo, ayant auparavant chargé 177 tonnes de charbon;

Considérant que cette relation du journal de bord se trouve confirmée en tous points par une lettre du capitaine Caffarena, datée du 30 août 1884 au Consul d'Italie à Saint-Vincent (*pièce* n° 34) et par la réponse, datée du même jour, de Mr. J. V. Miller. vice-consul d'Allemagne, faisant fonctions de consul d'Italie, dans laquelle il rend compte des démarches tentées en vain auprès du Gouverneur général des îles de Cap Vert et auprès du délégué du service sanitaire pour obtenir le débarquement en quarantaine à Porto-Praia (*pièce* n° 35), qu'elle est encore confirmée par une requête envoyée le même jour par Henry Lubrano, passager à bord de l'*Adria*, venant de Gênes, à Mr. le délégué de la junta de santé à Saint-Vincent, à l'effet de n'être pas forcé de faire le voyage avec sa famille à l'Amérique du Sud, notamment au Brésil, où la fièvre jaune existait (*pièce* n° 37); et par une protestation signée par neuf sujets italiens, résidant à Saint-Vincent, dont les signatures ont été légalisées par Mr. C. Martins, agent consulaire d'Italie a Saint-Vincent, le 6 septembre 1884, se plaignant de ce que leurs compatriotes, les voyageurs à bord de l'*Adria*, s'étaient vu refuser la permission de débarquer avec leurs bagages et marchandises, quoique le navire eût une patente nette et que l'existence du choléra en Italie ne fût pas constatée, tandis que le même jour, les mêmes autorités à Saint-Vincent avaient donné la permission à plusieurs voyageurs, arrivés à bord du vapeur *Elbe* venant d'Angleterre, de débarquer avec leurs bagages dans une goëlette louée à cet effet pour les conduire à Porto-Praia, et ce quoique les ports d'Angleterre fussent officiellement déclarés infectés du choléra (*pièce* n° 36), et enfin par une protestation datée du 30 août 1884, signée par Lavarello lui-même, Michel et Henry Lubrano et L. Germanetti, tous passagers à bord de l'*Adria*, adressée au consulat italien à Saint-Vincent et légalisée comme ci-dessus, contenant plainte de ce qu'en dépit des lois et traités existants, on leur refusait de purger leur quarantaine et qu'ils allaient être forcés, à leur grand dommage pécuniaire, à faire un voyage à l'Amérique du Sud et à remporter leurs marchandises (*pièce* n° 38);

Considérant que Lavarello a produit un connaissement daté à Gênes le 18 août 1884 et signé R. Piaggio & fils, portant que lui Lavarello avait chargé sur l'*Adria*, avec destination à Saint-Vincent, 37 colis de marchandises, savoir: 2 caisses marbre ouvré, 1 caisse bouchons, 1 caisse biscuits, 6 colis chemises de coton, 1 beurre, 1 fût de vin, 4 colis de sucre, 20 comestibles divers, et 1 cuisine en fer (*pièces* n° 18); qu'il a encore prouvé par les comptes acquittés de fournisseurs à Gênes et autres lieux et par une déclaration des propriétaires de l'Adria, R. Piaggio & Fils (*pièces* n° 2 à 17 et 19), qu'il avait acheté et payé les dites marchandises pour des sommes se montant à 15,072,18 lires, et payé pour son voyage de Gênes à Saint-Vincent 250 lires: pour fret, idem, 369,75 lires; pour passage et fret de Saint-Vincent à Montevideo et retour 1000 lires; ensemble 16,719,56 lires.

Considérant que les dites marchandises ont été déchargées le 16 ou 17 octobre 1884 dans le schooner portugais *Maria*, transportées à Porto Praia, et de retour à Saint-Vincent, emmagasinées en douane le 27 et dédouanées le 28 du même mois avec déclaration de valeur totale de 207 $ 490 réis (équivalent à lires 1,151,62 ¹/₂) suivant la déclaration spécifiée du directeur de la douane J. H. D. Ferreira, datée à Saint-Vincent le 22 Février 1886 à son chef, le secrétaire général du Gouvernement à Praia *(Mémoire pour le Gouvernement Portugais*, documents, p. 112 à 115).

Considérant que le compte de vente de ces marchandises manque; mais que: 1° le directeur de la douane, d'après la déclaration citée, s'est contenté d'une évaluation à une valeur vénale de beaucoup inférieure au prix coûtant et certifié que du moins 10 colis (de fruits) étaientg âtés; 2° que suivant les déclarations faites par cinq sujets italiens résidant à Saint-Vincent, par devant l'agent consulaire d'Italie, à diverses dates en 1885, les comestibles apportés par Lavarello en août 1884 sont arrivés en mauvais état en octobre de la même année et que les autres marchandises ne pouvaient plus rapporter que 50 pour cent de moins qu'elles n'auraient pu valoir en août; notamment le négociant C. B. Figari a déclaré que quelques-unes de ces marchandises avaient été apportées de Gênes en commission pour lui Figari, et qu'en août il les aurait prises pour lires 10,000, mais que deux mois plus tard, elles avaient 50 pour cent moins de valeur :

Considérant, que de tout ce qui précède il résulte que les autorités de Saint-Vincent ont causé des dommages et préjudices à M. A. Lavarello par leurs actes en août 1884, et qu'ainsi, la première question du compromis doit être résolue affirmativement ;

Considérant quant à la deuxième et la troisième question du compromis : que les traités existant entre les Hautes Parties ne contiennent aucune stipulation spéciale à l'égard des mesures sanitaires en cas d'épidémie; que par conséquent les sujets et les navires d'une nation amie doivent se soumettre à la loi locale des ports et autres lieux où ils se trouvent en pays ami, et qu'en revanche ils ont le droit d'être traités impartialement et à l'égal d'autres étrangers ou nationaux ; que le traité de commerce entre l'Italie et le Portugal du 15 juillet 1872 garantit en général la liberté de commerce et de navigation aux sujets italiens sur le territoire portugais (article 1er) et bien que selon l'article 26 tous les autres articles du traité sont applicables seulement dans la métropole et les îles adjacentes, cependant ce même article garantit dans les colonies portugaises aux navires italiens le traitement de la nation la plus favorisée; et conséquemment ce traité est incompatible avec des mesures qui entraveraient exceptionnellement ou arbitrairement la liberté de commerce de navires et voyageurs italiens dans ces colonies;

Considérant que le règlement du service de santé maritime du 12 novembre 1874, qui en 1884 était en vigueur aux îles de Cap Vert, prescrit dans l'article 94 que les navires provenant de ports non infectés avec patentes nettes seront admis en libre pratique, mais que le § 2 du même article admet une exception pour le cas où l'inspecteur en chef apprendra officiellement ou d'autre source authentique, que (entre autres) dans les ports de départ il s'est manifesté des cas de choléra morbus dans l'un des cinq jours qui auront suivi le départ de la même embarcation ; dans ce cas, la quarantaine devra être appliquée conformément aux autres articles du règlement ;

Considérant qu'au mois d'août 1884 la circonstance prévue par le § 2 s'est réalisée en effet à l'égard du port de Gênes; qu'ainsi les autorités civiles et sanitaires de Saint-Vincent ont légalement refusé la libre pratique à l'Adria et aux voyageurs à bord de ce navire; mais qu'en leur refusant l'occasion et en les mettant par conséquent dans l'impossibilité de se soumettre à la quarantaine, même de se rendre au lazaret de Porto-Praia, ces autorités de Saint-Vincent ont outrepassé les bornes de leur pouvoir légal ; qu'elles se sont notamment écartées des articles 87 et 99 du règlement cité ci-dessus; qu'il est vrai qu'un arrêté du 26 juillet 1884, émané du ministère de l'intérieur à Lisbonne, autorisa des mesures plus sévères pendant l'épidémie du choléra qui sévissait alors, notamment la défense de débarquer des personnes ou de décharger des marchandises appliquée aux navires provenant des ports infectés, mais que cet arrêté, d'après sa teneur, ne concernait que le continent et les îles adjacentes, non les provinces d'outre-mer, nommément les îles de Cap Vert;

Considérant qu'il suit de ce qui précède qu'on ne peut que répondre négativement à la deuxième et affirmativement à la troisième question du compromis;

Considérant que pour l'évaluation des dommages éprouvés par Lavarello par suite des mesures arbitraires prises à son égard par les autorités civiles et sanitaires de Saint-Vincent, les frais de voyage et le fret qu'il aurait épargnés, si on lui avait permis de débarquer ou de se rendre au lazaret de Porto-Praia en août 1884, sont de lires 1000; qu'il y a lieu d'admettre qu'il n'obtint en octobre 1884 et plus tard qu'un prix peu supérieur à la somme de lires 1125.62 1/2 à laquelle les marchandises furent évaluées lors du dénouement à la fin d'octobre; que cependant l'italien Figari, demeurant à Saint-Vincent, dont Lavarello a invoqué le témoignage, a déclaré plus tard, être prêt à payer encore lires 5000 telles de ces marchandises dont il aurait donné auparavant lires 10,000; qu'à défaut de données plus précises sur les pertes subies et la chance de gain manquée sur ces marchandises, il y a lieu d'évaluer les dommages, dont réparation est due à Lavarello, à lires 11,000.

Quant à la plainte *sub b:*

Considérant qu'il est avéré, que l'*Adria* étant revenue des ports du Rio de la Plata le 15 octobre 1884, au port de Saint-Vincent, a été soumis à la quarantaine sans autre motif donné que sa provenance de Gênes; que cette mesure paraît très rigoureuse après un voyage de cinquante-huit jours sans cas de maladie contagieuse à bord, mais que cette rigueur ne dépasse pas les termes du règlement, cité plus haut, notamment les articles 99 et 114; que d'ailleurs Lavarello et les autres voyageurs italiens à bord de l'*Adria* se sont soumis aux mesures quarantenaires en louant le schooner *Maria* pour se faire transporter avec leurs bagages à Porto Praia et deux gabares, afin de recevoir du maïs qui serait déchargé de l'*Adria* pour entrer ensuite en douane, et que nulle réclamation n'a été faite à cause de la mise en quarantaine;

Considérant que le sujet de la plainte portée est, que la permission donnée par les autorités du Port de Saint-Vincent pour décharger du maïs, appartenant à Lavarello, aurait été retirée arbitrairement par les mêmes autorités qui l'avaient donnée et que le navire aurait été forcé de partir; que ces faits sont contestés formellement par le gouvernement de Portugal;

Considérant que Lavarello a produit la preuve directe qu'il était chargeur et propriétaire de 512 sacs de maïs, qui ont été déchargés du 16 au 17 octobre 1884, savoir le connaissement *(pièce n° 44)* daté de Buenos Ayres le 25 septembre 1884 signé par le Capitaine de l'*Adria* (M. Caffarena) contenant le nom du chargeur E. Piaggio, celui du consignataire M. A. Lavarello, et en outre un endossement à F. Dias de Carvalho Braga en date du 30 octobre 1884, signé par M. A. Lavarello lui-même, et deux remarques signées par le greffier de la douane à Saint-Vincent, V. F. F. Vidal; que ce document fait preuve pleine et entière pour Lavarello de la propriété du maïs lors de l'arrivée de l'*Adria* à Saint Vincent selon les articles 558 et 559 du code de commerce italien;

Considérant que pareille pièce n'a pas été produite pour prouver que Lavarello était chargeur et propriétaire de 6,000 sacs de maïs destinés pour Saint-Vincent et que, selon les documents produits en janvier 1893, par le gouvernement d'Italie, de pareilles pièces n'existent pas et n'ont pas existé à l'égard des sacs de maïs non déchargés à Saint-Vincent; que probablement pour suppléer au manque de ces connaissements, M. A. Lavarello a produit deux comptes (pièces 26 et 32) émanant tous deux de la maison de

commerce Rocco et Piaggio & Fils de Gênes, le premier daté de Gênes le 4 novembre 1884, et portant facture pour l'achat de 1,270 sacs de maïs embarqués à Buenos Ayres, et 4,684 sacs de maïs embarqués à Montevideo, ensemble 5,954 sacs avec destination à Saint-Vincent de Cap Vert pour le compte de Lavarello, au prix de lire 45,349. 10 et pour fret, assurance et commission lire 10,623. 10, ensemble lire 55,972. 20 payables le 15 janvier 1885 à Gênes; le second daté de la même ville le 15 décembre 1884, et portant compte de vente 5,454 sacs de maïs ex *Adria* au prix de lire 41,721. 25, dont à déduire pour débarquement (de 4,000 quintaux) timbres, frais de douane, pesage (à 3,830 quintaux), courtage, commission et del credere lire 2,729. 70; à ajouter pour intérêt d'un mois lire 292. 45 faisant un produit net au 15 janvier 1885 de lires 39,284, de sorte que M. A. Lavarello y est débité pour le solde de lire 16,688. 20 à la même date; que la sincérité du résultat ou solde de ce dernier compte a été affirmée sous serment par M. Erasme Piaggio, chef de la maison Rocco Piaggio & Fils (en liquidation) devant un des prêteurs à Gênes, le 31 décembre 1892; que ces pièces quoique ne faisant pleine preuve qu'entre les parties elles-mêmes (Lavarello et Rocco Piaggio & Fils) offrent cependant une forte présomption pour affirmer que Lavarello avait à bord de l'Adria 5,954 sas de maïs à sa disposition;

Considérant que les documents cités laissent pourtant quelques doutes quant à la destination de ces sacs de maïs savoir: 1° D'après la pièce n° 26, le fret du chargement est porté au débit de Lavarello depuis les deux ports de la Plata à Saint-Vincent, mais d'après la pièce n° 32 aucun fret n'est porté à sa charge pour le voyage de Saint-Vincent à Gênes; 2° Parmi les documents justificatifs du *Mémoire pour le gouvernement Portugais,* page 112, on trouve la traduction d'un certificat de la douane de Gênes, portant spécification des chargements de maïs, débarqués ex *Adria* en novembre 1884, entrés en douane et dédouanés à Gênes, on y trouve, outre 2,009 sacs de maïs pour un autre chargeur, 1,258 ou 1,259 sacs de maïs chargés à Buenos Ayres, destinés pour Gênes, dont était chargeur E. Piaggio à ordre et 4,684 sacs de maïs chargés pareillement à Buenos Ayres, destinés pour Gênes, dont était chargeur E. Piaggio à lui-même; ces deux parties de maïs ont été dédouanées étant vendues à l'étranger; admettant que la différence de 1,258 ou 1,259 sacs, pour la première partie, à 1,270 sacs soit une quantité négligeable, et que la provenance de Buenos Ayres ait été notée par erreur (au lieu de Montevideo) pour la deuxième partie, on peut admettre l'identité de ces deux parties de maïs consignées à Gênes, ensemble 5,942 ou 5,943 sacs avec les 5,954 sacs dont l'achat est porté en compte à Lavarello par la pièce n° 36; alors Lavarello était le seul ayant droit sur ce chargement de maïs et on doit conclure en même temps que les 522 sacs de maïs déchargés du bord de l'Adria sur des gabares n'ont pas été déduits de ce chargement, mais se trouvaient en outre dans la possession de Lavarello; de là on devra tirer la conséquence; 3° Que Lavarello en faisant sa première réclamation le 25 octobre 1885, quelques mois après avoir apuré son compte avec Rocco Piaggio & Fils, se soit trompé étrangement à son propre désavantage, en soutenant qu'il avait (en octobre 1884) une quantité de 6,000 sacs de maïs à bord, et qu'il avait manqué d'en vendre à Saint-Vincent 5,488; tandis qu'en réalité il aurait eu 5,954 plus 512, soit 6,466 sacs de maïs, et aurait remporté 5,954 de Saint-Vincent; et 4° il reste inexpliqué pourquoi Rocco Piaggio & Fils, ayant reçu et vendu dans la douane de Gênes 5,954 (soit 5,942 ou 5,943) sacs de maïs, ne tenaient compte à Lavarello que de 5,454 sacs dans la *pièce* n° 32;

Considérant que, en admettant que Lavarello (en dehors des 512 sacs dont on a le connaissement) pouvait disposer, le 16 et 17 octobre 1884, d'une grande partie de maïs, se trouvant à bord de l'*Adria*, il est nécessaire de rechercher s'il a voulu le décharger le 16 ou 17 octobre 1884, s'il a tenté de le faire et s'il en a été empêché par les autorités de Saint-Vincent?

Considérant qu'à l'égard du fait, allégué par Lavarello, que les autorités de Saint-Vincent auraient empêché le déchargement de la plus grande quantité du maïs à bord de l'*Adria*, les Hautes Parties ont eu recours à l'épreuve testimoniale et ont produit plusieurs témoignages, qui se contredisent entre eux; mais en comparant et jugeant ces témoignages, il faut observer que les témoins n'ont jamais été entendus ensemble ni contradictoirement, ni même en vertu d'une commission rogatoire judiciaire, mais séparément par divers magistrats, dont chacun, ne connaissant pas l'affaire, n'était éclairé que par une des parties intéressées sur ce qu'il avait à demander au témoin; de sorte que, même quand la contradiction la plus apparente se produit entre deux ou plus de ces témoignages, il ne s'ensuit pas, que l'un des témoins ait dit toute la vérité, ni qu'un autre ait juré un faux serment;

Considérant que M. Caffarena, en 1884 capitaine, et trois autres témoins, alors officiers de l'*Adria*, ont déclaré le 20 août 1886 devant un des prêteurs de Gênes, entre autres, que le capitaine du port de Saint-Vincent et le médecin du service sanitaire, étant à bord de l'*Adria* le 16

octobre 1884, après s'être informés si M. A. Lavarello était à bord ont décidé que ce navire serait mis en quarantaine; que plus tard il lui fut permis de débarquer des voyageurs et du maïs, mais que, après que Lavarello et la famille Lubrano (de Livorno) et 512 sacs eussent été débarqués, on donna l'ordre (si intimó) au navire de partir le jour même et que l'*Adria* dut subir la violence qu'on lui faisait et remporter à Gênes les 5488 sacs de maïs restants *(pièces nᵒˢ 42 et 43)*; en faisant cette dernière déclaration ces témoins n'avaient évidemment pas présente à l'esprit la déclaration faite par Caffarena à la douane de Gênes en novembre 1884, suivant laquelle, environ 8000 sacs de maïs se trouvaient à bord de l'*Adria* lors de son départ; de sorte que le chiffre était inexact et ne pouvait être resté en leur mémoire que par ce qu'ils connaissaient depuis quelque temps la réclamation de Lavarello; d'ailleurs aucun d'eux ne précise, qui a donné l'ordre de repartir sans délai, ni si cet ordre fût verbal ou par écrit.

Considérant que trois témoins du nom de Morino, tous trois marins à bord de l'*Adria* en 1884, ont déclaré devant le prêteur de Recco, le 19 septembre 1885, entre autres, que l'autorité sanitaire de Saint-Vincent après avoir permis, le 16 octobre 1884, le débarquement des passagers, destinés aux îles de Cap Vert et du maïs fit cesser cette opération à peine commencée et ordonna au navire de partir après que les voyageurs avaient été débarqués pour se rendre à Porto Praia; de sorte qu'une grande quantité de maïs appartenant à Lavarello fût transportée à Gênes *(pièce nᵒ 40)*;

Considérant que Michel Lubrano, en 1884 voyageur à bord de l'*Adria* avec destination pour Saint-Vincent, a déclaré le 7 septembre 1886 devant un des prêteurs de Livorno, entre autres, que le débarquement des passagers pour se rendre à Porto Praia, et du maïs ayant été permis par l'autorité sanitaire, et après que lui déposant et sa famille et Lavarello eurent quitté l'*Adria* et se trouvaient à bord d'un allège avec les marchandises, la même autorité fit défense au capitaine Caffarena de continuer le déchargement du maïs et qu'on donna au dit capitaine l'ordre de partir, contre lequel le capitaine protesta *(pièce nᵒ 41)*; il est à remarquer que le témoin Lubrano, n'étant plus à bord de l'*Adria* n'a pu connaître que plus tard par ouï-dire ce dernier fait et que Caffarena n'en a rien déclaré;

Considérant que M. A. Annovazzi et trois dames Ravagli (artistes), ayant voyagé à bord de l'*Adria* de Buenos Ayres à Gênes, ont déclaré, le 17 septembre 1886, devant un des prêteurs de Milan qu'en vertu de la quarantaine imposée le 16 octobre 1884, il ne leur fut pas permis de quitter le navire à Saint-Vincent, mais que Lavarello et la famille Lubrano ont débarqué avec une partie des marchandises dans une allège et qu'on ne les a pas revus à bord; que plus tard, l'ordre a été donné de cesser le débarquement et de partir du port *(pièce n° 30)*.

Considérant qu'à ces témoignages le gouvernement de Portugal en a opposé d'autres, reçus sous serment en 1887 par une commission d'enquête administrative au sujet de toutes les plaintes de Lavarello, désignée par arrêté du gouverneur général de Cap Vert du 10 février 1886; entre autres ceux de cinq employés de la douane et de la santé maritime, un timonnier et deux rameurs du même service, qui ont tous accompagné le 16 et le 17 octobre 1884 le Dr A. M. da Costa Lereno, délégué du service sanitaire lors de ses visites à bord de l'*Adria*, déclarant: qu'ils n'ont entendu aucun ordre de cesser le déchargement du maïs, et que l'*Adria* est parti, quand le capitaine l'a voulu, après avoir pris des vivres et du charbon; un garde de la douane qui a été chargé ce surveillance du vapeur *Adria* pendant toute la durée du séjour de ce navire à Saint-Vincent le 16 et 17 octobre 1884 et de l'exécution des ordres touchant la quarantaine donnés par le Dr Lereno, lequel garde (Amado) a déclaré que nul ordre de cesser le déchargement du maïs n'a été donné si ce n'est qu'après le soleil couché ce travail a dû être cessé jusqu'au lendemain matin, comme c'est la règle dans le port de Saint-Vincent; que l'*Adria* n'a pas été forcé de partir, mais est parti quand cela lui a plu, après avoir pris des vivres et du charbon. *(Mémoire pour le gouvernement portugais, p. 90 à 96)*;

Considérant que devant la même commission d'enquête administrative sont comparus et entendus sous serment en juillet 1887 deux sujets italiens domiciliés à Saint-Vincent, dont le premier E. Galleano, a dit être négociant et associé avec M. A. Lavarello, et qu'il a été à bord de l'*Adria* le 17 octobre 1884, quand ce navire était en quarantaine; qu'alors Lavarello lui, ayant dit qu'il avait une partie de maïs à vendre, lui confia deux échantillons de cette marchandise pour savoir le prix qu'il en pourrait obtenir; que le témoin est retourné à bord et a dit à Lavarello que les négociants de l'île n'en voulaient donner qu'un très bas prix, vu que c'était du maïs étranger et que le maïs indigène ne manquait pas; qu'ensuite Lavarello, après avoir conféré avec Caffarena, lui a dit qu'il ne vendrait pas ce maïs et que tout irait en Italie; que cependant, le même jour, environ 500 sacs de maïs ont été transbordés dans des gabares louées de Cory Brothers; que Lavarello a débarqué tout ce qu'il a voulu et l'a consigné à F. Dias de Carvalho Braga, qui a vendu le maïs à bas prix; le second, G. Cavassa, négociant, a dit que, se trouvant en octobre 1884 dans une embarcation aux flancs de l'*Adria*, il a appris que Lavarello avait à bord une partie de maïs à vendre; qu'en effet environ 500 sacs de maïs ont été déchargés dans des gabares de Cory Brothers; qu'il n'a jamais entendu dire que la permission ait été refusée d'en débarquer davantage. *(Mémoire du gouvernement portugais*, p. 109, 110):

Considérant enfin, que le journal de bord de l'*Adria* mentionnant ce qui s'est passé le 16 et 17 octobre 1884 au port de Saint-Vincent, n'a pas été produit, et qu'il n'existe aucune demande ou requête adressée soit aux autorités de l'île, soit au consulat d'Italie à Saint-Vincent, ni de la part de Caffarena ni de celle de Lavarello, ayant rapport à l'empêchement allégué du déchargement de maïs ou au prétendu départ forcé de l'*Adria* en octobre 1884, comme les passagers et le capitaine n'avaient pas manqué de faire en août 1884, et cela quoique Lavarello soit resté encore plusieurs semaines aux îles de Cap Vert après le 17 octobre;

Considérant que comme conséquence de tout ce qui précède il n'est pas possible d'admettre comme certain et bien prouvé le fait dont Lavarello s'est plaint sub *b* et que la première question posée dans le compromis doit être résolue négativement;

Quant à la plainte *sub c* :

Considérant qu'il est avéré entre les deux Hautes Parties que 512 sacs de maïs, provenant de Buenos-Ayres, appartenant à Lavarello, ont été débarqués de l'*Adria* le 17 octobre 1884, dans deux gabares ouvertes appartenant à Cory Brothers pour être exposés à l'air pendant vingt-quatre heures et être emmagasinés ensuite le 16 octobre à Saint-Vincent; considérant que suivant le compte acquitté de Cory Brothers en date de Saint-Vincent le 17 décembre 1884, Lavarello a eu l'usage de ces gabares pendant trois jours du 16 au 19 octobre; que d'après les informations du Gouvernement portugais *(Mémoire*, p. 41 et 106) on ne peut affirmer que réellement la marchandise soit entrée en douane le 18, comme cela aurait dû se faire et comme le registre de la douane le porte; qu'il est possible que l'entrée en magasin se soit faite un ou deux jours plus tard; que de son côté Lavarello a produit un télégramme signé Cory et reçu par lui le 20 octobre à Porto Praia, où il se trouvait alors pour purger la quarantaine imposée, dans lequel on lui mande que le maïs se trouvait encore en quarantaine et qu'une partie des sacs était avariée par la pluie *(pièce n° 45)*; que, suivant les observations météorologiques fournies par le Gouvernement de Portugal, il n'a pas plu à Saint-Vincent le 17 et le 18, mais bien le 19 et beaucoup le 20 octobre, ce qui confirme en partie la teneur du télégramme; que, en vérité, l'authenticité du télégramme a été mise en doute, mais seulement: 1° parce que MM. Cory Brothers n'en ont pas tenu copie; 2° parce que la *Brasilian submarine telegraph company* n'a commencé son service à Praia que le 20 novembre 1884; objection futile, puisque le télégramme porte en tête le nom d'une compagnie d'entrepreneurs, qui évidemment avait posé le câble sous-marin, livré depuis à la *Brasilian*, savoir la *India rubber, gutta-percha and telegraph wire works company;*

Considérant que sur le connaissement des 512 sacs de maïs se trouve écrit en portugais (au recto): « sont entrés dans cette douane quatre cent soixante-quatorze (474) sacs de maïs; plusieurs de ces sacs étant mouillés et avariés en grande partie» (signé) V. F. F. Vidal. « Ce sont quatre cent soixante-quatorze (474) (signé) V.F.F. Vidal ». (A la première ligne on avait d'abord écrit: quatro centos noventa e sete (497), puis en surchargeant les mots: noventa e sete en les chiffres 97, on a écrit dessus: setenta e quatro et les chiffres 74; ensuite pour ne pas laisser de doute, on a de nouveau ajouté les vrais nombres et signé de nouveau).

Au verso du connaissement, sur la page imprimée, se trouve écrit, de la même main (en portugais): « Déclaration. Les sacs de maïs sont entrée dans la douane en mauvais état, une grande partie de ces sacs ayant beaucoup de manque causé par rupture, et d'autres se trouvant avec le maïs mouillé et en commencement de putréfaction. Douane de Saint-Vincent le 10 janvier 1885 (signé) V. F. F. Vidal » *(pièce n° 44);* que V. Ferreira de Fonseca Vidal, secrétaire du déchargement de la douane à Saint-Vincent, étant interrogé sous la foi du serment, le 25 juin 1887, par l'administrateur du district de Praia, île Santhiago, a d'abord déclaré ne pas avoir le moindre souvenir d'avoir écrit de pareilles notes et qu'elles seraient contraires à la vérité, mais en étant interrogé plus précisément, a répondu qu'il pourrait bien avoir écrit le nombre de 474 sacs, parce que les sacs avaient été comptés ainsi, mais ensuite on en avait trouvé 514; qu'il en était de même de la seconde déclaration; qu'il y avait bien du coulage et que 12 ou 15 sacs n'étaient peut-être pas pleins et 6 sacs seulement remplis à moitié; que s'il y avait eu du maïs gâté ou avarié, il aurait dû en référer à l'administration; que s'il avait cependant déclaré telle chose, ce n'avait été qu'une déclaration gracieuse.

Considérant que la déclaration de ce témoin ne peut faire d'autre impression morale que de son embarras d'avoir attesté des faits vrais, mais désagréables à ses chefs immédiats.

Considérant que la vérité des déclarations écrites par Vidal sur le connaissement est confirmée par le compte de vente de F. Dias de Carvalho Brago, négociant demeurant à Mindello, agent en douane, et ayant agi dans cette affaire comme fondé de pouvoir pour Lavarello, qui lui avait endossé le connaissement; dans ce compte daté de Saint-Vincent le 18 février 1885 *(pièce n° 31)* Brago porte à son débit 474 sacs de maïs, dont 2 qu'il avait remis à Lavarello personnellement; les 472 restants ont mesuré 3790 quartos (c'est-à-dire 9475 alqueires, lesquels, suivant une déclaration sous serment de Brago du 6 juillet 1887, pesaient environ 300 quintaux ou, si l'on évalue l'alqueire au poids de $\frac{1}{8}$ quintal, 315,8 quintaux) de maïs qui (avec 111 sacs vides, valant 100 réis chaque sac) ont obtenu un prix de 834 \$ 860 réis, dont à déduire 10 pour cent de commission 83 \$ 485 réis, droit d'entrée de 10 pour cent de la valeur calculée à 1 \$ 000 réis le sac de maïs, 47 \$ 400 réis; droit d'octroi de 3 pour cent de la même valeur, 14 \$ 240 réis (au juste 14 \$ 220 réis) et timbre de 700 réis; différences de monnaies, frais de transport dans les magasins et pour l'enchère et quatre mois de loyer de magasin, ensemble 25 \$ 700; en tout 171 \$ 525 réis; solde en faveur de Lavarello 663 \$ 335 réis; lequel compte a été apuré et Lavarello lui a donné quittance et décharge du solde *(Mémoire du Gouvernement portugais, p. 100).*

Considérant que l'on peut et doit induire de ces chiffres que Lavarello a éprouvé des dommages sur le maïs en question depuis que cette marchandise avait été reçue ou avait dû être reçue en douane:

Sur la *quantité*: les 5,954 sacs de maïs embarqués aux ports de la Plata pesaient 1,012,280 livres ou 465,602.80 kilogrammes, c'est-à-dire chaque sac en moyenne 78.2 kilogrammes; de la même cargaison 5,454 sacs débarqués à Gênes pesaient 380,387.5 kilogrammes, c'est-à-dire chaque sac en moyenne 69.8 kilogrammes; donc il y eut pendant le voyage de la Plata à Gênes un déchet d'environ 8.5 kilogrammes par moyenne de sac, ce qui correspond assez bien au compte de Braga donnant 8.03 quartas de mesure par sac; ainsi on trouve un extra déchet ou coulage de 6.3 kilogrammes par sac ou 2,973.6 kilogrammes sur les 472 sacs, et ensuite le poids probable de 38 sacs manquants donnant, à 63.5 kilogrammes la moyenne de sac, une quantité de 2,413 kilogrammes, ensemble 5,386.6 kilogrammes de manque:

Quant au *prix:* il résulte du compte de Braga que les 472 sacs n'ont rendu netto que 663 $ 335 réis, soit par sac 1 $ 405 réis, par quarta 175 réis, par alqueire 700 réis; or le prix de maïs étranger a été, suivant les mercuriales officielles d'octobre 1884 à janvier 1885, à Saint-Vincent, de 960 à 800 réis l'alqueire *(Mémoire du Gouvernement portugais,* p. 98, 99; à la page 36 du même mémoire ce prix courant est calculé par quintal, ce qui donnerait des prix ridicules); il y a donc eu perte sur la valeur des sacs de maïs vendus en douane, de 15 à 25 pour cent, ou en moyenne de 20 pour cent;

Considérant que par conséquent la première question du compromis doit être resolu affirmativement;

Considérant que d'après le rapport du délégué Dr da Costa Lereno, daté du 17 octobre 1884, c'est-à-dire du jour même du second départ de l'*Adria (Mémoire pour le Gouvernement portugais,* p. 66) il y eut doute et dissentiment, parmi des docteurs à Saint-Vincent, sur la question, si la quarantaine pouvait et devait être appliquée au pyroscaphe *Adria* et aux voyageurs et leurs bagages; que l'affirmative ayant été adoptée malgré le long voyage depuis le départ de Gênes et le bon état de santé à bord, l'autorité sanitaire ordonna que le maïs à débarquer resterait pendant vingt-quatre heures exposé à l'air sur une ou deux gabares ouvertes, et cela quoique ce maïs provînt d'un port indemne et que les céréales ne soient pas considérées comme susceptibles d'infection; même dans le lazaret elles ne peuvent être soumises qu'à une ventilation sous un hangar, suivant l'article 166 du règlement de santé maritime; que cette décision plus rigoureuse que ne le comportaient les articles 94 et 99 du règlement susdit, portait d'autant plus préjudice aux intérêts de Lavarello que celui-ci ne pouvait surveiller sa marchandise, vu qu'il devait forcément partir le jour même pour Porto Praia et que le procédé devint tout à fait injustifiable et irrégulier, lorsque le maïs ne fut pas emmagasiné en douane aussitôt après l'expiration des vingt-quatre heures prescrites mais un ou deux jours plus tard;

Considérant que par conséquent l'autorité de la douane est responsable envers Lavarello, comme propriétaire de la partie de maïs, pour le manque et les avaries que sa marchandise a éprouvées; et qu'en outre on n'a qu'à lire attentivement le rapport de J. H. Duarte Ferreira, directeur de la douane, daté du 11 juillet 1887 *(Mémoire pour le gouvernement portugais,* p. 100 à 104) pour se convaincre de l'incurie de cette administration à l'égard du maïs en question, le simple comptage des sacs ayant été fait négligemment, les sacs ayant été mêlés avec une autre quantité qui appartenait à un autre propriétaire, et un coulage

extraordinaire ayant été reconnu en magasin, que le directeur attribue aux charançons et aux rats;

Considérant qu'ainsi il y a lieu de répondre par la négative à la deuxième et par l'affirmative à la troisième question du compromis;

Considérant qu'il y a lieu de fixer le montant de la réparation des dommages pour le sujet de réclamation *sub c* à 20 pour cent du prix net obtenu pour les 472 sacs de maïs vendus, soit 132 $ 666 réis, ou lires 736. 30 et pour les 5,386,6 kilogrammes manquants un prix équivalant à la moyenne obtenue par kilogramme pour les sacs de maïs vendus à Gênes, en novembre 1884, savoir lires 11. 35 par 100 kilogrammes, faisant une somme de lires 611. 38; ensemble lires 1,357. 68;

Considérant que la demande n'étant reconnue bien fondée qu'en partie, il est juste de partager les frais du procès,

Nous arbitre, en vertu du pouvoir qui nous est attribué dans cette affaire, condamnons le gouvernement de Portugal à payer au gouvernement d'Italie au profit des ayant cause de feu Michel-angelo Lavarello, la somme de lires 12,347. 68 avec les intérêts moratoires à 5 pour cent par an depuis le 1er septembre 1891, date du compromis;

Déclarons la réclamation non fondée pour le reste;

Mettons à charge de chacune des Hautes Parties la moitié des frais, consistant uniquement dans le prix du papier timbré et les honoraires à fixer par le gouvernement des Pays-Bas.

Fait en double à la Haye le 12 mars 1893[1].

CVII. Etats Unis d'Amérique, Vénézuéla.
19 janvier 1892.

Lors de la guerre civile qui sévit au Vénézuéla vers 1871 les navires d'une compagnie de navigation américaine furent l'objet de saisies et les officiers de bord furent emprisonnés. Après vingt ans de correspondance diplomatique, un compromis fut signé et une indemnité de 142,400 $ fut accordée aux intéressés.

Convention to submit to arbitration the claims of the Venezuela Steam Transportation Company, concluded at Caracas, January 19, 1892.

The Government of the United States of America and the United States of Venezuela, being mutually desirous of removing all causes of difference between them in a manner honorable to both parties and in consonance with just rights

---

[1] J. B. MOORE. *History and Digest. . . .* p. 5021.

and interests, have resolved to submit to arbitration the claim of the «Venezuela Steam Transportation Company», and have respectively named as their plenipotentiaries to conclude a Convention for that purpose:

The President of the United States of America, William L. Scruggs, Envoy Extraordinary and Minister Plenipotentiary of the United States at Caracas;

And the President of the United States of Venezuela Doctor Rafael Seijas, legal adviser for the Department of Foreign Relations;

Who, after having exhibited their respective full powers, found in good and due form, have agreed upon the following articles:

ART. I. The high contracting parties agree to submit to arbitration the question whether any, and, if any, what indemnity shall be paid by the Government of the United States of Venezuela to the Government of the United States of America for the alleged wrongful seizure, detention and employment in war or otherwise of the steamships Hero, Nutrias and San Fernando, the property of the «Venezuela Steam Transportation Company», a corporation existing under the laws of the State of New York and a citizen of the United States, and the imprisonment of its officers, citizens of the United States.

ART. II. The question stated in Article I shall be submitted to the board of three Commissioners, one to be appointed by the President of the United States of America, one by the President of the United States of Venezuela, and the third who shall not be either an American or a Venezuelan citizen, to be chosen by the two appointed as aforesaid, but, if, within ten days from the time of their first meeting as hereinafter provided, they cannot agree upon the third Commissioner, the Secretary of State of the United States and the Venezuelan Minister of Washington shall forthwith request either the Diplomatic representative of Belgium or that of Sweden and Norway at that capital to name him subject to the restriction aforesaid.

The Commissioners to be chosen by the President of the United States of America and the President of the United States of Venezuela shall be appointed within a month from the date of the exchange of the ratifications of this Convention.

In case of the death, resignation or incapacity of any of the Commissioners, or in the event of any of them ceasing or omitting to act, the vacancy shall be filled in the same manner as is herein provided for the original appointment.

ART. III. The Commissioners appointed by the President of the United States of America

and the President of the United States of Venezuela shall meet in the city of Washington at the earliest convenient moment within three months from the date of the exchange of the ratifications of this Convention, and shall proceed to the selection of a third Commissioner.

When such Commissioner shall have been chosen, either by agreement between the two first named, or in the alternate manner hereinbefore provided, the three Commissioners shall meet in the city of Washington at the earliest practicable moment within five months from the date of the exchange of the ratifications of this Convention, and shall subscribe, at their first act, a solemn declaration to examine and decide the claim submitted to them in accordance with justice and equity and the principles of international law.

The concurrent judgment of any two of the Commissioners shall be adequate for the decision of any question that may come before them, and for the final award.

ART. IV. The Commissioners shall decide the claim on the Diplomatic correspondence between the two Governments relative thereto, and on such legal evidence as may be submitted to them by the high contracting parties within two months from the date of the first meeting of the full Commission. Their decision shall be rendered within three months at farthest from the date of the first meeting of the full Commission.

They shall hear one person as Agent in behalf of each Government and consider such arguments as either of such persons may present; and may, in their discretion, hear other counsel either in support of or in opposition to the claim.

ART. V. If the award shall be in favour of the United States of America, the amount of the indemnity, which shall be expessed in American gold, shall be paid in cash at the city of Washington, in equal annual sums, without interest within five years from the date of the award. the first of the five payments to be made within eight months from that date. Each Government shall pay its own commissionner and agent, and all other expenses including clerk hire shall be borne by the two Governments in equal moieties.

ART. VI. This Convention shall be ratified by the President of the United States of America by and with the advice and consent of the Senate thereof, and by the President of the United States of Venezuela, with the approval of the Congress thereof; and the ratifications shall be exchanged at Washington as soon as possible.

In witness whereof, the respective plenipotentiaries have signed and sealed the present Convention in duplicate in the English and Spanish languages.

Done at Caracas this nineteenth day of January, in the year of our Lord one thousand eight hundred and ninety two[1].

Award pronounced by the mixed commission at Washington, March 26, 1895.

Whereas by a convention between the United States of America and the United States of Venezuela, signed at Caracas the 19th of January 1892 and of which the ratifications by the two Governments were exchanged at Washington the 28th of July 1894 it was agreed and concluded that the high contracting parties should submit the claim of the 'Venezuela Steam Transportation Company' against the Government of Venezuela to the arbitration of a board of three commissioners, one to be appointed by the President of the United States of America, one by the President of the United States of Venezuela, and the third to be chosen by the two appointed as aforesaid; and

The President of the United States of America having appointed Gen. N. L. Jeffries commissioner: and

The President of the United States of Venezuela having appointed Señor Don José Andrade, venezuelan minister at Washington; and

The commissioners thus appointed having chosen Mr. A. Grip, envoy extraordinary and minister plenipotentiary of His Majesty the King of Sweden and Norway at Washington, as third commissioner; and

The board of commissioners, thus composed, having duly examined and considered the documents, evidence, and arguments submitted to them by the respective parties pursuant to the provisions of said treaty:

Now, we, the said commissioners:

Whereas the agent on the part of the United States of Venezuela has raised an exception to the jurisdiction of the commission over the portions of the claim stated in Articles XIX, XXI and XXV of the 'Statement of the case of the United States of America', filed by the agent on the part of the United States of America on the 16th of January last, do hereby unanimously declare ourselves competent on the said portions of the claims:

Do hereby, by a majority of the commission, award to the United States of America from the United States of Venezuela the sum of one hundred and forty-one thousand five hundred dollars

($ 141,500) in American gold, without interest, for the satisfaction in full of all the claims mentioned in Part I. Articles I to XXI inclusively, of the aforesaid statement of the case;

Do hereby unanimously disallow the claim mentioned in Part II. Article XXV of the aforesaid statement of the case.

Done in duplicate, at the city of Washington and signed by us this twenty-sixth day of March, in the year eigtheen hundred and ninety-five[1].

CVIII. Etats Unis d'Amérique, Grande-Bretagne.

29 février 1892.

Cette affaire, dont l'importance ressort des termes de la sentence intervenue, a eu spécialement pour objet de fixer les droits de jurisdiction des Etats Unis d'Amérique dans la mer de Behring et d'assurer la conservation des phoques à fourrure. Nous avons cru intéressant de reproduire également les actes d'exécution qui ont suivi le prononcé de la sentence.

Traité fixant les bases d'un arbitrage pour examiner le litige relatif aux pêcheries dans la mer de Behring, signé à Washington le 29 février 1892.

The United States of American and Her Majesty the Queen of the United Kingdom of Great Britain and Ireland, being desirous to provide for an amicable settlement of the questions which have arisen between their respective governments concerning to jurisdictional rights of the United States in the waters of Behring's Sea, and concerning also the preservations of the furseal in, or habitually resorting to, the said Sea, and the rights of the citiziens and subjects of either country as regards the taking of fur-seal in, or habitually resorting to the said waters, have resolved to submit to arbitration the questions involved, and to the end of concluding a convention for that purpose have appointed as their respective Plenipotentiairies:

The President of the United States of America, James G. Blaine, Secretary of state of the United States; and Her Majesty the Queen of the United Kingdom of Great Britain and Ireland, Sir Julian Pauncefote, G. C. M. G., K. C. B., Her Majesty's Envoy Extraordinary and Minister Plenipotentiary to the United States;

Who, after having communicated to each other their respective full powers which were found

---

[1] F. DE MARTENS. *Nouveau recueil général.* 2ᵉ série, t. XXII, p. 263.

[1] J. B. MOORE. *History and Digest...* p. 723.

to be in due and proper form, have agreed to and concluded the following articles.

ARTICLE I. The questions which have arisen between the Government of the United States and the Government of Her Britannic Majesty concerning the jurisdictional rights of the United States in the waters of Behring's Sea and concerning also the preservation of the fur-seal in or habitually resorting to the said sea, and the rights of the citizens and subjects of either country as regards the taking of fur-seal in or habitually resorting to the said waters, shall be submitted to a tribunal of arbitration, to be composed of seven Arbitrators, who shall be appointed in the following manner, that is to say: two shall be named by the president of the United States; two shall be named by Her Britannic Majesty; His Excellency the President of the French Republic shall be jointly requested by the High Contracting Parties to name one, His Majesty the King of Italy shall be so requested to name one and His Majesty the King of Sweden and Norway shall be so requested to name one. The seven Arbitrators to be so named shall be jurists of distinguished reputation in their respective countries; and the selecting Powers shall be requested to choose, if possible, jurists who are acquainted with the English language.

In case of the death, absence or incapicity to serve of any of either of the said Arbitrators, or in the event of any or either of the said Arbitrators, omitting or declining or ceasing to act as such, the President of the United States, or Her Britannic Majesty, or His Excellency President of the French Republic, or His Majesty the King of Italy, or His Majesty the King of Sweden and Norway, as the case may be, shall name, or shall be requested to name forthwith another person to act as arbitrator in the place and stead of the Arbitrator originally named by such head of a State.

And in the event of a refusal or omission for two months after receipt of the joint request from the High Contracting Parties of His Excellency the President of the French Republic, or His Majesty the King of Italy, of His Majesty the King of Sweden and Norway to name an Arbitrator either to fill the original appointment or to fill a vacancy as above provided, then in such case the appointment shall be made or the vacancy shall be filled in such manner as the High Contracting Parties shall agree.

ARTICLE II. The Arbitrators shall meet at Paris within twenty days after the delivery of the counter cases mentioned in Article IV and shall proceed impartially and carefully to examine and decide the questions that have been or shall be laid before them as herein provided on the part of the Government of the United States and Her Britannic Majesty respectively. All questions considered by the tribunal, including the final decision, shall be determined by a majority of all the Arbitrators.

Each of the High Contracting Parties shall also name one person to attend the tribunal as its Agent to represent it generally in all matters connected with the arbitration.

ARTICLE III. The printed case of each of the two parties, accompanied by the documents, the official correspondence, and other evidence on which each relies, shall be delivered in duplicate to each of the Arbitrators and to the Agent of the other party as soon as may be after the appointment of the members of the tribunal, but within a period not exceeding four months from the date of the exchange of the ratifications of this treaty.

ARTICLE IV. Within three months after the delivery on both sides of the printed case, either party may, in like manner, deliver in duplicate to each of the said Arbitrators, and to the Agent of the other party, a counter case, and additional documents, correspondence, and evidence in reply to the case, documents, correspondence and evidence so presented by the other party.

If, however, in consequence of the distance of the place from which the evidence is to be procured, either party shall, within thirty days after the receipt by its agent of the case of the other party, give notice to the other party that it requires additional time for the delivery of such counter case, documents, correspondence and evidence, such additional time so indicated, but not exceeding sixty days beyond the three months in this Article provided, shall be allowed.

If, the case submitted to the Arbitrators, either party shall have specified or alluded to any report or document in its own exclusive possession, without annex of a copy, such party shall be bound, if the other party thinks proper to apply for it, to furnish that party with a copy thereof: and either party may call upon the other, through the Arbitrators, to produce the originals or certified copies of any papers adduced as evidence, giving in each instance notice thereof within thirty days after delivery of the case; and the original or copy so requested shall be delivered as soon as may be and within a period not exceeding forty days after receipt of the notice.

ARTICLE V. It shall be the duty of the agent of each party, within one month after the expiration of the time limited for the delivery of the counter case on both sides, to deliver in duplicate to each of the said Arbitrators and to the Agent of the other party a printed argument showing the points and referring to the evidence upon which his Government relies, and either party may also support the same before the arbitrators by oral argument of counsel, and the arbitrators may, if they desire further elucidation with regard to any point, require a written or printed statement or argument, or oral argument by counsel upon it; but in such case the other party shall be entitled to reply either orally or in writing, as the case may be.

ARTICLE VI. In deciding the matters submitted to the Arbitrators, it is agreed that the following five points shall be submitted to them, in order that their award shall embrace a distinct decision upon each of the said five points, to wit:

1° What exclusive jurisdiction in the sea now known as the Behring's Sea, and what exclusive rights in the seal fisheries therein, did Russia assert and exercise prior and up to the time of the cession of Alaska to the United States?

2° How far were these claims of jurisdiction as to the seal fisheries recognized and conceded by Great Britain?

3° Was the body of water now known as the Behring's Sea included in the phrase « Pacific Ocean » as used in the Treaty of 1825 between Great Britain and Russia; and what rights, if any, in the Behring's Sea were held and exercised by Russia after said treaty?

4° Did not all the rights of Russia as to jurisdiction, and as to the seal fisheries in Behring's Sea east of the water boundary, in the treaty between the United States and Russia of the 30ᵗʰ March, 1867, pass unimpaired to the United States under that treaty?

5° Had the United States any right, and if so, what right of protection or property in the fur-seals frequenting the United States in Behring's Sea when such seals are found outside the ordinary three mile limit?

ARTICLE VII. In the determination of the foregoing questions as to the exclusive jurisdiction of the United States shall leave the subject in such position that the concurrence of Great Britain is necessary to the establishment of Regulations for the proper protection and preservation of the fur-seal, in or habitually resorting to the Behring's Sea, the Arbitrators shall then determine what concurrent Regulations outside the jurisdictional limits of the respective Governments are necessary, and over what waters such Regulations should extend, and to aid them in that determination the report of a Joint Com-

mission, to be appointed by the respective Governments, shall be laid before them, with such other evidence as either Government may submit.

The High Contracting Parties furthermore agree to cooperate in securing the adhesion of other Powers to such Regulation.

ARTICLE VIII. The High Contracting Parties having found themselves unable to agree upon a reference which shall include the question of the liability of each for the injuries alleged to have been sustained by the other or by its citizens, in connection with the claims presented and urged by it, and being solicitous that this subordinate question should not interrupt or longer delay the submission and determination of the main questions, do agree that either may submit to the Arbitrators any question of fact involved in said claims and ask for a finding thereon, the question of the liability of either Government upon the facts found to be the subject of further negotiation.

ARTICLE IX. The High Contracting Parties have agreed to appoint two Commissioners on the part of each Government, to make the joint investigation and report contemplated in the preceding Article VII, and to include the terms of the said Agreement in the present Convention, to the end that the joint reports and recommendations of said Commissioners may be in due form submitted to the Arbitrators, should the contingency therefore arise, the said Agreement is accordingly herein included as follows:

Each Government shall appoint two Commissioners to investigate, conjointly with the Commissioners of the other Government, all the facts having relation to seal life in Behring's Sea, and the measures necessary for its proper protection and preservation.

The four Commissioners shall, so far as they may be able to agree, make a joint report to each of the two Governments, and they shall also report, either jointly or severally, to each Government on any points upon which they may be unable to agree.

These reports shall not be made public until they shall be submitted to the Arbitrators, or it shall appear that the contingency of their being used by the Arbitrators can not arise.

ARTICLE X. Each Government shall pay the expenses of its members of the joint Commission in the investigation referred to in the preceding article.

ARTICLE XI. The decision of the Tribunal shall, if possible, be made within three months from the close of the argument on both sides.

It shall be made in writing and dated, and shall be signed by the Arbitrators who may assent to it.

The decision shall be in duplicate, one copy whereof shall be delivered to the Agent of the United States for his Government, and the other copy shall be delivered to the Agent of Great Britain for his Government.

ARTICLE XII. Each Government shall pay its own Agent and provide for the proper remuneration of the counsel employed by it and of the Arbitrators appointed by it, and for the expense of preparing and submitting its case to the Tribunal. All other expenses connected with the arbitration shall be defrayed by the two Governments in equal moieties.

ARTICLE XIII. The arbitrators shall keep an accurate record of their proceedings and may appoint and employ the necessary officers to assist them.

ARTICLE XIV. The High Contracting Parties engage to consider the result of the proceedings of the tribunal of arbitration as a full, perfect, and final settlement of all the questions referred to the Arbitrators.

ARTICLE XV. The present treaty shall be duly ratified by the President of the United States of America, by and with the advice and consent of the Senate, thereof, and by Her Britannic Majesty; and the ratifications shall be exchanged either at Washington or at London within six months from the date hereof, or earlier if possible.

In faith whereof we, the respective Plenipotentiaries, have signed this treaty and have hereunto affixed our seals.

Done in duplicate at Washington the twenty-ninth day of February, one thousand eight hundred and ninety-two [1].

Convention between the United States of America and Great Britain for the renewal of the existing « modus vivendi » in Behring's Sea, signed at Washington, April 18, 1892.

Whereas by a Convention concluded between the United States of America and Her Majesty the Queen of the United Kingdom of Great Britain and Ireland, on the twenty-ninth day of February one thousand eight hundred and ninety two, the High Contracting Parties have agreed to submit to Arbitration, as therein stated, the questions which have arisen between them con-

cerning the jurisdictional rights of the United States in the waters of Behring's Sea and concerning also the preservation of the fur-seal in, or habitually resorting to the said sea, and the rights of the citizens and subjects of either country as regards the taking of the fur-seal in, or habitually resorting to the said sea; and whereas the High Contracting Parties, having differed as to what restrictive Regulations for seal hunting are necessary, during the pendency of such Arbitration, have agreed to adjust such difference in manner hereinafter mentioned, and without prejudice to the rights of either party:

The said High Contracting Parties have appointed as their Plenipotentiaries to conclude a Convention for this purpose that is to say:

The President of the United States of America, James G. Blaine, secretary of State of the United States;

And Her Majesty the Queen of the United Kingdom of Great Britain and Ireland, Sir Julian Pauncefote, Knight Grand Cross of the Most Distinguished Order of Saint Michael and Saint George, Knight Commander of the Most Honorable Order of the Bath, and Envoy Extraordinary and Minister Plenipotentiary of Her Britannic Majesty to the United States who, after having communicated to each other their respective full powers, found in due and good form, have agreed upon and concluded the following articles:

ARTICLE I. Her Majesty's Government will prohibit, during the pendency of the Arbitration, seal killing in that part of Behring's Sea lying eastward of the line of demarcation described in Article n° I of the Treaty of 1867 between the United States and Russia, and will promptly use its best efforts to ensure the observance of this prohibition by British subjects and vessels.

ARTICLE II. The United States Government will prohibit seal-killing for the same period in the same part of Behring's Sea, and on the shores and islands thereof, the property of the United States (in excess of seven thousand five hundred to be taken on the islands for the subsistence of the natives) and will promptly use its best efforts to ensure the observance of this prohibition by United States citizens and vessels.

[1] *Parliamentary Paper*, United States, n° 1, 1893, p. 2-7.

ARTICLE III. Every vessel or person offending against this prohibition in the said waters of Behring's Sea outside of the ordinary territorial limits of the United States, may be seized and detained by the naval or other duly commissioned officers of either of the High Contracting Parties, but they shall le handed over as soon as practicable to the authorities of the Nation to which they respectively belong, who alone shall have jurisdiction to try the offence and impose the penalties for the same. The witnesses and proof necessary to establish the offence shall also be sent with them.

ARTICLE IV. In order to facilitate such proper inquiries at Her Majesty's Government may desire to make with a view to the presentation of the case and arguments of that Government before the Arbitrators, it is agreed that suitable persons designated by Great Britain will be permitted at any time, upon application, to visit or remain upon the Seal Islands during the sealing season for that purpose.

ARTICLE V. If the result of the Arbitration be to affirm the right of British sealers to take seals in Behring's Sea within the bounds claimed by the United States, under its purchase from Russia, then compensation shall be made by the United States to Great Britain (for the use of her subjects) for abstaining from the exercise of that right during the pendency of the Arbitration upon the basis of such a regulated and limited catch or catches as in the opinion of the Arbitrators might have been taken without and undue diminution of the sealherds; and on the other hand, if the result of the Arbitration shall be to deny the right of British sealers to take seals within the said waters, then compensation shall be made by Great Britain to the United States (for itself, its citizens and lessees) for this agreement to limit the island catch to seven thousand five hundred a season, upon the basis of the difference between this number and such larger catch as in the opinion of the Arbitrators might have been taken without an undue diminution of the sealherds.

The amount awarded, if any, in either case shall be such as under all the circumstances is just and equitable, and shall be promptly paid.

ARTICLE VI. This Convention may be denounced by either of the High Contracting Parties at any time after the thirty first day of October, one thousand eight hundred and ninety-three, on giving to the other Party two months notice of its termination; and at the expiration of such notice the Convention shall cease to be in force.

ARTICLE VII. The present Convention shall be duly ratified by the President of the United States, by and with the advice and consent of the Senate thereof, and by Her Britannic Majesty; and the ratifications shall be exchanged either at Washington or at London as early as possible.

In faith whereof, we, the respective Plenipotentariies have signed this Convention and have hereunto affixed our seals.

Done in duplicate at Washington, this eighteenth day of April one thousand eight hundred and ninety-two [1].

Sentence du Tribunal d'arbitrage constitué en vertu du traité conclu à Washington, le 29 Février 1892, entre les Etats-Unis d'Amérique et la Grande-Bretagne, prononcée le 15 août 1893.

Attendu que par un traité entre les Etats-Unis d'Amérique et la Grande-Bretagne, signé à Washington le 29 février 1892, et dont les ratifications par les Gouvernements des deux pays ont été échangées à Londres le 7 mai 1892, il a été, entre autres stipulations, convenu et réglé que les différends qui avaient surgi entre le Gouvernement des Etats-Unis d'Amérique et le Gouvernement de Sa Majesté Britannique, au sujet des droits de juridiction des Etats-Unis dans les eaux de la Mer de Behring et aussi relativement à la préservation des phoques à fourrure se trouvant dans les dites eaux où les fréquentent, seraient soumis à un Tribunal d'Arbitrage composé de sept Arbitres, qui seraient nommés de la manière suivante, savoir: deux Arbitres seraient désignés par le Président des Etats-Unis; deux Arbitres seraient désignés par Sa Majesté Britannique; Son Excellence le Président de la République Française serait prié, d'un commun accord par les Hautes Parties Contractantes de désigner un Arbitre; Sa Majesté le Roi d'Italie serait prié de la même manière de désigner un Arbitre; Sa Majesté le Roi de Suède et de Norvège serait prié de la même manière de désigner

---

[1] F. DE MARTENS, *Nouveau Recueil Général*, 2ᵐᵉ série, t. XVIII, p. 592.

un Arbitre: les sept Arbitres ainsi nommés devant être des jurisconsultes d'une réputation distinguée dans leurs pays respectifs, et les Puissances auxquelles leur désignation serait remise devant être priées de choisir autant que possible des jurisconsultes sachant la langue Anglaise;

Et attendu qu'il a été pareillement convenu, par l'Article II du dit Traité, que les Arbitres se réuniraient à Paris dans les vingt jours qui suivraient la remise des Contre-Mémoires mentionnés à l'Article IV, qu'ils examineraient et décideraient avec impartialité et soin les questions qui leur étaient ou leur seraient soumises dans les conditions prévues par le dit Traité, de la part des Gouvernements des Etats-Unis et de sa Majesté Britannique respectivement, et que toutes les questions examinées par le Tribunal, y compris la sentence finale, seraient décidées par les Arbitres à la majorité absolue des voix;

Et attendu que par l'Article VI du dit Traité, il a été pareillement convenu ce qui suit:

« En vue de la décision des questions soumises aux Arbitres il est entendu que les cinq points suivants leur seront soumis, afin que leur sentence comprenne une décision distincte sur chacun des dits cinq points, savoir:

« 1° Quelle juridiction exclusive dans la mer aujourd'hui connue sous le nom de Mer de Behring et quels droits exclusifs sur les pêcheries des phoques dans cette mer la Russie a-t-elle affirmés et exercés avant et jusqu'à l'époque de la cession de l'Alaska aux Etats-Unis?

« 2° Jusqu'à quel point la revendication de ces droits de juridiction en ce qui concerne les pêcheries des phoques a-t-elle été reconnue et concédée par la Grande-Bretagne?

« 3° L'espace de mer aujourd'hui connu sous le nom de Mer de Behring était-il compris dans l'expression « Océan Pacifique » telle qu'elle a été employée dans le texte du Traité conclu en 1825 entre la Grande-Bretagne et la Russie, et quels droits, si droits il y avait, la Russie a-t-elle possédés et exclusivement exercés dans la Mer de Behring après le dit Traité?

« 4° Tous les droits de la Russie en ce qui concerne la juridiction et en ce qui concerne les pêcheries de phoques, dans la partie de la Mer de Behring qui s'étend à l'est de la limite maritime déterminée par le Traité du 30 Mars 1867, entre les Etats-Unis et la Russie, ne sont-ils pas intégralement passés aux Etats-Unis en vertu de ce même Traité?

« 5° Les Etats-Unis ont-ils quelque droit, et, en cas d'affirmative, quel droit ont-ils, soit à la protection, soit à la propriété des phoques à fourrure qui fréquentent les îles appartenant aux Etats-Unis dans la Mer de Behring, quand ces phoques se trouvent en dehors de la limite ordinaire de 3 milles?

Et attendu que, par l'Article VII du dit Traité, il a été pareillement convenu ce qui suit:

« Si la décision des questions qui précèdent, en ce qui concerne la juridiction exclusive des Etats-Unis, laisse les choses en tel état que le concours de la Grande-Bretagne soit nécessaire pour l'établissement de Règlements en vue de la protection et de préservation convenables des phoques à fourrure habitant ou fréquentant la Mer de Behring, les Arbitres auront à déterminer quels Règlements communs sont nécessaires, en dehors des limites de la juridiction des Gouvernements respectifs, et sur quelles eaux ces Règlements devraient s'appliquer . . . .

« Les Hautes Parties Contractantes s'engagent en outre à unir leurs efforts pour obtenir l'adhésion d'autres Puissances à ces Règlements; »

Et attendu que par l'Article VIII du dit Traité, après avoir exposé que les Hautes Parties Contractantes n'avaient pu s'entendre sur une formule qui comprît la question des responsabilités à la charge de l'une d'elles, à raison des préjudices allégués avoir été causés à l'autre, ou aux citoyens de l'autre, à l'occasion des réclamations présentées et soutenues par la dite partie, et quelles « désiraient que cette question secondaire ne suspendît ou ne retardât pas plus longtemps la production et la décision des questions principales », les Hautes Parties Contractantes sont convenues que « chacune d'elles pourrait soumettre aux Arbitres toute question de fait impliquée dans les dites réclamations et demander une décision à cet égard, après quoi la question de la responsabilité de chacun des deux Gouvernements à raison des faits établis serait matière à négociations ultérieures; »

Et attendu que le Président des Etats-Unis d'Amérique a désigné l'Honorable John M. Harlan, juge de la Cour suprême des Etats-Unis et l'Honorable John T. Morgan, sénateur des Etats-Unis, pour être deux desdits Arbitres; que Sa Majesté Britannique a désigné le Très Honorable Lord Hannen et l'Honorable sir John Thompson, Ministre de la Justice et Attorney-Général pour le Canada, pour être deux desdits Arbitres; que son Excellence le Président de la République Française a désigné le Baron Alphonse de Courcel, sénateur, Ambassadeur de France, pour être un desdits Arbitres; que Sa Majesté le Roi d'Italie a désigné le Marquis Emilio Visconti Venosta, ancien Ministre des Affaires Etrangères et sénateur du royaume d'Italie, pour être un desdits Arbitres; et que Sa Majesté le Roi de Suède et de Norvège a désigné M. Gregers Gram, Ministre d'Etat, pour être un desdits Arbitres;

Et attendu que nous susnommés Arbitres, désignés et investis de la manière qui vient d'être relatée, ayant accepté de prendre la charge de cet Arbitrage, et nous étant dûment réunis à Paris; avons procédé avec impartialité et soin à l'examen et à la décision de toutes les questions qui ont été soumises à nous, Arbitres susnommés, en vertu dudit Traité, où à nous présentées, au nom des Gouvernements des Etats-Unis et de Sa Majesté Britannique respectivement, de la manière prévue par ledit Traité ;

Nous Arbitres susnommés ayant examiné avec impartialité et soin lesdites questions, décidons et prononçons de même, sur lesdites questions, par notre présente sentence, de la manière qui suit, à savoir :

En ce qui concerne les cinq points mentionnés dans l'article VI et sur chacun desquels notre jugement doit comprendre une décision distincte, nous décidons et prononçons ce qui suit :

Par l'Ukase de 1821 la Russie a revendiqué des droits de juridiction, dans la mer connue aujourd'hui sous le nom de Mer de Behring, jusqu'à la distance de cent milles italiens au large des côtes et îles lui appartenant; mais, au cours des négociations qui ont abouti à la conclusion des Traités de 1824 avec les Etats-Unis et de 1825 avec la Grande-Bretagne, elle a admis que sa juridiction dans ladite mer serait limitée à une portée de canon de la côte ; et il paraît que depuis cette époque jusqu'à l'époque de la cession de l'Alaska aux Etats-Unis, elle n'a jamais affirmé en fait ni exercé aucune juridiction exclusive dans la Mer de Behring, ni aucun droit exclusif sur les pêcheries de phoques à fourrure dans ladite mer, au delà des limites ordinaires des eaux territoriales.

Sur le second des cinq points susdits, nous, Arbitres susnommés, le Baron de Courcel, le juge Harlan, sir John Thompson, le Marquis Visconti Venosta, et M. Gregers Gram, constituant la majorité des Arbitres, décidons que la Grande-Bretagne n'a reconnu ni concédé à la Russie aucun droit à une juridiction exclusive sur les pêcheries de phoques dans la Mer de Behring, en dehors des eaux territoriales ordinaires.

Sur le troisième des cinq points susdits, et quant à la partie dudit troisième point où nous est soumise la question de savoir si l'espace de mer aujourd'hui connu sous le nom de Mer de Behring était compris dans l'expression « Océan Pacifique » telle qu'elle a été employée dans le texte du Traité de 1825 entre la Grande-Bretagne et la Russie, nous, Arbitres susnommés, décidons et prononçons à l'unanimité que l'espace de mer aujourd'hui connu sous le nom de Mer de Behring était compris dans l'expression « Océan Pacifique » telle qu'elle a été employée dans ledit Traité.

Et quant à la partie dudit troisième point d'après laquelle nous avons à décider quels droits, si droits il y avait, la Russie a possédé et exclusivement exercés après ledit Traité de 1825, nous Arbitres susnommés, le Baron de Courcel, le juge Harlan, Lord Hannen, sir John Thompson, le Marquis Visconti Venosta et M. Gregers Gram, constituant la majorité des Arbitres, décidons et prononçons que la Russie n'a possédé ni exercé après le Traité de 1825, aucun droit exclusif de juridiction dans la Mer de Behring ni aucun droit exclusif sur les pêcheries de phoques dans cette mer, au delà de la limite ordinaire des eaux territoriales.

Sur le quatrième des cinq points susdits, nous Arbitres susnommés décidons et prononçons à l'unanimité, que tous les droits de la Russie en ce qui concerne les pêcheries de phoques, dans la partie de la mer de Behring qui s'étend à l'est de la limite maritime déterminée par le Traité du 30 mars 1867, entre les Etats-Unis et la Russie, sont intégralement passés aux Etats-Unis en vertu de ce même Traité.

Sur le cinquième des cinq points susdits, nous Arbitres susnommés le Baron de Courcel, Lord Hannen, sir John Thompson, le Marquis Visconti Venosta et M. Gregers Gram constituant la majorité des Arbitres, décidons et prononçons que les Etats-Unis n'ont aucun droit de protection ou de propriété sur les phoques à fourrure qui fréquentent les îles appartenant aux Etats-Unis daus la Mer de Behring, quand ces phoques se trouvent en dehors de la limite ordinaire de 3 milles.

Et attendu que les décisions ci-dessus relatées, sur les questions concernant la juridiction exclusive des Etats-Unis mentionnées dans l'article VI laissent les choses en état tel que le concours de la Grande-Bretagne est nécessaire pour l'établissement de Règlements en vue de la protection et de la préservation convenables des phoques à fourrure habitant ou fréquentant la Mer de Behring, le Tribunal ayant décidé à la majorité absolue des voix sur chacun des articles des Règlements qui suivent, nous, Arbitres susnommés, le Baron de Courcel, Lord Hannen, le Marquis Visconti Venosta, et M. Gregers Gram, donnant notre assentiment à l'ensemble des articles des Règlements qui suivent, et constituant la majorité absolue des Arbitres, décidons et prononçons, d'après le mode prescrit par le Traité, que les Règlements communs qui suivent, applicables en dehors des limites de la juridiction des Gouvernements respectifs, sont nécessaires et qu'ils doivent s'étendre sur les eaux ci-après déterminées :

ART. I. Les Gouvernements des Etats-Unis et de la Grande-Bretagne interdiront à leurs citoyens et sujets respectifs de tuer, prendre ou poursuivre, en tout temps et de quelque manière que ce soit, les animaux appelés communément phoques à fourrure, dans une zone de 60 milles autour des îles Pribyloff, en y comprenant les eaux territoriales.

Les milles mentionnés dans le paragraphe précédent sont des milles géographiques de 60 au degré de latitude.

ART. II. Les deux Gouvernements interdiront à leurs citoyens et sujets respectifs de tuer, prendre ou poursuivre, les phoques à fourrure de quelque manière que ce soit, pendant la saison s'étendant chaque année du 1er mai au 31 juillet inclusivement, sur la haute mer, dans la partie de l'Océan Pacifique, en y comprenant la Mer de Behring, qui est sise au nord du 35e degré de latitude nord, et à l'est du 180e degré de longitude de Greenwich jusqu'à sa rencontre avec la limite maritime décrite dans l'article 1er du Traité de 1867 entre les Etats-Unis et la Russie, et ensuite à l'est de cette ligne jusqu'au détroit de Behring.

ART. III. Pendant la période de temps et dans les eaux où la pêche des phoques à fourrure demeurera permise, les navires à voiles seront seuls admis à l'exercer ou à s'associer aux opérations de cette pêche. Ils auront cependant la faculté de se faire assister par des pirogues ou autres embarcations non pontées, mues par des pagaies, des rames ou des voiles, du genre de celles qui sont communément employées comme bateaux de pêche.

ART. IV. Tout navire à voiles autorisé à se livrer à la pêche des phoques à fourrure devra être muni d'une licence spéciale délivrée à cet effet par le Gouvernement et devra porter un pavillon distinctif qui sera déterminé par le Gouvernement.

ART. V. Les patrons des navires engagés dans la pêche des phoques à fourrure devront mentionner exactement sur leurs livres de bord la date et le lieu de chaque opération de pêche des phoques à fourrure, ainsi que le nombre et le sexe des phoques capturés chaque jour. Ces mentions devront être communiquées par chacun des deux Gouvernements à l'autre à la fin de chaque saison de pêche.

ART. VI. L'emploi des filets, des armes à feu et des explosifs, sera interdit dans la pêche des phoques à fourrures. Cette restriction ne s'appliquera pas aux fusils de chasse quand cette pêche sera pratiquée en dehors de la Mer de Behring et pendant la saison où elle pourra être légitimement exercée.

ART. VII. Les deux Gouvernements prendront des mesures en vue de contrôler l'aptitude des hommes autorisés à exercer la pêche des phoques à fourrure ; ces hommes devront être reconnus aptes à manier avec une habileté suffisante les armes au moyen desquelles cette pêche pourra être faite.

ART. VIII. Les Règlements contenus dans les précédents articles ne s'appliqueront pas aux Indiens habitant sur les côtes du territoire des Etats-Unis ou de la Grande-Bretagne et pratiquant la pêche des phoques à fourrure dans des pirogues ou embarcations non pontées, non transportées par d'autres navires, ni employées à l'usage de ceux-ci, mues exclusivement à l'aide de pagaies, d'avirons ou de voiles, et manœuvrées chacune par cinq personnes au plus, de la manière jusqu'à présent usitée par les Indiens ; pourvu que ceux-ci ne soient pas engagés au service d'autres personnes, et qu'alors qu'ils chassent ainsi dans des pirogues ou embarcations non pontées, ils ne poursuivent pas les phoques à fourrure en dehors des eaux territoriales, en vertu d'engagements contractés pour la livraison de peaux à une personne quelconque.

Cette exception n'aura pas pour effet de porter atteinte à la législation nationale de l'un ou de l'autre des deux pays ; elle ne s'étendra pas aux eaux de la Mer de Behring, ni aux eaux des passes Aléoutiennes.

Aucune des dispositions qui précèdent n'a pour objet de s'opposer à ce que les Indiens soient employés comme chasseurs, ou à tout autre titre, ainsi qu'ils l'ont été jusqu'à présent, sur les navires se livrant à la poursuite des phoques à fourrure.

Art. IX. Les Règlements communs établis par les Articles précédents, en vue de la protection et de la préservation des phoques à fourrure, demeureront en vigueur jusqu'à ce qu'ils aient été en tout ou en partie abolis ou modifiés par un accord entre les Gouvernements des Etats-Unis et de la Grande-Bretagne.

Les dits Règlements communs seront soumis tous les cinq ans à un nouvel examen, pour que les deux Gouvernements intéressés se trouvent en mesure d'apprécier, à la lumière de l'expérience acquise, s'il y a lieu d'y apporter quelque modification.

Et attendu que le Gouvernement de Sa Majesté Britannique a soumis au Tribunal d'Arbitrage, par application de l'article VIII du dit Traité, certaines questions de fait. impliquées dans les réclamations dont il est fait mention au dit article VIII, et a soumis également à nous, formant le dit Tribunal, un exposé des faits dans les termes suivants :

« Conclusions de fait proposées par l'Agent de la Grande-Bretagne, acceptées par l'Agent des Etats-Unis, qui en admet l'exactitude, et soumises à l'examen du Tribunal d'Arbitrage.

« 1. Que les diverses visites et saisies de marchandises et les diverses arrestations de patrons et d'équipages, mentionnées dans l'Annexe au Mémoire Britannique (pages 1 à 60 inclusivement) ont été faites par autorité du Gouvernement des Etats-Unis ; les questions se rapportant à la valeur des dits navires ou de leur contenu, ensemble ou séparément, et la question de savoir si les navires désignés dans l'Annexe au Mémoire Britannique, ou certains d'entre eux, étaient en totalité ou en partie, la propriété de citoyens des Etats-Unis, ont été retirées et n'ont pas été l'objet de l'examen du Tribunal, sous cette réserve que les Etats-Unis gardent le droit de soulever ces questions ou quelqu'une entre elles, s'ils le jugent à propos dans toute négociation ultérieure pouvant engager la responsabilité du Gouvernement des Etats-Unis, en ce qui touche le payement des sommes mentionnées dans l'Annexe au Mémoire Britannique.

« 2. Que les susdites saisies, sauf en ce qui concerne le « Pathfinder » saisi à Neah Bay, ont été effectuées dans la mer de Behring aux distances de côte mentionnées au tableau ci-annexé sous la lettre (C).

« 3. Que les dites visites et saisies de navires ont été faites par des navires armés pour le service public des Etats-Unis, dont les Commandants avaient reçu, toutes les fois qu'elles ont eu lieu du Pouvoir Exécutif du Gouvernement, des instructions dont un exemplaire est reproduit en copie ci-après, Annexe (A), les autres exemplaires des dites instructions étant conformes à ce modèle sur les points essentiels ; que, dans toutes les occasions où des poursuites entamées devant les Cours de District des Etats-Unis ont été suivies de condamnations, ces poursuites ont débuté par le dépôt d'un acte d'accusation, dont un modèle est annexé ci-dessous, Annexe (B), les actes d'accusation déposés dans les autres procédures étant, en tous points essentiels, semblable à ce modèle ; que les actes ou délits allégués comme motifs de ces visites et saisies, ont été accomplis ou commis dans la mer de Behring, aux distances

de la côte déjà indiquées ; que dans tous les cas, où une condamnation a été prononcée, exceptés ceux où les navires ont été relâchés après condamnation, la saisie a été approuvée par le Gouvernement des Etats-Unis, et que dans les cas où les navires ont été relâchés, la saisie avait été opérée par autorité du Gouvernement des Etats-Unis ; que les amendes et emprisonnements ont été prononcés à raison d'infractions aux lois nationales des Etats-Unis, infractions toutes commises dans la mer de Behring, aux distances de la côte déjà indiquée.

« 4. Que les différents ordres mentionnés dans l'annexe ci-jointe sous la lettre (C) enjoignant à certains navires de quitter la mer de Behring, ou de ne pas y entrer, ont été donnés par des navires armés pour le service public des Etats-Unis, dont les commandants avaient toutes les fois qu'ils ont donné ces ordres, des instructions conformes à celles mentionnées ci-dessus sous le n° 3, et que les navires qui ont reçu ces injonctions étaient occupés à la chasse ou faisaient route pour entreprendre cette chasse ; et que cette façon de procéder a été sanctionnée par le Gouvernement des Etats-Unis.

« 5. Que les Cours de district des Etats-Unis, devant lesquelles des poursuites ont été entamées ou suivies pour obtenir des condamnations contre les navires saisis dont il est fait mention dans l'Annexe au Mémoire de la Grande-Bretagne (pages 1 à 60 inclusivement), avaient tous droits de juridiction et pouvoirs appartenant aux Cours d'Amirauté, y compris la juridiction de Tribunaux de Prises, mais que, dans chaque cas particulier, la sentence prononcée par la Cour s'appuyait sur les causes mentionnées dans l'acte d'accusation.

ANNEXE A.

(Traduction.)

« Département du Trésor, Cabinet du Secrétaire.

« Washington, 21 avril 1886.

« Monsieur, comme suite à une lettre du Département, en date de ce jour, vous enjoignant à vous diriger avec le vapeur du service des douanes « Bear » placé sous votre commandement, vers les îles aux phoques, vous êtes par les présentes investi de tous les pouvoirs nécessaires pour assurer l'exécution de la Loi dont les termes sont contenus dans la Section 1956 des Statuts Revisés des Etats-Unis, et ordre vous est donné de saisir tout navire et d'arrêter et livrer aux autorités compétentes tout individu ou toutes personnes que vous trouveriez agissant en violation de la Loi susmentionnée, après qu'un avertissement suffisant leur aura été donné.

« Vous saisirez également tous spiritueux et armes à feu que l'on chercherait à introduire dans le pays sans une permission en règle, en exécution de la Section 1955 des Statuts Revisés et de la Proclamation du Président en date du 4 février 1870.

.(signé) C. S. Fairchild — Sre. par intérim.

« Au Capitaine M. A. Healy. Commandant le vapeur du service des Douanes « Bear » à San Francisco (Californie). »

ANNEXE B.

(Traduction.)

« Devant la Cour de district des Etats-Unis pour le District d'Alaska. Session (Special Term) d'août 1886.

« A l'Honorable Lafayette Dawson, Juge de la dite Cour de district.

« Le réquisitoire à la fin d'information par lequel M. D. Ball, Attorney des Etats-Unis pour le District d'Alaska, poursuivant au nom des Etats-Unis et présent ici devant la Cour, en sa personne, comme Représentant des Etats-Unis et en leur nom, contre la goëlette Thornton, ses agrès, apparaux, embarcations, cargaison et matériel, et contre toutes personnes intervenant comme ayant des intérêts engagés dans ce navire, en poursuite à fin de confiscation, présente les allégations et déclarations suivantes:

« Que Charles A. Abbey, officier du service des Douanes maritimes des Etats-Unis, chargé d'une mission spéciale dans les eaux du District d'Alaska, antérieurement au présent jour, à savoir le 1ᵉʳ août 1886, dans les limites du territoire d'Alaska, à savoir dans l'étendue des cours de cette partie de la mer de Behring qui appartient au dit district, dans les eaux navigables pour des navires venant de la haute mer et jaugeant 10 tonneaux ou au-dessus, a saisi le vaisseau ou navire communément dénommé goélette, le « Thornton », ses agrès, apparaux, embarcation, cargaison et matériel lesquels étaient la propriété d'une ou de plusieurs personnes inconnues du dit attorney et les a confisqués au profit des Etats-Unis pour les causes ci-après:

« Que le dit navire ou goëlette a été trouvé se livrant à la destruction des phoques à fourrure, dans les limites du territoire d'Alaska et de ses eaux, en violation des dispositions de la Section 1956 des Statuts Revisés des Etats-Unis.

« Et le dit attorney déclare que toutes les propositions ci-dessus énoncées et chacune d'elles sont et étaient vraies, et qu'elles tombent sous la juridiction maritime et d'amirauté de cette Cour,

et que pour cette raison, et en exécution des Statuts des Etats-Unis établis et édictés pour de tels cas, le navire ou la goëlette mentionnée et décrite ci-dessus jaugeant plus de 20 tonneaux, ses agrès, apparaux, embarcations, cargaison et matériel ont été et sont confisqués au profit des Etats-Unis, et que la dite goëlette se trouve maintenant dans le district susdit.

« Ce pourquoi le dit attorney demande que l'honorable Cour de justice procède et avise comme d'usage en cette affaire et que toutes personnes ayant un intérêt dans la dite goëlette ou navire soient citées par voie d'assignation géné-. rale ou spéciale, afin de répondre aux propositions susénoncées, et que, à la suite de la procédure à ce nécessaire, le dit navire ou goëlette, ses agrès, apparaux, embarcations, cargaison et matériel soient condamnés pour la dite cause ou tout autre qu'il apparaîtrait juste, par arrêt formel et décret de cette honorable Cour et confisqués au profit des dits Etats-Unis, selon la forme des Statuts des dits Etats-Unis, établis et édictés pour de tels cas.

(Signé) M. D. Ball,

« Attorney des Etats-Unis pour le district d'Alaska. »

ANNEXE C.

« La table ci-dessous contient les noms des navires Britanniques employés à la chasse des phoques qui ont été saisis ou avertis par les croiseurs du Service des Douanes des Etats-Unis, de 1886 à 1890 et la distance approximative de la terre où ces saisies ont eu lieu. Ces distances sont indiquées, en ce qui concerne les navires « Carolena », « Thornton » et « Onward » d'après le témoignage du Commandant Abbey de la marine des Etats-Unis (voir 50ᵉ Congrès, 2ᵉ session Sénat, Documents exécutifs, n° 106, pp. 20, 30 et 40). Elles sont indiquées en ce qui concerne les navires « Anna Beck », « W. P. Sayward », « Dolphin » et « Grace », d'après le témoignage du Capitaine Shepard, de la Marine du Trésor des Etats-Unis (Livre Bleu, Etats-Unis, n° 2, 1890, pp. 80—82. Voir « Appendice au Mémoire Britannique », vol. 111.) [1]»

Et attendu que le Gouvernement de Sa Majesté Britannique a demandé à nous, Arbitres susnommés, de décider sur les dites questions de fait telles qu'elles résultent de l'exposé susmentionné; que l'Agent et les Conseils du Gouvernement des Etats-Unis ont, en notre présence et s'adressant à nous, déclaré que le dit exposé des faits était confirmé par les dépositions des témoins, et qu'ils

---

[1] La table dont il est question dans cette annexe se trouve reproduite à la page suivante.

Nom du navire	Date de la saisie	Distance approximative de terre au moment de la saisie	Navire des Etats Unis qui a fait la saisie
Carolena	1ᵉʳ aout 1886	75 milles	Corwin
Thornton	1ᵉʳ » 1886	70 milles	Idem
Onward	2 » 1886	115 milles	Idem
Favourite	2 » 1886	Averti par le Corwin à peu près dans la même position que l'Onward	—
Anna Beck	2 juillet 1887	66 milles	Rush
W. P. Sayward . . .	9 » 1887	59 milles	Idem
Dolphin	12 » 1887	40 milles	Idem
Grace	17 » 1887	96 milles	Idem
Alfred Adams . . .	10 août 1887	62 milles	Idem
Ada	25 » 1887	15 milles	Idem
Triumph	4 » 1887	Averti par le Rush de ne pas entrer dans la mer de Behring	Idem
Juanita.	31 juillet 1889	66 milles	Idem
Pathfinder.	29 » 1889	50 milles	Idem
Triumph	11 » 1889	Averti par le Rush d'avoir à quitter la mer de Behring. Position au moment de l'avertissement?	—
Black Diamond . . .	11 juillet 1889	35 milles	Idem
Lily	6 août 1889	65 milles	Idem
Ariel	30 juillet 1889	Averti par le Rush d'avoir à quitter la mer de Behring	—
Kate	13 août 1889	Idem	—
Minnie.	15 juillet 1889	66 milles	Idem
Pathfinder.	27 mars 1890	Saisie dans la Baie de Neah	Corwin

s'étaient mis d'accord avec l'Agent et les Conseils de Sa Majesté Britannique pour s'en remettre à nous Arbitres de dire et prononcer, véritable, en tant que nous le jugerions à propos, le dit exposé des faits.

Nous, Arbitres susnommés, disons et prononçons à l'unanimité que les dits faits tels qu'ils se trouvent dans le dit exposé sont véritables.

Et attendu que toutes et chacune des questions qui ont été examinées par le Tribunal ont été décidées à la majorité absolue des voix.

Nous, le Baron de Courcel, Lord Hannen, le Juge Harlan, Sir John Thompson, le Sénateur Morgan, le Marquis Visconti Venosta et M. Gregors Gram, étant entendu que les arbitres qui se sont trouvés en minorité sur certaines questions, ne retirent pas leur votes, déclarons que le présent acte contient la décision finale et la sentence écrite du Tribunal, conformément aux prescriptions du Traité.

Fait en double à Paris, et signé par nous, le 15ᵉ jour d'août de l'année 1893 [1].

[1] *Parliamentary Paper*, c-7107.

Proclamation of April 9, 1894, giving effect to the award rendered by the Tribunal of Arbitration at Paris, under the treaty between the United States and Great Britain, concluded at Washington, February 29, 1892.

Whereas an Act of Congress entitled 'An Act to give effect to the award rendered by the Tribunal of Arbitration at Paris, under the treaty between the United States and Great Britain, concluded at Washington, February 29, 1892, for the purpose of submitting to arbitration certain questions concerning the preservation of the furseals' was approved April 6, 1894, and reads as follows:

Whereas the following articles of the award of the Tribunal of Arbitration constituted under the treaty concluded at Washington the twenty-ninth of February, eighteen hundred and ninety-two, between the United States and Her Majesty the Queen of the United Kingdom of Great Britain and Ireland were delivered to the agents of the respective Governments on the fifteenth day of August, eighteen hundred and ninety three:

ARTICLE I. The Governments of the United States and Great Bretain shall forbid their citizens and subjects respectively to kill, capture or pursue at any time and in any manner whatever, the animas commonly called fur-seals within a zone of sixty miles around the Pribilow Islands, inclusive of the territorial waters.

The miles mentioned in the preceding paragraph are geographical miles, of sixty two a degree of latitude.

ARTICLE II. The two Governments shall forbid their citizens and subjects respectively to. kill, capture or pursue, in any manner whatever, during the season extending, each year, from the first of May to the thirty first of July, both inclusive, the furseals on the high Sea, in the part of the Pacific Ocean, inclusive of the Behring Sea, which is situated to the north of the thirty-fifth degree of north latitude, and eastward of the one hundred and eightieth degree of longitude from Greenwich till it strikes the water boundary described in Article 1 of the treaty of eighteen hundred and sixty-seven between the United States and Russia, and following that line up to Behring's Straits.

ARTICLE III. During the period of time and in the waters in which the fur-seal fishing is allowed, only sailing vessels shall be permitted to carry on or take part in fur-seal fishing operations. They will however be at liberty to avail themselves of the use of such canoes or undecked boats, propelled by paddles, oars, or sails, as are in common use as fishing boats.

ARTICLE IV. Each sailing vessel authorized to fish for fur-seals must be provided with a special licence issued for that purpose by its Governments, and shall be required to carry a distinguishing flag to be prescribed by its Government.

ARTICLE V. The masters of the vessels engaged in fur-seal fishing shall enter accurately in their official log book the date and place of each fur-seal fishing operation and also the number and sex of the seals captured upon each day. These entries shall be communicated by each of the two Governments to the other at the end of each fishing season.

ARTICLE VI. The use of nets, firearms and explosives shall be forbidden in the fur-seal fishing. This restriction shall not apply to shotguns when such fishing takes place outside of Behring Sea, during the season when it may be lawfully carried on.

ARTICLE VII. The two Governments shall take measures to control the fitness of the men authorized to engage in fur-seal fishing; these men shall have been proved fit to handle with sufficient skill the weapons by means of which this fishing may be carried on.

ARTICLE VIII. The regulations contained in the preceding articles shall not apply to Indians dwelling on the coast of the territory of the United States or of Great Britain, and carrying on fur-seal fishing in canoes or undecked boats not transported by or used in connection with other vessels and propelled wholly by paddles, oars or sails and manned by not more than five persons each in the way hitherto practiced by the Indians, provided such Indians are not in the employment of other persons and provided that, when so hunting in canoes or undecked boats, they shall not hunt fur-seals outside of territorial waters under contract for the delivery of the skins to any person.

This exemption shall not be construed to affect the municipal law of either country, nor shall it extend to the waters of Behring Sea or the waters of the Aleutian Passes.

Nothing herein contained is intended to interfere with the employment of Indians as hunters or otherwise in connection with fur-sealing vessels as heretofore.

ARTICLE IX. The concurrent regulations hereby determined with a view to the protection and preservation of the fur-seals, shall remain in force until they have been, in whole or in part, abolished or modified by common agreement between the Governments of the United States and of Great Britain.

The said concurrent regulations shall be submitted every five years to a new examination, so as to enable both interested governments to consider whether, in the light of past experience, there is occasion for any modification thereof.

Now therefore be it enacted by the Senate and House of Representatives of the United States of America in Congress assembled:

Sec. 1. That no citizen of the United States, or person owing the duty of obedience to the law or the treaties of the United States nor any person belonging to or on board of a vessel of the United States, shall kill, capture, or pursue, at any time, or in manner whatever, outside of territorial waters, any fur-seal in. the waters surrounding the Pribilov Islands within a zone of sixty geographical miles (sixty to a degree of latitude) around said Islands, exclusive of the territorial waters.

Sec. 2. That no citizen of the United States, or person above described in Section I of this Act, nor any person belonging to or on board of a vessel of the United States shall kill, capture, or pursue, in any manner whatever, during the season extending from the first day of May to the thirty-first day of July, both inclusive, in each year, any fur-seal on the high seas outside of the zone mentioned in section one, and in that part of the Pacific Ocean, including Behring Sea, which is situated to the north of the thirty fifth degree of north latitude and to the east of the one hundred and eightieth degree of longitude from Greenwich till it strikes the water boundary described in article one of the treaty of eighteen hundred and sixty seven. between the United States and Russia, and following that line up to Behring Straits.

Sec. 3. No citizen of the United States or person above described, in the first section of this Act, shall, during the period and in the waters in which by section two of this Act the killing of fur-seals is not prohibited, use or employ any vessel, nor shall any vessel of the United States be used or employed, in carrying on or taking part in fur-seal fishing operations, other than a sailing vessel propelled by sails exclusively, and such canoes or undecked boats, propelled by paddles, oars or sails as may belong to, and be used in connection with such sailing vessels; nor shall any sailing vessel carry on or take part in such operations without a special license obtained from the government for that purpose, and without carrying a distinctive flag prescribed by the Government for the same purpose.

Sec. 4. That every master of a vessel licensed under this act to engage in fur-seal fishing operations shall accurately enter in his official log book the date and place of every such operation, and also the number and sex of the seal captured each day, and on coming into port, and before landing cargo, the master shall verify, on oath, such official log book as containing a full and true statement of the number and character of his fur-seal fishing operations, including the number and sex of seals captured; and for any false statement willfully made by a person so licensed by the United States in this behalf he shall be subject to the penalties of perjury; and any seal skins found in excess of the statement in the official log book shall be forfeited to the United States.

Sec. 5. That no person or vessel engaging in fur-seal fishing operation under this Act shall use or employ in such operations, any net, firearm, airgun or explosive: Provided however, that this prohibition shall not apply to the use of shotguns in such operations outside of Behring Sea during the season when the killing of fur-seals is not there prohibited by this Act.

Sec. 6. That the foregoing sections of this Act shall not apply to Indians dwelling on the coast of the United States and taking fur-seals in canoes or undecked boats propelled wholly by paddles, oars, or sails and net transported by or used in connection with other vessels, or manned by more than five persons, in the manner heretofore practiced by the said Indians; provided however, that the exception made in this section shall not apply to Indians in the employment of other persons, or who shall kill, capture, or pursue fur-seals outside of territorial waters under contract to deliver the skins to other persons, nor to the waters of Behring Sea or of the passes between the Aleutian Islands.

Sec. 7. That the President shall have power to make regulations respecting to special license and the distinctive flag mentioned in this Act and regulations otherwise suitable to secure the due execution of the provisions of this act, and from time to time to add to, modify, amend, or revoke such regulations as in his judgement may seem expedient.

Sec. 8. That, except in the case of a master making a false statement under oath in violation of the provisions of the fourth section of this Act, every person guilty of a violation of the provisions of this Act, or of the regulations made thereunder, shall for each offense be fined not less than two hundred dollars, or imprisoned not more than six months, or both; and all vessels, their tackle, apparel, furniture and cargo, at any time used or employed in violation of this Act, or of the regulations made thereunder, shall be forfeited to the United States.

Sec. 9. That any violation of this Act, or of the regulations made thereunder, may be prosecuted either in the district court of Alaska or in any district court of the United States in California, Oregon or Washington.

Sec. 10. That if any unlicensed vessel of the United States be found within the waters to which this Act applies and at a time when the killing of fur-seals is by this Act there prohibited, having on board seal skins or bodies of seals, or apparatus or implements suitable for killing or taking seals; or if any licensed vessel shall be found in the waters to which this Act applies, having on board apparatus or implements suitable for taking seals, but forbidden then and there to be used, it shall be presumed that the vessel in the one case and the apparatus or implements in the other was or were used in violation of this Act until it is otherwise sufficiently proved.

Sec. 11. That it shall be the duty of the President to cause a sufficient naval force to cruise in the waters to which this Act is applicable to enforce its provisions, and it shall be the duty of the commanding officer of any vessel belonging to the naval or revenue service of the United States, when so instructed by the President, to seize and arrest all vessels of the United States found by him to be engaged, used, or employed in the waters last aforesaid in violation of any of the prohibitions of this Act, or of any regulations made thereunder, and to take the same with all persons on board thereof, to the most convenient port in any district of the United States mentioned in this Act, there to be dealt with according to law.

Sec. 12. That any vessel or citizen of the United States, or person described in the first section of this Act, offending against the prohibitions of this Act or the regulations thereunder, may be seized and detained by the naval or other duly commissioned officers of Her Majesty the Queen of Great Britain, but when so seized and detained they shall be delivered as soon as practicable with any witnesses and proofs on board, to any naval or revenue officer or other authorities of the United States whose courts alone shall have jurisdiction to try the offense and impose the penalties for the same: Provided, however, that British officers shall arrest and detain vessels and persons as in this section specified only after, by appropriate legislation, Great Britain shall have authorized officers of the United States duly commissioned and instructed by the President to that end to arrest, detain and deliver to the authorities of Great Britain vessels and subjects of that Government offending against any statutes or regulations of Great Britain enacted or made to enforce the award of the treaty mentioned in the title of this Act.

Now, therefore, be it known that I, Grover Cleveland, President of the United States of America, have caused the said Act specially to be proclaimed to the end that its provisions may be known and observed; and I hereby proclaim that every person guilty of a violation of the provisions of said Act will be arrested and punished as therein provided; and all vessels so employed their tackle, apparel, furniture and cargo will be seized and forfeited.

In testimony whereof, I have hereunto set my hand and caused the seal of the United States to be affixed.

Done at the City of Washington this 9th day of April in the year of our Lord one thousand eight hundred and ninety-four, and of the Independence of the United States the one hundred and eighteenth. [1]

Act of Parliament, to provide for carrying into effect the Award of the Tribunal of Arbitration constituted under a Treaty between Her Majesty the Queen and the United States of America.

Whereas by a Treaty between Her Majesty the Queen and the Government of the United States of America various questions which had arisen respecting the taking and preservation of the fur-seals in the North Pacific were referred to Arbitrators as mentioned in the Treaty:

And whereas the award of such Arbitrators (in this Act referred to as the Behring Sea Arbitration award) dated the 15th day of August, 1893, contained the provisions set out in the first schedule to this Act; and it is expedient to provide for carrying the same into effect.

Be it therefore enacted, by the Queen's Most Excellent Majesty, by and with the advice and consent of the Lords Spiritual and Temporal, and Commons, in this present Parliamentary assembled, and by the authority of the same as follows:

1. (1). The provisions of the Behring Sea Arbitration Award set out in the First Schedule to this Act shall have effect as if those provisions (in this Act referred to as the scheduled provisions) were enacted by this Act; and the Acts directed by Articles 1 and 2 thereof to be forbidden were expressly forbidden by this Act.

(2). If there is any contravention of this Act, any person committing, procuring, aiding, or abetting such contravention shall be guilty of a misdemeanour within the meaning of the Merchant Shipping Act, 1854, and the ship employed in such contravention and her equipment and everything on board thereof, shall be liable to be forfeited to Her Majesty as if an offence had been committed under Section 103 of the said Act; Provided that the Court, without prejudice to any other power may release the ship, equipment, or thing, on payment of a fine not exceeding 500 l.

(3). The provisions of the Merchant Shipping Act, of 1854, with respect to official logs (including the penal provisions) shall apply to every vessel engaged in fur seal fishing.

(4). Every person who forges or fraudulently alters any licence or other document issued for the purpose of Article 4 or of Article 7 in the

[1] F. DE MARTENS, *Nouveau Recueil Général*, 2ᵉ série, t. XXII, p. 557.

First Schedule to this Act, or who procures any such licence or document to be forged or fraudulently altered, or who knowing any such licence or document to be forged or fraudulently altered uses the same, or who aids in forging or fraudulently altering any such licence or document, shall be guilty of a misdemeanour within the meaning of the Merchant Shipping Act, 1854.

(5). Subject to this Act, the provisions of Sections 103 and 104 and Part 10 of the Merchant Shipping Act, 1854, and of Section 34 of the Merchant Shipping Act, 1876, which are set out in the Second Schedule to this Act, shall apply as if they were herein re-enacted, and in terms made applicable to an offence and forfeiture under this Act; and any commissioned officer on full pay in the naval service of Her Majesty the Queen may seize the ship's certificate of registry.

2. (1). Where an officer seizes, under this Act, a ship's certificate of registry, he shall either retain the certificate and give a provisional certificate in lieu thereof, or return the certificate with an indorsement of the grounds on which it was seized, and in either case shall direct the ship, by an addition to the provisional certificate or to the indorsement, to proceed forthwith to a specified port, being a port where there is a British Court having authority to adjudicate in the matter, and if this direction is not complied with, the owner and master of the ship shall, without prejudice to any other liability, each be liable to a fine not exceeding 100 l.

(2). Where in pursuance of this section a provisional certificate is given to a ship, or the ship's cirtificate is indorsed, any Officer of Customs in Her Majesty's dominions or British Consular Officer may detain the ship until satisfactory security is given for her appearance in any legal proceedings which may be taken against her in pursuance of this Act.

3. (1). Her Majesty the Queen in Council may make revoke, and alter Orders for carrying into effect the scheduled provisions, and this Act, and every such Order shall be forthwith laid before both Houses or Parliament and published in the « London Gazette », and shall have effect as if enacted in this Act.

(2). If there is any contravention of any regulation made by any such Order, any person committing, procuring aiding, or abetting such contravention shall be liable to a penalty not exceeding 100 l.

(3). An Order in Council under this Act may provide that such officers of the United States

of America as are specified in the Order may, in respect of offences under this Act, exercise the like Powers under this Act as may be exercised by a commissioned officer of Her Majesty in relation to a British ship, and the equipment and certificate thereof, or such of those powers as appear to Her Majesty in Council to be exerciseable under the law of the United States of America against ships of the United States ; and that such British officers as are specified in the Order may exercise the powers conferred by this Act, with any necessary modifications specified in the Order, in relation to a ship of the United States of America, and the equipment and certificate thereof.

4. (1). Where any offence under this Act has been committed by some person belonging to a ship, or by means of a ship, or the equipment of a ship, the master of the ship shall be deemed guilty of such offence, and the ship and her equipment shall be liable to forfeiture under this Act.

(2). Provided that if it is proved that the master issued proper-orders for the observance, and used due diligence to enforce the observance of this Act, and the regulations in force thereunder, and that the offence in question was actually committed by some other person without his connivance, and that the actual offender has been convicted, or that he has taken all proper means in his power to prosecute such offender, if alive, to conviction, the master of the ship shall not be liable to any penalty or forfeiture other than such sum as will prevent any profit accruing by reason of the offence to the master or crew or owner of the ship.

5. The expression « equipment » in this act includes any boat, tackle, fishing, or shooting instruments and other things belonging to a ship.

6. This act may be cited as « The Behring Sea Award Act 1894 ».

7. (1). This Act shall come into operation on the 1ˢᵗ day of May, 1894, provided that Her Majesty in Council, if at any time it appears expedient so to do, having regard to the circumstances which have then arisen in relation to the scheduled provisions or to the enforcement thereof may suspend the operation of this Act or any part thereof during the period mentioned in the Order, and the same shall be suspended accordingly.

(2). Where on any proceeding in any Court against a person or ship in respect of any offence under this Act it is proved that the ship sailed from its port of departure before the provisions of the award mentioned in the First Schedule to this Act were known there, and that such person or the master of the ship did not, after such sailing and before the alleged offence, become aware of those provisions, such person shall be acquitted, and the ship shall be released and not forfeited.

8. This Act shall remain in force so long as the scheduled provisions remain in force and no longer; Provided that if by agreement between Her Majesty the Queen and the Government of the United States of America, the scheduled provisions are modified then Her Majesty in Council may order that this Act shall, subject to any modifications specified in the order, apply, and the same shall accordingly apply, to the modified provisions in like manner as if they were set out in the First Schedule to this Act [1].

CIX. Grande-Bretagne, Etats-Unis d'Amérique.

5 juin 1854.

Cet arbitrage a eu pour objet de fixer exactement les parties des côtes appartenant aux deux pays et réservées aux pêcheurs nationaux. La commission arbitrale réunie en 1855 ne termina ses travaux, interrompus à diverses reprises, qu'en 1866. Lors du traité du 8 mai 1871, il fut formellement stipulé, par l'article 20, que les décisions de la commission susdite conserveraient leur pleine autorité.

Treaty extending the right of fishing, signed at Washington, June 5, 1854.

The Government of the United States being equally desirous with Her Majesty the Queen of Great Britain to avoid further misunderstanding between their respective citizens and subjects in regard to the extent of the right of fishing on the coasts of British North America, secured to each by Article I of a convention between the United States and Great Britain signed at London on the 20th day of October 1818; and being also desirous to regulate the commerce and navigation between their respective territories and people, and more especially between Her Majesty's possessions in North America and the United States, in such manner as to render the same reciprocally beneficial and satisfactory, have, respectively, named Plenipotentiaries to confer and agree thereupon, that is to say:

The President of the United States of America, William M. Marcy, Secretary of State of the

[1] HERTSLET. A complete collection ...., t. XIX, p. 925.

United States, and Her Majesty the Queen of the United Kingdom of Great Britain and Ireland, James, Earl of Elgin and Kincardine, Lord Bruce and Elgin, a peer of the United Kingdom, Knight of the most ancient and most noble Order of the Thistle and Governor General in and over all Her Britannic Majesty's provinces on the continent of North America, and in and over the Island of Prince Edward;

Who, after having communicated to each other their respective full powers, found in good and due form, have agreed upon the following articles:

ARTICLE I. It is agreed by the high contracting parties that in addition to the liberty secured to the United States fishermen by the abovementioned convention of October 20, 1818, of taking, curing, and drying fish on certain coasts of the British North American Colonies therein defined, the inhabitants of the United States shall have, in common with the subjects of Her Britannic Majesty, the liberty to take fish of every kind, except shell-fish, on the sea-coasts and shores, and in the bays, harbors, and creeks of Canada, New-Brunswick, Nova Scotia, Prince Edward's Island, and of the several islands thereunto adjacent, without being restricted to any distance from the shore, with permission to land upon the coasts and shores of those colonies and the islands thereof, and also upon the Magdalen Islands, for the purpose of drying their nets and curing their fish; provided that, in so doing, they do not interfere with the rights of private property, or with British fishermen, in the peaceable use of any part of the said coast in their occupancy for the same purpose.

It is understood that the above-mentioned liberty applies solely to the sea fishery, and that the salmon and shad fisheries, and all fisheries in rivers and the mouths of rivers, are hereby reserved exclusively for British fishermen.

And it is further agreed that, in order to prevent or settle any disputes as to the places to which the reservation of exclusive right to British fishermen contained in this article, and that of fishermen of the United States contained in the next succeeding article, apply, each of the high contracting parties, on the application of either to the other, shall, within six months thereafter, appoint a Commissioner. The said Commissioners, before proceeding to any business, shall make and subscribe a solemn declaration that they will impartially and carefully examine and decide, to the best of their judgment, and according to justice and equity, without fear, favor, or affection to their own country, upon all such places as are intended to be reserved and excluded from the common liberty of fishing under this and the next succeeding article, and such declaration shall be entered on the record of their proceedings.

The Commissioners shall name some third person to act as an Arbitrator or Umpire in any case or cases on which they may themselves differ in opinion. If they should not be able to agree upon the name of such third person, they shall each name a person and it shall be determined by lot which of the two persons so named shall be the Arbitrator or Umpire in cases of difference or disagreement between the Commissioners. The person so to be chosen to be Arbitrator or Umpire shall, before proceeding to act as such in any case, make and subscribe a solemn declaration in a form similar to that which shall already have been made and subscribed by the Commissioners, which shall be entered on the record of their proceedings.

In the event of the death, absence, or incapacity of either of the Commissioners, or of the Arbitrator or Umpire, or of their or his omitting, declining, or ceasing to act as such Commissioner, Arbitrator, or Umpire, in the place and stead of the person so originally appointed or named as aforesaid, and shall make and subscribe such declaration as aforesaid.

Such Commissioners shall proceed to examine the coasts of the North American provinces and of the United States, embraced within the provisions of the first and second articles of this treaty, and shall designate the places reserved by the said articles from the common right of fishing therein.

The decision of the Commissioners and of the Arbitrator or Umpire shall be given in writing in each case, and shall be signed by them respectively. The high contracting parties hereby solemnly engage to consider the decision of the Commissioners conjointly or of the Arbitrator or Umpire, as the case may be, as absolutely final and conclusive in each case decided upon by them or him respectively.

ARTICLE II. It is agreed by the high contracting parties that British subjects shall have, in common with the citizens of the United States, the liberty to take fish of every kind, except shell-fish, on the eastern sea coasts and shores of the United States north of the 36th parallel of north latitude, and on the shores of the several islands thereunto adjacent, and in the bays, harbors, and creeks of the said sea coast and shores of the United States and of the said islands, without being restricted to any distance from the shore, with permission to land upon the said coasts of the United States and of the

islands aforesaid, for the purpose of drying their nets and curing their fish:

Provided, that in so doing, they do not interfere with the rights of private property, or with the fishermen of the United States, in the peaceable use of any part of the said coasts in their occupancy for the same purpose.

It is understood that the above-mentioned liberty applies solely to the sea fishery and that salmon and shad fisheries in rivers and mouths of rivers, are hereby reserved exclusively for fishermen of the United States.

. . . .

ARTICLE VII. The present treaty shall be duly ratified, and the mutual exchange of ratifications shall take place in Washington within six months from the date hereof, or earlier if possible.

In faith whereof we, the respective Plenipotentiaries, have signed this treaty and have hereunto affixed our seals.

Done in triplicate, at Washington, the fifth day of June, anno Domini one thousand eight hundred and fiftyfour[1].

Les commissaires prononcèrent cinquante-six sentences presque toutes identiques. Seule la sentence du surarbitre a examiné les questions litigieuses en la cause.

Award of the umpire dated at Sanct John, New Brunswick, April 8, 1858.

By the third Article of the Treaty of 1783 between Great Britain and the United States it was stipulated, 'That the people of the United States should continue to enjoy unmolested the right to take fish of every kind in the Grand Bank, and on all the other Banks of Newfoundland; also in the Gulph of Saint Lawrence, and at all other places in the sea where the inhabitants of both countries used at any time theretofore to fish. That the inhabitants of the United States shall have liberty to take fish of every kind on such part of the coast of Newfoundland as British fishery shall use (but not to cure or dry them on the island) and also on the coasts, bays and creeks of all His Majesty's dominions in America. And that the American fishermen shall have liberty to dry and cure fish in any of the unsettled bays, harbours and creeks in Nova Scotia, Magdalen Islands and Labrador, so long as the same shall remain unsettled: but so soon as the same or either of them shall be settled, it shall not be lawful for the said fishermen to dry or

---

[1] *Treaties and Conventions . . .*, 1889, p. 448.

cure fish at such settlement, without a previous agreement for that purpose, with the inhabitants, proprietors, or possessors of the ground.' The War of 1814 between Great Britain and the United States, was held by the former to have abrogated this stipulation, and the declaration of peace, and Treaty of Ghent, which subsequently followed, were entirely silent on the point. This silence was intentional — during the negotiations the question had been expressly raised — and the claim of the United States to the continued enjoyment of the rights secured by that stipulation denied. By the Convention of the 20th October 1818, the privilege of the Fisheries within certain limits was again conceded to the United States — and the United States by that Convention 'renounced any liberty before enjoyed or claimed by them, or their inhabitants, to take, dry or cure fish, on or within three marine miles of any of the coasts, bays, creeks, or harbours of any of the British dominions of America, not included within that part of the Southern Coast of Newfoundland extending from Cape Ray to the Rameau Islands; on the Western and Northern Coast of Newfoundland, from Cape Ray to the Quirpon Islands — on the shores of the Magdalen Islands — and also on the coasts, bays, harbours, and creeks, from Mount Jolly on the South of Labrador, to and through the Straits of Bellisle, and thence Northerly along the Coast'. This concession was to be without prejudice to any of the exclusive rights of the Hudson Bay Company, and the American Fishermen were also to have the liberty, forever, to dry and cure fish in any of the unsettled bays, harbours, and creeks of the Southern part of the Coast of Newfoundland therein described, and of the Coast of Labrador, but so soon as the same or any portion thereof should be settled, it should not be lawful for the said Fishermen to dry or cure fish at such portion so settled without previous agreement for such purpose with the inhabitants, proprietors or possessors of the ground; and was further subject to a proviso, that the American Fishermen should be permitted to enter the bays and harbours in His Britannic Majesty's dominions in America, not included within those limits, for purpose of shelter, and of repairing damages therein, of purchasing wood and obtaining water, and for no other purpose whatever.

But they should be under such restrictions as might be necessary to prevent their taking, drying or curing fish therein, or in any other manner whatever abusing the privileges thereby reserved to them.

A difference arose between the two countries, Great Britain contending that the prescribed limits 'of three marine miles', the line of exclusion should be measured from headland to headland, while the United States Government contended it should be measured from the interior of the bays and the sinuosities of the coasts.

The mutual enforcement of these positions led to further misunderstandings between the two countries.

To do away with the causes of these misunderstandings, and to remove all grounds of future embroilment, by the treaty of Washington, June 5th, 1854, it was by Article 1st agreed: 'That in addition to the liberty secured to the United States Fishermen by the above-mentioned Convention of October 20th, 1818, of taking, curing and drying fish on certain coasts of the British North American Colonies therein defined, the inhabitants of the United States shall have, in common with the subjects of Her Britannic Majesty, the liberty to take fish of every kind (except shell fish) on the sea coasts and shores, and in the bays, harbours and creeks of Canada, New Brunswick, Nova Scotia, Prince Edward Island, and of the several Islands thereunto adjacent, without being restricted to any distance from the shore, with permission to land upon the coasts and shores of those Colonies, and the Islands thereof, and also upon the Magdalen Islands, for the purpose of drying their nets and curing their fish; provided that in so doing, they do not interfere with the rights of private property, or with British Fishermen in the peaceable use of any parts of the said Coast, in their occupancy for the same purpose.

'It is understood that the above-mentioned liberty applies solely to the Sea Fishery, and that the Salmon and Shad Fisheries, and all Fisheries in Rivers, and the mouths of Rivers, are hereby reserved exclusively for British Fishermen'.

By Article the 2nd: —

'It is agreed by the high contracting parties, that British subjects shall have, in common with the citizens of the United States, the liberty to take fish of every kind (except shell fish), on the eastern sea coasts and shores of the United States, North of the 36th parallel of North Latitude, and on the shores of the several Islands thereunto adjacent, and in the bays, harbours and creeks of the said sea coasts and shores of the said United States, and of the said Islands, without being restricted to any distance from the shore, with permission to land upon the said coasts of the United States, and of the Islands aforesaid for the purpose of drying their nets and curing their fish: provided that in so doing they do not interfere with the rights of private property, or with the fishermen of the United

States in the peaceable use of any part of the said coasts in their occupancy for the same purpose. It is understood that the above mentioned liberty applies solely to the Sea Fishery; and that the Salmon and Shad Fisheries, and all Fisheries in Rivers, and the mouths of Rivers, are hereby reserved exclusively for Fishermen of the United States'.

By the 1st Article it was also further agreed: — 'That in order to prevent or settle any dispute as to the places to which the reservation of exclusive right to British Fishermen contained in this Article, and that of Fisherman of the United States, contained in the second Article, should apply—each of the high contracting parties, on the application of either to the other, shall, within six months thereafter, appoint a Commissioner. The said Commissioners before proceeding to any business, shall make and subscribe a solemn declaration that they will impartially and carefully examine and decide to the best of their judgment, and according to justice and equity, without fear, favour, or affection to their own country, upon all such places as are intended to be reserved and excluded from the common liberty of fishing under the said two articles. In case·of disagreement, provision is made for an umpire, and the high contracting parties solemnly engage to consider the decision of the commissioners conjointly, or of the arbitrator or umpire, as the case may be, absolutely final and conclusive in each case decided upon by them, or him, respectively'.

By Article 5, the Treaty was to 'take effect as soon a sthe laws required to carry it into operation should be passed by the Imperial Parliament of Great Britain, and by the Provincial Parliaments of those British North American Colonies which are affected by this Treaty, on the one hand, and by the Congress of the United States on the other'.

It is understood that in making this last Treaty, neither Government admitted itself to have been in error, with reference to the position it had before maintained. The Treaty was emphatically an arrangement for the future: 'The Government of the United States being equally desirous with Her Majesty the Queen of Great Britain (as declared in the preamble) to avoid further misunderstanding between their respective citizens and subjects, in regard to the extent of the right of fishing on the coasts of British North America, secured to each by Article I of a Convention between the United States and Great Britain, signed at London on the 20th day of October 1818'.

The Commissioners appointed under the provisions of this Treaty, proceeded to examine and decide upon the places intended to be reserved and excluded from the common liberty of fishing under the 1st and 2nd Articles. They differed in opinion as to the places hereinafter named, and it has been submitted to me as umpire under the provisions of that Treaty, to determine those differences.

The copies of the Records of disagreement between the Commissioners, transmitted to me, are as follows:

RECORD N° 1. We, the undersigned, Commissioners respectively on the part of Great Britain and the United States, under the Reciprocity Treaty concluded and signed at Washington on the 5th day of June, A. D. 1854, having met at Halifax, in the Province of Nova Scotia, on the 17th day of August, A. D. 1855, thence proceeded to sea in the British Brigantine "Halifax" and passing through the Strait of Canso, first examined the River Buctouche, in the Province of New Brunswick.

A survey was made of the mouth of the said River Buctouche by the surveyors attached to the Commission, Geoge H. Perley, on the part of Great Britain, and Richard D. Cutts, on the part of the United States, a plan of which, marked N° 1, and signed by the Commissioners respectively, will be found in Récord Book N° 2. We, the Commissioners, are unable to agree upon a line defining the mouth of said River.

Her Majesty's Commissioner claims that a line from Glover's Point to the Southern extremity of the Sand Bar (marked in red upon the foresaid Plan N° 1) designates the mouth of the said River Buctouche; the United States Commissioner claims that a line from Chapel Point, bearing South, 4° West (magnetic), marked in blue on the aforesaid Plan N° 1, designates the mouth of said river; and of this disagreement record is here made accordingly.

Dated at Buctouche, in the Province of New Brunswick, this 19th day of September, A. D. 1856.

RECORD N° 2. We, the undersigned Commissioners respectively, on the part of Great Britain and the United States, under the reciprocity Treaty concluded and signed at Washington on the 5th day of June, A. D. 1854, having examined the river Miramichi, in the Province of New Brunswick, are unable to agree upon a line defining the mouth of said River.

Her Majesty's Commissioner claims that a line connecting Fox and Portage Islands, marked in red, Plan 2, Record Book N° 2, designates the mouth of the Miramichi River. The United States Commissioner claims, that a line from Spit Point to Moody Point, marked in blue on

Plan N° 2, Record Book N° 2, designates the mouth of said River; and of this disagreement record is here made accordingly.

Dated at Chatham, on the Miramichi, in the Province of New Brunswick, on this 27ᵗʰ day of September A. D. 1855.

RECORD N° 9. We, the undersigned, Commissioners under the Reciprocity Treaty between Great Britain and the United States, signed at Washington on the 5th day of June, A. D. 1854, having examined the Elliot River, emptying into Hillsborough Bay, on the Coast of Prince Edward Island, one of the British North American Colonies, do hereby agree and decide, that a line bearing North, 85° East (Magnetic) drawn from Block House Point, to Sea Trout Point, as shown on Plan 7, Record Book N° 2, shall mark the mouth, or outer limit, of the said Elliot River; and that all the waters within, or to the Northward of such line, shall be reserved and excluded from the common right of fishing therein, under the first and second articles of Treaty aforesaid.

Her Majesty's Commissioner, in marking the above line, claims the same as defining the joint mouth of the Elliot, York, and Hillsborough Rivers.

The United States Commissioner agrees to the above line as the mouth of the Elliot River only, not recognizing or acknowledging any other River.

Dated at Bangor, in the State of Maine, United States, this twenty-seventh day of September, A. D. 1856.

RECORD N° 10. We, the undersigned, Commissioners under the Reciprocity Treaty between Great Britain and the United States, signed at Washington on the 5th day of June, A. D. 1854, having examined the Montague River, emptying into Cardigan Bay, on the Coast of Prince Edward Island, one of the British North American Colonies, do hereby agree and decide, that a line bearing North, 72° East (magnetic), drawn from Grave Point to Cardigan Point, as shown on Plan 7, Record Book N° 2, shall mark the mouth, or outer limit, of the said Montague River; and that all the waters within, or to the Westward of such line, shall be reserved and excluded from the common right of fishing therein, under the first and second Articles of the Treaty aforesaid.

Her Majesty's Commissioner, in marking the above line, claims the same as defining the joint mouth of the Montague and Brudenell Rivers.

The United States Commissioner agrees to the above line, as marking the mouth of the Montague only, not recognizing, or acknowledging any other River.

Dated at Bangor, in the State of Maine, United States, this twenty-seventh day of September, A. D. 1856.

RECORD N° 11. We, the undersigned, Commissioners under the Reciprocity Treaty between Great Britain and the United States, signed at Washington on the 5th day of June, A. D. 1854, having examined the Coasts of Prince Edward Island, one of the British North American Colonies, are unable to agree in the following respect:

Her Majesty's Commissioner claims, that the undermentioned places are Rivers, and that their mouths should be marked, and defined, under the provisions of the said Treaty:

Vernon, Orwell, Seal, Pinnette, Murray, Cardigan, Boughton, Fortune, Souris, Sᵗ Peter's (designated Sᵗ Peters Bay on the Map of the Island), Tryon, Crapaud, Winter, Hunter, Stanley, Ellis, Foxley, Pierre Jacques, Brae, Percival, Enmore, Ox, Haldiman, Sable.

The United States Commissioner denies that the above-mentioned places are Rivers, or such places as are intended to be reserved and excluded from the common liberty of fishing.

Dated at Bangor, in the State of Maine, United States, this twenty-seventh day of September, A. D. 1856.

It will thus be seen that the differences between the Commissioners resolve themselves into two divisions:

1st. — Whether the twenty-four places named in Prince Edward Island, or any of them, as is contended by Her Majesty's Commissioner, are to be deemed Rivers, and therefore reserved and excluded from the common liberty of the Fishery? Or whether, as is contended by the United States Commissioner, these places, or some of them, are not Rivers, and therefore open to the common liberty of the Fishery?

2nd. — The Miramichi and Buctouche in New Brunswick, being admitted to be Rivers, by what lines are the mouths of those Rivers respectively to be determined?

In coming to any conclusion on these points, it is unquestionably the duty of the Umpire, to look at the spirit and object of the Treaty,— the causes of difficulty it was intended to remove, —the mode of removal proposed.

The classes of fish sought for in the deep sea Fisheries strike within 'three marine miles' from the shore; the 'Bays' within the headlands are their places of resort, but unlike the salmon or the shad, they do not ascend the Rivers, or particularly seek their entrances. To prosecute the Mackerel Fishery with success, the right of fishing 'on the sea coast and shores' within three marine miles, and within the 'Bays' with the privilege of landing for drying nets and curing fish was absolutely necessary; the convenience of a 'Harbour', and the right of fishing therein, desirable.

A 'creek', which Webster and Maunders both define to be, according to English usage and etymology, 'a small inlet, bay or cove, a recess in the shore of the sea, or of a river', and which though in some of the American States, 'meaning a small River, Webster says, is contrary to English usage, and not justified by etymology', would also in many instances afford accommodation. A right to the 'sea coast and shores' — to the 'Harbours' and the 'Creeks' would thus afford the fisherman all that he would require, and leave to the Rivers, rising far in the interior of the respective countries, and flowing by the homes and the hearths of a different nation, the sacred character which would save them from the stranger's intrusion.

PART FIRST.

The question then that first presents itself, are the twenty-four places named, or any, and which of them, in Prince Edward Island, to be deemed Rivers?

It is difficult to lay down any general proposition the application of which would determine the question. There is no limitation as to size or volume; the Mississippi and the Amazon roll their waters over one fourth of the circumference of the earth. The 'Tamar', the 'Ex' and the 'Tweed' would hardly add a ripple to the St Lawrence; yet all alike bear the designation, are vested with the privileges, and governed by the laws and regulations of Rivers. It is not the absence of prevalence of fresh or salt water; that distinction has been expressly ignored in the celebrated case of Horne against McKenzie on appeal in the House of Lords. It is not the height or lowness of the banks; the Rhine is still the same River, whether flowing amid the mountains of Germany or fertilizing the low plains of Holland. It is not the rise or fall of tide, or the fact that there may be little, or any water, when the tide is out. The Stour and Orwell in England, are dry at low water, yet they have always been recognized and treated as Rivers. The Petitcodiac in New Brunswick, the Avon in Nova Scotia, owe their width, their waters, their utility, entirely to the Bay of Fundy; yet their claim to be classed among Rivers has never been doubted. The permanent or extraordinary extent of the stream, in cases where not at all or but little influenced by the tides is no criterion. The periodical thaws and freshets of Spring and Autumn in America make rivers of vast magnitude, useful for a thousand commercial purposes, in places where, when those thousand freshets have passed away, their dry beds are visible for weeks. The term 'flottable' applied to such streams, is well recognized in the Courts of the United States, classing them among rivers, and clothing the inhabitants upon their banks with the rights of riparian proprietors, and the public at large with the privilege of accommodation.

An important test may be said to be the existence or nonexistence of bars at the mouths of waters or streams running into the sea. The existence of such bars necessarily presupposes a conflict of antagonistic powers. An interior water forcing its way out, yet not of sufficient strength to plough a direct passage through the sands accumulated by the inward rolling of the sea, would necessarily diverge, and thus leave a bar in front of its passage, just at that distance where the force of its direct action would be expended. Some rivers, such as the Mississippi and the Nile, make deltas, and run into the sea.

In this cases, the extreme land would give a natural outlet. Others again run straight into the sea, without any delta, and without any estuary. In these cases, the bar at the mouth would give a natural limit; but the bar at the mouth is equally characteristic of its being a river. There are cases again, where the estuary gradually widening into the sea, leaves neither bar nor delta to mark its outlet, or determine its character. In such cases, for the latter object, other grounds must be sought on which to base a decision; and in making the former, the exercise of a sound discretion could be the only guide.

The decision upon any such question must, after all, be more or less arbitrary. The physical features of the surrounding country, the impressions created by local inspection, the recognized and admitted character the disputed places have always borne, constitute material elements in forming conclusion. The possibility that the privileges conceded by this Treaty may be abused, can have no weight. There will doubtless be found in both countries men who will disregard its solemn obligations, and take advantage of its concessions, to defraud the revenue, violate local laws, and infringe private rights, and in thus disgracing themselves, affect the character of the nation to which they belong; they will, however, meet with no consideration at the hands of the honourable and right thinking people of either country. The framers of this Treaty would not permit such minor difficulties to stand in the way of the great object they had in view, to cement the alliance, and further the commercial prosperity of two Empires. Such difficulties can be obviated, if necessary, by national or local legislation.

The Rivers of Prince Edward Island, whether one or one hundred in number, must, as to length, necessarily be small. The Island is in no part much over thirty miles in width, and the streams run through it, more or less transversely, not longitudinally. Captain (now Admiral) Bayfield, the accomplished hydrographer, and Surveyor of the Gulf of S⁺ Lawrence, thus describes it:

'Prince Edward Island, separated from the Southern shore of the Gulf of the S⁺ Lawrence by Northumberland straits, is one hundred and two miles long, and in one part about thirty miles broad ; but the breadth is rendered extremely irregular by large Bays, inlets, and rivers, or rather sea creeks, which penetrate the Island, so that no part of it is distant more than seven or eight miles from navigable water. Its shape is an irregular crescent, concave towards the Gulf, the Northern shore forming a great Bay, ninety-one miles wide and twenty-two miles deep, out of which, the set of the tides and the heavy sea render it very difficult to extricate a ship, when caught in the Northeast gales which frequently occur towards the fall of the year, occasionally blowing with great strength and duration, and at such times proving fatal to many vessels.'

This passage has been particularly called to my attention in a very elaborate and able statement of his views, placed before me by the United States Commissioner, who further adds, that Sir Charles A. Fitzroy, the Lieut. Governor of the Island of Prince Edward, in an official communication to the British Government, calls the Island Rivers 'strictly speaking, narrows arms of the sea'; and that Lord Glenelg. in his reply, alludes to them as 'inlets of the sea'.

On examining the Records referred to by the Commissioner, I find the first to be a Dispatch (in January, 1858) from Sir Charles Fitzroy, to the Colonial Secretary, Lord Glenelg, with reference to the reserves for Fisheries, contained in the original grants in the Island, arising out of the Order in Council, under which those grants were issued, and which was as follows: 'That in order to promote and encourage the Fishing, for which many parts of the Islands are conveniently situated, there be a clause in the grants of each Township that abuts upon the sea shore, containing a reservation of liberty to all Her Majesty's subjects in general, of carrying on a free fishery on the coasts of the said Townships, and of erecting stages and other necessary buil-

dings for the said fishery, within the distance of five hundred feet from high water mark.'

He then states he enclosed for the information of the Government — 'a return showing the several reserves for this purpose contained in the different Townships, from which it will appear that the reservation as contemplated in the Order of Council has been strictly followed in only twelve Townships. In thirty-two Townships the reservation is as follows — "and further saving and reserving for the disposal of His Majesty, his heirs and successors, five hundred feet from high water mark, on the coast of the tract of land hereby granted, to erect stages and other necessary buildings for carrying on the Fishery": of the remaining twenty-three Townships, eighteen contain no fishery reservation ; and of five no grants whatever are on record '. And he then remarks: — 'By reference to a plan of the Island annexed to the return, your Lordship will perceive that several of the Townships which do contain reservations abut upon rivers only, or more strictly speaking, narrow arms of the Sea.'

Lord Glenelg, in his reply (May, 1858), says: 'It appears to me that the reservation made of lands adjacent to the sea coast, or to the shores of inlets from the sea, for the purpose of fishing, so far as the right has been reserved to the Queen's subjects collectively, constitute(s) a property, over which the power of the Crown is exceedingly questionable.'

It does not appear to me that these passages bear the construction put upon them, or were intended to designate the Island rivers generally, or in any way determine their character. Is it not rather a mere qualified mode of expression used at the time, without any definite object, or perhaps if any, to avoid being concluded by either term? But if the use of a term by one or two of the local authorities is to be deemed of such weight, of how much more weight would be the continued use by the legislature for years of a contrary term? There are Acts of the Assembly vesting rights, imposing penalties, and creating privileges with reference to these waters, under the name and designation of Rivers, to a series of which I call attention, namely : 10 Geo. IV., c. 11 ; 2 Wm. IV., c. 2 and 13 ; 3 Wm. IV., c. 8, 9 and 10 ; 5 Wm. IV., 3 and 7 ; 6 Wm. IV., c. 25 ; 7 Wm. IV., c. 23 ; 1 Vic., c. 19 ; 2 Vic., c. 10 ; 3 Vic., c. 12 ; 4 Vic., c. 16 ; 4 Vic., c. 18 ; 5 Vic., c. 9 : 7 Vic., c. 3 ; 8 Vic., c. 20 ; 12 Vic., c. 18, 35 and 22 ; 15 Vic., c. 34 : 16 Vic., c. 28. Also to the various reports of the Annual Appropriations and Expenditures, to be found in the Journals of the Legislature.

On an examination of these Acts, it will be found that the Legislature of the Island has by a continued series of enactments, extending over a period of thirty years, legislated upon the 'Rivers', 'Bays', 'Creeks', 'Harbours' and 'lesser streams' of the Island, recognizing their existence and difference, appropriating the local revenues to their improvement, establishing rights, and creating private interests with reference to them, entirely inconsistent with their being aught but the internal waters and rivers of the Island, and directly at variance with the terms and character of legislation, which would have been used had they been considered 'arms' or mere 'inlets in the sea'. Such Acts by the Congress of the United States, or by the respective Legislatures of the several States, on any matter within their juridiction would be regarded as conclusive of the character of the subject legislated upon. The legislation of Prince Edward Island, in *pari materia*, is entitled to the same consideration. The British Government at the present day, neither legislates away, nor interferes with the local administration of the affairs of the Colonies. This very treaty is depended upon the action of the Provincial Parliaments, and based upon the preservation of private rights. Can it be contended, or shall it be admitted, that this Treaty abrogates the Legislation of years, ignores the Laws of the Island, and by implication annuls rights and privileges the most sacred a Colony can possess? Certainly not. If it be desirable from the peculiar conformation of this Island and its waters, that the latter should be viewed in a light different from that in which they have been hitherto regarded, the local Legislature can so determine.

In a very important decision of the Supreme Court of Iowa, reported in the American Law Register, issued at Philadelphia, in August 1857, it was determined, 'that the real test of navigability in the United States was ascertained by *use*, or by *public act of declaration*; and that the Acts and Declarations of the United States, declare and constitute the Mississippi River, a public highway, in the highest and broadest intendment possible'. Shall not therefore the public Acts and Declarations of the Legislature of Prince Edward Island be considered of some authority in determining what are the Rivers of that Island? And particularly when those Acts and Declarations were made long anterior to the present question being raised? But might it not also be assumed, that where a country had, by a long series of public documents, legislative enactments, grants and proclamations, defined certain waters to be rivers, or spoken of them as such, or defined where the mouths of certain rivers were, and

another country subsequently entered into a Treaty with the former respecting those very waters, and used the same terms, without specifically assigning to them a different meaning, nay, further stipulated that the Treaty should not take effect in the localities where those waters were, until confirmed by the local authorities, might it not be well assumed that the definitions previously used, and adopted, would be mutually binding in interpreting the Treaty, and that the two countries had consented to use the terms in the sense in which each had before treated them in their public instruments, and to apply them as they had been previously applied in the localities where used? I think it might.

Admiral Bayfield did not intend by the term 'sea creeks', as he informs me in reply to a communication on this subject, to convey the impression contended for by the United States Commissioner, that they were not Rivers. He says, under date of 3d September, 1857: 'With reference to the term "sea creeks", to which your attention has been called as having been used by me at page 92, and various other parts of the Directions, I have used that term in order to distinguish the inlets from the small streams (disproportionably small in summer) that flow through them to the sea.

'In the instances referred to, I mean by "sea creeks", inlets formed by the combined action of the Rivers and the Tides, and through which those rivers flow in the channels, more or less direct, and more or less plainly defined by shoals on either side. Wherever there are bars across the inlets, as is very generally the case, I consider the channels through those bars, to form the common entrances from the sea to both Inlets and Rivers; for it appears to me that a River is not the less a River, because it flows through a creek, an inlet, or an estuary. The point where the fresh water enters the estuary, and mixes with the tide waters, may be miles inland, but it does not, I think, cease to be a River until it flows over its bar into the sea.'

This view of Admiral Bayfield, that such waters do not lose their character of Rivers because flowing through an inlet, or an estuary, is confirmed by the principles laid down to determine what are 'navigable' Rivers, in the technical sense of the term, as distinguished from its common acceptation. To the extent that fresh waters are backwardly propelled by the ingress and pressure of the tide, they are denominated navigable *Rivers;* and to determine whether or not a River is navigable both in the common law, and in the Admiralty acceptation of the term, regard must be had to the ebbing and flowing of the tide. In the celebrated case of the River Bann, in Ireland, the Sea is spoken of as *ebbing and flowing in the River*. These principles are recognized in the Courts of the United States, and the authorities collated, and most ably commented upon by Angel.

Indeed, it would seem that the Commissioners themselves have not attached to this term 'sea creek' as used by Admiral Bayfield, the force or character which it is now alleged it should bear, as they have by their Record N° 10, under date of 27ᵗʰ of September 1856, transmitted to me, with the other official documents in this matter, pronounced the 'Montague' to be a River and determined upon its mouth, though Captain Bayfield, in his Sailing Directions, before referred to, page 123, speaks of it as a 'sea creek'. It has been urged, that if these places are declared to be Rivers, and not creeks or harbours, then where are the creeks and harbours, contemplated by the Treaty. To this it may be answered, that this treaty does not contemplate Prince Edward Island alone—and even though none such might be found within its narrow circle—yet they may be found in numbers along the five thousand miles of coast, exclusive of Newfoundland, which this Treaty covers, extending from 36th parallel of north latitude in the United States, to the furthest limits of Labrador.

With these preliminary observations, I shall take up the disputed places in Prince Edward Islands, and proceed to decide upon them, in the order in which they have been submitted.

[Then follow the 24 awards deciding that the Vernon, Orwell, Seal, Murray, Cardigan, Boughton, Fortune, Souris, Tryon, Winter, Hunter, Stanley, Ellis, Foxley, Pierre Jacques, Percival, Enmore, Haldiman and Sable are rivers and that the Pinnette, Saint Peter, Crapaud, Brae and Ox are not rivers.]

PART SECOND.

I now come to the second division, namely: the Miramichi and the Buctouche, being admitted to be Rivers, which of the lines pointed out by the Commissioners shall respectively designate the mouths of those Rivers?

THE MIRAMICHI. — I, the undersigned, Arbitrator or Umpire under the Reciprocity Treaty, concluded and signed at Washington on the 5th day of June, A. D. 1854, having proceeded to and examined the mouth of the Miramichi, in the Province of New Brunswick, concerning which a difference of opinion had arisen between Her Britannic Majesty's Commissioner and the Commissioner of the United States, and disclosed in

Record N° 2 of their proceedings, declare as follows : --

With reference to the Miramichi, it will be seen by Record N° 2 — Her Majesty's Commissioner claims, that a line connecting Fox and Portage Islands (marked in red, Plan N° 2, Record Book N° 2) designates the mouth of the Miramichi River. The United States Commissioner claims, that a line from Spit Point to Moody Point (marked in blue, Plan N° 2, Record Book N° 2) designates the mouth of said River.

By the Treaty it is provided, that 'the above mentioned liberty applies solely to the sea fishery; and that the salmon and shad Fisheries, and all Fisheries in Rivers, and mouths of Rivers, are reserved exclusively, etc. etc.'

The preceding portion of Article 1st gives the right to fish 'on the sea coasts and shores, and in the bays, harbours and creeks'.

The Inner Bay of the Miramichi, and the Harbour of Buctouche, are among other grounds, claimed as coming within the definition of 'Bays and Harbors', and it has been urged, that the clause just referred to, is conclusive in favor of that claim, whether such bay or harbour does or does not constitute the mouth of a River.

It is therefore necessary, before deciding which of the lines above designated as the mouth of the Miramichi, is the correct one, to dispose of this preliminary question, namely: — Does the mouth of a River forfeit its exclusive character, under this Treaty, because it may constitute a bay, or harbour? Is the restriction imposed, limited to particular fish, or locality? The spirit with which this Treaty was made, and the object it has in view, demand for it the most liberal construction; but, consistently with the most liberal construction, there are many wise and judicious reasons why the exception should be made. The joint, or common Fishery in those places where the forbidden fish resort, would be a prolific cause of dispute. The very fact, that after the forbidden fish are named, there should follow the significant expression that *all* fisheries in those places should be reserved, is conclusive as to the idea predominant in the minds of the framers of the Treaty. They wanted peace; they would not put the fishermen of the two nations together, on the same ground, where they would have unequal rights. Considerations of a national, administrative, or fiscal character, may have determined them to exclude the entrances of the great thoroughfares into the respective countries, from common possession. There are large and magnificent bays and harbours, unconnected with Rivers; there are bays and harbours dependent upon and formed by mouths of Rivers. The terms are not indicative of locality. Bays and harbours may be found far up in the interior of a country; in lakes or in rivers, and on the sea board. The 'mouths of Rivers' are found only in one locality, namely, in that part of the River by which its waters are discharged into the sea or ocean, or into a lake, and that part of the River is by the express language of this Treaty excluded. Is the use of a term which may be applicable to many places, to supersede that which can only be applied to a particular place, when the latter is pointedly, *eo nomine*, excluded? But why should such a construction be required, when the object of the Treaty can be obtained without it?

The cause of the difficulty was not the refusal to permit a common fishery within the mouths of Rivers, but within three marine miles of the sea coast. That difficulty is entirely removed, by the liberty to take fish 'on the sea coast and shores, and in the bays, harbours and creeks, without being restricted to any distance from the shore'.

The position taken by the Commissioner of the United States, is further pressed upon the ground, — 'That the terms of a grant are always to be construed most strongly against the granting party'. The application of that principle to the present case is not very perceptible. This is rather the case of two contracting parties exchanging equal advantages; and the contract must be governed by the ordinary rules of interpretation. Vattel says, — 'In the interpretation of Treaties, compacts, and promises, we ought not to deviate from the common use of the language, unless we have very strong reasons for it'. And, 'When we evidently see what is the sense that agrees with the intention of the contracting parties, it is not allowable to wrest their words to a contrary meaning.' It is plain that the framers of this Treaty intended to exclude the 'mouths of Rivers' from the common possession.

Ought we, by construing the terms of the Treaty most strongly against the nation where the River in dispute may happen to be, to 'wrest their words to a contrary meaning'? I think not. Mr. Andrews, for many years the United States Consul in New Brunswick and in Canada, a gentleman whose great researches and untiring energies were materially instrumental in bringing about this Treaty and to whom the British Colonies are much indebted for the benefits they are now deriving and may yet derive from its adoption, thus speaks of the Miramichi in his Report to his Government in 1852: — 'The extensive harbour of Miramichi is formed by the estuary of the beautiful River of that name, which is two hundred and twenty miles in length. At its entrance into the Gulf this River is nine miles in width.

'There is a bar at the entrance of the Miramichi, but the River is of such great size, and pours forth such a volume of water, that the bar offers no impediment to navigation, there being sufficient depth of water on it at all times for ships of six and seven hundred tons, or even more. The tide flows nearly forty miles up the Miramichi, from the Gulf. The River is navigable for vessels of the largest class full thirty miles of that distance, there being from five to eight fathoms of water in the channel; but schooners and small craft can proceed nearly to the head of the tide. Owing to the size and depth of the Miramichi, ships can load along its banks for miles.'

In Brook's Gazetteer, an American work of authority, the width of the Potomac, at its entrance into the Chesapeake, is given at seven and a half miles.

In the same work, the mouth of the Amazon is given at 'one hundred and fifty-nine miles broad'.

In Hárper's Gazetteer (Edition of 1855), the width of the Severn, at its junction with the Bristol Channel, is given at ten miles across. That of the Humber, at its mouth, at six or seven miles: and that of the Thames, at its junction with the North sea at the Nore, between the Isle of Sheppey and Foulness Point, or between Sheerness and Southend, at fifteen miles across. And the Saint Lawrence, in two different places in the same work, is described as entering 'the Gulf of Saint Lawrence at Gaspe Point, by a mouth one hundred miles wide'. And also that 'at its mouth, the Gulf from Cape Rosier to Mingan settlement in Labrador, is one hundred and five miles in length'.

Thus width is no objection. The real entrance to the Miramichi is, however, but one and a half miles wide. Captain Bayfield may, apparently, be cited by both Commissioners as authority. He says, pages 30, 31 and 32: —

'Miramichi Bay is nearly fourteen miles wide from the sand-bars off Point Blackland to Point Escumenac beacon, and six and a half miles deep from that line across its mouth to the main entrance of the Miramichi, between Portage and Fox Islands. The bay is formed by a semicircular range of low sandy islands, between which there are three small passages and one main or ship channel leading into the inner bay or estuary of the Miramichi. The Negowac Gully, between the sand bar of the same name and a small one to the S. W., is 280 fathoms wide and 3 fathoms deep; but a sandy bar of the usual mutable character lies off it, nearly a mile to the S. S. E., and had about 9 feet over it at low water at the time of our survey. Within the Gully a very narrow channel only fit for boats or very small craft, leads westward up the inner bay. The shoal water extends 1¼ miles off this Gully, but there is excellent warning by the lead here and everywhere in this bay, as will be seen by the chart. Shoals nearly dry at low water extend from the Negowac Gully to Portage Island, a distance of 1¼ miles to the S. W. Portage Island is 4 miles long in a S. W. by S. direction; narrow, low, and partially wooded with small spruce trees and bushes. The ship channel between this Island and Fox Island, is 1½ miles wide.

'Fox Island, 3¾ miles long, in a S. S. E. direction, is narrow and partially wooded, like Portage Island; it is formed of parallel ranges of sand hills which contain imbedded drift timber, and have evidently been thrown up by the sea in the course of ages. The islands are merely sand-bars on a large scale, and nowhere rise higher than 50 feet above the sea. They are incapable of agricultural cultivation, but yet they abound in plants and shrubs suited to such a locality, and in wild fruits, such as the blueberry, strawberry and raspberry. Wild fowl of various kinds are also plentiful in their season; and so also are salmon, which are taken in nets and weirs along the beaches outside the islands, as well as in the gullies.

'The next and last of these islands is Huckleberry Island, which is nearly 1½ miles long, in a S. E. direction. Fox Gully between Huckleberry and Fox Islands is about 150 fathoms wide at high water, and from 2 to 2½ fathoms deep, but there is a bar outside with 7 feet at low water. Huckleberry Gully, between the island of the same name and the mainland, is about 200 fathoms wide, but is not quite so deep as Fox Gully. They are both only fit for boats or very small craft; and the channels leading from them to the westward, up a bay of the main within Huckleberry Island or accross to the French river and village, are narrow and intricate, between flats of sand, mud and eel-grass, and with only water enough for boats. Six and a quarter miles from the Huckleberry Gully, along the low shore of the mainland, in an E. S. E. ½ E. direction, brings us to the beacon at point Escumenac, and completes the circuit of the bay.

The Bar of Miramichi commences from the S. E. end of Portage Island, and extends accross the main entrance and parallel to Fox Island, nearly 6 miles in a S. E. by S. direction. It consists of sand, and has not more than a foot or two of water over it in some parts, at low spring tides.'

He also says pp. 37 and 39:

'The Inner Bay of Miramichi is of great extent, being about thirteen miles long from its entrance at Fox Island to Sheldrake Island (where the river may properly be said to commence) and 7 or 8 miles wide. The depth of water accross the bay is sufficient for the largest vessels that can cross the inner bar being 2¾ fathoms at low water in ordinary springtides, with muddy bottom. Sheldrake Island lies off Napan Point, at the distance of rather more than 3 quarters of a mile, and bears from Point Cheval N. W. by W. 1¾ miles. Shallow water extends far off this island in every direction, westward to Bartiboque Island, and eastward to Oak Point. It also sweeps round to the south and southeast, so as to leave only a very narrow channel between it and the shoal, which fills Napan Bay, and trending away to the eastward past Point Cheval, forms the Middle Ground already mentioned. Murdoch Spit and Murdoch Point are two sandy points, a third of a mile apart, with a cove between them, and about a mile W. S. W. of Sheldrake Island. The entrance of Miramichi River is 3 quarters of a mile wide between these points and Moody Point, which has a small Indian church upon it, and is the east Point of entrance of Bartiboque River, a mile N. W. by W. ½ W. from Sheldrake Island.'

But a strong, and I may add, a conclusive point in showing the passage between Fox and Portage Islands, to be the main entrance, or mouth of the Miramichi, is the peculiar action of the tides. It is thus described by Bayfield p. 35:

'The stream of the tides is not strong in the open bay outside the bar of Miramichi. The flood draws in towards the entrance as into a funnel, coming both from the N. E. and S. E. alongshore of Tabisintac, as well as from Point Escumenac. It sets fairly through the ship channel at the rate of about 1½ knots at the black buoy increasing to 2 or 2½ knots in strong springtides between Portage and Fox Islands, where it is strongest. The principal part of the stream continues to flow westward, in the direction of the buoys of the Horse Shoe Shoal, although some part of it flows to the northward between that shoal and Portage Island.'

The effect of this is thus singularly felt. A boat leaving Negowac to ascend to Miramichi with the flood tide is absolutely met by the tide flowing northerly against it until coming abreast of the Horse Shoe Shoal, or in the line of the main entrance; and the boat at the Horse Shoe Shoal, steering for Negowac, with the ebb tide making, would have the current against it, though Negowac is on a line as far seaward as the entrance to the Portage and Fox Islands; thus showing conclusively that the main inlet and outlet of the tidal waters, to and from the mouth or entrance of the Miramichi, is between Portage and Fox Islands.

As such Arbitrator or Umpire, I decide that a line connecting Fox and Portage Islands (marked in red, Plan N° 2, Record Book N° 2) designates the mouth of the Miramichi River.

THE BUCTOUCHE. — I, the undersigned, Arbitrator or Umpire under the Reciprocity Treaty, concluded and signed at Washington on the 5th day of June, A. D. 1854, having proceeded to and examined the mouth of the River Buctouche, in the Province of New Brunswick, concerning which a difference of opinion had arisen between Her Britannic Majesty's Commissioner and the Commissioner of the United States, as disclosed in Record N° 1 of their proceedings. With reference to the Buctouche it will be seen by Record N° 1: Her Majesty's Commissioner claims, that a line from Glover's Point to the Southern extremity of the Sand Bar, marked in red on the Plan N° 1, designates the mouth of the said River Buctouche. The United States Commissioner claims, that a line from Chapel Point, bearing South 4° West (magnetic), marked in blue on said Plan N° 1, designates the mouth of said River.

On the subject of this River the United States Commissioner addresses me as follows: 'The red line extending from Glover's Point, to the Point of the Sand Bar, is the line marked by Her Majesty's Commissioner as designating the mouth of the River ; in that line I could not concur because it excludes from the common right of fishing the whole of Buctouche Harbour in contravention of the express words of the Treaty. If it had been the duty and office of the Commissioners to indicate the point which constitutes the mouth of the Harbour, I should have been disposed to acquiesce in the point and line thus denoted ; but from the proposition that it marks the entrance of these Rivers, or any one of them, into the Sea or Bay, or Harbour, and constitutes their mouth, I entirely dissent.'

With the views I have already expressed that the mouth of a River does not lose its treaty character because it constitutes a harbour, it becomes important to determine which is the principal agent in forming this harbour. the River or the Sea. If it is a mere indentation of the coast, formed by the sea, a creek, a bay, or harbour, unformed by and unconnected with any River, one of those indentations in a coast, indebted to the sea mainly for its waters, then plainly it is not intended or entitled to be reserved ; but if on the contrary it is formed by the escape of waters from the interior, by a River seeking its outlet to the deep, showing by the width and depth of its channel at low water that it is not to the sea it owes its formation,

then plainly it is the mouth of a River and intended to be reserved.

Captain Bayfield describes the Buctouche as follows, pp. 53 and 54: 'Buctouche Roadstead, off the entrance of Buctouche River and in the widest part of the channel within the outer bar, is perfectly safe for a vessel with good anchors and cables ; the ground being a stiff tenacious clay, and the outer bar preventing any very heavy sea from coming into the anchorage. It is here that vessels, of too great draft of water to enter the river, lie moored to take in cargoes of lumber.

'Buctouche River enters the sea to the S. E., through the shallow bay within the Buctouche sand-bar, as will be seen in the chart. The two white beacons which I have mentioned, as pointing out the best anchorage in the roadstead, are intended to lead in over the bar of sand and flat sandstone, in the best water, namely, 8 feet at low water and 12 feet at high water in ordinary spring tides. But the channel is so narrow, intricate, and encumbered with oyster beds, that written directions are as useless as the assistance of a pilot is absolutely necessary to take a vessel safely into the River. Within the bar is a wide part of the channel in which vessel may ride safely in $2\frac{1}{2}$ and 3 fathoms over mud bottom ; but off Giddis Point the channel becomes as difficult, narrow, and shallow as the bar. It is in its course through the bay that the Buctouche is so shallow and intricate ; higher up its channel being free from obstruction, and in some places 5 fathoms deep. Having crossed the bar, a vessel may ascend about 10 miles further, and boats 13 or 14 miles to where the tide water ends.'

By an examination of the Channel we find miles up this River a deep continuous channel of twelve, fifteen, twenty, twenty-four and thirty feet, down to Priest Point, varying from eighteen to twenty-four feet to Giddis Point, and thence to a line drawn across from the Sand Bar to Glover's Point, from seven to twenty feet, but of greater width. On the outside of this channel, which is clearly defined, and between the Sand Bar and the channel, we find mud flats with dry patches and oyster beds, 'flats of mud and ell-grass, with dry patches at low water'; with depths from Priest Point to the Sand Bar, varying from four to six feet and from the channel of Giddis Point to the bar, from one foot to three. On the other side of the channel, from Priest Point and Giddis Point we find 'flats of mud and weeds, with dry patches and oyster beds'. What has given depth and breadth to this channel ? The tide rises in this vicinity about four feet ; would that rise create a channel of the average depth above named ? Can there be any doubt that it is created by the great body of the river water finding its way to the sea ? The line from 'Glover's Point to the southern extremity of the Sand Bar, marked in red on plan Nº 1', is claimed by Her Majesty's Commissioner as the mouth of the River, and admitted by the United States Commissioner as the month of the Harbour ; but if there no River here, would there be any harbour at all ? I think not, and this line therefore, while it constitutes the mouth of the harbour, also constitutes the mouth of the River.

This conclusion is consonant with the conclusion at which the Commissioners themselves arrived in the cases of the Elliot and Montague Rivers in Prince Edward Island, as shown by Records Nᵒˢ 9 and 10. The harbours of Charlottetown und Georgetown are clearly within the lines they have marked and designated as the mouths of those Rivers respectively, and thus within the lines of exclusion ; but if the express words of the Treaty gave a right to such harbours, because 'harbours', then why did the Commissioners exclude them? And why should not the same principle which governed the Commissioners in their decision with regard to those 'harbours', not (sic) also govern with regard to Buctouche Harbour ?

As Arbitrator or Umpire, I decide that a line from Glover's Point to the southern extremity of the Sand Bar, marked in red on Plan Nº 1, in Record Nº 2, designates the mouth of the River Buctouche.

It may not come within the exact line of my duty, but I cannot forbear remarking, that the true benefits of this Treaty can only be realized to the inhabitants of both countries by a course of mutual forbearance, and enlightened liberality. Captious objections, fancied violations and insults, should be discountenanced ; and above all, there should be an abstinence from attributing to either nations or people, as a national feeling, the spirit of agression which may occasionally lead individuals to act in direct contravention of its terms. Every friend of humanity would regret further misunderstanding between Great Britain and the United States. The march of improvement which is to bring the broad regions of North America, between the Atlantic and Pacific, within the pale of civilization, is committed by Providence to their direction ; fearful will be the responsibility of that nation which mars so noble a heritage.

Dated at Saint John, in the Province of New Brunswick, this 8ᵗʰ day of April, 1858 [1].

[1] J. B. MOORE, *History and Digest...*, p. 449-473.

CX. Equateur, Etats-Unis d'Amérique.

28 février 1893.

Dans cette affaire il s'agissait d'une indemnité réclamée par un sieur Santos, originaire de l'Equateur, mais naturalisé citoyen américain, du chef d'une arrestation opérée en 1884 et maintenue pendant 226 jours.

Convention to refer to the decision of an arbitrator the claim in behalf of Julio R. Santos, concluded at Quito, February 28, 1893.

The United States of America, and the Republic of Ecuador, being desirous of removing all questions of difference between them, and of maintaining their good relations, in a manner consonant to their just interests and dignity, have decided to conclude a convention and for that purpose have named as their respective Plenipotentiaries, to wit:

The President of the United States: Rowland Blennerhassett Mahany, Envoy Extraordinary and Minister Plenipotentiary of the United States to Ecuador ; and

The President of Ecuador: Honorato Vazquez, Plenipotentiary ad hoc, of that Republic; who having communicated to each other their respective Full Powers found in good and due form, have agreed upon the following articles:

ART. I. The two governments agree to refer to the decision of an arbitrator, to be designated in the manner hereinafter provided, the claim presented by the Government of the United States against that of the Republic of Ecuador, in behalf of Julio R. Santos, a native of Ecuador and naturalized as a citizen of the United States in the year 1874; the said claim being for injuries to his person and property, growing out of his arrest and imprisonment by the authorities in the years 1884 and 1885.

ART. II. 1. In order to secure the services of a competent and impartial arbitrator, it is agreed that the government of Her Britannic Majesty be requested to authorize its diplomatic representative in Quito, to act in that capacity; or in case of his absence from the country, that this permission be given to his successor.

2. In case of the failure of the diplomatic representative of Her Britannic Majesty's Government, or of the successor of the said representative, to act as such arbiter, then the said representative, or his successor be requested to name an arbitrator who shall not be a citizen either of the United States or of Ecuador,

3. Any vacancy in the office of Arbitrator, to be filled in the same manner as the original appointment.

ART. III. 1. As soon as may be, after the designation of the Arbitrator, not to exceed the period of ninety days, the written or printed case of each of the contracting parties accompanied by the documents, the official correspondence and other evidence on which each relies, shall be delivered to the Arbitrator, and to the agent of the other party; and within ninety days after such delivery and exchange of the cases of the two parties, either party may, in like manner, deliver to the Arbitrator, and to the agent of the other side, a counter-case to the documents and evidence presented by the other party, with such written or printed argument as may, by each, be deemed proper. And each government shall furnish upon the request of the other or its agent, such papers in its possession as may be deemed important to the just determination of the claim.

2. Within the last named period of ninety days, the Arbitrator may also call for such evidence as he may deem proper, to be furnished within the same period; and shall also receive such oral and documentary evidence as each Government may offer. Each Government shall also furnish, upon the requisition of the Arbitrator, all documents in its possession, which may be deemed by him as material to the just determination of the claim.

3. Within sixty days after the last mentioned period of ninety days the Arbitrator shall render his opinions and decisions in writing, and certefy the same to the two Governments. These decisions and opinions shall embrace the following points, to wit:

a) Whether, according to the evidence adduced, Julio R. Santos by his return to and residence in Ecuador did or did not, under the provisions of the Treaty of Naturalization between the two Governments, concluded May 6, 1872, forteit his United States citizenship as to Ecuador, and resume the obligations of the latter country.

b) If he did not so forfeit his United States citizenship, whether or not it was shown by the evidence adduced, that Julio R. Santos has been guilty of such acts of unfriendliness and hostility to the Government of Ecuador, as, under the Law of Nations, deprived him of the consideration and protection due to a neutral citizen of a friendly Nation.

ART. IV. 1. In case either one or the other of the points recited in clauses (*a*) and (*b*) of the last preceding article, should be decided in favor of the contention of the Government of Ecuador, said Government shall be held to no further responsibility to that of the United States for arrest, imprisonment, and other acts of the authorities of Ecuador towards Julio R. Santos, during the years 1884 and 1885.

2. On the other hand, should the Arbitrator decide the above recited points against the contention of Ecuador, he shall, after a careful examination of the evidence touching the injuries and losses to the person and property of the said Santos, which shall have been laid before him concerning the arrest and imprisonment of said Santos, and other acts of the authorities of Ecuador towards him, during the years 1884 and 1885, award such damages for said injuries and losses as may be just and equitable; which shall be certified to the two Governments and shall be final and conclusive.

ART. V. 1. Both Governments agree to treat the decisions of the Arbitrator and his award as final and conclusive.

2. Should a pecuniary indemnity be awarded, it shall be specified in the gold coin of the United States and shall be paid to the Government thereof within sixty days after the beginning of the first session of the Congress of Ecuador, held subsequent to the rendition of the award and the said award shall bear interest at six per centum from the date of its rendition.

3. The Government of Ecuador, however, reserves the right to pay, before the expiration of the above stated time, the whole amount to the Government of the United States, with interest at six per centum from the date of the announcement of the award till the date of the payment thereof.

ART. VI. 1. Each Government shall pay its own agent and counsel, if any, for the expenses of preparing and submitting its case to the Arbitrator.

2. All other expenses including reasonable compensation to the Secretary, if any, of the Arbitrator, shall be paid upon the certificates of the Arbitrator, by the two Governments in equal moieties.

ART. VII. The present convention shall be ratified by the President of United States, by and with the advice and consent of the Senate thereof; by the Congress of Ecuador and by the President thereof; and the ratifications exchanged at Washington as soon as possible.

In faith whereof, the Plenipotentiaries have signed and sealed this convention in duplicate, in the City of Quito, this twenty-eight day of

February, in the year of our Lord one thousand eight hundred and ninety three[1].

L'arbitre désigné fut prié simplement, par suite de l'arrangement direct avenu entre le sieur Santos et le général Alfaro, président de la République de l'Equateur, de prononcer une sentence de pure forme, destinée à donner un caractère authentique à la transaction acceptée par l'intéressé.

Award of M. St. John, arbitrator in the case Santos, between Ecuador and the United States of America, pronounced on September 22, 1896.

The undersigned, nominated arbitrator in conformity with section 2 of Article II of the convention between the United States and the Republic of Ecuador, concluded in Quito on the 28th of February 1893, to decide the claim of Mr. Julio R. Santos against the Government of Ecuador on account of the acts done by the authorities of the Republic of Ecuador in the years 1884 and 1885, in view of the transaction which is presented and that has intervened between Mr. Julio R. Santos and the special agent of the Ecuadorian Government, duly approved by said government and the representative of the United States at Quito, and in which they solicit that there may be pronounced judgment in favor of the claimant for the sum of $ 40,000 gold, payable by installements semiannually without interest, decides that the government of Ecuador shall pay to the Government of the United States in four semiannual installements of $ 10,000, the sum of $ 40,000 gold of the United States without interest, the first dividend to be paid within sixty days, counting from the first session of the Congress of Ecuador subsequent to the notification of this judgment in conformity with section 2 of Article V of the above-mentioned treaty of 1893[2].

CXI. Chili, Grande-Bretagne.

26 septembre 1893.

Relatif aux indemnités réclamées par des citoyens anglais à raison des dommages causés par la guerre civile, cet arbitrage donna lieu à de nombreuses décisions. Un rapport fait à son gouvernement par le Ministre des Etats-Unis d'Amérique résume les opérations

de la commission et nous avons cru intéressant de le reproduire. La commission siégea du 24 octobre 1894 jusqu'au 4 mars 1896 et accorda 7548 £ 18 sh. 2 d. et $ 135,079. 30. Il avait été réclamé 191,928 £ 9 sh. 7 d. et $ 594,295. 06.

Convention d'arbitrage, signée à Santiago, le 26 Septembre 1893.

S. Exc. le Président de la République du Chili et S. M. la Reine du Royaume-Uni de la Grande-Bretage et d'Irlande, afin de mettre un terme amical aux réclamations formulées par la Légation de S. M. B. au Chili, au sujet de la guerre civile qui s'est produite le 7 Janvier 1891, ont décidé de conclure une Convention d'arbitrage et, à cet effet, ont nommé pour leurs plenipotentiaires savoir:

Sa Majesté Britannique, John Gordon Kennedy, Esq., Ministre résident de sa Majesté au Chili; et

Son Exellence le Président de la République du Chili, Don Ventura Blanco Viel, Ministre des Affaires Etrangères.

Lesquels, après s'être communiqué l'un à l'autre leurs pleins pouvoirs respectifs, trouvés en bonne et due forme, sont convenus des articles suivants:

ART. 1. Un tribunal arbitral décidera, en la forme et d'après les termes fixés dans l'article V de cette Convention, sur toutes les réclamations motivées par des actes et des opérations exécutés par les forces de mer et de terre de la République pendant la guerre civile qui commença le 7 Janvier 1891 et se termina le 28 Août de la même année, et sur celles qui seront motivées par des événements postérieurs qui, d'après les termes énoncés dans le dit article V, seraient de nature à engager la responsabilite du Gouvernement du Chili.

Les réclamations devront être placées sous le patronage de la Légation de S. M. B. et présentées dans le délai de six mois à partir de la date de l'installation du tribunal.

ART. 2. Le tribunal se composera de trois membres, le premier nommé par S. E. le Président de la République du Chili, le deuxième par S. M. la Reine Victoria et le troisième par les deux hautes parties contractantes. Ce choix ne pourra porter ni sur un citoyen chilien, ni sur un sujet de S. M. B.

ART. 3. Le tribunal admettra les preuves et les moyens d'investigation qui, selon le jugement et le juste discernement de ses membres seraient de nature à apporter le plus de lumière sur les faits litigieux et spécialement sur la qualification

---

[1] F. DE MARTENS, *Nouveau Recueil général*, 2ᵉ série, t. XXII, p. 375.
[2] *Foreign Relations of the U. S.*, 1896, p. 109.

de l'état et du caractère de neutralité du réclamant.

Le tribunal admettra aussi les allégations verbales ou écrites des deux Gouvernements ou de leurs agents ou défenseurs respectifs.

ART. 4. Chaque Gouvernement pourra constituer un agent qui veille sur ses intérêts particuliers et pourvoie à leur défense, présente des documents, des pétitions, des interrogatoires, prenne ou repousse des conclusions, appuie ses charges ou réfute celles des adversaires, fournisse des preuves et expose devant le tribunal par lui-même ou par l'organe d'un avocat, verbalement ou par écrit, conformément aux règles de procédure et aux voies que le même tribunal établira au début de ses fonctions, les doctrines, principes légaux ou précédents qui répondent à son droit.

ART. 5. Le tribunal décidera sur les réclamations en raison des preuves formulées et d'accord avec les principes de droit international et les usages et la jurisprudence établis par les tribunaux analogues modernes qui ont le plus d'autorité et de prestige et rendra, des jugements interlocutoires ou définitifs à la majorité des votes.

Le tribunal exposera brièvement dans chaque jugement définitif les faits et les raisons de la réclamation, les motifs allégués en sa faveur ou contre elle et les règles de droit international qui justifient ses décisions. Les décisions et décrets du tribunal seront écrits et signés par tous ses membres et légalisés par le secrétaire. Les originaux seront laissés avec les dossiers respectifs au Ministère des Relations Extérieures du Chili; des expéditions seront données aux parties qui le solliciteront.

Le tribunal tiendra un registre sur lequel se noteront les procédures, les demandes des réclamants et les arrêts et décisions rendus.

Le tribunal siégera à Santiago.

ART. 6. Le tribunal aura la faculté de se pourvoir de secrétaires, rapporteurs et autres employés qu'il jugera nécessaires pour le bon exercice de ses fonctions.

Il appartient au tribunal de proposer les personnes qui devront respectivement remplir les fonctions et de désigner les salaires ou rémunérations qui devront leur être attribués.

La nomination des dits employés sera faite par S. E. le Président de la République du Chili.

Les arrêts du tribunal qui devront être exécutés au Chili auront l'appui de la force publique comme ceux rendus par les tribunaux ordinaires du pays.

Ceux qui devront être exécutés à l'étranger le seront conformément aux règles et usages du droit international privé.

ART. 7. Le tribunal aura pour accomplir son mandat concernant toutes les réclamations soumises à sa connaissance et à sa décision le délai d'un an à partir du jour où il se déclarera installé.

Passé ce délai, le tribunal aura la faculté de prolonger ses fonctions pour une nouvelle période qui ne pourra excéder six mois en cas où, pour cause de maladie ou empêchement temporaire de quelqu'un de ses membres ou pour d'autres motifs de gravité notoire, il ne serait pas parvenu à remplir sa tâche dans le délai fixé au paragraphe précédent.

ART. 8. Chacun des Gouvernements contractants paiera les dépenses de sa propre procédure et les honoraires de ses agents ou défenseurs respectifs.

Les honoraires des membres du tribunal courront du jour où il commencera à fonctionner.

Les frais d'organisation du tribunal, les honoraires de ses membres, les soldes de secrétaires, rapporteurs et autres employés ainsi que les autres dépenses et coûts du service commun seront payés par moitié par les deux Gouvernements; mais si des sommes ont été attribuées par jugement aux réclamants, on en déduira les dits frais et dépenses communs autant qu'ils n'excéderont pas les 6% des valeurs que le Trésor chilien aurait à payer pour la totalité des réclamations qui auraient reçu satisfaction.

Les sommes qu'un jugement du tribunal attribuera aux réclamants seront remises par le gouvernement du Chili au gouvernement de S. M. B. par l'intermédiaire de la Légation à Santiago ou de la personne que celle-ci désignera, dans le délai d'une année à compter de la date de la décision respective, sans que, pendant ce délai, les dites sommes rapportent un intérêt quelconque en faveur des réclamants précités. Le gouvernement du Chili déduira de toutes sommes qu'il aura à payer pour satisfaire les réclamations soumises au tribunal, soit que le paiement se fasse par ordre du tribunal ou en vertu d'un arrangement privé, les sommes stipulées dans le troisième paragraphe de cet article, les dites sommes devant être retenues et employées pour le paiement des dépenses communes d'arbitrage.

ART. 9. Les hautes parties contractantes s'obligent à considérer les jugements du tribunal organisé par cette Convention comme une conclusion satisfaisante, parfaite et irrévocable, des difficultés dont le règlement est ainsi fait, de sorte que toutes les réclamations des sujets de S. M. B. présentées ou non dans les conditions signalées par les articles précédents soient tenues pour décidées et jugées définitivement et de manière que, sous aucun prétexte, elles ne puissent donner lieu à un nouvel examen ou à une nouvelle discussion.

Art. 10. Si les hautes parties contractantes n'arrivent pas à un accord concernant le troisième arbitre, elles demanderont à S. M. le Roi des Belges de faire cette désignation et, dans ce cas, la période dans laquelle le tribunal devra commencer ses travaux, sera de six mois à compter de la date de l'échange des ratifications de cette Convention.

Art. 11. La présente Convention sera ratifié par les hautes parties contractantes et l'échange des ratifications aura lieu à Santiago.

En foi de quoi, les soussignés plénipotentiaires du Chili et de S. M. Britannique ont signé ad referendum et en double exemplaire la présente Convention rédigée en espagnol et en anglais et y ont opposé le cachet de leurs armes.

Fait à Santiago, le 26 du mois de septembre de l'an de Notre Seigneur 1893 [1].

Rules of Procedure of the Anglo-Chilian Tribunal of Arbitration, Santiago, November 16, 1894.

Art. I. The Claimant, his Attorney or his legal representative, shall present to the Tribunal of Arbitration, within the time specified in Article I of the Convention of September 26, 1893, a memorial accompanied by all the documents and proofs in support of his claim. When the Claimant shall think fit to produce oral testimony of witnesses he must state in his memorial, or in an annex to it, the facts he proposes to establish as well as the name, profession, nationality, and residence of each witness.

The Tribunal shall have the right to authorise, during the proceedings, the attestation of new facts, and the examination of new witnesses.

The memorial must be transmitted through Her Britannic Majesty's Legation in Santiago, or presented by the agent named in accordance with Article IV of the Convention of Arbitration. In this latter case it will be deemed presented through the British Legation, thus complying with the requisite established by paragraph 2 of Article I of the Convention.

Art. II. The memorial, as well all documents annexed in support of the claim, must be presented in the Spanish language, accompanied by a faithful translation into English. In this form the answers must also be presented.

Art. III. The Memorial must contain the name and surname, profession and actual residence of the Claimant, the place and year of his birth, and the place of his residence at the time when the occurrences originating the claim took place. The Memorial and translation must be in print and 12 copies of each must be deposited in the Secretaries' Office.

Art. IV. The Memorial must also state whether the Claimant is British by birth or naturalisation, and must contain the information required by Article III for the establishment of the status and neutral character of the Claimant; it must also state whether he took part, directly or indirectly, in the Civil War which began on the 7th January, 1891, and terminated on the 28th August of that year, and whether he was, during that period, in the service or pay of either of the contending parties.

Art. V. If the claim is made in the name of a Company or firm which is not a Joint Stock Company, the nationality, and domicile of the Company or firm, and the names of all the parties interested in it must be given. When the claimant is not the person who has suffered damages but only the attorney or legal representative of that person, he must prove his personality and quality as such to the satisfaction of the Tribunal.

Art. VI. The Claimant must state in his Memorial whether he has received any money or compensation on account of his claim and from whom, and whether such claim had been previously presented to any other Tribunal.

Art. VII. The memorial must contain a clear and detailed statement of the claim, that is to say, its amount, the place and acts which have originated it, the quantity and value of the property lost, destroyed, or damaged and all the facts and circumstances having any relations to the loss and damage for which indemnity is claimed; and also, in so far as may be possible, the name, rank and position of the persons who committed the acts which have occasioned the claim.

If any receipt or any written declaration has been given to the Claimant, he must present it, and in case of not doing so he must explain the motives which render its presentation impossible.

Art. VIII. The Memorial must specify with precision the sum demanded, making a distinction between capital and interest, and stating the kind of money, which represents the value of the damages.

Art. IX. The Memorial must be accompanied by a declaration in which the Claimant ratifies under oath, or under a solemn declaration,

---

[1] F. de Martens, *Nouveau Recueil Général*, 2ᵐᵉ série, t. XXI, p. 649.

everything he has stated: this declaration must be received and legalised by a Diplomatic or Consular functionary, or in their default by the competent local authority.

ART. X. When a Memorial is presented, a written receipt shall be given by the secretaries to the agent presenting it. It will then be inscribed in the respective register of the Secretaries' office, noting down on the Memorial itself the date of its reception and the numerical order of its inscription.

The Secretaries shall then immediately notify the agent of the Chilian Government of the fact of the presentation. The agent of the Chilian Government shall have a term of 30 days, after being notified of the presentation of the Memorial, to reply to it, taking the exceptions he may deem necessary, and refuting the proofs of the Claimant with such counter-proofs as he may think relevant to his case, accompanied by all documents justifying his reply, and indicating the testimony of witnesses he may tend to produce in the course of his defence.

The Secretaries shall notify the agent of the British Government of this reply, who shall be allowed 30 days after the notification to answer it, presenting new documents, new petitions, and naming counter-proofs of witnesses, and he may also rectify and complete the requisites of the preceding Articles.

Notification of this presentation shall be given by the Secretaries to the Chilian Agent, who in his turn will be allowed 30 days to reply under the same conditions. His reply shall be notified to the British Agent.

In case the British Agent should renounce his right to answer the first reply of the Chilian Agent, he shall so notify the latter through the Secretaries, in which case the Chilian Agent will not have the faculty of making a second reply.

ART. XI. Whenever the oral testimony of witnesses is to be taken, the party offering it shall notify the facts he proposes to prove by this means, and he shall state, when possible, the names, residence, profession, and nationality of such witnesses. The residence of the witness must in all cases be given.

Whenever circumstances permit, the testimony of witnesses shall be taken before the Tribunal. When this is shown to the satisfaction of the Tribunal to be impossible, the Tribunal will decide how the evidence shall be taken, and will name a competent authority to take it.

The Agents, or their delegates, may be present at the examination of the witnesses and may cross-examine them. The witness shall testify under oath, or solemn declaration, and he shall state if he has any interest in the claim, if he is related to the Claimant, if he is a creditor or partner, whether he is at that moment in the employ of the Chilian Government, or was in the service of the said Government at the time that the act which originated the claim took place and if he took part directly or indirectly in the Civil War of 1891.

ART. XII. As soon as the last notification prescribed by Article X of these rules, or the time for presentation of proof has elapsed, whether this should have been taken or the party interested should have failed so to do within the limit of time, the Secretaries shall inscribe the Claim on the list of Claims for hearing, and the Secretaries shall notify the same within 48 hours to the agents of both Governments. Between this notification and the hearing not less than 10 days shall elapse.

The Tribunal, after hearing the case, may pronounce sentence if it should consider that no further investigation be necessary, or, on the contrary, it may of its own will, or on the petition of either Agent of either Government, order such further investigation as it may think proper, fixing the time and place when these investigations should be made.

ART. XIII. The Agents, Secretaries, Relator and the Advocates named by the parties according to Articles IV and V of the Convention are the only persons that may attend the sittings of the Tribunal. In no case shall any person be present during the deliberations of the Tribunal.

ART. XIV. The Secretaries shall keep, besides the register mentioned in Article X, a book in which they shall note down an extract of the proceeding in each case, another in which they will copy sentences, and a third in which they will transcribe the protocols of the sittings.

The extract of the proceedings in each case, the decrees and sentences, and the protocols of the sittings, shall be kept in duplicate, one copy in Spanish and the other in English. When the Tribunal has completed its labours the documents in the Spanish language will be delivered to the agent of the Chilian Government, and those in English to the agent of the British Government.

ART. XV. The Secretaries shall remit to each Agent a legalised copy of each decree, or sentence, as soon as pronounced, and the said Agent personally, or by means of a person specially delegated to do so, shall be allowed to inspect any documents he may require, and take copies of them by and with previous consent of the Tribunal.

The Tribunal reserves to itself the right to order or permit the publication of the documents deposited in the Secretaries' Office.

ART. XVI. The archives will be in charge of the Secretaries and without permission of the Tribunal it is prohibited to remove any document, paper or book from the Secretaries' Office.

ART. XVII. The Tribunal reserves the right to suppress, modify or augment the provisions of the preceding Articles when experience may indicate the advisability of doing so. It may likewise authorise the rectification of all errors of facts which the parties may have incurred in good faith [1].

Parmi les réclamations produites se trouvaient celles présentées par MM. W. E. Egerton et Barnett. Tous deux exigeaient des indemnités assez fortes, l'une de deux mille piastres et l'autre de neuf cents livres sterling. Dans les deux affaires les arbitres se décidèrent par les motifs suivants.

Sentence prononcée le 15 Septembre 1895 par le tribunal arbitral anglo-chilien formé en exécution du traité du 26 Septembre 1893.

. . . .

Attendu que la bataille de Placilla, qui eut pour résultat la chute définitive du président Balmacéda fut livrée le 28 août 1891 et à environ six kilomètres de la ville de Valparaiso ; que la nouvelle de la victoire du parti congressiste y fut connue très dix heures du matin, ainsi qu'il ressort du bulletin adressé à l'Amirauté par le capitaine de vaisseau Saint-Clair qui commandait le navire de guerre « Champion » mouillé alors dans la baie de Valparaiso (Blue Book, Correspondance relative à la Révolution du Chili, n° 1892, n° 1, p. 253) ; que les soldats de l'armée vaincue se réfugièrent à Valparaiso, ainsi que le constate le consul général d'Angleterre M. Servis Joel dans une communication adressée le 1er septembre au Foreign Office (loc. cit., p. 250) ;

Attendu que vers onze heures et demie du matin, l'intendant de Valparaiso, contre-amiral Viel, convaincu de son impuissance à continuer la résistance et à garantir l'ordre, s'adressa spontanément aux commandants des escadres mouillées dans le port et leur demanda de débarquer une partie de leurs forces et d'intervenir dans la reddition de la place au parti victorieux (Télégramme du contre-amiral de Valois à l'Amirauté

allemande, Livre blanc n° 243) ; que, depuis le milieu du jour, des marins des escadres allemande, anglaise, française et des Etats-Unis débarquèrent et se distribuèrent entre les divers quartiers principalement habités par les étrangers ; que le consul général d'Angleterre, dans sa communication, évalue ces forces à 700 hommes ;

Attendu que c'est seulement après le débarquement de ces forces et après une entrevue, qu'il avait lui-même sollicitée, avec les commandants des escadres et au moment même de l'entrée de l'avant-garde de l'armée victorieuse que l'amiral Viel se réfugia à bord du navire allemand « Leipsick » (Blue Book, loc. cit.); que dans l'après-midi, deux bataillons d'infanterie et un détachement de cavalerie occupèrent la ville et que, vers quatre heures, l'état-major installa son quartier général dans les bâtiments de l'Intendance :

Attendu que, d'après les communications officielles du commandant de l'escadre anglaise et du consul général anglais, l'ordre ne fut pas troublé durant le reste de la journée du 28 août et que ce fut seulement à la tombée de la nuit que des soldats démoralisés et la populace commirent des excès aux extrémités de la ville et incendièrent quelques maisons, et se livrèrent à des excès jusqu'au jour ; qu'il ressort de la communication du capitaine anglais Saint-Clair, que le peuple s'était emparé des fusils abandonnés par les soldats vaincus, et que ceux-ci dans leur fuite se dépouillèrent de leurs uniformes, afin de ne pas être reconnus et faits prisonniers ; que tous ces faits sont confirmés par le contre-amiral George Brown, de la marine des Etats-Unis (Correspondance officielle relative au Chili -- Washington 1892, p. 284), de même que par le contre-amiral allemand de Valois et le consul allemand à Valparaiso dans ses communications du 1er septembre 1895 (Livre blanc, n° 261 et 259), que le même amiral de Valois constate que « durant toute la nuit on entendit des décharges de fusils plus ou moins nourries faites principalement par les patrouilles contre les auteurs de pillage à main armée et les incendiaires » ;

Attendu que le Gouvernement du parti vainqueur nomma sans retard un intendant nouveau, M. Altamirano, qui entra immédiatement en fonctions et adressa le 29 août une proclamation aux habitants de Valparaiso ;

Attendu qu'il résulte de toutes ces circonstances, constatées officiellement par les autorités étrangères présentes, que si, malgré les mesures prises, des désordres graves se sont produits à Valparaiso dans la nuit du 28 au 29 août 1891, on ne peut en rejeter la responsabilité sur le

---

[1] HERTSLET. *A complete collection...*, t. XIX, p. 142.

Gouvernement, puisque, dans les circonstances difficiles où il se trouvait après une bataille sanglante qui mettait fin à une guerre civile qui avait surexcité les esprits, il a pris toutes les mesures à sa portée ; que la résolution extrême de solliciter des commandants des escadres le débarquement de marins étrangers prouve suffisamment qu'il n'y a pas eu de sa part une négligence ou une imprévoyance de nature à engager sa responsabilité ;

Attendu que le réclamant se borne à dire que la maison qu'il habitait a été envahie par une bande de soldats sans préciser si ces soldats étaient sous la surveillance de leurs chefs et sans prouver qu'ils appartenaient à l'armée régulière : qu'il résulte au contraire des communications officielles précitées qu'il est très vraisemblable, ainsi que le disent également le commandant de l'escadre anglaise, le consul général anglais et d'autres fonctionnaires étrangers, que les excès commis le furent par des soldats fugitifs et la populace armée, excès que l'autorité était alors dans l'impossibilité de réprimer d'une manière complète et efficace ;

Attendu que lorsqu'un Gouvernement est temporairement incapable de contenir sur son territoire une partie de la population ou des individus qui se sont soustraits à son autorité et se sont soulevés contre elle, en cas de rebellion, de guerre civile ou de troubles locaux, il n'est pas responsable des préjudices subis par des étrangers ;

Attendu que si le droit international prescrit aux autorités militaires d'un pays belligérant de faire tout ce qui est en leur pouvoir pour assurer le respect de la propriété des habitants pacifiques par les personnes qui sont sous leurs ordres, il n'y a rien qui prouve que les désordres relatifs dont la ville de Valparaiso a eu à souffrir aient été le fait des soldats de l'armée victorieuse, les seuls sur lesquels les chefs eussent encore conservé leur autorité ; qu'il est d'ailleurs admis par la doctrine et la jurisprudence que les faits de maraude et de pillage commis par des soldats débandés et hors de la surveillance de leurs chefs n'engagent pas la responsabilité de leurs Gouvernements ; que de tels faits sont considérés comme des délits de droit commun, sujets seulement à la répression pénale ordinaire (William Edward Hall, Traité de Droit International, 3ᵉ édition, 1890, Oxford, p. 218. — Bluntschli, le Droit International codifié, art. 280ᵇⁱˢ. — Dudley Field, Code International, p. 249 et 721. — Revue générale de Droit International, année 1895, n° 3, mai-juin. — Tribunal arbitral anglo-chilien de 1884, sentence n° 50, p. 351. — Tribunal arbitral italo-chilien de 1884, sentence n° 96, p. 305).

Pour ces motifs, le Tribunal arbitral, à la majorité des voix, le vote de l'arbitre anglais étant contraire, déclare le Gouvernement chilien irresponsable des pertes subies par le réclamant.

Santiago, le 25 septembre 1895 [1].

Une autre sentence, également intéressante, mérite d'être reproduite.

Decision of Belgian and British arbitrators on claim of bark „Chépica". Santiago, December 12, 1895.

Considering that the convention of arbitration of September 26, 1893, only submits to the jurisdiction of this tribunal « claims based upon acts or operations executed by the land and sea forces of the Republic during the civil war which began on January 7, 1891, and ended on August 28 of the same year»;

Considering that the refusal on the part of the authorities of the port of Valparaiso to permit the bark *Chépica* to set sail for Tocopilla on March 7, 1891, because the latter port was at that time occupied by revolutionary forces does not partake of the character of an act executed by the land forces of the Republic, but an act of the de jure Government of the country executed in accordance with law ; that article 7 of the act of December 26, 1872, authorizes the President of the Republic « to close temporarily one or more ports to commerce whenever extraordinary circumstances require it »; that such a measure dictated as a measure of urgency when the forces of the Congressional party occupied the ports of the north was ratified by supreme decree dated April 1, 1891, which declared the eight first-class ports of the north, from Chanaral to Pisagua, as well as the intermediate harbors, closed to commerce; that the fact that this measure, which, from the point of view of an internal public law, is entirely legal, had been taken by the de jure Government of the country during the civil war, is not sufficient to give it the character of an act executed by the land forces of the Republic against the bark *Chépica*;

Considering that article 17 of the treaty of amity, commerce, and navigation, concluded on October 4, 1854, between Chile and Great Britain, stipulates that whenever in case of war, and when the interests of the State are so seriously affected as to necessitate such action, one of the contracting parties shall decree the general embargo or closing of ports, merchant vessels can only claim certain stipulated indemnities if the detention or closing exceeds the

---

[1] F. DE MARTENS, *Nouveau Recueil Général*, 2° série, t. XXI, p. 652.

period of six days; that by this clause Great Britain recognizes that the Chilean Government has the right to detain vessels and to close ports in case of war, but on condition of granting certain indemnities ; that the claim being based upon measures taken in time of war, we must examine whether this tribunal has jurisdiction to apply the provisions of the treaty of October 4, 1854, to the case in question, since, by the very terms of the convention, it must observe the rules of international law, which comprises the general law of nations and the special law of nations established by treaties (A. Merignhac, Traité Théorique et Pratique de l'Arbitrage International, Paris, 1895, p. 289 ; Calvo, Le Droit International Théorique et Pratique, vol. III, p. 1768) ;

Considering that the measure taken by the Government of President Balmaceda regarding the bark *Chépica*, destined to a port in the north of Chile, is invested with the character of a ruler's decree (arrêt de prince), which is but one of the forms of embargo, as is admitted by the agent of the Chilean Government (Calvo, Le Droit International, vol. III, p. 1277 ; — Carlos Testa, Le Droit Public International Maritime, Paris, 1886, p. 128) ; that if the Government has the right in time of war, in the interest of its own defense, to detain neutral vessels in its ports, and refuses them authorization to proceed to certain ports which are declared closed, the exercise of this right not only involves its moral responsibility, but also its real responsibility, whenever the case has been provided for in an international treaty, a circumstance which exists in the present case ; that otherwise there would result, at least as regards vessels which are in ports of the country that are not closed and destined for ports which are closed, the establishment of a paper blockade prohibited by modern international law ;

Considering besides that the decree of April 1, 1891, promulgated by President Balmaceda, and placing upon a regular basis the measures of urgency which had already been taken, declares that the eight first-class ports situated between Chanaral and Pisagua, as well as the intermediate harbors, are closed to commerce ; that as this measure, which is applicable to an extended coast, and to all vessels without distinction of nationality which may be anchored in the ports still in possession of the Government, may be considered as a general closure of the ports provided for by article 17 of the treaty of 1854 ; that a belligerent can not without exposing himself to responsibility, especially when the measure is provided for in the treaties concluded by such belligerent, declare one or several ports over

which he has lost all control to be closed pending the duration of a war, except on the condition of employing force to prevent access to them, and for imposing in this way an effective blockade, « In the case where a revolution or civil war breaks out in a country », says Lord John Russel, quoted by Hall, « the Government can not declare ports which are in possession of the insurgents to be closed, and such a measure would be a violation of the laws of blockade » (W. E. Hall, A Treatise on International Public, p. 75) ;

Considering that if the measure taken by President Balmaceda in reference to the bark *Chépica* falls under article 17 of the treaty of 1854, which regulates the question of indemnity in case of embargo or general closing of ports, the same article provides for the appointment of special arbitrators whose duty it is, in case of disagreement, to fix the amount of indemnities, and that consequently this tribunal has no jurisdiction to give a decision in this case.

For these reasons the tribunal of arbitration unanimously declares that it has no jurisdiction to decide the present case, the Chilean arbitrator having declared that he does not accept, for the reasons stated in his dissenting opinion, the second ground upon which the tribunal declares itself without jurisdiction.

Santiago, December 12, 1895[1].

Report on the arbitration of British claims growing out of civil war, made to his government by the Minister of the United States of America. Santiago, April 23, 1896.

I have the honor to report that the Anglo-Chilean tribunal of arbitration closed its labors some weeks ago.

The tribunal was composed of Monsieur Camille Janssen, appointed by the King of the Belgians, president of the tribunal ; Mr. Alfred St. John, Her Britannic Majesty's consul at Callao, British arbitrator ; and señor Luis Aldunate, Chilean arbitrator.

The decisions are being published from time to time in the Official Journal (Diario official). I have, however, secured a statement of the result of the arbitration.

The claims may be divided into the following classes, according to the grounds on which they were presented and the principles on which they were decided :

I. For loss of property by the fire in Iquique on February 19, 1891, twenty claims, amounting to £ 17,319 9 s. 4 d. and $ 24,359. Disallowed,

---

[1] *Foreign Relations of U. S.*, 1896, p. 38.

the British arbitrator dissenting on the ground that the fire was caused by the bombardment, which was considered a legitimate act of warfare.

II. For loss of property by fire in Pisagua on April 6, 1891, five claims, amounting to £ 4,013 18 s. 2 d. and $ 4,016.98. Disallowed unanimously on the same ground as the preceding class.

III. Loss of property by fire and pillage on the entry of the congressional troops into Valparaiso, August 28, 1891, five claims, amounting to £ 1,150 and $ 44,273. 50. Disallowed, the British arbitrator dissenting on the ground that the authorities were powerless to prevent the disorder.

IV. Loss of property by the sacking of Santiago on August 29, 1891, one claim, amounting to $ 30,393. 95. Disallowed unanimously on the same ground as the preceding class.

V. Loss of property through pillage by Government troops at Miramar in August, 1891, four claims, amounting to £ 4,787 19 s. and $ 3,679. 15.

An agreement was made between the British and Chilean agents by which the Chilean Government paid a lump sum of £ 2,097 12 s. in settlement of these claims. This action was probably due to the decision of the commission of the United States and Chile at Washington in favor of W. S. Shrigley, Nº 4, which belonged to this class.

VI. For murder near Valparaiso, one claim, presented by the widow of the victim, for £ 20,000. Dismissed unanimously for want of jurisdiction, because there was no evidence that the murder had been committed by military forces.

VII. For illegal imprisonment, two cases, amounting to £ 5,400. Dismissed unanimously for want of jurisdiction, because there was no evidence to show that the imprisonment complained of was by order of the Chilean military forces.

VIII. For illegal imprisonment and cruelty, two claims, amounting to £ 25,000. Dismissed unanimously for want of jurisdiction, on two grounds: First, because the imprisonment was not by the military authorities, and second, because the acts complained of had taken place after the time fixed by the convention, which embraced the period from January 7 to August 28, 1891. The two cases of this class were Patrick Shields and Andrew Mc. Kinstrey, respectively Nºˢ 23 and 24, before the commission at Washington.

IX. For seizure of mules, horses, etc., in different parts of the Republic, eighteen claims, amounting to £ 19,586 4 s. 1 d. and $ 48,263.97. Four claims were awarded, the Chilean arbitrator dissenting in all but one case, $ 15,572. 82. Twelve claims were disallowed for want of evidence, and on two claims the tribunal came to no decision.

X. For damage to railway lines and interruption of traffic, two claims, amounting, respectively, to £ 1,310 4 s. 8 d. and $ 200,000. The tribunal awarded, respectively, the Chilean arbitrator dissenting, £ 9,542 and $ 111,721. 85.

XI. Services rendered by railways to the Government by conveyance of troops, war material, etc., two claims, amounting to £48,775 19 s. 5 d. and $ 40,011.98. Dismissed, with the dissenting vote of the British arbitrator, for want of jurisdiction, as being proper subjects for the courts of the country.

XII. Forced discharge of cargo arriving for railway company at Antofagasta, one claim, amounting to £ 184 0 s. 7 d. Disallowed for want of evidence.

XIII. For refusal to grant clearance papers to vessels and their consequent detention, twelve cases, amounting to £ 8,984 19 s. 6 d. Dismissed for want of jurisdiction, on two grounds : First, because the act complained of was the result of an administrative order and not the act of military forces ; second, because the indemnity is provided for by the treaty of amity, commerce and navigation of 1854 between Great Britain and Chile. The refusal of the Chilean arbitrator to sign these decisions is the subject of my following dispatch of this date.

XIV. For demurrage, twenty one claims, amounting to £ 19,584 2 s. 11 d. Eighteen were unanimously disallowed because the delay was caused in consequence of warlike operations and the general state of affairs during the revolution. The remaining were dismissed for want of jurisdiction, because the damage complained of was the result of the action of the civil authorities.

XV. For preventing a vessel from communicating with people on shore at the port into which she had put in distress, one claim for £ 450 8 s. 4 d. Dismissed for want of jurisdiction, because it was the act of the civil authorities.

XVI. For dead freight through vessels being prevented from loading their full cargo because military forces had blown up the loading apparatus at Lobos de Afuera, five claims, amounting to £ 7,382 15 s. 6 d.; four claims were awarded, £ 3,960 6 s. 2 d. The remaining claim was dismissed for want of jurisdiction on account of there being no evidence that it was the act of military forces.

XVII. For breach of charter party by Government through inability to furnish cargo on account of destruction by troops of loading apparatus at Lobos de Afuera, one claim, amounting to £ 4,218. Awarded, Chilean arbitrator dissenting, £ 1,500.

XVIII. For injury to vessels and delay in consequence of bombardment, four claims, amounting to £ 2,518 19 s. 4 d. Disallowed; acts complained of being those of legitimate warfare.

XIX. For notification of vessel on high sea of the existence of a blockade which was only a paper blockade, and causing her to proceed to a different port, one claim, amounting to £ 989 1 s. 2 d. Disallowed for want of evidence.

The general result of the arbitration on these cases between Great Britain an Chile was, therefore, as follows : 101 claims presented, amounting to £ 191.928 9 s. 7 d. and $ 594,295.06; claims disallowed, £ 57,267 4 s. 1 d. and $ 114,978.18; claims dismissed for want of jurisdiction, £ 111,473 15 s. 2 d. ; claims allowed, £ 7,548 18 s. 2 d. and $ 135,079.30; claims withdrawn, £ 439 19 s. and $ 199,295.90; claims on which the members of the tribunal arrived at no decision, £ 5,861 13 s. 4 d. Number of claimants, 101. Interest at the rate of 6 per cent per annum was allowed in almost all the awards[1].

CXII. Grande-Bretagne, Transvaal.

11 juillet 1894.

Après une correspondance qui prit naissance au cours de l'année 1884, le Haut Commissaire du Cap consentit, par lettre du 21 mars 1894, à accepter le principe de l'arbitrage au sujet des difficultés nées de l'immigration au Transvaal de personnes de couleur originaires des Indes anglaises. Le Volksraad acquiesça à cet arbitrage par délibération du 11 juillet 1894.

Letter from the High Commissioner, Capetown, March 21, 1894, in the case of British Indians.

With reference to the question of arbitration in the case of British Indians, resident in the South African Republic, I have the honour to acquaint you that Her Majesty's Government assent to the principle of arbitration and agree

to the selection of the Chief Justice of the Orange Free State if that gentleman can be induced to act. Her Majesty's Government assume that the arbitration will apply to any arboriginal of Asia who may be a British subject. Will Your Honour obtain from the President and Chief Justice of the Orange Free State the necessary approval and consent for the Chief Justice to act as arbitrator or shall I do so[1].

Volksraadbesluit dd. 11 Juli 1894 in de kwestie van Aziatische gekleurde personen.

De Eerste Volksraad, gelet hebbende op De Regeeringsmissive, dd. 28. 5. 1894, voorstellende de koelie-kwestie te onderwerpen aan arbitrage; gelet hebbende op de correspondentie omtrent den arbiter gevoerd ; gelet hebbende dat de keuze voor arbiter gevallen is op den Hoofdrechter van den Oranje Vrystaat; besluit : zich met die keuze te vereenigen en de H. Ed. Regeering de macht te geven, indien Z. Ed. Gest. de Hoofdrechter van de Oranje Vrystaat zich de keuze laat welgevallen, hem als arbiter in deze te laten optreden[2].

Award of the arbitrator with reference to the matters in controversy, relative to article 14 of the Convention of London of 1884, pronounced to Bloemfontein, April 2, 1895.

Whereas certain questions have arisen between the Government of the South African Republic and the Government of Her Majesty the Queen of the United Kingdom of Great Britain and Ireland, with reference to the fourteenth article of a certain Convention entered into in London, on the 27th day of February, 1884, by the representatives of the said Governments on behalf of the said Governments respectively, with reference to Law N° 3, of 1885, enacted and in the year 1886 amended, by the Volksraad of the South African Republic, and with reference to certain dispatches thereunto relating ;

And whereas the said Governments have agreed to submit the said questions to arbitrator, and have nominated me, the undersigned, Melius de Villiers, as arbitrator, to decide and determine the matters in controversy between the said Governments; and, I, the arbitrator so nominated, have taken upon myself the burden of such arbitration ;

And whereas it has been agreed on behalf of the said Governments, that the arbitrator, taking into consideration the statements of the

[1] J. B. Moore, History and Digest..., p. 4931.

[1] Groenboek, 1894, II, bldz 92.
[2] Groenboek, 1899, III, bldz 3.

case, put forward by the Government of the South African Republic and Her Majesty's Government respectively, and of the correspondence therein cited, might decide as to him, the arbitrator, should appear to be equitable and just;

And whereas Her Majesty's Government, in their statement of the case, claim:

a. That the Indian and other Asiatic traders, being British subjects, be allowed to reside in the towns of the South African Republic, in some quarters, (wards and streets) which for sanitary purposes may be assigned to them;

b. That they may be allowed to carry on their trade or business in shops or stores in any part of the town;

And whereas the Government of the South African Republic, in their statement of the case, claim:

a. That the South African Republic is fully entitled to make such regulations concerning Coolies, Arabs, Malays and Mohammedan subjects of the Turkish Empire as it may think fit;

b. That Her Majesty's Government is not entitled to object when the Government of the South African Republic prohibit Coolies, Arabs, Malays and Mohammedan subjects of the Turkish Empire from having business premises in villages and towns on other places than those assigned by the Government.

And whereas I, the said arbitrator, have heard the counsels, instructed on behalf of the said Governments respectively, and considered their arguments, and have carefully investigated the aforesaid questions and documents relating thereto;

And whereas it was agreed and understood that I, the said arbitrator, should give my award on the aforesaid questions in writing, in duplicate, to be communicated to the Governments before mentioned respectively;

Now, therefore I, the said arbitrator, do make this my award in writing, in manner following, that is to say:

a. The claims of Her Majesty's Government and of the South African Republic respectively, are disallowed, save and except to the extent and degree, following that is to say:

b. The South African Republic is bound and entitled in its treatment of Indian and other Asiatic traders, being British subjects, to give full force and effect to Law No. 3 of 1885 enacted, and in the year 1886 amended by the Volksraad of the South African Republic, subject (in case of objections being raised by or on behalf of any such persons to any such treatment as not being in accordance with the provisions of the said law as amended) to sole and exclusive

interpretation in the ordinary course by the tribunals of the country.

In witness whereof, I, the said Melius de Villiers, have hereunto set my hand this second day of April 1895.

Reasons of the Arbitrator for his award with reference to the matters in controversy, relative to Article 14 of the Convention of London of 1884.

§ 1. The questions in controversy between Her Majesty's Government and the Government of the South African Republic, relate to the interpretation and effect of the fourteenth Article of the Convention of London, entered into by the two Governments; of the terms in which assent was given by the British Government to legislation on the part of the South African Republic, on certain matters in connection whit that article of Law No. 3 of 1885, enacted by the Volksraad of the South African Republic, and consequently amended by that legislative body; of the terms in which assent was given by the British Government to this enactment, and of the dispatches which passed between the two Governments on the. subjects to which the above mentioned Article of the Convention and Law No. 3 of 1885, as subsequently amended, refer.

§ 2. Article 14 of the Convention of London is to the following effect:

All persons, other than natives, conforming themselves to the laws of the South African Republic:

a. Will have full liberty with their families, to enter, travel or reside in any part of the South African Republic;

b. Will be entitled to hire or possess houses, manufactories, warehouses, shops and premises;

c. May carry on their commerce either in person or by any agents whom they may think fit to employ;

d. Will not be subject in respect of their persons or property, or in respect of their commerce or industry, to any taxes, whether general or local, other than those which are or may be imposed upon citizens of the said Republic.

§ 3. In the same year that the Convention of London was signed, an agitation was set on foot in the South African Republic, against the threatened invasion of « Asiatics, such as already has commenced at Pretoria », and memorials were sent in to the Volksraad, strongly urging that the influx of such Asiatics should be restricted by law.

In a petition (of this document and of some others that originally appeared in Dutch, the translation is my own), signed by T. W. Beckett and 86 others, the memorialists say amongst other things:

‹ We fear that if His Lordship (Lord Derby, then Secretary of State) should be of opinion, that Asiatics should enjoy the same privileges as Europeans who came to settle in this State, this would be in conflict with our constitution, which recognises only two races of men, white and coloured; and the clause in the constitution relative to this matter remained unaltered during the time of the British Government.

. . . .

‹ Our knowledge of South African affairs and of the use and meaning of the word 'native', creates the conviction, that the representatives of the South African Republic and of Great Britain could only and exclusively have meant by the words:

I. ‹ All persons, all Europeans and their descendants ›. II. ‹ Natives, the aboriginal races of South Africa and their descendants ›.

Indeed, the meaning of the two expressions used in the Conventions of Pretoria and of London was quite limited in intention and applications to the conditions of Southern Africa; and it would be equally incorrect to suppose that the aboriginal races of Asia, America and Australia are included in the expression of the Convention ‹ Natives › as to suppose that they would be included under the expression of the Convention ‹ all persons ›.

‹ The Aborigines of Asia, America and Australia are out of the questions and have nothing to do with our conditions. ›

After adducing a number of arguments against Asiatic races being allowed freely to settle in the territory of the South African Republic, the petition ends with the following words:

‹ Lastly, and with further reference to the 14th Article of the Convention of London, we have the honour to observe, that if the Right Honourable Lord Derby should be of opinion that our reading . . . . is not the correct one, it then becomes evident, that the well educated Christian natives of South Africa, under the constitution of this Republic, are held to occupy a lower and far less advantageous position in this State, than the common Hindoo-Coolies and the other aborigines of the other parts of the world.

‹ We hope and trust that the Right Honourable Lord Derby shall be willing to devote such attention to this matter, as its importance so urgently demands, and that he shall be willing to elucidate and declare the substance of Article 14 of the London Convention in such a

manner, that you will be enabled to take such steps as may seem to you to be requisite to protect the joint interests of the subjects of Her Majesty and of the citizens of this State. ›

§ 4. Another petition addressed to the Volksraad stated:

‹ That the population of the Arabians and Coolies is much increasing in this town and in this State. That your memorialists after extensive and careful investigation, founded upon the experience and acts of legislative bodies of other countries, are of opinion, that the present system by which Arabians and Coolies are permitted to settle in any part of the towns of this Republic, and more especially in the centres and principal streets, should be abolished in the interest of the inhabitants of this State, and this for the following reasons:

a. ‹ Your petitioners are in a position to prove, that all sanitary measures are neglected in the extreme in the dwelling-houses of the Arabians and Coolies, and that their mode of living is loathsome.

b. ‹ Your petitioners further wish to bring to your notice that at a meeting of the most influential inhabitants of the town, it has been stated by the District Surgeon, that by allowing the Arabians and Coolies to live amidst a white population, the development and spreading of epidemics and of the consequent deaths are much accelerated. And it is apparent, that if these Arabians and Coolies are isolated within their own locations, quite separated from the white population, such epidemics can be counteracted sooner and with more effect, not only for the welfare of the Arabians and Coolies themselves, but also in the interest and for the protection of the white inhabitants. ›

§ 5. A counter-petition was also presented to the Volksraad by certain Arab merchants, in which they draw attention to the difference between themselves and Coolies, Chinese, &c., contradict certain assertions made in the petitions presented by the white inhabitants, and pray that their demands might not be acceded to.

§ 6. A letter, dated 6th January 1885 (G. B. I, No. 9, p. 21) was thereafter sent by the Government of the South African Republic to Lord Derby on the subject of the petitions, which were inclosed therewith. In this letter the writer referred amongst other things, to the fact, that a few years since Orientals had emigrated from Asia or Northern Africa, nearly all of them being storekeepers, and had settled in the Republic, and that gradually an agitation had been begun against these persons, which had found expression in the newspapers, in a certain pamphlet and in numerously signed petitions to the Volksraad, which went mainly to shew their unsuitability as residents in the country and the detrimental effect that would follow their being allowed to trade in competition with whites, and he continued by stating that the Volksraad was not unwilling to meet the wishes of the white petitioners, entirely or partly; for example, by assigning to the Orientals thus immigrated locations or wards within certain prescribed limits. The letter here referred to ended thus:

« The view taken in this last petition (that set out in § 3 above) is to the effect that the London Convention does not relate to the persons against whom the petitioners raised their complaints.

« I beg to request that Your Lordship will be so good as to acquaint this Government as to the views of Her Majesty's Government on the subject, that is, whether in the opinion of Her Majesty's Government, this Government is at liberty under the Convention now in force, to frame such regulations relative to the coloured persons referred to, as may appear to it to be in the interests of the inhabitants of this Republic and if not, whether Her Majesty's Government by its assent will empower this Government to meet either entirely or partly the wishes of the petitioners of European descent. »

§ 7. His Excellency the High Commissioner Sir Hercules Robinson, in forwarding this letter to the Secretary of State, in an accompanying dispatch, dated 28th January, 1885 (G. B. 1, p. 27) wrote as follows: —

I. « I have the honour to enclose a letter from the State Secretary of South African Republic, which has been forwarded to me for transmission to Your Lordship.

II. « Mr. Bok encloses petitions and other documents relating to the position of Asiatics in the South African Republic and in connection with the question raised, asks what meaning is attached by Her Majesty's Government to Article 14 of the London Convention.

III. « . . . .
The point raised is whether Arabs, Indian Coolies, Malays, Chinese and other Asiatics are to be considered « Natives » or whether they are included amongst the persons other than natives, to whom certain specified rights are secured.

IV. « Article 14 of the London Convention (with the exception of the substitution of the words 'South African Republic' for 'Transvaal State'), is the same as Article 26 of the Convention of Pretoria. The latter article as originally drafted by the Royal Commission and

agreed to by the representatives of the Boers, ran as follows: —

« The subjects of Her Majesty conforming themselves to the laws &c., &c. — When this article was telegraphed to Lord Kimberley, he, in his message of the 27th July, 1881, instructed me to omit the subjects of Her Majesty, and insert all persons other than natives, which was done. »

. . . .

VII. « As it was doubtless not the intention of Lord Kimberley, to prohibit the Transvaal Government from adopting, if necessary, special legislation for the regulation of Indian or Chinese Coolie Immigrants, I should be disposed to recommend that the Government of the South African Republic be informed that Her Majesty's Government will be willing to amend Article 14 of the Convention, by asserting the words African natives or Indian or Chinese Coolies immigrants. »

The article would then run as follows:
« All persons, other than African natives or Indian or Chinese Coolie immigrants, conforming themselves to the laws of the South African Republic, will have full liberty with their families to enter, travel or reside, &c. »

VIII. « The article as amended would still leave the few Arab traders at present in Pretoria, entitled to liberties secured under the existing article to all persons other than natives, and I can see no sufficient grounds for their being deprived of their rights. »

§ 8. It may be conveniently noticed here, in the first place, that the point raised was not quite that which it was understood by Sir Hercules Robinson to be;

The contention was rather that there had not been any intention on the part of the parties to the Convention to include Asiatics amongst either other persons than natives, or amongst natives.

This was also later the contention of counsel for the South African Republic before the Arbitrator. This contention amounted in fact to this: That the representatives of Her Majesty's Government had solely in view the interests of European or white settlers in the South African Republic; and that at the time the Convention of London was signed, and still more so at the time the Convention of Pretoria (Article 26 of which, slightly modified as stated by His Excellency in his dispatch last referred to, became Article 14 of the later Convention) was signed, there was as yet no such general influx of foreign coloured natives that the exclusion of any but the natives of South Africa from the privileges granted in that Article should have been thought of as necessary.

In the second place it may be remarked that the reference in the concluding passage of Sir Hercules Robinson's dispatch to the few Arab traders at present in Pretoria, left it not quite clear whether His Excellency wished only to safeguard the rights of those few Arab traders whom he stated to be then at Pretoria; and what, in prospect of the threatened invasion of Asiatics, such as had already commenced at Pretoria, as alleged in the petitions above referred to, his views were as to Arabs who might subsequently settle in that country.

§ 9. The Secretary of State, Lord Derby, replied on the 19th March 1885, in a dispatch to the High Commissioner (G. B. I, p. 29) in the following terms:

« I have carefully considered your suggestion as to the amendment of the Convention, and if you are of opinion that it would be preferable and more satisfactory to the Government of the South African Republic, to proceed as you propose, Her Majesty's Government will be willing to amend the Convention as suggested. It seems to deserve consideration, however, whether it would not be more correct for the Volksraad to legislate in the proposed sense having received an assurance that Her Majesty's Government will not desire to insist upon any such construction of the terms of the Convention as would interfere with reasonable legislation in the desired direction. »

This dispatch was communicated to the Government of the South African Republic, together with the dispatch of the High Commissioner, to which it was a reply.

§ 10. It will be seen hereafter that the construction subsequently placed by the Government of the South African Republic upon the concluding words of this dispatch differed from that placed upon them by Her Majesty's Government. The former held that the words legislation in the desired direction should be read in connection with the letter forwarded by that Government to Lord Derby on the 6th January, 1885 (§ 5 above), and were intended to mean legislation in which the Volksraad had expressed a desire to legislate; the latter held that these words should be explained as referring to the High Commissioner's dispatch of 28th January, 1885 (§ 7 above), and meant the same as « legislation in the proposed sense »; that is to say « special legislation for the regulation of Indian or Chinese Coolie immigrants ».

§ 11. Acting however, it seems, upon what they conceived to be the purport of Lord Derby's dispatch above referred to, and having before them the correspondence which had passed between the two Governments on the subject, Government of the South African Republic prepared and laid before the Volksraad a draft-law, which with some slight modifications was adopted by the Volksraad as Law N° 3 of 1885. This enactment was to the following effect: —

I. « This law applies to persons belonging to any of the aboriginal races of Asia, including thereunder the so-called Coolies, Arabs, Malays and Mahommedan subjects of the Turkish Empire. »

II. « With respect to the persons referred to in Section I, the following provisions shall be in force:

a. « They shall not acquire citizenship in the South African Republic; »

b. « They shall not be owners of landed property in the Republic. This provision has no retroactive effect; »

c. « Those who settle in the Republic with the object of trading, &c., shall have to be inscribed in a Register, to be specially kept for that purpose by the Landdrosts of the respective districts, according to a model to be prescribed by the Government.

« With this registration, which shall have to be effected within eight days after arrival, the sum of £ 25 (twenty five pounds) sterling shall be payable. Contravention of the provisions contained in c, shall be punishable by a fine of from £ 10 (ten) to £ 100 (one hundred pounds) sterling for which shall be substituted in default of payment imprisonment for not less than fourteen days and not more than half a year.

« The registration above referred to, shall be effected without payment in the case of those who have settled in the Republic before the date upon which this law shall come into operation, provided that they shall have announced themselves to the Landdrosts, in the case of Pretoria within eight days, and in the case of other districts within thirty days after such date. »

d. « The Government shall have the right to assign to them special streets, wards and locations for habitation.

« This provision shall not apply to those who reside with the masters in whose service they are. »

§ 12. On 9th October 1885, Mr. Michell, Joint General Manager of the Standard Bank of South Africa, sent a communication to His Excellency the High Commissioner, Sir Hercules Robinson (G. B. I, p. 36), in which he complained of the operation of the law N° 3 of 1885, passed in respect of Coolies, Arabs, and Asiatics generally. On the 16th of that month the Imperial Secretary in Cape Town wrote a letter to the State Secretary of the South African Republic, in which (G. B. 1, N° 22, p. 36), after referring to the complaints thus made, he says: —

« His Excellency desires me to refer you to the last paragraph of his dispatch to the Secretary of State, a copy of which was forwarded to you in my letter, and to point out that the new law relating to Asiatics, if Mr. Michell has correctly apprehended its effect, is a breach of the understanding upon which Her Majesty's Government waived their right to insist upon the strict interpretation of the terms of the Convention of London.

« It was expressly understood by the Secretary of State that the proposed legislation was not to apply to Arab traders or merchants, but to Indian or Chinese Coolie immigrants. »

His Excellency trusts therefore that the Government of the South African Republic will be able to assure him that merchants or traders of the class mentioned in Mr. Michell's letter, and especially such as are British subjects, will enjoy the same privileges as are secured by the Convention of London to « all persons other than natives ».

§ 13. With reference to the last preceding letter it was pointed out to the arbitrator by Counsel for the South African Republic, that the Secretary of State had, as a matter of fact, not given any express intimation that the proposed legislation should not apply to Arab traders or merchants. The Imperial Secretary's reference however undoubtedly is to the general assent given by the Secretary of State on 19th March, 1885 (v. § 9 above), to the suggestions of Sir Hercules Robinson contained in his dispatch of 28th January (v. § 7 above) which, as before stated, he concluded by saying that article 14 of the Convention if amended as proposed by His Excellency, would not apply to the few Arab traders at Pretoria, at the time when His Excellency wrote.

§ 14. Again on 24th October, 1885, the Imperial Secretary to the High Commissioner Sir Hercules Robinson, wrote a letter (G. B. 1, N° 23, p. 38) to the State Secretary of the South African Republic, in which, referring to certain disabilities complained of by a certain Mr. Cronwright, as having been imposed upon Arab merchants, he expressed His Excellency's view that such disabilities constituted a breach of the understanding on which Her Majesty's Government waived their right to insist on a strict interpretation of the terms of the Convention of London, and intimated that His Excellency would

be glad to receive an early assurance that merchants of that class had been relieved from those disabilities.

§ 15. Amongst other further correspondence the Government of the South African Republic, in a letter of 23rd December, 1885, signed by the State Secretary (G. B. 1, N° 26, p. 41), defended its action with respect to Law N° 3 of 1885, and submitted that the law passed had no wider application than that proposed in the dispatch from that Government of 6th January 1885 (v. § 6 above), and stated that the law had been passed only after the Government had gratefully received the assurance of Her Majesty's Government contained in Lord Derby's dispatch of 19th March, 1885 (v. § 9 above).

§ 16. On 20th January, 1886, the High Commissioner forwarded a dispatch to the British Government, asking for instructions upon this subject. No copy of this dispatch was served upon the Government of the South African Republic, and it is therefore not necessary to recite any part of it.

§ 17. On the 24th February, 1886, the Secretary of State (Lord Granville, who had succeeded Lord Derby), wrote to the High Commissioner, requesting the latter to inform the Government of the South African Republic, that he was unable to accept the explanation offered in the State Secretary's letter of 23rd December 1885, (v. § 15 above) and that he must desire that the law in question may be revised « as it is in direct opposition to the views of Her Majesty's Government, and in its present form is a contravention of the Convention of London » (G. B. 1, p. 43).

§ 18. In a letter of 6 September, 1886 (G. B. 1, N° 32, p. 45), to the High Commissioner, the State Secretary, on behalf of the Government of the South African Republic, expressed its regret that the provisions of the Law N° 3 of 1885 were not quite in accordance with the views of Her Majesty's Government, and that there had been an apparent misconception as to the understanding upon which the British Government had waived its right to insist upon the strict interpretation of the Convention of London. « It appears » (it is remarked), « that there likewise exists a misconception in respect of the object with which the law referred to was made.

« It was for the sake of the general sanitary conditions, with a view to the experience gained in other countries and colonies, and also already in this country, very desirable and necessary to take measures of a sanitary nature in respect of those foreign Orientals who have settled themselves here in increasing numbers, and that first *after* the Pretoria Convention was signed, and selected their residences everywhere in the midst of the white population. It was to meet this necessity and the wishes in accordance therewith expressed by the memorialists (most of them British subjects) and already brought to the notice of Her Majesty's Government, that the law referred to was passed.

‹ This Government is not disinclined to let that object appear more clearly and to meet the views of Her Majesty's Government It has therefore asked and obtained from the Volksraad authorisation to amend Law No. 3 of 1885 on the following bases:

I. ‹ That after the first division of section 2 *b* of Law No. 3 of 1885, shall be added these words: 'Excepting in those streets, wards and locations which the Government shall assign to them for sanitary purposes' › ;

II. ‹ That the sum of £ 25, mentioned in the second division of section 2 *c* of the said law, shall be brought down to £ 3 › ;

III. ‹ That section 2 *d* of the said law shall read as follows: The Government shall have the right for sanitary reasons to assign to them definite streets, wards and locations for habitation. This provision does not apply to those who live with their masters. According to these amendments, the Orientals mentioned in the law shall not be prevented from acquiring landed property in the Republic. ›

‹ This Government conceives that when these amendments have been effected, those objections will fall away, which may have existed with Her Majesty's Government, and that his views shall be met thereby.

‹ It will be a pleasure to this Government to be informed of the conformation thereof from Your Excellency. ›

§ 19. On the 24th September, 1886, a letter was sent to the Government of the South African Republic by Sir Hercules Robinson (G. B. 1, N° 33, p. 46), acknowledging receipt of the letter notifying the changes which the Volksraad had authorized the Government to make in the law, and ending with these words:

‹ Although the amended law is still a contravention of the 14th Article of the Convention of London, I shall not advise Her Majesty's Government to offer further opposition to it in view of Your Honour's opinion that it is necessary for the protection of the public health. ›

Receipt of this letter was duly acknowledged on 29th October, 1886 (G. B. 1, N° 34, p. 46).

§ 20. Thereafter, on the 4th November, the Secretary of State (then Mr. Stanhope), withdrew his objections to the law which had been under

discussion, in a dispatch to the Acting High Commissioner (G, B. 1, p. 48) in the following terms: —

‹ I have the honour to .... inform you that Her Majesty's Government do not see occasion any longer to object to the legislation of the South African Republic, in regard to Asiatic traders, having regard to the amendments which the Volksraad has introduced into the Laws of 1885. I have to request that a communication in this sense may be addressed to the Government of the Republic. ›

This dispatch was duly communicated to the Government of the South African Republic.

§ 21. On the 26th January, 1887, the law as amended was promulgated in the *Gouvernements Courant* of that date. Article 2 *b* of law N° 3 of 1885 was now made to read as follows: —

‹ They shall not be owners of landed property in the Republic, except in those streets, wards and locations that the Government shall for sanitary purposes assign (aanwyzen) to them. ›

Article 2 *d* was altered thus: —

‹ The Government shall have the right for sanitary purposes to assign (aanwyzen) to them special (bepaalde) streets, wards and locations for habitation. ›

Therewith it was supposed by the legislature of the South African Republic, that the matter was finally settled (G. B. 1, p. 51).

§ 22. Thereafter, however, fresh difficulties arose out of the action of the Government of the South African Rèpublic. It appears, in short, that in cases where locations had been assigned to the Asiatic natives, the authorities in that Republic, acting, it is alleged, under the provisions of Law No. 3 of 1885, as amended, required certain Indian merchants, claiming to be British subjects, to conduct their trade within such locations, and refused them licences to do so elsewhere.

§ 23. In August, 1888, the firm of Ismael Suliman & Co (Arab merchants), applied to the High Court for an order to compel the Landdrost to issue to them a licence for trading purposes in the town of Midelburg. The Court refused to grant this order, in a judgment given on the 18th of the month. To this judgment it will be necessary to refer again.

§ 24. Complaints having been made to the British Government on behalf of Indian merchants in the Republic, correspondence ensued between the two Governments with reference to the position of these persons. The South African Republic, in the statement of its case (§ 9 *b* & *c*), places much reliance upon a certain letter from

59

the British Agent at Pretoria of 14th December 1888 (G. B. 2, N° 8, p. 5) and annexure thereto, a letter of 5th January, 1889 (G. B. 2, N° 11, p. 7), a telegram of 8th August, 1889 (G. B. 2, N° 19, p. 12), and a letter of even date with annexures (G. B. 2, N° 20, p. 13) as shewing that up to towards the end of the year 1889, the British Government and its representatives virtually admitted the right of the Government of the South African Republic to act as it had done by urging on the latter to defer any action in respect to the Indian traders till the meeting of the Volksraad, and that licences prior to the laws of 1885 should be renewed, and « to postpone· putting the law into effect until sufficient time has elapsed for a consideration of the question by the Raad. » In the lastnamed letter, Sir Hercules Robinson writes :

« Whilst fully appreciating the difficulties of Your Honour's Government in this matter, *I trust that you will be able to meet in some respect the wishes of Indian traders.*

« *It appears to me that the traders may reasonably claim that the law should respect vested interests,* and should not apply to persons who acquired rights previous to the enactment of the law, on the faith of the protection accorded by the Conventions of Pretoria and London. » Also in the annexure, being a dispatch from Lord Knutsford to Sir Hercules Robinson, of 1st April 1889, this passage occurs :

« Her Majesty's Government fully appreciate the difficulty which the President may feel in *interfering with the execution of the law,* but they trust that it may yet be found possible in some way to meet to a greater extent than at present the wishes of the Indian traders and not to press the law in its full strictness against any reasonable objections which they may make. » (I have underlined the passages specially relied upon.)

§ 25. It was urged before the Arbi rator, on behalf of the Government of the South African Republic, that Her Majesty's Government was bound to the standpoint alleged to have been once assumed by them and could not be heard to allege, that the law did not apply, and only asked that action upon it might be stayed till the next session of the Volksraad, and that the Government and Volksraad of the South African Republic were justified in acting upon such admission.

On the other side it was contended, that Her Majesty's Government were merely at the time not inclined to press for the full effect of the law, properly construed, but that this was at a time when it was thought that the Volks-

raad was going to sit, and that the matter would then be conveniently settled.

§ 26. On the 14th February, 1890, a letter, dated the 13th was received by the Government at Pretoria, from the British Agent there (G. B. 2, N° 27, p. 22) with an enclosed dispatch from Lord Knutsford to Sir Henry Loch, who had then been appointed High Commissioner, which relates to further complaints continuing to be made by Indian traders and contains the following passage:

« The right of residing, trading, &c., under the London Convention, appears to be restricted, as regards Asiatics, by the Law of 1885, amended in 1886, by requiring residence in certain localities selected for sanitary reasons, and by registration, but not otherwise; and if trading licences are granted to other persons on application, Indian traders have clearly a right to obtain them.

« Moreover, the law only prescribes locations for habitation, and there does not appear to be any prohibition as to the trading in places other than location. »

§ 27. After some further correspondence, a lengthy communication, dated 18th February, 1890, was despatched by the State Secretary of the South African Republic to the High Commissioner (G. B. 2, N° 38, p. 30). It is unnecessary to cite this communication in full. In view however of·the fact, that the Government of the South African Republic appeals to the judgment given by the High Court of that country, in the matter of the application of Ismael Suliman & Co, which has already been referred to, as one of the grounds for its claims, as set forth in the statement of its case, and in view of the remarks it will be incumbent upon me hereafter to make with reference to this point, it is necessary to cite that portion of this communication that refers to this judgment, and also to cite further correspondence relative to it.

§ 28. The writer in the communication of 18th February 1890, just referred to, says:

« . . . . I have the honour to refer to a certain judgment of the High Court of this State, given towards the end of the year 1888.

« This judgment was the result of an action to order the Landdrost of Middelburg to issue a licence to Ismael Suliman & Co, to carry on business on a certain premises, N° 148, situated within the town just mentioned.

« The applicants had, in order to obtain this licence, tendered £ 7 10 s. to the Landdrost.

« He refused to issue it, but pointed out a place for which the licence could be obtained.

« After the arguments had been heard, the Chief Justice said that the application could not be granted. › ‹ As the Chief Justice remarked, Law N° 3 of 1885 made provision, that the Government had the right for sanitary purposes to assign locations where Coolies could live, and the question was, whether this signified that they could only live there or also carry on business.

‹ An Arab, the Chief Justice remarked, could live at several places, for he has in many cases more than one wife.

‹ The Chief Justice left no difficulty about the expression 'for habitation' and can therefore make no distinction between places where persons carried on business, and those where they lived.

‹ The Government is bound to respect this judgment (heeft deze uitspraak te eerbiedigen) and has also no reasons for not agreeing therewith, especially with a view to the requirements demanded from it in respect of the promotion of sanitary conditions. ›

§ 29. In a reply to the above letter addressed to the State President and dated 3rd March 1890 (G. B. 2, N° 39, p. 33) the High Commissioner wrote as follows:

‹ I observe that you quote the judgment of the Chief Justice of the High Court, who stated that he had no difficulty as to the expression 'for residence' and could make no distinction between places of 'trade' and 'residence', but it is clear from the context, that the Chief of Justice intended to speack of places of trade which were inhabited by a portion of the family of the trader, for he explained that an Arab has in many instances more than one family, and could therefore reside in several places.

‹ The judgment, quoted therefore, does not apply to the contention urged in the Secretary of State's dispatch that an Indian trader may inhabit (or as I would interpret the expression, sleep) in a location, and yet be lawfully entitled to trade in the town.

‹ But whatever may be the true interpretation of the judgment of the High Court, and Her Majesty's Government would, in this, as in all matters, desire to give weight to the opinions of the High Court of the Republic, it must be borne in mind, that Her Majesty's Government are entitled to define the interpretation of the law which was intended and contemplated when they assented to the deviation from the provisions of the Convention. ›

§ 30. An answer to the foregoing was sent on 30th April 1890 (G. B. 2, N° 42, p. 35) in which the State Secretary of the South African Republic wrote:

‹ The Government regrets that it finds it impossible to adopt your reading of this judgment...

‹ ... The Chief Justice... declared, that, basing his view on the existing law, he could make no distinction between places where persons carried on business, and those where they lived, and did not grant the application. This Government is grateful to Your Excellency for the declaration, of which indeed they never had any doubt, that Her Majesty's Government would desire in this as in all other matters to give weight to the opinions of the High Court of this Republic. It naturally is open for the Indian traders, just as to any other person, to continue applying to that Court, when they consider themselves aggrieved, and it would undoubtedly put an end to the existence of a twofold interpretation of the judgment which has been given, if parties in similar circumstances again betook themselves to the High Court.

‹ The Government feels quite assured, that then also it would appear, that its interpretation of the judgment is the correct one.

‹ Your Excellency's second remark relates to the right of Her Majesty's Government assented to the deviations from the provisions of the Convention. › Setting aside the principle, which in the opinion of this Government is a correct one, that the Lawgiver, when any doubt arises as to the interpretation of existing laws, is the person indicated to give such interpretation, this Government must with reference to this contention again refer to what it tried to make evident in its letter of February last, etc., etc. ›

§ 31. In the *Staatscourant* of the S. A. Republic of 27th September 1893, appeared a resolution of the Volksraad, of 8th September (G. B. 2, N° 105, p. 79) to the effect that Law N° 3 of 1885 should be strictly applied, in such manner that all Asiatics and persons falling under the law should have to confine themselves in respect both of habitation and of trade to the locations assigned to them, with the exception of those whose leases (entered into before the locations had been assigned) had as yet not expired. A Government circular embodying this resolution was subsequently published (G. B. 2, N° 113, p. 85). Other correspondence besides that to which reference has already been made, also took place (more particularly between the British Resident at Pretoria, and the Government of the South African Republic), but as it is not relied upon by either of the Governments concerned, it needs not be further noticed.

§ 32. No satisfactory settlement of the questions at issue between the two Governments having been arrived at, it was agreed to submit them to arbitration.

§ 33. In the statement of the case drawn up on behalf of Her Majesty's Government, the claims put forward were:

a. That the Indian and other Asiatic traders, being British subjects, be allowed to reside in the towns of the S. A. Republic, in some quarter (« wards and streets ») which for sanitary purposes may be assigned to them; and

b. That they be allowed to carry on their trade or business in shops or stores in any part of the town.

§ 34. In the statement of the case drawn up on behalf of the Government of the South African Republic, the claims put forward on behalf of that Government were:

a. That the South African Republic has full liberty to make such regulations in respect of Coolies, Arabs, Malays and Mohammedan subjects of the Turkish Empire, as it may think fit; and

b. That Her Majesty's Government have no ground of objection, should the Government of the South African Republic prohibit Coolies, Arabs, Malays and Mohammedan subjects of the Turkish Empire, from having business premises upon any places in towns or villages, other than those assigned to them by Government.

§ 35. It was agreed on 16th March 1885, on behalf of the two Governments in terms of paragraph XI of the statement of claim of the South African Republic « that the arbitrator taking into consideration the statements of the case put forward by Her Majesty's Government and the Government of the South African Republic respectively, and of the correspondence therein cited, might decide as to him the arbitrator should appear to be equitable and just ».

§ 36. The facts of the case being thus far stated, I propose now to deal with the arguments advanced on both sides, *so far as they appear to me to be of matter and importance* to the case, and to state the ground for the conclusions at which I have arrived. The arguments thus advanced relate to the interpretation and effect of article 14 of the Convention of London, and the position of the two Governments with reference thereto; to the terms in which Her Majesty's Government expressed their willingness to waive any such interpretation of the Convention as would interfere with reasonable legislation, and the effect of such waiver; to the terms in which Her Majesty's Government withdrew their objections to Law No. 3 of 1885 as amended in 1886, and the effect of such withdrawal, and to

the construction and effect of the amended Law N° 3 of 1885 itself.

§ 37. It was contended in the first place on behalf of the South African Republic, that it was not the intention of the parties to the Convention of London to include in the words « all persons other than natives », Coolies, Arabs, Malays and Mohammedan subjects of the Turkish Empire; and that the Convention should be interpreted accordingly.

§ 38. In support of this contention it was argued that if the literal interpretation of article 14, as claimed by the British Government, were adopted, it would lead to certain unreasonable consequences which could never have been in the contemplation of the contracting parties.

§ 39. The arguments favourable to this Contention may be summarized as follows:

I. That inasmuch as the Constitution of the South African Republic, the terms of which could not have been unknown to the British Government, lays down that no equality between the white and coloured races shall be tolerated, it cannot be supposed that there was any intention on the part of the delegates of the South African Republic to assent to, or on the part of the British Government to insist upon any such breach of the constitution as would be involved (with a literal reading of the Convention) in placing upon a footing of equality Europeans and foreign coloured races.

II. That it cannot be presumed that it was the purpose of the contracting parties to place christianized, civilized and educated natives of the country in a far worse position than foreign heathen coloured races, such as Polynesians, Papuans and Hindoos; as would actually be the case if a literal interpretation were adopted.

III. That every European nation or nation of European origin has an absolute and defeasable right to exclude alien elements which it considers to be dangerous to its development and existence, and more especially Asiatic elements from settling within its territory; and that there is a strong presumption against any intention on the part of the delegates of the South African Republic to surrender this right, or on the part of Great Britain to insist upon a surrender of this right, more especially in favor of foreign coloured races who are not presumed to be the subjects of international rights (since international law is not supposed to exist otherwise than between civilized European races), and in some of whom (such as Polynesians, Papuans, etc.) Great Britain has absolutely no concern.

§ 40. In favor of a restrictive interpretation of the Convention, moreover, it was argued that with the possible exception with a few Arab settlers who came into the country after the Convention of Pretoria, the influx of Arabs after the Convention of London was a newly emergent circumstance which the parties to the Convention never had in contemplation and to which their attention could never have been directed ; that the *ratio legis* for the exclusion of natives of South Africa, applied, with as much if not greater force, to Asiatic natives, and that this *ratio legis* must be taken into consideration in the interpretation of article 14 of the Convention.

§ 41. It is possible and indeed seems probable from the terms of His Excellency the High Commissioner's letter of 28th January 1885 (v. § 7 above) that in making use of the expression « persons other than natives », the representatives of Her Majesty Government had as a matter of fact in view solely the interests of white or European persons settling in the South African Republic, and that other coloured races than those native to South Africa were not thought of. And that in a country where a sharp line of demarcation is drawn between white and coloured races generally (as is apparent from the constitution of the South African Republic), apparently no efforts should have been made by its representatives to have the terms of exclusion made of wider application than to merely natives of South Africa, seems also to lend some support to such a supposition. Moreover it does not seem probable on the one hand that the South African Republic would willingly have agreed without remonstrance to surrender, in favour of foreign coloured races, one of the most precious privileges of a young community, that of deciding for itself of what materials the future nation shall be built up ; nor on the other hand that the British Government would deliberately have placed educated, christianized and civilized natives of South Africa, in a worse position than foreign heathen coloured races.

Nevertheless, when Her Majesty's Government insisted upon a literal interpretation of article 14 of the Convention, I am bound to hold that they were within their rights. For it is impossible to surmise what the Governments concerned would have done or would not have done, had the subject of foreign coloured races expressly been brought to their notice. They might have made no stipulations in favour of Papuans and Polynesians, who now enjoy certain privileges if included under the term « all persons other than natives » according to a strict interpretation of the Convention ; on the other hand the British

Government might have insisted upon protecting the Indian and other Asiatic traders, whom alone in the present instance the British Government claim to protect. Accordingly I do not feel at liberty to apply the alleged *ratio legis* for the exclusion of African natives to the case of foreign coloured races, and feel bound therefore to decide, as I do against the general contention of the South African Republic, that article 14 of the Convention of London does not stand in the way of its making such legislative provisions as it may think fit, in respect of Coolies, Arabs, Malays and Mohammedan subjects of the Turkish Empire. And I do not consider that under the Convention the South African Republic is entitled to enact exceptional legislation in restriction of the liberty of Indian and Arab traders to have or to hire shops wherever they may like.

§ 42. It was argued on behalf of the South African Republic, that even if Law No. 3 of 1885 had been in conflict with the provisions of article 14 of the convention, yet the South African Republic would have been justified in passing that law, inasmuch as by International Law a treaty becomes voidable so soon as it is absolutely dangerous to the welfare of the State in a manner that had not been intended, and that this was the case here. I cannot admit the force of this contention in the present instance, supposing the principle of International Law to be such as here laid down.

§ 43. It was further argued on behalf of the South African Republic that the dispatch of Lord Derby of 19th March 1885 (v. § 9 above), read together with the letter of the High Commissioner of 28th January 1885 (v. § 7 above) constituted an admission that the literal interpretation of the Convention of London was not in accordance with the intention of the parties thereto, and that the British Government cannot withdraw from this admission after the South African Republic had acted upon it by adopting legislation to meet a case which, it followed from such admission, was really not provided for in the Convention.

§ 44. To me there does not seem to be any such admission, at all events not any admission that would justify the position taken up on behalf of the South African Republic. In the passage from the High Commissioner's letter, « it was doubtless not the intention of Lord Kimberley to prohibit » may mean no more than « to refuse to allow ». If this passage meant that the South African Republic should be entitled under the Convention, without reference to the British Government, to place Indian and Chinese Coolie Immigrants under the same disabilities as natives of South Africa, it would not have been necessary to amend Article 14 of the Convention in a manner suggested by His Excellency. With this view of mine on the contention just referred to, it is not necessary for me to express any opinion, as to what would have been the effect of any such admission as alleged on the part of the High Commissioner, or to dwell longer on this point.

§ 45. As to the contention of the South African Republic, that Law No. 3 of 1885 was passed only after the assent of the British Government had been given to reasonable legislation in the direction desired by itself (v. § 10 above), I am of opinion that the British Government merely assentet to reasonable legislation, such as had been suggested by the High Cummissioner, namely, « special legislation for the regulation of Indian or Chinese Coolie Immigrants ». In view, however, of the assent later given by Her Majesty's Government to the legislation actually· effected, any expression of opinion on this point can be of but little importance.

§ 46. As regards the terms upon which Her Majesty's Government gave their assent to Law No. 3 of 1885 (as subsequently amended), after that the law had been passed, it was contended on behalf of the South African Republic, that after such assent had been given in the manner in which it was given, Her Majesty's Government could no longer raise the objection that that law was not in conformity with the 14th article of the convention of London.

I concur with this view entirely.

§ 47. The contention was advanced on behalf of Her Majesty's Government that in the execution of Law No. 3 of 1885, it must be considered that there are imported into the Law, the conditions under which the assent of that Government was given to that Law. These conditions I understood it to be asserted, were such : that (1) any action taken under the law must not be unreasonable; and (2) any action taken under the law must be necessary for the protection of the public health. This leaves the question open who in every individual case is entitled to decide whether any act is reasonable or unreasonable, or absolutely necessary for the protection of the public health, or not necessary; but this is a question which it does not appear to me to be necessary now to discuss.

§ 48. As regards the alleged requirement of reasonableness, I do not consider that it was imported into the Law, in any special degree by virtue of the assent given to the law by the British Government. That Government having at first intimated that they would not oppose reasonable legislation in a certain direction, had the opportunity of satisfying themselves when the enactment came before them, as to whether its provisions were reasonable or not; they might have refused to give assent to it, if they considered that it was not such legislation as they had declared they would not oppose; but having subsequently assented, no investigation can be further made as to whether it is reasonable or not. If any act that was done in strict accordance with the law is impeached, it is a sufficient answer to say that it was so done in strict accordance with the law; and there may be no after enquiry at the instance of the British Government as to whether the act is reasonable or otherwise.

§ 49. It does not seem to me either to be a very practical proposal to read this requirement in a special degree into the law passed by the Volksraad of the South African Republic, inasmuch as « reasonableness » in itself is such an abstract and relative term that it would be difficult to lay down in any particular case what is reasonable or otherwise. In the present instance of course this requirement would have relation to the circumstances of the South African Republic, and would have to be judged of in the light of those circumstances; and it has been argued that since the legislature of that country were in a far better position to form a correct judgment as to what was reasonable or unreasonable with reference to local circumstances than a foreign Government could be, the endorsement by the Volksraad of the proceedings of the Government goes far to show the reasonable nature of such proceedings. It was also remarked that since by the terms of the Convention, the South African Republic had the right to exclude entirely from its territory native races, a right of exclusion which Sir Hercules Robinson was willing to extend also to Indian and Chinese Coolie Immigrants, it could not be so unreasonable in the case of other coloured immigrants to exercise the smaller right of controlling their methods of trade.

It is alleged that the methods of trade of the Asiatic races, generally, are such that it is most desirable for sanitary reasons that they should be entirely isolated. Of this I have no means of judging. Independently, however, of sanitary reasons, I must confess that I would not wish to undertake to say that there is anything unreasonable in itself, in restrictions being imposed upon Asiatic trading in competition with that of white persons, supposing the allegations set forth in the various petitions to the Volksraad to be correct. The question as to whether anything is reasonable or unreasonable in any case, entirely depends upon the circumstances of that case. To those accustomed to the habits of thought prevalent in countries where a certain state of things does not present itself as a pressing danger, that may appear unreasonable which, in another country where this state of things threatens the welfare of the community, may appear to be an absolutely necessary act of national self-preservation. Things too may appear in a very different light to the doctrinal theorist, and the man of practical experience.

I need hardly point out the numerous instances where principles theoretically unreasonable have been adopted as the basis of practical legislation, as where in some of the States of the American Union intermarriage between white and blacks, and education in common schools of white and black children are prohibited by the Constitution; or where laws for the exclusion of Chinese have been passed in Australia and Canada.

In these cases it cannot be supposed that the legislation was under the special circumstances of each particular case unreasonable. And in connection with this point I may here cite the remarks of a recent writer who shows a wide knowledge of the subject with which he deals, in preference to putting forward any opinion of my own with regard to the United States Chine Exclusion Act. He writes as follows :—

‹ The justice of Chinese exclusion is clear when we once apprehended that it is a matter of life and death to the European race to keep to itself those temperate regions, such as the United States and Australia, in which alone they can live in health.... That the industrial extermination of the white labourer is the inevitable result of unrestricted Chinese immigration has been proved beyond question in America and Australia. It is understating the case to say that the standard of existence of the white labourer is lowered by Chinese competition. The white labourer cannot subsist on the wages of the Chinese, whose wants are fewer, as a result chiefly of his lower stage of civilization, and partly of the fact that unlike the white man, he has no family to support. The white labourer is simply starved out of existence, or driven out of the country. In a word, justice to Europeans demands Chinese exclusion. › *(Law Quarterly Review, vol. 10, p. 269. ‹ Recent questions of International Law. ›)* Very similar arguments are used by the memorialists in the petitions to which I have already referred with regard to Arab and Indian competition in business, and they are possibly not quite unfounded.

§ 50. With regard to the alleged requirement of reasons of public health for any act done under Law No. 3 of 1885, I hold that no such requirement is imported into Law No. 3 of 1885, through the terms of the assent of the British Government; but that sanitary reasons are required only so far as that law itself in express terms requires them. If the law was not explicit enough, the British Government could have withheld their assent thereto; having given their assent they cannot object to proceedings, supposing these to be in strict accordance with the law, because unforeseen consequences have ensued.

§ 51. With respect to the assent given by Her Majesty's Government to Law No. 3 of 1885, it is clear that it was given without reserve, condition or qualification. Two letters relate to it. In the first Sir Hercules Robinson says: that in view of the opinion of the State President of the South African Republic, that the law was necessary for the protection of the public health, he would not advise Her Majesty's Government to offer further opposition to it. Supposing that notwithstanding the later communication made on behalf of Her Majesty's Government to the Government of the South African Republic, this letter must be regarded as affecting the position of the latter Government, I fail to see that His Excellency reserved any right to object to any act purporting to be done under the provisions of Law No. 3 of 1885, and actually so done, on the ground that in the opinion of himself or of Her Majesty's Government, it is not necessary for the public health. His Excellency's motives in recommending the concession cannot effect the fact that the concession was actually made. If it were requisite in the execution of the law to have a regard to what was in the mind of the British Government or their representatives on the one side, it might be as necessary also to discover from the correspondence what was in the mind of the State President of the South African Republic, on the other side, when he suggested that the proposed legislation was necessary for the sake of the public health; and it is not impossible that it might then be argued that he had in view that complete ‹isolation› of Arabs and Coolies that was sought by some of the memorialists, whose petitions had been forwarded by the Government of the South African Republic to Her Majesty's Government, and were referred to in the State Secretary's letter of 6th January, 1885 (v. § 6 above).

§ 53. Be this, however, as it may, it is clear that in the second letter, referring to this subject, the assent given by the British Government to the enactment as amended was unqualified. It may be that Her Majesty's Government, in assenting, attached the same value to His Honour the

State President's opinion as His Excellency the Commissioner did; it may also be that they acted on their own judgment as to the merits of the law after it had been amended. It may be that they adopted His Excellency's motives, it may be that they acted upon distinctly different motives. In any case a simple intimation was made «that Her Majesty's Government do not see occasion any longer to object to the legislation of the South African Republic in regard to Asiatic traders, having regard to the amendments which the Volksraad has introduced into the Law of 1885».

It is obvious then, that in so far as Law No. 3 of 1885 (as amended) derogated from the provisions of Article 14 of the Convention of London, such derogation was effected with the full approval of Her Majesty's Government.

§ 54. Law No. 3 of 1885 was purely a municipal law of the South African Republic, and nothing that had occurred between the Government of that State and Her Majesty's Government, could in any way affect its character as a purely municipal law. It is clear that being such, all the ordinary incidents of a municipal law (in so far as such incidents are not expressly or by necessary implication excluded), must attach to Law No. 3 of 1885.

§ 55. I hold that when the British Government assented to the legislation effected by the Volksraad of the South African Republic, they were bound by the indisputable principle that the legislative enactments of a country are subject to the exclusive interpretation of the tribunals of that country; and they must be held to have acquiesced in that principle. I do not here refer to the so-called «authentic» interpretation by the legislative body itself, for though no doubt a legislative body, constituted of the same members as when it passed a law, would best know what it meant when it passed such law, yet such «authentic interpretation» must be considered as more in the nature of fresh legislation than of explanation of previous legislation.

§ 56. It would be impossible for me in any way to the contention put forward in the letter of His Excellency Sir Henri Loch, in his letter of 3rd March 1890 (v. § 29 above) to the effect that Her Majesty's Government are entitled to define the interpretation of the law, which was intended and contemplated when they assented to the deviation from the provisions of the Convention. Nor, in fact, do I understand that this contention is now insisted upon on the part of Her Majesty's Government.

§ 57. It is perfectly clear that persons who settle in a foreign country are not only subject to its laws, but also to the interpretation of those laws by the legally appointed tribunals. When access to such tribunals is refused to them or justice is in any other way denied to them, they may have a right to carry their complaints to the Government of the country of which they are subjects, and their Governments may have a right to remonstrate; this also may be the case were the tribunals of the country are incompetent to declare the law as over against the Government of the country, or were the Government to act in opposition to the decision of its highest tribunals; but nothing of the kind is here asserted; in fact, the Government of the South African Republic, in these dispatches, themselves suggest, that the persons concerned should have recourse to the Courts of the country; they rely upon a judgment of the High Court in defence of the position taken up by themselves, and declare themselves bound to respect that judgment.

It would be a calamitous and intolerable position that aliens in any country should be allowed to complain to their own Governments, that the local tribunals have erred in the interpretation of the law of the country. The judgments of such tribunals over matters within their jurisdiction are final and conclusive force everywhere; there can be no concurrent jurisdiction in any extraneous body to interpret the law; nor can any appel lie from such tribunals to any foreign body or Government. Nor can it be supposed, that the Volksraad in acquiescing in the assent given by Her Majesty's Government, and in enacting the law or in any subsequent proceeding. contemplated the possibility of the law, by itself, being subject to interpretation by any tribunal but those lawfully appointed in accordance with the constitution of the South African Republic.

§ 58. Her Majesty's Government cannot reasonably insist upon greater rights and privileges on behalf of Her Majesty's subjects themselves are entitled to claim. I hold therefore, that on questions that have arisen, and on the various questions which may possibly still arise in the application of Law No. 3 of 1885, as amended in 1886, with reference to the interpretation and effect of that law, the decision of the competent tribunals of the South African Republic must be considered as decisive, both in respect of the individuals affected thereby, and of Her Majesty's Government.

§ 59. The further questions raised relate to the interpretation of Law No. 3 of 1885, as subsequently amended. These I may merely mention as having been mooted (with a few remarks that it seems to me not improper to make) as

I hold it to be incompetent for me to give any decision therein.

§ 60. On the side of the Government of the South African Republic it was maintained:—

That the proceedings of that Government in regard to Asiatic Residents in that country, which proceedings Her Majesty's Government complain of, were in conformity with the law passed in 1885, amended in 1886, and agreed to by the British Government.

That the words « for habitation » used in sections 2 b and 2 d of the amended law have reference as well to places of business as to places for sleeping; and that therefore the Government of the South African Republic has the right to prohibit the coloured persons mentioned in the law to carry on business in towns, in other places than those assigned to them for that purpose. That the word « location » used in the law referred to has reference not only to pieces of ground reserved for coloured races outside of proclaimed towns but also to pieces of ground reserved for places of abode for such coloured persons, on town lands, and that word « Coolie » means in South Africa any person belonging to or descended from the native races of Asia.

§ 61. On behalf of Her Majesty's Government, on the other hand it was maintained, that there is nothing in the law of 1885, which prevents Her Majesty's Asiatic subjects from carrying on their business or trade in any portion of a town.

That the words for « sanitary purposes » and « for habitation » should be construed as referring to the dwelling places of such traders and not to places of business.

That the words « streets and wards » have reference to the special quarter of the town which may be assigned to such persons who may be residing in the town; the word « locations » has reference to a special place which may be assigned to such persons who may be residing not in towns but in country places.

§ 62. With reference to the contention put forward on behalf of Her Majesty's Government, that the word « locations » has reference to special places which may be assigned to such persons who may be residing not in towns but in country places, I am not aware that this any longer be insisted upon; should it in any specific case be insisted upon, the matter may have to be decided by the Courts of Law of the South African Republic.

§ 63. As regards the question whether the words « for habitation » and « for sanitary purposes » have reference only to dwelling places and not to business premises, I would feel myself bound by any decision the High Court of the South African Republic may have given on the subject, were it necessary for me to give a decision thereon. It is indeed said that no actual decision on that point was given by the High Court. It is not for me to give an interpretation of the decision of the High Court, but if it be so that no such decision has actually been given, the point is one that may at any time arise, and then it will be with the tribunals of the South African Republic to give the necessary decision thereon.

§ 64. As regards the contention of the South African Republic, that its proceedings in regard to the Asiatics were in conformity with the law, it is clear that if the High Court of the South African Republic has decided that they were in conformity with the law, they must be deemed to be such. In every specific case where proceedings alleged to have been undertaken in execution of the law are impeached, it will be for the tribunals of the South African Republic to declare in how far such proceedings shall have been lawful or not.

§ 65. With regard to the meaning of the words « Coolies », Counsel of Her Majesty's Government fully admitted that in popular parlance no fine or very accurate discrimination is made between the different classes of Indian races, and that it is generally also applied to Arabs. This, however, is a matter on which I need give no decision.

§ 66. It may be proper here to remark that it was observed by counsel for Her Majesty's Government that in the present arbitration Her Majesty's Government insisted upon what they considered to be the true effect of the law taken into consideration with the dispatches relating thereto, only so far as it affected British subjects, without prejudice to their right to object to this law (which related generally to the native races of Asia, including thereunder the « so-called Coolies », Arabs, Malays and other Mohammedan subjects of the Turkish Empire), in respect of the manner in which it affected other than British subjects.

§ 67. After consideration of the whole matter I come to the conclusion (and upon this conclusion my award is based) that the claims of neither of the two Governments concerned, can be fully sustained, and that in fact, they must be disallowed in so far as they are not in accordance with the following principle which, under the circumstances, I hold to be equitable and just; that is to say, that the South African Republic is bound and entitled in its treatment of Indians and other Asiatic traders, being British subjects, to give full force and effect to the provisions of Law No. 3 of 1885 enacted, and in the year 1886 amended, by the Volksraad of the South African Republic, subject (in case of objections being raised by or on behalf of any such persons to any such treatment as not being in accordance with the provisions of the said law as amended), to sole and exclusive interpretation in ordinary course by the tribunal of the South African Republic.

§ 68. It remains only for me to remark with regard to the resolution of the Volksraad of the South African Republic, of 8th September 1893, marked Article 1353 (G. B. 2, N° 105, p. 79) that in terms of my award, Her Majesty's Government may rightly object to that resolution and to any similar amplification by the legislature of the South African Republic, of Law No. 3 of 1885, as also to the circular of December 1893, embodying that resolution. That resolution does not merely convey instructions to its own functionaries as to the execution of the above mentioned law; it virtually also has the effect of establishing a legislative interpretation of that law which may or may not be in accordance with judicial decision but which at all events the tribunals of the Country will no doubt consider themselves bound in future to adopt, and to recognize as having force of law, so long as it remains in existence [1].

CXIII. Chili, Etats-Unis d'Amérique.

7 août 1892.

Réclamations réciproques de citoyens des deux pays, soumises à un conseil d'arbitrage de trois membres.

Convention for the settlement of certain claims of the citizens of either country against the other, signed at Santiago, August 7, 1892.

The United States of America and the Republic of Chile, animated by the desire to settle and adjust amicably the claims made by the citizens of either country against the Government of the other, growing out of acts committed by the civil or military authorities of either country, have agreed to make arrangements for that purpose, by means of a Convention and have named as their Plenipotentiaries to confer and agree thereupon as follows:

The President of the United States of America, Patrick Egan, Envoy Extraordinary and Minister Plenipotentiary of the United States at Santiago,

[1] GROENBOEK, 1899, III, bldr. 22—53.

and the President of the Republic of Chile, Isidoro Errázuriz, Minister of Foreign Relations of Chile;

Who, after having communicated to each other their respective full powers, found in good and true form, have agreed upon the following articles:

ART. I. All claims on the part of corporations, companies or private individuals, citizens of the United States upon the Government of Chile, arising out of acts committed against the persons or property of citizens of the United States not in the service of the enemies of Chile, or voluntarily giving aid and comfort to the same, by the civil or military authorities of Chile; and on the other hand, all claims on the part of corporations, companies or private individuals, citizens of Chile, upon the Government of the United States, arising out of acts committed against the persons or property of citizens of Chile, not in the service of the enemies of the United States, or voluntarily giving aid and comfort to the same, by the civil or military authorities of the Government of the United States, shall be referred to three Commissioners, one of whom shall be named by the President of the Republic of Chile, and the third to be selected by mutual accord between the President of the United States and the President of Chile.

In case the President of the United States and the President of Chile shall not agree within three months from the exchange of the ratifications of this Convention to nominate such third Commissioner, then said nomination of said third Commissioner shall be made by the President of the Swiss Confederation.

ART. II. The said Commission, thus constituted, shall be competent and obliged to examine and decide upon all claims of the aforesaid character presented to them by the citizens of either country.

ART. III. In case of the death, prolonged absence or incapacity to serve of one of the said Commissioners, or in the event of one Commissioner omitting, or declining, or ceasing to act as such, then the President of the United States, or the President of the Republic of Chile, or the Swiss Confederation, as the case may be, shall forthwith proceed to fill the vacancy so occasioned by naming another Commissioner within three months from the occurrence of the vacancy.

ART. IV. The Commissioners named as hereinbefore provided shall meet in the city of Washington at the earliest convenient time within six months after the exchange of ratifications of this Convention, and shall, as their first act in so meeting, make and subscribe a solemn declaration that they will impartially and carefully examine and decide, to the best of their judgment and according to public law, justice and equity, without fear, favor or affection, all claims within the description and true meaning of Articles I and II, which shall be laid before them on the part of the Governments of the United States and of Chile respectively; and such declaration shall be entered on the record of their proceedings; provided, however, that the concurring judgment of any two Commissioners shall be adequate for every intermediate decision arising in the execution of their duty and for every final award.

ART. V. The Commissioners shall, without delay after the organization of the Commission, proceed to examine and determine the claims specified in the preceding articles, and notice shall be given to the respective Governments of the day of their organization and readiness to proceed to the transaction of the business of the Commission. They shall investigate and decide said claims in such order and in such manner as they may think proper, but upon such evidence or information only as shall be furnished by or on behalf of the respective Governments. They shall be bound to receive and consider all written documents or statements which may be presented to them by or on behalf of the respective Governments in support of, or in answer to, any claim, and to hear, if required, one person on each side whom it shall be competent for each Government to name as its Counsel or Agent to present and support claims on its behalf, on each and every separate claim. Each Government shall furnish at the request of the Commissioners, or of any two of them, the papers in its possession which may be important to the just determination of any of the claims laid before the Commission.

ART. VI. The concurring decisions of the Commissioners, or of any two of them, shall be conclusive and final. Said decisions shall in every case be given upon each individual claim, in writing, stating, in the event of a pecuniary award being made, the amount or equivalent value of the same in gold coin of the United States; and in the event of interest being allowed on such award, the rate thereof and the period for which it is to be computed shall be fixed, which period shall not extend beyond the close of the Commission; and said decision shall be signed by the Commissioners concurring therein.

ART. VII. The High Contracting Parties hereby engage to consider the decision of the Commissioners, or of any two of them, as absolutely final and conclusive upon each claim decided upon them, and to give full effect to such decisions without any objections, evasions, or delay whatever.

ART. VIII. Every claim shall be presented to the Commissioners within a period of two months reckoned from the day of their first meeting for business, after notice to the respective Governments as prescribed in Article V of this Convention. Nevertheless, where reasons for delay shall be established to the satisfaction of the Commissioners, or of any two of them, the period for presenting the claim may be extended by them to any time not exceeding two months longer.

The Commissioners shall be bound to examine and decide upon every claim within six months from the day of their first meeting for business as aforesaid; which period shall not be extended except only in case of the proceedings of the Commission shall be interrupted by the death, incapacity, retirement or cessation of the functions of any one of the Commissioners, in which event the period of six months herein prescribed shall not be held to include the time during which such interruption may actually exist.

It shall be competent in each case for the said Commissioners to decide whether any claim has, or has not been duly made, preferred, and laid before them, either wholly, or to any and what extent, according to the true intent and meaning of this Convention.

ART. IX. All sums of money which may be awarded by the Commissioners as aforesaid, shall be paid by the one Government to the other, as the case may be, at the capital of the Government to receive such payment, within six months after the date of the final award, without interest, and without any deduction save as specified in Article X.

ART. X. The Commissioners shall keep an accurate record and correct minutes or notes of all their proceedings, with the dates thereof; and the Governments of the United States and of Chile may each appoint and employ a Secretary versed in the languages of both countries, and the Commissioners may appoint any other necessary officer or officers to assist them in the transaction of the business which may come before them.

Each Government shall pay its own Commissioner, Secretary, Agent or Counsel, and at the same equivalent rates of compensation, as near as may be, for like officers on the one side as on the other. All other expenses, including compensation of the third Commissioner, which latter shall be equal or equivalent to that of the other Commissioners, shall be defrayed by the two Governments in equal moieties. The whole expenses of the Commission, including contingent expenses, shall be defrayed by a ratable deduction on the amount of the sums awarded by the Commissioners, provided always that such deductions shall not exceed the rate of five per centum on the sum so awarded. If the whole expenses shall exceed this rate, then the excess of expense shall be defrayed jointly by the two Governments in equal moieties.

ART. XI. The High Contracting Parties agree to consider the result of the proceedings of the Commission provided for by this Convention as a full, perfect and final settlement of any and every claim upon either Government within the description and true meaning of Articles I and II; and that every such claim, whether or not the same may have been presented to the notice of, made, preferred or laid before the said Commission, shall, from and after the conclusion of the proceedings of the said Commission, be treated and considered as finally settled, concluded and barred.

ART. XII. The present Convention shall be ratified by the President of the United States, by and with the advice and consent of the Senate thereof and by the President of the Republic of Chile, with the consent and approbation of the Congress of the same, and the ratifications shall be exchanged at Washington, at as early a day as may be possible within six months from the date thereof.

In testimony whereof the respective Plenipotentiaries have signed the present Convention, in the English and Spanish languages, in duplicate and hereunto affixed their respective seals.

Done at the city of Santiago the seventh day of August, in the year of our Lord one thousand eight hundred and ninety-two [1].

Final award of the Chilean claims commission given at Washington, April 9, 1894.

We, the undersigned, commissioners appointed under and in pursuance of Article I of the Convention between the United States of America and the republic of Chile, signed at Santiago, August 7, 1892, do now make this our final award of and concerning the matters referred to us by said convention which we have been able to consider within the time limit of the treaty as follows :

I. We award that the Government of the republic of Chile shall pay to the Government of the United States of America, within six months from the date hereof, the sum of two hundred and forty thousand five hundred and sixty-four dollars and thirty-five cents ($ 240,564.35)

without interest, in accordance with the provisions of Article IX of the convention aforesaid, for and in full satisfaction of the several claims on the part of corporations, companies, or private individuals citizens of the United States, upon the Government of the republic of Chile, arising out of acts committed against the persons and property of citizens of the United States by the civil or military authorities of Chile, which have been determined by us, said sum being the aggregate of the principal sums and interest allowed to certain claimants by the several separate awards to that effect made in writing and signed by us, or such of us as assented to said separate awards, which are among the records of this commission, and are hereby referred to for more definite information.

II. All claims on the part of citizens of Chile against the United States, and on the part of citizens of the United States against the republic of Chile, which have been disallowed or dismissed in manner and form as will appear in the records of the commission by the several separate judgments in writing concerning the same, are hereby remitted, without consideration on their merits and without any result or determination by the commission to the respective Governments of the United States and Chile for further action and disposition, for the reason that the time limit of the convention under which this commission is acting is too short as to prevent the hearing, consideration, and determination of the same by this Commission.

III. We refer to the separate awards made and signed as aforesaid, as part of this final award in the cases which we have been able to consider, and to a list and statement thereof hereto attached giving the number of each claim, the name of each claimant, the character of the claim, the time when it arose, the amount claimed, the disposition of the claim and where an allowance has been made, the sum allowed in each case.

Signed at Washington, D. C., this 9th day of April, A. D. 1894 [1].

CASES CONSIDERED AND DETERMINED BY THE COMMISSION.

Claim N° 1, Central and South American Telegraph Company v. Chile, for damages to telegraph line, etc., in 1891, during Congressional Revolution ; amount claimed, $ 163,858. 55 ; award against Chile for $ 40,725. 89, Commissioner Gana dissenting.

---

[1] F. DE MARTENS, *Nouveau Recueil Général*, 2ᵐᵉ série, t. XXII, p. 339.

[1] J. B. MOORE, *Digest and History...*, p. 1475.

Claim N° 2, Edward C. Du Bois v. Chile, for damages and destruction of railroad property at Chimbote in 1880-1882, during war with Peru; amount claimed, $ 2,451,155. 58; award against Chile for $ 155,232, Commissioner Gana dissenting.

Claim N° 4, Winfield S. Shrigley v. Chile, for destruction of property in 1891, during Congressional Revolution; amount claimed $ 12,717.51; award against Chile for $ 5,086.

Claim N° 5, Eugène L. Didier et al. v. Chile, for breach of contract with Chile in 1817; amount claimed, $ 1,111,760. 63 ; dismissed on demurrer, Commissioner Goode dissenting.

Claim N° 6, John L. Thorndike v. Chile, for damages to railroad property at Mollendo in 1880, during war with Peru ; amount claimed, $ 190,361. 34 ; dismissed on hearing, Commissioner Goode dissenting.

Claim N° 9, Gilbert Bennet Borden v. Chile, for damages, false arrest, and detention of ship in 1883 ; amount claimed, $ 32,209. 10 ; award against Chile for $ 9,187. 50, Commissioner Gana dissenting.

Claim N° 10, Wells, Fargo & Co. v. Chile, for seizure of Peruvian money tokens in 1880 ; amount claimed, $ 58,389. 97 ; compromise award for $ 29,194. 98.

Claim N° 11, Charles G. Wilson v. Chile, for destruction of property in 1891, during Congressional Revolution ; amount claimed, $ 142,487 ; dismissed on demurrer.

Claim N° 13, Jennie R. Read v. Chile, for destruction of property in 1891, during Congressional Revolution ; amount claimed, $ 8,253. 40, award against Chile for $ 1,137.98.

Claim N° 15, Charles Watson v. Chile, for destruction of property in 1880, during war with Peru ; amount claimed $ 278,205. 84 ; dismissed for failure to amend, Commissioner Goode dissenting on demurrer.

Claim N° 16, Grace Brothers & Co. v. Chile, for damage to 200 bags of sugar in 1883 ; amount claimed, $ 14,521. 68 ; dismissed for want of jurisdiction, Commissioner Goode dissenting.

Claim N° 17, Frederick Selway v. Chile, for personal damages in 1847, amount claimed, $ 50,000 with interest at 6 per cent from 1847; dismissed on merits.

Claim N° 19, Grace Brothers & Co. v. Chile, for detention of vessel in 1880, during war with Peru; amount claimed $ 15,593. 74; dismissed for want of jurisdiction, Commissioner Goode dissenting.

Claim N° 20, Grace Brothers & Co. v. Chile, for seizure of cargo of coal in 1879, during war with Peru; amount claimed $ 3,989. 20; dismissed for want of jurisdiction, Commissioner Goode dissenting.

Claim N° 21, Grace Brothers & Co. v. Chile, for illegal seizure of guano and nitrate deposits in 1879, during war with Peru; amount claimed $ 240,940. 26; dismissed for want of jurisdiction, Commissioner Goode dissenting.

Claim N° 22, William R. Grace & Co. v. Chile, for seizure of nitrate deposits in 1879; amount claimed $ 1,076,764. 67; dismissed for want of jurisdiction, Commissioner Goode dissenting.

Claim N° 23, Patrick Shields v. Chile, for personal damages in 1891 ; amount claimed $ 100,000 and interest on the award; dismissed on demurrer, for want of jurisdiction.

Claim N° 24, Andrew McKinstry v. Chile, for personal damages in 1891; amount claimed $ 25,000; dismissed on demurrer for want of jurisdiction.

Claim N° 29, Grace Brothers & Co. v. Chile, for loss of shares in nitrate company of Peru in 1879 during war with Peru; amount claimed $ 866,945. 99; dismissed for want of jurisdiction, Commissioner Goode dissenting.

Claim N° 34, Stephen M. Chester v. Chile, for personal damages in 1881, during war with Peru; amount claimed $ 86,000; dismissed for want of evidence.

Claim N° 36, Elizabeth C. Murphy et al. v. Chile, for destruction of property in 1881, during war with Peru; amount claimed $ 17,122. 50; dismissed on hearing, Commissioner Goode dissenting.

Claim N° 38, John C. Landreau v. Chile, for damages for seizure of certain guano deposits in 1881, during war with Peru; amount claimed $ 5,000,000 with interest at 6 per cent from 1882; dismissed on demurrer, Commissioner Goode dissenting.

Claim N° 39, T. Ellet Hodgskin v. Chile, for damages for seizure of certain guano deposits in 1881, during war with Peru; amount claimed $ 3,333,000 with interest at 6 per cent from 1882; dismissed on demurrer, Commissioner Goode dissenting (Claims N°s 38 und 39 are different claimants for the same subject-matter).

Claim N° 43, Frederick H. Lovett v. Chile, for personal damages, detention and loss of bark *Florida* in 1852; amount claimed $ 225,800; dismissed on demurrer.

Claim N° 48, Ricardo L. Trumbull v. The United States, for personal damages in 1891; amount claimed $ 32,500; dismissed on demurrer.

Ainsi que les termes de la sentence finale l'indiquent, il fut statué sur une partie seulement des réclamations, et notamment 25 réclamations à charge du Chili et 1 réclamation à charge des Etats-Unis. Le nombre des premières avait été de 40, d'un import total de $ 26,042,976. 96 et celui des seconds de 3, d'un import total de $ 264,740. Les deux gouvernements intéressés se décidèrent à conclure une nouvelle convention.

Convention to revive the convention of August 7, 1892, to adjust the claims of citizens of either country against the other, signed at Washington, May 24, 1897.

The Convention between the United States of America and the Republic of Chile, signed August 7, 1892, having expired, and the Commission thereunder established to adjust amicably the claims made by the citizens of either country against the Government of the other having failed, through limitation to conclude its task, leaving certain claims duly presented to the said commission unadjudicated, the Government of the United States of America and the Government of the Republic of Chile, desiring to remove every cause of difference in the friendly relations that happily exist between the two Nations have agreed to revive the said convention of August 7, 1892, and for that purpose have named as their Plenipotentiaries, to wit:

The President of the United States of America, the Honorable John Sherman, Secretary of State of the United States; and

The President of the Republic of Chile, Señor Don Domingo Gana, Envoy Extraordinary and Minister Plenipotentiary of Chile in the United States of America: Who have agreed upon the articles following:

ARTICLE I. The High Contracting Parties agree to revive the Convention of August 7, 1892, between the United States of America and the Republic of Chile, and that the commission thereunder created shall be allowed for the transaction of its business a period of four months, to be reckoned from the day of its first meeting for business, and conforming, in other respects, with the provisions of the second paragraph of Article VIII of the said Convention.

Nevertheless, if the period of four months before stipulated shall prove insufficient for the settlement of the claims, the Commissioners are authorized to extend, at their discretion, such period to one or two months more.

It is expressly stipulated that this article shall in no wise extend or change the period designated by the first paragraph of Article VIII of the said Convention for the presentation of the claims; so that the new Commission shall be limited to considering the claims duly presented to the former Commission in conformity with the terms of the Convention and with the Rules that governed its labors, excepting claim No 7 of the North and South American Construction Company, which was subsequently withdrawn, a direct and final settlement thereof having been arrived at by the interested parties.

ARTICLE II. The present convention shall be ratified by the President of the United States of America, by and with the advice and consent of the Senate thereof and by the President of the Republic of Chile, with the approbation of the National Congress thereof and the ratifications shall be exchanged at Washington, at as early a day as possible.

In testimony whereof we have signed the present convention in the English and Spanish languages, in duplicate, affixing thereto our respective seals, the Plenipotentiary of Chile declaring that he signs the same «ad referendum».

Done at the city of Washington, the 24th day of May in the year of Our Lord eighteen hundred and ninety-seven.

CXIV. Honduras, Nicaragua.

7 octobre 1894.

Le traité reproduit a pour objet de confier à une commission mixte la fixation des limites des deux pays et, en cas de désaccord entre les commissaires, à une commission arbitrale de trois membres.

Convencion sobre Demarcacion de Limites Territoriales celebrada el 7 de Octubre de 1894 entre los Gobiernos de Honduras y Nicaragua.

Los Gobiernos de las Repúblicas de Honduras y Nicaragua deseosos de terminar de una manera amigable sus diferencias acerca de la demarcación de límites divisorios que hasta hoy no ha podido verificarse, y deseosos también de que tan enojoso asunto se resuelva a satisfacción de ambos, con toda cordialidad y con la deferencia que corresponde á pueblos hermanos, vecinos y aliados, han creido conveniente celebrar un Tratado que llene esas aspiraciones; y al efecto han nombrado á sus respectivos Plenipotenciarios:

El señor Presidente de la República de Honduras, al señor Doctor don César Bonilla, su Secretario de Estado en el Despacho de Relaciones Exteriores; y el señor Presidente de la

República de Nicaragua, al señor don José Dolores Gómez, su Enviado Extraordinario y Ministro Plenipotenciario ante las Repúblicas de Centro-América; quienes habiendo examinado y encontrado bastantes sus respectivos plenos poderes, han convenido en los artículos siguientes:

ARTICULO I. Los Gobiernos de Honduras y Nicaragua, nombrarán comisionados que, con la autorización correspondiente, organisen una Comisión Mixta de Límites, encargada de resolver de una manera amigable, todas las dudas y diferencias pendientes, y de demarcar sobre el terreno la línea divisoria que señale el límite fronterizo de ambas Repúblicas.

ARTICULO II. La Comisión Mixta, compuesta de igual número de miembros por ambas partes, se reunirá en una de las poblaciones fronterizas, que ofrezca mayores comodidades para el estudio, y allí principiará sus trabajos, ateniéndose á las reglas siguientes:

1ª Serán límites entre Honduras y Nicaragua, las líneas en que ambas Repúblicas estuviesen de acuerdo ó que ninguna de las dos disputare.

2ª Serán también límites de Honduras y Nicaragua las líneas demarcadas en documentos públicos no contradichos por documentos igualmente públicos de mayor fuerza.

3ª Se entenderá que cada República es dueña del territorio que á la fecha de la Independencia constituía, respectivamente, las provincias de Honduras y Nicaragua.

4ª La Comisión Mixta para fijar los límites, atenderá al dominio del territorio plenamente probado, y no le reconocerá valor jurídico á la posesión de hecho que por una ú otra parte se alegare.

5ª En falta de la prueba del dominio, se consultarán los mapas de ambas Repúblicas y los documentos geográficos ó de cualquiera otra naturaleza, públicos ó privados, que puedan dar alguna luz, y serán límites entre ambas Repúblicas los que con presencia de ese estudio fijare equitativamente la Comisión Mixta.

6ª La misma Comisión Mixta, si lo creyere conveniente, podrá hacer compensaciones y fijar indemnizaciones para procurar establecer, en lo posible, límites naturales bien marcados.

7ª Al hacer el estudio de los planos, mapas y demás documentos análogos que presenten ambos Gobiernos, la Comisión Mixta preferirá los que estime más racionales y justos.

8ª En caso de que la Comisión Mixta no pudiese acordarse amigablemente en cualquier punto, lo consignará por separado en los libros especiales, firmando una doble acta detallada, con cita de lo alegado por ambas partes, y continuará su estudio sobre los demás puntos de la línea de demarcación con prescindencia del punto indicado, hasta fijar el término divisorio el último extremo de la misma línea.

9ª Los libros á que se refiere la cláusula anterior serán enviados por la Comisión Mixta, uno á cada Gobierno de los interesados, para su custodia en los archivos nacionales.

ARTICULO III. El punto ó los puntos de demarcación que la Comisión Mixta de que habla el presente Tratado, no hubiese resuelto, serán sometidos, á más tardar, un mes después de concluidas las sesiones de la misma Comisión, al fallo de un arbitramento inapelable que será compuesto de un Representante de Honduras y otro de Nicaragua, y de un miembro del Cuerpo Diplomático extranjero acreditado en Guatemala, electo este último por los primeros, ó sorteado en dos ternas propuestas, una por cada parte.

ARTICULO IV. El arbitramento se organizará en la ciudad de Guatemala, en los veinte días siguientes á la disolución de la Comisión Mixta, y dentro de los diez días immediatos principiará sus trabajos, consignándolos en un libro de actas, que llevará por duplicado, siendo ley el voto de la mayoría.

ARTICULO V. En el caso de que el Representante Diplomático extranjero se excusare, se repetirá la elección en otro, dentro de los diez días inmediatos, y así sucesivamente. Agotados los miembros del Cuerpo Diplomático extranjero, la elección podrá recaer, por convenio de las comisiones de Honduras y Nicaragua, en cualquier personaje público, extranjero ó centroamericano; y si este convenio no fuere posible, se someterá el punto ó los puntos controvertidos, á la decisión del Gobierno de España, y en defecto de éste á la de cualquiera otro de Sud-América, en que convengan las Cancillerías de ambos países.

ARTICULO VI. Los procedimientos y términos á que deberá sujetarse el arbitramento, serán los siguientes:

1º Dentro de los veinte días siguientes á la fecha en que la aceptación del tercer árbitro fuere notificada á las partes, éstas la presentarán, por medio de sus Abogados, sus alegatos, planos, mapas y documentos.

2º Si hubiere alegatos, dará traslado de ellos á los respectivos Abogados contrarios, dentro de los ocho días siguientes á la presentación, concediéndoles diez días de término para rebatirlos y presentar los más documentos que creyeren del caso.

3º El fallo arbitral será pronunciado dentro de los veinte días siguientes á la fecha en que se hubiere vencido el término para contestar alegatos, háyanse ó no presentado éstos.

ARTICULO VII. La decisión arbitral, votada por mayoría, cualquiera que sea, se tendrá como Tratado perfecto, obligatorio y perpetuo entre las Altas Partes Contratantes, y no admitirá recurso alguno.

ARTICULO VIII. La presente Convención será sometida en Honduras y Nicaragua á las ratificaciones constitucionales, y el canje de éstas se verificará en Tegucigalpa ó en Managua, dentro de los sesenta días siguientes á la fecha en que ambos Gobiernos hubieren cumplido con lo estipulado en este articulo.

ARTICULO IX. Lo dispuesto en el articulo anterior, no obsta en manera alguna para la organización inmediata de la Comisión Mixta, que deberá principiar sus estudios, á más tardar, dos meses después de la última ratificación, de conformidad con lo que se ha dispuesto en la presente Convención, sin perjuício de hacerlo antes de las ratificaciones, si éstas se tardasen, para aprovechar la estación seca ó del verano.

ARTICULO X. Inmediatamente después del canje de esta Convención, háyanse ó no principiado los trabajos de la Comisión Mixta, serán nombrados por los Gobiernos de Honduras y Nicaragua, los representantes que en conformidad del articulo IX, deben formar el arbitramento, para que, organizándose en junta preparatoria nombren el tercer árbitro y lo comuniquen á los Secretarios de Relaciones respectivos, á fin de recabar la aceptación del nombrado. Si éste se excusase, se procederá en seguida al nombramiento de un nuevo tercer árbitro en la forma estipulada, y así sucesivamente hasta quedar organizado el arbitramento.

ARTICULO XI. Los plazos señalados en el presente Tratado para nombramiento de árbitros, principio de estudios, ratificaciones y canje, lo mismo que cualesquiera otros términos en él fijados, no serán fatales ni producirán nulidad de ninguna especie. Su objeto ha sido dar precisión al trabajo; pero si por cualquiera causa no pudieran atenderse, es la voluntad de las Altas Partes Contratantes que la negociación se lleve adelante hasta terminarla en la forma aquí estipulada, que es la que creen más conveniente. A este fin, convienen en que este Tratado tenga la duración de diez años, caso de interrumpirse su ejecución, en cuyo término no podrá reverse ni modificarse en ninguna manera, ni podrá tampoco dirimirse la cuestion de límites por otro medio.

En fe de lo cual, los Plenipotenciarios de las Repúblicas des Honduras y Nicaragua firman, en dos ejemplares que autorizan con sus respectivos sellos, en la ciudad de Tegucigalpa, á los siete días del mes de octubre de mil ochocientos noventa y cuatro, año septuagésimo cuarto de la Independencia de Centro-América[1].

CXV. Chili, France.

19 octobre 1894.

Convention similaire à celle que la Grande-Bretagne et le Chili avaient conclue le 26 septembre 1893. Un arrangement amiable mit fin à l'arbitrage moyennant le paiement d'une indemnité de 5000 £.

Convention d'arbitrage destinée à mettre un terme aux réclamations faites par la France à raison des actes posés et opérations accomplies pendant la guerre civile de 1891, signée à Santiago, le 19 octobre 1894.

S. E. le Président de la République française et S. E. le Président de la République du Chili, désirant mettre amicalement un terme aux réclamations introduites par la Légation de France au Chili et motivées par la guerre civile qui s'est produite le 7 janvier 1891, ont résolu de conclure une convention d'arbitrage et à cet effet ils ont nommé pour leurs plénipotentiaires respectifs, savoir :

S. E. le Président de la République française, le sieur Comte Balny d'Avricourt, Envoyé extraordinaire et Ministre plénipotentiaire de la République française ;

S. E. le Président de la République du Chili, le sieur Mariano Sanchez Fontecilla, Ministre des Relations extérieures,

Lesquels plénipotentiaires, après avoir exhibé leurs pouvoirs et les avoir trouvés en bonne et due forme, sont convenus des stipulations contenues dans les articles suivants :

ART. 1. Un tribunal arbitral jugera en la forme et selon les termes établis dans l'article 5 de cette convention toutes les réclamations motivées par les actes et opérations accomplies par les forces de mer et de terre de la République, pendant la guerre civile qui a commencé le 7 janvier 1891 et qui s'est terminée le 28 août de la même année, ainsi que celles motivées par des actes postérieurs, qui, selon les termes dénoncés dans l'article 5, seront de la responsabilité du Gouvernement du Chili.

Les réclamations devront être placées sous le patronage de la Légation de France et pré-

---

[1] *Tratados celebrados por el Gobierno de Honduras,* 1895, p. 29.

sentées dans le délai de six mois compté depuis la date de l'installation du tribunal.

ART. 2. Le tribunal se composera de trois menibres, l'un nommé par S. E. le Président de la République française, l'autre par S. E. le Président de la République du Chili et le troisième par les deux Parties contractantes.

La nomination du troisième membre ne pourra être faite en faveur d'un citoyen français ni d'un citoyen chilien.

ART. 3. Le tribunal accueillera les moyens probatoires ou d'investigation qui, d'après l'appréciation et le juste discernement de ses membres, pourront le mieux conduire à l'éclaircissement des faits controversés et spécialement à la détermination de l'état et du caractère neutre du réclamant. Le tribunal recevra également les allégations verbales ou écrites des deux Gouvernements, de leurs agents ou défenseurs respectifs.

ART. 4. Chaque Gouvernement pourra constituer un agent qui veille aux intérêts de ses commettants et en prenne la défense ; qui présente des pétitions, documents, interrogatoires ; qui pose des conclusions ou y réponde ; qui appuie ses affirmations et réfute les affirmations contraires, qui en fournisse les preuves, et qui, devant le tribunal, par lui-même ou par l'organe d'un homme de loi, verbalement ou par écrit, conformément aux règles de procédure et aux voies que le tribunal lui-même arrêtera en commençant ses fonctions, expose les doctrines, principes légaux ou précédents qui conviennent à sa cause.

ART. 5. Le tribunal jugera les réclamations d'après la valeur de la preuve fournie, et conformément aux principes de droit international et à la pratique de la jurisprudence établie par les tribunaux récents analogues ayant le plus d'autorité et de prestige, en prenant ses résolutions tant interlocutoires que définitives à la majorité des votes.

Dans chaque jugement définitif, le tribunal exposera brièvement les faits et causalités de la réclamation, les motifs allégués à l'appui ou en contradiction, et les bases de droit international sur lesquelles s'appuient ses résolutions.

Les résolutions et jugements du tribunal seront écrits et signés par tous ses membres et revêtus de la forme authentique par son secrétaire.

Les actes originaux resteront, avec leurs dossiers respectifs, au Ministère des Relations extérieures du Chili où il sera délivré des copies certifiées aux parties qui le demanderont. Le tribunal tiendra un livre d'enregistrement dans lequel on inscrira la procédure suivie, les demandes des réclamants et les jugements et décisions rendus.

Le tribunal fonctionnera à Santiago.

ART. 6. Le tribunal aura la facilité de se pourvoir de secrétaires, rapporteurs et autres employés qu'il estimera nécessaires pour le bon accomplissement de ses fonctions.

Il appartient au tribunal de proposer les personnes qui auront à remplir respectivement ces emplois et de fixer les traitements et rémunérations à leur assigner.

La nomination de ces divers employés sera faite par S. E. le Président de la République du Chili.

Les jugements du Tribunal qui devront être exécutés au Chili auront l'appui de la force publique de la même manière que ceux rendus par les tribunaux ordinaires du pays. Les jugements qui auront à être exécutés à l'étranger sortiront leurs effets conformément aux règles et aux usages du droit international privé.

ART. 7. Le tribunal aura pour terminer sa mission à l'égard de toutes les réclamations soumises à son examen et décision un délai d'une année à compter du jour où il se sera déclaré installé. Passé ce délai, le tribunal aura la faculté de proroger ses fonctions pour une nouvelle période qui ne pourra excéder six mois dans le cas que, pour cause de maladie ou incapacité temporaire de quelqu'un de ses membres ou pour tout autre motif de gravité reconnue, il ne serait pas parvenu à terminer sa mission dans le délai fixé au premier paragraphe.

ART. 8. Chacun des Gouvernements contractants pourvoira aux frais de ses propres gestions et aux honoraires de ses respectifs agents ou défenseurs.

Le paiement des appointements des membres du tribunal courra du jour où ils commenceront leurs fonctions.

Les dépenses d'organisation du tribunal, les honoraires de ses membres, les appointements des secrétaires, rapporteurs et autres employés, et tous frais et dépenses de service commun seront payés de moitié par les deux gouvernements ; mais s'il y a des sommes allouées en faveur des réclamants, il en sera déduit lesdits frais et dépenses communes en tant qu'ils n'excèdent pas le 6 % des valeurs que le trésor du Chili aurait à payer pour la totalité des réclamations admises.

Les sommes que le tribunal assignera en faveur des réclamants seront versées par le Gouvernement du Chili au Gouvernement français par l'entremise de sa Légation à Santiago, ou de la personne à ce désignée, dans le délai d'un an à compter de la date de la résolution y afférente, sans que durant ce délai lesdites sommes soient passibles d'aucun intérêt en faveur du réclamant. Le Gouvernement du Chili déduira de toute somme qu'il aurait à payer pour satisfaire les réclamations soumises au tribunal, soit que le paiement se fasse par ordre du tribunal ou en vue d'un arrangement privé, les sommes stipulées dans le troisième paragraphe de cet article, lesdites sommes devant être retenues et employées pour le paiement des dépenses communes de l'arbitrage.

ART. 9. Les Hautes Parties contractantes s'obligent à considérer les jugements du tribunal organisé par la présente Convention, comme une solution satisfaisante, parfaite et irrévocable, des difficultés qu'il a eu en vue de régler ; et il est bien entendu que les réclamations des citoyens français présentées ou non présentées dans les conditions signalées aux articles précédents, seront tenues pour décidées et jugées définitivement, et de manière que, pour aucun motif ou prétexte, elles ne puissent être l'objet d'un nouvel examen ou d'une nouvelle discussion.

ART. 10. Si les Hautes Parties contractantes n'arrivaient pas à un accord, relativement au choix d'un troisième arbitre, il sera sollicité de S. M. le roi des Belges qu'il en fasse le choix et dans ce cas, la période pendant laquelle le tribunal doit commencer ses travaux sera de six mois à compter de la date de l'échange des ratifications de cette Convention.

ART. 11. La présente Convention sera ratifiée par les Hautes Parties contractantes et l'échange des ratifications s'effectuera à Santiago. En foi de quoi les soussignés, plénipotentiaires de France et du Chili, ont signé ad referendum la présente Convention en double exemplaire et dans les langues française et espagnole, et l'ont scellée de leurs sceaux respectifs.

Fait à Santiago, le dix-neuvième jour du mois d'octobre de l'année de N. S. 1894 [1].

Convention additionnelle à la Convention du 19 octobre 1894, signée à Santiago le 12 octobre 1895 ; suivie d'un règlement de procédure du tribunal arbitral Franco-Chilien.

Les plénipotentiaires soussignés, dûment autorisés par leurs gouvernements respectifs, dans le but d'activer la solution des réclamations déférées au tribunal arbitral franco-chilien institué par la Convention du 19 octobre 1894, ont arrêté ce qui suit :

Les délais stipulés aux articles 1 et 7 de ladite Convention seront réduits de moitié. En conséquence les réclamations devront être pré-

[1] F. DE MARTENS. *Nouveau Recueil Général*, 2ᵐᵉ série, t. XXIII, p. 152.

sentées dans le délai de trois mois, à dater de l'installation du tribunal, au lieu des six mois indiqués dans l'article 1.

La durée des fonctions du tribunal, primitivement fixée à une année à partir du jour où le tribunal se sera déclaré installé suivant l'article 7, est réduite à six mois.

Dans les cas prévus au deuxième paragraphe du même article, le délai éventuel de prorogation est réduit de six mois à trois mois.

En foi de quoi, les ministres plénipotentiaires ont signé le présent accord additionnel.

Fait en double exemplaire, en espagnol et en français, à Santiago, le 12 octobre 1895.

Règlement de procédure du tribunal arbitral Franco-Chilien, adopté à Santiago, le 17 octobre 1895.

ART. 1. Toute partie réclamante, son mandataire ou son représentant légal, présentera au tribunal franco-chilien, dans le délai prévu dans l'article 1 de la Convention du 19 octobre 1894, modifiée par la Convention additionnelle du 12 octobre 1895, un mémoire accompagné de tous les documents et pièces justificatives de sa réclamation. Quand elle jugera utile d'administrer la preuve testimoniale, elle devra indiquer dans le mémoire ou dans une pièce annexée, les faits qu'elle se propose d'établir, ainsi que les nom, prénoms, profession, nationalité et résidence des témoins. Le tribunal aura toujours le droit d'autoriser dans le cours de procédure, la preuve de faits nouveaux et l'audition de nouveaux témoins. La présentation du mémoire devra être faite par l'intermédiaire de la Légation de France à Santiago ou par l'agent qu'elle aura désigné, en conformité de l'article 4 de la Convention d'arbitrage.

Dans ce dernier cas, les réclamations présentées par l'agent du Gouvernement français seront censées avoir été présentées par la Légation de France au Chili et, par ce fait, les conditions prévues dans l'alinéa 2 de l'article 1 de la Convention du 19 octobre 1894 seront tenues pour remplies.

ART. 2. Le mémoire et tous les documents présentés à l'appui de la réclamation seront rédigés en langue espagnole et accompagnés d'une traduction fidèle en langue française ; il en sera de même du mémoire de défense.

ART. 3. Le mémoire devra contenir les nom, prénoms, profession, et la résidence actuelle de la partie réclamante, le lieu et l'année de sa naissance, ainsi que le lieu de la résidence à l'époque où se sont passés les faits qui donnent lieu à sa réclamation. Le mémoire et sa traduction devront être déposés en double exemplaire au secrétariat du tribunal.

ART. 4. Le mémoire établira également si l'auteur de la réclamation est sujet français par naissance ou par naturalisation et fournira les renseignements exigés par l'article 3 de la Convention pour établir la qualité et le caractère de neutralité du réclamant et dira notamment s'il a pris part directement ou indirectement à la guerre civile qui a commencé le 7 janvier 1891, pour prendre fin le 28 août de la même année, comme aussi s'il était durant cette période au service de l'une des parties en cause ou recevait un salaire de l'une d'elles.

ART. 5. Si la réclamation est faite au nom d'une société qui n'est pas une société anonyme ou d'une firme sociale, le mémoire doit indiquer le lieu de son domicile, les noms de tous les associés et intéressés et fournir, autant que possible, eu égard à chaque associé ou intéressé, les renseignements exigés par les articles 3 et 6 ci-dessus.

Quand la partie réclamante n'est pas la personne qui a souffert le préjudice, mais son mandataire ou représentant légal, elle devra, en outre, justifier de sa personnalité à la satisfaction du tribunal.

ART. 6. La partie réclamante doit déclarer dans le mémoire si elle a reçu quelque somme d'argent ou compensation à compte de la réclamation et de qui; et si sa réclamation a déjà été portée devant un autre tribunal.

ART. 7. Le mémoire doit contenir une exposition détaillée et claire de la réclamation, c'est-à-dire son montant, le lieu où se sont passés les faits qui lui ont donné naissance, l'espèce, la quantité et la valeur de la propriété perdue, détruite ou endommagée, tous les faits et circonstances qui se rapportent à la perte ou au préjudice pour lequel on réclame une indemnité, et aussi pour autant que ce soit possible, les noms, grades et fonctions des personnes qui ont posé les actes donnant lieu à la réclamation.

Si quelque reçu ou déclaration par écrit ont été donnés à la partie réclamante, elle devra les présenter et, au cas où elle ne les possède pas, elle devra expliquer le motif qui rend cette présentation impossible.

ART. 8. Le mémoire doit spécifier avec précision la somme réclamée en faisant une distinction entre le capital et les intérêts et indiquer la qualité de la monnaie qui représente la valeur du préjudice.

ART. 9. Le mémoire doit être confirmé par une déclaration assermentée ou solennelle par laquelle la partie réclamante ratifie tous les faits qu'elle a avancés.

Cette déclaration doit être reçue et légalisée par un fonctionnaire diplomatique ou consulaire ou, à son défaut, par l'autorité locale compétente.

ART. 10. Dès qu'un mémoire sera présenté, les secrétaires l'inscriront dans le registre à ce destiné, puis le déposeront dans les archives après avoir fait mention du fait de sa réception sur le mémoire même et lui avoir donné un numéro d'ordre correspondant à celui du registre; ils délivreront un certificat de réception à l'agent qui aura déposé le mémoire.

Ces prescriptions accomplies, les secrétaires notifieront, dans les cinq jours, le fait de la réception du mémoire à l'agent du Gouvernement chilien; ce dernier, dans un délai de trente jours à compter de cette notification, présentera la défense à ce mémoire, y opposera toutes les exceptions et demandes, qui incombent à son droit, présentant tous les documents justifiant son opposition et offrant les preuves testimoniales contraires qu'il se propose de produire dans l'intérêt de sa défense.

Ce mémoire de défense sera signifié dans les cinq jours par les secrétaires à l'agent du Gouvernement français qui, dans un délai de dix jours depuis ladite notification, aura à son tour la faculté de présenter une réplique, de nouveaux documents, de nouvelles requêtes et d'indiquer les preuves testimoniales contraires dont il se propose de faire usage et de modifier ou rectifier les formalités indiquées dans les articles précédents.

La présentation de cette réplique sera notifiée dans les cinq jours par les secrétaires à l'agent du Gouvernement chilien, lequel, à son tour et dans le délai de dix jours, aura la faculté de répliquer dans les mêmes conditions. Cette dernière réplique sera notifiée par les secrétaires à l'agent du Gouvernement français.

Au cas où l'agent du Gouvernement français renoncerait à la faculté à lui accordée par le 3e alinéa du présent article, il le fera notifier à l'agent du Gouvernement chilien par l'intermédiaire des secrétaires, et, en ce cas, ce dernier ne jouira pas de la faculté qui lui est accordée par l'alinéa précédent.

ART. 11. Chaque fois qu'il y aura lieu d'administrer la preuve testimoniale, la partie qui l'offrira devra préciser les faits qu'elle se propose d'établir et indiquer les noms, profession et nationalité des témoins qu'elle veut faire entendre; elle devra toujours renseigner la résidence exacte des témoins.

Le tribunal décidera dans chaque cas séparé, comment se feront les interrogatoires des témoins et, le cas échéant, quels seront les fonctionnaires propres à recevoir les témoignages. Toutefois, chaque fois que les circonstances le permettront, l'interrogatoire des témoins se fera devant le tribinal même.

Les agents ou leurs délégués pourront interroger et contreinterroger les témoins.

Le témoin déposera sous serment ou après avoir fait une déclaration solennelle et il devra préalablement déclarer s'il a quelque intérêt dans la déclaration, s'il est parent, créancier ou associé de la partie réclamante ou employé par le Gouvernement chilien, soit actuellement, soit à l'époque où se sont passés les faits donnant lieu à la réclamation, ou s'il a pris part directement ou indirectement à la guerre civile de 1891.

ART. 12. Dès que la dernière notification prévue par l'article 10 aura été faite ou que les enquêtes seront terminées, soit qu'on y ait procédé ou que les parties intéressées aient négligé de le faire dans les délais fixés, les secrétaires inscriront la réclamation au rôle destiné à recevoir les affaires qui sont en état d'être portées devant le tribunal arbitral. Le tribunal fixera l'audience dans laquelle les parties seront entendues et les secrétaires notifieront cette résolution dans les quarante-huit heures aux agents des deux Gouvernements. Entre la date de cette notification et le jour de l'audience il devra s'écouler un délai d'au moins six jours.

Le tribunal, après avoir entendu le plaidoyer des parties, pourra prononcer la sentence s'il juge qu'il n'a pas besoin d'autres éclaircissements que ceux qui ont été présentés; au cas contraire, il pourra ordonner, d'office ou à la demande d'un des agents des deux Gouvernements, qu'il soit procédé à toutes les nouvelles diligences qu'il jugera nécessaires, fixant la forme et le lieu de leur exécution.

ART. 13. Les agents, ainsi que les secrétaires, rapporteurs et jurisconsultes nommés par les agents en conformité des articles 4 et 5 de la Convention, pourront seuls assister aux audiences du tribunal. Personne ne pourra, en aucun cas, assister aux délibérations du tribunal.

ART. 14. Les secrétaires, indépendamment du registre mentionné à l'article 10, tiendront un registre dans lequel ils inscriront les minutes de la procédure, un autre dans lequel ils copieront les décisions et les jugements et un troisième dans lequel ils inscriront les procès-verbaux des audiences.

Les minutes de la procédure, les décisions et les jugements, ainsi que les procès-verbaux des audiences, seront rédigés en langue espagnole et accompagnés d'une traduction en langue française.

Dès que le tribunal aura terminé ses travaux, les documents rédigés en langue française seront remis à l'agent du Gouvernement français.

ART. 15. Les secrétaires remettront à chaque agent une copie certifiée conforme de chaque décision et jugement dès qu'ils auront été prononcés, et lesdits agents pourront, soit par eux-mêmes ou par une personne expressément déléguée à cette fin, prendre connaissance des documents qu'ils désirent consulter et en prendre copie avec l'autorisation préalable du tribunal.

Le tribunal se réserve le droit d'ordonner ou d'autoriser la publication des documents déposés au secrétariat.

ART. 16. Les archives sont à la garde des secrétaires auxquels il est défendu de laisser sortir n'importe quel document au dehors sans l'autorisation préalable du tribunal.

ART. 17. Le tribunal se réserve la faculté de supprimer, modifier ou augmenter les prescriptions contenues dans les articles précédents quand l'expérience en aura montré la nécessité, comme aussi de permettre la rectification de toute erreur de fait que les parties auraient pu commettre de bonne foi.

Santiago, le 17 octobre 1895[1].

Arrangement ayant pour but de mettre fin à toutes les réclamations présentées au Tribunal arbitral institué par la convention du 19 octobre 1894, signé à Santiago le 2 février 1896.

M. Léopold Fernand Balny d'Avricourt, envoyé extraordinaire et ministre plénipotentiaire de France, officier de l'ordre national de la Légion d'honneur, etc. etc., et M. Adolfo Guerrero, ministre des affaires étrangères, étant réunis au département des affaires étrangères du Chili, et dûment autorisés à cet effet, sont convenus de mettre fin, conformément aux bases ci-après indiquées, à toutes les réclamations des citoyens français ayant pour cause la guerre civile et qui ont été présentées au tribunal d'arbitrage compétent.

Premièrement. Il est mis fin au fonctionnement du tribunal franco-chilien institué par la Convention du 19 octobre 1894, pour connaître et décider des réclamations formulées par les citoyens français contre le Gouvernement du Chili.

Deuxièmement. Toutes les réclamations françaises qui ont été présentées au tribunal et dont la somme totale s'élève, d'une part, à 344,041 piastres, et d'autre part, à 424,356 fr., seront considérées comme complètement payées et éteintes quels que soient leur nature, leurs antécédents et leur situation actuelle devant le tribunal, moyennant la somme de 5000 livres sterling que le

---

[1] F. DE MARTENS, *Nouveau Recueil Général*, 2ᵐᵉ série, t. XXIII, p. 155.

Gouvernement du Chili payera au représentant diplomatique de France à Santiago, dans les quinze jours qui suivront l'approbation de cet accord par le Congrès de la République. Ladite somme de 5000 livres sterling sera distribuée entre les réclamants par le Gouvernement français suivant la proportion et la forme qu'il jugera convenable, sans qu'une pareille distribution puisse affecter d'une manière quelconque la responsabilité du Gouvernement du Chili.

Troisièmement. Il est expressément convenu que le Gouvernement du Chili a conclu cet arrangement amical dans le but de mettre fin aux réclamations pendantes et sans que cet accord affecte ni directement ni indirectement les principes et la jurisprudence que le Gouvernement du Chili a défendus et soutenus devant les tribunaux arbitraux.

En foi de quoi, l'envoyé extraordinaire et ministre plénipotentiaire de France et le ministre des affaires étrangères du Chili ont signé ce protocole en double expédition et l'ont revêtu de leurs sceaux respectifs à Santiago du Chili le deux du mois de février de mil huit cent quatre-vingt-seize [1].

CXVI. Grande-Bretagne, Portugal.

7 janvier 1895.

Question de délimitation qui donna lieu à une remarquable sentence de M. P. H. Vigliani, favorable en majeure partie aux prétentions de la Grande-Bretagne.

Déclaration signée à Londres, le 7 janvier 1895, à l'effet de soumettre à l'arbitrage la question des frontières des possessions africaines de la Grande-Bretagne et du Portugal.

Le 11 juin 1891, un Traité a été signé entre Sa Majesté la Reine du Royaume-Uni de la Grande-Bretagne et d'Irlande, Impératrice des Indes, et Sa Majesté Très-Fidèle le Roi de Portugal et des Algarves, lequel Traité détermina la question des frontières de leurs possessions et de leurs zones d'influence dans l'Afrique Orientale et Centrale.

L'Article II de ce Traité contient la démarcation de la frontière au sud du Zambèze; c'est-à-dire, du point sur la rive de ce fleuve vis-à-vis de l'embouchure de l'Aroangoa ou Loangwa, jusqu'au point où s'entrecoupent la frontière du Swaziland et le fleuve Maputo.

Des différends ayant surgi à l'égard de la signification de certaines phrases dans ledit Article,

les deux Gouvernements ont décidé à recourir à l'arbitrage de Son Excellence M. Paul Honoré Vigliani, ancien Premier Président de Cour de Cassation, Sénateur et Ministre d'Etat du Royaume d'Italie.

Ils ne proposent pas, cependant, que l'arbitrage porte sur toute la ligne indiquée ci-dessus.

On peut considérer la frontière au sud du Zambèze comme divisée en trois sections : —

1º Du Zambèze jusqu'au 18º 30´ de latitude sud.

2º Du 18º 30´ de latitude sud jusqu'au point où le fleuve Sabi et le Lunde ou Lunte se rencontrent.

3º A partir de ce point jusqu'au fleuve Maputo.

Il n'est pas jugé nécessaire de soumettre à l'arbitrage le tracé des sections 1 et 3; les différends ne regardent que la 2º section.

Les négociations ont eu lieu à Londres. Le texte du Traité fut rédigé en anglais et parafé par le Marquis de Salisbury, alors Ministre des Affaires Etrangères, et par M. de Soveral, Ministre du Portugal. Le Traité ayant été comparé avec le texte parafé à Londres, fut signé à Lisbonne par le Comte Vallom, Ministre des Affaires Etrangères du Portugal, et par Sir George Petre, Ministre de Sa Majesté Britannique à Lisbonne.

La partie de l'Article qui traite de la 2º section de la frontière est conçu dans les termes suivants :

« De là » (c'est-à-dire de l'intersection du 33º degré de longitude est de Greenwich avec le 18º 30´ parallèle de latitude sud) « elle suit, vers le sud, la partie supérieure du versant oriental du plateau de Manica jusqu'au milieu du chenal principal du Sabi, et elle suit ce chenal jusqu'au point où il rencontre le Lunte...

« Il est entendu qu'en traçant la frontière le long du versant du plateau, aucune partie de territoire à l'ouest du 32º 30´ de longitude est de Greenwich ne sera comprise dans la zone Portugaise, ni aucune partie de territoire à l'est du 33º de longitude est de Greenwich dans la zone Britannique. Toutefois, le cas échéant, la ligne sera détournée de manière à laisser Mutassa dans la zone Britannique et Massi-Kessi dans la zone Portugaise. »

Les termes, en Anglais et en Portugais, sont les suivants :

"...Thence it follows the upper part of the eastern slope of the Manica plateau southwards to the centre of the main channel of the Sabi, follows that channel to its confluence with the Lunte, whence it strikes	"... D'ahi accompanha a crista da vertente oriental do planalto de Manica na sua direcção sul até á linha media do leito principal do Save, seguindo por elle até á sua confluencia com o Lunde, d'onde corta di-

---

[1] F. DE MARTENS, *Nouveau Recueil Général*, 2ᵐᵉ série, t. XXIII, p. 231.

direct to the north eastern point of the frontier of the South African Republic, and follows the eastern frontier of the Republic, and the frontier of Swaziland, to the River Maputo.

"It is understood, that, in tracing the frontier along the slope of the plateau no territory west of longitude 32° 30' east of Greenwich shall be comprised in the Portuguese sphere, and no territory east of longitude 33° east of Greenwich shall be comprised in the British sphere.

The line shall, however, if necessary, be deflected so as to leave Mutassa in the British sphere and Massi-Kessi in the Portuguese sphere."

reito ao extremo nordeste da fronteira da Republica Sul Africana, continuando pelas fronteiras orientaes d'esta Republica e da Swazilandia até ao Rio Maputo.

"Fica entendido ao traçar a . fronteira ao longo da crista do planalto, nenhum territorio a oeste do meridiano de 32° 30' de longitude leste de Greenwich será comprehendido na esphera Portugueza, e que nenhum territorio a leste de 33° de longitude leste de Greenwich ficará comprehendido na esphera Britannica.

Esta linha soffrerá comtudo, sendo necessario, a inflexão bastante para que Mutassa fique na esphera Britannica e Macequece na esphera Portugueza."

Au mois de Juin 1892, les Commissaires des deux Gouvernements ont tâché de tracer la ligne frontière d'après les stipulations précitées ; mais un différend s'est élevé entre eux, le règlement duquel ils ont référé à leurs Gouvernements. Des pourparlers directs entre le Ministère des Affaires Etrangères de Lisbonne et le Foreign Office ont eu lieu ; mais, toute entente ayant paru impossible, les deux Gouvernements ont décidé à recourir à l'arbitrage.

Ces pourparlers diplomatiques et les travaux techniques des Commissaires ont laissé la question de la démarcation dans la situation suivante :

1° Pour ce qui regarde le territoire compris entre le 18° 30' parallèle et un point situé à une distance de quelques milles au sud du défilé de Chimanimani chaque Commissaire a proposé une ligne-frontière, et chaque Gouvernement a adopté la ligne proposée par son Commissaire ; d'où il s'est ensuivi une divergence de vues qu'on n'a pas encore trouvé moyen de concilier.

2° Pour ce qui regarde le territoire compris entre un point situé à une distance de quelques milles au sud du défilé de Chimanimani et le 20° 42' 7" de latitude sud, le Commissaire Britannique et un Délégué du Commissaire Portugais, pour autant qu'il s'y trouvait autorisé, sont convenus d'une ligne frontière dont l'examen par les deux Gouvernements est resté inachevé.

3° Pour ce qui regarde le territoire qui s'étend du 20° 42' 7" de latitude sud jusqu'au point où se rencontrent les fleuves Sabi et Lunte, aucun projet de démarcation n'a été discuté par les deux Gouvernements.

Dans ces circonstances, les deux Gouvernements sont convenus de prier l'Arbitre de prendre en considération les documents, les comptes rendus des pourparlers, et les résultats des travaux techniques, d'apprécier les arguments des deux Gouvernements à l'appui de leurs opinions respectives et de se prononcer sur la ligne qui devra séparer la zone d'influence Portugaise en Afrique de celle de la Grande-Bretagne à partir du parallèle 18° 30' jusqu'au point où se rencontrent le Lunte et le Sabi.

En foi de quoi les Soussignés, dûment autorisés par leurs Gouvernements respectifs, ont signé la présente déclaration qu'ils ont revêtue du sceau de leurs armes.

Fait à Londres, le 7 Janvier 1895 [1].

Décision de Monsieur Paul Vigliani, arbitre entre la Grande-Bretagne et le Portugal, relativement à la frontière du Manica, prononcée le 30 Janvier 1897.

Nous, Paul Honoré Vigliani, ancien Premier Président de la Cour de Cassation de Florence, Ministre d'Etat et Sénateur du Royaume d'Italie, Arbitre entre la Grande-Bretagne et le Portugal au sujet des questions relatives à la délimitation de leurs zones d'influence dans l'Afrique Orientale.

Vu la déclaration signée à Londres le 7 janvier 1895, par Lord Kimberley et M. Luiz de Soveral, qui contient l'Acte de Compromis dont la teneur suit : . . . . . . [2]

Après que nous avons accepté les fonctions d'Arbitre, il a été convenu, entre nous et les deux Gouvernements, que les travaux de l'Arbitrage auraient lieu à Florence, notre résidence, et que les actes de l'arbitrage seraient rédigés en langue Française.

Nous avons invité alors les deux Gouvernements à nous présenter chacun de sa part un Mémoire contenant sa demande motivée avec les pièces à l'appui et avec une carte géographique contenant le tracé de la ligne-frontière réclamée par lui ; et nous nous sommes réservés de les prier, après l'examen des pièces, d'envoyer auprès de nous des Délégués techniques chargés de nous fournir tous les éclaircissements et les explications

---

[1] *Parliamentary Paper*, C. 8434.

[2] L'arbitre reproduit *in terminis* la convention du 7 janvier 1895, dont le texte a été donné plus haut par nous.

utiles pour la pleine connaissance des faits et des lieux concernant les questions à décider.

Pour la rédaction des actes de la procédure et pour les autres travaux de l'arbitrage nous avons nommé notre Secrétaire M. le Marquis Alexander Corsi, Professeur de Droit International à l'Université de Pise.

Vu et examiné le Mémoire présenté par le Gouvernement de la Grande-Bretagne le 16 Mars, 1896, avec cinq cartes, dont celle indiquée par la lettre D contient le tracé de la ligne de frontière réclamée par la Grande-Bretagne.

Les conclusions de ce Mémoire sont celles qui suivent:

Quant à la première section de la frontière contestée:

1. Que la ligne de partage des eaux qui s'étend entre le bassin du Sabi et ceux du Pungwe et du Busi, laquelle ligne de partage des eaux a été proposée comme frontière par M. du Bocage, a été définitivement rejetée pendant les négociations qui précédèrent la conclusion de la Convention.

2. Qu'un grand accroissement de territoire a été assigné au Portugal au nord du Zambèze pour le dédommager de l'abandon de ses prétentions à la ligne de partage des eaux.

3. Que le plateau mentionné dans le IIe Article de la Convention Anglo-Portugaise existe réellement à peu près tel qu'il est marqué sur des cartes publiées avant la conclusion de cette Convention, quoique son escarpement oriental soit çà et là moins clairement défini qu'on ne l'a alors supposé.

4. Que la demande de la Grande-Bretagne laisse le plateau, conformément à l'intention des négociateurs, dans la zone Britannique et toute la pente qui le rattache à la plaine, dans la zone Portugaise.

5. Qu'en suivant le bord supérieur du plateau et en traversant les bouches des ravins, la ligne réclamée par le Gouvernement de Sa Majesté Britannique est en harmonie avec le texte de la Convention et est absolument celle prévue par les négociateurs Britanniques et les négociateurs Portugais.

6. Que le détour fait à Massi-Kessi par la ligne réclamée par le Gouvernement de Sa Majesté Britannique remplit pleinement les conditions requises.

Quant à la deuxième section de la frontière:

7. Que la ligne agréée par le Major Leverson et le Capitaine d'Andrade est celle qui doit être adoptée.

Quant à la troisième section de la frontière:

8. Que, jusqu'au point où la frontière touche le Sabi, il faut qu'elle aille vers le sud entre les limites de longitude 32° 30′, et de longitude 33° est de Greenwich.

9. Que la frontière sera également en accord avec le texte et l'esprit de la Convention, soit qu'elle suive le Sabi en amont ou en aval, vu que ce fleuve sert uniquement de moyen par lequel puisse arriver la frontière au confluent du susdit fleuve avec le Lunte, endroit choisi comme point fixe d'où la ligne continue jusqu'à l'extrémité nord-est de la République Sud-Africaine.

Vu et examiné de même le Mémoire présenté le 10 Juin, 1896, au nom du Gouvernement Portugais avec un volume du Livre Blanc et trois cartes, dont celle marquée par la lettre C contient le tracé de la ligne qu'il réclame.

Les conclusions de ce Mémoire sont celles qui suivent:

1. Que la frontière, depuis le parallèle de 18° 30′ sud jusqu'au défilé de Chimanimani, doit suivre le tracé proposé par le Commissaire Portugais;

2. Qu'à partir de Chimanimani, vers le sud, cette frontière peut suivre jusqu'à Mapunguana le tracé projeté par le Commissaire Britannique et accepté par le Délégué Technique Portugais Freire d'Andrade;

3. Qu'entre Mapunguana et le parallèle de 20° 30′ sud environ, le projet de délimitation arrêté entre le Commissaire Britannique et le Délégué Portugais doit être rectifié, la frontière suivant de Mapunguana par le mont Xerinda vers la montagne située, sous le dit parallèle, entre les bassins du Zona et du Chinica;

4. Que, n'existant plus de plateau au sud du parallèle de 20° 30′ sud, il semble juste et rationnel que, de ce parallèle, la frontière se rende au Save par les monts Mero et Zunone et par la Rivière Lacati, suivant ensuite le cours du Save jusqu'à son confluent avec le Lunde.

Sur notre invitation, les deux Gouvernements ont envoyé à Florence et mis à notre disposition leurs Délégués, savoir: M. le Major Julian John Leverson de la part de la Grande-Bretagne; son Excellence le Conseiller Antoine Ennes et M. le Capitaine Alfred Freire d'Andrade, pour le Portugal.

Les Délégués des deux Gouvernements, après avoir reçu le 16 et 18 Juin, 1896, communication réciproque de ces Mémoires, et des cartes relatives, dans une série de conférences qui ont eu lieu auprès de nous, et dont il a été dressé procès-verbal, nous ont exposé largement les circonstances et les arguments à l'appui des demandes de leurs Gouvernements respectifs ; et par leurs discussions, ils nous ont fourni les éclaircissements et les explications les plus soigneuses et détaillées, que nous avons jugé utile de leur demander, sur les doutes et les difficultés que la nature et la configuration inattendue du plateau montagneux et irrégulier de Manica opposent à une application exacte et littérale du texte de l'Article II de la Convention du 11 Juin, 1891, au territoire qu'il s'agit de délimiter.

Dans le cours de ces discussions, nous furent présentées le 9 Juillet, 1896, des « Observations sur le Mémoire Britannique » par MM. Ennes et d'Andrade, et des « Notes sur le Mémoire Portugais » par Mr. Leverson, et puis encore des « Observations sur le Contre-Mémoire Britannique » par M. d'Andrade, aussi bien que des répliques manuscrites produites d'un côté et de l'autre, des cartes et des profils démonstratifs rédigés avant la clôture des conférences par M. d'Andrade, et une carte topographie présenté le 14 Juillet par Mr. Leverson pour modifier deux petites parties de la première partie de la frontière réclamée par son Gouvernement.

Enfin, après la clôture des conférences, le 17 Août, Mr. Leverson nous a remis ses « Observations finales », de même que M. Freire d'Andrade nous a fait parvenir sous la date du 21 Août, 1896, ses « Conclusions ». Toutes ces productions imprimées ont été notifiées par notre Secrétaire à chacun des Délégués, de manière que l'échange de chaque pièce d'une partie à l'autre a été, autant que possible, contemporaine. Les manuscrits et les cartes ont été mises en même temps à leur disposition.

I. — Questions Préalables.

Dans l'étude des documents et dans les discussions, des questions préalables se présentèrent d'abord à notre examen. Elles se rapportent au texte du Traité du 11 Juin, 1891.

Il résulte de l'Acte de Compromis, que le Traité fut rédigé premièrement en Anglais et parafé le 14 Mai, 1891, par le Marquis de Salisbury, Ministre des Affaires Etrangères de la Grande-Bretagne, et par M. de Soveral, Minister Plénipotentiaire du Portugal à Londres ; qu'ensuite le texte Portugais ayant été comparé avec le texte Anglais parafé à Londres, il fut signé dans le double texte Anglais et Portugais à Lisbonne par le Comte de Valbom, Ministre des Affaires Etrangères du Portugal, et par Sir George Petre, Ministre de Sa Majesté Britannique à Lisbonne le 11 Juin, 1891.

Ces circonstances se trouvent confirmées par les Mémoires des deux Gouvernements. (Voir Mémoire Anglais, 1er Partie, et Mémoire Portugais, page 43.) Il n'a été nulle part déclaré lequel des deux textes, l'Anglais ou le Portugais, doit être considéré comme l'original du Traité.

Il en suit que chacun des deux textes contenus dans le Protocole signé à Lisbonne le 11 Juin, 1891, peut aspirer à l'honneur d'être considéré l'original ; tandis que le texte Anglais parafé à Londres constitue proprement la première « Minute ». En tout cas, on ne peut mettre en doute que chacun des deux doit servir également à l'interprétation du Traité.

Au double texte de l'original on vient d'ajouter une version Française de l'Article II du Traité insérée dans l'Acte de Compromis, l'usage de cette langue ayant été convenu pour les actes de l'arbitrage. Mais comme à la suite de cette traduction Française on y trouve reproduit le double texte Anglais et Portugais du même Article II, on doit croire que les Hautes Parties ont considéré cette version en tout point conforme au double texte de l'original.

Néanmoins, l'emploi de deux langues dans la rédaction du même acte pouvait facilement engendrer, ainsi qu'il est arrivé, notamment dans le monde scientifique à Lisbonne, des doutes et des divergences dans son interprétation ; et cela a été une des causes principales de la nécessité de recourir à l'arbitrage (Mémoire Britannique, § 1).

On s'est demandé principalement : (1) quelle a été la portée de la dénomination de « plateau de Manica » ; (2) quelle était la signification des mots, « la partie supérieure du versant oriental » (« the upper part of the eastern slope » — « a crista da vertente oriental ») ; (3) qu'est-ce qu'on a entendu par le mot de « plateau », lorsqu'on l'a opposé aux mots de « pente » ou « versant » ; (4) si ces derniers mots « pente » et « versant » ont été employés comme synonymes, quelle est la surface *(table, terrasse, ou esplanade)* du plateau proprement dit ; quelle en est la *pente* ou le *versant*, et quel le *bord*, ou *l'escarpement* ; (5) si l'expression « vers le sud » de la version Française équivaut à celle de « southwards » du texte Anglais, et de « na direcção sul » du texte Portugais, et si ces trois expression signifient la direction exacte du sud, ou simplement *à peu près vers le sud* entre l'est et l'ouest ; (6) enfin, si la phrase « suit ce chenal » (du Save) signifie indistinctement suivre ce fleuve en aval ou en amont, ou bien, si elle doit nécessairement signifier le *suivre en aval*.

Tous ces doutes, et les disputes dont elles furent l'objet, ont eu leur retentissement devant l'Arbitre au moyen des Mémoires des deux Parties et dans les discussions de leurs Délégués. Mais on peut heureusement affirmer que, après de loyales explications, ces doutes désormais ont perdu toute importance.

En effet, les Parties ont été amenées par leurs déclarations à reconnaître, que par la dénomination de « plateau de Manica » les négociateurs de la Convention de 1891, en laissant de côté les définitions beaucoup plus restreintes des géographes, ont eu l'intention bien claire et concord[ant]e de comprendre non seulement le district administratif de Manica, borné par les fleuves Munene et Sucuwa, mais tout le territoire qui s'étend, au sud du Zambèse, depuis le parallèle 18° 30′ jusqu'au confluent du Save avec le Lunte, savoir toute la région dont la délimitation a été tracée par la Commission Anglo-Portugaise, et qui forme l'objet de discussion devant l'Arbitre.

C'est en réalité à toute l'étendue de ce territoire, composé d'une suite de hautes terres jointes à l'ancien plateau de Manica, que les cartes géographiques publiées dans les deux pays intéressés, à l'époque où le Traité a été stipulé, ont appliqué la désignation de « plateau » de Manica, se rapportant soit au texte de l'Article, soit à l'intention des négociateurs.

Le Gouvernement Portugais dans son Mémoire (page 70) avec une loyauté qui l'honore, a fait cette déclaration :

« Il est donc incontestable que le négociateur Portugais avait admis que le plateau ne [se] terminait pas au parallèle de 19°; et si son projet du 19 Avril ne l'eût prouvé avec assez d'évidence, la démonstration en serait complétée par les instructions télégraphiques qu'il transmit plus tard au Ministre à Londres, et qui ont été publiées dans le Livre Blanc de 1891, page 196, document No. 260. Cette pièce, à elle seule, tranche la question. ,Comme dernière tentative', disait M. du Bocage, ,il convient de proposer encore: partager le plateau par le parallèle de 20°, en nous laissant à nous la partie méridionale.' Quel était ce plateau, qui atteignait le parallèle 20° et le dépassait encore vers le sud? Evidemment c'était celui de Manica, puisqu'il n'a jamais été question d'aucun autre, pendant la durée des négociations. »

Cette franche déclaration, qui se trouve raffermie dans le Mémoire Portugais par d'autres observations et raisonnements d'une grande valeur, ne permet plus de douter que le plateau de Manica auquel se rapporte le Traité de 1891 n'est nullement le petit pays de Manica des anciens géographes, mais il embrasse toutes les hautes terres comprises entre le parallèle 18° 30′ et le confluent du Save avec le Lunte; c'est-à-dire tout l'ancien royaume ou plateau de Manica réuni avec le plateau couvert d'herbe, et avec l'autre de 2000 à 3000 pieds au-dessus du niveau de la mer, qu'on remarque à la suite du plateau de Manica sur la Carte de M. Maund, qui a été certainement sous les yeux des négociateurs (Mémoire Britannique, § 20).

Quant à la vraie signification de la phrase « partie supérieure » (the upper part » — « a crista ») du versant oriental, les Parties sont facilement tombées d'accord, qu'elle ne peut avoir dans le Traité d'autre sens que celui de la ligne, le long de laquelle, et d'une façon générale et bien marquée, le plateau commence à descendre vers la plaine; ou bien, c'est le bord supérieur qui sépare la table (ou surface) du versant (ou pente) du plateau, et non pas la partie supérieure du versant du plateau au-dessus de la ligne moyenne de sa plus grand altitude. C'est précisément sur cette ligne ou sur ce bord que la frontière doit être tracée (Mémoire Britannique, § 21, et notes du Délégué Britannique, § 19 — Mémoire Portugais, pages 71, 72 et 73). Le mot « il suit » (« it follows » — « accompanha ») perdrait sa signification propre, si au lieu de se rapporter à une ligne qu'on doit longer autant que possible, il se rapportait à une zone susceptible, à son tour, d'être délimitée par d'autres bornes.

Cette interprétation, conforme certes à l'esprit de la Convention, identifie les deux textes et fait disparaître toute différence entre les expressions « upper part » et « crista » du versant; elles ne peuvent exprimer, et n'expriment en effet, autre chose qu'une ligne, et cette ligne ne pourrait être que celle qui sépare la table de la pente ou du versant du plateau.

Les disputes sur la signification des mots: « plateau », « terrasse », ou « esplanade du plateau » — bord ou escarpement du plateau » — ont été terminées par les définitions qu'on en a données et qui ont été admises de part et d'autre.

Ainsi le Délégué Portugais, M. le Capitaine d'Andrade, nous a donné une exacte et complète définition applicable en général à tous les plateaux en ces termes: « Une vaste étendue de terrain qui domine d'une manière nettement définie, et sur un ou plusieurs côtés, les régions qui l'environnent, et qui est réunie à ces régions par des versants dont l'inclinaison est plus forte que celle du plateau lui-même ». Une définition semblable avait été proposée par le Délégué Britannique dans son Mémoire (§ 37) d'après l'autorité de l'illustre géographe M. Elysée Réclus. Et les autres écrivains plus distingués dans cette matière ne s'en éloignent pas.

Il n'est donc pas nécessaire, d'après la géographie moderne, que la surface du plateau soit une plaine unie et régulière, ainsi que son nom semble l'indiquer. Mais elle peut être, et même elle est souvent, inégale, irrégulière, accidentée, hérissée de montagnes, de pics et collines, traversée par des vallées, déchirée par de profonds ravins, sillonnée par des fleuves et des rivières, dont quelques-unes ne sortent point de sa surface ou table, d'autres se déversent le long des versants et sont nécessairement entrecoupées par les bords des versants mêmes.

Telle est la configuration du plateau nommé de Manica. Il est connu comme un des plus irréguliers et des plus montagneux. M. Réclus, suivant la description de l'ingénieur Kuss, qui a exploré récemment cette région et à qui se rapportent aussi les Mémoires des deux Parties, nous apprend que c'est un *groupe de montagnes,* ayant l'aspect d'un plateau (E. Réclus, « La Terre », Paris, 1888, vol. xiii, pages 618 et 619).

Chaque plateau a sa *table* ou *esplanade,* et sa *pente* ou *versant.*

On s'accorde à appeler *table* ou *esplanade* tout le terrain qui, quoique incliné et inégal à cause de l'existence de montagnes ou de collines, maintient toutefois une hauteur à peu près constante et uniforme sur le niveau des terres environnantes, et où les eaux coulent, plus ou moins rapidement sur la surface plus ou moins inclinée, dans leur direction naturelle pour s'y arrêter et former quelquefois des lacs, ou pour se verser plus souvent le long des versants.

On considère comme *pente* ou *versant* du plateau (ces deux derniers mots ayant été employés comme synonymes), tout le terrain fortement incliné qui relie la table du plateau à la plaine adjacente. Le plateau, en effet, d'après sa définition plus correcte, pouvant être incliné aussi d'un côté que l'autre, il est évident qu'une inclinaison quelconque ne suffit pas à déterminer le commencement de la pente, mais il faut qu'elle soit bien marquée et générale.

La ligne qui sépare la *table* du plateau de son versant, c'est-à-dire celle qui marque la fin de la table et le commencement de la pente ou du versant, prend le nom de « bord » ou « crête du versant ». Entendu dans ce sens, « la partie supérieure du versant », dont parle l'Article II du Traité, est un synonyme des mots « upper part of the slope », ou « crista da vertente ».

L'expression Anglaise «southwards », qu'on lit dans le même Article, ne doit pas être entendue dans le sens qu'elle signifie constamment la direction précise du sud, mais plutôt dans le sens large de *direction du côté sud,* ou *à peu près vers le sud.* Dans ce sens elle est acceptée par les deux Parties et elle s'adapte parfaitement au dit Article, d'après lequel la frontière depuis le parallèle 18° 30′ jusqu'au Sabi, renserrée entre le 32° 30 et le 33° de longitude, devant suivre les inflexions sinueuses du bord du versant oriental du plateau, elle ne peut se diriger en ligne droite au sud, mais elle doit se plier tantôt à sud-est, tantôt à sud-ouest. (Voir Mémoire Portugais, page 82, et notes Leverson, No 31.)

Quant à la dernière question, celle de savoir si lorsque dans une Convention de délimitation on dit: *suivre un cours d'eau,* on doit nécessairement entendre: le *suivre en aval,* comme les deux Parties continuent à se trouver en désaccord, nous nous réservons de la résoudre dans la dernière partie de notre décision.

Ayant ainsi éliminé les questions que nous avons qualifié préalables, nous allons examiner les deux lignes de frontière réclamées par chacune des Parties.

II. — *Conditions Générales de la Frontière suivant l'Article II du Traité.*

Nous devons avant tout reconnaître, quelles sont les règles établies par la Convention du 11 Juin, 1891, pour la délimitation du Manica.

L'Article II de cette Convention dispose que: la frontière en partant de l'intersection du 33° longitude est de Greenwich avec le parallèle 18° 30′ de latitude

a) Suit vers le sud la partie supérieure du versant oriental du plateau de Manica ; .

b) Jusqu'au milieu du chenal principal du Sabi ;

c) Puis elle suit ce chenal jusqu'au point où il rencontre le Lunde ;

d) En traçant la frontière, le long de la pente du plateau, aucune partie de territoire à l'ouest du 32° 30′ de longitude est de Greenwich ne sera comprise dans la zone Portugaise, ni aucune partie de territoire à l'est du 33° de longitude est de Greenwich dans la zone Britannique ;

e) Le cas échéant, la ligne sera détournée de manière à laisser Mutassa dans la zone Britannique et Massi-Kessi dans la zone Portugaise.

Le résultat final de la délimitation doit être, que tout le *plateau,* savoir la table ou l'esplanade, soit attribué à la Grande-Bretagne, et toute la *pente,* ou le versant oriental soit réservé au Portugal.

Cette règle fondamentale ne se trouve pas écrite dans le Traité ; mais elle a été admise par ceux qui l'ont rédigé comme une conséquence naturelle et comme une condition essentielle et nécessaire, ainsi que M. le Marquis de Salisbury l'a déclaré par une formule nette et caractéristique dans sa réponse à M. de Soveral le 22 Avril, 1891 : « Le plateau pour nous » (la Grande-Bretagne) « et la pente pour vous » (le Portugal).

Cette réponse a été transmise par M. de Soveral dans sa dépêche du 22 Avril à son Gouvernement, qui en a pris connaissance (voir Livre Blanc Portugais de 1891, page 188) et qui, non seulement n'a pas protesté contre cette proposition, mais il n'a pas même suggéré des expressions qui prouvent qu'il avait des intentions différentes.

En outre, comme la Société Géographique de Lisbonne, quelque temps après, avait soulevé des doutes à cet égard, M. le Conseiller Ennes, Commissaire Portugais pour le règlement des questions relatives à la Convention, s'est chargé de les dissiper en déclarant dans une lettre qu'il adressa le 25 Janvier, 1894, au Président de la même Société (voir Mémoire Britannique, § 19) que: « l'idée était de faire la partition du Manicaland de façon que le plateau, ou à mieux parler, l'esplanade, resterait dans la zone Britannique, tandis que la pente serait dans la zone Portugaise ».

Il ne reste donc aucun doute que la formule « le plateau à la Grande-Bretagne et la pente au Portugal » a été clairement admise comme une règle directive pour la délimitation du Manicaland selon le Traité de 1891.

Or, nous allons voir comment ces règles ont été appliquées et interprétées par les deux Gouvernements.

Ce que nous avons dit de la configuration montagneuse et irrégulière du haut massif à qui on a donné le nom du plateau de Manica, et la circonstance que les personnages qui en réglaient de Londres et de Lisbonne la délimitation, n'en pouvaient avoir qu'une connaissance bien vague et imparfaite, peuvent suffire à expliquer le grave désaccord survenu lorsqu'il s'est agi d'appliquer l'Article II du Traité à des terrains qui présentaient à chaque pas des surprises, des inconnus, et des conditions topographiques bien éloignées de l'attente et de la supposition, soit des auteurs du Traité, soit de la Commission de Délimitation.

Le plus grand esprit de conciliation à peine aurait pu suffir à vaincre toutes les causes de divergence. Ce bon esprit, il faut l'avouer, n'a pas fait complètement défaut; et on peut en remarquer les effets dans la partie, qui n'est pas petite, de la ligne de démarcation qui a été concordée entre le Major Leverson et le Capitaine Freire d'Andrade. Toutefois le désaccord, malgré de longs pourparlers, subsiste dans la première et la plus importante partie de la frontière, ainsi que dans d'autres.

Aussi, pour résoudre tous les points de question qui ont surgi, nous allons suivre l'ordre indiqué dans l'Acte de Compromis. Nous partagerons donc la ligne-frontière soumise à notre arbitrage en trois sections, savoir: —

1. De l'intersection du parallèle 18° 30′ avec le 33° longitude est de Greenwich jusqu'à un point situé sur ce méridien à une distance de quelques milles au sud du défilé de Chimanimani. Dans cette section chaque Gouvernement a adopté la ligne proposée par son Commissaire dans les travaux de délimitation et il l'a réclamée devant l'Arbitre.

2. De l'extrémité méridionale de la première section jusqu'au point où le bord du versant du plateau coupe le 32° 30′ longitude est de Greenwich. Cette section ayant été concordée entre les Commissaires des deux Gouvernements, la Grande-Bretagne demande qu'elle soit adoptée entièrement. Le Portugal n'accepte la ligne concordée qu'en partie; pour le reste il propose une nouvelle ligne.

3. Du point où termine la deuxième section, jusqu'au confluent des fleuves Save et Lunde. Pour cette troisième section aucun projet de démarcation n'ayant été discuté entre les Parties, la Grande-Bretagne dans son Mémoire réclame une ligne qui irait vers le sud jusqu'au centre du chenal principal du Save et puis suivrait ce chenal en amont jusqu'à son confluent avec le Lunde. La direction dans laquelle la ligne devrait être tracée, est laissée à la décision de l'Arbitre, mais elle ne devrait en aucun cas dépasser à l'ouest le 32° 30′ et à l'est le 33° de longitude. Le Portugal refuse cette ligne et en réclame pour des raisons spéciales une autre qui, en s'écartant des règles établies par le Traité, irait vers l'ouest jusqu'au Save.

Aucune carte géographique n'a été annexée au Traité, ni au Compromis. Et, de notre avis, il n'y en a aucune qui puisse être adoptée comme preuve sûre et complète des intentions des négociateurs du Traité.

Pas même la carte publiée par M. Maund dans les « Proceedings of the Royal Geographical Society », produite par l'Angleterre sous la lettre A, et qui fait l'objet de sa troisième conclusion, ne pourrait être considérée comme une carte reconnue exacte, surtout dans ses détails, pendant les négociations.

Enfin, pendant la procédure de l'arbitrage, on n'a produit aucune carte qui ait été reconnue entièrement exacte par les deux Parties. Elles ont beaucoup discuté sur l'importance et l'exactitude de leurs cartes; mais malheureusement ces discussions n'ont abouti à une conclusion bien arrêtée sur la valeur qu'on peut attribuer à l'une plus qu'à l'autre dans les différents traits de la frontière.

C'est un inconvénient des plus regrettables; car, au défaut d'une base solide et constante pour la discussion, nous sommes obligés à suivre minutieusement les deux Parties sur le terrain des arguments qu'elles ont produits, et à rechercher, section par section, les intentions des négociateurs, pour les coordonner avec le texte du Traité, et avec les faits qui résultent établis par l'examen comparé que nous avons fait de ces cartes différentes, et par les observations impartiales d'un tiers expert.

III. — *Première Section de la Frontière.*

En entreprenant l'examen des lignes réclamées par les Hautes Parties dans la première section, nous observons d'abord que dans cette section (qui est la plus importante et la plus contestée en vue de la valeur qu'on attache à ce territoire), les deux Gouvernements n'ayant réussi à se mettre d'accord, ni pendant, ni après les travaux des Commissaires pour la délimitation, ils réclament maintenant des lignes tout à fait différentes, et très éloignées l'une de l'autre.

En effet, la Grande-Bretagne réclame une ligne qui, d'après la définition donnée par le Commissaire Britannique dans un premier Mémorandum du 29 Avril, 1893 (Mémoire Portugais, page 38) « est en quelques endroits la ligne des crêtes des montagnes, et en d'autres la ligne qui unit les sommets des pics orientaux des chaînes qui s'allongent vers l'est de la ligne principale de partage des eaux », et plus spécialement, quant au trait entre le mont Vumba et les montagnes Mabata, le Commissaire Britannique déclare que sa frontière « est une ligne courant presque directement vers le sud, et unissant les bords des contreforts montagneux qui s'avancent dans une direction orientale ». (Voir Procès-verbal, 27 Juin, 1892, reproduit dans le Mémoire Portugais, page 22).

Les montagnes principales que la ligne Britannique atteint depuis le parallèle 18° 30', sont celles de Panga, Gorongue, Shuara, Vengo, Saddle-Hill, Vumba, un pic au nord du fleuve Mazongue (2350 p.), un autre pic sur le Mussapa R. (5100 p.) et le col de Chimanimani. Tous ces points de différentes hauteurs sont réunis par des lignes droites, que le Commissaire Britannique justifie par l'observation, que les lignes droites entre des points naturels bien marqués forment, à son avis, une bonne frontière pratique.

Le Commissaire Portugais objecte à cette ligne : —

1. Qu'elle n'est pas une ligne naturelle, elle ne suit aucun bord marqué sur le sol, ni un accident quelconque du terrain, qu'elle est toute artificielle, tracée à la règle sur la carte, et non d'après là nature du plateau.

2. Qu'elle n'atteint pas le sommet des montagnes où elle passe, mais elle traverse les bords des contreforts qui s'étendent à l'est plus que la masse générale du plateau, et par une conséquence nécessaire elle passe sur le versant oriental.

3. Qu'en traçant les lignes droites qui lient des contreforts ou éperons des montagnes ou des pics, elle coupe plusieurs cours d'eau, des bouches de ravins, et des vallées larges et profondes, comme celle de l'Inhamucarara ; qu'aussi elle n'est pas continue, tandis qu'elle s'avance souvent sur le versant, et elle descend parfois aux terres basses, notamment entre Vumba et Chimanimani.

4. Qu'une telle ligne ne peut pas être conforme à l'Article II du Traité qui veut une ligne naturelle, tracée le long de la partie supérieure, ou du bord du versant du plateau.

5. Qu'une ligne droite peut bien être abstraitement et en règle générale une bonne frontière pratique, mais elle n'est pas admissible dans le cas qu'une autre direction soit déterminée par une Convention.

6. Qu'enfin le détour que la ligne fait pour comprendre Massi-Kessi dans la zone Portugaise, ne laisse pas autour de ce village, selon l'esprit de la Convention, un territoire suffisant au développement de sa vie commerciale et industrielle, anisi qu'à sa défense militaire.

Après que ces objections ont été produites, le Délégué Britannique, par une carte qu'il a présentée dans la Conférence du 14 Juillet, et contresignée sous cette date, a introduit dans sa ligne deux petites modifications, dont l'une élève sur le parallèle 18° 30' le point de son départ pour monter au sommet du contrefort septentrional du mont Panga, et l'autre supprime entre le mont Shuara et le mont Vengo le détour vers Shiromiro qui ne résultait pas justifié.

La ligne Portugaise suit une direction tout à fait différente. Elle est tracée sur la crête des hautes montagnes qui forment le partage des eaux entre le bassin du Save et les bassins du Pungwe et du Busi, et, partant du mont Samanga, elle suit le partage des eaux jusqu'à Chimanimani. Le Commissaire Portugais soutient que cette ligne coïncide avec le bord du versant oriental du plateau ; le table, ou l'esplanade, resterait ainsi à l'ouest, et le versant à l'est, de la ligne de partage des eaux.

Il observe, en outre, que la frontière réclamée par le Portugal passe par les plus hauts points du plateau sans se plonger dans des vallées, ni les couper ainsi que leurs rivières ; qu'à l'est de cette ligne le terrain s'affaisse et de nombreux cours d'eau en découlent vers la plaine avec une rapidité parfois torrentielle ; que c'est justement la déclivité du sol et la direction des rivières, qui déterminent le commencement de la pente et le bord du versant.

La Grande-Bretagne oppose à la ligne de partage des eaux les raisons suivantes : —

1. Elle a le vice de confondre la crête la plus élevée du plateau avec le bord de son versant, en supposant qu'on ne puisse trouver ce bord que lorsqu'on arrive au sommet de ses plus hautes chaînes de montagnes ; tandis que toutes les chaînes de montagnes du Manica, qu'elles soient

tournées à l'est ou à l'ouest, forment partie du plateau montagneux.

2. Le pays immédiatement à l'est de la ligne de partage des eaux étant composé de chaînes de montagnes, et sillonné par des rivières et par des vallées profondes, suivant la nature d'un plateau montagneux, ne représente pas un versant dont il n'a pas les caractères. Il est vrai qu'on y voit couler des cours d'eau plus ou moins rapides ; mais la grande irrégularité et inégalité de la table du plateau suffit à expliquer le cours plus ou moins rapide de ses rivières, et à démontrer qu'elles parcourent encore la table ou surface du plateau avant d'arriver au bord, qui nécessairement les entrecoupe. De même, comme il est question ici d'une table montagneuse, on conçoit sans peine qu'elle ait une certaine déclivité, avant d'arriver au commencement de la pente, ou au versant, que l'on ne doit reconnaître que par une déclivité bien marquée et générale.

3. Ce qui est plus essentiel, le partage des eaux comme frontière n'est nullement conforme au texte de la Convention, qui n'en fait aucune mention, pas même indirectement. Le silence de la Convention sur un point si important à la plus grande valeur ; car il faut considérer que le partage des eaux est une ligne de frontière si usuelle et préférable dans un pays montagneux, que si les Hautes Parties avaient voulu l'admettre, elles en auraient fait une mention explicite, ainsi qu'elles l'ont fait dans l'Article I de la même Convention, où le partage des eaux est mentionné comme frontière en quelques points au nord du Zambèze.

Mais il y a plus que le silence de la Convention ; il y a un refus formel de la Grande-Bretagne. Pendant le cours des négociations la ligne de partage des eaux fut proposée comme ligne de frontière par le projet que M. du Bocage, Ministre du Portugal, présenta le 19 Avril, 1891 ; et elle fut refusée par M. le Marquis de Salisbury, Ministre Britannique, qui insista sur son projet du 3 du même mois, contenant la proposition du bord du escarpement est comme ligne de frontière. Ce refus suffit à exclure la possibilité que M. le Marquis de Salisbury, au moment de la conclusion du Traité, ait considéré comme identiques la ligne de partage des eaux, et le méridien 33°. Car entre ces deux lignes (quelle que soit l'idée exprimée par méprise dans la dépêche de Lord Salisbury du 4 Février 1891) il existe une distance de plusieurs milles.

En sorte que le Portugal invoque inutilement les expressions contenues dans ce document, d'autant plus qu'il a repoussé la proposition de suivre approximativement le 33° degré de longitude est, qui était l'objet principal de la conversation rapportée dans la dite dépêche du 4 Février.

Il faut observer, en outre, que c'est précisément pour assurer à la Grande-Bretagne la bande de terrain entre la ligne de partage des eaux et la ligne du bord du versant oriental que Lord Salisbury à porté de 18,000 à 60,000 kilom. carrés, la compensation ou le dédommagement proposé au nord du Zambèze au Portugal, qui l'a accepté (Mémoire Britannique N° 17).

4. Si on admet avec le Portugal que toute la partie du plateau de Manica qui se trouve à l'est du partage des eaux soit un versant *oriental*, on doit également appeler versant *occidental* la partie située à l'ouest de cette ligne de partage, vu qu'elle coupe en deux la table montagneuse qui s'étend aussi bien à l'ouest qu'à l'est. Il en découlerait la conséquence absurde que le plateau de Manica n'aurait point de table, puisqu'elle serait absorbée par les deux versants.

Le Portugal a toujours fondé sa défense sur l'existence d'une grande étendue de terrain à l'ouest de la ligne de partage des eaux, se rapportant à ses cartes qui présentent la Rivière de l'Odzi dans le Détroit de l'Umtali (Mutari Port) à la distance de 40 kilom. de cette ville. Mais au cours des discussions M. le Major Leverson a fait constater, et M. le Capitaine Andrade n'a pu contester, que l'Odzi n'est séparé de l'Umtali que par une distance à peu près de 15 kilom. (Observations finales de M. le Major Leverson, note au N° 7.)

L'étendue du plateau à l'ouest de la ligne de partage n'est donc pas aussi considérable, et cette ligne n'est qu'une crête centrale du plateau, dont la table doit nécessairement s'étendre des deux côtés aussi bien à l'est qu'à l'ouest.

IV. — Examen du Rapport du Tiers Expert.

En présence d'un tel désaccord sur l'intelligence et sur l'exactitude des cartes présentées par les deux Parties — en vue de la gravité des arguments d'un caractère essentiellement technique, que l'un et l'autre en déduisait — tous nos efforts pour rendre possible un arrangement amiable étant restés sans effet — pour mieux assurer notre conscience, nous avons reconnu l'extrême convenance de recourir, avec le consentement des deux Parties, à l'avis d'un Expert spécialement compétent en matière de géographie et de topographie.

A cet effet nous nous sommes adressés à la Direction de l'Institut Géographique Militaire d'Italie, siégeant à Florence, et suivant la proposition qu'elle nous à faite, nous avons nommé Expert M. le Chevalier Raphaël Vinaj, Major d'Etat-Major, Chef de la Division Topographique du dit Institut. Nous lui avons communiqué toutes les pièces et les cartes présentées au nom des deux Parties, aussi bien que les procès-verbaux des Conférences, et nous lui avons soumis les questions suivantes :

Quelle est depuis l'intersection du parallèle 18° 30′ avec le 33° longitude est de Greenwich jusqu'au col de Chimanimani, la ligne de frontière qui suit la partie supérieure du versant oriental du plateau de Manica selon l'Article II du Traité de Délimitation du 11 Juin, 1891 ? Est-elle en tout, ou en partie, la ligne tracée sur la carte D du Gouvernement Britannique ? Est-elle en tout, ou en partie, la ligne tracée sur la Carte C du Gouvernement Portugais ? Est-elle en tout, ou en partie, une autre ligne ?

Dans ce dernier cas, quelle est la ligne, qui par rapport à l'une et à l'autre des dites cartes, devrait être tracée pour être conforme à l'Article II du Traité du 11 Juin, 1891 ?

En lui proposant ces questions, par notre lettre du 10 Octobre, 1896, nous l'avons invité à tenir présent ce qui suit : —

1. Que la ligne de partage des eaux, ayant été proposée par le Portugal et refusée par la Grande-Bretagne pendant les négociations, et n'ayant pas été admise dans le texte du Traité elle ne pourrait être approuvée comme ligne de frontière établie d'accord par les Hautes Parties, si ce n'est que, et pour autant qu'il résulterait qu'elle coïncide avec la partie supérieure du versant oriental et avec les autres prescriptions de l'Article II du Traité.

2. Que par les documents échangés pendant les négociations il résulte avoir été consenti par les Hautes Parties que la délimitation se fit de manière que, suivant l'expression de Lord Salisbury, le plateau restât à la Grand-Bretagne et la pente au Portugal.

L'Expert ayant soigneusement rempli son mandat, en date du 19 Décembre, 1896, il nous a remis un Rapport qui nous a prouvé combien étaient fondés les doutes que nous avions conçus sur la justesse de chacune des lignes réclamées, eu égard au texte du Traité et aux intentions déclarées des Parties.

Nous croyons devoir en rendre compte en détail pour en apprécier les conclusions.

Après avoir examiné avec la plus grande diligence les divers caractères que peuvent avoir les plateaux, les versants supérieurs et inférieurs (appelés par les géographes *couchés* ou *debout*) et leurs escarpements, et les différentes acceptions de ces mots dans la science, dans l'étude pratique des terrains et dans les actes soumis à l'arbitrage, — M. le Major Vinaj pose comme base de son vote les quatre postulats, ou principes géographiques, qui suivent : —

1. La partie supérieure, ou *table* d'un plateau, ainsi que, dans le sens le plus large du mot, l'envisagent les géographes modernes, peut réussir d'autant plus irrégulière, qu'elle est plus étendue, c'est-à-dire, qu'elle peut comprendre des pics, des montagnes, et des chaînes montagneuses, et être sillonnée par des vallées, et même par de profonds ravins.

2. La séparation entre la partie supérieure, ou *table*, d'un plateau et ses versants (pris dans le sens des surfaces qui unissent le plateau à la région basse, c'est-à-dire cette partie du versant général, qui se distingue par le nom de *versant debout*) peut en général être constituée par une ligne (bord, ou crête plus ou moins marquée) à partir de laquelle le terrain s'affaisse plus rapidement et d'une manière bien définie vers la région inférieure.

3. Cette ligne peut être discontinue à cause des vallées, ou des ravins, produisant de vraies entailles, qui seraient le prolongement de celles, ou de ceux qui sillonnent le plateau.

4. La surface qui constitue le versant n'est pas nécessairement toujours unie et régulière, mais elle peut aussi être composée de terrains divers, formés soit par des chaînes transversales au cours longitudinal du bord du plateau, soit par des vallées et chaînes parallèles, qui s'abaissent toutefois graduellement ; et cette variété de versants réguliers ou irréguliers peut se trouver dans le même plateau, notamment s'il a une étendue considérable.

Ensuite M. le Major Vinaj, passant à examiner les questions qui lui ont été adressées, adopte sur la première question les conclusions, qu'il dit concord[ant]es, des deux Commissaires, d'après lesquelles la frontière doit suivre la ligne qui constitue le bord, ou la crête, qui indique la séparation de la table du plateau de son versant oriental.

C'est dans la recherche de cette ligne de séparation que le désaccord entre les deux Commissaires se manifeste. Il faut donc examiner partie par partie les deux lignes réclamées. Les raisons qui justifient cette opinion ayant été longuement développées et discutées par les Commissaires dans leurs productions écrites et dans les Conférences orales, il se borne à résumer celles qu'il juge les plus graves.

A l'égard de la ligne Britannique modifiée, il observe que, sauf son premier trait à partir du 18° 30′ jusqu'au mont Venga, et le dernier trait tout près de Chimanimâni, elle est presque une ligne artificielle, qui n'est justifiée que par la préférence que le Commissaire Britannique accorde aux lignes droites entre des points naturels bien définis.

Mais cette préférence n'ayant pas été consacrée par un accord, qui aurait été autorisé par l'Article VII du Traité, on doit se borner à voir si elle est conforme à son Article II. Et il est d'avis qu'elle ne l'est pas, parce qu'elle ne suit aucun accident naturel topographique, tel que le bord du versant; mais joignant en ligne droite des points qui s'avancent, parfois considérablement, sur la surface qui s'abaisse et forme le versant, elle coupe souvent ce dernier et descend même quelquefois dans la région qu'on peut dire des terres basses au-dessous du plateau. Il en déduit, que la ligne Britannique entre le mont Venga et la hauteur signée par la cote de 5100 ps. sur la rive gauche du Petit Mussapa (Carte D) n'est pas conforme à l'Article II du Traité.

Quant à la ligne Portugaise, l'expert remarque qu'elle suit constamment dans son parcours, exceptée la partie au nord modifiée (voir les procès-verbaux des Conférences du 13 et 14 Juillet) la crête d'une chaîne qui forme le vrai partage des eaux dans toute la région de cette section. En général, le bord d'un plateau ne coïncide point avec la ligne de partage des eaux, ainsi qu'il résulte de la définition même du plateau qui a été donnée par M. le Capitaine d'Andrade (voir ci-dessus le § 1, questions préalables), sauf dans le cas que, depuis la ligne de partage des eaux, le terrain s'abaisse d'une manière marquée et presque uniforme, ou bien, qu'il s'abaisse graduellement, même avec de courts éperons détachés, ou avec des chaînes et des vallées parallèles, vers les terres basses.

Or ces conditions, d'après l'examen attentif des cartes et des levés topographiques expédiés Anglais et Portugais, ne se réalisent qu'en deux seuls traits, savoir, autour du bassin où se trouve Massi-Kessi, et entre Inyamatumba et un point situé précisément à l'ouest du mont Guzane (Carte Portugaise) sur la rive gauche du Petit Mussapa.

La chaîne du partage des eaux, qui est plus élevée particulièrement dans la partie méridionale, comprend dans son ensemble presque toujours les altitudes [les] plus prononcées du pays, et, à l'exception des deux traits mentionnés ci-dessus, elle est entourée, non seulement à l'ouest, mais à l'est, par un terrain d'une élévation remarquable, surtout dans sa partie septentrionale au-dessus du mont Venga, où se trouvent réellement les cimes les plus hautes.

La prétention de tracer la délimitation, pour toute l'étendue de cette section, précisément sur la crête de partage des eaux, ne semble pas con-

forme à la définition du plateau et du versant donnée par M. le Capitaine d'Andrade, car on arriverait à considérer comme versant tout le terrain qui est incliné dans le même sens; tandis que suivant cette définition, la table du plateau peut être inclinée et le bord du versant ne commencer que là où l'inclinaison du terrain devient bien marquée et générale.

Et on ne peut soutenir que cette crête coïncide, dans toute la section, avec le bord du versant oriental; parce que dans sa plus grande partie, immédiatement après la crête, il y a, aussi à l'est, une pente assez douce qui, à un certain point dans sa descente, devient beaucoup plus raide (monts Vumba-Inyamatumba), et qui constitue ainsi, ce que le Colonel de la Noë (« Les Formes du Terrain », Paris, 1888) a appelé *versant debout* ou inférieur, par opposition au *versant couché* ou supérieur, qui fait encore partie de la table du plateau.

La ligne Portugaise donc ne correspond non plus dans son ensemble au texte de l'Article II du Traité.

Ainsi, arrivé à l'examen de la dernière question, M. l'Expert, à l'aide d'une suite de profils équidistants de 2' 30" tracés, au mieux possible, sur les cartes, et tout en observant qu'il lui manquaient des éléments nécessaires pour cette espèce de travaux, il démontre que la ligne conforme au Traité est en partie différente des deux lignes réclamées par chacun des Gouvernements, il la divise en quatre parties, et il la trace ainsi qu'il suit : —

1re *Partie*. — En partant du parallèle 18° 30' sud, près du confluent du Garura avec l'Honde, qui correspond à l'étroite gorge entre le mont Mahemasemika et le contrefort septentrional du Panga dans la Carte Britannique, et précisément au-dessous de la cote de 760 m. signée un peu au-dessus du parallèle dans la Carte Portugaise, la ligne remonte au sommet du dit contrefort jusqu'au Panga. Puis, suivant la Carte Britannique, elle se dirige vers le sud-est (cote de 3890 p.) en traversant la Rivière Inhamucarara jusqu'à la hauteur de la cote 6740 p. au nord du Gorongoe, tandis que, suivant la Carte Portugaise, elle va du Panga vers sud-est (cote 1257 m.) en traversant l'Inhamucarara jusqu'à la hauteur au nord du Gorongoe (cote 1810 m.). De là elle suit la crête du Gorongoe par le mont Shuara (cote 5540 p. C. B.) jusqu'au Monga ou Vengo (C. P. et B.).

Cette partie de la section se justifie observant que le bassin de la Honde, depuis ses sources jusqu'à la gorge bien marquée par les contreforts de Mahemasemika au nord et du Panga au sud, fait partie du plateau, parce qu'il a une altitude générale remarquable, et il est environné par un terrain assez étendu et élevé qui fait évidemment partie du plateau. La gorge d'où sort la Honde doit être considérée comme une vraie entaille du bord du plateau après laquelle le versant descend par une pente presque uniforme jusqu'à la région de la Rivière Pungwe.

En descendant à l'est de la ligne Portugaise, il n'y a pas de pente générale, mais le terrain, après un certain abaissement, remonte vers la région très élevée du Punga et du Gorongoe. C'est donc seulement au delà de cette montagne que commence le vrai versant oriental du plateau avec une pente assez raide.

Les massifs du Pungwa-Panga et du Venga-Shuara-Gorongoe ne peuvent pas être regardés comme des chaînes parallèles faisant partie intégrale du versant oriental, puisque leur hauteur et leur importance, ainsi que l'élévation générale des terres et des vallées que ces montagnes renferment, indiquent évidemment qu'elles appartiennent encore à la surface du plateau.

Et en effet la haute vallée de l'Inhamucarara, renfermée entre ces deux chaînes, ne peut être considérée comme un cours d'eau du versant oriental, attendu que, indépendamment de son élévation générale, par son lit étroit et peu praticable, elle a tout l'aspect d'une vraie et profonde entaille de la table du plateau; et sa direction nord-nord-est est bien différente de celle orientale du versant.

L'objection que cette ligne part d'un point très bas sur le parallèle 18° 30′ et que ce point de prime abord ne semble pas situé sur le bord ou la crête qu'on cherche, n'a pas de valeur, parce que ici le hasard a voulu que le parallèle 18° 30′ corresponde précisément à une des plus fortes entailles qui puissent rendre le bord discontinu.

2ᵉ Partie. — En partant du mont Venga, elle se dirige par la crête qui va vers le nord-ouest-ouest et vers la cote 6200 p. du Gomoriyangani (C. B.), ou à l'est de la cote 1620 m. du Mabonde (C. P.) De là, se tenant à la Carte Britannique, elle suit la ligne colorée en bleu, qui longeant la crête du dit Gomoriyangani, atteint le mont Snuta (cote 5570), le mont Chenadombue (cote 4700) et la hauteur de la cote 4510, jusqu'aux sources du Menini où se trouve marqué le col par la cote de 3750, et où passe le chemin indiqué avec le nom « Selous Road »; tandis que, se tenant à la Carte Portugaise, elle suit la crête du Mabonde, atteint le Mugudo, le Lapulare (cote 1600), le Chitumbo (cote 1530), et passe à l'est du Bumbuli jusqu'au point où se détache vers l'ouest le contrefort de l'Thamazire. De ce point, faisant un arc de cercle avec

la concavité à peu près vers le nord-est, elle rejoint le contrefort qui va vers le mont Vumba (ou Serra-Chitumba de la C. P.) coupant la haute vallée du Munene ou Menini.

Cette partie est ainsi motivée. Elle contourne la région de Massi-Kessi depuis le mont Venga jusqu'au mont Vumba, laissant ainsi dans la zone Portugaise les hautes vallées du Révué, du Zambusi, et du Menini, qui, étant plus ouvertes et séparées par des contreforts étroits avec une pente plus raide, font partie du versant oriental.

Les contreforts entre le Révué et son affluent le Chua, celui qui se détache du Chenadombue et finit au Saddle Hill (C. B.) ou Maritza (C. P.), et celui du Clarke's Hill, peuvent être classés parmi les contreforts mentionnés dans le 4ᵉ postulat ci-dessus rapporté, et doivent faire partie du versant.

Enfin la ligne proposée, partant du col [dé]signé par la cote 3750 sur la Carte Britannique, se porte vers le Vumba, parce que à sa droite, et au sud de la vallée du Menini commence un tel rehaussement général du terrain, qu'il faut le considérer comme appartenant au plateau.

3ᵉ Partie. — En partant du Vumba la ligne fait plusieurs inflexions afin de suivre vers le sud la crête de la pente plus raide ; elle coupe les hautes vallées du Zombi ou Zombe, du Mazongwe ou Zomoe, elle atteint le mont Matura à la cote de 4495 p. (C. B.), ou le point trigonométrique qui est marqué sur la carte Portugaise à la distance de 2500 mètres à l'ouest de la cote 596 m. en continuation de la Serra Chaura, et ensuite elle va couper les hautes vallées du Mangwene et Pambe, ou Inhamatoca, du Litanti ou Bonde, et l'Inyamangwene jusqu'à l'extrémité orientale du mont Inyamatumba à la cote de 4650 p. (C. B.), c'est-à-dire, jusqu'au sud-ouest du Chabua (C. P.).

Cette partie de la section est justifiée par l'observation qu'entre elle et la ligne Portugaise est compris tout le haut terrain qui commence un peu au sud du Menini, et dans lequel se trouvent les hautes vallées et les surfaces d'écoulement des torrents déjà cités, et qui fait partie sans doute de la table du plateau, tandis que tout au long de cette ligne il y a un échelon ou changement sensible d'inclinaison, qui indique le vrai bord d'où commence le versant oriental proprement dit. En observant attentivement la carte Britannique D on aperçoit facilement la différence caractéristique du terrain situé entre les cours d'eau du Zombi, Mazongwe, Mangwene, &c., et celui compris entre les étroits contreforts du Saddle Hill et du Clarke's Hill, entre le Révué, le Zambusi, et le Menini, qui appartiennent au versant.

4ᵉ *Partie.* — Depuis le mont Inyamatumba, la ligne, en remontant le contrefort de ce massif vers l'ouest, va rejoindre de nouveau la ligne Portugaise, et la suit le long du mont Kokoboudira (C. B.) ou Choanda (C. P.) jusqu'à la cote 1500 mètres (C. P.), c'est-à-dire au nord-ouest de la cote 5100 pieds (C. B.). De ce point se dressant vers l'est, elle va couper la haute vallée du Petit Mussapa, et atteint le mont Guzane (C. P.) pour rejoindre, en écornant l'angle fait par la ligne Anglaise, le 33° longitude est de Greenwich, et le suivre jusqu'à Chimanimani, après avoir dépassé le Grand Mussapa.

Cette dernière partie de la ligne proposée est justifié ainsi que suit : —

Les mêmes raisons par lesquelles le Révué, le Zambusi, et le Menini ont été reconnus comme des cours d'eau du versant, obligent à juger que le Mangwingi (C. B.) ou Munhinga (C. P.) ne peut être un cours d'eau du plateau. On doit en dire autant des autres torrents plus au sud jusqu'au Petit Mussapa, ce dernier exclu ; parce que la vallée supérieure du Petit et du Grand Mussapa est compris dans une région qui est beaucoup surélevée, et qui appartient au plateau de l'aveu même des deux Parties.

La ligne, une fois arrivée au méridien 33°, le suit vers le sud, selon la prescription de l'Article II de la Convention, qui défend que la ligne dépasse ce méridien au profit de la Grande-Bretagne.

Le savant et diligent Rapport de l'honorable Expert a mis ainsi en relief tout ce qu'il y a d'irrégulier dans les lignes des deux Gouvernements, et, en les rectifiant, il nous a proposé une troisième ligne, qui, ayant été par nous examinée avec le plus grand soin, et comparée avec celles des deux Parties, nous paraît exempte des vices que nous avions toujours entrevus dans chacune d'elles, et qui nous ont empêché de nous prononcer pour l'une ou pour l'autre.

Nous avons en effet dans la proposition de l'Expert une ligne naturelle, qui dans son cours tortueux se conforme, autant qu'il est possible, à la configuration montagneuse du plateau, et suivant les hauteurs qui le dessinent, et qui en forment le versant oriental, elle longe la partie supérieure ou le bord de ce versant. Elle ne coupe ainsi que les cours d'eau et les vallées qui par l'élévation du terrain doivent faire partie de la table du plateau ; et elle laisse dans la pente les autres d'un niveau inférieur et d'une inclinaison plus raide.

Ajoutons que cette ligne fait une juste application du Traité, puisqu'elle n'adopte comme frontière le partage des eaux, si ce n'est dans les endroits où il est constaté, qu'il coïncide avec le bord du versant, ce qui est conforme à la lettre et à l'esprit de l'Article II.

Ainsi nous voyons que dans son ensemble cette ligne n'empiète ni sur la surface du plateau, ni sur celle de la pente ; mais elle remplit, autant que l'irrégularité du Manica le consent, et pour autant que les cartes produites le permettent, le but final de la délimitation, résumé dans les mots, « le plateau à la Grande-Bretagne et la pente au Portugal ».

En outre cette ligne laisse dans la zone Portugaise toute la région de Massi-Kessi, suivant les sommets de cette espèce de cirque montagneux, que la nature semble avoir établi comme une limite territoriale, et comme un rempart vers l'ouest.

Les aspirations du Portugal à cet égard n'avaient [pas] dans le texte du Traité une garantie suffisante, et les intentions des négociateurs n'avaient pas été manifestées assez nettement pour servir de base à une définition judiciaire. Mais nous avons néanmoins reconnu que ces aspirations trouvent leur fondement dans une correspondance heureuse entre une ligne tracée par la nature et les inspirations de l'équité.

Pour toutes ces considérations la ligne proposée par l'Expert nous semble présenter tous les caractères que l'Article II exige dans la frontière entre les zones d'influence des deux pays, et nous apparaît la seule conforme à la lettre et à l'esprit du Traité. Par conséquent nous serions disposé à l'adopter dans son ensemble avec une pleine conviction.

Seulement nous avons réfléchi que le tracé de la ligne proposée par l'Expert, depuis le mont Vumba jusqu'à l'Inyamatumba, bien qu'il soit techniquement exact, toutefois — par ses nombreuses inflexions et par la difficulté d'en préciser le cours sur des cartes si peu détaillées, soit par leur échelle trop petite, soit pour le genre de la levée tout à fait expédiée — il pourrait facilement donner occasion sur un terrain aussi irrégulier, à des doutes et à des divergences qu'il faut soigneusement prévenir.

En conséquence nous avons jugé convenable d'inviter le même Expert à nous indiquer dans cet endroit une ligne mieux marquée et plus pratique.

Secondant notre invitation, dont il a reconnu l'opportunité, l'Expert nous a signalé de légères modifications à introduire dans son tracé en substituant quelques lignes presque droites et mieux définies aux inflexions naturelles du bord du versant, de manière que la quantité du terrain qui revient à chacune des Parties, par la substitution des lignes droites à la rigoureuse démarcation du bord, demeure presque équivalente.

Il propose en conséquence, que du mont Vumba la frontière suive en ligne droite jusqu'à un point trigonométrique qui se trouve entre 4 ou 5 kilom. à l'est du partage des eaux (Serra Chaura), et de ce point, elle continue en ligne droite, jusqu'à la hauteur [dé]signée par la cote 4650 à l'extrémité orientale de l'Inyamatumba. De là elle remonterait cette montagne et se rattacherait ainsi à la ligne déjà proposée.

Ces modifications nous ayant paru correspondre au but de rendre plus facile, plus pratique et mieux déterminée la délimitation, nous y avons conformé notre décision.

Suivant la division tracée dans le Compromis, nous ajoutons, pour compléter la première section de la frontière, qu'après Chimanimani la frontière continue à suivre, sans contestation, le méridien 33° jusqu'au point [dé]signé A sur la Carte Britannique, à quelques milles au sud du défilé de Chimanimani.

V. — Deuxième Section de la Frontière.

L'Acte de Compromis nous apprend, que sur la seconde section de la frontière il est intervenu un accord entre le Major Leverson, Commissaire Britannique, et le Capitaine d'Andrade, Délégué du Commissaire Portugais, sur les lieux mêmes qu'ils devaient délimiter.

Cet accord est constaté dans les Mémoires que les deux Parties nous ont présentés; mais avec cette différence, que le Gouvernement Britannique le maintient et il en réclame intégralement l'adoption; tandis que le Gouvernement Portugais, s'appuyant sur l'Article 15 du Règlement pour les travaux de délimitation, signé à Mozambique le 24 Octobre, 1891, par les Commissaires des deux pays, soutient que l'acceptation de l'accord signé par M. le Capitaine d'Andrade, Délégué Technique, ne pouvait être définitive et obligatoire pour lui, que moyennant son approbation, qu'il n'a pas donnée avant l'arbitrage.

En effet, ce n'est que dans le Mémoire présenté à l'Arbitre, que le Commissaire Portugais a déclaré que le Portugal approuve l'accord Leverson-d'Andrade *seulement en partie*, savoir, depuis Chimanimani jusqu'à Mapunguana (Mémoire Portugais, page 98).

A l'appui de cette approbation partielle le Commissaire Portugais observe que dans la partie qu'il a acceptée la délimitation concordée est rigoureusement conforme à l'Article II du Traité jusqu'au parallèle 20° à peu près; qu'au sud de ce parallèle, et jusqu'au 20° 30′ de latitude environ, le relief du sol devient tellement irrégulier qu'il est très difficile d'y appliquer les règles de l'Article II; que *la table et le versant* du plateau y sont si mal caractérisés, à cause de l'irrégu-

larité du régime des eaux et de l'absence de lignes générales bien nettes dans la configuration du sol, qu'il est presque impossible de determiner avec précision quelle est la ligne qui les sépare, c'est-à-dire le bord du versant oriental. Seulement par esprit de conciliation, d'après lui, on a éliminé les questions bien graves qui se présentent dans la délimitation, parce que « le terrain se prête à être *compris* de différentes manières » (Mémoire Portugais, page 93). Enfin, dans cette partie, la ligne concordée, de l'avis même de ceux qui l'ont tracée, ne suit point la crête du versant (voir Observations sur le Contre-Mémoire Britannique, N° 32 *et seq.*); en sorte qu'on n'a appliqué ici les règles de l'Article II qu'autant qu'il était possible.

En d'autres termes, bien que cette démarcation ne soit peut-être pas rigoureuse, le Gouvernement Portugais reconnaît que le pays, dans ce trait, n'en admet pas une autre dont l'exactitude soit moins contestable.

Mais il pense qu'on ne puisse en dire autant du prolongement de la ligne depuis Mapunguana jusqu'au parallèle 20° 42′ 17″, et c'est pourquoi il refuse cette dernière partie de l'accord et il propose d'y substituer une ligne nouvelle qui suivrait les montagnes Xerinda jusqu'au mont Zuzunye, et qui, touchant les hauteurs de 990, 1150, et 960 mètres qui séparent le bassin du Zona et du Chinica, serait naturellement déterminée par le relief orographique. Cette ligne, ajoute le Portugal (Observations sur le Mémoire Britannique. N° 68), évite le détour inutile de la ligne concordée, qui de Mapunguana court vers le sud-est, à travers l'Inhamazi, pour se rendre à une hauteur de 1100 mètres, et descendre ensuite à des cotes de 670 et 760 mètres. Et tandis qu'elle est presque rectiligne, elle conserve une altitude moyenne de 1110 mètres, et une régularité plus grande que la ligne concordée.

Le Gouvernement Britannique, ainsi que nous l'avons dit, maintient en tout l'accord d'après lequel la ligne, arrivée à Mapunguana (point [dé] signé H sur la C. B.), fait un angle aigu se dirigeant vers le sud-est, et va droit à une colline bien marquée à l'est du fleuve Zoma ou Zona, et puis se prolonge jusqu'à un point situé sur la chaîne qui sépare la vallée du Zoma de celle du Sheneyka ou Chinici, et enfin se dirigeant presque directement vers l'ouest, arrive en ligne droite au sommet du mont Zuzunye.

Contre l'adoption de la rectification réclamée par le Portugal, la Grande-Bretagne oppose deux objections, l'une juridique et l'autre technique.

L'exception juridique consiste dans le caractère spécial de l'accord Leverson-d'Andrade. Il est admis d'un côté et de l'autre, que cet accord représente dans son ensemble une transaction discutée et acceptée sur le terrain même, et moyennant des concessions mutuelles, par des techniciens qui avaient acquis la connaissance des lieux et qui étaient bien compétents pour juger de leurs caractères topographiques.

La description ci-dessus rapportée, que le Portugal a fait du terrain très irrégulier et accidenté que parcourt la ligne concordée jusqu'à Mapunguana, nous fait assez clairement comprendre à combien d'arrangements a dû donner lieu le tracement de cette ligne. Le Commissaire Britannique déclare que par le désir d'arriver à une solution immédiate, il s'est décidé à accepter les modifications apportées à ses premières propositions par le Capitaine d'Andrade, bien qu'il fût convaincu que la première ligne correspondait plus exactement aux termes de l'Article II du Traité.

L'étendue des concessions faites par le Commissaire Britannique résulte de la dite Carte Britannique D sur laquelle la ligne rouge ponctuée représente la frontière qu'il avait d'abord proposée dans les endroits où elle ne coïncide pas avec la ligne concordée, savoir depuis la lettre *C* jusqu'à la lettre *K*. On voit par cette carte, que la partie *acceptée* par le Délégué Portugais est bien importante; il déclare lui-même dans son Mémoire (page 93) que c'est *la plus grande partie de la demarcation* arrêtée. C'est là précisément que lui ont été faites les plus larges concessions dont il entend de profiter.

Au reste, la manière dont ce compromis a été formé, nous est expliquée même par le Capitaine d'Andrade en des termes qu'il est utile de rapporter: « La ligne Leverson-d'Andrade (dit-il au No. 109 des Observations sur le Mémoire Britannique) a été tracée en se faisant des concessions réciproques; il y avait la ligne Leverson et la ligne d'Andrade, et après des discussions prolongées sur le terrain, pour faire preuve d'un esprit de conciliation d'un côté et de l'autre, on est arrivé à la ligne ci-dessus indiquée, quoique d'un côté et de l'autre on était persuadé que chacune des deux lignes était plus conforme au texte de la Convention. »

Le langage des Délégués des deux Gouvernements met ainsi en évidence, que toute la ligne concordée a été l'effet d'un compromis ou d'une transaction, qu'on ne pourrait scinder sans aller contre les intentions de ses auteurs et sans blesser la justice aux dépens de l'une ou de l'autre Partie. C'est le cas de dire de cet accord, qu'il est à tout prendre ou à tout laisser. Le Portugal qui accepte la partie plus grande qui lui est avantageuse, ne peut rejeter l'autre au désavantage de la Grande-Bretagne, sans que la balance de la justice soit évidemment troublée et l'équilibre dérangé entre les Parties.

Le défaut de pleins pouvoirs du Délégué d'Andrade, sur lequel le Portugal appelle notre attention dans plusieurs Mémorandums rapportés dans son Mémoire, quand même il était démontré d'une manière irréfutable, ne pourrait être admis comme un argument en faveur du Portugal, que dans le cas que ce dernier refusât l'accord tout entier pour refaire toute la ligne concordée.

Mais le Portugal prétend qu'il ne fait dans ce trait que conformer sa ligne à la Convention.

La Grande-Bretagne conteste cette affirmation par la seconde exception, que nous avons qualifiée technique. Son Délégué au No. 15 de ses *Observations finales* observe que la ligne Portugaise depuis Mapunguana jusqu'au mont Zuzunye *est bien une ligne de crête naturelle, mais c'est une crête qui se trouve sur le plateau et non pas le bord du plateau.* En examinant, en effet, la carte anglaise D on voit que la pente depuis cette crête au nord-ouest vers l'Unswilizi est beaucoup plus rapide, que la pente générale de l'autre côté vers le sud-est, et le district de l'Unswilizi (ou Moussurize), même d'après le Capitaine d'Andrade, est une vraie rivière du plateau à ne pas en douter. (Observations sur le Contre-Mémoire Britannique, No. 68).

Le Gouvernement Portugais cherche ici, à ce qu'il paraît, comme dans la première section, le bord du versant sur les altitudes les plus saillantes et il confond encore une crête du plateau avec la crête ou le bord de son versant. Si la ligne du bord oriental descend davantage dans cet endroit, c'est l'effet naturel de l'abaissement graduel de tout le plateau de Manica qu'on remarque à l'ouest de la ligne en allant du Lusitu vers le sud. Cette pente générale du pays, et de la table du plateau lui-même, ne doit pas être confondue avec la pente ou le versant qui s'abaisse naturellement avec l'abaissement du plateau.

Il faut, au surplus, avoir présent cet aveu des Parties (que nous avons déjà mis en relief), que cette section de la ligne est le résultat de concessions mutuelles. En sorte que, si dans son parcours il y a quelque trait moins régulier et moins conforme à l'exacte application de l'Article II du Traité, ces irrégularités se compensent mutuellement; et si après Mapunguana il y a quelque avantage pour la Grande-Bretagne, le Portugal trouve une large compensation dans les concessions qui lui ont été faites dans la partie bien plus grande qui précède Mapunguana et dans celle qui suit.

Nous estimons donc fondées les deux exceptions de la Grande-Bretagne. Quoiqu'elles soient essentiellement distinctes, elle s'entr'aident, et les deux réunies nous portent à conclure que l'acceptation partielle de l'accord, et la conséquente modification proposée par le Portugal entre le point *H* et le point *M* est aussi contraire aux principes de justice, qu'aux règles de l'Article II du Traité. C'est pourquoi l'accord doit, à notre avis, être maintenu jusqu'au mont Zuzunye.

Quand à la dernière partie de cette section jusqu'au point *O*, nous en parlerons en examinant la troisième section, à laquelle cette partie a été réunie par la discussion des Délégués.

VI. — *Troisième Section de la Frontière.*

La ligne, une fois portée par les Délégués des deux Gouvernements au sommet du mont Zuzunye, donne lieu à une grave divergence sur la manière d'interpréter et d'appliquer la Convention au terrain qui reste à délimiter pour atteindre le fleuve Save.

Pour le Gouvernement de la Grande-Bretagne, en partant du sommet du mont Zuzunye (point marqué *M* sur la carte D), la ligne traverse la vallée de l'Umswilizi jusqu'à un point élevé de la ligne de partage des eaux qui sépare la vallée de Nyamgamba de celle d'autres affluents de l'Umswilizi (qui sont tous des fleuves du plateau), et elle suit la ligne de l'accord jusqu'au point *O*, où elle rencontre le méridien 32° 30′.

Cette petite partie de la frontière est le complément de la ligne concordée entre le Major Leverson et le Capitaine d'Andrade, et on doit conséquemment y appliquer toutes les observations que nous avons faites ci-dessus, sur l'indivisibilité de l'accord proposé comme une transaction bilatérale qui ne supporte la moindre altération. L'abaissement sensible de tout le plateau dans cette partie, et son détour vers le sud-ouest, oblige naturellement la ligne, qui suit son bord oriental, à fléchir vers l'ouest jusqu'au méridien 32° 30′; ensuite s'arrêtant à ce méridien, fixé comme limite extrême par l'Article II du côté de l'ouest, elle le suit jusqu'au Save, laissant dans la zone Portugaise tout le territoire qui se trouve à l'est du même méridien.

Nous jugeons à propos de remarquer ici que l'accord ayant fait reculer la ligne à l'ouest, a pour résultat, dans son parcours du point *M* au point *N*, de faire entrer dans la zone Portugaise le triangle *LMN*, dont l'importance est visible sur la carte D., et qui est compris entièrement dans le district de l'Umswilizi placé sur le plateau. C'est donc une autre concession considérable au profit du Portugal.

Enfin, la ligne Anglaise, dans l'ensemble de cette dernière section, serait conforme aux deux conditions exigées par le Traité, savoir, la direction vers le sud, suivant les déviations du bord du plateau, et la limitation du parallèle 32° 30′ du côté de l'ouest.

Le Gouvernement Portugais, au contraire, se croit autorisé, par la configuration du terrain dans cet endroit, à suivre une toute autre direction, et à s'écarter des règles fixées par le Traité.

En se fondant sur la supposition que l'abaissement des terres après le parallèle du mont Zuzunye jusqu'au chenal du Save est tellement marqué, que le plateau de Manica et son versant au sud viennent à cesser complètement, il en tire la conséquence que la frontière ne peut plus longer son bord oriental vers le sud. Il se produit, dit-il, un cas non prévu ou omis dans le Traité, car celui-ci suppose que le plateau se prolonge au sud jusqu'au Save. Dès lors, les règles établies par l'Article II cessant d'être applicables, il faut y suppléer en faisant recours aux principes généraux d'herméneutique diplomatique, d'après lesquels, lorsque dans une Convention de délimitation il est dit qu'une ligne doit se rendre d'un point à un autre, sans en déterminer le parcours, elle doit s'y rendre directement, soit par la voie la plus courte.

En appliquant cette règle au cas supposé, le Commissaire Portugais soutient que la frontière ne pouvant se diriger au Save *vers le Sud*, ainsi qu'exige le Traité, elle doit y aller du côté de l'ouest par la voie la plus courte, afin de suivre son cours en aval jusqu'à son confluent avec le Lunde. Il ajoute que cela serait conforme, soit à l'intention des négociateurs, qui n'ont eu en vue que de laisser tout le plateau à la Grande-Bretagne, soit aux principes de justice et d'équité qui militent en faveur du Portugal, soit enfin aux expressions du Traité « suit ce chenal jusqu'à son confluent avec le Lunde », puisque *suivre un cours d'eau*, d'après lui, signifie plus proprement le *suivre en aval* et non pas *en amont*, ainsi que le ferait la ligne Anglaise.

Par ces arguments en rejetant la ligne proposée par la Grande-Bretagne le Portugal croit *juste et rationnel*, que la frontière depuis le 20° 30′ environ, se rende au Save par les monts Nero et Zuzunye et par la Rivière Lacati, suivant ensuite le cours du Save jusqu'à son confluent avec le Lunde.

Et comme cette ligne dépasserait le méridien 32° 30′, il cherche d'écarter cette difficulté en observant « que les méridiens du 33° à l'est et du 32° 30′ à l'ouest ne figurent dans le Traité qu'avec le rôle de limites que la frontière dans son cours ne doit jamais dépasser, lorsqu'il s'agit de la tracer au long du bord du versant oriental du plateau ; donc » (il conclut) « ces limites n'ont rien à voir dans la délimitation d'une contrée, où précisément le plateau et le versant font défaut ». (Mémoire Portugais, page 97.)

Les raisonnements que nous venons de résumer nous paraissent plus spécieux que solides, n'étant essentiellement fondés ni en fait, ni en droit. Deux sont les questions qu'ils soulèvent dans leur ensemble, savoir : (1) si le plateau de Manica cesse réellement au sud avant d'arriver au Save ; (2) si dans le cas affirmatif, il soit permis d'en tirer les conséquences qu'on en déduit.

1. Nous remarquerons avant tout que les officiers topographes qui ont arrêté d'accord la frontière depuis le point *M*, sommet sur le mont Zuzunye, jusqu'au point *O* où le bord coupe le 32° 30', ont dû reconnaître dans ce parcours l'existence du plateau et du versant, condition nécessaire de ce tracé.

Le Major Leverson observe (No. 30 de ses Notes), que la supposition du Traité, que le versant du plateau, sans cesser d'être versant oriental, s'étende jusqu'au Save, était parfaitement justifiée par la Carte de M. Maund, dans laquelle on voit que le bord de ce plateau, après avoir coupé le méridien de 32° 30', suit une direction à peu près sud-ouest jusqu'au Save ; qu'en effet l'examen du terrain a démontré que la déflexion générale donnée au bord à l'ouest de ce méridien par cette carte n'est pas très inexacte. Il ajoute, qu'il n'admet aucunement que le plateau n'existe plus au sud du mont Zuzunye, puisque cette montagne se trouve, dit-il, même à l'est de la grande ligne de partage des eaux et précède le triangle *LMN* entièrement compris dans le district de l'Umswilizi (ou Moussurise) qui, de l'aveu même du Capitaine d'Andrade, ainsi que nous l'avons déjà remarqué, est une vraie rivière du plateau.

L'abaissement considérable des hautes terres de Manica avant d'arriver au Save serait, d'après le Portugal, la preuve que le plateau existe plus et qu'on y trouve la plaine.

Mais tout en reconnaissant qu'il y a un abaissement, nous estimons qu'il n'arrive pas à effacer les caractères du plateau.

Il ne faut pas oublier en premier lieu, que le plateau de Manica (ainsi que les autres plateaux d'Afrique en général) est, d'après l'aveu des Parties et les observations des géographes et des voyageurs, plus élevé à l'est et s'affaisse graduellement vers le sud et l'ouest. Mais cet abaissement naturel n'ôte point aux plateaux leur caractère. En effet, le Délégué Britannique en reconnaissant que la partie du plateau de Manica au sud du parallèle de l'intersection de son bord par le 32° 30' est moins élevée que le pays au nord, il soutient que cela n'empêche pas qu'on doive le considérer encore comme partie de la table du plateau ; il explique et appuie bien cette proposition en remarquant, que la diminution dans l'altitude générale du pays à l'ouest,

en allant du Lusitu vers le sud, est causée par l'abaissement graduel de tout le plateau depuis Mapunguana et par la façon dont, en approchant du Limpopo, il recule vers le sud-ouest ; mais cette inclinaison générale du terrain n'autorise pas à y voir la partie d'une pente extérieure, c'est-à-dire, le versant qui rattache le plateau à la plaine, et encore moins le commencement de la plaine.

Il est admis par les géographes, que la surface d'un district élevé peut avoir une pente générale de cette espèce sans cesser nécessairement, et à cause de cela, d'être un plateau. L'autorité de M. Élysée Reclus en fournit un exemple dans son œuvre déjà cité («La Terre», tome 1, 2ᵉ éd., p. 137), où il nous apprend que « la plupart des hautes terres de l'Afrique sont peu élevées et leurs pentes offrent un accès facile ; ainsi les plateaux de la Colonie du Cap, dont la hauteur moyenne est au sud de 200 mètres à peine, s'élèvent par degrés vers le nord jusqu'à une altitude qui va de 600 à 1,000 mètres au-dessus du niveau de la mer».

Cette observation s'applique parfaitement aux hautes terres de Manica, qui, sans contredit, s'élèvent vers le nord à plus de 1,000 mètres, tandis que vers le sud, un peu avant d'arriver au Save, leur altitude n'est pas de beaucoup supérieure à 300 mètres. (Observations sur le Contre-Mémoire Britannique, No. 12, et Conclusions du Délégué Portugais, No. 4.)

Une autre observation complète cette démonstration. Il est généralement reconnu, même par M. le Capitaine d'Andrade (Observations sur le Mémoire Britannique, No. 71) que «la définition du plateau est susceptible d'une certaine élasticité à cause de l'application peu restreinte qu'on fait de ce mot». La géographie ne fixe donc point le *minimum* de son altitude ; ce *minimum* dépend des terres qui l'environnent et des conditions particulières de chaque région. Nous venons de rappeler que, suivant le témoignage de M. Réclus, la hauteur de 200 mètres en Afrique suffit à constituer un plateau. Cette opinion nous la trouvons partagée par M. Ritter (cité avec nombre d'autres auteurs dans le Mémoire Portugais, page 48) qui considère l'élévation de 500 pieds (160 mètres environ) comme étant la limite la plus basse du niveau d'un plateau. De même le Capitaine d'Andrade dans ses Conclusions (No. 4) reconnaît que, d'après le même Réclus, il peut y avoir des plateaux à l'altitude de 50 mètres, et que d'après l'illustre géographe Italien Marinelli, l'altitude minime d'un plateau est de 200 mètres. (Marinelli, «La Terra», vol. 1, page 302.)

Dans notre cas, la règle d'herméneutique légale — suivant laquelle les expressions employées dans un contrat doivent être prises dans le sens le plus conforme à l'intention des parties qui l'ont stipulé et le plus favorable au but du contrat — nous oblige à donner au mot de plateau la signification la plus large possible, c'est-à-dire à exiger seulement le minimum de son altitude normale, afin de pouvoir constater son existence jusqu'au Save, telle que l'avaient supposée les Hautes Parties, et afin de rendre possible ainsi l'application du texte de l'Article II du Traité. Suivant ainsi, au point de vue du droit, une règle d'interprétation universelle, et, au point de vue technique, l'opinion des plus illustres géographes auxquels se rapportent aussi les deux Parties, nous concluons, que le plateau de Manica, bien qu'il s'abaisse graduellement vers le sud et se réduise à des proportions minimes, conserve toutefois une hauteur suffisante pour admettre (ainsi que l'ont supposé les rédacteurs du Traité) qu'il existe encore jusqu'au Save.

2. Enfin, pour examiner la question sous toutes ses faces, nous supposerons avec le Portugal, que le plateau, contre la prévision des auteurs du Traité, vienne à cesser à une distance plus ou moins grande avant d'arriver au Save. Les conséquences qui s'ensuivraient ne seraient certainement pas celles que le Portugal croit d'en tirer.

La direction que la ligne doit avoir vers le sud ne cesserait pas, et les limites des méridiens qu'elle doit garder dans sa marche, resteraient invariables ; aussi on ne pourrait pas même dire qu'il se vérifie un cas omis, ou une lacune dans la Convention.

En effet, quant à la direction de la ligne vers le sud, il suffit de réfléchir, qu'elle est la seule qui se trouve établie dans l'Article II du Traité comme règle générale pour le tracé de toute la frontière entre le 18° 30′ et le Save. Les mots « southwards to the centre » du texte Anglais, ainsi que les mots « na sua direcção sul até á linha media » du texte Portugais, signifient « vers le sud jusqu'au centre » et non seulement « vers le Sabi ». (Voir Observations du Major Leverson, No. 18.) Il est vrai que l'Article dit en même temps que la ligne « suit la partie supérieure de la pente orientale du plateau ». Mais par ces mots on n'a pas voulu dire que la ligne n'ira vers le sud que si, et *pour autant que*, elle pourra suivre le bord de ce versant, ainsi que le Délégué Portugais estime ; mais tout simplement que la frontière en allant vers le sud au Save, doit suivre le cours naturellement tortueux du bord et non pas y aller en ligne droite.

Ce n'est là évidemment qu'une condition imposée au tracé et non à la direction de la ligne qui doit surtout aller vers le sud : seulement en allant vers le sud au Save, elle doit suivre le bord du versant oriental. Il est donc bien entendu qu'elle suit ce bord tant qu'il existe dans son parcours. Or si le bord, que le Traité suppose se prolonger jusqu'au chenal du Save, cesse avant d'y arriver, cette modalité du tracé cesse nécessairement avec le bord même, comme une condition remplie ; et depuis le point où le bord finit, la ligne, restant dégagée de tout lien, doit aller directement au Save suivant la règle générale de sa direction vers le sud, dont l'application, en fait, ne trouve aucun empêchement. Seulement elle ne pourra dépasser à l'est le 33°, ni à l'ouest le 32° 30′ de longitude, ainsi que nous allons bientôt expliquer.

Cette interprétation est la seule raisonnable, la seule conforme au texte de l'Article II et à l'intention de ses auteurs.

L'objection que ce texte suppose que le plateau arrive jusqu'au Save ne pourrait aucunement secouer cette conviction.

Les rédacteurs du Traité, de l'aveu des Parties, n'avaient qu'une connaissance imparfaite du plateau qu'ils délimitaient. Or s'ils se sont trompés, cette erreur qui ne tombe sur une condition substantielle, mais sur une modalité dans le tracé de la ligne, ne pourrait changer en rien sa direction finale vers le sud qui peut et qui doit être suivie tout de même.

D'ailleurs, cette persuasion des négociateurs que le plateau arrivait jusqu'au Save, quoique erronée, fournirait la preuve évidente, que par les mots « la *frontière suit vers le sud* » la partie supérieure du versant oriental jusqu'au Save », ils n'ont voulu dire autre chose que la frontière va vers le sud jusqu'au Save *en toute son étendue* qui, pour eux, s'identifiait avec l'étendue du bord.

Quant à la limitation du 32° 30′ de longitude, nous estimons que le Portugal n'aurait non plus le droit de s'en émanciper en supposant que le plateau cesse avant le Save.

Si on recherche la cause et les raisons de cette limitation, on comprend aisément qu'elle est en tout cas indépendante de la continuité du bord jusqu'au Save.

Il résulte de l'histoire des négociations qui ont précédé la rédaction du Traité, que M. le Marquis de Salisbury avait d'abord proposé de fixer la frontière au 33° de longitude depuis le 18° 30′ jusqu'au Save ; que le Portugal, n'ayant pas accepté cette proposition, a pourtant déclaré par M. le Ministre du Bocage, qu'il pourrait agréer comme ligne divisoire le 32° 30′, pourvu qu'on eût égard aux modifications exigées par les conditions géographiques. (Mémoire Britannique, No. 13.) Les deux propositions réduisaient la différence entre les deux lignes à la bande de terrain existante entre le 32° 30′ et le 33° de longitude. Ce fut alors que, pour concilier la différence, Lord Salisbury présenta une espèce de transaction, qui établissait comme ligne frontière la partie supérieure, ou le bord du versant oriental, depuis le 18° 30′ jusqu'au confluent du Save avec le Lunde.

Ce moyen de conciliation a été accueilli par le Portugal et adopté par l'Article II du Traité.

Mais prévoyant naturellement que le bord du versant d'un plateau montagneux irrégulier, tel que celui de Manica, serait tortueux dans son développement, les négociateurs ont jugé nécessaire d'établir que la frontière, suivant le bord dans son cours sinueux, n'aurait jamais dû dépasser les limites proposées par chacune des Parties, savoir le méridien 33° à l'est, proposé par l'Angleterre, et le méridien 32° 30′ à l'ouest, proposé par le Portugal.

Ainsi la ligne venait à être, pour ainsi dire, renserrée dans l'ornière des deux méridiens, dans le double but de ne pas sortir de la bande du terrain disputé, et de ne pas assigner aux Parties plus qu'elles n'avaient demandé.

C'est ce qui a été précisément convenu par le paragraphe de l'Article II : « *Il est entendu qu'en traçant la frontière* le long de la pente du plateau, aucune partie de territoire à l'ouest du 32° 30′ de longitude ne sera comprise », &c. La ligne donc *dans tout son tracé* ne pourra dépasser les limites sus-indiquées ; si on y fait mention du tracement le long du versant, ce n'est que pour la simple raison ci-dessus mentionnée, que les négociateurs du Traité étaient pleinement persuadés que le bord du versant se prolongeait, autant que la ligne, vers le Save. Si, par hasard, on a trouvé qu'il s'arrête avant de l'atteindre, cette circonstance n'empêche pas que la limite des deux méridiens ait toute sa raison d'être, et que la ligne, en allant directement au Save, après la cessation supposée du bord, reste dans l'ornière que les Parties lui ont fixée par ces expressions qui contiennent une prohibition claire et absolue.

L'impossibilité de tracer la ligne entre ces bornes (ainsi qu'il a été observé par le Délégué Britannique) serait la seule raison qui pourrait être invoquée pour les franchir ; mais une telle impossibilité est si loin d'avoir été prouvée, qu'elle n'a pas même été alléguée par le Portugal.

Le seul effet que la cessation du plateau avant le Save peut produire à l'avantage du Portugal, est celui de donner à la zone Portugaise vers l'ouest la plus grande étendue, en la poussant jusqu'à toucher la limite extrême du 32° 30′. Mais, comme la Grande-Bretagne immédiatement au sud de Chimanimani a reconnu qu'elle ne peut suivre le plateau dans son détour au delà du 33°, de même le Portugal ne peut prétendre de suivre le versant, ou la pente, ou

la plaine, au delà du 32° 30′, contre la défense explicite du Traité.

Enfin, il ne faut pas oublier que la Grande-Bretagne pour s'assurer que la frontière ne dépasserait [pas] le 32° 30′ vers l'ouest et n'irait jamais empiéter sa zone au delà de cette limite, a fait, comme nous avons plus d'une fois remarqué, la concession d'une large étendue de territoire au nord du Zambèse au Portugal pour le dédommager de la perte qu'il aurait subie sur le plateau de Manica. Or, il serait contraire aux principes de justice, que, sous un prétexte quelconque, le Portugal, en dépassant cette même limite, reprît une partie du territoire en échange duquel il a accepté la dite compensation. Il est vrai, qu'à l'égard de cette concession, ou, pour mieux dire, de cet arrangement, le Portugal devant l'Arbitre n'a manqué de soulever des exceptions, soit sur sa valeur, soit sur les droits de la Grande-Bretagne à l'égard du territoire cédé. Mais nous devons répéter, ce que nous avons déjà eu l'occasion d'observer, que le Portugal, après avoir accepté par le Traité ce territoire comme une compensation équitable, il n'est plus recevable à opposer des exceptions, dont, au surplus, il n'a fourni aucune justification, s'étant borné à de simples allégations.

Il ne reste que le dernier argument du Portugal, tiré de la phrase « la frontière suit le chenal du Save jusqu'au point où il rencontre le Lunde » qu'il croit devoir signifier, que la frontière va au Save *en aval* du confluent avec le Lunde et que par conséquent elle doit l'atteindre avant son arrivée au Lunde. Cet argument est détruit par le fait, que selon la Convention la ligne devant entrer dans le Save avant le méridien 32° 30′ et ce méridien coupant le Save après son confluent avec le Lunde, il s'ensuit qu'on a entendu nécessairement qu'on doit remonter le Save pour aller au confluent du Lunde.

Mais, à part la question si la phrase « suivre une rivière en amont » soit rigoureusement exacte au point de vue philologique, il est certain que dans le langage diplomatique et technique des Conventions de délimitation, suivre un fleuve, une rivière, se dit aussi bien dans le sens de suivre *en amont*, que de suivre *en aval*.

M. le Délégué Britannique, dans ses Notes (No. 39) en a fourni une preuve par la citation de l'Acte de Délimitation de la Frontière Turco-Grecque signé à Constantinople par la Commission Mixte Européenne le 15 (27) Novembre, 1891. (Voir dans le vol. iii de la *N. Raccolta dei Trattati e delle Convenzioni fra il Regno d'Italia e i Governi Esteri*, Turin, 1890, pages 99 et seq. les Articles I et II de la dite Convention), où évidemment les mots « suit » et « suivre » le *thalweg* d'une rivière sont employés pour signifier suivre *en amont*.

Bien d'autres exemples pourraient être rapportés ; mais il est superflu, une fois que le Délégué Portugais lui-même dans ses Observations sur le Contre-Mémoire Britannique (No. 32 *h*) déclare, que si l'interprétation naturelle des mots « suivre une rivière » est celle de la suivre *en aval*, « cela n'est pas absolument nécessaire ».

En résumé, nous croyons que la prétention du Portugal de pouvoir mettre de côté l'Article II de la Convention depuis le mont Zuzunye, et d'y substituer des principes généraux en fait de délimitation, n'est justifiée ni en fait, ni en droit ; et que la ligne qui doit être adoptée dans cette section est celle tracée sur la Carte D de la Grande-Bretagne, telle qu'elle avait été concordée par les Délégués des deux Gouvernements jusqu'à la rencontre du 32° 30′. La continuation de la ligne jusqu'au Save suivant ce méridien, n'en est qu'une conséquence nécessaire.

Par ces motifs :

Nous déclarons que, d'après l'Article II du Traité signé à Lisbonne le 11 Juin, 1891, la ligne qui doit séparer les zones d'influence de la Grande-Bretagne et du Portugal dans l'Afrique Orientale au sud du Zambèze, depuis le parallèle 18° 30′ jusqu'au confluent du Save (ou Sabi) avec le Lunde (ou Lunte), doit être tracée ainsi qu'il suit :

1. Quant à la première section de la frontière contestée telle qu'elle est désignée par le Compromis, la ligne en partant du point où le parallèle 18° 30′ coupe le 33 degré longitude est de Greenwich, va vers l'ouest jusqu'à un point qui se trouve à l'intersection du 18° 30′ avec une ligne droite tirée entre le *stone pinnacle* sur la crête de Mahemasemika (ou Massimique) et une hauteur sur le contrefort septentrional du mont Panga qui est [dé] signée par la côte de 6340 p. Depuis ce point d'intersection sur le parallèle, monte en ligne droite jusqu'à la dite côte de 6340 p. ; d'où, suivant la ligne de partage des eaux jusqu'à la côte de 6504 p., elle va en ligne droite au sommet du mont Panga (6970 p.). Depuis cette côte en ligne droite elle va à la côte de 3890 p., et d'ici elle va directement en traversant la Rivière Inyamkarara (ou Inhamucarara) à la côte de 6740 p. au nord du mont Gorongoe.

Elle parcourt ensuite la ligne de partage des eaux par les côtes de 4960 p. et 4650 p. jusqu'au sommet du mont Shuara ou Chuara (côte de 5540 p.) ; et de là en suivant la ligne de partage des eaux entre l'Inyamkarara et le Shimezi (ou Chimeza, côte de 3700 p.), elle arrive au signal trigonométrique marqué sur le mont Venga (ou Vengo, côte de 5550 p.).

Depuis le mont Venga, elle suit la ligne de partage des eaux entre la haute vallée de l'Inyamkarara et le Révué, et puis celle entre le Révué et l'Odzi, jusqu'au point où se détache le contrefort qui forme la ligne de partage des eaux entre le Menini (ou Munene) et le Zombi (ou Zombe), d'où elle suit la crête du dit contrefort jusqu'au mont Vumba (côte de 4950 p.).

Du mont Vumba elle va en ligne droite au point trigonométrique qui se trouve sur le Serra Chaura entre 4 et 5 kilomètres à l'est de la grande ligne de partage des eaux, et de là en ligne droite jusqu'au point qui se trouve à l'extrémité orientale de Serra Inyamatumba (côte de 4650 p.).

De là elle suit la ligne de partage des eaux qui renferme au nord la vallée du Mangwingi (ou Munhinga) jusqu'à ce qu'elle rejoint la grande ligne de partage entre le Save et le Révué. Elle suit cette ligne jusqu'au point d'où se détache le petit contrefort qui renferme au nord la haute vallée du Little Mussapa (ou Mussapa Pegueno) et elle en suit la crête jusqu'au point de côte 5100, d'où elle va directement vers le vrai est en traversant le Petit Mussapa et atteignant la crête du versant oriental du mont Guzane, qu'elle suit jusqu'au méridien 33° longitude est de Greenwich ; elle suit enfin ce méridien en coupant le Grand Mussapa (défilé de Chimanimani) jusqu'au point marqué *A* sur la carte ci-jointe.

2. Quant à la deuxième section de la frontière comprise entre la fin de la section précédente, et le point où la partie supérieure du versant oriental du plateau coupe le 32° 30′ de longitude est de Greenwich, la frontière suit la ligne qui est indiquée sur la carte ci-jointe par les lettres *A, B, C, D, E, F, G, H, I, J, L, M, N, O*, arrivant ainsi à la rencontre du méridien 32° 30′ à peu près au parallèle 20° 42′ 17″.

3. Quant à la troisième section qui regarde le territoire qui s'étend de la rencontre du bord du versant oriental avec le 32° 30′ à peu près au 20° 42′ 17″, jusqu'au point où se rencontrent les fleuves Save et Lunde, la ligne suivant le dit méridien 32° 30′ va directement au milieu du chenal principal du Save, et puis elle suit ce chenal en amont jusqu'à son confluent avec le Lunde, où [se] termine la frontière soumise à notre Arbitrage.

Une carte qui contient le tracé de la ligne de délimitation conforme à notre décision, signée par nous et munie de notre sceau, est annexée à chacun des deux originaux de notre arrêt dont elle forme partie intégrante.

Fait à Florence, en double original, ce 30 Janvier, 1897 [1].

[1] *Parliamentary Paper*, c. 8434.

CXVII. Honduras, Salvador.

. 19 janvier 1895.

Cette convention, similaire à celle conclue entre les gouvernements du Honduras et du Nicaragua, prévoit également une commission mixte, et subsidiairement une commission arbitrale.

Convencion de limites celebrada entre Honduras y el Salvador, el 19 de Enero 1895.

Los gobiernos de las Repúblicas de Honduras y El Salvador, deseosos de terminar de una manera amigable sus diferencias acerca de la demarcación de límites divisorios que hasta hoy no ha podido verificarse, y á fin de que tan enojoso asunto se resuelva á satisfacción de ambos con toda cordialidad y con la deferencia que corresponde á pueblos hermanos, vecinos y aliados, han creido conveniente celebrar un tratado que llene esas aspiraciones, y al efecto han nombrado á sus respectivos Plenipotenciarios: el señor Presidente de la República de Honduras al señor General don Manuel Bonilla, Enviado Extraordinario y Ministro Plenipotenciario, y el señor Presidente de la República de El Salvador al señor Dᵣ don Jesús Velasco, actual Subsecretario de Relaciones Exteriores, Encargado del Despacho; quienes, habiendo examinado y encontrado bastantes sus respectivos plenos poderes, han convenido en los artículos siguientes:

ARTICULO I. Los Gobiernos de Honduras y El Salvador nombrarán comisionados que, con la autorización correspondiente, organicen una Comisión Mixta de Límites encargada de resolver de una manera amigable todas las dudas y diferencias pendientes, y de demarcar sobre el terreno, la línea divisoria que señale el límite fronterizo de ambas Repúblicas.

ARTICULO II. La Comisión Mixta, compuesta de igual número de miembros por ambas partes, se reunirá en una de las poblaciones fronterizas que ofrezca mayores comodidades para el estudio, y allí principiará sus trabajos, ateniéndose á las reglas siguientes:

1ª Serán límites entre Honduras y El Salvador las líneas en que ambas Repúblicas estuviesen de acuerdo ó que ninguna de las dos disputaren.

2ª Serán también límites entre Honduras y El Salvador, las líneas demarcadas en documentos públicos no contradichos por documentos igualmente públicos de mayor fuerza.

3ª Se entenderá que cada República es dueña del territorio que á la fecha de la independencia constituia respectivamente las provincias de Honduras y El Salvador.

4ª La Comisión Mixta, para fijar los límites, atenderá al dominio del territorio plenamente probado. A la posesión solamente deberá darse valor en lo que tenga de justo, legitimo y fundado, conforme á los principios generales del derecho y á las reglas de justicia que sobre el particular tiene sancionadas el Derecho de Gentes.

5ª En falta de la prueba del dominio se consultarán los mapas de ambas Repúblicas y los documentos geográficos ó de cualquiera otra naturaleza públicos ó privados que puedan dar alguna luz; y serán límites entre ambas Repúblicas, los que con presencia de ese estudio fijase equitativamente la Comisión Mixta.

6ª La Comisión Mixta, si lo creyere conveniente, podrá hacer compensaciones y aun fijar indemnización para procurar establecer en lo posible, límites naturales bien marcados.

7ª Al hacer el estudio de los planos, mapas y demás documentos análogos que presenten ambos Gobiernos, la Comisión Mixta preferirá los que estime más racionales y justos.

8ª En caso de que la Comisión Mixta no pudiese acordarse amigablemente en cualquier punto, lo consignará per separado en dos libros especiales, firmando una doble acta detallada con cita de lo alegado por ambas partes y continuará su estudio sobre los demás puntos de la línea de demarcación, con prescindencia del punto indicado, hasta fijar el término divisorio en el último extremo de la misma línea.

9ª Los libros á que se refiere la cláusula anterior, serán enviados por la Comisión Mixta uno á cada Gobierno de los interesados para su custodia en los Archivos Nacionales.

ARTICULO III. El punto ó los puntos de demarcación que la Comisión Mixta, de que habla el presente tratado, no hubiese resuelto, serán sometidos á más tardar un mes después de concluidas las sesiones de la misma Comisión, al fallo de un arbitramento inapelable que será compuesto de un representante de Honduras y otro de El Salvador y un miembro del Cuerpo Diplomático extranjero acreditado en Guatemala, electo este último por los primeros ó sorteados en dos ternas propuestas una por cada parte.

ARTICULO IV. El arbitramente se organizará en la ciudad de Guatemala en los veinte días siguientes á la disolución de la Comisión Mixta, y dentro de los diez días inmediatos principiará sus trabajos, consignándolos en un libro de actas que llevará autenticado, siendo ley el voto de la mayoría.

ARTICULO V. En el caso de que el Representante Diplomático extranjero se excusare, se repetirá la elección en otro, dentro de los diez

64

días inmediatos y así sucesivamente. Agotados los miembros del Cuerpo Diplomático extranjero, la elección podrá recaer por convenio de los comisionados de Honduras y El Salvador en cualquier personaje público, extranjero ó centroamericano; y si este convenio no fuere posible se someterá el punto ó los puntos controvertidos á la decisión del Gobierno de España y en defecto de éste á la de cualquier otro de Sud-America, en que convengan la Cancillerias de ambos países.

ARTICULO VI. Los procedimientos y terminos á que deberá sujetarse el arbitramento serán los siguientes:

1° Dentro de los veinte días siguientes á la fecha en que la aceptación del tercer árbitro fuese notificada á las partes, éstas le presentarán por medio de sus abogados sus alegados, planos, mapas y documentos.

2° Si hubiese alegatos, dará traslado de ellos á sus respectivos abogados contrarios dentro de los ocho días siguientes á la presentación, concediendoles diez días de término para rebatirlos y presentar los demás documentos que creyeren del caso.

3° El fallo arbitral será pronunciado dentro de los veinte días siguientes á la fecha en que se hubiere vencido el término para contestar alegatos, háyanse ó no presentado éstos.

ARTICULO VII. La decisión arbitral, adoptada por mayoría, cualquiera que sea, se tendrá como tratado perfecto, obligatorio y perpetuo entre las Altas Partes Contratantes y no admitirá recurso alguno.

ARTICULO VIII. La presente convención será sometida en Honduras y El Salvador á las ratificaciones constitucionales, y el canje de éstas se verificará en Tegucigalpa ó en San Salvador dentro de los sesenta días siguientes á la fecha en que ambos Gobiernos hubiesen cumplido con lo estipulado en este artículo.

ARTICULO IX. Lo dispuesto en el artículo anterior no obsta en manera alguna para la organización inmediata de la Comisión Mixta, que deberá principiar sus estudios á mas tardar dos meses después de la ultima ratificación, en conformidad con lo que se ha dispuesto en la presente convención, sin perjuicio de hacerlo antes de las ratificaciones, si éstas se tardasen para aprovechar la estación seca ó del verano.

ARTICULO X. Inmediatamente después del canje de esta convención, háyanse ó no principiado los trabajos de la Comisión Mixta, serán nombrados por los Gobiernos de Honduras y El Salvador los representantes que, en conformidad con el artículo cuarto, deben formar el arbitra-

mento; para que organizándose en junta preparatoria, nombren el tercer árbitro y lo comuniquen á los Secretarios de Relaciones respectivos á fin de recabar la aceptación del nombrado.

Si se excusase se procederá en seguida al nombramiento de un nuevo tercer árbitro, en la forma estipulada y así sucesivamente hasta quedar organizado el arbitramento.

ARTICULO XI. Los plazos señalados en el presente tratado para nombramiento de árbitros, principio de estudios, ratificaciones y canjes, lo mismo que cualesquiera otros términos en el fijados no serán fatales, ni producirán nulidad de ninguna especie. Su objeto ha sido dar precisión al trabajo; pero si por cualquiera causa no pudieren atenderse, es á voluntad de las Altas Partes Contratantes que la negociación se lleve adelante, hasta terminarla en la forma aquí estipulada que es la que creen más conveniente. A este fin convienen en que este tratado tenga la duración de diez años, caso de interrumpirse su ejecución, en cuyo término no podrá reverse ni modificarse de ninguna manera, ni podrá tampoco dirimirse la cuestión de límites por otro medio.

En fe de lo cual, los Plenipotenciarios de las Repúblicas de Honduras y El Salvador firman en dos ejemplares que autorizan con sus respectivos sellos en la ciudad de San Salvador, á los diez y nueve días del mes de enero de mil ochocientos noventa y cinco [1].

CXVIII. Guatemala, Honduras.

1 mars 1895.

L'arbitrage ici organisé est tout éventuel, pour le cas où les deux gouvernements intéressés ne parviendraient pas à s'entendre sur les limites communes de leurs territoires respectifs.

Convencion de Limites celebrada en la ciudad de Guatemala el primero de Mayo 1895 por Plenipotenciarios de las Repúblicas de Honduras y Guatemala.

Los Gobiernos de las Repúblicas de Honduras y Guatemala, deseosos de establecer, de una manera definitiva, la demarcación de los límites divisorios entre ambos países, que hasta hoy no ha podido verificarse, lo cual da lugar á difficultades que al común interés importa remover, y deseosos también de que tan enojoso asunto se resuelva á satisfacción de ambas partes, con toda cordialidad y con la deferencia que corres-

[1] *Tratados celebrados por el Gobierno de Honduras*, 1895, p. 83.

ponde á pueblos hermanos, vecinos y amigos, han creído conveniente celebrar una Convención que llene esas aspiraciones; y al efecto, han nombrado á sus respectivos Plenipotenciarios, el señor Presidente de la República de Honduras, al señor Doctor don Juan Angel Arías, su Secretario de Estado en el Despacho de la Gobernación, y actualmente Enviado Extraordinario y Ministro Plenipotenciario de su Gobierno cerca del de Guatemala; y el señor Presidente de la República de Guatemala, al señor Licenciado don Jorge Muñoz, su Secretario de Estado en el Despacho de Relaciones Exteriores; quienes, habiendo examinado sus respectivos plenos poderes, han convenido en los artículos siguientes:

ARTICULO I. Los Gobiernos de Honduras y Guatemala nombrarán una Comisión técnica mixta, compuesta de igual número de miembros por cada parte, para que se encargue de estudiar todos los antecedentes, documentos y datos que existan sobre los límites entre ambas Repúblicas.

ARTICULO II. Tan pronto como dicha Comisión este organizada, dará principio á sus estudios; y podrá hacer sobre el terreno mismo de la frontera todos los reconocimientos, operaciones y trabajos, teniendo, como punto de reunion, la ciudad de Ocotepeque.

ARTICULO III. La Comisión consignará el resultado de sus estudios y observaciones en actas razonadas que se extenderán en un libro que para ese fin deberá llevarse por dublicado. Si en alguno ó algunos de los puntos de que se ocupe la Comisión, no pudieren sus miembros ponerse de acuerdo, consignarán la divergencia en el acta ó actas respectivas, exponiendo cada uno los fundamentos de su opinión; y hecho esto, continuarán el estudio de los puntos restantes hasta concluir su cometido.

ARTICULO IV. Al terminar la Comisión sus trabajos, enviará los libros de actas á los respectivos gobiernos y les propondrá las bases que, á su juicio, deban adoptarse para celebrar un tratado que fije definitivamente los límites entre ambas Repúblicas, acompañando un plano en que se halle trazada la línea divisoria tal como juzgue que deba marcarse según el resultado de sus estudios.

ARTICULO V. En vista de las bases que proponga la Comisión, los Gobiernos Contratantes procederán á discutirlas y á definir en un tratado los límites entre Honduras y Guatemala. Para este efecto, ambos Gobiernos nombrarán sus representantes, los que se reunirán, para llenar su misión, en Tegucigalpa ó en Guatemala, á más tardar 60 días después de concluidos los trabajos de la Comisión mixta.

ARTICULO VI. Para tomar las resoluciones del caso, los Gobiernos Contratantes después que la Comisión mixta haya presentado el resultado de sus trabajos, tendrán en cuenta: las observaciones y estudios de la misma Comisión; las líneas demarcadas en documentos públicos no contradichos por otros de igual clase y de mayor fuerza, dando á cada uno el valor que le corresponda según su antigüedad y eficacia jurídica; la comprensión del territorio que constituia las antiguas provincias de Honduras y Guatemala á la fecha de su independencia; las disposiciones de la Real ordenanza de Intendentes que entonces regía y, en general, todos los documentos, mapas, planos, etc., que conduzcan al esclarecimiento de la verdad, dándose la preferencia á los que por su naturaleza deban tener más fuerza por razon de antigüedad, de ser mas claros, justos é imparciales, ó por cualquier otro motivo fundado, según los principios de justicia.

A la posesión solamente deberá darse valor en lo que tenga de justo, legítimo y fundado, conforme á los principios generales del derecho y á las reglas de justicia que sobre el particular tiene sancionadas el Derecho de Gentes.

ARTICULO VII. Al convenir en la fijación de la línea divisoria entre Honduras y Guatemala, pueden los respectivos Gobiernos, si lo creen necesario ó conveniente, adoptar el sistema de compensaciones equitativas, ateniéndose á las reglas y usos establecidos en las prácticas internacionales.

ARTICULO VIII. Una vez determinada definitivamente por las dos Altas Partes Contratantes la línea divisoria entre ambas Repúblicas, se establece desde ahora que las propiedades nacionales que deban quedar á uno ú otro lado de ella, pertenecerán respectivamente á la República en cuyo territorio resulten comprendidas; y que las propiedades particulares que existan legitimamente tituladas con anterioridad al presente Convenio, deberán ser respetadas como corresponde y gozarán de todas las garantías que para la de sus nacionales establezcan la Constitución y las leyes de cada uno de los dos países, á cuyas leyes estarán en un todo sometidas dichas propiedades.

ARTICULO IX. Si los Gobiernos no pudieren ponerse de acuerdo en alguno ó algunos de los puntos en discusión, convienen en someter su decisión á un árbitro, que será cualquiera de los Presidentes de las otras Repúblicas de Centro-America, en este orden sucesivo: El Salvador, Nicaragua y Costa-Rica. El nombramiento de árbitro deberá hacerse dentro de 60 días de publicado por el periódico oficial la nota en que uno de los Gobiernos Contratantes excita al otro á dicho nombramiento.

ARTICULO X. En caso de excusa ó impedimento de los Presidentes de las Repúblicas Centroamericanas, se someterá el punto ó puntos discutidos á la decisión de S. M. el Rey de España y en defecto de éste á la de cualquiera de los Presidentes de las Repúblicas de Sud-America, en que convengan las Cancillerías de ambos países.

ARTICULO XI. Los procedimientos y términos á que deberá sujetarse el juicio arbitral serán los siguientes:

1º Dentro de los 60 días posteriores á la fecha en que la aceptación del árbitro fuese notificado á las dos Altas Partes, éstas le presentarán sus alegatos, planos, mapas y documentos;

2º El árbitro comunicará al representante de cada Gobierno el alegato del contrario, dentro de los ocho días siguientes á su presentación;

3º Cada Gobierno tendrá derecho á rebatir el alegato de la parte contraria dentro de los 90 días que sigan á la fecha en que el respectivo alegato le fuese comunicado y con ambas réplicas podrán también presentarse documentos, planos y mapas;

4º El árbitro deberá pronunciar su fallo dentro de los 180 días siguientes á la fecha en que se hubiere vencido el término para contestar alegatos, háyanse ó no presentado éstos.

5º El árbitro podrá delegar sus funciones para la tramitación y estudio del asunto; pero deberá emitir directa y personalmente la sentencia definitiva.

ARTICULO XII. El laudo arbitral, cualquiera que sea, se tendrá como tratado perfecto, obligatorio y perpetuo entre las Altas Partes Contratantes y no se admitirá contra él recurso alguno.

ARTICULO XIII. La presente Convención será sometida en Honduras y Guatemala á las ratificaciones constitucionales de ley, y el canje de éstas verificará en Tegucigalpa ó en Guatemala dentro de los 60 días posteriores á la fecha en que ambos Gobiernos hubiesen cumplido con lo estipulado en este artículo.

ARTICULO XIV. Lo dispuesto en el artículo anterior no obsta en manera alguna para la organización inmediata de la Comisión mixta, que deberá principiar sus estudios, á más tardar, dos meses después de la última ratificación, en conformidad con lo que se ha dispuesto en el presente convenio, sin perjuicio de hacerlo antes de las ratificaciones, si éstas se tardasen, para aprovechar en los trabajos de campo la estación seca ó del verano.

ARTICULO XV. Inmediatamente después del canje de esta Convención, háyanse ó no principiado los trabajos de la Comisión mixta, será designado por los Gobiernos de Honduras y Guatemala, el árbitro que, en conformidad al art. 9º, deberá emitir su fallo sobre el punto ó puntos en que dichos Gobiernos puedan llegar á estar en desacuerdo, recabando al efecto su aceptación ó no aceptación. En caso de excusa se procederá á designar otro árbitro según el orden establecido en el art. 10.

ARTICULO XVI. Ninguno de los plazos señalados en este tradado ha el carácter de fatal, ni dará lugar á nulidad de ninguna especie.

El fin con que se han fijado es el de dar precisión al trabajo; pero si por cualquiera causa no fueren suficientes para su objeto, es la voluntad de las Altas Partes Contratantes que la negociación se lleve adelante hasta terminarla en la forma estipulada, que es la que creen más conveniente. A este fin consienten en que el presente convenio tenga la duración de diez años, en caso de interrumpirse su ejecución, durante cuyo término no podrá reverse ni modificarse de ninguna manera, salvo estipulación en contrario, ni podrá tampoco dirimirse la cuestión de límites por otro medio.

En fe de lo cual, los Plenipotenciarios de Honduras y Guatemala, firman en dos ejemplares que autorizan con sus respectivos sellos en la ciudad de Guatemala, á primero de marzo de mil ochocientos noventa y cinco, año septuagésimo cuarto de la independencia de Centro-América [1].

CXIX. Guatémala, Mexique.

1 avril 1895.

Cette affaire se rattache à la délimitation des deux pays. Le gouvernement guatémalien fit occuper par sa force armée le territoire de la rive occidentale du Rio Lacantum et causa par ce fait des dommages à des citoyens méxicains établis en ces parages. Bien que son droit à occuper ce territoire ait été implicitement reconnu, il consentit cependant à indemniser les personnes atteintes et à faire évaluer les indemnités par un arbitre.

Convencion de arbitraje e de límites firmada en Mexico, el 1 de Abril de 1895.

Los infrascritos debidamente autorizados, después de la correspondencia que se ha cambiado entre ellos y de las conferencias que han tenido con el fin de arreglar, de un modo pacífico

---

[1] *Tratados celebrados por el Gobierno de Honduras*, 1895, p. 59.

y honroso para Guatemala y México, las difficultades que entre ambos países ha causado el ejercicio de actos de soberanía dentro del territorio que se extiende al Oeste del río Lacantum, han convenido en los artículos siguientes:

I. Guatemala declara, como ya lo ha hecho antes, que, creyendo hacer uso de su derecho, ha ejercido actos de soberanía dentro del territorio que se extiende al Oeste del río Lacantum y por lo mismo no ha sido su intención ofender á México al ejecutarlos.

II. No obstante esto, en obsequio de la buena armonía el Gobierno de Guatemala conviene, por un sentimiento de equidad, en indemnizar á los perjudicados por sus agentes del valor de las propiedades ocupadas ó destruidas y de los perjuicios que se les hayan causado directamente por esa ocupación ó destrucción. Un árbitro nombrado de común acuerdo fijará el monto de esas indemnizaciones . . . .

. . . .

VII. El presente convenio se someterá á la aprobación del Senado de los Estados Unidos Mexicanos y de la Asamblea Nacional Legislativa de Guatemala, sin perjuicio de que desde luego se publique en los órganos oficiales de ambos Gobiernos. El canje de las ratificaciones se verificará en la ciudad de México antes del treintiuno de mayo próximo.

Hecho y firmado en dos ejemplares, en la ciudad de México, hoy primero de abril de mil ochocientos noventicinco [1].

Saisi par une demande des 26 et 28 mai 1897, le Ministre Plénipotentiaire d'Espagne à México termina sa mission le 15 janvier 1898.

Nos	Noms des réclamants	Sommes réclamées	Sommes accordées
1	Policarpo Valenzuela e hijos	$ 936,654. 14	$ 28,352. —
2	Nabor Cordoba Manzanilla	» 8,000. —	
3	Romano y Comp.Secesores	» 371,771. 38	» 31,650. —
4	Transito Mejenes . . .	» 10,000. —	
5	Miguel Torruco (Monteria Egipto)	» 92,272. 05	» 3,157. 80
6	Miguel Torruco (Monteria Agua Azul)	» 44,746. —	» 23,500. —
7	Sebastian Torruco. . .	» 10,000. —	
8	Federico Schindler . .	» 388,100. —	—
	Totaux	$ 1,861,543. 57	$ 86,659. 80

Boletin oficial de la Secretaria de Relaciones Exteriores (Mexico), t. V, p. 292-316.

---

[1] *Memoria . . . Ministerio de Relaciones Exteriores* (Guatemala), 1896, Anexo V, p. 1.

CXX. Grande-Bretagne, Pays-Bas.

16 mai 1895.

Il s'est agi dans cette affaire de l'arrestation illégale d'un capitaine de baleinier par les autorités coloniales néerlandaises. L'arbitre désigné accorda au total, à titre d'indemnité, une somme de 8550 £.

Traité d'arbitrage destiné à mettre fin au différend né de la détention préventive du capitaine du baleinier «Costa Rica Packet», signé à La Haye, le 16 mai 1895.

Sa Majesté la Reine du Royaume-Uni de la Grande-Bretagne et d'Irlande, Impératrice des Indes, et Sa Majesté la Reine-Régente du Royaume des Pays-Bas:

Considérant que le Gouvernement Britannique a adressé au Gouvernement des Pays-Bas des réclamations du chef de l'arrestation et de la détention préventive aux Indes Néerlandaises du sieur Carpenter, capitaine du baleinier « Costa Rica Packet » de Sydney; que ces réclamations concernent non seulement les dommages qui, d'après le Gouvernement Britannique, ont été soufferts par ledit capitaine personnellement, mais encore ceux qui ont été subis par les officiers, l'équipage et les propriétaires dudit bâtiment, et qui doivent être considérés comme étant les conséquences nécessaires de la détention préventive du capitaine;

Considérant que le Gouvernement des Pays-Bas conteste le bien-fondé en droit, de chacune de ces réclamations, estimant qu'aucune indemnité ne saurait être portée à la charge du Gouvernement des Pays-Bas du chef de l'arrestation ou de la détention préventive dudit capitaine, ni en faveur du capitaine, ni, à plus forte raison, en faveur d'autres personnes qui allèguent avoir souffert des dommages qui devraient être considérés comme étant les conséquences nécessaires de cette détention préventive, que, même, si de telles réclamations pouvaient être admises en droit comme devant tomber à la charge du Gouvernement des Pays-Bas, il n'en résulterait nullement que les dommages susmentionnés prétendûment soufferts, soit par le capitaine, soit par les officiers, l'équipage et les propriétaires dudit bâtiment, devraient être considérés comme suffisamment justifiés;

Désirant mettre fin à l'amiable au différend survenu de ce chef,

Ont nommé pour leurs Plénipotentiaires, savoir:

Sa Majesté la Reine du Royaume-Uni de la Grande-Bretagne et d'Irlande, Impératrice des Indes, Sir Horace Rumbold, Baronet du Royaume de la Grande-Bretagne, Chevalier Grand-Croix de l'Ordre Très Distingué des Saint-Michel et

Saint-Georges, etc., etc., son Envoyé Extraordinaire et Ministre Plénipotentiaire à la Cour des Pays-Bas ; et Sa Majesté la Reine-Régente du Royaume des Pays-Bas, les sieurs Jonkheer Joan Röell, Chevalier de l'Ordre du Lion Néerlandais, Ministre des Affaires Etrangères ; et Jacques Henri Bergsma, Chevalier de l'Ordre du Lion Néerlandais, Ministre des Colonies ;

Lesquels, après s'être communiqué leurs pleins pouvoirs, trouvés en bonne et due forme, sont convenus des Articles suivants :

ART. 1. Le Gouvernement de Sa Majesté la Reine du Royaume-Uni de la Grande-Bretagne et d'Irlande, et le Gouvernement de Sa Majesté la Reine des Pays-Bas, conviennent d'inviter le Gouvernement d'une Puissance tierce à désigner parmi ses sujets un jurisconsulte d'une réputation incontestée pour prononcer comme Arbitre dans le différend mentionné ci-dessus.

Art. 2. Cet Arbitre aura à prendre connaissance des réclamations d'indemnité susmentionnées formulées par le Gouvernement Britannique à charge du Gouvernement des Pays-Bas, tant en faveur du capitaine du baleinier « Costa Rica Packet », qu'en faveur des officiers, de l'équipage et des propriétaires de ce bâtiment.

ART. 3. La Partie demanderesse remettra à l'Arbitre, dans un délai de trois mois après l'échange des ratifications de la présente Convention, un Mémoire à l'appui de sa demande, et en fera parvenir immédiatement une copie à la partie défenderesse.

En déans trois mois après la réception de cette copie la Partie demanderesse pourra, si elle le juge utile, remettre à l'Arbitre un nouveau Mémoire, dont elle fera parvenir immédiatement une copie à la Partie défenderesse, qui pourra également, en déans trois mois après la réception de cette copie, remettre à l'Arbitre un nouveau Mémoire, dont il fera parvenir une copie à la partie demanderesse.

L'Arbitre est autorisé à accorder à chacune des Parties qui le demanderait une prorogation d'un mois par rapport à tous les délais mentionnés dans cet Article.

ART. 4. Après l'échange de ces Mémoires, aucune communication, ni écrite, ni verbale, ne sera faite à l'Arbitre, à moins que celui-ci ne s'adresse aux Parties pour obtenir d'elles, ou de l'une d'elles, des renseignements ultérieurs par écrit.

La Partie qui donnera ces renseignements en fera parvenir immédiatement une copie à l'autre Partie, et celle-ci pourra, si bon lui semble, en déans un mois après la réception de cette copie, communiquer par écrit à l'Arbitre les observations auxquelles ils lui donneront lieu. Ces observations seront également communiquées immédiatement en copie à la Partie adverse.

ART. 5. L'Arbitre décidera de toutes les questions qui pourraient surgir relativement à la procédure dans le cours du litige.

ART. 6. Dans sa sentence, qui sera communiquée par lui aux deux Parties contractantes, l'Arbitre, tout en tenant compte des principes du droit des gens, décidera à l'égard de chaque réclamation formulée à charge du Gouvernement des Pays-Bas, si elle est bien fondée et, dans l'affirmative, si les faits sur lesquels chacune de ces réclamations est basée sont prouvés.

Dans ce cas l'Arbitre fixera le montant de l'indemnité due par le Gouvernement des Pays-Bas du chef des dommages soufferts par le capitaine du « Costa Rica Packet » personnellement ; de même que du chef des dommages qui auront été justifiés avoir été soufferts par les officiers, l'équipage et les propriétaires dudit bâtiment comme conséquences nécessaires de la détention préventive du capitaine. Sans préjudice de l'obligation incombant à la partie demanderesse de justifier les dommages soufferts, l'Arbitre pourra s'il le juge opportun, inviter chaque Gouvernement à désigner un expert commercial pour l'aider en sa dite qualité, à fixer le montant de l'indemnité.

ART. 7. L'Arbitre fixera également dans sa sentence le montant des frais nécessaires occasionnés par l'arbitrage, et décidera laquelle des Parties aura à les supporter. Ces frais dont il est bien entendu que le montant devra être limité autant que possible, pourront être compensés en tout ou en partie.

ART. 8. Les Hautes Parties Contractantes s'engagent à accepter comme jugement en dernier ressort la décision prononcée par l'Arbitre dans les limites de la présente Convention, et à s'y soumettre sans aucune réserve.

ART. 9. La présente Convention sera ratifiée et entrera en vigueur immédiatement après l'échange des ratifications qui aura lieu à La Haye aussitôt que possible après que la Convention aura reçu l'approbation des Etats Généraux des Pays-Bas.

En foi de quoi, les Plénipotentiaires respectifs ont signé la présente Convention, qu'ils ont revêtue de leurs cachets.

Fait en double à La Haye, le 16 Mai 1895.

Sentence de M. Martens en date du 13/25 février 1897, en cause du « Costa Rica Packet ».

En vertu des hautes fonctions d'Arbitre conférées, par ordre suprême de mon auguste Maître, Sa Majesté l'Empereur Nicolas II de Toutes les Russies, à moi, F. de Martens, Conseiller Privé,

Membre Permanent du Conseil du Ministère des Affaires Etrangères de Russie, et Professeur émérite, conformément à la Convention du 16 mai, 1895, conclue entre le Gouvernement de S. M. la Reine de Grande-Bretagne et d'Irlande, Impératrice des Indes, et le Gouvernement de Sa Majesté la Reine des Pays-Bas, au sujet du différend survenu entre les deux Gouvernements du chef de la détention du sieur Carpenter, capitaine du baleinier Australien « Costa Rica Packet ».

Ayant dûment examiné et mûrement pesé les documents qui ont été produits de part et d'autre concernant l'indemnité réclamée par le Gouvernement de S. M. Britannique du Gouvernement Royal des Pays-Bas au profit du capitaine Carpenter, ainsi qu'au profit des officiers, de l'équipage et des propriétaires du navire « Costa Rica Packet ».

Animé du désir sincère de répondre par une décision impartiale et scrupuleuse au grand honneur qui m'a été dévolu, et

En tenant compte des principes du droit des gens applicables au différend survenu entre les deux Hauts Gouvernements en litige, afin de fixer le montant de l'indemnité due par le Gouvernement des Pays-Bas du chef des dommages soufferts par le capitaine Carpenter du « Costa Rica Packet » personnellement, de même que du chef des dommages qui auront été justifiés avoir été soufferts par les officiers, l'équipage et les propriétaires dudit bâtiment comme conséquences nécessaires de la détention préventive du sieur Carpenter.

Je prononce la sentence arbitrale suivante :

Considérant que le droit de souveraineté de l'Etat sur la mer territoriale est déterminée par la portée du canon à partir de la laisse de basse mer ;

Qu'en haute mer, même les navires marchands, constituent les parties détachées du territoire de l'Etat dont ils portent le pavillon, et, en conséquence, ne sont justiciables des faits commis en haute mer qu'aux autorités nationales respectives ;

Que l'Etat a non seulement le droit, mais encore le devoir de protéger et de défendre, par tous les moyens qu'autorise le droit international, ses nationaux à l'étranger, lorsqu'ils sont l'objet de poursuites arbitraires ou de lésions commises à leur préjudice ;

Que la souveraineté de l'Etat et l'indépendance de ses autorités judiciaires ou administratives ne sauraient prévaloir jusqu'à supprimer arbitrairement la sécurité légale qui doit être garantie tant aux étrangers qu'aux régnicoles sur le territoire de tout pays civilisé ;

Attendu que la pirogue (prauw) flottant à l'abandon en mer et arrêtée en janvier 1888 par le sieur Carpenter, capitaine du « Costa Rica Packet » fut saisie par celui-ci incontestablement en dehors de la mer territoriale des Indes Néerlandaises ;

Que l'appropriation de la cargaison de ladite pirogue, par le sieur Carpenter, ayant eu lieu en pleine mer, n'était justiciable que des Tribunaux Anglais, mais nullement des Tribunaux Hollandais ;

Que même, l'identité de l'épave susmentionnée et de la pirogue perdue du sieur Frieser n'est nullement prouvée ;

Que les autorités des Indes Néerlandaises, lesquelles avaient arrêté le sieur Carpenter en Novembre 1891 sous l'inculpation du fait commis en 1888 en dehors des eaux territoriales des Indes Néerlandaises, ont renoncé spontanément par l'Arrêt du Conseil de Justice de Macassar, du 28 Novembre 1891, à la poursuite du prévenu, et ont par là même irréfutablement constaté l'illégitimité de sa détention, ainsi que de son transport forcé de Ternate à Macassar ;

Que tous les documents et actes produits prouvent le manque de cause sérieuse pour l'arrestation du sieur Carpenter, et confirment le droit de celui-ci à une indemnité pour les dommages qu'il a soufferts ;

Que le traitement infligé au sieur Carpenter dans la prison de Macassar ne paraît pas justifié à l'égard d'un sujet d'un Etat civilisé qui se trouve en état de détention préventive, et que, par conséquent, ce traitement lui donne droit à un juste dédommagement ;

Attendu que la détention non justifiée du capitaine Carpenter lui a fait perdre la meilleure partie de la saison pour la chasse aux baleines ;

Attendu que, d'autre part, le sieur Carpenter une fois relâché, aurait pu retourner à bord du navire « Costa Rica Packet » au plus tard en Janvier 1892, et qu'aucune preuve concluante n'a été produite de sa part, pour établir la nécessité dans laquelle il se serait trouvé de laisser son navire jusqu'en Avril 1892 dans le port de Ternate sans maître, ni encore moins de le vendre à vil prix ;

Que les propriétaires ou le capitaine d'un navire étant obligés, pour le cas d'un accident quelconque survenant au capitaine, de pourvoir à son remplacement, le premier officier du « Costa Rica Packet » devait être capable de prendre le commandement et d'exercer l'industrie de la chasse des baleines ;

Et qu'ainsi les dommages soufferts en suite de la détention du sieur Carpenter par les propriétaires du bâtiment « Costa Rica Packet », les officiers et l'équipage, ne sont pas *uniquement* des conséquences nécessaires de cette détention préventive ;

Attendu, en ce qui concerne l'indemnité à payer au capitaine Carpenter, aux officiers, à l'équipage et aux propriétaires du bâtiment « Costa Rica Packet » que les documents produits et spécialement l'expertise à laquelle il a été procédé à Bruxelles, fournissent les éléments nécessaires pour en fixer le chiffre, et qu'en allouant au capitaine Carpenter la somme de 3,150 £, aux officiers et à l'équipage la somme de 1,600 £, et aux propriétaires du navire « Costa Rica Packet » la somme de 3,800 £, il leur sera alloué une indemnité suffisante :

Par ces motifs :

Je déclare le Gouvernement de Sa Majesté la Reine des Pays-Bas responsable, et je fixe, en conséquence, l'indemnité à payer :

Au capitaine Carpenter à la somme totale de 3,150 £ ;

Aux officiers et à l'équipage à la somme totale de 1,600 £ ;

Aux propriétaires du bâtiment « Costa Rica Packet » à la somme totale de 3,800 £ ;

Avec intérêts pour tous les dommages à raison de 5 pour cent par an à partir du 2 Novembre, 1891, date de l'arrestation illégale du capitaine Carpenter, et je mets les dépens à la somme totale de 250 £ à la charge du Gouvernement de Sa Majesté la Reine des Pays-Bas.

Fait à St-Pétersbourg, en double original, le 13 (25) Février, 1897.

CXXI. Colombie, Venezuela.

14 septembre 1881.

Arbitrage relatif aux limites des deux pays, fort important à raison des longs malentendus qui divisèrent ce à propos les deux gouvernements. Ce fut la Reine Régente d'Espagne que trancha le différend par une sentence rendue en 1891.

Tratado sobre arbitramento juris entre los Estados Unidos de Colombia y los Estados Unidos de Venezuela, de 14 de Septiembre de 1881.

Los Estados Unidos de Colombia y los Estados Unidos de Venezuela, y en su nombre sus respectivos Presidentes constitucionales, deseando poner término á la cuestión de límites territoriales que por el espacio de cincuenta años ha venido dificultando sus relaciones de sincera amistad y natural y antigua é indispensable fraternidad, con el objeto de alcanzar una verdadera delimitación territorial de derecho, tal como existía por los mandamientos del antiguo común Soberano, y

alegados por una y otra parte, durante tan largo periodo, todos los títulos, documentos, pruebas y autoridades constantes en sus archivos, en repetidas negociaciones, sin haber podido ponerse de acuerdo en cuanto á los respectivos derechos ó *Uti possidetis juris* de 1810; animados de los más cordiales sentimientos, han convenido y convienen en nombrar sus respectivos Plenipotenciarios para negociar y concluir un Tratado de arbitramento *juris*, y han nombrado para negociarlo y concluirlo, el Gobierno de Colombia á su Ministro residente en Caracas, Dr Justo Arosemena, y el de Venezuela, al ilustre Prócer Antonio L. Guzmán, Consultor del Ministerio de Relaciones Exteriores; los cuales, reconocidos sus poderes respectivos en la debida forma, y de conformidad con sus instrucciones, han convenido en los artículos siguientes :

ART. I. Dichas Altas Partes contratantes someten al juicio y sentencia del Gobierno de S. M. el Rey de España, en calidad de árbitro, Juez de derecho, los puntos de diferencia en la expresada cuestión de límites, á fin de obtener un fallo definitivo é inapelable, según el cual todo el territorio que pertenecía á la jurisdicción de la antigua Capitanía general de Caracas por actos regios del antiguo Soberano, hasta 1810, quede siendo territorio jurisdiccional de la República de Venezuela, y todo lo que por actos semejantes, y en esa fecha, perteneció á la jurisdicción del Virreinato de Santa Fe, quede siendo territorio de la actual República llamada Estados Unidos de Colombia.

ART. II. Ambas Partes contratantes, tan luégo como sea canjeado este Tratado, pondrán en conocimiento de S. M. el Rey de España la solicitud de ambos Gobiernos para que S. M. acepte la jurisdicción ya expresada, y esta solicitud se hará por medio de Plenipotenciarios y simultáneamente ; y ocho meses después, los mismos ú otros Plenipotenciarios, presentarán á S. M., ó al Ministro á quien S. M. comisione, una exposición ó alegato en que consten sus pretensiones y los documentos en que las apoyan.

ART. III. Desde ese día los Plenipotenciarios, representando á sus propios Gobiernos, quedarán autorizados para recibir los traslados que el augusto Tribunal jusgue conveniente pasarles, y complirán el deber ó deberes que se les impongan por tales providencias para esclarecer la verdad del derecho que representan, y esperarán la sentencia que, recibida que sea, la comunicarán á sus respectivos Gobiernos, quedando ejecutoriada por el hecho de publicarse en el periódico oficial del Gobierno que la ha dictado, y obligatoriamente establecida para siempre la delimitación territorial de derecho de ambas Repúblicas.

ART. IV. Este Tratado, después de aprobado por los Gobiernos de Colombia y de Venezuela, tan pronto como sea posible, y ratificado que sea por los Cuerpos Legislativos de una y otra República en sus próximas sesiones, será canjeado en Caracas, sin dilación alguna, en el término de la distancia.

En fe de lo cual, los Plenipotenciarios de los Estados Unidos de Colombia y de los Estados Unidos de Venezuela, lo hemos convenido y firmado, y sellado con nuestros sellos particulares, por duplicado, en Caracas, á catorce de Septiembre de mil ochocientos ochenta y uno.

Acta-Declaración de París, de 15 Febrero de 1886.

Los infrascritos, á saber: Dr Carlos Holguin, Enviado Extraordinario y Ministro Plenipotenciario de los Estados Unidos de Colombia en España y la Gran Bretaña, y General Guzmán Blanco, Enviado Extraordinario y Ministro Plenipotenciario de Venezuela en España, la Gran Bretaña, etc., reunidos en París con el objeto de examinar la cuestión de si la lamentable muerte de S. M. D. Alfonso XII ha podido afectar de algun modo la jurisdicción que al Gobierno del Rey de España tienen conferida sus respectivos Gobiernos por Tratado de 14 de Septiembre de 1881, para decidir como árbitro de derecho el litigio pendiente sobre límites territoriales entre las dos Repúblicas, trajeron á la vista dicho Pacto, y juzgaron que su articulo 1º es suficientemente claro para afirmar que tanto el espíritu como la letra de aquella estipulación confieren al actual Gobierno de España la misma jurisdicción que en virtud de él tenían los Gobiernos que existieron bajo S. M. D. Alfonso XII, desde la fecha del canje de sus ratificaciones, para continuar conociendo de la expresada cuestión de límites hasta dar el laudo que las dos partes se han comprometido á respetar y á cumplir. Con efecto, ven que en ese articulo las dos partes designan como árbitro no á S. M. D. Alfonso XII, sino al Gobierno del Rey de España, sin expresar siquiera quién le fuese á la sazón, como para significar que cualquier Gobierno que hubiese en España, ya presidido por D. Alfonso XII, ya por alguno de sus sucesores, había de tener jurisdicción bastante para conocer y decidir de las disputas sometidas á su fallo, y asimismo recuerdan que la elección del Gobierno Español para juez en este caso, se debió particularmente á la circunstancia de haber sido España dueña de los territorios que se disputan las dos Repúblicas, y de existir en los archivos de aquélla los documentos de donde emanan los titulos alegados por ambas; además de tener la Península muchos hombres ilustrados en estas cuestiones americanas. En tal virtud, hacen la presente declaración, que dirigirán al actual Gobierno de S. M. Dª Cristina la Reina Regente, manifestándole que, aun cuando en concepto de los abajo firmados el punto es claro, someterán este Protocolo á la ratificación de sus respectivos Gobiernos, á fin de evitar dudas ó desacuerdos en lo futuro acerca del derecho aquí reconocido. También han convenido los suscritos en que el árbitro en cuyo conocimiento lo pondrán con esta declaratoria, puede fijar la línea del modo que crea más aproximado á los documentos existentes, cuando respecto de algún punto de ella no arrojen toda la claridad apetecida.

En fe de lo cual firman esta acta en París, á quince de Febrero de mil ochocientos ochenta y seis [1].

Sentence arbitrale de la Reine Régente d'Epagne, en cause de la Colombie et du Venezuela, prononcée le 16 mars 1891.

Don Alfonso XIII por lo gracia de Dios y la Constitución Rey de España y en su nombre y durante su menor edad Doña María Cristina Reina Regente del Reino;

Por cuanto: hallándose sometida á Mi Gobierno la cuestión de límites pendiente entre la República de Colombia y los Estados Unidos de Venezuela, en virtud y al tenor de lo dispuesto en el Tratado de Caracas de 14 de Septiembre de 1881 y del Acta-declaración de París de 15 de Febrero de 1886;

Inspirada en los deseos de corresponder á la confianza que por igual han otorgado á la antigua Madre Patria las dos citadas Repúblicas, sometiendo á su decisión asunto de tanta importancia, y que en ocasiones ha comprometido los fraternales vínculos que las unen;

Resultando que al efecto y por Real decreto de 19 de Noviembre de 1883 se nombró una Comisión técnica encargada de estudiar detenidamente el litigio y proponer las conclusiones que estimará procedentes;

Resultando que las Altas Partes interesadas presentaron á su debido tiempo los alegatos en apoyo de sus respectivos derechos, y la Comisión, en cumplimiento de las instrucciones que le fueron comunicadas, procedió al detenido exámen de dichos alegatos y de los documentos que obran en los Archivos nacionales y extranjeros referentes á este asunto;

Resultando que por Convenio de las Altas Partes interesadas, el laudo ha de fijar los límites que separaban el año de 1810 la antigua Capi-

[1] *Anales diplomaticos y consulares de Colombia*, Tomo I, p. 94—97.

tanía general de Venezuela, hoy Estados Unidos del mismo nombre, del Virreinato de Santa Fe, hoy República de Colombia;

Resultando que las atribuciones de derecho concedidas al árbitro por el Tratado de Caracas de 14 de Septiembre de 1881 fueron ampliadas por el Acta-declaración de París de 15 de Febrero de 1886, para poder fijar la línea de frontera « del modo que crea más aproximado á los documentos existentes, cuando respecto de algún punto de ella no arroje toda la claridad apetecida »;

Resultando que los territorios en litigio forman una ancha zona, que partiendo más al norte de los 12° de latitud en la Peninsula de Goajira, llega poco más de un grado distante del Ecuador á la Piedra del Cocuy, y puede para los efectos de la demarcación considerarse dividida en seis secciones, á saber: 1ª, La Goajira; 2ª, línea de las Sierras de Perijaá y de Montilones; 3ª, San Faustino; 4ª, línea de la Serranía de Tamá; 5ª, línea del Sarare, Arauca y Meta; y, 6ª, línea del Orinoco y Río Negro;

Considerando que en lo referente á las secciones 1ª y 3ª la Real Cédula de 8 de Septiembre de 1777, la Real Orden de 13 de Agosto de 1790, y las Actas de entrega y demarcación de Sinamaica en 1792, por lo que respecta á la Goajira, y la Real Cédula de 13 de Junio de 1786, la Real Orden de 29 de Julio de 1795 y la ley general 1ª, título 1°, libro V, de la Recopilación de Indias, en lo relativo á San Faustino, fijan de una manera clara y precisa los límites que ha de determinar el árbitro, ateniendose á las facultades *juris* que le asignó el Tratado de Caracas de 1881;

Considerando que en lo referente á las secciones 2ª y 4ª las Altas Partes interesadas han decidido de común acuerdo la frontera en litigio, y es por lo tanto innecesaria la intervención del árbitro;

Considerando que la Real Cédula de creación de la Comandancia de Barinas de 15 de Febrero de 1786, que ha de servir de base legal para la determinación de la línea de frontera de la 5ª sección, suscita dudas por citarse lugares desconocidos al presente, á saber: *las Barrancas del Sarare y el Paso Real de los Casanares;*

Considerando que por esta razón el árbitro se encuentra en uno de los casos previstos en el Acta-declaración de París de 1886, según la cual ha de fijar la línea de frontera dal modo que estime más aproximado á los documentos existentes;

Considerando que si bien, como queda dicho, se ignora el emplazamiento preciso de los Barrancas del Sarare, por deducciones, y principalmente por lo que en su alegato exponen los Estados Unidos de Venezuela, pueden fijarse

para los effectos del laudo en la « comunicación del Sarare con el Arauca »;

Considerando que el curso del río Arauca traza un límite natural, pero que es preciso desviarse de él en un punto del mismo para vi á buscar el Antiguo Apostadero en el río Meta, por expresa indicación de la mencionada Real Cédula de 1786;

Considerando que procede fijar el punto de esta desviación en aquél que por estar próximamente á cuatro jornadas de ciudad de Barinas y de las referidas Barrancas, como requiere de un modo expreso la mencionada Real Cédula de 1785, debe suponerse, con fundamento, que es el lugar donde en otros tiempos estuvo situado el *Paso Real de los Casanares;*

Considerando que el punto que reúne la expresada condición es el del río Arauca, que se halla equidistante de la villa del mismo nombre y de aquél en que el meridiano de la confluencia del Masparro y del Apure intersecta también el mismo río Arauca;

Considerando que para mayor claridad puede subdividirse la sección 6ª en dos trozos, á saber: del Meta à Maipures y de Maipures à la Piedra del Cocuy;

Considerando que respecto al primero de los trozos citados, la Real Cédula de nombramiento de D. Carlos Sucre y Pardo, Gobernador de Cumaná; la carta oficio del mismo de 30 de Abril de 1735; la Representación á S. M. de D. Gregorio Espinosa de los Monteros, Gobernador también de dicha provincia, de fecha 30 de Septiembre de 1743; los mapas, estados de población y correspondencia oficial del Comandante de las Nuevas Poblaciones, D. Manuel Centurión; el informe del P. Manuel Román, superior de las misiones de yesuitas del Orinoco, de fecha 3 de Diciembre de 1749; el señalamiento del territorio de la Tenencia de la Guayana en 1761, por D. José Digujá y Villagómez, Gobernador asimismo de Cumaná; la carta oficio de éste de 10 Julio de 1761; el proyecto de informe sobre demarcación de la Guayana en 1760, por D. Eugenio Alvarado, segundo Comisario de la expedición de Iturriaga; el informe de D. José Solano, Gobernador de Caracas, de 11 de Mayo de 1762; los mapas ó planos geográficos del Virreinato de Santa Fé, por D. José Antonio Perelló, D. Luis Surville, D. Antonio de la Torre, y el de D. Francisco Requena del año 1796, y los modernos de Codazzi y Ponce de León, y por último, el expediente instruído con motivo del viaje que D. Antonio de la Torre hizo en los años de 1782 á 1783 de orden y por comisión del Illmo. Arzobispo Virrey de Santa Fé, fijan de una manera clara la línea de frontera dentro de las facultades *juris;*

Considerando que el punto de partida y la base legal para la determinación de la línea de frontera en el segundo trozo de la 6ª sección es la Real Cédula de 5 de Mayo de 1768, sobre cuyo sentido hay disparidad de pareceres entre las dos Altas Partes interesadas;

Considerando que los términos de la mencionada Real Cédula no son tan claros ni precisos como requiere esta clase de documentos, para poder fundar exclusivamente en ellos una decisión *juris*;

Considerando, por tanto, que el árbitro está en el caso previsto en el Acta-declaración de París, ya citada;

Considerando que los Estados Unidos de Venezuela poseen de buena fe territorios al occidente del Orinoco, Casiquiare y Río Negro, ríos que forman los límites asignados por este lado en la mencionada Real Cédula de 1768 á la provincia de la Guayana;

Considerando que en dichos territorios existen cuantiosos intereses venezolanos, fomentados en la leal creencia de hallarse establecidos en los dominios de los Estados Unidos de Venezuela;

Y considerando, por último, que los ríos Atabapo y Negro trazan una frontera natural, clara y precisa con la sola interrupción de algunos kilómetros de Yávita á Pimichin, respetándose así los términos respectivos de estos dos pueblos;

De acuerdo con mi Consejo de Ministros, y oído el parecer del Consejo de Estado en pleno;

Vengo en declarar que la línea de frontera en litigio entre la República de Colombia y los Estados Unidos de Venezuela queda determinada en la forma siguiente:

Seccion 1ª. — Desde los Mogotes llamados los Frailes, tomando por punto de partida el más inmediato á Juyachi en derechura á la línea que divide el valle de Upar de la provincia de Maracaibo y Río de la Hacha, por el lado de arriba de los montes de Oca, debiendo servir de precisos linderos los términos de los referidos montes, por el lado del valle de Upar y el Mogote de Juyachi, por el lado de la Serranía y orillas de la mar.

Seccion 2ª. — Desde la línea que separa el valle de Upar de la Provincia de Maracaibo y Río de la Hacha, por las cumbres de las Sierras de Perijáa y de Motilones, hasta el nacimiento de río Oro, y desde este punto à la boca del Grita en el Zulia: por el trayecto del *statu quo* que atraviesa los ríos Catatumbo, Sardinata y Tarra.

Seccion 3ª. — Desde la embocadura del río de la Grita en el Zulia, por la curva reconocida actualmente como fronteriza, hasta la quebrada de Don Pedro, y por ésta bajando hasta el río Táchira.

Seccion 4ª. — Desde la quebrada de Don Pedro, en el río Táchira, aguas arriba de este río hasta su origen, y de aquí por la Serranía y Páramo de Tamá, hasta el curso del río Oirá.

Seccion 5ª. — Por el curso del río Oirá hasta su confluencia con el Sarare por las aguas de éste atravesando por mitad la laguna del Desparramadero hasta el lugar en que entran en el río Arauca, aguas abajo de éste hasta el punto equidistante de la villa de Arauca y de aquel en que el meridiano de la confluencia del Masparro y del Apure intersecta también el río Arauca, desde éste punto en línea recta al Apostadero del Meta, y por las aguas de éste río hasta su desembocadura en el Orinoco.

Seccion 6ª, Trozo 1º. — Desde la desembocadura del río Meta en el Orinoco por la vaguada de éste río hasta el raudal del Maipures. Pero teniendo en cuenta que desde los tiempos de su fundación el pueblo de Atures se sirve de un camino situado en la orilla izquierda del Orinoco, para salvar los raudales desde frente al citado pueblo de Atures hasta el embarcadero sito al mediodía de Maipures, frente al cerro de Macuriana y en dirección al norte de la boca del Vichada, queda expresamente consignada en favor de los Estados Unidos de Venezuela la servidumbre de paso por el mencionado camino, entendiéndose que dicha servidumbre cesará á los veinticinco años de publicado el presente laudo, ó cuando se construya un camino por territorio venezolano, que haga innecesario el paso por el de Colombia, reservando entre tanto á las Partes la facultad de reglamentar de común acuerdo el ejercicio de esta servidumbre.

Trozo 2º. — Desde el raudal de Maipures por la vaguada del Orinoco hasta su confluencia con el Guaviare; por el curso de éste hasta la confluencia del Atabapo; por el Atabapo aguas arriba hasta 36 kilómetros al norte del pueblo de Yávita, trazando desde allí una recta que vaya á parar sobre el río Guainia, 36 kilómetros al Occidente del pueblo de Pichimin, y par el cauce del Guainia, que más adelante toma el nombre de Río Negro, hasta la piedra del Cocuy.

Dado en el Real Palacio de Madrid por duplicado á diez y seis de marzo de mil ochocientos noventa y uno[1].

---

[1] F. DE MARTENS, *Nouveau Recueil Général*, 2ª série, t. XXIV, p. 110.

CXXII. Chili, Suède et Norvège.

6 juillet 1895.

Par la convention reproduite, les Gouvernements du Chili et de la Suède et de la Norvège soumirent au tribunal anglo-chilien, constitué par le traité du 26 septembre 1893, deux réclamations d'un import de $ 61,592.12. Les deux demandes furent écartées.

Convencion entre la República de Chile i el Reino de Suecia i Noruega firmada en Santiago, Julio 6, 1895.

Su Majestad el Rei de Suecia i Noruega i S. E. el Presidente de la República de Chile, deseando arreglar amistosamente las reclamaciones presentadas por la Legacion de Su Majestad en Chile, orijinadas por la guerra civil que comenzó el 7 de Enero de 1891 i terminó el 28 de Agosto del mismo año, han convenido en celebrar una Convencion de Arbitraje i con tal objeto han nombrado sus respectivos plenipotenciarios, á saber: Su Majestad el Rei de Suecia i Noruega al señor Jens Martin Bolstad, su Ministro Plenipotenciario en Mision Especial cerca del Gobierno de Chile, i S. E. el Presidente de la República de Chile, al señor don Luis Barros Borgoño, Ministro de Relaciones Esteriores de la República, quienes, despues de haberse exhibido sus Plenos Poderes i de haberlos encontrado en debida forma, han convenido en lo siguiente:

ART. I. — El Tribunal Arbitral creado por la Convencion celebrada entre Chile i Gran Bretaña con fecha 26 de Setiembre de 1893, para solucionar las reclamaciones provenientes de la guerra civil de 1891 será solicitado para resolver, en la forma i de acuerdo con los términos prescritos en los articulos 3°, 4° i 5° de dicha Convencion, todas las reclamaciones acerca de las cuales pudiera afectar al Gobierno de Chile alguna responsabilidad por los actos u operaciones ejecutadas por las fuerzas de mar i tierra de la República durante la guerra civil que comenzó el 7 de Enero de 1891 i terminó el 28 de Agosto del mismo año, i todas aquellas que provenientes de actos posteriores, puedan ser tambien de responsabilidad del Gobierno de Chile de conformidad con las disposiciones del citado articulo 5°.

Las reclamaciones deberán ser patrocinadas por la Legacion de Su Majestad el Rei de Suecia i Noruega i deberán ser presentadas al Tribunal dentro del plazo de setenta i cinco dias, que se contará desde la fecha de la promulgacion del presente Convenio.

ART. 2. — Cada uno de los Gobiernos contratantes sufragará los gastos de sus propias jestiones, i los honorarios de sus respectivos ajentes i defensores.

Todas las espensas que imponga la decision de las reclamaciones por el Tribunal Arbitral serán pagadas entre ambos gobiernos por mitad; pero si hubiere cantidades juzgadas en favor de los reclamantes, se deducirán de éstas las antedichas espensas i gastos comunes en cuanto no excedan del seis por ciento de los valores que haya de pagar el Tesoro de Chile por la totalidad de las reclamaciones aceptadas.

Las sumas que el Tribunal juzgue en favor de los reclamantes, serán entregadas por el Gobierno de Chile al Gobierno de Su Majestad el Rei de Suecia i Noruega por intermedio de su Legacion en Santiago o de la persona que Su Majestad designase con este propósito, dentro del plazo de un año a contar desde la fecha de su respectiva resolucion, sin que durante este término devenguen dichas sumas interes alguno en favor de los espresados reclamantes. El Gobierno de Chile deducirá de cualesquiera sumas que pague en satisfaccion de las reclamaciones sometidas al Tribunal, sea que el pago se haga por orden del Tribunal ó en vista de un arreglo privado, las cantidades estipuladas en el inciso segundo de este articulo, debiendo ser retenidas i empleadas dichas cantidades en el pago de las espensas comunes de arbitraje.

ART. 3. — Las Altas Partes Contratantes se obligan a considerar los juzgamientos del Tribunal Arbitral como una terminacion satisfactoria, perfecta é irrevocable, de las dificultades cuyo arreglo se ha tenido en mira i en la intelijencia de que todas las reclamaciones de los súbditos de Suecia i Noruega presentadas u omitidas en las condiciones señaladas en los articulos precedentes, se tendrán por decididas i juzgadas definitivamente i de modo que, por ningun motivo o pretesto puedan ser materia de nuevo examen o discusion.

En fé de lo cual, los infrascritos Plenipotenciarios de Suecia i Noruega i de Chile firman, en doble ejemplar, el presente Convenio i lo sellan con sus sellos respectivos, en Santiago de Chile, a los seis dias del mes de Julio del año 1895 [1].

CXXIII. Grande-Bretagne, Nicaragua.

1 novembre 1895.

Il s'est agi dans cette affaire d'indemnités réclamées par des citoyens anglais victimes d'une émeute survenue dans la réserve des Mosquitos. Il nous a été impossible de savoir quelle suite a été donnée à cet arbitrage.

---

[1] *Memoria del Ministro de Relaciones esteriores*, 1895, p. XLV.

Convention between Great Britain and Nicaragua for the settlement of claims arising out of the disturbances in the Mosquito reserve, concluded at London, November 1, 1895.

Her Majesty the Queen of the United Kingdom of Great Britain and Ireland, Empress of India, and His Excellency the President of the Republic of Nicaragua, desiring to adjust amicably the claims of certain British subjects in respect of injury caused to them or their property or goods in the Mosquito Reserve, owing to the action of the Nicaraguan authorities in the course of the year 1894, have agreed to conclude a Convention for the settlement of such claims, and have for that purpose named as their respective Plenipotentiaries :

Her Majesty the Queen of the United Kingdom of Great Britain and Ireland, Empress of India, the Most Honourable Robert Arthur Talbot Gascoyne Cecil, Marquess of Salisbury, Earl of Salisbury, Viscount Granborne, Peer of the United Kingdom, Knight of the Most Noble Order of the Garter, Member of Her Majesty's Most Honourable Privy Council, Her Majesty's Principal Secretary of State for foreign Affairs, etc., etc. ;

And His Excellency the President of the Republic of Nicaragua, Señor Don Crisanto Medina, Commander of the Legion of Honour, Envoy Extraordinary and Minister Plenipotentiary of the Republic of Salvador in charge of the Legation of the Republic of Nicaragua at the United Kingdom, etc., etc.

Who have agreed upon the following Articles:

ART. 1. — A mixed Commission shall be constitued to · fix the amount due to British subjects in respect of injury caused to them or their property or goods in the Mosquito Reserve owing to the action of the Nicaraguan authorities in the course of the year 1894. It shall be composed of a British Representative (who must be well acquainted with the Spanish language), a Nicaraguan Representative (who must be well acquainted with the English language), and a jurist, not a citizen of any American State. This third person, who shall be President of the Commission, shall be selected by agreement between Her Britannic Majesty's Government and the Government of Nicaragua, and, failing such agreement, the President of the Swiss Confederation shall be requested to name a person.

In case of the death, absence, resignation, or incapacity of either the British or the Nicaraguan Commissioner, or in the event of either of them omitting or ceasing to act, the Government of Her Britannic Majesty or the Government of Nicaragua, as the case may be, shall forthwith proceed to fill the vacancy.

In similar circumstances another third Commissioner shall be appointed in the same manner as hereinbefore provided.

ART. 2. — The Commissioners shall sit in the city of Bluefields at the earliest convenient period after they shall have been respectively appointed, and they shall proceed with and conclude the business of the Commission with the utmost despatch possible.

ART. 3. — The Commission shall admit such methods of proof and inquiry as may, in the judgment of the majority of its members, conduce most effectually to the elucidation of the matters in dispute.

The Commission shall also admit written and verbal statements made by each Government through their Commissioners, or by the several claimants, or their counsel or agent.

ART. 4. — The Commission shall decide the claims according to the evidence tendered, and in accordance with the principles of international law, and the practice and jurisprudence established by such analogous modern Commissions as enjoy the best reputation, and shall give its decisions by majority of votes.

The Commission shall express shortly in each award the facts and origin of the claim dealt with, the arguments alleged for and against it, and the principles on which the decision is based.

The decisions and awards of the Commission shall be in writing, and shall be signed by all the members. The originals, together with the documents belonging to each claim, shall be deposited in the British Consulate at Bluefields, and copies shall be given to the parties at their request.

ART. 5. — The Commissioners shall fix a reasonable time which shall not exceed three months, within which all claims must be submitted to them, and they shall give public notice of the period so fixed.

ART. 6. — The Commission shall, for the final discharge of its duties in regard to all claims submitted to its consideration and decision, be allowed a term of six months from the date on which it shall declare itself validly constitued. When this term shall have expired, the commission shall have power to prolong its existence for a further period, which may not exceed six months, in case the illness or temporary incapacity of any of its members, or any other event of acknowledged gravity may have prevented it from fulfilling the duties intrusted to it within the term fixed under the first paragraph of this Article.

ART. 7. — The decisions of the Commission shall be final, and the amounts awarded shall in every case be paid by the Government of Nicaragua to Her Britannic Majesty's Government, through such person as may be designated for the purpose by Her Majesty, within three months of the conclusion of the labours of the Commission.

ART. 8. — The Commissioners may, if necessary, appoint and employ a Clerk to assist them in the transaction of their business.

The salary of the British and Nicaraguan Commissioners shall be paid by their respective Governments and shall commence only from the date of their labours.

Any salary or gratuity, paid to the third Commissioner and to the Clerk, and any contingent expenses shall be defrayed in moieties by the two Governments.

The above-mentioned expenses and costs shall be deducted proportionately from any sums of money awarded to the claimants, in so far as they shall not exceed 6 per cent of the total amounts respectively to be paid by the Nicaraguan Treasury on account of such claims as may be admitted.

The amount so deducted shall be applied, firstly, towards payment of the common expenses; and, secondly, towards defraying, in equal parts, the salaries of the British and Nicaraguan Commissioners.

The Government of Nicaragua will deduct from any sums paid directly by them in satisfaction of claims, without the intervention of the Commission, the sums stipulated in the fourth paragraph of this Article such amounts to be similarly applied towards payment of the expenses of the Commission.

ART. 9. — The present Convention shall be ratified, and the ratifications shall be exchanged at London as soon as may be within three months from the date hereof.

In witness whereof the Undersigned have signed the present Convention and have affixed thereto their seals.

Done at London, this first day of November, 1895 [1].

CXXIV. Brésil, Italie.

3 décembre 1895.

Des réclamations de nature diverse et d'une valeur considérable avaient été formulées par le gouvernement italien, au nom

---

[1] HERTSLET. *A complete collection* ..., t. XX, p. 818.

---

de citoyens émigrés au Brésil. Ces réclamations furent soumises à une double juridiction arbitrale, l'une instituée par la convention ici reproduite, l'autre par une convention du 12 février 1896, à laquelle nous consacrerons un paragraphe spécial.

Protocollo fatto nella città del Rio de Janeiro, 3 Dicembre 1895, per la soluzione definitiva a tutt' i reclami italiani.

I sottoscritti, Ministro di Stato per le Relazioni Estere della Repubblica degli Stati Uniti del Brasile, e Inviato Straordinario e Ministro Plenipotenziario di Sua Maestà il Re d' Italia, allo scopo di dare una soluzione definitiva a tutt'i reclami Italiani e di stringere vie più i legami di amicizia felicemente esistenti fra i due paesi, hanno stipulato quanto segue.

Tutt'i reclami predetti saranno deferiti al Giudizio arbitrale del Presidente degli Stati Uniti di America, senza limitazione alcuna al suo mandato. Si non fosse da Lui accettato, i due Governi s'intenderanno per la scelta di un altro Arbitro.

I sottoscritti firmano il presente Protocollo con la riserva, l'uno dell' approvazione del suo Governo e l'altro di quella del Congresso Nazionale.

Fatto in doppio originale nella città del Rio de Janeiro addi tre del mese de Dicembre dell'anno mille ottocento novanta cinque [1].

Le 12 février 1896 cette convention un peu sommaire fut complétée par un acte plus détaillé.

Protocollo firmato nella città di Rio de Janeiro el 12 Febbraio 1896 concernente i reclami italiani.

I sottoscritti, Dottor Carlo Augusto de Carvalho, Ministro di Stato per le Relazioni Esteriori della Repubblica degli Stati Uniti del Brasile, e conte Roberto Magliano di Villar San Marco, Inviato Straordinario e Ministro Plenipotenziario di Sua Maestà il Re d' Italia, — debitamente autorizzati dai loro rispettivi Governi: animati del desiderio di semplificare ed affrettare una definitiva amichevole soluzione di ogni difficoltà concernente i reclami Italiani tuttora pendenti, e preso in considerazione il Protocollo firmato il giorno tre del mese di Dicembre del 1895 tra il predetto Ministro delle Relazioni Esteriori del Brasile e il precedente Titolare di questa Real Le-

---

[1] *Relatorio do Ministerio das Relaçôes exteriores*, 1896, Annexo I, p. 150.

gazione d'Italia, sono addivenuti alle seguenti stipulazioni:

1ª I reclami che, previo esame *ex æquo et bono*, siano già stati o possono essere riconosciuti come sufficientemente fondati dal Governo del Brasile, in via di amichevole transazione, saranno senz'altro soddisfatti mediante il pagamento delle indennità da concordarsi.

2ª Per la soluzione di tutti i reclami che, entro il termine di due mesi dalla data d'oggi, non saranno stati, di mutuo accordo, soddisfatti od altrimenti eliminati, i due Governi, appena scaduto tale termine e tosto che il presente accordo sarà stato approvato dal Congresso Nazionale del Brasile e dal Governo Italiano, rivolgeranno a Sua Eccellenza il Presidente della Repubblica degli Stati Uniti d'America la preghiera di voler assumere l'ufficio di Giudice Arbitro.

A ciascuno dei due Governi è però riservata la facoltà di dare immediatamente preventiva ufficiosa comunicazione del presente Protocollo alla Segretaria di Stato in Washington.

3ª Il Governo Italiano, entro sei mesi dal giorno in cui il Presidente degli Stati Uniti d'America avrà dichiarato di accettare l'alto mandato, comunicherà al Segretario di Stato in Washington la lista dei reclami deferiti al Giudizio arbitrale, unitamente ai documenti ed alle osservazioni prodotte in loro appoggio, facendo in pari tempo eguale comunicazione al Governo Brasiliano, il quale a partire dalla data di siffatta comunicazione avrà sei mesi di tempo per presentare all'arbitro le sue contra osservazioni nonchè i documenti relativi alla difesa delle proprie ragioni. Eguale comunicazione verrà fatta in pari tempo dal Governo del Brasile a quello d'Italia.

Nella lista dei reclami deferiti al Giudizio arbitrale potranno essere inclusi tutti quelli che il Governo Italiano crederà di appoggiare, purchè siano stati originati da fatti anteriori alla data del presente Protocollo.

4ª L'arbitro darà il suo giudizio nel tempo e nel modo che stimerà convenienti, anche con facoltà di giudicare *ex æquo et bono*, da nessuna limitazione dovendosi intendere vincolato il mandato che gli è conferito; e le sue decisioni saranno dalle Alte Parti Contraenti considerate come una soluzione soddisfacente, perfetta ed irrevocabile di tutti i reclami contemplati nella precedente stipulazione, di guisa chè per niun motivo possano i medesimi essere argomenti di nuove discussioni.

5ª Riguardo ai reclami che venissero ulteriormente elevati, per fatti posteriori alla data d'oggi, si osserverà la norma: che, in materia di reclami o lagnanze d'individui privati, riferentisi all'ordine penale, civile ed amministrativo, gli Agenti diplomatici o consolari devono astenersi dall'intervenire, eccettuati soltanto i casi in cui, dopo che per parte degl'interessati siano stati esauriti i mezzi legali, venga a risultare che si tratti di denegata giustizia o di ritardo straordinario od illegale nel fare giustizia o di altra qualsiasi violazione dei principii del Diritto internazionale generalmente riconosciuti dalle Nazioni civili.

Ai detti agenti rimane però sempre conservato, senz'alcuna restrizione, il diritto dell'amichevole intervento ufficioso inteso a prevenire o spianare difficoltà e dissidii.

6ª Il presente Protocollo avrà da essere approvato dal Congresso Nazionale del Brasile e dal Governo d'Italia, rimanendo impegnati i sottoscritti a sollecitare tale approvazione nel più breve tempo possibile.

Fatto e firmato in doppio originale esteso in lingue portoghese e italiana, nella città di Rio de Janeiro, il giorno dodici del mese di Febbraio dell'anno mila ottocento novanta sei[1].

La convention du 12 février 1896 ne fut pas approuvée par le Congrès national des Etats-Unis du Brésil et une nouvelle convention transactionnelle fut conclue entre les gouvernements intéressés et acceptée par le parlement brésilien sous la date du 19 novembre 1896.

Accordo firmato nella città di Rio de Janeiro, 19 Novembre 1896, per liquidare finalmente tutt'i reclami italiani.

I Governi del Brasile e d'Italia, riconoscendo la difficoltà d'intendersi sul merito di alcuni dei Reclami Italiani che, sembrando all'una delle Parti ingiusti e all'altra giusti, furono l'oggetto di discussione, convengono che sieno liquidati mediante un solo atto, che non importi l'abbandono per Essi dei principii sostenuti; e a questo effetto il Ministro di Stato delle Relazioni Estere della Repubblica degli Stati Uniti del Brasile e l'Inviato Straordinario e Ministro Plenipotenziario di Sua Maestà il Re d'Italia, sottoscritti, debitamente autorizzati dei loro Governi, hanno stipulato quanto segue:

1º Il Ministro di Stato per le Relazioni Estere della Repubblica degli Stati Uniti del Brasile verserà non appena il presente Accordo sarà approvato dal Congresso Nazionale, al Rappresentante del Reale Governo d'Italia, la somma di quattromila contos di rèis, moneta corrente.

---

[1] *Relatorio do Ministerio* . . ., 1896, p. 156.

2° Col pagamento della predetta somma il Governo Brasiliano sarà liberato da ogni intervento del Governo Italiano pei reclami presentati sino alla data del presente Accordo dalla Regia Legazione d'Italia nel Brasile al Ministro Federale delle Relazioni Estere, ed ai quali non fu data, o pei quali non fu stipulata sinora un' altra soluzione; di modo che per nessuna causa o razione quei reclami potranno mai più essere ripresentati o sostenuti.

3° Il Governo Italiano, rimanendo solo ed esclusivo Giudice della validità dei reclami, avrà piena ed illimitata facoltà di distribuire la predetta somma per proprio conto ed a suo beneplacito senza che il Governo Brasiliano entri nello esame del modo della distribuzione, ni dei reclami che saranno o non saranno ammessi ad indennità.

4° In caso qualche reclamante rifiutasse la indennità che gli sarà attribuita dal Governo Italiano, la somma rifiutata sarà restituita al Tesoro della Repubblica e il reclamante conservarà il suo diritto di ricorrere ai Tribunali Brasiliani competenti, senza, bene inteso, qualsiasi ulteriore intervento del Governo Italiano.

5° Il Governo di Sua Maestà il Re d'Italia ha già data la sua approvazione al presente Accordo e il Governo della Repubblica lo sottometterà alla approvazione al Congresso Nazionale entro l'attuale sessione.

Fatto e firmato in doppio originale esteso in lingue portoghese e italiana nella città Rio de Janeiro il giorno deciannove del mese di novembre mila ottocento novanta sei[1].

CXXV. Etats-Unis d'Amérique, Grande-Bretagne.

8 février 1896.

Cette contestation a eu pour but de fixer les indemnités dues à des citoyens britanniques, du chef des arrestations de navires armés pour la pêche des phoques à fourrures. Le présent arbitrage est une suite de celui qui a été conclu entre les deux gouvernements sous la date du 29 février 1892.

Convention for the settlement of claims, presented by Great Britain against the United States in virtue of the Convention of February 29, 1892, concluded at Washington, February 8, 1896.

Whereas by a Treaty between the United States of America and Her Majesty the Queen of the United Kingdom of Great Britain and Ireland, signed at Washington on February 29,

[1] *Relatorio do Ministerio...* 1897, Annexo III, p. 44.

1892, the questions which had arisen between their respective Governments concerning the jurisdictional rights of the United States in the waters of Behring Sea, and concerning also the preservation of the fur-seal in, or habitually resorting to the said Sea, and the rights of the citizens and subjects of either country as regards the taking of fur-seal in, or habitually resorting to the said waters, were submitted to a Tribunal of Arbitration as therein constituted;

And whereas the High Contracting Parties having found themselves unable to agree upon a reference which should include the question of the liability of each for the injuries alleged to have been sustained by the other, or by its citizens, in connection with the claims presented and urged by it, did, by Article VIII of the said Treaty, agree that either party might submit to the Arbitrators any questions of fact involved in said claims and ask for a finding thereon, the question of the liability of either Government on the facts found to be the subject of further negotiations;

And whereas the Agent of Great Britain did in accordance with the provisions of said Article VIII, submit to the Tribunal of Arbitration certain findings of fact which were agreed to as proved by the Agent of the United States, and the Arbitrators did unanimously find the facts so set forth to be true, as appears by the Award of the Tribunal rendered on the 15th day of August 1893;

And whereas in view of the said findings of fact and of the decision of the Tribunal of Arbitration concerning the jurisdictional rights of the United States in Behring Sea and the right of protection or property of the United States in the fur-seals frequenting the islands of the United States in Behring Sea, the Government of the United States is desirous that in so far as its liability is not already fixed and determined by the findings of fact and the decision of said Tribunal of Arbitration, the question of such liability should be definitively and fully settled and determined, and compensation made, for any injuries for which, in the contemplation of the Treaty aforesaid, and the award and findings of the Tribunal of Arbitration, compensation may be due to Great Britain from the United States;

And whereas it is claimed by Great Britain, though not admitted by the United States, that prior to the said award certain other claims against the United States accrued in favor of Great Britain on account of seizures of or interference with the following named British sealing vessels, to wit, the *Wanderer*, the *Winifred*, the *Henrietta* and the *Oscar and Hattie*, and it is for the mutual interest and convenience of both the High Contracting Parties that the liability of the United States, if any, and the amount of compensation to be paid, if any, in respect of such claims and each of them should also be determined under the provisions of this Convention—all claims by Great Britain under article V of the Modus Vivendi of April 18, 1892, for the abstention from fishing of British sealers during the pendency of said arbitration having been definitively waived before the Tribunal of Arbitration ;

The United States of America and Her Majesty the Queen of the United Kingdom of Great Britain and Ireland, to the end of concluding a Convention for that purpose, have appointed as their respective Plenipotentiaries :

The President of the United States, the Honorable Richard Olney, Secretary of State ; and Her Majesty the Queen of the United Kingdom of Great Britain and Ireland, the Right Honorable Sir Julian Pauncefote, G. C. B., G. C. M. G., Her Majesty's Ambassador Extraordinary and Plenipotentiary to the United States ;

Who, after having communicated to each other their respective full powers, which were found in due and proper form, have agreed to and concluded the following Articles :

ARTICLE I. The High Contracting Parties agree that all claims on account of injuries sustained by persons in whose behalf Great Britain is entitled to claim compensation from the United States and arising by virtue of the Treaty aforesaid, the award and the findings of the said Tribunal of Arbitration, as also the additional claims specified in the 5th paragraph of the preamble hereto, shall be referred to two Commissioners, one of whom shall be appointed by the President of the United States, and the other by Her Britannic Majesty, and each of whom shall be learned in the law. Appended to this Convention is a list of the claims intended to be referred.

ARTICLE II. The two Commissioners shall meet at Victoria, in the Province of British Columbia, Canada, as soon as practicable after the exchange of the ratifications of this Convention, and after taking an oath that they will fairly and impartially investigate the claims referred to them and render a just decision thereon, they shall proceed jointly to the discharge of their duties.

The Commission shall also sit at San Francisco, California, as well as Victoria, provided either Commissioner shall so request if he shall be of opinion that the interests of justice shall so require, for reasons to be recorded on the minutes.

ARTICLE III. The said Commissioners shall determine the liability of the United States, if any, in respect of each claim and assess the amount of compensation, if any, to be paid on account thereof—so far as they shall be able to agree thereon—and their decision shall be accepted by the two Governments as final.

They shall be authorized to hear and examine, on oath or affirmation which each of said Commissioners is hereby empowered to administer or receive, all suitable authentic testimony concerning the same ; and the Government of the United States shall have the right to raise the question of its liability before the Commissioners in any case where it shall be proved that the vessel was wholly or in part the actual property of a citizen of the United States.

The said Commission, when sitting at San Francisco or Victoria, shall have and exercise all such powers for the procurement or enforcement of testimony as may hereafter be provided by appropriate legislation.

ARTICLE IV. The Commissioners may appoint a secretary and a clerk or clerks to assist them in the transaction of the business of the Commission.

ARTICLE V. In the cases, if any, in which the Commissioners shall fail to agree they shall transmit to each Government a joint report stating in detail the points on which they differ, and the grounds on which their opinions have been formed ; and any such difference shall be referred for final adjustment to an Umpire to be appointed by the two Governments jointly, or in case of disagreement, to be nominated by the President of the Swiss Confederation at the request of the two Governments.

ARTICLE VI. In case of the death, or incapacity to serve, from sickness or any other cause, of either of the two Commissioners, or of the Umpire, if any, his place shall be filled in the manner herein provided for the original appointment.

ARTICLE VII. Each Government shall provide for the remuneration of the Commissioner appointed by it.

The remuneration of the Umpire, if one should be appointed, and all contingent and incidental expenses of the Commission, or of the Umpire, shall be defrayed by the two Governments in equal moieties.

ARTICLE VIII. The amount awarded to Great Britain under this Convention on account of any claimant shall be paid by the Government of the United States to the Government of Her Britannic Majesty within six months after

66

the amount thereof shall have been finally ascertained.

ARTICLE IX. The present Convention shall be duly ratified by the President of the United States of America, by and with the advice and consent of the Senate thereof, and by Her Britannic Majesty; and the ratifications shall be exchanged either at Washington or at London within six months from the date thereof, or earlier, if possible.

In faith whereof, we, the respective Plenipotentiaries, have signed this Convention and have hereunto affixed our seals.

Done in duplicate at Washington, the eight day of February, 1896 [1].

Award of the Behring Sea Damage Commission, given at Victoria, December 17, 1897.

Whereas by a convention between the United States of America and Great Britain, signed at Washington on February 8, 1896, it was, among other matters, agreed and concluded that all claims on account of injuries sustained by persons in whose behalf Great Britain is entitled to claim compensation from the United States, and arising by virtue of a certain treaty between the United States and Great Britain, signed at Washington on February 29, 1892, the award and the findings of the tribunal of arbitration constituted thereunder, as also certain additional claims specified in the preamble of the convention first above mentioned should be referred to two commissioners, one of whom should be appointed by the President of the United States and the other by Her Britannic Majesty, and each of whom should be learned in the law, and it was further agreed and concluded in the convention first herein named, that said commissioners should determine the liability of the United States, if any, in respect of each claim, and assess the amount of compensation, if any, to be paid on account thereof;

And whereas the President of the United States of America appointed the Honorable William L. Putnam, a judge of the circuit court of the United States for the first circuit, one of said commissioners, and Her Britannic Majesty appointed the Honorable George Edwin King, a justice of the supreme court of Canada, the other of said commissioners; and we, the said commissioners, having met at Victoria, in the province of British Columbia, Canada, on the twenty-third day of November, A. D. 1896, and our respective powers having been found to be

duly authenticated, and each of us having duly taken the oath prescribed by the convention, proceeded jointly to the discharge of our duties thereunder; and having heard and examined on oath or affirmation every question of fact not found by the tribunal of arbitration under the treaty between the United States of America and Her Britannic Majesty, signed at Washington on the 29th of February 1892, and having received all suitable authentic testimony concerning the same, and being attended by counsel on behalf of the United States and by counsel on behalf of Great Britain, who were duly heard before us, and having impartially and carefully examined the questions submitted to us:

Now therefore we, the said commissioners, do hereby determine, adjudge, and award as follows:

The rate of interest awarded by us is six per cent per annum, being the statutory rate at Victoria, British Columbia, during the period covered, but being less than the current rate thereat.

As to the claim in respect of the vessel *Carolina*, it is determined that the United States are liable to Great Britain in respect thereof, and we assess the amount of compensation to be paid on account thereof to Great Britain on behalf of the owner, master, officers, and crew of the vessel, as follows: Thirteen thousand three hundred and forty-one dollars and seventy-two cents ($ 13,341. 72), with interest from September 10, 1886, until this day, amounting to nine thousand and twenty dollars and seventy-one cents ($ 9,020. 71), and making a total of principal and interest of twenty-two thousand three hundred and sixty-two dollars and forty-three cents ($ 22,362. 43).

As to the claim in respect of the vessel *Thornton*, it is adjudged and determined that the United States of America are liable to Great Britain in respect thereof, and we assess and award the amount of compensation to be paid on account thereof to Great Britain on behalf of the owners, master, officers, and crew of the vessel, as follows, that is to say, thirteen thousand five hundred and twenty-one dollars and ten cents ($ 13,521. 10), with interest from September 10, 1886, until this day, amounting to nine thousand one hundred and forty-two dollars and fifty-three cents ($ 9,142. 53), and making a total of principal and interest of twenty-two thousand six hundred and sixty-three dollars and sixty-three cents ($ 22,663. 63).

As to the claim in respect of the vessel *Onward*, it is adjudged and determined that the United States of America are liable to Great Britain in respect thereof, and we assess and

---

[1] HERTSLET. *A complete collection...*, t. XX, p. 935.

award the amount of compensation to be paid on account thereof to Great Britain, on behalf of the owners, master, officers and crew of the vessel (exclusive of the net interest of Alexander McLean, who at the time of the convention was a citizen of the United States and domiciled therein and has so remained), as follows, that is to say, nine thousand three hundred and seventy-six dollars ($ 9,376), with interest from September 10, 1886, until this day, amounting to six thousand three hundred and thirty-nine dollars and seventy-four cents ($ 6,339. 74), and making a total of principal and interest of the sum of fifteen thousand seven hundred and fifteen dollars and seventy-four cents ($ 15,715. 74).

As to the claim in respect of the vessel *Favourite*, it is adjudged and determined that the United States of America are liable to Great Britain in respect thereof, and we assess and award the amount of compensation to be paid on account thereof to Great Britain, on behalf of the owners, master, officers, and crew of the vessel (exclusive of the net interest of said Alexander McLean), as follows, that is to say, three thousand two hundred and two dollars ($ 3,202), with interest from September 10, 1886, until this day, amounting to two thousand one hundred and sixty-five dollars and eight cents ($ 2,165. 08), and making a total of principal and interest of the sum of five thousand three hundred and sixty-seven dollars and eight cents ($ 5,367. 08).

As to the claim in respect of the vessel *W. P. Sayward*, it is adjudged and determined that the United States of America are liable to Great Britain in respect thereof, and we assess and award the amount of compensation to be paid on account thereof to Great Britain, on behalf of the owners, master, officers, and crew of the vessel, as follows, that is to say, twelve thousand five hundred and thirty-seven dollars and fifty cents ($ 12,537. 50), with interest from September 10, 1887, until this day, amounting to seven thousand seven hundred and twenty-five dollars and twenty-two cents ($ 7,725. 22), and making a total of principal and interest of the sum of twenty thousand two hundred and sixty-two dollars and seventy-two cents ($ 20,262. 72).

As to the claim in respect of the vessel *Anna Beck*, it is adjudged and determined that the United States of America are liable to Great Britain in respect thereof, and we assess and award the amount of compensation to be paid on account thereof to Great Britain, on behalf of the owners, master, officers, and crew of the vessel, as follows, that is to say, twenty-one thousand six hundred and ninety-two dollars and fifty cents ($ 21,692. 50), with interest from September 10, 1887, until this day, amounting to

thirteen thousand three hundred and sixty-six dollars and nineteen cents ($ 13,366. 19), making a total of principal and interest of the sum of thirty-nine thousand and fifty-eight dollars and sixty-nine cents ($ 35,058. 69).

As to the claim in respect of the vessel *Alfred Adams*, it is adjudged and determined that the United States of America are liable to Great Britain in respect thereof, and we assess and award the amount of compensation to be paid on account thereof to Great Britain on behalf of the owners, master and officers, and crew of the vessel, exclusive of the net interest of Alexander Frank, who at the time of the convention was a citizen of the United States and domiciled therein, and has so remained, as follows, that is to say, ten thousand one hundred and twenty-four dollars, with interest from September 10, 1887, until this day, amounting to six thousand two hundred and thirty-eight dollars and seven cents ($ 6,238. 07), and making a total of principal and interest of the sum of sixteen thousand three hundred and sixty-two dollars and seven cents ($ 16,362. 07).

As to the claim in respect of the vessel *Grace*, it is adjudged and determined that the United States of America are liable to Great Britain in respect thereof, and we assess and award the amount of compensation to be paid on account thereof to Great Britain, on behalf of the owners, master, officers and crew of the vessel, as follows, that is to say, twenty-six thousand two hundred and thirteen dollars and fifty cents ($ 26,213. 50), with interest from September 10, 1887, until this day, amounting to sixteen thousand one hundred and twenty-five dollars and sixty-seven cents ($ 16,125. 67), and making a total of principal and interest of forty-two thousand three hundred and thirty-nine dollars and seventeen cents ($ 42,339. 17).

As to the claim in respect of the vessel *Dolphin*, it is adjudged and determined that the United States of America are liable to Great Britain in respect thereof, and we assess and award the amount of compensation to be paid on account thereof to Great Britain, on behalf of the owners, master, officers and crew of the vessel, as follows, that is to say, thirty-one thousand four hundred and eighty-four dollars ($ 31,484), with interest from September 10, 1887, until this day, amounting to the sum of nineteen thousand three hundred and ninety-nine dollars and thirty-eight cents ($ 19,399. 38), and making a total of principal and interest of the sum of fifty thousand eight hundred and eighty-three dollars and thirty-eight cents ($ 50,883. 38).

As to the claim in respect of the vessel *Ada*, it is adjudged and determified that the United

States of America are liable to Great Britain in respect thereof, and we assess and award the amount of compensation to be paid on account thereof to Great Britain, on behalf of the owners, master, officers and crew of the vessel, as follows, that is to say, twenty thousand, nine hundred and two dollars and sixty-nine cents ($ 20,902. 69), with interest from September 10, 1887, until this day, amounting to twelve thousand eight hundred and eighty dollars and one cent ($ 12,880. 01), and making a total of principal and interest of the sum of thirty-three thousand seven hundred and eighty-two dollars and seventy cents ($ 33,782. 70).

As to the claim in respect of the vessel *Triumph*, warned or seized August 4, 1887, it is adjudged and determined that the United States of America are liable to Great Britain in respect thereof, and we assess and award the amount of compensation to be paid on account thereof to Great Britain, on behalf of the owners, master, officers, and crew of the vessel, as follows, that is to say, seventeen hundred and fifty dollars ($ 1,750), with interest from September 10, 1888, until this day, amounting to one thousand and seventy-eight dollars and twenty-nine cents ($ 1,078. 29), and making a total of principal and interest of the sum of two thousand eight hundred and twenty-eight dollars and twenty-nine cents ($ 2,828. 29).

As to the claim in respect of the vessel *Juanita*, it is adjudged and determined that the United States of America are liable to Great Britain in respect thereof, and we assess and award the amount of compensation to be paid on account thereof to Great Britain, on behalf of the owners, master, officers, and crew of the vessel, as follows, that is to say, eleven thousand four hundred and ninety-three dollars ($ 11,493), with interest from September 10, 1889, until this day, amounting to five thousand seven hundred and two dollars and forty-four cents ($ 5,702. 44), and making a total of principal and interest of the sum of seventeen thousand one hundred and ninety-five dollars and forty-four cents ($ 17,195. 44).

As to the claim in respect of the vessel *Pathfinder*, seized or warned July 29, 1889, it is adjudged and determined that the United States of America are liable to Great Britain in respect thereof, and we assess and award the amount of compensation to be paid on account thereof to Great Britain, on behalf of the owners, master, officers, and crew of the vessel, as follows, that is to say, thirteen thousand seven hundred and ninety-six dollars ($ 13,796), with interest from September 10, 1889, until this day, amounting to six thousand eight hundred and forty-five

dollars and twelve cents ($ 6,845. 12), and making a total of principal and interest of the sum of twenty thousand six hundred and forty-one dollars and twelve cents ($ 20,641. 12).

As to the claim in respect of the vessel *Triumph*, seized or warned July 11, 1889, it is adjudged and determined that the United States of America are liable to Great Britain in respect thereof, and we assess and award the amount of compensation to be paid on account thereof to Great Britain, on behalf of the owners, master, officers, and crew of the vessel, as follows, that is to say, fifteen thousand four hundred and fifty dollars ($ 15,450) with interest from September 10, 1889, until this day, amounting to seven thousand six hundred and sixty-five dollars and seventy-seven cents ($ 7,665. 77), and making a total of principal and interest of the sum of twenty-three thousand one hundred and fifteen dollars and seventy-seven cents ($ 23,115. 77).

As to the claim in respect of the vessel *Black Diamond*, seized or warned July 11, 1889, it is adjudged and determined that the United States of America are liable to Great Britain in respect thereof, and we assess and award the amount of compensation to be paid on account thereof to Great Britain, on behalf of the owners, master, officers and crew of the vessel, as follows, that is to say, fifteen thousand one hundred and seventy-three dollars ($ 15,173), with interest from September 10, 1889, until this day, amounting to seven thousand five hundred and twenty-eight dollars and thirty-two cents ($ 7,528. 32), and making a total of principal and interest of the sum of twenty-two thousand seven hundred and one dollars and thirty-two cents ($ 22,701. 32).

As to the claim in respect of the vessel *Lily*, it is adjudged and determined that the United States of America are liable to Great Britain in respect thereof, and we assess and award the amount of compensation to be paid on account thereof to Great Britain, on behalf of the owners, master, officers and crew of the vessel, as follows, that is to say, eleven thousand seven hundred and thirty-nine dollars ($ 11,739), with interest from September 10, 1889, until this day, amounting to five thousand eight hundred and thirty-two dollars and forty-eight cents ($ 5,832. 48), and making a total of principal and interest of the sum of seventeen thousand five hundred and seventy-one dollars and forty-eight cents ($ 17,571. 48).

As to the claim in respect of the vessel *Ariel*, it is adjudged and determined that the United States of America are liable to Great Britain in respect thereof, and we assess and award the amount of compensation to be paid on account thereof to Great Britain, on behalf of the owners, master, officers and crew of the vessel, as follows, that is to say, three thousand and fifty dollars ($ 3,050), with interest from September 10, 1889, until this day, amounting to one thousand five hundred and thirteen dollars and thirty-one cents ($ 1,513. 31), and making a total of principal and interest of the sum of four thousand five hundred and sixty-three dollars and thirty-one cents ($ 4,563. 31).

As to the claim in respect of the vessel *Minnie*, it is adjudged and determined that the United States of America are liable to Great Britain in respect thereof, and we assess and award the amount of compensation to be paid on account thereof to Great Britain, on behalf of the owners, master, officers, and crew of the vessel, as follows, that is to say, eighty-four hundred and sixty dollars ($ 8,460), with interest from September 10, 1889, until this day, amounting to four thousand one hundred and ninety-seven dollars and fifty-seven cents ($ 4.197. 57), and making a total of principal and interest of the sum of twelve thousand six hundred and fifty-seven dollars and fifty-seven cents ($ 12,657. 57).

As to the claim in respect of the vessel *Pathfinder*, seized March 27, 1890, it is adjudged and determined that the United States of America are liable to Great Britain in respect thereof, and we assess and award the amount of compensation to be paid on account thereof to Great Britain, on behalf of the owners, master, officers and crew of the vessel, as follows, that is to say, eight hundred dollars ($ 800), with interest from March 27, 1890, until this day, amounting to three hundred and seventy dollars and sixty-seven cents ($ 370. 67), and making a total of principal and interest of the sum of eleven hundred and seventy dollars and sixty-seven cents ($ 1,170. 67).

As to the claim in respect of the vessel *Wanderer*, it is adjudged and determined that there is no liability on the part of the United States of America in respect of such claim.

As to the claim in respect of the vessel *Winnifred*, it is adjudged and determined that the United States of America are liable to Great Britain in respect thereof, and we assess and award the amount of compensation to be paid on account thereof to Great Britain, on behalf of the owners thereof, as follows, that is to say, three thousand two hundred and eighty-three dollars and five cents ($ 3,283. 05), with interest from July 27, 1892, until this day, amounting to one thousand and sixty-one dollars and fifty-two cents ($ 1,061. 52), and making a total of principal and interest of the sum of four thousand three hundred and forty-four dollars and fifty-seven cents ($ 4,344. 57).

As to the claim in respect of the vessel *Henrietta*, it is adjudged and determined that the United States of America are liable to Great Britain in respect thereof, and we assess and award the amount of compensation to be paid on account thereof to Great Britain on behalf of the owners, master, officers, and crew of the vessel, as follows, that is to say, nine thousand five hundred and ninety-nine dollars and eighty-five cents ($ 9,599. 85), with interest on twenty-four hundred and thirty-seven dollars from September 2, 1892, until this day, and upon the balance from February 17, 1894, until this day, making the entire interest two thousand four hundred and twenty-one dollars and nineteen cents ($ 2,421. 19), making a total of principal and interest of the sum of twelve thousand and twenty-one dollars and four cents ($ 12,021. 04).

As to the claim in respect of the vessel *Oscar and Hattie*, it is adjudged and determined that the United States of America are liable to Great Britain in respect thereof, and we assess and award the amount of compensation to be paid on account thereof to Great Britain, on behalf of the owners thereof, as follows, that is to say, two thousand two hundred and fifty dollars ($ 2,250), with interest from August 30, 1892, until this day, amounting to seven hundred and fifteen dollars and five cents ($ 715. 05), and making a total of principal and interest of the sum of two thousand nine hundred and sixty-five dollars and five cents ($ 2,965. 05).

As to the personal claims we adjudge and determine that the United States of America are liable on account of the following persons, and assess and award the amount of compensation to be paid to Great Britain on account of each of them, as follows:

Daniel Monroe, master of the *Onward*, the principal sum of tree thousand dollars ($ 3,000), with interest from September 10, to this day, making a total amount of five thousand and twenty-eight dollars and fifty cents ($ 5,028. 50).

John Margotich, mate of the *Onward*, the principal sum of twenty-five hundred dollars ($ 2,500), with interest from September 10, 1886, to this day, making a total amount of four thousand one hundred and ninety dollars and forty-two cents ($ 4,190. 42).

Hans Guttormsen, master of the *Thornton*, the principal sum of three thousand dollars ($ 3,000), with interest from September 10, 1886, to this day, making a total amount of four thousand one hundred and ninety dollars and forty-two cents ($ 4,190. 42).

Harry Norman, mate of the *Thornton*, the principal sum of twenty-five hundred dollars ($ 2,500), with interest from September 10, 1886, to this day, making a total amount of four thousand one hundred and ninety dollars and forty-two cents ($ 4,190. 42).

James Ogilire, master of the *Carolina*, the principal sum of three thousand dollars,with interest from September 10, 1886, to this day, making a total amount of five thousand and twenty-eight dollars and fifty cents ($ 5,028. 50).

James Blake, mate of the *Carolina*, the principal sum of twenty-five hundred dollars ($ 2,500), with interest from September 10, 1886, to this day, making a total amount of four thousand one hundred and ninety dollars and forty-two cents ($ 4,190. 42).

James D. Warren, master of the *Dolphin*, the principal sum of two thousand dollars ($ 2,000), with interest from September 10, 1887, to this day, making a total amount of three thousand and two hundred and thirty-two dollars and thirty-three cents ($ 3,323. 33).

John Reilly, mate of the *Dolphin*, the principal sum of fifteen hundred dollars ($ 1,500), with interest from September 10, 1887, to this day, making a total amount of two thousand four hundred and twenty-four dollars and twenty-five cents ($ 2,424. 25).

George P. Fesey, master of the *W. P. Sayward*, the principal sum of two thousand dollars($ 2,000), with interest from September 10, 1887, to this day, making a total amount of three thousand two hundred and thirty-two dollars and thirty-three cents ($ 3,232. 33).

A. B. Laing, mate of the *W. P. Sayward*, the principal sum of fifteen hundred dollars ($ 1,500), with interest from September 10, 1887, to this day, making a total amount of two thousand four hundred and twenty-four dollars and twenty-five cents ($ 2,424. 25).

Louis Olsen, master of the *Anna Beck*, the principal sum of two thousand dollars ($ 2,000), with interest from September 10, 1887, making a total amount of three thousand two hundred and thirty-two dollars and thirty-three cents ($ 3,232. 33).

Michael Keefe, mate of the *Anna Beck*, the principal sum of fifteen hundred dollars ($ 1,500), with interest from September 10, 1887, to this day, making a total amount of two thousand four hundred and twenty-four dollars and twenty-five cents ($ 2,424. 25).

W. Petit, master of the *Grace*, the principal sum of two thousand dollars ($ 2,000), with interest from September 10, 1887, to this day, making a total amount of three thousand two hundred and thirty-two dollars and thirty-three cents ($ 3,232. 33).

C. A. Lundberg, mate of the *Ada*, the principal sum of one thousand dollars ($ 1,000), with interest from September 10, 1887, to this day,

making a total amount of one thousand six hundred and sixteen dollars and seventeen cents (1,616. 17).

As to 'costs in *Sayward* Case', it is adjudged and determined that there is no liability on the part of the United States of America in respect of such claim.

Her Majesty also presented for our consideration the following claims, that is to say in behalf of the *Black Diamond* warned by the collector at Unalaska on July 1, 1886, and also in behalf of James Gaudin, master of the *Ada*, as to each of which we determine and award that we have no jurisdiction, and we dismiss the same.

Made in duplicate and signed by us this seventeenth day of December, A. D. 1897 [1].

L'ensemble des indemnités mises à charge du Gouvernement des Etats-Unis de l'Amérique du Nord s'est monté à $ 473,151. 26.

CXXVI. Brésil, Italie.

12 février 1896.

L'entente intervenue entre les deux gouvernements a eu surtout pour objet les réquisitions faites par les autorités brésiliennes au cours des opérations contre les troupes fédéralistes ; contrairement à ce qui avait été soutenu par lui, lors de la convention du 3 décembre 1895, le gouvernement brésilien ne nia pas, pour les réquisitions susdites, sa responsabilité ; il ne s'agissait plus dès lors que d'établir l'importance des dommages soufferts.

Protocollo firmato nella città di Rio de Janeiro, 12 Febbraio 1896, per la soluzione dei reclami italiani originati da requisizioni.

I sottoscritti, Ministro di Stato per le Relazioni Esteriori della Repubblica degli Stati Uniti del Brasile e Inviato Straordinario e Ministro Plenipotenziario di Sua Maestà il Re d'Italia, per la soluzione dei reclami italiani originati da requisizioni di animali, viveri ed altri oggetti o valori per le forze del Governo in operazione contro i federalisti, atteso che, essendo riconosciuto in principio l'obbligo a risarcimento, è necessario fissare l'ammontare di ciò che è realmente ed effettivamente dovuto, hanno convenuto quanto segue :

[1] J. B. MOORE. *History and Digest...*, p. 2123.

ART. I. Il Presidente dello Stato di Rio Grande e il Console del Regno d'Italia in Porto Alegre, personalmente o per mezzo di loro rispettivi Delegati, esamineranno e risolveranno *ex æquo et bono* i reclami di tale categoria originati da atti effettuatisi in quello Stato, fissando le corrispondenti indennità e nel caso di disaccordo si remetteranno alla decisione del Console dell'Impero Germanico in quella città, il quale verrà opportunamente invitato ad assumere l'ufficio di arbitro.

ART. II. Nei casi in cui la suddetta commissione mista venga a trovare non sufficientemente comprovata l'origine o la qualità degli autori delle requisizioni od appropriazioni di valori, i reclami saranno rimessi al Rappresentante diplomatico del Regno d'Italia presso il Governo del Brasile, affinchè venga seguito il procedimento adottato nella soluzione degli altri reclami italiani.

ART. III. La liquidazione dei reclami dovrà essere compiuta entro sei mesi dalla data d'oggi, ed il pagamento delle indennità dovrà essere effettuato prima della fine dell'anno in corso.

ART. IV. Riguardo ai reclami per fatti della stessa natura verificatisi nello Stato di Santa Caterina la relativa liquidazione verrà eseguita dal Presidente dello stesso Stato e dal Console del Regno d'Italia in Florianopolis (Desterro) o personalmente o per mezzo di loro rispettivi Delegati, venendo altresì, in caso di disaccordo, assunto come arbitro lo stesso prefato Console dell'Impero Germanico, ed egualmente applicandosi le disposizioni degli articoli II et III.

E per tanto i sottoscritti firmano, apponendovi il proprio sigillo, il presente Protocollo, redatto in doppio esemplare a ciascun originale in lingua portoghese e italiana.

Fatto nella città di Rio de Janeiro addi dodici del mese di Febbraio dell'anno mille ottocento novanta sei [1].

Pour éviter toute confusion entre l'arbitrage ici examiné et celui institué par le protocole du 3 décembre 1895, une déclaration spéciale fut échangée entre les deux gouvernements.

Dichiarazione firmata nella città di Rio de Janeiro, 19 Novembre 1896.

Nell'atto di firmare l'accordo in data d'oggi che risolve le difficoltà esistenti tra i Governi del Brasilio e d'Italia, ad evitare ogni possibile malinteso avvenire, il Ministro di Stato per le

Relazioni Estere della Repubblica degli Stati Uniti del Brasile et l'Inviato Straordinario e Ministro Plenipotenziario di Sua Maestà il Re d'Italia, debitamente autorizzati dai loro Governi, dichiarano quanto segue:

ART. 1. Pei reclami originati da requisizioni di animali, viveri ed altri oggetti o valori per le forze del Governo negli Stati di Rio Grande do Sul e di Santa Caterina, rimane in vigore la soluzione pattuita dal Protocollo delli 12 Febbraio di questo anno, e però questi reclami non vanno inclusi nel numero di quelli che saranno soddisfatti con la somma indicata nel Articolo Primo del predetto accordo.

ART. 2. I casi a cui si riferisce l'Articolo Secondo di quel Protocollo, invece di essere l'oggetto di nuovi negoziati tra i due Governi, saranno senz'altro deferiti al Giudizio Arbitrale del medesimo Console di Germania che è di già instituito Arbitro dal Protocollo, e in tutti i casi pei quali egli giudicherà che danni furono in un qualunque modo cagionati dalle forze del Governo, le indennità saranno fissate *ex bono et æquo* da questo Arbitro medesimo, e alle sue sentenze sarà data piena e completa esecuzione dal Governo Federale, essendo bene inteso che anche queste indennità non sono incluse nella somma pattuita dall'Accordo in data d'oggi.

ART. 3. Essendosi constatato che il termine dell'Articolo terzo del predetto Protocollo fissato per la liquidazione dei reclami non era sufficiente, questo termine è esteso di altri sei mesi dalla data di oggi, ed il pagamento delle indennità dovrà essere dal Governo Federale effettuato prima della fine dell'anno 1897. In caso che una delle commissioni per qualche causa di forza maggiore non potesse aver compiuto i suoi lavori neanche entro il periodo di tempo qui sopra fissato, una nuova dilazione potrà essere stabilita di comune accordo fra i commissarii medesimi, o, questo accordo mancando, dell'Arbitro. Se la causa dispendisse dall'Arbitro, il periodo di tempo che trascorrerà non sarà compiutato. In caso che una interruzione dipendesse da malattia, da partenza o da qualunque altra incapacitazione di uno dei commissarii, il periodo di tempo, che non dovrà superare i tre mesi, neanche sarà compiutato. È infine inteso che alle Alte Parti Contraenti è devoluto il diritto di procedere alla sostituzione di quel Commissario che per una causa qualunque fosse incapacitato di proseguire l'opera sua, ma questa sostituzione dovrà essere compiuta entro tre mesi.

ART. 4. Per la liquidazione delle successioni è confermata la intesa stabilita dalle note del Ministro Federale delle Relazioni Estere e del Ministro d'Italia in data delli 3 Dicembre 1895.

Art. Addizionale. La presente dichiarazione è, per quella parte che concerne l'ampliamento dei poteri dell'Arbitro, subordinata al grazioso consenso di Sua Eccellenza l'Inviato Straordinario e Ministro Plenipotenziario di Sua Maestà l'Imperatore di Germania presso del Governo della Repubblica degli Stati Uniti del Brasile.

Fatto e firmato in doppio originale esteso in lingue portoghese e italiana, nella città di Rio de Janeiro, il giorno diciannove del mese di Novembre mille ottocento novanta sei [1].

Les commissions arbitrales terminèrent leurs travaux vers la fin de 1897 : celle de Porto Alegre statua sur 376 affaires, dont 57 furent écartées, 3 furent renvoyées au surarbitre et 316 donnèrent lieu à l'attribution d'une somme totale de Rs. 750 : 404 $ 620 ; celle de Florianopolis statua sur 63 affaires, dont 26 furent écartées, 2 furent renvoyées au surarbitre et 35 donnèrent lieu à l'attribution d'une somme totale de Rs. 4 : 780 $. Les 5 affaires renvoyées donnèrent lieu à des arrangements transactionnels en date du 18 juin 1898, pour un import total de Rs. 59 : 882 $ 500.

CXXVII. Costa-Rica, Nicaragua.

27 mars 1896.

Cette affaire n'est qu'une suite à celle du 24 décembre 1886. La convention intervenue invite le Président des Etats-Unis de l'Amérique du Nord à désigner un arbitre, Ce dernier rendit cinq sentences sous les dates des 30 septembre et 20 décembre 1897, 22 mars 1898, 26 juillet 1899 et 10 mars 1900.

Convencion entre las Republicas de Costa Rica y Nicaragua para el trazado y amojonamiento de la linea fronteriza, firmada en San Salvador, Marzo 27, 1896.

Habiendo sido aceptada la mediación del Gobierno de El Salvador por los Excelentísimos señores Presidentes de Costa Rica y Nicaragua para arreglar el trazo de la línea divisoria de las dos Repúblicas, han nombrado, respectivamente, Enviados Extraordinarios y Ministros Plenipotenciarios, á sus Excelencias los señores Licenciado don Leonidas Pacheco y don Manuel C. Matus, quienes, después de varias conferencias

tenidas en presencia del señor Ministro de Relaciones Exteriores, Doctor don Jacinto Castellanos, autorizado especialmente para representar al Gobierno de El Salvador, encontrándose en buena et debida forma sus plenos poderes, y con assistencia del Excelentísimo señor Presidente de la República, general don Rafael A. Gutiérrez, quien ha tenido la deferencia de concurrir, para dar mayor solemnidad al acto, han celebrado el siguiente Convenio.

Art. I. — Los Gobiernos Contratantes se obligan á nombrar cada uno una comisión compuesta de dos Ingenieros ó agrimensores, con el objeto de trazar y amojonar debitamente la línea divisoria entre las Repúblicas de Costa Rica y Nicaragua, según lo establece el Tratado de 15 de abril de 1858 y el Laudo arbitral del señor Presidente de los Estados Unidos de Norte América, Mr. Gróver Cléveland.

Art. II. — Las Comisiones que por el artículo anterior se crean, serán integradas por un Ingeniero, cuyo nombramiento será solicitado por ambas Partes del señor Presidente de los Estados Unidos de América, y cuyas funciones se concentran á lo siguiente : cuando en la práctica de las operaciones estuvieren en desacuerdo las Comisiones de Costa Rica y Nicaragua, se someterá el punto ó puntos discutidos al juicio del Ingeniero del señor Presidente de los Estados Unidos de América. El Ingeniero tendrá amplias facultades para decidir cualquier clase de dificultades que surjan, y conforme á su fallo se ejecutarán ineluctablemente las operaciones de que se trate.

Art. III. — Dentro de los tres meses siguientes al canje de la presente Convención, ya debidamente ratificada por los respectivos Congresos, los Representantes en Wáshington, de ambos Gobiernos Contratantes, procederán, de común acuerdo á solicitar del señor Presidente de los Estados Unidos de Norte América que acceda á nombrar el Ingeniero á que antes se hizo referencia y que verifique su elección. Si por falta de Representante en Wáshington de cualquiera de los dos Gobiernos ó por cualquiera otro motivo que sea, dejare de hacerse la solicitud conjuntamente en el plazo enunciado, una vez vencido éste, podrá cualquiera de los Representantes de Costa Rica ó Nicaragua en Wáshington, hacer por separado tal solicitud, la cual surtirá todos sus efectos, como si hubiese sido presentada por ambas Partes.

Art. IV. — Verificado el nombramiento del Ingeniero norteamericano, y dentro de los tres meses siguientes á la fecha de ese nombramiento, se procederá á la demarcación y amojonamiento de la línea fronteriza, lo cual deberá estar ter-

---

[1] *Relatorio do Ministerio...*, 1897, p. 150.

minado dentro de los veinte meses siguientes á la fecha de inauguración de los trabajos. Las Comisiones de las Partes Contratantes se reunirán en San Juan del Norte, dentro de los términos fijados al efecto, é iniciarán sus trabajos en el extremo de la línea divisoria que, según el Tratado y Laudo antes referidos, parte de la costa atlántica.

ART. V. — Las Partes Contratantes convienen en que si, por cualquier motivo, el día de iniciar los trabajos faltare en el lugar designado alguna de las Comisiones de las Repúblicas de Costa Rica ó Nicaragua, se dará principio á los trabajos por la Comisión de la otra República que se halle presente, con la concurrencia del señor Ingeniero del Gobierno norteamericano, y será válido y definitivo lo que en tal forma se haga, y sin lugar á reclamo por parte de la República que haya dejado de enviar sus Comisionados. Del mismo modo se procederá si se ausentaren algunos de los Comisionados, ó todos, de cualquiera de las Repúblicas Contratantes, una vez iniciadas las obras ó si rehuyeren la ejecución de ellas en la forma en que señalan el Laudo y Tratado aquí referidos ó con arreglo á la decisión del Ingeniero del señor Presidente de los Estados Unidos.

ART. VI. — Las Partes Contratantes convienen en que el plazo fijado para la conclusión del amojonamiento no es perentorio, y por tanto será válido lo que después de su vencimiento se hiciere, bien por haber sido aquel plazo insuficiente para la práctica de todas las operaciones, ó bien por haber convenido los Comisionados de Costa Rica y Nicaragua entre sí y de acuerdo con el Ingeniero norteamericano, en suspender temporalmente las obras y no bastar para concluirlas el plazo que quede del fijado.

ART. VII. — Caso de suspensión temporal de los trabajos de amojonamiento, se tendrá lo hecho hasta entonces por definitivo y concluído, y por fijados materialmente los límites en la parte respectiva, aun cuando, por circunstancias inesperadas é insuperables, dicha suspensión continuase indefinidamente.

ART. VIII. — El libro de actas de las operaciones, que se llevará por triplicado y que firmarán y sellarán debitamente los Comisionados, será, sin necesidad de aprobación ni de ninguna otra formalidad por parte de las Repúblicas signatarias, el título de demarcación definitiva de sus límites.

ART. IX. — Las actas á que se refiere el artículo anterior se extenderán en la siguiente forma : se consignará todos los días, al concluir las obras, minuciosa y detalladamente todo lo hecho, expresándose el punto de partida de las operaciones del día, la clase de mojones construídos ó adoptados, la distancia á que queden unos de otros, el arrumbamiento de la línea que determina el común lindero, etc. Caso de que hubiere discusión entre las Comisiones de Costa Rica y Nicaragua respecto de algún punto, se consignará en el acta respectiva la cuestión ó cuestiones debatidas y la resolución del Ingeniero norteamericano. Las actas se llevarán por triplicado : la Comisión de Costa Rica conservará uno de los ejemplares. otro lo de Nicaragua, y el tercero el Ingeniero norteamericano, para depositarlo, una vez concluídas las operaciones, en el Departamento de Estado de Washington.

ART. X. — Los gastos que se ocasionen con motivo del envío y permanencia del señor Ingeniero norteamericano, así como los sueldos que le correspondan durante todo el tiempo que dure en el ejercicio de sus funciones, serán pagados, por mitades, por las dos Repúblicas signatarias.

ART. XI. — Las Partes Contratantes se comprometen á recabar las ratificaciones de esta Convención de sus respectivos Congresos, dentro de seis meses, á contar de esta fecha, aunque para ello deba hacerse convocatoria extraordinaria de aquellos Altos Cuerpos, y el canje subsiguiente se verificará dentro del mes siguiente á la fecha de la última de las ratificaciones indicadas, en San José de Costa Rica ó en Managua.

ART. XII. — El trascurso de los términos de que antes se ha hablado, sin la ejecución de los actos para los cuales han sido estipulados, no produce la caducidad de la presente Convención, y se tratará de llenar la omisión por parte de la República a que corresponda verificarlo, dentro del más breve término posible.

En fe de lo cual firman y sellan por duplicado la presente Convención, en la ciudad de San Salvador, á los veintisiete días del mes de marzo de mil ochocientos noventa y seis [1].

First award rendered, to San Juan del Norte, by the umpire, M. E. P. Alexander, on September 30, 1897, in the boundary question, between Costa Rica and Nicaragua.

San Juan del Norte, Nicaragua,
September 30, 1897.

In pursuance of the duties assigned me by my commission as engineer-arbitrator to your two bodies, with the power to decide finally any points of difference, that may arise in tracing and marking out the boundary line between the two republics, I have given careful study and

---

[1] *Memoria de Relaciones exteriores* (Costa Rica), 1897, p. 28.

consideration to all arguments, counter arguments, maps, and documents submitted to me in the matter of the proper location of the initial point of the said boundary line upon the Caribbean coast.

The conclusion at which I have arrived and the award I am about to make do not accord with the views of either commission. So, in deference to the very excellent and earnest arguments so faithfully and loyally urged by each commission for its respective side, I will indicate briefly my line of thought and the considerations which have seemed to me to be paramount in determining the question: and of these considerations the principal and the controling one is that we are to interpret and give effect to the Treaty of April 15, 1858, in the way in which it was mutually understood at the time by its makers.

Each commission has presented an elaborate and well argued contention that the language of that treaty is consistent with its claims for a location of the initial point of the boundary line at a place which would give to its country great advantages. The points are over six miles apart, and are indicated on the map accompanying this award.

The Costa Rican claim is located on the left-hand shore or west headland of the harbor; the Nicaraguan on east headland of the mouth of the Taura branch.

Without attempting to reply in detail to every argument advanced by either side in support of his respective claim, all will be met and sufficiently answered by showing that those who made the treaty mutually understood and had in view another point, to wit, the eastern headland at the mouth of the harbor.

It is the meaning of the men who framed the treaty wich we are to seek, rather than some possible meaning which can be forced upon isolated words of sentences. And this meaning of the men seems to me abundantly plain and obvious.

This treaty was not made hastily or carelessly. Each State had been wrought up by years of fruitless negotiations to a state of readiness for war in defense of what it considered its rights, as is set forth in article 1. In fact, war had actually been declared by Nicaragua on November 25, 1857, when, through the mediation of the Republic of Salvador, a final effort to avert it was made, another convention was held, and this treaty resulted. Now, we may arrive at the mutual understanding finally reached by its framers by first seeking in the treaty as a whole for the general idea or scheme of compromise upon which they were able to agree. Next, we

must see that this general idea of the treaty as a whole harmonizes fully with any description of the line given in detail, and the proper names of all the localities used, or not used, in connection therewith, for the non use of some names may be as significant as the use of others. Now, from the general consideration of the treaty as a whole, the scheme of compromise stands out clear and simple.

Costa Rica was to have as a boundary line the right or southeast bank of the river, considered as an outlet for commerce, from a point 3 miles below Castillo to the sea.

Nicaragua was to have her prized *sumo imperio* of all the waters of this same outlet for commerce, also unbroken to the sea.

It is to be noted that this division implied also, of course, the ownership by Nicaragua of all islands in the river and of the left or north-west bank and headland.

This division brings the boundary line (supposed it to be traced downward along the right bank from the point near Castillo) across both the Colorado and the Taura branches.

It can not follow either of them, for neither is an outlet for commerce, as neither has a harbor at its mouth.

It must follow the remaining branch, the one called the Lower San Juan, through its harbor and into the sea.

The natural terminus of that line is the right-hand headland of the harbor mouth.

Next let us note the language of description used in the treaty telling whence the line is to start and how it is to run, leaving out for the moment the proper name applied to the initial point. It is to start « at the mouth of the river San Juan de Nicaragua, and shall continue following the right bank of the said river to a point three English miles from Castillo Viejo».

This language is evidently carefully considered and precise, and there is but one starting point possible for such a line, and that is at the right headland of the bay.

Lastly, we come to the proper name applied to the starting point, «the extremity of Punta de Castillo». This name Punta de Castillo does not appear upon a single one of all the original maps of the bay of San Juan which have been presented by either side, and which seem to include all that were ever published before the treaty or since. This is a significant fact, and its meaning is obvious. Punta de Castillo must have been, and must have remained, a point of no importance, political or commercial, otherwise it could not possibly have so utterly escaped note or mention upon the maps. This agrees entirely with the caracteristics of the mainland and the headland on the right of the bay. It remains until to-day obscure and unoccupied, except by the hut of a fisherman. But the identification of the locality is still further put beyond all question by the incidental mention, in another article of the treaty itself, of the name Punta de Castillo.

In Article V Costa Rica agrees temporarily to permit Nicaragua to use Costa Rica's side of the harbor without payment of port dues, and the name Punta de Castillo is plainly applied to it. Thus we have, concurring, the general idea of compromise in the treaty as a whole, the literal description of the line in detail, and the verification of the name applied to the initial point by its incidental mention in another portion of the treaty, and by the concurrent testimony of every map maker of every nation, both before the treaty and since, in excluding this name from all other portions of the harbor. This might seem to be sufficient argument upon the subject, but it will present the whole situation in a still clearer light to give a brief explanation of the local geography and of one special peculiarity of this Bay of San Juan.

The great feature in the local geography of this bay, since our earliest accounts of it, has been the existence of an island in its outlet, called on some early maps the island of San Juan. It was an island of such importance as to have been mentioned in 1820 by two distinguished authors, quoted in the Costa Rican reply to Nicaragua's argument (page 12), and it is an island to-day, and so appears in the map accompanying this award.

The peculiarity of this bay, to be noted, is that the river brings down very little water during the annual dry season. When that happens, particularly of late years, sand bars, dry at all ordinary tides, but submerged more or less and broken over by the waves at all high ones, are formed, frequently reaching the adjacent headlands, so that a man might cross dry-shod.

Now, the whole claim of Costa Rica is based upon the assumption that on April 15, 1858, the date of the treaty, a connection existed between the island and the eastern headland, and that this converted the island into mainland, and carried the initial point of the boundary over to the western extremity of the island. To this claim there are at least two replies, either one seeming to me conclusive.

First, the exact state of the bar on that day can not be definitely proven, which would seem to be necessary before drawing important conclusions.

However, as the date was near the end of the dry season, it is most probable that there was such a connection between the island and the eastern Costa Rican shore as has been described. But even if that be true, it would be unreasonable to suppose that such temporary connection could operate to change permanently the geographical character and political ownership of the island. The same principle, if allowed, would give to Costa Rica every island in the river to which sand bars from her shore had made out during that dry season. But throughout the treaty the river is treated and regarded as an outlet of commerce. This implies that it is to be considered as in average condition of water, in which condition alone it is navigable.

But the overwhelming consideration in the matter is that by the use of the name of Punta de Castillo for the starting point, instead of the name Punta Arenas, the makers of the treaty intended to designate the mainland on the east of the harbor. This has already been discussed, but no direct reply was made to the argument of Costa Rica quoting three authors as applying the name Punta de Castillo to the western extremity of the before-mentioned island, the point invariably called Punta Arenas by all the naval and other officers, surveyors, and engineers who ever mapped it.

These authors are L. Montufar, a Guatemalan, in 1887 : J. D. Gamez, a Nicaraguan, in 1889, and E. G. Squier, an American, date not given exactly, but subsequent to the treaty. Even of these, the last two merely used, once each, the name Punta de Castillo as an alternate for Punta Arenas. Against this array of authoriry we have, first, an innumerable number of other writers clearly far more entitled to confidence ; second, the original makers of all the maps, as before pointed out, and third, the framers of the treaty itself, by their use of Punta de Castillo in Article V.

It must be borne in mind that for some years before the making of this treaty Punta Arenas had been by far the most important and conspicuous point in the bay. On it were located the wharves, workshops, offices, etc., of Vanderbilt's great transit company, conducting the through line from New-York to San Francisco during the gold excitement of the early fifties. Here the ocean and river steamers met and exchanged passengers and cargo. This was the point sought to be controlled by Walker and the filibusters.

The village of San Juan cut no figure at all in comparison, and it would doubtless be easy to produce, by hundreds, references to this point as Punta Arenas by naval and diplomatic officers of all prominent nations, by prominent residents and officials, and by engineers and surveyors constantly investigating the canal problem, and all having a personal knowledge of the locality.

In view of all these circumstances, the jealousy with which each party to the treaty defined what it gave up and what it kept, the prominence and importance of the locality, the concurrence of all the original maps in the name, and its universal notoriety, I find it impossible to conceive that Nicaragua had conceded this extensive and important territory to Costa Rica, and that the latter's representative had failed to have the name Punta Arenas appear anywhere in the treaty. And for reasons so similar that it is unnecessary to repeat them, it is also impossible to conceive that Costa Rica should have accepted the Taura as her boundary and that Nicaragua's representative should have entirely failed to have the name Taura appear anywhere in the treaty.

Having then designated generally the mainland east of Harbor Head as the location of the initial point of the boundary line, it now becomes necessary to specify it more minutely, in order that the said line may be exactly located and permanently marked. The exact location of the initial point is given in President Cleveland's award as the extremity of Punta de Castillo, at the mouth of the San Juan de Nicaragua River, as they both existed on the 15th day of April 1858.

A careful study of all available maps and comparisons between those made before the treaty and those of recent date made by boards of engineers and officers of the canal company, and one of to-day made by ourselves to accompany this award, makes very clear one fact: The exact spot which was the extremity of the headland of Punta de Castillo April 15, 1858, has long been swept over by the Caribbean Sea, and there is too little concurrence in the shore outline of the old maps to permit any certainty of statement of distance or exact direction to it from the present headland. It was somewhere to the northeastward, and probably between 600 and 1600 feet distant, but it can not now be certainly located. Under these circumstances it best fulfills the demands of the treaty and of President Cleveland's award to adopt what is practically the headland of to-day, or the northwestern extremity of what seems to be the solid land, on the east side of Harbor Head Lagoon.

I have accordingly made personal inspection of this ground, and declare the initial line of the boundary to run as follows, to wit:

Its direction shall be due northeast and southwest, across the bank of sand, from the Caribbean Sea into the waters of Harbor Head Lagoon. It shall pass at its nearest point, 300 feet on the northwest side from the small hut now standing in that vicinity. On reaching the waters of Harbor Head Lagoon the boundary line shall turn to the left, or southeastward, and shall follow the water's edge around the harbor until it reaches the river proper by the first channel met. Up this channel, and up the river proper, the line shall continue to ascend as directed in the treaty [1].

Segundo Laudo sobre límites entre las Repúblicas de Nicaragua y Costa Rica, firmado en San Juan del Norte, Diciembre 20 de 1897.

En cumplimiento otra vez de mis deberes como Ingeniero Arbitro entre los dos Honorables Cuerpos de Ustedes, he sido llamado para decidir la cuestión sometida á mí en el acta del 7 del presente mes, como se manifesta en el siguiente páraffo del libro de sesiones, á saber: « Propuso la Comisión Costaricense que se proceda á medir la línea que continúo desde el punto inicial y sigue por la margen de Harbour Head, y después por la del caño mas próximo hasta encontrar el río propio de San Juan, siguiendo la de éste hasta el punto que diste tres millas abajo del Castillo Viejo; que se levante el plano de dicha línea y que se incorpore todo en las actas día por día en las sesiones. La de Nicaragua manifesto que el trabajo de la medida y levantamiento del plano en esa parte de la línea no tiene valor ni objeto útil porque, según el Tratado y el Laudo del General E. P. Alexander, el límite divisorio lo forma la margen derecho del Harbour y del río, y que siendo así, es variable y no línea fija; y por tanto el plano y los datos que se obtengan no corresponderán nunca á la verdadera línea divisoria. En tal estado determinan ambas Comisiones oír la decisión del señor Arbitro sobre este punto, á cuyo fin le presentarán sus respectivos fundamentos dentro del término de ocho días. »

Han sido recibidos y debidamente considerados los referidos argumentos de cada parte. Debe de hacerse notar para una clara inteligencia de la cuestión propuesta que en la parte baja de su curso el río San Juan corre al través de un delta llano y arenoso, y que son evidentemente posibles no solamente acrecimientos ó disminuciones graduales en sus márgenes, sino cambios enteros de sus caños. Estos cambios pueden ser más o menos rápidos y repentinos por causas no siempre aparentes y aún sin la concurrencia de factores especiales tales como terremotos ó grandes tempestades. Son abundantes los ejemplos de caños anteriores ahora abandonados, y de márgenes que están cambiando hoy día por graduales acrecimientos ó disminuciones.

---

[1] *Monthly Bulletin of the Bureau of the American Republics,* 1897, vol. V, p. 909.

La línea divisoria de hoy debe ser necesariamente afectada en lo futuro más ó menos, por todos estos cambios graduales ó repentinos. Pero el efecto en cada caso puede ser determinado solamente por las circunstancias del mismo caso, como él acontezca, según los principios de las leyes internacionales que puedan ser aplicables.

La medida y demarcación propuesta de la línea divisoria no producerá ningún efecto sobre la aplicación de estos principios.

El hecho de que ella haya sido medida y demarcada no aumentará ni disminuirá cualquiera estabilidad legal que ella pudiera tener como si no hubrera sido medida ni demarcada.

El solo efecto que se obtiene de la medida y demarcación es que el cáracter y extensión de los cambios futuros pueden ser más fácil y definitivamente determinados.

No se puede negar que hay una cierta ventaja contigente en esta futura capacidad de encontrár siempre la línea primitiva. Pero bien puede existir una diferencia de opinión sobre cuanto tiempo y gastos actuales deben invertirse para obtener esa ventaja contingente. Esta es la diferencia que existe ahora entre las dos Comisiones.

Costa Rica desea tener esa facilidad futura. Nicaragua considera que il beneficio contingente no vale el gasto actual.

Para decidir cual de estas opiniones debe prevalecer, me debo atener á la letra y al espíritu del Tratado de 1858, si hay en cualquiera de ellos lo que es aplicable á la cuestión. Yo encuentro ambas cosas en el artículo 3º.

El artículo 2º describe toda la línea divisoria desde el mar Caribe hasta el Pacífico, y el artículo 3º sigue así: « Se practicarán las medidas correspondientes á esta línea divisoria en el todo ó en parte por Comisionados de los Gobiernos, poniéndose éstos de acuerdo para señalar el tiempo en que haya de verificarse la operación. Dichos Comisionados tendrán la facultad de desviarse un tanto de la curva del rededor del Castillo, de la paralela á las márgenes del río y y el lago, ó de la recta astronómica ente Sapoá y Salinas, caso que en ello puedan acordarse para buscar mojones naturales. »

Todo este artículo está dedicado á prescribir la exactitud con que los Comisionados deberán ejecutar la obra. El permite apartarse de algunos·detalles, porque dice que la línea puede ser medida en todo ó en parte, y permite apartarse de la exactitud si por eso es posible encontrar mojones naturales. Pero la condición expresamente estipulada en el último caso y claramente comprendida tambien por el primero, es que ambas Comisiones estén de acuerdo.

De otro modo la línea debe medirse en el todo, y con todo la exactitud prácticamente realizable como está descrita en el artículo 2º.

Claramente, pues, la consecuencia de cualquiera desavenencia sobre la cuestión de más ó menes exactitud en la medida, ha de ser que prevalezca la opinión de la parte que desea hacerla más perfecta.

Yo, por consiguiente anuncio como mi Laudo en ésta materia que las dos Comisiones procederán enseguida á la medida de la línea desde el punto inicial hasta el punto tres millas abajo del Castillo Viejo, como se propuso por Costa Rica [1].

Tercero Laudo sobre límites entre las Republicas de Nicaragua y Costa Rica, firmado en San Juan del Norte, 22 de Marzo de 1898.

Al manifestar las razones que obraron en mi para emitir mi Laudo Nº 2, me referi brevemente al hecho de que, según los preceptos bien conocidos del Derecho Internacional, la exacta localización de la línea divisoria, que ahora define esta Comisión sobre la margen derecha del rio San Juan, puede ser alterada en lo futuro por los cambios posibles en las márgenes ó en los canales del río.

Me suplica ahora el Comisionado nicaragüense que en la actualidad funciona en su cargo, que complete este Laudo con una declaración mas exacta del cáracter legal y permanente, ó estabilidad de este línea como ahora se está definiendo y midiendo día á día.

Se me pride que prácticamente declare que esta línea mantendrá su cáracter como la exacta línea divisoria solamente mientras las aguas del río mantengan su nivel actual, y que la línea divisoria en acalquiera día futuro será derterminada por la altura del agua en ese día.

El argumento emitido para sostener esta proposición, es como sigue :

« No creo necesario hacer aquí una disertación minuciosa acerca de la significación del *cauce ó lecho* de un río; que es toda la zona del territorio por donde corre el agua en mayor ó menor volumen ; pero si recordare la doctrina de los Expositores del Derecho de Gentes, la cual está reasumida por don Carlos Calvo en su obra 'Le Droit International théorique et pratique' Lib. 40, § 295, Pag. 385, con estas palabras : — « Las fronteras marcadas por las corrientes de aguas estan sujetas á variar cuando el lecho de ella recibe cambios . . . »

« Y hago presente que coinciden con esta doctrina los Códigos modernos al disponer que el

[1] *Memoria [de Relaciones Exteriores]*, Nicaragua, 1899, p. 228.

terreno que cubre y descubre un río ó un lago periódicamente, no accede al terreno vecino porque es el lecho de les aguas. Así se ve en el Código Civil hondureño en estos términos: « El suelo que el agua ocupa y desocupa alternativamente en sus crecientes y vaciantes periódicas no accede mientras tanto á las heredades contiguas » (Art. 728).

« Es, pués, cosa evidente que la línea matemática obtenida y la que se sigue obteniendo en la forma referida, servirá para ilustración y referencia más ó menos útil, pero no para tenerla como la exacta expresión del límite divisorio, que es y será siempre la margen derecha del río en la forma en que se encuentre en cualquier momento dado. »

Este argumento del comisionado, considerado en relación con la solicitud que contiene su oficio, como se menciona arriba, indica un concepto equivocado que importa corregir.

Es estrictamente cierto que la « margen derecha del río en cualquier forma que pueda estar » fijará siempre la línea divisoria; pero el Comisionado evidentemente concibe falsamente que la localización legal de la línea, que define la margen de un río, variará con la altura de las aguas en el río.

En verdad, la palabra « margen » con frecuencia se aplica en conversación vagamente al primer terreno seco que se levanta sobre el agua; pero la impropriedad de tal uso viene á ser aparente si nosotros consideramos los casos por donde los ríos inundan sus márgenes por muchas millas, ó donde sus lechos se secan totalmente. Tal uso indefinido de la palabra no es lícito en la interpretación de un Tratado que define una línea divisoria. El objeto de todo límite es asegurar la paz evitando los conflictos de jurisdicción. Para llenar esto debe poseer toda la estabilidad posible.

Claramente sería este estado de cosas una situación intolerable para los residentes y para los dueños de propriedades cerca de los límites de los dos países, si la línea que determina á que país debe su obediencia y tasas, y cuyas leyes rigen todos sus asuntos, pudieran alternativamente estar en vigor ó no, porque tal línea sería creada para producir disturbios en lugar de evitarlos. No es necesario ilustrar las dificultades que surgirían, por ejemplo, si ciertas tierras y bosques, y sus dueños y residentes ó gente empleada en cualquiera manera en ellos, fueran intimados á ser costaricenses en tiempo seco y nicaragüenses en tiempo de lluvias y alternativamente el uno y el otro en los tiempos intermedios. Pero exactamente tales dificultades serían inevitables, si la línea divisoria entre estos dos países fuera el cambio diario de la margen donde

se levanta primero la tierra seca sobre el agua al lado de Costa Rica. Porque en la estación de lluvias las aguas del río inundan la tierra por muchas millas en ciertas localidades.

Es por estas razones que los escritores sobre Derecho Internacional mantienen expresamente, que las inundaciones temporales no dan título á las tierras inundadas. Esa es la verdadera inteligencia de la cita hecha por el Comisionado nicaragüense, del Código de Honduras. Aplicado á este caso es como si se leyera así: « El terreno (de Costa Rica) que las aguas (de Nicaragua) alternativamente ocupan y desocupan en su periodo de crecientes y vaciantes, no será accesorio de las contiguas heredades (de Nicaragua). En comprobación de esta regla, si el tiempo me permitiera traer ejemplos, podría citar un gran numero de casos de los Estados Unidos donde hay muchos procesos de los Estados separados por ríos, siendo una de las márgenes, y no el hilo de la corriente su límite divisorio. Con uno de tales casos estoy familiarizado personalmente, en donde la margen izquierda del río Savannah constituye la línea divisoria entre Georgia en el lado derecho y la Carolina del Sur en el izquierdo. En tiempos de crecientes el río cubre millas del territorio de la Carolina del Sur, pero esta circunstancia no lleva el poder ó jurisdicción de Georgia más allá del límite que antes tenia, marcado por las aguas bajas ordinarias. Al hacerlo así, no daría ventaja ninguna á Georgia y será un grave inconveniente para la Carolina del Sur. Ni puedo creer que exista en el mundo un ejemplo de tal límite movible.

Claramente, pues, donde quiera que un Tratado designe, que la margen de un río será tomado como un límite, lo que es entendido no es la orilla temporal de tierra firme discubierta en estados extraordinarios de las aguas altas ó bajas, sino la margen en el estado ordinario de las aguas. Y cuando sea una vez definida per Convenio vendrá á ser permanente como la superficie del suelo en donde ella corre. Si la margen se retira, retrocede; si la margen aumenta hacia la corriente, avanza.

Las llenas y vaciantes periódicas de las aguas no la afectan. Y esto es enteramente de acuerdo con el precepto de don Carlos Calvo citado por el Comisionado nicaragüense. « Las fronteras marcadas por corrientes de aguas están sujetas á variar cuando sus lechos reciben cambios. » En otras palabras es el lecho el que gobierna y no el nivel del agua en el, sobre él, ó bajo él.

Respecto á los cambios futuros posibles del lecho ó de las márgenes y sus efectos, sería vano querer discutirlos todos, y también sería extraviado discutir alguno cualquiera que pudiera ocurrir.

No es la función de esta Comisión dar reglas por las contingencias futuras, sino definir y marcar el límite en el día presente.

Para reasumir, pues, brevemente, y para la inteligencia clara de toda la materia, y también en conformidad con los principios enunciados en mi primer Laudo, que, en la interpretación practica del Tratado de 1858, el río San Juan debe ser considerado como un río navegable, por consiguiente declaro ser la exacta línea de división entre la jurisdicción de los dos países, el borde de las aguas sobre la margen derecha, cuando el río se halla en su estado ordinario, navegable por las embarcaciones y botes de uso general. En este estado toda porción de las aguas del río esta en jurisdicción de Nicaragua. Toda porción de la tierra en la margen derecha está en jurisdicción de Costa Rica. La medida y localización hecha ahora por las partes en el campo día por día determina puntos sobre esta línea á convenientes intervalos, pero la línea divisoria entre estos puntos no corre por línea recta sino por el borde de las *aguas en el estado navegable* como arriba *se dijo, marcando así una línea curva de irregularidades innumerables* que son de pequeño valor, y que exigirían un gran gasto para trazarse minuciosamente.

Las variaciones del nivel del agua no alterarán la localización de la línea divisoria, pero los *cambios de las márgenes ò de los canales del río la alterarán* como puede ser determinado por los preceptos de las Leyes Internacionales aplicables á cada caso según ellos acontezcan [1].

Fourth Award made to Greytown, July 26, 1899, in the question of the limit between Costa Rica and Nicaragua.

As the arbitrator of whatever points of difference may arise between your two bodies in tracing and marking the boundary lines between the Republics you represent, I am called upon to decide the following question:

What level of its waters shall be taken to determine the shore line of Lake Nicaragua, parallel to which and 2 miles distant therefrom the boundary line must be traced, from near the San Juan River to the Sapoa?

It will facilitate discussion to define in advance the principal levels which must be frequently referred to. Under the influence of rainy seasons of about seven months and dry seasons of about five the level of Lake Nicaragua is in constant

fluctuation. We shall have to discuss five different stages.

First. Extreme high water, the level reached only in years of maximum rainfall or some extraordinary conditions.

Second. Mean high water, the average high level of average years.

Third. Mean low water, the average low level of average years.

Fourth. Extreme low water, the lowest level reached in years of minimum rainfall or other extraordinary conditions.

Fifth. Mean water, the average between mean high water and mean low water.

The argument presented to me in behalf of Nicaragua claims that the level to be adopted in this case should be the first level named, to wit, extreme high water. It argues that this line, and this alone, is the true limit of what the argument calls the bed of the lake. Costa Rica claims the adoption of the third level, to wit, mean low water. This is argued principally upon two grounds: First, it is shown by a great number of legal decisions that in most States all water boundaries are invariably held to run at either extreme or mean low water. Second, it is claimed that in case of any doubt Costa Rica is entitled to its benefit, as she is conceding territory geographically hers.

I will begin with Costa Rica's first argument. The equity of adopting a low water line in the case of all water boundaries is readily admitted, even though instances of contrary practice exist.

Between all permanent lands and permanent waters usually runs a strip of land, sometimes dry and sometimes submerged. We may call it, for short, semisubmerged. Its value for ordinary purposes is much diminished by its liability to overflow, but, as an adjunct to the permanent land, it possesses often very great value. If the owner of the permanent land can fence across the semisubmerged he may save fencing his entire water front. He also can utilize whatever agricultural value may be in the semisubmerged land in dry seasons. Both of this values would be destroyed and wasted if the ownership were conferred upon the owner of the water. Therefore equity always, and law generally, confers it upon the owner of the permanent land.

I recognized and followed this principle in my award No. 3, where I held that the boundary line following the right bank of the San Juan River, below Castillo, follows the lowest water mark of a navigable stage of river. And, if now the lake shore were itself to be the boundary of Costa Rica, I would not hesitate to declare that the semisubmerged land went with

[1] *Memoria* [*de Relaciones Exteriores*], Nicaragua, 1899, p. 232.

the permanent land and carried her limits at least to the mean low water line.

But this case is not one of a water boundary, nor is it at all similar, or on all fours with one, for none of the equities above set forth have any application. It is a case of rare and singular occurrence and without precedent within my knowledge. A water line is in question, but not as a boundary. It is only to furnish starting points whence to mesure off a certain strip of territory. Clearly the case stands alone, and must be governed strictly by the instrument under which it has arisen. That is the treaty of 1858, and its language is as follows :

« Thence the line shall continue toward the river Sapoa, which discharges into the Lake Nicaragua, following a course which is distant always 2 miles from the right bank of the river San Juan, with its sinuosities, up to its origin at the lake, and from the right bank of the lake itself up to the said river Sapoa, where this line parallel to the said bank will terminate. »

The principles, upon which the language and intent of treaties are to be interpreted, are well set forth in the Costa Rica argument by many quotations from eminent authors. All concur that words are to be taken as far as possible in their first and simplest meanings—« in their natural and obvious sense, according to the general use of the same words », « in the usual sense, and not in any extraordinary or unused acceptation ».

We must suppose that the language of the treaty above quoted suggested to its framers some very definite picture of the lake with its banks and of the 2 miles strip of territory. It evidently seemed to them all so simple and obvious that no further words were necessary. Let us first call up pictures of the lake at different levels and see which seems the most natural, obvious and reasonable.

The very effort to call up a picture of the lake at either extreme high water or at extreme low water seems to me immediately to rule both of these levels out of further consideration. Both seem unatural conditions, and I must believe that had either been intended, additional details would have been given.

Next, is the mean low water mark the first, most obvious and natural picture called up by the expression « the bank of the lake » ? It seems to me decidedly not. During about eleven months of the year this line is submerged, invisible and inaccessible. It seems rather a technical line than a natural one. The idea of a bank is of water limited by dry land with some elements of permanency about it. Even during the brief period when the line is uncovered the idea of it is

suggestive far more of mud and aquatic growths than of dry land and forest growths.

To my mind, the natural, simple and obvious idea of the bank of a lake in this climate is presented only by the line of mean high water. Here we would first find permanent dry ground every day of an average year. Here an observer, during every annual round of ordinary seasons, would see the water advance to his very feet and then recede, as if some power had drawn the line and said to the waters, « Hitherto shalt thou come, but no further ». Here the struggle between forest growths and aquatic vegetation begins to change the landscape. Here lines of drift, the flotsam and jetsam of the waves, naturally suggest the limits of the « bed of the lake ».

One level of the lake remains for discussion, the mean level, or average of all waters. In a different climate, where the rainfall is more uniformly distributed throughout the year, the mean high water and mean low water lines, with all their respective features, would approach each other, tending to finally merge in the line of mean water. But, where wet and dry seasons prevail, as in the present case, the line of mean water is destitute of all obvious features, and is submerged for many months of the year. It is purely a technical and not a natural line, and is not to be understood where not expressly called for.

In argument against Nicaragua's claim of the extreme high water line, Costa Rica appeals to the general custom of geographers and scientific men in making ordinary topographical maps, who never adopt the extreme lines of overflows for the outlines of lakes. This argument of general custom has great weight, but it is equally against Costa Rica's claim for the mean low water line. Wherever wet and dry seasons prevail, general custom treats mean high water as the normal state, always to be understood where no other level is expressed, and its line is assumed as the lake boundary in all ordinary topographical maps. Two quotations from Commander Lull's report of his Nicaraguan Canal survey will illustrate (Report Secretary of the Navy, 1873, p. 187) :

« In a survey made by Mr. John Baily, many years since, that gentleman professed to have found a pass with but 56 feet above the lake level, but the most of his statements are found to be entirely unreliable... For example, he finds Lake Nicaragua to be 121 feet above mean tide in the Pacific, while the true difference of level is but 107 feet. » (Ibid., p. 199.)

« The surface of Lake Nicaragua is 107 feet above mean tide in either sea. »

From comparison of this level with the levels found by other surveys, there is no question that this figure was Lull's estimate of mean high water, as shown by his line of levels.

From every consideration of the lake, therefore, I am driven to conclude that the shore line of the lake contemplated in the treaty is the mean high water line.

I am led to the same conclusion also from the standpoint of the 2 miles strip of territory. The treaty gives no intimation as to the purpose of this concession, and we have no right to assume one, either political or commercial. We have only to observe the two conditions put upon the strip in the treaty. Under all ordinary conditions it must be land, and 2 miles wide. This would not be the case if we adopted the line of either mean low water or mean water. In the former case the strip would be too narrow for about eleven months of an ordinary year; in the latter case for about five months.

Without doubt, then, I conclude that mean high water mark determines the shore of the lake; and it now remains to designate that level and how it shall be found.

Several surveys of the proposed Nicaraguan Canal route, besides that of Commander Lull above quoted, have been made within the last fifty years. Each found a certain mean high level of the lake, and it might seem a simple solution to take an average of them all, but, as each adopted its own bench mark on the ocean and ran its own line of levels to the lake, I have no means of bringing their figures to a common standard. It seems best, therefore, to adopt the figures of that one which is at once the latest and most thorough, which has enjoyed the benefit of all of the investigations of all of its predecessors, and whose bench marks on the lake are known and can be referred to. That is the survey, still in progress, under the direction of the United States Canal Commission. Its results have not yet been made public, but, by the courtesy of Rear Admiral J. G. Walker, President of the Commission, I am informed of them in a letter dated July 10, 1899, from which I quote: « In reply I am cabling you to-day as follows: 'Alexander, Greytown, six,' the six meaning, as per your letter, 106 as mean high level of lake. This elevation of 106 is, to the best of our knowledge (Mr. Davis, our hydrographer) the mean high water for a number of years... The highest level of the lake in 1898 was 106.7, last of November. The elevation of our bench mark on inshore end of boiler at San Carlos is 109.37. »

A complete copy of this letter will be handed you, and also blue prints of the maps made by the Commission of the lower end of the lake, which may facilitate your work.

As this Commission is the highest existing authority, I adopt its finding and announce my award as follows:

The shore line of Lake Nicaragua, at the level of 106 feet, by the bench marks of the United States Nicaragua Canal Commission, shall be taken as the bank of said lake referred to in the treaty of 1858[1].

Fifth Arbitral Award in the question of limits between Costa Rica and Nicaragua, rendered to Greytown, March 10, 1900.

In the discharge of my duties as Arbitrator of whatever differences may arise in your works of tracing and marking the boundary line between the countries you represent, I was called upon in October last, by the Nicaraguan Commission, to declare what point in Salinas Bay should be taken as its center, in laying out the final course of the boundary, from its meeting with the Sapoa River to its ending upon this bay. The work in the field at that time was near San Carlos with some months of work ahead before it could reach the Sapoa River, but the decision was asked in advance to allow time for argument and yet avoid any delay when the work arrived at that point.

The Nicaraguan Commission, along with its request that I should fix the central point of the bay, submitted a statement of its views in the matter and some extracts from the proceedings of a former joint commission, which in 1890 considered this subject and seemed not far from an amicable agreement, but finally dissolved, without effective action.

This exposition of its views by the Nicaraguan Commission was immediately transmitted to the Costa Rica Commission, who were invited to make such reply as they saw fit.

Both Commissions were also informed that, as an amicable agreement seemed possible, I would delay making any award in the matter as long as that possibility seemed to exist, and I asked to be informed from time to time of progress.

No such agreement has been arrived at. Nor has the Costa Rican Commission submitted any statement or comments upon the views of the Nicaraguan Commission above referred to.

Meanwhile the working parties in the field will soon reach the Sapoa River, and must then suspend work until the central point of Salinas Bay is determined before they can fix the direction of the final course of the boundary line.

---

[1] *Monthly Bulletin of the Bureau of the American Republics*, 1899, vol. VII, p. 877.

To avoid this delay, and its consequent expense to both Governments, I can no longer suspend my award in this matter; but, it is proper to point out in this connection, that my award has no effect to prevent amicable agreement from being even yet arrived at.

Power is given the Commissioners in the Treaty of 1858 « to diverge from the straight astronomical line between Sapoa and Salinas, provided they can agree upon this, in order to adopt natural landmarks ».

This power is in no way restricted or abridged by my award, which only determines where a straight astronomical line will run. Having therefore duly considered the whole matter, I announce my award as follows:

The provisions of the Treaty of 1858 bearing upon this matter are these:

From Article II: « From the point where the boundary touches the river Sapoa, which, as before said, must be 2 miles from the lake, a straight astronomical line shall be projected to the central point of the Bay of Salinas in the sea of the south, at which place will terminate the demarcation of the territory of the contracting Republics. »

From Art. IV: « The Bay of San Juan del Norte, as well as that of Salinas shall be common to both Republics and consequently their advantages and the obligation to unite for their defense shall be common also. »

The interpretation of this treaty upon all doubtful points was submitted to President Cleveland in 1888, and his award upon this matter was in the following very clear provisions:

« 2. The central point of the Bay of Salinas is to be fixed by drawing a straight line across the mouth of the bay and determining mathematically the center of the closed geometrical figure formed by such straight line and the shore of the bay at low-water mark.

« 3. By the central point of Salinas Bay is to be understood the center of the geometrical figure formed as above stated. The limit of the bay toward the ocean is a straight line drawn from the extremity of Punta Arrauca Barba nearly true south to the westernmost portion of the land about Punta Zacate. »

In the argument made by the Nicaraguan Commission it is submitted to me that the true limit of the bay should be a line between Punta Zacate and Punta Mala. This would be between 1 and 2 miles inside of the line fixed by President Cleveland's award. It is unnecessary to discuss the merits of this claim.

By the Matus Pacheco Treaty, made at San Salvador, March 27, 1896, this award was adopted as the law for this Commission.

The first article of that treaty is as follows: « The contracting Governments are bound to appoint a Commission, respectively, each composed of two engineers, or surveyors, for the purpose of duly defining and marking out the dividing line between the Republics of Nicaragua and Costa Rica according to the stipulations of the Treaty of 15th April, 1858, and the award of the President of the United States of North America, Mr. Grover Cleveland. »

The powers of arbitration given me in the second article of this treaty, to decide whatever kind of difficulties may arise, are plainly to be exercised only within the limits set by Article 1. Where the meaning of President Cleveland's award is not in question, I have no authority to set it aside.

As to the unfinished work and partial agreements of 1890, they were all set aside by this treaty of 1895. It may be noted that the territory which would have accrued to Nicaragua by the proposed amicable adoption of the line from Punta Zacate to Punta Mala as the limit of the bay would be about three fourths of a mile of shore front.

It is further set forth in the Nicaraguan argument that the line from Sapoa to the center of the bay loses its character as a dividing or boundary line where it leaves the shore and enters upon the waters of the bay. This, indeed, seems to follow from Article IV of the Treaty of 1858, already quoted, which declares the waters of the bay to be common, and from the fact that the line is terminated at the center of the bay, and not extended to the ocean.

But, in my opinion, the functions of this Commission are limited in the *defining and marking out* of the dividing line between the Republics. The legal character of that portion of the line upon the water, and perhaps some questions of jurisdiction which might arise, are at least beyond the scope of the present inquiry, which is merely the location of the center of Salinas Bay as described in the award of President Cleveland.

The Bay of Salinas was carefully surveyed and mapped by officers of the United States navy in 1883, and a map of the same is published in the United States Naval Hydrographic Office, N° 1025. I have adopted this map, with the consent of both Commissions, as correctly representing the outline of the bay. In shape it is a curved pocket starting east and bending southward, about 5 miles long and about one-half of that in average width. Its outline a little resembles the rounded handle or butt of a pistol, with some irregular projections and indentations.

It is desired to find the mathematical center of this figure, closed by the straight line joining the headlands of the bay.

The mathematical center of an irregular figure, is the mid position of its area. All mechanical centers, such as the center of gravity or of equilibrium, etc., in which the actions of any force is concerned must be excluded from consideration.

This will readily appear if we consider for a moment the case of a bay in the shape of a crescent. The center of gravity of its figure would not fall upon the water of the bay at all, but upon the promontory of land embraced by the water. This, of course, could not be considered as the center of the bay.

Neither is any general mathematical process applicable, such as that of the method of least squares. This method will find the center of any group of random spots, but were they disposed in crescent form the center would be, not among them, but within the convex space which they partially surround.

Other methods must therefore be devised for finding the mid position of irregular and restricted areas, and many might be suggested more or less applicable to different figures; but it will be sufficient here to indicate only the method which I have adopted as best suited to the figure in hand, possessing, as this does, something of a curved or crescent shape.

I have supposed a vessel to enter the bay from the ocean at a point midway between its headlands, and to sail a course as nearly as possible equidistant between the opposite shores, on the right and left, until it has penetrated to the remotest point of the bay. This course, being carefully platted upon the map, although curved, may be taken as the long axis of the bay.

At right angles to it, at different points, I have drawn straight lines reaching across the bay from shore to shore and, by use of a planimeter, I have determined the position of such a line which will exactly divide the whole area of the bay into equal parts. This line may be taken as the corresponding short axis of the bay, and its intersection with the long axis will be the center of the bay.

When at that point a line drawn across the bow of the supposed vessel, perpendicular to her course, would have one-half of the waters of the bay in front of it and one-half behind it.

Having carefully located the point in this manner, I have determined from the scale of the map its distance from the summit point of the small island in the bay, whose latitude and longitude are given upon the map as follows:

Latitude, 10° 03′ 10″, longitude, 85° 43′ 38″.

It proves to be 37 seconds to the northward and 14 seconds to the eastward of this point.

I therefore fix the position of the center of Salinas Bay to be

Latitude, 11° 03′ 47″ north; longitude, 85° 43′ 52″ west.

Toward this point the boundary line must run, from its meeting with the Sapoa River, unless the two commissioners can agree upon a line with natural landmarks[1].

CXXVIII. Argentine, Chili.

17 avril 1896.

Des discussions prolongées ont divisé les deux républiques de l'Argentine et du Chili au sujet de leurs frontières communes, notamment en ce qui concernait les abords du détroit de Magellan. Par l'article 39 du traité du 30 avril 1856, le recours à l'arbitrage avait été conventionnellement stipulé et à deux reprises différentes, les 18 janvier et 6 décembre 1878, des tentatives furent faites pour arriver à l'acceptation d'un compromis.

Proyecto de tratado entre Argentina y Chile, firmado en Buenos Aires, Enero 18, 1878.

El Gobierno de la República Argentina y el Gobierno de la República de Chile, deseando poner fin á la cuestion de límites pendiente entre una y otra República, han convenido en celebrar un tratado con este objeto, y al efecto han nombrado Ministros Plenipotenciarios:

S. E. el señor Presidente de la República Argentina al Exmo. señor Ministro de Relaciones Exteriores, Dr. D. Ruffino de Elizalde, y S. E. el señor Presidente de la República de Chile al Exmo. señor Enviado Extraordinario y Ministro Plenipotenciario de Chile en Mision Especial D. Diego Barros Arana. Quienes despues de haberse comunicado sus plenos poderes, cangeado copias authenticas, y habiéndolas encontrado bastantes y en buena forma, han convenido en lo siguiente:

ART. 1. — La República Argentina está dividida de la República de Chile por la Cordillera de los Andes, corriendo la línea divisoria por sobre los puntos mas encumbrados de ella, pasando por entre los manantiales de las vertientes que desprenden á un lado y al otro. Las dificultades que pudieran suscitarse por la existencia de ciertos valles de Cordillera, en que

[1] *Monthly Bulletin . . . .* vol. IX, p. 294-298.

no sea perfectamente clara la línea divisoria de las aguas, se resolverán siempre amistosamente por medio de peritos.

ART. 2. — Estando pendientes reclamaciones deducidas por la República Argentina y reclamaciones deducidas por la República de Chile sobre el Estrecho de Magallanes y sobre otros territorios en la parte austral de este continente, y estando estipulado en el artcíulo 39 del Tratado de 1856 que en caso de no arribar los Gobiernos Argentino y de Chile al completo arreglo de ellas, se someterían á arbitraje de una nacion amiga, el Gobierno de la República Argentina y el de la República de Chile declaran : que ha llegado el caso previsto en la última parte del artículo citado. En consecuencia el Gobierno de la República Argentina y el de Chile someten al fallo del árbitro que mas adelante se designará, la siguiente cuestion? Cuál era el *uti possidetis* de 1810 en los territorios que se disputan : es decir, los territorios disputados pertenecian en 1810 al Vireynato de Buenos Aires ó á la Capitania General de Chile?

ART. 3. — Habiendo convenido las Repúblicas Argentina y de Chile en el artículo 39 del Tratado antes citado, que ambas Partes Contratantes reconocen como límites de sus respectivos territorios los que poseían como tales al tiempo de separarse de la dominacion española el año de 1810, y habiendo sostenido los Gobiernos de ambas Repúblicas que sus títulos al dominio del territorio austral del Continente son claros, precisos é incontestables ; el árbitro deberá tener presente para pronunciar su fallo, la siguiente regla de derecho público americano, que los Gobiernos Contratantes aceptan y sostienen. Las Repúblicas Hispano-Americanas han sucedido al Rey de España en los derechos de posesion y de dominio que él tenía sobre toda la América Española. En consecuencia no hay en ésta territorios que puedan reputarse *res nullius*, y los territorios disputados en el presente caso tienen que declararse de la República Argentina ó de Chile con arreglo á los derechos preferentes de una ú otra.

ART. 4. — El árbitro tendrá el carácter de árbitro *juris*, que ambos Gobiernos le confieren. El árbitro fallará en ese carácter y con sujecion :

1º A los actos y documentos emanados del Gobierno de España, de sus autoridades y agentes en América y á los actos y documentos procedentes de los Gobiernos de la República Argentina y de Chile.

2º Si todos estos actos y documentos no fuesen bastante claros para resolver por ellos las cuestiones pendientes, el árbitro podrá resolverlas aplicando tambien los principios de Derecho Internacional.

ART. 5. — Dentro del plazo de doce (12) meses despues de ratificado este Tratado, el Gobierno Argentino entregará al de Chile en Santiago y el de Chile al Argentino en Buenos Aires, una memoria sobre las pretensiones respectivas y las razones en que las fundan, estando obligados á comunicarse reciprocamente los antecedentes que invoquen y que se pidiesen por uno ú otro. Seis (6) meses despues y en la misma forma anterior, se entregarán las contra memorias.

Constituido el arbitraje ambos Gobiernos podrán hacerse representar ante el árbitro por los Plenipotenciarios que crean conveniente, para dar los informes que se les pida, para gestionar los derechos de sus paises respectivos y para asistir á las discusiones á que puedan ser invitados por el árbitro.

ART. 6. — Los principios ó hechos en que estén de acuerdo las Altas Partes Contratantes, en sus memorias y contra memorias, se tendrán por definitivamente resueltas y en consecuencia, el árbitro al pronunciar su fallo, lo hará en la forma siguiente :

1º Declarará cuales son los principios ó hechos en que las Altas Partes Contratantes estan de acuerdo y los pondrá fuera de decision arbitral.

2º Establecerá los hechos que cada una de las Altas Partes pretenda constituir en derecho y pronunciará su fallo.

ART. 7. — La sentencia del árbitro tendrá la autoridad de cosa juzgada. Ambas Partes se someterán á ella sin ulterior recurso.

ART. 8. — El árbitro será S. M. el Rey de los Belgas. Los Gobiernos Contratantes solicitarán su beneplacito á la brevedad posible.

Los Plenipotenciarios de estos deberán encontrarse en el lugar en que reside el árbitro, cuatro meses despues de recibidas las contra memorias mensionadas en el art. 5. Si desgraciadamente el árbitro elejido no aceptase el cargo, ambas Partes Contratantes designarán otro de comun acuerdo.

ART. 9. — Por un protocolo anexo se resuelven las cuestiones pendientes por incidentes que han dificultado la solucion de la cuestion de límites. Ese protocolo forma parte integrante de este Tratado.

ART. 10. — Para evitar las dificultades que puedan suscitarse por cuestiones de jurisdiccion en los territorios disputados, mientras el árbitro dicta su sentencia, regirá entre ambos paises el siguiente arreglo provisorio.

La República Argentina ejercerá jurisdiccion sobre los territorios bañados por el Atlántico, comprendidos hasta la Boca Oriental del Estrecho de Magallanes y la parte de la Tierra del Fuego bañada por el mismo mar. Las islas situadas en el Atlántico estarán igualmente sometidas á la misma jurisdiccion.

La República de Chile ejercerá jurisdiccion en todo el Estrecho con sus canales é islas adyacentes.

Ambas Partes Contratantes se obligan á defender unidas los territorios sometidos á arbitraje contra toda ocupacion estranjera celebrando los acuerdos que fuesen necesarios para el cumplimiento de esta estipulacion.

Este arreglo provisorio no dá derecho alguno á ninguna de las dos Partes; las cuales no podrán invocarlo ante el árbitro como título de posesion.

ART. 11. — El presente Tratado será ratificado y las ratificaciones canjeadas en el término de siete (7) meses ó antes si fuese posible, en esta ciudad.

En fé de lo cual los Plenipotenciarios respectivos han firmado este Tratado y le han puesto sus sellos en la ciudad de Buenos Aires á los 18 dias del mes de Enero del año de 1878.

Protocolo sobre la Jeanne Amélie, firmado en Buenos Aires, Enero 21, 1878.

Reunidos en el Ministerio de Relaciones Exteriores el Exmo. señor Ministro de Relaciones Exteriores Dr. D. Rufino de Elizalde y el Exmo. señor Enviado Extraordinario y Ministro Plenipotenciario de Chile en mision especial, D. Diego Barros Arana, plenamente autorizados por sus respectivos Gobiernos.

El Exmo. señor Elizalde espuso — que con arreglo á lo convenido, era necesario dirimir el incidente de la Barca francesa « Jeanne Amélie », sobre el cual existe pendiente una reclamacion deducida por su Gobierno. Que escusa entrar á manifestar la gravedad que este incidente tiene para el Gobierno Argentino, por que el asunto ha sido detenidamente tratado en la correspondencia oficial á que habia dado lugar.

El Exmo. señor Barros Arana espuso : que como lo habia dicho en notas y conferencias anteriores, y como lo habia declarado su Gobierno, este creia que su conducta fundado en declaraciones generales que hizo en años atrás, estaba justificada en sus comunicaciones ; pero que debia ademas espresar — que el Gobierno de Chile habia deplorado sinceramente este incidente, por cuanto por desgracia tuvo lugar en los momentos

en que despues del cambio de correspondencia entre ambos Gobiernos á mediados de 1875, todo hacia creer, que la cuestion de límites marchaba á un desenlace amistoso. Que su Gobierno no pudo preveer, que despues de esa correspondencia ocurriese un incidente de esa naturaleza.

Que aún despues de ocurrido creyó, á la vista de los papeles del buque, que el Gobierno Argentino cuando conociese las irregularidades de la espedicion que se han señalado en la discusion, no le daria una importancia capaz de embarazar la marcha tranquila de la negociacion. Que el mismo Comandante de la Corbeta « Magallanes », que en virtud de órdenes espedidas en años atras al Gobernador de Punta Arenas, ejecutó la detencion del buque, se persuadió de que éste no habia arreglado su conducta á las leyes argentinas, y que aun las habia violado. Que nada habia estado mas lejos de su animo que inferir ofensa alguna al Gobierno Argentino. Y por, último — que siendo este acto un incidente de la cuestion de límites podia someterse esta negociacion á la decision del árbitro que habia de decidir aquella.

El Exmo. señor Ministro de Relaciones Exteriores manifestó : que despues de lo espuesto, y desde que la negociacion sobre lo principal habia llegado á un término feliz, no tenía inconveniente en aceptar el arbitrio propuesto, reservando á su Gobierno poder esponer ante el árbitro cuanto á sus derechos correspondiese, sobre lo espuesto anteriormente por el Exmo. señor Barros Arana.

En consecuencia, de comun acuerdo, quedó establecido que la reclamacion deducida sobre el referido incidente y sus antecedentes, fuera sometida á la decision del árbitro á cuyo fallo se presente la cuestion principal. La discusion de este incidente debe hacerse en la misma forma y en las mismas memorias en que se trate aquella.

Y lo firmaron en Buenos Aires á 21 de Enero de 1878[1].

Proyecto de convención de arbitraje firmado en Santiago el 6 de diciembre de 1878.

Animadas la República de Chile y la República Arjentina del propósito de solucionar dignamente la controversia que han sostenido sobre límites i sus incidencias, i sinceramente convencidas de que el respeto recíproco es el vínculo que mas afianza las relaciones, como la justicia es el fundamento mas sólido de la civilizacion i

---

[1] *Cuestion de límites con Chile.* Buenos Ayres, impr. de la Sociedad Anonyma, 1878, p. 66.

cultura de dos pueblos, llamados por nobles intereses i por antecedentes históricos a vivir en la armonía fecunda del trabajo i de la paz; i queriendo sus Gobiernos dar cumplimiento al artículo 39 del Tratado de 1856 con actos de recíproca confianza i fraternidad, han resuelto celebrar una Convencion que obedezca a esos sentimientos, i nombrado para el efecto Plenipotenciarios, a saber:

S. E. el Presidente de la República de Chile a don Alejandro Fierro, Ministro de Estado en el Departamento de Relaciones Exteriores, i S. E. el Presidente de la República Arjentina a don Mariano E. de Sarratea, Cónsul Jeneral de esta República en Chile;

Quienes, despues de haberse manifestado sus respectivos Plenos Poderes i encontrádolos en buena i debida forma, han convenido en los artículos siguientes:

ART. I. — Los Gobiernos de Chile i de la República Arjentina nombrarán respectivamente, dentro del término de treinta dias contados desde que esta Convencion será canjeada, dos ciudadanos chilenos i dos arjentinos, los cuales formarán un Tribunal Misto que resolverá las cuestiones relativas al dominio de los territorios disputados entre ámbas naciones.

Este tribunal decidirá tambien las demandas que cualesquiera de las dos Potencias deduzca para obtener las reparaciones que crea debidas a su dignidad, derechos i intereses.

ART. II. — Los Gobiernos de ámbas Repúblicas nombrarán, dentro del término de tres meses contados desde la fecha en que esta Convencion sea firmada por sus plenipotenciarios, dos Ministros ad hoc, uno por cada parte, quienes acordarán los territorios i las cuestiones que han de someterse al fallo del Tribunal, las formas del procedimiento a que éste haya de sujetarse i el lugar i dia de su instalación.

ART. III. — Si tres meses despues de afecto el canje de esta Convencion, los Gobiernos no se hubiesen puesto de acuerdo respecto de los territorios i cuestiones que hayan de someterse al fallo de los árbitros, o si habiendo celebrado una transaccion, ésta no estuviese aprobada por los respectivos Congresos, el Tribunal queda ámpliamente facultado para proceder a desempeñar sus funciones fijando las reglas de procedimiento que deban observar i entrando en seguida a conocer i decidir todas las cuestiones i sus incidencias en el estado en que se encontrasen.

ART. IV. — El Tribunal iniciará sus tareas, designando un estadista americano, que no sea chileno ni arjentino, o un Gobierno amigo que,

como *arbitro juris*, resuelva los casos en que los jueces estuviesen en desacuerdo.

ART. V. — El Tribunal fallara con arreglo a derecho i adoptará como fundamento de su sentencia, tanto el principio establecido por las dos Partes Contratantes en el Artículo 39 del Tratado que celebraron el año de mil ochocientos cincuenta i seis, reconociendo como límites de sus territorios los que poseián al tiempo de separarse de la dominación española en mil ochocientos diez, como tambien el principio de derecho público americano, según el cual no existen en la América que fué española territorios que puedan considerarse *res nullius*, de manera que los disputados deben declararse *de Chile* o de la *República Arjentina*.

ART. VI. — Miéntras el Tribunal no resuelva la cuestion de límites, la República de *Chile* ejercerá jurisdicción en el mar i costas del Estrecho de Magallanes, canales e islas adyacentes, i la República Arjentina en el mar i costas del Atlántico e islas adyacentes.

ART. VII. — La jurisdicción establecida en el artículo anterior no altera los derechos de dominio que tuviesen cada una de las dos naciones, i en ella no se fundarán títulos que puedan invocarse ante el Tribunal.

ART. VIII. — El *statu quo modus vivendi*, designado en el artículo IV, durará catorce meses contados desde el dia en que esta Convencion sea aprobada definitivamente, i este plazo podrá ser prorogado un año mas, si el Tribunal lo juzga necesario para dar su sentencia.

ART. IX. — Las cuestiones que suscitase la intelijencia que las Partes Contratantes atribuyan a este Pacto, serán resueltos por el Tribunal.

ART. X. — Sea cual fuere la resolucion de los árbitros i la condición internacional en que puedan encontrarse las resoluciones de ámbos paises, la navegacion del Estrecho de Magallanes será libre para todas las banderas.

ART. XI. — La sentencia del Tribunal servirá de antecedente para la celebración de un Tratado de Amistad, Comercio i Navegacion entre ámbas Repúblicas, en el que se establecerá el réjimen que ha de observarse en las fronteras a fin de evitar las depredaciones de las tribus indíjenas i obtener su completa pacificacion.

ART. XII. — Las ratificaciones de esta Convencion serán canjeadas en el término de ocho meses o ántes si fuere posible i el canje tendrá lugar en la ciudad de Santiago o Buenos Aires.

En fé de lo cual, los Plenipotenciarios de la República de Chile i de la República Arjentina firmaron i sellaron con sus respectivos sellos, en doble ejemplar la presente Convencion, en Santiago, a seis dias del mes de diciembre del año N. S. mil ochocientos setenta i ocho [1].

Les deux projets furent repoussés par la législature et les rapports des deux pays furent fort tendus pendant plusieurs années. A l'intervention des Ministres des Etats-Unis de l'Amérique du Nord accrédités auprès des deux gouvernements, une convention fut signée le 23 juillet 1881, qui détermina les limites litigieuses et en confia la description détaillée à des commissaires. Des conventions complémentaires furent encore conclues sous les dates des 20 août 1888, 1er mai 1893 et 6 septembre 1895. Ce ne fut que par une convention du 17 avril 1896 que le gouvernement de la Grande-Bretagne fut désigné pour nommer éventuellement un tribunal arbitral. Les commissaires chargés de la délimitation résumèrent, dans trois procès-verbaux des 29 août, 1er et 3 septembre 1898, les constatations faites par eux et déterminèrent les points au sujet desquels l'accord ne put s'établir. Le 23 novembre 1898 le Gouvernement de la Grande-Bretagne fut officiellement saisi de la contestation et un tribunal composé de trois membres fut organisé par lui.

Acuerdo de los gobiernos de la República Argentina y de la República de Chile, firmado en Santiago de Chile, Abril 17, 1896.

En la ciudad de Santiago de Chile, á diez y siete días del mes de abril de mil ochocientos noventa y seis, reunidos en la sala del despacho del ministerio de relaciones exteriores, el señor don Norberto Quirno Costa, enviado extraordinario y ministro plenipotenciario de la República Argentina en Chile, y el señor don Adolfo Guerrero, ministro del ramo, expusieron que: los gobiernos de la República Argentina y de la República de Chile, deseando facilitar la leal ejecución de los tratados vigentes que fijan un límite inconmovible entre ambos países, restablecer la confianza en la paz y evitar toda causa de conflicto, persiguiendo, como siempre, el propósito de procurar soluciones por avenimientos directos, sin perjuicio de hacer efectivos los otros recursos conciliatorios que esos mismos pactos prescriben, han llegado al acuerdo que contienen las bases siguientes:

[1] *Memoria de Relaciones Exteriores*, Chile, 1879, p. 239.

Primera. — Las operaciones de demarcación del límite entre la República Argentina y la República de Chile, que se ejecutan en conformidad al tratado de 1881 y al protocolo de 1893, se extenderán en la cordillera de los Andes hasta el paralelo veinte y tres de latitud austral, debiendo trazarse la línea divisoria entre este paralelo y el veintiseis grados, cincuenta y dos minutos y cuarenta y cinco segundos, concurriendo á la operación ambos gobiernos y el gobierno de Bolivia, que será solicitado al efecto.

Segunda. — Si ocurriesen divergencias entre los peritos al fijar en la cordillera de los Andes los hitos divisorios al sur del paralelo veintiseis grados, cincuenta y dos minutos y cuarenta y cinco segundos y no pudieran allamarse amigablemente por acuerdo de ambos gobiernos, quedarán sometidas al fallo del gobierno de Su Majestad Británica, á quien las partes contratantes designan, desde ahora, con el carácter de árbitro encargado de aplicar estrictamente en tales casos las disposiciones del tratado y protocolo mencionados, previo el estudio del terreno, por una comisión que el árbitro designará.

Tercera. — Los peritos procederán á efectuar el estudio del terreno en la región vecina al paralelo cincuenta y dos de que trata la última parte del artículo segundo del protocolo de 1893, y propondrán la línea divisoria que allí debe adoptarse si resultar el caso previsto en dicha estipulación. Si hubiere divergencia para fijar esta línea, será tambien resuelta por el árbitro designado en este convenio.

Quarta. — Sesenta días después de producida la divergencia, en los casos á que se refieren las bases anteriores, podrá solicitarse la intervención del árbitro por ambos gobiernos de común acuerdo, ó por cualquiera de ellos separadamente.

Quinta. — Convienen ambos gobiernos en que la actual ubicación del hito de San Francisco entre los paralelos veintiseis y veintisiete, no sea tomado en consideración como base ó antecedente obligatorio para la determinación del deslinde en esa región, estimandose las operaciones y trabajos efectuados en ella en diversas épocas como estudios para la fijación definitiva de la línea, sin perjuicio de realizarse otros que los peritos tuvieron á bien disponer.

Sexta. — Los peritos, al reanudar sus trabajos en la próxima temporada, dispondrán las operaciones y estudios á que se refieren las bases primera y tercera de este acuerdo.

Septima. — Convienen asimismo ambos gobiernos en ratificar el acuerdo tercero del acta de 6 de septiembre de 1895 para la prosecusión de los trabajos de demarcación, en el caso que se presentará algun desacuerdo, á fin de que estos trabajos, como es el propósito de las partes contratandes, nunca sean interrumpidos.

Octava. — Dentro del término de sesenta días despues que hubiere sido firmado el presente acuerdo, los representantes diplomáticos de la República Argentina y de la República de Chile, acreditados cerca del gobierno de Su Majestad Británica, solicitarán conjuntamente de este la aceptación del cargo de árbitro que se le confiere, á cuyo efecto los respectivos gobiernos impartirán las instrucciones necesarias.

Novena. — Los gobiernos de la República Argentina y de la República de Chile, abonarán por mitad los gastos que requiera el cumplimiento de este acuerdo.

Los ministros infrascritos, en nombre de sus respectivos gobiernos y debitamente autorizados, firmaron el presente acuerdo en dos ejemplares, uno para cada parte, y les ponen sus sellos [1].

CXXIX. Colombie, Grande-Bretagne.

31 juillet 1896.

Il s'est agi dans l'espèce des différends survenus à la suite des conventions conclues entre MM. Punchard, McTaggart, Lowther & Co. et la Republique de Colombie, en 1892 et 1893, en vue de la construction du chemin de fer de Medellin au fleuve Magdalena. Il fut accordé aux intéressés une somme de 40,000 £; ils en reclamaient 642,309.

Convention to submit to a Tribunal of Arbitration the differences touching the import, validity, interpretation and mode of execution of certain contracts, concluded at London, Juli 31, 1896.

Whereas certain Contracts were entered into between the Government of the Department of Antioquia, the Government of Columbia, and Messrs. Punchard, McTaggart, Lowther and Co., a mercantile co-partnership in London, for the construction of a railway to connect the city of Medellin with the Magdalena River, which Contracts are designated and dated as follows:

Contract N° 80 of the 24th September, 1892
Contract N° 81 of the 10th November, 1892
Contract N° 82 of the 24th September, 1892
Contract N° 2 of the 5th January, 1893
Contract N° 6 of the 9th January, 1893:

---

[1] *Memoria de Relaciones Exteriores*, Argentina, 1896, p. 22.

And whereas differences have arisen between the parties to the said Contracts touching their import, validity, interpretation, and mode of execution:

Now, therefore, the Governments of Her Britannic Majesty and of the Republic of Colombia, being desirous that all such differences between the parties to said Contracts should be settled in a just and equitable manner, have agreed, that is to say, the Government of Her Britannic Majesty for and on behalf of the said copartnership of Punchard, McTaggart, Lowther and Co., and the Government of the Republic of Colombia, that the differences referred to shall be submitted to the examination of a Tribunal of Arbitration.

To this end, the Government of the Swiss Confederation having consented as a friendly office to the Governments of Her Britannic Majesty and of Colombia, to lend their services towards the constitution and establishment of such a Tribunal of Arbitration, the Undersigned, to wit: The Most Honourable the Marques of Salisbury K. G., Her Majesty's Principal Secretary of State for Foreign Affairs, and Don José M. Hurtado, Envoy Extraordinary and Minister Plenipotentiary of Colombia to Her Britannic Majesty, duly authorized and empowered by their respective Governments, have agreed as follows : --

ART. I. — As soon as the Government of the Swiss Confederation shall have been notified of the exchange of ratifications of the present Convention, the Swiss Federal Council shall proceed to select and appoint three Swiss jurists, fully qualified in the judgment of the Council to act as impartial and competent arbitrators under this Convention, who, upon their acceptance of the trust, shall collectively constitute the Tribunal of Arbitration to which this Convention has reference. The Tribunal shall meet as soon as possible thereafter at a place in Switzerland to be designated by the Arbitrators.

ART. II. — The Tribunal of Arbitration being so constituted, it will stand vested with the necessary and sufficient authority to frame and adopt its own rules, regulations, and mode of procedure.

ART. III. — The Tribunal shall be competent to take cognizance of, examine and decide upon all allegations, questions and issues both of law and of fact, which may present themselves in the course of the inquiry, provided that in the judgment of the Tribunal such questions and issues arise out of, or are pertinent to the matter of the Contracts hereinbefore referred to. And the Tribunal is specially authorized and empowered to determine the amount of the indemnity which either the defendants or the plaintiffs may, in the judgement of the Tribunal, be entitled to claim and receive from the other. All questions considered by the Tribunal, including the final Award, shall be decided by a majority of the Arbitrators.

ART. IV. — The amount of indemnity (if any) which, in the judgment of the Tribunal, either the defendants or the plaintiffs may be entitled to claim and receive from the other party being determined, its equivalent in good and lawful money of the Swiss Confederation shall be ascertained and declared by the Tribunal in the form of an Award, which the Contracting Governments undertake for themselves and for the parties interested to accept as final and without appeal, in regard to all points and matters submitted to the Tribunal. And the Award shall provide that the party liable for the payment of the indemnity shall pay into the Political Departement of the Swiss Confederation the amount thereof in lawful money of the Swiss Confederation, within six months from the date of the Award, and the sum shall be held at the disposal of the Government of the party entitled to receive the indemnity.

ART. V. — Each party to the suit shall be represented before the Tribunal of Arbitration by an Agent, who shall enjoy the privileges usually accorded to plaintiffs and defendants in Courts of Justice, without prejudice, however, to the Rules, Regulations, and procedure which may be adopted by the Tribunal.

ART. VI. — If at any time before the case be decided any one or more of the Arbitrators should cease to act as such, from other than temporary causes, the remaining arbitrator or arbitrators shall forthwith make known the circumstance to the Swiss Federal Council, who shall thereupon proceed to appoint a substitute or substitutes for the arbitrator or arbitrators having so ceased to act, who thenceforth shall become *functus officio*.

ART. VII. — The emoluments of the Arbitrators shall be fixed by the Swiss Federal Council at a specified sum, of which one third part will be paid to them before the suit is brought on, and the remaining two thirds of the emolument at the close of the proceedings of the Tribunal.

The emolument of the Arbitrators and the salary of such officers and employers as the Board of Arbitrators may deem proper to employ under remuneration, together with all expenses incurred by order of the Tribunal, shall be borne share and share alike by the parties to the suit. But each party shall pay the salary of its agent and defray all expenses incurred for its special benefit; provided always that nothing contained in this Article shall prevent the Tribunal from condemning one party to the suit to pay such portion of the joint costs and expenses of the Arbitration as, in the judgment and discretion of the Tribunal, may seem fit and proper.

ART. VIII. — A period of three months, reckoned from and after the day appointed by the Arbitrators for the commencement of the proceedings, shall be allowed to the plaintiffs, that is to say, to Messrs. Punchard, McTaggart, Lowther and Co., to present through their Agent their case to the Tribunal, and upon the close of the preliminary case for the plaintiffs a period of three months shall be granted to the defendants, that is to say, the Government of the Republic of Colombia, to put in their answer through their Agent. The Tribunal will determine what other and subsequent periods of time shall be allowed for the production of proofs, rebutting evidence, reply and rejoinder: having in view the earliest possible termination of the suit that may be found consistent with the ascertainement and elucidation of facts material to the ends of justice.

The Arbitrators may call upon the parties to the suit to produce in Court any and all papers and documents the examination of which, in their opinion, would promote the ends of justice. In cases of non-compliance with such requests, the Tribunal shall limit its action in the matter to drawing its own inferences or conclusions from such non-compliance.

ART. IX. — The present Convention shall be ratified by the Vice-President of the Republic of Colombia upon its approval by the National Congress and the exchange of ratifications shall take place in London four months from the date thereof, or sooner if possible.

In witness whereof the respective Plenipotentiaries have signed the same and have affixed thereto the seals of their arms.

Done at London the thirty-first day of July in the year of our Lord one thousand eight hundred and ninety-six.

Sentence arbitrale relative au chemin de fer d'Antioquia, prononcée à Berne, le 17 octobre 1899.

Le litige dont le Tribunal arbitral est appelé à connaître, se réduit, en substance, à trois questions principales.

1° Les contrats passés entre parties ont-ils été valablement conclus ou ont-ils été d'emblée viciés par une cause de nullité?

2° Dans l'hypothèse de la validité, laquelle est-ce des parties qui les a violés et qui, par ce fait, a donné à la partie adverse un juste motif de résiliation ?

3° Quid des dommages et intérêts ?

Quant au droit applicable à la solution de ces trois questions, le Tribunal constate que les parties sont d'accord pour appliquer le droit colombien, ce qui est d'ailleurs conforme aux principes du droit international.

1° CAUSES DE NULLITÉ.

La partie défenderesse conclut à ce que les contrats passés entre parties soient déclarés nuls et de nul effet par défaut de cause et comme étant entachés de dol.

a. Défaut de cause.

Aux termes de l'art. 1524 du code civil colombien (qui dérive des articles 1131 à 1133 du code civil français) « une obligation ne peut pas exister là où il n'existe pas *une cause réelle*», c'est-à-dire « un motif qui induit à l'acte ou contrat ».

Cette cause maîtresse ou ce motif, au dire de la partie défenderesse, aurait, dans l'espèce, consisté dans le fait que les demandeurs se sont présentés en qualité de capitalistes assez puissants pour fournir de leurs propres deniers les fonds nécessaires à l'exécution de l'œuvre, objet du contrat de construction. Or, il y avait, en réalité, *manque de cause* ou *fausse cause*, partant obligation nulle, puisque — toujours au dire de la partie défenderesse — il serait établi que cette qualité de capitalistes capables de procurer les fonds nécessaires, les demandeurs se l'étaient faussement attribuée et qu'ils ne la possédaient point.

Ce raisonnement repose sur une confusion du mobile psychologique, de la cause impulsive, avec le motif ou la cause juridique. Il se peut, et il est même assez plausible que l'un des mobiles qui ont déterminé le gouvernement d'Antioquia à contracter avec la maison Punchard ait été la confiance en la puissance financière de cette maison, mais le motif juridique, c'est-à-dire l'objet *immédiat* recherché par lui, le but direct qu'il avait en vue, en contractant, était d'obtenir, en échange de son propre engagement, l'engagement correspondant de l'autre partie contractante. Or, ce but immédiat il l'a réellement atteint et réalisé par la conclusion même du contrat bilatéral, puisque, en vertu de ce contrat, la maison Punchard prenait, de son côté, l'engagement de construire la ligne et de fournir les fonds nécessaires. Peu importait, pour la validité de cet engagement, que la maison Punchard fût ou ne fût pas en état de le tenir. De toute façon, elle était liée, et le motif du contrat ayant précisément été, pour la partie colombienne, *de lier* l'autre partie, la conclusion même du contrat répondait exactement à ce que voulait le Gouvernement d'Antioquia : l'engagement qu'il obtenait ainsi de l'autre partie contractante était la cause de son propre engagement, et vice-versa.

Et l'on peut dire, d'une manière générale, que tout contrat bilatéral, par le fait même qu'il est bilatéral, est un contrat dont la cause gît et apparaît dans le contrat lui-même et résulte de ses propres termes : cette cause, pour chacune des parties, n'étant autre que l'obligation de l'autre partie.

b. Dol.

Le dol viciant les contrats, consiste, au dire de la partie défenderesse, dans deux ordres de faits distincts imputables aux demandeurs : leurs actes de corruption et le fait de s'être attribué faussement une capacité financière qu'ils ne possédaient pas.

Pour ce qui est des actes de corruption, il y a lieu de distinguer entre les contrats *ad referendum*, les contrats définitifs de 1892 et les contrats additionnels de 1893. Les faits de corruption qui ont accompagné la conclusion des contrats *ad referendum*, pour établis qu'ils puissent être, sont sans pertinence juridique parce que ces contrats ne furent point ratifiés et que les contrats définitifs qui leur furent substitués en diffèrent sur des points essentiels.

Ainsi que l'a reconnu, dans sa déposition du 26 décembre 1893, l'un des adversaires les plus décidés des contrats *ad referendum*, M. Pedro Bravo, les contrats signés à Medellin entre le Gouvernement départemental et M. Ridley contenaient « des modifications très favorables (pour la Colombie) à celui conclu à Londres par M. Barrientos, modifications si avantageuses qu'elles permettaient à des ennemis déclarés de l'ancien contrat d'être devenus partisans du nouveau».

Quant aux contrats définitifs de 1892, il n'apparaît pas que la corruption ait joué un rôle dans leur conclusion : à considérer leur contenu, beaucoup plus onéreux et à certains égards même très embarrassant pour les entrepreneurs, il est manifeste que, dans les négociations qui précédèrent leur signature, les fonctionnaires colombiens ont consciencieusement défendu les intérêts nationaux et que la corruption, si tant est qu'elle ait été tentée — ce qui n'est point établi — n'a pas eu prise sur eux, de l'aveu même de la partie défenderesse.

Telle fut bien aussi l'opinion de M. Caro, vice-président de la République, lorsque, un an après, dans sa lettre du 2 septembre 1893 au ministre de l'intérieur, il s'exprimait en ces termes : « Le contrat qui fut mené à bonne fin peut être considéré comme distinct du premier, par les *différences essentielles* qui se remarquent entre les deux, de sorte que plusieurs qui s'étaient opposés au premier, appuyèrent le second et celui-ci obtint le vote favorable de la plus grande partie des conseils municipaux du Département. »

Restent les deux contrats additionnels de 1893 pour l'obtention desquels des sommes auraient été promises et même versées par le canal de M. Perez Triana. Mais, ici aussi, il n'est point établi, il est même contesté par la partie défenderesse que ledit M. Perez Triana, dépourvu lui-même, à ce moment-là, de tout caractère officiel, ait été de connivence avec les fonctionnaires qui ont coopéré à la conclusion de ces contrats. Et l'eût-il été, que les effets de cette prétendue connivence n'apparaissent guère : le chiffre de £ 37,500 auquel a été porté le montant annuel de la subvention nationale est conforme à la loi nº 67 de 1890, et les avantages concédés aux entrepreneurs par le contrat nº 6 de 1893 ne constituent pas, à proprement parler, des *nova* : ils ne font que préciser des points dont l'interprétation, dans les contrats de 1892, prêtait le flanc à la controverse.

La partie défenderesse allègue, d'autre part, que les demandeurs l'auraient trompée, en se faisant passer faussement pour des capitalistes possédant eux-mêmes ou pouvant du moins se procurer, par leur crédit ou par leurs relations, les fonds nécessaires pour l'exécution de l'entreprise dont ils se chargeaient aussi en qualité de constructeurs.

« La maison Punchard — dit à ce propos la défenderesse — était dans l'impossibilité matérielle de se couvrir ou de procurer l'emprunt contracté, et elle connaissait mieux que personne cette impossibilité, en sorte que c'est le sachant, le voulant, qu'elle a promis une chose qu'elle ne possédait pas. »

Et pour donner le change sur sa situation réelle, la maison Punchard aurait, au surplus, trompé la partie défenderesse en prétendant avoir exécuté au moyen de ses propres ressources les travaux pour la construction du port et du brise-lames de la Guayra, au Vénézuéla.

Ces assertions de la partie défenderesse méritent d'être prises en considération, car il est vrai, en principe, que l'affirmation sciemment fausse d'une qualité essentielle peut vicier le consentement de l'autre partie qui, si elle n'avait été induite à croire à l'existence de cette prétendue qualité, n'eût pas contracté.

Mais il n'est point établi que les demandeurs aient jamais affirmé posséder eux-mêmes, dans leur patrimoine, les fonds nécessaires pour couvrir l'emprunt ou pour construire la ligne, pas plus qu'en affirmant avoir fourni eux-mêmes le capital nécessaire aux travaux de la Guayra, ils ne prétendaient l'avoir fourni de leurs propres deniers. Encore que l'art. VII du contrat nº 80 de 1892 leur réserve la faculté de « couvrir eux-mêmes, de leurs propres deniers », l'emprunt à contracter, il résulte des dispositions circonstanciées contenues dans les deux contrats de 1892, au sujet de l'émission de cet emprunt, que l'éventualité d'un emprunt couvert sans émission, par les propres fonds des entrepreneurs, n'était visée pour ainsi dire que pour la forme seulement, et que les deux parties se rendaient parfaitement compte qu'il faudrait bien en venir à faire appel au crédit public pour réunir les fonds nécessaires à la construction.

Le tout est donc de savoir, si la maison Punchard, en s'attribuant assez de crédit pour émettre un emprunt de cette importance, était, oui ou non, de mauvaise foi.

Qu'elle ait commis une grande imprudence en prenant un pareil engagement, on ne saurait le nier, et les appréhensions exprimées par la maison elle-même, dans sa lettre du 18 novembre 1892 à son représentant M. Ridley, attestent qu'elle n'était elle-même pas sans inquiétude à cet égard. Mais de là à la convaincre de mauvaise foi, il y a encore un pas. Les demandeurs étaient en relations avec une banque importante, et ces relations, d'un grand secours pour eux, ils les eussent vraisemblablement conservées si les certificats de travaux, donnés en nantissement à la banque, eussent été réglés par qui de droit.

D'autre part, les ressources mises à la disposition des demandeurs pour le service des intérêts : traites sur les fermiers de l'impôt sur les alcools, bons sur la douane, rendement de la ligne à construire, paraissaient, à première vue du moins, offrir au public des garanties assez sérieuses pour l'engager à souscrire un emprunt offert à un taux d'intérêt très rémunérateur. Tout dépendait, il est vrai, des dispositions futures et incertaines du marché monétaire, et il y avait dans toutes ces prévisions une large part d'aléa, mais il n'apparaît pas qu'en trop comptant sur leur propre crédit, sur les bonnes dispositions du marché et en s'exagérant la valeur des garanties offertes par les gouvernements d'Antioquia et de Colombie, les demandeurs aient été de mauvaise foi. Il est plus probable que la perspective du bénéfice à réaliser sur le contrat de construction ait provoqué chez eux un état d'esprit optimiste, sous l'empire duquel les difficultés à surmonter, et surtout celles des débuts, leur ont paru moins grandes qu'elles ne l'étaient en réalité.

Il résulte de ce qui précède, que les contrats doivent être tenus pour valablement conclus et qu'ils ne sauraient être réputés nuls d'emblée, ni pour défaut de cause, ni en raison du dol dont leur conclusion aurait été entachée.

2° VIOLATION DES CONTRATS.

a. Par la partie demanderesse.

La partie demanderesse, au dire de l'Etat défendeur, aurait non seulement violé, mais rompu le contrat, par la cessation des travaux et par ses lettres des 4 et 5 octobre 1895 à MM. Cisneros et Bruce.

Il y a en effet dans ces deux lettres la phrase : « toutes les responsabilités provenant pour nous des contrats ont pris fin », qui semble indiquer nettement l'intention de rompre. Mais, ni M. Bruce, ni M. Cisneros n'avait qualité pour recevoir au nom de la partie adverse une déclaration de cette nature. Les fonctions de ces deux ingénieurs étaient celles d'arbitres techniques appelés à trancher tous les conflits d'ordre technique : aucun d'eux n'avait pour mission de recevoir au nom d'une partie et de transmettre à celle-ci les déclarations de l'autre partie contractante. Il n'apparaît pas d'ailleurs que l'un ou l'autre de ces messieurs ait transmis au gouvernement défendeur la déclaration dont il s'agit ; ils ne semblent même pas l'avoir tenue pour définitive et irrévocable, puisqu'ils ont continué à traiter ensemble les questions relatives à la construction du chemin de fer.

Aussi bien convient-il de ne considérer dans cette affaire que les actes et les paroles de M. Spencer, le représentant attitré des demandeurs à Medellin, qui seul a agi et seul a correspondu en cette occurrence avec le gouvernement défendeur. M. Spencer a arrêté les travaux ; mais sa lettre au gouverneur, du 9 octobre 1893, énonce clairement qu'il n'entendait pas, pour autant, rompre ou résilier le contrat : il voulait seulement faire trancher par la voie arbitrale les différends qui divisaient les parties et suspendre les travaux jusqu'à droit connu.

D'où il appert que, par leur attitude en octobre 1893, les demandeurs n'ont pas rompu le contrat ; ils en ont seulement suspendu l'exécution.

Cette suspension était-elle légitime ?

Le code colombien, à son article 1609, a consacré la règle du droit romain et du droit français, d'après laquelle « dans les contrats bilatéraux, l'un des contractants n'est pas en de-

meure par défaut d'exécution de ce qu'il a promis, aussi longtemps que l'autre ne s'exécute pas, pour sa part, ou ne se met pas en mesure de le faire dans la forme et dans le temps fixé ».

La question est donc de savoir si, au moment où les entrepreneurs suspendirent leurs travaux, l'autre partie contractante avait failli à ses propres engagements. Parmi les griefs articulés à cet égard par les demandeurs, il suffit de retenir celui qu'ils invoquèrent à l'époque même de la suspension des travaux, à savoir l'ordre donné par le gouverneur à l'un des dépositaires de Medellin de refuser le paiement du solde des certificats n°ˢ 1 et 2 et de récupérer sur les certificats subséquents ce qui avait été payé sur les deux premiers.

La partie défenderesse invoque deux raisons pour justifier cette mesure : elle affirme, d'une manière générale, que les demandeurs n'avaient aucun droit au paiement de leurs certificats tant qu'ils n'avaient pas fourni l'emprunt, et elle allègue plus spécialement le caractère irrégulier des deux premiers certificats qui, à son avis, la dispensait de les tenir pour valables.

Quant au premier moyen :

La clause XXVII du contrat n° 80 de 1892 stipule expressément que « jusqu'à ce que la première émission de l'emprunt soit effectuée, les certificats qui seront délivrés en faveur des entrepreneurs seront payés à Medellin et par les dépositaires de cette ville ». Il est vrai que la clause XII du dit contrat qualifie d'exceptionnel cet emploi du produit de l'impôt sur les alcools. Exceptionnel, il devait l'être en effet, puisque les contractants considéraient apparemment l'état de choses précédant la première émission de l'emprunt comme un état exceptionnel et transitoire, l'emprunt devant être émis le plus tôt possible.

A l'époque dont il s'agit, les parties se trouvaient donc précisément encore dans le cas « exceptionnel » visé par la clause XII et les demandeurs étaient, en droit de se prévaloir de la clause XXVII. L'art. 3 du contrat explicatif, n° 6 de 1893, loin de modifier cette clause, l'avait au contraire confirmée en statuant que « les dépositaires de Medellin doivent appliquer au paiement des certificats de travail et de matériel toute cette partie du produit de l'impôt sur les alcools et de la subvention nationale qui n'est pas nécessaire au paiement des intérêts échus des séries déjà émises de l'emprunt ».

Il est évident, en effet, que tant qu'aucune série de l'emprunt n'avait encore été émise, rien du produit de l'impôt sur les alcools n'était nécessaire au paiement des intérêts de la future dette ; car point n'était besoin d'accumuler des fonds en vue de ce service à venir, puisque les annuités courantes des subventions départementale et nationale devaient largement suffire pour couvrir les intérêts d'une première émission d'emprunt, qui devait être limitée à £ 550,000 au maximum. Le tout pouvait donc être affecté au paiement des certificats. Ce raisonnement est corroboré par le fait, qu'à l'époque dont il s'agit le gouvernement défendeur n'a jamais songé à contester, en principe, aux demandeurs leur droit d'affecter les fonds en dépôt à Medellin au paiement de leurs certificats. Cette faculté ne leur a été contestée qu'après coup, au cours du procès.

Quant au second moyen tiré du caractère spécial des deux premiers certificats :

Ces certificats ont été émis pour « *frais préliminaires* ». Ils l'ont été en vertu de la clause XXV, qui statuait expressément que « le coût des frais préliminaires » serait remboursé sur le vu des certificats. L'Ingénieur-Conseil et l'Agent officiel, à qui il appartenait de délivrer ces certificats, exerçaient à cet égard — suivant la lettre et l'esprit du contrat de construction — une sorte de juridiction : leurs décisions liaient et les parties et les dépositaires.

A la forme, le gouvernement n'avait donc aucune qualité pour interdire à un dépositaire de solder sur les fonds provenant de l'impôt sur les alcools, des certificats régulièrement ordonnancés par l'Ingénieur-Conseil et l'Agent officiel.

Cette mesure n'était pas davantage justifiée au fond. La somme de £ 10,000 pour frais préliminaires, ne représentant que le 0,8 % du prix total de l'œuvre, n'avait rien d'exorbitant ; elle est conforme aux habitudes et il n'est pas d'usage non plus de fournir des états détaillés pour les dépenses multiples rentrant dans cette catégorie, et qui ne relève d'aucun tarif.

Si l'Etat défendeur allègue aujourd'hui, pour expliquer sa façon d'agir, que l'attitude des demandeurs lui faisait craindre que ceux-ci n'exécutassent pas le contrat, et que l'argent qu'il leur aurait payé risquait ainsi d'être perdu, cet argument, si plausible qu'il soit en fait, est sans valeur juridique : tant que les demandeurs n'avaient pas été constitués en demeure, la partie défenderesse n'avait pas le droit de surseoir unilatéralement à l'accomplissement d'une obligation échue.

Il résulte de l'exposé ci-dessus que le Gouvernement d'Antioquia n'avait pas le droit de l'interposer pour empêcher le paiement des certificats 1 et 2 ; que ce faisant il a commis une violation du contrat, qui autorisait la partie adverse à suspendre, de son côté, l'exécution de ses engagements.

b. Par la partie défenderesse.

La partie défenderesse, de son côté, a interrompu l'exécution du contrat par sa résolution du 19 octobre 1893, notifiée le 24 octobre suivant à la partie adverse.

Elle prête aujourd'hui à cette manifestation le caractère d'une simple suspension d'exécution. Mais, à la lumière de ses actes et de ses paroles d'alors, la mesure prise le 19 octobre 1893 par le gouvernement d'Antioquia apparaît comme ayant eu une portée plus considérable : elle était et elle voulait être une résiliation du contrat. Cela résulte notamment des termes du chiffre 2 : « Il opte *dès à présent*, pour la résolution des contrats », termes qui furent corroborés peu après par des faits tels que l'accaparement des fonds en dépôt, de la ligne et du materiel. De pareils faits apparaîtraient comme des actes de pure spoliation s'ils n'eussent été la manifestation de la conviction que les contrats avaient pris fin et étaient définitivement résiliés en fait et en droit.

Pour juger la légitimité de la résolution du 19 octobre 1893 et des actes dont elle fut suivie, il y a donc lieu d'examiner si, à ladite époque, la partie colombienne était en droit de résilier le contrat.

L'art. 1546 du code civil de Colombie dispose :

« Dans les contrats bi-latéraux est impliquée « la condition résolutoire dans le cas où ce qui « est stipulé ne serait pas accompli par un des « contractants.

« Mais dans ce cas, l'autre contractant pourra « demander à son choix, ou la résolution ou « l'accomplissement du contrat avec indemnité de « dommages-intérêts ».

La question est donc, ici aussi, de savoir si, au moment où le gouvernement d'Antioquia opta « pour la résolution » du contrat, l'autre partie contractante lui avait fourni un juste motif de résiliation en manquant à ses engagements.

La partie défenderesse a dressé, au cours du procès, toute une liste de ces prétendus manquements ; à l'époque de la rupture, elle n'en avait invoqué que deux ; l'inaction des entrepreneurs sur le terrain et l'omission de fournir l'emprunt.

1. L'inaction des entrepreneurs sur le terrain.

Les opérations sur le terrain ne pouvaient être entreprises sérieusement qu'après la confection et l'adoption des plans.

Or, la plupart des plans n'arrivèrent à Londres que vers la fin du mois de juin 1893; ils ne furent soumis à l'Agent officiel (soit à son représentant) que vers la fin de juillet.

Etant donné que les entrpreneurs avaient pu se mettre à l'œuvre dès le mois d'octobre 1892, le laps de temps employé pour l'élaboration des plans peut paraître long. Mais il y a lieu de tenir compte de la controverse qui surgit au sujet de l'emploi du *système Abt*: suivant l'issue qu'aurait ce différend, le tracé variait considérablement et l'on ne pouvait exiger des entrepreneurs qu'ils exécutassent les plans de détail en double, pour l'une et l'autre des variantes en présence. Or, l'Ingénieur-Conseil et l'Agent officiel s'étant déclarés d'emblée favorables au système Abt, dont l'emploi constituait en effet la solution la plus rationnelle au point de vue technique, les entrepreneurs ont eu raison de tenir bon sur ce point et de ne pas céder à l'opposition de l'Ingénieur officiel, subordonné de l'Agent officiel et dont l'avis, encore qu'il dût être requis, ne pouvait prévaloir sur celui de son chef; cela en dépit du 2ᵉ alinéa de l'art. 2 (chap. II, titre 1ᵉʳ) du cahier des charges, où l's du pluriel du mot « *ingénieurs* » dans la phrase « *s'il y avait désaccord* (au sujet des pentes et moyens de traction) *entre tels ingénieurs et agent* » si elle n'est pas due à une simple erreur de plume, est certainement — comme le dit M. Cisneros, dans son rapport du 1ᵉʳ juillet 1896 (Doc. Col., nº C. C. 1) — « en opposition avec ce que dit cet article, avec l'esprit de tout le contrat de construction et du cahier des charges lui-même, esprit qui est que l'Ingénieur-Conseil et l'Agent officiel soient juges en toutes les questions techniques et que les ingénieurs résident et officiel soient leurs aides, subordonnés à eux, en toutes questions techniques ».

Il est à remarquer, d'ailleurs, que le contrat de construction ne stipule aucune date, ni pour la présentation des plans, ni pour le commencement des travaux de terrassement, etc.; il se borne à fixer en bloc le délai imparti pour la construction. Si les entrepreneurs avaient perdu du temps, ils étaient donc quittes à le rattraper dans la suite en forçant les travaux. Ce n'est qu'une fois les plans définitivement adoptés, ce qui ne fut le cas que vers la fin d'octobre 1893, qu'on aurait pu déduire d'une inaction prolongée de leur part qu'ils ne voulaient ou ne pouvaient pas achever l'ouvrage dans le délai stipulé. Et encore eût-il fallu alors constater ce défaut de vouloir ou de pouvoir par une mise en demeure préalable.

A l'époque où intervint la rupture, les choses n'en étaient pas encore là, puisque la plupart des plans ne furent signés à Londres que quelques jours après.

2. *Omission de fournir l'emprunt.*

Aux termes des clauses VII du contrat nº 80 et IV du contrat nº 82 de 1892, les entrepreneurs étaient tenus de fournir, soit de leurs propres deniers, soit par voie d'emprunt, les fonds nécessaires à « l'exécution totale de l'œuvre ». Cette obligation devait être remplie « *dans le plus bref délai possible* » et, en tout cas, « *en temps opportun* », « le manque de fonds » ne pouvant « en aucun moment être allégué par les entrepreneurs comme un fait les exemptant de l'accomplissement régulier de leurs engagements » (clause VIII du contrat nº 82 de 1892).

Le « temps opportun » dont il est ici question est évidemment le temps indiqué par les exigences de l'ouvrage à construire. Faire l'apport des fonds en « temps opportun » cela veut dire les apporter assez tôt pour qu'aucun manque de fonds ne puisse jamais entraver ni retarder la marche des travaux.

On ne saurait donc admettre avec les demandeurs qu'ils fussent libres de choisir, dans la limite de quatre années, le moment où il leur conviendrait d'apporter les fonds. Mais l'on ne saurait prétendre non plus avec l'Etat défendeur que le premier apport de fonds, par émission d'emprunt ou autrement, eût dû être opéré dès le début de l'année 1893. N'avait-il pas été expressément stipulé, afin de laisser aux entrepreneurs une certaine latitude, que pendant une période transitoire le montant des certificats de travail et de matériel pourrait être soldé sur les fonds provenant des subventions, en dépôt à Medellin?

Cette période transitoire avait été prolongée par les discussions relatives aux plans, qui avaient retardé l'ouverture des travaux de construction; mais à la vérité, en octobre 1893, elle touchait à sa fin; car, pour peu que, les plans une fois adoptés, les entrepreneurs se fussent mis sérieusement à l'œuvre, comme c'était leur devoir, les fonds de Medellin eussent été épuisés très rapidement.

Aussi bien, le gouvernement d'Antioquia était-il parfaitement fondé, à l'époque dont il s'agit, à se préoccuper de la façon dont les entrepreneurs entendaient s'acquitter de l'obligation leur incombant à titre de bailleurs de fonds, et l'attitude prise à cet égard par ces derniers; les nouvelles reçues de M. Cisneros, etc., avaient bien de quoi émouvoir et inquiéter l'autre partie contractante. Le moment était certes venu pour elle de constater que « le temps opportun » nécessitant un premier apport de fonds était là et pour sommer péremptoirement les entrepreneurs à s'exécuter à cet égard. Le gouvernement a cru pouvoir se passer de cette formalité. Il a considéré de prime abord les entrepreneurs comme étant en demeure et les a traités en conséquence. Cette façon d'agir serait justifiée, selon lui, par l'article 1608 du code civil de Colombie statuant que « le débiteur est en demeure : 1° quand il n'a pas accompli l'obligation *dans le terme stipulé* ».

Le défaut de ce raisonnement, c'est que dans l'espèce, il n'y avait pas, à proprement parler, de « terme stipulé ». Le terme de « temps opportun » est un terme élastique ; il ne correspond pas à une date fixe ou à une donnée objective précise ; il laisse une marge à l'appréciation individuelle. La partie qui juge le « temps opportun » venu ne saurait supposer d'emblée que l'autre partie contractante partage ce sentiment. Même à défaut d'une disposition expresse de la loi, le bon sens et la bonne foi veulent qu'en pareil cas, le débiteur ne soit constitué en demeure qu'après une interpellation du créancier, lui indiquant que le moment de remplir son obligation paraît être venu et lui fixant suivant les circonstances un délai pour s'exécuter.

Ce mode de procéder eût été d'autant plus indiqué dans le cas particulier que les demandeurs, encore qu'ils eussent dû tenir pour légitime la réclamation et la mise en demeure émanant de la partie colombienne, auraient cependant été fondés à formuler, de leur côté, certaines conditions : ils eussent pu exiger le paiement préalable des deux certificats en souffrance et la remise intégrale, aux dépositaires de Medellin, des bons de la subvention nationale, ne s'étant prêtés que temporairement au *modus vivendi* qui avait consisté à mettre ces bons en dépôt à la Banque nationale.

N'ayant été ni interpellés, ni mis en mesure de formuler leurs observations ou leurs exigences légitimes, les demandeurs en leur qualité de bailleurs de fonds ne sauraient être tenus pour avoir été *ipso facto* en demeure au moment où le gouvernement colombien les a traités comme tels sans avertissement préalable.

3. Autres griefs.

Quant aux autres reproches adressés, au cours du procès, à la partie demanderesse, aucun d'eux n'implique à sa charge un cas de *demeure* nettement caractérisé.

La prétendue incapacité financière des demandeurs ne constituait pas l'inexécution, dont la portée a été appréciée à propos des causes de nullité.

L'omission de désigner le dépositaire de Londres était sans importance tant que, faute de fonds, ce personnage n'avait encore aucune fonction à remplir.

Les tentatives de se faire délivrer des certificats pour des sommes indues, à les supposer réelles, eussent simplement constitué, non des infractions, mais simplement des réclamations injustifiées dont les ingénieurs du contrôle, seuls juges en la matière, n'avaient qu'à faire justice en les repoussant.

Le fait d'avoir levé des plans en vue du système Abt et en faisant abstraction des tunnels, est également couvert par l'approbation des ingénieurs du contrôle compétents. Les prescriptions du cahier des charges, relatives aux tunnels, n'avaient qu'une portée éventuelle ; il est généralement admis que le cahier des charges, pièce auxiliaire, n'a point pour but d'imposer des travaux d'art déterminés ; il ne vise qu'à indiquer les conditions d'exécution des différents travaux d'art possibles qui viendraient à être imposés par le tracé et par les plans. La copie des plans Jones, si elle a eu lieu, était une chose licite, les entrepreneurs étant libres d'utiliser pour la levée de leurs plans, sous leur propre responsabilité et à leurs risques, n'importe quelles données se trouvant à leur disposition.

La prétendue détérioration de la ligne de Puerto-Berrio à Pavas et de son matériel eût simplement obligé les entrepreneurs à pourvoir à la réfection avant la remise de la ligne ; elle était sans portée pendant la période de construction.

Le cautionnement a été fourni en vertu d'une convention passée le 28 juin 1893 avec le Représentant de la Colombie à Londres. Il n'a pas été établi que la partie défenderesse ait désavoué son mandataire ; elle est donc réputée avoir agréé le cautionnement tel qu'il fut constitué.

Enfin la cessation des travaux de la part des entrepreneurs fut, comme il a été démontré ci-dessus, un acte légitime.

Il faut conclure de ce qui précède, que les demandeurs n'étaient en demeure, au sens juridique de ce terme, avec aucun de leurs engagements à l'époque où le gouvernement d'Antioquia résilia le contrat ; que, par conséquent, le dit gouvernement, en prononçant de son chef cette résiliation et en procédant en conséquence, a violé, lui, le contrat qui liait les parties.

Celles-ci étant d'accord dans leurs conclusions pour maintenir cette résiliation comme un fait accompli, la violation commise par la partie défenderesse doit se résoudre non par une remise en vigueur du contrat, mais, en application de l'article 1546 du code civil colombien, par l'allocation de dommages et intérêts à la partie demanderesse qui a été lésée par la rupture du contrat.

3° DÉTERMINATION DES DOMMAGES ET INTÉRÊTS.

Le dommage causé à une partie par la rupture illicite du contrat, comprend, en principe, d'une part, toutes les dépenses qu'elle a faites en pure perte dans l'accomplissement de ses obligations contractuelles *(damnum emergens)* et d'autre part, tous les bénéfices que l'exécution régulière du contrat lui aurait rapportés *(lucrum cessans)*.

Il en serait ainsi, dans l'espèce, si, sans l'acte de rupture de l'autre partie, les demandeurs eussent, eux, exécuté le contrat jusqu'au bout et que, agissant ainsi, ils en eussent réellement retiré un bénéfice.

Or, cette supposition ne cadrerait pas avec les faits de la cause.

Tout porte à croire, au contraire, que, dans le cas particulier, loin de priver les demandeurs d'un bénéfice, la rupture est venue à point pour les tirer d'embarras et pour les dispenser de s'avouer, eux-mêmes, incapables de remplir le plus essentiel de leurs engagements : celui de fournir de leurs deniers ou par voie d'emprunt les fonds nécessaires à la construction de l'ouvrage.

Il est hors de doute, en effet, que les demandeurs — leur lettre du 4 octobre 1893 à M. Cisneros, à défaut d'autres nombreux indices, suffirait à le prouver — ne disposaient pas personnellement des fonds considérables que le contrat d'emprunt les obligeait à fournir. Force était donc pour eux de faire appel au crédit, et ils n'eussent plus pu éluder ou différer de longtemps l'accomplissement de cette obligation. Or, il y a tout lieu de penser qu'une tentative entreprise dans ce sens aurait échoué ; les appréhensions énoncées à ce sujet, déjà une année auparavant, par les demandeurs eux-mêmes, dans leur lettre à M. Ridley, du 18 novembre 1892, n'étaient que trop fondées. Le moment de lancer l'emprunt venu, MM. Bruce et Cisneros déclarèrent à l'unisson que toute émission était impossible et que, si l'on voulait maintenir l'entreprise, il fallait recourir à une nouvelle combinaison ; or, rien n'obligeait la Colombie à s'y prêter ; elle pouvait persister à exiger purement et simplement l'accomplissement du contrat dans toutes ses clauses ; perspective si peu rassurante pour les demandeurs, que, dans leur lettre à M. Spencer, du 18 octobre 1893, ils semblent lui tracer comme ligne de conduite d'esquiver avant tout l'obligation d'accomplir le contrat.

La promptitude avec laquelle les demandeurs avaient suspendu leurs travaux, en raison de la contestation de deux certificats de £ 5000 chacun, alors que ce différend eût pu être réglé arbitralement sans suspension de travaux, est un indice de plus du peu d'empressement qu'ils mettaient à exécuter un contrat, devenu pour eux, selon toute apparence, plus onéreux que profitable.

Mais à supposer qu'ils eussent surmonté toutes les difficultés, qu'ils eussent triomphé des mauvaises dispositions du marché financier et réussi à placer l'emprunt, ce résultat n'eût pu être obtenu qu'au prix de sacrifices excessifs, sacrifices qui eussent rendu tout profit illusoire ; ayant d'ailleurs déjà perdu pas mal de temps, contraints de se presser outre mesure pour arriver à terme, ils eussent vu le plus clair de leurs bénéfices absorbé par le loyer usuraire de l'argent et par les excédents de frais provenant de la nécessité de forcer les travaux.

Il serait dès lors abusif d'allouer aux demandeurs en de telles circonstances une somme quelconque à titre de *lucrum cessans* pour un fait, qui, vraisemblablement, ne les a privés d'aucun lucre appréciable.

L'indemnité à accorder doit donc viser simplement à mettre les demandeurs dans la situation où ils se trouveraient s'ils n'avaient jamais passé de contrat avec la partie adverse ; elle doit les indemniser du dommage éprouvé, non pas du fait de la rupture, mais du fait de la conclusion et de l'accomplissement partiel du contrat. C'est dire que la réparation doit être limitée au *damnum emergens*, au remboursement des dépenses effectives.

Appelé à déterminer le montant de ces dépenses, le Tribunal reconnaît que la méthode de détermination qui, à l'origine du conflit, eût fourni les données les plus certaines, à savoir la vérification des travaux sur les lieux, est aujourd'hui impracticable pour la simple raison que le *statu quo* d'alors n'existe plus. Il n'eût pas été possible au Tribunal d'ordonner une visite locale avant 1898, soit avant l'échange des deux premières pièces de procédure. Or, à cette époque, cinq années s'étaient déjà écoulées depuis la naissance du différend : d'autres travaux avaient été exécutés dans l'intervalle, le temps avait fait son œuvre, et il eût été matériellement impossible d'établir, par une inspection du théâtre des opérations, l'état de choses tel qu'il existait vers la fin de 1893 et la somme de travail, de matériel et d'argent dépensé, qu'il représentait.

A défaut d'une inspection locale, le Tribunal eût pu recourir à une expertise des livres de la partie demanderesse, telle que la réclamait l'Etat défendeur. Mais cette expertise comptable lui a paru superflue, attendu que, quel qu'en eût été le résultat, sa force probante eût pu être mise en doute, la preuve tirée des livres de la partie même qui les invoque n'étant point une preuve absolument concluante.

Les choses étant ainsi, le Tribunal a cru devoir s'en tenir aux éléments d'appréciation qui lui sont fournis par les faits avérés de la cause, par le relevé de compte intitulé « statement A » que les demandeurs ont produit, et par l'expérience en matière technique.

Le statement A, en particulier, fournit à cet égard des données qui, sans être probantes à la forme, constituent, en fait, une base d'une certaine valeur pour l'appréciation et le raisonnement des arbitres.

Cet état accuse, jusqu'à fin 1893, les dépenses réparties en vingt rubriques et s'élevant au total à £ 31,053. 10. 11; dont à défalquer £ 13,687. 6. 10 que les demandeurs reconnaissent avoir touchés; différence à leur actif: 17,366. 4. 1. Les dépenses faites dans les années suivantes sont indiquées à £ 11,168. 14. 1.

Les postes les plus importants mentionnés dans le statement sont: le poste n° 6, de £ 12,878 pour réparation de la ligne existante, et le poste n° 18, de £ 5822 pour levée des plans.

Les pièces au dossier établissent suffisamment que ces deux postes ne sont point exagérés. Nous invoquerons notamment la reconnaissance résultant de l'approbation, par les organes compétents. du certificat n° 3 de l'Ingénieur-Conseil et de l'Agent officiel, du 27 mars 1893, et celle qui s'exprime par les relevés mensuels contresignés par les organes du contrôle: la majeure partie des sommes alléguées se trouve justifiée par ces diverses pièces.

Cette considération, plutôt de forme, est corroborée par le fait que pour la mise en état de la ligne, d'une longueur de 30 milles, de Puerto Berrio à Pavas, y compris la levée des plans, une dépense de £ 12,878 n'a rien d'exagéré. Et quant au chiffre de dépenses indiqué pour la levée des autres plans, il est couvert par des reconnaissances expresses. La somme de £ 5822 n'a d'ailleurs, en fait, rien d'exorbitant, même si les plans sont imparfaits et incomplets, comme il y a lieu de le supposer. Pour un travail soigné et achevé elle serait considérablement inférieure d'après les tarifs usités en Europe; à plus forte raison paraît-elle justifiée par rapport aux circonstances difficiles dans lesquelles de pareils travaux s'exécutent en Colombie.

Quant aux autres postes du « statement A » pour l'année 1893, ils ont tous trait à des chefs de dépenses qui paraissent plausibles et que toute entreprise de ce genre doit entraîner dans sa suite: frais de transport et de voyage, frais préliminaires salaires, frais d'avocats, d'administration, de câblegrammes, mobilier, instruments, etc. Les sommes indiquées pour ces différentes rubriques ne sont pas hors de proportion avec l'importance de l'ouvrage et la durée des travaux.

Et comme il s'agit dans l'espèce d'allouer une somme ronde à titre d'indemnité globale, le tribunal, jugeant ex æquo et bono, estime, qu'il possède dores et déjà les éléments suffisants pour une appréciation approximative, la seule possible, et il juge inutile de requérir des justifications minutieuses pour les différents postes figurant dans les livres de la maison demanderesse.

Aux dépenses occasionnées à la partie demanderesse par l'exécution du contrat, viennent s'ajouter les montants ci-après:

1° Les intérêts à 6 % l'an pour six années, de 1893 à 1899.

2° Une indemnité supplémentaire pour pertes indirectes (frais postérieurs à 1893, résiliation de contrats avec des sous-traitants, des employés, etc.).

3° Une part — la moitié environ — des frais causés aux demandeurs par les arbitrages de Bogotá et de Lausanne, et les tractations qui les ont précédés.

Tous ces éléments combinés portent l'indemnité, à allouer en raison du damnum emergens, à la somme ronde de £ 40,000, soit un million de francs en monnaie suisse.

La partie défenderesse ne saurait taxer cette appréciation d'exagérée, puisque c'est elle qui par des mesures arbitraires et par ses atermoiements a rendu impossible toute vérification sur les lieux, et puisque, il convient de le rappeler ici, dans des négociations transactionnelles qui eurent lieu en 1895, un de ses fonctionnaires, le sous-secrétaire aux finances de Colombie, M. Justiniano Cañon, avait émis lui-même l'avis motivé que si la maison Punchard se contentait de £ 50,000 « on pourrait arriver amiablement à un arrangement convenable » (Doc. P. n° 79).

Il est entendu que la somme allouée aux demandeurs comprend aussi le prix de la levée des plans et que, par conséquent, l'Etat de Colombie aura le droit de réclamer, en échange, la livraison des plans en possession de la partie demanderesse. Si ce droit ne se trouve pas consacré expressément dans le dispositif ci-après, c'est uniquement en raison de ce qu'il n'a été formulé aucune conclusion à son égard.

Pour ce qui est finalement des dépens et frais communs de l'arbitrage, il est juste et convenable, par application de l'art. 17 du compromis, d'en mettre la partie prépondérante, 60 %, à la charge de la partie défenderesse puisqu'elle est condamnée, mais d'en faire supporter

70

une notable part, 40 %, par les demandeurs, attendu que la somme que le présent jugement leur reconnaît est de beaucoup inférieure à celle qu'ils ont réclamée dans leurs conclusions principales.

Par ces motifs le tribunal arbitral prononce :

1° Les six contrats passés entre les parties, du 24 septembre 1892 au 26 janvier 1893, et dont la résiliation est demandée par chacune d'elles, sont déclarés résiliés.

2° Le Gouvernement de la République de Colombie, tant en son nom personnel qu'en celui du Département d'Antioquia, est condamné à payer aux demandeurs, MM. Punchard, McTaggart, Lowther & Co., la somme de un million de francs en monnaie légale suisse.

En conformité de l'article IV du compromis arbitral, cette somme devra être versée dans les six mois du prononcé de la présente sentence, entre les mains du Département politique de la Confédération Suisse, qui la transmettra, pour le compte des ayants droit, au Gouvernement de la Grande-Bretagne.

A défaut de paiement dans le délai imparti, la dite somme deviendra productive d'intérêts moratoires au taux de six pour cent l'an, à dater de l'expiration du délai de paiement.

3° Tous cautionnements consentis par la partie demanderesse ou par ses représentants pour l'exécution de ses engagements en faveur du Département d'Antioquia et de la République de Colombie sont déclarés caducs et le billet de £ 10,000 remis à ce titre à MM. Schlocs frères d'Ethelburga House à Londres, devra être restitué à la partie demanderesse.

4° Quant aux frais:

Les dépens des parties sont compensés.

Les frais de l'arbitrage, comprenant les émoluments des arbitres, le salaire du secrétaire et les dépenses du tribunal arbitral, le tout suivant état qui sera fourni ultérieurement, seront supportés par les parties dans les proportions suivantes :

60 % par la Colombie.

40 % par les demandeurs.

5° Les conclusions des deux parties, pour autant qu'elles diffèrent du dispositif ci-dessus, sont écartées.

6° La présente sentence sera communiquée au Conseil fédéral suisse et, par son intermédiaire, aux deux parties en cause.

Ainsi délibéré en séance du Tribunal arbitral à Lausanne le 27 juillet 1899, et prononcé le 17 octobre 1899 [1].

---

[1] *Tribunal arbitral international du Chemin de fer d'Antioquia.* Sentence arbitrale. Berne, impr. Stæmpfli & Cⁱᵉ.

CXXX. Grande-Bretagne, Vénézuéla.

2 février 1897.

Une des contestations multiples auxquelles donnèrent lieu les frontières incertaines des diverses Guyanes. Bien que la question souleva de vives discussions dans la presse, le compromis qui institua l'arbitrage et la sentence intervenue ont un caractère absolument normal et n'appellent aucun commentaire.

Treaty of arbitration signed at Washington, February 2, 1897, to determine the boundary line between the Colony of British Guiana and the United States of Venezuela.

Her Majesty the Queen of the United Kingdom of Great Britain and Ireland, and the United States of Venezuela, being desirous to provide for an amicable settlement of the question which has arisen between their respective Governments concerning the boundary between the Colony of British Guiana and the United States of Venezuela, have resolved to submit to arbitration the question involved, and to the end of concluding a Treaty for that purpose have appointed as their respective Plenipotentiaries :

Her Majesty the Queen of the United Kingdom of Great Britain and Ireland, the Right Honourable Sir Julian Pauncefote, a Member of Her Majesty's Most Honourable Privy Council, Knight Grand Cross of the Most Honourable Order of the Bath and of the Most Distinguished Order of Sᵗ Michael and Sᵗ George, and Her Majesty's Ambassador Extraordinary and Plenipotentiary to the United States ;

And the President of the United States of Venezuela, Señor José Andrade, Envoy Extraordinary and Minister Plenipotentiary of Venezuela to the United States of America ;

Who, having communicated to each other their respective full powers, which were found to be in due and proper form, have agreed to and concluded the following Articles :

ARTICLE I. — An Arbitral Tribunal shall be immediately appointed to determine the boundary line between the Colony of British Guiana and the United States of Venezuela.

ARTICLE II. — The Tribunal shall consist of five jurists; two of the part of Great Britain nominated by the members of the Judicial Committee of Her Majesty's Privy Council, namely, the Right Honourable Baron Herschell, Knight

Grand Cross of the Most Honourable Order of the Bath, and the Honourable Sir Richard Henn Collins, Knight, one of the Justices of Her Britannic Majesty's Supreme Court of Judicature; two on the part of Venezuela, nominated, one by the President of the United States of America, namely, the Honourable Melville Weston Fuller, Chief Justice of the United States of America, and one nominated by the Justices of the Supreme Court of the United States of America, namely, the Honourable David Josiah Brewer, a Justice of the Supreme Court of the United States of America; and of a fifth jurist to be selected by the four persons so nominated, or in the event of their failure to agree within three months from the date of the exchange of ratifications of the present Treaty, to be selected by His Majesty the King of Sweden and Norway. The jurist selected shall be President of the Tribunal.

In case of the death, absence, or incapacity to serve of any of the four Arbitrators above named, or in the event of any such Arbitrator omitting or declining or ceasing to act as such, another jurist of repute shall be forthwith substitued in his place. If such vacancy shall occur among those nominated on the part of Great Britain, the substitute shall be appointed by the members for the time being of the Judicial Committee of Her Majesty's Privy Council, acting by a majority, and if among those nominated on the part of Venezuela, he shall be appointed by the Justices of the Supreme Court of the United States, acting by a majority. If such vacancy shall occur in the case of the fifth Arbitrator, a substitute shall be selected in the manner herein provided for with regard to the original appointment.

ARTICLE III. — The Tribunal shall investigate and ascertain the extent of the territories belonging to, or that might lawfully be claimed by the United Netherlands or by the Kingdom of Spain respectively at the time of the acquisition by Great Britain of the Colony of British Guiana, and shall determine the boundary line between the Colony of British Guiana and the United States of Venezuela.

ARTICLE IV. — In deciding the matters submitted, the Arbitrators shall ascertain all facts which they deem necessary to a decision of the controversy, and shall be governed by the following Rules, which are agreed upon by the High Contracting Parties as Rules to be taken as applicable to the case, and by such principles of international law not inconsistent therewith as the Arbitrators shall determine to be applicable to the case :

RULES.

a) Adverse holding or prescription during a period of fifty years shall make a good title. The Arbitrators may deem exclusive political control of a district, as well as actual settlement thereof, sufficient to constitute adverse holding or to make title by prescription.

b) The Arbitrators may recognize and give effect to rights and claims resting on any other ground whatever, valid according to international law, and on any principles of international law which the Arbitrators may deem to be applicable to the case, and which are not in contravention of the foregoing rule.

c) In determining the boundary line, if territory of one party be found by the Tribunal to have been at the date of this Treaty in the occupation of the subjects or citizens of the other Party, such effect shall be given to such occupation as reason, justice, the principles of international law, and the equities of the case shall, in the opinion of the Tribunal, require.

ARTICLE V. — The Arbitrators shall meet at Paris, within sixty days after the delivery of the printed arguments mentioned in Article VIII, and shall proceed impartially and carefully to examine and decide the questions that have been, or shall be, laid before them, as herein provided, on the part of the Governments of Her Britannic Majesty and the United States of Venezuela respectively. Provided always that the Arbitrators may, if they shall think fit, hold their meetings, or any of them, at any other place which they may determine.

All questions considered by the Tribunal, including the final decision, shall be determined by a majority of all the Arbitrators.

Each of the High Contracting Parties shall name one person as its Agent to attend the Tribunal, and to represent it generally in all matters connected with the Tribunal.

ARTICLE VI. — The printed Case of each of the two Parties, accompanied by the documents, the official correspondence, and other evidence on which each relies, shall be delivered in duplicate to each of the Arbitrators and to the Agent of the other Party as soon as may be after the appointment of the members of the Tribunal, but within a period not exceeding eight months from the date of the exchange of the ratifications of this Treaty.

ARTICLE VII. — Within four months after the delivery on both sides of the printed Case, either Party may in like manner deliver in duplicate to each of the said Arbitrators, and to the Agent of the other Party, a Counter-Case, and additional documents, correspondence, and evidence, in reply to the Case, documents, correspondence, and evidence 'so presented by the other Party.

If in the Case submitted to the Arbitrators either Party shall have specified or alluded to any report or document in its own exclusive possession, without annexing a copy, such Party shall be bound, if the other Party thinks proper to apply for it, to furnish that party with a copy thereo', and either Party may call upon the other, through the Arbitrators, to produce the originals or certified copies of any papers adduced as evidence, giving in each instance notice thereof within thirty days after delivery of the case, and the original or copy so requested shall be delivered as soon as may be, and within a period not exceeding forty days after receipt of notice.

ARTICLE VIII. — It shall be the duty of the Agent of each Party, within three months after the expiration of the time limited for the delivery of the Counter-Case on both sides, to deliver in duplicate to each of the said Arbitrators, and to the Agent of the other Party a printed argument showing the points, and referring to the evidence upon which his Government relies, and either Party may also support the same before the Arbitrators by oral argument of Counsel; and the Arbitrators may, if they desire further elucidation with regard to any point, require a written or printed statement or argument, or oral argument by Counsel upon it; but in such case the other Party shall be entitled to reply either orally or in writing, as the case may be.

ARTICLE IX. — The Arbitrators may, for any cause deemed by them sufficient, enlarge either of the periods fixed by Articles VI, VII and VIII by the allowance of thirty days additional.

ARTICLE X. — The decision of the Tribunal shall, if possible, be made within three months from the close of the argument on both sides.

It shall be made in writing and dated, and shall be signed by the Arbitrators who may assent to it.

The decision shall be in duplicate, one copy whereof shall be delivered to the Agent of Great Britain for his Government, and the other copy shall be delivered to the Agent of the United States of Venezuela for his Government.

ARTICLE XI. — The Arbitrators shall keep an accurate record of their proceedings, and may employ the necessary officers to assist them.

ARTICLE XII. — Each Government shall pay its own Agent and provide for the remuneration of the Counsel employed by it, and of the Arbitrators appointed by it or in its behalf, and for the expense of preparing and submitting its case to the Tribunal. All other expenses connected with the Arbitration shall be defrayed by the two Governments in equal moieties.

ARTICLE XIII. — The High Contracting Parties engage to consider the result of the proceedings of the Tribunal of Arbitration as a full, perfect, and final settlement of all the questions referred to the Arbitrators.

ARTICLE XIV. — The present Treaty shall be duly ratified by Her Britannic Majesty and by the President of the United States of Venezuela, by and with the approval of the Congress thereof, and the ratifications shall be exchanged in London or in Washington within six months from the date hereof.

In faith whereof, we, the respective Plenipotentiaries, have signed this Treaty and have hereunto affixed our seals.

Done in duplicate, at Washington, the second day of February, one thousand eight hundred and ninety-seven [1].

Award of the Tribunal of Arbitration pronounced in Paris, October 3, 1899, fixing the line of delimitation between British Guiana and Venezuela.

Whereas, on the 2nd day of February, 1897, a Treaty of Arbitration was concluded between Her Majesty the Queen of the United Kingdom of Great Britain and Ireland and the United States of Venezuela in the terms following : —

. . . .

And whereas the said Treaty was duly ratified, and the ratifications were duly exchanged in Washington on the 14th day of June, 1897, in conformity with the said Treaty ;

And whereas since the date of the said Treaty, and before the arbitration thereby contemplated had been entered upon, the said Right Honourable Baron Herschell departed this life ;

And whereas the Right Honourable Charles Baron Russell of Killowen, Lord Chief Justice of England, Knight Grand Cross of the Most Distinguished Order of S[t] Michael and S[t] George, has, conformably to the terms of the said Treaty, been duly nominated by the members of the Judicial Committee of Her Majesty's Privy Council to act under the said Treaty in the place and stead of the said late Baron Herschell ;

And whereas the said four Arbitrators, namely : the said Right Honourable Lord Russel of Kil-

---

[1] HERTSLET, *A complete collection...*, t. XX, p. 943.

loven, the Right Honourable Sir Richard Henn Collins, the Honourable Melville Weston Fuller, and the Honourable David Josiah Brewer, have conformably to the terms of the said Treaty, selected his Excellency Frederic de Martens, Privy Councillor, Permanent Member of the Council of the Ministry of Foreign Affairs in Russia, LL. D. of the Universities of Cambridge and Edinburgh, to be the fifth Arbitrator ;

And whereas the said Arbitrators have duly entered upon the said Arbitration, and have duly heard and considered the oral and written arguments of the Counsels representing respectively Her Majesty the Queen and the United States of Venezuela, and have impartially and carefully examined the questions laid before them, and have investigated and ascertained the extent of the territories belonging to or that might lawfully be claimed by the United Netherlands or by the Kingdom of Spain respectively at the time of the acquisition by Great Britain of the Colony of British Guiana;

Now, we the undersigned Arbitrators do hereby make and publish our decision, determination, and award of, upon and concerning the questions submitted to us by the said Treaty of Arbitration, and do hereby, conformably to the said Treaty of Arbitration, finally decide, award and determine that the boundary line between the Colony of British Guiana and the United States of Venezuela is as follows :

Starting from the coast at Point Playa, the line of boundary shall run in a straight line to the River Barima at its junction with the River Mururuma, and· thence along the mid-stream of the latter river to its source, and from that point to the junction of the River Haiowa with the Amakuru, and thence along the mid-stream of the Amakuru, to its source in the Imataka Ridge, and thence in a south-westerly direction along the highest ridge of the spur of the Imataka Mountains to the highest point of the main range of such Imataka Mountains opposite to the source of the Barima, and thence along the summit of the main ridge in a south-easterly direction of the Imataka Mountains to the source of the Acarabisi, and thence along the mid-stream of the Acarabisi to the Cuyuni, and thence along the northern bank of the River Cuyuni westward to its junction with the Wenamu, and thence following the mid-stream of the Wenamu to its westernmost source, and thence in a direct line to the summit of Mount Roraima, and from Mount Roraima to the source of the Cotinga, and along the mid-stream of that river to its junction with the Takutu, and thence along the mid-stream of the Takutu to its source, thence

in a straight line to the westernmost point of the Akarai Mountains, and thence along the ridge of the Akarai Mountains to the source of the Corentin called the Cutari River.

Provided always that the line of delimitation fixed by this Award shall be subject and without prejudice to any questions now existing, or which may arise, to be determined between the Government of Her Britannic Majesty and the Republic of Brazil, or between the latter Republic and the United States of Venezuela.

In fixing the above delimitation the Arbitrators consider and decide that in times of peace the Rivers Amakuru and Barima shall be open to navigation by the merchantships of all nations, subject to all just regulations and to the payment of light or other like dues : Provided that the dues charged by the Republic of Venezuela and the Government of the Colony of British Guiana in respect of the passage of vessels along the portions of such rivers respectively owned by them shall be charged at the same rates upon the vessels of Venezuela and Great Britain, such rates being no higher than those charged to any other nation : Provided also that no customs duties shall be chargeable either by the Republic of Venezuela or by the Colony of British Guiana in respect of goods carried on board ships, vessels, or boats passing along the said rivers, but customs duties shall only be chargeable in respect of goods landed in the territory of Venezuela or Great Britain respectively.

Executed and published in duplicate by us in Paris this 3rd day of October 1899[1].

Il est utile de rappeler que les Etats-Unis de l'Amérique du Nord intervinrent énergiquement en faveur du Vénézuéla. Une convention préliminaire fut signée par eux avec la Grande-Bretagne le 12 novembre 1896. Nous croyons intéressant de la reproduire.

Heads of proposed treaty between Venezuela and Great Britain for settlement of Venezuela boundary question as agreed upon between Great Britain and the United States, November 12, 1896.

I. An arbitral tribunal shall be immediately appointed to determine the boundary line between the colony of British Guiana and the Republic of Venezuela.

II. The tribunal shall consist of two members nominated by the judges of the Supreme Court

---

[1] *Parliamentary Paper*, [C-9533].

of the United States and two members nominated by the judges of the British supreme court of Justice and of a fifth juror selected by the four persons so nominated, or, in the event of their failure to agree within three months from the time of their nomination, selected by His Majesty the King of Sweden and Norway.

The person so selected shall be president of the tribunal. The persons nominated by the judges of the Supreme Court of the United States and of the British supreme court of Justice, respectively, may be judges of either of said courts.

III. The tribunal shall investigate and ascertain the extent of the territories belonging to or that might lawfully be claimed by the United Netherlands or by the Kingdom of Spain, respectively, at the time of the acquisition by Great Britain of the colony of British Guiana and shall determine the boundary line between the colony of British Guiana and the Republic of Venezuela.

IV. In deciding the matters submitted the arbitrators shall ascertain all the facts which they deem necessary to a decision of the controversy and shall be governed by the following rules, which are agreed upon by the high contracting parties as rules to be taken as applicable to the case, and by such principles of international law not inconsistent therewith as the arbitrators shall determine to be applicable to the case.

RULES.

a) Adverse holding or prescription during a period of fifty years shall make a good title. The arbitrators may deem exclusive political control of a district, as well as actual settlement thereof, sufficient to constitute adverse holding or to make title by prescription.

b) The arbitrators may recognize and give effect to rights and claims resting on any other ground whatever, valid according to international law, and on any principles of international law which the arbitrators may deem to be applicable to the case and which are not in contravention of the foregoing rule.

c) In determining the boundary line, if territory of one party be found by the tribunal to have been at the date of this treaty in the occupation of the subjects or citizens of the other party, such effect shall be given to such occupation as reason, justice, the principles of international law, and the equities of the case shall, in the opinion of the tribunal, require[1].

---

[1] *Foreign Relations of U. S.*, 1896, p. 254.

CXXXI. Etats-Unis d'Amérique, Mexique.

2 mars 1897.

Cette affaire, fort simple, a eu pour objet une demande d'indemnité, réclamée par deux citoyens américains. Cette demande fut repoussée.

Convenio para someter á un árbitro las reclamaciones de Charles Oberlander y Bárbara M. Messenger, firmado en Washington, Marzo 2, 1897.

Los Estados Unidos Mexicanos y los Estados Unidos de América, por medio de sus representantes Matías Romero, Enviado Extraordinario y Ministro Plenipotenciario de los Estados Unidos Mexicanos, y Richard Olney, Secretario de Estado de los Estados Unidos de América, han convenido y firmado el siguiente protocolo :

Considerando que los Estados Unidos de América, en nombre de Charles Oberlander y Bárbara M. Messenger, ciudadanos de los Estados Unidos de América, han reclamado del Gobierno de México una indemnización por ciertos hechos ilegales que, segun se alega, fueron ejecutados por funcionarios mexicanos en perjuicio de Oberlander y la Messenger ; y considerando que los Estados Unidos Mexicanos niegan los hechos alegados en que se fundan estas reclamaciones y el derecho de los Estados Unidos de América para demandar una indemnización en favor de cualquiera de los quejosos. En esta virtud, los dos Gobiernos convienen con el consentimiento de dicho Oberlander y la Messenger, dado por conducto de sus respectivos apoderados, en lo siguiente :

I. — Las cuestiones de hecho y de derecho que se han discutido entre los dos Gobiernos respecto de estas reclamaciones, se someterán á la decisión del Sr. D. Vicente G. Quesada, Ministro de la República Argentina en Madrid, á quien se autoriza plenamente por este Convenio para que proceda como árbitro.

II. — Cada Gobierno someterá al árbitro, dentro de tres meses contados desde el día en que ambos Gobiernos reciban la notificación oficial del Sr. D. Vicente G. Quesada, de que acepta el arbitraje, previo el permiso respectivo de su Gobierno, copias de la correspondancia, documentos y pruebas que ha sometido á la consideración del otro Gobierno, respecto de las dos reclamaciones ; y el árbitro tomará en consideración, para dar su fallo, solamente aquellas cuestiones de derecho ó de hecho que resultan de esa correspondencia y de los documentos ó pruebas.

III. — Cada Gobierno podrá someter, con los documentos antes descritos, un alegato en que funde su manera de ver los dos casos; pero el árbitro no será requerido ni estará facultado para oir alegatos orales ó recibir nuevas pruebas, á no ser que, después de examinados los documentos que se le sometan, considere necesario pedir pruebas ó alegatos para dilucidar algún punto especial que no encuentre claro.

IV. — El árbitro pronunciará su decisión dentro de seis meses, contados desde la fecha en que se le sometan las pruebas, documentos, etc., por ambas partes. Decidirá con fundamento de las pruebas y alegatos que se le someten, si el dicho Oberlander ó la dicha Messenger tienen ó no derecho á una indemnización por parte del Gobierno de México; y en caso de que decida ese punto afirmativamente, ya respecto de ambos ó de uno de los dos reclamantes, fijará el monto de la indemnización á que cada uno ó alguno de ellos tenga derecho; pero á condición de que esa indemnización no excederá, en ningún caso, de la suma demandada por cada quejoso en los documentos sometidos por cada uno de ellos á los Estados Unidos.

V. — Se pagará al árbitro una retribución equitativa, y ese gasto y los demás que fueren de carácter común ocasionados por el arbitraje, seran cubiertos, por mitad, por cada Gobierno.

VI. — El laudo pronunciado por dicho árbitro será final y decisivo; y si fuere en favor de los reclamantes ó de uno de ellos, y de la manera de ver la cuestión de los Estados Unidos de América, el Gobierno de México pagará el monto de la indemnización fijada tan pronto como el Congreso mexicano autorice el gasto; pero dentro del plazo de dos años contados desde la fecha del laudo.

Hecho por duplicado, en Washington, el día 2 de Marzo de 1897 [1].

Laudo pronunciado por Vicente G. Quesada en Madrid, Noviembre 19, 1897.

Yo, D. Vicente G. Quesada, Enviado Extraordinario y Ministro Plenipotenciario de la República Argentina, nombrado árbitro único por los Excelentísimos Gobiernos de los Estados Unidos de América y de los Estados Unidos Mexicanos, según consta en el Convenio celebrado en la ciudad de Washington el día 2 de Marzo de 1897, por medio de sus Representantes Mr. Richard Olney, Secretario de Estado de los Estados Unidos de América, y D. Matías Romero, Enviado Extraordinario y Ministro Plenipoten-

ciario de los Estados Unidos Mexicanos, convenio por el cual las Altas Partes contratantes señalan la materia del arbitraje y el procedimiento que deberá observar el árbitro en el cumplimiento de sus funciones, á fin de fallar definitavamente las reclamaciones que Mr. Charles Oberlander y la Sra. Bárbara M. Messenger han deducido contra el Gobierno de México por intermedio del Secretario de Estado de los Estados Unidos de América y por la vía diplomática.

Animado del sincero deseo de corresponder, por una decisión imparcial y escrupulosa, al grande honor que me ha sido dispensado:

Habiendo debidamente examinado y estudiado con madurez los documentos y exposiciones que han sido presentados por intermedio de las Legaciones de aquellos Excelentísimos Gobiernos en esta Corte, lugar designado para pronunciar mi fallo dentro del plazo prescrito, prorogado por convenio de las altas partes contratantes;

Resultando en cuanto á los hechos:

Que Charles Oberlander, en el memorial que dirigió al Presidente de los Estados Unidos de América en 10 de Enero de 1893, presentó como documento justificativo, entre otros, la declaración por él prestada ante Notario publico de los Estados Unidos de América, en la cual confiesa que el objeto que tuvo cuando pasó al territorio mexicano, fué procurar pruebas para servir en una causa criminal seguida por Crossthwaite contra el mexicano Cruz, á quien se acusaba de plagio, y por lo tanto en servicio de un interés privado;

Que fué preso en 20 de Mayo de 1892, en Tijuana, territorio mexicano, según lo reconoce Mr. Ryan, Ministro de los Estados Unidos en México, por telegrama dirigido en 24 de Mayo del mismo año al Secretario de Estado de los Estados Unidos, Mr. Blaine;

Que el Vicecónsul de los Estados Unidos en Ensenada, México, con fecha 27 de Mayo del citado año, en nota oficial, reproduce el telegrama que envió al Ministro de los Estados Unidos en México, informándole que Oberlander había sido arrestado en territorio Mexicano, sin duda alguna: afirmaciones de carácter oficial y concluyentes;

Que Oberlander desempeñaba á la sazón el cargo de subalguacil en San Diego, agente de Policia de la Alta California, y llevaba en su bolsillo la orden de prisión expedida por el Juez de Township contra el mexicano Donaciano Cruz, acusado precisamente por la persona en cuyo interés había sido Oberlander á buscar pruebas al territorio mexicano;

Que fué preso por las autoridades mexicanas y en territorio mexicano, por haber intentado, se dice, ejecutar el arresto de Cruz en cumplimiento de la orden que llevaba;

[1] *Foreign Relations of U. S.*, 1897, p. 378.

Que preso y registrado por la autoridad territorial, se le encontró efectivamente la citada orden de prisión, una pistola y cartuchos;

Que las esposas de nickel que se ponen en las manos á los presos, tanto en México como en algunos Estados de los Estados Unidos de América, se emplean por los agentes de policía para asegurar á los detenidos, pero en manera alguna con la mira de martirizarlos;

Que Oberlander, si juzgaba ilegal la prisión, debió entablar las acciones criminales y civiles ante los tribunales territoriales, para pedir el castigo de los culpables y la indemnización de los daños que se le hubieran causado, y en caso omiso, renunciaba su derecho;

Que en vez de ejercitar las acciones legales ante los tribunales del territorio, confesó en la declaración prestada en Tijuana, en 25 de Mayo de 1892, ante el Juez mexicano, declaración que por la naturaleza de los hechos era una denuncia ó acusación, «que en la noche del sábado, como entre siete y ocho, despachó á comprar cigarros á un tal Melon Santos, que no conoce, y que le servía de custodia ó guardián, y se quedó con un francés que también lo vigilaba, y aprovechando esa oportunidad salió corriendo del cuarto, dándole un empujón con el cuerpo al francés, escapándose de esa manera con dirección á la línea; que con la precipitación de la carrera se cayó en el camino, causándose los rasponces que tiene en el cuerpo...» y en cuanto á la captura, dice:... «que lo sujetaron trayéndolo preso de nuevo..., que lo han maltratado en la prisión... que además de los rasponces de que habló, se dió un golpe en la cabesa por querer salir por una ventana del cuarto que le sirvió de prisión...»;

Que la fuga, empleando la fuerza y violencia contra el guardia de la autoridad judicial de México, constituye por sí un nuevo delito que agravaba la causa de la prisión, aunque ésta hubiera sido en su origen injusta é ilegal;

Que esta declaración de Oberlander lo fué con posterioridad á la licencia para ausentarse, que le concedió el Juez de 1ª instancia de Ensenada, bajo la simple promesa de que volvería á prestar declaración, pasando al territorio de California, donde permaneció veinticuatro horas, y desde ahí volvió al de México, como lo había prometido, sin coacción ni temores de amenazas de muerte por parte de los que le aprehendieron, declarando, en efecto, ante el Juez territorial;

Que quien tuvo libertad y seguridad para declarar ante el Juez territorial, la tuvo evidentemente para ejercitar las acciones criminales y civiles contra sus aprehensores;

Que ante el Juez territorial, único competente para conocer y resolver sobre la prisión y sus incidencias, no especificó los actos de violencia, ni quiénes le martirizaron, como ha pretendido probarlo después en informaciones extraoficiales y en el extranjero; y no especificando cargos ni designando personas, imposibilitaba la averiguación de la verdad y el castigo de los culpables si los hubiera;

Que pretende que la noche de su fuga llegó á territorio de los Estados Unidos de América, y que ahí, en casa de Messenger... «se metieron los que le perseguían y lo tomaron preso...» hechos cuya pruebas á él incumbía, y ésta solo es admisible y legal ante el Juez de México, quien seguia la causa contra sus aprehensores, por cuánto no hubo imposibilidad ni fuerza que le impidiese hacerlo;

Que ante dicho Juez y en la misma declaración, que el Secretario de Estado de los Estados Unidos de América, Mr. Olney reconoce como «la verdadera declaración», porque... «sin peligro podía decir la verdad» (Mr. Olney, al Ministro Ramson — Departamento de Estado — Washington, Noviembre 30 de 1895), el citado Oberlander agrega... «que en el camino lo llevaron en su carruaje y no sufrió maltrato...»;

Que afirma en el mismo acto... «que la esposa de Messenger no presentió la manera como la tomaron...»;

Que el testigo José Messenger es inhábil para declarar, por el interés que tiene en la causa, por pretender su mujer y él, como dueño de la casa, una indemnización de cincuenta mil pesos; que su dicho es tachable por esa razón legal, con arreglo á las leyes de México, y además, ineficaz, por declarar... «que ignora la manera cómo fué aprehendido aquel (Oberlander) y por qué motivo...»;

Que la testigo Sra. Bessie Mosser lo es de referencia, disiendo... «que Oberlander habló con un hijo de la declarante en la puerta... que ignora á qué hora y de qué manera ó modo fué aprehendido el referido Oberlander;

Que el testigo Sirl declara... «que vió que bajaba de la loma allí cercano, gente que no conoció, pues sólo veía bultos; que no sabe qué pasaría y de la manera y modo como fué aprehendido Oberlander...»;

Que el Juez de la Ensenada de Todos Santos consideró que no había mérito para que continuare la detención de Oberlander, y por los indicios que resultaban de la sumaria ordenó la prisión preventiva de los acusados de haber aprehendido á Oberlander en territorio de los Estados Unidos, consignándolos al Juez del Distrito de la Baja California como presuntos reos del delito contra la seguridad exterior de México;

Que el auto de prisión es, por su naturaleza, interlocutorio y apelable;

Que siendo confirmado por el Tribunal de Circuito de México, los indiciados usaron del derecho que las leyes territoriales les acuerdan para solicitar la excarcelacion bajo fianza, mientras se seguía la causa criminal;

Que seguida la causa en el Juzgado 2º de Distrito de la Baja California, el Juez mandó sobreseer respecto del primero de los acusados y absolvió á los cuatro restantes;

Que esta sentencia fué confirmada por el Tribunal de Circuito de México, previos los trámites establecidos por la ley territorial:

Que acusado Oberlander por Donaciano Cruz de cónato de plagio en territorio mexicano, y acusado Cruz y otros por Oberlander, de plagio en el territorio de los Estados Unidos de América, el Juez territorial recibió la prueba sobre ambos extremos, declarando ó acusando el mismo Oberlander, y juzgó y aplicó la ley territorial según lo alegado y probado y esta sentencia fué confirmada y quedó firme y valedera;

Que por último, se alega por la parte de México que Charles Oberlander fué preso por orden judicial en Brewerton, hace ocho años, acusado de robo, fugándose á California;

Que fué después acusado por atentados contra el pudor en las jovenes Kattie Kehve y Luisa Hawing, y por estupro de la joven Nellie Dagwell, todas del Asilo de Huérfanas de Monte Tabor;

Que en esa causa criminal se pidió, judicialmente, se nombrase una comisión de médicos por suponer que había perdido la rázon;

Que el Juez Row, de Nueva York, nombró tres médicos; y los Dres. Kaufman y Walsh, como testigos, declararon haber conocido á Oberlander desde la niñez, que no está en su juicio y que su conducta ha sido siempre la de un trastornado;

Que en virtud de las pruebas dadas en la referida causa, el Procurador Fiscal y el abogado de Oberlander han sostenido que el trastorno ó locura de Oberlander comenzó desde la niñez, habiéndose observado esa enfermedad en la escuela, y la que ha continuado después sin interrupción; que padece la monomanía de las persecuciones;

Que las conclusiones del dictamen facultativo en esa causa fueron... «que Oberlander sufre una enfermedad mental que se desarrolla especialmente en las personas que heredan una inteligencia desequilibrada, y que continúa durante la vida, la cual se conoce como una forma de demencia con el nombre de *paranoia*...»;

Que en mérito de estos antecedentes el Juez Row declaró que Oberlander no era responsable de los delitos por los cuales fué acusado, y ordenó que se le condujera al Asilo de dementes de Utica, y no al de dementes criminales de Manteawan.

Resultando respecto á la Sra. Bárbara M. Messenger:

Que por nota de la Legación de los Estados Unidos en México, fecha 9 de Abril de 1895, dirigida por Mr. Butler al Ministro de Relaciones Exteriores de los Estados Unidos Mexicanos, se establece terminantemente que: «El Departamento está dispuesto á confesar la exactitud del juicio expresado por el Gobierno Mexicano, que en cuanto á la enfermedad de la Sra. Messenger, fué causada no tanto por la invasión á viva fuerza de la casa, como por su misma conducta al perseguir á los plagiarios, y que por esto no es probablemente acreedora á la considerable indemnización que reclama; pero tiene, por cierto, que el hecho de que *su casa ó la de su marido* fuese allanada y el que su huésped fuese extraido por la fuerza, indudablemente les da motivo para demandar adecuada indemnización...»;

Que en mérito de la precedente limitación en la demanda, no es pertinente examinar lo alegado sobre la pretendida enfermedad de la Sra. Messenger;

Que por la exposición hecha por la Secretaría de Relaciones Exteriores de México en 15 de Julio de 1895, y oficialmente remitida á la Legación de los Estados Unidos por nota de 16 de Julio del mismo año, se establece, evacuando la demanda: «Con relación á la demanda de Bárbara Messenger, es satisfactorio que el Gobierno de los Estados Unidos haya convenido con el de México en que la enfermedad de dicha mujer fué causada no tanto por la supuesta invasión á su casa, cuanto por su conducta al perseguir á los llamados plagiarios, y que por esto no es acreedora á la indemnización que reclama. Pero en seguida indica que el hecho de que su casa ó la de su marido fué allanada y su huésped extraido por la fuerza, les da motivo para demandar adecuada indemnización...»;

Que el Gobierno de México niega el hecho del allanamiento de la casa, y por tanto, este hecho, contradicho entre las dos Altas Partes, es fundamental y debe ser apreciado jurídicamente en el laudo;

Que Mr. Ramson, Ministro de los Estados Unidos en México, en nota dirigida al Sr. Mariscal, Ministro de Relaciones Exteriores de los Estados Unidos Mexicanos, fecha 11 de Diciembre de 1895, manifiesta terminante y decisivamente que la demanda de su Gobierno la constituye la nota antes citada de Mr. Butler y la que él dirige, con su anexo; por consiguiente, queda con claridad establecida la materia que motivo las dos

71

reclamaciones y sobre cuyo mérito debe recaer el fallo arbitral.

Considerando :

Que es doctrina de derecho internacional « que dentro de los límites jurisdiccionales de cada Estado soberano los agentes de la autoridad son personalmente responsables en la medida establecida por el derecho público interno de cada Estado. Cuando faltan á sus deberes, excediendo sus atribuciones ó violando la ley, crean, según las circunstancias, á aquellos cuyos derechos han sido lesionados, un recurso legal por las vías administrativas ó judiciales ; pero respecto de los terceros, nacionales ó extranjeros, la responsabilidad del Gobierno que los ha nombrado queda puramente moral, y no podría convertirse en directa y efectiva, sino en el caso de complicidad ó de denegación de justicia » (Calvo, Le Droit International, etc., 4ª edic., vol. 3, página 120) ;

Que en el presente caso el Gobierno demandante ha declarado... « no tiene observación que hacer sobre los procedimientos seguidos contra los aprehensores de Oberlander, si tales procedimientos son considerados como asunto puramente doméstico... » (El Secretario de Estado Mr. Richard Olney al Ministro de los Estados Unidos en México, Mr. Ransom — Washington, 30 de Noviembre de 1895) ;

Que en mérito de este reconocimiento del demandante, no hubo complicidad ni denegación de justicia ; por lo tanto, la sentencia de los jueces territoriales, que establece que no se ha probado que la captura de Oberlander fuese en territorio de la soberanía de los Estados Unidos, queda firme y valedera dentro del territorio mexicano, en virtud de ser ésta la verdad legal, contra la cual no puede proceder el Poder Ejecutivo ni el Legislativo sin cometer atentado contra la independencia del Poder Judicial ;

Que aun cuando el demandante niega que la excepción de cosa juizgada opuesta por el demandado no tiene fuerza extraterritorial para extinguir acciones civiles, en el presente caso no se cuestiona que esa sentencia de los tribunales mexicanos será cumplida en el territorio de los Estados Unidos, sino por el contrario, que no hay reclamación diplomática que tenga atribuciones de casación para rever esa sentencia y pretender por la vía diplomática que dentro del territorio de la soberanía de los tribunales, se acepten informaciones para destruir el efecto jurídico de la cosa juzgada, y disponer precisamente de las contribuciones que pagan los habitantes, que es « asunto doméstico » por su naturaleza, en beneficio de extranjeros que no quisieron, por mala fe, ignorancia ó conveniencia,

recurrir ante los tribunales territoriales á fin de hacer valer sus pretendidos derechos, como era de su deber ;

Que sería ofensivo á la independencia y soberanía de las naciones que las informaciones de testigos, levantadas ante notarios en el extranjero, sin sujeción á ninguna de las garantías y trámites que establecen las leyes de procedimientos en los tribunales de justicia, produciendo aquellas libremente en diversas épocas, declarando el marido en favor de la mujer, el hijo en favor de la madre, la criada en favor de su anca y los mismos interesados en suproprio favor, puedan alegarse por la vía diplomática como fundamento para darles fuerza jurídica extraterritorial que anule la validez legal de la cosa juzgada ;

Que es doctrina de derecho internacional : « que todo lo que las otras naciones pueden pedir á un Gobierno, es que se muestre penetrado de un profundo sentimiento de justicia y de imparcialidad ; recuerde á sus subditos, por todos los medios en su poder, el respeto á las obligaciones internacionales ; no deje impunes las transgresiones que hayan podido cometer ; en fin, que obre en todo con buena fe y conforme á los preceptos del derecho natural ; ir más allá, sería elevar una injuria privada á la altura de una ofensa pública, imputar á una nación entera la falta de uno de sus miembros » (Calvo, obra citada, página 134, v. 3) ;

Que es doctrina de derecho internacional : « que los lazos morales que unen los pueblos son del mismo orden é implican un carácter absoluto de solidaridad : un Estado no podría legítimamente ni revindicar en los otros una situación privilegiada que él no estuviese dispuesto á que gocen los extranjeros, ni reclamar para sus subditos ventajas superiores á lo que constituye el derecho común de los habitantes del país » (Obra citada) ;

Que las Altas Partes contratantes reconocieron como principios de derecho internacional los terminantemente expresadas por la Comisión Mixta que funcionó en Washington, en virtud del Tratado de 4 de Julio de 1868, la cual, al fallar el caso del pueblo de Cenecú, estableció como doctrina de derecho convencional entre los Estados Unidos y México : « Soló pueden ser asuntos de reclamación · de una nación contra otra, aquellos agravios ó injusticias que proceden de la autoridad suprema de un país, contra la cual no se puede recurrir á ninguna otra autoridad del mismo país ; ó los que, cometidos en su origen por autoridades subalternas, no hayan sido reparados por los superiores á quienes correspondiera hacerlo, habiéndoseles pedido que lo hiciesen de la manera que prescriben las leyes locales. Están, pués, reducidos á dos capítulos los casos en que la injuria hecha á un ciudadano de un país puede prestar materia á una reclamación internacional; ó la injuria ha sido hecha por autoridad tan elevada que no hay en la legislación de su país ningún remedio establecido para reparar sus actos ó evitar el perjuicio que provenga de ellos, ó existe el remedio, se ha intentado y no ha producido efecto, porque quienes debieran corregir el yerro lo confirman ó se niegan á enmendarlo y lo hacen así irremediable. Donde no ha habido ni acción soberana é irresponsable, dentro del país, del poder supremo, ni denegación de justicia que se ha solicitado diligentemente, no hay razón para reclamación internacional » ;

Que en el presente caso tanto Oberlander, que denunció el hecho por declaración prestada ante el Juez territorial, como la Sra. Messenger, cuyo marido prestó libre y espontáneamente declaración ante el mismo Juez, no entablaron las acciones criminales y civiles que les correspondía ante los tribunales territoriales, sino que se han acogido á la acción diplomática sin causa que lo autorice ni derecho ni privilegio para pretender un procedimiento excepcional, en oposición á las doctrinas de derecho internacional antes citadas ;

Que el Gobierno demandante ha establecido precedentes en esta materia, oponiéndose á las pretensiones de extranjeros que demandaron indemnización, protegidos y apoyados por reclamación diplomática, como consta en el caso del Presidente Cleveland en su Mensaje al Congreso, fecha 6 de Mayo de 1886, con motivo de las reclamaciones entabladas por la Legación de la Gran China, quíen negó y rechazó la intervención diplomática aun cuando reconoció como ... « escandalosos sucesos los ocurridos en Rock Springs en el territorio de Wyoming ... » y agregaba que los hechos evidenciados eran ... « que un número de súbditos chinos, en Septiembre último (1885), fueron asesinados en Rock Springs, que muchos otros resultaron heridos y que todos fueron despojados de sus bienes, después de echados de sus habitaciones los infelices supervivientes ... » ;

Que en ese documento declaró el Presidente Cleveland que el Gobierno de Estados Unidos no estaba obligado á indemnizar las perdidas causadas por tales crímenes y delitos, desatendiendo, en consecuencia, la reclamación de la Legación de China.

Que las palabras del Presidente Cleveland en ese Mensaje son terminantes y decisivas, diciendo: « Mientras el Ministro chino, en virtud de sus instrucciones, haga de estas la base de un llamamiento á los principios y convicciones de la humanidad, no hay lugar á reparo alguno. Pero cuando va más allá, y tomando como precedente el proceder del Gobierno Chino en casos pasados, en los que se han comprometido bienes de ciudadanos americanos en China, sostiene que hay una reciproca obligación de parte de los Estados Unidos á indemnizar á los súbditos chinos damnificados en Rock Springs, se hace necesario prevenir esta argumentación y negar con todo énfasis las conclusiones que trata de deducir el Ministro respecto á la existencia de semejante responsabilidad, y el derecho del Gobierno Chino de insistir en ello ... » ;

Que en mérito de lo expuesto oficialmente por el Presidente de los Estados Unidos y precedentes considerandos, esa es la doctrina de derecho internacional que debe aplicarse al caso presente.

Por estos fundamentos definitivamente fallando: Declaro que el Gobierno de los Estados Unidos Mexicanos no está obligado á pagar indemnización de ninguna especie á Mr. Charles Oberlander ni à la Sra. Bárbara M. Messenger.

Dado en Madrid, á 19 días del mes de Noviembre de 1897 en dos ejemplares del mismo teñor [1].

CXXXII. France, Brésil.

10 avril 1897.

Contestation des plus importantes par l'étendue des territoires contestés. Les prétentions de la France furent repoussées par le Conseil Fédéral Suisse, choisi comme arbitre.

Traité pour soumettre à un arbitrage la question des frontières du Brésil et de la Guyane française, signé à Rio de Janeiro, le 10 avril 1897.

Le gouvernement de la République des Etats-Unis du Brésil et le gouvernement de la République française, désirant fixer définitivement les frontières du Brésil et de la Guyane française, sont convenus de recourir dans ce but à la décision arbitrale du gouvernement de la Confédération suisse.

L'arbitre sera invité à décider quelle est la rivière Yapoc ou Vincent-Pinson et à fixer la limite intérieure du territoire.

Pour la conclusion du traité, les deux gouvernements ont nommé leurs plénipotentiaires, savoir :

Le Président de la République des Etats-Unis du Brésil a nommé le général de brigade Dio-

[1] *Boletín oficial*, t. V, p. 129.

nysio Evangelista de Castro Cerqueira, ministre d'Etat aux affaires étrangères ;

Le Président de la République française a nommé Stephan Pichon, envoyé extraordinaire et ministre plénipotentiaire de la même République au Brésil ;

Lesquels après avoir échangé leurs pleins pouvoirs, qui ont été trouvés en bonne et due forme, ont arrêté les articles suivants :

ART. I. — La République des Etats-Unis du Brésil prétend que, conformément au sens précis de l'article VIII du traité d'Utrecht, la rivière Yapoc ou Vincent-Pinson est l'Oyapoc qui débouche dans l'Océan à l'ouest du cap Orange et que la ligne de démarcation doit être tracée par le thalweg de cette rivière.

La République française prétend que, conformément au sens précis de l'article VIII du traité d'Utrecht, la rivière Yapoc ou Vincent-Pinson est la rivière Araguary (Araouary) qui débouche dans l'Océan au sud du cap Nord et que la ligne de démarcation doit être tracée par le thalweg de cette rivière.

L'arbitre résoudra définitivement les prétentions des deux parties en adoptant, dans sa sentence qui sera obligatoire et sans appel, une des deux rivières réclamées comme limite, ou, s'il le juge bon, quelqu'une des rivières comprises entre elles.

ART. II. — La République des Etats-Unis du Brésil prétend que la limite intérieure dont une partie a été reconnue provisoirement par la Convention de Paris du 28 août 1817, est le parallèle 2° 24′ qui, partant de l'Oyapoc, va aboutir à la frontière de la Guyane hollandaise.

La France prétend que la limite intérieure est la ligne qui, partant de la source principale du bras principal de l'Araguary, court à l'ouest parallèlement au fleuve des Amazones jusqu'à la rive gauche du Rio Branco et suit cette rive jusqu'à sa rencontre avec le point extrême de la montagne Acarary.

L'arbitre décidera définitivement quelle est la limite intérieure en adoptant dans sa sentence, qui sera obligatoire et sans appel, une des lignes revendiquées par les deux parties ou en choisissant comme solution intermédiaire à partir de la source principale de la rivière adoptée comme étant le Yapoc ou Vincent-Pinson jusqu'à la frontière de la Guyane hollandaise, la ligne de partage des eaux du bassin des Amazones, qui, dans cette région, est constituée en presque totalité par le faîte des monts Tumuc-Humac.

ART. III. — Afin de mettre l'arbitre à même de prononcer sa sentence, chacune des parties devra, dans le délai de huit mois après l'échange des ratifications du présent traité, lui présenter un mémoire contenant l'exposé de ses droits et les documents à l'appui. Ces mémoires imprimés seront en même temps communiqués aux parties contractantes.

ART. IV. — A l'expiration du délai prévu dans l'article III chacune des parties aura un nouveau délai de huit mois pour présenter à l'arbitre, si elle le juge convenable, un second mémoire en réponse aux arguments de l'autre partie.

ART. V. — L'arbitre aura le droit d'exiger des parties les éclaircissements qu'il jugera nécessaires et de régler les termes non prévus de la procédure d'arbitrage et les incidents occurrents.

ART. VI. — Les dépenses de la procédure d'arbitrage établies par l'arbitre seront partagées par moitié entre les parties contractantes.

ART. VII. — Les communications entre représentants des parties contractantes se feront par l'intermédiaire du département des affaires étrangères de la Confédération suisse.

ART. VIII. — L'arbitre se prononcera dans le délai maximum d'un an à compter du dépôt des premiers mémoires ou des seconds si les parties ont répliqué.

ART. IX. — Ce traité, les formalités légales une fois remplies, sera ratifié par les deux gouvernements et les ratifications seront échangées dans la capitale fédérale des Etats-Unis du Brésil dans le délai de quatre mois ou avant s'il est possible.

En foi de quoi les plénipotentiaires respectifs signent le dit traité et y apposent leur sceau [1]).

Sentence rendue par le Conseil Fédéral Suisse dans la question des frontières de la Guyane, prononcée à Berne le 1 décembre 1900.

I. Le traité d'arbitrage.

1. — Le 10 avril 1897, a été signé à Rio de Janeiro entre le Gouvernement de la République française et le Gouvernement de la République des Etats-Unis du Brésil un traité par lequel les deux Etats ont chargé le Conseil fédéral suisse de fixer définitivement, par décision arbitrale, les frontières du Brésil et de la Guyane française.

Dans ce traité, les parties ont défini comme suit les questions à résoudre, ainsi que la nature et l'étendue de la mission de l'arbitre . . . . . [2])

---

[1] F. DE MARTENS, *Nouveau Recueil Général*, 2me série. t. XXV, p. 335.

[2]) La sentence reproduit les deux premiers articles du traité que nous avons publié plus haut.

L'article 8 du traité d'Utrecht du 11 avril 1713, visé dans la convention d'arbitrage, est ainsi conçu :

« Afin de prevenir toute occasion de discorde qui pouroit naitre entre les sujets de la Couronne de France et ceux de la Couronne de Portugal, Sa Majesté tres Chrestienne se desistera pour toujours, comme elle se desiste des a present par ce Traité dans les termes les plus forts, et les plus authentiques, et avec toutes les clauses requises, comme si elles étoient inserées icy, tant en son nom, qu'en celuy de ses hoirs, successeurs et heritiers, de tous droits et pretentions, qu'elle peut ou pourra pretendre sur la proprietté des terres appellées du Cap du Nord, et situées entre la riviere des Amazones, et celle du Japoc, ou de Vincent Pinson, sans se reserver ou retenir aucune portion desdites terres, afin qu'elles soient desormais possedées par Sa Majesté Portugaise, ses hoirs, successeurs, et heritiers avec tous les droits de souveraineté, d'absolue puissance, et d'entier domaine, comme faisant partie de ces Etats, et qu'elles luy demeurent a perpetuité, sans que Sadite Majesté Portugaise, ses hoirs, successeurs et heritiers puissent jamais estre troublés dans ladite possession par Sa Majesté tres Chrestienne ny par ses hoirs, successeurs et heritiers. »

2. — La convention distingue par conséquent entre la limite extérieure qui, partant de l'Océan, suit un cours d'eau à déterminer, et la limite intérieure, qui, partant de ce cours d'eau, continue dans l'intérieur du pays. En ce qui concerne la première, l'arbitre décidera quel est le cours d'eau que désigne l'article 8 du traité d'Utrecht ; en ce qui concerne la limite intérieure, l'arbitre adoptera ou bien l'une des frontières revendiquées par les parties, ou bien, partant de la source principale du cours d'eau qu'il aura choisi comme frontière extérieure, il adoptera comme limite jusqu'à la Guyane hollandaise la ligne de partage des eaux du bassin de l'Amazone, qui, dans cette région, est constituée dans sa presque totalité par la ligne de faite des monts Tumuc-Humac.

Quant à la limite extérieure, l'arbitre désignera soit l'un des cours d'eau revendiqués par les parties comme frontière, soit, à son choix, une des rivières comprises entre ces deux cours d'eau. Quant à la limite intérieure, l'arbitre choisira entre les frontières revendiquées par les parties et la ligne de partage des eaux des monts Tumuc-Humac, qui aura un point de départ différent selon que l'Araguary ou l'Oyapoc ou un des cours d'eau intermédiaires sera adopté comme limite maritime.

La sentence de l'arbitre déterminant les limites intérieure et maritime sera obligatoire pour les parties et sans appel.

Quelque simples et claires que paraissent ces dispositions, elles n'en ont pas moins donné lieu, dans les mémoires des parties, à des commentaires et parfois à des controverses qui doivent être mentionnées ici.

1. En ce qui concerne la limite *extérieure*, que les parties appellent aussi « limite maritime », le Brésil soutient, dans son premier mémoire, que l'arbitre est libre d'adopter comme frontière un des cours d'eau intermédiaires, « pourvu que le cours d'eau choisi soit, *selon lui*, le Japoc ou Vincent Pinçon de l'article 8 du Traité d'Utrecht ». Suivant cette opinion, l'arbitre ne peut donc choisir une des rivières qui coulent entre l'Araguary et l'Oyapoc comme cours d'eau frontière que s'il tient cette rivière pour le Japoc ou Vincent Pinçon de l'article 8 du traité d'Utrecht.

Dans sa réplique, la France fait observer à cet égard : « Nous sommes.... amenés à adhérer à l'interprétation brésilienne sur ce point et nous convenons que l'arbitre, devant statuer conformément aux stipulations d'Utrecht, ne pourra prendre comme frontière que le cours d'eau qui lui paraîtra représenter le plus exactement le Japoc ou Vincent Pinçon prévu par ce traité. Mais c'est à lui seul à désigner librement la rivière qu'il adopte comme telle dans la pleine souveraineté de sa conscience. »

Il n'est pas besoin de rechercher si cette interprétation répond au texte du traité, attendu que l'examen de la question a conduit l'arbitre à adopter une solution précise sur le point de savoir quel est le cours d'eau visé dans le traité d'Utrecht sous le nom de Japoc ou Vincent Pinçon. Il sera permis de relever toutefois que si l'arbitre s'était vu obligé d'admettre que le Japoc et le Vincent Pinçon sont deux fleuves différents et que, par conséquent, les rédacteurs du traité d'Utrecht se trouvaient dans l'erreur lors de la conclusion de cet acte, il lui serait impossible sur la base de ladite interprétation, de rendre une sentence fixant la frontière.

2. Selon cette convention, la France revendique comme limite *intérieure* la ligne « qui, partant de la source principale du bras principal de l'Araguary, *continue par l'Ouest parallèlement à la rivière des Amazones* » ...

Il y a lieu de remarquer à ce sujet :

Le Brésil se fondant sur les explorations auxquelles il a fait procéder en 1891 et 1896 par le capitaine d'état-major *Felinto Alcino Braga Cavalcante*, prétend que le cours supérieur de l'Araguary se dirige du nord au sud, qu'il faut chercher la source principale de cette rivière à proximité de la source principale de l'Oyapoc et non pas dans la direction de l'ouest. La France conteste la valeur de cette exploration isolément entreprise par le Brésil ; lors de la signature de la convention d'arbitrage, explique-t-elle, l'opinion dominante était que l'Araguary coulait de l'ouest à l'est ; il est donc conforme au compromis que l'Araguary ne constitue la limite extérieure que dans la partie de son cours qui vient de l'ouest, laquelle a été explorée scientifiquement, et que, par conséquent, on fasse commencer à la Grande Pancada la limite intérieure se dirigeant vers l'ouest. Les deux parties ont fait dresser des cartes à l'appui de leur démonstration. Au moyen d'une des cartes annexées à son mémoire, le Brésil expose comment, dans son opinion, la frontière qui, partant de la source de l'Araguary et se dirigeant vers l'ouest parallèlement à l'Amazone, se confondrait presque avec la ligne de partage des eaux des monts Tumuc-Humac. La France oppose à cette démonstration deux cartes annexées à sa réplique et dont la première a pour but d'établir qu'étant admise l'hypothèse du Brésil quant à la source de l'Araguary, la frontière serait déplacée beaucoup plus au sud que ne la fixe le Brésil ; la deuxième représente en son entier le territoire réclamé par la France. Par note du 27 juillet 1900, l'Ambassade de France a communiqué à l'arbitre une rectification de la deuxième de ces cartes, où la frontière partant également de la source de l'Araguary se dirige vers l'ouest, de sorte que cette carte n° 2 se rapproche sensiblement de la carte n° 1 de R. F. [1] ; la seule différence qu'on constate entre elles porte sur le tracé du cours supérieur de l'Araguary. L'Ambassadeur de France dit dans sa note que cette carte n° 2, rectifiée, « a ... été établie d'une manière exactement conforme à la Convention ». La France ne maintient donc plus la manière de voir qu'elle a exposée dans sa réponse au sujet du point de départ de la limite intérieure.

3. La France prétend dans sa réplique que la convention d'arbitrage règle et met hors de contestation un point de fait, savoir la position du *Cap de Nord*. L'article 1er désigne l'Araguary comme étant le cours d'eau *qui se jette dans l'Océan au Sud du Cap Nord*. Le Cap Nord serait donc le promontoire au sud duquel l'Araguary se jette dans la mer. La France ajoute que les deux parties ont reconnu expressément par là que l'Araguary se jette dans l'Océan et qu'il n'est par conséquent pas un affluent de l'Amazone.

Mais il est impossible d'attribuer cette portée à la convention d'arbitrage. Bien que le texte en ait été arrêté d'accord entre les parties, le traité ne saurait à l'évidence déterminer ce qui, à

diverses époques et d'après différents auteurs, a été considéré comme l'embouchure de l'Amazone, ou comme appartenant encore ou n'appartenant plus à cette embouchure. On n'a pas pu davantage décider une fois pour toutes que, d'après les données géographiques et l'opinion des auteurs sur la situation du Vincent Pinçon ou Oyapoc, le Cap de Nord devait être le cap qui est immédiatement au nord de l'embouchure de l'Araguary. Imposer cette interprétation à l'arbitre serait l'obliger à adopter des conclusions manifestement inexactes dans le cas où il est établi, sans doute possible, que, par Cap de Nord, il faut entendre le cap de l'île de Maraca et non pas le cap de l'embouchure de l'Araguary. Aussi importe-t-il de maintenir que toute liberté est laissée à l'arbitre d'examiner et de trancher cette question sans être lié par la terminologie employée par la convention.

4. Un désaccord plus profond s'est manifesté entre les parties au sujet de l'étendue des pouvoirs de l'arbitre.

Nous lisons à ce sujet dans le mémoire de la France : « D'après ce traité (le traité d'arbitrage), le Gouvernement de la Confédération suisse est appelé à connaître de tous les éléments du litige. Ses pouvoirs ne sont pas bornés à l'appréciation de formules irréductibles et invariables. Il peut, soit dire le droit tel qu'il lui paraît découler des textes, soit arbitrer *ex æquo et bono* telle décision transactionnelle qui lui semblerait justifiée. Si nous avons cru devoir investir le Gouvernement de la Confédération suisse de ces pouvoirs illimités, ce n'est point par défiance de notre cause, c'est pour donner à l'arbitre un témoignage éclatant de notre confiance dans sa justice, dans son impartialité et dans l'élévation de ses vues. Désirant avoir une solution complète, nous n'avons pas voulu entraver son jugement en l'enfermant dans des bornes trop étroites ; nous avons tenu à lui fournir tous les moyens d'exercer librement sa mission et de décider, sans appel et sans restriction, soit sur le terrain du droit, soit sur celui de la convenance et de l'équité. »

La France entend par conséquent donner à l'arbitre le droit de baser sa sentence sur des motifs tirés de la convenance ou de l'équité.

Dans sa réplique, le Brésil s'est élevé contre cette manière de voir que ne justifient, d'après lui, ni la lettre, ni l'esprit, ni la genèse du traité d'arbitrage. Les parties ont voulu s'en remettre non pas à un *médiateur*, mais à un véritable *arbitre appelé seulement à dire le droit*.

Le premier projet de traité d'arbitrage rédigé par le Gouvernement français et remis en janvier 1896 par la Légation de France à Rio de

---

[1] Les lettres R. F. signifient : Réponse du Gouvernement de la République française.

Janeiro au Ministre des Relations Extérieures, Monsieur Carlos de Carvalho, contenait cette clause :

Art. 2. L'Arbitre réglera définitivement la question, soit qu'il adopte entièrement dans sa sentence le tracé de frontière qui lui sera proposé par l'une ou l'autre des deux Puissances, soit qu'il choisisse toute autre solution intermédiaire qui lui paraîtrait plus conforme au sens précis de l'article VIII du Traité d'Utrecht.

Le 20 mars 1896, M. Berthelot, Ministre des affaires étrangères de France, remettait au Ministre du Brésil à Paris un second projet dans lequel le même article était rédigé comme suit :

L'Arbitre réglera définitivement la délimitation dont il s'agit, soit qu'il adopte dans sa sentence la ligne de frontière qui lui sera proposée par l'une ou l'autre des deux Parties, soit qu'il choisisse toute autre solution intermédiaire, les Parties entendant donner à l'Arbitre les pouvoirs les plus étendus afin d'arriver à une solution équitable de la difficulté.

Le Ministre du Brésil répondit le 25 mars :

« J'étudierai avec soin ces deux pièces (c'est-à-dire un projet de compromis arbitral du 20 mars et un projet de convention relative à la constitution d'une police mixte) et j'aurai l'honneur de soumettre prochainement à Votre Excellence un contre-projet de traité d'arbitrage, mais, dès maintenant, et pour ce qui est de l'article 2 du nouveau projet, je prends la liberté de rappeler à Votre Excellence que l'arrangement amiable à intervenir, c'est-à-dire l'arrangement définitif des limites par un Arbitre, ne saurait être fait que « conformément au sens précis de l'article VIII du Traité d'Utrecht et aux stipulations de l'Acte du Congrès de Vienne », ainsi qu'il a été convenu à Paris le 28 août 1817.

« Dans l'entretien auquel Votre Excellence fait allusion, j'ai eu l'honneur de la prier de vouloir bien préciser par écrit les limites réclamées par la France. Il importe que le Traité établisse clairement les lignes prétendues par les deux Parties ; et cette délimitation préalable du territoire contesté, ainsi que les pouvoirs à conférer à l'Arbitre constituent certainement les deux questions délicates à discuter et à résoudre dans la négociation du Traité. »

Le Brésil expose ensuite comment la convention définitive n'a pas repris la clause, inacceptable pour lui, autorisant l'arbitre à statuer en équité, tandis qu'elle a maintenu le renvoi à l'article 8 du traité d'Utrecht, malgré l'opposition des négociateurs français ; elle oblige au contraire l'arbitre à fixer la limite maritime selon le sens précis de l'article 8 du traité d'Utrecht exclusivement.

L'arbitre est lié par la convention d'arbitrage telle qu'elle a été signée par les parties le 10 avril 1897 et ratifiée le 6 août 1898. Aux termes de cette convention, il doit dire quel est le cours d'eau appelé Japoc ou Vincent Pinçon par l'art. 8 du traité d'Utrecht, comme il doit aussi fixer la frontière intérieure des deux Etats limitrophes.

La frontière intérieure doit forcément être fixée d'après la limite maritime qui sera tout d'abord déterminée ; pour la frontière intérieure, l'arbitre ne peut que choisir entre les prétentions des parties et une solution intermédiaire que prévoit la convention. Sur ce point, l'arbitre n'est pas lié par une convention, invoquée par les parties et qu'il aurait à interpréter. Il lui serait en conséquence loisible de tenir compte de motifs d'équité en ce qui concerne la limite intérieure.

Mais, en revanche, pour ce qui concerne la limite maritime, le compromis arbitral l'oblige à rechercher et à fixer le sens précis de l'article 8 du traité d'Utrecht. Il s'agit donc d'interpréter le traité et pour résoudre le problème, il lui faudra recourir aux données scientifiques que lui fournissent l'histoire et la géographie. La nature des choses exclut toute interprétation du traité d'Utrecht tirée de motifs d'équité ou de convenance ; on ne saurait, en effet, déduire de considérants de cet ordre quelle fut, lors de la signature du traité, l'intention de ses auteurs.

3. — Pour plus de clarté, il y a lieu d'expliquer ici l'article 2 de la convention d'arbitrage. Le Brésil prétend que la limite intérieure, *dont une partie a été reconnue provisoirement par la convention du 28 août 1817*, est sur le parallèle de 2° 24' latitude nord, entre l'Oyapoc et la frontière de la Guyane hollandaise. Il se réfère à la *convention de Paris*, conclue à cette date entre la France et le Portugal et dont l'article premier est ainsi conçu :

« Sa Majesté Très Fidèle étant animée du désir de mettre à exécution l'article 107 de l'Acte du Congrès de Vienne, s'engage à remettre à Sa Majesté Très Chrétienne dans le délai de trois mois, ou plus tôt si faire se peut, la Guyane française jusqu'à la Rivière d'Oyapock, dont l'embouchure est située entre le quatrième et le cinquième degré de latitude septentrionale et jusqu'au trois cent vingt-deuxième degré de longitude à l'Est de l'île de Fer, *par le parallèle de deux degrés vingt-quatre minutes de latitude septentrionale.* »

Incontestablement l'Oyapoc que mentionne cet article est le cours d'eau que le Brésil désigne aujourd'hui comme étant le Japoc ou Vincent Pinçon du Traité d'Utrecht et qu'il revendique pour frontière maritime. L'article 2 de la convention de Paris dit en ce qui concerne la limite intérieure :

« On procédera immédiatement des deux parts à la nomination et à l'envoi de Commissaires pour fixer définitivement les limites des Guyanes française et portugaise, conformément au sens précis de l'article VIII du traité d'Utrecht, et aux stipulations de l'acte du Congrès de Vienne. Lesdits commissaires devront terminer leur travail dans un délai d'un an, au plus tard, à dater du jour de leur réunion à la Guyane. Si, à l'expiration de ce terme d'un an, lesdits Commissaires respectifs ne parvenaient pas à s'accorder, les deux hautes Parties contractantes procéderaient à l'amiable à un autre arrangement sous la médiation de la Grande-Bretagne, et toujours conformément au sens précis de l'article VIII du Traité d'Utrecht, conclu sous la garantie de cette puissance. »

Cette disposition resta sans exécution. Aussi la France s'empare-t-elle du fait pour affirmer que la question est demeurée entière et qu'il faut, pour la trancher, interpréter définitivement l'article 8 du traité d'Utrecht, ainsi que le disait Guizot dans une dépêche qu'il adressait le 5 juillet 1841 au Ministre de France à Rio de Janeiro et qui fut communiquée au Gouvernement brésilien : « Je vous ai entretenu, le 21 octobre précédent, des circonstances qui avaient empêché la nomination de commissaires français pour la démarcation des limites de la Guyane du côté de Para. J'ai à vous parler aujourd'hui des motifs qui nous font regarder cette nomination comme inutile, parce que, dans notre opinion, la réunion de commissaires français et brésiliens serait peu propre à conduire à un résultat complet et définitif. Il ne s'agit point, en effet, d'un travail ordinaire de démarcation, suite naturelle d'une négociation où la limite qui doit séparer deux territoires a été convenue en principe, pour être réalisée ensuite sur le terrain. Avant que la question soit arrivée à des termes aussi simples, il faut d'abord s'entendre sur l'interprétation de l'article 8 du traité d'Utrecht et déterminer une base de délimitation ; il faut, ce qui ne peut se faire que par une négociation entre les deux Cabinets, vider d'abord la question des traités et définir les droits respectifs avant d'arriver à l'application pratique de ces mêmes droits. »

Le Brésil s'est dans la suite rangé à cette manière de voir, ce qui explique pourquoi l'article premier du compromis d'arbitrage stipule que l'arbitre désignera le cours d'eau qui est le Japoc ou Vincent Pinçon du traité d'Utrecht, en se basant exclusivement sur le sens précis de ce traité et sans recourir à la convention de Paris. Et dans son premier mémoire, le Brésil déclare à réitérées fois, qu'en ce qui concerne la fron-

tière maritime, il s'agit uniquement d'interpréter l'article 8 du traité d'Utrecht. Aucun désaccord ne règne entre les parties sur ce point, de sorte que l'arbitre peut se dispenser d'examiner si, par la convention de Paris, les parties n'entendaient pas reconnaître l'Oyapoc actuel pour le Japoc ou Vincent Pinçon de l'article 8 du traité d'Utrecht.

Mais si la convention de Paris n'a pas désigné définitivement le cours d'eau frontière, elle doit, en ce qui concerne la limite intérieure, avoir d'autant plus un caractère provisoire, puisque la fixation de cette limite dépend de celle de la limite maritime, qui est à déterminer tout d'abord.

Il est vrai que la convention de Paris a essayé de formuler une norme constitutive de la frontière intérieure et c'est peut-être ce qui aura engagé le Brésil à en invoquer le texte. Le Brésil reconnaît d'ailleurs lui-même, dans sa prétention, que la démarcation de 1817 n'avait été fixée que *provisoirement*.

II. La Procédure.

1. — Le traité d'arbitrage contient quant à la procédure les dispositions essentielles ci-après :

Chacune des parties doit, dans le délai de huit mois après l'échange des ratifications du traité, présenter à l'arbitre un mémoire contenant l'exposé de ses droits et les documents qui s'y rapportent. Ces mémoires sont en même temps communiqués aux parties contractantes. Passé ce premier délai de huit mois, chacune des parties en aura un nouveau, de même durée, pour présenter à l'arbitre, si elle le juge nécessaire, un second mémoire en réponse aux allégations de l'autre partie. L'arbitre a le droit d'exiger des parties les éclaircissements qu'il juge nécessaires ; il règle les cas non prévus par la procédure de l'arbitrage et les incidents pouvant survenir. Les frais du procès arbitral sont déterminés par l'arbitre et partagés également entre les parties contractantes. Les communications entre les parties contractantes ont lieu par l'intermédiaire du Département politique de la Confédération suisse. Enfin l'arbitre décidera dans le délai maximum d'un an à compter de la remise des répliques.

2. — L'échange des ratifications a eu lieu le *6 août 1898*, à Rio de Janeiro et le 8 septembre 1898 le Conseil fédéral, sur la demande des deux parties, accepta la mission que lui confiait la convention du 10 avril 1897.

Les Etats-Unis du Brésil désignèrent pour les représenter dans le litige Monsieur Paranhos do Rio-Branco qui présenta le 6 avril 1899 au Président de la Confédération ses lettres de créance comme Envoyé extraordinaire et Ministre plénipotentiaire en mission spéciale.

La France se fit représenter par son Ambassadeur accrédité auprès du Conseil fédéral, feu le comte de Montholon, puis par son successeur Monsieur Paul-Louis-Georges Bihourd, auxquels furent adjoints comme conseillers en mission spéciale le Marquis de Ripert-Monclar, Ministre plénipotentiaire, et Monsieur Albert Grodet, Gouverneur des colonies de première classe.

Le 4 avril 1899, l'Ambassadeur de la République française remit au Président de la Confédération, pour être communiqués au Conseil fédéral :

1. Un Mémoire contenant l'exposé des droits de la France dans la question des frontières de la Guyane Française et du Brésil : deux volumes, dont le premier contient l'exposé de la demande, le deuxième les documents et pièces justificatives.

2. Un atlas, contenant des reproductions de cartes du territoire contesté.

Le 6 avril 1899, le Ministre du Brésil remit au Président de la Confédération, pour être communiqués au Conseil fédéral :

1. Un Mémoire présenté par les Etats-Unis du Brésil au Gouvernement de la Confédération Helvétique, Arbitre choisi selon les stipulations du Traité conclu à Rio de Janeiro, le 10 avril 1897, entre le Brésil et la France ; trois volumes, dont le premier contient l'exposé de la demande du Brésil, le second des documents et le troisième des documents et procès-verbaux relatifs aux négociations qui ont eu lieu à Paris en 1855 et 1856 (Mission spéciale du Vicomte do Uruguay à Paris, 1855-1856) ;

2. L'ouvrage : L'Oyapoc et l'Amazone, question Brésilienne et Française, par Joaquim Caetano da Silva, deux volumes ;

3. Un atlas contenant des reproductions de cartes du territoire contesté ;

4. Un atlas contenant les relevés géographiques de la Commission brésilienne d'exploration du haut Araguary, sous la direction du capitaine d'état-major Felinto Alcino Braga Cavalcante.

Le Département politique de la Confédération remit aux parties le nombre convenu d'exemplaires de ces diverses pièces.

On constata lors du dépôt des premiers mémoires que les parties différaient d'avis quant au calcul du délai de huit mois. Pour lever tout doute à cet égard, le Conseil fédéral décida, le 5 juin 1899, que le délai prévu à l'article 4 du traité d'arbitrage du 10 avril 1897 expirait le 6 décembre 1899, à 6 heures après midi, heure de l'Europe centrale, ce dont avis fut donné aux deux parties.

Le 6 décembre 1899, les deux parties ont remis leurs répliques au Président de la Confédération ; le mémoire du Brésil est accompagné de trois tomes contenant des documents, d'un atlas et d'un volume renfermant le fac-similé de toute une série des pièces imprimées dans les tomes annexes.

3. — Dans l'intervalle, l'Ambassade de France avait fait au Conseil fédéral les communications ci-après :

a) Par note du 30 mars 1900, il fut expliqué que M. F. I, pages 171 et 175[1]), contenait une erreur, en ce que deux passages d'une lettre de Pontchartrain à Lefebvre d'Albon, du 19 décembre 1714, y sont mentionnées, qui sont en réalité empruntées à deux documents différents. L'erreur a passé dans le volume contenant les pièces justificatives où l'on trouve, sous le titre de « Lettre de Pontchartrain, Ministre de la Marine, à l'ordonnateur de la Guyane, Lefebvre d'Albon » un document qui est visiblement composé de deux pièces différentes. Selon la première partie, en effet, le traité d'Utrecht n'est encore ni ratifié ni publié, tandis que suivant la seconde, ce traité serait en voie d'exécution. Vérification faite, il a été constaté que la première partie est un extrait d'une lettre du Secrétaire d'Etat de la Marine, d'avril 1713, tandis que les passages subséquents sont la reproduction d'une lettre du même Secrétaire d'Etat, du 19 décembre 1714.

b) Par note du 21 mai 1900, en réponse à une question posée par le Conseil fédéral, il a été fourni des éclaircissements sur les rapports, de 1688, de M. de Ferrolles, qui fut plus tard Gouverneur de Cayenne. La question concernait la controverse qui s'est élevée entre les parties au sujet de la lettre de Ferrolles, du 22 septembre 1688, adressée à « Monsieur et Madame de Seignelay », et reproduite dans M. F. II, pages 155 et suivantes, et des passages qu'en donne M. F. I, pages 163 et suivantes, d'après les Archives des Colonies, t. LXIII.

La note du 21 mai 1900 expose que c'est par erreur qu'il est renvoyé au t. LXIII des Archives des Colonies « pour ce qui concerne le voyage de Ferrolles à l'Araguary. Le rédacteur travaillait sur des notes réunies par divers employés, et l'inexactitude vient de ce que le volume LXIII a été plus particulièrement consulté. Mais il ne renferme rien sur le voyage de Ferrolles en 1688. » De plus, la lettre à Monsieur et Madame de Seignelay n'est pas une pièce originale, mais une copie, dont il existe deux exemplaires, le premier, le meilleur, aux Archives des Colonies, volume II de la Correspondance générale (Guyane) fol. 44 et suiv., le deuxième, défectueux, aux Archives nationales, K 1232, n° 54 ; en outre, la lettre était adressée non à

---

[1]) Les lettres M. F. signifient: Mémoire de la France.

Monsieur et Madame, mais au Ministre de Seignelay. L'original de la lettre de Ferrolles n'a pu être retrouvé, mais aucune des deux copies ne contient les mots : « à la rivière du Cap d'Orange ». Ces deux copies ont été remises à l'arbitre en expédition authentique, en partie en reproduction photographique.

c) Enfin, l'Ambassade de France a, comme il est dit ci-dessus, communiqué au Conseil fédéral par note du 27 juillet 1900, une rectification de la carte n° 2 annexée à R. F., sur laquelle la frontière méridionale revendiquée par la France est tracée non plus à partir de la Grande Pancada, mais de la source de l'Araguary dans la direction de l'ouest.

Sur la demande du Conseil fédéral, le Représentant des Etats-Unis du Brésil a, le 11 juillet 1900, produit les pièces ci-après :

a) Une copie du « Compendio das mais substanciaes Razões e argumentos que evidentemente provam que a Capitania chamada do Norte situada na boca do rio das Amazonas legitimamente pertence á Coroa de Portugal, etc. » légalisée par le conservateur de la Bibliothèque royale de Ajuda à Lisbonne, M. Rodrigo V. d'Almeida.

b) Des extraits de l'ouvrage d'Enciso « Suma de geographia, etc. » Séville 1519, que le représentant du Brésil déclare conformes au texte de l'exemplaire qui se trouve à la Bibliothèque nationale de Paris.

4. — La réponse de la France, page 20, dit quant au droit de réplique accordé aux parties par le traité d'arbitrage : « Nous tenons... à dire un mot de la signification que nous donnons à l'article 4 (du traité d'arbitrage) relatif au droit de réplique. Après avoir imposé à chacune des deux parties, dans l'article 3, l'obligation de présenter un mémoire imprimé contenant l'exposé de ses droits et les documents s'y rapportant, le compromis ouvre à chacune d'elles la faculté d'adresser à l'arbitre un second mémoire en réponse aux allégations de l'autre partie. Il ne s'agit plus, comme on le voit, que d'une réponse aux dires de l'adversaire. Il nous semble résulter de ce texte qu'en principe les seconds mémoires doivent être consacrés à la discussion des premiers. Ceci est plus amplement démontré encore par ce fait qu'après l'expiration du second délai de huit mois la procédure écrite est close. Le juge peut encore demander des éclaircissements; mais les parties n'ont plus le droit d'argumenter l'une contre l'autre : on est entré dans la période finale d'une année pendant laquelle l'arbitre a la parole pour élaborer et rendre sa sentence. Mettre au jour pour la première fois dans le second mémoire des systèmes tenus jusque-là en réserve, et qui ne pourront plus être contrôlés, nous

paraîtrait contraire à l'esprit du compromis. C'est évidemment une question de mesure et de bonne foi ; en combattant un argument adverse, on est tout naturellement et très légitimement entraîné à des raisonnements nouveaux et à des justifications nouvelles. Mais nous pensons que, d'une façon générale, le second mémoire doit être essentiellement une réponse, et c'est dans ces termes que nous nous sommes efforcés de nous maintenir. »

Le Brésil ne se prononce pas sur la question, mais il a joint à sa réplique une si grande quantité de moyens de preuve nouveaux qu'on est tenté de croire qu'il ne se place pas au même point de vue que la France.

L'arbitre estime qu'il n'est pas réduit à s'en tenir aux allégations des parties et aux moyens de preuve qu'elles invoquent. Il ne s'agit pas, pour lui, de trancher un différend de droit civil, selon les voies de la procédure civile, mais d'établir un fait historique ; il doit rechercher la vérité par tous les moyens qui sont à sa disposition. Il ne tiendra compte des allégations des parties et des documents produits, sur lesquels la partie adverse n'aura pas pu s'expliquer, que si leur exactitude et leur authenticité lui paraissent hors de doute.

III. Exposé des motifs.

1. — Le traité d'arbitrage conclu le 10 avril 1897 entre la République française et les Etats-Unis du Brésil, qui a pour objet de faire fixer définitivement les frontières de la Guyane française et du Brésil, soumet deux points litigieux à la décision de l'arbitre choisi par les parties : le premier concerne la frontière extérieure ou maritime, soit la question de savoir quelle est « conformément au sens précis de l'article 8 du traité d'Utrecht » la rivière « Japoc ou Vincent Pinçon » : le second est relatif à la frontière intérieure, l'arbitre ayant pour mission de la déterminer.

La tâche de l'arbitre diffère essentiellement selon qu'il a à juger l'une ou l'autre des questions. Le traité d'arbitrage le fait ressortir très nettement. Dans cet acte, les parties formulent leurs prétentions tant en ce qui concerne la frontière extérieure que la frontière intérieure. Pour déterminer la première, l'arbitre doit rechercher quelle est, d'après le sens précis de l'article 8 du traité d'Utrecht, la rivière Japoc ou Vincent Pinçon. La rivière qu'il aura adoptée comme telle sera la rivière frontière et son thalweg formera la ligne frontière, que cette rivière soit celle indiquée par la France, ou celle indiquée par le Brésil, ou un troisième cours d'eau. En revanche, pour résoudre quelle est la limite intérieure, s'il n'admet comme fondée la prétention ni de l'une ni de l'autre des parties, il prononcera selon la « solution intermédiaire » que les parties d'un commun accord ont déterminée dans le traité d'arbitrage ; il tracera en conséquence la frontière intérieure qui partira du point extrême de la limite extérieure.

La première question a donc exclusivement pour objet d'interpréter les termes « Japoc ou Vincent Pinson » de l'article 8 du traité d'Utrecht ; la seconde concerne uniquement l'examen de la légitimité des prétentions de chacune des parties.

2. — L'arbitre, considérant que la fixation de la frontière intérieure dépend de la solution qui sera donnée à la question de la frontière extérieure, constate, sur la base des données détaillées fournies par l'exposé historique et géographique que « conformément au sens précis de l'article 8 du traité d'Utrecht » la rivière « Japoc ou Vincent Pinson » de cet article 8 est l'Oyapoc actuel qui se jette dans l'Océan entre le 4ᵉ et le 5ᵉ degré de latitude nord immédiatement à l'ouest du Cap d'Orange.

Pour déterminer quelle est la rivière Japoc ou Vincent Pinçon du traité d'Utrecht du 11 avril 1713, il faut rechercher préalablement si les pièces contemporaines de la conclusion du traité établissent d'une manière précise quel sens les parties contractantes ont entendu attribuer et ont effectivement attribué à la dénomination « Japoc ou Vincent Pinson » dont se sert l'acte diplomatique.

En procédant à cette recherche, l'arbitre a été amené à étudier non pas seulement les négociations qui ont immédiatement abouti à l'adoption de l'article 8 et des autres dispositions connexes du traité d'Utrecht, mais encore les traités de 1700, 1701 et 1703. Le traité provisionnel du 4 mars 1700 a, en effet, revêtu une telle importance lors de la discussion du traité d'Utrecht qu'il a fallu admettre d'emblée qu'il existait un certain rapport d'identité entre le Japoc ou Vincent Pinçon du traité d'Utrecht et la « Riviere d'Oyapoc dite de Vincent Pinçon » (Rio de Oiapoc ou de Vicente Pinson) du traité provisionnel.

Les délibérations dont est sorti le traité provisionnel de 1700 ont été précédées en 1698 et 1699 de tout un échange d'explications écrites par lesquelles les parties, la France d'un côté, le Portugal de l'autre, ont développé dans leurs moindres détails les questions qui les divisaient, chacune s'efforçant à l'aide de faits, de documents, de considérations tirées de l'histoire et de la géographie, de convaincre sa partie adverse du bien-fondé de ses prétentions. Pour arriver à apprécier sainement les mémoires si importants de 1698 et 1699, qui ont exercé une incontestable

influence même sur les thèses soutenues par les parties dans le litige actuel, et à bien comprendre les documents qui sont en connexité plus ou moins étroite avec ces mémoires, il a été nécessaire de se livrer à une étude complète des faits et des pièces.

C'est pourquoi l'arbitre a eu pour tâche d'examiner toute l'histoire du contesté, du territoire en litige qui va de l'Amazone jusqu'à l'Oyapoc actuel à l'ouest du Cap d'Orange, depuis les premiers voyages de découverte effectués dans l'Amérique du sud ; il a dû notamment se former une opinion sur la valeur des revendications du contesté fondées sur des concessions de terrains octroyées par des gouvernements d'Europe et voir jusqu'à quel point de semblables concessions ont été suivies de l'occupation effective du pays.

Il eût d'ailleurs été impossible d'omettre cette étude approfondie de l'histoire du contesté depuis l'origine de sa découverte par des Européens, cela d'autant moins que les parties ont invoqué dans leurs mémoires l'historique de la question et que le nom de la rivière frontière, Vincent Pinçon, se rattachait à l'évidence à Vicente Yañez Pinzon, qui découvrit l'embouchure de l'Amazone et le littoral du continent au sud-est et au nord-ouest de celle-ci. C'est précisément pourquoi les questions d'ordre purement géographique que soulève l'identification de la rivière Vincent Pinçon avec un des cours d'eau du littoral brésilien-guyanais ne pouvaient pas être tranchées à l'aide seulement des cartes datant de l'époque du traité d'Utrecht ; il a fallu examiner ces questions dans leur relation avec l'histoire, et c'est ainsi qu'on est parvenu au cœur de l'étude de ce problème scientifique aussi intéressant que controversé du développement de la cartographie de la côte sud-est de l'Amérique en général, du littoral du contesté en particulier.

3. — Cela posé, il y a lieu de relever les points ci-après :

Ce n'est qu'à la fin du XVIᵉ siècle et au commencement du XVIIᵉ siècle que divers Etats d'Europe se préoccupent du territoire côtier situé au nord-ouest de l'embouchure de l'Amazone. A cette époque, les Portugais s'établissent et restent fixés à l'embouchure et sur les rives du fleuve, non pas seulement en vertu du titre historique créé par le partage du monde fait par le Pape entre l'Espagne et le Portugal, mais plutôt en vertu d'une domination effective et d'une possession défendue à main armée contre quiconque cherchait à la troubler ou à la restreindre.

Seule l'Espagne aurait pu disputer cette contrée au Portugal en se fondant sur le traité de Tordesillas, mais le conflit fut écarté grâce à la réunion des deux Couronnes qui dura jusqu'en 1640. A la fin du XVIe et au commencement du XVIIe siècle, l'opinion généralement accréditée chez les auteurs espagnols et portugais semble avoir été que la frontière entre l'Espagne et le Portugal, l'ancienne « linea de demarcacion » passait au nord-ouest de l'embouchure de l'Amazone et qu'en particulier la rivière Vincent Pinçon qui se jette dans la mer au nord-ouest du « Cabo del Norte » formait la limite du Brésil portugais et des possessions espagnoles au nord. Il n'est pas besoin de rechercher comment cette opinion a pu se former ; il suffira de constater que le roi d'Espagne Philippe IV, troisième du nom en Portugal, avait par ordonnance du 13 juin 1621 partagé les possessions portugaises dans l'Amérique du sud en deux grands arrondissements administratifs dont l'un, l'Estado de Maranhão, situé au nord-ouest, s'étendait au delà de l'embouchure de l'Amazone jusqu'à la frontière du territoire espagnol. Or cette frontière était la rivière Vincent Pinçon.

A la même époque des Brésiliens relevant du Portugal avaient entrepris de chasser du territoire de l'embouchure de l'Amazone les ressortissants des nations européennes, notamment les Hollandais, les Anglais et les Français, et de se défendre contre toute intrusion étrangère ; cette entreprise, ils la menèrent à bien.

Il ne s'agit plus aujourd'hui de décider si c'est le Portugal ou toute autre puissance européenne dont la prétention à posséder le territoire de l'embouchure de l'Amazone était la mieux fondée en droit, mais uniquement de constater qu'effectivement les Portugais devinrent les maîtres du pays et qu'ils assurèrent également leur domination sur la rive gauche du fleuve en refoulant toutes les autres nations européennes ; puis, que la Couronne de Portugal partagea le territoire en « Capitaineries » et qu'en 1637 elle fit donation de la « capitania do cabo do norte » à Bento Maciel Parente, un des Conquistadores portugais. Le long du littoral cette Capitainerie avait une étendue de 30 ou 35 à 40 leguas comptées du Cabo do Norte. A lui seul le texte de l'acte de donation montre que cette concession n'était pas une « commission de découverte » : le fait que Parente dressa procès-verbal officiel de la prise de possession de sa Capitainerie, que celle-ci passa à ses héritiers, et la présence d'agents de Parente dans le territoire, prouvent bien que la donation fut suivie d'exécution.

Ce n'est que depuis 1676 que les Français ont pris définitivement possession de Cayenne. A partir de ce moment-là, ils tentèrent de donner à leur colonie le développement que lui attribuaient les concessions des rois de France. Ces concessions assignaient à la France Equinoxiale les territoires entre l'Amazone et l'Orénoque. Le lieutenant-général de ce pays, Lefebvre de la Barre, dans sa description de la contrée, fait ressortir la différence qui existe entre les concessions et l'occupation effective des Français. Il désigne le pays situé entre l'embouchure de l'Amazone et le Cap d'Orange, où débouche la rivière Yapoco, comme étant la Guyane indienne à laquelle il oppose, comme formant la Guyane française, le pays compris entre le Cap d'Orange et la rivière Maroni. C'est ce dernier territoire et non l'autre qui est possession française. Et encore pour Lefebvre de la Barre la Guyane indienne est-elle susceptible d'être occupée. Lorsque les Français s'appliquèrent à procéder à l'occupation du Cap d'Orange jusqu'au fleuve des Amazones, en se prévalant des concessions de leur roi et « pour le maintien et l'augmentation de la Colonie de Cayenne », comme il est dit dans les instructions du Président Rouillé, en date du 11 décembre 1697, ils se heurtèrent aux Portugais. Ceux-ci s'opposèrent à la pénétration des Français dans leur territoire qui, selon le Portugal, s'étendait au delà de l'Amazone et du Cap de Nord jusqu'à la rivière de Vincent Pinçon. Ils se mirent à construire des forts pour défendre leur possession où ils avaient déjà quelques missions. Le conflit entre la France et le Portugal ne tarda pas à éclater.

Tout d'abord les Français, venant de Cayenne et rencontrés aux alentours du Cap de Nord, sont pris par les Portugais et expulsés du pays, pendant qu'à Cayenne les autorités continuent à autoriser des Français à se rendre dans ce territoire jusqu'au fleuve des Amazones, et notamment à y faire le commerce avec les Indiens. Le conflit s'aggrave du moment que les Français élèvent leurs protestations contre l'établissement des forts construits par les Portugais sur la rive gauche de l'Amazone, qu'ils demandent la destruction des ouvrages de défense, l'abandon du territoire par les Portugais « attendu que toute la rive septentrionale de l'Amazone appartient de droit à Sa Majesté Très Chrétienne », tandis que les Portugais songeaient à de nouvelles mesures pour protéger leurs possessions. Pierre-Eléonor de la Ville de Ferrolles qui en 1688 alla de Cayenne remettre la « sommation » de la France au commandant du fort portugais sur la rive gauche de l'Araguary, relate en ces mots l'accueil qu'il y reçut : « Il me demanda ensuite ce que j'estois venu faire. Je dis que j'estois venu scauoir pourquoy ils s'establissoient sur les terres du Roy qui estoient separées des leurs par le fleuve des Amazones. Ce qui l'estonna, disant que le capitaine-major de Para auoit encore des ordres de construire des forts plus prez de nous, et que les terres du Roy son maistre s'estendoient jusques a la Riviere Pinson, que nous appelons Ouyapoque. » L'attaque infructueuse tentée par de Ferrolles en mai 1697 contre les forts portugais sur l'Amazone marque la phase aiguë de la querelle.

Sur ces entrefaites, on recourut aux voies diplomatiques pour mettre fin au litige ; en même temps les parties, après avoir recueilli des données historiques et géographiques, exposaient leurs prétentions dans les mémoires de 1698 et 1699.

Le traité du 4 mars 1700 régla provisoirement la question. Il s'agissait de « l'affaire de la rivière des Amazones », ainsi que le faisait remarquer fort bien le négociateur français, le Président Rouillé ; aussi son mémoire de janvier 1698, qu'il remit au gouvernement portugais, était-il intitulé : « Mémoire contenant les droits de la France sur les pays scituez à l'oüest de la rivière des Amazones. » Ce n'était donc pas la frontière de la rivière Vincent Pinçon, appelé « Ouyapoque » par les Français de Cayenne, qui aux yeux de la France formait l'objet du litige, mais bien la frontière de l'Amazone ; et l'instruction remise à l'Ambassadeur de France à Lisbonne lui recommandait d'obtenir des Portugais qu'ils reconnussent « que la rivière des Amazones serve de borne aux deux nations et que les Portugais laissent aux François la possession libre de la partie occidentale de ses bords ». Le Portugal opposait à cette prétention la revendication de la rive gauche de l'Amazone jusqu'au « Rio de Oyapoca ou Vincente Pinson, como querem os Castelhanos, ou Rio Fresco como mostrão muitos roteiros e cartas ».

Les mémoires ainsi que les documents et cartes communiqués à l'arbitre établissent à l'évidence que lors de la conclusion du traité du 4 mars 1700 les Etats contractants, par Rivière d'Oyapoc dite de Vincent Pinçon, n'ont pas entendu désigner et n'ont pas en fait désigné d'autre cours d'eau que l'Oyapoc actuel, immédiatement à l'ouest du Cap d'Orange.

Les différences d'orthographe du nom Oyapoc n'avaient aucune importance ; en effet, l'Oyapoca ou Oyapoc de la réponse du Portugal de 1698, s'appelle Yapoco dans la réplique de la France de février 1699, probablement parce que de la Barre et d'autres auteurs français le dénommaient ainsi, tandis que la duplique du Portugal écrit : Ojapoc (Oyapoc) ou Oviapoc (Wiapoc ou Yapoc) ; c'est le même cours d'eau qui figurera dans le traité d'Utrecht sous le nom Japoc, que de Ferrolles écrit Ouyapoc ou Ouyapoque, tandis que les Hollandais et les Anglais employaient plutôt les expressions Wiapago, Wiapoco, Wyapogo, Wayapoco, Wajabego, etc. Or, pour les Français, cet Oyapoc était l'Oyapoc actuel du Cap d'Orange. De Ferrolles le dit clairement dans son rapport du 20 juin 1698, quand, voulant établir la différence entre l'île d'Ouyapoc (Hyapoc) et la rivière de ce nom, il fait observer au sujet de celle-ci : elle « est dans la Guyane au deça du Cap de Nord à quinze lieues de nos habitations de Cayenne ». Déjà même, en 1688, dans son rapport sur son expédition vers l'Araguary, il avait décrit exactement sous le nom d'Ouyapoque le fleuve qui se jette dans l'Océan à l'ouest du Cap d'Orange, sans connaître ni nommer aucun autre cours d'eau de ce nom dans le contesté entre Cayenne et l'Amazone. Bien plus, il n'eut aucune objection quelconque à faire, ainsi qu'il résulte de son entretien avec le commandant portugais du fort sur l'Araguary, contre l'identification du Pinson, la rivière frontière portugaise (Vincent Pinçon) et de son propre Ouyapoc (c'est-à-dire l'Oyapoc du Cap d'Orange). Son objection ne visait pas cette identification, mais simplement la fixation de la frontière à l'Oyapoc du Cap d'Orange, parce qu'il revendiquait pour la France la frontière de l'Amazone.

Des délibérations qui eurent lieu entre 1698 et 1700 se dégage la même conclusion. A la revendication par les Portugais de la frontière Oyapoc-Vincent-Pinçon, les Français n'opposent pas cette objection : il n'y a pas d'identité entre l'Oyapoc et le Vincent Pinçon, car l'Oyapoc est la rivière qui coule près du Cap d'Orange et le Vincent Pinçon est un cours d'eau plus rapproché de l'Amazone. Les Français s'attachent plutôt à démontrer que le Vincent Pinçon est une rivière imaginaire ; les Portugais, disent-ils, n'ont aucun droit à revendiquer l'Oyapoc comme rivière frontière ; en outre, cette frontière serait inutile et insuffisante ; il existe d'ailleurs dans l'Amazone une île du nom d'Oyapoc (Yapoco), elle peut servir de frontière entre le Portugal et la France. On voit clairement que pour les Français, lorsqu'ils ont à s'occuper de la frontière de la rivière d'Oyapoc, il s'agit de l'Oyapoc d'eux connu, de l'Oyapoc du Cap d'Orange et non d'une autre rivière. Aussi les Portugais se bornent-ils à répondre dans leur duplique : il n'existe pas d'île d'Oyapoc dans l'embouchure de l'Amazone, les auteurs et les cartes signalent l'existence d'une rivière Vincent Pinçon qui n'est autre que l'Oyapoc : cette frontière de l'Oyapoc n'est d'ailleurs, à l'égard même de la France, ni inutile ni insuffisante, pas plus qu'elle ne le fut autrefois lorsqu'elle constituait la limite de l'Espagne et du Portugal.

Il importe toutefois de retenir que les Portugais étaient loin d'être renseignés avec exactitude sur la position de l'Oyapoc du Cap d'Orange, pour eux le Vincent Pinçon. Mais on attachait si peu d'importance à connaître exactement la position de la rivière revendiquée comme frontière par les Portugais, que le mémoire français de janvier 1698 ne contient sur la latitude aucune des indications figurant dans le mémoire sur lequel il se basait.

On conçoit que les Français connussent l'Oyapoc mieux que les Portugais, puisque pour atteindre l'Amazone, ils devaient passer près de l'Oyapoc et du Cap d'Orange ; pour les Portugais en revanche, cette rivière frontière était fort éloignée.

Une fois que les négociations eurent abouti à obliger les Portugais à raser tous leurs forts sur la rive gauche de l'Amazone et que la possession du Contesté fut déclarée « indecise entre les deux Couronnes », la France n'avait plus d'intérêt à ne pas délimiter le Contesté de manière à lui donner l'Amazone pour frontière méridionale, conformément à sa propre revendication, et l'Oyapoc (Ojapoc) ou Vincent Pinçon pour frontière septentrionale et occidentale, conformément à la revendication du Portugal. La France avait atteint le but qui lui importait le plus, le libre accès de l'Amazone. Elle n'avait pas à redouter que les Portugais avançassent vers Cayenne. Mais rien n'indique que l'Oyapoc ou Vincent Pinçon du traité provisionnel du 4 mars 1700 fut un autre cours d'eau que celui que les débats préliminaires font connaître sous ce nom, savoir l'Oyapoc d'aujourd'hui.

4. — On s'en tint à la convention du 4 mars 1700. L'article 9 du traité avait prévu que la question des frontières, Amazone ou Oyapoc-Vincent-Pinçon, serait éclaircie et définitivement tranchée selon les nouvelles données qui devaient être recueillies, mais cette disposition resta lettre morte, et le 18 juin 1701 le traité provisionnel de l'année précédente fut converti en un traité définitif et perpétuel.

La France considérait cet acte comme une concession qu'elle devait faire au Portugal à cause de la situation politique générale. Aucune réserve ou exception n'ayant été stipulée, il faut admettre que la dénomination adoptée en 1701 « terres du Cap de Nord, confinant à la rivière des Amazones » (article 15, première rédaction, ou article 6, seconde rédaction du traité), ne peut pas viser autre chose que le territoire du Contesté, tel que le délimitait le traité provisionnel, auquel on se référait expressément.

Ce que le Portugal avait en vain demandé à la France en 1701, savoir la renonciation de cette puissance « à toute prétention des terres du Cap de Nord confinant à la rivière des Amazones », et s'étendant « jusqu'à la rivière de Vincent Pinson autrement dit de Oyapoc », il se

le fit garantir le 16 mai 1703 dans son traité d'alliance avec l'Empereur, l'Angleterre et les Pays-Bas. L'article 22 de ce traité d'alliance stipule expressément : « ... pax fieri non poterit cum Rege Christianissimo, nisi ipse cedat quocumque Jure, quod habere intendit in Regiones ad Promontorium Boreale vulgo Caput de Norte pertinentes et ad ditionem Status Maranonii spectantes, jacentesque inter Fluvios Amazonium et Vincentis Pinsonis ». Le Portugal désignait la rivière devant servir de frontière septentrionale sous le nom qu'il lui donnait d'habitude, rien ne l'engageait à y ajouter la dénomination adoptée par les Français pour la même rivière. La désignation « Regiones ad Promontorium Boreale vulgo Caput de Norte pertinentes » est la traduction aussi exacte que possible du terme « Terres du Cap de Nord ».

Le traité de 1703 donne au Contesté la même étendue que les traités de 1700 et de 1701, et le traité d'Utrecht du 11 avril 1713 ne peut être interprété différemment.

Cela ressort directement des articles 8 et 9 du traité d'Utrecht, où le traité provisionnel de 1700 est déclaré nul et de nulle vigueur, où le même territoire dont avait disposé ce traité provisionnel est définitivement attribué au Portugal et où ce territoire, le Contesté, est désigné selon les mêmes termes que ceux dont s'étaient servis les traités antérieurs « terres appellées du Cap du Nord et situées entre la riviere des Amazones et celle de Japoc ou de Vincent Pinson ». Cette opinion est corroborée par l'article 12 qui fait défense aux Français « de passer la riviere de Vincent Pinson, pour negocier... dans les terres du Cap du Nord » ; cette dénomination ne vise pas d'autre territoire que celui délimité par l'article 8. En conséquence, les terres françaises de Cayenne commencent sur la rive gauche et nordouest du Vincent Pinçon des Portugais ou du Japoc des Français et c'est pourquoi l'article 12 précité stipule en outre : « Sa Majesté Portugaise promet... qu'aucuns de ses sujets n'iront commercer à Cayenne ».

L'origine des articles du traité d'Utrecht que l'arbitre doit interpréter est expliquée dans toute une série de documents dignes de foi : l'arbitre a puisé dans toutes ces pièces la conviction que par le Japoc ou Vincent Pinson de l'article 8, on ne peut pas entendre une autre rivière que celle à laquelle se rapportent les traités de 1700 et de 1703, donc pas d'autre cours d'eau que l'Oyapoc actuel du Cap d'Orange.

Au fond, les parties sont d'accord pour reconnaître qu'il ne saurait être attaché aucune importance à la différence d'orthographe de Japoc et d'Oyapoc ; dans les délibérations qui ont abouti à la conclusion du traité, on a écrit indifféremment Yapoco, Oyapoco, Oyapoc (Ojapoc). La dénomination Japoc est due probablement à ce que les plénipotentiaires portugais à Utrecht, qui connaissaient la rivière sous le nom de Vincent Pinçon, rédigèrent les articles du traité, et, d'après la forme usuelle pour eux, firent alors du Yapoco des cartes françaises un Japoc.

Il résulte des négociations que l'intervention de l'Angleterre a valu au Portugal des clauses favorables, en premier lieu l'attribution du Contesté et l'interdiction faite aux Français de naviguer sur l'Amazone. Cette ligne de conduite était dictée aux Anglais par leur propre intérêt et aussi par le respect des obligations que le traité de 1703 leur imposait à l'égard du Portugal.

Dès le début des négociations, le Portugal, se prévalant du traité d'alliance de 1703, et ce nonobstant le traité du 4 mars 1700, demandait que la France renonçât à son profit à toute prétention sur les « Terres du Cap du Nord situées entre la Rivière des Amazones et celle de Vincent Pinson » ; sa demande avait incontestablement pour objet le territoire dont, en 1700, la possession avait été déclarée « indecise entre les deux Couronnes » et dont la frontière vers Cayenne était formée par l'Oyapoc actuel du Cap d'Orange. La France, en revanche, entendait d'abord maintenir l'état de choses antérieur à la guerre et observait : « quant aux domaines de l'Amérique, s'il y a quelques différends à régler, on tâchera d'en convenir à l'amiable » ; plus tard, les plénipotentiaires français au congrès d'Utrecht avaient pour instruction de réclamer la frontière de l'Amazone et, au cas où ils ne pourraient pas l'obtenir, d'insister sur ce point « que les François auront la liberté entière de la Nauigation dans la Riviere des Amazones », en même temps que le traité provisionnel de 1700 resterait en vigueur « jusqu'à ce qu'on soit convenu deffinitivement des Limites de la Province de la Guyanne » : mais si cette convention venait à ne pas être conclue dans le délai d'une année à partir du traité de paix, le fleuve des Amazones deviendrait la frontière.

Le Portugal qui avait complètement confié la défense de ses intérêts à l'Angleterre fut soutenu par cette Puissance. Lord Bolingbroke fit savoir au Marquis de Torcy, ministre français des Affaires étrangères, que la reine d'Angleterre avait pris à l'égard du roi de Portugal « par traité des engagements plus solides qu'à l'égard de tout autre allié » ; à Londres, ce fut principalement le ministre portugais José da Cunha Brochado qui fit valoir avec succès les prétentions du Portugal ; il exposa combien le traité provisionnel de 1700 avait été préjudiciable au Portugal, en imposant au roi de Portugal de « s'abstenir de l'ancienne Possession et de la

jouissance des Terres, qu'il possedoit, situées depuis la Riviere appelée Yapoco jusques au Cap du Nort de la Riviere des Amazones inclusive », « au grand prejudice de son ancien Domaine, avec si peu de seureté pour le reste du Maragnan » ; il faisait ressortir que le maintien de ce traité de 1700 amènerait de nouvelles disputes et de nouvelles querelles. L'Angleterre était disposée à prendre contre la France la défense de la prétention du Portugal sur le Contesté, cela en ce sens « que les Français abandonnent totalement ces terres-là, pour les éloigner du voisinage du Brésil », mais les égards qu'elle avait pour la France firent qu'elle ne mit toute son énergie à soutenir cette prétention que du moment où, au cours des négociations, la France réclama pour ses ressortissants la libre navigation sur l'Amazone et présenta cette demande comme étant pour elle la plus importante.

Les rapports sur la mémorable conférence d'Utrecht, du 9 février 1713, à laquelle ont pris part les plénipotentiaires français, portugais et anglais, démontrent — et cela mérite d'être relevé — que la contestation au sujet de la latitude de l'embouchure de la rivière frontière aurait pu naître alors, si l'on avait attaché quelque importance à connaître exactement cette latitude. Mais comme tel n'était pas le cas, la question ne devint pas aiguë. Il faut toutefois insister sur ce point : en 1713, pas plus qu'en 1700 et dans les années précédentes, la question actuellement litigieuse n'existait et elle n'existait pas par cette raison : l'on était d'accord sur l'identité du Japoc (Oyapoc) et du Vincent Pinçon et d'accord aussi que, sous ce nom, il fallait entendre une seule et unique rivière et cette rivière était l'Oyapoc d'aujourd'hui, l'Oyapoc du Cap d'Orange.

La discussion du 9 février 1713 montra bien que les Français et les Portugais n'étaient pas du même avis touchant la latitude de l'embouchure de ce cours d'eau. Deux prétentions étaient en présence : le Brésil réclamait le Contesté, la France le maintien du traité provisionnel de 1700, subsidiairement le partage du Contesté, avec la clause que la libre navigation de l'Amazone serait garantie aux ressortissants français. Et quand le partage fut discuté, les Portugais déclarèrent l'accepter en principe : ils exigeaient cependant que le traité même traçât la ligne frontière de manière que celle-ci atteignît la côte par $3^{3}/_{4}$° de latitude nord : partant du point de vue que leur carte, qui donnait au Vincent Pinçon ou Oyapoc une latitude nord de $3^{3}/_{4}$°, était plus exacte et plus précise que les cartes françaises, qui plaçaient la rivière beaucoup plus au nord, ils estimaient que ce partage leur vaudrait non seulement tout le Contesté, mais encore une frontière sûre et indiscutable à l'avenir. Mais les Français étaient opposés à ce mode de partage : en premier lieu, un partage immédiat ne leur convenait pas ; ils préféraient un partage auquel il aurait été procédé après la conclusion de la paix, sur place ou ailleurs, par des commissaires des deux Etats ; en outre, ils n'agréaient pas le projet, parce que la part qu'il attribuait au Portugal leur paraissait trop grande. Parlant des plénipotentiaires portugais, ils rapportent : « Ils... se reservèrent toujours, non seulement la plus grande partie des costes jusqu'au cap de Nort, mais encore tous les bords de la riviere des Amazones, jusqu'au fort le plus reculé, qu'ils avoient avant 1700. »

Ce qui importait le plus aux Français, c'était la libre navigation de l'Amazone. Leurs plénipotentiaires le disent clairement dans le rapport qu'ils adressaient à Louis XIV sur la conférence du 9 février 1713 : « La première chose que nous demandames fut la liberté de la navigation pour les sujets de Vostre Majesté dans la riviere des Amazones. » Et Louis XIV qualifie la liberté de navigation sur l'Amazone de « condition fondamentale » qui seule le déterminera à entrer en matière sur le projet de partage du Contesté. La divergence des opinions sur la latitude de la rivière frontière perdit toute importance, du moment que la France, au lieu d'obtenir la libre navigation fut obligée d'y renoncer expressément ensuite de l'ultimatum de l'Angleterre, des 17 février—6 mars 1713, en même temps qu'elle devait abandonner au Portugal tout le Contesté tel qu'il avait été délimité par les précédents traités. Les Français acceptèrent le Japoc (Oyapoc) ou Vincent Pinçon comme étant le cours d'eau frontière visé par le traité de 1700, cela sans restriction ni réserve. La réserve que Louis XIV fit stipuler, lors de la signature du traité d'Utrecht, concernait non l'identité du Vincent Pinçon et de l'Oyapoc actuel, mais la liberté de navigation de l'Amazone ; c'était là le but qu'il se proposait, il ne tenait pas à une ligne frontière au sud-est de l'Oyapoc actuel et qui n'eût pas atteint l'Amazone.

5. — Le litige, tel qu'il existe actuellement entre les parties, est né depuis la conclusion du traité d'Utrecht, en un espace de temps relativement court.

Le conflit surgit lorsqu'en 1723, le Gouverneur français de Cayenne, Claude d'Orvilliers, tout en reconnaissant encore l'Oyapoc actuel comme étant la frontière adoptée par le traité d'Utrecht, revendiqua pour la France le territoire entier de l'embouchure de ce cours d'eau, par la raison que le traité d'Utrecht avait attribué au Portugal les terres du Cap de Nord seulement et non pas celles du Cap d'Orange. Il estimait qu'on pouvait d'un commun accord prendre le Cachipour pour limite. De son côté, João da Maya da Gama, gouverneur portugais à Pará, soutenait, en invoquant la découverte faite en 1723 par João Paes do Amaral d'une borne frontière entre les possessions espagnoles et portugaises sur la Montagne d'Argent, qui est sur la rive gauche de l'Oyapoc, que « les territoires du Roi Très-Chrétien commencent à la dite pointe appelée Comaribô, qui se trouve à l'Ouest de la rivière de Vicente Pinçon et non pas au Cap d'Orange... attendu que celui-ci se trouve à l'Est, et que toute l'embouchure de la rivière de Vicente Pinçon laquelle est et forme la limite des deux territoires appartient au Roi mon Maître ». Les deux parties partent donc du même cours d'eau comme cours d'eau frontière, c'est-à-dire de l'Oyapoc du Cap d'Orange, mais non pas du thalweg de ce cours d'eau ; elles revendiquent par contre le territoire sis de l'autre côté.

Tandis que le Portugal renoncera tôt après à toute prétention sur la rive gauche de l'Oyapoc, il n'en sera pas de même de la part des autorités françaises à Cayenne. En 1726 déjà, d'Orvilliers tire argument de la « Baie de Vincent Pinson » qui devient pour la suite du litige d'une grande importance ; il considère la frontière du Cachipour comme une concession à faire au Portugal et motive son opinion en ces termes : « Quoique la Baie de Vincent Pinson soit plus au Sud que la Rivière de Cachipour, je conviendrai, pour le Roi mon Maître, que nos limites soient à la Rivière de Cachipour ; cette Rivière ne dépend nullement des terres dites du Cap du Nord, qui sont celles que le Roi a cédées par le dernier traité au Roi de Portugal ; mais comme la Rivière de Vincent Pinson, autrement nommée Oyapoc, est petite, je crois que le Roi ne désapprouvera pas que nous placions la limite à la Rivière de Cachipour, qui est une grande rivière ».

L'exposé historique a démontré que cette argumentation ne peut pas se concilier avec l'article 8 du traité d'Utrecht ; il suffit d'avoir signalé les premiers faits auxquels se rattache le litige actuel. Ceux-ci ne sauraient rien changer aux constatations qui se dégagent des débats qui ont précédé le traité d'Utrecht et qui fixent le sens véritable et précis de son article 8. L'histoire des rapports qu'ont entretenus depuis 1713, au sujet de la question de la frontière, les autorités françaises de Cayenne et les autorités brésiliennes de Pará d'une part, puis, d'autre part, le Gouvernement français et le Gouvernement portugais, remplacé plus tard par le Gouvernement brésilien, n'a d'autre intérêt pour l'arbitre que de démontrer avec une entière clarté, quelle est l'origine du litige actuel et de quelle manière les parties, au cours du conflit, ont formulé et défendu leurs prétentions. Il n'est pas nécessaire de revenir encore sur cette partie de l'histoire de la contestation, pas plus que sur les œuvres cartographiques sur lesquelles elle exerça son influence ; ces points ont été examinés d'une manière approfondie dans l'exposé historique et géographique.

6. — Après qu'en 1822, le Brésil se fut séparé du Portugal pour devenir un Etat indépendant et eut été reconnu comme tel par les puissances, il se trouva à l'égard de la France, en ce qui concerne le Contesté, dans la même situation que le Portugal jusqu'alors. Aucun désaccord n'existe sur ce point entre les parties.

7. — L'examen auquel l'arbitre s'est livré l'a conduit à adopter, en conformité de la demande formulée par le Brésil dans l'article 1er du traité d'arbitrage, l'Oyapoc d'aujourd'hui comme devant former la frontière extérieure ou maritime entre la Guyane française et le Brésil. Cette décision entraîne le rejet de la revendication par la France de la frontière de l'Araguary. Il y a lieu de même d'écarter comme frontière tout autre cours d'eau coulant entre l'Araguary et l'Oyapoc. Ce résultat se trouve confirmé, sous tous les rapports, par l'examen de chacune des questions d'ordre purement géographique.

L'exposé géographique a montré comment un seul et même cours d'eau a reçu des noms différents, le nom de Vincent Pinçon de la part des Espagnols et des Portugais, le nom d'Oyapoc, très diversement orthographié d'après la dénomination primitive d'origine indienne, de la part des Anglais, des Hollandais et des Français. Il montre aussi que les indications de la latitude de cette rivière variaient beaucoup selon les divers géographes et les diverses cartes géographiques, mais que l'identité du cours d'eau n'en peut pas moins être établie grâce aux « montagnes » qui, situées à l'ouest de son embouchure, le signalent, grâce aussi à la détermination de sa position et à la nomenclature reproduite dans les cartes.

Il reste acquis pour l'arbitre que la cartographie espagnole et portugaise du XVIe siècle, depuis le Padron real de Chaves de 1536, entend par le Rio de Vicente Pinzon accompagné de « Montañas », l'Oyapoc actuel du Cap d'Orange. Vers le milieu du XVIe siècle, un fleuve nouveau et important fut introduit dans les cartes, en premier lieu par Nicolas Desliens et Sebastiano Cabotto, qui l'empruntèrent à la relation qu'Orellana avait donnée de son voyage. Il figura sur les cartes comme un cours d'eau distinct du Marañon déjà connu et au nord-ouest de celui-ci. Or

les cartes identifiaient le Marañon connu avec l'Amazone d'aujourd'hui, lui donnaient une position presque analogue, et le nouveau fleuve étant également identifié avec l'Amazone, il s'ensuit que la position du nouveau fleuve était inexacte ; il devait forcément être déplacé trop au nord-ouest, parce que le reste du littoral n'avait subi aucun changement. Le Rio de Vicente Pinzon, abstraction faite du fleuve nouvellement introduit, garda l'ancienne position que lui avait donnée Chaves, il était en conséquence beaucoup plus rapproché du nouveau cours d'eau que de l'ancien Marañon. Mais quelques géographes reconnurent bientôt l'erreur ainsi commise, et en 1558 déjà Diogo Homem remet le Rio de Vicente Pinzon, avec les Montañas, à la distance primitive et exacte du fleuve des Amazones. Le représentant le plus autorisé de la cartographie portugaise de la seconde moitié du XVIe siècle, Vaz Dourado, se rallia à cette opinion, ainsi que Gerardus Mercator dans ses mappemondes, établies d'après les cartes de l'école de Séville, qui firent connaître universellement et transmirent au XVIIe siècle le nom du Rio de Vicente Pinzon.

La description que donna B. M. Parente vers 1630 et la donation qui lui fut octroyée en 1637, démontrent avec une assez grande certitude, ainsi que l'explique l'exposé géographique, que le Rio de Vicente Pinzon et l'Oyapoc sont un seul et même cours d'eau. En revanche, les cartes de João Teixeira ne peuvent pas servir à déterminer la position du cours d'eau frontière, par le motif qu'elles ne figurent cette partie du littoral que d'une manière absolument insuffisante.

L'exposé géographique réfute aussi les divers arguments développés par la France à l'appui de la frontière de l'Araguary. Il est démontré que cette prétention n'est pas fondée, par la raison qu'il est impossible d'établir que l'Araguary ait eu autrefois une seconde embouchure et qu'il n'a pas été constaté de fait permettant d'admettre l'identification du Rio de Vicente Pinzon avec un bras septentrional, aujourd'hui disparu, de l'Araguary. L'Araguary a son embouchure au sud du Cap de Nord, tandis qu'incontestablement le Rio de Vicente Pinzon se jette dans l'Océan au nord-ouest du Cap de Nord. Et de tout temps, on a fait une distinction entre ces deux cours d'eau.

C'est ensuite d'une fausse combinaison que la Baie de Vincent Pinçon figure sur la carte dressée en 1703 par Guillaume de l'Isle et plus tard notamment sur celle de La Condamine, au débouché septentrional du Canal actuel de Carapaporis : cette erreur provient, d'après les documents versés aux débats, de celle qu'a commise Robert Dudley dans son interprétation du rapport que Keymis avait fait de son voyage, et des fausses notions qu'avaient au sujet de l'Amazone Desliens, Cabotto et d'autres.

Outre les mémoires de 1698 et 1699, ce sont notamment la carte dressée par le père Fritz en 1691 et la description du père Pfeil qui montrent que le Portugal, à la fin du XVIIe siècle et lors de la conclusion du traité de 1700, identifiait le Rio de Vicente Pinzon et l'Oyapoc d'aujourd'hui. Sur la carte du père Fritz, qui suit en général la nomenclature indienne, le Rio de Vicente Pinzon prend la place de l'Oyapoc; le père Pfeil identifie expressément le Vincent Pinzon avec l'Oyapoc, en relevant que c'est toujours le même cours d'eau, qu'on l'appelle Rio Pinçon ou Wiapoc, ou Yapoc, ou Vaiabogo, ou Oyapoc. La rivière dont il parle est l'Oyapoc d'aujourd'hui, car il dit : il se jette dans la mer en formant une belle baie et son eau douce se perd entre les deux célèbres promontoires du Mont-d'Argent et du Cabo d'Orange. Il est d'ordre secondaire que le père Pfeil, à l'exemple de tant d'autres géographes, indique une latitude inexacte, car c'est le cours d'eau et non la latitude qui revêt de l'importance.

8. — A teneur du traité d'arbitrage et en conformité des explications ci-dessus, la frontière extérieure ou maritime va jusqu'à la source principale de l'Oyapoc d'aujourd'hui, à moins que le Brésil ne puisse donner un fondement juridique à la prétention qu'il a articulée aux fins d'obtenir une frontière intérieure passant par le parallèle de 2° 24'. Mais le Brésil n'a pas réussi à justifier sa prétention, par la raison que le seul argument qu'il invoque est tiré de la convention de Paris du 28 août 1817; mais ce moyen, de l'aveu général, n'est pas définitif; il n'est que provisoire. Or comme il s'agit en l'espèce de la revendication d'une frontière définitive, la convention de Paris doit être écartée du débat.

Il y a lieu de remarquer en outre qu'une ligne frontière déterminée d'après un parallèle, constitue une limite artificielle, que l'arbitre ne saurait adopter si elle ne peut pas se fonder sur un titre.

La limite intérieure que la France revendique dans le traité d'arbitrage, et qui devrait suivre une ligne parallèle au cours de l'Amazone jusqu'au Rio Branco, manque, elle aussi, de base juridique.

Il est exact que la ligne parallèle qu'elle revendique aujourd'hui, la France l'a déjà en principe réclamée sous la forme de la « ligne de M. de Castries »; mais pour que l'arbitre pût attribuer à la France cette ligne parallèle, il serait nécessaire qu'elle fût basée sur une convention ou sur un autre acte incontestable.

Ce titre fait défaut; car c'est à tort que la France estime que l'article 10 du traité d'Utrecht n'a cédé au Portugal qu'une bande de terres relativement étroite le long des bords, tandis que le vaste territoire qui se trouve derrière cette bande serait resté à la France.

Le traité d'Utrecht se borne à édicter : « les deux bords de la rivière des Amazones, tant le meridional que le septentrional, appartiennent... à Sa Majesté Portugaise ». Il ne parle pas d'une bande de terrain le long des bords, mais des bords même; il ne stipule pas davantage que le territoire qui s'étend derrière la bande côtière appartient à la France, pas plus qu'il ne dit que les terres qui sont derrière les bords sont cédées au Portugal. Il dispose en termes identiques des deux bords; une interprétation restrictive du terme « bords » ne parait admissible ni pour l'un ni pour l'autre côté du fleuve.

L'allégation de la France qu'elle est fondée à revendiquer, en vertu d'une possession effective, les territoires qui sont limités par la frontière intérieure qu'elle propose, n'est pas confirmée par des faits.

Par ces motifs, l'arbitre doit, en ce qui concerne la frontière intérieure, adopter la « solution intermédiaire » convenue par les parties dans l'article 2 du traité d'arbitrage.

IV. Sentence.

Vu les faits et les motifs ci-dessus, le Conseil fédéral suisse, en sa qualité d'arbitre appelé par le Gouvernement de la République française et par le Gouvernement des Etats-Unis du Brésil, selon le traité d'arbitrage du 10 avril 1897, à fixer la frontière de la Guyane française et du Brésil, constate, décide et prononce :

I. — Conformément au sens précis de l'article 8 du traité d'Utrecht, la rivière Japoc ou Vincent Pinçon est l'Oyapoc qui se jette dans l'Océan immédiatement à l'ouest du Cap d'Orange et qui par son thalweg forme la ligne frontière.

II. — A partir de la source principale de cette rivière Oyapoc jusqu'à la frontière hollandaise, la ligne de partage des eaux du bassin des Amazones qui, dans cette région, est constituée dans sa presque totalité par la ligne de faîte des monts Tumuc-Humac, forme la limite intérieure.

Ainsi arrêté à Berne dans notre séance du 1er décembre 1900.

La présente sentence, revêtue du sceau de la Confédération suisse, sera expédiée en trois exemplaires français et trois exemplaires allemands. Un exemplaire français et un exemplaire allemand seront communiqués à chacune des deux parties par les soins de notre Département politique; le troisième exemplaire français et le troisième exemplaire allemand seront déposés aux Archives de la Confédération suisse.

CXXXIII. Chili, France.

3 juillet 1897.

Réclamation basée sur l'inexécution de certaines clauses d'un contrat relatif à un marché de nitrates. Les héritiers du réclamant transigèrent pour une somme de 200,000 $.

Protocolo para someter al arbitraje la reclamacion del ciudadano Carlos Fréraut, celebrado en Santiago, Julio 3, 1897.

Reunidos en el Departamento de Relaciones Esteriores de Chile el Ministro del ramo señor don Carlos Morla Viceña, i el Encargado de Négocios *ad interim* de Francia, Conde de Saint-Aulaire, con el fin de poner término á la reclamacion del ciudadano frances señor Carlos Fréraut, motivada, segun establece el reclamante, por inejecucion de varios contratos relacionados con la oficina salitrera « Barrenechea » convinieron en los siguientes artículos.

ART. I. — Los Gobiernos de Chile i Francia designan al señor don Eduardo H. Strobel para que, como Arbitrador i amigable componedor, decida con plenos poderes, procediendo *ex æquo et bono* sobre los puntos siguientes :

A. Es o nó justa en todo o en parte la reclamacion del ciudadano frances señor Carlos Fréraut, presentada contra el Gobierno de Chile con el patrocinio diplomático de la Legacion de Francia ?

B. Si es justa, en todo o en parte, qué cantidad debe el Gobierno de Chile pagar al señor Fréraut o a quien sus derechos represente, como indemnizacion i completa cancelacion de dicho reclamo ?

ART. 2. — Las Partes Contratantes convienen ademas en que el señor don Eduardo H. Strobel decida las anteriores cuestiones, en virtud de los antecedentes que han mediado entre los representantes de los dos Gobiernos en Santiago i de los documentos i pruebas aducidas durante la controversia sobre la materia de esa reclamacion, i en vista de un memorial o alegato que uno i otro podrán presentar si lo estiman conveniente.

ART. 3. — Se fija el plazo de tres meses como término dentro del cual la reclamacion del señor don Carlos Fréraut debe quedar fallada en definitiva por el Arbitro que se designa por el presente Convenio.

ART. 4. — La sentencia arbitral, que será inapelable, deberá, sin embargo, establecer que las sumas que pudieran ser atribuidas al reclamante, serán pagadas por el Gobierno de Chile en cinco anualidades iguales sin intereses, debiendo efec-

tuarse el pago de la primera anualidad seis meses despues de la fecha de la sentencia.

ART. 5. — Las Partes Contratantes acuerdan remunerar los servicios del Arbitro con un honorario de quinientas libras esterlinas (£ 500), que le será abonado totalmente por el Gobierno de Chile si el fallo arbitral no acordará al reclamante indemnizacion alguna i por mitad entre éste i el mismo Gobierno, si el fallo favoreciera al reclamante en algun sentido.

Hecho en Santiago de Chile, en doble ejemplar i en los idiomas español i frances, á los 3 dias del mes de julio de 1897 [1].

CXXXIV. Etats-Unis d'Amérique, Siam.

26 juillet 1897.

Il s'est agi dans cette affaire d'importantes concessions forestières accordées par le Siam à un citoyen américain et mises en péril par suite des agissements des autorités de ce pays. Il fut accordé par l'arbitre une indemnité de 706,721 ticals.

Protocol of an agreement for submission to an arbitrator of mutual claims in the case of the late Marion A. Cheek, signed at Bangkok, July 26, 1897.

His Majesty the King of Siam and the United States of America, through their representatives, His Royal Highness Prince Devawongse Varopraker, minister for foreign affairs of His Majesty the King of Siam, and John Barrett, minister resident and consul general of the United States of America, have agreed upon and signed the following protocol :

Whereas the United States of America, on behalf of the late Marion A. Cheek, have claimed indemnity from the Government of Siam for arbitrary, unjustifiable, and other injurious action alleged to have been taken against the said Marion Cheek by the Government of Siam ; and whereas the Government of Siam denies either the allegations of fact or contentions of law on which the claims of the other party are based, or the right of the other party to demand indemnity on account of such facts and contentions of law, and holds that in any case said Marion A. Cheek's liabilities to the Siamese Government, eventually including the amount of damages that might be awarded to Siam in consequence of the injurious action of said Marion A. Cheek or of the administrator of his estate (which injurious action is denied by the other

---

[1] *Memoria de Relaciones Exteriores*, 1897, p. 347.

party) exceeds the amount of damages that might be awarded to said Marion A. Cheek, or his estate, in consequence of the injurious action of the Government of Siam ; it is therefore agreed between the two Governments, with the consent of the administrator of the estate of Marion A. Cheek :

I. That every matter of dispute, both facts and law, brought into issue between the two parties shall be referred to the decision of Sir Nicholas J. Hannen, Her Britannic Majesty's chief justice and consul general at Sanghaï, who is hereby authorized as arbitrator, and who has given to both Governments official notice that he has accepted this office by permission of his Government.

II *a*. That the parties to this agreement shall jointly have printed, not later than the 25th day of september, 1897, copies of the correspondence, documents, evidence, proofs and other matter which have passed between them or which have been submitted by one of said parties to the other party in the consideration or discussion of said case ; and each party shall be provided with six copies of said printed matter, and two signed copies shall be immediately forwarded to the arbitrator through the British representative in Bangkok.

b. That on, or not later than, the 20th day of November, 1897, the parties hereto shall exchange with each other, and file with the British representative in Bangkok to be immediately forwarded to the arbitrator, such pleadings, statements of fact, claims for compensation or damages, and other matter pertaining to the case as shall be deemed necessary by the party filing the same for a proper presentation of his case.

c. That when the court of arbitration opens both parties may file answers to the respective pleadings, statements of fact, claims for compensation or damages, and other matter pertaining to the case referred to in the above paragraph « *b* », and the arbitrator may permit either or both parties to file further pleadings or statements or not, as he deems advisable. Both parties may present evidence in support of the allegations contained in the various pleadings and statements filed in the case.

III. That the arbitration court shall sit in Bangkok from and after the 1st day of February, 1898, unless another date shall be agreed upon between the arbitrator and the two Governments, and the arbitrator, after examining the statements, pleadings, documents, evidence, proofs, and other matter submitted, may permit arguments and call for any additional evidence.

IV. That the arbitrator shall render his decision within three months after having left Bangkok. He shall decide on the statements, pleadings, evidence, proofs, and arguments submitted to him whether, and for what sum, the Government of Siam is indebted to the estate of Marion A. Cheek, or the estate of Marion A. Cheek to the Government of Siam, provided that, if the award is made in favour of the Government of Siam, it shall be against the estate of Marion A. Cheek only and not against the United States.

V. Reasonable compensation to the arbitrator and the other common items of expense attending to the hearing of the case by the arbitrator shall be paid in equal moieties by the two Governments.

VI. Any award made by the arbitrator shall be final and conclusive, and the amount so awarded shall be paid, as the case may be, either by the Government of Siam or by the estate of Marion A. Cheek, not later than four months from the date of such award.

VII. Should either party to this protocol fail to comply with its provisions the effect thereof shall be determined by the arbitrator.

Done in duplicate at Bangkok this twenty-sixth day of July 1897 [1].

Award of Nicholas J. Hannen, rendered on March 21, 1898, in the case of Dr. Cheek, between Siam and the United States of America.

Whereas by an agreement dated the 6th day of July 1897 between His Royal Highness Prince Devawongse Varoprakar, minister for foreign affairs of His Majesty the King of Siam, and John Barrett, minister resident and consul general of the United States of America, it was agreed to refer every matter of dispute, both facts and law, brought into issue between the Siamese Government and the estate of the late Marion A. Cheek to the decision of me, Sir Nicholas John Hannen, knight, chief justice of Her Britannic Majesty's supreme court for China and Japan ; and

Whereas in conformity with Article III of the said agreement I sat in Bangkok on the 1st day of February 1898 and on nine subsequent days and examined the statements, pleadings, documents, proofs and other matter submitted to me, and also listened to the arguments presented to me on behalf of the parties ; and

Whereas all other preliminary matters referred to in the said agreement were duly carried

---

[1] *Foreign Relations of the U. S.*, 1897, p. 479.

out by the parties. Now having fully taken into consideration the said agreement and also the cases, counter-cases, documents, evidence, and arguments, and likewise all other communications made to me by the parties during the progress of the sittings, and having impartially and carefully examined the same, I have arrived at the decision embodied in the present award:

Whereas on and after the 20th day of August 1892 the Siamese Government seized and entered into possession of property in the possession of and under the control of Marion A. Cheek: and

Whereas I am of opinion that such seizure and entry into possession was a violation of the second article of the treaty of 1856 between the United States of America and the Kingdom of Siam; and

Whereas in justification of the said seizure and entry into possession it has been alleged that the said Dr. Marion A. Cheek made default in the performance of certain conditions of certains agreements made between him and the Siamese Government, one of which conditions was alleged to be the payment of interest upon a loan made by the Siamese Government to the said Dr. Marion A. Cheek upon the 31st day of March of each year; and

Whereas it is necessary that before default in the performance of a condition can be proved, the existence of the condition in the contract must first be demonstrated; and

Whereas I am of opinion that it was not proved to my satisfaction that the said contracts contained, or that their wording necessarily implied, in the minds of the parties, such a condition as was alleged to have been broken; and

Whereas it has not been proved to my satisfaction that the said Dr. Marion A. Cheek did make default in the performance of any other of the conditions alleged to have been contained in the said agreement so as to justify the Siamese Government in its action; and

Whereas on the 15th day of July 1893 the Siamese Government issued or permitted to be issued an order, alluded to in the correspondence and at the hearing as the Chieng Mai order, which was in my opinion unjustifiable and which said order was calculated to and did greatly injure the said Dr. Marion A. Cheek; and

Whereas I am of opinion that the estate of the late Dr. Marion A. Cheek should as far as possible be placed in the same position as it would have been in had not the Siamese Government seized the property in the control and possession of Dr. Cheek in August 1892 and had not the said government issued or permitted to be issued the Chieng Mai order, I hereby

award to the estate of the late Dr. Marion A. Cheek the sum of ticals 706,721 (seven hundred and six thousand seven hundred and twenty-one) as the indemnity to be paid by the Siamese Government for the satisfaction of all claims referred to my consideration, and I further award that the « bill of sale mortgage » of the 23d April 1889 is now void, the amount of the loan, together with the interest for which it was given, having been taken into account by me in reckoning the sum due by the Siamese Government to the Cheek estate, and the property by the said bill of sale; and

Whereas it was alleged by the said Dr. Marion A. Cheek and by his representatives that the Siamese Government had promised to grant to the said Dr. Cheek the lease of certain forests in the correspondence and at the hearing referred to as « The Nan Forest » and compensation for the nonfulfillment of the said promise was claimed by the Cheek estate; and

Whereas it was not proved to my satisfaction that any such promise was ever made, I hereby decide and award that the Cheek estate shall not recover anything from the Siamese Government upon this portion of their claim.

In testimony whereof this present decision and award has been made in duplicate and signed by me this 21st day of March 1898 at Shanghaï in the Empire of China [1].

CXXXV. Belgique. Grande-Bretagne.

19 mars 1898.

Il s'est agi, dans cette espèce, de l'arrestation et de l'expulsion d'un citoyen anglais. L'arbitre reconnut à la Belgique le droit qu'elle s'était arrogé.

Convention entre la Belgique et la Grande-Bretagne concernant l'arbitrage en cause du sieur Ben Tillett, signé à Bruxelles le 19 Mars 1898.

Sa Majesté la Reine du Royaume-Uni de la Grande-Bretagne et d'Irlande, Impératrice des Indes, et Sa Majesté le Roi des Belges, considérant que le 21 août 1896, Mr. Ben Tillett, sujet Britannique, a été arrêté à Anvers, en exécution des ordres donnés par le ministre de la Justice de Belgique, qu'il a été détenu et ensuite expulsé du pays:

Qu'il est allégué par le dit Ben Tillett que cette détention lui a occasionné des dépenses et une perte de temps; qu'elle a été accompagnée

---

[1] J. B. MOORE, *History and Digest* ..., p. 5068.

de mesures rigoureuses et inconvenantes qui ne peuvent se justifier, et que sa santé a souffert par suite du traitement auquel il a été soumis :

Considérant que le Gouvernement de Sa Majesté Britannique, tout en ne contestant pas au Gouvernement de Sa Majesté le Roi des Belges le droit d'expulser Mr. Ben Tillett, et de le détenir pour autant qu'il serait raisonnablement nécessaire en vue d'assurer l'expulsion, est cependant d'avis que l'arrestation et la détention du dit Ben Tillett n'ont pas été nécessaires, et que certaines circonstances rigoureuses dont elles ont été entourées excèdent absolument tout ce qui peut être justifié comme une conséquence du droit d'expulsion, et que, par conséquent, l'expression d'un regret ainsi qu'une compensation matérielle sont dues à Mr. Ben Tillett par le Gouvernement Belge ;

Considérant que le Gouvernement de Sa Majesté le Roi des Belges estime, de son côté, qu'il n'y a lieu à aucune réparation ou indemnité pécuniaire, les mesures dont se plaint Mr. Ben Tillett ayant été prises dans les limites de l'exercice de la souveraineté de l'Etat ;

Sa Majesté Britannique et Sa Majesté le Roi des Belges, désirant mettre fin d'une manière juste et équitable à la divergence d'opinion qui s'est élevée entre leurs Gouvernements, sont convenus de soumettre cette divergence à l'examen et à la décision d'un Arbitre, et à cet effet ont nommé pour leurs Plénipotentiaires, savoir :

Sa Majesté la Reine du Royaume-Uni de la Grande-Bretagne et d'Irlande, Impératrice des Indes, l'Honorable Sir Francis Plunkett, G. C. M. G., son Envoyé Extraordinaire et Ministre Plénipotentiaire près Sa Majesté le Roi des Belges ; et Sa Majesté le Roi des Belges, M. Paul de Favereau, Chevalier de l'Ordre de Léopold, Membre de la Chambre des Représentants, son Ministre des Affaires Etrangères :

Lesquels après avoir échangé leurs pleins pouvoirs, trouvés en bonne et due forme, sont convenus des Articles suivants :

ARTICLE I. — Le Gouvernement de Sa Majesté Britannique et le Gouvernement de Sa Majesté le Roi des Belges conviennent d'inviter un jurisconsulte étranger à exercer les fonctions d'Arbitre dans le différend dont il s'agit.

ARTICLE II. — L'Arbitre aura à examiner si la réclamation d'une indemnité pécuniaire émise par le Gouvernement Britannique en faveur de Mr. Ben Tillett est fondée et, dans l'affirmative, à déterminer le montant de cette indemnité.

ARTICLE III. — Le Gouvernement de Sa Majesté Britannique fera parvenir à l'Arbitre, par la voie diplomatique, dans l'espace d'un mois après l'échange des ratifications de la présente Convention, un mémoire à l'appui de sa réclamation en faveur de Mr. Ben Tillett et dans le même délai il en fournira une copie au Gouvernement de Sa Majesté le Roi des Belges.

Dans le délai d'un mois après la réception de cette copie, le Gouvernement de Sa Majesté le Roi des Belges transmettra un contre-mémoire dont il fournira en même temps une copie au Gouvernement de Sa Majesté Britannique.

En déans les trois semaines qui suivront la réception de cette copie, le Gouvernement de Sa Majesté Britannique, s'il le juge utile, transmettra à l'Arbitre une réplique dont il fournira en même temps une copie au Gouvernement de Sa Majesté le Roi des Belges.

Le Gouvernement de Sa Majesté le Roi des Belges pourra, à son tour, dans le délai de trois semaines après la réception de la dite copie, faire parvenir à l'Arbitre une réponse à cette réplique, sauf à en transmettre en même temps une copie au Gouvernement de Sa Majesté Britannique.

ARTICLE IV. — Après l'échange de ces Mémoires, aucune communication ni écrite ni verbale ne sera faite à l'Arbitre, à moins que ce dernier ne s'adresse lui-même aux Parties Contractantes pour obtenir par écrit de l'une d'elles ou de toutes deux des renseignements ultérieurs.

La Partie Contractante qui aurait à donner de semblables renseignements en transmettra immédiatement une copie à l'autre Partie Contractante, et celle-ci, si elle le juge convenable, en déans le mois de la réception de cette copie, communiquera par écrit à l'Arbitre les observations auxquelles ce document pourra donner lieu. Ces observations seront également, et en même temps, transmises en copie à l'autre Partie Contractante.

L'Arbitre pourra, s'il le juge opportun, réclamer qu'il lui soit fourni, de la manière qu'il indiquera, la preuve de l'un des faits sur lesquels porte le différend.

ARTICLE V. — L'Arbitre rendra sa sentence aussitôt que possible, et il fixera le montant des frais nécessaires résultant de l'arbitrage ; il déterminera celle des Parties Contractantes qui aura à les supporter. Ces frais, dont il est bien entendu que le montant sera limité autant que possible, pourront être mis pour le tout ou partiellement à la charge de l'une des Parties Contractantes.

ARTICLE VI. — Les Hautes Parties Contractantes s'engagent à accepter comme définitive la décision prononcée par l'Arbitre dans les limites de la présente Convention et à s'y soumettre sans aucune réserve.

ARTICLE VII. — Si, à un moment quelconque, avant que la sentence ne soit rendue, l'Arbitre venait à cesser ses fonctions pour un autre motif qu'une cause temporaire, les Hautes Parties Contractantes s'entendront pour désigner un autre Arbitre, qui procédera à la solution du différend à sa place.

ARTICLE VIII. — Le montant de l'indemnité qui serait éventuellement allouée par l'Arbitre sera payé au Gouvernement de Sa Majesté Britannique en déans le mois qui suivra le vote, par les Chambres Belges, du crédit nécessaire à cet effet.

ARTICLE IX. — La présente Convention sera ratifiée et les ratifications seront échangées à Bruxelles aussitôt que faire se pourra.

En foi de quoi les Plénipotentiaires respectifs ont signé cette même Convention et y ont apposé le sceau de leurs armes.

Fait à Bruxelles, le 19e jour du mois de Mars de l'an de grâce 1898 [1].

Sentence Arbitrale dans l'Affaire Ben Tillett, prononcée à Paris, le 26 Décembre 1898.

M'acquittant des fonctions d'Arbitre qui m'ont été conférées avec l'autorisation du Gouvernement Français, en vertu de la Convention du 19 Mars 1898, conclue entre le Gouvernement de Sa Majesté le Roi des Belges et le Gouvernement de Sa Majesté Britannique, au sujet du litige international suscité par l'expulsion de Mr. Ben Tillett, sujet Anglais, du territoire Belge.

Ayant examiné soigneusement et mûrement pesé les documents qui ont été produits de part et d'autre concernant l'indemnité réclamée par le Gouvernement de Sa Majesté Britannique au Gouvernement de Sa Majesté le Roi des Belges au profit de Mr. Ben Tillett.

M'étant en outre transporté, le 15 Août 1898, à Anvers pour résoudre en pleine connaissance de cause certaines questions qui me paraissent douteuses, et ayant procédé à une enquête dans la prison même d'Anvers.

Je prononce la Sentence Arbitrale suivante:

A. Sur le droit d'expulsion envisagé dans son principe:

Attendu que l'on ne saurait contester à un Etat la faculté d'interdire son territoire à des étrangers quand leurs menées ou leur présence lui paraissent compromettre sa sécurité:

Qu'il apprécie, d'ailleurs, dans la plénitude de sa souveraineté la portée des faits qui motivent cette déclaration.

B. Quant à la surveillance exercée sur la personne de Ben Tillett à la suite du meeting

[1] *Parliamentary Paper*, C. 9235.

du 21 Août 1896, et jusqu'à l'incarcération de ce sujet Anglais dans la Maison de Sûreté d'Anvers;

Attendu qu'en reconnaissant à l'Etat le droit d'expulser on ne saurait lui dénier les moyens d'assurer l'efficacité de ses injonctions;

Qu'il doit pouvoir surveiller les étrangers dont la présence lui paraît dangereuse pour l'ordre public, et s'il craint que ceux auxquels il interdit son territoire n'échappent à cette surveillance, les garder en vue;

Attendu, en fait, que Ben Tillett s'était rendu en Belgique pour y organiser la fédération internationale des dockers et pour y fomenter une grève jugée par le Gouvernement Royal tout à la fois préjudiciable aux intérêts du port d'Anvers, et menaçante pour la tranquillité publique;

Attendu qu'il existait pour le Gouvernement Belge des motifs plausibles de penser que Ben Tillett avait une première fois harangué les ouvriers du port au « Werker » dans la soirée du 22 Juillet 1896, et s'était habilement soustrait, après ce discours, aux recherches de la police;

Que ce Gouvernement ne sortait pas de son rôle, et n'excédait pas son droit en s'appliquant à ne pas perdre de vue Ben Tillett dans l'après-midi du 21 Août, par suite à s'assurer de sa personne après la réunion tenue dans la cour du cabaret Schram;

Attendu, il est vrai, qu'aucune mesure d'expulsion n'avait encore été prise contre Ben Tillett au moment où il fut conduit au bureau de police le 21 Août 1896, vers 4 heures de l'après-midi; mais que la dépêche ministérielle du 9 Juillet 1896 (visée dans le réquisitoire, en date du 21 Août, du Commissaire de Police de la Cinquième Section, Sud, à Anvers), relative aux étrangers arrivant à Anvers pour y donner des meetings en faveur d'une union universelle des marins et ouvriers des ports, ne laissait subsister aucun doute sur les volontés du pouvoir central; que la police Anversoise ne pouvait, sans désobéir à ses instructions, s'abstenir de mettre à la disposition du Gouvernement les étrangers qui viendraient prendre une part active à l'agitation provoquée depuis le mois de Juin 1896, pour organiser la fédération internationale;

Qu'au surplus, d'après les documents de la cause, notamment d'après un rapport de l'Adjoint-Commissaire Bucan, daté du 31 Août 1896, Ben Tillett avait été formellement avisé des instructions ministérielles; qu'aux termes de la déposition du même Bucan, entendu par moi sous la foi du serment le 15 Août 1898, Ben Tillett savait absolument à quoi s'en tenir; on l'avait officiellement avisé, dès son débarquement, que, s'il voulait donner le meeting public bruyamment annoncé dans le « Seamen's Chronicle du 8 Août 1896 », il n'avait qu'à quitter le territoire Belge ; autrement il s'exposait à être arrêté et reconduit par la force armée à la frontière ;

Que dans cet état des faits, des agents du Pouvoir Exécutif ont pu retenir Ben Tillett au bureau de police pendant un peu plus de trois heures en vue d'assurer l'exécution d'une mesure d'expulsion arrêtée en principe dans les Conseils du Gouvernement et dont la réalisation était imminente ;

Que, les arrêtés d'expulsion ne précédant pas en général les événements qui les motivent, si l'on ne peut employer des moyens de coercition pour garder à vue pendant quelques heures, jusqu'à ce que la mesure soit officiellement prise, un étranger dont la conduite est devenue une cause de trouble, ce personnage aura le temps de se dérober à la police et le Gouvernement se trouvera désarmé ;

C. Sur l'incarcération dans une Maison de Sûreté ;

Attendu que le Gouvernement Britannique reproche aux autorités Belges d'avoir extrait Ben Tillett du bureau de police pour le conduire dans une prison où il s'est trouvé confondu avec des hommes condamnés pour délits de droit commun ou prévenus de délits de droit commun ;

Attendu, en fait, que Ben Tillett a été écroué le 21 Août 1896, à 8 heures du soir, dans la Maison de Sûreté d'Anvers pour être, aux termes du réquisitoire du 21 Août, 1896, « tenu à la disposition de la gendarmerie » et de là « reconduit hors du royaume » ;

Que les autorités Belges se sont assurément conformées au règlement de cet établissement pénitentiaire, selon lequel la maison de dépôt est affectée non seulement aux prévenus, mais encore aux « étrangers à la disposition de l'Administration de la Sûreté Publique et à ceux dont l'extradition est demandée par les Gouvernements étrangers », qu'il s'agit uniquement de savoir si le Gouvernement Royal, en internant Ben Tillett dans un quartier simultanément affecté à ces diverses classes de prisonniers n'a pas enfreint une obligation de l'ordre international ;

Mais attendu, d'une part, en fait, que Ben Tillett a été successivement enfermé dans deux cellules de ce quartier ;

Attendu, d'autre part, en droit, qu'il est impossible d'astreindre un Etat souverain soit à construire des établissements particuliers exclusivement affectés à la détention provisoire des étrangers depuis leur arrestation jusqu'au moment où la mesure d'expulsion peut être exécutée, soit même à leur réserver dans les maisons déjà construites un quartier spécial, que le Gouvernement Belge en isolant Ben Tillett, par suite en l'empêchant de subir le contact des prévenus, a satisfait aux exigences de la courtoisie internationale ;

D. Sur la durée de la détention totale :

Attendu, en fait, que Ben Tillett, écroué à la prison d'Anvers le 21 Août, à 8 heures du soir, n'en a été extrait que le lendemain, 22 Août, à 6 heures du soir, pour être conduit au bateau « Harwich » partant pour l'Angleterre à 7 heures ; qu'il s'est donc écoulé vingt-six [sic] heures depuis le moment où ce sujet Anglais a été consigné au bureau de police jusqu'au moment où il a été mis à même de regagner son pays ;

Mais attendu qu'on ne pouvait astreindre le Gouvernement Belge à faire repartir Ben Tillett par le bateau « Harwich » dès le 21 Août, à 7 heures du soir ; que la police Anversoise devait se concerter avec le Gouvernement, par suite communiquer avec Bruxelles, que les instructions attendues par le témoin Winne, adjoint au Commissaire de Police d'Anvers, par nous entendu sous la foi du serment, ne lui étaient pas encore parvenues à 7 heures ;

Qu'on ne peut, sans mesurer avec un excès de rigueur aux Représentants du Gouvernement Belge l'emploi de leur temps, soutenir que ces instructions devaient nécessairement parvenir avant 7 heures aux agents de la police Anversoise ;

Que d'autres bateaux partaient, il est vrai, pour l'Angleterre, soit dans la nuit du 21 au 22 Août, soit dans la matinée du 22 Août, et que le Gouvernement Britannique demande, dans son dernier Mémoire, pourquoi l'on n'a pas utilisé un de ces divers moyens de transport ;

Mais attendu qu'il résulte des documents produits et des dépositions par nous recueillies dans la prison d'Anvers le 15 Août, 1898 :

1. Que Ben Tillett en s'embarquant pour Anvers sur le bateau « Harwich », avait pris un coupon d'aller et retour valable pour trente jours ;

2. Qu'il comptait, pour utiliser ce billet, employer la même ligne dans le trajet de retour ;

3. Qu'il avait exprimé formellement au témoin Winne son intention de revenir par le bateau « Harwich » :

Que dans ces circonstances de fait, en embarquant Ben Tillett le 22 Août à 7 heures, c'est-à-dire par le plus prochain départ de ce bateau, le Gouvernement Belge n'a commis aucune faute ;

E. Sur le traitement subi dans la maison de sûreté :

Attendu que j'ai requis, à Anvers même, le 15 Août 1898, M. van Calster, Directeur de la

— 585 —

Maison de Sûreté, de me faire ouvrir les cellules 6 et 29 successivement occupées les 21 et 22 Août par Ben Tillett ;

Que je les ai trouvées non humides, suffisamment aérées, propres, sans odeur ; que les lits étaient d'une dimension suffisante ; que leur couverture unique, en laine, m'a paru suffire aux habitants des cellules, eu égard à la température du mois d'Août ; qu'un séjour de vingt-deux heures dans l'une ou dans l'autre pièce, à cette époque de l'année, ne m'a pas semblé pouvoir compromettre la santé d'un détenu :

Que, les cellules 6 et 29 pouvant avoir été aménagées en prévision de mon transport, je me suis fait ouvrir les cellules 8, 12 et 21 ; que ces trois autres pièces étaient installées dans les mêmes conditions ;

Que, d'après un extrait officiel des registres de la prison d'Anvers placé sous mes yeux, il a été payé par l'Administration, pendant les sept premiers mois de l'année 1896, 801 journées de badigeonnage, 259 journées de maçon, 334 journées de peintre, 117 journées de matelassier; que cette maison était évidemment entretenue en 1896 comme elle l'est en 1898 ;

Que Ben Tillett avait, d'ailleurs, toutes les facilités pour se procurer un supplément de nourriture si l'ordinaire de la prison lui paraissait insuffisant ;

Que d'après l'affirmation très énergique du Directeur de la prison, entendu par moi sous la foi du serment, les prévenus et les étrangers à la disposition de l'administration de la Sûreté Publique ne sont jamais contraints de porter le costume de la prison, si ce n'est dans le cas de malpropreté manifeste, et par mesure d'hygiène; que l'Article 81 du Réglement de la Maison de Sûreté se borne à dire « le prisonnier est revêtu du costume de la prison, s'il est malpropre », que l'usage même du capuchon d'après la Circulaire Ministérielle du 24 Août 1891, n'est imposé ni aux prévenus, ni aux accusés, ni aux détenus pour dettes ; enfin que d'après la déposition du témoin Gillade, Ben Tillett n'a pas été revêtu du costume de la prison par application de l'Article 81 du Règlement ; qu'il n'est pas établi en fait que cette humiliation lui a été infligée ;

F. Sur la relation entre le séjour de Ben Tillett dans la prison d'Anvers et l'état de sa santé ;

Attendu qu'il n'est pas établi qu'il existe un lien de cause à effet entre cette détention de vingt-deux heures, et l'état morbide signalé par deux certificats de médecins ;

Qu'un de ces certificats rattache d'ailleurs les troubles nerveux dont se plaint Ben Tillett à un

« surmenage mental prolongé » ; que cet orateur a poursuivi, en effet, dès le 29 Août et pendant tout le mois de Septembre une campagne de meetings avec la plus grande ardeur et la plus grande activité ;

Par ces motifs :

Je décide que le Gouvernement de Sa Majesté Britannique est mal fondé dans sa demande et je l'en déboute.

Je le condamne aux frais par application de l'Article V de la Convention du 19 Mars 1898, en supposant qu'il y ait des frais à payer ; mais je déclare n'avoir, en ce qui me concerne, ni honoraires ni déboursés à réclamer.

Fait à Paris en double original, le 26 Décembre, 1898 [1].

CXXXVI. Argentine, Chili.

2 novembre 1898.

Ainsi qu'il fut spécifié dans l'arbitrage convenu le 17 avril 1896, le Gouvernement Britannique n'avait à se prononcer que sur la partie de la frontière située au sud du 26° 52′ 45″. Toute la partie située au nord de ce point jusqu'au 23°, et connue sous le nom de Puna d'Atacama, fut déterminée par un tribunal arbitral dont le surarbitre fut M. Buchanan, Ministre des Etats-Unis de l'Amérique du Nord à Buenos Aires.

Actas firmadas en Santiago, a los 2 de Noviembre 1898, conviniendo en celebrar una conferencia y una comision en Buenos Aires con el objeto de trazar la linea divisoria en la Puna d'Atacama.

En la ciudad de Santiago de Chile, á los dos dias del mes de noviembre de mil ochocientos noventa y ocho, reunidos en la sala de despacho del ministerio de relaciones exteriores el señor don Alberto Blancas, encargado de negocios y plenipotenciario ad hoc de la República Argentina, según credencial telegráfico que será ratificada posteriormente en la forma de estilo, y el señor ministro del ramo don Juan José Latorre, expusieron que deseando los gobiernos de la República Argentina y de la República de Chile llegar á un acuerdo sobre todos los asuntos que afectan ó puedan afectar, directa ó indirectamente, á los dos países, estableciendo así de una manera completa, franca y amistosa las relaciones que glorias comunes impusieron desde los momentos mismos de su emancipación política, convinieron:

[1] *Parliamentary Paper*, C. 9235.

74

Primero. — Celebrar en la ciudad de Buenos Aires una conferencia con los objetos siguientes:

A. Trazar la línea divisoria entre los paralelos veintitres grados y veintiseis grados, cincuenta y dos minutos y cuarenta y cinco segundos de latitud austral, en cumplimiento de lo establecido en la base primera del acuerdo de diez y siete de abril de mil ochocientos noventa y seis, teniendo en consideración todos los documentos y antecedentes de su referencia.

B. Estudiar y proyectar las soluciones que correspondan en los asuntos que puedan interesar directa ó indirectamente á los dos países y que sean sometidos expresamente á su deliberación.

Segundo. — La conferencia se compondrá de diez delegados, siendo cinco designados por la República Argentina y cinco por la República de Chile. La designación que cada gobierno hará de sus delegados y la fijación de la fecha inicial de la conferencia serán materia de un acta posterior.

Tercero. — La conferencia empezará por ocuparse del primer punto á que se refiere la base primera. Si los delegados llegaren á un acuerdo sobre dicho punto, ya sea por unanimidad ó por mayoría, quedará trazada definitivamente la línea divisoria así acordada y se comunicará inmediatamente á los gobiernos para que, poniéndolo en conocimiento del gobierno de Bolivia, se proceda á establecer en el terreno los hitos divisorios en los puntos de aquella línea que se consideren necesarios. Si los delegados no llegaren á un acuerdo, lo avisarán á sus gobiernos respectivos á fin de que se lleve á efecto el procedimiento establecido en otra acta de esta misma fecha.

Cuarto. — Cumplido lo determinado en la base anterior, la conferencia procederá á ocuparse de los demás puntos á que se refiere la base primera. Las resoluciones que adoptaren los delegados no tendrán cáracter obligatorio para los gobiernos respectivos ; pero una vez que les fueren comunicadas deberán dichos gobiernos pronunciarse sobre ellas de una manera definitiva.

Quinto. — La conferencia deberá terminar su cometido diez dias después de su primera sesión, á no ser que los gobiernos de comun acuerdo resolvieran prorrogar dicho término.

Sexto. — Si después de tres sesiones no hubiera hecho la conferencia el trazado de la línea entre los paralelos veintitres grados y veintiseis grados, cincuenta y dos minutos y cuarenta y cinco segundos de latitud austral, la comisión demarcadora á que se refiere el acta de esta misma fecha comenzará á desempeñar su cometido.

Para constancia los infrascriptos, en nombre de sus respectivos gobiernos, firman el presente acuerdo en dos ejemplares, uno por cada parte, y le ponen sus ellos.

En la ciudad de Santiago de Chile, á los dos días del mes de noviembre de mil ochocientos noventa y ocho, reunidos en la sala de despacho del ministerio de relaciones exteriores el señor don Alberto Blancas, encargado de negocios y plenipotenciario ad hoc que será ratificada posteriormente en la forma de estilo, y el señor ministro del ramo don Juan José Latorre, con el objeto de continuar la conferencia á que se refiere el acta de 17 de septiembre último, después de un cambio de ideas convinieron :

Primero. — Designar á un delegado argentino y á otro chileno y al ministro actual de los Estados Unidos de Norte América acreditado en República Argentina para que, en calidad de demarcadores y en vista de los documentos y antecedentes de la cuestión, procedan par mayoría á trazar de una manera definitiva la línea divisoria á que se refiere la base primera del acuerdo de diez y siete de abril de mil ochocientos noventa y seis.

Segundo. — Trazada la línea divisoria, la comisión demarcadora lo pondrá en conocimiento de los gobiernos respectivos á fin de que se comunique al de Bolivia y se proceda á establecer en el terreno los hitos divisorios en los puntos de aquella línea que se consideren necesarios.

Tercero. — La comisión demarcadora se reunirá en la ciudad de Buenos Aires y empezará á llenar su cometido cuarenta y ocho horas después que los gobiernos respectivos comuniquen á sus miembros que ha llegado el caso previsto en el acuerdo de esta misma fecha. Tres dias después de la primera sesión, deberá quedar terminada la demarcación de la línea divisoria.

Cuarto. — Si hubiere disidencia en cuanto á la solución adoptada, el miembro disidente podrá hacerla constar firmando como tal, pero no podrá determinar los fundamentos que le motivan.

Para constancia los infrascriptos, en nombre de sus respectivos gobiernos, firman el presente acuerdo en dos ejemplares, uno por cada parte, y le ponen sus ellos [1].

Comme la teneur des actes reproduits l'établit, une conférence internationale devait se réunir avant qu'un recours au tribunal

[1] *Memoria de Relaciones Exteriores*, Argentina, 1899, p. 94-97, 118-127.

arbitral puisse avoir lieu. Cette conférence siégea en effet les 1er et 9 mars 1899 sans parvenir à s'entendre sur la démarcation contestée. Le tribunal arbitral fut dès lors appelé à départager les deux gouvernements : il consacra quatre séances, du 21 au 24 mars 1899, à l'examen du litige. Aucune sentence ne fut, à proprement parler, rendue par lui : il se contenta de déposer dans des actes succincts le résultat de ses délibérations et formula les conséquences à en tirer, dans le procès-verbal du 24 mars 1899. Le texte consiste uniquement dans la description de la frontière définitivement adoptée [1].

CXXXVII. Argentine, France,

29 octobre 1840.

Arbitrage convenu pour évaluer les indemnités dues à des citoyens français. Le total des indemnités allouées a été fixé à 173,725 piastres fortes.

Convention conclue à Buenos Ayres, le 29 octobre 1840, pour régler les différends survenus entre la France et le Gouvernement de la Confédération Argentine.

Sa Majesté le Roi des Français et Son Excellence le Gouverneur et Capitaine Général de la Province de Buenos Ayres, Chargé des Relations Extérieures de la Confédération Argentine, dans la vue de régler et terminer les différends malheureusement survenus entre la France et le dit Gouvernement, ont nommé, à cet effet pour leurs Plénipotentiaires, savoir :

Sa Majesté le Roi des Français, M. Ange-René-Armand de Mackau, Baron de Mackau, Grand Officier de l'Ordre Royal de la Légion d'Honneur, Vice-Amiral, Commandant en chef des forces navales françaises employées dans les mers de l'Amérique du Sud.

Et son Excellence le Gouverneur et Capitaine Général, son Excellence le Ministre des Relations Extérieures du dit Gouvernement, Caménisté Docteur Don Philippe Arana.

Lesquels après s'être communiqué leurs pleins pouvoirs respectifs qu'ils ont trouvés en bonne et due forme, sont convenus de ce qui suit :

ARTICLE I. — Sont reconnues par le Gouvernement de Buenos Ayres les indemnités dues aux Français qui ont éprouvé des pertes ou souffert des dommages dans la République Argentine, et le chiffre de ces indemnités, qui

reste seul à déterminer, sera réglé dans le délai de six mois, par la voie de six arbitres nommés d'un commun accord, et trois pour chaque partie, outre les deux Plénipotentiaires.

En cas de dissentiment, le règlement des dites indemnités sera déféré à l'arbitrage d'une Tierce Puissance, qui sera désignée par le Gouvernement Français.

. . . .

ARTICLE VII. — La présente Convention sera ratifiée, et les ratifications en seront échangées à Paris, dans le délai de huit mois ou plus tôt si faire se peut, par l'intermédiaire d'un Ministre Plénipotentiaire du Gouvernement de la République, qui sera accrédité, à cet effet, près du Gouvernement de Sa Majesté le Roi de France.

En témoignage de quoi, les Plénipotentiaires respectifs l'ont signée et scellée de leurs sceaux.

Fait à bord du brick parlementaire français *La Boulonnaise*, le vingt-neuf Octobre mil huit cent quarante [1].

Accord conclu à Buenos Ayres, le 26 avril 1841, entre les commissaires français et argentins, pour régler l'exécution de l'article I de la Convention du 29 octobre 1840 en ce qui concerne le payement des indemnités.

Les soussignés, membres de la commission d'arbitrage créée en exécution de la convention du 29 octobre 1840 entre la France et la Confédération Argentine, dont la teneur suit :

. . . .

Sont convenus de ce qui suit :

ART. I. — Le Gouvernement de la Confédération Argentine mettra à la disposition du Chargé d'Affaires de France à Buenos-Ayres la somme de 173,725 piastres fortes, moyennant quoi l'article premier de la convention du 29 octobre 1840 aura reçu son exécution.

ART. II. — Le payement de la somme ci-dessus mentionnée aura lieu comme suit, savoir :

25,000 piastres fortes le 1er juin 1841 avec les intérêts d'un mois, calculés à raison de 12 pour cent par an ;

Les 148,725 piastres fortes restant à payer, par termes mensuels de 4000 piastres fortes à partir du 1er juin 1841, époque à laquelle aura lieu le versement du premier terme.

Au montant de chacun des termes mensuels de 4000 piastres fortes seront ajoutés les intérêts

---

[1] DE CLERCQ, *Recueil des Traités de France*, t. IV, p. 591.

à 12 pour cent par an tant du terme échu que des termes à échoir. Ces intérêts seront calculés à partir du 1ᵉʳ mai 1841.

Art. III. — Le Gouvernement Argentin conservera la faculté d'anticiper sur les termes de payement fixés par la présente convention, avec déduction des intérêts correspondants des sommes ainsi payées par avance, mais sans rien changer aux échéances mensuelles qui devront suivre sans aucune interruption, et de manière à rapprocher seulement l'époque de parfait acquittement de la somme totale.

Buenos-Ayres, le 26 avril 1841 [1].

CXXXVIII. Equateur, Pérou.

16 mars 1853.

L'ancien président de l'Equateur, Don Juan José Flores, avait dirigé contre son pays une expédition armée. Les navires qui constituèrent cette expédition se réfugièrent dans le port de Paita, situé sur le territoire du Pérou. La question de savoir si ces navires, avec leurs armes et munitions, appartenaient au Pérou ou à l'Equateur, fut soumise au jugement arbitral du Chili.

Tratado de paz, amistad i arbitraje, entre Peru i Ecuador, celebrado Marzo 16, 1853.

. . . .

Art. 5. — La adjudicacion i pertenencia de los buques, armas, municiones i pertrechos que, habiendo pertenecido al armamento de D. Juan José Flores, se refujiaron al puerto de Paita, se someteran a la decision arbitral del Gobierno de Chile, quedando ambas Partes Contratantes sujetas a lo que este decidiere como arbitro [2].

Nous ignorons la suite qui a été donnée à cet arbitrage.

CXXXIX. Grande-Bretagne, Guatemala.

30 avril 1859.

Question de limites confiée à deux commissaires avec un surarbitre. Il ne nous a pas été donné de constater si la convention a été exécutée, ni de relever le résultat auquel elle a abouti.

[1] De Clercq, *Ibid.*, t. IV, p. 594.
[2] Perú. *Coleccion de los Tratados,* vol. V, p. 132.

Convention between Great Britain and Guatemala relative to the Boundary of British Honduras, signed at Guatemala, April 30, 1859.

Whereas the boundary between Her Britannic Majesty's settlement and possessions in the Bay of Honduras, and the territories of the Republic of Guatemala, has not yet been ascertained and marked out; Her Majesty the Queen of the United Kingdom of Great Britain and Ireland, and the Republic of Guatemala, being desirous, with a view to improve and perpetuate the friendly relations which happily subsist between the two countries, to define the boundary aforesaid, have resolved to conclude a Convention for that purpose, and have named as their Plenipotentiaries, that is to say:

Her Majesty the Queen of the United Kingdom of Great Britain and Ireland, Charles Lennox Wyke, Esquire, Her Britannic Majesty's Chargé d'Affaires to the Republic of Guatemala;

And His Excellency the President of the Republic of Guatemala, Don Pedro de Aycinena, Councillor of State, and Minister for Foreign Affairs;

Who, after having communicated to each other their respective full powers, found in good and due form, have agreed upon and concluded the following articles:

Art. I. — It is agreed between Her Britannic Majesty and the Republic of Guatemala that the boundary between the Republic and the British settlement and possessions in the Bay of Honduras, as they existed previous to and on the 1st day of January, 1850, and have continued to exist up to the present time, was and is as follows:

Beginning at the mouth of the River Sarstoon in the Bay of Honduras and proceeding up the mid-channel thereof to Gracias a Dios Falls; then turning to the right and continuing by a line drawn direct from Gracias a Dios Falls to Garbutt's Falls on the River Belize, and from Garbutt's Falls to north until it strikes the Mexican frontier.

It is agreed and declared between the High Contracting Parties that all the territory to the north and east of the line of boundary above described, belongs to Her Britannic Majesty, and that all the territory to the south and west of the same belongs to the Republic of Guatemala.

Art. II. — Her Britannic Majesty and the Republic of Guatemala shall within 12 months after the exchange of the ratifications of the present Convention, appoint each a Commissioner for the purpose of designating and marking out the boundary described in the preceding article.

Such Commissioners shall ascertain the latitude and longitude of Gracias a Dios and of Garbutt's Falls, and shall cause the line of boundary between Garbutt's Falls and the Mexican territory to be opened and marked where necessary, as a protection against future trespass.

ART. III. — The Commissioners mentioned in the preceding article shall meet at such place or places as shall be hereafter fixed, at the earliest convenient period after they shall have been respectively named, and shall, before proceeding to any business, make and subscribe a solemn declaration that they will impartially and carefully examine and decide, to the best of their judgment, and according to justice and equity, without fear, favour or affection to their own country, upon all matters referred to them for their decision; and such declaration shall be entered on the record of their proceedings.

The Commissioners shall then, and before proceeding to any other business, name some third person to act as arbitrator or umpire in any case or cases in which they may themselves differ in opinion. If they should not be able to agree upon the choice of such third person, they shall each name a person; and in each and every case in which the Commissioners may differ in opinion as to the decision which they ought to give, it shall be determined by lot which of the two persons so named shall be the arbitrator or umpire in that particular case. The person or persons so to be chosen shall, before proceeding to act, make and subscribe a solemn declaration, in a form similar to that which shall already have been made and subscribed by the Commissioners, which declaration shall be entered on the record of the proceedings. In the event of the death, absence or incapacity of either of such Commissioners, or of either of such arbitrators or umpires, or of his omitting, or declining, or ceasing to act, another person shall be named, in the same manner, to act in his place or stead, and shall make and subscribe such declaration as aforesaid.

Her Britannic Majesty and the Republic of Guatemala shall engage to consider the decision of the two Commissioners conjointly, or of the arbitrator or umpire, as the case may be, as final and conclusive on the matters to be respectively referred to their decision, and forthwith to give full effect to the same.

ART. IV. — The Commissioners hereinbefore mentioned shall make to each of the respective Governments a joint report or declaration, under their hands and seals, accompanied with a map or maps in quadriplicate (two for each Government), certified by them to be true maps of the boundary defined in the present treaty, and traversed and examined by them.

ART. V. — The Commissioners and the arbitrator or umpire shall keep accurate records and correct minutes or notes of all their proceedings, with the dates thereof, and shall appoint and employ such surveyors, clerk or clerks, or other persons, as they shall find necessary to assist them in the transaction of the business which may come before them.

The salaries of the Commissioners shall be paid by their respective Governments. The contingent expenses of the Commission, including the salary of the arbitrator or umpire, and of such surveyors and clerks, shall be defrayed in equal moieties by the two Governments.

. . . .

ART. VIII. — The present Convention shall be ratified, and the ratifications shall be exchanged at London or Guatemala as soon as possible within the space of six months.

In witness whereof, the respective Plenipotentiaries have signed the same, and have affixed thereto the seals of their arms.

Done at Guatemala, the 30th day of April, in the year 1859[1].

CXL. Orange, Transvaal.

30 octobre 1869.

Cette contestation peu connue a eu pour objet la fixation de la frontière entre les deux républiques. Il nous a été impossible de reproduire le texte du compromis, mais les termes en semblent introduits dans le préambule de la sentence.

Uitspraak gedaan door R. W. Keate in zake der grensscheiding tusschen de Zuid Afrikaansche Republiek en de Oranje Vrijstaat, te Pietermaritzburg, 19 February 1870.

Aan allen die deze acte zal toekomen, Ik, Robert William Keate, Schildknaap, Luitenant-Gouverneur van Natal, Salut.

Nademaal eene overeenkomst gemaakt is op den dertigsten dag van October 1869, tusschen Zijn H. Edelen Marthinus Wessel Pretorius in zijne hoedanigheid als President van de Zuid-Afrikaansche Republiek en Zijn Hoog Edelen Johannes Hendrikus Brand in zijne Capaciteit als President van den Oranje Vrijstaat, te kennen

---

[1] HERTSLET, *A complete collection...*, vol. XI, p. 345.

gevende dat eertyds te weten : den 16den dag van Januari, in het jaar onzes Heeren Een Duizend Acht Honderd en Twee en Vijftig eene Conventie gesloten was te Zandrivier tusschen Harer Britsche Majesteits Assistent Commissarissen Hogge en Owen en eene Deputatie van Emigratie Boeren, wonende ten Noorden van de Vaalrivier, bestaande uit Commandant Generaal Pretorius en anderen, welke gezedge Conventie later, te weten op den 15den dag van April 1852 bekrachtigd en goedgeheurd was te King Williamstad door Zijn Excellentie Sir George Cathcart, Luitenant Generaal en Harer Britsche Majesteits Hooge Commissaris, en dat door de gezedge Conventie het regt was gewaarborgd van de zijde van het Britsch Gouvernement aan de Emigranten Boeren over de Vaalrivier, bewonende het gebied, nu bekend onder den naam van de Zuid-Afrikaansche Republiek, om hunne eigene zaken te bestieren en zichzelven te regeren, en verder te kennen gevende, dat door eene Conventie, ingegaan te Bloemfontein op den 23sten dag van Februarij 1854, tusschen Sir George Russel Clerk, Harer Majesteits Speciale Commissaris ter regeling en in orde brenging per zaken van het Oranje Rivier Grondgebied en de Vertegenwoordigers daarvan, het Gouvernement van het Oranje Rivier Grondgebied was overgemaakt aan de Vertegenwoordigers, afgevaardigd door de Inwoners daarvan om het te ontvangen en de aanstaande onafhankelijkheid van dat land te waarborgen van de zijde van Haar Majesteits Gouvernement, en welke gezegd grondgebied nu bekend staat onder den naam van den Oranje Vrijstaat en verder te kennen gevende, dat het overeengekomen en bedongen was, dat, indien er eenig misverstand later mogt ontstaan met betrekking tot de ware meening van de woorden de Vaalrivier, dit verschil, voor zooverre zij betrof de lijn van den oorsprong van de rivier over den Drakenberg, vereffend en geregeld zoude worden door Commissarissen te worden gekozen door beide partijen, en verder te kennen gevende, dat geschillen ontstaan zijn tusschen het Gouvernement van de gezegde Zuid-Afrikaansche Republiek en van den gezegden Oranje Vrijstaat met betrekking tot de ware meening van den oorsprong van Vaalrivier, de grensscheiding tusschen de gezegde Zuid-Afrikaansche Republiek en den Oranje Vrijstaat en dat de genoemde Gouvernementen verschillende vruchtelooze pogingen aangewend hebben voornoemd geschil tusschen zichzelven te vereffenen, en verder te kennen gevende, dat de partijen, in deze overeenkomst, beide verlangend zijn het verschil tusschen hen, betreffende de gezegde betwiste grensscheiding, naauwkeurig, vriendschappelijk en spoedig te vereffenen, hebben Zijn Excellentie

Robert William Keate, Schildknaap, Luitenant Gouverneur van de Colonie Natal verzocht als Scheidsregter het gezegd verschil te onderwerpen aan de uitspraak, order en finaal besluit van den gezegden Robert William Keate, Schildknaap, en dat de gezegde Robert William Keate, Schildknaap, ingewilligd heeft de taak van de gezegde arbitratie op zich te nemen, met dien verstande dat de gezegde partyen respectievelijk zoodanig zullen handelen als noodig mogt zijn om den gezegden Robert William Keate, Schildknaap, in staat te stellen eene juiste uitspraak te doen, en dat geen van beiden door woord of daad iets doen zal om de uitspraak van den gezegden Robert William Keate, Schildknaap, te vertragen of te verhinderen, de gemelde partyen overeengekomen zijnde respectievelijk voor en ten behoeve hunner respective Gouvernementen en Volk, de uitspraak welke gemaakt zoude worden in de voornoemde zaak door den gezegden Robert William Keate, Schildknaap, te ondersteunen, daarin te berusten en te houden.

Zij het dus kennelijk, dat ik alle zoodanige Documenten en bewijzen, die voor mij gebracht werden door de respectieve gezegde partyen, ten volle onderzocht, overdacht en overwogen, de partyen voornoemd gehoord, met betrekking tot deze zaak, overwogen zoodanige Correspondentien en andere Documenten, mij ten dienste staande, betreffende dat onderwerp, en de plaats in kwestie onderzocht en naauwkeurig bezien te hebben laten onderzoeken en bezien; het mij gebleken is, dat de ware bedoeling en beteekenis van de bepaling, vervat in de Conventie van den 16den dag van Januarij 1852, met betrekking tot de lijn van den oorsprong van de Vaalrivier over de Drakenberg als uitgelegd wordt door eene Correspondentie, die plaats vond over dit onderwerp tusschen Luitenant Gouverneur Pine en Sir George Cathcart en Hare Majesteits Assistent Commissarissen in 1852 en door de Proclamatie te kennen gevende de afstand van de Souvereiniteit van het Oranje Rivier Grondgebied aan de inwoners daarvan in 1854, was dat de Vaalrivier, welke volgens de Conventie, de Noordelijke Grenslijn maakt van het Oranje Rivier Grondgebied, nu de Oranje Vrijstaat, ook, voor zooverre zulks mogelijk is, de verbindende schakel zou moeten formeeren tusschen hetzelve en de Drakenbergsketen, welke laatste, volgens Conventie, de Oostelijke Grenslijn van dat Gebied of Staat vormt, en, dat het kleine overblijvende gedeelte, gelaten ter latere arbitratie in de rigting van het punt waar zoodanige Grenslijnen elkander natuurlijk zouden snijden, te worden bepaald door Commissarissen te worden gekozen tot dien einde, die, voor zooverre mogelijk, zouden nemen, den oorsprong van Vaalrivier, loopende over den

Drakensberg, als zoodanig verbindende schakel tusschen, of vereeiniging van zoodanige scheidingslijn, en dat het mij verder gebleken is, dat de Vaalrivier, geen rivier is die zijn ontstaan heeft uit eenige enkelen oorsprong over de Drakensberg, doch zou, als aangewezen door Luitenant Gouverneur Pine in de Correspondentie, reeds aangehaald, verscheidene oorsprongen of zamenvloeijing heeft, van welke de Wilgerivier, als zijnde de meest Westlijke en als komende over den Drakensberg geeigend wordt door het Gouvernement der Zuid-Afrikaansche Republiek als de ware oorsprong van de Vaal, beschouwd in de Conventie, en verder, dat dat gedeelte van de Vaal, welke volgens de Conventie, de Noordelijke Grenslijn van de Souvereiniteit, nu de Oranje Vrijstaat, formeert, eene rivier is, het gevolg van de zamenvloeijing van twee hoofdtakken gelegen ten Oosten van de Wilgerivier eene waarvan haar ontstaan heeft in het effen veld hoog op in den rand, die de waters scheid, welke Oost en Westwaarts vloeyen, en in haar loop door de Inboorlingen de Likwa en door de Hollanders de Kapok genoemd worden, tot op een zeker punt en van daar de Vaal en wordt gevoed door stroomen van zoodanig verdeelenden rand, van welke de meest voornaamste inloopt op dat punt waar haar Hollandsche naam van de Kapok veranderd in de Vaal en door de inboorlingen de kleine Likwa en de Hollanders de Bokspruit genoemd wordt, en in haar loop Wakkerstroom distrikt van de Zuid-Afrikaansche Republiek snijdende, welke, als zijnde de meest Oostelijke zamenvloeijing van de Vaal, geeigend wordt door het Gouvernement van den Oranje Vrijstaat als de ware oorsprong van de Vaalrivier, als beschouwd door de Conventie, terwijl de andere voorname tak haar ontstaan heeft uit verscheidene kleine stroomen vlietende uit de Drakensbergketen, ter zuiden van of nabij de noordelijke grensscheiding van Natal in dat gedeelte van de keten, welke, volgens de Conventie de Oostelijke Grensscheiding van het Oranje Gebied of Vrijstaat maakt en door de Hollanders de Kliprivier genoemd wordt en daar het mij verder gebleken is, bij verwijzing naar wat gehouden werd, de Drakensbergketen te vormen, bij gelegenheid van de Grenslijnen van de Kolonie van Natal bepaald door Harer Majesteit's Order in Rade gedateerd den 3den Februarij 1858, waarin de eerste toevloed, ontvangen door de Buffelrivier van die reeks, bepaald was als de noordelijke Grenslijn daarvan, dat eene verlenging van afgezonderde Bergen in eene Noord-Oostelijke rigting van die reeks van waar het ophoudt eene aaneengeschakelde keten te zijn, in welke verlenging andere oorsprongen van de Buffelrivier, zoowel als van andere rivieren, inloopende in de Vaalrivier, gevonden worden, niet gehouden kunnen worden als zoodanig te zijn, maar, dat, met het doel van eene Scheidingslijn tusschen den Oranje Vrijstaat en de Zuid-Afrikaansche Republiek, het woord Drakensberg moet genomen worden in dezelfde zin, als die waarin het genomen was met het doel voor eene grenslijn tusschen de laatstgenoemde en de Kolonie van Natal, en dat het mij verder gebleken is dat het Britsche Gouvernement voor de overgave van den Oranje Rivier Souvereiniteit, beschouwende de Drakensberg als de Oostelijke Grenslijn daarvan, voortging plaatsen uittegeven tot aan die reeks, en dat eenige dier plaatsen aldus uitgegeven, dwars over eenige dier stroomen, die de bovenste · waters van de klip of zuidelijken tak van de Vaalrivier formeeren of in de tusschenruimte van zoodanige stroomen in de bergketen, uit welke zij ontstaan, liggen, en dat het mij verder gebleken is, dat, sedert den afstand van de Souvereiniteit het Gouvernement van den Oranje Vrijstaat van tijd tot tijd andere plaatsen toegekend hebben in en omtrent dezelfde localiteit, en dat het mij daarenboven gebleken is, dat aan de andere zijde, nadat de toevlugt tot vijandelijkheden zijn genomen door de twee Gouvernementen, belanghebbenden in de betwiste scheidings-lijn, welke vijandelijkheden opgevolgd werden door een verdrag, gedateerd den 1sten Junij 1867, waarbij iedere partij zich verbonden heeft onder anderen, zich te houden in deze zaak van de grensscheiding aan de Conventie van den 16den dag van Januari 1852.

Het Gouvernement der Zuid-Afrikaansche Republiek onmiddelijk daarna, en van tijd tot tijd plaatsen uitgaf langs de oostelijke oevers zoowel van de Noordelijke als Zuidelijke takken van de Vaalrivier en verscheidene jaren de zaken van het land, waarin zoodanige plaatsen gelegen waaren, algemeen administreerde zonder verzet of verhindering van, of eenige protest aangeteekend is door het Gouvernement van de Oranje Vrijstaat,

Zoo is mijne uitspraak, order en uitwijzing, dat, nu voortaan en voor het vervolg, de grenslijn tusschen de Zuid-Afrikaansche Republiek en den Oranje Vrijstaat, op het punt, alwaar het ter arbitratie gelaten was, door de Conventie van den 18den en Januari 1852, zal beginnen : op een punt in de grenslijn van de Kolonie Natal onmiddelijk over en naast bij die oorsprong van den stroom genoemd Gansvallei, welke haar oorsprong neemt op de kortste afstand van de Noordelijke baken van de gezegde Kolonie, van daar langs den gezegden stroom tot aan deszelfs zamenvloeijing met de Kliprivier en van daar langs den loop van de Kliprivier tot waar zij zich met de Vaalrivier vereenigt.

Aldus gedaan en gegeven onder mijn zegel te Pietermaritzburg dezen negentienden dag van Februarij, 1870, en deze uitspraak op denzelfden dag in duplo bekend gemaakt, door eene te zenden aan zijn Hoog Edelen den President van den Oranje Vrijstaat en de andere aan Zijn Hoog Edelen den President van de Transvaal Republiek [1].

CXLI. Chili, Pérou.

20 octobre 1883.

Lors du traité qui termine la guerre entre le Chili et le Pérou, il fut stipulé que les indemnités dues à des citoyens chiliens du chef de cette guerre seraient réglées par la voie de l'arbitrage. C'est en 1897 seulement que cet arbitrage fut organisé: les résultats en sont encore inconnus à l'heure actuelle.

Tratado de paz y amistad entre las Republicas del Peru y Chile, firmado en Lima, Octubre 20, 1883.

. . . .

ARTICLE XII. — Las indemnizaciones que se deban al Perú á los Chilenos que hayan sufrido perjuicios con motivo de la guerra, se juzgarán por un Tribunal arbitral ó Commission mixta internacional nombrada inmediatamente despues de ratificado el presente tratado, en la forma establecida por Convenciones recientes, ajustadas entre Chile y los Gobiernos de Inglaterra, Francia é Italia [2].

Convención de Arbitraje para juzgar las indemnizaciones que se deban á Chilenos, firmada en Lima, Abril 5, 1897.

Su Excelencia el Presidente de la República del Perú i Su Excelencia el Presidente de la República de Chile, deseando dar cumplimiento á la estipulación contenida en el artículo 12° del Tratado de Paz y Amistad celebrado entre ambas Repúblicas el 20 de octubre de 1883, según la que, las indemnizaciones que se deban á Chilenos que hayan sufrido perjuicios con motivo de la guerra, deben juzgarse por un tribunal analogo á los mixtos internacionales establecidos en Chile, para conocer de los reclamos de subditos ingleses é italianos i de ciudadanos franceses, han acordado celebrar una Convención de Arbitraje, para lo cual han nombrado por sus Plenipotenciarios respectivos: Su Excelencia el Presidente de la República del Perú, al señor don Enrique de la Riva-Agüero, Ministro de Relaciones Exteriores de la República; i Su Excelencia el Presidente de la República de Chile, al señor don Maximo R. Lira, Enviado Extraordinario i Ministro Plenipotenciario de Chile en el Perú.

Los cuales Plenipotenciarios, despúes de haber examinado i canjeado sus poderes i de hallarlos en buena i debida forma, han convenido en los siguientes articulos:

I. Un Tribunal Arbitral ó comisión mixta internacional, que funcionará en Lima, juzgará, en la forma que se establece en la presente Convención, todas las reclamaciones de indemnización que, con el patrocinio del Gobierno de Chile, deduzcan contra el Gobierno del Perú los Chilenos que hayan sufrido perjuicios con motivo de la guerra á que puso término el tratado de 20 de octubre de 1883.

II. El Tribunal ó comisión mixta se compondrá de tres miembros, uno nombrado por S. E. el Presidente de la República del Perú, otro nombrado por S. E. el Presidente de la República de Chile i el tercero por S. M. la Reina de los Paises Bajos.

En los casos de muerte, ausencia ó inhabilitacion por cualquier motivo, de alguno ó algunos de los miembros de la comisión mixta, se procederá á su riemplazo en la forma i condiciones expresadas en este articulo.

III. Tanto el Gobierno del Perú como el Gobierno de Chile constituirán un agente que vigile el interés de su parte y atienda á su defensa, presente peticiones, documentos, interrogatorios, ponga i absuelva posiciones, apoye sus cargos ó redarguya los contrarios, rinda pruebas i exponga ante la Comisión, por si ó por el órgano de un letrado, verbalmente ó por escrito, en conformidad á las reglas del procedimiento i tramitacion que el mismo Tribunal acordase al iniciar sus funciones, las doctrinas, principios legales ó procedentes que convengan á su derecho.

Ninguna reclamación será aceptada si no la formula, declarando patrocinada por su Gobierno, el Agente del Gobierno de Chile, quien, antes de que comience el Tribunal á funcionar, pasará al Ministerio de Relaciones Exteriores una razón de las reclamaciones que apoye, con el indicación de su respectivo monto.

IV. El Agente de Chile deberá presentar las reclamaciones al Tribunal dentro de los tres meses siguientes al día en que registre El Peruano el aviso por el que se anuncie la instalación de aquél.

V. El Tribunal ó Comisión mixta aceptará los medios probatorios ó de investigación que, según el criterio ó discernimiento de sus miem-

---

[1] La copie de cette sentence nous a été communiquée par la gracieuse entremise de M. Canneel, Vice-Consul de la République Sud Africaine à La Haye.

[2] Perú. *Coleccion de los Tratados*, t. IV, p. 658.

bros, fuesen conducentes al mejor esclarecimiento de los hechos controvertidos i en especial á la calificación i carácter de chileno del reclamante.

La Comisión admitirá asimismo las alegaciones verbales ó escritas de ambos Gobiernos ó de sus respectivos agentes o defensores.

VI. La Comisión mixta decidirá las reclamaciones en mérito de la prueba rendida i con arreglo á los principios del derecho internacional i á las prácticas i jurisprudencia establecidas por los tribunales análogos modernos de mayor autoridad i prestigio, librando sus resoluciones interlocutarias ó definitivas por mayoría de votos.

La Comisión mixta expondrá brevemente en cada juzgamiento definitivo los hechos i causales de la reclamación, los motivos alegados en su apoyo ó en su contradicción i los fundamentos de derecho internacional que justifiquen sus resoluciones.

Las resoluciones y decretos de la Comisión serán firmados por todos sus miembros i autorizados por su secretario i se dejarán originales con su respectivo expediente en el Ministerio de Relaciones Exteriores del Perú, dándose à las partes las copias que solicitaren.

VII. La Comisión mixta llevará también un libro en que se anoten sus procedimientos, las peticiones que reciba i los decretos i resoluciones que pronuncie.

VIII. El Tribunal ó Comisión mixta tendrá la facultad de proveerse de secretarios, relatores i demás oficiales que estime necesarios para el buen desempeño de sus funciones.

Corresponde á la Comisión proponer á las personas que hayan de desempeñar respectivamente aquellas funciones i designar los sueldos ó remuneraciones que deban percibir.

El nombramiento de los expresados oficiales se hará por S. E. el Presidente de la República del Perú.

IX. Los decretos de la Comisión mixta que hayan de cumplirse en el Perú, tendrán el auxilio de la fuerza pública como los expedidos por los tribunales ordinarios del país. Los que hayan de ejecutarse en el extranjero se llevarán á efecto conforme á las reglas i usos del derecho internacional privado.

X. La Comisión tendrá para evacuar su encargo, en todas las reclamaciones sujetas á su conocimiento i decisión, el plazo de un año, contado desde el día de su instalación. Trascurrido este plazo, tendrá facultad de prorrogar sus funciones por un nuevo término que no podrá exceder de tres meses, en el caso de que, por enfermedad ó inhabilitación temporal de alguno de sus miembros ó por otro motivo de calificada gravedad, no hubiese alcanzado á desempeñar su cometido dentro del término de un año.

XI. Cada uno de los Gobiernos contratantes sufragará los gastos de sus propias gestiones i los honorarios de sus respectivos agentes ó defensores.

Las expensas de la organización de la Comisión mixta, los honorarios de sus miembros, los sueldos de los secretarios, relatores i demás empleados, i los gastos i costas del servicio común serán pagados entre ambos Gobiernos por mitad; pero, si hubiese cantidades juzgadas á favor de los reclamantes, se deducirán de éstas las antedichas expensas i gastos comunes, en cuanto no excedan del seis por ciento de los valores que haya de pagar el Tesoro del Perú por la totalidad de las reclamaciones aceptadas.

Las sumas que la Comisión mixta juzgue en favor de los reclamantes serán pagadas por el Gobierno del Perú en la forma, modo i tiempo que, dentro del término de tres meses á contar desde la fecha en que terminen las funciones del tribunal arbitral, acuerde con el de Chile en vista de la cantidad á que ascienda el total de ellas i sin que, entretanto, devenguen intereses.

XII. Las Altas Partes contratantes se obligan á considerar los juzgamientos de la Comisión mixta que se organiza por esta Convención, como una terminación satisfactoria, perfecta é irrevocable de las dificultades cuyo arreglo se ha tenido en mira, quedando entendido que todas las reclamaciones presentadas ó no presentadas en las condiciones señaladas en los articulos precedentes, se tendrán por decididas i definitivamente juzgadas, de manera que por ningún motivo ó pretexto puedan ser materia de nuevo examen ó discusión. En consecuencia, los que no usaren de su derecho ante el Tribunal, en los términos señalados, lo tendrán definitivamente perdido i no podrán deducirlo más tarde, en ninguna forma, contra el Gobierno del Perú.

No se tendrán por decididas ni definitivamente juzgadas, las reclamaciones respecto de las cuales el Tribunal se declare incompetente por estimarlas extrañas al objeto de esta Convención, pudiendo en tales casos los reclamantes deducir sus derechos contra el Gobierno del Perú en el tiempo i forma que estimen más conveniente.

XIII. La presente Convención será ratificada por las Altas Partes contratantes i el canje de las ratificaciones se verificará én Lima.

En fe de lo cual, los Plenipotenciarios de la República del Perú i de la República de Chile, han firmado la presente Convención en doble ejemplar i puesto en ella sus sellos respectivos.

Hecha, en Lima, á los cinco días del mes de abril año de mil ochocientos noventa y siete[1].

¹ *Memoria del Ministerio de Relaciones Exteriores* (Perú), 1897, p. 66.

CXLII. Chili, Grande-Bretagne, France, Pérou.

20 octobre 1883.

Peu d'arbitrages ont été plus pénibles à établir que celui que nous avons à examiner ici. Lorsque la guerre sévissait entre le Chili et le Pérou, le gouvernement chilien, par un décret du 9 février 1882, mit en vente un million de tonnes de guano à prendre sur le territoire des provinces péruviennes, alors occupées par les troupes ennemies. Ce décret toutefois, dans ses articles 13 à 19, reconnaissait les droits des porteurs de bons péruviens, garantis précisément par le produit de l'exploitation du guano. Ce décret prévoyait notamment la constitution d'un tribunal arbitral, chargé d'attribuer certaines sommes déposées dans la Banque d'Angleterre et provenant de la vente prémentionnée. Lors de la conclusion de la paix, le traité du 20 octobre 1883 confirma le décret unilatéral du 9 février 1882 et la clause d'arbitrage devint contractuelle.

Decreto de 9 de Febrero de 1882 para la vendida de 1,000,000 de toneladas de guano.

. . . .

ART. 13. — El precio liquido del guano, deducidos los gastos de extracción, ensaye, peso, embarque, sueldos de empleados que vigilen estas operaciones y los demás que se causen hasta dejar las especie al costado del buque cargador, se distribuirá por partes iguales entre el Gobierno de Chile y aquellos acreedores del Gobierno del Perú cuyos titulos de crédito aparecen sustentados con la garantia de esta sustancia.

ART. 14. — Para que los acreedores del Gobierno del Perú puedan ejercitar el derecho que les otorga el articulo precedente, deberán constituir, por acuerdo previo de todos los que se acogieren á los beneficios de esta concesión, un tribunal de árbitros que solucione las diversas dificultades á que pueda dar origen la liquidación, legitimidad o validez de sus títulos y la prioridad con que deban ser cubiertos de sus creditos respectivos.

ART. 15. — Se concede un plazo de 180 dias, contado desde la fecha de este decreto, para que los mencionados acreedores del Gobierno del Perú pongan en conocimiento del Ministerio de Hacienda la designación que hubiesen hecho del tribunal de árbitros á que se refiere el articulo precedente.

Si trascurrido este plazo no se hubieren puesto de acuerdo para verificar la designación de los árbitros, el Gobierno de Chile lo hará por si mismo.

ART. 16. — El Gobierno de Chile depositará en el Banco de Inglaterra el importe liquido del precio del guano que corresponda al 50 % que se destina á los acreedores del Perú.

ART. 17. — A mérito de las gestiones hechas por Mr. John Procter con el poder bastante del Comité de tenedores de bonos peruanos, reconocido en este carácter por el fallo de 7 de Junio de 1881, expedido por la alta Corte de Justicia del *Master of the Rolls* — division de Cancillería — téngase desde luego á los expresados tenedores de bonos peruanos como aceptantes de la concesión que otorga este decreto, quedando desde esta fecha sin efecto ni valor alguno, la que en favor de esos mismos acreedores se hizo en el bando de 22 de febrero de 1880, dictado por el General en jefe del Ejercito de operaciones y aprobado por decreto supremo de 2 de marzo de ese mismo año.

ART. 18. — Archívese en el Ministerio de Hacienda el poder conferido al señor John Procter como mandatario y delegado en los territorios de Chile y otros de Sud-América, del Comité de tenedores extranjeros de bonos peruanos. Dicho poder datado en Londres, está fechado en 30 de mayo de 1881, autorizado en el mismo día por el notario público de aquella ciudad señor William W. Venn, y visado en el Consulado de Chile. Del mandato expresado, consta que el total de bonos registrados que Procter representa asciende á la cantidad de 25,838,270 libras esterlinas, aun cuando en la elección del Comité solo hubieran tomado parte 21,243,040 libras esterlinas que votaron en 8008 listas diferentes.

ART. 19. — El depósito de los fondos en el Banco de Inglaterra, á que se refiere el artículo 16, se hará á la orden del tribunal de arbitros inmediatamente que éste sea designado por las partes interesadas ó por el Gobierno de Chile en subsidio, en el caso previsto en el artículo 15.

Si antes de verificarse la designación de los árbitros se acumularen fondos procedentes de la enagenación de los guanos, aquél depósito se pondrá provisoriamente á la orden conjunta del funcionario que designe el Gobierno de Chile y del Comité de tenedores extranjeros de bonos peruanos.

A medida que otras categorias de acreedores del Gobierno del Perú vayan acogiéndose á los beneficios de esta concesión, se hará extensivo también á su orden el depósito provisorio de los fondos [1].

---

[1] *Memoria del Ministerio de Relaciones Exteriores* (Perú), 1896, p. 402.

. . . .

Art. IV. — En conformidad á lo dispuesto en el supremo decreto de 9 de Febrero de 1882, por el cual el Gobierno de Chile ordenó la venta de un million de toneladas de guano, el producto líquido de esta sustencia deducidos los gastos y demas desembolsos á que se refiere el artículo 13 de dicho decreto, se distribuirá por partes iguales entre el Gobierno de Chile y los acreedores del Perú, cuyos títulos de crédito aparecieren sustentados con la garantia del guano.

Terminada la venta del million de toneladas á que se refiere el inciso anterior, el Gobierno de Chile continuará entregando á los acreedores peruanos el cincuenta por ciento del producto líquido del guano, tal como se establece en el mencionado artículo 13, hasta que se extinga la deuda ó se agoten las covaderas en actual explotacion.

Los productos de las covaderas ó yacimientos que se descubran en lo futuro en los territorios cedidos, pertenecerán exclusivamente al Gobierno de Chile.

. . . .

Art. VI. — Los acreedores peruanos á quienes se concede el beneficio á que se refiere el artículo 4°, deberán someterse para la calificacion de sus títulos y demas procedimientos, á las reglas fijadas en el supremo decreto de 9 de Febrero de 1882.

AII. VII. — La obligacion que el Gobierno de Chile acepta, segun el artículo 4°, de entregar el cincuenta por ciento del producto líquido del guano de las covaderas en actual explotacion, subsistirá, sea que esta explotacion se hiciere en conformidad al contrato existente sobre venta de un million de toneladas, sea que ella se verifique en virtud de otro contrato ó por cuenta propia del Gobierno de Chile . . . . [1].

Depuis lors un nouveau traité fut conclu entre le Chili et le Pérou sous la date du 8 janvier 1890, et les deux gouvernements furent en désaccord sur la validité du traité antérieur, notamment en ce qui concernait la constitution du tribunal arbitral.

D'autre part, le Chili concluait avec la France, sous la date du 23 juillet 1892, un traité spécial par lequel toutes les difficultés, relatives à l'extraction du guano et à la distribution des sommes provenues ou à provenir de cette extraction, seraient soumises au jugement du Président du Tribunal Fédéral de la Confédération Suisse.

Reunidos en este Departamento los señores Don Isidoro Errazuriz, Ministro de Relaciones Exteriores de la República de Chile, y Don Enrique de Bacourt, Enviado Extraordinario y Ministro Plenipotenciario de la República Francesa, provistos ambos de los plenos poderes de sus respectivos Gobiernos, después de cambiar ideas respecto á la situación en que se hallan los acreedores franceses en presencia del Tratado de Ancón, y resumiendo las negociaciones posteriores que ha habido entre las Cancillerías de Francia y de Chile, han acordado protocolizar el siguiente Convenio :

Art. I. — El Gobierno de Chile, deseoso de hacer desaparecer los inconvenientes que han frustrado hasta aquí las concesiones que en Enero de 1890 hizo espontánea y gratuitamente al Perú para el arreglo de su deuda externa, y teniendo presente, por una parte, que al firmarse el Protocolo de 8 de Enero de 1890, por el cual Chile otorgó las expresadas concesiones, no estaba, ni pudo estar, en el ánimo de los Gobiernos que lo subscribieron el propósito de arrebatar á las sumas que se hallan en depósito en el Banco de Inglaterra, procedente del 50 por ciento del producto de la venta de guanos, el caracter de propiedad de las acreedores del Perú, cuyos títulos de crédito se encuentran sustentados por la garantía del guano, que les atribuyeron los artículos 13 y 16 del decreto de 9 de Febrero de 1882, incorporado en el Tratado de Ancón — teniendo presente, por otra parte, que en el final de la cláusula A del mencionado Protocolo se dispone que el 50 por ciento depositado en el Banco de Inglaterra será distribuido en conformidad á los artículos 4°, 7° y 8° del Tratado de Ancón, en el primero de los cuales se reconoce el derecho á dicho 50 por ciento á los acreedores del Perú cuyos títulos de crédito aparecieren sustentados con la garantia indicada — declara que, en cumplimiento de la cláusula A del Protocolo del 8 de Enero de 1890, tendrán opción al depósito proveniente del 50 por ciento del producto líquido de la venta del millón de toneladas de guano que se ordenó por el decreto de 9 de Febrero de 1882, todos los acreedores del Perú, cualesquiera que sea su nacionalida, cuyos títulos de crédito se encuentran sustentados con la garantía del guano.

---

[1] Peru. *Coleccion de los Tratados*, t. IV, p. 656.

ART. II. — En consecuencia el Gobierno de Chile en cumplimiento de lo dispuesto en las cláusulas 4ª, 6ª y 7ª del Tratado de Ancón y en los artículos 14 y 15 del supremo decreto de 9 de Febrero de 1882, que está incorporado á aquél, y teniendo en consideración los deseos expresados en diversas ocasiones por Gobiernos extranjeros, en representación de los principales grupos de los acreedores del Perú, estima que debe proceder á la brevedad posible á constituir el Tribunal de Arbitros.

ART. III. — Los fondos depositados en el Banco de Inglaterra, á qui se refiere la cláusula A citada del Protocolo de Enero de 1890, serán distribuidos entre los acreedores á virtud de las resoluciones que el indicado Tribunal transmita directamente á dicho Banco.

ART. IV. — Queda ratificada la designación del Presidente de la Suprema Corte de Justicia de la Confederazión Suiza como Arbitro llamado á calificar los derechos que cada cual creyere tener á á distribuir la suma depositada en el Banco de Inglaterra.

· ART. V. — Resumiendo las negociaciones seguidas entre las Cancillerías de Francia y de Chile desde el año 1888, el Gobierno de Chile cede definitivamente á favor de los acreedores franceses del Perú, cuyos titulos hubieren obtenido un fallo favorable del Arbitro indicado en el artículo precedente, y hasta la concurrencia de las sumas que dicho Tribunal reconozca, lo que sigue :

El 20 por ciento de todo el producto líquido de la venta del guano que Chile ha percibido desde el 9 de Febrero de 1882 hasta el 8 de Enero de 1890, y reitera las ofertas hechas al Gobierno de Francia en diversas ocasiones, esto es, en 1888, en 1889 (misión confidencial á Lima) y en 1890 (nota reservada de 12 de Abril), al efecto de que, siempre con el propósito de facilitar á un país vecino y amigo el arreglo de sus difficultades financieras, podría elevar á cuatro millones de pesos, plata, la indemnización que, según el artículo 3º del Tratado de 20 de Octubre de 1883, habiá el Perù de recibir de Chile, dado caso de que queden definitivamente incorporados al dominio y soberanía chilenos los territorios de Tacna y Arica.

ART. VI. — Estas concesiones espontáneas de parte del Gobierno de Chile, y hechas con el mismo espíritu que le guió al estipular el Protocolo de 8 de Enero citado, es decir, para facilitar al Perú la completa extinción de su deuda externa, y para asegurar igualmente en la costa del Pacífico la paz y la tranquilidad de que Chile, por su parte, necesita para el desenvolvimiento de sus intereses y seguridad de su

comercio y navigacion, no menoscaban los derechos que los acreedores franceses tuvieran que hacer valer en algún caso cerca del Gobierno del Perú, dado el evento de que las sumas cedidas por Chile no fuesen suficientes para cancelar totalmente los créditos á que los acreedores franceses tuvieran derecho por la resolución arbitral, quedando bien establecido que el Gobierno de Chile sólo responderá al pago de las acreencias reconocidas hasta la concurrencia de las cantidades que espontaneamente ha cedido y ofrecido en este Protocolo.

El Gobierno de Chile, por su parte, se compromette á apoyar tanto cuanto le sea posible al Gobierno Francés, en el sentido de que sean sometidas al arbitraje todas las reclamaciones de los acreedores franceses de la deuda externa peruana, dado caso de que aún no esté convenido entre el Perú y Francia el seguir esta línea de procedimiento.

En fe de lo cual ambos Plenipotenciarios han firmado ad referendum el presente Protocolo, complementario del Convenio de 8 de Enero de 1890, que está conforme al caracter al espíritu de las negociaciones seguidas entre las Cancillerías de Francia y de Chile, como también con los arreglos sobre los cuales estaban de acuerdo desde que fué firmado y ratificado aquel documento.

Queda bien establecido que la aprobación del Gobierno Francés del presente acuerdo, envuelve ipso facto el retiro de la oposición que creyó de su deber hacer á la ejecución de las cláusulas del Protocolo de 8 de Enero de 1890.

Santiago, veintitrés de Julio de mil ochocientos noventa y dos [1].

La convention du 23 juillet 1892 souleva, elle aussi, les protestations du Pérou, qui n'était pas partie à cet acte, alors qu'il s'agissait pourtant de créances à sa charge ; de plus, le Pérou soutenait que les créances visées n'avaient aucun rapport avec les bons péruviens et qu'elles n'étaient nullement, comme ces derniers, garanties par les produits de la vente du guano.

Le Conseil Fédéral de la Suisse, saisi par la France et le Chili de la demande d'arbitrage contenue dans le traité du 23 juillet 1892, proposa le 24 mars 1894 de confier l'arbitrage à trois arbitres, membres du Tribunal Fédéral, et stipula en outre quelles seraient la mission

---

[1] Recopilación de Tratados y Convenciones (Chili), 1894, t. II, p. 366 ; — Colección de los Tratados (Perú), t. IV, p. 720.

et la compétence spéciales du tribunal arbitral. Le Chili, la Grande-Bretagne, la France et le Pérou acquiescèrent à cette proposition et le tribunal se trouva dès lors régulièrement constitué. Nous ne reproduisons que les conclusions du mémoire du Conseil Fédéral.

Memorandum explicatif transmis aux gouvernements intéressés par le gouvernement suisse. Berne, le 24 mars 1894 [1].

El tribunal arbitral será compuesto, como queda dicho, del señor doctor Hafner, Presidente actual, y de dos miembros del Tribunal Federal. Este instituirá el procedimiento que ha de seguirse; estatuirá sobre su propia competencia y sobre todas las cuestiones prejudiciales, tendrá la facultad de decidir en todas las intervenciones y de proceder á los llamamientos en juicio que juzgue necesarios. En una palabra, fijará todas las condiciones del arbitraje.

Sobre estas bases es que el Consejo Federal ha creido necesario dirigir la presente comunicación á los Gobiernos de Francia y Chile, firmantes del compromiso de 23 de julio de 1892, de la Gran Bretaña y el Perú, así como al señor abogado Forrer, apoderado de la Compania consignataria del guano en los Estados Unidos de América.

Par divers actes des 16 avril 1895 et 20 janvier 1896, le tribunal arbitral fixa les règles à observer par les parties en cause.

Règles de procédure du tribunal arbitral franco-chilien, adoptées le 16 avril 1895 [1].

Considerando:

I. Que por decreto de 9 febrero de 1882, el Gobierno de la República de Chile ordenó la venta, en pública subhasta, de un millón de toneladas de guano, proveniente de los yacimientos situados en aquella parte del territorio del Perú á la sazón ocupada por las tropas de Chile, y dispuso que la mitad del producto neto de la venta fuese depositada en el Banco de Inglaterra, para ser distribuida entre aquellos de los acreedores del Gobierno del Perú, cuyos créditos estuviesen garantidos por el guano.

II. Que habiendo sido instituido el tribunal arbitral franco-chileno por los Gobiernos de Chile, de Francia y de la Gran Bretaña, "con el objeto

---

[1] Nous nous voyons obligés de donner la traduction espagnole des documents qui suivent; cette traduction seule a été publiée.

de determinar quiénes son los que tienen derecho á la suma depositada en el Banco de Inglaterra, y repartir entre ellos dicha suma", el Presidente del tribunal arbitral, mediante una circular de 22 de enero de 1895, invitó, so pena de exclusión, á todos los acreedores del Perú, cuyos créditos estuviesen garantidos por el guano, como arriba se indicó y que desearen hacer uso de sus derechos sobre el expresado depósito en el Banco de Inglaterra, para que anunciasen sus nombres hasta el 31 marzo de 1895, con indicación exacta y suscinta del título y monto de los créditos.

III. Las personas, que en seguida se expresan, han anunciado su reclamación al tribunal arbitral, antes de la circular citada de 22 de enero de 1895.

1. *Dreyfus frères & Cie.*, banqueros de París, representados por los señores Dupraz y Correvón, abogados de Lausanne, y Waldeck-Rousseau, abogado de París.

2. *Société générale pour favoriser le développement du commerce et de l'industrie*, establecida en París, y representada por los señores Dupraz y Correvón, abogados de Lausanne, y Waldeck-Rousseau, abogado de París.

3. *Compagnie Financière et Commerciale du Pacifique*, establecida en París, representada por les señores Meuron y Mayer, abogados de Lausanne.

4. *Peruvian Corporation Limited*, establecida en Londres, representada por los señores Charles Boiceau, abogado de Lausanne; Carlos Wiesse, peruano; R. A. Germaine, miembro del foro inglés; y Sir Richard Webster, M. P.

5. *Compagnie Consignataire du guano aux Etats-Unis d'Amérique*, establecida en Lima, representada por el señor Luis Forrer, abogado de Winterthour.

6. *J. L. Domis*, de Londres, representado por los señores Dubrit y Secretan, abogados de Lausanne.

7. Señor *Bouillet*, 44, rue des Ecuries-d'Artois, París.

IV. Antes de la espiración del plazo fijado en la circular de 22 de enero de 1895, se anunciaron:

8. *Compagnie Financière et Commerciale du Pacifique*, establecida en París, representada por el señor Dubois, abogado de Lausanne, por un crédito reconocido por el Gobierno del Perú, el 31 diciembre de 1892, ascendente á la suma de 5,935,922 francos 82 cts.

9. *Banque de l'Ouest*, establecido en París, representado por los señores Dubrit y Secretan,

abogados de Lausanne, por once obligaciones del empréstito peruano de 1870 (série F) de 500 francos cada una.

10. Viuda *Alice Belny*, residente en Nanterre (Francia) representada por los señores Dubrit y Secretan, abogados de Lausanne, por una obligación del empréstito peruano de 1870 (série C) de 500 francos.

11. Viuda *Philon Bernal*, residente en Biarritz, Francia, representada por los señores Dubrit y Secretan, abagados de Lausanne, por

8 obligaciones (série A) frs. 25,000 cada una
2 » (» B) » 12,000 » »
10 » (» C) » 50,000 » »
24 » (» E) » 1,250 » »
90 » (» F) » 500 » »
del empréstito peruano de 1870.

12. *Auguste Gilliard*, vecino de Lyon, representado por los señores Dubrit y Secretan, abogados de Lausanne, por diez obligaciones (série E) del empréstito peruano de 1870, de 500 francos cada una.

13. Señor *Ciron*, residente en Sainte-Mère-l'Eglise (Manche), Francia, por

2 obligaciones (série B) frs. 1250 cada una
4 » (» F) » 500 » »
del empréstito peruano de 1870.

14. *Emile Dutoit*, abogado de Lausanne, por diez obligaciones del empréstito peruano de 1870 (série F), de 500 francos cada una.

15. *J. Pezet*, arquitecto, vecino de Villars en Arthies (Seine-et-Oise), Francia, por seis obligaciones del empréstito peruano de 1870 (série F) de 500 francos cada una.

16. Dr. *Drognat-Landré*, 84, boulevard Saint-Michel, París, por un bono de la Peruvian Corporation, n° 1594 de 2000 libras esterlinas.

17. *L. Cauvin*, propietario, residente en Montmartin-sur-Mer (Manche), Francia, por 48 acciones de una libra esterlina, privilegiadas, y 60 acciones de £ 1 ordinarias, convertidas en bono n° 12,404.

18. *P. Schwægel*, abogado, 303, avenue de Neuilly (Seine), Francia, por 4 titulos de £ 50, números 43,423 à 44,426, dos titulos de £ 20, números 62,103 y 62,104, sean £ 240 ó 6000 francos con los intereses.

19. *A. Delmas*, vecino de la villa Fauvette, Rodez (Seine), Francia, por dos certificados de la Peruvian Corporation Limited.

20. Señora *Layous*, 54, Bellavista, cerca de Lima (Perú), por 19 negociaciones Dreyfus, de 1000 francos cada una.

21. Viude *Novis Page*, 38, rue Claudot en Nancy, Francia, por titulos en los empréstitos peruanos de 1870 y 1872, convertidos: número

6162, £ 300 — 6.126, 1. 4; 10 fractionnal certificate chilian bonds of the 4 % of 1893, 7490 reg. número 4.529, 1. 90 ordinarios, 7999 reg. número 4.625, 1. 72 privilegiados.

V. Después de la espiración del plazo fijado en la circular de 22 de enero de 1895, y por cartas fechas 4 y 9 de abril de 1895, *Charles Quantin*, vecino de Rouffiac-Plassac (Charente), Francia, y *Marie Quantin*, esposa de *Bernard Raynaud*, 20, Clos de la Bruyère, Limoges, tanto en nombre propio come en el de *Célestin Landreau*, tío de ellos, en Washington, han expuesto que Jean Théophile Landreau, hermano de Célestin Landreau, de quien son herederos, descubrió yacimientos de guano en el Perú, los cuales se explotaron en los años de 1858 à 1862, perteneciéndole de derecho el 33 por ciento del producto de dicha explotación, derecho que le fué reconocido por el decreto del tribunal, pero que aún no se le ha entregado su parte.

VI. Los Gobiernos de Chile y del Perú han declarado intervenir en este incidente, y han designado para que los representen:

El Gobierno de Chile al señor Francisco Gandarillas, 45, rue des Belles-Feuilles, Paris.

El Gobierno del Perú al señor Georges Favey, abogado de Lausanne.

Resuelve:

I. Admitese la reclamación de Charles Quantin, Marie Raynaud, nacida Quantin, y Célestin Landreau, reservandose á las otras partes el derecho de oponerse á la admisión de aquella.

II. Se concede un plazo hasta el 30 de setiembre de 1895, á todos los demandantes para que presenten su demanda.

III. La demanda comprenderá: 1° la relación de los hechos; 2° las pruebas que la asisten; 3° la exposición de los medios de derecho; 4° las conclusiones.

IV. Las demandas no serán admitidas siempre que los demandantes no hubieren presentado la demanda, los alegatos, medios de prueba y de derecho que los asiste, y las conclusiones, dentro del plazo señalado en el párrafo segundo.

Los demandantes que dentro de dicho plazo no hubieran presentado escrito alguno, serán considerados como que han renunciado á todo derecho á la suma depositada en el Banco de Inglaterra, y, además, que desisten de la pretensión aducida por ellos á la repartición de dicho depósito.

V. Dentro del mismo plazo que vence el 30 de setiembre de 1895 deberán igualmente los demandantes, so pena de ser excluídos, presentar el original ó la copia debidamente certificada, todos los medios de prueba que posean ó que puedan proporcionarse ellos mismos, así como todos los actos legislativos (leyes, decretos, resoluciones, etc.) en los cuales quieran apoyarse y que aún no obran en el expediente de la materia.

VI. La demanda y las pruebas deberán remitirse al Presidente del tribunal arbitral, al Palacio del Tribunal Federal en Lausanne (Suiza) en 35 ejemplares impresos en lengua francesa ó alemana.

VII. Después de recibidas las demandas serán comunicadas éstas á las partes contrarias y á los Gobiernos de Chile y del Perù. Se fijará un plazo para entregar las respuestas.

VIII. Después de comunicar las respuestas, el tribunal arbitral reglará los procedimientos judiciales ulteriores.

IX. Los demandantes que no estén domiciliados en Suiza, y que aún no han constituido su representante domiciliado en Suiza, debidamente acreditado, deben hacerlo antes del 30 de setiembre de 1895; lo contrario se les dirigirá las comunicaciones del tribunal por la posta, de su cuenta y riesgo.

Las decisiones serán remitidas en un ejemplar impreso á todas las partes interesadas ó á sus representantes en Suiza, quienes otorgarán el correspondiente recibo [1].

[1] *Memoria de Relaciones Exteriores*, Perú, 1896, p. 460.

Règles de procédure du tribunal arbitral franco-chilien, adoptées le 20 janvier 1896.

I. Vistas las demandas interpuestas por:

1. Los señores Dreyfus frères & Cie de Paris, representados por los señores Dupraz y Correvón, abogados de Lausanne, y Waldeck-Rousseau, abogado de París;

2. La Société générale pour favoriser le développement du commerce et de l'industrie, representada por los abogados señores Dupraz y Correvon de Lausanne, y Waldeck-Rousseau, de París;

3. La Compagnie Financière et Commerciale du Pacifique, conjuntamente con los señores Pierre, Louis y Henri Gautreau, de Paris, representados por el abogado S. Meuron, de Lausanne;

4. La Peruvian Corporation Limited de Londres, representada por los abogados señores Boiceau y Wiesse de Lausanne, R. J. Reid, Q. C. y R. A. Germaine de Londres;

5. La Compagnie consignataire de guano en los Estados Unidos de América, de Lima, representada por el abogado señor Forrer de Winterthour;

6. La Compagnie Financière et Commerciale du Pacifique, de Paris, representada por el abogado señor S. Dubois de Lausanne;

7. La Banque de l'Ouest, de Paris, representada por los abogados señores Dubrit y Gross de Lausanne;

8. La señora viuda Philon Bernal de Biarritz (Francia), representada por los abogados señores Dubrit y Gross de Lausanne;

9. El señor Augusto Gilliard de Lyon, representado por el abogado señor Gross de Lausanne;

10. El señor E. Dutoit de Lausanne, representante del señor Dumaray de Ginebra, representado por los abogados señores Dubrit y Gross de Lausanne;

11. Señores J. C. Landreau de Rollins (Carolina del Norte), Ch. Quantin de Rouffiac-Plassac (Charente), Bernard Raynaud de Limoges, y consortes, en calidad de herederos de don Juan Teófilo Landreau, representados por los abogados señores Carrard y Thélin de Lausanne;

12. El señor J. C. Landreau de Rollins, representado por los abogados señores Carrard y Thélin de Lausanne;

13. Los esposos Coichot, en calidad de herederos de Alejandro Coichot, llamado Cochet, representados por los abogados J. C. Marnand de Valence (Drôme), Carrard y Thélin de Lausanne;

14. Los herederos testamentarios de don José Vicente Oyague de Lima, representados por el abogado doctor Roclli de Berna.

II. Vista la solicitud de 19 de diciembre de 1895, del Bank für Handel und Industrie de Darmstadt, y de otras catorce personas ó casas alemanas (coparticipantes del finado S. Premsel, banquero de París, de un sindicato formado por los señores Dreyfus frères & Cie) á efecto de que el tribunal arbitral disponga que su parte proveniente de la suma que sea asignada á los señores Dreyfus, del deposito de Londres, sea directamente entregada á prorrata á los solicitantes, quienes declaran estar en aptitud de probar su derecho.

III. Vista la solicitud del doctor Forrer, sobre que se le conceda á la Compania consignataria de guano en los Estados Unidos, un plazo suplementario para presentar los documentos siguientes, cuyas copias obran en el expediente: 1° un certificado autentico de los textos de las leyes citadas (codigo civil y de comercio del Perú), del procedimiento civil y reglamento del Tribunal de Cuentas del Perú; 2° el original del contrato de 22 de noviembre de 1869; 3° la traducción de este instrumento en aleman ó en frances; 4° la cuenta de intereses detallada.

IV. Vista la declaración del señor Drognat-Landré de 17 de mayo de 1895, de que no entabla demanda, porque considera que sus intereses no son distintos de los de la Peruvian Corporation, y

Considerando:

1º Que las solicitudes indicadas bajo el nº I han sido presentadas dentro del plazo fijado, y con arreglo á lo prescrito en los decretos del tribunal arbitral de 16 de abril y de 17 de julio de 1895.

2º Que los recursos de los señores Domis y Bouillet no están aparejados en la forma prescrita, según decreto de 16 de agosto de 1895; que habiendo sido presentados en un solo ejemplar, no pueden ser comunicados á las demás partes interesadas; que al tribunal arbitral no le es dado subsanar de oficio aquellas irregularidades, sin detrimento del derecho de igualdad entre las partes; que además, á los señores Domis y Bouillet asisten todos los derechos que podrían tener como pertenecientes al uno ó al otro de los grupos de acreedores indicados bajo el nº I, y la facultad de hacer valer estos derechos anté los tribunales ordinarios, caso de serles disputados por otros acreedores pertenecientes á estos grupos.

3º Que el Bank für Handel und Industrie de Darmstadt y compartes declaran pertenecer al grupo de acreedores representado por los señores Dreyfus frères y Cie.; que su solicitud tiene por objeto probar su participación á la suma que fuere asignada á este grupo, en virtud de la sentencia del tribunal arbitral; y á la distribución de esta suma entre ellos y los demás participantes; que no es de la atribución del tribunal arbitral las controversias entre los que forman parte del mismo grupo de acreedores; que estas controversias son exclusivamente del dominio de los tribunales ordinarios.

4º Que el pedido de un plazo suplementario hecho por el doctor Forrer lo justifican las circunstancias que expone en su solicitud, muy particularmente el fallecimiento del representante de la Compañía Consignataria, y el termino de la distancia, por cuyas razones puede concederse esto sin paralizar la instrucción de la causa.

Se resuelve:

I. Tomase en consideración la declaración del señor Drognat-Landré.

II. Los reclamantes que se apersonaron antes del 31 marzo de 1895, no han presentado recurso alguno dentro del plazo fijado por las resoluciones de 16 de abril y 17 de julio de 1895, y son:

1º La señora viuda Alice Belny de Nanterre,
2º E. Pezet, arquitecto, de Villars en Arthies,
3º L. Cauvin de Montmartin-sur-Mer,
4º P. Schwægel de Neuilly,
5º A. Delmas de Rodez,
6º La señora viuda Nobis Page de Nancy,
7º Señora Layous de Lima,
los cuales estan considerados como habiendose desistido de la causa.

III. No se les ha dado curso á las reclamaciones presentadas por los señores Domis, Bouillet, el Bank für Handel und Industrie y compartes.

IV. Un plazo suplementario que vence el 31 de mayo de 1896 se ha concedido á la Compañía Consignataria de guano en los Estados Unidos, para que exhiban los documentos mencionados en su solicitud de 31 de diciembre de 1895.

V. Las reclamaciones indicadas bajo el nº I de los considerandos de hecho y los comprobantes serán comunicados á las partes que figuran activamente en la causa, y á los Gobiernos de Chile y del Perú, mediante la remisión de un ejemplar impreso á sus representantes en Suiza.

VI. Se les concede á las partes y á los Gobiernos de Chile y del Perú, un plazo que vence el 31 de agosto de 1896 á fin de que presenten su réplica ó su memoria.

VII. Las réplicas ó la memoria deberán contener:

1º La calificación de los hechos, los medios de prueba, las conclusiones principales y los incidentes de las reclamaciones.

2º Todos los medios de defensa con que cuentan.

3º La indicación de los medios probatorios que han de ser empleados, sea para debatir los hechos alegados en las reclamaciones, sea para justificar las excepciones.

4º Las conclusiones.

VII. Los hechos, medios probatorios y conclusiones principales ó incidentes que no hayan sido expresamente contestados, serán considerados como admitidos.

VIII. Las partes serán excluídas de hacer valer los medios probatorios y conclusiones que no se hubiesen presentado dentro del plazo fijado para hacerlo.

IX. Dentro del mismo plazo que vence el 31 de agosto de 1896, deberán las partes, so pena de ser excluídas, exhibir, en original ó en copia debidamente certificada, los titulos que invocan como medios probatorios y que no hayan sido ya exhibidos, por cuanto estos titulos están en poder de los interesados ó puedan proporcionárselos.

X. Las réplicas, memorias y comprobantes deberán ser dirigidos al Presidente del tribunal arbitral, y depositados en el Palacio del Tribunal Federal en Lausanne, en 35 ejemplares impresos en lengua francesa ó alemana.

XI. Estas resoluciones serán comunicadas á todas las partes interesadas, mediante un ejemplar impreso que se remitirá á sus representantes en Suiza, bajo recibo. Al señor Domis se le devolverán los documentos que hubiere presentado [1].

CXLIII. Chine, Etats-Unis d'Amérique.

.... 1884.

Il s'est agi d'un conflit au sujet d'une pêcherie concédée à un citoyen américain et dont ce dernier avait été dépouillé par suite des agissements des autorités chinoises. Le Ministre Plénipotentiaire des Etats-Unis d'Amérique se mit d'accord avec le Taotai de la Province de Kuangtung pour soumettre le différend à un arbitrage. Il est difficile de juger si le fonctionnaire chinois avait le pouvoir de lier son gouvernement, car le compromis intervenu n'a pas été publié, pour autant qu'il en soit intervenu un.

Award given by the consuls of Great Britain and Netherlands in the Ashmore Fishery question, at Swatow, May 24, 1884.

We, George Philips, Her Britannic Majesty's Consul, officiating at Swatow, and Robert Hunter Hill, Her Netherland Majesty's Consul, at Swatow, having been requested by His Excellency the Honorable J. Russell Young, Envoy Extraordinary and Minister Plenipotentiary of the United States at Peking, and Chang, Taotai of the Hui Chao Kia Intendancy in the Province of Kuang Tung, to arbitrate in a matter as to the sum of money that the Rev. Dr. Ashmore, a United States citizen, residing at Swatow, is held to be entitled to receive from the Chinese Government, for giving up to them his title deeds to a certain fishery ground, from which he for many years has received an income of four hundred dollars a year.

We, after deliberately and carefully weighing the facts of this case, hold it as our opinion, that the Rev. Dr. Ashmore should receive from the Chinese Government for giving up his right and title to the said fishery ground, the sum of four thousand six hundred dollars.

We hold Dr. Ashmore to be entitled to that sum for the following reasons: Dr. Ashmore, by giving up his deeds to this fishery ground, loses four hundred dollars per annum, and he should in justice be paid a sum which would without difficulty give him in a like venture the same amount of interest.

The Chinese authorities admit that for two years Dr. Ashmore has not received the rental of the fishery ground, which amounts to eight hundred dollars. This sum we consider he is entitled to receive.

The fact that Dr. Ashmore was not willing to part with his deeds, and that he is for the moment deprived of a good investment, should be taken into consideration, and in estimating the value of the fishery, a certain sum has to be added to the purchase money. This we have done, and we have fixed the sum to be due Dr. Ashmore on the three counts, viz.: the loss of two years rental, the value of the property, and recompense for compulsory sale at $ 4,600.

In arriving at this decision, we think we, on the one hand, have dealt fairly with the Chinese Government, for we argue that if Dr. Ashmore could get a rental of $ 400 a year for the fishery ground, the Chinese Government will on receipt of the deeds be in a position to relet it for a like amount; we think, on the other hand, that taking into consideration the nature of the property, we could not in fairness award Dr. Ashmore a larger amount than we have done, which amount with the interest attainable upon investments of a kindred character in China will always bring him in the amount of which he has been deprived, and at the same time cover all that can be fairly claimed. This amount of $ 4,600 to be paid two months from to-day the 24th May, 1884.

Given under our hands and seals of office this twenty fourth day of May, 1884 [1].

CXLIV. Allemagne, Grande-Bretagne.

1 juillet 1890.

Dans la convention reproduite, il n'est question d'arbitrage qu'à titre éventuel et il nous a été impossible de vérifier si, depuis 1890, l'arrangement direct, qui devait écarter le recours à l'arbitrage, est intervenu en réalité.

---

[1] *Memoria de Relaciones Exteriores*, (Peru) 1896, p. 479.

J. B. MOORE. *History and Digest* ..., p. 1858.

Agreement between Great Britain and Germany, respecting Zanzibar, Heligoland, and the spheres of influence of the two countries in Africa. Signed at Berlin, July 1, 1890.

. . . .

ARTICLE III. In South-West Africa the sphere in which the exercise of influence is reserved to Germany is bounded —

1. To the south by a line commencing at the mouth of the Orange River, and ascending the north bank of that river to the point of its intersection by the 20th degree of east longitude.

2. To the east by a line commencing at the above-named point, and following the 20th degree of east longitude to the point of intersection by the 22nd parallel of south latitude, its runs eastwards along that parallel to the point of its intersection by the 21st degree of east longitude; thence it follows that degree northward to the point of its intersection by the 18th parallel of south latitude: it runs eastward along that parallel till it reaches the River Chobe; and descends the centre of the main channel of that river to its junction with the Zambesi where it terminates.

It is understood that under this arrangement Germany shall have free access from her Protectorate to the Zambesi by a strip of territory which shall at no point be less than 20 English miles in width.

The sphere in which the exercise of influence is reserved to Great Britain is bounded to the west and northwest by the above-mentioned line. It includes Lake Ngami. The course of the above boundary is traced in general accordance with a map officially prepared for the British Government in 1889.

The delimitation of the southern boundary of the British territory of Walfish Bay is reserved for arbitration, unless it shall be settled by the consent of the two Powers within two years from the date of the conclusion of this Agreement. The two Powers agree that, pending such settlement, the passage of the subjects and the transit of goods of both Powers through the territory now in dispute shall be free; and the treatment of their subjects in that territory shall be in all respects equal. No dues shall be levied on goods in transit. Until a settlement shall be effected the territory shall be considered neutral. [1]

CXLV. Haïti, République Dominicaine.

3 juillet 1895.

Cet arbitrage, confié à Sa Sainteté le Pape, a pour objet la fixation définitive de la fron-

tière entre les deux républiques. Aucune décision n'est encore intervenue, à notre connaissance, dans ce conflit.

Convention d'arbitrage signée à Santo Domingo le 3 juillet 1895.

Le Président de la République d'Haïti, dans l'exercice de ses attributions constitutionnelles,

Et le Président de la République Dominicaine, spécialement autorisé par le plébiscite des un et deux juin mil huit cent quatre-vingt-quinze ;

Vu le traité en vigueur du neuf novembre mil huit cent soixante-quatorze, en son article 4 ainsi conçu :

« Art. 4. — Les hautes parties contractantes s'engagent formellement à établir de la manière la plus conforme à l'équité et aux intérêts réciproques des deux peuples, les lignes frontières qui séparent leurs possessions actuelles. Cette nécessité fera l'objet d'un traité spécial et des Commissaires seront respectivement nommés le plus tôt possible à cet effet. »

Vu l'interprétation opposée donnée au dit article quatre, par les deux Gouvernements ;

D'une part, le Gouvernement haïtien soutenant que l'*uti possidetis* de mil huit cent soixante-quatorze, est celui qui a été conventionnellement accepté et consacré pour le tracé de nos lignes frontières ; qu'en effet, le terme de possessions actuelles veut dire les possessions occupées à l'époque de la signature du traité ;

D'autre part, le Gouvernement dominicain soutenant que l'*uti possidetis* de mil huit cent soixante-quatorze n'est pas conventionnellement accepté ni consacré dans ledit article quatre, parce que, par possessions actuelles, on ne peut entendre que ce qui, en droit, pourrait appartenir à chacun des deux Gouvernements, c'est-à-dire les possessions fixées par le *statu quo post bellum* en mil huit cent cinquante-six, uniques *(sic)* que peut avoir en sa faveur l'*uti possidetis* auquel peut raisonnablement se référer la clause de l'article quatre ;

Désireux de donner une solution amiable à la difficulté existant entre leurs Gouvernements respectifs au sujet de l'interprétation contraire susdite,

Ont résolu de soumettre à un arbitrage la difficulté en question et, dans le but de conclure une convention à cet effet, ont institué comme Plénipotentiaires respectifs :

Le Président de la République d'Haïti :

M. Dallémar, Jean-Joseph, Envoyé Extraordinaire et Ministre plénipotentiaire d'Haïti, à Santo-Domingo ;

Le Président de la République dominicaine :

M. Enrique Henriquez, ministre des Relations Extérieures de la République dominicaine ;

---

[1] HERTSLET, *A complete Collection* . . . , t. XVIII, p. 457.

Lesquels après avoir échangé leurs pleins-pouvoirs et les ayant trouvés en bonne et due forme, ont agréé et conclu les articles suivants :

ART. 1. — La difficulté qui a surgi entre le Gouvernement d'Haïti et le Gouvernement dominicain au sujet de l'interprétation de l'article quatre du Traité de mil huit cent soixante-quatorze sera soumis à l'arbitrage de Sa Sainteté le Pape, à la bonté paternelle et impartiale duquel il sera demandé de décider si le dit article quatre du Traité de mil huit cent soixante-quatorze a le sens et donne le droit que lui suppose le Gouvernement dominicain.

ART. 2. — Chacune des hautes parties contractantes désignera l'agent spécial ou les agents qui seront chargés de produire les notes et explications nécessaires à l'examen de la question, telle qu'elle est posée à l'article précédent.

ART. 3. — Le mémoire de chacune des deux parties, accompagné de documents qu'il y aura lieu d'y joindre à l'appui, sera soumis, en double, au Souverain Pontife et à l'agent de l'autre partie, aussitôt que possible, après que le Saint Père aura daigné consentir à être juge-arbitre, mais dans un délai ne dépassant pas deux mois, du jour de l'échange des ratifications du présent Traité.

ART. 4. — Dans le délai d'un mois après la remise réciproque du mémoire, chaque partie pourra, de la même manière, remettre en double au Souverain Pontife et à l'agent de l'autre partie un contre-mémoire, et, s'il y a lieu, des documents additionnels en réponse aux contre-mémoire et documents ainsi présentés par l'autre partie.

ART. 5. — La décision rendue par écrit, en double, datée et signée comme le Très Saint Père sera prié de le faire, une copie sera remise à l'agent de la République dominicaine pour son Gouvernement.

ART. 6. — Chaque gouvernement paiera son propre agent et pourvoira aux dépenses de préparation et de présentation de son affaire devant le Tribunal arbitral. Toutes les autres dépenses possibles relatives à l'arbitrage seront supportées également par moitié par les deux Gouvernements.

ART. 7. — Les hautes parties contractantes s'engagent à considérer le résultat de l'arbitrage comme la solution complète et définitive de la difficulté sur l'interprétation ci-dessus indiquée de l'article 4 du Traité de 1874.

ART. 8. — Si le point est résolu en faveur de la nation haïtienne, le Gouvernement dominicain s'oblige à tracer la ligne frontière définitive de manière que restent en faveur d'Haïti toutes les possessions occupées par elle dans l'année 1874.

ART. 9. — Si l'arbitrage décide la question suivant l'interprétation soutenue par le Gouvernement dominicain, alors que celui-ci, considérant que Haïti a toujours occupé et peuplé le territoire en litige depuis laps de temps et que la République dominicaine serait aujourd'hui dans l'impossibilité d'indemniser les propriétaires haïtiens des biens situés et établis dans le dit territoire, comme aussi elle se trouverait dans l'impossibilité de l'occuper et de le peupler de familles dominicaines, s'oblige à convenir avec le gouvernement haïtien, usant pour cela de l'autorisation expresse que lui a conférée le peuple souverain, pour laisser Haïti en possession, avec droit parfait, du territoire qu'elle occupait èn 1874, moyennant juste compensation pécuniaire.

ART. 10. — Le présent Traité sera soumis à l'approbation et sanction des autorités compétentes respectives et les ratifications seront échangées à Santo-Domingo dans le délai de deux mois, à compter de cette date, ou plus tôt si c'est possible.

En foi de quoi les Plénipotentiaires des parties contractantes ont signé la présente convention et ont apposé leurs sceaux respectifs.

Fait en double original, en langue française et espagnole, dans la ville de Santo-Domingo, le trois du mois de juillet mil huit cent quatre-vingt-quinze [1].

CXLVI. Bolivie, Pérou.

26 août 1895.

Le territoire de la Bolivie avait, à trois reprises, été envahi par des troupes armées péruviennes sur le lac Titicaca, à Berenguela et à Desaguadero. Le Pérou ne se refusa pas à réparer les préjudices causés aux particuliers, mais prétendit ne pas devoir rendre au drapeau bolivien les honneurs spéciaux réclamés par le gouvernement de la Bolivie. Cette dernière question seule fut soumise à un arbitrage.

Acuerdo para someter al fallo arbitral de un gobierno amigo la cuestion de saludo á la bandera boliviana, firmado en Lima, Agosto 26, 1895.

Reunidos en el Ministerio de Relaciones Exteriores los infrascritos Melchor Terrazas, Enviado Extraordinario y Ministro Plenipotenciario de Bolivia, y Manuel Candamo, Ministro de Relaciones Exteriores del Perú, á mérito de los buenos

---

[1] F. DE MARTENS, *Nouveau recueil général*, 2me série, t. XXIII, p. 79 et t. XXVII, p. 17.

oficios interpuestos por los honorables representantes diplomáticos de la Santa Sede, Francia, Colombia (doctor don Anibal Gabindo) é Italia para solucionar las diferencias suscitadas últimamente entre ambos países, han convenido en lo siguiente :

1° Someter al fallo arbitral de un Gobierno sud-americano la siguiente cuestión : Los hechos lamentados por el Perú en 1890 fueron de la misma naturaleza y gravedad que los lamentados por Bolivia durante la última guerra civil peruana, hasta hacer necesaria igual satisfacción de saludo á la bandera ?

2° El Perú reparará los daños y perjuicios causados por los hechos consignados en la demanda formulada por la Legación de Bolivia en su nota de 12 de marzo del presente año, que estuviesen debitamente comprobados.

3° El Ministro Plenipotenciario del Perú en Bolivia expresara al Gobierno de esa República, en audiencia especial, el sentimiento de lo ocurrido y el propósito del Gobierno peruano de conservar inalterables las buenas relaciones entre ambos países.

4° Se someterá á juicio ó se continuaran los juicios existentes contra los ejecutores de los atropellos en que se fundan las reclamaciones bolivianas, para su castigo ó su destitución, si aún ejerciesen funciones oficiales.

En fé de lo cual firmaron el presente Protocolo, en doble ejemplar, y lo sellaron con sus sellos particulares en Lima, á veintiseis de agosto de mil ochocientos noventa y cinco.

Acuerdo para designar la persona del arbitro, firmado en Lima, Septiembre 7, 1895.

Reunidos en el Despacho de Rélaciones Exteriores los infrascritos Melchor Terrazas, Enviado Extraordinario y Ministro Plenipotenciario de Bolivia, y Manuel Candamo, Ministro del Ramo, para designar la persona del árbitro y demás condiciones del arbitraje establecido en el Protocolo de 19 de Agosto ultimo, han convenido en los artículos siguientes :

I. Desígnase en calidad de árbitro al Excmo. Gobierno de los Estados Unidos del Brasil, y si él no aceptare el cargo confiado á su alta rectitud, será sustituido por el de la República de .Colombia, sobre igual base y con las mismas informaciones, tan pronto como sea conocida su excusa.

II. Ratificado que sea el presente acuerdo por los dos Gobiernos interesados dirigirán al Arbitro la respectiva carta rogatoria, dentro de los treinta días siguientes, enviándole al propio tiempo, impresas y legalizadas en ambas Can

cillerías : 1° las demandas de Bolivia, con los comprobantes en que se apoyan ; 2° las contestaciones relativas de parte del Perú, y el consiguiente debate diplomático á que ellas dieron lugar, hasta 10 de Julio último, inclusive ; 3° el proceso de la reclamación sustentada el año 1890, por el Ministro doctor don Manuel María Rivas, ante el Gobierno de Bolivia, con las reparaciones, que lo terminaron.

III. El laudo será pronunciado dentro de los cien días siguientes á la aceptacion del arbitramento, á no ser que el Arbitro estimase necesario prorogar prudencialmente el término indicado.

IV. Si el laudo fuese favorable á la demanda del Gobierno de Bolivia, el del Perú realizará, de inmediato, la satisfacción del saludo militar á la bandera de aquella nación.

V. El Excmo. Arbitro se servirá comunicar su decisión á los Gobiernos discordes ó á sus representantes, si los hubiere acreditados ante él, para los fines consiguientes.

En fé de lo cual firmaron el presente, por duplicado, y lo sellaron con sus sellos particulares en Lima, á los siete días del mes de septiembre de mil ochocientos noventa y cinco [1].

CXLVII. Etats-Unis d'Amérique, Siam.

. . . . 1897.

La date du compromis, dans cette affaire, nous est demeurée inconnue. Seule la sentence a été publiée : elle est intéressante par ce fait qu'elle n'a condamné les autorités siamoises qu'à des mesures disciplinaires et à des excuses officielles.

Award rendered, September 20, 1897, by the arbitrators in the case between Siam and the United States of America.

Whereas we, the undersigned, have been duly appointed and authorized respectively by the United States and Siamese Governments to investigate a certain alleged assault upon the United States vice-consul-general, Mr. E. V. Kellett, at Chiengmai, in November 1896, and to arbitrate all questions of law, fact, and reparation of said alleged assault ;

Whereas we have held an investigation in both Bangkok and Chiengmai and have heard all evidence obtainable in this matter ;

Whereas from said investigation it appears that on the 19th of November, 1896, at about 7 p. m., after and following certain difficulties

---

[1] *Memoria de Relaciones Exteriores* (Bolivia), 1895, p. 401.

between the said vice-consul-general of the United States and soldiers of His Siamese Majesty's army acting as police, in regard to the arrest of a clerk of said vice-consul-general of the United States, the said vice-consul-general was assaulted in one of the main streets of Chiengmai by a number of said soldiers;

Whereas this unfortunate incident could have been avoided, or at least its gravity lessened, if the Nai Roi Ake—i. e. Captain—Luang Phuvanat, the officer in command of the soldiers who committed the said assault, had taken the steps which his duty and the circumstances required;

Whereas the Nai Roi Tri—i. e. Sublieutenant—Choi, under whose immediate command the soldiers who committed the said assault were placed and who was present when the said soldiers committed the assault, did nothing to prevent them from inflicting injuries upon the person of the vice-consul-general;

Whereas Nais Kram, Niem and Phun, ordinary soldiers, while obeying certain orders, are convicted of having transcended such orders, and of having struck several times the said vice-consul-general, using to that effect the butts of their rifles, and inflicting bruises upon his body;

Whereas the conduct of the said officers and soldiers is, to a certain extent, excusable from the excitement resulting from the unusual and imprudent steps taken by the vice-consul-general in this matter;

Therefore we have agreed on the following:

I. The Nai Roi Ake—i. e. Captain—Luang Phuvanat, shall be recalled to Bangkok without delay after the publication of this decision; he shall be reprimanded in the presence of an official of the United States legation in Bangkok and a Siamese official of equal rank; he shall lose the grade he holds in His Siamese Majesty's army, and shall be reduced to the grade of Nai Roi Toh—i. e. Lieutenant—from which he shall not be promoted for a period of two years from date of reprimand; he shall be suspended from the army without pay for a period of one year from date of reprimand; he shall not return to Chiengmai within five years from date of this decision.

II. The Nai Roi Tri—i. e. Sublieutenant—Choi, shall be recalled to Bangkok without delay after the publication of this decision; he shall be reprimanded in the presence of an official of the United States legation in Bangkok and a Siamese official of equal rank; he shall not be open to promotion for a period of eighteen months from date of reprimand; he shall be suspended from the army without pay for a period of six months from date of reprimand; he shall not return to

Chiengmai within five years from the date of this decision.

III. Nais Kram, Niem and Phun shall be recalled to Bangkok without delay after the publication of this decision; they shall be reprimanded in the presence of an official of the United States legation in Bangkok and a Siamese official of equal rank; they shall be deprived of their pay during three months from date of reprimand; they shall not return to Chiengmai within five years from date of this decision.

We have also agreed:

A. His Siamese Majesty's Government shall express its official regrets to the United States Government, through the latter's representative in Bangkok, that soldiers of His Siamese Majesty's army committed an assault upon the person of a consular official of the United States, and shall duly instruct the chief commissioner of the Monthon Laochieng, Phya Song Suradij, to take such steps as will prevent a repetition of such an incident.

B. That copies of this decision shall be published in the official gazettes of both Governments within a reasonable time after their acquaintance with the same, and one shall be posted on the gateway of the police station in Chiengmai for not less than three weeks and within seventy-five days of the date of said decision.

Done in duplicate at Chiengmai this twentieth day of September, eighteen hundred and ninety-seven [1].

CXLVIII. Grèce, Turquie.

22 novembre 1897.

Le recours à l'arbitrage avait été prévu par l'article 15 du traité de paix conclu à Constantinople le 22 novembre/4 décembre 1897. Or, parmi les clauses de ce traité figurait un article 11 qui prévoyait la conclusion d'une convention consulaire à réaliser, aux termes d'un protocole spécial, dans un délai de deux ans à paitir de l'échange des ratifications du traité de paix. Entamées le 12/24 mars 1898, les négociations ne purent aboutir et le 1/14 mai 1900 le gouvernement hellénique se décida à recourir à l'arbitrage collectif prévu.

**Traité de paix signé à Constantinople,
le 22 novembre/4 décembre 1897.**

· · · · · · · · · ·

ARTICLE 15. — En cas de divergences dans le cours des négociations entre la Grèce et la

---

[1] J. B. MOORE, *History and Digest ...*, p. 1857.

Turquie, les points contestés pourront être soumis, par l'une ou l'autre des parties intéressées, à l'arbitrage des Représentants des Grandes Puissances à Constantinople, dont les décisions seront obligatoires pour les deux gouvernements.

Cet arbitrage pourra s'exercer collectivement ou par désignation spéciale des intéressés, et soit directement, soit par l'entremise de délégués spéciaux.

En cas de partage égal des voix, les arbitres choisiront un surarbitre.

CXLIX. Guatemala, Italie.

18 mars 1898.

Le compromis avenu entre les deux gouvernements n'a pas été publié. La sentence intervenue a condamné le Guatemala au payement d'une indemnité de 5800 $. Il s'agissait dans l'espèce d'une institutrice italienne, engagée par le gouvernement du Guatemala et brusquement renvoyée par lui.

Laudo arbitral pronunciado por el senor F. Garcia Gomez de la Serna, Madrid, Octubre 12, 1898.

Nombrado por V. E. para representar á España como Arbitro en la controversia surgida entre el Gobierno de S. M. el Rey de Italia y el de la República de Guatemala, con motivo de la reclamación de la señorita María Cedroni, paso á dar cuenta á V. E. del resultado de la misión con que se servió honrarme.

ANTECEDENTES. — El 11 de abril de 1892 el Gobierno de Guatemala, accediendo á lo solicitado en el mes anterior por la señorita Cedroni, le concedió, por cinco años, el uso de una casa para establecer en ella una « Academia superior de señoritas » en la inteligencia de que se sujetaría á la inspección de la Secretaría de Instrucción Pública, se obliga á educar y preparar para profesoras á cinco niñas, designadas por la misma secretaría, debiendo devolver á los cinco años la casa cedida con todos los útiles y enseres del establecimiento, que quedarían á beneficio del Gobierno.

En 28 de junio del mismo año concedió el Gobierno á la señorita Cedroni 250 pesos por trimestre para la educación de las cinco niñas mencionadas, á razón de 50 pesos cada una y se le designarón nominalmente las que debián ingresar.

En 23 de junio recibió la señorita Cedroni, como Directora del « Instituto Froebeliano », una circular *autografica* del secretario de Instrucción Pública, excitando á concurrir á una Junta para deliberar acerca de la representación de la Instrucción Pública de Guatemala en la Exposición de Chicago. No habiendo encontrado el que suscribe, entre los documentos facilitados por las partes interesados, ninguno que demuestre que la señorita Cedroni recibiera encargo especial de preparar tales ó cuales trabajos para Chicago.

Habiéndose quejado la señorita Cedroni de las condiciones insalubres de la casa que se le había cedido, y después de un informe del Consejo de Higiene, fechado el 10 de octubre (según dice la misma), el Gobierno guatemalteco, en 29 de noviembre, subvencionó el establecimiento con la cantidad que costará el alquiler del local que tomase, no excediendo de 200 $ mensuales.

Antes de pasar los nueve meses de inaugurado el establecimiento, fijó la señorita Cedroni, según dice, el día 18 de diciembre de 1892 para los exámenes públicos, de lo cual dió anticipado conocimiento al señor Secretario de Instrucción Pública, que, según oficio del 10 del mismo mes, designó para presidir dichos exámenes á tres personas, que la señorita Cedroni se negó á recibir por conceptuarlas enemigas de su naciente Instituto, según manifiesta ella misma en 12 de diciembre.

Pocos días después, y por Decreto Presidencial de 28 del mismo diciembre, se acordó « retirar toda subvención al Instituto Froebeliano », declarando insubsistentes los acuerdos de 11 de abril y 27 de junio de aquel año, fundándose en que, no obstante la protección del Gobierno, dicho Instituto no había correspondido á las esperanzas que se tuvieron en mira ; « que eran muchos los informes desfavorables que se tenían con respecto á la Dirección, y que el Ejecutivo no estaba en el caso de tolerar las expresiones injuriosas con que la misma Dirección calificaba al país ».

Este decreto viene á reiterarlo una carta del señor Presidente de la República, fecha del día siguiente, en que, contestando á otra que sin duda le dirigió la señorita Cedroni, le dice : « que el interés y empeño espontáneo y liberal que el Gobierno había demostrado por el « Instituto Froebeliano », unidos á la protección que le había dispensado, le daban perfecto derecho para nombrar el jurado que había de presenciar los exámenes de fin de año, para juzgar del resultado ; que sin tomar esto en cuenta se había permitido la señorita Cedroni dirigir á las personas nombradas cartas insultantes, y que esta circunstancia y los informes de algunos padres de familia, le habían impulsado á retirar toda protección, debiendo hacer formal entrega de los muebles y útiles que se le proporcionaron para el Instituto. »

En 3 de enero de 1893 acordó el señor Presidente de la República que : « Habiéndose retirado la subvención, se entreguen á la señorita Cedroni $ 300 para viaje. »

Ya en Italia acudió le interesada á su Gobierno, que desde 1894 procuró obtener del de Guatemala que accediera á indemnizar á la señorita Cedroni, reduciendo unas veces á 15,000 libras italianas la compensación de sus gastos y perjuicios y llegando otras á los 61,600 pesos que hoy solicita ; pero no habiendo podido en cuatro años ponerse de acuerdo los dos Gobiernos (cuya correspondencia llegó á ser un tanto agria) decidieron someter la cuestión al arbitraje de otro país ; y de ahí el protocolo de 18 de marzo último y su adicional de 23 del mismo mes y año.

Estos dos protocolos limitan la misión del árbitro á las dos cuestiones siguientes :

1ª Puede ó no la señorita Cedroni pedir al Gobierno de Guatemala que le dé alguna indemnización por derechos que aquélla hubiere adquirido y conservado legítimamente ?

2ª En caso afirmativo, á cuanto monta el importe de dicha indemnización, ó sea de los perjuicios que á la expresada señorita se le hayan seguido por la inejecución de aquellos mismos derechos ?

El laudo arbitral, que será inapelable, se dará conforme á las pruebas y alegaciones que se presenten por ambas partes, y versará sobre la justicia ó injusticia de las dos únicas cuestiones antes indicadas.

Para la presentación de pruebas se dieron de plazo tres meses, que terminaron en 18 de junio último ; para la réplica ó contradeducción, otros tres meses, fenecidos en 18 de septiembre próximo pasado, y para pronunciar el laudo se concede un mes, que vence en 18 del corriente. Las pruebas y réplicas han venido á poder del que suscribe con toda regularidad dentro de los plazos señalados, y ahora sólo le toca emitir su humilde opinión sobre las dos cuestiones sometidas el arbitraje.

De lo que queda expuesto se deduce lo siguiente :

RESUMEN. — La señorita Cedroni, de *mútuo proprio* y buscando (según manifiesta Guatemala) valiosas recomendaciones, *solicitó* la protección necesaria (local 1ª) para establecer un instituto docente, y el Gobierno de aquella República *accedió* á sus ruegos, imponiéndole, como consecuencia, varias condiciones.

Era una de ellas someterse á la inspección de la Secretaría de Instrucción Pública, y en su virtud este Centro delegó á tres personas para que presenciaran los primeros exámenes que anunció la señorita Cedroni, pero ésta, al saber quienes eran las designadas, se dirigió á las tres, manifestándoles en cartas cuya redacción dió lugar á fuertes quejos, que no las admitiría á los citados exámenes. El Gobierno guatemalteco, por esta negativa que conceptúa como falta grave á una de las condiciones de la concesión y además por otras razones, revocó de un golpe la expresada concesión, sin pedir ni dar lugar á que la interesada tratara de justificarse.

Existen, pues, en sentir del que escribe, dos faltas, una por cada parte, estímese ó no como contrato bilateral ó cuasi contrato el mutuo compromiso contraido entre Guatemala y la señorita Cedroni ; porque si bien es cierto que ésta no deb'a haberse dirigido personalmente á los examinadores ó delegados de la Secretaría de Instrucción Pública, que es con quien únicamente debía entenderse la reclamante, también parece innegable que procedía oírla (y no consta que se le haya siquiera amonestado) antes de despojarla repentinamente de las bases más principales de su establecimiento, cuando aún apenas había tenido tiempo para resarcirse de los gastos (mayores ó menores) que fundada en la esperanza de 5 años de residencia había hecho.

PRIMERA CUESTIÓN. — La señorita Cedroni promueve su reclamación por los conceptos y las cantidades siguientes :

1º Por planteamiento del Instituto . . . . $	2,000. 00
2º Por trabajos para la Exposición de Chicago . . . »	2,000. 00
3º Por la asignación de $ 200 mensuales durante cuatro años . . . . »	9,600. 00
4º Por lucro cesante . . . »	48,000. 00
Total $	61,600. 00

La discusión de esta cuestión principal versa, entre las dos partes, sobre un punto exclusivamente jurídico. Sostiene la parte italiana que las concesiones, aunque hayan sido graciosas, desde el momento en que son aceptadas por el favorecido, con ciertas condiciones recíprocas y han tenido un principio de ejecución, toman un carácter contractual que lleva consigo todas las obligaciones de un contrato bilateral. Fundados en esto dicen los alegatos de la señorita Cedroni :

Cierto es que ella solicitó casa y auxilios para establecer el Instituto docente, pero desde el momento en que el Gobierno de Guatemala accedió á su petición y le concedió los auxilios *con determinadas condiciones*, se crearon recíprocas obligaciones de que ninguna de las dos partes podía eximirse á capricho ; y como no encuentran en el Decreto Presidencial de 28 de diciembre de 1892 razón bastante para justificar la revocación de lo concedido sin oír ni discutir antes con la parte perjudicada las razones alegadas en el decreto expresado, el contrato subsistente y sus consiguientes obligaciones quedan en pié por el término de cinco años en él estipulado.

Contesta Guatemala negando en absoluto el carácter contractual de una concesión absolutamente graciosa que conceptúa como un mero acuerdo gubernativo, revocable à voluntad del Poder Ejecutivo, sobre todo cuando á su juicio la parte agraciada ha faltado á algunas de las principales condiciones.

Esta controversia sobre el carácter de las concesiones voluntarias acordadas por un Gobierno á petición de parte, entraría de lleno, en sentir del que suscribe, en la competencia de los Tribunales de Justicia; pero ya que se le ha conferido el carácter de árbitro, se cree en el deber de apreciar, como tal Árbitro, tanto el aspecto jurídico de la cuestión como la parte de equidad, que sin faltar á la justicia pueda aplicarse en la resolución de este asunto. Forzoso le parece, pues, examinar el espíritu y letra de los decretos de concesión y retirada de las subvenciones.

El Gobierno de Guatamala ni mandó abrir ni obligó á la señorita Cedroni á cerrar su Academia. Lo que hizo fué autorizar la apertura, ofreciendo subvenciones durante cinco años, á cambio de ciertas obligaciones por parte de la interesada, y después limitarse á retirar las subvenciones, perjudicando así, es cierto, á la reclamante, pero dejándola en libertad de continuar con su Instituto.

Expone la señorita Cedroni que, cuando en 29 de noviembre de 1892 se le concedió la subvención de, á lo más, doscientos pesos mensuales para alquiler de casa, y nada se le dijo respecto á su conducta y á la marcha de su establecimiento, es prueba que no iba mal, pues de lo contrario, ó no se le hubiera otorgado la subvención, ó por lo menos se le hubieran hecho observaciones.

Cierto es que esa subvención parecía confirmar las concesiones anteriores por el plazo de cinco años y no podía preparar el ánimo de la reclamante para recibir, un mes después, el acuerdo, suprimiendo todo apoyo.

No ignora el que suscribe, pues los cargos que ha desempeñado en su ya larga vida se lo han demostrado, que hay momentos en que la autoridad gubernativa no puede excusarse de tomar ciertas medidas que, para quien no conoce el fondo de la cuestión, digámoslo así, para la generalidad de las gentes, revisten carácter dictatorial: pero parece equitativo que en estos casos se procure evitar perjuicio de tercero, hasta donde posible sea.

Es indudable que, si la señorita Cedroni al saber que se le iba á pagar el alquiler de casa hubiera arrendado una, abonando la cantidad que en Guatemala sea costumbre (uno ó más meses anticipados) era de toda equidad que el Gobierno, al revocar la concesión pagará esa candidad. No consta que la interesada hiciera desembolso por este concepto; pero sí es presumible que, confiada en el plazo de 5 años, haya invertido sumas más ó menos crecidas para instalarse.

Si el Gobierno de Guatemala hubiera prevenido ó amonestado á la señorita Cedroni con alguna anelación de que su Academia no correspondía á los propósitos de él y que en su visto eso iba á retirarse el apoyo que se le prestaba, entonces podría ella haber corregido los defectos que se le hubieran señalado, haber practicado gestiones para sincerarse, y por último, dada la voz de alerta, haber tomado precauciones para el porvenir, reclamar entonces sus gastos de instalación etc. Como lo primero no tuvo lugar y lo segundo por consiguiente no pudo tenerlo, cree el que suscribe que es de equidad conceder por las razones antes indicadas una indemnización á la señorita Cedroni, como compensación de los gastos que fiada en el plazo de cinco años pudo hacer.

Respecto á los trabajos que preparó para la Exposición de Chicago, la cuestión varia, pues no aparece entre la documentación que el que suscribe ha tenido á la vista (según queda dicho antes) que se le encargaron á la reclamante determinados trabajos para aquel Certamen, y existe, por el contrario, una nota ó comunicación del Presidente Interino que fué de la Comisión para la Exposición de Chicago, que dice no recordar que se hiciera á la señorita Cedroni encargo alguno; que no presentó trabajos para dicha Exposición, y que si bien solicitó cierta cantidad para ejecutarlos, no se le abonó.

En tal situación le es difícil al Árbitro hallar el fundamento de la reclamación de 2000 pesos que presenta la interesada por trabajos para la Exposición de Chicago, no obstante haberlos ella dado á conocer aquí. Esto último prueba, si, que trabajos, con ó sin encargo, los ejecutó la señorita Cedroni, y el no haberlos presentado en la Exposición, ha sido evidentemente perjudicial para ella. Ahora bien, la no remisión de ellos á Chicago ha sido culpa del Gobierno guatemalteco? .... Teniendolos ya pronto no podía la interesada enviarlos como expositora? ....; á esto nada puede contestar fundamentalmente el que suscribe y tiene que hacer caso omiso de la reclamación de los dos mil pesos.

Solicita en 3er lugar la señorita Cedroni 9600 pesos por cuatro años de la subvención de $ 200 mensuales que dice se le asignaron por el establecimiento y dirección de su Instituto: pero no aparece entre los presentados, documento alguno decretando este auxilio, y la misma interesada confiesa « que no le fué oficialmente comunicado este acuerdo ». Sin embargo, en una comunicación del señor Secretario de Instrucción Pública (n° 3 f. 7) se hace mención de él, como teniendo fecha 27 de junio de 1892. Nada se pagó á la reclamación por este concepto, y siendo cierto que se le había prometido, según el señor Secretario citado, como auxilio ó subvención para el Establecimiento, también lo es que la agraciada obraría y haría probablemente gastos, fundada en esta pensión: parece pues, de equidad, que reciba una parte prudencial de ella.

Queda por último la 4ª reclamación de la señorita Cedroni, sean 48,000 pesos por lucro cesante, y este es el punto más delicado y difícil de apreciar. Parece el distinguido letrado señor don Luis Silvela en su por muchos extremos notable alegato, querer englobar en esta elevado partido la indemnización que haya de darse á la interesada por haberla difamado: y hace notar con este motivo que en todos los países, excepto España, los ataques á la conducta moral de una persona, cuando no resultan probados de una manera categórica y decisiva, se castigan y penan con una fuertísima indemnización. Pero tiene razón el señor Silvela cuando dice que en lo caballeresca tierra del Quijote no ha llegado aún á tasarse, á lavarse con vil metal, la honra mancillada: y el Árbitro que estima que tratándose de una señorita, hasta discutir este punto la empaña, prefiere pasar por alto las acusaciones fundadas en documentos que el señor Silvela califica de extemporáneos y dejar de lado la defensa para no ocuparse de extremo tan delicado y vidrioso.

Veamos únicamente si de haber seguido el establecimiento era probable que la reclamante hubiera ganado 48,000 pesos líquidos y si el Gobierno de Guatemala es responsable de esa ú otra suma por la pérdida de tal beneficio.

Observa el señor Representante de Guatemala, como ampliación al alegato suyo, que si la señorita Cedroni fundaba tan buenas esperanzas en su establecimiento, debió haberlo conservado y continuar al frente de él, para obtener así los ópimos frutos que prometía: pero ha de tenerse presente que la retirada de la protección oficial causa siempre una impresión de gran trascendencia para el establecimiento ó persona que la sufre, y es indudable que si bajo la égida del Gobierno no consiguió la señorita Cedroni (según dice este) gran número de discípulas en los

pocos meses que funcionó el Instituto, menos había de tener cuando se hiciera público que el mismo Gobierno le retiraba de pronto su apoyo, es decir, que desaprobaba de una manera terminante la marcha de la Academia.

Debe también tomarse en cuenta que una empresa del género de que se trata no puede empezar á dar frutos en los primeros meses, ni aún tal vez en el primer año. Las certificaciones ó declaraciones que presenta el Alegato guatemalteco acerca de algunos profesores, dan por cierto las más favorables, pues teniendo una subvención de 200 pesos mensuales, podría ganarse, á lo sumo, la cantidad que representa esta subvención, y como esto es lo que la señorita Cedroni reclama en su 3ª petición puesta también en duda por Guatemala, no parece deba repetirse.

En todo caso el lucro cesante es de dificilísima apreciación y es menester que esté muy justificado para poder admitirlo.

Todo el expediente ofrece dudas y dificultades, y la señorita Cedroni, que es lo que pide, estaba obligada á comprobar y esclarecer los hechos que, desgraciadamente para ella, no han podido ponerse en claro, perjudicándola hasta la misma exageración que evidentemente muestra en la cantidad que reclama.

No es posible in justo, por consiguiente, tomar en cuenta esta parte de su reclamación.

SEGUNDA CUESTIÓN. — De lo expuesto resulta que dos son únicamente las cantidades discutibles en la reclamación de la señorita Cedroni; la primera, de dos mil pesos por gastos de planteamiento del Instituto, y la tercera, de 9600 pesos por la asignación prometida de 200 pesos mensuales durante cuatro años.

Ahora bien, si hubiera podido demostrarse que la falta de cumplimiento de lo pasado, había sido una de las partes solamente, justo era que esa parte fuese la que sufriera todas consecuencias de la falta: pero como según queda dicho antes, ambas partes faltaron en sentir del que suscribe, las dos deben soportar la pérdida consiguiente, partiendo por mitad las dos cantidades que quedan expresadas.

En este supuesto, el Gobierno de Guatemala debe abonar á la reclamante señorita María Cedroni:

Por el primer concepto . . . . . $ 1000
Y por el segundo . . . . » 4800

Sean en junto . . . . $ 5800

(cinco mil ochocientos pesos). Respecto á la moneda en que deba satisfacerse esta cantidad, no cabe la menor duda. En Guatemala se pidió y obtuvo la concesión, allí mismo se prestó el servicio que tuvo lugar y se hubiera prestado todo al no haberse interrumpido, y alli se hubiera ganado ó gastado lo que en último término hubiera de gastarse ó ganarse. Claro es, por consiguiente, que allí, y en moneda de allí, debe hacerse el pago que corresponda por virtud de este laudo.

CONCLUSIÓN. — En suma y para concluir el que suscribe, honrado por Vuestra Excelencia para representar á España como Arbitro en la controversia surgida entre el Gobierno de su Majestad el Rey de Italia y el de la República de Guatemala en la presente contienda, después de bien examinados los antecedentes y pesadas todas las circunstancias, cree que el Gobierno de Guatemala debe abonar á la señorita Maria Cedroni, cinco mil ochocientos pesos en Guatemala y en moneda de plata corriente en Guatemala.

Madrid, 12 de octubre de 1898 [1].

CL. Chili, Pérou.

16 avril 1898.

Le 20 octobre 1883, le Gouvernement du Pérou consentit à ce que l'occupation des provinces de Tacna et d'Arica fût maintenue par le Chili pendant une durée de dix années, à l'expiration desquelles la population serait consultée par un plébiscite sur l'attribution définitive du territoire à l'une ou à l'autre des deux nations intéressées. L'organisation de ce plébiscite donna lieu à de sérieuses difficultés et c'est à leur occasion que le présent arbitrage fut institué.

Nous croyons utile de faire précéder le texte du compromis du texte de l'article qui fut la cause de la contestation.

Tratado de paz y amistad entre las Republicas del Peru y Chile, firmado en Lima a 20 de Octubre, 1883.

. . . .

ART. III. — El territorio de las provincias de Tacna y Arica, que limita por el Norte con el rio Sama, desde su nacimiento en las cordilieras limitrofes con Bolivia hasta su desembocadura en el mar; por el Sur con la quebreda y rio de Camarones: por el Oriente con la Republica de Bolivia, y por el Poniente con el mar Pacifico, continuara poseido por Chile y sujeto

· [1] *Memoria presentada por la Secretaria de Relaciones Exteriores*, Guatemala, 1899. p. 5 15

á la legislacion y autoridades chilenas durante el termino de diez años contados desde que se ratifique el presente tratado de paz. Espirado este plazo, un plebiscito decidira en votacion popular si el territorio de las provincias referidas queda definitivamente del dominio y soberania de Chile, o si continua siendo parte del territorio peruano. Aquel de los dos paises a cuyo favor queden anexadas las provincias de Tacna y Arica, pagara al otro diez millones de pesos moneda chilena de plata o soles peruanos de igual ley y peso que aquella.

Un protocolo especial, que se considerara como parte integrante del presente tratado, establecera la forma en que el plebiscito deba tener lugar y los terminos y plazos en que hayan de pagarse los diez millones por el pais que quedo dueño de las provincias de Tacna y Arica [1].

Tratado relativo a la cuestion de Tacna y Arica, firmado en Santiago, Abril 16, 1898.

Los gobiernos de la Republica de Chile i de la Republica del Peru, deseosos de llegar a una solucion definitiva respecto al dominio i soberania de los territorios de Tacna i Arica, en conformidad al Tratado de Paz de 20 de octubre de 1883, i de estrechar las relaciones de amistad entre ambos pueblos eliminando una cuestion que los ha preocupado desde hace tiempo, despues de examinar i calificar sus respectivos poderes i de encontrarlos bastantes, ajustaron la siguiente convencion, destinada a dar cumplimiento al articulo III del aludido Tratado de 20 de octubre de 1883.

ART. I. — Quedan sometidos al fallo del Gobierno de Su Majestad la Reina Rejente de España, a quien las Altas Partes Contratantes designan con el caracter de Arbitro, los puntos siguientes:

1º Quienes tienen derecho a tomar parte en la votacion plebiscitaria destinada a fijar el dominio i soberania definitivos de los territorios de Tacna i Arica, determinando los requisitos de nacionalidad. sexo, edad, estado civil, residencia o cualesquiera otros que deban reunir los votantes.

2º Si el voto plebiscitario debe ser publico o secreto.

ART. II. — Una Junta Directiva compuesta de un representante del Gobierno de Chile, de un representante del Gobierno del Peru i de un tercero designado por el Gobierno de España, presidira los actos i tomara las resoluciones necesarias para llevar a cabo el plebiscito. Tendra

[1] Perú, *Coleccion de los Tratados*, t. IV, p. 656.

el carácter de Presidente de la Junta el Tercero designado por el Gobierno de España . . . . .

. . . .

ART. XVII. - Dentro del termino de sesenta dias contados desde que queden canjeadas las ratificaciones de la presente Convencion, los representantes diplomaticos de la Republica de Chile i de la Republica del Peru cerca del Gobierno de España solicitaran conjuntamente de este la aceptacion del cargo a que se refiere el articulo 1° i el nombramiento del Tercero que prescribe el articulo 2°.

ART. XVIII. — Dentro del plazo de cuarenta dias, contados desde que el arbitro acepte el cargo, cada una de las Altas Partes Contratantes fundara su derecho en una esposicion escrita que presentara por medio de su Plenipotenciario para que, con ella i en vista de las disposiciones del Tratado de 20 de octubre de 1883 i de la presente Convencion, espida aquel su fallo.

La presente Convencion sera ratificada por los respectivos Congresos i las ratificaciones, canjeadas en Santiago de Chile dentro del mas breve plazo posible [1].

Le parlement chilien refusa d'accepter la convention et des pourparlers sont actuellement en cours au sujet de ce différend.

CLI. Costa Rica, République de l'Amérique centrale.

26 avril 1898.

Il s'est agi dans l'espèce de réclamations réciproques relatives aux relations des deux pays. Déja la guerre était sur le point d'éclater, lorsque le Guatemala interposa sa médiation. Il nous a été impossible de vérifier si la convention arbitrale intervenue a été ratifiée. Dès 1899 la République de l'Amérique centrale avait cessé d'exister.

Tratado de Paz, firmado en aguas neutrales del Oceano Pacífico, el 26 de Abril 1898.

En aguas neutrales del Océano Pacífico, á bordo del navío de guerra de los Estados Unidos *Alert*, generosamente ofrecido para este acta por el Excelentísimo señor don William L. Merry, Ministro Plenipotenciario de los Estados Unidos ante el Gobierno de la República de Costa Rica, hallándose á la altura de Cabo Blanco en el

9° 26' 45" N. latitud y 85° 3' 30" O. longitud, los infrascritos, Ricardo Pacheco, Plenipotenciario de la República de Costa Rica, Manuel Coronel Maltus, Plenipotenciario de la República Mayor de Centro América, y Francisco Lainfiesta, en concepto de amistoso Mediator, Plenipotenciario de la República de Guatemala, canjeados y examinados sus plenos poderes, y hallando los en debida forma, hacen constar en los términos más solemnes : que estando previamente estipulado por las Partes respectivas, concluir por medio de la amistad las desavenencias que disgraciadamente han sobrevenido entre la República de Costa Rica y el Estado de Nicaragua, correspondiente á la República Mayor de Centro América, desavenencias que han dado margen al peligro inminente de la guerra, bajo todos respectos deplorable, hallándose en disposición de llevar á efecto las miras civilizadoras y honrosas que han provocado la presente reunión, formulan y acuerdan los siguientes puntos de avenencia hermanable y pacifica, en virtud de los cuales cesa desde este momento, de una y otra parte de los contendientes, todo intento de hostilidad por medio de las armas y se reblece la buena inteligencia y armonia en que les corresponde existar para bien de los dos pueblos hermanos y honra de Centro América. Por tanto, declaren y convienen :

ARTICULO I. — La República de Costa Rica y la República Mayor de Centro América, respectivamente, defiriendo al amistoso ruego del Gobierno de Guatemala y al justo reclamo de los intereses generales de Centro América, no menos que á las conveniencias de los dos pueblos hermanos de Costa Rica y Nicaragua, hoy en desacuerdo, aceptan libremente el recurso de un convenio pacífico y amigable, que ponga término honroso al conflicto que les ha conducido á tomar las armas.

. . . .

ARTICULO III. - - Ocurriendo al medio civilizador y culto del arbitramento que aun los pueblos guerreros recomiendan para dirimir las cuestiones internacionales, las altas Partes contratantes convienen en someter las mutuas quejas y reclamos que les asistan, al fallo de un Tribunal compuesto de tres centroamericanos, uno nombrado por la República de Costa Rica, uno por la República Mayor de Centro América y un tercero por la República de Guatemala, en su carácter de pacífica mediator.

ARTICULO IV. — Dichos Arbitros se reunirán en la capital de la República de Guatemala dentro del término de un mes después de ratificado este convenio por ambas Partes, para el efecto de organizarse convenientemente y pro-

[1] *Memoria de Relaciones Exteriores*, Chile. 1898. p. 41.

ceder al cumplimiento de su encargo, ajustándose en cuanto á procedimientos arbitrales á las siguientes reglas :

1. Dentro del mes siguiente á la fecha de la instalación del Tribunal, las Partes contratantes, por medio de sus representantes, presentarán por escrito y detalladamente sus respectivas quejas y reclamaciones :

2. El día en que venza el plazo á que se refiere la regla anterior, los Arbitros entregaren á cada Representante de las Partes signatarias copia exacta de las demandas contrarias que les hayan sido sometidas, á efecto de que, dentro del plazo de un mes, contesten lo que á bien tengan :

3. Pasado dicho plazo y presentadas ó no las contestaciones, el Tribunal concederá á las Partes el plazo de un mes para la prueba de los hechos que la requieran ;

4. Vencido este último término y dentro de los dos meses siguientes, dictará el Tribunal su veredicto ;

5. A petición de cualquiera de las Partes ó de oficio, podrá el Tribunal de Arbitros, en cualquier estado del juicio, pedir á cualquiera de las Partes que suministre los documentos, datos ó informes que se soliciten ó se juzgue necessario ó conveniente tener á la vista.

El Tribunal, de acuerdo con ambas Partes, podrá acortar ó ampliar los plazos indicados, para la más pronta terminación del juicio ó para el mejor esclarecimiento de los hechos.

ARTÍCULO V. — Las reclamaciones que una y otra de las Partes tengan que hacerse, sea cual fuere su carácter y alcance, serán sometidas libremente al Tribunal arbitral para que las considere y falle, conforme al Derecho de Gentes, en los términos que considere justos y equitativos.

ARTÍCULO VI. — Ambas Partes declaran que no serán objeto de reclamaciones ante el Arbitro, las cuestiones de límites resueltas en el Tratado de 15 de abril de 1858, en el laudo arbitral del señor Presidente Cleveland ó en la Convención de San Salvador de 1896.

ARTÍCULO VII. — Los jueces de ese Tribunal conocerán y fallarán en el carácter de árbitros arbitradores y amigables componedores, teniendo en cuenta la benevolencia con que cumple sean considerados los incidentes enojosos ocurridos entre hermanos y los beneficios que una transacción inmediata, dictada por la amistad, habrá de derramar sobre los intereses comunes de Centro América.

Ambas Partes contratantes se obligan de la manera más formal y solemne á observar y

cumplir fielmente la sentencia arbitral en lo que á cada una de ellas corresponda, sin dar lugar á reclamación de ninguna especie.

. . . .

ARTÍCULO X. — Este convenio será sometido inmediatamente á la aprobación de las Legislaturas de la República de Costa Rica y del Estado de Nicaragua para el efecto de obtener la aprobación de aquellos altos Cuerpos en lo tocante al sometimiento de las respectivas quejas y reclamaciones á un fallo arbitral, para proceder sin tardanza, después de emitida aquella superior autorización, al cumplimiento de lo establecido en los artículos respectivos de este convenio.

ARTÍCULO XI. — Las Representaciones de Costa Rica y de la República Mayor, á nombre de sus Gobiernos, consignan un voto de gracias al Gobierno de Guatemala por su eficaz cooperación en el avenimiento amigable de las Partes, y á su digno Representante el Honorable señor Ministro Francisco Lainfiesta, que tan noblemente ha sabido interpretar los sentimientos fraternales de su comitente.

En fe de lo cual y de entera conformidad, firmamos y sellamos tres ejemplares de un tenor. como queda dicho, á bordo del navío de guerra de la Marina de los Estados Unidos *Alert* y en presencia de su Capitán E. H. C. Leutzé, que firma igualmente, certificando la posición del buque en aguas neutrales del mar Pacífico, á las cuatro de la tarde del día veintiséis de abril del año de mil ochocientos noventa y ocho [1].

CLII. Etats-Unis d'Amérique, Pérou.

17 mai 1898

Cette affaire a eu pour objet les indemnités dues à un citoyen américain pour la destruction d'un chemin de fer et les violences faites à sa personne. Il lui fut accordé 40,000 $ par une sentence du 15 octobre 1898 qui n'a pas été publiée.

Convencion para someter a arbitraje los perjuicios demandados por Victor H. MacCord, firmado en Washington, el 17 de Mayo de 1898.

La República del Perú y los Estados Unidos de América por medio de sus Representantes. doctor don Victor Eguiguren, Enviado Extraordinario y Ministro Plenipotenciario de la República del Perú, y William R. Day, Secretario de

---

[1] *Memorias de Relaciones Exteriores*, Costa Rica, 1898, p. 103.

Estado de los Estados Unidos de América, han acordado y firmado el siguiente protocolo:

Por cuanto los Estados Unidos de América, en protección del ciudadano de los Estados Unidos de América, Victor H. MacCord, han reclamado una indemnizacion del Gobierno del Perú, por las injurias inflijidas contra aquel, en Arequipa, Perú, en 1885: se ha acordado entre los dos Gobiernos:

I. Que la cuestión del monto de dicha indemnización se someta al muy honorable Sir Samuel Henry Strong P. C. Justicia Mayor de la Suprema Corte del Canadá, á quien por la presente se nombra árbitro para que conozca de dicha causa y determine el monto de la expresada indemnización.

II. El Gobierno de los Estados Unidos de América presentará al árbitro las pruebas del reclamante y las que han sido presentadas por el Gobierno del Perú. El Gobierno de los Estados Unidos proporcionará al Ministro del Perú una lista de esas pruebas.

III. Habiendo condescendido el Gobierno del Perú, como un acto de deferencia á los Estados Unidos, en excluir del arbitraje la cuestión de su responsabilidad ó irresponsabilidad, el árbitro limitará su decisión y fallo al siguiente punto que es el único que se somete á su decisión: determinar, en vista de las pruebas que le serán presentadas, el monto de la indemnización pecuniaria que ha de pagarse á Mr. Victor H. MacCord, por los actos cometidos contra él en Arequipa, Perú, en 1885. Habiendo el Gobierno de los Estados Unidos negádose á someter á arbitraje ninguna otra cuestión que no sea el monto de los perjuicios que deban indemnizarse, el Gobierno del Perú ha accedido á poner de un lado la cuestión de su irresponsabilidad, y á permitir que el árbitro tome conocimiento del asunto para determinar la suma que cree que debe darse á MacCord, asumiendo el Gobierno del Perú la obligación de pagar esa suma. Las pruebas serán presentadas al árbitro el 1º de julio de 1898 ó antes: y el fallo se expedirá en el término de dos meses, de la fecha de la presentación de las pruebas.

IV. Cada Gobierno podrá presentar al árbitro, un alegato, antes del 10 de agosto de 1898: pero el árbitro no está obligado por tal motivo a demorar su decisión.

V. El Gobierno del Perú pagará la suma fijada por el árbitro, tan pronto como el Congreso del Perú autorice el pago: pero en ningún caso podrá demorar más de 6 meses contados desde la fecha del fallo.

VI. Una rasonable compensación por el árbitro y los demás gastos del arbitraje se pagarán por mitad por ambos Gobiernos.

VII. El fallo del árbitro será final y definitivo.

Hecho por duplicado, en Washington, hoy 17 de mayo de 1898[1].

CLIII. Allemagne, Etats-Unis d'Amérique. Grande-Bretagne.

7 novembre 1899.

Simple question d'indemnités réclamées par des citoyens des trois pays respectivement à raison des événements survenus à Samoa.

Convention between the United States of America, Germany and Great Britain relating to the settlement of certain claims in Samoa by Arbitration, done at Washington, November 7, 1899.

The President of the United States of America, His Majesty the German Emperor, King of Prussia, in the name of the German Empire, and Her Majesty the Queen of the United Kingdom of Great Britain and Ireland, being desirous of effecting a prompt and satisfactory settlement of the claims of the citizens and subjects of their respective countries resident in the Samoan Islands on account of recent military operations conducted there, and having resolved to conclude a Convention for the accomplishment of this and by means of arbitration, have appointed as their respective plenipotentiaries:

The President of the United States of America the Honorable John Hay, Secretary of State of the United States:

His Majesty the German Emperor, King of Prussia His Minister in Extraordinary Mission, Dr. Jur. Mumm von Schwarzenstein, Privy Councilor of Legation; and

Her Majesty the Queen of the United Kingdom of Great Britain and Ireland, Mr. Reginald Tower, Her Britannic Majesty's Chargé d'Affaires ad interim:

Who, after having communicated to each other their full powers, which were found to be in due and proper form, have agreed to and concluded the following articles:

ARTICLE I. — All claims put forward by American citizens or German or British subjects respectively, whether individuals or companies, for compensation on account of losses which they allege that they have suffered in consequence of unwarranted military action, if this be shown to have occurred, on the part of American, German or British officers between the first of January last and the arrival of the Joint Commission in Samoa shall be decided by Arbitration in conformity with the principles of International Law or considerations of equity.

ARTICLE II. — The three Governments shall request His Majesty the King of Sweden and Norway to accept the office of Arbitrator. It shall also be decided by this Arbitration whether and eventually to what extent, either of the three Governments is bound, alone or jointly with the others, to make good these losses.

ARTICLE III. — Either of the three Governments may, with the consent of the others, previously obtained in every case, submit to the King for Arbitration, similar claims of persons not being natives, who are under the protection of that Government, and who are not included in the above mentioned categories.

ARTICLE IV. — The present Convention shall be duly ratified by the President of the United States of America, by and with the advice and consent of the Senate thereof, and by His Majesty the German Emperor, King of Prussia : and by Her Majesty the Queen of the United Kingdom of Great Britain and Ireland : and the ratifications shall be exchanged at Washington four months from the date hereof, or earlier if possible.

In faith whereof, we, the respective Plenipotentiaries, have signed this Convention and have hereunto affixed our seals.

Done in triplicate at Washington the seventh day of November, one thousand eight hundred and ninety-nine[1].

CLIV. Italie, Pérou.

25 novembre 1899.

Dans cette affaire il s'est agi d'indemnités réclamées par des citoyens italiens pour dommages soufferts pendant la guerre civile de 1894-1895. La mission de juger le différend fut confiée au Ministre d'Espagne.

Acuerdo diplomático para el arreglo de las reclamaciones italianas, firmado, en Lima, á los 25 días del mes de noviembre 1899.

Reunidos los señores doctor don Manuel M. Gálvez, Ministro de Relaciones Exteriores del Perú, y Giuseppe Pirrone, Enviado Extraordinario y Ministro Plenipotenciario de Italia, para

---

[1] *Treaty series*, 1900, n° 10.

tratar nuevamente de las reclamaciones de los súbditos italianos residentes en el Perú, por daños ocasionados en la última guerra civil de 1894-1895, y no habiendo sido posible llegar á una inteligencia respecto del modo de transigirlas directamente, han convenido en dar forma al acuerdo á que se refieren las notas cambiadas entre ambos, para someter al arbitraje del Representante de España en este país, la solución definitiva de las mencionadas reclamaciones, y han fijado las bases siguientes :

ART. I. — El Enviado Extraordinario y Ministro Plenipotenciario de España en este país, don Ramiro Gil de Uribarri, queda ampliamente facultado para fallar ó transigir como árbitro, en conformidad con la cláusula 2ª de este acuerdo, todas las reclamaciones que, presentadas al Ministerio de Relaciones Exteriores del Perú, por la Real Legación de Italia dentro del plazo fijado en el decreto peruano de 21 de marzo de 1896, y patrocinadas por ella, tienen por causa los daños y perjuicios ocasionados a los súbditos italianos residentes en el Perú, durante la guerra civil de 1894-1895.

ART. II. — El señor Ministro de España juzgará y resolverá los reclamos citados :

a. Con arreglo al tratado vigente entre Perú é Italia, á los principios del derecho internacional y á las prácticas y jurisprudencia establecidas :

b. En vista y en mérito de los expedientes ya organizados y que existen en el Ministerio de Relaciones Exteriores y que éste le entregará desde luego ;

c. Tomando en consideración las alegaciones, simplemente expositivas, que las partes deberán presentarle ; y

d. Solicitando las demás pruebas y referencias que estime necesarias.

El árbitro exigirá, previamente, la comprobación de la nacionalidad y carácter neutral del reclamante, y cuando éste actúe como mandatario, la justificación de su personería.

Es entendido que no existe, para los reclamantes, el derecho de presentar nuevos expedientes ó pruebas, sino cuando ellas fuesen solicitadas por el árbitro para aclarar ó ilustrar su juicio.

ART. III. — El Gobierno del Perú se reserva el derecho de nombrar un personero, representante, abogado ó agente, que atienda á la defensa, ante el árbitro, de sus intereses, en todas ó cada una de las reclamaciones citadas. La Real Legación de Su Majestad, ó los respectivos reclamantes, conservan igual derecho.

ART. IV. — El señor Ministro de España queda en libertad de emplear, en el desempeño de su encargo, en calidad de secretario ó empleado, á la persona ó personas que estime precisas.

ART. V. — Queda reservado al árbitro el derecho de juzgar y fallar las reclamaciones, ó de resolverlas, á medida que lo estime conveniente.

ART. VI. — Los fallos del Enviado Extraordinario y Ministro Plenipotenciario de España, serán inapelables, y tanto el Ministro de Relaciones Exteriores del Perú, como el Enviado Extraordinario y Ministro Plenipotenciario de Italia, declaran, que tales decisiones se respeterán de un modo absoluto, feneciendo con ellas las reclamaciones de que se trata.

ART. VII. — Los gastos que este compromiso ocasione se abonarán, preferentemente, de las cantidades juzgadas en favor de los respectivos reclamantes, en la proporción que el árbitro fije.

No se considera entre esos gastos el pago de honorarios á los defensores ó agentes, que el Gobierno del Perú y los reclamantes sufragarán por su cuenta.

ART. VIII. — El total de las sumas que pudiera resultar reconocido en favor de uno ó mas reclamantes, se abonará por el Gobierno del Perú á la Real Legación de Italia, en tres dividendos anuales consecutivos, comenzando desde el año próximo, y quedando la Real Legación facultada para preferir en el pago ó applicación de esos dividendos, á los reclamantes mas menesterosos.

ART. IX. — El árbitro tendrá, para evacuar su encargo, el plazo de seis meses, que se prorrogará, por grave motivo, á juicio del mismo.

En fe de lo cual, firman este acuerdo, por duplicado, y lo sellan con sus sellos respectivos, en Lima, á los veinticinco dias del mes de noviembre de mil ochocientos noventa y nueve[1].

CLV. Etats-Unis d'Amérique, Guatemala.

23 février 1900.

Il s'est agi, en l'espèce, d'une réclamation faite par un citoyen américain. Ni le compromis originaire, ni la sentence n'ont été publiés.

Supplemental protocol to the Agreement of February 23, 1900, signed at Washington, May 10, 1900.

Whereas a protocol was signed at Washington, February 23, 1900, between the Secretary of State of the United States and the Envoy Extraordinary and Minister Plenipotentiary of the

[1] *Memoria de Relaciones Exteriores*, Perú. 1900. p. 645.

Republic of Guatemala for submission to an arbitrator of certain issues involved in the claim and counterclaim of Robert H. May and Guatemala as specified in said protocol; and

Whereas it is stipulated in Article II of said protocol as follows, to wit:

« That within thirty days from the date of the signing of this protocol, each party shall furnish to the other and to the arbitrator a copy of the memorial on which its own claim is based: and within ninety days after such signing each Government shall furnish to the other and to the arbitrator copies of all the documents, papers, accounts, official correspondence and other evidence on file at their respective Foreign Offices relating to these claims, and of all affidavits of their respective witnesses relating thereto: Provided, the said arbitrator may request either Government to furnish such additional proof as he may deem necessary in the interests of justice, and each Government agrees to comply with said request as far as possible: but he shall not for such purpose delay his decision »: and

Whereas it is stipulated by Article III of said protocol as follows, to wit:

« That each Government by its counsel, and said May by his attorney, may severally submit to said arbitrator an argument in writing touching the questions involved within sixty days from the date limited for the submission of the evidence: but the Arbitrator shall not for such purpose nor in any event delay his decision beyond four months from the date of the submission to him of the evidence aforesaid »:

Whereas it is stipulated by Article IV of said protocol as follows, to wit:

« It shall be the duty of said arbitrator to decide both cases upon such evidence as may have been filed before him and solely upon the issues of law and fact presented by claim and counterclaim and upon the consideration of said entire controversy he shall render an award in favor of the party entitled thereto: which shall not exceed the amount claimed by said party as shown by the evidence, and interest thereon from the time said sums were due until the date of the award, and said award shall bear six per cent interest from said date until paid. »

It is agreed between the two Governments that said Article II be, and the same is hereby, amended to read as follows, to wit : —

« That within ninety days from the date of the signing of the original protocol each party shall have furnished to the arbitrator and to the other a copy of the memorial on which its own claim is based: and within one hundred and fifty days after such signing each Government shall furnish to the arbitrator and to the other copies of all the documents, papers, accounts, official correspondence and other evidence on file at their respective Foreign Offices relating to these claims, and of all affidavits of their respective witnesses relating thereto: Provided, that said arbitrator may request either Government to furnish such additional proof as he may deem necessary in the interest of justice, and each Government agrees to comply with said request as far as possible. »

It is agreed that said Article III, be, and it is hereby, amended to read as follows, to wit:

« That each Government by its counsel, and said May by his attorney, may severally submit to said arbitrator an argument in writing touching the questions involved within ninety days from the date limited for the submission of the evidence: but the arbitrator shall not for such purpose nor in any event delay his decision beyond six months from the date of the submission to him of the evidence aforesaid. »

It is agreed that said Article IV be, and it is hereby amended to read as follows:

« It shall be the duty of said arbitrator to decide both cases upon such evidence as may have been filed before him and solely upon the issues of law and fact presented by the claim and upon the consideration of said entire controversy, he shall render an award in favor of the party entitled thereto: which shall not exceed the amount claimed by said party and interest at the rate of six per cent per annum thereon from the time said sums were due until the date of the award, and said award shall bear six per cent interest per annum from said date until paid. »

Done in duplicate in English and Spanish at Washington this 10th day of May, 1900.

CLVI. Etats-Unis d'Amérique, Nicaragua.

22 mars 1900.

Cette affaire a également pour objet des réclamations de citoyens américains à charge du gouvernement du Nicaragua. La sentence n'a pas été publiée encore.

Agreement for the arbitration of the claims of Orr and Laubenheimer and the Post-Glover Electric Company, signed at Washington, March 22, 1900.

The United States of America and the Republic of Nicaragua, through their representatives, John Hay, Secretary of State of the United States of America and Luis F. Corea, Envoy Extraordi-nary and Minister Plenipotentiary of the Republic of Nicaragua have agreed upon and signed the following protocol.

Whereas the said Orr and Laubenheimer, citizens of the United States of America, have claimed through the Government of the United States from the Government of Nicaragua indemnity on account of damages sustained through the alleged seizure and detention by Nicaraguan authorities of said Orr and Laubenheimer's steam launches the « Buena Ventura » and the « Alerta »: and

Whereas the said Post-Glover Electric Company, a citizen of the United States of America, has claimed through the Government of the United States from the Government of Nicaragua indemnity on account of the alleged seizure at Bluefields of certain goods and chattels of the Post-Glover Electric Company:

It is agreed between the two Governments:

I. — That the question of the amount of the indemnity in each of said cases shall be referred to General E. P. Alexander, who is hereby appointed as Arbitrator to hear said cases and to determine the respective amounts of said indemnities.

II. — The Government of the United States will lay before the arbitrator and before the Nicaraguan Government a copy of all the correspondence sent and received by and on file in the Department of State in relation to said claims.

III. — The Government of the United States having declined to submit any matter in dispute herein to arbitration, except the amount of indemnity to be awarded in each of said cases, the Government of Nicaragua, as an act of deference to the United States, waives its denial of liability in said cases and agrees that said Arbitrator may award such sum as he believes said Orr and Laubenheimer and said Post-Glover Electric Company may be justly entitled to: but the award shall not exceed the amount claimed in the memorials filed in the Department of State in each case.

IV. -- The said evidence is to be submitted to the Nicaraguan Government and to the arbitrator on or before the first day of May 1900, who may if he deems it necessary in the interests of justice, require the production of further evidence and each Government agrees to comply with said request so far as possible: but he shall not for that purpose delay his decision beyond July 1, 1900.

V. — Each Government may furnish to the arbitrator an argument or brief not later than

June 1, 1900, but the arbitrator need not for that purpose delay his decision.

VI. — The Government of Nicaragua shall pay the indemnity fixed by the arbitrator, if any, in American gold or its equivalent in silver, at the General Treasury at Mangua, as soon as the Legislative Assembly of Nicaragua shall authorize the payment, but the time thus allowed shall in no case exceed six months from the day the decision is pronounced, unless an extension of time of its payment should be granted by the Government of the United States.

VII. — Reasonable compensation to the arbitrator is to be paid in equal moieties by both Governments.

VIII. — Any award given by the arbitrator shall be final and conclusive.

Done in duplicate at Washington this 22d day of March 1900.

CLVII. Brésil, Etats-Unis d'Amérique.

15 octobre 1842.

Il s'est agi, dans cette affaire, de la saisie du schooner John S. Bryan, opérée dans la province de Para, en juin 1836. Des commissaires furent désignés par les deux gouvernements le 15 octobre 1842 pour fixer les indemnités à allouer. Le 12 juin 1843 ils accordèrent une somme de 26 contos de reis[1].

CLVIII. Etats-Unis d'Amérique, Salvador.

4 mai 1864.

Un citoyen américain, Henry Savage, avait importé au Salvador, en 1851, une certaine quantité de poudre, lorsqu'en 1852 un décret transforma en monopole gouvernemental le commerce de ce produit. Le gouvernement du Salvador se refusa à tout arrangement avec l'importateur dont le négoce se trouva paralysé. Il fallut l'intervention officielle du gouvernement américain pour aboutir à l'acceptation d'un arbitrage ; la sentence, rendue le 21 février 1865, accorda une indemnité de 4497 $ 50 plus les intérêts à six pour cent depuis le 10 décembre 1852.

Ni le compromis, ni la sentence n'ont été publiés[2].

CLIX. Chili, Grande-Bretagne.

4 juin 1875.

Il n'existe au sujet de cette affaire qu'un document parlementaire anglais du 10 juillet 1874, d'après lequel il résulte que la perte du navire Tacna, due au chargement intempestif du pont, aurait été imputable aux autorités locales de Valparaiso, pour avoir permis le départ de ce navire malgré la situation dangereuse dans laquelle il se trouvait.

Des pourparlers diplomatiques auraient abouti au choix, comme arbitre, de l'Empereur d'Allemagne[1].

CLX. Colombie, Equateur.

28 juin 1884.

Cette affaire aurait eu pour objet la fixation des indemnités dues à des citoyens colombiens. Le tribunal arbitral se serait réuni à Quito le 11 février 1887. Il accorda 16 indemnités au total de 78,598 $ 76 ; 10 furent repoussées, 4 retirées et 7 réservées[2].

CLXI. Espagne, Grande-Bretagne.

... avril 1887.

Demande d'indemnité à raison d'une collision maritime occasionnée par le Don Jorge Juan et subie par la Mary Mark. La sentence serait du 5 décembre 1887[3].

CLXII. Congo, Portugal.

7 février 1890.

Par deux notes identiques, datées l'une de Bruxelles et l'autre de Berne, le 7 février 1890, les gouvernements intéressés demandèrent au Conseil fédéral suisse d'accepter les fonctions d'arbitre éventuel pour les différends qui sur-

---

[1] J. B. MOORE, *History and Digest . . .*, p. 4613 donne les quelques renseignements reproduits par nous. Il nous a été impossible de les vérifier.

[2] J. B. MOORE, *History and Digest...*, p. 1855.

[1] *Foreign affairs of United States*, 1875-1876, p. 199.

[2] *Informe de relaciones exteriores*, Colombie, 1888, p. 38 ; 1890, p. 16 ; 1892, p. 13.

[3] J. B. MOORE, *History and Digest . . .*, p. 5017.

giraient entre eux à l'occasion de la détermination de leurs confins en Afrique. Dès le 18 février, le Conseil fédéral répondit affirmativement. Les difficultés survenues furent réglées directement entre les parties par une convention signée à Bruxelles le 25 mai 1891[1].

CLXIII. France, Grande-Bretagne.
.... 1892.

Relatif à la frappe de la monnaie de Zanzibar concédée à un sieur Greffülhe, cet arbitrage donna lieu à une sentence rendue par un membre du Parlement anglais, M. Martin, le 19 juillet 1893. Seules les plaidoiries ont été publiées[2].

CLXIV. Chili, France.
.... 1897.

Arbitrage relatif à un transport d'émigrants opéré par le vapeur Cheribon. Les arbitres désignés auraient été MM. Decrais et Blest Gana, et le surarbitre, M. Edmond Monson. Une somme de 200,000 francs aurait été allouée[3].

CLXV. Grande-Bretagne, Honduras.
... mars 1899.

Il s'est agi, dans cette affaire, de l'arrestation du capitaine du schooner Lottie May et de la détention de ce navire pendant six jours. L'arbitre choisi fut le Chargé d'affaires des Etats-Unis d'Amérique[4].

CLXVI. Etats-Unis d'Amérique, Russie.
8 septembre 1900.

Arbitrage consacré à la capture de navires dans la Mer de Behring. Confié à M. Asser, membre du Conseil d'Etat des Pays-Bas, il est actuellement pendant devant lui. Ces navires, les schooners James Hamilton Lewis, C. H. White, Kate and Anna et le baleinier Cape Horn Pigeon se livraient à la chasse aux phoques à fourrures. C'est par l'échange de déclarations identiques que l'arbitrage fut institué.

Ces déclarations ont eu pour objet de régler la procédure dans les conditions suivantes :

Parmi les preuves à fournir par les parties pourront être comprises toutes preuves déjà présentées dans la correspondance entre les représentants officiels des deux hautes parties contractantes.

L'échange des memorandums et contre-memorandums entre les parties est réglé conformément à l'usage qui s'est établi pour les arbitrages internationaux.

Après l'échange des memorandums aucune communication, ni écrite, ni verbale, ne pourra être adressée à l'arbitre, à moins que celui-ci ne s'adresse lui-même aux parties ou à l'une d'entre elles pour obtenir des renseignements supplémentaires. La partie qui donnera des renseignements à l'arbitre fera parvenir immédiatement une copie de ces renseignements à l'autre partie et celle-ci pourra, si bon lui semble, en déans un mois après la réception de cette copie, transmettre par écrit à l'arbitre ses observations sur le contenu de cette communication.

Il appartient à l'arbitre de statuer sur toutes les questions qui pourraient surgir relativement à la procédure, dans le cours de l'arbitrage.

Dans sa sentence, qui sera rendue, dans toutes les clauses soumises à sa décision, dans un délai de six mois à partir de la réception du dernier memorandum, l'arbitre se réglera sur les principes généraux du droit des gens et sur l'esprit des accords internationaux applicables à la matière, qui étaient en vigueur et obligatoires pour les parties impliquées dans le litige, au moment où la saisie des navires a eu lieu.

L'arbitre déclarera à l'égard de chaque réclamation formulée à la charge du Gouvernement Impérial de Russie si elle est bien fondée et, dans l'affirmative, il fixera le montant de l'indemnité due.

Sans dispenser la partie demanderesse de l'obligation de justifier les dommages soufferts, l'arbitre pourra, s'il le juge opportun, inviter chaque gouvernement à désigner un expert commercial pour l'aider à fixer le montant de l'indemnité.

Chaque gouvernement prend à sa charge toutes les dépenses faites ou à faire pour soutenir son point de vue dans l'affaire et la moitié des honoraires de l'arbitre.

La sentence de l'arbitre, prononcée dans les limites du compromis sera acceptée comme jugement en dernier ressort par les deux parties, qui s'y soumettront sans aucune réserve.

La langue française est reconnue comme la langue officielle de l'arbitrage et la sentence sera rendue dans cette langue.

---

[1] *Feuille fédérale*, Suisse, 1890, vol. I, p. 644; — *Rapport du Conseil fédéral*, 1891, p. 126.
[2] J. B. MOORE, *History and Digest . . .*, p. 4939.
[3] *Memoria de Relaciones Exteriores*, Chili, 1897, p. 99 et 1899, p. 73.
[4] *Foreign Relations of the United States*, 1899, p. 371.

ADDENDA.

IV. Etats-Unis d'Amérique, Grande-Bretagne.

20 octobre 1818.

La sentence dont nous donnons le texte plus loin, n'a été publiée, à notre connaissance, que traduite en anglais.

His Imperial Majesty's Award in the difference between the United States of America and Great Britain, done at St. Petersburg, 22d April, 1822.

Invited by the United States of America and by Great Britain to give an opinion, as Arbitrator, in the differences which have arisen between these two Powers, on the subject of the interpretation of the first article of the treaty which they concluded at Ghent, on the 24th December, 1814, the Emperor has taken cognizance of all the acts, memorials, and notes in which the respective Plenipotentiaries have set forth to his administration of foreign affairs the arguments upon which each of the litigant parties depends in support of the interpretation given by it to the said article.

After having maturely weighed the observations exhibited on both sides :

Considering that the American Plenipotentiary and the Plenipotentiary of Britain have desired that the discussion should be closed;

Considering that the former, in his note of the 4th (16th) November, 1821, and the latter, in his note of the 8th (20th) October, of the same year, have declared that it is upon the construction of the text of the article as it stands, that the Arbitrator's decision should be founded, and that both have appealed, only as a subsidiary mean, to the general principles of the law of nations and of maritime law ;

The Emperor is of opinion that the question can only be decided according to the literal and grammatical sense of the first article of the Treaty of Ghent.

As to the literal and grammatical sense of the first article of the Treaty of Ghent :

Considering that the stipulation upon the signification of which doubts have arisen, is expressed as follows :

‹ All territory, places, and possessions whatsoever, taken by either party from the other during the war, or which may be taken after the signing of this treaty, excepting only the islands hereinafter mentioned, shall be restored without delay, and without causing any destruction or carrying away any of the artillery or other public property *originally captured in the said forts or places, and which shall remain therein upon the exchange of the ratifications of this treaty*, or any slaves, or other private property ; and all archives, records, deeds, and papers, either of a public nature, or belonging to private persons, which, in the course of the war, may have fallen into the hands of the officers of either party, shall be, as far as may be practicable, forthwith restored and delivered to the proper authorities and persons to whom they respectively belong.›

Considering that, in this stipulation, the words *originally captured, and which shall remain therein upon the exchange of ratifications*, form an incidental phrase, which can have respect, *grammatically*, only to the substantives or subjects which precede ;

That the first article of the Treaty of Ghent thus prohibits the contracting parties from carrying away, from the places of which it stipulates the restitution, not only the public property *which might have been originally captured there, and which should remain therein upon the exchange of the ratifications*, but that it prohibits the carrying away from these same places *any private property* whatever :

That, on the other hand, these two prohibitions are solely applicable to the places of which the article stipulates the restitution ;

The Emperor is of opinion :

That the United States of America are entitled to a just indemnification, from Great Britain, for all private property carried away by the British forces ; and as the question regards slaves more especially, for all such slaves as were carried away by the British forces, from the places and territories of which the restitution was stipulated by the treaty, in quitting the said places and territories ;

That the United States are entitled to consider, as having been so carried away, all such slaves as may have been transported from the above-mentioned territories on board of the British vessels within the waters of said territories, and who, for this reason, have not been restored ;

But that, if there should be any American slaves who where carried away from the territories of which the first article of the Treaty of Ghent has not stipulated the restitution to the United States, the United States are not to claim an indemnification for the said slaves.

The Emperor declares, besides, that he is ready to exercise the office of mediator, which has been conferred on him beforehand by the two States, in the negotiations which must ensue between them in consequence of the award which they have demanded.

Done at St. Petersburg, 22d April, 1822[1].

XI. Etats-Unis d'Amérique, Nouvelle Grenade.

10 septembre 1857.

Nous donnons ci-dessous le texte de la convention de 1864 à laquelle nous avons fait allusion plus haut, p. 35.

Convention between the United States of America and the United States of Columbia to extend the time for the adjustment of claims, done at Washington, 10th February, 1864.

Whereas a Convention for the adjustment of claims was concluded between the United States of America and the Republic of New Granada, in the city of Washington, on the tenth of September, 1857, which convention, as afterward amended by the contracting parties, was proclaimed by the President of the United States on the 8th November, 1860 ;

And whereas the Joint Commission organized under the authority conferred by the preceding mentioned convention did fail, by reason of uncontrollable circumstances, to decide all the claims laid before them under its provisions, within the time to which their proceedings were limited by the 4th article thereof ;

The United States of America and the United States of Colombia, the latter representing the late Republic of New Granada, are desirous that

the time originally fixed for the duration of the commission should be so extended as to admit the examination and adjustment of such claims as were presented to but not settled by the joint commission aforesaid, and to this end have named Plenipotentiaries to agree upon the best mode of accomplishing this object, that is to say :

The President of the United States of America, William H. Seward, Secretary of State of the United States of America, and the President of the United States of Colombia, senor Manuel Murillo, Envoy Extraordinary and Minister Plenipotentiary of the United States of Colombia ;

Who, having exchanged their full powers, have agreed as follows :

ARTICLE I. — The high contracting parties agree that the time limited in the convention above referred to for the termination of the commission, shall be extended for a period not exceeding nine months from the exchange of ratifications of this convention, it being agreed that nothing in this article contained shall in any other wise alter the provisions of the convention above referred to ; and that the contracting parties shall appoint commissioners anew, and an umpire shall be chosen anew, in the manner and with the duties and powers respectively expressed in the said former convention.

ARTICLE II. — The present convention shall be ratified, and the ratifications shall be exchanged at Washington as soon as possible.

In witness whereof the respective Plenipotentiaries have signed the same, and have hereunto affixed their seals.

Done at Washington this tenth day of February, in the year of our Lord one thousand eight hundred and sixty-four[1].

XIII. Etats-Unis d'Amérique, Paraguay.

4 février 1859.

Nous reproduisons ci-dessous la sentence intervenue dans la présente affaire ainsi que les motifs sur lesquels elle a été basée. La somme réclamée se montait à 402,250 $ 37.

Award given the 13th of August, 1860, in the arbitration between the United States of America and the Republic of Paraguay.

And now, on this thirteenth day of August, anno Domini one thousand eight hundred and sixty, the undersigned, commissioners appointed and empowered respectively, as appears fully in the aforegoing record, having heard and maturely

---

[1] J. B. MOORE, *History and Digest . . .*, p. 360.

[1] *Treaties and Conventions between the United States and other Powers*, 1776-1887, p. 213.

considered the 'proofs of the charges and defenses of the contending parties', in respect of the 'claims of the United States and Paraguay Navigation Company—a company composed of citizens of the United States—against the Government of Paraguay', and having conferred together and deliberated upon the same and upon the printed arguments of counsel thereupon, in virtue of the powers invested in them by the convention in this record recited and set forth, do hereby determine and award :

That the said claimants, 'The United States and Paraguay Navigation Company', have not proved or established any right to damages upon their said claim against the government of the Republic of Paraguay ; and that, upon the proofs aforesaid, the said government is not responsible to the said company in any damages or pecuniary compensation whatever, in all the premises.

In testimony whereof, the said commissioners have hereunto subscribed their names and directed the attestation of the secretary and interpreter the day and year aforesaid [1].

The United States and Paraguay Navigation Company had been organized by an association of enterprising citizens of Rhode Island in the fall of 1852, and chartered by the legislature of that State in June 1853. The capital was one hundred thousand dollars, with liberty to increase it to a million, for the general purposes of trade.

M[r] E. A. Hopkins, who had been mainly instrumental in getting up the company, became its general agent for the transaction of its business south of the equator, with a salary of two thousand dollars per annum, and by the same contract entitled to five per centum on its profits, until his share of the profits should reach thirty thousand dollars, when he was to be paid ten thousand dollars in cash, and the other twenty thousand dollars in stock of the company at par. He had been likewise appointed the consul of the United States for Paraguay.

M[r] Hopkins had resided many years in that country. His favorable accounts of the valley of the La Plata, of the fertility of its soil, its salubrious climate, the absence of industry and entreprise among its citizens, their total ignorance of the mechanical arts, commerce, and agricultural pursuits, presented to his associates a field for entreprise that promised, in their estimation, unbounded wealth, such as had· never been realized, except by British merchants in the East Indies.

Paraguay was selected as the chief theater of their operations ; but the contract with

[1] J. B. MOORE, *History and Digest* . . . , p. 1501.

M[r] Hopkins constituted him their agent for all parts south of the equator indicating a more extended field.

For thirty years the government of that country, nominally a republic, had been, under the control of Doctor Francia, an absolute despotism. His policy had excluded foreigners, and prohibited all intercourse with foreign nations ; had paralyzed the industry of the country, and rendered its population entirely subservient to his will.

Upon his death, which occurred nearly twenty years ago, Carlos Antonio Lopez had been selected as his successor, under a modified government, and with the title of President. He had the sagacity to see the evil influences experienced by the people from the policy adopted by the dictator, and patriotism enough to seek a remedy. He encouraged the arts and industry by the most liberal patent laws, securing rights for inventions, improvements, and the introduction of new and useful machines, thereby promoting agricultural and mechanical industry ; and still more, by opening to commerce the great rivers Parana and Paraguay, which nearly surround the country. In the efforts to improve the condition of the citizens, long accustomed to oppression and injustice, he could not fail to perceive that such a change in their condition, to be permanently beneficial, must necessarily be gradual.

He found the republic surrounded by states constantly in agitation, at war with each other and among themselves ; all was anarchy and disorder. Under such circumstances it was no easy task to establish order and peace and to promote industry and the arts among his own people. It could only be accomplished by a firmness, vigor, and energy in his administration which would be regarded in other countries (more enlightened and more accustomed to self-government) as tyrannical and oppressive. It could scarcely be expected that the ideas of rights of person and property, of political and civil liberty, and the administration of justice, as understood and practiced in the States of this Union, could be at once introduced and put into successful operation in the infancy of a republic like Paraguay.

That a more rapid advancement of industry and civilization has been attained under his administration is generally conceded. Proceeding in this spirit he seems to have hailed with alacrity the prospect of friendly relations with the United States.

Captain Page, in his narrative of the scientific expedition under his command, says that the government extended to him a serie of national courtesies, which commanded his respect. « Indeed (he says), government hospitalities represent a characteristic of the Paraguayans. A more generous, singlehearted people it is impossible to find, and they have a native tact which rarely offends even the conventional ideas of those who have associated more with the outer world. »

The kindest treatment was extended to him and his officers until the rupture with Hopkins. Upon the arrival of Consul Hopkins and his employees, which took place in the fall of 1853, they were received with the utmost cordiality, and every possible aid generously extended to them. The soldiers of the republic were turned out of a barrack for their accommodation, without any compensation for its use. Aid was cheerfully given to Mr Hopkins for the selection of suitable sites for the works he contemplated. Laborers were selected and ordered into his service, for a very moderate compensation: and when President Lopez found the company embarrassed with disasters, and with the debts they contracted, he liberally and generously extended to them an accommodation of ten thousand dollars for two years, from the treasury.

Stronger evidence of a desire to cultivate the good will of the company, and to secure the confidence and respect of the citizens of the United States, could not have been given than was exhibited in the conduct of President Lopez, and the citizens generally, in courtesies and favors freely and cheerfully extended to Captain Page, his officers and men, and to the agent and servants of the United States and Paraguay Navigation Company.

Many of these acts, so beneficial to these claimants, were of a nature peculiar to a government of strong powers, and a people unaccustomed to question their extent, and without which the establishment could not have been put in operation. Mr Hopkins in his letter to Governor Marcy, of 22d August 1854, says, I knew well enough its [the government's] arbitrary character, and believed the people to be unfit to govern themselves.

Mr Hopkins, then, with a full knowledge of the institutions and laws, the customs and habits of the people, voluntarily selected for himself and employees that country as a residence and place of business. Thus they became entitled, as citizens of the United States resident in Paraguay, to all the immunities, rights, and privileges granted to the people of that State by their laws, and made themselves equally liable with them to the penalties and punishments imposed for an infraction of those laws. And more, as citizens of the United States, they owed it to themselves and to their own country, as well as to the infant republic just emerging from tyranny and oppression, to have set an example of forbearance, moderation, and justice that would have reflected honor upon the institutions of their own country, and have inspired the people of Paraguay with new zeal and energy in their struggles to secure for themselves institutions producing such results.

Whilst the company were indulging in golden dreams of untold wealth seldom if ever realized, there seems to have been lurking in the mind of their agent, Hopkins, an enthusiasm for progress and civilization and reform approaching fanaticism, which led him to censure other institutions than those of his own country, and to condemn the conduct of other public officers with whom he was brought into connection by his consular position, whose ideas did not conform to his visionary notions.

Mr Hopkins continued to act as general agent of the company, as a partner, and as consul of the United States, until the 1st September 1854, when his exequatur was withdrawn by President Lopez and he and his employees abandoned the country, alleging that they *were expelled, their business broken up,* and their property confiscated by him. For these alleged wrongs and injuries heavy damages are demanded.

A question arose, upon the opening statements of the counsel for the claimants and the republic of Paraguay respectively, touching the jurisdiction and duty of the commission to inquire into the origin and nature of the transactions upon which this claim was based, so as to determine whether, in fact and law, the republic of Paraguay owed any pecuniary satisfaction whatever to the claimants.

The question was discussed orally by counsel, after the reading of their opening papers, and was again treated to some extent on both sides in the concluding arguments. It has received the most deliberate consideration.

On the part of the claimants, it is fully presented in their summing up of the case. They say :

« In this case, the wrong is beyond question. It appears from the memorials of the company, from the recorded judgments of the Department of State under two administrations, from the messages of the President, from the solemn action of both branches of Congress, and from the treaty itself, which assumes the wrong, and constitutes a commission to assess the damages.

« It is a peculiarity of this commission that it is formed with reference to a single case and for a single purpose. Ordinarily, a claim commission is authorized to consider and determine all such claims of a certain character as may have been presented within a given time. In such cases the treaty assumes only certain general facts, such as the previous existence of a war, the appropriation of a sum of money, or some general principle of liability. Neither of these assumptions would be inquired into by a commission. In this case, the whole subject-matter of the negotiation which led to the treaty having been a single claim, it was easy to make this convention definite, and to confine the duties of the commission to a single point. This has been done. The treaty assumes the wrong committed, and the liability of Paraguay, and only authorizes the commissioners to assess the amount of damages. It is a simple question of how much?

« If there was any ambiguity in the convention on this point, it could not fail to be removed by a reference to the proceedings which led to the convention.

« The first application of the company to their government was dated January 15, 1855, and requested that such measures may be taken as to him (the President) may seem meet and proper, to demand of the government of Paraguay, and enforce the payment, as indemnity for our losses and the destruction of our business in that country, the sum of $ 935,000.

« The statement of Mr Gallup (see his letter to Mr Bradley of July 8, 1855) shows that Mr Marcy, the Secretary of State, 'although at first somewhat prejudiced against it (the claim), at the last interview I had with him, expressed himself satisfied that a great outrage had been committed upon our citizens by the President of the republic of Paraguay, and that he should make a demand upon his government for indemnity'.

« On the 2d of June 1858 Congress adopted a resolution authorizing the President to adopt such measures and use such force to secure justice from Paraguay as he might think necessary. »

On the part of the Republic of Paraguay, the counsel, in his opening statement, said:

« I. The counsel for the claimants assume as a foregone conclusion that wrong and injury in the transactions upon which this claim is based have been done by the republic of Paraguay.

« This is utterly denied. And it will be respectfully insisted that it will be for this honorable commission not to take for granted, but to require to be here proven and established, in fact and law, the allegation that by reason of any matter or thing done or permitted by the Republic of Paraguay in the premises any responsibility in damages to these claimants rests upon it.

« This commission is organized under the law of nations and the terms of a treaty or convention between sovereigns of equal dignity

in the view of that code. The instructions given by one of these high contracting parties to its minister, its executive messages, the reports of committees, or other proceedings of its legislature, referred to in the opening statement, can have no other weight or value than as exhibiting in an imposing form the claim which is here made, and is here to be established or rejected. They are not even entitled to be regarded as the deliberate conclusions of the government from whom they emanated, since they are founded exclusively upon the case as made *ex parte* by those whose interests and feelings may have naturally colored their representations. By the solemn act of the United States in entering into this convention it is stipulated that this claim shall be here « *investigated* » and « *adjusted* », and « *its amount determined* », « *upon sufficient proof of the charges and defenses of the contending parties* » (Convention, Art. II). »

This is the general outline of the argument.

The question which it presents seemed to be altogether of a technical nature and quite too narrow and unsubstantial to be of any practical importance in a matter of public law. Nevertheless, it is very evident that from a very early period in the history of this claim the claimants steadily looked to the foreclosure of all inquiry into *the foundation of the claim*, and labored to place the republic of Paraguay in the condition of a defendant in an ordinary suit at law who had suffered judgment to pass, reserving only the right to have an inquisition of damages. If this could be admitted—and it would be certainly an anomaly in international affairs—the result would be practically unimportant; because, in order to ascertain the damages, especially where they are claimed to be punitory or vindictive, there must necessarily be an investigation into all the facts and circumstances, so as to determine the animus and every other element properly entering into measure of damages.

Such an inquiry, conducted according to the municipal law, might possibly result in merely nominal damages. But a formal award, made by a mixed commission, under treaty, giving to the claimants one cent damages, would be simply ridiculous. Such a technicality would be unbecoming the dignity of nations and repugnant to the spirit of the public law.

There was no difference of opinion between the commissioners upon the question. They concurred in holding that their respective commissions, the oaths which they had taken as prescribed by the third article of the convention, the language of that convention in all its parts referring to the matter, and the nature of the subject submitted to them, required a full and unrestricted examination of the claim. To ascertain the amount of the claim necessarily obliged them to determine between o and the highest amount which figures could express, according to the exigencies of the proofs.

Any other view of the subject would seem to be equally irreconcilable with the terms of the convention as with justice and fair dealing.

By the first article of the convention, « the government of the republic of Paraguay *binds itself* for the *responsibility* in favor of the United States and Paraguay Navigation Company *which may result* from the decree of the commissioners, who, it is agreed, shall be appointed as follows ». By this article the liability of Paraguay was distinctly admitted, no doubt. But *what* liability? The article answers, « the responsibility which *may result* from the decree of the commissioners ». Can this be understood as a stipulation that the commissioners shall at all events fix *some* responsibility to *some* amount upon that republic? If so, *what* amount was to be this minimum? If it were not fixed by the terms of the convention (and it was not), in what other mode was it to be arrived at? The second article answers « by sufficient *proofs* of the charges and defenses of the contending parties »; and the third article requires that the commissioners shall be sworn « fairly and impartially to investigate the said claims and a just decision thereon render, to the best of their judgment and ability ». It then necessarily follows that the whole matter of this claim was submitted to the *decree* of this commission.

Before entering upon an investigation of the accounts submitted, it seemed desirable to ascertain the precise demand made by the company, and for this purpose all the papers on file in the Department of State were carefully examined. The following statement will show the claims set up at different times:

The letter of Mr Hopkins to the Secretary of State, dated 30th of August 1854, advises him that « if the extraordinary avarice of this *old man Lopez* should be compelled to pay *two or three hundred thousand dollars* for our *reclamations*, expenses, etc., all would go well for years to come ». And again, in a communication to the Secretary, of 2d September 1854, he tells him:

« The *delay* in having the claim settled; the entire ruin of their commercial operations; the expenditure of $ 116,000, shown in their last balance sheet; the destruction of their credit; the destruction of my own personal, official, and mercantile character: the calumnies of the press —*all will not be satisfied, principal and interest, by the payment of a less sum than four hundred thousand dollars* ».

So the claim for damages stood, until their memorial of 15th January 1855 was presented to the President of the United States, claiming $ 935,000.

No specification of items accompanied the memorial but there was filed in the Department of State, under date of 31st January 1855, by Messrs Arnold and Gallup, the following statement, exhibiting the items upon which the claim was founded:

For property in Paraguay, being real estate in Asuncion and San Antonio, with costly improvements made there, sundry mills, heavy machinery, tools, etc., confiscated, seized, and rendered worthless by the arbitrary conduct of the government, valued as per the accompanying deposition of Georges M. Boyd, and certificate of Lieutenant James H. Moore . . . . $ 500,000

Property at the mouth of the river, being a clipper schooner, two river steamboats, built for the upper waters, a large sawmill, and other machinery and general merchandise, costing the claimant nearly $ 80,000 in cash, and rendered useless to the company by the acts of said government, valued, as per aforesaid deposition and certificate, at . . . . » 100,000

For interest from 1st September 1853 to 1st May 1855 (average time) upon $ 350,000, the present cash liabilities of the company, at 6 per cent per annum. . . . . » 35,000

The actual damages sustained in the interruption of business in Paraguay, destruction of commercial interests along the river, and entire loss of credit, upon the sudden and wanton outrage committed upon the company by the Government of Paraguay, estimated at a moderate consideration of 50 per cent upon the valuation above of $ 600,000, which was accompanied by the affidavit of George M. Boyd and a certificate of Lieutenant James H. Moore . . . . » 300,000

$ 935,000

Governor Marcy replied, 7th March 1855, stating to them the propriety, if not the necessity, when making a demand on a foreign government, that the claim should be just « *and the amount of losses and damages should be fairly estimated*» *In this latter respect particularly, the proofs sub-* mitted by you are very inadequate. There is no evidence filed of the company's title to the property, no evidence as to the nature and character of the grants, and no reliable evidence as to the quantity or value of the property owned by the company ». He further informes them that, « the actual cost *of the property, and not only the amount, but the items of the expenditure on improvements, with a particular description of the improvements, ought to be given ».*

On the 14th March M'Gallup, in the absence of M' Arnold, replies to this letter, vindicating the demand as presented, and informing him that there was « no other testimony in the country as to the value of the property than the deposition of Boyd and the certificate of Moore: *that the title, deeds, grants, and other evidences of property, are all in the possession of our agent in South America, retained by him for use before the commissioners, when the claims shall be finally adjudicated ».*

On the 16th March the company filed with the Secretary a statement of their treasurer, Bailey, exhibiting the liabilities and assets of the company, which is annexed to this report, marked B, viz. :

Liabilities of the company in the United
States . . . . $ 361,103. 10
And their assets . . . . » 23,854. 54

This was the extent of their response to M' Marcy's requisition.

The company continued, from time to time, to urge upon the Department some action in their behalf, in various supplemental memorials accompanied by affidavits from themselves or employees not materially varying the proof, and not paying that respect to the suggestions of Governor Marcy which they merited. They, however, furnished a statement, in connection with these memorials, of the expenditures of the company, which is annexed to this report, marked A and No. 3, by which the expenditures appear to have exceeded the receipts by the sum of $ 402,520. 37, and which statement, it may be observed, furnishes no dates for the respective transactions; and a supplemental statement, marked No. 1, is also exhibited.

These demands were twice sent to an agent of the Department in South America, with instructions for their settlement, but without any satisfactory result.

A serious misunderstanding took place between that government and the United States in relation to the attack upon the *Water·Witch*, and other indignities alleged to have been offered to citizens of the United States, which induced Congress to authorize the Executive to send a commissioner, accompanied by a naval force, to demand satisfaction for the insults and wrongs complained of, against the United States flag and citizens. He was instructed to have the claims of this company adjusted; his authority being limited to the reception of $ 500,000, in accor-

dance, it is supposed, with the wishes of the company.

Commissioner Bowlin was selected for this mission, and found no difficulty in adjusting all the demands of this government, without resorting to force, except the claims of this company, which President Lopez regarded as unjust. Nevertheless, M' Bowlin says, in a dispatch, that he could have secured a large sum in cash, by way of compromise, if he had not been restricted, but further adds: « *It is due to President Lopez to say, whatever offer he made was avowedly to purchase his peace, protesting the smallness of his liability, if any at all »,* upon the claim of this company.

The company also instructed M' Bowlin in a *private* letter to receive $ 500,000, in satisfaction, if it should be paid without resort to force, but if coercion became necessary, to insist upon $ 1,000,000. They also sent a memorial to him, setting forth their claim to patent rights for the new machinery claimed to have been introduced by them under the decree of 20th May 1845, and representing at not less than $ 5,000,000 the value that these alleged rights would have been to them if the government, without interruption, had permitted their use.

The foundation on which were erected such golden dreams of untold wealth as seem to have been constantly present to the mind of M' Hopkins, and more or less of his associates, will be best understood by their representations to M' Bowlin of the immense value placed upon their favorite machines, and then exhibiting the facts as proven before the commission.

They inform M' Bowlin that the company had in operation the first and only steam saw mill in that country, which at the time of our interruption by the Government of Paraguay, produced seven hundred feet, or two hundred and forty-seven Spanish varas per day, valued at the mill at fifty to sixty-two cents per vara, say fifty cents per vara, is $ 123. 50. The cost of logs in South Carolina or Maine, with labor at one dollar per day, to produce the above quantity would be five dollars, and labor sawing two dollars and seventy-five cents, making the whole cost of seven hundred feet per day seven dollars and seventy-five cents. Three hundred working days per annum would yield $ 34,725 net profit of one saw per year, and for ten years, $ 347,250.

Similar and more extravagant calculations were gone into for the purpose of showing the extraordinary profits of the cigar factory, which had been established, and the brickmaking machine which they proposed to put into operation. Their statements accompany this report, marked E and G.

Similar claims were alleged to exist for patents. for other machinery and agricultural implements, but no estimates are given of the profits antici-pated from their ·use. From all these advantages secured to them, as they allege, by the decree of 20th May 1845, they expected to realize *a wealth akin to that which the great commercial companies of Europe have realized in the East Indies*.

Such are the claims and demands made by the company upon the Government of Paraguay, and for which the Government of the United States was urged to enforce payment, even to the extent of a war with that new and feeble republic.

Neither the original estimate of damages by Mᴿ Hopkins, the items furnished to the Secretary of State of 31st January 1855, nor the statement of capital by Mʳ Bailey, the treasurer, now seem to be relied on as the basis upon which da-mages are to be estimated; but only the losses of the company as exhibited in the annexed papers A and C. The former, as has been said, is somewhat remarkable in having furnished no dates to most of its items; the proofs, however, enables us to decide upon each of them with all the accuracy necessary for this report. The paper C deserves a passing remark upon a few of the largest items, as illustrating the mode by which the claim has grown to its present size. It will be observed that the accounts embrace the whole expenditures of the company, and the profits and losses from its origin to the present year; a period of over six years, embracing travelling expenses, the fees of counsel, etc.

The first two items, amounting to about $ 114,000, constitute the cost of the vessel *El Paraguay* and its cargo, which sailed from New York about the 20th March 1852, and cleared for *Montevideo and a market*, and which vessel, after encountering storms, and having cost large sums for repairs, was finally abandoned on the coast of South America near Maranham, was taken into port, condemned as unseaworthy, and sold, with a part of the damaged cargo, before reaching her destination at Montevideo. So much of the cargo as had been saved was reshipped to Montevideo, and then forwarded by the steamer *Fanny*, chartered for that purpose, to Asuncion, the capital of Paraguay, where the cargo was examined by the officers of the governement, and a statement made of each article by Mʳ Hopkins himself, and was valued by the regular appraisers, and the *ad valorem* duties paid by Mʳ Hopkins.

The value of the whole cargo amoun-ted to . . . . $ 15,300
On the 3d February 1854 there was reship-ped, out of the country, and drawback allowed Mʳ Hopkins . . . . » 3,726

$ 11,574
February 7th, afterwards, he imported other goods, valued at . . . . » 291

$ 11,865

These were all the goods ever taken into the country by the company, exclusive of the ma-chinery, sawmills, etc.

It does not appear from the evidence that President Lopez had any connection with the company, or even knew of the proposed enterprise, until the arrival of the *Fanny*, in October 1853, with a part of the cargo of the steamer *El Paraguay*. This steamer is proved to have cost from sixty-five to seventy thousand dollars. What became of the residue of the cargo beyond what was shipped by the Fanny and taken into Paraguay, is not satisfactorily shown. Nor does this seem at all important; for it may be justly said there would seem to be as much propriety in charging the loss upon the ship and cargo to the govern-ment at Montevideo, to which place the goods had been shipped, or to Buenos-Ayres, where the company afterward had a trading house, as to Paraguay. Whatever might have been the tyranny and oppression practiced by that govern-ment toward Mʳ Hopkins and his employees, after their arrival and during their stay, surely can form no excuse for charging the losses which occurred by the dangers of the sea before their arrival.

Under this same head belong the charges on account of what is called the second expedition to wit, the schooner *E. T. Blodget*, with merchan-dise and two small steamers in detached pieces on board, and which never entered Paraguay. The schooner was wrecked above Buenos-Ayres, at the Tigre River, and had no insurance to that point. The wreck was sold. The cargo, so far as saved, was taken to other countries, and disposed of in other markets by the company. This ground of claim is charged in the statement of 31ˢᵗ January 1855 at $ 100,000.

The whole amount of property taken into Paraguay was either sold or taken away by Mʳ Hopkins when he left the country, except the mills, machinery, and agricultural implements, and some personal property of little value left in San Antonio, and the effects in the cigar factory in the city.

All the property left, including the real estate and a large portion of that taken off by him, was under mortgage to the Government of Paraguay to secure the loan of ten thousand dollars.

Nevertheless, as is stated by Captain Page, in his dispatch of 26th September 1854, President Lopez satisfied him, «there was no intention on the part of the Government to prevent Mr Hopkins taking out of the country any of his effects, merchandise, or property, notwithstanding the indebtedness of the company to the government to the amount of ten thousand dollars, for the payment of which he would not hold the property». At the time Mr Hopkins was ordered to leave the cuartel (barracks) at San Antonio he was requested to remove all the property. He removed some of the articles, declining to remove others. They were removed by the government an inventory having been taken and an appraisement made. These articles—a list of which, together with the proceedings, will be found in the papers sent—were stored in the city, they having been thrown on the hands of the governement by Mr Hopkins, and will be sold; the money given to Mr Hopkins if he will receive it, and if not, will be put into the treasury for the benefit of his creditors or for the company. — (Captain Page's dispatch.)

Another item of loss, not less extraordinary, grew out of the mode adopted by the company of increasing their capital stock by issuing their bonds for $ 100,000, bearing interest, and selling them to the stockholders of the company at a loss of over $ 57,000. Such losses, and other like losses and expenditures of the company, can, upon no principle of law or equity, be made chargeable to the republic of Paraguay.

There is no evidence showing any encouragement held out by Paraguay to this company to induce them to go into that country as new settlers, or for the employment of their agricultural implements, machinery, etc., or to engage in trade generally, other than the patents law of 1845. The enterprise was undertaken upon their own judgment, conducted by their own officers, in their own way. If they desired to avail themselves of patents, as offered by that law, they must necessarily be compelled to comply with its provisions. Patent laws, giving exclusive privileges, are always made not only with a view to the interests of the patentees, but also of the people after the expiration of the patent; and hence they generally require, as the decree of 28th May 1845 did, that explanations must be made to the proper officer, in *writing, setting forth* the *particular invention* or *improvement*, or, as in this case, the *new machinery* to be introduced. The officer is then to judge of its importance and utility, decide upon the propriety of its allowance, and the time for which it should be allowed: and then it is for him to issue the patent. Until the patent is granted no right accrues, under the law, to any person.

The opinion or recommendation of Senor Gelly, no doubt honestly made, and with the best motives, can have no more influence upon the construction of the decree than the opinion of any other private citizen, and could by no means be holden to excuse a noncompliance with the provisions of a law of the republic. But he says distinctly that the President would have no authority to do so, and that the granting of other monopolies than those provided for in the law would be unjust.

If the company had been induced by the liberal provisions of the decree of 1845 to engage in so important an enterprise, in which so much of their capital had been invested, it is remarkable that no effort was made, for eight or ten months, to secure the patents authorized by it, and which are now esteemed of such immense value.

The shipments made by the steamer *El Paraguay* and the *E. T. Blodget*, and the claims now set up for the losses sustained in these respects, present the naked question of the liability of a foreign government for shipments made to its territory, under the expectation of profits, which are lost by the perils of the sea before reaching the port of destination. If such liability exists, then favorable commercial regulations, liberal laws for settlers, or favoring immigration into any country, would make the government the insurer not only against the perils of the seas, but also for the prudence and discretion of officers having charge of the vessels. The character of the government of the country to which such shipments are made can have nothing to do with the question of its liabilities for such enterprises. Whatever of tyranny or oppression may have been practiced (it may well be repeated) after the arrival of Hopkins and his employees in Paraguay, could have no influence in producing the disasters which caused them such heavy losses.

Surely no one can believe that the loss of $ 57,000 on the bonds of the company can, with any propriety, be chargeable to that government. Again, interest on the debts of the company, amounting to thousands of dollars, is charged against Paraguay. which, for the reasons before suggested, is wholly inadmissable.

To cap the climax, the extraordinary sum of $ 300,000 is demanded as a remuneration for the trouble, anxiety, and loss of credit growing out of the imputed misconduct of President Lopez.

Such are the details of the claim of $ 935,000, so often and so earnestly pressed upon the consideration of Congress, and the executive government of the United States, and the spirit in which the same has been presented will be seen in the letter of their counsel, Mr C. S. Bradley, to General Cass, Secretary of State, hereto annexed, marked *F.*

The commissioners did not entertain a doubt that the Government of Paraguay could not, in any view of the case, be holden liable for any losses or expenses incurred by the company before October 1853, when they took up their residence in Paraguay.

Nor can that government be justly holden responsible for any expenses or losses which they sustained in the business or trade prosecuted by them with other governments in South America, after they had abandoned Paraguay, which trade was continued for three or four years, at a very heavy loss to the company, as shown by the accounts exhibited with their memorials.

The remaining question, and the only one upon which the claimants have made even a plausible case, arises upon the allegation that their business was wrongfully broken up, their property confiscated, and their agents expelled from the country, and involves the inquiry whether such wrongful acts were done, and if so, what damages should be allowed in the way of compensation for actual losses, or in addition by way of punishment.

Upon this branch of the case it is proper to say that as to the alleged wrongful acts of Paraguay, the evidence adduced by the company consists in the main of the productions directly or indirectly of their agent, Mr Hopkins, in his character of consul, evidently influenced by that of general agent and partner of the company. His correspondence with the Secretary of State, and the papers inclosed in his dispatches, all bear the impress of his own peculiar character and mind, and are little calculated to have weight before any tribunal of a judicial character; indeed, it may be truly said that upon a critical examination they furnish strong internal evidence against the justice or validity of the claim. Among these may be noted the formal proceedings of a regularly organized meeting, consisting of himself and five or six persons connected with the company, at which certain resolutions were passed, condemning the conduct of Lieutenant Page and President Lopez in terms equally violent and vague, and a paper purporting to have been drawn up for publication in answer to charges against Mr Hopkins in the newspaper at Asuncion, but which appears only to have been used as a defence of Mr Hopkins's consular conduct with the Secretary of State, to impugn the character of President Lopez, and to advance the interests of the company in this claim. Of the same nature are certain depositions of some six or eight Paraguayans, resident in Buenos-Ayres, who are shown to be refugees, and members of a revolutionary club in that city, for the overthrow of President Lopez's government, none of whom profess to have knowledge of any fact upon which this claim is founded, but who denounce in strong language the personal and political character of President Lopez, and the general operations of his government, to which they attribute an influence, descending to the most minute affairs in the private life of the humblest citizens.

This kind of evidence; the action of Congress, or the executive officers of the Government, upon the *ex parte* statements of those most deeply interested in this claim; the public opinion in the adjoining States, which may have been formed by the misrepresentations and falsehoods of those whose interests are involved and who may be entitled to the profits arising from the successful prosecution of this claim — do not seem to be a safe foundation upon which heavy damages are to be awarded. The acts of tyranny and oppression should be shown, which, as is alleged, expelled the company and broke up their business; the value of the property confiscated should be exhibited as the best, if not the only, means of ascertaining the true amount of damages.

The company, aware of the necessity of some such proof as suggested by Secretary Marcy, have shown that the brother of the consul, C. E. Hopkins, was stricken on the back by a soldier with the flat side of his sword, for which, according to the affidavits of C. E. Hopkins and Mrs Guillemot (who was in company with him), there was no excuse whatever, not act done or word uttered by him to produce the blow, but which, according to the affidavits of the soldier and his two companions, C. E. Hopkins had provoked, by riding into the herd of cattle which he was driving, dispersing them and causing him much trouble in gathering them together; and *this* after he had been notified not to do so.

The consul, Hopkins, became greatly excited to find that his brother had been stricken by a common soldier, and instead of having the case brought before a judicial tribunal of the district in which the offense had been committed, and having the soldier punished according to the laws of the country, made it a national case: his dignity as consul had been assailed in the attack upon his brother; the rights of an American citizen had been trampled upon; and the Government of Paraguay was to be made responsible for the outrage! He accordingly addressed the government an angry and offensive note, demanding punishment of the soldier, and satisfaction for the offense to his brother, and alluded in the most offensive terms to other alleged indignities suffered by the American citizens from those of Paraguay. This led to a correspondence between him and the Secretary of State.

President Lopez, upon examining the case, seems to have entertained the idea that the brother of the consul had not in reality much cause of complaint against the soldier, as he had probably committed the first wrong; yet it was held to be the duty of the soldier to have reported the conduct of Hopkins to his superior officer, instead of redressing the injury when perpetraded, and therefore the soldier was ordered to be punished with three hundred lashes.

This transaction, which occurred 22ᵈ July 1854, Mʳ Hopkins states in his letter to the Secretary of State, to have been the commencement of the difficulties between himself and the President.

Some newspaper publications on the subject seem to have produced violent language on the part of Mʳ Hopkins against President Lopez, wholly unbecoming the position he occupied.

The other charges to which he alluded in his letter seem to have been of petty annoyances, rude and improper language addressed by some of the populace in the city to Mʳ Hopkins and some of his companions, whose supercilious and haughty conduct toward the people, as well as the government, had rendered them very odious, and occasioned harsh words to be used in the streets, throwing missiles such as orange peelings, pieces of cigars, and sand into the door and windows of their houses, by day as well as by night, and which is attributed to the influence, if not direct sanction, of the President or his officers, and not to any misconduct or provocation on their own part; and yet when the complaint was made, without designating any offender, a guard of soldiers was stationed at their house for their protection. The annoyances are alleged to have continued, and become even worse; yet no individual could be named, so as to enable the police officers to punish them.

Such acts of incivility and rudeness toward the consul of the United States and his family resident in the city deserved punishment, which would undoubtedly have been inflicted on the offenders if they could have been discovered. Mʳ Hopkins could not ascertain their names, at least made no report of any to the government, at the same time most injudiciously imputing to the officers of the government a knowledge of their commission, and strongly intimating a connivance at the conduct of the offenders.

It never seems to have occurred to Mʳ Hopkins or his associates that his own arrogance and presumption, his haughty and overbearing conduct among the citizens, his violent and denunciatory language toward the government and officials, were well calculated to arouse the hostile feelings of the people against them, and produce the annoyances of which he complained. Mʳ Falcon, the Secretary of State, in his letter to Governor Marcy of 2d September 1854, speaks of «the *repeated complaints* made by the officers of the districts *against the conduct of Mʳ Hopkins* and *his servants*; the want of *respect and civility* to the justices, *his shocking expressions* against any who dared to complain of his conduct, his disregard of *port regulations*, and *contempt toward the police officers*». And further telling him, when speaking of the excesses of Mʳ Hopkins, « *they have been repeated by a series of rudenesses, and bitter recriminations against the most excellent government of the republic*, which has for some time been *astonished* at the audacious provocations of Mʳ Hopkins »; and concludes by telling him, « *If Mʳ Hopkins had accepted the consulate for the express purpose of discrediting the worthy government of the United States, and his fellow-citizens, he could not have done more to create disaffection.* »

When speaking of the punishment of the soldier Sylveire, Captain Page says, « Had Mʳ Hopkins been content with making a *simple statement* of the affair, and not have accompanied his *communication with irrelevant remarks, passing censure upon the government and people of Asuncion*, I am informed by the President that the difficulty would not have occurred ». And again, he says, in his letter of 1st September, « If Mʳ Hopkins expects to involve me and the *Water Witch* in the *disgraceful affair between the Government of Paraguay and himself*, he deludes himself with very false hopes. » Referring to the publications in the *Seminario*, he says, « By a most impolitic and unauthorized course, he has brought upon himself the wrath and indignation of a Government which has the power, because of its peculiar relations with its people, to embarrass and render profitless the entire enterprise of those American citizens who have so unwisely put him at its head. This may be most effectually accomplished (if such be the disposition of the government), without infringing one single article of the treaty between the two nations, or committing one single overt act which would form the basis of complaint. Lieutenant Powell, among the most intelligent officers of the navy, says of him, Mʳ Hopkins was well known in the navy as an egotistical and presuming man, and one who had constantly embroiled himself in all kinds of difficulties while in it. »

Mʳ Ferguson, the millwright, who had been in the employment of the company all the time in Paraguay, whose good sense, modesty, and frankness before this commission made a most favorable impression, says, when speaking of the deportment of Mʳ Hopkins while there, « *I think his conduct was scandalous, according to my ideas of morality, and shocked even the people of that country* ». And being further interrogated as to his course generally among the people, and officially, whether it was kind and conciliatory, answers, « *It was quite the reverse. It was overbearing and tyrannical.* He had a *swaggering, bullying way* with him *in all his relations* of life, and his deportment was always tyrannical and overbearing. »

Such conduct on the part of the consul toward the government and the people of Asuncion, was well calculated to produce an unfavorable impression toward him and his associates, as well as their countrymen, who were but little known except through them, and to lead to the petty annoyance of which they complain. His conduct seems to have made a not less unfavorable impression upon the officers under the command of Captain Page. Mʳ Hopkins, in his letter to Secretary Marcy, 25th August 1854, says: « In the midst of these affairs and publications, the five or six officers of the navy who are now here *continue to cut my house and presence,* thereby causing *infinite moral aid and comfort to President Lopez.* »

So wholly forgetful did he seem to be of that dignity and propriety of conduct which should characterize a representative of the United States, and of the respect and courtesy due and always extended to the chief officers of another government that it was made a matter of boast that he had forcibly entered the audience chamber of President Lopez in his riding dress, whip in hand, despite the remonstrance of the guard and in violation of the rules adopted in that country of intercourse between the President and citizens, as if designedly to bring into contempt the authority of the President among his people.

Such conduct toward the people of Paraguay and their President, *without reference to his moral conduct,* which Ferguson designates as *scandalous,* may be supposed to account more satisfactorily for the *indignities* and *annoyances* of which so much complaint has been made than any supposed interference or encouragement of them by the President or his officers.

In relation to this whole subject of the alleged *insults* and *outrages* complained of by the company in their memorials, and which could not fail, (coming from a respectable source) to attract the attention of the executive and of Congress, it is proper to make a few remarks.

In the first place, no complaints of this sort appear to have been made until the occurrence between Mʳ C. E. Hopkins and the soldier on the 22d July 1854. The letter addressed by Mʳ Consul Hophins to the Paraguayan Secretary of State on the 25th of the same month asserts in general terms that such things had taken place. The affidavits of Boyd, Morales, Hines and his wife, all made subsequently, make the same accusations. Giving to these affidavits all the weight that can possibly be claimed for them, it would seem that nothing had occurred to which private persons are not liable under the oldest and best ordered governments, if there should be any provocation in their own personal deportment and intercourse with the people. There is nothing in the evidence tending to show a denial of justice to any person who had recourse to the ordinary tribunals under such circumstances, and surely there can be no propriety or pretext of right in claiming for the persons engaged in this speculation a status different from that of the citizens of the country generally. No claim whatever is set up on account of these supposed insults and outrages. The persons who may have been annoyed by them make no claim, but appear as witnesses for the company upon the claim made by it in its corporate capacity.

All this part of the case, therefore, even if it were satisfactorily made out by the proofs (which it is not), could have no effect beyond that of aggravating and giving color to the charges of expulsion, confiscation and breaking up of the business of the company.

As to the *expulsion,* it is perfectly clear that nothing of the kind took place. If there had been an expulsion of the company generally, or of any person in particular, without doubt there would have been some explicit or intelligible evidence of the fact. Not only is there no affirmative evidence of it adduced by the company, but there is clear evidence to the contrary. The conclusion arrived at by Mʳ Marcy upon the official dispatches and the first memorial and proofs of the company is abundantly sustained by the thorough examination of the whole case before the commission. In his letter to Messrs. Arnold and Gallup, 7th March 1855, he says:

« It is evident throughout the whole correspondence that the opposition of the Government of Paraguay was confined solely to Mʳ Hopkins; and Lieutenant Commander Page, in his dispatches on the subject to the Navy Department, while condemning in strong terms the arbitrary and oppressive conduct of the Government, confirms the opinion that the hostility was to Mr Hopkins, and not to the company of which he was the agent; and Mr Falcon, in a letter to Mr Hopkins, wherein he informs him of the resolution of President Lopez to decline any further communication with him in his capacity of agent, holds the following language: « It is, however, to be well understood that any other person of better conduct toward the government of the republic can make such propositions as time shall render proper. »

But even as to Mr Hopkins there was no expulsion. The account given by Captain Page on the spot, in his dispatch to the Secretary of the Navy, dated Asuncion, 26th September 1854, is relied on as truthful and accurate. The following extracts are deemed important to the proper understanding of this pretended expulsion :

« Mr Hopkins declined allowing any one of the persons under him to carry on these works, and came to the conclusion that the course for him to pursue was to throw the responsibility on this government, and look to a reclamation being made by the government at home... The opposition of the government was confined to himself and a Mr Morales, who had made himself odious to the government by some very imprudent and ridiculous remarks...

« Acting Lieutenant Powell used his best endeavors, both for the interest of this company and to avoid collision with the government. He desired to know from Mr Hopkins if he would allow another to act in his stead, stating that to this the government had no objection. He declined doing so...

« I called on the President on my arrival. He expressed himself as having been outraged by the remarks, the communications, and conduct of Mr Hopkins and Mr Morales, and said that matters had gone to such a length that he would not now permit Mr Hopkins to do any more business here. *I requested to be informed if other Americans belonging to the company would not be allowed to do business. He said that any Americans would be allowed to do business with the same privileges that were accorded to other foreigners, and that his objections were confined to Mr Hopkins and Mr Morales.* I stated to him that some of the persons of this company had said they did not feel themselves protected, and desired to know if they would not receive every protection from insult and injury. He said they should.

« The day following I saw Mr Hopkins on board this vessel, having sent him word to meet me at a certain hour, for I had expected to have seen him the day before. He explained the circumstances involved in this difficulty, stating to me that he had thrown all the work they had

in hand on the responsibility of this government, having been compelled to do so because of its action *toward him,* and that he *required or demanded of me* to join him in a protest to this government for the outrages that had been committed. His tone and manner were *in his usual style of presumption,* and I promptly informed him that his requisition and demand would not be granted. I assume this, in my humble judgment, as the proper course for me to pursue, because I could see no good resulting from such an empty boast, Mr Hopkins having taken *such steps before my arrival* as to preclude any action on my part toward a continuation of the operations of the company. *I stated to him the nature of my interviews with the President,* and at the same time assured him that if he or any American citizen residing on shore considered himself unprotected from insult or injury, he or they would find protection on board of the *Water Witch.* He said he desired to leave the country, *with those who were attached to the company,* and to take with him such effects and merchandise as he had in store and in his dwelling house ; but that he apprehended no merchant captain would consent to receive him on board, lest he should incur the displeasure of the government. I informed him that I would see the President on the subject and if I could not procure him a passage with his effects, I would take himself, company, and effects on board of the *Water Witch* to Corrientes, where he desired to go.

« I called to see the President—singular as it may appear, nothing is done in this country without his knowledge and assent—and learned from him that he was willing and desirous that Mr Hopkins should leave the country, and said that he would instruct the captain of the port to procure a vessel. No captain of a vessel would decline taking Mr Hopkins on board, with his company and merchandise, if requested to do so by the captain on the port, because he would be assured that by so doing he would be acting in accordance with the wishes of the President...

« *This, Mr Hopkins is aware of,* and for the interest of his company he should have withdrawn himself actively from its operations, and *have made a trial, at least, of the sincerity of the government in its professions of friendly disposition toward the company...*

« I should have mentioned in another part of this letter, that I ascertained from the President there was no intention on the part of the government to prevent Mr Hopkins taking out of the country any of his effects, merchandise, or property, notwithstanding the indebtedness of the company to the government to the amount of

$ 10,000, for the payment of which he would not hold the property.

‹ At the time Mr Hopkins was ordered to leave the cuartel at San Antonio, he was requested to remove all the property. He removed some of the articles, declining to remove others. They were removed by the government, an inventory having been taken and an appraisement made. These articles, a list of which, together with the proceedings, will be found in the papers sent, were stored in the city, they having been *thrown on the hands of the government by Mr Hopkins*, and will be sold, the money given to Mr Hopkins, if he will receive it, and if not, will be put in the treasury for the benefit of his creditors, or for the company.

‹ The operations of the cigar factory were stopped because Mr Hopkins would not take out a licence, in accordance with a decree of the government. These are arbitrary acts, and show the power of this Government, but still, it is its mode of proclaiming the laws, and all have to abide by them. ›

There is no proof in the case, putting any other face upon the transaction than that which is here given by Captain Page. On the contrary, it is supported by all the evidence.

The passeports were made out the very same day on which they were applied for, the 29th September; and although some difficulty occurred as to their delivery from the custom house, as reported by Morales to Captain Page, they were delivered, in fact, before the sailing of the *Water Witch*, and no obstacle interposed to the shipment of the goods, or the departure of the vessel; which was attributable, in a great degree, to the prudence and judgment of Captain Page. The President might justly and properly have insisted that the mortgaged goods should remain in the republic until the debt was paid. By the practice in most of the States of this Union, an attachment, or other process, in such case holds the mortgaged property until the maturity of the debt. The property sold corresponded with the valuation made, and the opinion given of its value by Ferguson as nearly as might be expected; and in the opinion of the commission, from all the evidence before them, *for its full value*. It is evident, therefore, that there was neither *expulsion* nor *confiscation* unless it be *expulsion* to require foreigners to conform to the laws, or *confiscation* to retain and take care of the property which they refuse to remove with them, though freely authorized to remove it, while under mortgage to the State.

But it may be proper, even at the hazard of repetition, to review more particularly, and under a distinct head, the effective property of the company in Paraguay, and the disposition which was made of it.

Setting aside the privileges, patents, and monopolies, which we have seen had no legal existence or foundation in justice, the remainder consists of the cigar factory in Asuncion, and the San Antonio establishment. For the cigar factory, it is in evidence, as before remarked, that the sum of $ 2,500. 75 was paid, and there was a licence duly issued by the government, authorizing this property to be transferred to and held by aliens. This establishment was in operation about ten months. It is proven by the claimants themselves that it could not have been carried on without the active aid of the government. The people of the country, according to this testimony, were unwilling to labor regularly, and would only have engaged themselves for a few days at a time; and thus no valuable progress could be made in the projected improvement upon their mode of making cigars, which required regular instruction and practice. This appears at page 51 of the record, in the testimony of C. E. Hopkins.

By the orders of the government this difficulty was avoided, and the necessary labor was supplied, *under compulsion*. Upon this point it will suffice to quote from the affidavit of a single witness, which, besides being in the record, is appended to the Senate report (No. 60, 35th Congress, 1st session) made by Mr Douglas, upon the difficulties with Paraguay. Mr Hines, the general cashier of the company, says: ‹ Upon first commencing in Paraguay, the government, through the judge of *peons*, provided us with *peons* for our mechanical department (meaning the establishment at San Antonio), women and other laborers for our cigar factory. › This point is clearly and very carefully made out by the claimants; indeed, it is insisted on in their memorial (Senate report, p. 66), in order to show that when these facilities were withdrawn by the government the failure of the enterprise necessarily followed. But it is not perceived that there was any pretext of vested right in these facilities. It has been seen that the company founds its claims upon the decree of 1845—the patent law—and the letter of Mr Gelly written to Mr Hopkins in the year 1848, more than four years before the incorporation of the company. There is not a particle of evidence of any other inducements or invitations or promises, expressed or implied, leading to the enterprise of the company. In neither of these papers (the decree or the letter) is there anything upon which to found a claim for the exercise by the government of its practically absolute powers (if they be so) to compel the *peons*, or laborers, to work for the company. It can not be said, therefore, that the company proceeded upon any implied agreement that these powers should be exercised for their benefit at all, still less that they should be continued to be exercised any longer than the Paraguayan Government should find it consistent with the public order and its own policy and institutions to do so. These remarks apply to both the establishments of the company, that at San Antonio, as well as the cigar factory in Asuncion.

It appears by the evidence from the books of the claimants that during the whole period of the existence of this factory it produced a little over five hundred thousand cigars, and that the sales of cigars made by the company amounted to $ 3,382.51, viz., in the United States, $ 1,895.71, and in South America, $ 1,480.80. The whole amount, and all the particulars, of the goods, chattels, and effects in that factory at the time it was closed, appear in the judicial proceedings put in evidence on the part of Paraguay ; and no attempt has been made to contradict, impeach, or discredit the inventory or appraisement, notwithstanding that Morales was in attendance before the commission as a witness for the company, and was several times examined. These values may therefore be safely taken to be unquestionably correct. In addition to these, the company claim that they would have made large profits by carrying on the factory with the privileges of the decree of 1845 ; but it has been shown already that no rights were acquired under that decree. It has been asserted and argued that President Lopez had dispensed with the terms of that decree, so as to give the company all its benefits, without a compliance with any of its corresponding obligations ; but there is no evidence whatever in support of this; or is it at all reasonable or probable.

The circumstances under which this factory was closed have been made the ground of claim: but it appears distinctly in the evidence that the licence required by law had not been taken for the factory. If, as has been stated, but not proven, the delay in taking it had been assented to, or even procured by the government, yet by the thirteenth article of the decree of August 1854 it was provided : « *13. Every industrial or commercial factory unlicensed will be shut, if the persons interested do not take out a licence within three days.* » [Senate report, p. 79; Record, p. 55.] The testimony of Morales, the company's witness, shows that this factory was unlicensed, and C. E. Hopkins proves that the cost of the license was that of the stamped paper only upon which the application was made. Morales further shows that upon the publication of this decree,

Mr Hopkins made application for the license for the cigar factory and the San Antonio mill, thereby recognizing the obligation to take out such license, and his previous omission to do so.

But in the same decree, article 14, the use of *any foreign commercial title* in the republic, without express permission of the government, was forbidden. This prohibition may seem absurd, as well as arbitrary, tested by the institutions and circumstances of our own country. But whether it was expedient and proper at that time in Paraguay, is a question which it was for that government alone to determine. And if it were never so unnecessary and arbitrary, it is difficult to see how it could possibly affect the interests of the company. Mr Hopkins had used the *foreign commercial title* of *General Agent of the United States and Paraguay Navigation Company.* It is alleged that this article of the decree was directed specially to prohibit *him* from further using that title. Doubtless this is true. But if it be so, what was Mr Hopkins's duty ? Manifestly to conform to the decree, which could in no wise affect the interests of his principal or himself. But upon the first knowledge of the decree, he gave notice to the government that he was *General Agent of the United States and Paraguay Navigation Company* (a fact well known before), and immediately thereafter, without waiting for any reply, he makes the application for the licenses, *carefully using the prohibited title.* The application was returned to him, with the explanation that it could not be entertained, as in it he violated the decree referred to. Now, it may be repeated, that all this importance attached to the use of this title is entirely foreign to American usages and ideas. But can the claimants sincerely believe that the internal policy of the country where they had established themselves was to yield to them, and not they to it, in a matter of this sort ? Were they to take all the advantages of this species of Government—such as the impressment of laborers for their benefit—and yet claim exemption from a decree forbidding the use of any foreign commercial title ? This seems to be the theory of this part of the case, for no other application was made for the license. Mr Hopkins preferred to have the license refused upon this ground, and to submit to the terms of article 13 of the decree, which provided that every industrial or commercial factory unlicensed should be closed unless the license should be taken out in three days. The cigar factory was accordingly closed by the chief of police in execution of this decree. The deposition of Morales shows that he was required by the chief of police to carry the sign to the station house. Morales proves by his own deposition (and no objection has been made to this proof), that he is a naturalized citizen, a native of Cuba. This fact of obliging him to carry the sign was well calculated to produce a feeling of indignation and resentment. But it is not perceived how it could affect the claims of the company, or alter the fact that the closing of the cigar factory was in pursuance of a law to which all persons in Paraguay owed obedience.

The evidence shows that there was no seizure or confiscation of the property. It was perfectly competent for the company to have reopened the factory on the same day, by merely complying with the terms of the law, which imposed no other obligation than that of applying for the license required in all cases, and paying $ 16 for the stamp, without at the same time defying the government by using the prohibited title.

The sawmill at San Antonio was in the same condition with respect to this law. But in addition to this, there were other and more serious difficulties, provoked entirely by the indiscreet and unjustifiable conduct of the company's agent, Mr Hopkins. In this connection it may be proper to make an extract from the statement or memorial of the company, which is appended to the Senate report, at page 66. They say :

‹ Notwithstanding unforeseen delays, upon the arrival of the expedition at Asuncion, the capital of Paraguay, in October 1853, the agents of the company were received with the greatest favor. Permission to purchase land was conceded by the President ; the use of the government barracks was granted to the company, free of expense, for the use of their employees ; a loan of money was made upon the credit of the company for a term of two years ; a large number of persons were impressed by the government, and paid by the company, to work in their cigar factory and other establishments.

‹ The President Lopez accepted, in his official capacity, the presents sent him by the company, and granted many other extraordinary facilities for their operations. In verification of these statements, we refer to the affidavit of W. E. Hines, general cashier of the company in Paraguay, hereunto annexed.

‹ The Government of Paraguay has never denied, but makes a boast of the facts. We give an instance of its decrees for our benefit, and also the letter accepting and returning presents.

‹ The justice of peace of Ipiane will select from the natives of the suppressed community ten men, bachelors or married, of good conduct and assiduous in labor, and will deliver them to the citizen of the United States, Mr Edward Augustus Hopkins, to be destined to work for him during one year in his establishment at San Antonio, with the monthly wages of three dollars, which he offers to pay, and providing victuals, upon the condition that every Saturday, after concluding the labors of the day, they can retire to their lodgings, and will present themselves the following Monday at daybreak : and that they will receive said salary every two months, on condition, also, that if any one of the ten individuals should happen not to be of good character required, they will be withdrawn, with less wages for the days they have had hire in proportion to that assigned to men of labor, and will be supplied by men capable of performing the labors of the contract, it being recommended to said justice of peace to make the best choice of workmen. The same order will be understood on the same terms by the justice of peace of Guarambaré. ›

This is the account which the claimants themselves give of the reception they met with. It appears by the evidence (and there is no contrariety on this point) that Mr Hopkins, acting for the company, attempted to procure a title to the government barrack and appurtenances, which he was then occupying by favor. All the proceedings are appended to the record, as well those under which Mr Hopkins claimed as those subsequently instituted by the Government. They speak for themselves. Without recapitulating them minutely, it might suffice to say that Mr Hopkins never applied for, or obtained, any license or permission to purchase the land, which was necessary, in the case of aliens, even where the government was not directly concerned, as in the instance of property occupied as a national barrack ; that he never had any official survey, but of is own authority directed the line to be run so as to include the barrack ; that he actually inclosed it, and with it a public road, the only one leading to the port; and that he refused to evacuate the barrack when requested so to do by the government, which had gratuitously loaned it to him.

The proceedings instituted by the government resulted in a decree, declaring the land where the barrack stood to be the property of certain infants, from whose mother, the widow Bedoya, Mr Hopkins had purchased it for the sum of *seventyfive dollars*. That this was the whole purchase money has not been denied. The requisite steps were not taken to divest the infants of their title, or to authorize the holding of the land by aliens.

The real estate of the company was also embraced in the beforementioned mortgage and consisted of about twelve acres of land at San Antonio, purchased from different individuals, costing $ 237. 50, and also the cigar factory at

Asuncion, costing $ 2,500.75. To the factory the title had been perfected by deed registered and possession given, and the assent of the President indorsed thereon, authorizing them as foreigners to hold the land, as required by the laws of Paraguay.

The President esteemed the position of the barrack as an important point for the defense of the State against the incursions of the Indians from the opposite side of the river, and thought the most ready mode of getting out of the difficulty with Mr Hopkins was to pay him back double the consideration money, which was submitted to him. He (Hopkins) desired time to consider of the subject, that he might himself make some proposition. Before he did so the irregularity of the title was made known to the President, and a decree was passed declaring his deed void and that the property was necessary for public use, and directing the money to be refunded. It was offered to him and declined. The President then took possession of it as public property for the reestablishment of the barrack and it was immediately occupied by his soldiers.

Whether the decree and other proceedings were right or wrong, so far as it concerned the rights of the widow and children, it could not be considered unjust to the company; *their titles had not been perfected, and could not have been, except with the assent of the President,* and besides they were his tenants in the barrack, by sufferance, and could set up no opposing claim to his title, and they had mortgaged the lands to secure the payment of a much larger sum than they were worth and their title was sold under a decree made according to the laws of Paraguay, and the full value applied toward the payment of the mortgage debt, leaving a balance of the loaned money still due and unpaid, of over *six thousand dollars.*

It is further alleged that they were indirectly compelled to give up their business and leave the country by the tyrannical and oppressive decrees of President Lopez. One of the most complained of was the prohibiton of « all meetings of foreigners except for the ostensible purpose of visiting and innocent diversions, are forbidden by day or night ». This was evidently designed to prevent the assemblage in the city of sailors and others accompanying the ships in port, which often ended in riots and bloodshed, and not for the purpose of preventing foreigners from meeting and transacting their ordinary business, as is alleged. There is no allegation that any such meeting for business or for any lawful purpose was in fact interrupted. Of the same character was the prohibition of any persons from wearing

arms, or being out of their houses after night without carrying a lamp.

These were mere police regulations, which President Lopez had an undoubtet right to establish, and it was the duty of the citizens of the United States, resident in Paraguay, to obey them; which might have been done with but little trouble.

It was known to Mr. Hopkins that the objection of the President was to himself and Morales, on account of their misconduct, and that no objection would be made to any other citizen of the United States. It is strange that decrees so easily complied with should have been made an excuse for abandoning the interests of the company now represented so valuable, and that the voluntary abandonment of such of the property as Hopkins could not conveniently take with him, or convert into money, should now be made the basis of heavy damages against Paraguay.

It has also been urged that President Lopez offered to pay a large sum of money ($ 250,000), and that the amount of damages could not fall short of that sum. It appears from the statement of Commissioner Bowlin, already alluded to, that when the offer was made President Lopez declared *there was little or nothing due the company, and that the offer was made to buy his peace.*

Propositions for a compromise of contests between contending parties are not and ought not to be considered as an admission of the liability of the party for anything, much less the amount offered and rejected, in any subsequent stage of the proceedings.

It should be a source of gratification to the Government of the United States, as well as its citizens, that Commissioner Bowlin, after having received prompt and full satisfaction for the insult offered the flag of the United States and the injury done to our citizens on board the *Water Witch,* consented to a reference of this pecuniary demand of the United States and Paraguay Navigation Company to arbitration, where justice would be more likely done to the parties, than by an attempt to coerce the payment of such a claim with musket and sword.

It has been painful to observe, in the course of this examination, the ingenuity displayed in making so strong a case *prima facie* for the consideration of Congress and the executive government, founded upon *ex parte* representations of those most deeply interested in the claim, by a studied perversion of the laws and decrees of the republic of Paraguay, and by the enormous, if not criminal exaggeration of the demands of this company, constantly growing larger by the skillful preparation of their accounts, and the studied and malignant assaults upon the President and people of Paraguay, and that, too, for the mere purpose of putting money into the pockets of those claimants.

It has always been the pride and glory of the government and citizens of the United States to submit to nothing wrong from any government or people, but at the same time to demand of them nothing but what is right; and the day is far distant, as I sincerely hope, when East India fortunes are to be accumulated, with their approbation and sanction, by the plunder of feeble States, extorted from them at the cannon's mouth.

For the reasons above given, I am clearly of opinion that the award should be in favor of the republic of Paraguay, and against the claimants, who have not established any right to damages upon their claim [1].

XXVIII. Espagne, États-Unis d'Amérique.

27 octobre 1795.

Contrairement à ce qui est affirmé dans le recueil officiel des traités, publié par les Etats-Unis d'Amérique, cet arbitrage s'est terminé régulièrement. La commission arbitrale a jugé quarante affaires et a accordé 325,440 $ 07 1/2 d'indemnités. Nous reproduisons le texte d'une des décisions intervenues.

Sentence rendue le 27 Décembre 1797 par la Commission d'arbitrage organisée aux termes du traité du 27 Octobre 1795.

To all to whom these presents shall come Greeting.

The Commissioners duly appointed for carrying into effect the twenty-first Article of the Treaty of Friendship, Limits and Navigation between His Catholic Majesty and the United States of America, dated at San Lorenzo Real the twenty seventh day of October one thousand seven hundred and ninety five, having attentively examined the claim of Abel Harris of Portsmouth in the State of New Hampshire, Merchant, a Citizen of the United States, together with the several Accounts and Documents exhibited by him in support thereof for Detention, Freight and Primage in the case of the Ship Rooksby whereof Nathaniel Jones was Master, captured on or about the seventeenth day of August one thousand seven hundred and ninety three by His Catholic Majesty's Frigate Santa Catalina commanded by Don Diego Choquet, do award that the sum of

fifteen thousand five hundred and thirty five Dollars and seventy nine Cents with Interest thereon at the rate of six per Centum per Annum from the twentieth day of April one thousand seven hundred and ninety six until the same be discharged, shall be paid to the said Claimant his lawful Attorney Executors, Administrators or Assigns in Specie without deduction at the City of Cadiz in the Kingdom of Spain within three months after this Award shall have been exhibited at the Royal Treasury at Madrid.

Given under the hands and seal of the said Commissioners, at the City of Philadelphia in the State of Pennsylvania the twenty-seventh day of December one thousand seven hundred and ninety seven. Having signed this award together with a Duplicate and Triplicate thereof either of which being paid the others to be void [1].

XXXV. Grande-Bretagne, Portugal.

13 novembre 1840.

Outre les règles de procédure reproduites par nous, les plénipotentiaires des deux Etats ont adopté, sous la date du 22 juin 1841, des règles spéciales pour la réception, la classification et l'adjudication des demandes.

General Rules for the Reception, Classification and Adjudication of Claims by the Mixed British and Portuguese Commission, adopted June 22nd, 1841.

PREAMBLE. — The Mixed British and Portuguese Commission appointed by the British and Portuguese Governments, to examine and to decide upon the claims of British subjects who served in the Portuguese army and navy, during the late war for the liberation of Portugal, will commence the reception and registry of claims from the 10th day of July, 1841. The following rules will govern the proceedings of the Commission, and are published for the guidance of the claimants.

ART. I. — *Contract for Navy.* — All officers, non-commissioned officers, sailors and marines who served in Her Most Faithful Majesty's navy, will base their claims upon the « Sartorius » contract.

ART. II. — *Contracts for Army prior to January 8, 1834.* — All officers, non-commissioned officers, and soldiers who served in the army, but left it, either voluntarily or compulsorily, before the 8th day of January, 1834, will

---

[1] J. B. MOORE, *History and Digest* . . ., p. 1502—1528.

[1] J. B. MOORE, *History and Digest...*, p. 1004.

base their claims upon the « Sartorius » Contract, or « Cotter's » Contract.

ART. III. — *Contract for those who rejected the « Saavedra » conditions.* — All officers, non-commissioned officers, and privates, who left the service because they would not submit to the « proposals » or new terms (called the « Saavedra » Contract), or who opposed its introduction, and did not in effect serve under it, although detained in the country, will claim under the provisions of the « Sartorius » Contract.

ART. IV. — *Conditions for those remaining in the Service after 8th January, 1834.* — All officers, non-commissioned officers, and privates, who served in the army from or after the 8th of January, 1834, and are not included in Articles I and V, are allowed, individually, the option of choosing on which of the 2 Contracts (« Sartorius » or « Cotter » and « Saavedra's »), they will found their claims.

ART. V. — *Exception to Articles I, II, III, IV.* — Are excepted from Articles I, II, III and IV, all those individuals who may have had an especial and formal contract, or who may, voluntarily and of their own accord, have proposed to serve under other and special conditions; provided such propositions shall have been accepted by the Portuguese Government, and any conditions thereto annexed by the party proposing them have been duly fulfilled.

ART. VI. — *Object of claim and period of claiming.* — The Commission will recognize a claim for whatever rates of pay, officers, non-commissioned officers, and privates may have been entitled to, for the respective periods they may have remained in the service, as late as November, 1835.

ART. VII. — *Provision for Claimants detained before Settlement.* — The Commission will recognize a claim on the part of officers, non-commissioned officers, and privates for pay, but not for allowances, for any intervening period between the date of their leaving the service, and that of the Portuguese Government tendering a settlement. The Commission, however, will consider the Portuguese Government as having tendered a settlement, in every case, in which that Government shall have tendered to the claimant, at or near to, or at some time subsequent to, the close of his service, a large sum or account, in one instalment, and either in money or by « Titulo ».

ART. VIII. — *Exceptions from the provisions of Article VII.* — Are excepted from Article VII:

Those who left the service during the war.

1. Those who left the service during the war, and not on account of the « Saavedra » contract being proposed. These will be entitled to claim « pay » only to the period and date of their leaving the service.

Those who were themselves the cause of delay.

2. Those of whom it can be satisfactorily shown that they themselves were the willful cause of delay, more especially by refusing, or delaying, to give such accounts of public money disbursed by them, as, notwithstanding the circumstances of the service, it ought still to have been within their means to render, and which they were legally and fairly liable to render, according to the rules and regulations of military service; or, by refusing or delaying to give such information as they might be able to give, and which might be reasonably excepted and justly required from them: provided, always, that it be shown, that such information was formally demanded by competent authority, and that it was within the scope of the duty of such claimants to furnish it.

Those who made no formal application for settlement.

3. Those who made no formal application for settlement to the Portuguese Government, or to the authorities constituted to receive such application, and to adjudicate upon the claims.

The heirs or representatives of those who died.

4. The heirs or representatives of those who died during the service, who are entitled to claim pay to the date of the decease of the party whose heir or representative they are.

ART. IX. — *Conditions for those who continued to serve after November, 1835.* — Those who continued in the Portuguese service after November, 1835, will be considered as entitled only to the pay and allowances of the Portuguese army, unless they can prove that they continued beyond such period under any specific agreement with the Portuguese Government, establishing other terms.

ART. X. — *Claims for Prize Money.* — Claims will be received for share of prizes made by the squadron, or by any of the ships of Her Most Faithful Majesty.

ART. XI. — *Claims for Pensions, etc.* — Claims will be received for compensation or pension for wounds received in action; and, if the Commission find the claim well founded, the parties will be examined before the British Army or Navy Medical Board; and the decision of the British authorities will determine the amount to which each shall be entitled, according to the regulations of the British service. Before such Medical Board shall be granted by the Commission, satisfactory proof must be given of the wound, or wounds, having been received in action in the service of Her Most Faithful Majesty; and a certificate to that effect from a medical officer of the ship, or regiment, and of the commanding officer, will be required wherever such documents are attainable.

ART. XII. — *Claims for Arrears of Pensions.* — Claims for arrears of pensions already granted by Her Most Faithful Majesty's Government will be received, provided such pensions shall be decided to be in conformity with the British regulations. This shall apply alike to the wounded, and to the widows or heirs of those deceased.

ART. XIII. — *Compensation for Delay.* — A compensation of 5 per cent per annum on the amount found due is awarded for delay to claimants (by the « Minute of Instructions », Article VI) to commence from the day on which such claimant ceased to receive pay from the Portuguese Government.

ART. XIV. — *Exceptions to Article XIII in reference to the Provisions of Article VII.* — Whereas the Commission, by the decision recorded in Article VII of these « Rules », has awarded to all claimants, who were detained after their dismissal, before a settlement was offered to them by the Portuguese authorities, a daily rate of pay for such intervening period; the Commission (also keeping in view that the 5 per cent allowed in Article VI of the « Minute of Instruction », is therein defined to be a « Compensation for delay ») has decided that no claim can be admitted for the 5 per cent compensation for such intervening period; namely that elapsing between the time when a settlement was tendered. Neither, after the date of the tender of a settlement, will 5 per cent be allowed upon the amount of daily pay which thus, by an act of the Commission, is added to the amount of arrears which may be found to have been otherwise due when such settlement was tendered.

ART. XV. — *Exceptions to Articles XIII and XIV.* — Are excepted from the rate of compensation specified in Articles XIII and XIV, those claimants whose cases are defined by Sections 2 and 4 of Article VIII.

ART. XVI. — *British Regulations, 1831 to 1834, in force.* — The claims founded upon British regulations shall be calculated according to the regulations in force for the British land and sea forces in the years 1831, 1832, 1833, 1834.

ART. XVII. — *Period of service of Officers.* — The period of service of officers claiming shall commence from the date at which it can be shown that they were employed on duty by competent authority; provided always, that if more than one month intervened between the appointment of any officer and his embarkation for Portugal, such officer shall give satisfactory evidence of his having been detained on duty.

ART. XVIII. — *Exceptions to Article XVII.* — Are excepted from Article XVII:

1. Those who served under Cotter's contract, who, it is therein stipulated, can claim only from the date of their disembarkation.

2. Any officer serving under a special agreement or contract not herein specified, if any clause in such agreement should otherwise define the period of commencing service.

ART. XIX. — *Period of Service of Non-Commissioned Officers and Privates.* — The period of service for all non-commissioned officers and privates (excepting sailors and those engaged in the First Marine Battalion and who joined the fleed), shall commence from the date of their disembarkation in Portugal.

ART. XX. — *Form of Claim.* — Every officer, non-commissioned officer, private, or sailor, shall present his claim in duplicate, according to the Form (No. 1), which will be delivered to each claimant on his applying at this office, either personally or by letter. And all documents or supporting vouchers are to be forwarded, together with a fair copy of the same signed by the claimant or his representative, by letter, and to be delivered at the office of the Commission. All letters addressed to the Commission must be prepaid, or they will not be taken in.

ART. XXI. — *Receipt of Claim.* — On the delivery of a claim, if in regular form, a receipt will be given for it, on which will be stated the day on which it was received, and the number attached to it on the register of claims.

ART. XXII. — *Registry of Claims.* — All claims will be entered in the register in the order in which they are received, and they will be successively taken into consideration by the Commission in that same order.

ART. XXIII. — *Days of Registry.* — Tuesdays, Thursdays, and Saturdays shall be allotted, exclusively, for the registration of claims; and no claim will be registered on any other day. Fridays will be allotted for the delivery of the titulos to the claimants.

ART. XXIV. — *Periods of reception of Claims.* — The claims of persons residing in London must be sent in within 2 months from the 10th of July, 1841; those of persons resident elsewhere in the United Kingdom, within 4 months from the same date; those of persons resident in any other part of Europe, within 8 months; and those of persons resident in any other part of the world, within 12 months from the above specified date.

ART. XXV. — *Agents*. — No agent will be allowed to present more than 10 claims for registration on any one day; but, at the end of each of the respective periods of 2, 4, 8 and 12 months, severally assigned in the next preceding Article (XXIV), a grace of 10 additional days will be allowed for the reception of all claims, not previously registered, of parties residing within the limits to which each of such prescribed periods applies.

ART. XXVI. — *Final Limitation of such Periods*. — When the periods defined in Article XXIV, and the 10 additional days mentioned in Article XXV, shall respectively have elapsed, no additional claims of persons residing within those limits will be registered for adjudication by the Commission.

ART. XXVII. — *Evidence before the Commissioners*. — The Commission will decide, in each case, whether they will or will not receive vivâ voce evidence or explanations from claimants; and in no case will any claimant or his representative be admitted to a personal interview with the Commission, unless the Commission shall have previously made an appointment with him for that purpose.

ART. XXVIII. — *Change of Residence of Claimant or his Agent*. — Any change of residence on the part of a claimant or his agent, while his claim is pending before the Commission, must be immediately communicated to the joint secretaries to the Commission.

ART. XXIX. — *Officers receiving Public Money for Disbursement*. — All officers who may have received public money, and have become responsible for the disbursement of such money, by the usages and regulations of military service, will be called upon by the Commission to render a satisfactory account of the application thereof, before their claims shall be taken into consideration, unless they shall have been recognized by the Portuguese Government as having already rendered such an account.

ART. XXX. — *Notice to Claimants of amount found due*. — Before the final adjudication of any claim, each claimant or his representative shall receive notice of the amount which the Commission shall have found due, upon the evidence before them, in order that, if such claimant or his agent should conceive that he is entitled to a different award, he or his agent may have an opportunity of stating the grounds upon which such an opinion on their part is founded. The Commission, after due consideration of such grounds, will give their final decision, and will direct their award to be prepared for delivery to the claimant.

ART. XXXI. — *Titulos*. — A document or titulo will be delivered by the Commission to each claimant, payable to the claimant, or to his order, by such financial agent in London as Her Most Faithful Majesty may appoint; in which document the total amount awarded, and the interest which that amount bears, until paid, will be stated.

ART. XXXII. — *Minute of Award, and its Grounds*. — A minute of the award and of its amount will be entered on the minutes of the Commission on the day it is given. The award shall state the different amounts found due, and the grounds of each decision; such award, together with the claim and the various documents appertaining thereto (or authenticated copies thereof), made out in duplicate, will be preserved by each commissioner, for the information of the British and Portuguese Governments.

ART. XXXIII. — *Proofs of Identity*. — If the claimant be on the spot, he will be required to prove his identity; if he be an officer, by producing his commission, and by otherwise satisfying the commissioners by such means as may seem to them in each case necessary. Petty officers and sailors, non-commissioned officers and privates will be required to prove their identity by the presentation of their discharge, or by any other document or certificate of service which may be in their possession, and by a declaration made before a magistrate or justice of the peace, by some respectable housholder established in London, attesting his personal knowledge of the claimant, and containing a description of the said claimant's person (according to the form, Nr. 2, which will be supplied at the office of the Commission on application), and the claimants will be required to give such further proof of their identity as the commission may in each case deem necessary.

ART. XXXIV. — *Absence of Claimant*. — If the claimant cannot appear in person before the Commission, his identity must be substantiated by a declaration to be made before a magistrate or justice of the peace by 2 respectable householders residing in the same town or parish with the claimant; and by the certificate of the minister of the parish, or of some municipal or parochial authority of the district, within which the said claimant is residing, which certificate should state that the parties signing it know of their own knowledge that the person making such claim is the person whom he signs himself to be. The forms containing the particulars referred to in this and the preceding Articles, will be forwarded from the office to claimants, upon application by letter.

ART. XXXV. — *Authentic Credentials to be produced by Heirs or Representatives, claiming under Probates of Wills.* — The heirs of British subjects, who served in Her Most Faithful Majesty's army or navy, will be required, if claiming under a will, to produce the probate of such will or an authenticated copy of probate; and, in case of intestacy, payment will be made to the personal representative to whom letters of administration shall have been granted, and on whom the duty of distribution among the next of kin is imposed by such letters of administration.

ART. XXXVI. — *Authority to Agents.* — Agents or representatives of claimants must produce an explicit and formal written authority, according to the form Nr. 3, from the claimant, attested before a magistrate, and giving such agent the necessary powers. The agent will also be required to produce the evidence of identity of the party, indicated in Article XXXIII or XXXIV.

ART. XXXVII. — *Authorities given to 2 Agents by 1 Claimant.* — If 2 such authorities to act for a claimant are presented by different parties, that bearing the latest date will be acted upon; and the representative under the former authority will be made acquainted with the presentation of the more recent authority. A claimant, in person, will take precedence of any party to whom he may have given a power of attorney or other written authority, provided he delivers to the Commission a formal and attested revocation of such power previously given by him to another person, according to form Nr. 4.

ART. XXXVIII. — *Legal Questions to be referred to the Law Officers.* — In the event of any legal question arising in reference to the foregoing points, such question will be referred to the decision of the law officers of the crown.

London, 22nd June, 1841 [1].

XLIX. Espagne, Etats-Unis d'Amérique.

12 février 1871.

Protocole relatif à la conservation des archives de la commission arbitrale, et intéressant à ce point de vue spécial.

---

[1] HERTSLET, *A complete collection . . .*, vol. VI, p. 732. The text is followed by the forms alluded to in the articles.

Protocol of an agreement concluded between Mr. John Davis, acting Secretary of State of the United States, and Don Francisco Barca, Envoy Extraordinary and Minister Plenipotentiary of His Majesty the King of Spain, signed the 2nd day of June 1883.

The undersigned, in view of the Spanish-American Commission of arbitration having concluded its labors on the 31st of December last in conformity with the provisions of the protocol of the 6th of May 1882, after having conferred on the subject, and being sufficiently empowered thereto by their respective governments, have agreed upon the following:

First: The Department of State of the United States will preserve in its archives the originals of the judgments pronounced by the Commission of Arbitration, giving a duly certified copy of each one of said judgments to the Legation of Spain.

The books, reports and other documents of the dissolved Commission shall be divided between the Department of State and the Legation of His Majesty the King of Spain.

Second: On the 30th day of the present month of June, Mr. Eustace Collett, late Secretary of the said Commission, and who at the present time is charged with the arrangement and division of its papers, shall complete its labors, delivering to each of the respective governments the documents, books and papers referred to in the preceding paragraph first.

Third: The Governments of the United States of America and of His Majesty the King of Spain recognizing the zeal, uprightness, and impartiality with which Count Lewenhaupt has given his services during nearly three years as Umpire, hereby agree that the Government of His Majesty the King of Spain shall pay to Count Lewenhaupt the salary or compensation to which he is entitled according to the 6th article of the agreement of February 12, 1871, and that the Government of the United States will give to him a suitable present, both of these, the salary as well as the present, to be given in the name of the two contracting parties.

Fourth: The Government of the United States and that of His Catholic Majesty desiring at the same time to present a testimonial of their thanks to Baron Carl Lederer, Mr. A. Bartholdi and Baron A. Blanc, for the zeal, impartiality and uprightness with which they in turn filled in past years the same delicate office of Umpire, hereby agree to offer to each of the three gentlemen mentioned a present consisting of a work of silver or of art, the cost of which shall be defrayed in equal moieties by the two governments.

Fifth: The payment of salary due to Count Lewenhaupt and the presents which are to be made to him as well as to his predecessors shall not prejudice in any manner the question touching the payment of the expenses of the dissolved Spanish and American Commission of Arbitration, or any other question pending between the two countries.

In testimony whereof, the undersigned have signed and sealed the present Protocol in the city of Washington, this 2nd day of June, A. D. 1883 [1].

CXLVIII. Grèce, Turquie.

22 novembre 1897.

Nous croyons devoir reproduire la sentence intervenue dans cette affaire. Elle est remarquable par ce fait qu'elle ne contient guère de motifs et qu'elle formule le texte de la convention consulaire litigieuse telle que les arbitres estiment qu'il importe qu'elle soit rédigée.

Décision arbitrale des Ambassadeurs des six Grandes Puissances, prononcée à Constantinople, le 20 mars/2 avril 1901.

Les soussignés, Ambassadeurs d'Autriche-Hongrie, d'Italie, d'Allemagne, de Russie, d'Angleterre et de France à Constantinople,

Considérant l'article III des Préliminaires de Paix· signés entre les Grandes Puissances et l'Empire Ottoman, le 6/18 Septembre 1897, ainsi conçu :

« Sans toucher au principe des immunités et privilèges, dont les Hellènes jouissaient avant la guerre sur le même pied que les nationaux des autres Etats, des arrangements spéciaux seront conclus en vue de prévenir l'abus des immunités consulaires, d'empêcher les entraves au cours régulier de la justice, d'assurer l'exécution des sentences rendues et de sauvegarder les intérêts des sujets ottomans et étrangers dans leurs différends avec les sujets hellènes, y compris les cas de faillite. »

Considérant l'article V, § b, des dits Préliminaires, qui prescrit la conclusion entre l'Empire Ottoman et le Royaume de Grèce, d'une « Convention Consulaire dans les conditions prévues par l'article III » ;

Considérant l'article XI des Préliminaires de Paix, ainsi conçu :

[1] J. B. MOORE, *History and Digest . . .*, p. 4807.

« En cas de divergences dans le cours des négociations entre la Turquie et la Grèce, les points contestés pourront être soumis, par l'une ou l'autre des parties intéressées, à l'arbitrage des Représentants des Grandes Puissances à Constantinople, dont les décisions seront obligatoires pour les deux Gouvernements. Cet arbitrage pourra s'exercer collectivement ou par désignation spéciale des intéressés, et soit directement, soit par l'entremise de délégués spéciaux.

« En cas de partage égal des voix, les arbitres choisiront un surarbitre. »

Considérant que, par une lettre adressée aux Représentants des Grandes Puissances à Constantinople, le 1/14 Mai 1900, les Délégués Hellènes, d'ordre de leur Gouvernement, ont invoqué l'arbitrage sur les points, au sujet desquels une entente n'a pu s'établir dans le cours des négociations sur la dite Convention Consulaire ;

Considérant que les Représentants des Grandes Puissances dûment autorisés par leurs Gouvernements respectifs ont, par leurs Notes du 4 Juin 1900, accepté le mandat collectif d'arbitrage sollicité sur les points contestés ;

Considérant les demandes des deux Parties et les Mémoires présentés à l'appui de ces demandes ;

Considérant que l'article III des Préliminaires maintient et confirme le principe des immunités et privilèges, dont les sujets hellènes jouissaient avant la guerre, et qu'il n'est pas besoin de spécifier dans la Convention Consulaire tous les droits qui découlent de ce principe relativement aux attributions administratives et judiciaires des Consulats helléniques ;

Considérant que les stipulations du Traité de Canlidja, conclu entre l'Empire Ottoman et le Royaume de Grèce le 27 Mai 1855, restent en vigueur, en tant qu'elles ne sont pas modifiées par les décisions arbitrales ci-dessous ;

Considérant que la validité du protocole annexé à la loi Ottomane du 7 Séfer 1284 (18 Juin 1867) et signé par la Grèce le 12/24 Février 1873, n'a pas été atteinte par l'état de guerre entre l'Empire Ottoman et le Royaume de Grèce ;

Considérant qu'il n'y a lieu d'arbitrer que sur les points contestés, qui ont trait aux arrangements spéciaux prévus par l'article III des Préliminaires de Paix ;

DÉCIDENT :

Les dispositions suivantes qui règlent les points contestés entre les Délégués Ottomans et Hellènes chargés de la négociation de la Convention Consulaire, ou qui constatent leur accord sur un certain nombre d'autres points où la question de durée était seule litigieuse, entreront en vigueur à l'expiration d'un délai de six mois à compter de la signification de la présente décision arbitrale à chacune des deux Parties:

ARTICLE 1. — Chacune des deux Hautes Parties Contractantes aura la faculté de nommer des Consuls Généraux, Consuls et Vice-Consuls dans tous les ports, villes et localités des Etats de l'autre Partie, à l'exception de ceux où le Gouvernement territorial verrait inconvénient à admettre de tels Agents.

Cette réserve, toutefois, ne sera pas appliquée dans les localités où se trouveraient des offices consulaires d'autres Puissances.

PROTOCOLE-ANNEXE. — Il est entendu que les deux Hautes Parties contractantes auront pleinement la faculté de maintenir les Offices Consulaires qui — reconnus d'un commun accord — auraient fonctionné au moment de la rupture des relations diplomatiques en 1897, entre les deux pays, ou à une date antérieure ne remontant pas au delà de l'année 1890.

Les Agents honoraires cesseront leurs fonctions et les deux Hautes Parties contractantes se réservent de les remplacer par des fonctionnaires de carrière.

ARTICLE 2. — Aucun sujet hellène ne pourra être nommé Consul Général, Consul ou Vice-Consul de Turquie en Grèce, ni aucun sujet ottoman ne pourra être nommé Consul Général, Consul ou Vice-Consul de Grèce en Turquie.

Ces fonctionnaires Consulaires seront choisis, de part et d'autre, parmi ceux de carrière, c'est-à-dire qu'ils seront des Agents rétribués s'occupant exclusivement de leur mission consulaire.

Toutefois, les sujets ottomans et les sujets hellènes pourront être employés comme drogmans et cavass (huissiers) par les Consuls Ottomans et Hellènes, suivant les règlements en vigueur dans les pays respectifs, et jouiront du traitement y établi, en tant qu'il n'y serait pas dérogé par la présente Convention.

ARTICLE 3. — Les Consuls Généraux, Consuls et Vice-Consuls des deux Hautes Parties contractantes seront réciproquement admis et reconnus, après avoir présenté leurs provisions, selon les règles et formalités établies dans les pays respectifs.

L'exequatur ou les Berats et Firmans ou autres pièces nécessaires pour le libre exercice de leurs fonctions, leur seront délivrés sans frais, et, sur la production des dites pièces, l'autorité supérieure du lieu de leur résidence prendra immédiatement les mesures voulues pour qu'ils puissent s'acquitter des devoirs de leur charge et qu'ils soient admis à la jouissance des ex-emptions, honneurs, immunités, et privilèges qui leur reviennent.

ARTICLE 4. — Les Consuls Généraux, Consuls et Vice-Consuls jouiront spécialement de l'exemption des logements et des contributions militaires, ainsi que de toutes contributions directes, personnelles, mobilières ou somptuaires imposées par une autorité quelconque des pays respectifs.

Il est entendu que les dits fonctionnaires ne seront aucunement exempts des impôts sur les immeubles qu'ils possèderaient dans le pays où ils résident.

ARTICLE 5. — Les Consuls Généraux, Consuls ou Vice-Consuls ne seront pas tenus de comparaître comme témoins devant les tribunaux du pays où ils résident.

Quand la justice locale aura à recevoir d'eux quelque déposition, elle devra se transporter à leur domicile ou déléguer, à cet effet, un fonctionnaire compétent pour y dresser, après avoir recueilli leurs déclarations orales, le procès-verbal nécessaire, ou bien elle leur demandera une déclaration par écrit.

ARTICLE 6. — Les Consuls Généraux, Consuls et Vice-Consuls des Hautes Parties contractantes jouiront réciproquement, dans les Etats de l'autre partie — en ce qui concerne leurs personnes, leurs fonctions et leurs habitations — des mêmes honneurs et égards, privilèges et immunités, droits et protection qui sont accordés aux fonctionnaires consulaires du même rang des nations les plus favorisées, mais, bien entendu, dans les limites de la présente Convention.

ARTICLE 7. — Seront exempts des droits d'entrée, après vérification douanière, les effets et objets importés à l'adresse et destinés à l'usage personnel ou de la famille du chef d'un Consulat Général, d'un Consulat ou d'un Vice-Consulat hellène établi en Turquie, en tant que le droit d'importation ne dépasse pas 2500 piastres or par an.

Il en sera de même pour les objets et effets importés à l'adresse et destinés à l'usage personnel ou de la famille d'un fonctionnaire consulaire hellène, quand ces objets et effets sont introduits lors de la première installation de ce fonctionnaire ou de sa famille en Turquie.

D'autre part, les Consuls Généraux, Consuls et Vice-Consuls de Turquie jouiront, en Grèce, des mêmes franchises de droit que les fonctionnaires du même rang et de la même qualité des autres Puissances.

PROTOCOLE-ANNEXE. — En ce qui concerne l'article 7, il est entendu que les autorités douanières ne percevront aucun droit sur les registres, papiers à en-tête, cahiers à souche, passeports, passavants, certificats, timbres et autres documents publics, ainsi que sur toute fourniture officielle de bureau, expédiés à l'adresse des fonctionnaires consulaires respectifs, ou envoyés par eux aux Administrations de leur pays.

ARTICLE 8. — Les Consuls Généraux, Consuls et Vice-Consuls pourront placer au-dessus de la porte extérieure de la maison consulaire leur écusson national avec une inscription indiquant leur caractère officiel.

Ils pourront également arborer le pavillon de leur pays sur la maison consulaire aux jours de solennités publiques, ainsi que dans d'autres circonstances d'usage.

ARTICLE 9. — En cas d'empêchement, d'absence ou de décès des Consuls Généraux, Consuls ou Vice-Consuls, le Chancelier ou l'un des Secrétaires, sujet de l'Etat qui l'a nommé, qui aura antérieurement été présenté en la dite qualité aux Autorités respectives, ou à défaut d'un Chancelier ou Secrétaire, un autre fonctionnaire consulaire de carrière envoyé comme remplaçant, sera admis, de plein droit, à exercer, par *interim*, et d'une manière provisoire, les fonctions consulaires, sans que les autorités locales puissent y mettre obstacle.

La gérance intérimaire de ce fonctionnaire de carrière, envoyé comme remplaçant, ne devra pas dépasser le délai de six mois.

Ces fonctionnaires jouiront, pendant la durée de leur gestion intérimaire, de tous les droits, immunités et privilèges qui appartiennent aux titulaires.

ARTICLE 10. — Les Chancelleries et Archives Consulaires seront inviolables en tout temps. Les autorités locales ne pourront les envahir sous aucun prétexte ni, dans aucun cas, visiter ou saisir les papiers qui y seront enfermés.

ARTICLE 11. — Les Consuls des deux Hautes Parties Contractantes auront le droit de s'adresser aux autorités compétentes de leur circonscription consulaire, pour réclamer contre toute infraction aux Traités et Conventions existant entre la Turquie et la Grèce, et pour protéger les droits et les intérêts de leurs nationaux.

S'il n'était pas fait droit à leurs réclamations, les dits Agents pourront recourir à leurs Légations respectives.

ARTICLE 12. — Les Consuls des deux Parties contractantes, ainsi que leurs Chanceliers et Secrétaires, auront le droit de recevoir, dans leurs Chancelleries, au domicile des Parties et à bord des navires de leur nation, les déclarations que pourront avoir à faire les capitaines, les gens de l'équipage, les passagers, les négociants et les autres sujets de leur pays.

Ils seront également autorisés à recevoir :

1° Les dispositions testamentaires de leurs nationaux et tous actes de droit civil qui les concernent et auxquels on voudrait donner une forme authentique.

2° Tous les contrats par écrit et actes conventionnels passés entre leurs nationaux ou entre ces derniers et d'autres personnes du pays où ils résident, et, de même, tout acte conventionnel concernant ce dernier pays seulement, pourvu, bien entendu, que les actes susmentionnés aient rapport à des biens situés ou à des affaires à traiter sur le territoire de la Partie contractante qui a nommé les dits fonctionnaires, et

3° Dans la mesure de la législation du pays de leur résidence, tous actes notariés destinés à l'usage dans ce pays, passés soit entre leurs propres nationaux, soit entre ces nationaux et d'autres étrangers.

Les déclarations et attestations contenues dans les actes ci-dessus mentionnés qui auront été reconnus authentiques par les dits fonctionnaires et revêtus du sceau du Consulat Général, Consulat et Vice-Consulat auront en justice dans le territoire de l'Empire Ottoman comme en Grèce la même force et valeur que si ces actes avaient été passés par devant d'autres employés publics de l'une ou de l'autre des Parties Contractantes, pourvu qu'ils aient été rédigés dans les formes requises par les lois de l'Etat qui a nommé les fonctionnaires consulaires et qu'ils aient ensuite été soumis au timbre et à l'enregistrement, ainsi qu'à toutes les autres formalités qui régissent la matière dans le pays où l'acte doit recevoir son exécution.

Dans les cas où l'authenticité d'un document public enregistré à la Chancellerie de l'une des Autorités consulaires respectives serait mise en doute, la confrontation du document en question avec l'acte original ne sera pas refusée à la personne y intéressée, qui en ferait la demande et qui pourra, si elle le juge utile, assister à cette confrontation.

Les Consuls pourront légaliser toute espèce de documents émanant des autorités ou fonctionnaires de leur pays et en faire des traductions qui auront, dans le pays où ils résident — en tant que les lois des Etats respectifs le permettent — la même force et valeur que si elles avaient été faites par les fonctionnaires compétents du pays de leur résidence.

ARTICLE 13. — Les sujets de l'un des Etats Contractants établis dans les Etats de l'autre, seront, réciproquement, affranchis de toute espèce de service militaire, tant sur terre que sur mer et seront exempts de l'impôt militaire, et de toute prestation pécuniaire ou matérielle imposée par compensation pour le service personnel, tout comme des réquisitions militaires, à l'exception de celle des logements et des fournitures pour les militaires de passage, qui seraient également exigées, selon l'usage du pays, des sujets indigènes et des étrangers.

ARTICLE 14. — Les effets et valeurs appartenant aux marins et passagers, sujets de l'une des Parties Contractantes, morts à bord d'un navire de l'autre Partie, seront envoyés au consul de la nation respective, pour être remis à qui de droit, conformément aux lois en vigueur dans les pays respectifs.

ARTICLE 15. — En cas de naufrage sur une des côtes des territoires des Hautes Parties Contractantes, d'un navire ottoman ou hellène, les Consuls respectifs jouiront de toutes les prérogatives accordées aux Consuls des autres Puissances, en matière de sauvetage des navires de leur pavillon.

Les navires abandonnés, dragues, embarcations, bouées, etc., dont la nationalité ottomane ou hellène est apparente et qui auraient été trouvés en mer et consignés aux autorités locales, seront remis, dans le port de remorque, entre les mains du Consul ottoman ou hellène le plus proche, s'il en fait la demande. Il est bien entendu, toutefois, que le dit fonctionnaire consulaire aura à verser à qui il appartient, avant d'entrer en possession des navires, embarcations ou autres susénoncés, les droits de sauvetage et remorque, conformément aux lois et règlements en vigueur dans les Etats des Hautes Parties Contractantes.

ARTICLE 16. — Les Consuls des deux Hautes Parties Contractantes auront à exercer une stricte surveillance pour empêcher, au besoin par des représentations à qui de droit, le changement du pavillon des navires de leur nation contre le pavillon de l'autre Etat, s'il est prouvé que ce changement a pour but de frustrer les droits des créanciers sujets de la nation qui a nommé le consul.

ARTICLE 17. — Les Consuls respectifs pourront aller personnellement ou envoyer des délégués à bord des navires de leur pays, après leur admission à la libre pratique, interroger le capitaine et l'équipage, examiner les papiers de bord, recevoir les déclarations sur le voyage, la destination du bâtiment et les incidents de la traversée, dresser les manifestes et faciliter l'expédition du navire.

ARTICLE 18. — En cas de décès d'un sujet ottoman en Grèce ou d'un sujet hellène dans les Etats de Sa Majesté Impériale le Sultan, l'Autorité Consulaire, de la juridiction de laquelle dépendra le décédé, prendra possession de la succession de celui-ci pour la transmettre à ses héritiers. En l'absence de l'autorité consulaire sur les lieux, le juge compétent de la localité sera tenu de transmettre l'inventaire et le produit de la succession à l'autorité consulaire la plus proche, sans réclamer aucun droit.

La succession aux biens immobiliers sera régie par les lois du pays, dans lequel les immeubles sont situés, et la connaissance de toute demande ou contestation concernant les successions immobilières, appartiendra exclusivement aux tribunaux de ce pays.

Pour ce qui concerne les successions mobilières laissées par les sujets de l'une des deux Parties contractantes dans le territoire de l'autre Partie — soit qu'à l'époque du décès ils y fussent établis ou simplement de passage, soit qu'ils fussent décédés ailleurs — les réclamations reposant sur le titre d'hérédité ou de legs, seront jugées par les Autorités ou tribunaux compétents du pays, auquel appartenait le défunt, et conformément aux lois de ce pays.

ARTICLE 19. — Les sujets ottomans auront en Grèce le même droit que les nationaux, de posséder toute espèce de propriété immobilière, de l'acquérir et d'en disposer par vente, échange, donation, testament ou de toute autre manière, sans payer de taxes ou impôts autres ou plus élevés que les nationaux.

ARTICLE 20. — Les droits de juridiction des consuls hellènes en Turquie en matière civile, commerciale et pénale, ainsi que les autres immunités et privilèges dont les consuls et sujets hellènes jouissaient en Turquie avant l'année 1897, sont maintenus, conformément aux stipulations des Préliminaires de Paix signés entre les Grandes Puissances et l'Empire Ottoman le 6/18 Septembre 1897 et à celles du Traité de Paix définitif signé entre la Turquie et la Grèce le 22 Novembre (4 Décembre) 1897 — et ce, en tant que lesdits droits de juridiction et lesdits immunités et privilèges ne sont pas modifiés par la présente convention.

ARTICLE 21. — Les intérêts des créanciers ottomans ou étrangers dans les faillites des sujets hellènes en Turquie seront représentés par un ou deux syndics, tant provisoires que définitifs. L'autorité consulaire hellénique compétente pour le règlement des dites faillites, nommera ces syndics sur la désignation qui lui en sera faite par les créanciers susdits, ottomans ou étrangers.

ARTICLE 22. — L'assistance consulaire devant les autorités et tribunaux ottomans étant maintenue pour les sujets hellènes, les Consuls hellènes sont tenus d'envoyer avec toute diligence leur délégué devant les autorités et tribunaux compétents.

En cas d'absence de ce délégué, les tribunaux surseoiront à l'examen de l'affaire et enverront une nouvelle invitation par écrit. Si, nonobstant cette seconde invitation, le délégué consulaire s'abstient de paraître, ils auront dans ce cas la faculté de ne plus attendre sa présence et pourront rendre leur jugement, sentence ou arrêt.

ARTICLE 23. — Les pièces judiciaires ou extra-judiciaires destinées à être signifiées aux sujets hellènes en Turquie, seront remises contre récépissé à l'autorité hellénique compétente, qui devra pourvoir à leur signification et devra retourner en temps utile l'acte de signification dûment signé par le destinataire. A cet effet, les dites pièces devront contenir des indications suffisantes, pour qu'il ne puisse y avoir erreur sur la personne à laquelle l'acte est destiné ; à défaut de quoi, la pièce pourra être retournée à l'autorité ottomane pour être complétée.

Dans les cas où l'acte de signification dûment signé par le destinataire ne serait pas restitué à l'autorité Ottomane dans un délai de quinze jours à partir de la remise de la pièce à l'autorité Consulaire Hellénique, la signification sera considérée comme faite à la partie elle-même, à moins que l'autorité Consulaire ne prévienne l'autorité Ottomane que la personne à laquelle la pièce était destinée, ne se trouve pas dans sa circonscription consulaire.

ARTICLE 24. — Les autorités consulaires helléniques procéderont en toute diligence à l'exécution des jugements, sentences ou arrêts rendus, en observation des droits reconnus aux autorités consulaires, contre les sujets hellènes par les autorités et les tribunaux compétents ottomans.

Si l'autorité consulaire refusait de mettre à exécution les dits jugements, sentences ou arrêts dans un délai maximum de deux mois, les autorités compétentes ottomanes auront la faculté de procéder elles-mêmes à cette exécution, en prévenant au préalable et par écrit l'autorité consulaire du jour et de l'heure où elles procéderont à ladite exécution.

ARTICLE 25. — En cas de perquisition, descente ou visite dans la demeure d'un sujet hellène, les fonctionnaires et agents de police à ce commis aviseront le consulat hellénique et lui feront connaître les motifs de la mesure, à l'effet qu'il envoie sans retard un délégué.

S'il s'écoule plus de six heures entre l'instant où le consulat aura été prévenu, et l'instant de l'arrivée du délégué, les fonctionnaires et agents de police ottomans procéderont à leur commission et aviseront ensuite le consulat, en lui com-

muniquant une copie légalisée du procès-verbal constatant l'absence du délégué consulaire.

ARTICLE 26. — En cas de visite à bord des navires helléniques autre que les visites de la santé, les autorités ottomanes attendront le délégué consulaire hellénique pendant un délai de trois heures à compter du moment de la remise de l'avis au consulat, et si le délégué se refuse ou tarde à venir, elles procéderont à leur commission et aviseront le consulat, en lui communiquant une copie légalisée du procès-verbal constatant l'absence du dit délégué.

ARTICLE 27. — En cas de flagrant délit, les autorités ottomanes pourront procéder à l'arrestation d'un sujet hellène sans attendre l'arrivée du délégué consulaire requis à cet effet ; mais elles devront aviser sans délai l'autorité consulaire hellénique.

Fait à Constantinople, le vingt Mars (deux Avril) mil neuf-cent-un [1].

CLXVI. Etats-Unis d'Amérique, Russie.

8 septembre 1900.

L'arbitre, choisi dans ce contesté, vient de rendre une sentence préparatoire, dont nous reproduisons le texte.

Sentence préparatoire dans le différend entre les Etats-Unis d'Amérique et la Russie, prononcée à La Haye, le 19 Octobre 1901.

Le soussigné Tobie Michel Charles Asser, Membre du Conseil d'Etat des Pays-Bas, exerçant les fonctions d'Arbitre qu'il a eu l'honneur de se voir conférées par le Gouvernement des Etats-Unis d'Amérique et par le Gouvernement Impérial de Russie, pour juger les différends relatifs aux affaires des schooners « James Hamilton Lewis », « C. H. White », « Kate and Anna » et du navire baleinier « Cape Horn Pigeon » a rendu, en ladite qualité, le jugement suivant.

L'Arbitre,

Attendu que dans les déclarations échangées entre les deux Gouvernements précités, à Saint-Pétersbourg le 26 Août/8 Septembre 1900, l'Arbitre a été chargé de statuer sur toutes les questions qui pourraient surgir entre les Hautes Parties dans le cours de l'arbitrage, relativement à la procédure ;

Attendu qu'il est constant en fait que le Gouvernement des Etats-Unis d'Amérique, partie demanderesse dans les différends indiqués ci-dessus,

---

[1] Cette sentence nous a été gracieusement communiquée par le Ministre de Turquie à Bruxelles

a nommé Monsieur Herbert H. D. Peirce, Premier Secrétaire de l'Ambassade de Saint-Pétersbourg, son agent et conseil dans la procédure arbitrale et a notifié cette nomination à la partie adverse ;

Attendu qu'une différence de vues s'étant manifestée entre les parties par rapport à la nature et aux conséquences juridiques de cette nomination, la partie demanderesse a présenté à l'Arbitre, sous la date du 18 Juin 1901, un Memorandum, dans lequel elle soumet à sa décision les trois qûestions suivantes :

I. La partie défenderesse ne doit-elle pas reconnaître l'Agent et Conseil nommé par la partie demanderesse pour la représenter dans l'arbitrage ?

II. La partie défenderesse ne doit-elle pas accepter comme officielles les communications émanant de l'Agent et Conseil de la partie demanderesse et, de même, ne doit-elle pas transmettre ses réponses à ce dit Agent ?

III. La partie défenderesse ne doit-elle pas accepter de l'Agent et Conseil de la partie demanderesse, comme officiellement livrées, les copies des memorandums ou des autres documents transmis à l'arbitre et livrer de même directement à l'Agent et Conseil de la partie demanderesse ses copies officielles des réponses aux memorandums ou des autres documents qu'elle transmettra à l'Arbitre ?

questions, auxquelle la partie demanderesse donne une réponse affirmative ;

Attendu que la partie défenderesse, dans un contre-memorandum, adressé à l'Arbitre sous la date du 12/25 Juillet 1901, en réponse au memorandum de la partie demanderesse, après avoir combattu le système exposé dans ce memorandum, déclare se remettre à l'Arbitre de décider si à l'avenir copie des contre-memorandums russes devra être envoyée au gouvernement américain par l'intermédiaire de l'Ambassadeur de Russie à Washington, ou bien devra être remise au Conseil et Agent du Gouvernement des Etats-Unis ;

Attendu que par une lettre du 13 Septembre 1901 la partie demanderesse a fait savoir à l'Arbitre qu'elle n'avait plus de pièces à lui soumettre et qu'elle le priait de rendre sa sentence sur l'incident ;

Attendu que dans une procédure arbitrale chaque partie a incontestablement le droit de nommer un Agent ou Conseil, chargé de la représenter au procès, à moins que cela n'ait été expressément défendu par le compromis, ce qui n'est pas le cas dans l'arbitrage actuel ;

qu'un tel Agent ou Conseil devant être considéré comme le mandataire spécial de la partie qui l'a nommé, les actes accomplis par lui dans les limites de son mandat ne sont pas moins valables que s'ils avaient été accomplis par le mandant ;

que, par conséquent, dans l'espèce, les mémoires et autres documents, transmis par ou à l'Agent de la partie demanderesse, doivent être censés transmis par ou à cette partie même ;

que, toutefois, ces conséquences légales de la nomination d'un mandataire, ni prévue ni réglée par le compromis, n'ôtent pas à la partie adverse la faculté de transmettre à la partie même, qui a nommé l'Agent — *in casu* le Gouvernement des Etats-Unis d'Amérique — les mémoires et documents dont il s'agit (conformément à ce qui a été stipulé dans la Convention précitée du 26 Août/8 Septembre 1900), ou, en général, de s'adresser directement à cette partie et non à son mandataire spécial ;

qu'à l'appui de l'opinion contraire, la partie demanderesse invoque la terminologie diplomatique, d'après laquelle les représentants ordinaires et permanents des gouvernements (ambassadeurs, ministres, chargés d'affaires) sont indiqués par l'expression : « Agents Diplomatiques » ;

que, toutefois, on ne saurait déduire de cette terminologie, que les agents nommés pour représenter une des parties dans une procédure arbitrale, doivent être assimilés aux agents diplomatiques, tandis que, même si tel était le cas, il n'en résulterait pas que la partie adverse n'aurait pas le droit de s'adresser directement au gouvernement qui a nommé l'agent ;

que la partie demanderesse a encore invoqué, à l'appui de son système, l'art. 37 de la Convention de la Haye du 29 Juillet 1899 pour le règlement pacifique des conflits internationaux, qui donne aux parties litigantes le droit de nommer auprès du Tribunal arbitral des délégués ou agents spéciaux, avec la mission de servir d'intermédiaires entre elles et le Tribunal et qui en outre autorise les parties à charger de la défense de leurs droits et intérêts devant le Tribunal, des conseils ou avocats, nommés par elles à cet effet ;

que, toutefois, en admettant même que d'après cet Article la nomination d'un Agent puisse avoir toutes les conséquences indiquées par la partie demanderesse, on ne saurait appliquer les dispositions de la Convention du 29 Juillet 1899 à l'arbitrage actuel, qui a été réglé par un compromis spécial, antérieurement à la mise en vigueur de ladite Convention ;

Par ces motifs

Faisant droit sur l'incident,

Déclare :

I. La Partie Défenderesse est tenue de reconnaître l'Agent et Conseil nommé par la

Partie Demanderesse pour la représenter dans l'arbitrage.

II. La Partie Défenderesse doit accepter comme officielles les communications émanant de l'Agent et Conseil de la Partie Demanderesse, mais elle n'est pas tenue de transmettre ses réponses à ce dit Agent.

III. La Partie Défenderesse doit accepter de l'Agent et Conseil de la Partie Demanderesse, comme officiellement livrées, les copies des memorandums et des autres documents transmis à l'Arbitre, mais elle n'est pas tenue de livrer de même directement à cet Agent et Conseil ses copies officielles des réponses aux memorandums ou des autres documents qu'elle transmettra à l'Arbitre.

Ainsi jugé à La Haye, le 19 Octobre 1901.

CLXVII. Honduras, Salvador.

18 décembre 1880.

Différend de frontière confié à l'arbitrage de Don Joaquim Zavala, président de la République du Nicaragua. La suite donnée à cette affaire ne nous est pas connue.

Convención preliminar para el arreglo arbitral y definitivo de las cuestiones sobre propiedad de terrenos. Diciembre 18 de 1880.

ART. I. — Las Altas Partes Contratantes se comprometen á someter las cuestiones de limites entre Opatoro y Colorós y Santa Elena ó Cuguara y Arambala, Perquin y San Fernando, á la resolución definitiva de un arbitro nombrado por ambas partes.

. . . .

ART. III. — Cada uno de los Gobiernos Contratantes, directamente ó por medio de un comisionado especial, deberá presentar al arbitro nombrado, dentro de sesenta días contados desde la fecha de la última ratificación del convenio, una exposición de los puntos cuestionados, con los documentos justificativos de su derecho y el protocolo de las conferencias celebradas por sus respectivos comisionados, en el mes de Junio del corriente año.

ART. IV. — Los documentos referidos serán la prueba preferente sobre que deba descansar el laudo; y si una de las Partes Contratantes omitiese verificar su presentación en el termino fijado en el artículo anterior, el arbitro se atendrá á los documentos que presente la otra parte, siendo estos atendibles, tanto por su legalidad y fuerza, como por referirse directamente á los objetos ó puntos en cuestión.

ART. V. — Si la prueba instrumental fuese insuficiente en algunos puntos ó originase algunas dudas para decidir por ellas los limites jurisdiccionales que disputan los pueblos referidos, el arbitro podrá resolver los puntos dudosos de la manera que jusgue más equitativa y conveniente, tomando en consideración las necesidades peculiares de los respectivos pueblos, y especialmente el que se concilien de un modo satisfactorio sus opuestas pretensiones, asegurando, como por medio de una transacción, su acquiescencia y tranquilidad [1].

CLXVIII. Equateur, Italie.

28 mars 1898.

Cette contestation a eu pour objet de dédommager les pères salésiens des conséquences de l'expulsion qu'ils avaient eu à subir de la part des autorités équatoriennes.

Protocolo nombrando arbitros arbitradores para que resuelvan la reclamacion de los padres salesianos, firmado en Quito, á 28 de Marzo de 1898.

Reunidos en el Despacho de Relaciones Exteriores del Ecuador los señores: Dr. D. Rafael Gomez de la Torre, Ministro del ramo, y Sr. D. Antonio Diaz Miranda, Encargado de Negocios de España y encargado de la proteccion de los intereses italianos en el Ecuador, han convenido en lo siguiente:

1º — Se nombrarán arbitros arbitradores, amigables conponedores, á los Sres. Jenaro Larrea y Francisco Andrade Marin para que resuelven la reclamacion de los padres salesianos, despues de haber oído á ambas partes, las cuales se haran representar por medio de personas idoneas, provistas de los respectivos datos, pruebas y documentos necesarios para el buen exito de su commision.

2º — Los arbitros fallarán conforme á las reglas de equidad y conveniencia publica, sin sujetarse á leyes ni procedimientos judiciales.

3º — El laudo estará debidamente fundado y sera inapelable.

4º — En caso de que los arbitros no logren ponerse de acuerdo, nombrarán un tercero dirimente con las mismas facultades.

En fe de lo cual el Ministro de Relaciones Exteriores del Ecuador y el Sr. Encargado de Negocios de España, firmaron y sellaron por

---

[1] *Algunos datos sobre Tratados de Arbitraje*, p. 28.

duplicado el presente protocolo en Quito, á 28 de Marzo de 1898 [1].

Le 21 juin 1899, un protocole additionnel fut conclu dans le but de permettre aux arbitres de juger la demande reconventionnelle formulée par le Gouvernement de la République de l'Equateur. Ce protocole n'a pas été publié.

CLXIX. Bolivie, Chili.

31 mai 1900.

Arbitrage similaire à celui conclu antérieurement avec divers gouvernements européens et relatif aux dommages causés à des boliviens au cours de la guerre civile de 1891.

Acuerdo diplomático para solucionar las reclamaciones de los súbditos bolivianos por daños sufridos durante la guerra civil de 1891, hecho en Santiago á los 31 días del mes de mayo 1900.

Reunidos en el Ministerio de Relaciones Exteriores de Chile, el señor Enviado Extraordinario y Ministro Plenipotenciario de Bolivia doctor don Claudio Pinilla, y el señor Ministro del Ramo don Rafael Errázuriz Urmeneta, expresaron que, deseando eliminar todas controversias que sustentan ambas cancellerías, para propender á la mejor y más cordial inteligencia de sus respectivos paises, han resuelto solucionar de una manera amistosa y sencilla las reclamaciones de los súbditos bolivianos por daños y perjuicios sufridos durante la guerra civil de 1891, y tramitadas ante su Gobierno, bajo el patrocinio de la Legación boliviana, han convenido en los siguientes articulos:

---

[1] *Informe de Relaciones Exteriores*, Ecuador, 1898, p. 135; 1899, p. 48.

Primero. —. Las reclamaciones pendientes de los súbditos bolivianos por daños y perjuicios que les hayan irrogado las fuerzas militares o las autoridades de Chile durante la guerra civil de 1891, patrocinadas por la Legación de Bolivia, se someteran á la decisión arbitral del Representante diplomático de Su Majestad Británica residente en Santiago, para que falle sobre su procedencia y legalidad, y fige el monto de las indemnizaciones a que hubiere lugar.

Segundo. — Para el efecto y una vez que sea aceptado el cargo, se pondrán en conocimiento del referido Representante de Su Majestad Británica, los expedientes tramitados ante el Gobierno de Chile, con más las pruebas, documentos y exposiciones que estimaren necesarias los interesados.

Tercero. — Esta prueba deberá ser rendida en el término perentorio de tres meses.

Cuarto. — El Arbitro designado en el presente acuerdo, fallará las antedichas reclamaciones en el término que estime necessario, intersándose ambos Gobiernos por que sea á la brevedad posible.

Quinto. — Si por cualquier motivo el Representante de Su Majestad Británica, no pudiere ejercer el cargo de Arbitro qui aquí se le confía, se procederá inmediatamente á reemplazarlo con otro agente diplomático nombrado de común acuerdo.

Sexto. — Las indemnizaciones reconocidas por el Arbitro, serán canceladas por el Gobierno de Chile, en el término de seis meses, á los reclamantes ó á quienes sus derechos representen.

En fé de lo cual los infrascritos han firmado el presente acuerdo en doble ejemplar y le han puesto sus sellos.

Hecho en Santiago, á los 31 días del mes de Mayo del año 1900 [1].

---

[1] *Informe de Relaciones Exteriores*, Bolivie, Anexos, p. 162.

TABLES

TABLE CHRONOLOGIQUE

---><—-

La présente table comprend, dans leur ordre de date, la liste de tous les compromis, de toutes les sentences et des divers incidents relevés dans la Pasicrisie. Les compromis seuls sont numérotés d'une manière continue et les dates et les noms des pays intéressés en sont imprimés en caractères gras. Les dates des incidents et des sentences, ainsi que les noms des pays y relatifs sont imprimés en caractères italiques. Les nombres en chiffres romains renvoient aux paragraphes de l'ouvrage, consacrés chacun à un ou plusieurs arbitrages. Les nombres de la dernière colonne renvoient aux pages.

No	DATE	ETATS EN CAUSE	OBJETS	No	Pages
1	1794—11—19	**Etats-Unis d'Amérique, Grande-Bretagne** .	Différend de frontière . . .	I A	1
2	1794—11—19	**Etats-Unis d'Amérique, Grande-Bretagne** .	Créances irrécouvrables . . .	I B	3
3	1794—11—19	**Etats-Unis d'Amérique, Grande-Bretagne** .	Réclamations réciproques . .	I C	4
4	1795—10—27	**Espagne, Etats-Unis d'Amérique**	Prises maritimes	XXVIII	79
	1797—12—27	*Espagne, Etats-Unis d'Amérique*	Sentence dans 1795—10—27 .	XXVIII	636
	1798—10—26	*Etats-Unis d'Amérique, Grande-Bretagne* . .	Sentence dans 1794—11—19 .	I A	2
	1802—01—08	*Etats-Unis d'Amérique, Grande-Bretagne* . . .	Transaction dans 1794—11—19	I B	4
	1802—01—08	*Etats-Unis d'Amérique, Grande-Bretagne* . .	Confirmation dans 1794—11—19	I C	5
5	1802—08—11	**Espagne, Etats-Unis d'Amérique**	Réclamations réciproques . .	II	6
	1804—08—24	*Etats-Unis d'Amérique, Grande-Bretagne* . .	Protocole final dans 1794-11-19	I C	6
6	1814—05—30	**France, Russie**	Réclamations réciproques . .	XLI	112
7	1814—12—24	**Etats-Unis d'Amérique, Grande-Bretagne** .	Territoire contesté	III A	7
8	1814—12—24	**Etats-Unis d'Amérique, Grande-Bretagne** .	Différend de frontière . . .	III B	8
9	1814—12—24	**Etats-Unis d'Amérique, Grande-Bretagne** .	Différend de frontière . . .	III C	15
10	1815—06—09	**Auvergne, Rohan**	Succession ducale	XL	112
11	1815—11—20	**France, Grande-Bretagne**	Réclamations particulières . .	XXXVII	101
12	1815—11—20	**France, Grandes Puissances**	Réclamations particulières . .	XXXVIII	104
13	1815—11—20	**France, Pays-Bas**	Intérêts arriérés	XXXIX	111
	1816—07—01	*Auvergne, Rohan*	Sentence dans 1815—06—09 .	XL	112
	1816—09—27	*France, Russie*	Exécution dans 1814—05—30	XLI	112
	1816—10—16	*France, Pays-Bas*	Sentence dans 1815—11—20 .	XXXIX	111
14	1817—07—28	**Grande-Bretagne, Portugal**	Prises maritimes	XXXI	84
	1817—11—24	*Etats-Unis d'Amérique, Grande-Bretagne* . .	Sentence dans 1814—12—24 .	III A	8
	1818—04—25	*France, Grande-Bretagne*	Transaction dans 1815—11—20	XXXVII	103
	1818—04—25	*France, Grandes Puissances*	Transaction dans 1815—11—20	XXXVIII	107
15	1818—10—20	**Etats-Unis d'Amérique, Grande-Bretagne** .	Réclamations particulières . .	IV	17
	1819—02—22	*Espagne, Etats-Unis d'Amérique*	Annulation dans 1802—08—11	II	7
	1819—02—22	*Espagne, Etats-Unis d'Amérique*	Annulation dans 1795—10—27	XXVIII	79
	1822—04—22	*Etats-Unis d'Amérique, Grande-Bretagne* . .	Sentence dans 1818—10—20 .	IV	17
	1822—06—18	*Etats-Unis d'Amérique, Grande-Bretagne* . .	Sentence dans 1814—12—24 .	III C	16
	1822—06—30	*Etats-Unis d'Amérique, Grande-Bretagne* . .	Compromis nouv. d. 1818-10-20	IV	17
16	1823—03—12	**Espagne, Grande Bretagne**	Réclamations réciproques . .	XXXII	88
	1826—11—13	*Etats-Unis d'Amérique, Grande-Bretagne* . .	Arrangement dans 1818-10-20	IV	20

N°	DATE	ÉTATS EN CAUSE	OBJETS	N°	Pages
	1827—09—29	*Etats-Unis d'Amérique, Grande-Bretagne* . .	Choix de l'arbitre d. 1814-12-24	III B	9
	1828—10—28	*Espagne, Grande-Bretagne*	Liquidation dans 1823—03—12	XXXII	89
17	1829—05—05	**Brésil, Grande-Bretagne**	Prises maritimes	XXXIII	91
18	1830—07—19	**Argentine, Grande-Bretagne**	Réclamations particulières . .	XXXIV	92
	1831—01—10	*Etats-Unis d'Amérique, Grande-Bretagne* . .	Sentence dans 1814—12—24 .	III B	11
19	1839—03—09	**France, Mexique**	Actes de guerre	V	20
20	1839—04—11	**Etats-Unis d'Amérique, Mexique**	Réclamations particulières . .	VI	21
21	1840—10—29	**Argentine, France**	Réclamations particulières . .	CXXXVII	587
22	1840—11—13	**Grande-Bretagne, Portugal**	Service militaire	XXXV	93
23	1840—11—17	**Deux-Siciles, Grande-Bretagne**	Monopole du soufre	XXXVI	97
	1841—04—26	*Argentine, France*	Sentence dans 1840—10—29 .	CXXXVII	587
	1841—06—22	*Grande-Bretagne, Portugal*	Procédure dans 1840—11—13	XXXV	636
	1841—12—24	*Deux-Siciles, Grande-Bretagne*	Sentence dans 1840—11—17 .	XXXVI	99
	1842—08—09	*Etats-Unis d'Amérique, Grande-Bretagne* . .	Arrangement dans 1814-12-24	III B & C	15
	1842—08—26	*Grande-Bretagne, Portugal*	Liquidation dans 1840—11—13	XXXV	96
24	1842—10—15	**Brésil, Etats-Unis d'Amérique**	Prise maritime	CLVII	617
25	1842—11—14	**France, Grande-Bretagne**	Etablissement d'un blocus . .	VII	24
	1843—01—09	*Etats-Unis d'Amérique, Mexique*	Renouvellement d. 1839-04-11	VI	23
	1843—06—12	*Brésil, Etats-Unis d'Amérique*	Sentence dans 1842—10—15 .	CLVII	617
	1843—11—30	*France, Grande-Bretagne*	Sentence dans 1842—11—14 .	VII	25
	1844—08—01	*France, Mexique*	Sentence dans 1839—03—09 .	V	21
	1848—02—02	*Etats-Unis d'Amérique, Mexique*	Transaction dans 1839—04—11	VI	23
26	1850—07—06	**Grande-Bretagne, Grèce**	Perte de documents	XLII	113
27	1851—02—15	**Espagne, France**	Prises maritimes	VIII	26
28	1851—02—26	**Etats-Unis d'Amérique, Portugal** . . .	Destruction de corsaire . . .	IX	30
	1851—05—05	*Grande-Bretagne, Grèce*	Sentence dans 1850—07—06 .	XLII	114
	1852—04—13	*Espagne, France*	Sentence dans 1851—02—15 .	VIII	27
	1852—11—30	*Etats-Unis d'Amérique, Portugal*	Sentence dans 1851—02—26 .	IX	30
29	1853—02—08	**Etats-Unis d'Amérique, Grande-Bretagne** .	Réclamations réciproques . .	X	31
30	1853—03—16	**Equateur, Pérou**	Prises maritimes	CXXXVIII	588
31	1854—06—05	**Etats-Unis d'Amérique, Grande-Bretagne** .	Pêcheries	CIX	437
	1854—07—17	*Etats-Unis d'Amérique, Grande-Bretagne* . .	Prorogation dans 1853—02—08	X	33
32	1855—07—09	**Grande-Bretagne, Portugal**	Réclamation particulière . .	CI	371
	1856—02—07	*Grande-Bretagne, Portugal*	Sentence dans 1855—07—09 .	CI	373
33	1857—06—23	**France, Grande-Bretagne, Uruguay** . . .	Actes de guerre	XLIII	115
34	1857—08—05	**Pays-Bas, Vénézuéla**	Territoire contesté	LI	151
35	1857—09—10	**Etats-Unis d'Amérique, Nouvelle Grenade** .	Voies de fait	XI	34
	1858—04—08	*Etats-Unis d'Amérique, Grande-Bretagne*. .	Sentence dans 1854—06—05 .	CIX	438
36	1858—06—02	**Brésil, Grande-Bretagne**	Réclamations réciproques . .	XLIV	117
37	1858—08—21	**Argentine, France, Grde.-Bretagne, Sardaigne**	Actes de guerre civile . . .	XLV	120
38	1858—11—10	**Chili, Etats-Unis d'Amérique**	Saisie d'une somme d'argent .	XII	35
39	1859—02—04	**Etats-Unis d'Amérique, Paraguay** . . .	Actes de guerre	XIII	37
40	1859—04—30	**Grande-Bretagne, Guatemala**	Différend de frontière . . .	CXXXIX	588
	1859—08—18	*Argentine, France, Grande-Bretagne, Sardaigne*	Modification dans 1858-08-21	XLV	121
41	1859—11—28	**Grande-Bretagne, Honduras**	Réclamations particulières . .	XLVI	121
42	1860—01—28	**Grande-Bretagne, Nicaragua**	Concessions de terres . . .	XXI	54
43	1860—07—02	**Costa-Rica, Etats-Unis d'Amérique** . .	Réclamations particulières . .	XIV	38
	1860—08—13	*Etats-Unis d'Amérique, Paraguay*	Sentence dans 1859—02—04 .	XIII	620
44	1861—03—08	**Grande-Bretagne, Portugal**	Réclamations particulières . .	CII	377
	1861—10—31	*Grande-Bretagne, Portugal*	Sentence dans 1861—03—08 .	CII	378
	1862—02—15	*Espagne, France*	Transaction dans 1851—02—15	VIII	29
	1862—06—28	*France, Grande-Bretagne, Uruguay* . . .	Transaction dans 1857—06—23	XLIII	116
	1862—09—27	*Grande-Bretagne, Nicaragua*	Interprétation dans 1860-01-28	XXI	56

N°	DATE	ÉTATS EN CAUSE	OBJETS	N°	Pages
45	1862—11—25	Equateur, Etats-Unis d'Amérique	Réclamations réciproques . .	XV	40
46	1862—12—20	Etats-Unis d'Amérique, Portugal	Prises maritimes	XVI	41
47	1863—01—05	Brésil, Grande-Bretagne.	Arrestation arbitraire. . . .	XVII	42
48	1863—01—12	Etats-Unis d'Amérique, Pérou	Réclamations réciproques . .	XVIII	43
	1863—05—15	Chili, Etats-Unis d'Amérique	Sentence dans 1858—11—10 .	XII	36
	1863—06—18	Brésil, Grande-Bretagne	Sentence dans 1863—01—05 .	XVII	42
49	1863—07—..	Grande-Bretagne, Pérou	Arrestation arbitraire. . . .	XX	46
50	1863—07—01	Etats-Unis d'Amérique, Grande-Bretagne	Territoire repris	XIX	44
	1864—01—..	Etats-Unis d'Amérique, Pérou	Refus d'arbitrer dans 1862-12-20	XVI	41
	1864—02—10	Etats-Unis d'Amérique, Colombie	Prorogation dans 1857—09—10	XI	620
	1864—04—18	Grande-Bretagne, Pérou	Sentence dans 1863—07—..	XX	47
51	1864—04—21	Egypte, Canal de Suez	Réclamation particulière. . .	XLVII	123
52	1864—05—04	Etats-Unis d'Amérique, Salvador	Monopole gouvernemental . .	CLVIII	617
	1864—07—06	Egypte, Canal de Suez	Sentence dans 1864—04—21 .	XLVII	123
53	1864—07—15	Argentine, Grande-Bretagne	Réclamations particulières . .	XXIII	61
	1865—01—18	Argentine, Grande-Bretagne	Choix de l'arbitre d. 1865-01-18	XXIII	62
	1865—02—21	Etats-Unis d'Amérique, Salvador	Sentence dans 1864—05—04 .	CLVIII	617
	1865—06—30	Pays-Bas, Vénézuéla	Sentence dans 1857—08—05 .	LI	152
54	1866—04—25	Etats-Unis d'Amérique, Vénézuéla . . .	Réclamations particulières . .	XXII	56
55	1866—06—16	Grande-Bretagne, Mexique	Réclamations particulières . .	XXIV	68
56	1868—03—04	Espagne, Grande-Bretagne	Destruction de navire . . .	XXV	69
57	1868—07—04	Etats-Unis d'Amérique, Mexique	Déprédations des Indiens . .	XXVI	70
58	1869—09—21	Grande-Bretagne, Vénézuéla	Réclamations particulières . .	XXVII	78
59	1868—12—04	Etats-Unis d'Amérique, Pérou	Réclamations réciproques . .	XXIX	79
60	1869—01—13	Grande-Bretagne, Portugal	Territoire contesté . . .	XXX	81
	1869—09—10	Etats-Unis d'Amérique, Grande-Bretagne	Sentence dans 1863—07—01 .	XIX	46
61	1869—10—30	Orange, Transvaal	Différend de frontière . . .	CXL	589
	1869—11—16	Grande-Bretagne, Vénézuéla	Protocole final dans 1868-09-21	XXVII	78
	1870—02—19	Orange, Transvaal	Sentence dans 1869—10—30 .	CXL	589
62	1870—03—14	Etats-Unis d'Amérique, Brésil	Perte de navire	XLVIII	129
	1870—04—21	Grande-Bretagne, Portugal	Sentence dans 1869—01—13 .	XXX	83
63	1870—06—16	Espagne, Etats-Unis d'Amérique.	Détention de navire	LII	154
	1870—07—11	Etats-Unis d'Amérique, Brésil	Sentence dans 1870—03—14 .	XLVIII	131
	1870—08—01	Argentine, Grande-Bretagne	Sentence dans 1864—07—15 .	XXIII	62
	1870—11—..	Espagne, Etats-Unis d'Amérique	Sentence dans 1870—06—16 .	LII	154
64	1871—02—12	Espagne, Etats-Unis d'Amérique.	Insurrection cubaine	XLIX	134
	1871—04—19	Etats-Unis d'Amérique, Mexique	Prorogation dans 1868—07—04	XXVI	73
65	1871—05—08	Etats-Unis d'Amérique, Grande-Bretagne	Armement de corsaire . . .	L A	138
66	1871—05—08	Etats-Unis d'Amérique, Grande-Bretagne	Réclamations réciproques . .	L B	144
67	1871—05—08	Etats-Unis d'Amérique, Grande-Bretagne	Pêcheries	L C	148
68	1871—05—08	Etats-Unis d'Amérique, Grande-Bretagne	Différend de frontière . . .	L D	149
	1871—06—10	Espagne, Etats-Unis d'Amérique	Procédure dans 1871—02—12	XLIX	137
69	1871—08—12	Brésil, Suède et Norvège	Abordage	LIII	155
70	1871—09—27	Chili, Pérou	Dépenses communes	LIV	156
	1871—09—27	Etats-Unis d'Amérique, Grande-Bretagne	Procédure dans 1871—05—08	L B	145
71	1872—01—09	Brésil, Paraguay	Réclamations particulières . .	LV	167
	1872—03—26	Brésil, Suède et Norvège	Sentence dans 1871—08—12 .	LIII	155
	1872—09—14	Etats-Unis d'Amérique, Grande-Bretagne	Sentence dans 1871—05—08 .	L A	141
72	1872—09—25	Grande-Bretagne, Portugal	Territoire contesté . . .	LVI	170
	1872—10—21	Etats-Unis d'Amérique, Grande-Bretagne	Sentence dans 1871—05—08 .	L D	151
	1872—11—27	Etats-Unis d'Amérique, Mexique	Prorogation dans 1868—07—04	XXVI	73
73	1872—12—05	Bolivie, Chili	Exploitations minières . . .	LXIII	220
74	1872—12—14	Colombie, Grande-Bretagne	Déni de justice	LVII	173

No	DATE	ÉTATS EN CAUSE	OBJETS	No	Pages
	1895—09—07	*Bolivie, Pérou*	Choix de l'arbitre d. 1895-08-26	CXLVI	603
	1895—09—25	*Chili, Grande-Bretagne*	Sentence dans 1893—09—26	CXI	455
	1895—10—12	*Chili, France*	Complément dans 1894-10-19	CXV	482
	1895—10—17	*Chili, France*	Procédure dans 1894—10—19	CXV	482
149	1895—11—01	**Grande-Bretagne, Nicaragua**	Faits insurrectionnels.	CXXIII	516
150	1895—12—03	**Brésil, Italie**	Réclamations particulières	CXXIV	518
	1895—12—12	*Chili, Grande-Bretagne*	Sentence dans 1893—09—29	CXI	456
	1896—01—20	*Chili, France, Grande-Bretagne, Pérou*	Procédure dans 1883—10—20	CXLII	599
	1896—02—02	*Chili, France*	Transaction dans 1894—10—19	CXV	484
151	1896—02—08	**Etats-Unis d'Amérique, Grande-Bretagne**	Pêcheries de phoques	CXXV	520
152	1896—02—12	**Brésil, Italie**	Réquisitions militaires	CXXVI	527
	1896—02—12	*Brésil, Italie*	Confirmation dans 1895-12-03	CXXIV	518
153	1896—03—27	**Costa Rica, Nicaragua**	Différend de frontière	CXXVII	528
154	1896—04—17	**Argentine, Chili**	Différend de frontière	CXXVIII	543
155	1896—07—31	**Colombie, Grande-Bretagne**	Construction de chemin de fer	CXXIX	544
	1896—09—22	*Equateur, Etats-Unis d'Amérique*	Sentence dans 1893—02—28	CX	451
	1896—11—04	*Colombie, Costa Rica*	Renouvellement d. 1880-12-25	CIV	395
	1896—11—12	*Grande-Bretagne, Vénézuéla*	Préliminaires dans 1897-02-02	CXXX	557
	1896—11—19	*Brésil, Italie*	Transaction dans 1895—12—03	CXXIV	519
	1896—11—19	*Brésil, Italie*	Confirmation dans 1896-02-12	CXXVI	527
	1896—12—30	*France, Vénézuéla*	Sentence dans 1891—02—24	XCVIII	344
156	1897—..—..	**Chili, France**	Transport d'émigrants	CLXIV	618
157	1897—..—..	**Etats-Unis d'Amérique, Siam**	Voies de fait	CXLVII	604
	1897—01—30	*Grande-Bretagne, Portugal*	Sentence dans 1895—01—07	CXVI	486
158	1897—02—02	**Grande-Bretagne, Vénézuéla**	Différend de frontière	CXXX	554
	1897—02—25	*Grande-Bretagne, Pays-Bas*	Sentence dans 1895—05—16	CXX	510
159	1897—03—02	**Etats-Unis d'Amérique, Mexique**	Arrestation illégale	CXXXI	558
	1897—03—02	*Colombie, Italie*	Sentence dans 1886—05—24	LXXXV	297
	1897—04—06	*Chili, Pérou*	Complément dans 1883-08-20	CXLI	592
160	1897—04—10	**Brésil, France**	Différend de frontière	CXXXII	563
	1897—05—24	*Chili, Etats-Unis d'Amérique*	Complément dans 1892-08-07	CXIII	478
161	1897—07—03	**Chili, France**	Marché de nitrates	CXXXIII	579
162	1897—07—26	**Etats-Unis d'Amérique, Siam**	Concession forestière	CXXXIV	579
	1897—09—20	*Etats-Unis d'Amérique, Siam*	Sentence dans 1897—..—..	CXLVII	604
	1897—09—30	*Costa Rica, Nicaragua*	Sentence I dans 1896—03—27	CXXVII	529
	1897—11—19	*Etats-Unis d'Amérique, Mexique*	Sentence dans 1897—03—02	CXXXI	559
163	1897—11—22	**Grèce, Turquie**	Convention consulaire	CXLVIII	605
	1897—12—17	*Etats-Unis d'Amérique, Grande-Bretagne*	Sentence dans 1896—02—08	CXXV	522
	1897—12—20	*Costa Rica, Nicaragua*	Sentence II dans 1896—03—27	CXXVII	532
	1898—01—15	*Guatemala, Mexique*	Sentence dans 1895—04—01	CXIX	509
164	1898—03—18	**Guatemala, Italie**	Retrait d'emploi	CXLIX	606
165	1898—03—19	**Belgique, Grande-Bretagne**	Arrestation arbitraire	CXXXV	581
	1898—03—21	*Etats-Unis d'Amérique, Siam*	Sentence dans 1887—07—26	CXXXIV	580
	1898—03—22	*Costa Rica, Nicaragua*	Sentence III dans 1896—03—27	CXXVII	533
166	1898—03—28	**Equateur, Italie**	Expulsion arbitraire	CLXVIII	647
167	1898—04—16	**Chili, Pérou**	CI. Plébiscite	CI.	610
168	1898—04—26	**Costa Rica, République Centrale**	Réclamations réciproques	CLI	611
169	1898—05—17	**Etats-Unis d'Amérique, Pérou**	Destruction de chemin de fer	CLII	612
	1898—10—12	*Guatemala, Italie*	Sentence dans 1898—03—18	CXLIX	606
	1898—10—15	*Etats-Unis d'Amérique, Pérou*	Sentence dans 1898—05—17	CLII	612
170	1898—11—02	**Argentine, Chili**	Différend de frontière	CXXXVI	585
	1898—12—26	*Belgique, Grande-Bretagne*	Sentence dans 1898—03—19	CXXXV	583
171	1899—03—..	**Grande-Bretagne, Honduras**	Rétention de navire	CLXV	618

TABLE GÉOGRAPHIQUE

Cette table permet de se renseigner sur le nombre des recours à l'arbitrage réalisés par les diverses nations civilisées. Toutes les contestations sont indiquées par leur date, l'objet en est spécifié et les chiffres de la dernière colonne renvoient aux pages où les documents relatifs à chaque conflit sont reproduits.

TABLE MÉTHODIQUE

————◦◉◦————

Dans cette table, nous avons énuméré les objets et les faits qui ont donné lieu aux divers arbitrages. Les mots y relatifs sont imprimés en caractères majuscules gras. Les caractères majuscules ordinaires ont été réservés pour les noms des Chefs d'État choisis comme arbitres, et les caractères italiques pour les noms des personnes, des localités et des navires au sujet desquels des différends sont nés. Les chiffres renvoient aux pages.

---◦◦◦◦---

Corrigenda.

Page 325, col. 1, ligne 12, lire: *XC* au lieu de *XL*.
Page 435, col. 2, ligne 7, ajouter: *April 28, 1894.*
Page 435, col. 2, ligne 23, lire: *Parliament,* au lieu de *Parliamentary.*
Page 455, col. 1, ligne 22, lire: *25* au lieu de *15.*

---◦◦◦◦---

POST SCRIPTUM. — *Nous désirons remercier ici tous ceux qui ont bien voulu nous aider dans les recherches souvent pénibles qu'il nous a fallu poursuivre, et plus particulièrement M. A. Germain, bibliothécaire du Ministère des Affaires étrangères de Belgique, dont le concours nous a été précieux.*

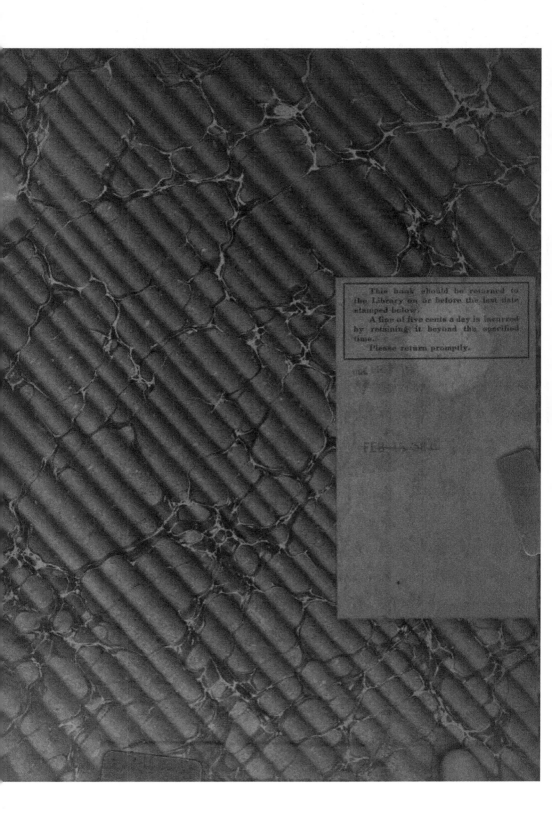

Lightning Source UK Ltd.
Milton Keynes UK
UKHW021838170822
407466UK00003B/154